Corporate Finance Law

Principles and Policy

Second Edition

Louise Gullifer
and
Jennifer Payne

·H A R T·
PUBLISHING
OXFORD AND PORTLAND, OREGON
2015

Hart Publishing
An imprint of Bloomsbury Publishing Plc

Hart Publishing Ltd
Kemp House
Chawley Park
Cumnor Hill
Oxford OX2 9PH
UK

Bloomsbury Publishing Plc
50 Bedford Square
London
WC1B 3DP
UK

www.hartpub.co.uk
www.bloomsbury.com

Published in North America (US and Canada) by
Hart Publishing
c/o International Specialized Book Services
920 NE 58th Avenue, Suite 300
Portland, OR 97213-3786
USA

www.isbs.com

HART PUBLISHING, the Hart/Stag logo, BLOOMSBURY and the
Diana logo are trademarks of Bloomsbury Publishing Plc

First published 2015

British Library Cataloguing-in-Publication Data
A catalogue record for this book is available from the British Library.

ISBN: HB: 978-1-84946-600-4

Typeset by Compuscript Ltd, Shannon
Printed and bound in Great Britain by CPI Group (UK) Ltd, Croydon CR0 4YY

To find out more about our authors and books visit www.hartpublishing.co.uk. Here you will find extracts,
author information, details of forthcoming events and the option to sign up for our newsletters.

PREFACE AND ACKNOWLEDGEMENTS

There have been a great many changes in corporate finance law since the first edition of this book was published in 2011. At that time the global financial crisis had obviously had significant effects on the markets, especially the market for debt, and the increase in regulation which has been a feature of the post-crisis period was beginning to be seen. Since 2011 the legal and regulatory changes designed to deal with the aftermath of the crisis have gathered pace. Within the EU there has been a slew of new directives and regulations aimed at tackling systemic risk and advancing the goal of a single financial market. Many of these have been focused on banks and financial institutions and impact on the material discussed in this book only indirectly but others have impacted very directly on ordinary commercial companies. Obvious examples include the 2014 Market Abuse Regulation and Market Abuse Directive, MIFIR/MiFID, the Short Selling Regulation, the Alternative Investment Fund Managers Directive and the Capital Requirements Directive and Regulation.

There have also been legislative changes at a domestic level that have important effects in this area, such as the Small Business, Enterprise and Employment Act 2015, the Financial Services Act 2012 and the amendments to Part 25 of the Companies Act 2006 concerning the registration of charges. There have also been many case law developments, of which some of the most significant have come from the Lehman insolvency, including the Supreme Court decision on the anti-deprivation principle, *Belmont Park Investments Pty Ltd v BNY Trustee Services Ltd*, the 'client money' case and the 'extended lien' case. Among other cases on debt financing, two on bondholder voting (*Assenagon Asset Management SA v Irish Bank Resolution Corporation Ltd* and *Azevedo v IMCOPA*) are particularly significant, as well as *Fons HF (In Liquidation) v Corporal Ltd* on the meaning of the word 'debenture'. The aftermath of the crisis has also led to an increase in regulatory enforcement actions and private lawsuits, including the launch of the first ever collective action under section 90 FSMA. Market practice has inevitably evolved too, with new forms of financing emerging, such as crowdfunding and peer-to-peer lending, as well as adaptations to existing structures as a result of economic conditions and these legal and regulatory developments. It has been an exciting time to be thinking about, researching and teaching corporate finance law.

In this second edition we have thoroughly updated the text to deal with these myriad, often very significant, developments and to reflect developments both in our own thinking and that of other academics. There are new sections to deal with material which has increased in importance (on subjects as diverse as the interpretation of commercial contracts, anti-assignment clauses and Islamic finance) or which has been brought into the regulatory spotlight in this period, such as the regulation of gatekeepers (particularly securities analysts and Credit Rating Agencies), short selling, crowdfunding, credit default derivatives and securitisation. The book has also been reorganised somewhat and contains two new chapters: chapter four which covers equity financing issues generally and brings together material which has been located in a number of different chapters in the first edition; and chapter twelve which deals with market misconduct and covers market abuse (previously covered in the chapter on secondary market regulation) as well as the new material on short selling regulation and a new section on high frequency and algorithmic trading. Other chapters, particularly seven and nine, have been internally reorganised to enable there to be greater focus on specific issues such as financial collateral, and the application of transfer techniques to loans and receivables. This book aims to state the law and major policy developments as at 1 May 2015.

As with the first edition, many of the issues discussed here have been shaped and developed by the Corporate Finance Law course which we teach in Oxford, and we would like to acknowledge and thank those alongside whom we have taught the course, and argued these points, especially Paul Davies, Ed Greene, Chris Hare, Jeremias Prassl and Richard Salter and the BCL/MJur/MLF classes who have taken the course. Special thanks are due to Chris Hale and Emma Watford for continuing to share their knowledge and expertise on Private Equity with us and with the students.

In writing this book we were assisted by a great many people, to whom we have a continuing debt, namely friends and colleagues in Oxford and beyond with whom we have continued to discuss corporate law and the issues arising out of this book, and we would like to acknowledge their advice and assistance. Particular thanks are due to Hugh Beale, Michael Bridge, Roy Goode, Niamh Moloney and Kristin van Zwieten. In preparing this second edition we have also been assisted by a number of excellent research assistants: Natalie Mrockova, Jenifer Varzaly, Elizabeth Howell and, in particular, Matteo Angelini, whose assistance was particularly invaluable. We would also like to thank Hart Publishing, and in particular Sinead Moloney and Ruth Massey (our really excellent copy editor), for overseeing the production of this book through its various stages with great care and skill.

Finally, we would like to thank our families for their unfailing patience and support during the writing of this book, and in particular to thank Robert and Nick (respectively) who have been sources of inspiration and encouragement and without whom this project could not have been completed. This second edition, like the first edition, is dedicated to them.

Louise Gullifer and Jennifer Payne
Oxford, July 2015

Handwritten notes at top:
2 Finance Options: Debt.
7: Proprietary
8: Debt Securities (372)
9: Transferred Debt

SUMMARY TABLE OF CONTENTS   15 ·

Preface and Acknowledgements..v
Detailed Table of Contents ix
List of Abbreviations...xxv
List of Common Texts..xxix
Table of Cases xxxi
Table of Legislation..lv

1. Introduction...1
2. Overview of Financing Options...8
3. The Relationship Between Equity and Debt..59
4. Issuing Shares...124
5. Legal Capital..146
6. Creditor Protection: Contractual..191
7. Creditor Protection: Proprietary..264
8. Multiple Lenders...360
9. Transferred Debt...423
10. Public Offers of Shares 473
11. Ongoing Regulation of the Capital Markets: Mandatory Disclosure 523
12. Ongoing Regulation of the Capital Markets: Market Misconduct...........578
13. Regulation of Debt..634
14. Takeovers..677
15. Schemes of Arrangement 729
16. Private Equity...764

Index 805

DETAILED TABLE OF CONTENTS

Preface and Acknowledgements.. v
Summary Table of Contents... vii
List of Abbreviations.. xxv
List of Common Texts.. xxix
Table of Cases... xxxi
Table of Legislation.. lv

1. **Introduction**.. 1

2. **Overview of Financing Options**.. 8
  2.1 Introduction... 8
  2.2 Equity Financing.. 8
      2.2.1 Different Types of Shares 10
            2.2.1.1 Ordinary Shares.. 11
            2.2.1.2 Preference Shares.. 13
      2.2.2 Sources of Equity Finance 14
  2.3 Debt Financing.. 19
      2.3.1 General.. 19
            2.3.1.1 Sources of Debt Finance... 19
            2.3.1.2 Choice of Debt Financing Transaction...................................... 20
            2.3.1.3 Protection of Creditors: Contractual and Proprietary 22
            2.3.1.4 Protection of Creditors: Regulation 25
            2.3.1.5 Multiple Lenders and Transfer of Debt 27
      2.3.2 Loans 28
            2.3.2.1 Bank Loans.. 28
            2.3.2.2 Multiple Lenders... 30
            2.3.2.3 Peer-to-Peer Lending.. 31
      2.3.3 Debt Securities.. 32
            2.3.3.1 General.. 32
            2.3.3.2 Securities versus Loan 33
            2.3.3.3 Who Issues Bonds? 35
            2.3.3.4 Debt Securities versus Equity... 36
            2.3.3.5 Varieties of Bonds... 36
      2.3.4 Finance Based on Assets.. 40
            2.3.4.1 Receivables Financing... 40
            2.3.4.2 Supply Chain Financing.. 42
            2.3.4.3 Asset-Based Lending... 42
            2.3.4.4 Devices Based on Retention of Title.. 43
                  2.3.4.4.1 Sale and Leaseback 44
                  2.3.4.4.2 Asset Finance 44
                  2.3.4.4.3 Stock Finance... 46
                  2.3.4.4.4 Sales on Retention of Title Terms................................ 46

 2.3.5 Specialised Forms of Finance 47
  2.3.5.1 Project Finance 47
  2.3.5.2 Financing of Group Companies 47
  2.3.5.3 Trade Finance 48
  2.3.5.4 Islamic Finance 48
 2.4 Hybrids 49
 2.5 Retained Profits 52
 2.6 The Debt/Equity Mix 55
 2.7 Conclusion 58

3. The Relationship Between Equity and Debt 59
 3.1 Introduction 59
 3.2 The Relationship Between Equity and Debt in a Solvent Company 61
  3.2.1 Position of Shareholders in a Solvent Company 62
   3.2.1.1 Ordinary Shares 63
    3.2.1.1.1 Rights to Capital 63
    3.2.1.1.2 Rights to Income 63
    3.2.1.1.3 Voting Rights 64
    3.2.1.1.4 Summary 65
   3.2.1.2 Preference Shares 66
    3.2.1.2.1 Rights to Capital 66
    3.2.1.2.2 Rights to Income 67
    3.2.1.2.3 Voting Rights 67
    3.2.1.2.4 Summary 68
   3.2.1.3 Role of Shareholders in a Solvent Company 69
    3.2.1.3.1 Section 172 of the Companies Act 2006 69
    3.2.1.3.2 Explaining the Pre-Eminence of Shareholders 70
    3.2.1.3.3 The Corporate Governance Role of Shareholders 77
  3.2.2 Position of the Creditors in a Solvent Company 78
   3.2.2.1 Non-Adjusting Creditors 80
   3.2.2.2 Risks to Creditors from the Operation of a Solvent Company 82
   3.2.2.3 Restrictions on the Company's Activities 84
   3.2.2.4 The Corporate Governance Role of Debt 86
    3.2.2.4.1 Debt Covenants 87
    3.2.2.4.2 Monitoring by Lenders 88
    3.2.2.4.3 Lender Influence on Breach 88
    3.2.2.4.4 Lenders as Directors? 91
    3.2.2.4.5 Is Lender Governance Efficient? 92
    3.2.2.4.6 Effect of Transfer of Risk by Lenders 93
    3.2.2.4.7 The Twilight Period before Insolvency 94
 3.3 The Relationship Between Debt and Equity in an Insolvent Company 95
  3.3.1 Order of Payment Out on a Winding Up or Distribution by
   an Administrator 97
   3.3.1.1 Holders of Proprietary Claims 98
   3.3.1.2 Order of Priority 99
    3.3.1.2.1 Liquidation or Administration Expenses 100
    3.3.1.2.2 Preferential Creditors 101
    3.3.1.2.3 The Prescribed Part 101
    3.3.1.2.4 General Unsecured Creditors 102
    3.3.1.2.5 The Shareholders 102

  3.3.2 Preservation of the Assets for Creditors on and During the Run-up
     to Insolvency 105
    3.3.2.1 Preventing Reduction of the Asset Pool 106
      3.3.2.1.1 Statutory Provisions 106
      3.3.2.1.2 The Anti-Deprivation Principle 107
    3.3.2.2 Preventing Uneven Distribution of the Assets.................................... 110
    3.3.2.3 Potential Overlap Between the Prevention of Reduction of the
      Asset Pool and the Prevention of Uneven Distribution of Assets.................. 111
    3.3.2.4 Protection of Creditors 113
  3.3.3 The Balance Between Creditors and Shareholders in an Insolvent Company 114
    3.3.3.1 Directors' Duties.. 114
    3.3.3.2 Lifting the Veil Between the Creditors and the Shareholders................ 116
      3.3.3.2.1 Common Law Mechanisms 116
      3.3.3.2.2 Statutory Mechanisms: Sections 213 and 214
         Insolvency Act 1986... 118
 3.4 Conclusion 122

4. Issuing Shares... 124
 4.1 Introduction... 124
 4.2 Shareholder Protection when Shares are Issued.. 124
  4.2.1 The Need for Shareholder Protection... 124
    4.2.1.1 Dilution of Existing Shareholders' Interests..................................... 125
    4.2.1.2 Misuse by the Directors of the Power to Issue New Shares................ 126
  4.2.2 Existing Company Law Mechanisms that Operate to Protect Shareholders 126
    4.2.2.1 Directors' Duties.. 126
    4.2.2.2 Minority Shareholder Protection 128
  4.2.3 Justification for Additional Protection in Relation to Share Issues........... 129
 4.3 Directors' Authority to Allot Shares.. 131
 4.4 Pre-Emption Rights... 132
  4.4.1 Scope of Pre-Emption Rights... 133
  4.4.2 Renounceable Letters of Allotment 135
  4.4.3 Waiver of Pre-Emption Rights 136
  4.4.4 Is the Current Balance Correct as Between Shareholder Protection and
    the Company's Capital-Raising Needs? 138
 4.5 Registration of Shares.. 139
 4.6 Methods of Holding Shares... 140
  4.6.1 Certificated Shares 140
  4.6.2 Uncertificated (Dematerialised) Shares... 141
  4.6.3 Bearer Shares.. 142
  4.6.4 Shares Held Through an Intermediary... 142
 4.7 Transfer of Shares.. 144
 4.8 Conclusion 145

5. Legal Capital... 146
 5.1 Introduction... 146
 5.2 Function of the Legal Capital Rules... 146
  5.2.1 Conflict Between Shareholders and Creditors 147
  5.2.2 Policy Response to the Conflict 148
  5.2.3 The UK's Legal Capital Regime.. 150

5.3 Rules Regulating the Amount of Money Paid In by Shareholders 151
    5.3.1 Entry Price for Limited Liability: Minimum Capital Rules........................... 151
    5.3.2 Measurement of Consideration: Payment for Shares 153
        5.3.2.1 Shares must have a Par Value 153
        5.3.2.2 'No Issue at a Discount' Rule........................... 155
            5.3.2.2.1 Cash Consideration........................... 155
            5.3.2.2.2 Non-Cash Consideration........................... 156
        5.3.2.3 Consequences of a Breach of the Provisions........................... 157
        5.3.2.4 Efficacy of the Rules as a Form of Shareholder Protection 160
        5.3.2.5 Efficacy of the Rules as a Form of Creditor Protection 161
5.4 Maintenance of Capital 162
    5.4.1 Dividend Payments........................... 163
        5.4.1.1 Potential Benefits of Dividend Payments........................... 163
        5.4.1.2 Constraints on Dividend Payments........................... 163
    5.4.2 Repurchases and Redemptions of Shares 165
        5.4.2.1 Potential Benefits of Repurchases and Redemptions of Shares 165
        5.4.2.2 Repurchases of Shares 166
            5.4.2.2.1 Rules Applicable to All Companies 166
            5.4.2.2.2 Additional Flexibility for Private Companies 167
        5.4.2.3 Redemption of Shares 169
    5.4.3 Reductions of Capital 170
        5.4.3.1 Potential Benefits of a Reduction of Capital 170
        5.4.3.2 Court Approval Route Available to All Companies........................... 171
        5.4.3.3 Solvency Statement Mechanism for Private Companies........................... 172
    5.4.4 Prohibition on Financial Assistance 173
    5.4.5 Efficacy of the Rules as a Form of Creditor Protection 176
5.5 Alternatives to the Legal Capital Rules 178
    5.5.1 Creditor Protection via Contract........................... 178
    5.5.2 Creditor Protection via Insolvency Law 180
    5.5.3 Solvency Statement Approach........................... 183
        5.5.3.1 The Test of Solvency........................... 184
        5.5.3.2 Liability of the Directors........................... 186
        5.5.3.3 Recovery of Unlawful Payments........................... 188
        5.5.3.4 Potential for Reform........................... 189
5.6 Conclusion 190

6. Creditor Protection: Contractual........................... 191
6.1 Introduction........................... 191
6.2 Interpretation of Commercial Contracts 192
    6.2.1 Introduction........................... 192
    6.2.2 Basic Principle........................... 192
    6.2.3 The Meaning of Words........................... 193
    6.2.4 Implication of Terms........................... 194
6.3 Contractual Rights Against the Borrower 195
    6.3.1 Restrictions on the Borrower's Activities........................... 197
        6.3.1.1 Restrictions on Borrowing........................... 197
        6.3.1.2 Restrictions on Asset Disposal........................... 197
        6.3.1.3 Restrictions on Dividend Payments........................... 198
        6.3.1.4 Change of Control Covenants 199
        6.3.1.5 Debt Buybacks........................... 200

6.3.1.6 Negative Pledge Clause.. 200

    6.3.1.6.1 Forms of Negative Pledge Clause 202

    6.3.1.6.2 Enforcement of Restrictive Covenants............................ 202

6.3.2 Rights to Information and Financial Covenants........................... 206

    6.3.2.1 Rights at the Time of Making the Loan............................... 207

    6.3.2.2 Ongoing Rights.. 209

6.3.3 Termination and Acceleration Rights 213

    6.3.3.1 Events of Default 214

    6.3.3.2 Effect of Wrongful Acceleration.. 215

    6.3.3.3 Validity of Acceleration Clauses.. 215

6.3.4 Set-Off.. 218

    6.3.4.1 Use of Set-Off and Flawed Asset Structures in Lending...... 219

    6.3.4.2 Independent Set-Off... 221

    6.3.4.3 Transaction Set-Off 221

    6.3.4.4 Banker's Right to Combine Accounts................................. 222

    6.3.4.5 Contractual Set-Off and Exclusion of Set-Off.................... 223

    6.3.4.6 Insolvency Set-Off... 226

        6.3.4.6.1 The Limits and Operation of Insolvency Set-Off............ 226

        6.3.4.6.2 The Mandatory and Exclusive Nature of
              Insolvency Set-Off... 227

        6.3.4.6.3 Policy Justifications for Insolvency Set-Off.................... 231

6.4 Contractual Rights Against Third Parties... 233

6.4.1 Guarantees, Indemnities and Performance Bonds 235

    6.4.1.1 Introduction 235

    6.4.1.2 Important Distinctions 236

    6.4.1.3 Guarantees 238

        6.4.1.3.1 Protection of the Third Party: Construction
              of the Guarantee.. 238

        6.4.1.3.2 Protection of the Third Party: Disclosure 238

        6.4.1.3.3 Protection of the Third Party: Discharge of
              the Third Party 239

        6.4.1.3.4 Protection of the Third Party: Third Party's
              Rights Against the Principal Debtor.............................. 241

    6.4.1.4 Indemnity and Performance Bond...................................... 241

6.4.2 Credit Insurance 245

6.4.3 Derivatives and Credit Default Swaps 247

    6.4.3.1 Management of Risk by the Use of Derivatives 247

    6.4.3.2 Credit Default Swaps.. 248

    6.4.3.3 Are Credit Default Swaps Insurance? 249

    6.4.3.4 Regulation of CDSs 252

6.4.4 Subordination 254

    6.4.4.1 Types of Subordination.. 256

        6.4.4.1.1 Turnover Trust... 256

        6.4.4.1.2 Contingent Debt... 260

        6.4.4.1.3 Contractual Subordination.. 260

        6.4.4.1.4 Structural Subordination... 262

6.5 Conclusion 263

7. Creditor Protection: Proprietary.. 264
  7.1 Introduction... 264
    7.1.1 Purpose of Obtaining Proprietary Rights 265
    7.1.2 Absolute Interests.. 267
    7.1.3 Distinctions in Relation to a Company's Assets.......................... 267
  7.2 Absolute and Security Interests... 270
    7.2.1 What is a Security Interest? 270
    7.2.2 Characterisation of Interests as Absolute or Security Interests...... 272
    7.2.3 Reasons for Choosing a Structure Based on an Absolute or
        a Security Interest 274
    7.2.4 Policy Considerations.. 276
    7.2.5 Process of Characterisation in Relation to Particular Structures...... 277
        7.2.5.1 Grant and Grant-Back... 278
        7.2.5.2 Grant 278
        7.2.5.3 Retention of Title.. 280
        7.2.5.4 Quistclose Trusts.. 281
  7.3 Types of Security Interest 282
    7.3.1 Introduction.. 282
    7.3.2 Non-Possessory Security Interests 283
        7.3.2.1 Security Over Future Property... 283
        7.3.2.2 Mortgage 286
        7.3.2.3 Charge 287
        7.3.2.4 Security Interest Over Lender's Own Indebtedness............ 288
    7.3.3 The Floating Charge 288
        7.3.3.1 Introduction 288
        7.3.3.2 Crystallisation.. 290
        7.3.3.3 Distinction Between Fixed and Floating Charges............. 295
            7.3.3.3.1 Introduction 295
            7.3.3.3.2 Defining Features of Fixed Charges and
                    Floating Charges... 295
            7.3.3.3.3 Methodology of Characterising a Charge as
                    Fixed or Floating 302
            7.3.3.3.4 Should Floating Charges be Treated Differently? 302
        7.3.3.4 The Future of the Floating Charge 308
    7.3.4 Security Financial Collateral Arrangements 310
        7.3.4.1 Introduction 310
        7.3.4.2 Current English Law.. 312
        7.3.4.3 Registration.. 315
  7.4 Registration and Priorities 316
    7.4.1 The Requirement of Registration 316
    7.4.2 The Registration Process 317
    7.4.3 The Effect of Registration 318
        7.4.3.1 Consequences of Failure to Register.................................. 318
        7.4.3.2 Registration as Notice... 319
    7.4.4 Priorities... 320
  7.5 Enforcement.. 326
    7.5.1 Methods of Enforcement: Security Interests................................ 329
        7.5.1.1 Foreclosure... 329
        7.5.1.2 Appropriation of Financial Collateral.............................. 329
        7.5.1.3 Possession and Sale... 330
        7.5.1.4 Appointment of a Receiver 331

7.5.2 Methods of Enforcement: Absolute Interests 334
    7.5.2.1 Devices Based on Retention of Title 334
    7.5.2.2 Devices Based on the Grant of an Absolute Interest 336
7.5.3 The Effect of Administration 336
7.6 Economic Arguments Concerning Secured Credit 338
  7.6.1 Means of Assessing a System of Secured Credit 339
  7.6.2 The Puzzle of Secured Credit 340
    7.6.2.1 Monitoring 340
    7.6.2.2 Signalling 342
    7.6.2.3 Non-Adjusting Creditors 342
7.7 Reform 347
  7.7.1 Attributes of an Ideal Law 348
  7.7.2 Unsatisfactory Aspects of English Law 349
  7.7.3 Options for Reform 350
  7.7.4 Outline of Notice Filing Scheme 351
    7.7.4.1 Functional Approach 351
    7.7.4.2 Registration 352
    7.7.4.3 Priorities 353
    7.7.4.4 Enforcement 355
  7.7.5 Assessment of Reform 356
7.8 Conclusion 359

8. Multiple Lenders 360
8.1 Introduction 360
8.2 Basic Concepts 362
  8.2.1 Trust 362
    8.2.1.1 Introduction 362
    8.2.1.2 Use of the Trust in Commercial Transactions 363
    8.2.1.3 The Three Certainties 365
      8.2.1.3.1 Certainty of Intention to Create a trust 365
      8.2.1.3.2 Certainty of Objects 365
      8.2.1.3.3 Certainty of Subject Matter 366
      8.2.1.3.4 Equitable Nature of an Interest Under a Trust 370
  8.2.2 Agency 371
8.3 Issue of Debt Securities 372
  8.3.1 Attracting Lenders 372
  8.3.2 Structure of Securities Issue 375
    8.3.2.1 Difference Between Bonds and Stock 375
    8.3.2.2 Stock 377
      8.3.2.2.1 Debt Owed to a Trustee 377
      8.3.2.2.2 Debt Contained in a Deed Poll 379
    8.3.2.3 Eurobonds 379
      8.3.2.3.1 Advantages and Disadvantages of the Trustee Structure 380
      8.3.2.3.2 Subject Matter of the Trust 383
      8.3.2.3.3 Bond Issue Without Trustee 390
  8.3.3 Ascertaining the Views of Holders 391
    8.3.3.1 The Decision-Making Process 391
    8.3.3.2 Protection of the Minority 392
    8.3.3.3 Schemes of Arrangement 394

        8.3.4 Trustees' Obligations 396
            8.3.4.1 Introduction 396
            8.3.4.2 The Functions of a Trustee... 396
                8.3.4.2.1 Modifications to the Terms of the Securities or
                           Trust Deed.. 396
                8.3.4.2.2 Receiving Information from the Issuer 397
                8.3.4.2.3 Taking Action on Event of Default 398
        8.3.5 Excluding Trustees' Duties 403
            8.3.5.1 Forms of Exclusion Clauses 403
            8.3.5.2 Contractual Construction of Clauses.................................... 405
            8.3.5.3 Unfair Contract Terms Act... 407
            8.3.5.4 Public Policy: Common Law Constraints 407
            8.3.5.5 Public Policy: Legislative Constraints? 410
            8.3.5.6 Conclusion.. 410
    8.4 Syndicated Loans 411
        8.4.1 Comparison Between Agency in Syndicated Loans and
              Trustee Structure in Bond Issues 411
        8.4.2 Finding Lenders 414
        8.4.3 Role of the Arranger 414
        8.4.4 Liability of the Arranger in Relation to False Statements in
              the Information Memorandum... 417
        8.4.5 Position of the Agent Bank... 420
        8.4.6 Majority Lenders.. 421
    8.5 Conclusion 422

9. Transferred Debt... 423
    9.1 Why is Debt Transferred? 423
    9.2 Methods of Transfer.. 426
        9.2.1 Novation... 427
        9.2.2 Assignment... 428
            9.2.2.1 Introduction 428
            9.2.2.2 Statutory Assignments 429
            9.2.2.3 Significance of Notice to the Debtor 430
            9.2.2.4 Equitable Assignment... 430
            9.2.2.5 Assignment of Equitable Interests 433
            9.2.2.6 Clauses Prohibiting Assignment... 434
                9.2.2.6.1 Introduction 434
                9.2.2.6.2 Construction of the Clause...................................... 434
                9.2.2.6.3 Where the 'Assignor' has been Paid by the Debtor 435
                9.2.2.6.4 Where the 'Assignor' has not been Paid by the Debtor.... 436
                9.2.2.6.5 Declaration of Trust 437
        9.2.3 Negotiable Instruments... 443
        9.2.4 Transfer of Loans 445
            9.2.4.1 Introduction 445
            9.2.4.2 The Use of Novation 446
                9.2.4.2.1 Consent in Advance... 446
                9.2.4.2.2 Restrictions on Transfer 447
                9.2.4.2.3 Consent not Unreasonably Withheld....................... 448
                9.2.4.2.4 Security for the Loan.. 449
                9.2.4.2.5 Novation Subject to Equities?.................................. 450

9.2.4.3 The Use of Assignment 450
9.2.5 Transfer of Receivables 452
9.2.5.1 The Use of Assignment in Receivables Financing 452
9.2.5.2 Anti-Assignment Clauses and Receivables Financing 453
9.2.5.3 Statutory Override of Anti-Assignment Clauses 454
9.2.6 Transfer of Securities 455
9.2.6.1 Transfer of Stock 456
9.2.6.2 Transfer of Intermediated Securities 457
9.2.6.3 Transfers via CREST 461
9.3 Structures which have a Similar Effect to Transfer 463
9.3.1 Sub-Participation 463
9.3.2 Credit Derivatives 466
9.3.3 Securitisation 467
9.4 Conclusion 472

10. Public Offers of Shares 473
10.1 Introduction 473
10.2 Why do Companies Go Public? 473
10.2.1 Advantages of Going Public 473
10.2.1.1 Opportunity to Raise Equity Finance from a Broader Range
of Investors 474
10.2.1.2 Providing an Exit for Existing Shareholders 474
10.2.1.3 Increased Flexibility and Value Attached to the Shares in
a Publicly Traded Company 475
10.2.1.4 Corporate Governance Improvements 476
10.2.1.5 Prestige 477
10.2.2 Disadvantages of Going Public 477
10.2.3 Summary 478
10.3 The Process of Going Public 478
10.3.1 Only Public Companies Can Offer their Shares to the Public 479
10.3.2 An Offer to the Public 479
10.3.2.1 Offer for Sale or Subscription 479
10.3.2.2 Placing 480
10.3.3 Admission to Listing or to Trading on a Public Market 481
10.3.3.1 Choice of UK Markets 482
10.3.3.2 Choice of International Markets 483
10.4 The Theory of Regulation of Public Offers 485
10.4.1 Objectives of Regulation 485
10.4.2 The Need for Regulation 486
10.4.3 Regulatory Strategies 488
10.4.3.1 Governance Strategies 488
10.4.3.2 Affiliation Strategies 489
10.4.3.3 Mandatory Disclosure 489
10.5 Regulation of Public Offers in the UK: Ex Ante Protection via
Mandatory Disclosure 493
10.5.1 Regulatory Structure 493
10.5.2 Mandatory Disclosure in the UK 494
10.5.2.1 Meaning of 'An Offer of Securities to the Public' 495
10.5.2.2 Form and Content of a Prospectus 496

10.6   Regulation of Public Offers in the UK: Enforcement of the
     Mandatory Disclosure Regime 499
     10.6.1   The Aims of Enforcement.. 500
          10.6.1.1   Encouraging the Accurate and Timely Disclosure
               of Information 500
          10.6.1.2   Providing Compensation to those who Suffer Loss................... 503
     10.6.2   Private Enforcement: Liability for Defective Prospectuses.................... 504
          10.6.2.1   Nature of the Claim Under Section 90 FSMA........................... 505
          10.6.2.2   Who can Claim?.. 508
          10.6.2.3   Who may be Liable?.. 510
          10.6.2.4   Remedy... 511
               10.6.2.4.1   Financial Compensation.................................. 512
               10.6.2.4.2   Rescission.. 514
          10.6.2.5   Summary... 515
     10.6.3   Public Enforcement.. 515
          10.6.3.1   Criminal Sanctions.. 515
          10.6.3.2   Administrative Sanctions.. 516
     10.6.4   Intensity of Enforcement 517
          10.6.4.1   Public Enforcement 517
          10.6.4.2   Private Enforcement 518
10.7   Regulation of Equity Crowdfunding.. 519
10.8   Conclusion... 521

11. **Ongoing Regulation of the Capital Markets: Mandatory Disclosure** 523
11.1   Introduction 523
11.2   Objectives of Regulating the Secondary Market.. 524
     11.2.1   Promoting an Efficient Market Price... 524
          11.2.1.1   Efficient Capital Markets Hypothesis 524
          11.2.1.2   Role of Mandatory Disclosure in Promoting
               Market Efficiency 527
     11.2.2   Promoting Corporate Governance.. 529
          11.2.2.1   Individual Investors 533
               11.2.2.1.1   Role of Individual Investors 533
               11.2.2.1.2   Effect of Intermediation 533
          11.2.2.2   Institutional Investors... 535
               11.2.2.2.1   Role of Institutional Investors........................... 535
               11.2.2.2.2   Encouraging Engagement by Institutional
                        Investors.. 538
               11.2.2.2.3   UK Stewardship Code.................................... 539
          11.2.2.3   Role of Mandatory Disclosure in Promoting
               Corporate Governance 539
          11.2.2.4   Summary... 540
11.3   Mandatory Disclosure in the Secondary Market.. 541
     11.3.1   Periodic Disclosures 542
          11.3.1.1   Annual Reports 542
               11.3.1.1.1   Obligation to Produce Annual Reports
                        and Accounts.. 542
               11.3.1.1.2   Directors' Report and Strategic Report................. 544
               11.3.1.1.3   Corporate Governance Statement........................ 546
          11.3.1.2   Half Yearly Reporting 546
          11.3.1.3   Function of Periodic Disclosures 547

11.3.2 Ad Hoc Disclosures 548
    11.3.2.1 Inside Information 548
    11.3.2.2 Disclosure of Directors' Shareholdings 551
    11.3.2.3 Disclosure of Major Shareholdings 552
    11.3.2.4 Disclosures Required by the Listing Rules 555
    11.3.2.5 Function of Ad Hoc Disclosures 557
11.4 Enforcement of Secondary Market Disclosure Obligations 558
    11.4.1 Private Enforcement 558
        11.4.1.1 Enforcement by Shareholders of Misstatements in
               Governance-Based Disclosures 558
        11.4.1.2 Enforcement by Shareholders and Other Investors of
               Misstatements in Investor-Focused Disclosures 560
            11.4.1.2.1 Background 560
            11.4.1.2.2 Scope of the Section 90A FSMA Provisions 562
            11.4.1.2.3 Comparison of Section 90A FSMA and
                    Section 90 FSMA 566
            11.4.1.2.4 Assessment of Section 90A FSMA 567
    11.4.2 Public Enforcement 569
        11.4.2.1 The FCA 569
        11.4.2.2 The Corporate Reporting Review 570
    11.4.3 Intensity of Enforcement 570
        11.4.3.1 Public Enforcement 571
        11.4.3.2 Private Enforcement 571
11.5 Regulation of Analysts 572
11.6 Conclusion 576

12. Ongoing Regulation of the Capital Markets: Market Misconduct 578
12.1 Introduction 578
12.2 The Regulation of Market Abuse 578
    12.2.1 Justifications for Regulating Market Abuse 579
        12.2.1.1 Justifications for Regulating Insider Dealing 579
            12.2.1.1.1 Relationship-Based Justifications vs
                    Market-Based Justifications 579
            12.2.1.1.2 Arguments Against the Regulation of
                    Insider Dealing 581
            12.2.1.1.3 Justifying the Market-Based Approach:
                    Enhancing Investor Confidence 582
        12.2.1.2 Justifications for Regulating Market Manipulation 584
    12.2.2 The Offences of Insider Dealing and Market Manipulation 586
        12.2.2.1 The Criminal Offence of Insider Dealing Under the
            Criminal Justice Act 1993 589
            12.2.2.1.1 Definition of an Insider 589
            12.2.2.1.2 Definition of Inside Information 590
            12.2.2.1.3 The Offence of Actual Dealing in Securities 592
            12.2.2.1.4 The Offence of Encouraging Another
                    Person to Deal 593
            12.2.2.1.5 The Offence of Disclosing Inside Information to
                    Another Person 593
            12.2.2.1.6 Penalties and Enforcement 593

12.2.2.2 The Criminal Offences of Market Manipulation Under
Sections 89–91 Financial Services Act 2012 595
12.2.2.2.1 Misleading Statements and Dishonest Concealment:
Section 89 Financial Services Act 2012 596
12.2.2.2.2 Misleading Impressions: Section 90 Financial
Services Act 2012 598
12.2.2.2.3 Misleading Statements etc in Relation to Benchmarks:
Section 91 Financial Services Act 2012 599
12.2.2.2.4 Penalties and Enforcement 600
12.2.2.3 The Regulatory Offence of Market Abuse Under
Section 118 FSMA 600
12.2.2.3.1 Insider Dealing 601
12.2.2.3.2 Market Manipulation 608
12.2.2.3.3 Levels of Enforcement Under Section 118 611
12.2.2.4 Private Enforcement of Market Abuse 613
12.2.2.5 Summary 616
12.3 The Regulation of Short Selling 616
12.3.1 Justifications for Regulating Short Selling 618
12.3.1.1 Short Selling Destabilises Orderly Markets 618
12.3.1.2 The Use of Short Selling to Manipulate Markets 620
12.3.1.3 Settlement Risk 621
12.3.2 Constraints Placed on Short Selling 622
12.3.2.1 Bans on Short Selling 623
12.3.2.2 Disclosure and Reporting Obligations 624
12.3.2.3 Circuit Breakers and Uptick Rules 626
12.3.2.4 Rules Designed to Mitigate Settlement Risk 627
12.3.2.5 The Role of National Authorities and ESMA 628
12.3.3 Summary 630
12.4 Algorithmic and High Frequency Trading 631
12.5 Conclusion 633

13. Regulation of Debt 634
13.1 Introduction 634
13.1.1 General Scope of Regulation 635
13.1.2 Methods of Regulation 637
13.1.3 Regulation by Disclosure Requirements 638
13.2 Regulation of Initial Issue of Debt Securities 641
13.2.1 Introduction 641
13.2.2 Factors Affecting the Disclosure Requirements 642
13.2.2.1 To whom the Securities are Offered 643
13.2.2.2 Trading on a Market 644
13.2.2.3 Denomination of Securities 645
13.2.2.4 Rationale of the Disclosure Regime 646
13.2.3 Information Required in a Prospectus 648
13.2.4 Disclosure Required for Listing on the PSM 650
13.2.5 Disclosure Requirements where Securities are not Listed 651
13.2.6 Restrictions on Financial Promotion 651

13.2.7 Enforcement of the Mandatory Disclosure Regime 653
    13.2.7.1 Claims Against the Issuer 653
    13.2.7.2 Claims Against Other Parties 654
13.2.8 Comparison of Protection by Regulation for Holders of Debt
    Securities and those Making Loans: Disclosure at the Initial Stage...................... 656
13.3 Ongoing Regulation by Disclosure.. 657
    13.3.1 Mandatory Ongoing Disclosure 657
    13.3.2 Enforcement of Ongoing Disclosure Requirements..................................... 659
    13.3.3 Comparison of Protection by Regulation for Holders of Debt
        Securities and those Making Loans: Ongoing Disclosure 660
13.4 Regulation of Market Misconduct 661
    13.4.1 Application of the Market Abuse Rules to the Debt
        Securities Markets 661
    13.4.2 Application of the Market Abuse Rules to the Making and
        Transfer of Loans... 663
    13.4.3 The Regulation of Short Selling.. 665
13.5 Accepting Deposits.. 666
13.6 Convertible Debt Securities... 667
13.7 Regulation of Credit Rating Agencies 668
13.8 Regulation of Peer-to-Peer Lending.. 671
13.9 Conclusion... 675

14. Takeovers 677
14.1 Introduction 677
    14.1.1 Objectives of the Takeover Regulation 678
    14.1.2 Comparative Aspects.. 680
14.2 The Regulatory Structure of Takeover Regulation in the UK............................... 681
    14.2.1 Historical Development... 682
    14.2.2 Implementation of the Takeover Directive 684
    14.2.3 Role and Status of the Takeover Panel.. 685
    14.2.4 Tactical Litigation 687
    14.2.5 Summary... 688
14.3 The Substance of Takeover Regulation in the UK 689
    14.3.1 The Procedure of a Bid... 689
        14.3.1.1 Initial Approach 689
        14.3.1.2 Formal Offer.. 690
        14.3.1.3 Squeeze-Out.. 693
        14.3.1.4 Sell-Out 694
        14.3.1.5 Further Offers 695
    14.3.2 Relationship Between the Target Directors and the Target Shareholders.............. 695
        14.3.2.1 Pre-Bid Defences 696
            14.3.2.1.1 Directors' duties 698
            14.3.2.1.2 Share Transfer Restrictions..................................... 700
            14.3.2.1.3 Removal of Directors and Staggered Boards 700
            14.3.2.1.4 The Role of Shareholders.. 702
            14.3.2.1.5 Summary 703
        14.3.2.2 Post-Bid Defences 704
            14.3.2.2.1 The No Frustration Principle 704
            14.3.2.2.2 Consequences of the UK's Adoption of the
                     No Frustration Principle... 708

14.3.3 Relationship Between the Target Directors and Other
Stakeholders in the Target..712
14.3.4 Relationship Between the Bidder and the Target Shareholders 716
14.3.4.1 Undistorted Choice...718
14.3.4.2 Protection of Minority Shareholders...............................722
14.3.4.2.1 Prevention of Oppression...........................723
14.3.4.2.2 An Exit Right..725
14.3.5 Relationship Between the Bidder Directors and Bidder Shareholders 726
14.4 Conclusion...727

15. Schemes of Arrangement 729
15.1 Introduction 729
15.2 The Mechanics of a Scheme of Arrangement.......................................730
15.2.1 Application to the Court for Meetings to be Summoned 730
15.2.2 Meeting(s) of the Members or Creditors 732
15.2.2.1 Who Needs to Consider the Scheme? 732
15.2.2.2 Separate Class Meetings: General....................................733
15.2.2.2.1 The General Test 734
15.2.2.2.2 Members' and Creditors' Rights.................735
15.2.2.2.3 Selecting the Correct Comparator 735
15.2.2.3 Separate Meetings for Shareholders.................................737
15.2.2.4 Separate Meetings for Creditors......................................738
15.2.2.5 Approval at the Class Meetings 741
15.2.2.5.1 The Majority in Value Requirement............741
15.2.2.5.2 The Majority in Number Requirement........741
15.2.3 The Sanction of the Court 743
15.2.3.1 Have the Statutory Provisions been Complied with?......744
15.2.3.2 Exercise of the Court's Discretion...................................745
15.2.3.3 Effect of the Scheme 746
15.3 Uses of Schemes of Arrangement..746
15.3.1 As an Alternative to a Takeover Offer 747
15.3.1.1 Advantages and Disadvantages of a Scheme rather
than a Takeover Offer to Effect a Change of Control..............748
15.3.1.2 Minority Protection in a Scheme 750
15.3.1.2.1 Concerns Regarding the Approval
Threshold for Schemes 751
15.3.1.2.2 Concerns Regarding the Bypassing of
Minority Protection in Takeover Offers....752
15.3.2 To Reorganise a Corporate Group..753
15.3.3 To Effect a Merger or Demerger 754
15.3.4 To Effect an Arrangement Between the Company and
its Creditors 757
15.3.4.1 Restructuring the Debts of Financially
Distressed Companies 758
15.3.4.2 Settling Claims within the Insurance Industry 761
15.4 Conclusion...763

16. Private Equity...764
16.1 Introduction 764
16.2 Historical Development...765

16.3 Private Equity Funds...768
  16.3.1 Structure of a Typical Private Equity Fund..768
  16.3.2 Sources of Funding for Private Equity Funds..771
  16.3.3 Why have Investors Wanted to Invest in Private Equity Funds? 772
16.4 Capital Structure of a Typical Private Equity Transaction......................................773
  16.4.1 Equity Financing 774
  16.4.2 Quasi-Equity...775
  16.4.3 Debt Financing 776
    16.4.3.1 Senior Debt 777
    16.4.3.2 Second Lien Debt..779
    16.4.3.3 Mezzanine Debt..779
16.5 Public-to-Private Transactions 780
  16.5.1 Financial Issues..781
  16.5.2 Recommendation by the Directors..782
  16.5.3 Equality Between Bidders 782
  16.5.4 Equality of Treatment of Shareholders 783
  16.5.5 Market Abuse...783
16.6 A Comparison of Private Equity Backed Companies and
      Non-Private Equity Backed Companies...784
  16.6.1 Ownership Structures 784
  16.6.2 Board/Management Structures..786
  16.6.3 Disclosure and Transparency..787
  16.6.4 Debt vs Equity Levels 788
    16.6.4.1 Employees 790
    16.6.4.2 Creditors..791
  16.6.5 Summary...793
16.7 Regulation..794
  16.7.1 The Need for Regulation 795
    16.7.1.1 Increased Transparency 795
    16.7.1.2 Systemic Risk...797
  16.7.2 The AIFMD..798
    16.7.2.1 Scope and Authorisation Requirements 798
    16.7.2.2 Regulation at the Fund Level...799
    16.7.2.3 Regulation at the Level of the Portfolio Company......................801
    16.7.2.4 Effect of the AIFMD on the Private Equity Industry..................802
16.8 Conclusion...803

Index 805

LIST OF ABBREVIATIONS

ABFA	Asset Based Finance Association
ABI	Association of British Insurers
ABS	Asset-Backed Securities
AGM	Annual General Meeting
AIF	Alternative Investment Fund
AIFM	Alternative Investment Fund Manager
AIFMD	Alternative Investment Fund Managers Directive 2011/61/EU
AIM	Alternative Investment Market
ASIC	Australian Securities and Investment Commission
BERR	Department for Business, Enterprise and Regulatory Reform (predecessor of BIS)
BIPRU	Prudential sourcebook for Banks, Building Societies and Investment Firms
BIS	Department for Business, Innovation and Skills
BVCA	British Venture Capital Association
CAMAC	Corporations and Markets Advisory Committee
CARD	Consolidated Admissions Requirements Directive
CASS	Client Assets Sourcebook
CCP	Central Counterparty
CDS	Credit Default Swap
CJEU	Court of Justice of the European Union (previously the ECJ)
CLR	Company Law Review
CMBOR	Centre for Management Buy-Out Research
COBS	Conduct of Business Sourcebook
CoCo	Contingent Convertible Securities
CRA	Credit Rating Agency
CRD	Capital Requirements Directive
CRR	Capital Requirements Regulation
CSD	Central Securities Depository
CVL	Creditors' Voluntary Liquidation
D&O	Directors and Officers
DISP	Dispute Resolution: Complaints Sourcebook
DTI	Department of Trade and Industry (predecessor of BIS)
DTR	Disclosure and Transparency Rules
EBITDA	Earnings Before Interest, Taxes, Depreciation and Amortisation
ECJ	European Court of Justice (now the CJEU)
ECLE	European Company Law Experts
ECMH	Efficient Capital Markets Hypothesis

EEA	European Economic Area
EMIR	European Markets Infrastructure Regulation (Regulation (EU) No 648/2012)
ESMA	European Securities and Market Authority
EU	European Union
EUI	Euroclear UK and Ireland Ltd
EURIBOR	Euro Interbank Offered Rate
EVCA	European Venture Capital Association
FCA	Financial Conduct Authority
FCARs	Financial Collateral Arrangements (No 2) Regulations (SI 2003/3226) as amended
FCD	Financial Collateral Directive 2002/47/EC as amended
FINMAR	Financial Stability and Market Confidence Sourcebook
FLA	Finance and Leasing Association
FRC	Financial Reporting Council
FRS	Financial Reporting Standard
FSA	Financial Services Authority (predecessor of the FCA)
FSB	Financial Stability Board
FSMA	Financial Services and Markets Act 2000
FUND	Investment Funds Sourcebook
GAAP	Generally Accepted Accounting Principles
GEFIM	Gilt-Edged and Fixed Interest Market
GENPRU	General Prudential Sourcebook
HFT	High Frequency Trading
IAS	International Accounting Standards
ICAEW	Institute of Chartered Accountants in England and Wales
ICAS	Institute of Chartered Accountants of Scotland
IFPRU	Prudential Sourcebook for Investment Firms
IFRS	International Financial Reporting Standards
IMA	Investment Management Association
INSPRU	Prudential Sourcebook for Insurers
IOSCO	International Organization of Securities Commissions
IPO	Initial Public Offering
ISDA	International Swaps and Derivatives Association
ISDX	ICAP Securities and Derivatives Exchange
LBO	Leveraged Buy-Out
LIBOR	London Interbank Offered Rate
LMA	Loan Market Association
LR	Listing Rules
LSE	London Stock Exchange
MAC	Material Adverse Change
MAR	Market Conduct Sourcebook
MBO	Management Buy-Out
MiFID	Markets in Financial Instruments Directive 2004/39/EC
MiFID II	Markets in Financial Instruments Directive 2014/65/EU

MiFIR	Markets in Financial Instruments Regulation (Regulation EU No 600/2014)
MTF	Multilateral Trading Facility
NAPF	National Association of Pension Funds
OFT	Office of Fair Trading
ORB	Online Retail Bond
OTC	Over the Counter
OTF	Organised Trading Facility
PERG	Perimeter Guidance Manual
PMSI	Purchase Money Security Interest
PPSA	Personal Property Security Act
PR	Prospectus Rules
PRA	Prudential Regulation Authority
PSM	Professional Securities Market
RBS	Royal Bank of Scotland
RINGA	Relevant Information Not Generally Available
RIS	Regulated Information Service
ROT	Retention of Title
SEC	Securities and Exchange Commission
SME	Small and Medium-Sized Enterprises
SPV	Special Purpose Vehicle
SSAP	Statements of Standard Accounting Practice
SUP	Supervision Manual
UCC	Uniform Commercial Code
UKLA	UK Listing Authority
USR	Uncertificated Securities Regulations 2001 (SI 2001/3755) as amended

LIST OF COMMON TEXTS

Andrews and Millett: Guarantees	G Andrews and R Millett, *Law of Guarantees*, 6th edn (London, Sweet & Maxwell, 2011)
Bamford: Financial Law	C Bamford, *Principles of International Financial Law*, 2nd edn (Oxford, Oxford University Press, 2015)
Benjamin: Financial Law	J Benjamin, *Financial Law* (Oxford, Oxford University Press, 2007)
Benjamin: Interests in Securities	J Benjamin, *Interests in Securities* (Oxford, Oxford University Press, 2000)
Chitty	H Beale (ed), *Chitty on Contracts*, 31st edn (London, Sweet & Maxwell, 2012)
Derham: Set-Off	R Derham, *The Law of Set-Off*, 4th edn (Oxford, Oxford University Press, 2010)
Encyclopaedia of Banking Law	P Cresswell, W Blair, G Hill and P Wood (eds), *Encyclopaedia of Banking Law* (London, LexisNexis Butterworths, 2014)
Fuller: Capital Markets	G Fuller, *The Law and Practice of International Capital Markets*, 3rd edn (London, LexisNexis Butterworths, 2012)
Fuller: Corporate Borrowing	G Fuller, *Corporate Borrowing: Law and Practice*, 4th edn (Bristol, Jordan Publishing Ltd, 2009)
Goode: Commercial Law	E McKendrick (ed), *Goode on Commercial Law*, 4th edn (London, LexisNexis UK, 2009)
Goode: Corporate Insolvency	R Goode, *Principles of Corporate Insolvency Law*, 4th edn (London, Sweet & Maxwell, 2011)
Goode: Credit and Security	L Gullifer (ed), *Goode on Legal Problems of Credit and Security*, 5th edn (London, Sweet & Maxwell, 2013)
Gower and Davies	P Davies and S Worthington (eds), *Gower and Davies: Principles of Modern Company Law*, 9th edn (London, Sweet & Maxwell, 2012)

Hudson: Finance

A Hudson, *The Law of Finance*, 2nd edn (London, Sweet & Maxwell, 2013)

Hughes: Banking

M Hughes, *Legal Principles in Banking and Structured Finance*, 2nd edn (Hayward's Heath, Tottel Publishing Ltd, 2006)

Law of Personal Property

M Bridge, L Gullifer, G McMeel and S Worthington, *The Law of Personal Property* (London, Sweet & Maxwell, 2013)

Mokal: Insolvency Law

R Mokal, *Corporate Insolvency Law: Theory and Applications* (Oxford, Oxford University Press, 2005)

Moloney: EU Regulation

N Moloney, *EU Securities and Financial Markets Regulation*, 3rd edn (Oxford, Oxford University Press, 2014)

Mugasha: Multi-Bank Financing

A Mugasha, *The Law of Multi-Bank Financing* (New York, Oxford University Press, 2007)

Paget

A Malek and J Odgers (eds), *Paget's Law of Banking*, 14th edn (London, LexisNexis UK, 2014)

Security and Title-Based Financing

H Beale, M Bridge, L Gullifer and E Lomnicka, *The Law of Security and Title-Based Financing*, 2nd edn (Oxford, Oxford University Press, 2012)

Smith and Leslie: Assignment

M Smith and N Leslie, *The Law of Assignment*, 2nd edn (Oxford, Oxford University Press, 2013)

Tennekoon: International Finance

R Tennekoon, *The Law and Regulation of International Finance* (London, Butterworths, 1991)

Tolhurst: Assignment

G Tolhurst, *The Assignment of Contractual Rights* (Oxford, Hart Publishing, 2006)

Treitel

E Peel (ed), *Treitel on the Law of Contract*, 13th edn (London, Sweet & Maxwell, 2011).

Valdez: Financial Markets

S Valdez, *An Introduction to Global Financial Markets*, 7th edn (Basingstoke, Palgrave Macmillan, 2013)

Wood: Loans and Bonds

P Wood, *International Loans, Bonds, Guarantees, Legal Opinions*, 2nd edn (London, Sweet & Maxwell, 2007)

Wood: Project Finance

P Wood, *Project Finance, Securitisations, Subordinated Debt*, 2nd edn (London, Sweet & Maxwell, 2007)

Wood: Set-Off and Netting

P Wood, *Set-Off and Netting, Derivatives and Clearing Systems* (London, Sweet & Maxwell, 2007)

TABLE OF CASES

United Kingdom

Abbey National Building Society v Cann [1991] 1 AC 56 (HL) 323
ABM AMRO Commercial Finance plc v McGinn [2014] EWHC 1674 (Comm) 242, 244
Actionstrength Ltd v International Glass Engineering IN.GL.EN SpA
    [2003] UKHL 17 237
Adams v Cape Industries plc [1990] Ch 433 (CA (Civ Div)) 117
AG of Belize v Belize Telecom Ltd [2009] UKPC 10 .... 10, 194
AG of Hong Kong v Nai-Keung [1987] 1 WLR 1339 (PC) 268
AG Securities v Vaughan [1990] 1 AC 417 (HL) 301
AG's Reference (No 1 of 1988) [1989] AC 971 (HL) 589, 590
Agnew v Commissioner of Inland Revenue (sub nom Brumark
    Investments Ltd, Re) [2001] UKPC 28 .... 252, 273, 295–300, 302
Agra and Masterman's Bank, Re (1866–67) LR 2 Ch App 391 457
Aiolos, The. *See* Central Insurance Co Ltd v Seacalf Shipping Corp
Airbase (UK) Ltd, Re: Thorniley v Revenue and Customs Commissioners
    [2008] EWHC 124 (Ch) 102
Aktieselskabet Dansk Skibsfinansiering v Brothers [2001] 2 BCLC 324 119
Alabama, New Orleans, Texas & Pacific Junction Rly Co, Re [1891]
    1 Ch 213 (CA) 739, 744, 745
Albazero, The. *See* Owners of Cargo Laden on Board the Albacruz v
    Owners of the Albazero
Aldrich v Norwich Union Life Insurance Co Ltd [1998] CLC 1621 (Ch D) 600
Allen v Gold Reefs of West Africa Ltd [1900] 1 Ch 656 (CA) 10, 63, 72, 74, 392, 538, 707, 757
Allen v Hyatt (1914) 30 TLR 444 616
Al-Nakib Investments (Jersey) Ltd v Longcroft [1990] 1 WLR 1390 509
American Express International Banking Corp v Hurley [1985] 3 All ER 564 .... 330, 332
Andrews v Mockford [1896] 1 QB 372 (CA) 509
Angelic Star, The. *See* Oresundsvarvet AB v Lemos
Anglia Television Ltd v Reed [1972] 1 QB 60 (CA) 512
Anglo American Insurance Co Ltd, Re [2001] 1 BCLC 755 .... 734, 737, 744, 758
Anglo Continental Supply Co Ltd, Re [1922] 2 Ch 723 744
Antaios Compania Naviera SA v Salen Rederierna AB [1985] AC 191 (HL) 193
Antaios, The. *See* Antaios Compania Naviera SA v Salen Rederierna AB
Apcoa Parking Holdings GmbH, Re [2014] EWHC 3849 (Ch) 743
Argo Fund Ltd, The v Essar Ltd [2005] EWHC 600 (Comm); aff'd
    [2006] EWCA Civ 241 .... 446–48, 451
Armitage v Nurse [1998] Ch 241 (CA) 364, 406–09
Armour v Thyssen Edelstahlwerke AG [1991] 2 AC 339 (HL) 271
Armstrong DLW GmbH v Winnington Networks Ltd [2012] EWHC 10 (Ch) 268
Arnold v Britton [2015] UKSC 36 193
Arthur D Little Ltd (In Administration) v Ableco Finance LLC [2002] EWHC 701 (Ch) 298
Ashborder BV v Green Gas Power Ltd [2004] EWHC 1517 (Ch) 198, 289, 324

Ashby v Blackwell (1765) 2 Eden 299 145
Ashpurton Estates Ltd, Re [1983] Ch 110 (CA) 317, 318
Assénagon Asset Management SA v Irish Bank Resolution Corp Ltd
    [2012] EWHC 2090 (Ch) 392–94, 740
Associated British Ports v Ferryways NV [2009] EWCA Civ 189 242
Associated Picture Houses Ltd v Wednesbury Corp [1948] 1 KB 223 (CA) 400
Astec (BSR) plc, Re [1998] 2 BCLC 556 .... 53, 723
Atlantic Computer Systems Ltd, Re [1992] Ch 505 (CA (Civ Div)) 298, 337, 338
Atlantic Medical Ltd, Re [1993] BCLC 386 298
Atwool v Merryweather (1867–68) LR 5 Eq 464 531
Augustus Barnett & Son Ltd, Re [1986] BCLC 170 119
Automatic Self-Cleaning Filter Syndicate Co Ltd v Cuninghame
    [1906] 2 Ch 34 (CA) 77, 696
Aveling Barford Ltd v Perion Ltd [1989] 1 WLR 360 .... 163, 188
Ayerst (Inspector of Taxes) v C & K (Construction) Ltd [1976] AC 167 (HL) 115
Azevedo v IMCOPA [2012] EWHC 1849 (Comm); [2013] EWCA Civ 364 .... 394, 399
Azur Gaz, The. *See* SHV Gas Supply & Trading SAS v Naftomar Shipping
    and Trading Co Ltd Inc
Bairstow v Queens Moat Houses plc [2001] EWCA Civ 712 187
Baker v Clark & Co (Transport) UK Ltd [2006] EWCA Civ 464 407
Bamford v Bamford [1970] Ch 212 (CA (Civ Div)) 127
Bank of Credit and Commerce International SA (No 3), Re [1993]
    BCLC 1490 (CA (Civ Div)) 758
Bank of Credit and Commerce International SA (No 8), Re [1996]
    Ch 245 (CA (Civ Div)) 219, 220, 227, 229, 288
Bank of Ireland v AMCD (Property Holdings) Ltd [2001]
    2 All ER (Comm) 894 29
Banque des Marchands de Moscou (Koupetschesky) v Kindersley
    [1951] Ch 112 (CA) 743
Barbados Trust Co Ltd v Bank of Zambia [2007] EWCA Civ 148 .... 435, 437–42, 451, 452
Barclays Bank Ltd v Quistclose Investments Ltd [1970] AC 567 (HL) 81, 281
Barclays Bank plc v British & Commonwealth Holdings plc [1995] BCC 19 162
Barclays Bank plc v HHY Luxembourg SARL [2010] EWCA Civ 1248 194
Barclays Bank plc v Kingston [2006] EWHC 533 (QB) 238, 240
Barclays Bank plc v Svizera Holdings BV [2014] EWHC 1020 (Comm) 415, 420
Barclays Bank plc v Unicredit Bank AG [2012] EWHC 3655 (Comm);
    [2014] EWCA Civ 302 .... 449, 471
Barleycorn Enterprises, Re [1970] Ch 465 (CA (Civ Div)) 100
Barnicoat v Knight [2004] EWHC 330 (Ch) 464 237
Barron v Potter [1914] 1 Ch 895 77
Bartlett v Barclays Bank Trust Co Ltd (No 2) [1980] Ch 515 .... 364, 403, 404
BAT Industries plc, Re (unreported, 3 September 1998) 743, 745
Bear Stearns Bank plc v Forum Global Equity Ltd [2007]
    EWHC 1576 (Comm) 445, 449
Belmont Finance Corp v Williams Furniture Ltd (No 2) [1980]
    1 All ER 393 (CA (Civ Div)) 175
Belmont Park Investments Pty Ltd v BNY Corporate Trustee Services Ltd
    [2011] UKSC 38 .... 107–10, 112, 217–20, 228
Bexhill UK Ltd v Abdul Razzaq [2012] EWCA Civ 1376 432
BG Global Energy Ltd v Talisman Sinopec Energy UK Ltd [2015] EWHC 110 (Comm) 449

Biggerstaff v Rowatt's Wharf Ltd [1896] 2 Ch 93 (CA) 325
Birch v Cropper (1889) LR 14 App Cas 525 (HL).................................63, 66, 67, 73, 102
Birmingham Citizens Permanent Building Society v Caunt [1962] Ch 883 330
Blakely Ornance Co, Re (1867) 3 Ch App 154.. 457
Blest v Brown, 45 ER 1225, (1862) 4 De GF & J 367 238
Blue Arrow plc, Re [1987] BCLC 585.. 724
Bluebrook Ltd, Re [2009] EWHC 2114 (Ch) 732, 733, 745, 760, 761
Bluecrest Mercantile BV; FMS Wertmanagement AÖR v
    Vietnam Shipbuilding Industry Group [2013] EWHC 1146 (Comm) 759
BNP Paribas v Wockhardt EU Operations (Swiss) AG [2009]
    EWHC 3116 (Comm)... 217
BNP Paribas SA v Yukos Oil Co [2005] EWHC 1321 (Ch) 215, 216, 401
BNY Corporate Trustee Services Ltd v Eurosail-UK 2007-3bl plc
    [2013] UKSC 28 ....61, 96, 184
Boardman v Phipps [1967] 2 AC 46 (HL) 364
BOC Group plc v Centeon LLC [1999] 1 All ER (Comm) 53 .... 225, 457
Bogg v Raper (The Times, 22 April 1998) 408
Bond v Barrow Haematite Steel Co [1902] 1 Ch 353.................13, 64, 67, 775, 792
Borax Co, Re [1901] 1 Ch 326 (CA) 289, 324
Borden (UK) Ltd v Scottish Timber Products Ltd [1981]
    Ch 25 (CA (Civ Div)) 46
Borland's Trustee v Steel Bros & Co Ltd [1901] 1 Ch 279 ....71, 108, 230
Bournemouth and Boscombe Athletic Football Club v Lloyds TSB
    Bank plc [2003] EWCA Civ 1755.. 401
Bradbury v English Sewing Cotton Co Ltd [1923] AC 744 (HL)............................... 71, 159
Bradford Third Equitable Benefit Building Society v Borders
    [1940] Ch 202 (CA).. 506, 509
Bradford Investments plc (No 1), Re [1990] BCC 740 68
Bradford Investments plc (No 2), Re [1991] BCC 379 157
Bradford Old Bank Ltd v Sutcliffe [1918] 2 KB 833 (CA) 222
Brady v Brady [1989] AC 755 (HL) 175
Brailey v Rhodesia Consolidated Ltd [1910] 2 Ch 95 756
Bratton Seymour Service Co Ltd v Oxborough [1992] BCC 471 .... 10, 72
Bray v Ford [1896] AC 44 (HL)... 364
Brice v Bannister (1878) 3 QBD 569 (CA) 430, 432, 436
Bridge v Campbell Discount Co Ltd [1962] AC 600 (HL) 217, 334
Briggs, Ex p (1866) LR 1 Eq 483... 514
Brightlife Ltd, Re [1987] Ch 200 290
Bristol Airport plc v Powdrill [1990] Ch 744 282
Bristol Groundschool Ltd v Intelligent Data Capture Ltd [2014]
    EWHC 2145 (Ch) 195
British American Nickel Corp Ltd v MJ O'Brien Ltd [1927] AC 369 (PC) 392, 757
British and American Trustee and Finance Corp v Couper [1894] AC 399 (HL)............... 63
British and Commonwealth Holdings plc (No 3), Re [1992]
    1 WLR 672 (Ch D)... 736
British Aviation Insurance Co Ltd, Re [2005] EWHC 1621 (Ch) 736, 740, 741, 744–46, 762
British Eagle International Air Lines Ltd v Compagnie Nationale
    Air France [1975] 1 WLR 758 (HL)...110, 228, 229, 256
British Gas Trading Ltd v Eastern Electricity plc [1996] EWCA Civ 1239........................ 449
Brogden, Re (1888) 38 Ch D 546 364

Bryan Court Ltd v National Westminster Bank plc [2012] EWHC 2035 (QB) 209
BSB Holdings Ltd, Re [1996] 1 BCLC 155 129
BTR plc, Re [1999] 2 BCLC 675; (leave to appeal) [2000]
    1 BCLC 740 (CA (Civ Div)) 735, 738, 745, 751
Buchler v Talbot [2004] UKHL 9 100
Bugle Press Ltd, Re [1961] Ch 270 (CA) 694
Bushell v Faith [1970] AC 1099 (HL) 13, 77
Business Computers Ltd v Anglo-African Leasing Ltd [1977] 1 WLR 578 .... 325, 436, 438
Buttle v Saunders [1950] 2 All ER 193 364
Camdex International Ltd v Bank of Zambia (No 1) [1998]
    QB 22 (CA (Civ Div)) 429
Campbell v Rofe [1933] AC 91 (PC) 63
Canada Inc v Financial Services Authority [2013] EWCA Civ 1662 .... 600, 609
Caparo Industries plc v Dickman [1990] 2 AC 605 (HL) 159, 507, 509,
                                                            530, 542, 547, 557–59, 561, 565, 691
Cape plc, Re [2006] EWHC 1316 (Ch) 745
Carey Group plc v AIB Group (UK) plc [2011] EWHC 567 (Ch) 447, 448
Carey Value Added SL v Grupo Urvasco SA [2010] EWHC 1905 (Comm) 242, 244
Cargill International SA v Bangladesh Sugar and Food Industries Corp
    [1998] 1 WLR 461 (CA (Civ Div)) 245
Carlill v Carbolic Smoke Ball Co [1893] 1 QB 256 (CA) 446
Carlton Communications plc v Football League [2002] EWHC 1650 (Comm) 237
Carlton Holdings Ltd, Re [1971] 1 WLR 918 (Ch D) 694
Carman v Bucci [2014] EWCA Civ 383 .... 61, 96
Carney v Herbert [1985] AC 301 (PC) 175
Carreras Rothmans Ltd v Freeman Mathews Treasure Ltd (In Liquidation)
    [1985] Ch 207 287
Cassa di Risparmio della Repubblica di San Marino SpA v Barclays
    Bank Ltd [2011] EWHC 484 (Comm) 194, 248, 420
Castle Holdco 4 Ltd, Re [2009] EWHC 1347 (Ch) 386, 395, 742
Caterpillar (NI) Ltd (Formerly Known as) FG Wilson (Engineering)
    Ltd v John Holt & Co (Liverpool) Ltd [2013] EWCA Civ 1232 280
Cator v Croydon Canal Co (1841) 4 Y & C Ex 405 .... 431, 434
Celestial Aviation Trading 71 Ltd v Paramount Airways Private Ltd
    [2010] EWHC 185 (Comm) 335, 336
Central Insurance Co Ltd v Seacalf Shipping Corp (The Aiolos)
    [1983] 2 Lloyd's Rep 25 (CA (Civ Div)) 432
Centre Reinsurance International Co v Curzon Insurance Ltd [2006] UKHL 45 337
Chaligne v Financial Services Authority [2012] All ER (D) 153 (Sep) 611
Chandler v Cape plc [2012] EWCA Civ 525 118
Chapman v Barclays Bank plc [1997] 6 Bank LR 315 (CA (Civ Div)) 29
Charge Card Services Ltd (No 2), Re [1987] Ch 150 288
Charles v Jones (1887) 35 Ch D 544 .... 276, 328
Chartbrook Ltd v Persimmon Homes Ltd [2009] UKHL 38 .... 193, 194
Charterhouse Capital Ltd, Re [2014] EWHC 1410 (Ch) 74
Chase Manhattan Equities Ltd v Goodman [1991] BCLC 897 615
Chaston v SWP Group plc [2002] EWCA Civ 1999 .... 174, 706
Chatterton v Maclean [1951] 1 All ER 761 237
Cheah Theam Swee v Equiticorp Finance Group Ltd [1992] 1 AC 472 (PC) 255, 321, 327
Chelsea and Walham Green Building Society v Armstrong [1951] 1 Ch 853 379

Cherry Tree Investments Ltd v Landmain Ltd [2012] EWCA Civ 736..194
Chez Nico (Restaurants) Ltd, Re [1992] BCLC 192 694
China & South Seas Bank Ltd v Tan [1990] 1 AC 536 (PC) 327
Chow Yoong Hong v Choong Fah Rubber Manufactory [1962] AC 209 (PC)..................................274
Chrysovalandou-Dyo, The. *See* Santiren Shipping Ltd v Unimarine SA
CIMC Raffles Offshore (Singapore) Ltd v Schahin Holding SA
   [2013] EWCA Civ 644 ....240, 244
Cine Bes Filmcilik ve Yapimcilik AS v United International Pictures
   [2003] EWCA Civ 1669 216
Citco Banking Corp NV v Pusser's Ltd [2007] UKPC 13 ....10, 74
Citibank NA v MBIA Assurance SA [2006] EWHC 3215 (Ch)..409
City and County Investment Co, Re (1879) 13 Ch D 475 (CA)...756
Clark v Cutland [2003] EWCA Civ 810 78
Clark v Urquhart [1930] AC 28, (1929) 34 Ll L Rep 359 (HL)..512, 513
Cleve v Financial Corp (1873) LR 16 Eq 363..756
Clinch v Financial Corp (1868–69) LR 5 Eq 450 756
Close Invoice Finance Ltd v Watts [2009] EWCA Civ 1182...245
Clough Mill Ltd v Martin [1985] 1 WLR 111 (CA (Civ Div)) 46, 271, 280
Coal Consumers Association, Re (1876) LR 4 Ch D 625 325
Coca-Cola Financial Corp v Finsat International Ltd (The Ira)
   [1998] QB 43 (CA (Civ Div))..225
Cochrane v Green (1860) 9 CB (NS) 448 222
Collins v Associated Greyhound Racecourse Ltd [1930] 1 Ch 1 (CA)..514
Collyer v Isaacs (1881) 19 Ch D 342 285
Colombiana, The. *See* Compania Colombiana de Seguros v
   Pacific Steam Navigation Co
Colonial Trusts Corp, ex p Bradshaw, Re (1879) 15 Ch D 465 292
Colt Telecom Group plc, Re [2002] EWHC 2815 (Ch)...402, 403
Commercial Union Assurance Co Ltd v TG Tickler Ltd (unreported,
   4 March 1959) 197
Compania Colombiana de Seguros v Pacific Steam Navigation Co
   (The Colombiana) [1965] 1 QB 101...434
Compania de Electricidad de la Provincia de Buenes Aires Ltd, Re [1980] Ch 146 ....64, 737
Company, ex p Glossop, Re a [1988] 1 WLR 1068 67
Company No 001418 of 1988, Re a [1990] BCC 526 118
Company, Re a [1985] BCLC 333...117
Company, Re a[1986] BCLC 382..707
Company, Re a[1987] BCLC 82...67
Compaq Computer Ltd v Abercorn Group Ltd (t/a Osiris) [1993] BCLC 603 ....46, 280, 429
Concord Trust v Law Debenture Corp plc [2004] EWHC 1216 (Ch);
   [2004] EWCA Civ 1001[2005] UKHL 27 .... 215, 398–401, 405
Contex Drouzhba Ltd v Wiseman [2006] EWHC 2708 (QB) 115
Continental Assurance Co of London plc, Re [2001] BPIR 733..120
Co-Operative Bank plc, Re [2013] EWHC 4074 (Ch) 395
Co-operative Group Ltd v Birse Developments Ltd (In Liquidation)
   [2014] EWHC 530 (TCC) 441
Cornhill Insurance plc v Improvement Services Ltd [1986]
   1 WLR 114 (Ch D)..14
Coroin Ltd, Re [2013] EWCA Civ 781 129
Cortefiel SA, Re [2012] EWHC 2998 (Ch) 743

Cosslett (Contractors) Ltd, Re [1998] Ch 495 (CA (Civ Div))... 271, 282
County Leasing Ltd v East [2007] EWHC 2907 (QB) 216
Cox Moore v Peruvian Corp Ltd [1908] 1 Ch 604 324
Craythorne v Swinburne, 33 ER 482, (1807) 14 Ves 160.. 241
Crimpfil v Barclays Bank plc [1995] CLC 385 (CA (Civ Div))... 29
Criterion Properties plc v Stratford UK Properties LLC [2002]
    EWHC 496 (Ch); [2002] EWCA Civ 1883;[2004] UKHL 28 ....127, 699, 702
Cuckmere Brick Co v Mutual Finance [1971] Ch 949 (CA (Civ Div))............................... 329–31
Cukurova Finance International Ltd v Alfa Telecom Turkey Ltd
    [2009] UKPC 19.. 329, 330
Cumbrian Newspapers Group Ltd v Cumberland & Westmorland
    Herald Newspapers & Printing Co Ltd [1987] Ch 1 .... 11, 62
Cumming v Shand (1860) 5 Hurl & N 95 28
Cunliffe Brooks & Co v Blackburn and District Benefit Building Society
    (1884) LR 9 App Cas 857 (HL) 28
Cunliffe Engineering Ltd v English Industrial Estates Corp [1994] BCC 972.......................... 286, 325
Curtain Dream Ltd, Re [1990] BCLC 925 .... 278, 470
D&G Cars Ltd v Essex Police Authority [2015] EWHC 226 (QB) 195
Dadourian Group International Inc v Simms [2009] EWCA Civ 169.. 565
Daimler Co Ltd v Continental Tyre and Rubber Co (Great Britain) Ltd
    [1916] 2 AC 307 (HL)... 272
Dallas, Re [1904] 2 Ch 385 (CA).. 456
Danka Business Systems plc (In Liquidation), Re [2013] EWCA Civ 92 226
Davies v Humphreys (1840) 6 M & W 153.. 236
Dawson International plc v Coats Paton plc (No 2) [1991] BCC 276 708
Dearle v Hall (1828) 3 Russ 1 ....312, 318, 321, 322,
                                                                        324, 349, 378, 429, 430, 456
Denney v John Hudson & Co [1992] BCLC 901 (CA (Civ Div))... 107
Denton's Estate, Re [1904] 2 Ch 178 (CA) 246
Deposit Protection Board v Barclays Bank plc [1994] 2 AC 367 (HL)................................ 431, 432
Derry v Peek (1889) 14 App Cas 337 (HL)............................490, 504, 506, 510, 511, 563
Diana Prosperity, The. *See* Reardon Smith Line Ltd v Hansen-Tangen
Don King Productions Inc v Warren (No 1) [2000] Ch 291 (Ch D and
    CA (Civ Div)).. 435, 437, 439–42
Doosan Babcock Ltd v Comercializadora de Equipos y Materiales
    Mabe Limitada [2013] EWHC 3201 (TCC)... 245
Downsview Nominees Ltd v First City Corp Ltd [1993] AC 295 (PC)....................................... 330
Duke of Norfolk's Settlement Trusts, Re [1982] Ch 61 (CA (Civ Div))..................................... 406
Dunderland Iron Ore Co, Re [1909] 1 Ch 446 .... 377, 395
Dunlop Pneumatic Tyre Co Ltd v New Garage & Motor Co Ltd [1915] AC 79 (HL) 216
Dunlop Tyres Ltd v Blows [2001] EWCA Civ 1032.. 301
Durham Bros v Robertson [1898] 1 QB 765 (CA).. 431
DX Holdings Ltd, Re [2010] EWHC 1513 (Ch)... 740
Eastern Counties Building Society v Russell [1947] 2 All ER 734 (CA).................................... 238
Ebrahimi v Westbourne Galleries Ltd [1973] AC 360 (HL) 78
Eckerle v Wickeder Westfalenstahl GmbH [2013] EWHC 68 (Ch) 387, 534
Edelstein v Schuler & Co [1902] 2 KB 144 444
Edmonds v Blaina Furnaces Co (1887) 36 Ch D 215.. 636
Ehrmann Bros Ltd, Re [1906] 2 Ch 697 (CA) 318
EIC Services Ltd v Phipps [2004] EWCA Civ 1069.. 155

Elektrim SA v Vivendi Holdings 1 Corp [2008] EWCA Civ 1178 402
Elliott International LP v Law Debenture Trustees Ltd [2006] EWHC 3063 .... 395, 403
ELS Ltd, Re [1995] Ch 11 .... 292, 325
EM Bowden's Patents Syndicate Ltd v Herbert Smith & Co [1904] 2 Ch 86 431
English and Scottish Mercantile Investment Co Ltd v Brunton
  [1892] 2 QB 700 (CA) 320, 324
Enron Europe Ltd (In Administration) v Revenue and Customs
  Commissioners [2006] EWHC 824 (Ch) 223
Equitable Life Assurance Society (No 2), Re [2002] EWHC 140 (Ch) 732, 734, 745, 746
Equitable Life Assurance Society v Hyman [2002] 1 AC 408 (HL) 194
Equitas Ltd v Walsham Bros & Co Ltd [2013] EWHC 3264 (Comm) 221, 222
Essentially Different Ltd v Bank of Scotland plc [2011] EWHC 475 (Comm) 402
Eurymedon, The. *See* New Zealand Shipping Co Ltd v AM Satterthwaite & Co Ltd
Evans v Rival Granite Quarries Ltd [1910] 2 KB 979 (CA) 290–92, 325
Explora Group plc v Hesco Bastion Ltd [2005] EWCA Civ 646 .... 441, 442
Export Credits Guarantee Department v Universal Oil Products Co
  [1983] 1 WLR 399 (HL) 215
Expro International Group plc, Re [2008] EWHC 1543 (Ch) 514 .... 687, 748
Facia Footwear (In Administration) v Hinchcliffe [1998] 1 BCLC 218 115
Falkonera Shipping Co v Arcadia Energy Pte Ltd [2012] EWHC 3678
  (Comm) 449
Fanshaw v Amav Industries Ltd [2006] EWHC 486 (Ch) 301
Fanti, The. *See* Firma C-Trade SA v Newcastle Protection and Indemnity Association
Fashoff (UK) Ltd v Linton [2008] EWHC 537 (Ch) 337
Fattal v Walbrook Trustees (Jersey) Ltd [2010] EWHC 2767 (Ch) 408
Feakins v Department for Environment Food and Rural Affairs [2005]
  EWCA Civ 1513 112
Fearns v Anglo-Dutch Paint & Chemical Co Ltd [2010] EWHC 2366 (Ch) 221
Federal Commerce & Navigation Co Ltd v Molena Alpha Inc (The Nanfri)
  [1978] QB 927 (CA (Civ Div)) 221, 222
Financial Services Authority v Anderson (No 1) [2010] EWHC 599 (Ch) 667
Financing No 3 Ltd v Excalibur Funding No 1 plc, Re [2011] EWHC 2111 (Ch) 193, 194
Firma C-Trade SA v Newcastle Protection and Indemnity Association
  (The Fanti) [1991] 2 AC 1 (HL) 243
Fiske Nominees Ltd v Dwyka Diamonds Ltd [2002] EWHC 770 (Ch) 694
Fletcher v Fletcher (1844) 4 Hare 67 384
Fletcher v Royal Automobile Club Ltd [2000] 1 BCLC 331 (CA (Civ Div)) 746
Flitcroft's Case (1882) LR 21 Ch D 519 .... 165, 187, 188
Florence Land and Public Works Co, Re (1878) 10 Ch D 530 (CA) 289
Foley v Hill, 9 ER 1002, (1848) 2 HL Cas 28 288
Folgate London Market Ltd v Chaucer Insurance plc [2011] EWCA Civ 328 108
Fons HF (In Liquidation) v Corporal Ltd [2014] EWCA Civ 304 .... 404, 636, 637, 652
Forster v Wilson (1843) 12 M & W 191 232
Foskett v McKeown [2001] 1 AC 102 (HL) 370, 406
Foss v Harbottle (1843) 2 Hare 461 700
Foster v Foster [1916] 1 Ch 532 77
Four-Maids Ltd v Dudley Marshall (Properties) Ltd [1957] Ch 317 330
Fraser v Oystertec plc [2004] EWHC 1582 (Ch) 220
Fulham Football Club Ltd v Cabra Estates plc [1994] 1 BCLC 363 (CA (Civ Div)) 708
Fuller v Happy Shopper Markets Ltd [2001] 1 WLR 1681 221

G & T Earle Ltd v Hemsworth (1928) 44 TLR 605 320

Gallery Capital SA, Re (unreported, Ch D, 21 April 2010) 395

Galoo Ltd v Bright Grahame Murray [1994] 1 WLR 1360 (CA (Civ Div)) 558, 561, 691

Gan Insurance Co Ltd v Tai Ping Insurance Co Ltd (No 2)
   [2001] EWCA Civ 1047 .... 195, 448

Gardom, ex p (1808) 15 Ves 286 236

Geldof Metaalconstructie NV v Simon Carves Ltd [2010] EWCA Civ 667 222

General Motor Cab Co Ltd, Re [1913] 1 Ch 377 (CA) 747

General Produce Co Ltd v United Bank [1979] 2 Lloyd's Rep 255 .... 237, 241, 243

George Fischer (Great Britain) Ltd v Multi Construction Ltd [1995]
   1 BCLC 260 (CA (Civ Div)) 559

George Inglefield Ltd, Re [1933] Ch 1 (CA) 40, 271, 274, 279

Gerald Cooper (Chemicals) Ltd, Re [1978] Ch 262 119

GHLM Trading Ltd v Maroo [2012] EWHC 61 (Ch) 116

Gilbert Ash (Northern) Ltd v Modern Engineering (Bristol) Ltd
   [1974] AC 689 (HL) 225, 457

Gilford Motor Co Ltd v Horne [1933] Ch 935 (CA) 117

Glencore Grain Ltd v Agros Trading Co Ltd [1999] 2 All ER (Comm) 288 221

Global Distressed Alpha Fund 1 Ltd Partnership v PT Bakrie Investindo
   [2011] EWHC 256 (Comm) 379

Global Trader Europe Ltd (In Liquidation), Re [2009] EWHC 602 (Ch) 258

Goker v NWS Bank plc (unreported, 1 August 1990) 335

Gold Coast Ltd v Caja de Ahorros del Mediterraneo [2001] EWCA Civ 1806 .... 242, 243

Goldcorp Exchange Ltd (In Receivership), Re [1995] 1 AC 74 (PC) 366, 367

Goodfellow v Nelson Line (Liverpool) Ltd [1912] 2 Ch 324 392

Graham v Every [2014] EWCA Civ 191 129

Graiseley Properties Ltd v Barclays Bank plc [2013] EWCA Civ 1372 .... 428, 450

Gramsci Shipping Corp v Lembergs [2013] EWCA Civ 730 117

Gray v G-T-P Group Ltd (Re F2G Realisations Ltd) [2010]
   EWHC 1772 (Ch) 299, 312, 313, 315

Greatship (India) Ltd v Oceanografia SA de CV [2012] EWHC 3468 (Comm) 194

Greenclose Ltd v National Westminster Bank plc [2014] EWHC 1156 (Ch) 195, 249

Greenhalgh v Arderne Cinemas Ltd [1951] Ch 286 (CA) 392

Gregory Love & Co, Re [1916] 1 Ch 203 .... 204, 206

Grey v Inland Revenue Commissioners [1960] AC 1 (HL) 459

Grimstead (EA) & Son Ltd v McGarrigan [1999] EWCA Civ 3029 420

Grimthorpe, Re [1958] Ch 615 399

Grupo Hotelero Urvasco SA v Carey Value Added SL [2013] EWHC 1039 (Comm) 211

Guardian Assurance Co, Re [1917] 1 Ch 431 (AC) 747

Habibson's Bank Ltd v Standard Chartered Bank (Hong Kong) Ltd
   [2010] EWCA Civ 1335 446

Hackney Empire Ltd v Aviva Insurance UK Ltd [2012] EWCA Civ 1716 240

Halesowen Presswork and Assemblies Ltd v National Westminster
   Bank Ltd [1971] 1 QB 1 222

Hall v Cable & Wireless plc [2009] EWHC 1793 (Comm) 561, 613, 669

Hall v Royal Bank of Scotland plc [2009] EWHC 3163 (QB) 29

Halpern v Halpern [2007] EWCA Civ 291 49

Halt Garage (1964) Ltd, Re [1982] 3 All ER 1016 .... 162, 163, 188

Halton International Inc (Holdings) Sarl v Guernroy Ltd [2005]
   EWHC 1968 (Ch) 406

Hampton v Minns [2002] 1 WLR 1 (Ch D) 237
Hanak v Green [1958] 2 QB 9 (CA).. 222
Hannam v Financial Conduct Authority [2014] UKUT 233 (TCC)..........................549, 591,
600, 601, 605, 606
Harman v BML Group Ltd [1994] 1 WLR 893 (CA (Civ Div)) 62
Harmer v Armstrong [1934] Ch 65 (CA) 438
Harmony Care Homes, Re [2009] EWHC 1961 (Ch)... 301
Harvard Securities Ltd (In Liquidation), Re [1997] 2 BCLC 369................................... 368
Harvey (John Spencer) v Dunbar Assets plc [2013] EWCA Civ 952 238
Hawk Insurance Co Ltd, Re [2001] EWCA Civ 241 ....730, 731, 734, 736–39, 744
Hayim v Citibank NA [1987] AC 730 (PC) 387
Heald v O'Connor [1971] 1 WLR 497 (QBD) 241
Hedley Byrne & Co Ltd v Heller & Partners Ltd [1964]
AC 465 (HL)..417, 505, 507, 510–13, 654
Helby v Matthews [1895] AC 471 (HL)...274, 277, 323
Hellenic and General Trust Ltd, Re [1976] 1 WLR 123 (Ch D) 735, 738, 751
Helstan Securities Ltd v Hertfordshire CC [1978] 3 All ER 262 (QBD) 440
Henderson v Merret Syndicates Ltd (No 1) [1995] 2 AC 145 (HL) 415, 416
Hendy Lennox (Industrial Engines) Ltd v Grahame Puttick Ltd
[1984] 1 WLR 485 (QBD) 280
Henry v Hammond [1913] 2 KB 515.. 259
Heron International Ltd v Lord Grade [1983] BCLC 244 (CA (Civ Div)) 706
Hickman v Kent or Romney Marsh Sheepbreeders Association
[1915] 1 Ch 881 72
Hilger Analytical Ltd v Rank Precision Industries Ltd [1984] BCLC 301................... 225, 457
Hill v Spread Trustee Co Ltd [2006] EWCA Civ 542 112
Hirsche v Sims [1894] AC 654 (PC)...127, 158, 698
HLC Environmental Projects Ltd, Re [2013] EWHC 2876 (Ch)........................... 114–16, 120
Hogg v Cramphorn Ltd [1967] Ch 254 .... 127, 131
Holme v Brunskill (1878) 3 QBD 495 (CA) 239–42, 244
Holroyd v Marshall (1862) 10 HL Cas 191..283, 284, 428, 436, 453
Hong Kong and Shanghai Banking Corp v Kloeckner & Co AG
[1990] 2 QB 514... 225
Hooper v Western Counties and South Wales Telephone Co Ltd
(1892) 68 LT 78 37
Horsley & Weight Ltd, Re [1982] Ch 442 (CA (Civ Div)) 115
Houldsworth v Glasgow City Bank (1879-80) LR 5 App Cas 317 (HL) 72
House of Fraser plc v ACGE Investments Ltd [1987] AC 387 (HL)............................... 66
Howard Smith Ltd v Ampol Petroleum Ltd [1974] AC 821 (PC) 127, 131, 698, 699
Hunter v Moss [1994] 1 WLR 452 (CA (Civ Div)) 258, 367–69
Hunting plc, Re [2004] EWHC 2591 (Ch) 14
Hydrodan (Corby) Ltd (In Liquidation), Re [1994] 2 BCLC 180 119
Hyundai Heavy Industries Co Ltd v Papadopoulous [1980] 1 WLR 1129 (HL).............. 237
Ian Chisholm Textiles Ltd v Griffiths [1994] 2 BCLC 291 ....46, 280
IFE Fund SA v Goldman Sachs International [2007] EWCA Civ 811........................ 418, 419
IG Index Ltd v Ehrentreu [2013] EWCA Civ 95... 457
IIG Capital LLC v Van Der Merwe [2008] EWCA Civ 542 .... 242, 244
ILG Travel Ltd (In Administration), Re [1995] 2 BCLC 128 259
In A Flap Envelope Co Ltd, Re [2003] EWHC 3047 (Ch) 186
Ind Coope & Co Ltd, Re [1911] 2 Ch 223.. 324

Inland Revenue Commissioners v Broadway Cottages Trust [1955] Ch 20 (CA) 365
Innovative Logistics Ltd (In Administration) v Sunberry Properties Ltd
   [2008] EWCA Civ 1321 337
Insurance and Financial Consultants Ltd, Re [2014] EWHC 2206 (Ch) 78
Interfoto Picture Library Ltd v Stiletto Visual Programmes Ltd [1989]
   QB 433 (CA (Civ Div)) 195
Internet Broadcasting Corp Ltd v MAR LLC [2009] EWHC 844 (Ch) 405
Investment Dar Co KSCC v Blom Developments Bank Sal [2009]
   EWHC 3545 (Ch) 49
Investors Compensation Scheme Ltd v West Bromwich Building Society
   (No 1) [1998] 1 WLR 896 (HL) 192, 193, 238
Ira, The. *See* Coca-Cola Financial Corp v Finsat International Ltd
Irvine v Irvine [2006] EWHC 406 (Ch) 67
It's A Wrap (UK) Ltd (In Liquidation) v Gula [2006] EWCA Civ 544 .... 164, 188
Jackson v Dear [2012] EWHC 2060 (Ch) 193
Jackson & Bassford Ltd, Re [1906] 2 Ch 467 .... 204, 206
Jacobs v Batavia and General Plantations Trust Ltd [1924] 2 Ch 329 (CA) 505
Jafari-Fini v Skillglass Ltd (In Administration) [2007] EWCA Civ 261 401
James Miller & Partners Ltd v Whitworth Street Estates (Manchester) Ltd
   [1970] AC 583 (HL) 193, 273, 301
Jeancharm Ltd v Barnet Football Club Ltd [2003] EWCA Civ 58 216
Jessel Trust Ltd, Re [1985] BCLC 119 731
Jetivia SA v Bilta (UK) Ltd (In Liquidation) [2015] UKSC 23 119
Jobson v Palmer [1893] 1 Ch 71 364
John Crowther Group Ltd v Carpets International [1990] BCLC 460 708
John Dee Group Ltd v WMH (21) Ltd [1998] BCC 972 (CA (Civ Div)) 230
John Smith's Tadcaster Brewery Co, Re [1963] Ch 308 128
Johns, Re [1928] Ch 737 217
Johnson v Gore Wood & Co (No 1) [2002] 2 AC 1 ....103, 159, 559
Jones v Farrell (1857) 1 De G & J 208 432
Jones v Lipman [1962] 1 WLR 832 (Ch D) 117
Joseph Holt plc, Re [2001] EWCA Civ 770 693
JP Morgan Chase Bank (formerly Chase Manhattan Bank) v
   Springwell Navigation Corp. *See* Springwell Navigation Corp v
   JP Morgan Chase Bank (formerly Chase Manhattan Bank)
Kapoor v National Westminster Bank [2011] EWCA Civ 1083 .... 432, 433
Karberg's Case [1892] 3 Ch D 1 514
Kaupthing Singer and Friedlander Ltd (In Administration), Re [2009]
   EWHC 740 (Ch) 225, 457, 462
Kayford Ltd (In Liquidation), Re [1975] 1 WLR 279 (Ch D) 81, 259, 365
Keenan Bros Ltd, Re [1986] BCLC 242 299
Kelly v Cooper [1993] AC 205 (PC) 406
Kensington International Ltd v Congo [2005] EWHC 2684 (Comm) 117
Kidner, Re [1929] 2 Ch 121 64
Kilnoore Ltd (In Liquidation) Unidare plc v Cohen [2005] EWHC 1410 (Ch) 145
King's Trust, Re (1892) 29 LR Ir 401 108
Kinlan v Crimmin [2006] EWHC 779 (Ch) 167
Kinloch Damph Ltd v Nordvik Salmon Farms Ltd (1999) Outer House Case, 30 June 1999 280
Kirby v Wilkins [1929] 2 Ch 444 140
Knight v Knight (1840) 3 Beav 148 365

Knightsbridge Estates Trust Ltd v Byrne [1940] AC 613 (HL) 636
Kudos Catering (UK) Ltd v Manchester Central Convention Complex
    Ltd [2013] EWCA Civ 38 405
Kuwait Asia Bank EC v National Mutual Life Nominees Ltd
    [1991] 1 AC 187 (PC) 91
Lagunas Nitrate Co Ltd v Schroeder & Co and Schmidt (1901) 85 LT 22 64
Langston Group Corp v Cardiff City Football Club Ltd [2008]
    EWHC 535 (Ch) 450
Law Debenture Trust Corp plc v Acciona SA [2004] EWHC 270 (Ch) 400, 401
Law Debenture Trust Corp plc v Concord Trust [2007] EWHC 1380 (Ch) 392
LB Re Financing No 3 Ltd (In Administration) v Excalibur
    Funding No 1 plc [2011] EWHC 2111 (Ch) 255
Lehman Bros International (Europe) (In Administration),
    Re [2009] EWHC 2545 (Ch) 258, 259, 369, 388
Lehman Bros International (Europe) (In Administration),
    Re [2009] EWCA Civ 1161 .... 318, 739, 746, 747
Lehman Bros International (Europe) (In Administration),
    Re [2010] EWHC 2914 (Ch) 143, 258, 369, 370
Lehman Bros International (Europe) (In Administration),
    Re [2011] EWCA Civ 1544 .... 369, 370
Lehman Bros International (Europe) (In Administration),
    Re [2010] EWCA Civ 917 .... 258, 369
Lehman Bros International (Europe) (In Administration),
    Re [2012] UKSC 6 .... 258, 370
Lehman Bros International (Europe) (In Administration),
    Re [2012] EWHC 2997 (Ch) 143, 220, 270, 311–14, 387, 459
Lehman Bros International (Europe) (In Administration),
    Re [2014] EWHC 704 (Ch) 102, 255, 261
Lemon v Austin Friars Investment Trust Ltd [1926] Ch 1 (CA) 636
Levison v Farin [1978] 2 All ER 1149 212
Levy v Abercorris Slate and Slab Co (1887) 37 Ch D 260 636
Lewis's of Leicester Ltd, Re [1995] BCC 514 259
Liberty Mutual Co (UK) Ltd v HSBC Bank plc [2002] EWCA Civ 691 238
Lind, Re [1915] 2 Ch 345 (CA) 284, 285
Linden Gardens Trust Ltd v Lenesta Sludge Disposal Ltd [1994] 1 AC 85 (HL) 434, 435
Lloyds & Scottish Finance v Cyril Lord Carpets Sales Ltd [1992] BCLC 609 (HL) 279
Lloyds Bank plc v Lampert [1999] 1 All ER (Comm) 161 (CA (Civ Div)) 29
Lloyds TSB Bank plc v Clarke [2002] UKPC 27 464
LNOC Ltd v Watford Association Football Club Ltd [2013] EWHC 3615 (Comm) 69, 698
Lomas v JFB Firth Rixson [2010] EWHC 3372 (Ch) 109, 249
Lomas v JFB Firth Rixson [2012] EWCA Civ 419 .... 107, 109, 219, 220
London Wine Co (Shippers) Ltd, Re [1986] PCC 121 .... 366, 367, 369
Lordsvale Finance plc v Bank of Zambia [1996] QB 752 .... 216, 217
Lovegrove, Re [1935] Ch 464 (CA) 279
Lowry (Inspector of Taxes) v Consolidated African Selection Trust Ltd
    [1940] AC 648 (HL) 158
MacJordan Construction Ltd v Brookmount Erostin Ltd [1994]
    CLC 581 (CA (Civ Div)) 258
Mackay, ex p (1873) LR 8 Ch App 643 217
MacPherson v European Strategic Bureau Ltd [2000] 2 BCLC 683 (CA (Civ Div)) 188

Madoff Securities International Ltd (In Liquidation) v Raven [2013]
    EWHC 3147 (Comm)..69
Magyar Telecom BV, Re [2013] EWHC 3800 (Ch) 743
Maidstone Building Provisions, Re [1971] 1 WLR 1085 Ch D) 118
Mair v Rio Grande Rubber Estates Ltd [1913] AC 853 (HL)..514
Makdessi v Cavendish Square Holdings BV [2013] EWCA Civ 1539 215–17
Mangles v Dixon (1852) 3 HL Cas 702..444
Manifest Shipping Co Ltd v Uni-Polaris Insurance Co Ltd (The Star Sea)
    [2001] UKHL 1 119
Manisty's Settlement, Re [1974] Ch 17..398
Mann Group plc, Re [2012] EWHC 4089 (Ch)..753
Manser v Dix (1857) 8 De GM & G 703 328
Marconi Corp plc v Marconi plc [2003] EWHC 663 (Ch)..744
Marconi, Re [2013] EWHC 324 (Ch) 395
Martinson v Clowes (1882) 21 Ch D 857 329
Marubeni Hong Kong and South China Ltd v Mongolia
    [2004] EWHC 472 (Comm)... 243, 244
Masri (Munib) v Consolidated Contractors International Co SAL
    [2007] EWHC 3010 (Comm)..439
Massey (David) v Financial Services Authority [2011] UKUT 49 (TCC) 606, 607
Maxwell Communications Corp plc (No 2), Re [1993]
    1 WLR 1402 (Ch D)..230, 260, 261
MBNA Europe Bank Ltd v Revenue and Customs Commissioners
    [2006] EWHC 2326 (Ch) 38, 467–70
MC Bacon Ltd (No 1), Re [1990] BCLC 324 (Ch D)... 112, 113
MC Bacon Ltd (No 2), Re [1991] Ch 127..100, 106
McConnel v Wright [1903] 1 Ch 546 (CA) 512
McEntire v Crossley Bros Ltd [1895] AC 457 (HL) 271, 274, 277, 280
McGuiness v Norwich and Peterborough Building Society [2011] EWCA Civ 1286 237
McHugh v Union Bank of Canada (No 2) [1913] AC 299 (PC) 330
Medforth v Blake [1999] EWCA Civ 1482..331, 332
Mediterranean Salvage & Towage v Seamar Trading & Commerce Inc
    (The Reborn) [2009] EWCA Civ 531 194
Mercantile Investment and General Trust Co v International Co of Mexico
    [1893] 1 Ch 484 393
Mercantile Trading Co, Schroeder's Case (1871) LR 11 Eq 13 155
Mercers of the City of London v New Hampshire Insurance Co Ltd
    [1992] 1 WLR 792 (CA (Civ Div))..240
Meridian Global Funds Management Asia Ltd v Securities Commission
    [1995] 2 AC 500 (PC)..119, 502
Meritz Fire, Marine Insurance Co Ltd v Jan de Nul NV [2010] EWHC 3362 (Comm) 238
Merrill Lynch International Bank Ltd (formerly Merrill Lynch Capital
    Markets Bank Ltd) v Winterthur Swiss Insurance Co [2007] EWHC 893 (Comm)......245
Metropolitan Coal Consumers' Association Ltd, Re (1890) 6 TLR 416.............................515
Metrovacesa SA, Re [2011] EWHC 1014 (Ch)...740
Michaels v Harley House (Marylebone) Ltd [1997] 1 WLR 967 (Ch D)...........................145
Mid Essex Hospital Services NHS Trust v Compass Group UK and
    Ireland Ltd [2013] EWCA Civ 200..195
Midland Coal, Coke & Iron Co, Re [1895] 1 Ch 267 (CA)..738
Mills v Sportsdirect.com Retail Ltd [2010] EWHC 1072 (Ch).................................141, 458

Minster Assets plc, Re [1985] BCLC 200 (Ch D) 732
Mistral Finance (In Liquidation), Re [2001] BCC 27 218
Modelboard Ltd v Outer Box Ltd (In Liquidation) [1992] BCC 945 (Ch D) 46, 280
Money Markets International Stockbrokers Ltd (In Liquidation) v
   London Stock Exchange Ltd [2002] 1 WLR 1150 (Ch D) 108
Monolithic Building Co, Re [1915] 1 Ch 643 (CA) 318
Moody v Condor Insurance Ltd [2006] EWHC 100 (Ch)... 379
Moorcock, The (1889) 14 PD 64 (CA) 194, 215
More OG Romsdal Fylkesbatar AS v Demise Charterers of the Jotunheim
   [2004] EWHC 671 (Comm).. 335
Morel (EJ) Ltd, Re [1962] Ch 21 222
Morgan Crucible Co plc v Hill Samuel & Co Ltd [1991] Ch 295 (CA (Civ Div)) 691
Morphitis v Bernasconi [2003] EWCA Civ 289.. 118
Morris v Bank of India [2005] EWCA Civ 693... 119
Morritt, Re (1886) 18 QBD 222 (CA)... 330
Moschi v Lep Air Services Ltd [1973] AC 331 (HL).. 237, 243
Mosely v Koffyfontein Mines Ltd [1904] 2 Ch 108 (CA).. 156
Mount I. *See* Raiffeisen Zentralbank Österreich AG v Five Star General Trading LLC
Mount Morgan (West) Gold Mines Ltd, Re (1887) 3 TLR 556 515
MS Fashions Ltd v Bank of Credit and Commerce International SA
   (In Liquidation) [1993] Ch 425 (CA (Civ Div)... 226, 227
MT Realisations Ltd (In Liquidation) v Digital Equipment Co Ltd
   [2002] EWHC 1628 (Ch) 174
Murray v Leisureplay plc [2005] EWCA Civ 963 215
Mutual Life Insurance Co of New York v Rank Organisation Ltd
   [1985] BCLC 11 (Ch D) 128, 129, 136, 154, 717, 723
Mytravel Group plc, Re [2004] EWHC 2741 (Ch).................................... 732–34, 736, 737
Myers (Dennis Edward) v Kestrel Acquisitions Ltd [2015] EWHC 916 (Ch) 195
Nanfri, The. *See* Federal Commerce & Navigation Co Ltd v Molena Alpha Inc
Nanwa Gold Mines Ltd, Re [1955] 1 WLR 1080 (Ch D) 259
National Bank Ltd, Re [1966] 1 WLR 819 (Ch D) 744, 747, 751
National Merchant Buying Society Ltd v Bellamy [2013] EWCA Civ 452.. 238
National Provincial and Union Bank of England v Charnley [1924] 1 KB 431 (CA)....................... 319
National Provincial Bank v Ainsworth [1965] AC 1175 (HL)... 362
National Westminster Bank v Jones [2001] 1 BCLC 98 (Ch D) 273
National Westminster Bank v Utrecht-America Finance Co [2001] EWCA Civ 658....................... 660
National Westminster Bank Ltd v Halesowen Presswork & Assemblies
   Ltd [1971] 1 QB 1 (CA (Civ Div)); [1972] AC 785 (HL)................................ 219, 222, 224,
                                                                      230, 232, 256, 261, 457
National Westminster Bank plc v Inland Revenue Commisssioners
   [1995] 1 AC 119 (HL)... 139
Nearfield Ltd v Lincoln Nominees Ltd [2006] EWHC 2421 (Ch) 237
Neath and Brecon Rly, Re [1892] 1 Ch 349 (CA).. 744
NEF Telecom Co BV, Re [2012] EWHC 2944 (Ch)... 740, 743
Nefeli, The. *See* Polaris Steamship Co SA v A Tarricone Inc
New Zealand Shipping Co Ltd v AM Satterthwaite & Co Ltd (The Eurymedon)
   [1975] AC 154 (HL).. 446
Newfoundland v Newfoundland Rly Co (1888) LR 13 App Cas 199 (PC)............................. 436, 438
NFU Development Trusts Ltd, Re [1972] 1 WLR 1548 (Ch D) 747
Norman Holding Co Ltd (In Liquidation), Re [1991] 1 WLR 10 (Ch D) 227

Nortel Companies, Re [2013] UKSC 52 ....102, 103, 226
North Central Wagon Finance Co Ltd v Brailsford [1962]
   1 WLR 1288 (Assizes) 278
North Shore Ventures Ltd v Anstead Holdings Inc [2011]
   EWCA Civ 230 .... 239, 244
North West Transportation Co Ltd v Beatty (1887)
   LR 12 App Cas 589 (PC)... 78, 531
Northern Engineering Industries plc, Re [1994] 2 BCLC 704 (CA (Civ Div)).......................... 128, 171
O'Neill v Phillips [1999] 1 WLR 1092 (HL) 14, 53, 74, 75, 724
Oakes v Turquand (1867) LR 2 HL 325 (HL).. 515
Oasis Merchandising Services Ltd (In Liquidation), Re [1998]
   Ch 170 (CA (Civ Div)) 105, 118, 120
OBG Ltd v Allan [2007] UKHL 21... 203, 563
Oceanic Steam Navigation Co Ltd, Re [1939] Ch 41 743
Offshore Ventilation Ltd [1989] 1 WLR 800 (CA (Civ Div)) 298
Olds Discount Co Ltd v John Playfair Ltd [1938] 3 All ER 275 .... 40, 279
On Demand Information plc (In Administration) v Michael
   Gerson (Finance) plc [2002] UKHL 13 335
Ooregum Gold Mining Co of India v Roper [1892] AC 125 (HL) 149, 153, 161
Opera Ltd, Re [1891] 3 Ch 260 (CA) 292, 325
Ord v Belhaven Pubs Ltd [1998] BCC 607 (CA (Civ Div)) 117
Oresundsvarvet AB v Lemos (The Angelic Star) [1988] 1 Lloyd's
   Rep 122 (CA (Civ Div)).. 216
Oriental Commercial Bank, Alabaster's Case, Re (1868–69) LR 7 273 756
Orion Finance Ltd v Crown Financial Management Ltd (No 1)
   [1996] BCC 621 (CA (Civ Div)) 274
Owen v Tate [1976] QB 402 (CA (Civ Div)) 241, 464
Owners of Cargo Laden on Board the Albacruz v Owners of the
   Albazero [1977] AC 774 (HL)... 117
Pacific Colocotronis, The. *See* UBAF Ltd v European American Banking Corp
Pain, Re [1919] 1 Ch 38 434
Palk v Mortgage Services Funding plc [1993] Ch 330 (CA (Civ Div)) 330
Pan Atlantic Insurance Co Ltd, Re [2003] EWHC 1969 (Ch) 762
Panama, New Zealand and Australian Royal Mail Co, Re (1870) 5 Ch App 318............................... 289
Pantone 485 Ltd, Re [2002] 1 BCLC 266 115
Parabola Investments Ltd v Browallia Cal Ltd [2010] EWCA Civ 486................................... 512, 513
Paragon Finance plc v Pender [2005] EWCA Civ 760... 38
Parker-Tweedale v Dunbar Bank plc (No 1) [1991] Ch 12 (CA (Civ Div))............................... 331
Partco Group Ltd v Wragg [2002] EWCA Civ 594... 691
Patel v Mirza [2014] EWCA Civ 1047... 589
Patrick & Lyon Ltd, Re [1933] Ch 786 119
Paulett v AG (1667) Hard 465 286
Paycheck Services 3 Ltd, Re; Revenue and Customs Commissioners v Holland
   [2010] UKSC 51..91, 163, 165
Peachdart Ltd, Re [1984] Ch 131 46
Peak (RW) (Kings Lynn) Ltd, Re [1998] BCC 596.. 167
Peek v Gurney (1873) LR 6 HL 377 (HL)... 509
Peekay Intermark Ltd v Australia and New Zealand Banking Group Ltd
   [2006] EWCA Civ 386 .... 276, 420
Peer International Corp v Termidor Music Publishers Ltd (No 1) [2002]
   EWHC 2675 (Ch) 285

Pender v Lushington (1877) LR 6 Ch D 70 .... 74, 538
Percival v Wright [1902] 2 Ch 421 .... 616, 700
Performing Right Society Ltd v London Theatre of Varieties [1924] AC 1 (HL) 432
Perpetual Trustee Co Ltd v BNY Corporate Trustee Services Ltd. *See*
    Belmont Park Investments Pty Ltd v BNY Corporate Trustee Services Ltd
Peskin v Anderson [2001] 1 BCLC 372 (CA (Civ Div)) 69, 530, 616, 700
Pfeiffer (E) Weinkellerei-Weineinkauf GmbH & Co v Arbuthnot
    Factors Ltd [1988] 1 WLR 150 (QBD) 46, 280, 318, 429
PTZFM Ltd, Re [1995] 2 BCLC 354 91
Phillips v Phillips (1861) 4 De GF & J 208 .... 444, 461
Photo Production Ltd v Securicor Transport Ltd [1980] AC 827 (HL) 405
Pitts v Jones [2007] EWCA Civ 1301 242
Polak v Everett (1876) 1 QBD 669 240
Polaris Steamship Co SA v A Tarricone Inc [1986] 1 Lloyd's Rep 339 240
Polly Peck International plc (In Administration) (No 4), Re [1996]
    2 All ER 433 (Ch D) 47, 274
Polsky v S and A Services [1951] 1 All ER 1062 (Note) (CA) 278
Porton Capital Technology Funds v 3M UK Holdings Ltd [2011]
    EWHC 2895 (Comm) 449
Possfund Custodian Trustee Ltd v Diamond [1996] 1 WLR 1351 (Ch D) 510
Potters Oils Ltd, Re [1986] 1 WLR 201 (Ch D) 331
Practice Statement (Ch D: Schemes of Arrangement with Creditors)
    [2002] 1 WLR 1345 731
Precision Dippings Ltd v Precision Dippings Marketing Ltd [1986]
    1 Ch 447 (CA (Civ Div)) 164, 165, 188
Prest v Petrodel Resources Ltd [2013] UKSC 34 .... 15, 61, 116, 117, 148
Primacom Holdings GmbH, Re [2011] EWHC 3746 (Ch) 740
Primacom Holdings GmbH, Re [2012] EWHC 164 (Ch) 743
Produce Marketing Consortium Ltd (In Liquidation) Ltd (No 2),
    Re [1989] 1 WLR 745 .... 116, 118, 120, 187
Progress Property Co Ltd v Moorgarth Group Ltd [2010] UKSC 55 163
Prudential Assurance Co Ltd v Chatterley-Whitfield Collieries Ltd
    [1949] AC 512 (HL) 171
Prudential Assurance Co Ltd v Newman Industries Ltd (No 2)
    [1982] Ch 204 (CA (Civ Div)) 559
Prudential Insurance Co v Commissioners of Inland Revenue [1904] 2 KB 658 250
Punt v Symons & Co Ltd [1903] 2 Ch 506 698
Purpoint Ltd, Re [1991] BCLC 491 (Ch D) 96, 120
Pym v Campbell (1856) 6 El & Bl 370 209
Queen's Moat Houses plc v Capita IRG Trustees Ltd [2004] EWHC 868 (Ch) 299
Quin & Axtens Ltd v Salmon [1909] AC 442 (HL) 72
R (on the application of Uberoi) v Westminster Magistrates' Court
    [2008] EWHC 3191 (Admin) 594
R v Aspinall (1875–76) 1 LR 730 584
R v Bailey and Rigby [2005] EWCA Crim 3487 597
R v Chester and North Wales Legal Aid Area Office, ex p Floods of
    Queensferry Ltd [1998] 1 WLR 1496 (CA (Civ Div)) 436
R v Clowes [1994] 2 All ER 316 (CA (Crim Div)) 259
R v De Berenger (1814) 3 M & S 67 (KB) 584, 597
R v Ghosh [1982] QB 1053 (CA (Crim Div)) 597

R v Goodman [1993] 2 All ER 789 (CA (Crim Div)) 593
R v Grunwald [1963] 1 QB 935 596
R v Kylsant [1932] 1 KB 442 .... 506, 564
R v Lockwood (1987) 3 BCC 333 597
R v McQuoid [2009] EWCA Crim 1301 .... 583, 594
R v Page [1996] Crim LR 821 (CA (Crim Div)) 596
R v Panel on Takeovers and Mergers, ex p Datafin plc [1987]
    QB 815 (CA (Civ Div)) 682, 687, 688
R v Panel on Takeovers and Mergers, ex p Fayed [1992]
    BCC 524 (CA (Civ Div)) 688
RAC Motoring Services Ltd, Re [2000] 1 BCLC 307 .... 743, 745
Rahman v HSBC Bank plc [2012] EWHC 11 (Ch) 213
Raiffeisen Zentralbank Österreich AG v Five Star General Trading
    LLC (The Mount I) [2001] EWCA Civ 68 .... 432, 436
Raiffeisen Zentralbank Österreich AG v Royal Bank of Scotland plc
    [2010] EWHC 1392 .... 419, 420
Railton v Wood (1890) LR 15 App Cas 363 (PC) 286
Rainy Sky SA v Kookmin Bank [2011] UKSC 50 ....193, 194, 238
Raja v Austin Gray (A Firm) [2002] EWCA Civ 1965 330
Rankin & Blackmore Ltd, Petitioners, 1950 SC 218 731
Reardon Smith Line Ltd v Hansen-Tangen (The Diana Prosperity)
    [1976] 1 WLR 989 (HL) 193
Reborn, The. *See* Mediterranean Salvage & Towage v Seamar Trading & Commerce
Redwood Master Fund Ltd v TD Bank Europe Ltd [2002]
    EWHC 2703 (Ch) 421, 422, 392, 393
Revenue and Customs Commissioners v Football League Ltd
    [2012] EWHC 1372 (Ch) 105, 107–10, 112, 219, 228, 261
Revenue and Customs Commissioners v Holland. *See* Paycheck Services 3 Ltd, Re
Rhodes v Allied Dunbar (Pension Services) Ltd [1989]
    1 WLR 800 (CA (Civ Div)) 298, 332
Rialto, The. *See* Yukong Line Ltd of Korea v Rendsburg Investments Corp of Liberia
Ridge Securities Ltd v Iland Revenue Commissioners
    [1964] 1 WLR 479 (Ch D) 162
Rights & Issues Investment Trust v Stylo Shoes Ltd [1965] Ch 250 74
Robbie (NW) & Co Ltd v Witney Warehouse Co Ltd
    [1963] 1 WLR 1324 (CA) 292
Robert Stephen Holdings Ltd [1968] 1 WLR 522 (Ch D) 737
Roberts (Liquidator of Onslow Ditchling Ltd) v Frohlich
    [2011] EWHC 257 (Ch) 96, 120
Roberts v Gill & Co [2010] UKSC 22 .... 432, 433
Robertson v French, 102 ER 779, (1803) 4 East 130 193
Robinson v Macdonnell, 105 ER 1034, (1816) 5 M & S 228 283
Robophone Facilities Ltd v Blank [1966] 1 WLR 1428 (CA) 215
Robson v Smith [1895] 2 Ch 118 325
Rodenstock GmbH, Re [2011] EWHC 1104 (Ch) 743
Rouse v Bradford Banking Co Ltd [1894] AC 586 (HL) 29
Roxburghe v Cox (1881) 17 Ch D 520 (CA) 430, 436, 438
Royal Bank of Scotland v Etridge (No 2) [2001] UKHL 44 239
Royscot Trust Ltd v Rogerson [1991] 2 QB 297 (CA (Civ Div)) 512, 513, 654
Rubin v Gunner [2004] EWHC 316 (Ch) 120

Sale Continuation Ltd v Austin Taylor & Co Ltd [1968] 2 QB 849...218
Salomon v Salomon & Co Ltd [1897] AC 22 (HL) 105, 115, 303
Saltdean Estate Co Ltd, Re [1968] 1 WLR 1844 (Ch D) 66
Saltri III Ltd v MD Mezzanine SA Sicar [2012]
    EWHC 3025 (Comm)...255, 406, 409, 415, 416, 420
Sam Weller & Sons Ltd, Re [1990] Ch 682 ....53, 67
Santiren Shipping Ltd v Unimarine SA (The Chrysovalandou-Dyo)
    [1981] 1 All ER 340 (QBD) 222
Santley v Wilde [1899] 2 Ch 474 (CA)...286
Saunders v Vautier (1841) 4 Beav 115... 442, 443
Savoy Hotel Ltd, Re [1981] Ch 351 .... 747, 750
Scandinavian Bank Group plc, Re [1988] Ch 87... 153
Scandinavian Trading Tanker Co AB v Flota Petrolera Ecuatoriana
    [1983] 2 AC 694 (HL)...334
Scaptrade, The. *See* Scandinavian Trading Tanker Co AB v Flota Petrolera Ecuatoriana
Schering Chemicals Ltd v Falkman Ltd [1982] QB 1 (CA (Civ Div))..616
Scholey v Central Rly of Venezuela (1869–70) LR 9 Eq 266...514
Schuler (L) AG v Wickman Machine Tool Sales Ltd [1974] AC 235 (HL) 301
Scottish Insurance Corp Ltd v Wilsons & Clyde Coal Co Ltd
    [1949] AC 462 (HL)...66, 102, 171
Scottish Lion Insurance Co Ltd v Goodrich Corp [2010] CSIH 6 757
Scottish Petroleum Co (No 2), Re (1883) 23 Ch D 413 (CA)..514
Seat Pagine Gialle SpA, Re [2012] EWHC 3686 (Ch) 740, 743
Seaton v Heath [1899] 1 QB 782 (CA) 242, 246
Secretary of State for Business, Innovation and Skills v Chohan
    [2013] EWHC 680 (Ch) 91
Secretary of State for Trade and Industry v Deverell [2001]
    Ch 340 (CA (Civ Div)) 91
Secure Capital SA v Credit Suisse AG [2015] EWHC 388 (Comm) 385–87, 389
Security Trustee Co v Royal Bank of Canada [1976] AC 503 (PC)..323
Severn and Wye and Severn Bridge Rly Co, Re [1896] 1 Ch 559..64
Shamil Bank of Bahrain EC v Beximco Pharmaceuticals Ltd
    [2004] EWCA Civ 19 .... 48, 49
Shamji v Johnson Matthey Bankers Ltd [1991] BCLC 36 (CA (Civ Div)) 330, 331
Sharpley v Louth and East Central Coast Rly Co (1876) 2 Ch D 663 (CA)...................................514
Shearer v Bercain Ltd [1980] 3 All ER 295 (Ch D)..125, 154, 160
Shiloh Spinners Ltd v Harding [1973] AC 691 (HL) 335
Shipton, Anderson & Co (1927) Ltd (In Liquidation) v Micks,
    Lambert & Co [1936] 2 All ER 1032m (KBD) 230
Shirlaw v Southern Foundries (1926) Ltd [1939] 2 KB 206 (CA)..194
Short v Treasury Commissioners [1948] AC 534 (HL) 71, 72, 717, 725
Shuttleworth v Cox Bros and Co (Maidenhead) Ltd [1927] 2 KB 9 (CA)...74
SHV Gas Supply & Trading SAS v Naftomar Shipping and Trading
    Co Ltd Inc (The Azur Gaz) [2005] EWHC 2528 (Comm)..212
Siebe Gorman & Co Ltd v Barclays Bank Ltd [1979] 2 Lloyd's Rep 142...320
Sigma Finance Corp (In Administration) [2009] UKSC 2.. 193, 255
Silven Properties Ltd v Royal Bank of Scotland plc [2003] EWCA Civ 1409...............................330–32
Sim Swee Joo Shipping Sdn Bhd v Shirlstar Container Transport Ltd
    [1994] CLC 188...432
Simm v Anglo-American Telegraph Co (1879) 5 QBD 188 (CA)..145

Simon Carves Ltd v Ensus UK Ltd [2011] EWHC 657 (TCC)...245
Simpson v Norfolk and Norwich University Hospital NHS Trust
    [2011] EWCA Civ 1149 428
Singh (Mahant) v Yi (U Ba) [1939] AC 601 (PC) 239
Skipton Building Society v Stott [2001] QB 261 240
Slavenburg's Bank NV v Intercontinental Natural Resources
    [1980] 1 WLR 1076 (QBD) 636
Slough Estates plc v Welwyn Hatfield DC [1996] 2 PLR 50 (QBD)..513
Smith v Chadwick (1884) 9 App Cas 187 (HL).................................506, 507, 563, 564, 567, 614
Smith (Administrator of Cosslett (Contractors) Ltd) v Bridgend
    CBC [2001] UKHL 58 ....204, 296, 318
Smith and Fawcett Ltd, Re [1942] Ch 304 (CA)................................69, 120, 149, 530, 698
Smith New Court Securities Ltd v Scrimgeour Vickers
    (Asset Management) Ltd [1997] AC 254 (HL)..513, 515, 565
Smith, Stone & Knight Ltd v Birmingham Corp [1939] 4 All ER 116 (QBD) 117
Smithton Ltd v Naggar [2014] EWCA Civ 939..91
SMP Trustees Ltd, Re [2012] EWHC 772 (Ch) 397
Sneath v Valley Gold Ltd [1893] 1 Ch 477 (CA) 421, 747
Snook v London and West Riding Investments Ltd [1967] 2 QB 786 (CA (Civ Div)) 273
Société Générale de Paris v Walker (1885) 11 App Cas 20 (HL) 456
Socimer International Bank Ltd (In Liquidation) v Standard
    Bank London Ltd (No 2) [2008] EWCA Civ 116...195
Soden v British & Commonwealth Holdings plc [1995] BCC 531 736
Soden v British & Commonwealth Holdings plc
    [1998] AC 298 (HL)..64, 104, 146, 180, 501, 567
Sovereign Life Assurance Co (In Liquidation) v Dodd [1892] 2 QB 573 (CA)......................734
Sovereign Marine and General Insurance Co Ltd, Re [2006] EWHC 1335 (Ch).....................736
Spectrum Plus Ltd (In Liquidation), Re [2005] UKHL 41 ....273, 277, 279, 292,
                                                                                                    295–99, 302, 307, 324, 465
Spread Trustee Co Ltd v Hutcheson [2011] UKPC 13..408, 409
Springwell Navigation Corp v JP Morgan Chase Bank
    (formerly Chase Manhattan Bank) [2008] EWHC 1186;
    [2010] EWCA Civ 1221 ....276, 398, 415, 419, 420, 655
Squires v AIG Europe Ltd [2004] EWHC 1760 (Ch);
    [2006] EWCA Civ 7 ....23, 256, 257, 260–62
SSSL Realisations, re. See Squires v AIG Europe Ltd Squires v AIG Europe Ltd
Stadium Finance Co Ltd v Helm (1965) 109 Sol Jo 471 242
Standard Chartered Bank v Pakistan National Shipping Corp
    (No 2) [2002] UKHL 43 115
Standard Chartered Bank v Walker [1982] 1 WLR 1410 (CA (Civ Div)) 332
Standard Manufacturing Co, Re [1891] 1 Ch 627 (CA) 292
Standard Rotary Machine Co Ltd (1906) 95 LT 829 320
Star Sea, The. See Manifest Shipping Co Ltd v Uni-Polaris Insurance Co Ltd
State Trading Corp of India Ltd v ED & F Man (Sugar) Ltd [1981]
    Com LR 235 (CA (Civ Div)) 245
Static Control Components (Europe) Ltd v Egan [2004] EWCA Civ 392................................238
Steel Wing Co Ltd, Re [1921] 1 Ch 349 ....258, 429, 432
Stein v Blake (No 2) [1998] 1 All ER 724 (CA (Civ Div))...559
Stein v Blake [1996] 1 AC 243 (HL)..226, 231, 232
Stewart v Scottish Widows and Life Assurance Society plc [2005] EWHC 1831 (QB)...................227

Stone & Rolls Ltd (In Liquidation) v Moore Stephens (A Firm) [2009] UKHL 39 114
Stopjoin Projects Ltd v Balfour Beatty Engineering Services
 (HY) Ltd [2014] EWHC 589 (TCC)...439, 441, 442
Sucden Financial Ltd v Fluxo-Cane Overseas Ltd [2010] EWHC 2133 (Comm) 213
Sumitomo v Banque Bruxelles Lambert SA [1997] 1 Lloyd's Rep 487 (QBD)................................ 418
Sunrise Radio Ltd, Re [2009] EWHC 2893 (Ch)..125, 129, 154, 160
Sutton & Co v Grey [1894] 1 QB 285 (CA).. 242
Swire v Redman (1876) 1 QBD 536 239
System Controls plc v Munro Corporate plc [1990] BCC 386 (Ch D).. 155
Szepietowski v National Crime Agency [2013] UKSC 65 328
T & N Ltd (No 2), Re [2005] EWHC 2870 (Ch) 731, 739
T & N Ltd (No 3), Re [2006] EWHC 1447 (Ch) 747
Taberna Europe CDO 11 plc v Selskabet [2015] EWHC 871 (Comm) 654
Tael One Partners Ltd v Morgan Stanley & Co International plc
 [2015] UKSC 12.. 446
Tailby v Official Receiver (1888) 13 App Cas 523 (HL) 283, 300, 370, 436, 453
Tancred v Delagoa Bay & East Africa Rly Co (1889) 23 QBD 239 453
Tatung (UK) Ltd v Galex Telesure Ltd (1989) 5 BCC 325 .... 46, 280
Taunton v Sheriff of Warwickshire [1895] 2 Ch 319 (CA)... 292
Taupo Totara Timber Co v Rowe [1978] AC 537 (PC) 701
TDG plc, Re [2008] EWHC 2334 (Ch)... 745, 751
Tea Corporation Ltd, Re [1904] 1 Ch 12 (CA).. 732, 733
Tele2 International Card Co SA v Post Office Ltd [2009] EWCA Civ 9... 213
Telewest Communications plc (No 1), Re [2004]
 EWHC 924 (Ch) 731, 732, 734, 737, 740, 759, 760
Tennent v City of Glasgow Bank (In Liquidation) (1879)
 4 App Cas 615 (HL) 515
Themehelp Ltd v West [1996] QB 84 (CA (Civ Div))... 245
Three Rivers DC v Bank of England (No 1) [1996] QB 292 (CA (Civ Div)) 432, 433, 439
Thundercrest Ltd, Re [1995] 1 BCLC 117.. 135
Titan Europe 2006-3 plc v Colliers International UK plc
 (In Liquidation) [2014] EWHC 3106 (Comm) 468
Titan Steel Wheels Ltd v Royal Bank of Scotland plc [2010]
 EWHC 211 (Comm)... 655
Titford Property Co Ltd v Cannon Street Acceptances Ltd
 (unreported, 25 May 1975) 29
Tolhurst v Associated Portland Cement Manufacturers (1900) Ltd
 [1902] 2 KB 660 (CA)... 428, 440
Tomlin v Luce (1889) 43 Ch D 191 (CA).. 330
Topland Portfolio No 1 Ltd v Smith News Trading Ltd [2014] EWCA Civ 18 239
Torkington v Magee [1902] 2 KB 427 .... 429, 434
Torre Asset Funding Ltd v Royal Bank of Scotland plc
 [2013] EWHC 2670 (Ch) 193, 255, 416, 420
Toshoku Finance UK plc (In Liquidation), Re [2002] UKHL 6 100
Total Gas Marketing Ltd v Arco British Ltd [1998] 2 Lloyd's Rep 209 (HL) 208
Trade Indemnity Co Ltd v Workington Harbour and Dock Board
 (No 1) [1937] AC 1 (HL)... 240
Tradigrain SA v State Trading Corp of India [2005] EWHC 2206 (Comm) 245
Trafalgar House Construction (Regions) Ltd v General Surety &
 Guarantee Co Ltd [1996] AC 199 (HL)... 238

Trans-Trust SPRL v Danubian Trading Co Ltd [1952] 2 QB 297 (CA) 208
Transag Haulage Ltd v Leyland DAF Finance plc [1994] 2 BCLC 88 (Ch D)................................ 335
Trendtex Trading Corp v Credit Suisse [1982] AC 679 (HL) 428
Trevor v Whitworth (1887) LR 12 App Cas 409 (HL) 165
Triodos Bank NV v Dobbs [2005] EWCA Civ 630.. 240
Trustor AB v Smallbone (No 2) [2001] 1 WLR 1177 (Ch D)... 117
Tse Kwong Lam v Wong Chit Sen [1983] 1 WLR 1349 (PC)... 330
Turcan, Re (1888) 40 Ch D 5 (CA) 435, 439
Twinsectra Ltd v Yardley [2002] UKHL 12.. 281
UBAF Ltd v European American Banking Corp (The Pacific Colocotronis)
    [1984] QB 713 (CA (Civ Div)).. 415
Ultraframe (UK) Ltd v Fielding [2005] EWHC 1638 (Ch) 91, 114, 119
Uniq plc, Re [2011] EWHC 749 (Ch) 174, 748, 782
Unisoft Group Ltd (No 3), Re [1994] BCC 766 Ch D) 129
US Bank Trustees Ltd v Titan Europe 2007-1 (NHP) Ltd
    [2014] EWHC 1189 (Ch) 255
Vandepitte v Preferred Accident Insurance Corp of New York
    [1933] AC 70 (PC)...................................... 378, 381, 385, 433, 438, 439, 441–43, 452
Vandervell v Inland Revenue Commissioners [1967] 2 AC 291 (HL) 459
Vietnam Shipbuilding Industry Groups, Re [2013] EWHC 2476 (Ch)... 743
Vivendi SA v Richards [2013] EWHC 3006 (Ch)... 91, 114
Vossloh AG v Alpha Trains (UK) Ltd [2010] EWHC 2443 (Ch)... 242, 244
VTB Capital plc v Nutritek International Corp [2013] UKSC 5.. 117
Wadham Stringer Finance Ltd v Meaney [1981] 1 WLR 39 (QBD) 216
Wait, Re [1927] 1 Ch 606 (CA) 367
Ward v Duncombe [1893] AC 369 (HL) 322
Ward v Royal Exchange Shipping Co Ltd (1887) 58 LT 174.. 324
Warner Bros Records Inc v Rollgreen Ltd [1976] QB 430 (CA (Civ Div)) 431
Washington Diamond Mining Co, Re [1893] 3 Ch 95 (CA) 224
Waste Recycling Group plc, Re [2003] EWHC 2065 (Ch)... 746
Watford Electronics Ltd v Sanderson CFL Ltd [2001] EWCA Civ 317... 420
Watson, Re (1890) 25 QBD 27 (CA).. 278
Watson v Mid Wales Rly Co (1866–67) LR 2 CP 593.. 436
Watteau v Fenwick [1893] 1 QB 346... 371
Watts v Shuttleworth (1861) 7 Hurl & N 353.. 239
Webb v Earle (1875) LR 20 Eq 556.. 67
Webb, Hale and Co v Alexandrina Water Co Ltd (1905) 21 TLR 572.. 142
Weddell v JA Pearce & Major (A Firm) [1988] Ch 26.. 431, 432
Wells (Sir Thomas), Re [1933] Ch 29 (CA) 286
Welsh Development Agency v Export Finance Co Ltd [1992]
    BCLC 148 (CA (Civ Div)) 22, 46, 273, 274, 278, 279, 307, 469
Welton v Saffery [1897] AC 299 (HL).. 66, 102
West Mercia Safetywear Ltd v Dodd [1988] BCLC
    250 (CA (Civ Div)) 60, 106, 114–16, 181, 182
Westdeutsche Landesbank Girozentrale v Islington LBC
    [1996] 1 AC 669 (HL).. 363
Western Credit Ltd v Albery [1964] 1 WLR 945 (CA).. 242
Wharfedale Brewery Co Ltd, Re [1952] Ch 913 67
Wheatley v Silkstone and Haigh Moor Coal Co (1885) 29 Ch D 715.. 324
White v Bristol Aeroplane Co [1953] Ch 65 (CA) 10, 63, 128

White v Davenham Trust Ltd [2010] EWHC 2748 (Ch) 327
Whitmore v Mason (1861) 2 John & H 204 108
William & Glyn's Bank Ltd v Barnes [1981] Com LR 205 29
William Brandt's Sons & Co v Dunlop Rubber Co Ltd [1905] AC 454 (HL) 432
Williams v Atlantic Assurance Co Ltd [1933] 1 KB 81 (CA) 431
Williams v Natural Life Health Foods Ltd [1998] 1 WLR 830 (HL) 115
Wilson v Kelland [1910] 2 Ch 306 .... 320, 323
Winkworth v Edward Baron Development Co Ltd [1986] 1 WLR 1512 (HL) 114–16
Winterflood Securities Ltd v Financial Services Authority [2010] EWCA Civ 423 600
Wittmann (UK) Ltd v Willdav Engineering SA [2007] EWCA Civ 824 240
Wood v Odessa Waterworks Co (1889) 42 Ch D 636 .... 64, 164
Woodroffes (Musical Instruments) Ltd, Re [1986] Ch 366 294
Wragg Ltd, Re [1897] 1 Ch 796 (CA) 156
Wright v Atlas Wright (Europe) Ltd [1999] 2 BCLC 301 (CA (Civ Div)) 167
Wright v National Westminster Bank plc [2014] EWHC 3158 (Ch) 366
Wuhan Guoyu Logistics Group Co Ltd v Emporiki Bank of Greece SA
    [2012] EWCA Civ 1629 244
Yagerphone, Re [1935] Ch 392 106
Yam Seng Pte Ltd v International Trade Corp Ltd [2013] EWHC 111 (QB) 195
Yenidje Tobacco Co Ltd, Re [1916] 2 Ch 426 (CA) 71
Yeoman Credit v Latter [1961] 1 WLR 828 (CA) 236, 242
Yorkshire Rly Wagon Co v Maclure (1882) 21 Ch D 309 (CA) 278
Yorkshire Woolcombers Association Ltd, Re [1903] 2 Ch 284 (CA) 295, 296
Yukong Line Ltd of Korea v Rendsburg Investments Corp of Liberia
    (The Rialto) [1998] 1 WLR 294 (QBD) 115, 117
Zanzibar v British Aerospace (Lancaster House) Ltd [2000]
    1 WLR 2333 (QBD) 420

Australia

ABM AMRO Bank NV v Bathurst Regional Council [2014] FCAFC 65 671
AMEV-UDC Finance Ltd v Austin (1986) 162 CLR 170 (HC) 216
Andrews v Australia & New Zealand banking Group Ltd [2012] HCA 30 (HC) 215, 334
Ankhar Pty Ltd v National Westminster Finance (Australia) Ltd (1987)
    162 CLR 549 (HC) 239
Ansett Australia Holdings Ltd v International Air Transport Association
    [2008] HCA 3 (HC) 229
Associated Alloys Pty Ltd v CAN 001 452 106 Pty Ltd (2000)
    202 CLR 588 (HC) 260, 276, 277, 280
Australian Securities and Investments Commission v Citigroup
    Global Markets Australia Ltd [2007] FCA 963 408
Australian Zircon NL v Austpac Resources NL [2011] WASC 186 439
Bathurst Regional Council v Local Government Financial Service
    Pty Ltd (No 5) [2012] FCA 1200 671
Beconwood Securities Pty Ltd v Australia and New Zealand Banking
    Group Ltd [2008] FCA 594 .... 274, 278
BP Refinery (Westernport) Pty Ltd v Shire of Hastings (1977) 180 CLR 266 194
Citicorp Australia Ltd v Hendry [1985] 4 NSWLR 1 (Sup Ct NSW CA) 242
Devefi Py Lt v Mateffy Perl Nagy Pty Ltd (1993) 113 ALR 225 439
Esanda Finance Corp Ltd v Plessing (1989) 166 CLR 131 (HC), (1989) 63 ALJ 238 216

Fire Nymph Products Ltd v The Heating Centre Pty Ltd (1992)
  7 ACSR 365 (Sup Ct NSW CA) 205
Gambotto v WCP Ltd (1995) 182 CLR 432 (HC) 73, 74
Gye v McIntyre (1991) 171 CLR 609 (HC) 226
Harlowe's Nominees Pty Ltd v Woodside Oil Co (1968) 121 CLR 483 (HC) 127
Hickory Developments Pty Ltd v Brunswick Retail Investment Pty Ltd [2012] VSC 224 240
Hospital Products Ltd v United States Surgical Corp (1984) 156 CLR 41 406
Jarass Pty Ltd, Re (1988) 13 ACSR 728 (Sup Ct NSW) 155, 161
King v Hussain 2411/05, 2005 NSWSC 1076 (Sup Ct NSW) 286
Kinsela v Russell Kinsela Pty Ltd (In Liquidation) (1986) 4 NSWLR 722
  (Sup Ct NSW) 115
Leveraged Equities Ltd v Goodridge (2011) 191 FCR 71 446
Lyford v Commonwealth Bank of Australia (1995) 17 ACSR 211 (Fed Ct) 291
Marra Developments Ltd v BW Rofe Pty Ltd (1977) 2 NSWLR 616 (Sup Ct NSW) 13, 68
McRae v Commonwealth Disposals Commission (1951) 84 CLR 377 512
Natwest Australia Bank Ltd v Tricontinental Corp Ltd, 1993 VIC LEXIS 743 418
NIAA Corp Ltd, Re (1993) 12 ACSR 141 (Sup Ct NSW) 256
North v Marra Developments (1982) 56 ALJR 106 599
O'Dea v Allstates Leasing Systems (WA) Pty Ltd (1983) 152 CLR 359 (HC) 216
Opes Prime Stockbroking Ltd (No 1), Re (2009) 73 ACSR 385 747
Palette Shoes Pty Ltd v Krohn (1937) 58 CLR 1 (HC) 279
Peters' American Delicacy Co Ltd v Heath (1939) 61 CLR 457 (HC) 74
Pilmer v Duke Group Ltd (2001) 75 ALJR 1067, (2001) 38 ACSR 121,
  [2001] 2 BCLC 773 (HC) 125, 158, 159
Pro-Image Studios v Commonwealth bank of Australia (1990–91)
  4 ACSR 586 (Sup Ct Victoria) 155, 161
Ring v Sutton (1980) 5 ACLR 546 (Sup Ct NSW) 116
Stephens Travel Service International Pty Ltd (Receivers & Managers
  Appointed) v Qantas Airways Ltd (1988) 13 NSWLR 331 (CA) 259
Tricontinental Corp Ltd v Federal Commissioner of Taxation (1987)
  73 ALR 433 (Queensland CA) 291
Turner Corp Ltd (In Liquidation), Re (1995) 17 ACSR 761 436
Westpac v Bell [2012] WASCA 157 120
White v Shortall [2006] NSWC 1379; [2007] NSWCA 372 .... 368, 369, 370

Bermuda

Validus Holdings Ltd v IPC Holdings Ltd and Max Capital Group Ltd
  [2009] SC (Sup Ct) 25 Civ (13 May 2009) 750

British Virgin Islands

Cukurova Finance International Ltd v Alfa Telecom Turkey Ltd [2009] 1 CLC 701 .... 329, 330

Canada

Air Canada v M & C Travel Ltd (1991) 77 DLR (4th) 536 (Sup Ct) 259
Caisse Populaire Desjardins de l'Est de Drummond v Canada [2009] SCC 29 (Sup Ct) 220, 231
R v Consolidated Churchill Copper Corp (1978) 90 DLR (3d) 357 291
Royal Bank of Canada v Radius Credit Union Ltd, 2010 SCC 48, 325 DLR (4th) 635 285
Teck Corp Ltd v Miller (1972) 33 DLR (3d) 288 (BC Sup Ct) 127

Cayman Islands

Weavering Macro Fixed Income Ltd v Peterson (26 August 2011,
   Grand Ct) (2015) CICA 10 of 2011 409

European Court of Human Rights

Grande Stevens v Italy, 4 March 2014 589

European Union

Alfred Hirmann v Immofinanz AG (C-174/12) 19 December 2013 104
Centros Ltd v Erhvervs-og Selskabsstyrelsen (C-212/97) [1999] ECR I-1459 .... 151, 178, 189
Geltl v Daimler AG (C-19/11) [2012] 3 CMLR 32 605–07
Siemens AG v Henry Nold (C-42/95) [1996] ECR I-6017 128
Spector Photo Group NV v Commissie voor het Bank-, Financie- en
   Assurantiewezen (CBFA) (C-45/08) [2009] ECR I-12073 .... 583, 600, 601
United Kingdom v Council and Parliament (C-270/12) EU: C:2013:562,
   [2014] 2 CMLR 44 629

Guernsey

Flightlease Holdings (Guernsey) v Flightlease (Ireland) (Judgment 3/2009,
   unreported 14 January 2009, Royal Ct) 23

Hong Kong

CA Pacific Finance Ltd (In Liquidation), Re [2000] 1 BCLC 494 368
PCCW Ltd, Re [2009] 3 HKC 292 742

Ireland

JD Brian Ltd (in liquidation), Re [2011] IEHC 283 294
Salthill Properties Ltd, Re [2004] IEHC 145 320
Welch v Bowmaker (Ireland) Ltd [1980] IR 251 (Sup Ct) 320, 324

New Zealand

Alexander v Perpetual Trustees WA Ltd [2001] NSWCA 240 408
Atwood & Reid Ltd v Stephens [1932] NZLR 1332 435
Coleman v Myers [1977] 2 NZLR 225 (Sup Ct NZ) 700
Hilton International Ltd v Hilton [1989] 1 NZLR 442 165
Hodder & Tolley Ltd v Cornes [1923] NZLR 876 435
Manurewa Transport Ltd, Re [1971] NZLR 909 (Sup Ct Auckland) 205
Nicholson v Permakraft (NZ) Ltd [1985] 1 NZLR 242 (CA) 115

Singapore

Asiatic Enterprises (Pte) Ltd, The v United Overseas Bank Ltd [2000] 1 SLR 300 204
DBS Bank v Tam Chee Chong [2011] SGCA 47 203
Electro-Magnetic (S) Ltd (Under Judicial Management) v Development
   Bank of Singapore Ltd [1994] 1 SLR 734 231

United States

Banco Español de Crédito v Security Pacific National Bank,
    763 F Supp 36 (SDNY, 1991); aff'd 973 F 2d 51 (2d Cir 1992) 417
Banque Arabe et Internationale D'Investissement v Maryland
    National Bank, 810 F Supp 1282 (SDNY, 1993); aff'd 57 F 3d 146 (2d Cir 1995)........................ 417
Basic v Levinson, 485 US 224 (1988) 614
Blackie v Barrack, 524 F 2d 891 (9th Cir 1975), 429 US 816 614
eBay Domestic Holdings Inc Newmark CA No 3705-CC (Del Ch, 9 September 2010) 709
Feldbaum v McCrory Corp, 18 Del J Corp L 630 402
Gallagher v Abbott Laboratories, Inc, 269 F2d 806 (7th Cir 2001) 550
Halliburton Co v Erica P John Fund, Inc Halliburton, 134 S Ct 2398 (June 23, 2014) 614
IBP Inc v Tyson Foods Inc, 789 A 2d 14 (Del Ch 2001) 212
Janus Capital Group v First Derivative Traders, 131 S Ct 2296 (13 June 2011).......................... 614
Kardon v National Gypsum Co, 69 F Supp 512 (ED Pa, 1946) 613
Kass v Eastern Airlines Inc [1986] WL 13008 (Delaware) 393
Katz v Oak Industries Inc, 508 A 2d 873 (1986) (Delaware) 393
Paramount Communications Inc v QVC Network, 637 A 2d 34 (Delaware, 1994)........................ 709
Paramount Communications Inc v Time Inc, 571 A 2d 1140 (Delaware, 1990)............................ 709
Quadrant Structured Products Co Ltd v Vertin (4 May 2015) 114
Revlon Inc v MacAndrews & Forbes Holdings Inc, 506 A 2d 173 (Delaware, 1986) 709
SEC v Cuban, 620 F 3d 551 (5th Cir, 2010) 580
SEC v Dirks, 346 US 646 (1983).. 580, 589
SEC v Lund, 570 F Supp 1397 (CD Cal, 1983) 580
Superintendent of Insurance v Bankers Life & Casualty Co, 404 US 6 (1971)............................. 613
Telegroup Inc, Re, 281 F 3d 133 (3rd Cir, 2002)... 104
Ultramares v Touche (1931) 255 NY 170 507
United States v Chiarella, 445 US 222 (1980).. 580
United States v Newman and Chiassion, No 13-1837 (2d Cir 2014) 580
United States v O'Hagan, 521 US 642 (1997)... 580
Unitrin Inc v American General Corp, 651 A 2d 1361 (Delaware, 1995) 709
Unocal Corp v Mesa Petroleum Co, 493 A 2d 946 (Delaware, 1985)................................ 708, 709

TABLE OF LEGISLATION

United Kingdom

Bills of Exchange Act 1882 (c 61)
s 29..444
s 31(4)...444
s 38(2)...444
Capital Allowances Act 2001 (c 2)
s 67..45
ss 70A–70YI...45
s 70G..45
Charging Orders Act 1979 (c 53) 266
Civil Liability (Contribution) Act 1978 (c 47)
s 1...237
Companies Act 1844 (c 110) 71
Companies Act 1900 (c 48) 303
Companies Act 1907 (c 50) 757
Companies Act 1947 (c 47) 404
Companies Act 1948 (c 38)
s 88...404
Companies Act 1980 (c 22) 131, 613
s 17...133
Companies Act 1985 (c 6) 131, 150, 555
s 14...10
s 80...131
s 89...133
ss 151–53 151
ss 153–55 781
ss 155–58 ....151, 174
s 192..404, 410
ss 324–29 552
s 428...706
s 459...723
ss 677–83 781
Companies Act 1989 (c 40) 293
Pt VII 230
s 100...293
s 115(1)..131
s 159..229, 230
Companies Act 2006 (c 46) 8, 10, 53, 63
Pt 10...91
Ch 4 556
Pt 11...501, 700, 713

Pt 15 543
  Ch 1 787
Pt 16 .... 543, 544
  Ch 2 556
  Ch 6 502
Pt 17 Ch 3 133
Pt 23 .... 173, 176
Pt 25 287
Pt 26 .... 731, 739, 743, 747, 748
Pt 27 754
Pt 28 681
  Ch 2 702
  Ch 3 693
s 3 8
s 4(2) 479
s 7 8
s 8 10
  (1)(b) 70
s 17 .... 10, 76
s 21 .... 10, 63, 72, 77, 702, 741, 751, 757
s 22 .... 63, 74
s 33 .... 10, 67, 72, 103, 508
s 39 49
s 40 .... 11, 49
  (3)(b) 11
ss 90–96 479
s 98 .... 387, 534
s 112 .... 72, 141, 737
  (2) 139
s 113 139
s 122(3) 141
s 125 135
s 126 .... 139, 378, 456, 533
s 127 145
s 145 535
s 146 535
s 152(1) 534
s 154 479
s 160 479
s 168 .... 77, 681, 701, 724
  (1) 77, 126, 530
  (5) 77
s 171 698
  (b) 126, 698
s 172 .... 69, 70, 120, 149, 180, 182, 530, 548, 698, 708, 712, 791
  (1) 59, 78, 120, 126, 180, 698, 791
    (a)–(f) 698
  (3) 69, 114, 149, 182
s 173(2) 708
s 174(2) 120

s 177...78
ss 177–87 ....529, 531
s 180...78, 531
ss 190–96 ....78, 531
s 197–214..78, 531
s 214...182
s 215(1)...701
  (2)...701
ss 217–18 701
s 219(1)..701
s 220(1)(a)...701
  (3)...701
s 221(1)(b)...701
s 222(3)..701
s 228...701
s 229...701
s 234...502
s 239...74, 78, 531, 707
s 251...91
s 252...78, 531
s 254...78, 531
ss 260–64 ....69, 78, 361
ss 265–69 ....69, 78, 361
s 270...479
s 271...479
s 284...64, 67
ss 284–85 535
s 288...479
ss 303–05 530
s 324...535
s 336...479, 543
ss 338–39 530
s 381...543
s 384(1)(a)...543
s 385...488
  (2)...543
    (a)...488
s 393(1)..543
s 395...544
s 396(4)..543
  (5)...543
s 403...544
s 404(4)..543
  (5)...543
ss 414A–14D..544
s 414C(1)...69, 544, 549
  (2)...544
  (7)...545
  (8)...540, 545
s 415...544

s 417 544
s 420 545
ss 420–21 .... 488, 531, 701
s 423(1) 547
ss 426–26A 544
s 430 796
ss 437–38 .... 479, 547
s 439 .... 531, 701
　(5) 548
ss 439–39A 488
s 439A 531, 701
s 442 543
　(2)(a) 796
　　(b) 796
ss 456–57 570
s 463 .... 501, 545, 566, 568
　(3) 501
　(4) 545
　(5) 545
s 464 544
s 475 544
s 476 543
s 477 543
s 495(1) 547
　(3) 544
s 496 544
s 497 544
s 541 72
s 542 153
　(2) 153
　(3) 153
　(4)–(5) 153
s 544 144
s 548 .... 65, 76
s 549 131
　(1) 131
　(2) 131
　(3) 131
　(4) 131
　(6) 131
s 550 .... 9, 131
s 551 ....9, 131, 702
　(2) 131
　(3) 132
　　(b) 132, 702
　(4) 132
　(6) 132
s 554 139
　(3) 139

s 560(1).. 133
(2).. 133
(3).. 133
ss 560–77 532
s 561 ....9, 17, 133, 160
(2).. 135
ss 561–77 16
s 562(2).. 133
(3).. 133
(5).. 133, 138
(6).. 133
s 563... 135
s 564... 133
s 565.. 133, 160
s 566... 133
s 567... 136
s 568... 136
ss 569–70 136
ss 569–71 9
s 570(3).. 136
ss 570–71 ....17, 136, 532, 702
s 571... 136
(3).. 136
(5)–(7)... 136
s 572... 136
s 582(1).. 155
s 583(3)(a)... 155
(b).. 155
(c) 155–57, 161
(d).. 155
(e) 155, 156
(4).. 156
(5).. 156
(6).. 156
s 584... 155
s 585... 157
(2)... 157, 158
s 586... 151
s 587... 155
(1).. 157
(2).. 158
s 588.. 157, 158
(2).. 158
s 589.. 157, 158
(1).. 158
(5).. 158
s 590... 158
s 591... 157
s 593... 156
(1)(c) 157

(2) 157
(3) 157, 158
ss 594–95 .... 156, 157
s 596 156
(3) 156
s 597 157
s 605 .... 157, 158
(3) 158
s 606 .... 157, 158
(4) 158
s 607 158
s 610 .... 154, 754
(2) 154
(3) 154
(4) 151
s 612 754
s 613 754
s 629 .... 11, 62
s 630 .... 128, 702
(4) 62
ss 630–35 .... 10, 62
s 631 128
s 641 171
(1) 172
(2) 172, 173
(6) 171
ss 642–43 753
ss 642–44 .... 184, 748
s 643 .... 172, 186
(1) 172, 185
(b)(i) 172
(2) 172, 184
(4) 172, 186
(5) 172, 186
s 644 172
(5) 172
(8) 172
(9) 172
s 645 753
(1) 171
(3) 171
(4) 171
ss 645–49 .... 748, 754
s 646 171
(2) 754
s 648 171
s 649 172
s 654 .... 170, 173
s 655 .... 72, 103, 505
s 656 152

s 658(1) 165
s 659 165
ss 670–80 706
s 677 174
   (1)(a) 175
     (b)(i) 175
       (ii) 175
     (c)(i) 175
     (d) 706
       (i) 175
ss 677–82 151
ss 677–83 174
s 678(1) 175
   (2) 175
   (3) 175
   (4) 175
s 680 175
   (2) 187
ss 681–82 175
s 684 169
   (2) 169
   (3) 169
ss 684–89 ....12, 62, 165
s 685 169
   (3) 169
   (4) 169
s 686 169
   (2) 169
s 687(1) 169
   (2) 169
s 688 169
s 690(1) 166, 167
   (2) 166
ss 690–708 165
ss 690–723 .... 12, 52
s 692(1)(b) 168, 169
   (2) 167
s 693(3)(a) 167
     (b) 167
   (4) 167
s 693A 167
s 694 167
   (2) 167
s 695(3) 167
   (5) 167
s 701 167
   (5) 167
ss 709–23 .... 172, 184
s 714 .... 168, 186
   (3) 168, 184

(4) 168, 184
(6) 168
s 715 .... 168, 186
s 716 168
s 717 168
s 718 168
s 719 168
ss 720A–720B 168
s 721 168
s 723 168
s 724 168
(1) 168
s 726(2)–(3) 168
s 727 169
s 729 169
s 731 169
s 733 169
(2) 167
(3) 168
(5) 151, 167
(6) 151
s 735 169
s 738 .... 404, 636
s 750 .... 398, 410
(1) 404
s 755 .... 16, 35, 124, 479, 638, 644
(1) 125
s 756 .... 124, 644
(3) 644
(4) 644
(5) 644
s 758(2) 125
(3) 125
s 760 125
s 761 151
s 763 479
(1) 9, 151
s 765(1) 153
s 769 141
s 770(1) 145
s 776 145
s 779 .... 142, 455
(2) 142, 144
ss 790D–90E 140
s 790F 140
ss 790G–90H 140
s 793 720
ss 793–96 .... 554, 555

s 830 .... 11, 13, 52, 198
  (1) 753
  (2) 73, 164
ss 830–31 775
s 831 .... 11, 13, 52, 164, 176, 198
  (2) 164
  (4) 164
s 836(1) 164
  (2) 164
s 837 164
ss 845–46 163
s 847(2) 164, 188
s 859A 205, 257, 315, 317, 465
  (6) 284, 316
  (7) 287, 316
s 859D 317
s 859E 285
s 859F 317
s 859G 317
s 859H 272, 301, 317–19
  (4) 319
s 859I 317
  (6) 317
s 860 294
s 893 353
s 895 .... 394, 743, 747
  (1) 729, 730
  (2) 729, 746
    (b) 743
s 896 730
  (1) 730
  (2) 730
s 897 .... 731, 750
  (1)(b) 731
  (3) 731
  (4) 731
  (5)–(8) 731
s 899(1) 395, 730, 733, 741, 744
  (2) 743
  (3) 743, 746
  (4) 730, 746
s 900 .... 753, 754
s 901 746
s 942(2) 688
ss 942–65 685
s 943 688
  (2) 686
  (3) 686

s 944(1) 686, 688
s 945 .... 686, 688
s 946 686
s 947(3) 686
ss 947–49 686
s 951 687
s 952 .... 686, 691
s 953 686
  (1) 686
s 954 .... 686, 691
s 955 686
s 956(1) 688
  (2) 688
s 961 688
  (3) 688
s 974 694
  (2) 693
  (3) 693
  (4) 693
s 975(1) 693
  (2) 693
s 977(1) 693
s 978 693
s 979(2) 706
  (a) 693, 749
  (b) 693
  (3) 693
  (4) 693
  (4)–(8) 693
ss 979–82 75
s 980(2)–(3) 693
  (4)–(8) 693
s 981(2) 694
  (5) 694
s 982 694
s 983(1) 694
ss 983–85 .... 694, 722, 750
s 984(1)–(4) 695
  (5)–(7) 695
s 985 695
s 986 695
  (1) 694
  (4) 694
s 993 118
  (1) 118
s 994 .... 53, 67, 72, 74, 78, 129, 723, 724
  (1) 724
ss 994–96 .... 487, 501
s 996 724
ss 1150–51 156

s 1266 555
s 1270 ....505, 560, 562
s 1277 538
s 1278 539
  (2) 539
s 1280(1) 539
s 1282 100
s 1296 174
Sch 1A 140
  paras 2–3 140
Sch 2 686
Companies Clauses Consolidation Act 1845 (c 16) 289
Companies (Consolidation) Act 1908 (c 69) 757
Company Directors Disqualification Act 1986 (c 46) 116, 122
  s 2 593
  s 6 122
  s 8 593
  s 15 .... 105, 116, 122
  s 15A 122
Consumer Credit Act 1974 (c 39) 46, 213
  s 8 46
Consumer Insurance (Disclosure and Representations) Act 2012 (c 6) 246
Contracts (Rights of Third Parties) Act 1999 (c 31) 379, 391, 407
  s 7(2) 407
County Courts Act 1984 (c 28)
  Pt V 266
Courts Act 2003 (c 39)
  Sch 7 paras 6–11 266
Criminal Justice Act 1993 (c 36) 550, 587, 589–95, 598, 602, 607, 615
  Pt V 661, 662
  s 52(1) 592, 601, 605
    (2)(a) 592, 593, 601
      (b) 592, 593, 601, 602
    (3) 592, 662
  s 53(1)(a) 592
      (b) 592
      (c) 592
    (2) 593
    (3)(a) 593
      (b) 593
    (4) 593
  s 54 592
  s 55 592
  s 56 590
    (1)(a) 590
      (b) 590
      (d) 591
  s 57 603
    (1) 590, 594

(2)(a)(i) 589
(ii) 589
(b) 589
s 58 590
(2)(a) 591
(c) 591
(d) 591
(3) 591
s 59 592
s 60(4) 590
s 61 593
s 62(1) 592
s 63(2) 593, 600, 615
Sch 1 593
Sch 2 592
Directors' Liability Act 1890 (c 64) 490, 504, 561
Employers' Liability (Compulsory Insurance) Act 1969 (c 57) 118, 179, 182
s 1 344
Employment Rights Act 1996 (c 18)
ss 182–86 345
Enterprise Act 2002 (c 40) 98, 101, 304, 327, 331
s 250 ....266, 327
s 251 101
Enterprise and Regulatory Reform Act 2013 (c 24)
s 79 ....531, 701
ss 79–82 488
Finance Act 2006 (c 25)
Pt 4 44
s 81(1) 45
Finance Act 2014 (c 26)
s 74 769
Sch 17 769
Financial Services Act 1986 (c 60)
s 47 ....584, 596
(1) 595
(2) 595
Financial Services Act 2010 (c 28)
s 8 618
Financial Services Act 2012 (c 21) 494, 518, 597
s 89 ....592, 595–98, 610
(1) 592, 596, 610
(c) 597
(2) 597
(3) 597
(a) 586, 596
(b) 596
(c) 596
(4) 595
ss 89–90 ....515, 570, 595, 599
ss 89–91 ....166, 587, 595–600, 661

s 90 ....586, 595, 598, 600, 609
  (2) 598, 609
  (3) 598
  (6)–(8) 598
  (9)(a) 598
    (b) 598
      (ii) 586, 596
    (c) 596, 598
    (d) 596, 598
  (10) 595
s 91 .... 588, 595, 599–601
  (1)(c) 599
  (2)(c) 599
  (3) 599
    (a) 586, 596
    (b) 596
    (c) 596
  (5) 595
  (6) 595
s 92(1) 600
s 93(3) 596, 661
  (4) 599
  (5) 596, 598, 661
s 95 595
Financial Services and Markets Act 2000 (c 8) 26, 251, 494, 550, 636, 663, 666, 674, 686
  Pt VI 494, 516, 569
  Pt XI 638
  s 5(2)(d) 485, 503, 568
  s 19 .... 247, 485, 520, 635, 637, 666, 768, 772
  s 21 .... 635, 651
  s 22 .... 247, 666
  s 55J 638
  s 56 611
  s 74 482
  s 75(5) 488
  s 79 650
  s 80(1) 650
  s 85 .... 515, 635
    (1) 494, 495
      (e) 496
    (2) 479, 494, 495, 642
    (3) 495, 515
    (4) 495
    (5) 496
      (a) 646
      (b) 495
    (6) 496
  s 86 515
    (1) 496, 643, 646
      (a) 643

(b)...496, 643
(c)..496
(d)...496, 645
(e)..645
(1A) 495, 644
(7) 496
s 87A...488, 499
(2) 496, 497, 649
(3) 490, 497
(5) 490, 497
(6) 490, 497, 505
(9) 505
(9)–(10) 497
s 87D..516
s 87G..496
s 87J...488, 516
s 87K..516
s 87L...516
s 87M...516
s 87N..516
s 89A(1)..553
(3)(a) 553
ss 89A–89G...555
s 90...103, 104, 402, 417, 505–08, 510–15, 518, 519, 563, 565–67,
572, 577, 615, 640, 653–55
(1) 615
(a) 508
(b)..505, 567, 615
(4) 508
(7) 508
(11) 505, 508
(12) 505, 508
s 90A 103, 104, 489, 503, 505, 506, 545, 558, 560,
562–68, 572, 577, 640, 659
(a) 563
(b) 563
s 91..610
(1)...569
(1A) 516
(1B)..569
(1ZA) 569
(2) 516, 566, 569
(3) 516, 569
s 92(7)..517
s 96B(1) 551
s 102...488, 688
s 102A(3) 563
s 102B 643, 645
(1) 495
(2) 495

(3) 495
(4) 495
s 118 .... 166, 570, 586–88, 590, 592, 598, 600–04, 607–13, 663
   (1) 569, 592, 601
   (2) 601, 602, 604, 607
   (3) 601, 602, 605, 607
   (4) 601–03
      (a) 602, 603
      (b).. 602
   (5) 609, 611
   (5)–(8) 601
   (6) 586, 609, 611
   (7) 586, 610, 611
   (8) 598, 603, 610, 611
      (a) 611
s 118A(5) 608
   (b)... 586
s 118B 603, 604
   (a)–(d)... 603
   (e) 604, 607
s 118C 591, 604, 605
   (2) 605
   (5) 605, 607
      (a) 606
      (b).. 606
   (6) 605, 606
s 123(1)(b)... 601
   (2) 586, 607–10
   (3) 611
s 124(2) 586, 607, 609, 610
s 130A 611
   (3) 603, 609
s 131 600
ss 212–24A.. 634
s 380.. 594, 600
s 381.. 611
s 382..569, 594, 600, 615
s 383.. 611
s 397.. 595–600
   (1) 595, 596
      (c) 596
   (2) 596, 597
   (3) 595, 598
   (4) 597, 598
   (5)(a) 598
s 401.. 515
s 402.. 594
Sch 2 para 12 635
   para 20... 247
Sch 6.. 638

Sch 10 para 1 506
  (2) 506
  para 2(2) 506
  para 6 .... 506, 567, 615
Sch 10A 562
  para 1 564
  para 3(1) 563, 564
    (a) 564
    (b) 563
    (2) 563, 566
    (3) 563, 564, 566
    (4) 567
  para 5 .... 563, 564
    (1)(a) 564
      (b) 563, 567
    (2) 566
  para 6 .... 563, 566
  para 7(1) 562, 565
    (2) 562, 565
    (3) 565
      (a)(v) 559
  para 8(1) 563
    (2) 563
    (5) 563, 566
Sch 11A 646
  para 9 .... 496, 646
Sch 11B 551
Gambling Act 2005 (c 19)
  s 335 249
Hire Purchase Act 1964 (c 53) 46
  Pt III 274
  s 27 323
  s 29(1) 272
Human Rights Act 1998 (c 42) 686
  s 6 488
    (1) 688
Income Tax Act 2007 (c 3)
  s 882 375
Insolvency Act 1986 (c 45) 101, 122, 181, 345, 402, 758
  ss 1–7 740
  s 11(3)(c) 337
  s 44 332
  s 72A 266, 327
  ss 72B–72GA 97, 327, 332
  s 74(2)(f) 64, 68, 103, 104, 180, 501, 567, 776, 779
  s 84(1)(b) 70
    (c) 70
  s 89 755
  s 90 755

s 107 .... 97, 105
s 110 .... 755, 756
  (3)(a) 755
  (5) 755
  (6) 755, 756
s 111 756
  (1) 756
  (2) 756
  (4) 756
s 122 70
  (1)(g) 67, 78
s 123 .... 95, 96, 106, 111, 756
  (1)(e) 61
  (2) 61
s 127 .... 106, 107
s 129 318
s 175 99
  (2)(b) 100
s 176A 99, 101, 102, 298, 346
  (6) 99
s 176ZA 99, 100, 102, 305, 346
  (2)(b)(ii) 99
s 183 326
s 189 102
s 212 .... 100, 115, 116, 118
s 213 .... 15, 61, 100, 105, 116, 118, 119, 121, 122, 181, 187
  (1) 118
  (2) 121
s 214 .... 15, 61, 91, 96, 100, 105, 114, 116, 118–22, 148, 176, 181–83, 187
  (1) 121, 187
  (2)(a) 119
    (b) 181
  (3) 96, 121
  (4) 120
  (6) 96, 119, 120
  (7) 91, 119
s 221 743
s 237 237
s 238 .... 100, 106, 108, 111–13, 121, 148, 203, 231, 262
s 239 .... 100, 111–13, 121, 201, 205, 228, 231
  (4) 111
  (5) 111
s 240(1) 111
  (2) 106, 111
  (3) 95
s 241 .... 106, 111
s 244 100
s 245 .... 113, 294, 295, 308, 347, 465
  (3) 113
s 246ZA 105

s 246ZB 105
s 251 .... 91, 119, 273, 291, 294, 300
s 410 293
s 423 .... 100, 106, 109, 112, 148
s 424(1)(a) 106
s 425 106
s 436 362
Sch A1 Pt III 758
Sch B1 para 3 .... 98, 333, 337
    (2) 333
    (4) 333
  para 10 318
  para 12 332
  para 14 .... 309, 327, 331
  paras 14–21 778
  para 19 318
  para 22 .... 327, 332
  para 31 318
  para 42 98
  paras 42–43 .... 758, 760
  para 43 .... 98, 266, 279, 327, 332, 336
    (2) 275, 337
    (3) 275, 337
    (4) 338
    (6) 338
  para 44 336
  para 49 337
  para 59 98
  para 65 .... 98, 327
    (2) 100
    (3) 327
  para 70 .... 101, 295, 305, 337
    (2) 101, 337
  para 71 305
    (1) 337
    (3) 337
  para 72(3) 337
  para 99 .... 99, 305
    (3) 100
    (4) 101
  para 111(1) 275, 337
Sch 6 345
Insurance Act 2015 (c 4) 81, 246
Pt 2 238
Sch 1 246
Joint Stock Companies Arrangement Act 1870 (c 104) 757
Judicature Act 1873 (c 66) 429
  s 25(6) 429
Land Charges Act 1972 (c 61) 317
Land Registration Act 2002 (c 9) 317

Law of Property Act 1925 (c 20)
  s 53(1)(c) 371, 378, 433, 458, 459
  s 94 325
  s 101 ....287, 328, 330–32
  s 103 287
  s 105 328
  s 109(2) 332
  s 136 .... 321, 428, 429, 434, 451, 453, 459
    (1) 429
  s 137(2) 456
  s 205(1)(xvi) 287
Life Assurance Act 1774 (c 48) 251
  s 3 251
Limitation Act 1980 (c 58)
  s 10 237
  s 32(1)(b) 416
Limited Liability Partnerships Act 2000 (c 12) 8
Limited Partnership Act 1907 (c 24) 768
  s 6(1) 769
Mercantile Law Amendment Act 1856 (c 97)
  s 5 .... 241, 464
Merchant Shipping Act 1995 (c 21)
  s 16 286
  Sch 1 .... 286, 317
Misrepresentation Act 1967 (c 7) 417, 506, 507, 510, 512, 513, 565
  s 2(1) 416, 419, 505, 506, 653–56
    (2) 514, 654
  s 3 ....419, 420, 654
Partnership Act 1890 (c 39) 768
Patents Act 1977 (c 37)
  ss 30–33 286
  s 33 317
Pensions Act 2004 (c 35)
  ss 43–51 716
Powers of Attorney Act 1971 (c 27)
  s 4 454
Powers of Criminal Courts Act 1973 (c 62)
  s 35 594
Preferential Payments in Bankruptcy Act 1888 (c 62) 303
Registered Designs Act 1949 (c 88)
  s 19 .... 286, 317
Road Traffic Act 1988 (c 52) 118, 179, 182
  s 143 344
  ss 157–58 344
Sale of Goods Act 1893 (c 71)
  s 16 .... 366, 367
  s 52 367
Sale of Goods Act 1979 (c 54)
  s 16 366
  s 17 .... 46, 81

s 21...323
ss 21–25...323
s 24...323
s 25...46, 323
  (1)..45
  (2)..46
s 27...46
s 41...81
s 44...81
s 62(4)...323
Small Business, Enterprise and Employment Act 2015 (c 26)...........................116, 378, 552
s 1...452, 454
s 2...454
s 5...31
s 81..533, 553
s 84..142, 455
s 89..91, 114
s 90...91
s 110..122
s 117...118, 121
s 118...114, 121
s 119..105, 106, 118
Sch 3...140, 533, 553
Sch 4..142
Social Security (Recovery of Benefits) Act 1997 (c 27)...344
Statute of Frauds 1677 (c 3)
s 4...236, 237
Statute of Frauds Amendment Act 1828 (c 14)
s 6...416
Statute of Uses 1535 (c 10)..363
Stock Transfer Act 1963 (c 18)..456
Theft Act 1968 (c 60)...597
Third Parties (Rights against Insurers) Act 2010 (c 10)................................81, 118, 179, 182, 344, 346
Trade Marks Act 1994 (c 26)
s 25..286, 317
Trustee Act 2000 (c 29)...404
s 1...403, 404
s 31(1)...399
Sch 1..404
  para 7..404
Unfair Contract Terms Act 1977 (c 50)..398, 404, 405, 654
s 1(1)...407
s 2..407, 420
  (2)..407, 419, 660
s 3...654
  (2)(b)..404
s 11..419
s 13..404, 420
Sch 1 para 1(e)..407

Statutory Instruments

Accounting Standards (Prescribed Body) Regulations (SI 2008/651) 544
Alternative Investment Fund Managers (Amendment) Regulations 2013 (SI 2013/1797) 764
Alternative Investment Fund Managers Order 2014 (SI 2014/1292) 764
Alternative Investment Fund Managers Regulations 2013 (AIFM
  Regulations 2013) (SI 2013/1773)...249, 764, 795, 799, 802
  Pt 2 799
  Pt 3 .... 36, 799
  para 4(4) 799
  para 5(3)(c) 799
  para 36 .... 787, 801
  para 38 787
    (1) 801
  para 39 .... 787, 802
  para 40 .... 787, 802
  para 42 .... 788, 802
  para 43 802
  para 68 801
Civil Procedure Rules (SI 1998/3132)
  r 16.6 221
  r 24 225
  Pt 72 266
  Pt 73 266
Companies Act 2006 (Amendment of Part 17) Regulations 2015 (SI 2015/472) 748, 749, 753
  reg 3 753
Companies Act 2006 (Amendment of Part 18) Regulations 2013 (SI 2013/999)........................ 166–68
Companies Act 2006 (Amendment of Part 18) Regulations 2015 (SI 2015/532)........................ 166–68
Companies Act 2006 (Commencement No 1, Transitional Provisions and
  Savings) Order 2006 (SI 2006/3428)
  Sch 3 555
  Sch 4 552
Companies Act 2006 (Commencement No 5, Transitional Provisions and Savings)
  Order 2007 (SI 2007/3495)
  para 52 174
Companies Act 2006 (Strategic Report and Directors' Report) Regulations 2013
  (SI 2013/1970)...69, 540, 544, 545
Companies and Limited Liability Partnerships (Accounts and Audit Exemptions
  and Change of Accounting Framework) Regulations (SI 2012/2301) 544
Companies (Cross-Border Mergers) Regulations 2007 (SI 2007/2974)... 754
Companies (Defective Accounts and Directors' Reports) (Authorised Person) and
  Supervision of Accounts and Reports (Prescribed Body) Order 2012 (SI 2012/1439)................. 570
Companies (Model Articles) Regulations 2008 (SI 2008/3229)
  Sch 1 ....53, 63, 64, 67, 77
  Sch 3 ....53, 63, 64, 67, 77
Companies, Partnerships and Groups (Accounts and Reports)
  Regulations 2015 (SI 2015/980) 543
Companies (Reduction of Share Capital) Order 2008 (SI 2008/1915) 173
  art 2 172
  art 3 170
    (2) 170

Companies (Share Capital and Acquisition by Company of its Own
   Shares) Regulations 2009 (SI 2009/2022) 133, 138, 167, 171
Companies (Shareholders' Rights) Regulations 2009 (SI 2009/1632)
   regs 2–3 535
   reg 4 530
Companies (Shares and Share Capital) Order 2009 (SI 2009/388)
   art 4 156
Conditional Fee Agreements Order 2013 (SI 2013/689) 519
Credit Rating Agencies (Civil Liability) Regulations 2013 (SI 2013/1637) 670, 671
   regs 10–12 672
Credit Rating Agencies Regulations 2010 (SI 2010/906) 670
Damages-Based Agreements Regulations 2013 (SI 2013/609) 519
Electricity and Gas (Market Integrity and Transparency)
   (Criminal Sanctions) Regulations 2015 (SI 2015/979) 586
Employment Rights (Increase of Limits) Order 2015 (SI 2015/226)
   Sch 1 345
Financial Collateral Arrangements (No 2) Regulations 2003
   (SI 2003/3226) (FCARs) 101, 270, 310–16, 338, 349, 445, 465
   reg 3 .... 224, 270, 310, 311, 315, 338, 445
   reg 4 .... 270, 310
      (2) 458
   reg 8 .... 100, 270, 300, 310, 338
   reg 10 .... 100, 107, 113, 270, 300, 310
   reg 12 .... 230, 270, 310
   reg 16 .... 276, 310
   regs 16–18 270
   reg 17 310
   reg 18(2) 329
      (3) 329
Financial Markets and Insolvency (Settlement Finality and Financial
   Collateral Arrangements) (Amendment) Regulations (SI 2010/2993) 270
Financial Markets and Insolvency (Settlement Finality)
   Regulations 1999 (SI 1999/2979)
   reg 14 .... 229, 230
Financial Services Act 2012 (Misleading Statements and
   Impressions) Order 2013 (SI 2013/637) 661
Financial Services and Markets Act 2000 (Financial Promotion)
   Order 2005 (SI 2005/1529) 673
   Sch 1 .... 635, 661
      para 4C 673
Financial Services and Markets Act 2000 (Liability of Issuers)
   Regulations 2010 (SI 2010/1192) 559, 560, 562–64, 568
Financial Services and Markets Act 2000 (Market Abuse)
   Regulations 2005 (SI 2005/381) 600
Financial Services and Markets Act 2000 (Market Abuse)
   Regulations 2014 (SI 2014/3081) 610
Financial Services and Markets Act 2000 (Official Listing of
   Securities) Regulations 2001 (SI 2001/2956)
   reg 6 .... 511, 655

Financial Services and Markets Act 2000 (Prescribed Markets and
  Qualifying Investments) Order 2001 (SI 2001/996)
  art 4.. 600, 661
  art 5.. 601, 661
Financial Services and Markets Act 2000 (Regulated Activities) (Amendment)
  (No 2) Order 2013 (SI 2013/1881)... 673
Financial Services and Markets Act 2000 (Regulated Activities) (Amendment)
  Order (SI 2015/369)... 596, 599
Financial Services and Markets Act 2000 (Regulated Activities) Order 2001
  (SI 2001/544) (Regulated Activities Order)
  art 5.. 637, 666
    (1) 666
    (2) 666
    (3) 666
  art 6.. 667
    (1)(c) 667
     (d).. 667
  arts 6–9 666
  art 9.. 667
    (2) 667
    (3) 667
  art 10.. 249
  art 17.. 637
  art 18.. 637
  art 25.. 485, 637
    (1) 520
    (2) 520
  art 34.. 637
  art 36H... 673
  art 37.. 485, 638
  art 53.. 485, 637
  art 77.. 635
Insider Dealing (Securities and Regulated Markets) Order 1994 (SI 1994/187) 592, 661
  reg 4 661
  reg 9 661
Insolvency Act 1986 (Prescribed Part) Order 2003 (SI 2003/2097)
  art 3.. 101
Insolvency (Amendment) Rules 2005 (SI 2005/527) 220
Insolvency (Amendment) Rules 2008 (SI 2008/737) 122
Insolvency Proceedings (Monetary Limits) Order 1986 (SI 1986/1996)
  para 4 345
Insolvency Rules 1986 (SI 1986/1925)
  Pt 2 ch 10... 98
  r 2.22... 332
  r 2.33(2).. 337
  r 2.69... 97, 105
  r 2.81... 226
  r 2.85... 226
    (2)(e) 426

    (4) 220, 226
        (c) 226
    (5) 226
    (8) 226
    r 2.88 102
    r 2.95 .... 110, 228
    r 4.75(1)(g) 99
    r 4.86 226
    r 4.90 226
        (2)(d) 426
        (4) 220, 226
            (c) 226
        (5) 226
        (8) 226
    r 4.128 100
    r 4.181 105
    r 4.218 122
    r 4.218A–E 100, 122
    r 11.13 217
    r 12.2 100
    r 12.3 102
        (1) 217, 226, 260
    r 13.12 217
International Tax Compliance (United States of America) Regulations
    2014 (SI 2014/1506) 795
Mortgaging of Aircraft Order 1972 (SI 1972/1268) 286, 317
Overseas Companies (Execution of Documents and Registration of Charges)
    (Amendment) Regulations 2011 (SI 2011/2194) 347
Overseas Companies Regulations 2009 (SI 2009/1801) 347
Prospectus Regulations 2011 (SI 2011/1668) 496
Prospectus Regulations 2012 (SI 2012/1538) 496
    reg 2(2) 495
Prospectus Regulations 2013 (SI 2013/1125) 495
Regulated Covered Bonds (Amendment) Regulations 2008 (SI 2008/1714) 638
Regulated Covered Bonds (Amendment) Regulations 2011 (SI 2011/2859) 638
Regulated Covered Bonds (Amendment) Regulations 2012 (SI 2012/2977) 638
Regulated Covered Bonds Regulations (SI 2008/346) 638
Small Companies (Micro-Entities' Accounts) Regulations 2013 (SI 2013/3008) 543
Transfer of Undertakings (Protection of Employment) Regulations 2006
    (SI 2006/246) 754
Uncertified Securities (Amendment) (Eligible Debt Securities) Regulations
    2003 (SI 2003/1633) 141, 461
Uncertified Securities (Amendment) Regulations 2007 (SI 2007/124) 141
Uncertified Securities (Amendment) Regulations 2013 (SI 2013/632) 141, 461
Uncertified Securities Regulations 2001 (SI 2001/3755) (USR) 141, 376, 461, 534
    reg 3 462
    regs 14–16 141
    reg 19 141
    reg 20 141
        (5) 141

reg 22 378
reg 23(3) 463
reg 24 463
   (2) 141, 377, 461
   (3) 141, 377, 461
reg 33 462
reg 35 463
   (2) 463
   (4) 463
   (5) 463
reg 38 378
   (5) 459
Sch 4 para 14 378
Unfair Terms in Consumer Contract Regulations 1999 (SI 1999/2083) 398

Australia

Company Law Review Act 1988 155
Corporations Act 2001
  s 254C 155
  s 411(d) 742
    (17) 750, 752
Personal Property Securities Act 2009 (APPSA) 290, 307, 316, 350, 355, 358
  Ch 4 355
  s 8(f)(vi)–(x) 351
  s 12(3) 351
  s 13 351
  s 14(1)(c) 354
    (3) 354
  s 17 354
  s 21(2) 352
    (c) 352
  s 25 316
  ss 25–29 352
  s 26 316
  s 27 316
  s 57 316
    (1) 354
  s 62 354
  s 64 355
  s 81 454
  s 109(1) 351
  s 111 356
  s 115 356
  s 131 356
  s 153 352
  s 157 353
  s 164(3) 353
  s 178 353
  s 275 353
  s 300 354

Canada

Bank Act 1991..285
Business Corporations Act 1985
  s 192...742
Ontario Personal Property Securities Act 1967 (OPPSA)........................350, 351, 358, 454
  Pt V..355
  s 1(1)..351
  s 2(c)..351
  s 4..351
  s 11..354
  s 22..352
  s 33..354
    (1)...354
  s 46(5)..354
    (6)...353
  s 56..353
  s 63(1)..356
Personal Property Securities Act...231, 350
Saskatchewan Personal Property Securities Act (SPPSA).........................351, 358, 454
  Pt V..355
  s 2(1)(qq)..351
  s 4(g)..351
    (h)...351
  s 12..354
  s 18..353
  s 24..352
  s 34..354
    (3)...354
  s 43(9)..353
    (12)...353
  s 47..354
  s 50..353
  s 55(2)(a)...351
  s 56(3)..356
  s 59(4)..356
  s 60(2)..356
  s 65(3)..356

European Union

Regulations
Regulation 1346/2000 Insolvency Regulation [2000] OJ L160/1 743
Regulation 44/2001 Judgments Regulation [2001] OJ L12/1 743
Regulation 1606/2002 on the Application of International Accounting
  Standards [2002] OJ L243/1...544
  art 4..544
Regulation 2273/2003 Buy Back and Stabilisation Regulation [2003] OJ L336/33............663
  recital 11 662
  art 8..663

arts 8–10 585
art 9 663
art 10 663
Regulation 809/2004 Prospectus Directive Regulation (PD Reg)
[2004] OJ L149/1 ....494, 497, 641, 649, 651
art 7 641
art 8 641
art 12 641
art 16 641
art 21(2) 641
Annex I 497, 649
  para 2.1 498
  para 4 ....498, 650
  para 5.1 497
  para 5.2.1 498
  para 6 650
  para 6.1.1 498
  para 6.2 498
  para 8 650
  para 8.1 498
  para 10 650
  para 12.1 498
  para 13 ....499, 500
  paras 13.2–13.3 499
  para 14.1 497
  para 15 650
  para 15.1 497
  para 17 ....497, 650
  para 18.1 497
  para 20.1 ....498, 649
  para 21 497
  para 21.2.3 497
  para 22 498
Annex IV 641
  para 3.1 649
  para 4 650
  para 5.2 649
  para 6 650
  para 8.2 649
  para 11 649
  para 13.1 649
Annex V 641
Annex VII 649
Annex VIII 649
Annex IX 641
  para 3.1 650
  para 5 650
  para 6 650
  para 11.1 649
Annex XIII 641

Regulation 1060/2009 on credit rating agencies (CRA I) [2009] OJ L302/1 ....670, 671, 798
    art 5a.. 670
    art 6b.. 670
    art 8.. 670
    art 35a.. 671
    Annex I 670
       section B para 4... 670
Regulation 1095/2010 establishing the European Securities and
  Markets Authority [2010] OJ L331/84798
Regulation 513/2011 on credit rating agencies (CRA II) [2011] OJ L145/30........................... 670, 671
Regulation 236/2012 Short Selling Regulation
  [2012] OJ L86/1 ....534, 618, 621–24, 630, 633, 666
    art 1.. 623
    art 2.. 623
    art 3(1).. 625
     (4) 625
    art 4.. 623, 666
    art 5.. 625, 626
     (2) 625
    art 6.. 625
     (2) 625
    art 7.. 624, 625
    art 8.. 624
    art 9(1).. 625
     (2) 625
     (4) 625
    art 10.. 625
    art 12.. 623
     (1)(a) 623
      (b) 623
      (c) 624
    art 13.. 623, 666
    art 14.. 623
    art 15.. 627
    art 16.. 623
    art 17.. 623
    art 18.. 628
    art 20.. 628
    art 23.. 627, 628
     (1) 627
     (2) 627, 628
    art 24.. 628
    art 27(1).. 629
     (3) 629
    art 28.. 627, 629
     (1) 629
     (2) 629
     (4) 629
     (11) 629
    art 29.. 629, 666

art 31.. 630
art 33.. 630
art 41.. 630
Regulation 486/2012 amending Regulation 809/2004 [2012] OJ L150/1 .... 494, 497
Regulation 648/2012 European Markets Infrastructure Regulation (EMIR)
  [2012] OJ L201/1 .... 233, 254
  art 4.. 254
  art 9.. 254
Regulation 826/2012 supplementing Regulation 236/2012 [2012] OJ L251/1 622
  arts 2–3 625
Regulation 827/2012 on public disclosure regarding short selling and
  credit default swaps [2012] OJ L251/11... 622, 624
  art 2.. 625
  art 6.. 624
  art 8.. 624
Regulation 862/2012 amending Regulation 809/2004 [2012] OJ L256/4 .... 494, 497
Regulation 918/2012 supplementing Regulation 236/2012 [2012] OJ L274/1 .... 622, 629
  arts 5–7 625
  art 10.. 625
  art 21.. 625
  art 24.. 628
  art 26.. 629
    (3).. 629
  art 27(2)... 629
Regulation 919/2012 supplementing Regulation 236/2012 [2012] OJ L274/16.......................... 622
Regulation 231/2013 supplementing Directive 2011/61 [2013] OJ L83/1 .... 800, 801
Regulation 462/2013 on credit rating agencies (CRA III) [2013] OJ L146/1 .... 670, 671
  art 35a.. 670
Regulation 575/2013 Capital Requirements Regulation
  (CRR) [2013] OJ L176/1 ....26, 152, 249, 471
  art 243.. 469
  art 244.. 469
  art 405.. 471
  art 406.. 471
  art 407.. 471
  art 409.. 471
Regulation 759/2013 amending Regulation 809/2004 [2013] OJ L213/1 497
Regulation 383/2014 496
Regulation 596/2014 Market Abuse Regulation
  [2014] OJ L173/1 ....484, 548, 549, 551, 552, 575, 587, 588, 600,
                                        603, 604, 606, 610, 611, 613, 616, 633, 646, 662, 663
  recitals 602
  recital 2 .... 580, 583
  recital 5 588
  recital 7 578
  recital 11 662
  art 1.. 578
  art 2.. 662
    (1) 588, 600, 663
      (a) 548, 551

(a)–(c) 588
(b) 548, 551
(d) 588, 601
(2)(a) 588, 601
(b) 588, 601
(c) 588, 595, 599, 601
(4) 588
art 3(1) 588
(19) 588
art 5 ....585, 608, 663
art 7 .... 548, 604
(1) 605
(b) 603
(c) 603, 604
(2) 605
(3) 605
(4) 605, 606
art 8(1) 603
(4) 603
art 11 608
art 12(1) 608, 611
(2) 588, 608, 611
(c) 609
art 14 ....588, 603, 612
art 15 ....589, 611, 612
art 16 588
art 17 .... 548, 589
(4) 549
art 18 549
art 19 551
(1) 551, 705
(1)–(3) 552, 584
(5) 552
(8) 552
(11) 552
(11) 575
art 20(1) 611
art 25 611
art 30 612
(2)(h) 612
(i) 612
(j) 612
art 31 612
art 32 588
art 34 612
Regulation 600/2014 MiFIR Markets in Financial Instruments
Regulation (MiFIR) [2014] OJ L173/84 .... 254, 455, 483, 541, 575, 646,
                                                                            657, 659, 660, 795
Title II 588, 600
art 3(1) 541
arts 3–5 541

art 4...541
  (1)(c) 541
art 6...541
art 8...659
art 10...659
art 11...659
art 18...659
art 21...659
art 23...455
art 26...626
Regulation 909/2014 on improving securities settlement in the
  EU and on central securities depositories [2014] OJ L257/1 627
  recital 11 377
  art 2(1)...628
  art 3..628
  art 7(2)..377, 534
    (3)–(8)..628
  art 76..377
Regulation 2015/848 Insolvency Regulation [2015] OJ L141/19 743

Directives

Directive 77/91 Second Company Law Directive [1977] OJ L26/1 ....9, 126, 130, 136, 139,
                                                                              148–52, 156, 189, 190
  art 10..156
  art 17..152
  art 21(1)...166
  art 29..131
  art 31(2)...156
    (3) 156
  art 33..133
Directive 77/187 Acquired Rights Directive [1977] OJ L61/26 754
Directive 85/611 on undertakings for collective investment in
  transferable securities [1985] OJ L375/3
  art 22(6)..638
Directive 98/26 Settlement Finality Directive [1998] OJ L166/45.......................................534
  art 3(2)..229
Directive 98/50 amending Directive 77/187 [1998] OJ L201/88 754
Directive 2001/23 Acquired Rights Directive [2001] OJ L82/16 754
Directive 2001/34 Consolidated Admissions Requirements Directive (CARD)
  [2001] OJ L184/1 ....482, 489, 493, 494
  art 5..482
  art 43..489
  art 44..489
  art 58..489, 498
Directive 2002/47 Financial Collateral Directive (FCD) [2002] OJ L168/43..............270, 310, 313, 315
  recital 3 270
  recital 5 ....270, 338
  recital 9 ....270, 311
  recital 10 ....270, 311

art 1(2)..315
art 2(1)(n) 224
    (2) 310
art 4..338
Directive 2002/65 on distance marketing of consumer
financial services [2002] OJ L271/16 674
Directive 2003/6 Market Abuse Directive [2003] OJ L96/16 ....548, 549, 551, 554, 569,
                                                                    587, 588, 600, 602–04, 610

recital 2 580
recital 12 ....578, 582
art 1... 548, 578
art 2..601
art 6..548
    (2) 549
    (3) 549
    (4) 551, 705
    (5) 575
art 8... 585, 608
Directive 2003/71 Prospectus Directive [2003] OJ L345/64 .... 124, 482, 484, 488, 493, 494,
                                                                    497, 516, 641, 645, 648, 668

art 2(1)(b) 667, 668
    (f)...497
art 3(2)...644
art 4(2)(b) 668
art 5(1)...490, 648, 649
    (2) 490, 497, 648
art 6..511
    (2) 500
art 7..668
    (2)(e) 497
art 13...488
art 17...643
art 24...497
Directive 2003/125 implementing Directive 2003/6 [2003] OJ L339/73 575
Directive 2004/25 Takeover Directive [2004] OJ L142/12 ....680, 681, 684, 685,
                                                                    688, 689, 696, 717, 722

Preamble para 7 687
art 1(1)..685
art 2(1)(a)..685
    (d)...692
art 3... 696, 717
    (1)(a) 722
art 4..687
    (1) 685
    (6) 687, 688
art 5..720
art 9...684, 702, 704
    (2) 705
art 11.. 684, 702

art 12..702

  (1)...704

art 15..693

art 16..694

Directive 2004/39 Markets in Financial Instruments Directive

  (MiFID) [2004] OJ L145..25, 541, 661

Title III..482

art 4..471

  (1)...635

  (18)...635

art 13(3)...575

art 16(10)...277

art 65..659

Annex II...799

Directive 2004/109 Transparency Directive [2004] OJ L390/38.................136, 483, 541–43, 547, 548,

                                                          553–55, 557, 562, 569, 571, 647

recital 1..557

art 4...543, 546

art 5...546–48

  (4)...546

art 6..547

art 7..562

art 9..553

  (1)...553, 705

art 28...571

art 28b..569, 571

Directive 2006/43 on statutory audits of annual accounts

  and consolidated accounts [2006] OJ L157/87...573

Directive 2006/48 Capital Requirements Directive [2006] OJ L177/1

  art 122a..472

  (3)...471

Directive 2006/68 amending Directive 77/91 [2006] OJ L69/27.................150, 156, 166, 189

Directive 2006/73 MiFID Level 2 Directive [2006] OJ L241/26.................................575

Directive 2007/36 Shareholder Rights Directive [2007] OJ L184/17.........531, 538, 555, 701

Directive 2009/44 amending Directive 98/26 [2009] OJ L146/37..............................270

Directive 2009/138 Solvency II Directive [2009] OJ L203/19.....................................794

Directive 2009/65 on undertakings for collective investment in

  transferable securities (UCITS) [2009] OJ L302/32...798

Directive 2009/102 on single-member private limited

  liability companies [2009] OJ L258/20..14

Directive 2009/111 Consolidated Admissions Requirements

  Directive (CRD2) [2009] OJ L302/97...471

Directive 2010/73 amending Directives 2003/71 and

  2004/109 [2010] OJ L327/1.............................124, 483, 496, 497, 641, 645

art 1(3)(a)(ii)...644

Directive 2011/61 Alternative Investment Fund

  Managers Directive (AIFMD).......................................471, 623, 764, 772, 773, 786,

                                                          787, 791, 795, 798–803

art 2..799

art 3... 799
    (2) 799
art 4(1)(a)... 798
art 5... 799
arts 6–8 799
art 7(3)(a)... 801
art 9(1).. 799
    (2) 799
    (3) 799
art 12... 800
    (1)(a) 800
        (b) 800
    (2) 800
art 13(1).. 800
arts 14–16 800
art 15(4).. 801
art 17... 471
art 20(1).. 800
art 21(1).. 799
art 22... 800
art 23... 801
arts 23–24 800
art 24.. 800, 801
    (5) 800
art 25(3).. 801
    (3)–(6)... 801
    (5) 801
    (6) 801
    (7) 801
    (8) 801
art 26(2)(a)... 801
    (5) 787, 801
art 27(1).. 787, 801
art 28(2).. 787, 802
    (4) 787, 802
art 29.. 788, 802
art 30... 802
art 31... 799
arts 31–33 799
art 32... 799
Annex II... 800
Directive 2012/6 on the annual accounts of micro-entities [2012] OJ L81/3....................542
Directive 2012/23 amending Directive 2009/138 [2012] OJ L249/1 794
Directive 2012/30 Second Company Law
    Directive (recast) [2012] OJ L315/74..126, 130, 139, 148–51,
                                                                                154–57, 162, 176, 189, 190
    art 6.. 9, 151
    art 7.. 157

art 8...154
　(1)..153
art 17(1)..164, 176
art 25...130, 174
art 31(3)..157
art 32..172
art 46..128, 136
Directive 2013/34 on the annual financial statements, consolidated
financial statements and related reports of certain types of
undertakings [2013] OJ L182/19 ....531, 538, 542, 543, 555, 701
art 20...546
Directive 2013/36 Consolidated Admissions Requirements
Directive (CRD IV) [2013] OJ L176/338...26, 27, 152, 249
Directive 2013/50 amending Directive 2004/109
[2013] OJ L294/13 ....136, 483, 542, 553, 647
art 1...547
　(3)(b)..543
　(4)..546
　(9)..553
　(20)..571
　(21)..569
Directive 2014/51 amending Directives 2003/71, 2009/138 and Regulations
1060/2009, 1094/2010 and 1095/2010 [2014] OJ L153/1 670
Directive 2014/57 Market Abuse Directive [2014] OJ L173/179 ....483, 587, 589, 662
Directive 2014/65 Markets in Financial Instruments Directive
(MiFID II) [2014] OJ L173/349 ....455, 482, 534, 541, 575,
632, 633, 646, 657, 659, 660, 795
art 2(1)(d) 632
　(j)..632
art 4(1)...632, 635, 663
　(15)...663
　(39)...632
　(40)...632
　(44)...635
art 16(3)..575
　(12)...575
art 17..632
　(1)..632
　(2)..633
　(3)..633
　(5)..632
Annex 1 section C..663
Directive 2014/91 UCITS Directive [2014] OJ L257/186 798

France

Code Civil, book IV
art 2333..283
art 2355..283

Germany

Aktiengesetz
§ 96 713
§ 101 713
§ 103–04 713
Commercial Code HGB
s 354(a) 454
Insolvency Statute, Insolvenzordnung (InsO)
§ 15a 120
§ 39(1) n 5 104
Übernahmegesetz
§ 33(1) 708

Greece

Civil Code
s 466(2) 454

Hong Kong

Companies Ordinance 2012, Cap 622
s 674 742
(2) 738, 750, 751
(3) 738

India

Companies Act 1956
s 391 742

Italy

Civil Code
s 1260(2) 454

Japan

Civil Code
s 466(2) 454

Jersey

Security Interests (Jersey) Law Act 351, 358

Korea

Civil Code
s 449(2) 454

New Zealand

Companies Act 1993
s 4 ....184, 185, 189
s 38 155

s 56(1) 189
Sch 7 cl 9 307
Personal Property Securities Act 1999 (NZPPSA) 290, 350, 351, 358
Pt 9 355
s 17(1)(b) 351
s 20 354
s 23(e)(viii)–(x) 351
s 40 354
s 41 352
s 74 354
s 105 351
s 107 356
s 110 356
s 142 352
s 148 353
s 152 353
s 162 353
s 177 353
Personal Property Securities Amendment Act 2001 350
Sch 1 307

Portugal

Civil Code
s 577(2) 454

South Africa

Companies Act No 71 of 2008
Ch 5 742

Spain

Civil Code
s 1112 454

United States

Bankruptcy Code
Ch 11 ....95, 729, 744, 761
§ 510(b) 104
Delaware General Corporation Law
§ 251 754
§ 252 754
Dodd-Frank Wall Street Reform and Consumer Protection Act 2010 .... 254, 471
s 1502 540
Model Business Corporation Act
§ 6.40 .... 184, 189
New York Business Corporation Law
§ 717(b) 714
Sarbanes-Oxley Act 2002 .... 484, 766
Securities Act 1933
r 175 545

Securities Exchange Act 1934 613
  § 9 586
    (a)(2) 584
  § 10(b) 580, 586
  § 13(d) 683
    (e) 683
  § 14(d)–(f) 683
Trust Indenture Act 1939
  s 316 393
Uniform Commercial Code
  Pt 6 355
  art 1-201(37) 351
  art 9 .... 315, 316, 340, 350, 351, 357
  art 9-103(b)(2) 354
  art 9-104 316
  art 9-109(d) 351
  art 9-203 354
  art 9-210 353
  art 9-312 352
    (b) 316
  art 9-313 352
  art 9-314 .... 316, 352
  art 9-324 354
    (b) 354
    (c) 354
  art 9-328 316
  art 9-331(c) 354
  art 9-406 454
  art 9-502(a) 352
  art 9-509 353
  art 9-518 353
  art 9-601(g) 351
  art 9-602 356
  art 9-610(b) 356
Williams Act 1968, 82 Stat 454, 15 USC 683
  § 78m(d)–(e) 683
  § 78n(d)–(f) 683

Table of International Instruments

European Convention on Human Rights 1950
  art 7 595
  Protocol 1 art 1 746
Hague Convention on the Law Applicable to Certain Rights in Respect of
  Securities Held with an Intermediary 2006 (Hague Securities Convention) 389
UN Convention on the Assignment of Receivables in International Trade 2002
  art 9(1) 454
UNIDROIT Convention on International Factoring 1988
  art 6(1) 454

UNIDROIT Convention on Substantive Rules regarding Intermediated
  Securities 2009 (Geneva Securities Convention) 389
    art 11(2) 459
    art 18 460
    art 19 460

Other

Corporate Governance Code 2014 .... 86, 477, 478, 483, 488,
                                                                                            530, 536, 546, 786
    A.2.1 478
    B.1 546
    B.1.2 478
    B.2.1 478
    B.7.1 531
    C.3.1 478
    D.2.1 478
CREST Rules 37, 225, 462, 463, 534
    r 7 para 3.2 .... 225, 457, 462
      para 5 457
FCA Handbook 25, 26, 494, 575, 637, 650, 802
  BIPRU (Prudential Sourcebook for Banks, Building Societies
    and Investment Fiems)
      BIPRU 3.1.5 26
      BIPRU 7.4 369
      BIPRU 7.13 369
      BIPRU 9 26
  CASS (Client Assets Sourcebook) 674
      CASS 5.5 259
      CASS 6.2 259
      CASS 7.4 259
  COBS (Conduct of Business Sourcebook) 673
      COBS 4 .... 651, 673
      COBS 4.2.1R(1) 673
      COBS 14.3.7A(1) 673
        (2) 673
        (8) 674
      COBS 4.4.7(3) 521
      COBS 4.4.7–4.4.10 521
      COBS 10 521
      COBS 12.4 575
      COBS 12.4.4(1) 575
        (2) 575
      COBS 12.4.5 576
      COBS 12.4.7 576
      COBS 12.4.10 575
        (4) 576
      COBS 18.5 800
  DISP (Dispute Resolution: Complaints Sourcebook) 675
      DISP 2.7.6R(12) 674

DTR (Disclosure and Transparency Rules) 136, 140, 477, 494, 542, 543,
547, 548, 562, 569, 597, 610, 658
DTR 1.3.4 .... 566, 569
DTR 1A.3.2 .... 566, 569
DTR 2 .... 548, 658
DTR 2.2 477
DTR 2.2.1 549
DTR 2.3.5 549
DTR 2.5.1 549
DTR 2.5.3 549
DTR 2.5.4 549
DTR 2.5.5A 549
DTR 2.8 549
DTR 3 .... 551, 658
DTR 3.1.2 .... 551, 705
DTR 3.1.3(7) 552
DTR 3.1.4 551
DTR 4 658
DTR 4.1 .... 544, 658
DTR 4.1.3 543
DTR 4.2 .... 546, 658
DTR 4.2.9 546
DTR 4.4.2 658
DTR 5 140
DTR 5.1 477
DTR 5.1.1(3) 553, 554
DTR 5.1.2 .... 477, 553, 705, 720
(1) 553
DTR 5.1.3(3) 553
DTR 5.1.4 553
DTR 5.8.1 .... 553, 554
DTR 5.8.3 553
(1) 553
DTR 5.8.12 .... 553, 554
DTR 6.1.3 136
DTR 6.2.2 .... 549, 551
DTR 6.3.4 549
DTR 7.2 546
FINMAR (Financial Stability and Market Confidence Sourcebook) 618
FINMAR 2.2 .... 620, 622
FUND (Investment Fund Sourcebook)
FUND 3.2.2 800
(j) 801
FUND 3.2.5–3.2.6 800
FUND 3.2.6(2) 801
FUND 3.3 800
FUND 3.4 800
FUND 3.4.5 801
FUND 3.7 800
FUND 3.7.7–3.7.9 801

FUND 3.9 800
FUND 3.11 799
GENPRU (General Prudential Sourcebook)
  GENPRU 2 26
  GENPRU 2.1.9 26
  GENPRU 2.1.10 26
  GENPRU 2.1.11 26
  GENPRU 2.2.31 26
  GENPRU 2.2.157 27
  GENPRU 2.2.158 27
  GENPRU 2.2.165 27
  GENPRU Annex 1 26
  GENPRU Annex 4 26
  GENPRU Annex 5 26
  GENPRU Annex 6 26
INSPRU (Prudential Sourcebook for Insurers)
  1.5.13 249
LR (Listing Rules) 65, 134–36, 144, 477, 478, 482, 483, 494, 511, 531, 532,
                              536, 537, 546, 548, 556, 557, 559, 569, 650–52, 658–700, 759
  LR 1.5.1 645
  LR 2.2.4 .... 681, 700
    (1) 16, 144, 475, 489
  LR 2.2.7(1)(a) 489, 645
    (b) 489, 645
  LR 2.2.9 489
  LR 2.2.12 667
  LR 4 650
  LR 4.1 505
  LR 4.2.4 651
    (1) 667, 668
  LR 6 483
  LR 6.1.3 .... 489, 498
  LR 6.1.4 489
  LR 6.1.16 489
  LR 6.1.17 489
  LR 6.1.18 489
  LR 6.1.19(1) 489
  LR 6.1.23–6.1.24 .... 142, 455
  LR 7.2 .... 475, 483
  LR 7.2.1 483
  LR 8 483
  LR 8.3.1 491
  LR 8.4.2 491
  LR 8.4.3 .... 491, 500
  LR 8.4.8 491
  LR 9.3.11–9.3.12 532
  LR 9.3.12 136
    (1) 532
  LR 9.5.4 135
  LR 9.5.7–9.5.8 135

LR 9.5.8A 135
LR 9.5.10 .... 134, 136, 489
LR 9.8.4 543
LR 9.8.6(5) 478
  (6) 478
LR 9.8.6–9.8.7 .... 546, 549
LR 9.8.7 478
LR 10 .... 483, 556, 559, 726, 727
LR 10.2.1 556
LR 10.2.2 531
LR 10.3.1 556
LR 10.3.2 556
LR 10.4 556
LR 10.4.1 .... 531, 556
LR 10.5.1 .... 532, 556
  (2) 556
  (3) 556
LR 10 Annex 1 556
LR 11 .... 483, 559
LR 11.1 555
LR 11.1.4 .... 532, 555
LR 11.1.5 555
LR 11.1.6 555
LR 11.1.7(1) 555
  (2) 555
  (4) 532, 555
LR 11 Annex 1R 555
LR 12 167
LR 13.4 556
LR 13.5 556
LR 17.3 658
LR 17.3.4 658
LR 17.3.9 658
LR 17.3.10 391
LR 17.3.12 391
MAR (Market Conduct) 596, 601, 602, 663
MAR 1.3.7–1.3.8 603
MAR 1.4.2E 602
MAR 1.4.5 602
MAR 1.6.15 609
MAR 1.7.2 610
MAR 1.9.2 611
MAR 2 .... 586, 596, 608
MAR 2.1.5 662
MAR 2.3 663
MAR 2.4 663
MAR 2 Annex 1 663
MAR 4.3 686

PERG (Perimeter Guidance Manual)
    6 251
    6.3 250
    6.5.4 251
    6.6.2 251
    6.6.8(1) 251
        (2) 252
        (3) 251, 252
        (4) 252
PR (Prospectus Rules) 477, 491, 494, 641, 643, 648–52
    PR 1.2 496
    PR 1.2.2 495
        (2) 690, 691
    PR 1.2.3 496
        (3) 690, 691
        (7) 667, 668
    PR 2.1.3 648
    PR 2.1.4 497
    PR 2.1.7 497
    PR 2.2.2 648
    PR 2.2.7 648
    PR 2.2.8 648
    PR 3.1 497
    PR 3.3.2 651
    PR 5.2 564
    PR 5.5 .... 511, 655
    PR 5.5.3(2) 566
        (a) 511
            (b)(i) 511
                (ii) 511
            (c) 511
            (f) 511
    PR 5.5.4(2)(b) 655
    PR 5.5.6 511
    PR 5.5.9 .... 511, 655
    PR App 1.1.1 667
    PR App 3 499
    PR App 3.1 500
PRIN (Principles for Businesses) 613
    PRIN 2 673
    PRIN 2.1 664
    PRIN 2.1.7 673
SUP (Supervision)
    16.12.4 674
SYSC (Senior Management Arrangements, Systems and Controls)
    4.1.8 674
LSE AIM Rules for Companies 2014 .... 477, 489, 494, 681
    para 18 543

r 1 482
r 5 494
r 11 548
rr 12–13 555
r 17 551
r 31 551
r 32 ....16, 475, 681, 700
Sch 2 494
Sch 5 551
Pre-Emption Group, Disapplying Pre-Emption Rights:
A Statement of Principles (2015) 137, 537, 703
Pt 1para 2 137
    para 3 137
Pt 2A 532
    para 1 .... 532, 703
    para 2 .... 137, 703
    para 3 ....137, 532, 703
Pt 2B para 1 137
    para 5 137
Pt 3 ....137, 532, 703
Takeover Code (City Code on Takeovers and Mergers) 127, 531, 537, 678,
                                                681–96, 703, 704, 706–08, 714, 715,
                                            717–22, 725, 727, 748, 750, 752, 780–83

Intro, A1 678
    A2 696
    A3–A5 685
    A3–A7 685
    A8 .... 682, 685
    A9 696
    A9–A10 686
    A10 686
    A12–A16 687
    A12–A17 684
    A16–A17 687
    A19 686
    A20–A21 686
GP 1 .... 717–19, 722, 750
GP 2 721
GP 3 ....127, 531, 696, 704, 705
GP 4 692
GP 5 .... 691, 781
GP 6 689
r 1(a) 690
r 2.1 690
r 2.2 690
rr 2.6–2.8 .... 690, 780
r 2.7 690
    (c) 781
    (d) 781
r 3 783

r 3.1..690, 705, 782
r 4.2..692
r 4.3..691
r 6..719
r 6.1..719
r 6.2..719
r 8..692
r 9..720
r 9.1..718, 720, 721, 750
r 9.2..720
r 9.3..721
r 9.5..721
r 10...692, 749
r 11..720
r 11.1...719, 720
  (c)..720
r 11.2..720
r 13..691
r 13.1..691
r 13.3..691
r 14..718
r 14.1..718
r 15..718
r 16...718, 783
r 16.2..783
r 19.1...691, 715
r 19.4..691
r 19.5..691
r 20.1..691
r 20.2...707, 782
r 20.3...704, 783
r 21...127, 531, 696, 704, 705
r 21.1...696, 702, 704
  (b)..705
r 21.2..706
r 23...690, 726
r 24...690, 752
r 24.2..715
r 24.3(f)...715
r 25..690
r 25.2...690, 704, 707, 709, 782
  (a)..715
r 26..715
r 28..691
r 28.1..705
r 29..690
r 30.1..690
r 31.1...692, 721
r 31.4..695
r 31.6..692

r 32.1 .... 692, 721
r 32.3 .... 692, 719
r 32.6 715
r 35.1 695
r 35.3 695
r 36 721
r 36.1 721
rr 36.1–36.8 721
r 36.5 721
r 37 721
App 1 721
App 7 685
   s 8 750

1

Introduction

The purpose of this book is to consider and analyse UK corporate finance law. We consider the principles and policy behind the law in this area, and examine the substantive provisions in light of that discussion. In particular we aim to consider both the debt and equity aspects of corporate finance law, and the interrelationship between the two. Before stating in more detail what we aim to achieve, it might also be helpful to set out some of the things we don't seek to achieve. First, although we hope that this book will be read by practitioners, as well as academics, students and policy-makers, and that practitioners will find it interesting and useful, this is not predominantly a how-to guide for practitioners. We don't aim to put the reader in a position to be able to carry out in practice the corporate finance transactions described here. By way of example, the chapter dealing with takeovers (chapter fourteen) does not provide a step-by-step guide as to how to conduct a takeover in the UK. Rather it considers why jurisdictions generally regulate takeovers, why different jurisdictions regulate this issue in different ways, how the UK system compares to other jurisdictions (principally, in that chapter, the US) and then, once the aims of the UK regulation have been established, assesses the UK regulations against that background.

This raises another point, namely that while the book's focus is UK corporate finance law, other regimes are considered, and this comparative analysis can have a number of benefits. Some aspects of UK corporate finance law can only be understood if other regimes are discussed. For example, in a number of areas UK law is very heavily influenced by European developments. An obvious example of this are the disclosure requirements for prospectuses, discussed in chapters ten and thirteen. The Prospectus Directive,[1] a maximum harmonisation directive, and its accompanying Regulation,[2] provide the substance of the UK's disclosure requirements. At other points we examine other jurisdictions as a comparison with the UK provisions in order to provide fresh insight as to the suitability and utility of the UK provisions. This is not intended to be a comparative text, but examining other jurisdictions can help us to better understand domestic provisions. For example, much of the jurisprudence on the policy issues relating to security interests comes from the US, and notice filing schemes such as the ones in Canada and New Zealand are discussed in the context of reform of the UK law on secured transactions.

Although we have said that the purpose of this book is to consider and analyse UK corporate finance law, it must be remembered that the UK consists of four countries: England, Wales, Scotland and Northern Ireland. While the law of England and Wales is the same for all relevant purposes, there are often significant differences between English and Scots law, and some between Northern Irish law and English law. The differences are most notable

---

[1] 2003/71/EC, as amended by Directive 2010/73/EU.
[2] Commission Regulation (EC) No 809/2004, as amended.

with regard to non-statutory law, such as property law and contract. Scots law, especially, comes from a different origin (the civilian tradition) and resembles, in some respects, the law in some European countries, although in other respects it resembles the English common law.[3] However, virtually all company law which is statute based is the same for the whole of the UK.[4] The same is true of most of the regulation discussed in this book, particularly securities regulation, much of which is now derived from European legislation. Other statutory provisions, though, are different as regards English law and Scots law.[5] The reader therefore needs to be aware of this issue. In general, in the debt sections of the book, the law discussed is that of England and Wales, while in the equity sections generally what is said is true for the whole of the UK.

Another general point is that this book is not intended to be comprehensive in any sense. The term 'corporate finance' is not a term of art, and can mean very different things to different people. In deciding what to include we have started from our own conception of what 'corporate finance' means and what it includes, which may well be different from that of others. In part we have also been guided by our interests, but, having taught this subject for a number of years, we have also been guided by what interests and stimulates others about this topic. We will no doubt have included some topics that others do not consider need to be present in a book dealing with corporate finance law, and left out other topics that others would wish to have seen included.

It might be helpful, therefore, to explain what our conception of corporate finance entails. Our starting point is that corporate finance primarily concerns how a company can obtain money to finance its operations, and therefore corporate finance law consists of the legal rules that govern these issues. However, the term 'corporate finance law' is misleading to some extent since it is not one single body of law. Indeed, as will be clear on reading this book, the law described here includes, variously, general contract law, property law, company law and corporate insolvency law as well as more specialist regulatory law dealing with securities, takeovers and other issues. We restrict our analysis to the financing of companies limited by shares. We don't consider unlimited companies or companies limited by guarantee.[6] Neither do we cover the financing of limited liability partnerships, partnerships more generally, sole traders, charities, mutual funds, trusts or other similar structures.

In relation to the financing of companies, there are three basic sources of finance: share issues, debt and retained profits. To a large extent, therefore, we concentrate in this book on the mechanisms by which companies can raise equity capital, and what use they can make of that capital once it has been raised, and on the different methods by which they can raise debt financing. Debt financing is broadly defined, so as to include both loans and debt securities, and also other forms of credit such as trade credit extended to a company by other

---

[3] See P Wood, *Law and Practice of International Finance* (London, Sweet & Maxwell, 2008) 3-24–3-26.

[4] The Companies Act 2006 creates a single company law regime for the whole of the UK (see Companies Act 2006, Part 45) although some differences are preserved within the Act, such as the different regimes regarding derivative actions (Companies Act 2006, ss 260–64 for England, Wales and Northern Ireland and ss 265–69 for Scotland).

[5] For example, different parts of the Unfair Contract Terms Act 1977 (see eg 8.3.5.3) apply, on the one hand, to England, Wales and Northern Ireland, and, on the other hand, to Scotland, and s 136 Law of Property Act 1925 (see eg 9.2.2.2) applies only to England and Wales.

[6] Companies Act 2006, s 3.

companies. However, it does not include all the money of which the company makes use, for example money which is owed by the company to a third party and which the company uses to finance its operations in the interim. One example of this might be a third party who has a tort claim against the company; another is someone who has a claim in respect of defective goods purchased from a company.

Thus, for the purposes of this book, we concentrate on the category of creditors who lend money or extend credit to the company and whose intention is to finance the company's activities, rather than on those who are not intending to become creditors, even though they may have chosen to contract, or otherwise deal, with the company. The additional category of creditors (not lenders) highlighted here, such as tort claimants, is not our predominant concern. This does not mean that they will be ignored in this book. They are of importance in policy discussions, since the contractual arrangements entered into between creditor-lenders and the company can impact on them. In general they are in a weak position to protect themselves (for example if they are involuntary creditors) and so the question arises as to whether the law should step in to protect them. The term 'lender' is used throughout the book generically to include all those who consciously lend to or extend credit to a company. In this context, the company is called the 'borrower'.[7] However, when wider issues about the protection of all those to whom the company owes money are discussed, the term 'creditor' is used to include both lenders and others such as tort and breach of contract claimants.

Any regulation imposed by the law will impact on those groups that are within the contemplation of this book, that is, those who buy shares or consciously lend or extend credit to a company. Generally speaking, investors in shares are protected primarily by regulatory law, although their contractual relationships, in particular with the company or with other shareholders, can be important. By contrast, those who lend or extend credit to a company are protected largely by contractual or proprietary rights for which they bargain, and only by regulatory law in certain specific circumstances.

It follows from this that this book concentrates on companies that are raising finance via equity and debt financing. There are companies (banks and other finance companies) whose business is predominantly to lend money to others. We are not concerned with those types of companies and the topic of banking regulation falls outside the remit of this book. However, the financing of companies that extend credit to other companies is discussed at various points.

As regards the companies that do fall within the ambit of this book, it is clear that there is considerable variety in terms of both the size of companies and the business of those companies, and this necessarily impacts on their financing needs and options. One point which we want to make clear from the outset is that there is not a one-size-fits-all approach to financing which will suit all companies in all situations.

The business in which a company engages will have a significant impact on its financing choices. Companies may be categorised in terms of what they do—for example financial companies, real property companies, construction companies, manufacturing companies, retail companies, services companies, investment companies, or special purpose vehicles (SPVs), engaged, for example, in project finance or securitisation. The type of business

---

[7] These terms are used even when the transaction is structured somewhat differently, for example where receivables are sold to a receivables financier.

conducted by the company will be crucial in determining, for example, whether it has assets over which security can be taken, whether it will depend on trade credit, or whether lenders can make use of some of the quasi-security devices such as retention of title clauses. There is likely to be all the difference in the world between the financing profile of the arche-typal company manufacturing and supplying widgets, a large listed pension fund company whose main business is investing in other companies, and an SPV set up to carry out a pro-ject finance operation. So, for example, a manufacturing company will have to raise finance to buy equipment and stock, as well as to meet employment and other running expenses. Its main assets will be tangible (land, equipment, stock) and intangible (receivables, maybe intellectual property and goodwill). It could be financed through loan finance, secured on its assets, or alternatively by asset-based finance, including receivables financing and reten-tion of title finance in relation to the acquisition of equipment and stock. The listed pen-sion fund company's assets will be equity and debt securities issued by other companies, and it will look to borrow in transactions using these as financial collateral. The project finance SPV will typically only have one asset, namely the revenue-generating contract, on the strength of which it will raise loan or bond finance. Another significant consideration might be whether the company operates within a group of companies and, if so, what role within the group that company performs.

As regards the size of companies, significant differences emerge according to whether the company in question is a private company or a publicly traded company, and whether it has a small group of shareholders who are heavily involved in the management of the company or a wide and dispersed shareholding profile. Consider, for example, a small private com-pany which is effectively an incorporated sole trader. The shareholders and directors are likely to be the same people. As regards financing, it is likely that the director/shareholders will put in a relatively small amount of equity, and that the majority of the financing will be via loans either from the shareholder/directors and/or a bank. The primary purpose of shares in such a company is likely to be their control function rather than any capital rais-ing device. Given the significant risk of insolvency for such a business, the bank will be very keen to protect against this eventuality. It is unlikely that the business itself will have signifi-cant assets, and usually the debts will be guaranteed by the director/shareholders personally and/or secured on their personal assets. In this situation, the relationship between the bank and the company is very important, and the bank will monitor the affairs of the company closely for signs of financial distress.

By contrast, in a somewhat larger private company, with some division between the shareholders and directors, shares become useful as finance-raising devices. However, the illiquidity of private company shares can make them unattractive as an investment, and therefore it may not be straightforward to persuade external investors to invest by way of share capital. One model is to seek a significant injection of equity capital from venture capital (discussed in chapter sixteen). The company is likely to still depend heavily on bank lending (an overdraft and maybe also a longer term loan) and again the bank will be keen to protect itself against the risk of insolvency by taking security (both fixed and floating charges) over the company's assets. The bank would decide to lend based on the previous and projected cash flow of the company, and there would still be an ongoing relationship between the bank and company, involving monitoring. However, such a company may also borrow using asset-based finance, where the amount lent is directly related to the amount of assets the company has. The assets may be sold to the lender (as in the case of receivables) or the lender will take a charge, fixed if possible, over available assets. Depending on the nature of the company's business it may rely on financing supplied via trade creditors, customers etc.

Ultimately, for companies looking to increase significantly their levels of external equity finance, there is the option of issuing the company's shares to the public (discussed in chapter ten). An offer of shares to the public allows the company to have access to outside investors who can participate substantially in the company. This access to significantly increased levels of equity capital is one of the major advantages of offering shares to the public, especially when combined with a listing. Obtaining a listing for the shares creates liquidity. Not only is there a ready market for the shares, but they must be freely transferable.[8] An alternative equity funding option for larger companies is the leveraged buy-out model, whereby a private equity fund injects significant equity financing and purchases a majority stake in the company.[9] Larger companies, whether public or private, will raise debt finance from a number of lenders. Thus loan finance may come from a syndicate of banks, and the company may decide to issue debt securities to a selected number of financial institutions or, in rare instances, to the public. Both of these techniques, which enable the risk of non-payment to be spread across many parties and therefore enable more debt finance to be raised, are discussed in chapter eight. Liquidity is available from the free transferability of debt securities, and, to a more limited extent, from the ability of the lender to novate or assign a syndicated loan or to transfer the risk by other techniques. Transfer of debt is discussed in chapter nine.

A final, general point regarding the aims of this book relates to tax. We recognise that tax law is an important driver in many of the decisions which a company may take about its financing choices, and indeed in the investment decisions taken by investors. We seek to highlight those instances in which tax has a particular impact on these issues, but this is not a book about tax law, and specialist books should be consulted in this regard.[10]

In terms of the scheme of the book, and following on from this discussion, in chapter two we provide an overview of the financing options that are available to companies, which operates to some extent as a menu of financing options for companies. We consider the options for equity financing, debt financing, and financing via retained profits. Those options are then considered in more detail in later chapters of the book. One of the strengths of this book, we hope, is the fact that we consider both the debt and the equity side of the equation for companies, including the interrelationship of these forms of financing, and the mix of debt and equity financing which a company may choose: these issues are explored in chapter two and throughout this book. In chapter three we continue to look at both debt and equity financing side by side, but this time from the perspective of the providers of the finance. In particular, chapter three examines the role that shareholders and lenders play in both solvent and insolvent companies.

Chapter four examines the issue of shares by a company, and specifically the constraints placed on directors of all companies regarding their ability to raise capital in this way (for public offers of shares there are additional regulatory constraints that are discussed in

---

[8] FCA Handbook, LR 2.2.4(1).

[9] See chapter 16.

[10] See eg GK Morse and D Williams, *Principles of Tax Law*, 7th edn (London, Sweet & Maxwell, 2012); J Tiley and G Loutzenhiser, *Revenue Law*, 7th edn (Oxford, Hart Publishing, 2012).

chapters ten, eleven and twelve). The purpose of these constraints is assessed (most notably the need for shareholder protection), and the main restrictions placed on directors, namely pre-emption rights and the need for them to have authority to allot, are considered. Chapter five then examines the issue of legal capital. This can be regarded as an aspect of equity financing—that is, how companies can raise finance from the shareholders and what they can then do with the capital that has been raised. It can also be regarded as a creditor protection issue, namely as a mechanism for providing a fund of capital available to creditors in certain circumstances. In this latter sense, chapter five links naturally with chapters six and seven, which also deal with creditor protection issues. When creditors lend to the company they are exposed to the risk that the company will not pay ongoing obligations of interest, or, even more seriously, that the company will be unable to pay the entire capital sum advanced. Chapter five relates to creditor protection by rules concerning the share capital of a company, chapter six to creditor protection by contractual means (relating both to contracts with the borrowing company and to contracts with third parties), and chapter seven to creditor protection by proprietary means (including both absolute and security interests). As mentioned above, creditors receive little protection from regulation. One exception is where there is a conflict between the interests of shareholders and creditors: thus the preservation of share capital is heavily regulated by company law rules, although the utility of this regulation is doubtful, as chapter five explains. On the other hand, creditors can bargain for considerable protection by contract, limited only by the general rules of contract law, as explained in chapter six. The purpose of regulation in this area is largely to protect third parties, such as other creditors (who receive some protection by the insolvency rules as discussed in chapter three) and third parties who themselves give contractual protection, such as guarantors, who are also protected to some extent by common law principles. In addition, of course, there is quite extensive regulatory protection for holders of debt securities, in both the primary and secondary markets: this is discussed in chapter thirteen. The ability of creditors to bargain for proprietary protection is also fairly unlimited, as explained in chapter seven: such regulation as there is relates largely to the protection of other creditors, and includes the requirement to register security interests, some protection from insolvency law (discussed in chapters three and seven) and rules relating to general property law.

Chapters eight and nine discuss more specific aspects of debt financing. Chapter eight discusses the problems that arise when there are multiple lenders, in terms of both organisational structure and decision-making procedures. The various techniques used to transfer debt, such as novation and assignment, are discussed in chapter nine. The chapter also considers the application of these legal techniques to loan transfers, the transfer of receivables and the transfer of debt and equity securities, as well as the transfer of the risk of debt by techniques such as securitisation and loan participation.

Chapters ten, eleven and twelve then return to equity financing issues. Chapter ten considers the issue of initial public offers for shares, discussing why companies might wish to float their shares on a public market, and why and how the law regulates this issue, in terms of both ex ante disclosure requirements and ex post enforcement mechanisms. Chapters eleven and twelve consider the next stage, namely the regulation of the secondary market. Chapter eleven examines the use of disclosure rules to regulate the secondary market, and in chapter twelve the use of rules designed to deal with market misconduct (such as market manipulation and short selling) is discussed. In each case both the ex ante and the ex post aspects of the regulatory regime are considered. Chapter thirteen returns to debt financing, but continues the themes of chapters ten to twelve by examining the regulation of the debt markets.

Chapters fourteen and fifteen consider a slightly different aspect of equity financing. Issuing shares is an important mechanism for raising finance, but holding shares in a company, particularly ordinary shares, provides the holder with voting rights, in addition to income and capital rights. As a result, holding shares has important consequences for the exercise of control within the company, and transferring shares can effect a change of control within a company. In these chapters we therefore consider two mechanisms for transferring control in a company via a transfer of shares. Takeovers are considered in chapter fourteen, and schemes of arrangement in chapter fifteen. These mechanisms are often used to achieve the same ends, and are seen as alternatives, but they operate in quite different ways. Schemes of arrangement are also used to rearrange a company's capital in other ways, and another common use of schemes is to reorganise the relationship between a company and its creditors, especially where the company is in financial distress. This use of schemes is also discussed in chapter fifteen.

Finally, in chapter sixteen, private equity transactions are examined. The growth of private equity as a mechanism for financing companies is considered, as is the content of a typical private equity transaction. Private equity grew enormously in the UK in the period up to 2008, to the point where it was said to rival the public markets as a source of financing in the UK. A comparison of private equity backed companies and publicly traded companies is undertaken in this chapter with a view to understanding this phenomenon, although it has been relatively rare in practice since the financial crisis. The increasing regulation of the private equity industry post-crisis is also considered in this chapter.

When the first edition of this book was written in 2010, the effects of the global financial crisis on the ways in which non-financial companies raised finance were considered. Two effects, in particular, were noted. The first was the severe reduction of available bank finance for all sorts of companies, and the second was the increase in regulation designed to ameliorate systemic risk. Nearly five years further on, the ramifications of the financial crisis continue to be felt. Although the equity and debt markets have largely recovered from the immediate aftermath of the crisis, the effects noted above still persist. There is still a lack of debt finance available from banks, and alternative providers have stepped in to fill the gap, often involving financing techniques other than straight loans.[11] There has been an enormous increase in regulation, with many of the changes being introduced by the EU, which has responded to the crisis both by following the global agenda of stability laid down by G20[12] and also by reforming its own regulatory regime in order to advance its goal of a single financial market.[13] It remains to be seen how much these regulatory changes have affected the raising of finance by non-financial companies, for example by increasing costs.

---

[11] See 2.3.1.1 and 2.3.1.2.

[12] This includes the regulation of short selling (see 12.3), of credit rating agencies (see 13.7), of alternative investment fund managers (16.7) and of the derivatives markets (see 6.4.3), as well as reforming the capital requirements regime (see 2.3.1.4).

[13] Such reforms include significant changes to the market abuse regime (see 12.2) and to the disclosure regime (see 11.3), but the scale of the change is enormous and almost no chapter of this edition is unaffected by the regulatory reforms. For discussion see Moloney: EU Regulation, 1.5; J Payne and E Howell, 'The Creation of a European Capital Market' in P Koutrakos and J Snell (eds), *Research Handbook on the Law of the EU's Internal Market* (Cheltenham, Edward Elgar, 2015).

2

Overview of Financing Options

2.1 Introduction

There are three basic sources of finance with which a company can finance its operations: share issues, debt and retained profits. This chapter provides an overview of these techniques,[1] introducing the issues that will be discussed in more detail in subsequent chapters. This chapter assesses, in particular, the different debt and equity financing options that are available to companies. It is, however, possible, and indeed common, for hybrid instruments to be created that combine elements of both debt and equity and that blur the distinctions between the two. These are discussed at 2.4 below. Finally, this chapter assesses the issue of the mix of financing options that a company should undertake.

2.2 Equity Financing

A company limited by shares, whether public or private, must have at least one issued share.[2] Although it is possible to set up both unlimited companies and companies limited by guarantee in the UK,[3] these types of companies are not commonly chosen by individuals setting up profit-making organisations.[4] In the case of companies limited by guarantee, they do not provide a simple mechanism for the sharing of profits,[5] and in the case of unlimited companies they forgo the benefit that is often regarded as providing the greatest advantage

---

[1] See eg BIS, *Financing a Private Sector Recovery* (Cm 7923, July 2010), ch 3. For current information on the availability and distribution of finance in the UK, see Bank of England, *Trends in Lending* (published quarterly), www.bankofengland.co.uk/publications/Pages/other/monetary/trendsinlending.aspx and the SME Finance Monitor, operated by BDRC continental, www.sme-finance-monitor.co.uk/. See also the Deloitte CFO survey at www.deloitte.com/view/en_GB/uk/research-and-intelligence/deloitte-research-uk/the-deloitte-cfo-survey/index.htm.

[2] A company limited by shares is formed by one or more persons subscribing their names to the memorandum of association and complying with the registration requirements of the Companies Act 2006: Companies Act 2006, s 7. By contrast, there is no requirement that a company must have any debt, although in practice very few companies will be able to operate without some form of debt financing.

[3] Companies Act 2006, s 3.

[4] Another form of business vehicle which is suited to raising finance and which can be utilised for profit-making ventures is the limited liability partnership, introduced by the Limited Liability Partnerships Act 2000. For discussion see PDavies, I Fletcher and G Morse, *Palmer's Limited Liability Partnership Law*, 2nd edn (London, Sweet & Maxwell, 2011. A discussion of this business form falls outside the parameters of the present book.

[5] Consequently, companies limited by guarantee are generally used for not-for-profit organisations.

to the corporate form, namely limited liability.[6] This book will therefore concentrate on companies limited by shares, which are by far the most numerous and most economically important business form in the UK.[7]

The options available for companies raising money via equity financing are more limited than those available for debt financing, discussed at 2.3 below. The company only has the option of issuing shares. The main variables are the type of shares issued and the sources of the company's equity finance. To a certain extent the options chosen by companies will be determined by their size and stage of development. Although companies limited by shares must have at least some equity capital, the levels may be very low; in particular, there is no minimum capital requirement for private companies in the UK.[8] It is common for small private companies to operate with very little equity capital, and for the majority of the financing to be via loans and retained profits.[9] In such circumstances the effect of equity financing on the company's operations will be slight. By contrast, equity financing tends to become more important as companies grow and develop, at which point external sources of funding start to become available, including venture capital, and, ultimately, access to the capital markets via an issue of the company's shares to the public.

Before discussing the main types of shares and sources of funding in more detail, however, it is important to consider who, within the company, has control of the process of issuing shares. Before directors can allot new shares they must have the authority to do so. For directors of private companies with only one class of shares the directors will have authority, unless the articles prohibit them from doing so.[10] For all other companies, directors can allot shares if they are authorised to do so by the company's articles or by ordinary resolution.[11] In addition, any proposed allotment of equity securities must first be offered to existing shareholders in proportion to the size of their existing holding (pre-emption rights).[12] This may be problematic if the directors wish to issue shares to anyone other than the existing shareholders: pre-emption rights can be disapplied, but that will require the consent of the shareholders.[13] Consequently, shareholders have the opportunity to exert control over directors in relation to the issue of new shares. This is less likely to be an issue in small 'quasi-partnership' companies where the directors and shareholders are often the same individuals. Once a differentiation between the directors and the shareholders in a company arises, however, these issues can become significant. For example, in publicly traded companies the operation of the Statement of Principles drawn up by the Pre-Emption Group means that if the directors want to raise new capital via a rights issue they

---

[6] See Gower and Davies, ch 1.

[7] See eg Statistical Tables on Companies Registration Activities 2013/14, which provide that 3,103,321 private companies limited by shares, 7,821 public companies, 91,879 companies limited by guarantee and 5,084 unlimited companies were on the register as at 31 March 2014.

[8] The minimum capital requirement for public companies is just £50,000: Companies Act 2006, s 763(1), implementing the Second Company Law Directive (EC) 77/91 [1977] OJ L26/1, recast as Directive 2012/30/EU, art 6 (although the Second Directive requires a minimum capital level of just €25,000). For further discussion see 5.3.1.

[9] See eg BIS, *Financing a Private Sector Recovery* (Cm 7923, July 2010), ch 3.7; BIS, *SME Access to External Finance*, January 2012.

[10] Companies Act 2006, s 550.

[11] Ibid, s 551. For further discussion see 4.3.

[12] Ibid, s 561. Pre-emption rights are discussed in detail at 4.4.

[13] Ibid, ss 569–71. For discussion see 4.4.3.

must first engage in a dialogue with existing shareholders.[14] This provides the share-holders, and particularly the institutional investors, with an opportunity to engage with the company, and can enable them to perform a monitoring role. Indeed, a positive relation between UK rights issues and managerial change has been found to exist.[15] For these reasons, financing the company with retained profits or debt finance may be a more attractive option to directors in some circumstances.

2.2.1 Different Types of Shares

Companies have a significant amount of flexibility as to the rights that they can attach to their shares. The rights are generally laid down in the articles of association, the predominant constitutional document for companies.[16] To an extent these rights are a matter of contract, although the articles form a contract of a peculiar kind.[17] The articles are a contract binding the company and its members, and the members inter se, as a result of section 33 of the Companies Act 2006. The binding force of this contract arises from the terms of the statute, rather than from any actual bargain struck between the parties. The rights attached to the shares may not be specifically negotiated or agreed to by a particular shareholder. When an investor buys a share in a company, he or she becomes bound by the terms of its articles in existence at that time, and these terms can subsequently be altered, potentially without that shareholder's permission, by a special resolution, ie a 75 per cent majority vote.[18] This contract is, therefore, quite unlike that between a creditor and the company, which complies with the usual rules of contract law and thus, for example, cannot be altered without the creditor's agreement.[19]

Shareholders can enter into an additional contractual arrangement: a shareholders' agreement. This is a conventional contract, which operates separate to and outside the articles of association. It can be used by the shareholders as an additional mechanism to

---

[14] See Pre-Emption Group, *Disapplying Pre-Emption Rights: Statement of Principles*, 2015. Although not technically binding, in practice this Statement has an important effect on the ability of public companies to raise new equity finance. For discussion see 4.4.3.

[15] J Franks, C Mayer and L Renneboog, 'Who Disciplines Management in Poorly Performing Companies?' (2001) 10 *Journal of Financial Intermediation* 209; D Hillier, SC Linn and P McColgan, 'Equity Issuance, CEO Turnover and Corporate Governance' (2005) 11 *European Financial Management* 515. For further discussion see 4.4.4.

[16] Companies Act 2006, s 17. Prior to the Companies Act 2006, a company's constitution comprised its memorandum of association and articles of association. Although Companies Act 2006 retains the concept of a memorandum of association, this document is now of marginal constitutional importance (s 8).

[17] *Bratton Seymour Service Co Ltd v Oxborough* [1992] BCC 471, 475 per Steyn LJ (in relation to Companies Act 1985, s 14, the similarly worded predecessor to Companies Act 2006, s 33); *AG of Belize v Belize Telecom Ltd* [2009] UKPC 10.

[18] The fact that articles can be altered by a special resolution of the company (Companies Act 2006, s 21) is subject to two provisos: (i) if the right comprises a class right, and the class right is being varied (see *White v Bristol Aeroplane Co* [1953] Ch 65), then the statute creates additional protections for the shareholder (Companies Act 2006, ss 630–35); and (ii) more generally, the courts have determined that for an alteration to be valid the shareholders must vote bona fide in the best interests of the company (*Allen v Gold Reefs of West Africa Ltd* [1900] 1 Ch 656; *Citco Banking Corp NV v Pusser's Ltd* [2007] UKPC 13).

[19] It is common for bond issues to provide that the terms of the contract can be altered by the agreement of 75% of the creditors (see chapter 8), but in such circumstances the creditors would have to agree to this arrangement upfront, when entering into the contract. A bond trustee is usually authorised to agree minor modifications without having to ask the permission of the bondholders (see 8.3.4.2.1).

order their relationship: a provision in a shareholders' agreement can have an effect similar to a provision in the articles.[20] A shareholders' agreement has an advantage over the articles in that it need not be registered at Companies House, and therefore remains private. It has the disadvantage, however, that new members of the company will not automatically be bound by its provisions, unless they specifically assent to it. Unless the terms of the agreement provide otherwise, it will only be possible to alter the provisions of a shareholders' agreement with the consent of all of the parties. Shareholders' agreements tend to be used in companies with relatively few shareholders, for example small quasi-partnership companies, joint venture companies and venture capital companies.

A company's ability to bargain with its shareholders as to the number and nature of the shares that it issues to shareholders, and the rights attached to those shares, is not entirely unconstrained. In particular, statute has intervened to prevent companies having complete freedom as to how and when they may issue new shares,[21] and to determine the rights that they may attach to those shares. For instance, even if the articles state that certain shares will have a guaranteed right to a specified dividend, this will be subject to the statutory rule that dividends can only be paid if the company has distributable profits.[22] These protections are sometimes put in place to protect the existing shareholders of the company,[23] and sometimes to protect the creditors of the company.[24] The restrictions contrast with the position regarding debt, where the parties are, in principle, free to make their own bargain.

There are three main rights that tend to be specified in relation to shares: income rights, capital rights and voting rights.[25] Beyond these rights, however, there are a wide range of other rights and entitlements which could potentially be attached to the share, a common one being the right to appoint one or more directors of the company.[26] The two most common types of shares that are issued by companies are ordinary shares and preference shares.[27]

2.2.1.1 Ordinary Shares

Ordinary shares are the default shares of companies: if a company has only one class of share then that class will be ordinary shares. Investors holding ordinary shares have no right to receive any fixed returns from the company. A company can only pay dividends to shareholders out of distributable profits.[28] Even where distributable profits exist, however, the

---

[20] Shareholders' agreements are included within the definition of the constitution of the company for the purposes of Companies Act 2006, s 40 (s 40(3)(b)).

[21] For example, new issues of shares are subject to pre-emption rights, discussed at 4.3.1.

[22] Companies Act 2006, ss 830–31 (for discussion see 5.4.1).

[23] For example, pre-emption rights, discussed at 4.3.1.

[24] For example, the minimum capital rules and maintenance of capital rules, discussed at 5.3 and 5.4.

[25] For discussion see 3.2.1.1 and 3.2.1.2.

[26] A right to appoint a director can, in theory, be a class right (for the definition of a class of shares see Companies Act 2006, s 629) if that right is attached to the shares (eg the right to appoint a director passes with the shares when they are sold) rather than attaching to the shareholder personally: see *Cumbrian Newspapers Group Ltd v Cumberland & Westmorland Herald Newspapers & Printing Co Ltd* [1987] Ch 1 per Scott J for a discussion of the definition of class rights in this context. For discussion see 3.2.1.1 and 3.2.1.2.

[27] See 3.2.1.1 and 3.2.1.2. It is also common for these to be issued as redeemable ordinary shares or redeemable preference shares.

[28] Companies Act 2006, ss 830–31, discussed further at 5.4.1.

holders of ordinary shares will have no absolute entitlement to demand that dividends be paid. The payment of dividends is governed by the company's articles, and these will usually leave it to the directors to recommend dividend payments to the shareholders in general meeting.[29] The right of ordinary shareholders to participate in the capital of the company is generally limited to their entitlement to any surplus left over after all the liabilities have been paid, ie they have no guarantee of any return on a winding up. They are the residual claimants of the company. They take the lion's share of the risk, but, in the good times, they will take the lion's share of the rewards. Indeed, investors in ordinary shares will generally expect a return that is adequate to compensate them for the risk that they will not be repaid in the event of a winding up. In terms of voting rights, they usually have one vote per share. They are generally the decision-makers of the company, to the extent that decisions need to be taken by the general meeting.[30]

There may be a number of reasons for issuing ordinary shares in a company. In some companies, particularly very small companies, the purpose of issuing shares may simply be to give the shareholders control of the company. It is common for shareholders to use their voting rights to appoint themselves directors of the company, or to appoint their representatives to that position. The amount of capital injected via the ordinary shares may be negligible, with most of the financing in the form of a bank loan and/or overdraft secured on the personal assets of the shareholder-directors. In such circumstances, the ordinary shares that are issued will have little or no financing role. In larger companies, however, even though the control aspect of ordinary shares often remains important, the use of ordinary shares as a capital-raising device cannot be ignored.[31]

Ordinary shares are a particularly flexible form of finance for companies. As long as the company is a going concern, the ordinary shareholders are not entitled to any particular level of return by way of dividend. In order to exit the company, shareholders may be able to sell their shares, but that is dependent on finding a buyer.[32] This will generally be difficult for shareholders in private companies since, by way of contrast to the shareholders in publicly traded companies, there is no ready market for their shares. Otherwise, shareholders cannot withdraw the contribution they have made in exchange for their shares without the company's consent. This consent may be given at the time of issue, as is the case where the company issues redeemable shares to the shareholder,[33] or may be given later, in the event that the company offers to repurchase its shares.[34] The capital provided by the shareholder can therefore be regarded as subject to a modified form of lock-in.

---

[29] For discussion see 3.2.1.1.

[30] Ibid.

[31] In private equity backed companies, for example, the amount of equity financing is by no means negligible, although the highly leveraged nature of these companies means that it is still outweighed by the amount of debt finance. Generally, today, private equity funds will hold the equity component of their investment by way of ordinary shares, but will also inject substantial financing by way of deeply subordinated debt. For further discussion see 16.4.2.

[32] Transfers of shares are discussed at 4.7.

[33] Companies Act 2006, ss 684–89 (for discussion see 5.4.2.3).

[34] Ibid, ss 690–723 (for discussion see 5.4.2.2).

2.2.1.2 Preference Shares

Ordinary shares can vary in form,[35] but the description set out above will be accurate for most purposes. By contrast, preference shares can exist in much greater variety. A reasonably common form of preference share, however, is one which is preferential as to a return of dividend,[36] and preferential as to a return of capital, but does not give the preference shareholder the right to participate in the surplus assets of the company. In addition, it is usual for preference shareholders to have a right to vote only in certain limited circumstances, such as where the preferential dividend has been in arrears for a specified period. These issues are discussed in detail in chapter three.[37] Consequently, preference shares are primarily an instrument of corporate finance, unlike ordinary shares which, as discussed, may perform other significant roles within the company.

There is no standard package of rights that attaches to all preference shares. Preference shares can be placed at numerous points on the continuum, which has the 'pure equity' of the ordinary shares at one end and debt at the other.[38] It is possible for a company to create a class of preferred ordinary shares, having a right to vote and to receive priority as to fixed income payments, but no priority as to the return of capital. Thus preference shareholders could be entitled to share in the surplus assets on a winding up, vote in a general meeting on all issues, but have a preference as to dividends and/or capital repayment. This form of preference share is rare.[39] It is more common for preference shares to be issued as a form of fixed interest security akin to debt.[40]

When debt is expensive, preference shares may be issued with a sufficiently attractive preferential dividend to tempt an investor, but with no rights to participate in the surplus and only minimal rights to vote. From the company's point of view this is attractive, since the preference shareholder has no guaranteed right to the dividend,[41] unlike creditors, who have a contractual right to receive interest payments, and often have a strong armoury of

---

[35] For example, non-voting ordinary shares are possible, though rare (particularly in public companies as they are unpopular with institutional investors: see generally Institutional Shareholder Services, Shearman & Sterling and European Corporate Governance Institute, *Report on the Proportionality Principle in the European Union* (May 2007), www.ecgi.org/osov/documents/final_report_en.pdf). More common are multiple voting rights in small quasi-partnership companies designed to entrench the shareholder-directors in their position on the board (see eg *Bushell v Faith* [1970] AC 1099).

[36] The dividend will still be subject to the company having distributable profits (Companies Act 2006, ss 830–31) and, generally, subject to the dividend having been declared (*Bond v Barrow Haematite Steel Co* [1902] 1 Ch 353). For discussion see 3.2.1.2.

[37] See 3.2.1.2.

[38] Discussed at 3.2.1.2.

[39] A variation on the standard preference share model that sometimes arises is a convertible preference share that entitles the holder of the preference share, at some point in the future, to convert it into another security of the company, commonly an ordinary share. This can allow the benefits of a preference share to be combined with the advantages of an ordinary share including, crucially in this instance, capital growth.

[40] For a discussion of preference shares as a form of hybrid security see 2.4.

[41] The preferential dividend entitlement is not a debt until declared, and therefore cannot be guaranteed: *Bond v Barrow Haematite Steel Co* [1902] 1 Ch 353. Even if the articles specify that the dividend does not need to be declared, and specify the date on which the dividend payment is due, the payment will still not be guaranteed, since it will remain conditional on distributable profits being available: see Companies Act 2006, ss 830–31. If no such profits are available then at best the right to payment will be suspended until there are sufficient distributable profits. This is the position in Australia (*Marra Developments Ltd v BW Rofe Pty Ltd* (1977) 2 NSWLR 616 (Sup Ct NSW)) and probably represents the English position, though there is no authority on this point.

weapons if they are unpaid.[42] The company, therefore, has maximum flexibility in terms of how to manage its business, with little or no interference from these capital-providers. The company may, however, need to offer an attractive rate of preferential dividend to tempt a potential investor. Consequently, once debt becomes cheaper, usually when interest rates go down, it is common for companies to then reduce their capital, repay the preference shares, and refinance the company using debt.[43]

2.2.2 Sources of Equity Finance

As discussed, for very small companies it is possible that issuing shares does not predominantly perform a financing role at all. In single-member companies,[44] or in so-called quasi-partnership companies,[45] it may well be that the amount of issued share capital is tiny. In these companies the primary value of the shares may be their control function, and in particular the ability of the shareholders to appoint themselves as directors and to protect themselves in that position. It is shares with voting rights attached, generally ordinary shares, that will be most valuable for this purpose.

This point highlights an interesting contrast between debt and equity. It is possible for a single creditor to finance a company, for example a single bank, or for multiple lenders to finance a company. Financing by multiple lenders raises a number of distinct issues, which are dealt with in chapter eight. By contrast, although it is possible for companies to have a single shareholder and therefore, technically, to be financed by a single shareholder, in practice, as discussed, in single-member companies the primary value of that share is not generally as a financing tool. In practice, to the extent that companies are financed by equity, they tend to be financed by multiple shareholders. It is an assumption of the equity financing issues discussed in this book that the financing is being provided by multiple shareholders.

As companies become larger, equity financing as a source of capital is likely to become more significant, and for most companies there will come a point at which the original shareholders cannot satisfy their equity financing. Of course, even for larger companies, one option is to continue to rely on debt rather than equity, but this may not always be possible or desirable. Bank debt typically requires businesses to make regular interest and principal payments. For some types of investment the expected stream of revenues may be uncertain and only available far into the future. Internet companies often fall into this category. Such companies will simply not generate adequate revenue to make the necessary

---

[42] For example, the creditors may be able to petition to wind up the company if the debt remains unpaid: *Cornhill Insurance plc v Improvement Services Ltd* [1986] 1 WLR 114. They are likely also to have contractual weapons, such as the right to accelerate the loan and terminate the contract: see 6.3.3.

[43] See eg *Re Hunting plc* [2004] EWHC 2591 (Ch) as an example of this in practice. For a discussion of the cost of debt see 2.6.

[44] An EU directive provides for limited harmonisation of the national company laws by requiring all EU Member States to allow companies to have a single shareholder and by regulating the powers of such single shareholder in relation to a company (Directive 2009/102/EC). In April 2014 the Commission published a provisional draft of a new directive on single-member private limited liability companies which aims to make it easier and less costly to set up private limited liability companies with a single shareholder across the European Union: European Commission, Proposal for a Directive of the European Parliament and of the Council on single member private limited liability companies, April 2014.

[45] The existence of these forms of companies does not appear in companies legislation, but is well recognised by the courts; see eg *O'Neill v Phillips* [1999] 1 WLR 1092.

interest and principal payments in the first few years after the loan is made. Banks also generally impose numerous covenants designed to protect their debt investment,[46] which may be undesirable to the company. There may also be good reasons for having a more balanced debt to equity ratio within the company, an issue which is discussed further in 2.6.

At some point, therefore, many businesses will seek additional capital in the form of equity. Equity financing has some benefits compared to debt, especially for companies that only expect to be profitable in the future. There are also downsides. From the perspective of the existing shareholders, bringing in more equity owners will dilute the potential upside return from the business, unless non-participating shares are issued, but these may not be attractive to potential investors. If the company wishes to increase its equity base in order to fund business expansion plans, to introduce new products or to reduce borrowings, it will need to consider how to attract additional equity investors, ie equity investors other than the original shareholders, and persuade them to put money into the company.

One possibility for such companies is to seek a significant injection of equity capital from a venture capital fund or a 'Business Angel' (ie a high net worth individual who provides early-stage venture capital to companies either alone or as part of a syndicate).[47] This option involves the existing shareholders potentially giving up a significant slice of their share ownership to the external investor. It avoids the need to go to the public markets, at least in the short term, although an offer of shares to the public may be the mechanism whereby the external investor exits the company in the future. The availability of this form of equity capital does not appear to be spread evenly across the market, and external equity finance of this kind appears to be more readily available in some sectors of the economy, and for companies of a certain size and stage of development, than others.[48] A variation on this model is the management buy-out or leveraged buy-out model, which usually occurs when the company is significantly larger, and indeed can occur when the shares in the company are publicly traded. This involves an injection of capital from the management of the company and from a private equity fund, together with substantial debt financing. Private equity is discussed in detail in chapter sixteen.

An alternative model for an expanding company seeking additional equity financing is to look for funding from 'external' shareholders, ie those who will not be involved in the management of the company. This form of financing can be problematic. The difficulty is not the fact that the shareholders may not be engaged in management. Limited liability allows shareholders to take no role in management and indeed, should they choose, not to monitor the management at all, secure in the knowledge that, as long as the principle of limited liability is upheld,[49] they know the full extent of their financial exposure to the company.[50]

---

[46] See 3.2.2.3 and 6.2.

[47] BIS, *Financing a Private Sector Recovery* (Cm 7923, July 2010), 3.46–3.48; BIS, *SME Access to External Finance*, January 2012.

[48] DTI, *A Mapping Study of Venture Capital Provision to SMEs in England* (DTI, Small Business Service, October 2005).

[49] There are mechanisms whereby limited liability can be set aside, some created by statute (eg Insolvency Act 1986, ss 213, 214), and some created by the courts (eg the doctrine of 'lifting the veil of incorporation': for discussion see eg *Prest v Petrodel Resources Ltd* [2013] UKSC 34).

[50] See SB Presser, 'Thwarting the Killing of the Corporation: Limited Liability, Democracy and Economics' (1992) 87 *Northwestern University Law Review* 148. Of course, limited liability is largely fictitious for the shareholders in quasi-partnership companies if they give personal guarantees to the company's creditors, and use their personal assets to secure the company's debts.

Without limited liability it is unlikely that a prudent investor would be prepared to invest in such a situation, or if they were prepared to invest they would expect a very high return to compensate them for the risks involved. Rather, the problem is generally that investors' contributions to private companies are locked in. Selling shares in a private company is not straightforward. In the majority of private companies, finding a buyer for the shares will often be very difficult. The existing shareholders[51] may not be interested in increasing their stake in the company, or may not have the resources to do so, and any new external investors will generally be hard to find. There is a potential liquidity problem for external investors in such companies.[52] The ability to transfer the shares may be the shareholder's only way of exiting the company and realising its investment.

For companies looking to increase significantly their levels of external equity finance, the option of issuing the company's shares to the public may therefore look attractive.[53] An offer of shares to the public allows the company to have access to outside investors who can participate substantially in the company. Such an offer can be attractive to investors, particularly when combined with a listing or an admission of the shares to trading, which will provide the shares with a secondary market and thereby create liquidity. Not only does this create a ready market for the shares, but requirements imposed by the stock exchanges mean that such shares must be freely transferable.[54] This has the consequence that the shares are no longer predominantly about a relationship between the shareholder and the company, but become items of property just like any other. Shares that are publicly traded also become valuable in other ways, both to investors[55] and to the issuing company.[56] These are not the only advantages of an offer of shares to the public,[57] but the access to significant levels of external equity finance that flow from an offer of shares to the public is one of the primary drivers in most such offers.[58]

An offer of shares to the public is not, however, something to be undertaken lightly. In order to offer shares to the public the company must be a public company.[59] Public companies face greater administrative burdens than private companies, and the legal capital

---

[51] Pre-emption rights will generally mean, of course, that the existing shareholders have to be offered the shares first: Companies Act 2006, ss 561–77. For discussion see 4.4.

[52] As far as venture capital and private equity investors are concerned, they tend to invest for a significant period of time and will generally have a clear exit strategy in mind, which might be a sale of the company or a flotation on the public markets. This is discussed in chapter 16. Generally, such investors will not invest unless they are comfortable that a viable exit strategy exists at the end of their anticipated hold period.

[53] It may be possible for the company to issue its shares to 'external' investors while avoiding the need for a full IPO prospectus if the offer does not fall within the definition of an offer of shares to the public (see 10.5.2.1) and if the securities are not admitted to listing on a regulated exchange (eg a placing of shares with institutional investors combined with a non-public offer, discussed further at 10.3.2.2). Non-public offers of debt securities are more common; see chapter 13.

[54] For shares admitted to listing the London Stock Exchange imposes this requirement via the Listing Rules: FCA Handbook, LR 2.2.4(1). For companies admitted to trading on AIM, this requirement is imposed by the admission rules for AIM: LSE, *AIM Rules for Companies*, May 2014, r 32.

[55] For example, investors may find that banks will accept listed shares as security for loans.

[56] Publicly traded shares can be used as a form of payment, for example as consideration in share-for-share acquisitions, thereby widening the company's financing options when compared to unlisted companies. The liquidity associated with such shares also provides greater scope for the company to offer remuneration packages that include shares and options.

[57] For a fuller discussion, see 10.2.1.

[58] For discussion see JC Brau, 'Why Do Firms Go Public?' in D Cumming (ed), *The Oxford Handbook of Enrepreneurial Finance* (Oxford, Oxford University Press, 2012).

[59] Companies Act 2006, s 755.

regime that they face is more burdensome.[60] In addition, in order to secure the liquidity gains involved in offering shares to the public, most offers will be accompanied by admission of the company's shares to trading on a public market.[61] Companies are generally able to raise money more easily and to obtain a better price if after the initial issue of shares there is a healthy secondary market available to investors on which they can sell their shares and realise their investment, if they so choose. There are a number of options available to the company in this regard. For example, within the UK, the London Stock Exchange offers the Main Market for well-established companies, and the Alternative Investment Market (AIM) for less well-established companies.[62] There is no obligation on UK companies to list their shares on a UK market, however, and a UK company has complete freedom to list its shares elsewhere, either as a primary listing or, more commonly, as a secondary listing.[63] The initial public offer of shares is discussed in detail in chapter ten, and the regulation of securities, once they have been listed on a UK public market, is discussed in chapters eleven and twelve. Once a company has its shares publicly listed, it can raise further equity capital via a fresh issue of shares. These may have to be offered first to the existing shareholders of the company in proportion to their existing shareholding in the company, in accordance with pre-emption rights.[64] Pre-emption rights can, however, be disapplied by special resolution,[65] and if this occurs the shares can be offered to external investors.

A further option that has emerged in recent years for companies wishing to acquire equity finance from external investors is crowdfunding.[66] Crowdfunding is a way of raising finance by asking a large number of people for a small amount of money, generally via an internet platform. Typically, those seeking funds set up a profile detailing their project on a website and may then use social media, alongside more traditional networks, to raise money. There are various different types of crowdfunding. One key distinction is between crowdfunding that aims at financial returns and crowdfunding that aims at non-financial returns. An example of the latter category is donation crowdfunding, whereby people invest simply because they believe in the cause, and may receive some return (for example acknowledgements on an album cover or tickets to an event), but may not. In this form of crowdfunding donors often have a social or personal motivation for putting their money in and expect nothing back, except perhaps to feel good about helping the project. Any returns are considered intangible. Another example is reward crowdfunding, which might involve someone effectively buying goods in advance. For example where a project involves

---

[60] See 10.3.1.

[61] See 10.3.3.

[62] The London Stock Exchange has no monopoly on the operation of public markets for securities within the UK and a number of alternatives now exist, such as ISDX (the ICAP Securities and Derivatives Exchange), which is an independent UK stock exchange regulated by the FCA and operated by ICAP plc. ISDX specialises in smaller and growing companies.

[63] See 10.3.3.2.

[64] Companies Act 2006, s 561. For discussion see 4.4.

[65] Ibid, ss 570–71. In publicly listed companies there is a further constraint on the directors' ability to issue shares to external investors. The Pre-Emption Group, an association representing institutional investors, has published a Statement of Principles providing guidance on the considerations that shareholders in such companies should take into account when deciding whether to vote in favour of a disapplication of pre-emption rights. For discussion see 4.4.3.

[66] See eg E Mollick, 'The Dynamics of Crowdfunding: An Exploratory Study' (2014) 29 *Journal of Business Venturing* 1.

the development of a new piece of technology the reward may be to receive one of the first versions of the product as and when it appears. Reward crowdfunding may also involve more established businesses providing their goods to investors, perhaps at a discount, as a reward for their investment.[67]

Crowdfunding that involves financial returns may be by way of debt[68] or equity.[69] Equity crowdfunding involves people investing in a business opportunity in exchange for shares in the company, which is unlisted. Investors invest via a platform, generally a website, which displays profiles of the companies seeking investment. Crowdfunding platforms do provide some investor protection as they carry out some vetting of the businesses listed on their platforms, although the extent of this vetting varies. On many equity crowdfunding platforms, including some of the largest, such as Crowdcube, the investors become direct shareholders in the relevant company, although some platforms hold the shares in the companies as nominees for the investors, and may charge a management fee for doing so. Generally, companies will seek a target amount within a stated period. Investors can select the companies and projects in which they wish to invest, and the amount they want to invest (the minimum may be as little as £10) via the platform's website. If the target is not reached within the stated period, then investors' funds are not taken from their bank accounts (although sometimes the period may be lengthened). If the target is achieved, then, in a typical scenario, investors will be emailed a copy of the adopted articles of association of the company and given seven working days to review them. During this period investors can ask any questions they might have, and edit or withdraw their investment if they wish. Once these seven working days have elapsed, the crowdfunding platform will capture payments from all investors and transfer funds to the entrepreneur. Subsequently, the share certificates will be issued to investors, generally available to download via the crowdfunding platform. At present, equity crowdfunding remains a relatively niche mechanism for raising equity capital, although it is a sector that grew rapidly in 2014.[70] It generates difficulties for regulators in terms of balancing companies' desire to access finance with the need to provide investors with protection.[71] This is an area in which regulation has been introduced, discussed further at 10.7.

---

[67] For discussion see P Belleflamme, T Lambert, A Schwienbacher, 'Crowdfunding: Tapping the Right Crowd' (2014) 29 *Journal of Business Venturing* 585.

[68] Debt crowdfunding involves investors receiving their money back with interest. This is also called peer-to-peer lending, and is discussed at 2.3.2 and 13.8.

[69] See eg P Belleflamme, T Lambert and A Schwienbacher, 'Crowdfunding: Tapping the Right Crowd' (2014) 29 *Journal of Business Venturing* 585; A Schwienbacher and B Larralde, 'Crowdfunding of Small Entrepreneurial Vehicles' in D Cumming (ed), *The Oxford Handbook of Entrepreneurial Finance* (Oxford, Oxford University Press, 2012).

[70] Equity crowdfunding grew by 201% in 2014: Z Zhang, L Collins and P Baeck, *Understanding Alternative Finance: The UK Alternative Finance Industry Report 2014*, www.nesta.org.uk/sites/default/files/understanding-alternative-finance-2014.pdf. See also IOSCO, *Crowdfunding: An Infant Industry Growing Fast*, February 2014.

[71] See 10.7. For a discussion of the FCA's approach see FCA, *The FCA's Regulatory Approach to Crowdfunding over the Internet, and the Promotion of Non-Readily Realisable Securities by Other Media*, Policy statement, PS 14/4, March 2014. For a discussion of the position in the US see CS Bradford, 'Crowdfunding and the Federal Securities Laws' [2012] *Columbia Business Law Review* 1.

2.3 Debt Financing

Very few companies have sufficient cash from equity capital or retained profits to meet every obligation as it falls due. Further, it would not be good business practice to do so. The operations of the company would be unduly restricted and the business would fail to grow. The company needs to borrow to expand its business, to invest in capital expenditure which will result in future income streams, and to enable it to meet current expenditure which is necessary in order to achieve future income. It will be seen that the need for debt finance is, therefore, at least in part, a question of cash flow. The company may have expectations of future profit (and in many cases these are more than expectations: money is actually due to the company in the future), but needs money upfront to meet its immediate obligations. This type of financing can only be achieved by debt financing. It is relatively short-term so that the capital circulates: equity financing is therefore unsuitable. In relation to long-term financing, the company has a genuine choice between debt and equity financing: the question of which to choose therefore becomes important. This question will arise in various forms throughout this chapter, especially where the distinction between debt and equity becomes blurred. Each form of financing has advantages and disadvantages: these will be outlined here and considered in more detail throughout the book.[72]

There is far more variety in the debt finance available to most companies as compared to the equity financing options on offer. Because more variety is available, far more thought needs to be given as to how the selection of the most appropriate forms of debt financing for each company is made. As this section indicates, the process of selecting the most appropriate debt financing will depend on a number of factors, including the size and nature of the company, its current financial position, the nature of its assets, the reason finance is needed, and the nature and requirements of the lender. In contrast to equity financing, where the shareholders have a potentially significant role, since they have the opportunity to exert control over directors in relation to the issue of new shares,[73] debt financing is a corporate decision taken solely by the directors.

2.3.1 General

2.3.1.1 Sources of Debt Finance

Twenty years ago, the main sources of debt finance were relatively limited. Leaving aside funding within a group of companies,[74] the main source of loan finance for companies was commercial banks, that is, banks that took deposits, while investors in corporate debt securities were institutional investors, including pension funds, insurance companies and other investment funds, together with some wealthy individuals and (occasionally) the wider retail market. There were also specialist financiers, including those who provided asset finance and receivables financing, although the latter was quite limited in scope.

---

[72] See eg the discussion of the roles of equity and debt in corporate governance in chapter 3.
[73] Discussed further at 4.3 and 4.4.
[74] 2.3.5.2.

More recently, and particularly since the financial crisis, the sources of debt finance have multiplied. Loan finance is available from what is called the 'shadow banking' sector, that is, entities that are not banks but which provide credit.[75] These include managed funds, such as hedge funds and private equity houses, institutional investors as mentioned above, and (perhaps surprisingly) individuals who are now able to lend through peer-to-peer lending.[76] Many of these entities also provide finance by purchasing receivables on online auction sites. Further, the UK Government's package of small business funding measures includes both lending through peer-to-peer sites and purchasing receivables through online auctions.[77]

2.3.1.2 Choice of Debt Financing Transaction

The term 'borrowing' is generally used to mean either borrowing by way of loan (usually from a bank)[78] or by way of debt securities.[79] However, debt in a wider sense can also include credit extended by those whom the company would otherwise have to pay immediately. Thus, when a company buys goods with payment due 30 days after delivery, or obtains services with payment due two months after the services have been supplied, the economic effect is the same as if the company had borrowed from the seller or supplier. Even closer in effect are situations where a company obtains equipment from a finance company on hire purchase or finance lease terms. The equipment is obtained immediately, yet the 'price' is paid in instalments over a long period. To understand how small and medium-sized companies (SMEs) are financed, it is important to realise both that this type of borrowing is widespread and that the companies selling the goods, supplying the services or financing hire purchase agreements or finance leases themselves need finance. In order to meet the market requirements of giving credit, these companies need cash upfront in order to meet the expenditure they have to make to provide the goods, the services or the equipment to the company that receives them. Even banks need to be financed by debt, as ultimately they cannot meet the cost of all the loans they make through equity financing, deposits (if they take them) and profits. This can also be the case for alternative providers of loan finance,[80] although often they will either be lending their own money (individuals, governments) or will be lending money they hold for investors, which is effectively like equity finance, in that the investors take the risk of loss (hedge funds, private equity houses). However, non-bank lenders may well enhance their returns by leverage—that is, debt finance.[81] Those providing

---

[75] The Financial Stability Board has described 'shadow banking' as 'credit disintermediation involving entities and activities outside the regular banking system': FSB, *Shadow Banking, Strengthening Oversight and Regulation* (27 October 2011), www.financialstabilityboard.org/publications/r_111027a.pdf. The focus of the FSB was on the raising of funds by the short-term asset paper and repo markets. However, the term 'shadow banking' can be used more widely to describe any type of debt financing which is not carried out by banks. The *Economist*, for example, has defined it as 'lending by anything other than a bank' (10 May 2014, special report on shadow banking).

[76] 2.3.2.2.

[77] Small Business Tranche of the Business Finance Partnership—see BIS, *SME Guide to Finance Schemes: Measures to Support Small and Medium Enterprise Growth*, www.gov.uk/government/publications/sme-access-to-finance-schemes-measures-to-support-small-and-medium-sized-enterprise-growth. Note that the Government is also providing SMEs with access to finance by guaranteeing bank loans, as described in the guide.

[78] But see now 2.3.1.1 on other sources of loans.

[79] Such as bonds, notes or commercial paper. See 2.3.3.

[80] See 2.3.1.1.

[81] For discussion see 16.6.5.

credit often use the repayment obligations owed to them to enable them to obtain debt finance, either by borrowing on the security of those obligations or by transferring them outright for a price.[82] Banks obtain much of their finance on the money markets, either by issuing short-term debt securities (commercial paper) or by using repos (structurally sale and repurchase, but economically the same as short-term borrowing).[83] The detail of these is beyond the scope of this book.

The type of debt financing used by any one company will depend on a number of factors. One very important factor is the size of the company: most SMEs are not in a position to issue debt securities, for example, and very large and creditworthy companies usually only borrow unsecured.[84] Another will be the purpose for which credit is needed. If it is for a one-off project, such as a new building, a company taking a loan is likely to want a term loan, while for recurrent expenditure it is likely to want a revolving facility such as an overdraft. Very specific purposes, such as the building of infrastructure or the purchase of high-value equipment, have such specific requirements that particular financing structures have developed to accommodate them.[85] The cost of finance is also very important: this will be determined partly by outside factors such as interest rates and partly by the type of finance required. Generally, finance which is riskier for the lender is more expensive than less risky finance; thus, secured borrowing is (at least in theory) cheaper than unsecured, and shorter-term finance is cheaper than long-term finance.[86]

The availability of types of finance will affect both the price and the choice of financial structure. For example, in a market where supply of goods on credit is common, no supplier can afford not to give credit and the credit is usually interest-free (though, of course, reflected in the overall price of the goods). Where credit is freely available, loans may be made and bonds issued with very few covenants[87] as a result of the competition between lenders to lend, but when credit becomes restricted such borrowing as there is will be on much harsher terms. A borrower also has to weigh up the advantages of flexibility, for example from an overdraft or other revolving facility[88] or by issuing short-term debt securities, against the security of long-term finance, such as a term loan or longer-term securities. The flexibility of a revolving facility means that the company only borrows when it needs to, and this keeps the costs of financing down. However, where the company needs a fairly continuous level of borrowing, short-term financing may not be so suitable. This is because it requires constant refinancing, which may be difficult if the company is in (temporary) difficulties, or if the market has changed so that finance is more expensive or no longer available. Paradoxically, taking short-term financing may be seen as a sign of confidence in the company's prospects since it shows that refinancing is viewed as likely to happen. Another relevant factor may be whether the company has any restrictions on its ability to

---

[82] This is broadly called receivables financing. See 2.3.4.1.

[83] Companies with spare cash may well invest it in the money markets, either in money-market mutual funds, in commercial paper or in repos. Thus they lend to banks on a short-term unsecured or secured basis—see *ACT Practical Steps to Investing in Repos*, May 2014, www.treasurers.org.

[84] BIS, *Financing a Private Sector Recovery* (Cm 7923, July 2010), 3.5–3.17.

[85] Some of these specialist forms of finance are discussed at 2.3.5.

[86] This is a generalisation, and in fact sometimes the opposite is true, for example because of outside factors such as interest rates set to achieve a particular government policy. See Valdez: Financial Markets, 151.

[87] Covenants are contractual obligations owed by the borrower to the lender, for the protection of the lender. See 6.3 for detailed discussion of loan covenants.

[88] Whereby the borrower can draw down finance when it needs it and repay it when it does not. See 2.3.2.1.

borrow (or to borrow in a certain way) in its articles or in its contracts with other lenders.[89] For example, this might lead to a company selling its receivables rather than taking out a loan secured on the receivables.[90] In many situations the regulatory and tax implications of certain types of financing will be critical factors. Finally, religious, cultural or ethical factors may be relevant, such as the restrictions on financing under Islamic law, which has led to a growth in Sharia-compliant financing structures.[91]

It should, of course, be pointed out that many companies will have more than one source of debt finance. Most very large companies will raise finance through a mixture of loans (often syndicated) and bonds, as well as often raising short-term finance by other means, while larger SMEs often have both bank lending and asset-based finance. The considerations mentioned above then apply to the choice of type of financing made by a company in a particular situation or at a particular time.

2.3.1.3 Protection of Creditors: Contractual and Proprietary

It is also necessary to consider what protection a creditor requires when lending or advancing credit, and how this affects the structure of the transaction. The first main concern of the creditor is credit risk, that is, the risk of non-payment.[92] This risk can be mitigated in a number of ways, mainly by the creditor obtaining rights as a result of its agreement with the borrower. These rights can be either contractual or proprietary. Contractual rights are merely against the contractual counterparty, while proprietary rights relate to assets. The main distinction between the two relates to the situation where the borrower is insolvent: a creditor with proprietary rights will have priority over the general class of unsecured creditors, while a creditor with merely contractual rights falls into the latter class. There are limited exceptions to this, such as set-off, which in many cases is effective on insolvency.[93]

Proprietary rights can be either absolute or security interests. The distinction between these two kinds of interests is discussed in detail in chapter seven. If the creditor has an absolute interest, it becomes, or remains, the absolute owner of the relevant asset. A security interest, by contrast, is a proprietary interest in an asset securing the obligation to repay. It extends only to the amount of that obligation, so that on enforcement there is an obligation to account to the borrower for any surplus value in the asset. Security interests vary in form: pledges and liens are possessory interests (and are not discussed in detail in this book). One type of non-possessory security interest is a mortgage. Here, the title to the asset passes to the lender, who is obliged to re-transfer the asset when the secured obligation is repaid. Another type is the charge, which entails no transfer of title but is an encumbrance on the asset. Charges can be fixed or floating. If a lender has a fixed charge, the borrower cannot dispose of the charged asset without the lender's consent. If the lender's charge is floating, the borrower can make such a disposition. Floating charges, therefore, are often taken over circulating assets and enable a lender to take security over all the assets of a company. These interests are discussed in more detail in chapter seven.

---

[89] Such restrictions in contracts include negative pledge clauses and are discussed at 6.3.1.6.
[90] *Welsh Development Agency v Export Finance Co Ltd* [1992] BCC 270. Most recently drafted negative pledge clauses, however, extend to sales as well as charges over receivables.
[91] See 2.3.5.4.
[92] For a more detailed discussion of the credit risk of creditors, see 3.2.2.
[93] 6.3.4.

Contractual rights are more varied. They can be divided into contractual rights against the borrower itself, and contractual rights against third parties. Both are discussed in detail in chapter six. Rights against a third party are obviously more valuable than rights against a borrower if the borrower becomes insolvent (unless the third party also becomes insolvent). Such rights include 'credit enhancement' transactions such as guarantees, insurance and credit default swaps. Broadly speaking, these transactions involve a promise by the third party to pay the lender if the borrower defaults, although the actual structures vary considerably.[94] The third party may be someone with a strong interest in the operation of the borrower, such as another company in the same group. Where the borrower is a small private company it is likely to be a director. In these cases the form of the transaction is likely to be a guarantee, and the third party takes on the liability without remuneration, although it would have a right to be indemnified by the borrower. Alternatively, the third party may be someone providing credit protection commercially for a fee: in this case the transaction is more likely to be an indemnity, a performance bond, credit insurance or a credit default swap.[95]

Rights against third parties also include an agreement made with another creditor to subordinate its claim to that of the protected creditor,[96] so that the subordinated creditor is not paid until the protected creditor has been paid in full. This has the effect of making it more likely that the protected creditor will be paid on the insolvency of the borrower, although, where the creditors are unsecured, it does not give priority over any creditor with a proprietary right. It is also very common for certain creditors to be subordinated to all other creditors, for example where there are different tranches of loans or bond issues,[97] or where hybrid securities are issued.[98] The indemnification rights of group companies and directors who give guarantees are usually subordinated to all other creditors.[99]

Contractual rights against the borrower (many of which are known as covenants) protect the position of the creditor in a number of different ways. Some covenants restrict activities of the borrower which may damage the creditors. Thus, dividend distribution, or the dissipation of assets or the grant of security, may be limited.[100] Other covenants seek to ensure that the creditor is properly informed about the credit risk it is undertaking: these include representations and warranties about the state of the company (or the assets transferred or given as security) at the time of the advance, and financial reporting covenants which oblige the company to give ongoing information and to maintain certain financial ratios.[101] Other types of clauses, such as acceleration or termination clauses on default, are often present to give the creditor the ability to force a restructuring, to terminate the lender's obligation (if there is one) to make further advances and, in the last resort, to enable the creditor to enforce the entire loan.[102] Where credit is extended on retention of title terms to enable the

---

[94] The details of the different structures are discussed at 6.4.

[95] See 6.4.1.4, 6.4.2 and 6.4.3.

[96] 6.4.4.

[97] For example, in a securitisation structure (see 9.3.3) or leveraged buy-outs (16.4.3).

[98] See 2.4.

[99] See eg *Re SSSL Realisations* [2006] EWCA Civ 7 and *Flightlease Holdings (Guernsey) v Flightlease (Ireland)* (Judgment 3/2009, unreported 14 January 2009, Royal Court of Guernsey).

[100] See 5.2.1.

[101] See 6.3.2.

[102] See 6.3.3.

borrower to acquire tangible assets, a termination clause enables the lender to repossess the asset.[103] Secured loans will include provisions enabling enforcement of security, although this is now often done in the context of the insolvency procedure of administration.[104]

Another type of provision gives rights based on set-off.[105] Set-off operates outside insolvency to prevent circularity of action and to enable transactions to be settled without transferring large sums. It operates under the general law, but is usually provided for in a contract to avoid any uncertainty as to when it applies. On insolvency, set-off, where there are mutual parties, is compulsory.[106] Its operation enables a creditor to be paid pound for pound, thus giving an equivalent protection to that of a security interest. Thus, it is provisions which give rise to set-off on insolvency (such as netting and close-out provisions or flawed asset provisions) that provide significant credit risk protection.

These main contractual provisions for reducing credit risk are discussed in chapter six. Not all financing agreements include all these provisions, and some may include others. This will depend on many factors, including the type of transaction in question (for example, whether it is an issue of securities or a loan), the market conditions and the bargaining power of the parties.[107] Many loans are made on standard terms, such as those of the Loan Market Association for use in syndicated loans, or those used by particular banks or financiers. The creditor may also wish to protect itself against risks other than credit risk, such as the risk of the transaction turning out to be less profitable than it hoped because it has to pay more for the money it borrows to fund the transaction, for market reasons or because of changes in tax or regulatory rules. Clauses dealing with such a situation are common in syndicated loan transactions.[108] Debt securities usually contain fewer covenants included by the issuer (and its advisers) as a result of what is seen as necessary to make the securities attractive to potential investors. In theory, investors buy debt securities on a 'take it or leave it' basis as there is no opportunity for negotiation of terms, although in reality potential investors are often consulted when the terms are fixed.[109]

The protection required by a creditor can, of course, have a profound effect on what types of financing are available to a particular borrower. For example, if a lender requires security in order to be persuaded to lend, a borrower who cannot give security will not be able to borrow (conversely, the provision of security may persuade a lender to lend who would not otherwise do so). It should, however, be borne in mind that most of the structures discussed in this book are, to some extent, standard in form with creditor protection already built in, so that the borrower will be choosing between different options rather than negotiating from scratch, although the detail of the documentation is usually negotiated, except in small-scale transactions. New forms of financing are developed all the time, of course, but this is often in relation to very large transactions, often involving financial institutions that are repeat players, and they usually develop out of and use structures and concepts already in existence. Since the financial crisis the development of alternative forms of

---

[103] See 2.3.4.3 and 7.5.2.1.
[104] See 7.5.3.
[105] See 6.3.4.
[106] See 6.3.4.6.2.
[107] See 3.2.2.3.
[108] 2.13; Fuller: Corporate Borrowing, 2.15.
[109] See 7.3.1.

finance for the lower end of the market has increased, particularly using online platforms, but even these, though innovative in the way lenders and borrowers are brought together, use existing concepts and structures for the actual agreement between the parties. With this in mind, this book will discuss the various legal issues that arise in the more common forms of debt corporate finance and will largely focus on devices which are for the protection of the creditor, although some benefit both parties, such as the appointment of a trustee in a bond issue.

2.3.1.4 Protection of Creditors: Regulation

Another way in which creditors can be protected is by regulation, that is, statutory provisions which impose conditions which have to be fulfilled before certain transactions can be entered into. These therefore limit the ability of borrowers and creditors to enter into whatever transactions they wish. Some areas of debt finance are more heavily regulated than others: in theory this is because they involve more risk to creditors, or more systemic risk to the market, although that is not entirely the case in practice. The issue of debt securities to the public is regulated in broadly the same way as an issue of equity securities.[110] This is to ensure that those buying the debt securities both on the primary and on the secondary market have accurate and detailed information about the credit risk they are taking on. However, an issue of bonds to professionals is more lightly regulated,[111] and the syndicated loan market is completely unregulated except by contract.[112] The same goes for other forms of lending and finance by banks and other financial institutions. However, lending by individuals via online platforms has now become regulated: here the lenders are seen as consumers, without the ability to protect themselves through enquiry and negotiation.[113] Another form of regulation is the requirement to register certain security interests so that other creditors know that they have been granted when they are considering lending to the borrower.[114] Sometimes particular transaction types are regulated, such as covered bonds.[115]

Of course, another purpose of regulation is to protect all participants in the financial markets from systemic collapse, and much of the regulation of banks and other financial institutions[116] is to this effect. This specific type of regulation is a specialist area, and is not covered in detail in this book.

However, one aspect of financial regulation that can be conveniently explained at this point is the requirement that banks and other financial institutions[117] retain a certain level of capital in order to cover the risk that their debtors will not repay. This is an ongoing

---

[110] For discussion see chapters 10 and 13.

[111] See chapter 13.

[112] Note that there is now some voluntary regulation of the secondary loan market; see 13.4.2.

[113] See 13.8.

[114] 7.4.

[115] See 13.1.1. The application of regulatory legislation to a particular credit product is a new departure. See C Oakley, 'Regulated Covered Bond Regulations: Issues arising from Interpretation of the UCITS Directive' [2008] *Journal of International Banking and Financial Law* 240.

[116] Such as the capital adequacy requirements and the 'soft law' promulgated by the FCA.

[117] These are credit institutions within the meaning of the Council Directive 2004/39/EC of 21 April 2004 on Markets in Financial Instruments [2004] OJ L145 (MiFID). In the interests of brevity, these will be called 'firms' in this section as that is the terminology used in the FCA Handbook. It should be noted that investment firms are subject to different rules from banks: the former are included in IFPRU and the latter in BIPRU. Both of these are part of the FCA Handbook.

requirement, and is in addition to the legal capital requirements discussed in chapter five. The capital adequacy requirement[118] balances the amount of credit risk against the amount of capital which needs to be held. Broadly speaking, the firm must retain capital amounting to 8 per cent of its risk exposure:[119] as this is an ongoing obligation, the firm must monitor constantly to ensure it is complying.[120] There are thus two separate calculations used to decide whether a firm is complying: the risk exposure of the firm, and the amount of capital it holds. Both are the subject of detailed regulation in the FCA Handbook, and only a very brief summary is given here. In addition to the 8 per cent requirement, the latest rules also introduce three capital buffers. Any one institution (depending on its size and function) will have to hold, in addition to the basic 8 per cent, capital complying with the capital conservation buffer, the countercyclical capital buffer and a buffer to protect against systemic risk;[121] these could significantly increase the amount and quality of capital that institutions have to hold.[122] Capital adequacy requirements are significant since the design of many transactions, particularly securities, has been heavily influenced by these requirements.

The risk exposure of the firm depends on the amount of money owed to that firm, and the risk weighting of each obligation. The risk weighting will be calculated on the basis of the creditworthiness of the debtor, which may depend on the type of debtor and also on its rating, any credit enhancement which makes it more likely that the debt will be repaid (such as a guarantee), and any collateral held against the debt.[123] A standardised approach based on these factors is used for unsophisticated firms; the more sophisticated firms are permitted to use an internal approach whereby they determine the risk levels themselves. Capital is also required to be held against some forms of operational risk, the measurement of which depends on the type of firm involved and its gross income.

The kind of capital a firm can hold is divided into two tiers, comprising equity and subordinated debt. Tier one is permanent capital, that is, capital that only has to be repaid on a winding up, and includes ordinary shares and retained capital, as well as certain types of hybrid instruments designed to achieve tier one status.[124] It can be used against any form

---

[118] Now found in CRR/CRD IV, which is the collective name for Directive 2013/36/EU and Regulation (EU) No 575/2013. These instruments, which came into force in January 2014, implement Basel III, which amends Basel II to take account of lessons learned from the global financial crisis. Basel II, in its turn, amended the original agreement, Basel I, inter alia to take account of risk-mitigation devices such as securitisation, credit derivatives, the use of security and netting. CRR/CRD IV is implemented in the UK by the Financial Services and Markets Act 2000 and in the FCA Handbook. In addition to capital requirements, it includes provisions on liquidity requirements, prudential regulation (found in the CRR), the build-up of leverage and corporate governance. For detailed discussion see Moloney: EU Regulation, IV.8.

[119] BIPRU 3.1.5. The FCA may require a higher ratio from particular firms (GENPRU 2.1.11).

[120] GENPRU 2.1.9. A firm must ensure that it can demonstrate its capital resources at any time if required to do so by the FCA (GENPRU 2.1.10).

[121] This buffer has various levels, depending on the systemic importance of the institution.

[122] For detailed discussion see Bank of England Prudential Regulatory Authority Policy Statement, 'Implementing CRD IV: Capital Buffers', PS 3/14 (2014), www.bankofengland.co.uk/pra/Documents/publications/ps/2014/ps314.pdf.

[123] Note that even 'off balance sheet' transactions such as securitisations (see 2.3.3.5) may be taken into account if the firm is still at some risk (BIPRU 9).

[124] See 2.4. Ordinary shares and retained profits form 'core' tier one capital (see GENPRU 2 Annex 1, 4, 5 or 6 depending on the firm). The amount of non-core tier one capital that can make up the tier one capital is limited. This is to ensure that most of the tier one capital of a firm is of the highest quality, that is, capable of maximum loss absorption (GENPRU 2.2.31).

of risk exposure, while there are limits as to the use of tier two capital.[125] Tier two capital comprises hybrid instruments which are structured like debt but have some of the loss absorbency of equity, for example by being deeply subordinated.[126] It includes both permanent instruments and dated instruments.[127]

2.3.1.5 *Multiple Lenders and Transfer of Debt*

Where the amount of debt financing required is large, a borrower will often seek funds from more than one lender. The loans may be consecutive, in which case issues of priority between lenders may arise.[128] However, in many cases a borrower will seek to raise funds from a number of lenders at once, such as in a syndicated loan[129] or bond issue.[130]

While accessing funds from a number of sources offers a borrower great advantages, there are also practical difficulties. For example, it is necessary to have some form of structure to enable decisions to be made in relation to the conduct of the borrowing relationship, such as whether modifications should be made to the terms of the loan, or whether the loan should be accelerated if a default has occurred. More prosaically, it is necessary to have one person who actually does the work required to administer the relationship, such as collecting payments from the borrower and distributing these to the lenders. There are two legal concepts that are used to overcome this problem: that of agency and that of trust. The main difference is that where there is an agent, he may act for the borrower or for the lenders, depending on context, whereas a trustee holds the obligation to repay, and any security, on trust for the lenders. Although an agent or trustee may have certain powers to make decisions, any important decisions have to be taken by the lenders, either unanimously, which may be hard to achieve, or by a majority. The structures arising from the use of agents or trustees, and the complex question of the extent of their rights and obligations, are discussed in chapter eight.

While a creditor may wish to retain a relationship with the borrower, and may be content to fund the loan or other credit from its own resources until it is repaid, in many cases a creditor will wish to divest itself of the asset represented by the debt, for a number of reasons. It may just be that it wishes to use the debt as collateral for a loan to itself, either by creating a security interest over it or by title transfer. In that case, the immediate credit risk of non-payment will be retained by the original lender. The lender may, however, wish to transfer the debt completely, so that the transferee takes on all risks in relation to the loan, including credit risk, in return for a price. A creditor may wish to do this to improve cash flow: it gets money upfront for a debt due in the future (for example, by securitisation or by discounting a bill of exchange). Alternatively, the creditor may be concerned about the ability of the debtor to pay in the future, and hopes to get some money now rather than

[125] The amount of tier one capital that has to be included in a firm's capital has been increased under CRD IV from 4% to 6%.

[126] GENPRU 2.2.158. See 2.4.

[127] GENPRU 2.2.157. Note that tier two instruments cannot contain any covenants which could lead to early repayment, such as a negative pledge clause or a cross-default clause (GENPRU 2.2.165).

[128] Priority questions between secured lenders are discussed at 6.4.3. Lenders may also agree the priority between them, whether the loans are consecutive or contemporaneous; see 7.4.4 and 6.4.4.

[129] See 2.3.2.2.

[130] See 2.3.3.

risk receiving nothing on the insolvency of the debtor (for example, by selling bonds). Or it may just be that there is a developed market for such debts and the sophisticated creditor can profit from movements in the market which are unrelated, or only loosely related, to the credit risk of the borrower. This is particularly true in relation to the most easily traded debt, that is, debt securities, where transfer is an integral part of the form of transaction. While most other debts can be sold, transfer may be less straightforward for a number of reasons, such as the presence of an anti-assignment clause in the original contract, or the fact that the lender is still obliged to make further advances. These problems have, to a large extent, been overcome by legal ingenuity, so that there is now a well-developed market in syndicated loans, and also in distressed debt, as well as extensive use of securitisation and receivables financing, both of which involve a sale of debts. Issues relating to the transfer of debt, including the methods of transfer, are discussed in chapter nine.

The following sections explain in outline the main types of debt financing, as defined above to include the provision of credit. Detailed consideration of relevant legal issues follow in the subsequent chapters.

2.3.2 Loans[131]

2.3.2.1 Bank Loans

Loans are usually made to companies by banks, either by one bank or a number of banks.[132] It is, of course, possible for a company to borrow from other parties, such as individuals (for example, directors) or from other companies (for example, parent companies or others in the same group). Such loans are quite likely to be subordinated,[133] but will still contain both contractual and maybe proprietary protection for the lender, as discussed below in relation to bank loans.

One main distinction to be drawn in relation to loans to companies is between committed and on-demand lending.[134] The most common example of on-demand lending is an overdraft, which, together with credit card finance, is the most common form of debt finance for SMEs.[135] Once agreed between the bank and the customer,[136] the customer can draw more money from its current account with the bank than it has paid in, up to the agreed limit. Normally, an overdraft is repayable on demand, although this can be varied by contrary agreement. Whether there is contrary agreement depends on the interpretation of

---

[131] See Fuller: Corporate Borrowing, ch 2; Tolley Company Law Service B5021–B5027; Benjamin: Financial Law, 8.1.2.2; Encyclopaedia of Banking Law, chs C13, F3150–F3210. For the critical importance of bank lending in corporate finance see BIS, *Financing a Private Sector Recovery* (Cm 7923, July 2010), 3.18–3.28.

[132] This would be a syndicated loan, which is discussed at 2.3.1.4 and 8.4.

[133] See 6.4.4.

[134] Tolley Company Law Service B5021.

[135] BDRC Continental SME Finance Monitor, report for Q2 2014 (www.sme-finance-monitor.co.uk) shows that about 18% of SMEs surveyed used overdraft finance and 15% used credit cards. However, 79% of credit card users reported that they usually paid off the balance at the end of each month, so that the credit card was used more as a payment mechanism than a form of finance. About 8% of SMEs used a bank loan (see next paragraph).

[136] Prior agreement is essential (*Cunliffe Brooks & Co v Blackburn & District Benefit Building Society* (1884) LR9 App Cas 857), but can be implied: *Cumming v Shand* (1860) 5 H & N 95.

the particular facility letter: the mere fact that the overdraft is available for a period of time does not mean that a provision that it is repayable on demand is ineffective.[137] This means that, unless the company takes specific steps to ensure appropriate wording in the overdraft documentation, it is in danger of the finance being withdrawn without notice when it is not itself in breach.[138] In theory this makes an overdraft a risky form of financing for a company, despite its popularity among small businesses.[139] There are, however, two ameliorating factors. First, generally a bank will not demand repayment of an overdraft without reason, and is, in fact, usually keen to continue the lending relationship with a company that is able to service its debts, since the interest payable on the overdrawn account is a source of income for the bank.[140] Second, the bank is obliged to honour cheques drawn on the account before demand.[141]

A committed facility is where the bank is committed to lend throughout a certain period, usually subject to the fulfilment of certain conditions.[142] It may be a term loan, where the amount lent is advanced all at once or in successive tranches, repayable in a single ('bullet') repayment or according to a payment schedule ('amortising').[143] It may have more flexibility, as in a revolving facility, which is similar to an overdraft in that the company can draw down, repay and draw down again, up to the date the facility ends, when the borrowings have to be repaid. A company is more likely to use a term loan for a one-off purchase, such as land, or in an acquisition, and a revolving facility to raise working capital.[144] An even more flexible loan is a standby credit[145] or 'swingline',[146] which is often used to support an issue of commercial paper.[147] This is a short-term advance which may not be used at all, but can be used to tide the company over if it has to repay some commercial paper but does not want to issue another batch immediately because of market conditions.

A loan is usually made in cash, but another method of advancing finance is for the bank to agree to accept a bill of exchange drawn on it by the company.[148] The company then sells the bill in the market (or the bank will do so and reimburse the company) so that the

---

[137] *Williams & Glyn's Bank Ltd v Barnes* [1981] Com LR 205; *Lloyds Bank plc v Lampert* [1999] 1 All ER 161, 167–68; *Bank of Ireland v AMCD (Property Holdings) Ltd* [2001] 2 All ER 894 [15]–[17]. There are also other cases where an express obligation on the bank to provide the facility for a period of time has been held to rebut the presumption that the overdraft is repayable on demand. See *Titford Property Co Ltd v Cannon Street Acceptances Ltd* (unreported, 25 May 1975) and *Crimpfil v Barclays Bank plc* (unreported, 20 April 1994). However, these authorities may be unreliable in the light of the later cases, or at least only explicable on the wording of the particular documentation.

[138] It also appears that, at least in the absence of very special circumstances, a bank does not owe a duty of care to a borrower when demanding repayment of an overdraft. See *Chapman v Barclays Bank plc* [1997] 6 Bank LR 315; *Hall v Royal Bank of Scotland plc* [2009] EWHC 3163 (Mercantile).

[139] See Benjamin: Financial Law, 8.17, citing R Cranston, *Principles of Banking Law*, 2nd edn (Oxford, Oxford University Press, 2002) 299.

[140] See 3.2.2.

[141] *Rouse v Bradford Banking Co Ltd* [1894] AC 586, 596; *Williams & Glyn's Bank v Barnes* [1981] Com LR 205.

[142] These are likely to be both conditions precedent and warranties; see discussion at 6.3.2.1.

[143] Term loans are relatively rare in small business finance. The BDRC Continental SME finance monitor, report for Q2 2014 shows that in the period 2012–14 the percentage of small businesses using bank loans was between 7% and 11%.

[144] Tolley Company Law Service B5024.

[145] Valdez: Financial Markets, 96.

[146] See Fuller: Corporate Borrowing, 2.6.

[147] See 2.3.3.1.

[148] See Fuller: Corporate Borrowing, 2.5.

company obtains money immediately. On the bill's maturity the bank, as acceptor, pays the person to whom the bill has been sold (the holder) and the company will then reimburse the bank for doing so.

All types of loans will include protection for the lender against the credit risk of the borrower. This may take the form of provision of contractual rights (as against the borrower or also against third parties), but may also be effected by the grant or retention of proprietary rights, that is, the provision of some sort of security or quasi-security interest. The possible types of security and the policy issues relating to the taking of security are discussed below in chapter seven.

2.3.2.2 *Multiple Lenders*

Where the loan required is large, the risk of making it is usually spread among a number of lenders, through syndication and/or through the use of subordination. Syndication involves one bank, mandated by the company to arrange the loan, preparing an information memorandum about the company and soliciting other banks to join it in making the loan. Each bank in fact makes a separate loan to the company, so that their liability is several. This has the effect that no bank is liable if another bank fails to lend or becomes insolvent,[149] and also enables individual banks to exercise set-off rights against individual borrowers. It also means that each bank can enforce the debt due to it itself. As mentioned above, the administrative duties of the syndicated loan are carried out by an agent (usually one of the banks making the loan). Syndicated loans are discussed in detail in 7.4 below.

In many financing structures, for example in an acquisition or leveraged buy-out, it is usual for the amount of finance available to be increased using subordination.[150] Subordination may be achieved by the junior creditor agreeing not to recover until the senior creditor has been paid in full, or that it will hold any recoveries on trust for the senior creditor.[151] The senior creditor is encouraged to lend more, as the junior debt provides a 'cushion' which will be lost first in the event of the insolvency of the borrower, and the junior creditors obtain a much higher interest rate, which compensates them for the extra risk they carry.[152] Sometimes the subordination is structural.[153] The junior debt layer may also be financed by the issuing of high-yield bonds rather than by a loan.[154]

It should be remembered that all debt can be sold, and so any bank making one of the loans described above can, if it wishes, pass on the credit risk of the loans it makes by transferring the debts represented by those loans. As mentioned above, there is a strong market in syndicated loans, and other loans can be disposed of by securitisation.[155] By transferring the loans they make, banks can obtain more capital to make more loans, and can reduce the amount of capital they have to hold under the capital adequacy requirements of Basel III.[156]

---

[149] Wood: Loans and Bonds, 3-006; Fuller: Corporate Borrowing, 2.17; Hughes: Banking, 9.2.
[150] See 16.4.3.
[151] 6.4.4.1.
[152] Wood: Project Finance, 10-008.
[153] See 6.4.4.1.4. Structural subordination is particularly important in private equity transactions, as discussed at 16.4.
[154] See 2.3.3.3.
[155] See chapter 9, especially 9.2.4.2 (novation of syndicated loans) and 9.3.3 (securitisation).
[156] See 2.3.1.3.

2.3.2.3 Peer-to-Peer Lending

As mentioned earlier, many companies now obtain funds through peer-to-peer lending. This is the generic name given to a number of online platforms which put potential lenders in touch with potential borrowers. Some platforms specialise in different areas, such as consumer lending, lending for property development secured on land, lending only by companies and high worth individuals, and so on.[157] Some also facilitate the sale of receivables by companies to those willing to buy them. The account of peer-to-peer lending given here is generalised, and relates to the platforms that involve lending to corporate businesses (though they may also lend to consumers and unincorporated businesses). Peer-to-peer lending is becoming an increasingly important source of finance for SMEs,[158] and is seen as a real alternative to bank finance by the Government, which is proposing to make it compulsory for banks to refer borrowers to alternative finance providers if they are turned down for a business loan.[159]

When a borrower applies to an online platform for a loan, the platform normally[160] carries out a vetting process: this can vary from a reasonably brief check to quite extensive due diligence. Typically, there is either an auction, whereby potential lenders indicate what interest rates they would be prepared to lend at, and borrowers accept those at which they are willing to borrow (the borrower actually pays a weighted average of the different rates accepted), or a market rate is set by the platform. A key feature is that, in either case, potential lenders can choose which companies they lend to (and, in the case of an auction, at what rates), although some sites also have a facility for allocating borrowers automatically to lenders according to an agreed risk profile.[161] Usually, the borrower enters into a loan agreement either with the company running the platform, acting as agent for the lenders, or with the lender direct, but through the intermediation of the platform. The loan agreement contains representations and warranties as well as covenants,[162] and the platform acts as agent for the lenders in enforcing the agreement if there is an event of default, although monitoring is usually limited to checking whether repayments have been made. Some loans are unsecured, although often backed by a personal guarantee, while others are secured by real security: this varies according to the platform but also according to the needs of the borrower.[163] Security is held by a company, usually related to the company running the platform, which acts as a security trustee.[164] Some platforms allow lenders to withdraw their money before the end of the term of the loan by transferring the loan to another lender in a

---

[157] See www.p2pmoney.co.uk/companies.htm for a comparison of a large number of online platforms.

[158] The UK peer-to-peer loan market was worth over £1.6 billion in 2014, and is predicted to be £2.5 billion in 2015 (see www.p2pmoney.co.uk/predictions.htm). See also N Harding, 'Why the UK Peer-to-Peer Loan Market Has Doubled in Size in Just Six Months', *International Business Times*, 13 September 2014.

[159] See www.gov.uk/government/news/plan-to-make-britain-global-centre-of-financial-innovation-set-out-by-government (press release of Chancellor's speech announcing this measure on 6 August 2014). A power to make regulations to this effect is included in Small Business, Enterprise and Employment Act 2015, s 5.

[160] The practice varies between different platforms.

[161] See eg www.moneyandco.com/faq.

[162] See chapter 6.

[163] See eg www.archover.com/solutions/ which offers trade loans secured against receivables, asset loans secured against existing assets, and purchase loans secured against the asset purchased. A similar spread of loans is offered by the more established Funding Circle: see https://www.fundingcircle.com.

[164] See chapter 8.

market run by the platform.[165] While most peer-to-peer platforms offer some form of loan, some offer finance by purchasing receivables,[166] and at least one enables companies to offer convertible debt securities.[167] Concern had been expressed regarding protection of lenders, particularly consumers, who lend using peer-to-peer platforms, and regulation has recently been introduced.[168] This is discussed in chapter thirteen.

2.3.3 Debt Securities

2.3.3.1 General

Debt securities are tradable instruments which a company can issue in order to raise money from a variety of lenders. Such lenders will be more numerous and more varied in type than the single bank or syndicate of banks that would otherwise make a loan to the company.[169] In theory, anyone can buy debt securities, although in most cases the target and actual investors are much more limited for a number of reasons.[170] Debt securities are issued, usually to a limited group of investors, in what is known as the primary market. The process of issuance is described in chapter eight.[171] Once issued, they can be traded in what is called the secondary market. Not all debt securities are traded: some are kept by the original owners until maturity: for example, loan notes issued as part of a private equity transaction fall within this category,[172] as do notes issued in the increasingly popular private placement market.[173] However, many are traded, and anything which adds to their tradability (liquidity) adds to their value.[174]

In this book we consider only debt securities issued by companies. However, it should be borne in mind that a vast number of debt securities are issued by governments: these are usually the most highly rated (though it does depend on the credit standing of the relevant government),[175] and the pricing of debt securities issued by companies is often tied to that of government securities.[176] The term 'debt securities' covers a number of different kinds of instruments. Companies, or banks, needing short-term finance can raise it by issuing commercial paper, a term meaning short-term securities (with a term up to 364 days) or, if the company is authorised to carry on deposit taking, certificates of deposit, which can have a term of up to five years. These are issued and traded in what are known as the money

---

[165] See eg www.moneyandco.com/loan-market.
[166] Eg http://marketinvoice.com and www.platformblack.com.
[167] https://crowdforangels.com/plc.
[168] See 13.8.
[169] Though the pool of potential lenders is now bigger than it was even five years ago; see 2.3.1.1.
[170] Many of reasons relate to regulatory issues, which are discussed in chapter 13.
[171] 8.3.1.
[172] 16.4.2.
[173] See 2.3.3.3.
[174] M Choudhry, *Corporate Bonds and Structured Financial Products* (London, Elsevier Butterworth-Heinemann, 2005) 59.
[175] See, for example, the weak position of Greek government bonds during 2010 and 2015.
[176] See M Choudhry, *Corporate Bonds and Structured Financial Products* (London, Elsevier Butterworth-Heinemann, 2005) 5.3, 128.

markets: this term refers to markets dealing with short-term securities with a term of one year or less.[177] Longer-term debt securities, which are issued and traded on the bond or capital markets, are called bonds or notes. Originally, notes were securities with a shorter term than bonds, but the terminology has now become more interchangeable, especially in the European markets. The term 'notes' is generally used, however, where the interest rate is floating, and also where securities are issued as part of a programme.[178]

It needs to be remembered when considering different types of securities (and different varieties of terms within the documentation) that these are dictated by the requirements of two people: the issuer and the potential investors. The potential investors are often not in a position to negotiate terms directly, and so it is usually the lead manager[179] who will advise the issuer what sort of bonds and what terms will be marketable at an interest rate the issuer wishes to pay, after taking soundings from those who might invest in the bonds. This will include the level of covenants. The issuer will want to ensure that the issue fulfils its requirements, for example as to the term of the financing (bearing in mind that the company will normally want to refinance on the maturity of the bond), the flexibility of the term (for example, whether the company has a call option)[180] and so on. When assessing the variety of the types of bonds available and the terms within the documentation, it is important to consider what features are for the protection of the lenders and what features are for the benefit of the issuer. In some cases, such as the use of a trustee, there are benefits for both parties.[181]

2.3.3.2 Securities versus Loan

As a general rule, it is cheaper for a company to raise money by issuing debt securities than by taking a loan. However, once they are issued the company cannot usually pay back the debt represented by the securities until the end of the term of the issue, so it is a less flexible form of financing than a revolving facility or overdraft.[182] Accordingly, it is probably more accurate to compare the merits of an issue of securities to those of a term loan. Why is this form of raising finance cheaper? The rate of interest payable on securities is determined by a combination of features, including market rates. However, it does not have to cover as many costs as the interest set by a bank in relation to a loan, such as the carrying out of due diligence and the costs of monitoring.[183] Further, bondholders are generally less risk averse than banks, and so charge less interest. However, the best mix of financing (from the point of view of the borrower) may well be to include some bank financing in addition to the issue of bonds. Bank financing indicates that the bank has, after due diligence enquiries,

---

[177] Fuller: Capital Markets, 1.01.
[178] See 8.3.1.
[179] See 8.3.1.
[180] See 2.3.3.5.
[181] For discussion of these, see 2.3.3.5.
[182] It is possible for the issuer to have a 'call' option to redeem early, or for the investors to have a 'put' option to require early redemption; see 2.3.3.5.
[183] Very little monitoring is done by the trustee of a bond issue; see 8.3.4.2.2.

decided that the company is a good credit risk. On the basis of this signalling, the bond issue can be at an even lower rate of interest.[184]

Although it will depend very much on the type of debt securities, covenants and warranties are generally fewer and less stringent than in a bank loan, mainly because of the problems involved in coordinating bondholders and the consequent difficulties of enforcement.[185] This can be seen as an additional advantage for the borrower. Another attractive feature of issuing debt securities for a company is that money is raised from a wider pool of lenders than is possible with a loan, even a syndicated loan, where the pool of lenders is confined to banks. Holders of debt securities may include institutional investors, such as pension funds, other companies, including insurance companies, and even private individuals. Since 2010 there has been considerable growth in the retail bond market in the UK. This is partly because of the unavailability of bank finance for medium-sized companies, and partly because of the low rates of interest offered by bank deposits and other non-equity investments. The London Stock Exchange launched an online retail bond (ORB) platform in 2010, and by October 2014 there were 35 retail bond issues amounting to nearly £3.7 billion.[186] Retail bonds attract a higher level of regulation than wholesale bonds,[187] which can add to the cost. Some companies have also issued retail bonds themselves: these are not traded on a market and are therefore illiquid.[188]

The wide pool of lenders not only taps sources of finance for the borrower which would be unavailable in the context of a loan, but corporate borrowers see individual bondholders as less likely to cause trouble on default than bank lenders, particularly if there is a bond trustee.[189] Further, finance by means of a bond issue may be available even when bank funds are limited, as was the case during the global financial crisis.[190] Debt securities are attractive to investors in that not only do they provide a steady stream of income,[191] but they are tradable on recognised markets. This means that the investor can easily realise its capital assets without waiting for the bond to mature, and can offload the risk of default onto someone else (although this will be reflected in the price at which the bond is sold). Some bonds are more liquid (that is, more easily traded on the capital markets) than others, and this is reflected in the price.[192] It should be noted, however, that in recent years the transfer of loans, or the transfer of risk of loans, using sub-participation or credit default swaps, has become very common.[193]

---

[184] A Morrison, 'Credit Derivatives, Disintermediation and Investment Decisions' (2005) 78(2) *Journal of Business* 621.

[185] See chapter 8.

[186] See www.londonstockexchange.com/prices-and-markets/retail-bonds/newrecent/newrecent.htm.

[187] See chapter 13.

[188] Self-issued retail bonds can also be very innovative, such as the bond issued by Hotel Chocolat which raised £4 million for the company involved the payment of 'interest' by delivery of boxes of chocolates to the bondholders (see www.hotelchocolat.com/uk/tasting-club/our-story/chocolate-bonds).

[189] D Petkovic, 'New Structures: "Whole Business" Securitisations of Project Cash Flows' [2000] *Journal of International Banking Law* 187.

[190] Bond issuance in the UK has been largely net positive since 2008, while the bank lending was strongly net negative until very recently (Q2 2014). See Bank of England, *Trends in Lending*, July 2014, p 5 fig 1.3.

[191] Unless they are zero coupon bonds or commercial paper, where interest is not payable.

[192] This is called the 'illiquidity premium' and is reflected in the price of, for example, bonds issued under a private placement, See Association of Corporate Treasurers, *PP15+ Working Group on Developing a UK Private Placement Market: Interim Report* (December 2012), 3.3.5 and 3.5.6.

[193] See chapter 9.

2.3.3.3 Who Issues Bonds?

Although it might seem to make sense for most companies to raise money by issuing debt securities, many cannot. First, there may be restrictions by virtue of the nature of the company itself—for example, a private company cannot offer debentures to the public.[194] Second, the company may not have a good enough credit rating for the securities to be marketable. A credit rating, which is given to a company by a credit rating agency,[195] is based on the likelihood that the company will default on its securities and is important in the bond market for several reasons. Investors are much more likely to buy bonds with a high credit rating. However, because the demand will be high, the issuer can offer a lower rate of interest than on a riskier bond with a lower credit rating.[196] The ratings (in theory at least) allow investors to match the amount of risk they are prepared to take with the amount of yield on bonds that they purchase. Certain investors, mainly financial institutions, are only permitted to buy bonds with an 'investment grade' rating. Thus, the market for investment grade rated bonds is much larger than for those with a lower rating. In fact, until relatively recently companies without such a rating could not issue bonds as no one would buy them. However, in the 1970s a phenomenon grew up in the US called 'junk bonds' (or, more respectably, 'high-yield' bonds)[197] which are very risky bonds issued by companies without an investment grade rating.[198] High yield bonds are usually subordinated to any senior debt (which is often in the form of loan finance); for example, they are used for mezzanine finance in leveraged buy-outs.[199]

Even so, bond issues are not appropriate for SMEs, which are much more likely to be looking at bank or asset-based lending as their main source of debt finance. Having said this, medium-sized companies are increasingly entering the 'private placement' market. 'Private placement' is a generic term used to refer to borrowing from non-banks (particularly insurance companies and pension funds), where the debt is not traded on the public markets, and is therefore illiquid. There is thus an illiquidity premium,[200] but costs are saved by the issue not having to be rated: investors tend to do their own investigations as to the creditworthiness of the company. In the US this borrowing is usually in the form of debt securities, while in Europe it can be either a loan or the issue of debt securities. In the past, companies accessed this form of borrowing by using the US private placement market, but increasing US regulation and a greater appetite on the part of both companies and investors for this type of finance have led to a greater demand in the UK and Europe. There are

---

[194] Companies Act 2006, s 755. See 13.2.1.1.

[195] The rating agencies are private companies that operate in both the domestic and international markets. The main agencies in the international markets are Moody's, Fitch and Standard & Poor's. Moody's grades are in the form Aaa to Baa3 (investment grade) and Ba1 to D (non-investment grade); the other two have grades in the form AAA to BBB (investment grade) and BB+ to D (non-investment grade). For discussion of the regulation of rating agencies see 13.7.

[196] M Doran, D Howe and R Pogrel, 'Debt Capital Markets: An Introduction' (2005) 16 *Practical Law Company* 21, 26.

[197] The polite term is now used much more frequently as such bonds have become more widespread.

[198] For accounts of the history of junk bonds see Valdez: Financial Markets, 181–82; Fuller: Capital Markets, 2.83–2.84. The high-yield market is very susceptible to market conditions: issuances declined dramatically during the global financial crisis but have increased reasonably steadily ever since.

[199] See Wood: Loans and Bonds, 2-015.

[200] See 2.5.3.2.

initiatives underway to increase the private placement market,[201] and barriers to entry are slowly being removed.[202]

2.3.3.4 Debt Securities versus Equity

Whether a company which needs money issues equity or debt securities depends on a number of factors.[203] One particular advantage of debt securities over equity securities is that the interest paid on debt securities is tax deductible for the company, unlike dividends, which cannot be deducted.[204] This makes debt a much cheaper option than equity, at least up to a certain point.[205]

In one sense, the tradability of debt securities makes them similar, from an investor's point of view, to equity securities. Debt securities are traded on the secondary market and are frequently listed on a stock market, although much of the trading takes place over the counter (OTC).[206] The big difference is that the owner of equity securities has a stake in the company and shares its profits and its losses. Another advantage of debt securities, particularly for private companies, is that the existing shareholders do not dilute their control of the company (or the value of their shares). The owner of debt securities does not share in the profits, and, as a creditor, ranks above shareholders if the company is insolvent. These issues are discussed further in chapter three. The exact priority of the owner of debt securities will depend on various matters, such as whether the securities are backed by security over other assets and whether they are the subject of a subordination agreement. There is also a twilight zone occupied by what are known as 'hybrid' instruments.[207] These are securities which have some characteristics of debt and some of equity, and are an attempt to give investors some of the best of both worlds, although, of course, they end up without the full benefits of either. For example, securities may be deeply subordinated, or perpetual, or convertible into equity.

2.3.3.5 Varieties of Bonds

Bonds in particular, as opposed to money market instruments such as commercial paper, come in all sorts of varieties, like ice cream. This similarity is reflected in the name given to

---

[201] This is spearheaded in the UK by the Association of Corporate Treasurers (see Association of Corporate Treasurers, *PP15+ Working Group on Developing a UK Private Placement Market: Interim Report* (December 2012)), and in Europe by the International Capital Markets Association (see ICMA press release, 12 June 2014, www.icmagroup.org/media/Press-releases/). The Loan Market Association has issued a standard template for private placement documentation, which should help to encourage the market: see www.lma.eu.com/press_releases_details.aspx?CID=2290.

[202] One potential barrier is that funds which invest in illiquid assets are regulated by the Alternative Investment Fund Managers Directive, and in some circumstances will have to comply with the UK National Private Placement Regime, which is set out in Chapter 3 of the Alternative Investment Fund Managers Regulations 2013 (SI 2013/1773).

[203] For a general discussion of the debt/equity mix in a company's capital structure, see 2.6.

[204] Discussed further at 2.6.

[205] For more discussion of the cost of capital, see 2.6.

[206] There are a far greater variety of debt securities than equity securities, and trades are usually larger and less frequent. Therefore, dealers often have to take a position onto their books and spend a number of days laying it off with different buyers. The market may change with the introduction of new rules on transparency of non-equity markets: see 13.2.1.4.

[207] See 2.4.

a typical unadorned bond: plain vanilla.[208] A plain vanilla bond is basically a promise by the issuer to pay both interest and, at maturity, the principal debt. The promise can be made to the bondholders or to a trustee acting on their behalf.[209] The documentation will, of course, include more than just the promise: it will include details of the interest rate payable (which is usually fixed but can be floating and can also be linked to an index), the details of payment and redemption and other administrative details, and covenants to protect the interests of the bondholders.

One variation is a 'zero coupon' bond. The terminology originated when bonds were bearer bonds, so that whoever held them owned them. The issuer would not necessarily know who the holders were, and so each bond had a number of detachable 'coupons' which related to each interest payment. When an interest payment was due, the holder at the time detached the relevant coupon, sent it to the issuer and claimed the interest. This is no longer the practice (very few bondholders actually hold bearer bonds now)[210] but the term 'coupon' for interest still remains. If a bond is 'zero coupon', this means that there is no interest payable. Instead, it is issued at a discount to its face value, that is, to the amount that is payable on maturity. The 'interest payments' are therefore paid at the end, when the bond matures. This used to have certain tax advantages, since the gain was seen as capital rather than income, but many jurisdictions have changed their tax legislation so that the gain is now seen as interest. Another variation relates to the time of payment and the possibility of prepayment. The issuer may be given the option to buy back or redeem some or all of the bonds before maturity. This is called a 'call' option;[211] an issuer would wish to exercise this if interest rates fell below the rate payable on the bond, so that it could issue another bond at a lower rate, that is, refinance. Conversely, the holders could have an option to require early redemption: this is called a 'put' option. Debt securities cannot be redeemed early unless this is specifically provided for in the terms of the issue.[212] Securities also may only be repayable after a very long time, or they may even be perpetual. These are seen as akin to equity for various purposes and are a type of hybrid security, which is discussed below.[213]

Yet another variation is whether the securities are domestic or international. Domestic stock[214] is issued by a UK issuer in sterling and is aimed at UK investors. Eurobonds are aimed at the international markets, and can be issued in any country, though they are often denominated in a currency other than that of the country in which they are issued. Domestic securities are also now often issued in the form of eurobonds. The main structural difference between the two is that stock is one single debt which is either held for the stockholders by a trustee, or contained in a deed poll for the benefit of all the stockholders,[215] which can be divided up into holdings of any size represented by one certificate (or CREST entry).[216] Eurobonds, on the other hand, are denominated in fixed amounts, and each bond

---

[208] This term is used to denote fixed rate securities with no special features. See Fuller: Capital Markets, 1.66.
[209] See chapter 8.
[210] See 8.3.2.3.2(a).
[211] M Choudhry, *Corporate Bonds and Structured Financial Products* (London, Elsevier Butterworth-Heinemann, 2005) 126.
[212] *Hooper v Western Counties and South Wales Telephone Co Ltd* (1892) 68 LT 78.
[213] 2.4.
[214] See Fuller: Corporate Borrowing, 3.3.
[215] See ibid, 3.6–3.10. For further discussion see 8.3.2.2.2.
[216] For a discussion of the CREST system see 4.6.2.

is an agreement between the bondholder and the company, although often there is a trustee who holds the benefit of the covenant to pay for the bondholders.[217] Both stock and eurobonds can be, and often are, listed on the London Stock Exchange.[218] Eurobonds are rarely issued to the public;[219] they are almost always issued to sophisticated institutional investors, and most trading is OTC—that is, away from the market and conducted between parties privately (usually over the telephone). The regulatory framework that governs listed debt issues is discussed below in chapter thirteen.

So far we have considered bonds which are issued by a company which is obliged to pay back the amount due from its trading income and, on maturity, from its own assets (or by reborrowing). The rating of the bond therefore depends on the creditworthiness of the company (plus any credit enhancement). However, it is also possible for bonds to be issued on the basis that repayment comes from a pool of income-producing assets, such as receivables. The effect is to turn illiquid assets (assets which may have a long repayment term) into liquid assets (the money paid by bondholders when they buy the bonds). This is the basic idea behind securities known as 'asset-backed securities' or 'ABS', where the bonds are issued not by the original owner of the receivables, but by a special purpose vehicle (SPV) which has bought the receivables from the original owner.[220] The original owner thus gets immediate cash in return for debts which are due in the future (and also, usually, acts as service provider for the SPV, that is, collects in the receivables and pays out proceeds to the bondholders, for which it receives a fee). Where the owner of the receivables is a trading (non-financial) company, it can be seen that this form of financing, known as securitisation, is therefore an alternative, for the owner of the receivables, to some forms of sale of the receivables to a financier (such as in invoice discounting),[221] or to taking a loan from a bank secured on the receivables (such as a term loan or overdraft secured by a floating or fixed charge).[222] It is usually only suitable where the company has a steady stream of receivables.[223] The rate paid on the asset-backed bonds is likely to be lower than the usual rate at which the company can borrow, since it will be determined based on the credit rating of the SPV, which depends solely on the quality of the assets (the receivables) rather than on the overall rating of the borrowing company. For this to work, the SPV has to be bankruptcy remote from the company, that is, it would be unaffected by the insolvency of the company. However, the cost of setting up the securitisation structure is considerable, and thus this form of financing is only suitable for reasonably large companies where the advantages of cheaper borrowing are not outweighed by these costs.[224]

---

[217] For further discussion of the structure of bonds and the position of the trustee, see 8.3.2.3.

[218] 13.2.1.2.

[219] Note that retail bonds are becoming more common, with the launch of the London Stock Exchange Order book for Retail Bonds (see text to n 187).

[220] See *Paragon Finance plc v Pender* [2005] EWCA Civ 760 [13] and [14]; *MBNA Europe Bank Ltd v Revenue and Customs Commissioners* [2006] EWHC 2326 (Ch) [46]–[48]. For more detailed discussion, see 9.3.3.

[221] 2.3.4.1.

[222] 2.3.2.

[223] Less consistent receivables are often the subject of a whole business securitisation; see below.

[224] For an analysis of the use of securitisation in financing non-financial companies in the US, see M Lemmon, L Liu, M Mao and G Nini, 'Securitization and Capital Structure in Nonfinancial Firms: An Empirical Investigation' (2014) 69 *Journal of Finance* 1787.

Securitisation is also used by financial companies, such as banks and credit card companies, to divest themselves of the loans they have made to others (such as home mortgage loans), in order to free up money for new loans and to get the existing loans off their balance sheets. Banks, of course, do securitise loans they have made to companies, and specialist finance companies (such as asset financiers) do the same. Thus, finance provided to small companies is, at one remove, finance by securitisation.

The basic structure has been developed in various ways. First, where it is not possible or desirable to sell receivables to an SPV (for example, where they arise from diverse contracts or where contracts generate cash revenues)[225] the SPV can, instead, make a loan to the company secured on those assets, and issue securities to fund the loan. This is known as a whole business securitisation. The assets remain on the issuer's balance sheet; it is a way of shifting credit risk, and raising immediate cash against later receipts, but it does not assist with taking assets off the borrower's balance sheet. Various features built into the structure, such as very rigorous covenants and the tranching of the bonds, may mean that the bonds are rated more highly than bonds issued by the originator company. It is used particularly in acquisition finance and project finance.[226] A concept similar to whole business securitisation is used in covered bonds, which are issued by the company itself but which are secured on a ringfenced pool of assets belonging to the company, so that the rating of the bonds depends on the quality of those assets rather than the overall credit rating of the company.

Where the motive behind securitising is removal of credit risk from the originator, another possibility is to transfer this synthetically to the SPV by means of a credit default swap or other derivative,[227] whereby the SPV agrees to pay the originator if there is default on the receivables, in return for a fee. The SPV issues securities in the same way as before, and invests the proceeds in some sort of safe investment. The payments that the SPV has to make on the securities are made partly from the interest from the safe investment and partly from the fee. Any payments that the SPV has to make to the originator under the credit default swap are made from the safe investment, thus reducing the amount available to pay the holders of the securities, who thus take the eventual credit risk on the receivables.[228] Synthetic securitisations are rarely used in relation to non-financial companies, and are often used as a form of speculation rather than for the transfer of genuine credit risk.

So far the structures described have been relatively simple, in that they only involve the originator, the SPV and the bondholders in one transaction and one allocation of risk. However, in the years leading up to 2008, the transactions became far more complex, and involved the layering of securitisations on top of one another. These structures, which on any view contributed to the global financial crisis, are unlikely to become popular again, and are not discussed further in this book.

---

[225] See D Petkovic, 'New Structures: "Whole Business" Securitisations of Project Cash Flows' [2000] *Journal of International Banking Law* 187, 188.

[226] Ibid, 187; M Brailsford, 'Securitisation-Creating Securities' (2004) 725 *Tax Journal* 15. Examples of businesses financed by whole business securitisations are London City Airport (1999), several pub companies such as Punch Taverns (2007), British Airports Authority (2007), Thames Water (2006), and Electricity North West (see C Barrett and A King, 'Electricity North West's High-Voltage Whole Business Securitisation' [2009] *Journal of International Banking and Financial Law* 590).

[227] For a discussion of credit default swaps see 6.4.3.

[228] See Fuller: Corporate Borrowing, 4.75; Wood: Loans and Bonds, 28-23; S Henderson, 'Synthetic Securitisation, Part 1: The Elements' [2001] *Journal of International Banking and Financial Law* 402.

2.3.4 Finance Based on Assets

This section considers a number of financing structures which are largely used for SMEs,[229] although large companies will also use big ticket asset finance. The common feature in all these structures is that the finance is given on the basis of specific collateral provided by the company. The financier has either an absolute interest (by way of sale or retention of title) or (in the case of some asset-based lending) a security interest.[230] It can be seen that there are some similarities with securitisation structures and covered bonds, but here the finance is provided not by the issue of securities but by the lender itself (which, of course, may well securitise its receivables from the financing). The use of finance based on assets (especially invoice discounting and asset-based lending) has increased greatly in recent times,[231] and is particularly popular when traditional bank lending is not available, either because of global conditions (as in the financial crisis) or where a company has already borrowed as much as the bank will permit.

2.3.4.1 Receivables Financing

Receivables financing provides upfront cash for a company which is owed money in the future. To that extent, it has the same economic effect as a loan which is paid back as and when the receivables are paid. In its pure financing form, the credit risk of the receivables is borne by the 'borrowing' company, so that if the receivables do not generate enough to 'repay' the loan, the company is liable for the rest.[232] The logical corollary of this would be that if the receivables generate more than is required to 'repay' then the company retains the excess, and this characteristic is also found in this form of receivables financing.[233]

This structure is usually called 'invoice discounting' and is achieved usually by a sale (an absolute assignment) of the receivables to the financier,[234] without notice to the debtors, so that the company continues to collect in the debts and holds the proceeds of sale on trust

---

[229] The BDRC Continental SME finance monitor, report for Q2 2014 shows that 34% of companies with between 50 and 249 employees had used leasing or hire purchase finance in that quarter, while 14% used invoice finance. Only 23% had a bank loan or commercial mortgage. Figures from the Asset Based Finance Association (ABFA) show that the amount in use at any one time in 2013 was £17.5 billion, of which 80% was invoice discounting and the other 20% asset-based financing. The latest figures from the Finance and Leasing Association (FLA) (for 2013) show that FLA members financed £22.4 billion of new assets to business and the public sector (29% of fixed capital investment), and of that £12.6 billion financed SMEs (see FLA annual review 2014, www.fla.org.uk/index.php/about-the-fla/annual-reports/).

[230] For further discussion of the distinction between the two, see 7.2.

[231] It is clear from the statistics produced by ABFA (www.abfa.org.uk/public/statistics.asp) that invoice discounting has risen reasonably steadily since 2000. For example, domestic invoice discounting rose from £34 million in Q1 2006 to £63 million in Q2 2014. Asset-based lending also rose, from £14.5 billion in Q1 2009 to £19 billion in Q2 2014, although the statistics are still not very reliable because of the difficult of defining this kind of lending. Asset finance has also seen steady growth (see FLA annual review 2014).

[232] As we shall see, this could be said to be one of the indicia of a charge (7.2.5.2).

[233] See *In re George Inglefield Ltd* [1933] Ch 1, 20; *Olds Discount Co Ltd v John Playfair Ltd* [1938] 3 All ER 275, 276–77.

[234] Despite the presence of the indicia of a charge, the courts have repeatedly held that this can be structured as a sale, and have refused to recharacterise the transaction. See 7.2.5.2.

for the financier.[235] The transaction is said to be 'with recourse', which means that the credit risk of the receivables is retained by the company: this is usually achieved by a contractual obligation on the company to repurchase receivables which are not paid.[236]

A receivables financing package can also include other services provided by the financier (for which, of course, the company pays). These include the transfer of the credit risk to the financier and the provision of a debt collecting service by the financier. Such a package is usually called 'factoring'. The company will sell the receivables to the financier by a statutory assignment, which means that the debtors are given notice and the financier can sue a non-paying debtor in its own name.[237]

As can be seen, from the company's point of view receivables financing is very similar to a traditional securitisation, especially where the credit risk is transferred to the financier. A securitisation structure will generally be cheaper for a company large enough to use it. This is because the company needs to pay only fees to the bank that sets it up, rather than paying the bank both interest (for the time value of money) and fees (for arranging the transaction). Further, usually, the cost of borrowing from the market by way of securities is cheaper than borrowing from a bank, especially when the securitisation structure means that the notes are more highly rated than the company itself.[238] The company also obtains a service charge for collecting in the receivables. However, normal receivables financing is more suitable for SMEs and for companies whose flow of receivables is less predictable or less consistent. The cost of setting up an invoice discounting agreement is lower than for setting up a securitisation, and although more has to be paid for the actual financing, it is much more flexible as the company only needs to 'borrow' what it requires.

The other alternative to receivables financing, for SMEs, is straight secured borrowing from a bank, either by way of a term loan or, more usually, by way of an overdraft. In the past this was very common, and banks took fixed charges over all the assets it could, including receivables. However, the possibility of taking a fixed charge over receivables has been greatly reduced by the *Spectrum* decision of 2005,[239] and this appears to be one of the factors that has led to a marked increase in invoice discounting (though not factoring).[240] Another reason may be the increase in flexibility of invoice discounting which has come from more sophisticated computerised methods of monitoring receivables and cash flow

---

[235] Even where the receivables are transferred by absolute sale, the financier usually takes a charge over other assets of the borrower. This is, in part, to catch any receivables which are not within the sale agreement. One reason might be that the receivable contains an anti-assignment clause (see 9.2.2.2.6). Although it depends on the construction of the clause, it is possible that some clauses will prohibit outright assignments but not charges. See N Ruddy, S Mills and N Davidson (eds), *Salinger on Factoring*, 4th edn (London, Sweet & Maxwell, 2006) 13.12.

[236] The borrower will also warrant that the amounts are due, so that it would be liable for the full amount if it were not paid by the account debtor, for example because there was a breach of the agreement giving rise to the receivable. For detailed discussion of these contractual rights see Security and Title-Based Financing, 7.127; for an example of a receivables financing agreement including such provisions see Goode: Commercial Law, 849.

[237] See 7.5.2.2.

[238] See 2.3.3.5.

[239] For discussion see 7.3.3.3.2.

[240] The figures published by ABFA show that the sale volume of clients using invoice discounting rose from £4 billion in 1995 to £40 billion in 2007 and £63 billion in 2014. The number of clients financed also rose, from 3,000 in 1995 to 16,500 in 2007 and 19,200 in 2014. Comparable figures for factoring are £1.85 billion in 1995, £5 billion in 2007 and £4.7 billion in 2014, with client numbers moving from 7,300 in 1995, peaking at 23,000 in 2007 and dropping to 17,600 in 2014.

on the part of financiers, which makes this form of financing a real alternative to an over-draft. Even more importantly, the reluctance of banks to lend to SMEs, arising out of the global financial crisis and the desire of the banks to reduce the risky assets on their balance sheets, has led to a significant increase both in traditional invoice discounting and in innovative forms, such as receivables purchased over an online platform.[241]

2.3.4.2 Supply Chain Financing

Supply chain financing is a variation on the theme of receivables financing, which is offered where a very large company is a customer of a number of smaller companies which require financing on the basis of their receivables. The customer arranges with a bank or other financial institution to buy receivables it owes to suppliers once they have been approved by the customer; in fact, in many cases, the customer will 'self-issue' invoices which are then assigned to the financier. The financier passes the purchase price to the supplier: the amount reflects a financing charge for the period between the date of financing and the date the invoice is due to be paid by the customer. The benefits for both parties are that the customer may obtain a longer period of credit than it could otherwise obtain from the supplier, and the supplier obtains cheaper financing, since the interest or discount rate is set on the basis of the credit rating of the customer and the fact that the customer often will be the client of the financier and has been for some time, so the financier can judge its credit record very accurately. Moreover, the customer avoids having to deal with an external financier in relation to a disputed invoice: only invoices it has itself approved are financed, and, in any event, the financier is one with whom it has a good relationship. The description of this model is generalised; there are many varieties.[242] Supply chain finance has been championed by the UK Government as a source of SME finance, and large companies have been encouraged to adopt it.[243] Further, the Government has itself adopted it in relation to National Health Service pharmacies. However, concern has been expressed that customers will be encouraged by the use of supply chain financing to demand longer credit periods, so that suppliers are forced to pay for longer periods of financing,[244] and that locking suppliers into supply chain financing deals can be anti-competitive.

2.3.4.3 Asset-Based Lending[245]

Asset-based lending originated in the US, and has only recently become popular in the UK. The term 'asset-based lending' is usually applied to financing against a wide variety of assets, including both revolving and fixed assets. Revolving assets include receivables,

---

[241] Eg http://marketinvoice.com/; and www.platformblack.com.

[242] See eg www.tungsten-network.com/TungstenBlog/post/2013/06/26/Dissecting-supply-chain-finance.aspx.

[243] See www.gov.uk/government/news/prime-minister-announces-supply-chain-finance-scheme.

[244] See www.telegraph.co.uk/finance/yourbusiness/9634184/Payment-concerns-over-supply-chain-finance-move.html; http://realbusiness.co.uk/article/15791-the-supply-chain-finance-scheme-hit-or-miss; www.selectfactoring.co.uk/supply-chain-finance-scheme.

[245] See C Swillman and A Cropley, 'Asset Based Lenders: Beneficiaries of the Credit Crunch?' [2007] *Journal of International Banking and Financial Law* 629; D Nash, 'ABL and Distressed Companies' (2008) 1(3) *Corporate Rescue and Insolvency* 104. We are very grateful to Steven Chait of Burdale Financial Ltd and Kate Sharp of ABFA (now of Metrobank plc) for discussion on the structure and scope of asset-based lending.

intellectual property and stock. Fixed assets include plant and machinery, and land. The entire transaction will involve different techniques for different assets: the financier will usually buy any receivables outright, but will take fixed charges over other assets if possible and, if not, floating charges.[246] The difference between this sort of financing and ordinary bank lending is that the asset-based financier assesses the credit risk purely in relation to the assets available as collateral, whereas the bank will look at the profitability of the business as a whole, and the cash flow of the company in particular. Thus the asset-based financier will only lend the amount it can be sure to obtain from enforcing its security and absolute interests if the company becomes insolvent, taking into account any other creditors which might have priority over it, such as suppliers on retention of title (where stock is taken as collateral), and the likely size of the prescribed part and liability to preferential creditors,[247] where its security is a floating charge. This method of financing often means that a company can raise more finance than is possible through the traditional bank lending route.

Where there are already other secured creditors, the asset-based lender will not lend unless it can obtain a subordination agreement so that it has priority over them. The significant proprietary protection for the financier means that there are likely to be fewer financial covenants than with a traditional bank loan. It also means that this financing is likely to be available in situations where banks will not lend, or where bank lending would be more expensive. This includes situations where companies appear to be failing but have substantial assets, where companies are refinancing, and in management buy-outs or buy-ins.[248] Asset-based lending proved popular during the financial crisis, when other forms of lending were becoming scarcer, and continues to grow steadily.[249] It can be used to provide finance to very large companies, and where the amounts are large the deal is often syndicated. In fact, since it is now very difficult for providers of syndicated loans to securitise their loan portfolio, asset-based lending is becoming a popular alternative.

2.3.4.4 *Devices Based on Retention of Title*

The receivables financier has proprietary protection against the credit risk of the company being financed, either by a security interest over the receivables or, more usually, by becoming the absolute owner of them. Another, similar, device for achieving proprietary protection is for the financier to have an absolute interest in tangible assets. The company can raise money on the basis of assets it already owns on this basis. The traditional method was by selling the assets to the financier and then leasing or buying them back.[250] Companies can

---

[246] The asset-based lender is likely to want a floating charge anyway, so that it can appoint an administrator: see 7.5.1.4. Fixed charges over stock are not uncommon, since the lender may use warehousing techniques or other information technology mechanisms to achieve the necessary degree of control. For discussion of the level of control required see 7.5.1.4 and 7.3.3.3.2.

[247] 3.3.1.2.2 and 3.3.1.2.3.

[248] Often the asset-based lending financing is only part of the total debt package.

[249] The balance of outstanding asset-based lending (including receivables financing) in Q2 2008 was £17 billion, of which about 17% was asset-based lending, and in Q2 2014 the balance was £19 billion, of which nearly 20% was asset-based lending.

[250] 2.3.4.4.1.

also acquire assets using this device, either from a financier, by way of a hire purchase, conditional sale or finance lease agreement,[251] or from a trader, by use of retention of title.[252]

In all these structures, except for sales on retention of title, the company obtains cash or the use of the item upfront, and makes periodic payments to the financier. In a sale on retention of title, the credit is short-term: the seller, of course, then needs to obtain finance from elsewhere in order to fund the extension of credit. This could be by an overdraft, or by some form of receivables financing.

2.3.4.4.1 Sale and Leaseback

This structure can be used if a company has fixed assets (land, plant or machinery) and wishes to raise cash while retaining and using the asset. Of course, the company could just take out a loan secured on the asset, either from a bank or by way of asset-based lending. However, a sale and leaseback may allow the company to borrow on cheaper terms, especially if there are tax advantages.[253] If the assets are plant or machinery, the lease can be either a finance lease or an operating lease: this will depend on whether the risks and rewards of the assets are with the financier or the company. It is also possible to have a sale and saleback, where the assets are 'bought' back by the company by way of hire purchase or, less likely, a conditional sale.[254]

2.3.4.4.2 Asset Finance[255]

If a company wishes to acquire machinery or vehicles or other large pieces of equipment, there are a number of options available to it other than having to pay the sale price out of existing assets. The company could borrow the price from a bank (unsecured or secured on all its assets or on the acquired item only) and buy the asset outright. It could hire the item under an operating lease, usually from a financier to whom the item has been sold by the seller. This kind of lease can be for any period of time, which means that the item can be hired just for the period it is needed, and can be updated very easily. The company never acquires ownership of the asset, which means that this structure is 'off balance sheet'.[256] The rental payments reflect the fact that the asset will eventually be returned to the financier. In between these two possibilities are the options of hire purchase and finance leasing. A finance lease is similar to an operating lease in that the company never acquires ownership

---

[251] 2.3.4.4.2.

[252] 2.3.4.4.3.

[253] This is likely to be the case where the leaseback is a finance lease (see below) or where land is sold to Real Estate Investment Trust (a tax transparent property holding company set up by Part 4 of the Finance Act 2006) and leased back to the company. In both cases the tax advantages to the financier are shared with the company in the form of lower rental payments.

[254] For a discussion of the characterisation of these transactions see 7.2.5.1.

[255] This is the term used in the industry to cover the acquisition of assets. This is a significant form of finance; for example, in 2009 almost £30 billion of finance was provided this way for businesses: BIS, *Financing a Private Sector Recovery* (Cm 7923, July 2010), 3.31.

[256] See Inland Revenue Leasing Manual BLM00060, BLM000725. The International Accounting Standards Board has been considering the accounting status of leases, and, after very considerable consultation, has decided to propose a new accounting standard with a single model of a lease, so that operating leases over one year will appear on the balance sheet (see www.ifrs.org/Current-Projects/IASB-Projects/Leases/Documents/Project-Update-Leases-August-2014.pdf). The revised accounting standard is due to be issued later in 2015—see www.ifrs.org/current-projects/iasb-projects/leases/Pages/leases.aspx.

of the asset,[257] but the lease is for a fixed period of time, and the periodic payments made by the company include the capital cost of the asset, spread out over that period of time, as well as payments for hire. At the end of the period, there is a second period during which the company can hire the item for just the hire cost. At any time after the end of the first period, the company can sell the item as agent for the financier and is usually allowed to retain a very high proportion (usually over 90 per cent) of the proceeds.[258] The chief advantage of a finance lease, as opposed to a hire purchase agreement, used to be the very favourable tax treatment it received, in that the financier (the lessor) could claim capital allowance for the asset, some of which benefit could be passed on to the company (the lessee) and the lessee could deduct the hire payments as revenue expenses.[259] This benefit has been altered, in relation to long-term finance leases (called 'long-funded leases' in the legislation), by the Finance Act 2006;[260] such leases are now taxed according to their economic substance, in a way very similar to loans.[261]

While they can be used for any sort of tangible asset, finance leases are often used for 'big ticket' items, such as aeroplanes[262] and large vehicles. An alternative, though similar, structure is hire purchase. Here the financier retains ownership of the item, but, as with a finance lease, all the risks and rewards are transferred to the company. The company (the 'hirer') makes periodic payments which in part reflect the hire charge and in part reflect the capital value of the item. At the end of the hire period the hirer has the option to purchase the item for a nominal fee. This structure does not attract the favourable tax and accounting treatment of a finance lease: the financier cannot claim capital allowance, and the payments made by the hirer are treated as partly rent (which is deductible from profits) and partly capital expenditure (on which capital allowance can be claimed).[263]

A similar structure, less common in the commercial sector than in the consumer sector, is conditional sale, where the owner agrees to sell at the beginning, but title is not transferred until the end of the agreed period, once all the instalment payments have been made.[264]

---

[257] The distinction between the two sorts of leases can be important for tax purposes—see Inland Revenue Leasing Manual BLM00035. Basically, a finance lease is defined as a lease which transfers all the risks and rewards of ownership to the lessee, while an operating lease is a lease which does not. Generally speaking, a financier that leases on an operating lease is concerned with the inherent value of the item leased as it has an 'equity stake' in the item, while a financier leasing on a finance lease is concerned only with the creditworthiness of the lessee (although this is not true where the last payment is to be funded by the proceeds from the sale of the item). See also UK GAAP, paragraph 15, SSAP 21 and IFRS IAS 17.

[258] This is because in a finance lease, the lessee has all the risks and rewards of the item, but cannot acquire it itself, as this would turn it into a hire purchase agreement.

[259] This is in reality a timing advantage rather than an absolute advantage, but depending on the tax position of both parties, the timing can be very significant. See Inland Revenue Leasing Manual BLM00710. There are also a large number of anti-avoidance provisions: see Inland Revenue Leasing Manual BLM01030.

[260] Finance Act 2006, s 81(1), which inserted ss 70A–70YI into the Capital Allowances Act 2001. The rules relating to long-funded leases apply only to leases of plant and machinery. See Capital Allowances Act 2001, s 70G.

[261] Thus capital allowances are available to the lessee not the lessor, but the amount of rental payments that can be deducted is reduced accordingly. Inland Revenue Leasing Manual BLM20015, BLM42005.

[262] The financing of aircraft and engines is the subject of a transnational commercial law convention providing for a central register of security interests, including finance leases and other retention of title devices. The convention, known as the Cape Town Convention on International Interests in Mobile Equipment (together with its Aircraft Protocol), is due to be ratified by the UK in the near future.

[263] Capital Allowances Act 2001, s 67. See Inland Revenue Leasing Manual BLM39010.

[264] One drawback of conditional sale, in the commercial context, is that if the buyer (in possession of the goods) makes an unauthorised sale to a third party, that party, if in good faith and without notice of the conditional sale agreement, can obtain good title under Sale of Goods Act, s 25(1). Conditional sales regulated by

2.3.4.4.3 Stock Finance[265]

Stock finance is a term that can cover a number of different structures based on the concepts already discussed. One, which is a variant of acquisition finance, involves the company entering into a hire purchase or conditional sale agreement as a temporary measure in order to fund the period between obtaining the item to display to potential customers and selling the item to a customer, rather than in order to own the item. This form of finance is usually provided in relation to motor vehicles, and the financier is likely to be a company associated with the manufacturer of the vehicles.

Another possible model is where, in order to 'lend' money against stock already owned by the company, the financier buys the stock from the company and the company sells it to customers as the undisclosed agent of the financier.[266] The company then holds the proceeds of sale on trust for the financier, in a similar way to an invoice discounting arrangement. Both of the arrangements discussed in this section are alternatives to a lender taking a charge over stock; while this will normally be floating, it may be fixed if sufficient control methods are put in place.[267]

2.3.4.4.4 Sales on Retention of Title Terms

The funding of the period between acquisition of raw materials or stock and the point at which these goods are disposed of (in their original state or after manufacture into something else) can be achieved, at least partly, by credit extended to the buyer by the seller. The seller is then exposed to the credit risk of the buyer. To protect itself, the seller will usually retain title to the goods in the sale agreement.[268] While the goods are in the possession of the buyer, if the buyer does not pay, the seller has the right to retake the goods, and, since the seller has a proprietary right, this will survive the buyer's insolvency. However, this form of protection has its limitations. Any attempt by a seller to gain proprietary protection in the products of the raw materials supplied,[269] or in the proceeds of sale[270] of the stock supplied, is very likely to be characterised as a charge and will therefore be registrable. Since it is impractical to register every sale agreement, this registrability means that the seller's proprietary protection is limited to an interest in the goods themselves.

Consumer Credit Act 1974 are excepted from this provision (s 25(2)) but this only includes sales to individuals and very small partnerships (Consumer Credit Act, s 8). Hire purchase agreements do not fall under s 25 Sale of Goods Act, although in relation to vehicles Hire Purchase Act 1964, s 27 has a similar effect where the sub-sale is to a private purchaser. This difference accounts for the preference for hire purchase agreements over conditional sales in the commercial context.

[265] See M Nield, 'Protecting Title in Stock Finance' [2007] *Journal of International Banking and Financial Law* 638.

[266] *Welsh Development Agency v Export Finance Co Ltd* [1992] BCLC 148.

[267] See Goode: Credit and Security, 4–18.

[268] In relation to the goods themselves, this is easily done as Sale of Goods Act, s 17 provides that property in the goods passes when the parties intend it to pass.

[269] See eg *Borden (UK) Ltd v Scottish Timber Products Ltd* [1981] 1 Ch 25; *Re Peachdart Ltd* [1984] Ch 131; *Clough Mill Ltd v Martin* [1985] 1 WLR 111; *Modelboard Ltd v Outer Box Ltd* [1992] BCC 945; *Ian Chisholm Textiles Ltd v Griffiths* [1994] BCC 96.

[270] *E Pfeiffer Weinkellerei-Weinein-kauf GmbH & Co v Arbuthnot Factors Ltd* [1988] 1 WLR 150; *Tatung (UK) Ltd v Galex Telesure Ltd* (1989) 5 BCC 325; *Compaq Computer Ltd v Abercorn Ltd* [1993] BCLC 602.

2.3.5 Specialised Forms of Finance

2.3.5.1 Project Finance

Project finance is a structure used to finance infrastructure projects, such as roads, pipelines, prisons and hospitals, whereby the lenders are paid out of the income generated by the project. The debt finance (which may be provided by way of loans or securities or a mixture of both) is made available to an SPV (owned by one or more 'sponsors') which is a party to a concession agreement with the relevant government entitling it to build the infrastructure. The SPV contracts out the construction work (which is paid for by the borrowings) and, when the infrastructure is built, receives the revenues from its operation, which may come in the form of tolls (in the case of roads) or government payments (in the case of prisons or hospitals). The revenues are distributed according to a contractual clause, known as a waterfall clause, which provides for scheduled repayment of the debt finance. The SPV is usually highly leveraged, so that the debt to equity ratio is high, and the lenders take upon themselves a certain amount of the risk that the project will not be completed, or will not make money. Although the lenders will take what security they can, this will often largely consist of a charge over the revenue-generating contract, since the SPV will normally not own the item built, nor will the item have much independent value aside from its revenue-generating value.

2.3.5.2 Financing of Group Companies

Lending to a company which is part of a group presents special problems for a lender, which may lead to complicated financing structures involving guarantees and also, maybe, set-offs or charge-backs.[271] Despite being part of a group, each company is treated as a separate entity by the law, and each has limited liability,[272] so that in order to have access to the assets of the group a lender will need to put in place contractual and proprietary protection by agreement. It will often be the case that the company that needs to borrow money does not have significant assets, since these are held by a parent company or another company in the group. In this situation, the lender may lend to the company that needs the money, and take a guarantee and security from the company with the assets (and probably all the other companies in the group). Alternatively, it may be another company in the group that has the ability to raise funds, for example by a bond issue or a loan, rather than the company which actually needs the funds. Here the company that can raise the money will on-lend the money to the other company, which will give a guarantee of the repayment obligations under the bonds or loan.[273] Quite often the company that gives the guarantee will have a credit balance with the lender. The lender will seek to ensure that, if necessary, the obligation under the guarantee can be enforced by set-off, both outside and within insolvency, but may also seek to protect itself by taking a charge-back or using a flawed asset structure.[274] Group companies may also lend to each other, or extend credit to each other, and external

---

[271] These issues are discussed in chapter 6.
[272] For discussion see 3.3.3.1.
[273] See, for example, the structure in *Re Polly Peck International plc (in administration)* [1996] 2 All ER 433.
[274] See 6.3.4.1.

lenders usually insist that inter-group liabilities are subordinated to the debts to external lenders.[275] It will be seen that the financing structure of a group can be very complicated, and can cause significant problems on insolvency. Further, the business is likely to be structured as a group for tax or some other cross-border purpose, in which case these issues will also impact on the financing structure.

2.3.5.3 Trade Finance

When goods are bought and sold internationally, there is a considerable period of time between shipping and receipt. The seller may well extend credit to the buyer, on retention of title terms, or the buyer may need to borrow in order to pay the seller, using the goods as security by way of a pledge of documents of title to the goods. The financing of international trade is a specialist area of the law, and is not dealt with further in this book.[276]

2.3.5.4 Islamic Finance[277]

There is now a large market in Islamic finance—that is, finance which complies with Sharia law: this is the law that governs Islamic societies.[278] There are three particular rules in Sharia law which relate to finance transactions: a prohibition on *riba* (interest), a requirement that uncertainty (*gharar*) should be avoided, and a requirement that the contract must not relate to immoral activities.[279] The prohibition on *riba* stems from the view that a profit cannot be made from merely lending money to another: all profit must be from commercial activity. Thus, Sharia-compliant finance contracts are either in the form of some sort of profit sharing (such as the partnership contracts, *musharaka* and *mudaraba*), sale (such as the *murabaha* contract,[280] which is a sale at a deferred price, which includes a profit mark-up for the seller to cover the cost of the deferred payment and is similar to a conditional sale)[281] or lease (such as the *ijarah*, which is similar to an operating lease, since the lessor must retain all the risks and rewards of ownership). The latter two types of contract can apply to both real estate assets and tangible personal property. The finance for these transactions is either provided by a bank or other finance company, or can be raised on the capital markets by the issuance of securities, known as *sukuk* certificates. The benefit of the underlying contracts is converted into securities by a securitisation process called *tawreeq*.[282] An SPV is created which owns the underlying assets. In a *musharaka* transaction, the SPV owns the shares in

---

[275] 6.4.4.

[276] For detailed discussion see Goode: *Commercial Law*, ch 35; *Security and Title-Based Financing*, 5.34–5.40 concerning pledges of documents of title to goods.

[277] For a full treatment see C Nethercott and D Eisenberg, *Islamic Finance* (Oxford, Oxford University Press, 2012).

[278] Sharia law is not seen, under English law, as law which can be the governing law of a contract: see *Shamil Bank of Bahrain v Beximco Pharmaceuticals Ltd* [2004] EWCA Civ 19.

[279] For discussion of these principles, see Fuller: *Capital Markets*, 6.19–6.25; O Salah, *Sukuk Structures: Legal Engineering under Dutch Law* (The Hague, Eleven International Publishing, 2014) 2.2.

[280] For an account of *murabaha* see *Shamil Bank of Bahrain EC v Beximco Pharmaceuticals Ltd* [2004] EWCA Civ 19 [13].

[281] See 2.3.4.4.2.

[282] See O Salah, *Sukuk Structures: Legal Engineering under Dutch Law* (The Hague, Eleven International Publishing, 2014) 4.2.

the *musharaka*; in a *murabaha* the SPV owns the tangible assets. The form of a *sukuk* based on *ijarah* can vary, but often the SPV owns the tangible asset that it leases to the originator, and the *sukuk* holders are paid the rent. In each case, if the structure is governed by English law, the SPV holds the asset on trust for the *sukuk* holders, and so the securities, rather than being debt securities, are similar to depositary receipts.[283]

Whether any particular transaction or structure is Sharia compliant depends on the application of Sharia principles by Islamic scholars. Usually, an opinion (*fatwa*) as to compliance is obtained before a transaction is finalised, and many banks and other finance institutions have their own board of Islamic scholars for this purpose.[284] Compliance can still be controversial, however, especially as some structures adhere to Sharia principles in form but not in substance.[285] It is not open to the parties to choose Sharia law as the law of the contract, but the parties can provide that the contract should be interpreted according to Sharia principles.[286] Thus, if the contract is valid under English law, the fact that it does not comply with Sharia principles will not render it void or voidable per se. If, however, one or both parties lacked capacity or authority to enter into a non-Sharia-compliant transaction, this could affect the validity of the contract.[287] It is also, presumably, possible for compliance with Sharia principles to be a condition precedent.[288]

2.4 Hybrids

A hybrid security combines some of the features generally associated with equity capital with some of those associated with debt capital. The idea behind hybrids is to obtain the best of all worlds, by designing a security that is treated as equity for some purposes and treated as debt for others. Hybrids come in a number of forms. Some are regarded as hybrid because their very nature contains elements associated with debt and equity, such as preference shares; others have both of those elements by design, such as deeply subordinated debt securities; and others, such as convertible securities, are regarded as hybrids because they start life as one type of capital (for example, debt) but have the ability to be converted into the other. Some forms of hybrid have existed for some considerable time, such as preference shares, while others have been developed more recently in response to particular issues, such as the regulatory capital requirements discussed in this section. The category of hybrids therefore comprises a variety of different devices, which may be utilised for a variety of reasons, the uniting feature being that these securities combine both debt and equity features.

---

[283] See Fuller: Capital Markets, 6.03.

[284] *Shamil Bank of Bahrain EC v Beximco Pharmaceuticals Ltd* [2004] EWCA Civ 19 [8].

[285] For an example see *The Investment Dar Company KSCC v Blom Developments Bank Sal* [2009] EWHC 3545 (Ch).

[286] *Shamil Bank of Bahrain EC v Beximco Pharmaceuticals Ltd* [2004] EWCA Civ 19; *Halpern v Halpern* [2007] EWCA Civ 291.

[287] Contracts entered into by a company incorporated in England will normally be enforceable by third parties despite lack of capacity or authority (see Companies Act 2006, ss 39 and 40), but this will not apply to public bodies or to foreign companies. See R Reed, 'The Application of Islamic Finance Principles under English and DIFC Law' [2014] *Journal of International Banking and Financial Law* 573.

[288] See 6.3.2.1.

Preference shares are a common form of hybrid security. A typical preference share-holder will have rights in the articles of the company which specify a fixed dividend[289] and a fixed return on capital, both generally payable in preference to the return on ordinary shares. Unlike ordinary shareholders, preference shareholders generally have no right to participate in the surplus, ie they are not residual claimants, and have no, or very limited, voting rights. The inclusion of rights to fixed returns on income and capital ahead of the ordinary shareholders means that preference shares to some extent resemble loan capital, although the rights of preference shareholders are generally weaker than those of creditors, and they continue to rank behind creditors in the order of payment on a winding up.[290] Preference shares remain, at law, shares. For accounting purposes, however, they may be classified as either equity or debt, depending on their precise terms.[291] Preference shares, then, are equity securities which have debt-like features. The attraction of preference shares over ordinary shares from the company's point of view, or, more particularly, that of the existing shareholders, is that they rarely contain general voting rights, and therefore they do not tend to disturb existing control rights. Their advantage over debt is that the return, though often expressed to be fixed, is not fixed in the same way as debt, and need not be paid in certain circumstances.[292] The advantage of preference shares for the holder is that they rank ahead of the ordinary shares for various purposes,[293] and that the preferential dividend should promise a higher return than the interest payment that could otherwise be obtained by that investor.

In contrast, many other effective hybrids are basically debt securities which have equity-like features; this structure is generally more tax effective. For tax purposes it is advantageous for the security to be treated as debt, so that payments made on it will be tax deductible.[294] Furthermore, the cost of issuing debt is considerably less than the cost of equity.[295] However, equity-like features are attractive for two reasons. One is that such features can enable the investor to share in the benefit if the company does well. Debt securities may, therefore, include an option to convert them into full equity ('convertible securities'), or to exchange them for equity securities in a third party held by the issuer ('exchangeable securities'), or to buy shares in the issuer at a particular price ('equity warrants'). From the point of view of the holder, a debt security with the addition of a right to convert it into an equity security gives it the best of both worlds, as it can take advantage of improvements in the company's performance without taking the initial risk of holding equity, and, until conversion, it gets a guaranteed fixed income from the security.[296] Thus, making securities convertible or exchangeable may make them more attractive to investors.

---

[289] This return is not guaranteed; it will always be subject to the company having the necessary distributable profits, and subject to the directors declaring the dividend, discussed at 2.2.1.2.

[290] See discussion at 3.2.1.2.4.

[291] For a discussion of whether preference shares should be treated as equity or debt see WW Bratton and ML Wachter, 'A Theory of Preferred Stock' (2013) 161(7) *University of Pennsylvania Law Review* 1815.

[292] See 3.2.1.2.

[293] Ibid.

[294] This is most advantageous if the holder of the security is receiving the payments in a jurisdiction where they are treated as dividends. See S Luder, 'Hybrid Financing' (2005) 810 *Tax Journal* 9.

[295] 'The Rise of the Hybrid' (April 2006) 37 *Euromoney* 2. For discussion of the different costs of capital, see 2.6.

[296] See Fuller: Capital Markets, 1.24.

Another reason for adding equity-like features to debt securities, which is particularly relevant to financial institutions, is that such features enable the security to be treated favourably from a regulatory capital point of view. Hybrids may be designed to help a financial institution meet its capital adequacy requirements.[297] An issuer that is a financial institution will benefit from a hybrid being treated as equity by qualifying for tier one regulatory capital. More generally, however, all issuers will benefit from the treatment of hybrids as equity in the rating agencies' assessment of the company's creditworthiness,[298] and they will likewise benefit if securities are treated as equity rather than debt in their balance sheets, as this makes it easier to comply with covenants which require a certain debt to equity ratio.[299] Convertible securities may be hybrids in the sense used above if the other features apply, but the convertibility itself does not give the securities the required equity rating: this will only be the case if the holder is obliged to convert.[300] In terms of regulatory capital requirements, however, the fact that debt securities are subordinated is enough for them to rank as tier two capital,[301] and such securities may be convertible so as to be attractive to investors.[302] Some debt securities issued by banks may also be convertible into equity securities on order to provide loss absorption in the event of failure: these 'contingent convertible securities' (also known as CoCos) have become popular since the financial crisis.[303]

One important feature from the point of view of the rating agencies and the regulatory capital requirements is that the security has a long maturity date. In order to gain tax treatment as debt, maturity has to be 'within the foreseeable future'. Many hybrid securities now have two maturity dates: a shorter 'scheduled' date of, for example, 30 years, and a longer 'final' maturity date of, for example, 80 years.[304] Another feature which makes such securities more 'equity-like' is an option, or, better still, an obligation on the issuer to repay by issuing equity securities, thus retaining or improving its debt to equity ratio.[305] A further feature is that the issuer has the ability to defer interest payments: this makes them similar to dividends, which the issuer has no obligation to pay.[306] The securities will also have to

---

[297] See 2.3.1.3.

[298] The rating agencies' willingness to do this was confirmed in February 2005 by Moody's, which published its 'Refinements to Moody's Tool Kit' setting out the precise criteria on which it would take into account the equity-like characteristics of hybrids. Standard and Poor's and Fitch followed later in 2005; see 'Hybrid Capital Goes from Strength to Strength' (April 2006) 37 *Euromoney* 4.

[299] See 'The Rise of the Hybrid' (April 2006) 37 *Euromoney* 2. For discussion of such covenants see 6.3.2.2.

[300] A Pinedo, 'Degree of Difficulty, 9; Style Points, 5 (or Understanding Hybrids)' [2007] *Journal of International Banking and Financial Law* 203. Financial institutions have recently begun to issue debt securities which convert into equity on certain stress triggers, so as to provide an 'equity cushion' when needed; these are called contingent capital (for example, these were issued by Lloyds Bank and the Royal Bank of Scotland in 2009). See T Humphreys and A Pinedo, 'Is it a Bird? A Plane? Exploring Contingent Capital' [2010] *Journal of International Banking and Financial Law* 67.

[301] See 2.3.1.3; Fuller: Capital Markets, 11.33.

[302] Ibid, 10.09.

[303] T Humphreys and A Pinedo, 'Is it a Bird? A Plane? Exploring Contingent Capital' [2010] *Journal of International Banking and Financial Law* 67.

[304] A Pinedo, 'Degree of difficulty, 9; Style Points, 5 (or Understanding Hybrids)' [2007] *Journal of International Banking and Financial Law* 203.

[305] Ibid. See also A Pinedo, 'Exceptionally Intelligent Design' [2008] *Journal of International Banking and Financial Law* 193.

[306] A Pinedo, 'Degree of Difficulty, 9; Style Points, 5 (or Understanding Hybrids)' [2007] *Journal of International Banking and Financial Law* 203.

be deeply subordinated. As explained in chapter three, on the insolvency of a company the unsecured creditors rank pari passu, with equity holders ranking behind them. Unsecured creditors can, however, agree to rank behind other unsecured creditors, in other words to be subordinated, and this is very common in various contexts. The more 'deeply' subordinated an issue of debt securities is—that is, the fewer creditors who rank below it—the more like equity it seems. It might be asked why investors would buy such debt securities, since the features set out so far would seem to make them very unattractive. The answer largely lies in the price, since holders are compensated for the greater risk of hybrid securities by the promise of a much larger return.[307]

2.5 Retained Profits

Retained profits are an internal source of finance for the company, the availability of which will depend upon the profitability of the company and the decisions taken by the company's directors as to whether to retain those profits or to return them to the shareholders, commonly by way of dividend payments or repurchases of the company's own shares. The ability of directors to distribute profits to the shareholders in this way is discussed in chapter five.[308] The capital maintenance rules discussed in that chapter impose some constraints on the circumstances in which returns can be made to shareholders, but where the company has distributable profits, these rules will cause little difficulty. Dividends can be paid as long as profits are available for the purpose,[309] and share repurchases can be made provided the appropriate procedure is followed.[310] It is predominantly a matter for the directors, acting in accordance with their directors' duties, whether the company will be best served by retaining its profits to finance its operations or returning some of those profits to its shareholders.

Benefits to the company can flow from returning profits to the shareholders. These benefits will differ depending on a number of factors, including the size of the company and the number and nature of its shareholders. In small quasi-partnership firms, share repurchases may not be regarded as a valuable option by shareholders, since the shares at this point may provide the shareholders with valuable control rights which they do not wish to forgo. This will change, however, where one or more of the shareholders wishes to leave the business. There is unlikely to be a ready market for the shares. If the other shareholders do not want to buy out the exiting shareholder, but there are funds available for the company to do so,[311] then a repurchase of the shares by the company may be a useful tool. Dividend payments are just one way for owner-managers to extract income from such companies; others are available. Shareholders in quasi-partnership companies are often employed by

---

[307] The same is also true of high-yield bonds, which are often subordinated to other debt. See 2.3.3.3.

[308] For discussion of these options see 5.4.1 and 5.4.2. Other methods of returning value to shareholders, which are less commonly used, include formal reductions of capital (5.4.3) and schemes of arrangement (see chapter 15).

[309] Distributions to shareholders can only be made out of profits available for the purpose: Companies Act 2006, s 830 (and s 831 for public companies). For discussion see 3.2.1.1.2.

[310] See 5.4.2.2.

[311] A private company can fund a repurchase of shares out of distributable profits, a fresh issue of shares or, in some circumstances, out of capital: Companies Act 2006, ss 690–723, discussed at 5.4.2.

the company, and so will be able to receive income by way of salary. They may also have lent money to the company, so that profits could be used to repay any capital sums outstanding. The decision as to which, if any, of these methods to use to return the company's profits to the shareholders will be determined by a variety of factors, and the decision will often be tax driven. The external funding options for a small quasi-partnership company are generally more limited than those for larger companies.[312] For small companies their primary form of external funding is likely to be a bank loan secured on the personal assets of the owner-managers. Profits are likely to be a key source of financing for the business.

Once external shareholders become involved, this may change: such shareholders may have expectations about the level of dividends that they should receive. Shareholders are not per se in a strong position to demand dividend payments. In general these are subject to the company having distributable profits and the dividends having been declared.[313] It may be that a failure to pay dividends could amount to unfairly prejudicial conduct, and thus allow a shareholder to bring a petition under section 994 of the Companies Act 2006, although this will be rare.[314] The shareholder would need to demonstrate that the failure to pay the dividends involved a breach of an agreement or understanding between the parties which it would be unfair to ignore.[315] This will often be an agreement arising, formally or informally, outside the constitutional documents of a company. Such an agreement is far more likely to arise in the context of small quasi-partnership companies than publicly traded companies.[316]

In publicly traded companies, shareholders usually do expect to receive regular dividends in respect of their shares. In general the dividends received by shareholders in publicly traded companies are kept at a fairly constant level, smoothed over time, and any increases in the dividend payments tend to reflect the underlying long-term prospects of the business.[317] As a result, directors in publicly traded companies tend to be conservative about their dividend policy. Dividends are kept relatively low, and any increases are contemplated only if the directors are confident about the sustained growth of the company.[318]

---

[312] See BIS, *Financing a Private Sector Recovery* (Cm 7923, July 2010), 3.7, discussed at 2.2.

[313] It is common for the articles to provide that final dividends are declared by the shareholders in general meeting (see Model Articles for Private Companies Limited by Shares, art 30; Model Articles for Public Companies, art 70: The Companies (Model Articles) Regulations 2008 (SI 3229/2008), Sch 1 and Sch 3) but subject to the recommendation of the directors. Since the shareholders generally cannot increase the level of dividend, and it is rare for them to declare less than recommended by the directors, this is largely a rubber stamping exercise.

[314] The courts have accepted that dividend policy can amount to unfairly prejudicial conduct: see eg *Re Sam Weller & Sons Ltd* [1990] 1 Ch 682.

[315] *O'Neill v Phillips* [1999] 1 WLR 1092. It is also possible to bring a section 994 petition in other circumstances, in particular where there has been a breach of a legal right held by the petitioner, but this is unlikely to be helpful in the context of dividends, since any 'right' to receive a dividend will be dependent on other factors, such as the fact that the company has made distributable profits.

[316] For discussion of the position regarding Companies Act 2006 and public companies see *Re Astec (BSR) plc* [1998] 2 BCLC 556.

[317] J Lintner, 'Distribution of Incomes of Corporations among Dividends, Retained Earnings, and Taxes' (1956) 46(2) *American Economic Review* 97; A Brav et al, 'Payout Policy in the 21st Century' (2005) 77 *Journal of Financial Economics* 483; F Bancel, UR Mittoo and N Bhattacharyya, 'Cross-Country Determinants in Payout Policy: A Survey of European Firms' (2004) 33 *Financial Management* 103; MT Leary and R Michaely, 'Determinants of Dividend Smoothing: Empirical Evidence' (2011) 24 *Review of Financial Studies* 3197.

[318] See Brav et al, 'Payout Policy in the 21st Century', ibid.

Corporate finance theory posits that in frictionless markets dividend policy should not affect the overall market value of the company's shares.[319] This is based on the idea that where the company retains profits and invests them in new profitable ventures, the shares will have a higher capital value than they would have if the company had paid a dividend and then had to raise further finance to fund the new venture. A shareholder can then realise this capital gain by selling the shares in the market, rather than by relying on the company to pay the dividend. This suggests that companies should only pay dividends after all investment decisions have been made. This theory does not, however, match the reality that is observable in the market. Markets are not frictionless and there is a cost involved in buying and selling shares. There is also a different tax treatment for dividends, which are taxed as income, and the capital gains made on the disposal of shares. In addition, investors may view the future gains to be made from new projects as more risky than dividends payable today, and so may undervalue shares in a company that pays low dividends,[320] or may simply prefer to receive steady dividends rather than to sell their shareholdings. In practice, directors do not generally conform to the model posited by this corporate finance theory. They tend to forgo positive investment opportunities or borrow to fund dividends, rather than reducing the existing levels of dividend payment. They do not, however, generally increase levels of dividend payment until all investment decisions have been made.[321]

Dividend policy in publicly traded companies can perform a signalling function regarding the state of the company. Paying healthy, consistent dividends is a way for managers to signal to the market that they have long-term confidence in the business.[322] In the environment of conservative dividend payments, a dividend increase makes a strong statement about the expected future profitability of the company, whereas a dividend cut may be taken as an indicator of a long-term problem within the company. A failure to meet shareholders' expectations is likely to have a negative effect on share price. Any benefits obtained by using dividend policy to signal to the market do, however, have to be weighed against the need for companies to finance their existing and future operations, and returning retained profits to shareholders may well mean that companies have to access external finance in order to fund these operations.[323]

In the UK, dividend conservatism is prevalent in publicly traded companies, so that, in general, retained profits will be used to fund relatively low levels of dividends that remain

---

[319] MH Miller and F Modigliani, 'Dividend Policy, Growth and the Valuation of Shares' (1961) 34 *Journal of Business* 411.

[320] MJ Gordon, 'Dividends, Earnings and Stock Prices' (1959) 41 *Review of Economics and Statistics* 99.

[321] A Brav et al, 'Payout Policy in the 21st Century' (2005) 77 *Journal of Financial Economics* 483.

[322] It has been suggested that directors can use dividend policy to make other signals to the market, for example in order to distinguish a company from its competitors (see eg MH Miller and K Rock, 'Dividend Policy under Asymmetric Information' (1985) 40 *Journal of Finance* 1031), but empirical evidence does not support this view: Brav et al, ibid.

[323] Some commentators suggest that it is good for shareholders if directors pay high dividends precisely because directors will then have to expose their business record and future plans for the company to the scrutiny of lenders in the market, and may have to submit to restrictive covenants in order to secure funds—ie that it can precipitate monitoring by lenders that can be beneficial to shareholders: M Jensen, 'Agency Costs of Free Cash Flow, Corporate Finance and Takeovers' (1986) 76 *American Economic Review* 323; FH Easterbrook, 'Two Agency-Cost Explanations of Dividends' (1984) 74 *American Economic Review* 650. However, managers do not appear to regard dividend policy as imposing discipline on themselves: A Brav et al, 'Payout Policy in the 21st Century' (2005) 77 *Journal of Financial Economics* 483.

fairly constant.[324] As a result, where directors have retained profits that they wish to return to the shareholders over and above existing dividend levels they may well do so via a repurchase of shares as these do not raise expectations about future payouts.[325] Returning profits to shareholders via a share buy-back can be very beneficial in circumstances where the company itself is unable to invest efficiently in profitable investment projects.[326] This can be a particularly valuable way to return profits to the shareholders as it can have a positive impact on the company's performance ratios (earnings per share and net assets per share) that are used to assess corporate performance, since these ratios assess the figures (earning or net profits) by reference to the number of equity shares in issue.[327]

2.6 The Debt/Equity Mix

A company's capital structure comprises its mix of debt and equity. The question then arises as to whether an optimal capital structure exists for all companies that will maximise every company's value.[328]

It is suggested by financial economists that a company's cost of capital, ie the total return expected by the providers of its debt and equity finance, is unaffected by its debt to equity ratio.[329] The Modigliani-Miller propositions suggest that no combination of debt and equity is better than any other, and that a company's overall market value is independent of its capital structure. Although borrowing increases the expected rate of return on shareholders' investments, adding debt to a company's capital structure increases the risk of insolvency, and shareholders, whose investment will be wiped out first in the event, require compensation for this risk. According to Modigliani and Miller, although debt financing can be regarded as a cheaper source of finance than equity, due to its reduced risk

---

[324] Some scholarship has associated dividend policy with levels of shareholder protection within a jurisdiction (R La Porta, F Lopez de Silanes, A Schleifer and R Vishny, 'Agency Problems and Dividend Policies Around the World' (2000) 55 *Journal of Finance* 1) but this is controversial (eg F Bancel, UR Mittoo and N Bhattacharyya, 'Cross-Country Determinants in Payout Policy: A Survey of European Firms' (2004) 33 *Financial Management* 103).

[325] Companies are also influenced by tax considerations: J Tiley, 'The Purchase by a Company of its Own Shares' [1992] *British Tax Review* 21.

[326] There is, of course, a danger that directors will decide to retain profits to expand the company's business into new ventures for reasons that are less to do with the growth to the company that may result and more to do with enhancing their personal reputation (eg V Brudney, 'Dividends, Discretion and Disclosure' (1980) 66 *Virginia Law Review* 85; DR Fischel, 'The Law and Economics of Dividend Policy' (1981) 67 *Virginia Law Review* 699; MC Jensen, 'Eclipse of the Public Corporation' [1989] *Harvard Business Review* 61). If this is correct, there may be some doubt as to the assessment of the company's ability to invest in profitable investment projects in this context.

[327] For a general discussion of share buy-backs, including some of the other reasons why directors may want to consider them, see 5.4.2.2.

[328] See eg SC Myers, 'The Capital Structure Puzzle' (1984) 39 *Journal of Finance* 574; M Bradley, GA Jarrell and EH Kim, 'On the Existence of an Optimal Capital Structure: Theory and Evidence' (1984) 39 *Journal of Finance* 857; S Titman and R Wessels, 'The Determinants of Capital Structure Choice' (1988) 43 *Journal of Finance* 1; M Harris and A Raviv, 'The Theory of Capital Structure' (1991) 46 *Journal of Finance* 297.

[329] F Modigliani and MH Miller, 'The Cost of Capital, Corporation Finance and the Theory of Investment' (1958) 48 *American Economic Review* 433; MH Miller, 'The Modigliani-Miller Propositions After Thirty Years' (1988) 2 *Journal of Economic Perspectives* 99; RA Brealey, SC Myers and F Allen, *Principles of Corporate Finance*, 10th edn (London, McGraw-Hill Higher Education, 2010) chs 17–18.

(for example, as a result of its prior ranking on insolvency), the additional return expected by equity investors as a result of the increased risk which they face exactly offsets this advantage. If this is correct then the amount of debt entered into by a company should be irrelevant and debt to equity ratios should vary randomly from company to company and from industry to industry. Yet this is not what is observed in practice. Almost all banks, for example, rely heavily on debt,[330] whereas in other sectors, such as pharmaceuticals and advertising, almost all companies have traditionally been mainly equity financed.[331]

Clearly, the original Modigliani-Miller propositions do not explain these observations. In part this is because the Modigliani-Miller model was developed on the basis of certain restrictive assumptions, including the existence of well-functioning capital markets[332] and the absence of taxes, transaction costs and insolvency costs. These assumptions are highly artificial. In practice these issues are important and will affect the relative cost of debt and equity to a company and are very likely to affect the debt to equity ratios within a company. In relation to taxes, for example, companies can deduct the interest payable on debt from their profits for the purpose of assessing corporation tax: dividends are not deductible in this way. Once these assumptions are relaxed, it becomes clear that some debt can be added to a company's capital structure without affecting the return expected by its shareholders.[333] As the proportion of debt in the company increases, however, it becomes more likely that the company will default and enter into insolvency. At a certain point these costs of distress will outweigh the tax benefit of debt. Financial distress and insolvency is costly, in terms of the direct costs of lawyers, courts and insolvency practitioners, as well as the reduction in the value of the company associated with insolvency. There are also the indirect costs attached to the difficulties of running a company while going through this process.[334] Even if the company avoids insolvency it will still face the costs of financial distress—for example, the suppliers may demand more protection, creditors may charge more and employees may leave and look for other jobs. When considering the costs of distress it is also important to have regard to the nature of the company's assets. If the assets are 'real', such as property, then there will be reduced distress costs because this will provide at least some of the creditors with the assurance that even if the company is distressed there are assets available which can be used to repay their debts. By contrast, in companies such as high tech companies where the principal assets are ideas and people, it is much more difficult on insolvency to cash in by selling off the assets. In order to understand the debt to equity ratio adopted by companies it is therefore relevant to consider not only the likelihood of insolvency, but also the value of the company that is likely to be realisable if insolvency occurs.[335]

---

[330] See eg H DeAngelo and RM Stultz, 'Liquid-Claim Production, Risk Management, and Bank Capital Structure: Why High Leverage is Optimal for Banks', ECGI Finance Working Paper No 356, October 2014.

[331] SC Myers, 'Capital Structure' (2001) 15 *Journal of Economic Perspectives* 81.

[332] For capital markets to be 'well functioning' for the purposes of this model, investors must be able to trade securities without restrictions and borrow and lend on the same terms as the company.

[333] F Modigliani and MH Miller, 'Corporate Income Taxes and the Cost of Capital: A Correction' (1963) 53 *American Economic Review* 261; H DeAngelo and RW Masulis, 'Optimal Capital Structure under Corporate and Personal Taxation' (1980) 8 *Journal of Financial Economics* 3.

[334] JB Warner, 'Bankruptcy Costs: Some Evidence' (1977) 26 *Journal of Finance* 337–48; LA Weiss, 'Bankruptcy Resolution: Direct Costs and Violation of Priority of Claims' (1990) 27 *Journal of Financial Economics* 285; EI Altman, 'A Further Investigation of the Bankruptcy Cost Question' (1984) 39 *Journal of Finance* 1067; G Andrade and SN Kaplan, 'How Costly is Financial (Not Economic) Distress? Evidence from Highly Leveraged Transactions that Became Distressed' (1998) 53 *Journal of Finance* 1443.

[335] See S Titman and R Wessels, 'The Determinants of Capital Structure Choice' (1988) 43 *Journal of Finance* 1.

The trade-off theory of capital structure recognises that investors will look for an enhanced return to compensate them for the increased risk of having to absorb these costs of financial distress. The addition of debt to a company's capital structure is beneficial, but only up to the point where the tax savings resulting from the debt are outweighed by the insolvency costs. The theoretical optimum is reached when the present value of the tax saving is just offset by increases in the value of the costs of financial distress. As a result the trade-off theory recognises that debt to equity ratios may vary from firm to firm. On this analysis, companies with safe, tangible assets and plenty of taxable income ought to have a lot of debt, whereas unprofitable companies with risky intangible assets ought to rely primarily on equity financing. In practice this theory can explain some industry differences in capital structure, but it does not explain, for example, why some very successful companies thrive with very little debt. In fact some of the most profitable companies borrow the least whereas the trade-off theory predicts the reverse.[336]

An alternative theory suggests that companies prefer to issue debt rather than equity only if internal finance is insufficient.[337] Internal finance is effectively retained profits, ie funds which could be paid out as dividends, but which are instead retained by the company to finance its projects. Retained profits can, therefore, be viewed as additional capital invested by the shareholders. Since internal finance does not send any adverse signals which may lower the share price, this is often the preferred choice of financing for companies. If external finance is required, firms will issue debt, because this is less likely to be interpreted by investors as a bad omen, and external equity financing is regarded as a last resort. As a result there is no optimum debt to equity mix because there are two kinds of equity: internal equity, which is top of the 'pecking order', and external finance, which comes last. This analysis may explain why the most profitable companies borrow less: they have access to the most internal finance and, therefore, do not need to rely heavily on external finance. This analysis is not without its difficulties, however. In particular, some studies suggest that companies do not always exhaust all sources of internal finance before turning to external sources,[338] and others suggest that some smaller, growth companies seem to rely on equity (in the form of venture capital) rather than debt when external financing is required.[339]

Other theories of capital structure have developed as variations on or refinements of these models, in order to try to explain the capital structures that are observable in practice.[340] It seems that capital structure does matter, but that there is no single optimal structure for all companies. It is necessary to consider the size and type of the company, the nature of its underlying assets, and the availability of internal finance. For individual companies these considerations will be important, but more specific details about the nature of the financing

---

[336] JK Wald, 'How Firm Characteristics Affect Capital Structure: An International Comparison' (1999) 22 *Journal of Financial Research* 161.

[337] SC Myers, 'The Capital Structure Puzzle' (1984) 39 *Journal of Finance* 575; L Shyam-Sunder and SC Myers, 'Testing Static Trade-Off Against Pecking-Order Models of Capital Structure' (1999) 51 *Journal of Financial Economics* 219; EF Fama and KR French, 'Testing Trade-Off and Pecking-Order Predictions about Dividends and Debt' (2002) 15 *Review of Financial Studies* 1; M Frank and V Goyal, 'Testing the Pecking Order Theory of Capital Structure' (2002) 67 *Journal of Financial Economics* 217.

[338] C Mayer and O Sussman, 'A New Test of Capital Structure', www.ssrn.com/abstract=509022.

[339] Eg L Shyam-Sunder and SC Myers, 'Testing Static Trade-Off against Pecking-Order Models of Capital Structure' (1999) 51 *Journal of Financial Economics* 219.

[340] Eg M Jensen and W Meckling, 'Theory of the Firm: Managerial Behaviour, Agency Costs and Ownership Structure' (1976) 3 *Journal of Financial Economics* 305; M Baker and J Wurgler, 'Market Timing and Capital Structure' (2002) 57 *Journal of Finance* 1.

on offer will often be determinative of the issue. For instance, issues such as the identity of the lender (trade credit, institutional lenders etc) and the contractual features of the debt, such as maturity, conversion rights, collateral, events of default and guarantees, will be important in determining the attractiveness of debt financing in a given scenario. On the equity side, the nature of the shares being issued (ordinary or preference, and whether or not they are redeemable), the rights attached to those shares, the price at which they are issued and whether pre-emption rights have been set aside will all be of importance. Further, general market conditions may well determine how much debt can be raised, as well as the means of raising it. This was made clear by the financial crisis, when bank financing became difficult to obtain. Larger companies turned to the bond and equity markets,[341] while smaller companies suffered from a lack of debt financing, although some turned to asset-based lending.[342]

2.7 Conclusion

Companies have a huge number of options to choose from when financing their operations. Almost all companies will utilise a mixture of equity and debt finance, as well as making use of retained profits, and this chapter has sought to explore the factors that influence this mix in different situations. The basic advantages of equity to a company are that the capital is less likely to be withdrawn, and dividends can only be paid when the company makes distributable profits; even then, shareholders rarely have the right to demand payment. Interest on debt, conversely, has to be paid whatever the state of the company's profits, and usually the capital has to be repaid at some stage. These two forms of finance are also treated differently for tax purposes. The extent to which these considerations influence companies' choice of financing has been discussed in this chapter.

Further, within the categories of equity and debt there are a number of variations, and this chapter has sought to explore the factors that lead companies to choose between them. Equity options are more limited than debt options, consisting largely of ordinary shares and different types of preference shares. The range of options for sources of equity finance depends largely on the size of the company. The options for debt financing are very wide, although most can be divided into either loans or issues of securities. The provision of trade credit is also significant, and itself requires financing. SMEs tend to rely on bank loans, although nowadays these are often supplemented or replaced by some sort of financing based on assets. Large companies will look to borrow from a number of banks or other lenders, or to issue securities to tap into the wider bond markets. Financial companies, and those with a steady stream of receivables, are likely still to consider securitisation, although the more exotic forms of this type of financing are unlikely to reappear in the near future. Since the financial crisis, however, innovative forms of finance have grown up, including equity crowdfunding and peer-to-peer lending, and the sources of loan finance have widened. This phenomenon is only likely to increase, as banks remain under regulatory pressure to retain capital and preserve liquidity.

---

[341] FSA Financial Risk Outlook 2010, 6; BIS, *Financing a Private Sector Recovery* (Cm 7923, July 2010), 3.40, 3.44.
[342] 2.3.4.3.

3

The Relationship Between Equity and Debt

3.1 Introduction

All companies need capital in order to function. As discussed in chapter two, companies can finance their operations via share issues, debt, retained profits or, more likely, a combination of these options. These financing options were examined from the company's point of view in chapter two. This chapter examines debt and equity financing from the point of view of those putting money into the company: the shareholders and creditors. There are certain fundamental differences between a shareholder's interest in a company and that of a creditor, which are explored in this chapter, although it is accepted that both concepts can be manipulated in order to make the contrast less stark in practice. Hybrid arrangements are discussed at 2.4.

This chapter analyses the respective roles that creditors and shareholders perform, the rights that they hold, and, therefore, the risks that they undertake, in both solvent and insolvent companies. Broadly, shareholders' interests dominate in the solvent company, whereas creditors' interests dominate in insolvency and in the twilight zone before insolvency actually commences. Determining the reasons for this dichotomy between the solvent and insolvent company scenario is important in order to understand the dynamics of company financing decisions, and also to understand the rationale for the law's regulation of these issues. The discussion in this chapter will also form the basis for the more specific discussions regarding equity and debt financing that will be undertaken in the remaining chapters of this book.

The thesis of this chapter is that shareholders are pre-eminent within the solvent company because they are the residual claimants of the company, and they therefore bear the lion's share of the risks and rewards of the company. The creditors' returns are fixed. They do not share proportionately in the upside of corporate decisions, and they only share in the downside if the company becomes insolvent. Their downside risk is different to that of the shareholders. It is particularly notable that the directors' general fiduciary duty to act in the best interests of the company is fundamentally shareholder-regarding while the company is solvent.[1] Whilst the company has significant shareholder funds, the creditors will normally favour projects which do not endanger this situation, even if a riskier project has a higher present value, because the creditors' position will not be materially enhanced by the higher value project. The danger of imposing creditor-focused duties on the directors while

---

[1] Companies Act 2006, s 172(1), discussed at 3.2.1.3.1.

a company is a profitable going concern is that the creditors will be primarily interested in excessively low-risk projects.[2] However, companies are vehicles for taking entrepreneurial risks. In order to maximise the firm's value when the company is solvent, directors' duties in that period need to be aligned with shareholders rather than creditors. Since the losses are borne by the shareholders first, when assessing strategic decisions directors should give paramount consideration to the risk profile of that group. An excessively risky project will impact most heavily on them, but they will share in the upside of any decision too.

In order to make these arguments, in 3.2.1 the position of shareholders in a solvent company is assessed. After an analysis of the rights that are typically held by shareholders, this section examines the main arguments in favour of the pre-eminence of shareholders in a solvent company. In line with the thesis set out above, it is suggested that these arguments are more compelling for certain shareholders than for others. In particular, the argument is stronger for those with a residual claim on the company, typically the ordinary shareholders. In 3.2.2 the position of creditors in a solvent company is examined. The risks faced by creditors in a solvent company are assessed. This section examines the features that are common to all creditors in a solvent company. In general, the creditors' relationship in this period is left to contract law.[3] This chapter suggests that most creditors are able to protect themselves through contract while the company remains solvent. The one group of creditors who may not be able to do so are the non-adjusting creditors, discussed at 3.2.2.1.

By contrast, when the company is insolvent, or nearing insolvency, it is the creditors' interests that dominate. It is notable that at this point the directors' general fiduciary duty to the company becomes creditor-focused rather than shareholder-focused.[4] This is also explicable by understanding where the risks fall at this point. Section 3.3.1 sets out the order of payment out on a winding up or a distribution by an administrator. This analysis makes it very clear that at this point creditors rank ahead of shareholders, but also that there is a distinct order of distribution in which some creditors rank ahead of others, either because they have bargained-for proprietary protection or because they fall into a category of creditors given limited protection by statute. Creditors are also protected by a number of statutory and common law provisions which, in certain circumstances before and after insolvency, prevent the diminution of the asset pool available for creditors and the uneven distribution of assets. These issues are discussed at 3.3.2.

The pre-eminence of creditors, as opposed to shareholders, at this point in time is entirely appropriate. Once the shareholders' funds in the company have been dissipated entirely, or at least reduced to a very low level, it is in the interests of the shareholders to encourage excessively risky projects.[5] This is because the shareholders will be interested entirely in the upside of the decision. The extent to which shareholders take any downside risk of business decisions once their funds in the company have evaporated will depend upon the extent to which the principle of limited liability is upheld within a jurisdiction.[6] As section 3.3.3.2

---

[2] MC Jensen and WH Meckling, 'Theory of the Firm: Managerial Behaviour, Agency Costs and Ownership Structure' (1976) 3 *Journal of Financial Economics* 305.

[3] The legal capital rules, discussed in chapter 5, also have the predominant aim of creditor protection, though the value of these rules as a creditor-protection device is questionable.

[4] *West Mercia Safetywear Ltd v Dodd* [1988] BCLC 250, discussed at 3.3.3.1.

[5] If the company is operating profitably, but its profits are fully distributed each year, the amount of shareholder funds in the company will be low, but the incentives for the directors to take on excessively risky projects will be weak, because the company's profit-making potential could be destroyed.

[6] DD Prentice, 'Creditor's Interests and Director's Duties' (1990) 10 *Oxford Journal of Legal Studies* 265.

examines, in the UK the principle of limited liability is upheld almost in its entirety at common law,[7] and although statutory exceptions do exist, most notably sections 213 and 214 of the Insolvency Act 1986, the levels of enforcement of these actions is extremely low.

If the directors acted in the shareholders' interests at this point,[8] therefore, this would create an incentive structure for directors which would positively favour excessively risky projects. In contrast to the solvent scenario, creditors cannot at this point rely on the 'shareholders first' rule in relation to losses to protect their interests, because shareholder-regarding directors can focus exclusively on the upside of potential projects, however remote the possibility of success might be. When comparing potential projects directors would be able to ignore the chances of a negative outcome. Shareholders at this point have little to lose from the downside of potential projects, but stand to gain enormously from the potential upside. It is therefore appropriate that the law protects the creditors at this point.

3.2 The Relationship Between Equity and Debt in a Solvent Company

In this section the rights and roles of shareholders and creditors in a solvent company are compared and contrasted. It is important to separate the solvent and insolvent scenarios because, as will become apparent, the positions of shareholders and of creditors in these two periods change markedly.

For these purposes a slightly more constrained view of solvency is adopted than is required if the strict legal definition is applied. A company is insolvent for the purposes of the law if it becomes unable to pay its debts.[9] There are two different approaches that can be adopted to determine when a company becomes unable to pay its debts. The first is the balance sheet test. This test measures the excess of liabilities over assets and considers whether the company's assets are insufficient to discharge its liabilities 'taking into account its contingent and prospective liabilities'.[10] The second is the cash flow test, which assesses the ability of the company to meet its debts and liabilities as they become due.[11] Both tests operate in the UK.[12] Nevertheless, it is recognised that there is likely to be a period prior to

---

[7] See eg *Prest v Petrodel Resources Ltd* [2013] UKSC 34 [36], discussed further at 3.3.3.2.

[8] For a discussion of the point in time at which the company shifts from being shareholder-focused to being creditor-focused see 3.3.

[9] Goode: Corporate Insolvency, ch 4.

[10] Insolvency Act 1986, s 123(2).

[11] Ibid, s 123(1)(e). This test involves an element of futurity: *BNY Corporate Trustee Services Limited v Eurosail-UK 2007-3bl plc* [2013] UKSC 28. However, any attempt to apply the cash flow test will become completely speculative once the court has moved beyond the reasonably near future, at which point the balance sheet test becomes the only sensible test: [37] per Lord Walker. For discussion see P Walton, 'Eurosail: From the Point of No Return to Crystal Ball Gazing' (2014) 26(8) *Insolvency Intelligence* 124; MS Wee, 'Misconceptions about the "Unable to Pay its Debts" Ground of Winding Up' (2014) 130 *Law Quarterly Review* 648.

[12] For discussion of the relationship between these two tests see *BNY Corporate Trustee Services Limited v Eurosail-UK 2007-3bl plc* [2013] UKSC 28; *Carman v Bucci* [2014] EWCA Civ 383. In systems that do not demand any significant minimum legal capital levels, such as the UK, the cash flow test may be more appropriate. This is because many companies without significant legal capital are often balance sheet insolvent from the moment they begin to trade, since they will usually have exchanged cash for business-specific assets whose market value may immediately begin to depreciate, or they may have borrowed more than the value of their current assets on the basis of their future cash flow.

formal insolvency when the roles of creditors and shareholders begin to change, and when the analysis entered into in this section will not necessarily be appropriate. A discussion of this twilight period prior to insolvency, and when that twilight period can be said to begin, is undertaken in the following section, 3.3. In this section, then, the concept of solvency is intended to encompass the scenario outside insolvency (as strictly defined), but also outside this twilight period; that is, for the purposes of this section solvency encompasses the scenario in which there remain significant shareholder funds within the company and the company remains a profitable going concern.

3.2.1 Position of Shareholders in a Solvent Company

In order to determine the position of shareholders in a solvent company, it is first necessary to understand the rights that are typically held by shareholders in such a company. The rights attaching to shares in a company are laid down in the company's constitution, in case law and in statute. It is usual for a company's share capital to comprise different classes of shares, the most common being ordinary shares and preference shares,[13] although a company under English law has practically unlimited freedom to create the capital structure that it wishes for itself.

The rights attached to shares can usefully be divided into three types: rights to capital, rights to income and voting rights. The capital, income and voting rights typically attached to ordinary and preference shares are discussed next. These rights will generally be class rights.[14] According to the Companies Act 2006, shares will be regarded as being of one class where the rights attached to them are uniform.[15] Consequently, preference shares carrying different rights to dividend and/or to capital will be treated as constituting a different class of shares from the ordinary shares. Equally, however, there may be different classes of ordinary shares, for example where some ordinary shares carry rights to vote but others do not, and different classes of preference shares, for example where different preference shares carry different entitlements to a particular dividend.

The significance of this differentiation is that there is a statutory procedure that needs to be followed where class rights are varied.[16] A class right found in the articles, for example, can only be changed by at least a 75 per cent majority of the class concerned.[17] Any other right found in the articles can prima facie be altered by a 75 per cent majority of all

---

[13] Another common class of shares is redeemable shares. All classes of shares may be issued as redeemable at the option of the company: Companies Act 2006, ss 684–89.

[14] Creditors of a company can also be divided into different classes. These may include secured and unsecured creditors, and tranches of creditors in a structured transaction where the classes are determined by subordination. The extent of these rights is determined predominantly by the contractual arrangements between the creditors and the company, but there may also be a role for the court in determining the classes of creditors, for example in relation to schemes of arrangement, discussed in chapter 15.

[15] Companies Act 2006, s 629. For a discussion of what constitutes class rights see *Cumbrian Newspapers Group Ltd v Cumberland & Westmorland Herald Newspaper & Printing Co Ltd* [1987] Ch 1; *Harman v BML Group Ltd* [1994] 1 WLR 893.

[16] Now contained in Companies Act 2006, ss 630–35.

[17] Ibid, s 630(4) (for companies having a share capital).

members.[18] This appears to provide significant protection to the holders of class rights. This potential protection is diminished, however, due to the extremely restrictive interpretation of the concept of 'variation' adopted by the courts for this purpose.[19] The courts have drawn a distinction between varying a right (in which case the statutory procedure must be followed) and merely varying the enjoyment of the right (in which case the procedure need not be followed). For example, the courts have determined that issuing new preference shares *pari passu* to existing preference shareholders might vary the enjoyment of the rights of the existing shareholders, but does not vary the right itself, and so the statutory procedure need not be followed.[20]

3.2.1.1 Ordinary Shares

An ordinary share is a default share, in the sense that the rights enjoyed by ordinary shares are those that attach to all shares unless contrary provision is made when the shares are issued, or by subsequent variation of the rights attaching to the shares.[21] If a company's shares are all of one class then these are necessarily ordinary shares, and if a company has share capital it must have at least one ordinary share. However, the power to issue shares with different rights usually appears in the articles of association.[22]

3.2.1.1.1 Rights to Capital

As regards capital rights, the default rule is that the surplus left after the paid-up capital has been repaid is distributable equally amongst the ordinary shareholders in proportion to the nominal value of their shares.[23] This principle can be modified by the company in its articles, but neither the Model Articles for Private Companies limited by shares nor the Model Articles for Public companies amend this default principle.[24] More generally, shareholders may seek to realise the capital growth in the value of their shares by selling them, something which will be easier where there is a secondary market for the shares, such as where the company's shares are publicly traded.

3.2.1.1.2 Rights to Income

The holder of an ordinary share does not have an absolute right to claim dividends.[25] The extent of any right to receive dividends will be set out in the company's articles, but

---

[18] Ibid, s 21, subject to the ability of shareholders to entrench rights in articles and to require a higher than 75% majority to alter those rights (s 22). This general right to alter the articles by special resolution is also subject to the constraint that in order to be valid the alteration must be bona fide in the best interests of the company (*Allen v Gold Reefs of West Africa Ltd* [1900] 1 Ch 656).

[19] Companies Act 2006 provides little, if any, detail as to the definition of 'variation' for this purpose, so it has been left to the courts to determine this issue.

[20] *White v Bristol Aeroplane Co* [1953] 1 Ch 65.

[21] A company that wants to issue shares with different rights must have the power to that effect in its constitution, so as to displace the presumption that all shareholders are to be treated equally: *Campbell v Rofe* [1933] AC 98; *British and American Trustee and Finance Corporation v Couper* [1894] AC 399, 416.

[22] See eg Model Articles for Private Companies Limited by Shares, art 22; Model Articles for Public Companies, art 43: Companies (Model Articles) Regulations 2008 (SI 3229/2008), Sch 1 and Sch 3.

[23] *Birch v Cropper* (1889) 14 App Cas 525.

[24] See Model Articles for Private Companies Limited by Shares; Model Articles for Public Companies: Companies (Model Articles) Regulations 2008 (SI 3229/2008), Sch 1 and Sch 3.

[25] For a discussion of dividend policy generally see 2.5.

shareholders only become entitled to receive a final dividend once that dividend has been declared,[26] at which point a debt is created.[27] By contrast, an interim dividend remains at the discretion of the board, so that a resolution to pay such a dividend does not create an immediate debt.[28] Dividends must be paid in cash unless the articles provide otherwise,[29] although it is very common for articles to authorise the payment of dividends in kind.[30] The articles will also set out the procedural aspects of dividend payments.[31] As amongst themselves the holders of the fully paid-up ordinary shares are entitled to share equally in dividends.[32]

A shareholder is a creditor in respect of any dividend that has been declared but not paid by the due date for payment.[33] If the company is in liquidation, however, any sum due to a member of the company by way of dividend will only be paid after all of the creditors' debts are paid in full.[34] The order of payment out on a winding up or distribution by an administrator ranks creditors' claims ahead of shareholders' claims.[35] Consequently, any debts due to members in their capacity as members, which would clearly include unpaid dividends, will only be paid after the unsecured creditors are paid in full. A distinction can, however, be drawn between these sums and sums due to the member in some other capacity, such as where the member brings a claim against the company relating to inaccuracies in a prospectus.[36]

3.2.1.1.3 Voting Rights

As regards voting rights, the default position is one vote per share, unless the articles make alternative provision.[37] Ordinary shares usually follow the default position, although different configurations can be created. It is possible to create different classes of ordinary shares with different voting rights—for example, non-voting ordinary shares can be issued,

---

[26] *Bond v Barrow Haematite Steel Co* [1902] 1 Ch 353.

[27] The debt is immediate if no date of payment is stipulated (*Re Severn and Wye and Severn Bridge Railway Co* [1896] 1 Ch 559), but the date when the dividend is due can also be specified, in which case the shareholder cannot enforce payment until that date arrives (*Re Kidner* [1929] 2 Ch 121). The six-year limitation period in respect of an unpaid dividend runs from the date when it is declared or any later date for payment: *Re Compania de Electricidad de la Provincia de Buenos Aires* [1980] 1 Ch 146.

[28] *Lagunas Nitrate Co Ltd v Schroeder & Co and Schmidt* (1901) 85 LT 22. If the directors resolve to pay an interim dividend at a future date, a shareholder has no enforceable right to demand payment prior to that date.

[29] *Wood v Odessa Waterworks Co* (1889) 42 Ch D 636.

[30] See eg Model Articles for Private Companies Limited by Shares, art 34; Model Articles for Public Companies, art 76: Companies (Model Articles) Regulations 2008 (SI 3229/2008), Sch 1 and Sch 3.

[31] See eg Model Articles for Private Companies Limited by Shares, art 30; Model Articles for Public Companies, art 70: Companies (Model Articles) Regulations 2008 (SI 3229/2008), Sch 1 and Sch 3. It is common for articles to provide that final dividends are declared by the shareholders in general meeting, but subject to the recommendation of the directors. Since the shareholders cannot increase the level of dividend, and it is rare for them to declare less than the amount recommended by the directors, this is largely a rubber-stamping exercise.

[32] Where the shares are partly paid the position may be more complicated. It will depend on whether the return available is calculated according to the nominal value or the amounts paid up on them.

[33] *Re Compania de Electricidad de la Provincia de Buenos Aires* [1980] 1 Ch 146.

[34] Insolvency Act 1986, s 74(2)(f).

[35] For discussion see 3.3.1.2.5.

[36] *Soden v British & Commonwealth Holdings plc* [1998] AC 298. For discussion see 3.3.1.2.5.

[37] Companies Act 2006, s 284.

although these are rare.[38] The ordinary shareholders, then, are the decision-makers in the company to the extent that matters need to be resolved by the general meeting.

3.2.1.1.4 Summary

One of the important features of ordinary shares is the control rights that they provide, via the right to vote. In some companies, particularly very small companies, the purpose of issuing shares may simply be to give the shareholders control of the company, for it is likely that the shareholders will use their voting rights as shareholders to appoint themselves, or their representatives, directors of the company. In such companies the amount of capital injected via the ordinary shares may be negligible,[39] and the predominant function of issuing ordinary shares will be to allocate control rights within the company. In larger companies, however, even though the control aspect of ordinary shares remains important, the use of ordinary shares as a capital-raising device cannot be ignored.[40]

The distinctive feature of the income and capital rights attaching to ordinary shares is that the returns are not fixed. This is clearly distinct from the position relating to debt,[41] but it also contrasts with preference shares, where, commonly, the rights in respect of dividends and/or capital may be in priority to the ordinary shares, but only for a fixed amount.[42] The definition of equity share capital within the Companies Act 2006 is 'its issued share capital excluding any part of that capital that, neither as respects dividends nor as respects capital, carries any right to participate beyond a specified amount in a distribution'.[43] The ordinary shares are, therefore, the purest form of equity within the company.[44] They are the residual claimants in the company, with no guarantee of any dividend payment, and no guarantee of any return on a winding up. Their entitlement to the surplus of the company means that, although the ordinary shareholders take the lion's share of the rewards, they also take the lion's share of the risk. In the event of winding up or administration, the right of the shareholders to be repaid is subject to the rights of the creditors, who get repaid in full ahead of the shareholders, so that the shareholders' right to repayment at that point will generally be worthless. This level of economic exposure explains the law's traditional willingness to give the shareholders control rights over the management of the company, at least while the company remains a going concern.

---

[38] Non-voting shares are not prohibited by the UK Listing Rules, but they are strongly discouraged by the London Stock Exchange and by the investment community and as a result they are rare: J Franks, C Mayer and S Rossi, 'Spending Less Time with the Family: The Decline of Family Ownership in the UK' in RK Morck (ed), *A History of Corporate Governance Around the World: Family Business Groups to Professional Managers* (Chicago, University of Chicago Press, 2005) 582–83.

[39] See eg BIS, *SME Access to External Finance*, January 2012. There are no minimum capital levels for private companies. For a discussion of minimum capital requirements see 5.3.1.

[40] For a discussion of the advantages of issuing ordinary shares, from the company's point of view, see 2.2.1.1.

[41] Discussed at 3.2.2.

[42] Preference shares are discussed further at 3.2.1.2.

[43] Companies Act 2006, s 548.

[44] It is possible to create participating preference shares with a right to share in the surplus (and a preferential return on dividends and/or capital), which would normally fall within the definition of equity capital, although such shares are rare.

3.2.1.2 Preference Shares

A preference share is a share which in respect of dividend and/or capital enjoys priority, for a limited amount, over the company's ordinary shares. The precise extent of the priority will depend upon the rights attached to the shares, primarily by way of provisions in the company's articles, although the courts do also play a part in determining the extent of the rights, through the application of a series of presumptions.[45]

3.2.1.2.1 Rights to Capital

As regards capital rights, there is a presumption that all shares rank equally with regard to the return of capital.[46] Any priority intended to be attached to preference shares regarding the return of capital must, therefore, be expressly stated. The fact that preference shares have priority as to dividends does not mean that the shares will be presumed to have priority as to a return of capital.[47] The sum repaid may be the par value of the shares, or the articles may provide for a higher sum. It is common to attach a Spens formula to preference shares, which provides that on a repayment of capital the holders of the share capital are expressly entitled to a premium if, during a defined period prior to repayment, the shares have been standing in the market at a figure in excess of their par value.[48]

As regards the right to share in the surplus capital of the company, where a share carries a preferential right to capital on a winding up this displaces the principle of equality, and it is presumed that the express preferential right to capital is the sum total of the entitlement.[49] It is for the preference shareholders to demonstrate that a provision in the company's constitution, or in the terms of issue of the shares, confers an entitlement to participate in any surplus assets.

The other occasion on which capital can be returned to the preference shareholders is on a reduction of capital.[50] The articles may specify expressly whether the preference shareholders are to be repaid in priority on a reduction, or the articles may be silent on this point. Where the articles provide that the shares have priority to capital on a winding up, but are silent regarding the position on a reduction, the courts have held that the rights on a reduction mirror those on a winding up.[51]

---

[45] The issues discussed in this section regarding the relationship between ordinary and preference shares are not unique to UK company law. See eg B Walther, 'The Peril and Promise of Preferred Stock' (2014) 39 *Delaware Journal of Corporate Law* 161 for a discussion of the position under Delaware law.

[46] *Welton v Saffery* [1897] AC 299, 309 per Lord Watson.

[47] *Birch v Cropper* (1889) 14 App Cas 525.

[48] For a discussion of par value see 5.3.2.1. The premium is usually ascertained by reference to the middle-market quotation in excess of par during the relevant period, subject to adjustments to take account of any accrued arrears of dividend which is reflected in the market price of the shares.

[49] *Scottish Insurance Corporation v Wilsons & Clyde Coal Co Ltd* [1949] AC 462, criticising the earlier suggestion (*Birch v Cropper* (1889) 14 App Cas 525, 546 per Lord Macnaghten) that preference shares were entitled to share in the surplus assets unless their terms contained an express and specific renunciation of the right.

[50] For discussion see 5.4.3.

[51] *Re Saltdean Estate Co Ltd* [1968] 1 WLR 1844, approved by the House of Lords in *House of Fraser plc v ACGE Investments Ltd* [1987] AC 387, although in that case the rights of preference shareholders on a reduction were expressly dealt with in the articles.

3.2.1.2.2 Rights to Income

In relation to dividend rights, again any rights to a preferential dividend need to be set out expressly in the articles. The mere fact that the share carries a right to priority in respect of capital does not mean that the courts will imply a priority as to the payment of a dividend.[52] It is usual, however, for preference shares to carry preferential rights in respect of both income and capital. Indeed, almost invariably the preferential rights attached to preference shares are income rights.

It is common for preferential dividends to be expressed as a specified percentage of the nominal value of the share, although other formulations are possible.[53] Preferential dividends are usually expressed to be payable only when declared,[54] but if no dividend is declared in a given year, or if the full entitlement is not paid, it is presumed that the unpaid amount is carried forward into subsequent years, unless the articles provide otherwise.[55] If the company goes into liquidation with the dividends still undeclared, there is a general presumption that the undeclared preferential dividends are not payable. However, the articles can, and often do, provide that on liquidation, or a reduction of capital, a sum equal to the unpaid dividends, whether declared or not, will be paid to the preference shareholders in priority to any payment to the ordinary shareholders.[56]

The preference shareholders are at the mercy of the directors, to the extent that the shareholders cannot declare a dividend in excess of the amount recommended by the directors.[57] If the directors do not recommend the full dividend in circumstances where the company has the necessary distributable profits, the preference shareholders' options for redress are rather limited. They may be able to petition for relief under section 994 of the Companies Act 2006, on the basis that the company's affairs are being managed in a way which is unfairly prejudicial to them, or they might be able to petition for a just and equitable winding up under section 122(1)(g) of the Insolvency Act 1986,[58] but neither option is guaranteed to produce the required result.[59]

3.2.1.2.3 Voting Rights

The default position on voting rights attaching to shares in a company is one vote per share, unless the articles make alternative provision.[60] Preference shares normally carry only limited voting rights. Typically, the right to vote will only arise where the preferential dividend

---

[52] *Birch v Cropper* (1889) 14 App Cas 525.

[53] For example, the preferential dividend can be expressed as a percentage of the amount paid up on the share.

[54] *Bond v Barrow Haematite Steel Co* [1902] 1 Ch 353.

[55] *Webb v Earle* (1875) LR 20 Eq 556.

[56] *Re Wharfedale Brewery Co Ltd* [1952] Ch 913.

[57] Model Articles for Private Companies Limited by Shares, art 30(2); Model Articles for Public Companies, art 70(2): Companies (Model Articles) Regulations 2008 (SI 3229/2008), Sch 1 and Sch 3.

[58] *Re A Company, ex p Glossop* [1988] 1 WLR 1068. It has also been suggested that the shareholders could bring an action against the directors for breach of the statutory contract under s 33 Companies Act 2006: *Re A Company* [1987] BCLC 82.

[59] See, for example, in relation to a petition under s 994 Companies Act 2006 for a failure to declare dividends, *Irvine v Irvine* [2006] EWHC 406 (Ch). In this case it was held that in the absence of some special arrangement minority shareholders have no legitimate expectation that dividends will be paid just because they are shareholders, even shareholders in a quasi-partnership company. See also *Re Sam Weller & Sons Ltd* [1990] BCLC 80.

[60] Companies Act 2006, s 284.

has been in arrears for longer than a specified period. This may include the position where the company has insufficient distributable profits to pay the dividend, if the articles provide a payment date and the date has passed.[61]

3.2.1.2.4 Summary

There is no standard package of rights that attaches to all preference shares. It is possible for a company to create preference shares having a right to vote and to receive a priority as to fixed income payments, but no priority as to the return of capital. This would be unusual. More likely are convertible preference shares that start life as preference shares of the more usual variety, ie fixed rights to income and capital in priority to the ordinary shares, limited voting rights and no entitlement to surplus, and which are subsequently convertible into another form of security in the company, such as ordinary shares, giving the holder the opportunity to participate in capital growth in the future.

However, more common is the issue of preference shares as a form of fixed interest security akin to debt:

> In relation to the commercial requirements of the modern company the preference share cannot now be said to have any unique and essential function. It is probable that the great majority of companies find, in principle, little to choose between preference or debenture securities as instruments of corporate finance.[62]

This statement, although more than 50 years old, remains accurate today.[63] While preference shares often have debt-like features, when compared to the ordinary shares, it is notable that the position of a preference shareholder will be inferior to that of the company's creditors in certain crucial respects. Unlike interest payments, the preferential dividend entitlement is not a debt until declared, and cannot be guaranteed. Even if the articles specify that the dividend does not need to be declared, and the articles specify the due date of the dividend, the payment will still be conditional upon distributable profits being available.[64] Preference shareholders have less security of capital than the company's creditors, who may have a charge on the assets of the company, and, on a winding up or administration, any sums due to preference shareholders (by way of unpaid dividends or capital repayment) will continue to rank behind the creditors in order of payment out.[65] As regards voting rights, which might be considered to counterbalance, to some extent, the greater capital and dividend rights of the creditors, such rights are generally only provided to preference shareholders when the preferential dividend payments are in arrears. The membership advantages conferred on most preference shareholders are extremely limited.

---

[61] *Re Bradford Investments plc* [1990] BCC 740.

[62] M Pickering, 'The Problem of the Preference Share' (1963) 26 *Modern Law Review* 499, 517.

[63] For a fuller discussion of the circumstances in which a company might make use of preference shares as a form of equity finance see 2.2.1.2. Because preference shares contain many of the same features of debt, they are often regarded as hybrid securities, as discussed at 2.4.

[64] If no such profits are available then at best the right to payment will be suspended until there are sufficient distributable profits. This is the position in Australia (*Marra Developments Ltd v BW Rofe Pty Ltd* (1977) 2 NSWLR 616 (Sup Ct NSW)) and probably represents the English position, though there is no authority on this point.

[65] Insolvency Act 1986, s 74(2)(f). For further discussion see 3.3.1.2.5.

3.2.1.3 Role of Shareholders in a Solvent Company

3.2.1.3.1 Section 172 of the Companies Act 2006

When the company is solvent, it is the shareholders, rather than the creditors, who dominate UK company law. In a solvent company directors have traditionally owed their duties to the shareholders as a whole.[66] Section 172 of the Companies Act 2006 now provides that a director must 'act in a way he considers, in good faith, would be most likely to promote the success of the company for the benefit of its members as a whole', ie a subjectively assessed obligation to operate the company in the interests of the shareholders as a whole, in line with the pre-existing common law obligation.[67] However, section 172 then requires that, in doing so, the director must have regard to a number of other stakeholder interests, such as the company's employees, suppliers, customers etc.[68]

The introduction of this provision into the Companies Act 2006 caused some concern. It was felt that section 172 might amend the existing common law obligation and give rise to significant additional duties for directors. In particular, the concern was that, when coupled with the new statutory derivative action,[69] directors might face an increase in the number of actions from minority shareholders unhappy with decisions taken by them.[70] These fears appear to have been misplaced. Litigation of this section remains relatively uncommon, and, indeed, the role of giving practical substance to section 172 may in fact lie with the extended reporting requirements to shareholders by directors, discussed in chapter 11.[71] Further, the courts have not found there to be any significant distinction between the common law duty and the statutory codification.[72]

Section 172 requires directors to have regard to the long-term interests of the shareholders, and in doing so the directors may take account of other stakeholder groups in order to determine what best ensures the long-term growth of the company. So, in a solvent company it is the long-term interests of the shareholders that remain the dominant concern, and the interests of other stakeholders are relevant only to the extent that they help to inform the directors' views of the long-term interests of the shareholders and the company. Notably, the interests of the creditors do not feature in this analysis at all.[73] The extent of the law's protection of creditors in a solvent company is the capital maintenance regime,

---

[66] Eg *Re Smith and Fawcett Ltd* [1942] Ch 304, 306 per Lord Greene MR. As a rule directors do not owe duties to individual shareholders, although they may do so in specific factual circumstances: *Peskin v Anderson* [2001] 1 BCC 874.

[67] See eg *LNOC Ltd v Watford Associated* [2013] EWHC 3615 (Comm).

[68] For a discussion of the implications of adopting such an approach see V Harper, 'Enlightened Shareholder Value: Corporate Governance Beyond the Shareholder-Stakeholder Divide' (2010) 36 *Journal of Corporation Law* 59; JR Macey, 'Corporate Social Responsibility: A Law and Economics Perspective' (2014) 17(2) *Chapman Law Review* 331.

[69] Companies Act 2006, ss 260–64 (England, Wales and Northern Ireland), ss 265–69 (Scotland).

[70] For discussion see D Ahern, 'Directors' Duties, Dry Ink and the Accessibility Agenda' (2012) 128 *Law Quarterly Review* 114.

[71] See Companies Act 2006 (Strategic Report and Directors' Report) Regulations 2013 (SI 2013/1970), which introduce a requirement for a strategic report to 'inform members of the company and to help them assess how directors performed their duty under section 172' (Companies Act 2006, s 414C(1)) (this requirement does not apply to small companies). For discussion see 11.3.1.1.2.

[72] See eg *Madoff Securities International Ltd (In Liquidation) v Raven* [2013] EWHC 3147 (Comm).

[73] Creditors are dealt with in Companies Act 2006, s 172(3), which confirms their existing statutory and common law rights once the company is insolvent, or close to insolvency. For a discussion of s 172(3) see A Keay, 'Directors' Duties and Creditors' Interests' (2014) 130 *Law Quarterly Review* 130.

discussed in chapter five. Otherwise, creditors must protect themselves via contract or other mechanisms.

The directors' role under section 172 is to assess what 'would be most likely to promote the success of the company for the benefit of its members as a whole'. A differentiation can be made between different kinds of members in this regard. The group most interested in the long-term success of the company will be those taking the lion's share of the risks and rewards, namely the residual claimants. The preference shareholders may be given the right to participate in the residual profits and losses of the company, but more likely they will be fixed claimants in a position akin to, but worse than, that of the creditors. To the extent that they are fixed claimants, their interests may be only marginally more relevant than the interests of the creditors when assessing what is in the long-term interest of the company. Other types of hybrid instruments could also be considered in this context, particularly convertible instruments which allow the holder to convert their securities from debt to equity in specified circumstances.[74]

3.2.1.3.2 Explaining the Pre-Eminence of Shareholders

This chapter began with an assertion that in a solvent company it is the shareholders that are pre-eminent. This section discusses the basis of that pre-eminence. One common explanation for this pre-eminence is based on the notion that shareholders are the owners of the company in some fundamental way. It is difficult to regard the shareholders as owners of the company in any meaningful sense, however, and although they can be regarded as holding some important rights in relation to the company, for example as regards income and capital, these do not seem to justify treating the shareholders, rather than the creditors, as being pre-eminent in this period. Rather, the pre-eminence of the shareholders flows from their role as residual claimants.

3.2.1.3.2(a) Shareholders as the Owners of the Company

The conventional explanation for the pre-eminence of shareholders in a solvent company is based on the shareholders' property rights as 'owners' of the company. One way in which shareholders could, potentially, be regarded as the owners of the company is via their ability to control the company. Some incidents of being a shareholder appear to provide support for this view. For example, it is the exclusive power of the shareholders to form a company. A company must have subscribers holding at least one share each,[75] whereas there is no equivalent requirement for the company to have creditors. Likewise, only shareholders can disband a company.[76] Unpaid creditors can only force a company into liquidation with the assistance of the court.[77] However, these differences do not seem to justify the pre-eminence of shareholders in any meaningful sense.

A potentially more compelling explanation for the pre-eminence of the shareholders rests on the idea that the shareholders can be said to be the owners of the company in some fundamental sense. This view was certainly prevalent at an earlier point in the history of the

---

[74] For discussion see 2.4.
[75] Companies Act 2006, s 8(1)(b).
[76] Insolvency Act 1986, ss 84(1)(b) and (c).
[77] Ibid, s 122. Note however that certain creditors (notably the floating charge holder) can appoint an administrator out of court. See chapter 7.

company. In the early nineteenth century there were two principal vehicles for the conduct of large-scale business ventures: the corporation and the joint stock company. The corporation owed its existence to either a Royal Charter or an Act of Parliament and had separate legal existence. The more important business vehicle, however, was the joint stock company, which was nothing more than a large partnership.[78] The joint stock company did not have a separate legal identity from its members. In regulating this vehicle the courts, unsurprisingly, employed the principles of partnership law.[79] The members, as partners, owned the assets, were jointly and severally liable for the debts incurred by the business, and had all the rights and powers that ownership implies.

In the intervening period, however, much has occurred to alter this view of the nature of shareholders' rights in a company. In particular, the concept of the company as a separate legal entity has developed.[80] The decision of the House of Lords in *Salomon v A Salomon & Co Ltd*[81] recognised that the separate legal personality of the company meant that a new person was created, to which the debts and liabilities of the company attached, and which was, crucially, in a position to hold the property of the company. By the beginning of the twentieth century, the idea had become established that shareholders have no direct interest in the company assets. The most famous formulation of this concept is that of Farwell J in *Borland's Trustees v Steel Brothers & Co Ltd*:

> A share is the interest of a shareholder in the company measured by a sum of money, for the purpose of liability in the first place, and of interest in the second, but also consisting of a series of mutual covenants entered into by all the shareholders inter se…[82]

So, it is clear that shareholders hold no direct interest in the assets of the company. This quotation suggests, however, that while shareholders do not own the assets of the company, they can nevertheless be said to own a share in the company itself. However, this view has subsequently been rejected by the courts, and the accepted view of the courts today is that shares are merely a piece of property conferring rights in relation to the income and capital of the company, and not a proportionate share in the company itself.[83] The importance of this view is illustrated by the facts of *Short v Treasury Commissioners*.[84] The entire share capital of the company was being compulsorily acquired by the Crown. In assessing the compensation payable it was suggested that, as all the shares were being acquired, the shareholders were entitled to the entire value of the company, which was greater than the aggregate value of the shares. The Court of Appeal rejected this suggestion. The shareholders were not entitled to compensation for the value of the company; they were only entitled to be compensated for the value of what was being expropriated, namely their

---

[78] L Sealy, 'Perception and Policy in Company Law Reform' in D Feldman and F Meisel (eds), *Corporate and Commercial Law: Modern Developments* (London, Lloyd's of London Press, 1996) 11–13.

[79] Eg P Ireland, 'The Triumph of the Company Legal Form 1856–1914' in J Adams (ed), *Essays for Clive Schmitthoff* (Abingdon, Professional Books, 1983) 31.

[80] Companies Act 1844 was the first to grant separate legal existence to any venture which complied with the statutory machinery set out in that Act, although for much of the remainder of the 19th century the company remained, in the eyes of the law, a peculiar kind of partnership, with the shareholders its collective owners. Concepts of partnership law were used to resolve company law problems even into the 20th century: *Re Yenidje Tobacco Co Ltd* [1916] 2 Ch 426.

[81] [1897] AC 22.

[82] [1901] 1 Ch 279, 288.

[83] See eg *Bradbury v English Sewing Cotton Co Ltd* [1923] AC 744, 767 per Lord Wrenbury.

[84] [1948] 1 KB 116.

shares: 'Shareholders are not, in the eyes of the law, part owners of the undertaking. The undertaking is something different from the totality of the shareholdings.'[85]

It seems clear, then, that shareholders do not own the assets of the company, nor do they hold a proportionate share of the company. What they own are the shares themselves.[86] This raises the next question, namely what ownership of a share constitutes in practice.

3.2.1.3.2(b)　*Shareholders as the Owners of a Capitalised Income Stream*

Once allotted, the shares in a company become the assets of the shareholders.[87] In many ways the proprietary nature of the ownership of shares is like the proprietary nature of debt securities,[88] in that shares can be transferred by the legal owner, they can be held on trust, and they survive the insolvency of a trustee or authorised transferee.[89]

Shares are a bundle of intangible property rights which shareholders receive from the company in return for their contribution of cash or non-cash assets to the company. The issue is to define the nature of this bundle of rights. One of the starting points for defining the rights attached to the shares is the company's constitution, primarily its articles. By virtue of section 33 of the Companies Act 2006, the articles form a contractual relationship between a company and its members,[90] and also between the members inter se. This is a peculiar form of contract.[91] Its binding force is derived from the terms of the statute, not from any bargain struck by the parties;[92] it is binding only so far as it affects the qua member interests of the members;[93] it can be altered by special resolution without the consent of all of the contracting parties;[94] it is not defeasible on the grounds of misrepresentation,

---

[85] Ibid, 122 per Evershed LJ. In some circumstances shareholders will be able to obtain more than just the market value of their individual shares at any given time, for instance where the number of shares held gives a shareholder effective control over the company's affairs. In that case, however, the shareholder is regarded as selling not merely the parcel of shares, but also that element of control, which has value. This does not interfere with the premise set out in *Short v Treasury Commissioners*. The holder of a block of shares in a company is in no real sense the owner of a proportionate part of the undertaking.

[86] Indeed there is Australian authority that a company has no proprietary rights in its own shares: *Pilmer v Duke Group Ltd (in liquidation)* (2001) 75 ALJR 1067, (2001) 38 ACSR 121, [2001] 2 BCLC 773 (High Court of Australia), discussed in DD Prentice and R Nolan, 'The Issue of Shares: Compensating the Company for Loss' (2002) 118 *Law Quarterly Review* 180. For further discussion see 5.3.2.3.

[87] Shares are treated as personal property despite the ownership of land by the company: Companies Act 2006, s 541.

[88] See 8.2.1.2.

[89] See generally the discussion in 8.2.1.

[90] The members are the original subscribers to the memorandum and those persons who subsequently agree to become members and whose names are entered on the register of members: Companies Act 2006, s 112.

[91] *Bratton Seymour Service Company Ltd v Oxborough* [1992] BCC 471, 475 per Steyn LJ.

[92] The shareholder may seek to enforce it by seeking a declaration or injunction against the company for breach of the statutory contract. It may be possible for a shareholder to obtain damages from the company (Companies Act 2006, s 655 which reverses *Houldsworth v Glasgow City Bank* (1879–80) LR 5 App Cas 317), although there is no clear authority that a damages claim would be allowed by the courts, given the special nature of the statutory contract. Breach of the provisions of the company's constitution may also give rise to an unfair prejudice claim under Companies Act 2006, s 994.

[93] *Hickman v Kent or Romney Marsh Sheepbreeders Association* [1915] 1 Ch 881; thus if an article purports to give someone the right to hold a position such as company solicitor or director those articles are not enforceable under the statutory contract. Cf *Quin & Axtens Ltd v Salmon* [1909] AC 442, which suggests that members should be able to enforce all the articles of the company, but the courts have tended to adopt the more restrictive approach.

[94] For example, the articles can be amended by special resolution (Companies Act 2006, s 21) subject only to the requirement that the power be exercised bona fide in the best interests of the company (*Allen v Gold Reefs of West Africa Ltd* [1900] 1 Ch 656).

common law mistake in equity, undue influence or duress; and it cannot be rectified on the grounds of mistake.

In addition to rights that may be specifically set out in the articles, or other constitutional documents, the interests of shareholders are also governed by statute and case law. For example, as we have seen, even if the articles state that the shareholders are entitled to a 7 per cent dividend per annum, this right will be subject to the provisions of the Companies Act 2006, which provide that dividends may only be paid out of a company's 'accumulated, realised profits … less its accumulated, realised losses'.[95] If that pot of money is not available in any given year, then no dividend can be declared. Likewise, the courts have created a number of presumptions that govern the rights attaching to shares, which will apply unless specifically disapplied by the articles. An example is the presumption that all shareholders are entitled to share equally in any surplus assets of the company that remain after all the debts and liabilities have been discharged and the nominal amount of the share capital has been repaid to shareholders.[96] These presumptions can be particularly important when new classes of shares are created.

It is clear, then, that the nature of the rights attached to shares can be found by examining the company's constitutional documents, and the general law governing companies. However, the question of the content of those rights is still unanswered. Returning to the statement of Farwell J quoted above, it is clear that the primary interest of a shareholder in a company is as an investor: a share is 'is an interest measured by a sum of money'. The shareholder pays a sum of money in the hope of earning a return. The primary interest of a shareholder in a company is, therefore, financial: a shareholder expects to earn a return on the investment in the form of dividends and capital growth. There may, of course, be other rights attached to the share as well, such as the right to vote, or the right to appoint a director. The question arises, however, as to whether these latter interests are core to a shareholder's rights in the company—that is, part of the default rights which form an intrinsic part of holding a share in a company—or whether shares can be regarded as merely a contractual entitlement to a portion of the income stream of the company.[97]

The idea that ownership of a share only gives the holder an entitlement to the capitalised income stream flowing from that share was rejected by the High Court of Australia in *Gambotto v WCP Ltd*.[98] The question for the High Court of Australia in that case was whether it was lawful for the majority shareholders to alter the articles of the company in order to acquire compulsorily the shares of the minority shareholders. The High Court held the expropriation to be unlawful on the basis that it was oppressive to the minority shareholder even though the price offered was fair taking account not only of the current market value of the shares but also of the dividends and future prospects of the company. It was also accepted that there were considerable tax and administrative advantages for the company if the expropriation was allowed to proceed. It is notable that the complainant in this case held just 0.2 per cent of the shares of the company. However, according to the court, to allow the expropriation would be to tilt the balance 'too far in favour of commercial expediency'.

---

[95] Companies Act 2006, s 830(2).

[96] *Birch v Cropper* (1889) 14 App Cas 525.

[97] HG Manne, 'Our Two Corporation Systems: Law and Economics' (1967) 53 *Virginia Law Review* 259; RM Buxbaum, 'Corporate Legitimacy, Economic Theory, and Legal Doctrine' (1984) 45 *Ohio State Law Journal* 515.

[98] (1995) 182 CLR 432, 447 (HC Aust).

The High Court stated that '[a] share is liable to modification or destruction in appropriate circumstances, but is more than a "capitalised dividend stream": it is a form of investment that confers proprietary rights on the investor'.[99]

This does not seem to be the correct approach. Although there may be additional rights and interests which shareholders regard as being an incident of their relationship with a company, especially in a small company, such as the right to be involved in the management of the company or the right to have a voice in setting company policy, these are rights and interests that are not protected by reason of holding a share in the company. They are not a part of the default package involved in being a shareholder in a company. Those rights need to be protected in other ways, for example via a separate contract, either a shareholders' agreement or a service contract, depending on the nature of the rights to be protected. They can also be protected via bargained-for amendments to the articles of association, and rights placed in the articles of association can be entrenched.[100] Even if the agreement is informal, the minority shareholder may be able to rely upon it to demonstrate that they have been unfairly prejudiced if the rights are subsequently removed.[101] Of course, minority protection of this kind will, in general, reduce the flexibility and freedom of the majority to run the company as they see fit, in accordance with the usual majority rule principle, and so is likely to have cost consequences. If minority shareholders want to bargain for these additional protections they are likely to have to pay for them. The more appropriate way to regard the default rights of a shareholder is as a capitalised income stream.

English law has not adopted the approach favoured by the High Court of Australia in *Gambotto*. In relation to alterations of articles cases the English courts apply the *Allen v Gold Reefs of West Africa Ltd*[102] test: that is, whether the alteration is bona fide in the best interests of the company.[103] They have adopted a subjective test of bona fides,[104] with the burden of proof on the person challenging the alteration.[105] It has been stated by Lord Hoffmann that the approach in *Gambotto* 'has no support in English authority'.[106] In practical terms, as long as 'there are grounds on which reasonable men could come to the same decision' as the majority shareholders, the minority will not succeed in overturning alterations of articles endorsed by the majority.[107] The more obvious, and possibly more appropriate, route for disgruntled minorities will often be via an unfair prejudice petition.[108]

---

[99] Ibid, 447.

[100] Companies Act 2006, s 22.

[101] Ibid, s 994. See *O'Neill v Phillips* [1999] 1 WLR 1092.

[102] [1900] 1 Ch 656.

[103] See eg *Re Charterhouse Capital Ltd* [2014] EWHC 1410 (Ch).

[104] *Citco Banking Corp NV v Pusser's Ltd* [2007] UKPC 13, approving Scrutton LJ in *Shuttleworth v Cox Brothers and Co (Maidenhead) Ltd* [1927] 2 KB 9, 23.

[105] Ibid, [18] endorsing *Peters' American Delicacy Company Ltd v Heath* (1939) 61 CLR 457, 482 per Latham CJ (HC Aust).

[106] Ibid, [20].

[107] *Shuttleworth v Cox Brothers and Co (Maidenhead) Ltd* [1927] 2 KB 9, 23 per Scrutton LJ. Interestingly, that majority decision can include the votes of the shareholders who are advantaged by the alteration (see *Citco Banking Corp NV v Pusser's Ltd* [2007] UKPC 13 [27]; cf the suggestion made in *Rights & Issues Investment Trust v Stylo Shoes Ltd* [1965] Ch 250 that these shares might have to be discounted). In this area of company law the general principle that a shareholder's vote is a piece of property that can be used as he or she sees fit remains good law (*Pender v Lushington* (1877) LR 6 Ch D 70) despite amendments to this principle introduced in relation to other aspects of company law (see Companies Act 2006, s 239 regarding voting to ratify a director's breach of duty).

[108] Companies Act 2006, s 994.

In *O'Neill v Phillips*,[109] however, Lord Hoffmann stated that, if the majority make an offer to buy out the minority at a fair price,[110] then any exclusion of the minority shareholder would not be unfair, and the respondent would be entitled to have the petition struck out as showing no reasonable cause of action.[111] Given that the most common remedy awarded by the courts is an order that the petitioner's shares be bought out at a fair price, this is a sensible approach, designed to reduce the costs of such petitions, which are notoriously large. This approach is also in accordance with the view that a share in a company per se comprises a sum of money, and nothing more. Provided that adequate compensation is offered for the removal of those shares, no wrong is done to the shareholder. A similar approach is followed in takeover situations. It is well accepted that once the offeror reaches the 90 per cent threshold then the remaining minority shareholder(s) can be required to sell their shares to the offeror on the same terms and, therefore, at the same price as the offer made for all the shares of the company, which will inevitably be at a premium to the market price (squeeze-out rights).[112]

3.2.1.3.2(c) Difficulties with Justifying Shareholders' Pre-Eminence Based on Ownership

The starting point for this discussion was the view that the pre-eminent position of shareholders in a solvent company can be justified by their ownership of the company. As discussed, however, shareholders do not own the assets of the company, or a part share of the company itself. They own their shares, which entitles them to a bundle of intangible property rights in return for their cash, or non-cash, contribution to the company. Further, these intangible rights primarily consist of rights to a capitalised income stream from the company. Any further rights, such as the right to be involved in management, need to be protected in other ways. This is not to suggest that shareholders do not have proprietary rights of some kind; clearly they do, albeit that those rights can be expropriated in certain circumstances. However, at least as a default position, what they appear to 'own' is a right to a sum of money (the capitalised income stream from their shares) in return for the payment of consideration for their shares. On this basis, they do not look dissimilar to creditors of the company. In one sense, then, they are merely the providers of one form of the company's capital,[113] although the fact that their entitlement is not fixed remains a key difference.

One theoretical model which has been developed in recent years denies the 'ownership' model of company law. This is the nexus of contracts theory of company law,[114] which treats the company as predominantly a web of contracts that link the various participants. On this analysis the function of company law is the facilitation of parties' bargains, and corporate personality is no more than convenient shorthand for the complex arrangements

---

[109] [1999] 1 WLR 1092.

[110] Lord Hoffmann provides guidance in *O'Neill* as to what this fair price includes in the context of an unfair prejudice petition (ibid, 1107). It will generally not be discounted for a minority holding, and where litigation has been commenced the reasonable offer should include an offer of costs as well.

[111] [1999] 1 WLR 1092, 1107.

[112] Companies Act 2006, ss 979–82. Squeeze-out rights are discussed in detail in 14.3.1.3

[113] EF Fama, 'Agency Problems and the Theory of the Firm' (1980) 88 *Journal of Political Economy* 288.

[114] See FH Easterbrook and DR Fischel, *The Economic Structure of Corporate Law* (Cambridge, MA, Harvard University Press, 1991) and 'The Corporate Contract' (1989) 89 *Columbia Law Review* 1416; MC Jensen and WH Meckling, 'Theory of the Firm: Managerial Behaviour, Agency Costs and Ownership Structure' (1976) 3 *Journal of Financial Economics* 305; B Cheffins, *Company Law: Theory Structure and Operation* (Oxford, Clarendon Press, 1997).

worked out between the various participants in the company. This theory reduces the company to the rights and duties of individuals, rights which require no further justification than that which already inheres in the notion of private rights.

This theory is problematic in a number of ways. In particular, it struggles to explain convincingly both the considerable amount of mandatory legislation that attaches to companies[115] and the basic fact of separate legal personality.[116] This theory also relies on an idea of contract in which the parties have personal autonomy and can fix their bargain as they please, which does not seem an accurate description of many typical relationships within a company. For example, as discussed, while technically a contract, the articles of association are heavily overlaid by statute, and cannot be regarded as a contract in any normal sense. In particular, the constitution of the vast majority of companies does not result from any real bargaining between the participants.[117] The shortcomings of the nexus of contracts theory, however, does not mean that contract is not important as a doctrinal explanation of the rights of shareholders in a company. Clearly, contract has played, and continues to play, an important role in UK company law, for example by providing the company's constitution with contractual status.[118]

The argument advanced here does not depend on the adoption of the nexus of contracts approach. What this discussion has sought to demonstrate, however, is that the shareholders cannot be said to own the company in any meaningful sense and that, further, ownership cannot provide a satisfactory explanation for their pre-eminent position in a solvent company.

3.2.1.3.2(d) Shareholders as Residual Claimants

The shareholders' pre-eminent position in the solvent company needs to be explained on another basis, namely that they are the residual claimants to the firm's income. The definition of equity share capital within the Companies Act 2006 is founded on the notion of residual claimants.[119] It is the holders of the equity capital, generally the ordinary shareholders rather than the creditors, who will benefit from the capital gains that flow from the company's success, but they will also lose first should the enterprise fail. The risk that the shareholders take is not merely the possibility that they will lose their initial stake, ie the price paid for their securities. In a successful company with undistributed reserves, the market value of the shares is likely to be higher than the price paid for the shares, and it is the risk of this loss that the shareholders face if things go wrong. These factors give the shareholders, in particular the ordinary shareholders, the incentive to monitor

---

[115] MA Eisenberg, 'The Structure of Corporation Law' (1989) 89 *Columbia Law Review* 1461, 1486. Proponents of the contractual approach tend to accept that some mandatory legislation may be justifiable but suggest that it should be kept to a minimum and where possible parties should be able to make their own bargain in accordance with prevailing market forces. See eg Easterbrook and Fischel, ibid, 21–22, and Cheffins, ibid, chs 3–4 where he considers the arguments for and against state intervention.

[116] For example, Cheffins concedes that the contractual characterisation is 'at odds with the legal conceptualisation of a company': see Cheffins, ibid, 32. This theory also fails to explain the processes by which company law is developed. It is clear that the courts and Parliament are motivated by considerations other than what, ex ante, the parties would have agreed to, when developing the law.

[117] MA Eisenberg, 'The Structure of Corporation Law' (1989) 89 *Columbia Law Review* 1461; V Brudney, 'Corporate Governance, Agency Costs and the Rhetoric of Contract' (1985) 85 *Columbia Law Review* 1403. Private equity companies are an exception: see chapter 16.

[118] Companies Act 2006, s 17.

[119] Ibid, s 548.

management, and it is for this reason that company law gives the shareholders a significant corporate governance role.

3.2.1.3.3 The Corporate Governance Role of Shareholders

The actual division of powers between the board and the shareholders is a matter for the articles,[120] but by far the most common scenario is the one in which substantial authority to manage the company is given to the board.[121] Nevertheless, shareholders have a number of important governance entitlements by which they can monitor the performance of the board. In very small companies where the shareholders and directors are effectively the same people, these governance rights are largely meaningless, and any monitoring of the directors will need to be achieved by other means, such as monitoring by the company's creditors, discussed at 3.2.2.4. Once there is a difference in identity between the directors and shareholders, then monitoring of the board by the shareholders becomes possible. If there is a single large shareholder that is not on the board then it is possible to introduce provisions into the articles giving substantial management powers (and perhaps veto rights) to that shareholder.[122] In private equity companies, discussed in chapter sixteen, the private equity fund is likely to have representation on the board of the company, but is also likely to strengthen its oversight of management via provisions in the articles.

One of the most significant governance rights held by the shareholders is the right to remove the directors at any time by an ordinary resolution.[123] This provision applies notwithstanding anything to the contrary in any agreement between the company and the director,[124] and potentially gives the shareholders significant influence in the affairs of the company. However, the provision itself acknowledges that directors can protect themselves by requiring compensation to be paid to them in the event of the termination of the service contract.[125] While this will not per se prevent removal, if the compensation is substantial enough it may help to entrench the director in practice. Further, in relation to private companies, the courts have authorised provisions which provide an indirect way around this section. For example, it is valid to include a provision in the articles attaching increased votes to a director's shares on a resolution to remove him, thus enabling him to defeat the resolution, thereby frustrating the object of this section.[126] It has also been recognised by the courts that the removal of a director in a 'quasi-partnership' company, ie a small private company that is a joint venture company, or possibly a company operating in effect an incorporated partnership, might constitute unfair prejudice, justifying a buy-out

---

[120] *Automatic Self-Cleansing Filter Syndicate Co Ltd v Cuninghame* [1906] 2 Ch 34. This is subject to a limited range of matters where statute requires the participation of shareholders in the decisions; for example alterations to the company's articles can only be made by a special resolution of the shareholders: Companies Act 2006, s 21.

[121] For both public and private companies the default provisions, stated in the model sets of articles, give substantial authority to the board: See Model Articles for Private Companies Limited by Shares, art 3; Model Articles for Public Companies, art 3: Companies (Model Articles) Regulations 2008 (SI 3229/2008), Sch 1 and Sch 3. Despite these provisions, the general meeting retains default powers in the event that the board cannot exercise its powers for some reason, such as where there is a deadlock on the board (*Barron v Potter* [1914] 1 Ch 895) or where an effective quorum cannot be obtained (*Foster v Foster* [1916] 1 Ch 532).

[122] See B Cheffins, 'The Undermining of UK Corporate Governance' (2013) 33(3) *Oxford Journal of Legal Studies* 503, who assesses the adequacy of minority shareholder protection provisions in the UK when applied to firms with a dominant shareholder.

[123] Companies Act 2006, s 168.

[124] Ibid, s 168(1).

[125] Ibid, s 168(5).

[126] *Bushell v Faith* [1970] AC 1099.

of shares,[127] or possibly even a compulsory winding up of the company.[128] Finally, once shareholdings become very dispersed it may be difficult for the shareholders to coordinate sufficiently to make this mechanism very valuable. In publicly traded companies there is also a problem of shareholder apathy, which might mean that shareholders do not exercise this governance right in any meaningful way. The corporate governance role of shareholders in publicly traded companies is discussed in detail at 11.2.2.

In addition to the right to remove directors, shareholders have other important governance rights. In a solvent company, as discussed above, directors owe their duties to the company, and the company for this purpose is regarded as comprising the long-term interests of the shareholders.[129] The shareholders have the right to ratify directors' wrongdoing,[130] and to litigate on behalf of the company in certain circumstances.[131]

Shareholders also have substantial control rights in relation to a number of corporate transactions. Company law requires that transactions to which the counterparty is a director or a connected party[132] be approved by the shareholders.[133] These include substantial property transactions[134] and corporate loans.[135] Additional governance rights are given to the shareholders in certain publicly traded companies.[136] These rights are potentially significant, although in the very smallest companies, where the directors and shareholders are the same people, the rights are meaningless, and in the very largest companies with dispersed share ownership, shareholder engagement in these issues may be limited. As discussed at 3.2.2.4, the corporate governance role of debt may in some circumstances be more significant than that of equity.

3.2.2 Position of the Creditors in a Solvent Company

As will be seen from the discussion in chapter two, there are many different types of creditors, who advance money to the company based on different contractual and proprietary structures. All creditors, however, have one thing in common: they are owed money by the company to which they have a legal right to payment at some time.[137] This right is usually,

---

[127] Companies Act 2006, s 994. See eg *Re Insurance and Financial Consultants Ltd* [2014] EWHC 2206 (Ch).

[128] In other words, a compulsory winding up on the just and equitable ground under Insolvency Act 1986, s 122(1)(g): *Ebrahimi v Westbourne Galleries Ltd* [1973] AC 360.

[129] Companies Act 2006, s 172(1), discussed at 3.2.1.3.1.

[130] *North-West Transportation Co Ltd v Beatty* (1887) LR 12 App Cas 589 and see now Companies Act 2006, s 239.

[131] It is generally the board that takes the decision to litigate, but the majority can prima facie control this decision via their control of the board. The minority may be able to make use of the derivative action procedure: Companies Act 2006, ss 260–64 (England, Wales and Northern Ireland), ss 265–69 (Scotland). There is also the possibility of using an unfair prejudice petition (Companies Act 2006, s 994) for this purpose (*Clark v Cutland* [2003] EWCA Civ 810), although the extent of that option is far from clear (see eg J Payne, 'Sections 459–461 Companies Act 1985: The Future of Shareholder Protection' [2005] *Cambridge Law Journal* 647).

[132] Companies Act 2006, ss 252, 254.

[133] Ibid, ss 177, 180.

[134] Ibid, ss 190–96.

[135] Ibid, ss 197–214.

[136] See 11.2.2.

[137] Even this is not entirely true. Those lenders who finance a company by purchasing its receivables (see 2.3.4.1) are actually owed nothing by the company so long as the proceeds from the assets are sufficient to cover the price. However, there is usually a contractual obligation for the company to make up any shortfall (see 7.2.5.2).

but not always, based on a pre-existing contract. Some creditors, such as trade creditors and tort claimants, have a right to a single payment, which they would like to be paid as soon as possible. However, most lenders who are in the business of providing finance do so in order to obtain an income stream, which, depending on the terms of the loan, will comprise interest or repayment of capital or a combination of both. In a sense, then, this contractual right to periodic payments can be compared and contrasted with the shareholders' right to a dividend, which is not contractually enforceable until the dividend is declared.[138]

Further, the payments to which the lender has a right are fixed, at least in the sense that they do not depend upon whether the company has made profits, although they may depend on other variables such as the current rate of interest. This means that, in relation to the lenders' right to income, they have no incentive for the company to engage in risky activity which increases profits, provided that sufficient profits are generated to meet the company's contractual obligations. In most financing structures, the profit which the lenders make comes from these periodic payments (here loosely called 'interest'), and so the lenders' incentive while the company is solvent is to keep the capital part of the loan outstanding for as long as possible so that they can make as much profit as possible. However, the lenders also have an incentive to ensure that the company remains solvent, since on insolvency it will lose not only the future profit of interest payments, but possibly also the capital repayment.

Many lenders will also have a long-term contractual right to repayment of capital. This may be deeply subordinated or have a very long maturity date, as in a hybrid security.[139] Conversely, capital may be repaid totally through periodic payments, but the lender will usually have the right to accelerate repayment of the whole amount due if the borrower company defaults.[140] If the company remains solvent, this capital debt will eventually have to be repaid (unlike the capital contributed by the shareholders). This will often be by refinancing, whereby the company just rolls over the debt with the same lenders or takes out new debt with different lenders. As mentioned above, most lenders do not have an incentive to seek early repayment, and would wish the lending relationship to go on for as long as possible if the company is solvent. However, the risk of losing the capital repayment if the company becomes insolvent is severe, and it is largely the protection against this risk that is discussed below. It is a risk which all creditors bear equally although their claims rank ahead of all shareholders. Creditors are not, on the whole, protected by the general law, although the legal capital rules, discussed in chapter five, are one significant exception to that principle. Creditors generally have the ability to protect themselves by a variety of means, which are discussed generally in chapter two, as well as in the discussion following and in more detail in chapters six and seven.

Proprietary means of protection, discussed in chapter seven, improve a creditor's ranking when assets of an insolvent company are distributed,[141] and certain classes of creditors are given improved ranking by the general law.[142] It is, of course, only when the company is insolvent that the ranking of claims really matters, and, as discussed below, on insolvency

---

[138] See 3.2.1.1.
[139] See 2.4.
[140] See 6.3.3.
[141] See 3.3.1.1.
[142] See 3.3.1.2.

not all creditors rank equally. When a company is solvent, ranking per se does not matter. We can see that from the two tests for insolvency under English law mentioned earlier.[143]

If a company is balance sheet solvent its assets are greater than its liabilities, so that (in theory) all creditors could be paid, and if it is cash flow solvent it can pay its debts as they fall due so again creditors can be paid in due course. If we exclude the twilight period before insolvency from our consideration of a solvent company,[144] it might be thought that creditors have no concerns about repayment while the company is solvent. However, as this section notes, this view is not entirely accurate.

As well as improving their ranking on insolvency by taking proprietary protection, creditors can protect themselves by various contractual means, which are discussed in chapter six, and can also adjust to the dangers of insolvency by other means, such as increasing their price or refusing to contract. The ability of creditors to adjust has meant that there is little protection for creditors from the general law. However, there are some creditors who are said to be unable to adjust and who therefore might need statutory or other protection.

3.2.2.1 Non-Adjusting Creditors[145]

To see who these non-adjusting creditors are, it is instructive to consider the types of creditor that exist. One could see creditors as falling into three categories: those who consciously extend credit to the company (whether in the form of loans or trade credit or otherwise); those who deal with the company without intending to extend credit, but who become creditors because the company becomes liable to them for breach of contract or otherwise (such as customers of goods or services); and those who have no prior contact with the company before becoming creditors (this category is mainly tort victims and the tax authorities).

The ability of some members of the first category (lenders, investors and other financiers) to protect themselves and to influence the company's activities is discussed extensively throughout this book. Two categories of lenders other than financiers or suppliers may also be present. Directors may extend loans to the company, particularly when it is in difficulties. Such loans are usually unsecured. Other companies in the same group may also lend to the company, and often this lending will be unsecured and, maybe, subordinated.[146] It should be remembered that directors and group companies may also guarantee loans to the company, and so will be unsecured creditors in any insolvency through their right of subrogation.[147]

Trade creditors also have means of protection at their disposal, although they may not be able to use them fully because of market pressure.[148] First, they can reflect the credit risks they face in the prices that they charge, either generally for all customers or in relation to

---

[143] See 3.2.

[144] See 3.2.

[145] The terminology 'adjusting' and 'non-adjusting' was first used in this context by L Bebchuk and J Fried, 'The Uneasy Case for the Priority of Secured Claims in Bankruptcy' (1996) 105 *Yale Law Journal* 857. For further discussion in the context of whether non-adjusting creditors should have some priority over secured creditors, see 7.6.2.3.

[146] We are indebted to Dr Sandra Frisby of the University of Nottingham for this information, which she drew from her extensive empirical research on insolvency.

[147] See 6.4.1.3.3.

[148] V Finch, 'Security, Insolvency and Risk: Who Pays the Price?' (1999) 62 *Modern Law Review* 633, 644.

a particular customer.[149] If they supply goods, they can protect themselves by the use of retention of title clauses, which are effective in relation to the goods themselves though not usually as regards the products of the goods or the proceeds of sale.[150] Certain protection is also afforded by the general law: under the Sale of Goods Act an unpaid seller has a lien on the goods before delivery,[151] and a right to stop the goods in transit if the buyer becomes insolvent.[152] These devices are not available to those who supply services, and they have to rely on more general measures (which are also available to those supplying goods). These include requiring payment in advance (if the market will bear this), spreading the risk of customer default by contracting with a wide number and variety of customers, and monitoring the credit of customers so that they can refuse to supply to a customer in difficulties. This latter device depends on the terms of the original contract: either the supplier has to protect itself with a term enabling it to terminate the contract if the customer gets into difficulties, or it has to operate on the basis of separate contracts for each supply, which involves the risk of losing the business for reasons other than the customer's financial position.

Those in the second category will find it much harder to protect themselves. A pre-paying customer could protect itself against non-delivery of goods by providing that property in the goods passes on payment rather than on delivery.[153] More contentiously, it is possible to ensure that payments in advance are held on trust for customers until the goods or services are provided.[154] Ongoing customers may be able to negotiate a retention fund, so that not all the price is paid until they are satisfied that the goods or services are of a certain quality. Further, customers who have not paid, or who have a running account with the company, may be protected by set-off.[155] Otherwise, customers just have to rely on diversification, so that they are exposed to the risk of non-payment by each contractual partner only to a small extent. They can also refuse to contract if they discover that the company is in difficulties, although, of course, they are not in a position to monitor and would have to rely on signals from lender creditors or possibly from the market. Employees are even less able to protect themselves, since they cannot diversify and are not usually in a position to change jobs quickly. Those providing services as independent contractors fall, at least in theory, into the first category.

Those in the third category are truly non-adjusting creditors and cannot protect themselves at all. The tax authorities are, however, in a slightly different position, since although they cannot refuse to 'do business' with the company, they can be proactive in enforcing the debt, or at least come to an arrangement with the company in relation to outstanding indebtedness. Tort victims are the least able to adjust, but they have some protection in the UK from the Third Party (Rights against Insurers) Act 2010.[156]

---

[149] The latter may be difficult as it depends on expensive information gathering which may not be economic for small creditors. However, it is possible that information may be obtained by free-riding on the monitoring activities of other lenders.

[150] See 7.2.5.3.

[151] Sale of Goods Act 1979, s 41.

[152] Ibid, s 44.

[153] Ibid, s 17.

[154] *Re Kayford Ltd* [1975] 1 WLR 279; *Barclays Bank Ltd v Quistclose Investments Ltd* [1970] AC 567.

[155] See 6.3.4.

[156] For further discussion see 7.6.2.3. This Act is not yet in force, but will be brought in when it has been amended in the manner provided for by the Insurance Act 2015.

3.2.2.2 *Risks to Creditors from the Operation of a Solvent Company*

The operations of a solvent company can create risk to a creditor. As discussed above, there is the risk that the company will in the future be unable to continue borrowing from the creditor and therefore cease to be a source of valuable profit. However, the more serious risk is that the company will, in the future but before the creditor is paid, become unable to pay the creditor's whole debt. These risks can be manifested in a number of ways. Some risks come from outside sources, such as an economic downturn which reduces the market for the company's products, or a sudden change in government policy. Other risks come from the conduct of the directors, who are managing the company. The directors may be fraudulent (and operating for their own gain) or incompetent. They can fail to react effectively to external events and forces, in a way which has a deleterious effect on the value of the company.[157] Alternatively, they may be acting in the best interests of the shareholders, but in a situation where the interests of the shareholders and the creditors diverge, thus creating what are called 'agency problems'.

In many ways, when the company is solvent, the interests of the creditors and the shareholders are broadly similar. However, because the shareholders benefit from any rise in the value of the company, they are likely to favour riskier projects which may increase that value, while creditors would be happier with lower risk projects which merely retain the status quo.[158] What the general law's response to this divergence of interest should be is discussed in chapter five; this section will discuss the responses that creditors can have by way of individual adjustment.

These risks could manifest themselves in a number of ways.[159] First, the company might, after borrowing from a creditor, incur further debts to others which do not result in an equivalent increase in assets. Supposing A Ltd borrows £100,000 from B and has £200,000 worth of assets. B at this point can be sure that it will be paid back. However, if A Ltd then borrows £100,000 from C, which it uses to pay its ongoing wages bill, B's position begins to look much more precarious. It is less of a problem if the money A Ltd borrows from C is used to buy a new machine worth £100,000, as A Ltd's assets rise to £300,000. However, even then, B's position is made worse as it will have to share the £100,000 'cushion' with C whereas before C came on the scene it had that cushion all to itself. This problem is called 'claim dilution'.[160]

---

[157] GG Triantis and RJ Daniels, 'The Role of Debt in Interactive Corporate Governance' (1995) 83 *California Law Review* 1073, 1075.

[158] See 3.1. This view, while representing orthodox finance theory, is not universally held, even in relation to the run-up to insolvency. See DG Baird and RK Rasmussen, 'Private Debt and the Missing Lever of Corporate Governance' (2006) 154 *University of Pennsylvania Law Review* 1209, 1246; F Tung, 'Leverage in the Board Room: The Unsung Influence of Private Lenders in Corporate Governance' (2009) 57 *UCLA Law Review* 115; JM Shepherd, F Tung and AH Yoon, 'What Else Matters for Corporate Governance? The Case of Bank Monitoring' (2008) 88 *Boston University Law Review* 991.

[159] See CW Smith and JB Warner, 'On Financial Contracting: An Analysis of Bond Covenants' (1979) 7 *Journal of Financial Economics* 117; J Day and P Taylor, 'Bankers' Perspectives on the Role of Covenants in Debt Contracts' [1996] *Journal of International Banking Law* 201, 202; W Bratton, 'Bond Covenants and Creditor Protection: Economics and Law, Theory and Practice, Substance and Process' (2006) 7 *European Business Organization Law Review* 39.

[160] CW Smith and JB Warner, 'On Financial Contracting: An Analysis of Bond Covenants' (1979) 7 *Journal of Financial Economics* 117, 118.

Second, the company might withdraw assets from the pool available to the creditors for repayment. Certain withdrawals are obviously necessary for the operation of the company (such as those for the payment of debts), but others may be less obviously in the interests of the creditors. This is particularly true where the recipients of the assets are the shareholders. One example is the payment of dividends; another is the return of capital. Even if the withdrawn assets do not go to the shareholders, they may go to fund risky projects, which, if they fail, mean that the asset pool is reduced. Third, the company might substitute the assets which it had when the creditor made the loan for other, more risky assets, which potentially benefit the shareholders if the risk pays off and the company increases in value, but will be detrimental to the creditors if the risk does not pay off.

There is also a risk of underinvestment, where the company is balance sheet insolvent (in that it has borrowed more than its assets) or near balance sheet insolvent. Here, growth in the value of the company is of real benefit to the creditors, but gives no benefit to the shareholders. Thus, the benefits of more investment accrue to the creditors rather than the shareholders, so that the shareholders do not have enough incentive to invest and maximise the potential gains.[161] If there is underinvestment, the creditors lose out on this benefit, and the shareholders have an incentive to divert value from the company to themselves so that they can use it for projects for which they will obtain all the benefit. However, the danger of underinvestment appears to recede the more solvent the company is.

Can the general law protect creditors against the risks identified above in any way? One possible method is by requiring a company to have a certain amount of capital. English law requires this in relation to public companies, and these rules are discussed below in chapter five.[162] Certain types of financial companies are required to have particular amounts and types of capital under the capital adequacy rules: these are described briefly in chapter two.[163] However, generally it is left to creditors to protect themselves, either by taking proprietary interests, discussed in chapter seven, or by the contractual means described below and in chapter six.

One very simple way in which creditors can protect themselves against these risks is by pricing the cost of debt in a way which reflects them. If it were possible to do this accurately, creditors would be indifferent to the risks and would take no steps to reduce them. There are, however, various reasons why this does not happen. The first is that companies would rather agree to restrictions on their activity than have to pay the full cost of the risks generated by their unrestricted activity. Another is that neither creditors nor companies can foresee everything that is going to happen and therefore pricing of risk can never be wholly accurate: it is much safer for creditors to agree to contractual or proprietary ways to mitigate at least some risks so that the degree of adjustment of price to mitigate risk is

---

[161] SC Myers, 'Determinants of Corporate Borrowing' (1977) *Journal of Financial Economics* 147; CW Smith and JB Warner, 'On Financial Contracting: An Analysis of Bond Covenants' (1979) 7 *Journal of Financial Economics* 117, 199; R Scott, 'A Relational Theory of Secured Financing' (1986) 86 *Columbia Law Review* 901, 920; W Bratton, 'Bond Covenants and Creditor Protection: Economics and Law, Theory and Practice, Substance and Process' (2006) 7 *European Business Organization Law Review* 39, 47.

[162] See 5.3.1.

[163] See 2.3.1.3.

limited.[164] Further, insolvency is costly to the company as well as to the creditors, so even if the creditors could be protected against a strong risk of insolvency by an adjustment in price, there is still a loss of overall value. This gives the company an incentive to agree to restrictions.[165] Another reason is that at least some creditors are not in a position to adjust the price or to impose restrictions on the company. The extent to which creditors can or cannot adjust is discussed elsewhere.[166]

3.2.2.3 Restrictions on the Company's Activities

Restrictions on the company's activities by creditors take the form of terms ('covenants') in the borrower/lender contract. Their actual content and operation are discussed in detail in chapter six. The grant of security by the company also has a restrictive effect, and this is discussed in detail in chapter seven. Certain important points about covenants can, however, be made here. Although the terms themselves are reasonably standard, the extent to which they are included in any given contract is a matter of the bargaining power of the parties, and what each party is able, and wants, to achieve. Lenders will want as much protection from restrictions as possible, while borrowers will want maximum flexibility of operation, and therefore as few restrictions as possible. In theory the level of restriction could be a direct trade-off against the price paid for the loan, so that the most expensive loan would be covenant-free, and the cheapest would include total restriction. In practice, other factors also play a part,[167] which are discussed in the rest of this section.

The credit risk of the borrower is critical, so that a borrower who is a poor credit risk will only be able to borrow on reasonably tight covenants, and lenders will not lend to such a borrower below a certain level of covenant protection, at whatever price. Conversely, a strongly creditworthy borrower will be able to borrow on the basis of few restrictions, and is likely to value flexibility of operation above the benefits of a very low interest rate.[168]

The number of lenders is also important. Where there is one lender (such as in a bank loan), covenants tend to be much stronger than where there are large numbers of lenders. Covenants in a syndicated loan are also stronger than those in a bond issue, particularly when the borrower is an investment grade company.[169] This is partly because banks are in a position to negotiate firm covenants from the start, while in a bond issue the level of

---

[164] A Keay, 'A Theoretical Analysis of the Director's Duty to Consider Creditor Interests: The Progressive School's Approach' [2004] *Journal of Corporate Law Studies* 307, 321. For a further gloss on this argument, see A Choi and G Triantis, 'Market Conditions and Contract Design: Variations in Debt Covenants and Collateral' (2013) 88 *New York University Law Review* 51, where it is argued that changes in the price of debt actually affect the severity of the covenants included, for reasons based on adverse selection and moral hazard.

[165] K Schmidt, 'The Economics of Covenants as a Means of Efficient Creditor Protection' (2006) 7 *European Business Organization Law Review* 89.

[166] See 3.2.2.1 and 7.6.2.3.

[167] W Bratton, 'Bond Covenants and Creditor Protection: Economics and Law, Theory and Practice, Substance and Process' (2006) 7 *European Business Organization Law Review* 39, 74–75.

[168] Ibid, 75. See the distinction between the LMA standard forms for investment grade and leveraged loans, and see 6.3.2.2.

[169] High-yield bond covenants tend to mirror those in leveraged loans, at least in relation to restrictive covenants, but there are typically fewer maintenance covenants, that is, covenants requiring ongoing compliance with financial ratios. See J Macdonald, 'High Yield Bonds: An Introduction to Material Covenants and Terms' [2014] *Journal of International Banking and Financial Law* 242.

protection is set by the issuer at the level it thinks (or is advised) the market will bear.[170] It is also partly because banks are in a better position to monitor and react to breaches of covenant, and can use such breaches as a trigger for renegotiation, whereas, despite the presence of a trustee, this process is much less easy for dispersed bondholders.[171] Another relevant reason is that bonds are tradable, and so the holders are able to exit more easily; they often would prefer to do this, rather than go through the process of enforcing covenants and renegotiating.[172] Further, bond investors can diversify their holdings and spread their risk, so they are less affected by the financial distress of one issuer.[173] In fact, an important function of bond covenants is to protect the value of the bond, rather than (directly) against the risk of non-payment.[174] However, where the issuer also has a considerable amount of loan debt, bondholders may not wish to be at a disadvantage compared to the lenders, and the bond covenants may go some way to reflect those in the loan agreements, at least to the extent that this is practicable.[175] It might be thought that as syndicated loans became more easily traded, this would lead to a reduction in covenants: this, however, does not appear to have been the case. Such evidence as there is suggests that covenants have been kept reasonably strict,[176] partly because the lead bank often retains its stake, partly to reassure purchasers of the quality of the loan purchased, and partly to enable purchasers either to monitor themselves or to rely on the lead bank's continued monitoring; there is also a possibility that the bondholders 'free-ride' on the monitoring of the banks.[177] The state of the market is

---

[170] This point is made forcefully by R Youard in 'Default in International Loan Agreements (Part 2)' [1986] *Journal of Business Law* 378, 382–83; cf P Wood, 'Bondholders and Banks: Why the Difference in Protection?' [2011] *Capital Markets Law Journal* 188, 193–94.

[171] J Markland, 'Cov-Lite—The New Cutting Edge in Acquisition Finance' [2007] *Journal of International Banking and Financial Law* 379. The use of a bond trustee may assist in the process of waiver of breach and renegotiation, but the costs are still considerable. Banks tend to be first to the negotiating table, but usually, in the end, have to include bondholders in the restructuring process, since they are likely to the have the power to accelerate the bonds themselves. See P Wood, 'Bondholders and Banks: Why the Difference in Protection?' [2011] *Capital Markets Law Journal* 188, 195–96.

[172] It should be pointed out, however, that not all the bondholders can exit: the more holders who sell the more the price will drop and in the end there may be no buyers at all on the market.

[173] A bank lender, of course, will also diversify to some extent, by lending to a large number of borrowers, and by limiting the amount lent to any one borrower by taking part in syndicated loans. Now that bank debt is more easily tradable, the ability of a bank to protect itself through diversification has increased. See CK Whitehead, 'The Evolution of Debt: Covenants, the Credit Market, and Corporate Governance' (2009) 34 *Journal of Corporation Law* 641, 653; E de Fontenay, 'Do Securities Laws Matter? The rise of the leveraged loan market' http://papers.ssrn. com/sol3/papers.cfm?abstract_id=2419668.

[174] This can be seen, for example, by the structure of the negative pledge covenant in a eurobond issue: see 6.3.1.6. The position is different where there is a significant credit risk, for example in high-yield bond issues, where covenants are likely to be stricter (for the distinction between investment grade bonds and high-yield bonds, see 2.3.3.3).

[175] M Hartley, 'Bondholder Protections Revisited' [2010] *Journal of International Banking and Financial Law* 219. Note that a group of four major investor organisations formed the Bond Covenant Group in 2010 and drew up model bond covenants: see www.ivis.co.uk/media/5984/model-covenants-in-sterling-and-euro-bond-issues-160610-1100am.pdf. It is not clear how far these are used in practice, however, as they had a very lukewarm reception. See J Hughes, 'Investors' Move on Covenants Rebuffed' *Financial Times*, 21 July 2010.

[176] S Drucker and M Puri, 'On Loan Sales, Loan Contracting, and Lending Relationships' (2008) 21 *Review of Financial Studies* 1, cited in F Tung, 'Leverage in the Board Room: The Unsung Influence of Private Lenders in Corporate Governance' (2009) 57 *UCLA Law Review* 115, 166; CK Whitehead, 'The Evolution of Debt: Covenants, the Credit Market, and Corporate Governance' (2009) 34 *Journal of Corporation Law* 641, 664.

[177] P Wood, 'Bondholders and Banks: Why the Difference in Protection?' [2011] *Capital Markets Law Journal* 188, 196 points out that bondholders do have the benefit of public information about the borrower (when the borrower is a publicly traded company) but cannot ask for more detailed information as this may cause them difficulties with the insider dealing rules. See 13.4.1.

also relevant to the strictness of the covenants. During the mid-2000s, when credit was very plentiful and borrowers were in a position to dictate terms, there was a growth in covenant-lite deals.[178] This situation changed considerably after the financial crisis,[179] but now seems to be reverting to the pre-2008 position in the high-yield bond market.[180]

3.2.2.4 *The Corporate Governance Role of Debt*

It is well recognised that corporate law faces a fundamental difficulty in giving broad discretion to the directors to run the company effectively, and yet constraining them from exercising that discretion in their own interests rather than in the interests of the shareholders and other stakeholders. In very small companies where the shareholders and the directors are effectively the same people, there is no danger of the directors abusing shareholder interests, although other stakeholders will not necessarily be protected. Once companies get larger, however, the separation of ownership and control means that the possibility of abuse does arise. The law has traditionally regarded shareholders as having an important monitoring role.[181] Whether shareholders operate as effective corporate monitors once the shareholding becomes very dispersed, for example in the context of publicly traded companies, is discussed at 11.2.2.[182] Other possible forms of corporate governance, once the company reaches this size, are the presence of non-executive directors,[183] and the role of takeovers to create a market for corporate control.[184] What has been less well recognised in the past is the possibility of a corporate governance role for creditors in a company.

Recently, however, more attention has focused on the role of creditors in influencing, and even controlling, the activities of the directors. Much of the literature in this area is from the US, and, although care has to be taken in transplanting the detailed arguments into a UK context, much of the theoretical discussion is relevant. The creditors have a close interest in how the company operates in the run-up to insolvency, when their financial interests are clearly prejudiced, and will seek to exercise their contractual and proprietary protection at that stage. What is examined here, however, is the extent to which creditors can influence the operation of a company when the company is solvent, as defined above. It should be

---

[178] J Markland, 'Cov-Lite—The New Cutting Edge in Acquisition Finance' [2007] *Journal of International Banking and Financial Law* 379. These forms of covenants were used particularly in the context of private equity transactions prior to the financial crisis. For discussion see 16.4.3.1.

[179] See eg M Hartley, 'Bondholder Protections Revisited' (2010) 25 *Journal of International and Financial Law* 219. For a theoretical explanation, see A Choi and G Triantis, 'Market Conditions and Contract Design: Variations in Debt Covenants and Collateral' (2013) 88 *New York University Law Review* 51, where it is argued that as debt capital becomes less available, covenants tighten because the quality of the pool of borrowers is lessened and because, as interest rates rise, shareholders have less stake in the company so more control by debt is required.

[180] K Clowry, 'European Credit Documentation Trends: Covenant-Lite or Covenant Empty?' [2014] *Journal of International Banking and Financial Law* 296.

[181] See 3.2.1.3.3.

[182] Whether the private equity backed companies operate as a more successful corporate governance model than other companies is assessed at 16.6.

[183] An obligation is placed on companies with a premium listing in the UK to disclose in their annual report the extent to which they have complied with the UK Corporate Governance Code. The Code sets out standards of good practice, including the existence and role of non-executive directors within a company: Financial Reporting Council, *UK Corporate Governance Code*, September 2014.

[184] Discussed further at 14.3.2.2.2.

remembered, of course, that only adjusting creditors who are in the first category discussed above[185] (lenders) are in a position to impose covenants and to have a significant role in corporate governance.[186]

Comparisons will be made to the corporate governance role of both shareholders[187] and non-executive directors. It should also be remembered that the mere existence of debt in a company's financial structure has a corporate governance function, since the directors have to run the company in such a way that the debt repayments can be made. Risky activity jeopardises the ability to make these payments, even though it may have potential benefits for shareholders.[188]

3.2.2.4.1 Debt Covenants

In order to protect a creditor from the agency conflicts discussed above, the covenants included in a typical debt contract will do a number of things.[189] First, certain activities will be prohibited, or prohibited under certain circumstances.[190] Thus a negative pledge will prohibit the grant of security over the borrower's assets,[191] and further borrowing may be prohibited if the borrower's debt to equity ratio rises beyond a certain prescribed level. Disposal of assets except in the ordinary course of business is likely to be prohibited, as is the declaration of dividends or other distributions to the shareholders beyond a certain percentage of net profits, and also substantial changes of business and mergers without the consent of the lender. There may also be limits on capital expenditure, or covenants which require repayment of debt on the occurrence of certain specified events. Secondly, the agreement will require the company to meet certain financial ratios in relation to cash flow and net worth.[192] Thirdly, it will require the company to furnish the lender with information about its financial position.[193] Fourthly, it will include a number of warranties as to the company's financial and legal position at the time of the agreement, which continue throughout the life of the loan.[194]

The agreement will specify events of default, which will include breaches of the terms of the agreement, but are likely also to include non-breach events such as default in relation to another agreement, the onset of any sort of insolvency or enforcement proceedings, and other events which might affect the borrower's ability to repay the loan. The lender will have the right to accelerate the loan and terminate the agreement if an event of default occurs.[195]

---

[185] See 3.2.1.1.

[186] Those making loans are in a stronger position than bondholders; see 3.2.2.3.

[187] Discussed at 3.2.1.3.3 in relation to companies generally and 11.2.2 in the context of publicly traded companies.

[188] See MC Jensen and WH Meckling, 'Theory of the Firm: Managerial Behaviour, Agency Costs and Ownership Structure' (1976) 3 *Journal of Financial Economics* 305, and see also the discussion at 16.6.5.2.

[189] See 6.3.

[190] See 6.3.1.

[191] See 6.3.1.6.

[192] See 6.3.2.2.

[193] See 6.3.2.

[194] See 6.3.2.1.

[195] See 6.3.2.2.

3.2.2.4.2 Monitoring by Lenders

These provisions put the lender in a strong position both to monitor the company's operations and to influence them. Let us first consider monitoring.[196] The borrower's obligation in the loan agreement to furnish financial and other information will vary according to the type of lender, as will the lender's ability to use information to monitor effectively. The lender in the best position to monitor is the single bank, which has a relationship with the borrower, and which is able to impose obligations on the borrower to provide financial information at very regular intervals.[197] Further, the bank may well also control the borrower's current account, and therefore be in a position to monitor its cash flow on a daily basis.[198] In some cases, the bank may also have the right to appoint a director of the borrowing company.[199] Thus, in many ways, it can be argued that a bank is in a better position to monitor than non-executive directors.[200] Bondholders, however, are less able to monitor effectively, because they are numerous and diverse. Even where there is a bond trustee, the terms of the trust deed normally exclude all active obligations to monitor and the trustee is only obliged to receive certificates of compliance from the issuer.[201] A single bank is therefore the most effective and the lowest cost monitor, although syndicated loans also provide a good monitoring structure, particularly where there is an effective agent bank.[202] Where a company raises finance from both bonds and from a bank or banks, it is usually more efficient for the banks to do the primary monitoring and for the bondholders (and other creditors) to rely on the signals generated by the bank monitoring and the resulting reaction.[203] The more liquid the syndicated loan market becomes, the less strong this argument is, as there is a correlation between illiquidity of a market and effective monitoring and governance. Instead, it has been argued, in a liquid market, changes in the position of the borrower will be factored into the price of the debt, which then serves as a proxy for monitoring.[204]

3.2.2.4.3 Lender Influence on Breach

Although the fact that the state of the company is being monitored is likely to make a difference to the behaviour of directors, monitoring by itself will not enable a lender to have a significant role in corporate governance. It is the restrictions contained in the covenants

---

[196] As pointed out by Triantis and Daniels, governance can be divided into two parts: monitoring and reaction. G Triantis and R Daniels, 'The Role of Debt in Interactive Corporate Governance' (1995) 83 *California Law Review* 1073, 1079.

[197] For a clear statement of the use made of monitoring by banks lending to small and medium sized businesses in the UK, see British Bankers Association, *Statement of Principles* (2009), 8–10.

[198] F Tung, 'Leverage in the Board Room: The Unsung Influence of Private Lenders in Corporate Governance' [2009] *UCLA Law Review* 115, 140.

[199] This is rare in the UK (E Ferran and LC Ho, *Principles of Corporate Finance Law*, 2nd edn (Oxford, Oxford University Press, 2014) 298), but appears to be common in the US (Tung, ibid, 139 citing RS Krozner and PE Strahan, 'Bankers on Boards: Monitoring, Conflicts of Interest, and Lender Liability' (2001) 62 *Journal of Financial Economics* 415, 436, who found that a third of large US firms have a banker on the board of directors).

[200] See Tung, ibid, 132.

[201] See 8.3.4.2.

[202] The agent bank may, however, have very limited duties: see 8.4.5.

[203] G Triantis and R Daniels, 'The Role of Debt in Interactive Corporate Governance' (1995) 83 *California Law Review* 1073, 1089.

[204] C Whitehead, 'Creditors and Debt Governance' in C Hill, J Krusemark, B McDonnell and S Robbins (eds), *Research Handbook on the Economics of Corporate Law* (Cheltenham, Edward Elgar Publishing, 2012) 74. For discussion of the liquidity of the syndicated loan market see chapter 9.

that restrain certain types of behaviour on the part of the directors and encourage other types of behaviour. Directors will, in general, wish to comply with the obligations and to avoid breach. This is partly in order to improve the company's reputation as a 'good' borrower, which may improve its ability to obtain cheaper finance in the future or finance with less restrictive covenants.[205] It is also partly to avoid the consequences of breach, which are discussed in the next paragraph.

The main way in which a lender can influence how a company is run is through the dialogue that arises if a covenant is breached. It may seem strange to see a breach as giving rise to a dialogue, since in theory it gives the lender power to accelerate the loan and terminate the contract.[206] This, however, is the 'nuclear weapon' that could well send the borrower into insolvency, and would at the very least terminate the relationship between the lender and the borrower. As pointed out above,[207] a lender does not wish to lose the profit resulting from the lending relationship, and will therefore wish to keep it going so long as its recovery of capital is not jeopardised by the risk of insolvency. Thus, although the threat of acceleration is always there in the background, and is used by lenders to give them 'leverage' over the borrower,[208] the actual influence is achieved by the renegotiation that follows a covenant breach, and the terms on which the lender agrees to waive the breach. Another similar way of exercising influence is where the finance is provided by a series of short-term loans, where the terms are renegotiated at regular intervals.[209] Where the loan is a revolving facility, the threat of a refusal to extend any further credit is often enough for the borrower to comply with the wishes of the lender.[210] Certain covenants may be tied to a pricing grid, so that if the lender's risk increases (for example, because the company's financial position has worsened) the interest rate rises, and if the risk decreases (for example, if the company's rating is upgraded) the interest rate reduces.[211]

The influence exerted by a lender through these means can have a number of effects on the operations of the company. It can affect the level of a company's borrowing,[212] and also from whom it borrows. It can also affect the level and direction of a company's investment. Thus, the covenants which restrict the directors' activities in this regard can be seen

---

[205] CK Whitehead, 'The Evolution of Debt: Covenants, the Credit Market, and Corporate Governance' (2009) 34 *Journal of Corporation Law* 641, 666.

[206] See 6.3.3. Triantis and Daniels explain that creditor 'reaction' can be divided into exit and voice. Exit, in the present context, would be acceleration and termination of the loan, while voice involves attempting to correct, rather than escape from, a state of affairs. See G Triantis and R Daniels, 'The Role of Debt in Interactive Corporate Governance' (1995) 83 *California Law Review* 1073, 1079, citing AO Hirschman, *Exit, Voice, and Loyalty: Responses to Decline in Firms, Organizations, and States* (Cambridge, MA, Harvard University Press, 1970) 10–15 as the origin of the ideas of exit and voice.

[207] See 3.2.2.

[208] F Tung, 'Leverage in the Board Room: The Unsung Influence of Private Lenders in Corporate Governance' [2009] *UCLA Law Review* 115, 216. 'Leverage' here is used in the sense of 'pulling the levers', a synonym for effective governance much used in the US literature (eg DG Baird and RK Rasmussen, 'Private Debt and the Missing Lever of Corporate Governance' (2006) 154 *University of Pennsylvania Law Review* 1209).

[209] Tung, ibid, 140.

[210] DG Baird and RK Rasmussen, 'Private Debt and the Missing Lever of Corporate Governance' (2006) 154 *University of Pennsylvania Law Review* 1209.

[211] See 6.3.2.2.

[212] See F Tung, 'Leverage in the Board Room: The Unsung Influence of Private Lenders in Corporate Governance' [2009] *UCLA Law Review* 115, 153, citing MR Roberts and A Sufi, 'Control Rights and Capital Structure: An Empirical Investigation' (2009) 64 *Journal of Finance* 1657 for evidence that a company's borrowing decreases after a covenant violation.

as a default position against which the directors and the lenders bargain. If the bargaining were costless, and each party were fully informed, this should lead to the company pursuing the most efficient projects from the point of view of both the shareholders (for whom the directors act) and the creditors. Of course, this ideal world does not exist, and in the real world there has to be a compromise between the strength of the restrictions imposed by the covenants and the costs of renegotiation. The stronger the covenants, the more the directors have to ask for permission for waiver, and the greater the ability of the lenders to demand changes as the 'price' of waiver. However, this can give rise to two problems.[213] One is that there is little incentive for the directors to investigate risky projects, even though these might enhance the value of the company, if these are going to be blocked by the lender. Secondly, if the lender's response to breach is always renegotiation, the borrower has less incentive to avoid breach.

There are other costs of renegotiation as well. For example the business routine is disrupted while the renegotiation is taking place, and the directors' time, which could, perhaps, be more profitably spent on other tasks, is lost.[214] Further, renegotiation is problematic when there are multiple lenders, particularly in bond issues: much will depend on the power of the trustee to deal with minor breaches and to negotiate on behalf of the bondholders.[215] The relative weakness of the renegotiation mechanism is another reason why covenants are usually weaker in bond issues than in bank loans, although even in the latter it will be seen that it is important to get the right balance between meaningful restriction, which gives the bank some leverage, and too much restriction, which can be costly.

The actual effects of lender influence, therefore, can be either the prevention of actions which the directors would otherwise take (such as further borrowing or the disposal or acquisition of assets) or the instigation of adjustments which the lender insists on as the 'price' for waiving a breach of covenant. It should be noticed that this 'price' could be achieved whether the breach consists of a prohibited activity, or the failure to meet a financial ratio (that is, an early warning sign of financial distress). Thus, the 'price' could be a change in strategy by the directors, but it could also be extra protection for the lender, such as the grant of additional security, a partial repayment of indebtedness, an increase in the cost of the loan or the imposition of more restrictive covenants.[216] It is harder to see these protective concessions as a form of corporate governance, or as externally valuable except to the extent that they send signals to other creditors of the possible weakness in the financial state of the company. Concessions which effect a change in corporate strategy, however, can realistically be described as a form of corporate governance.

One particularly significant effect that lender influence can have on corporate operations is the replacement of the top management of the company, such as the managing director. A lender is unlikely to insist on this unless the company is in financial distress, but a combination of the threat of acceleration of the existing indebtedness and the threat of

---

[213] K Schmidt, 'The Economics of Covenants as a Means of Efficient Creditor Protection' (2006) 7 *European Business Organization Law Review* 89.

[214] F Tung, 'Leverage in the Board Room: The Unsung Influence of Private Lenders in Corporate Governance' [2009] *UCLA Law Review* 115, 146.

[215] K Schmidt, 'The Economics of Covenants as a Means of Efficient Creditor Protection' (2006) 7 *European Business Organization Law Review* 89, and see 8.3.4.

[216] G Triantis and R Daniels, 'The Role of Debt in Interactive Corporate Governance' (1995) 83 *California Law Review* 1073, 1098.

refusal to extent fresh credit (particularly under a revolving facility) may give a lender sufficient leverage to effect this change if it considers it necessary.[217]

3.2.2.4.4 Lenders as Directors?

It should be pointed out that if a lender becomes too involved in the operation of a company, it risks liability for the decisions it makes and implements. The lender could be classified as a de facto director or as a shadow director. A de facto director is someone who undertakes the functions of a director, even though not formally appointed as such.[218]

Once someone is a de facto director then there is little doubt that the full range of directors' duties attach to them, including all of the general statutory duties now found in Part 10 of the Companies Act 2006. However, the risk of a lender becoming a de facto director is slight. Even if a bank is responsible for replacing a managing director, the bank, as nominator of the new incumbent, will not be responsible for that individual's actions, nor is it responsible for ensuring that the individual properly discharges his or her director's duties.[219]

By contrast, a shadow director is a person in accordance with whose directions or instructions the directors are accustomed to act.[220] A shadow director is someone who has real influence over the affairs of the company.[221] On the whole, the case law on this issue requires that the lender must step outside the usual lender–borrower relationship before they are likely to be held to be a shadow director.[222] It is clear that a bank is entitled to keep a close eye on what is done with its money, and to impose conditions on its support of the company, without being found to be a shadow director.[223] If a lender became a shadow director this could, for example, give rise to liability for wrongful trading under section 214 of the Insolvency Act 1986.[224]

It used to be unclear whether a shadow director is subject to the full range of directors' duties, or just to those, such as section 214, where the statute specifically extends liability to shadow directors.[225] This point has now been clarified by section 89 of the Small Business,

---

[217] DG Baird and RK Rasmussen, 'Private Debt and the Missing Lever of Corporate Governance' (2006) 154 *University of Pennsylvania Law Review* 1209; F Tung, 'Leverage in the Board Room: The Unsung Influence of Private Lenders in Corporate Governance' [2009] *UCLA Law Review* 115, 157, citing S Ozelge, 'The Role of Banks and Private Lenders in Forced CEO Turnovers' (15 January 2008), www.ssrn.com/abstract=1031814, and MS Weisbach, 'Outside Directors and CEO Turnover' (1988) 20 *Journal of Financial Economics* 431 as evidence that the turnover of Chief Executive Officers is higher in companies which have bank debt than in other companies, and that the influence of lenders in this regard is stronger even than that of independent boards.

[218] See *Revenue and Customs Commissioners v Holland; Re Paycheck Services 3 Ltd* [2010] UKSC 51.

[219] *Kuwait Asia Bank v National Mutual Life Nominees Ltd* [1991] 1 AC 187.

[220] Companies Act 2006, s 251 (as amended by Small Business, Enterprise and Employment Act 2015, s 90); Insolvency Act 1986, s 251. The two concepts of de facto director and shadow director are not necessarily mutually exclusive, although they will not overlap extensively: see *Revenue and Customs Commissioners v Holland; Re Paycheck Services 3 Ltd* [2010] UKSC 51 [80]; *Smithton Ltd v Naggar* [2014] EWCA Civ 939 [34]–[37]; *Secretary of State for Business Innovation and Skills v Chohan* [2013] EWHC 680 (Ch).

[221] *Secretary of State for Trade and Industry v Deverell* [2001] Ch 340.

[222] *Ultraframe (UK) Ltd v Fielding* [2005] EWHC 1638 (Ch); *Re PTZFM Ltd* [1995] 2 BCLC 354.

[223] *Ultraframe*, ibid, [1268].

[224] Insolvency Act 1986, s 214(7). See 3.3.3.

[225] See *Ultraframe (UK) Ltd v Fielding* [2005] EWHC 1638 (Ch) [1279] ff where Lewison J took the view that shadow directors do not owe the full range of directors' duties, while in *Vivendi SA v Richards* [2013] EWHC 3006 (Ch) Newey J considered that *Ultraframe* understated the fiduciary duties owed by shadow directors, and concluded that there are a number of reasons for thinking that shadow directors commonly owe fiduciary duties to at least some degree.

Enterprise and Employment Act 2015, which provides that the general duties apply to a shadow director of a company where and to the extent that they are capable of so applying. The Act also contains a power for the Secretary of State to make provision by regulation as to which general duties apply to shadow directors and which do not.

3.2.2.4.5 Is Lender Governance Efficient?

Much of the literature in this area considers the question of whether lender governance is efficient, in the sense that it improves the value of the company.[226] There are various ways in which this might be the case. First, creditors for whom monitoring and influence would be costly can 'free-ride' on the actions of a lender who can do this more cheaply.[227] Thus the reaction of the lender to early warnings of distress can signal that distress to the other creditors, who can then adjust or act accordingly. Secondly, if the lender's influence helps to overcome the agency conflicts between the shareholders and the creditors, this is also to the benefit of the other creditors. Thirdly, to the extent that the lender's influence prevents managerial incompetence, fraud, self-interest or failure to react to external changes, it enures for the benefit of the shareholders as well as other creditors.[228] Empirical studies carried out in the US seem to show that the prospect of bank monitoring adds value to a company's shares, and conclude that this means that lender influence adds value to the company.[229]

It is also clear from the foregoing discussion that the most effective and economically efficient monitoring and influence is exercised by a single bank lender, as compared to the situation where finance is provided to a company by many creditors,[230] such as where a number of creditors lend, each on the security of separate assets, or where a loan is syndicated or where finance is provided by a bond issue (or a combination of these). The single bank lender is most common in the case of small and medium sized enterprises. In the UK, banks make it clear to borrowers that they will monitor carefully and will expect to have a dialogue with the company throughout the course of the relationship, especially at any time of financial distress.[231] Even where finance is provided from a number of sources, however, it appears that the influence of a bank lender is still significant.[232]

The conclusion reached by many commentators is that, both as a matter of theory and as a description of fact, lenders contribute significantly to corporate governance. Some have then gone on to consider whether such creditors should owe fiduciary or similar duties to

---

[226] CW Smith and JB Warner, 'On Financial Contracting: An Analysis of Bond Covenants' (1979) 7 *Journal of Financial Economics* 117; DG Baird and RK Rasmussen, 'Private Debt and the Missing Lever of Corporate Governance' (2006) 154 *University of Pennsylvania Law Review* 1209; JM Shepherd, F Tung and AH Yoon, 'What Else Matters for Corporate Governance? The Case of Bank Monitoring' (2008) 88 *Boston University Law Review* 991.

[227] S Levmore, 'Monitors and Freeriders in Commercial and Corporate Settings' (1982) 92 *Yale Law Journal* 49.

[228] G Triantis and R Daniels, 'The Role of Debt in Interactive Corporate Governance' (1995) 83 *California Law Review* 1073, 1078.

[229] JM Shepherd, F Tung and AH Yoon, 'What Else Matters for Corporate Governance? The Case of Bank Monitoring' (2008) 88 *Boston University Law Review* 991.

[230] For discussion of this argument in relation to secured lending see R Scott, 'A Relational Theory of Secured Financing' (1986) 876 *Columbia Law Review* 901, and see 7.6.2.1.

[231] British Bankers Association, *Statement of Principles* (2009).

[232] G Triantis and R Daniels, 'The Role of Debt in Interactive Corporate Governance' (1995) 83 *California Law Review* 1073, 1080.

the company.[233] However, creditors do not act as fiduciaries; they act in their own interest, and it is by acting in accordance with their own interests that they act most efficiently. Further, if a creditor does step over the line and exercises the same degree of control as a manager, it may be liable under English law either as a de facto director or as a shadow director.[234] Thus there is no need to impose extra duties on them.

3.2.2.4.6 Effect of Transfer of Risk by Lenders

As discussed in chapter two, there has been a move in recent years for those who make loans to divest themselves of some or all of the credit risk. This can happen through the transfer of syndicated loans,[235] through loan participation (which transfers the risk but not the loan itself),[236] through securitisation,[237] or through the use of credit derivatives.[238] While these practices are less evident in a liquid bond market, since a bondholder can exit rather than have to transfer risk in another way, protection against risk by the use of credit derivatives is prevalent.

These practices potentially weaken the role of debt in corporate governance, as the person with the right to pull the levers of governance may not be the person who is exposed to the risk which incentivises the monitoring and governance. This can occur at several stages. First, the bank or other entity that makes the loan may have less incentive to perform strict due diligence if it is going to pass the risk on as soon as the loan is made.[239] Second, banks which are no longer at risk have little incentive to monitor corporate activity, or to intervene to control mismanagement.[240] Third, and perhaps most disturbingly, a lender may over hedge[241] its credit risk in respect of a loan, using a credit default swap, so that it is better off if the borrower defaults than if it pays. The lender then has the perverse incentive not to waive any breaches or to rescue the company,[242] and, in fact, could even take steps to acquire shares in the company, in order to use the voting rights to put the company into default.[243] Commentators have suggested several ways forward as a result of these concerns. It is pointed out that the dangers discussed above are rare in the market in syndicated

---

[233] F Tung, 'Leverage in the Board Room: The Unsung Influence of Private Lenders in Corporate Governance' [2009] *UCLA Law Review* 115, 170–73; M Hamer, 'Corporate Control and the Need for Meaningful Board Accountability' (2010) 94 *Minnesota Law Review* 541. This point has also arisen because 'activist' financiers (such as hedge funds) may hold hybrid instruments, so that the line between bondholders and shareholders is blurred.

[234] See 3.2.2.4.4.

[235] Discussed at 9.2.4.

[236] 9.3.1.

[237] 9.3.3.

[238] 6.4.3 and 9.3.2.

[239] Note the recent regulatory requirements that originators retain 'skin in the game' in a securitisation, discussed at 9.3.3.

[240] For evidence of this, see the account of the role of credit derivatives in the banks' lack of activity in relation to Enron: F Partnoy and DA Skeel, Jr , 'The Promise and Perils of Credit Derivatives' (2007) 75 *University of Cincinnati Law Review* 1019, 1032, and see also P Bolton and M Oehmke, 'Credit Default Swaps and the Empty Creditor Problem' (2011) 24 *Review of Financial Studies* 2617.

[241] For a discussion of credit default swaps and of hedging more specifically see 6.3.3.

[242] F Tung, 'Leverage in the Board Room: The Unsung Influence of Private Lenders in Corporate Governance' [2009] *UCLA Law Review* 115, 167–68; H Hu and B Black, 'Debt and Hybrid Decoupling: An Overview' [2008] *M&A Lawyer* 1, 7; V Finch, 'Corporate Rescue in a World of Debt' (2008) 8 *Journal of Business Law* 756, 764–65.

[243] See Hu and Black, ibid, 4, using the example of Bear Sterns.

loans.[244] Banks making loans which are to be transferred still investigate extensively before making the loan and monitor before transfer, so as to assure buyers that the loans are worth buying, and also to secure their own reputation as a seller of good quality loans.[245] Lead banks of syndicates also wish to maintain a reputation as arrangers, and will often not sell their stake, or at least will retain part of it.[246]

The chief concern had come from the use of credit derivatives. The lack of transparency in the market meant that it was not clear when a bank had hedged its exposure on a loan, nor were the disincentives to governance apparent to other creditors. It had been argued that greater transparency in the market, and the use of central clearing where appropriate, would improve the situation in relation to lender corporate governance.[247] These reforms are now put in place in Europe,[248] but it is too early to say whether there has been any improvement. It has also been argued that transparency would make the credit default swap market a better signal in relation to the credit risk of borrowers: if it were public that a lender had hedged its exposure, this would send a negative signal about the borrower. It might also damage the lender's reputation, and thus transparency could act as a disincentive to hedging, which could mitigate some of the dangers discussed above. Thus, the market in loans and credit derivatives could itself act as a means of corporate governance complementary to that of the actions of lenders.[249]

3.2.2.4.7 The Twilight Period before Insolvency

It is important to remember that the position of creditors changes extensively in the twilight period before insolvency. There is a far greater incentive for a creditor to protect its own interests in this period, and this can often involve using its rights to accelerate and terminate a loan, or to enforce security. However, there is considerable evidence that lenders attempt, at the first signs of distress, to help a company pull out of its difficulties, by using the governance strategies discussed above. For many years the banks in the UK operated a system called the 'London approach' which involved an agreement between the lending banks not to enforce their loans while investigations were made into the company's financial

---

[244] See also D Mengle, 'The Empty Creditor Hypothesis' ISDA research paper, www.isda.org/researchnotes/pdf/ISDa-research-notes3.pdf&gt, arguing that the empty creditor hypothesis is logically flawed, and that there is no evidence to show that the adverse effects are happening. However, for a table summarising potential incidences of the empty creditor problem from 2001 to 2010 see P Bolton and M Oehmke, 'Credit Default Swaps and the Empty Creditor Problem' (2011) 24 *Review of Financial Studies* 2617.

[245] F Tung, 'Leverage in the Board Room: The Unsung Influence of Private Lenders in Corporate Governance' [2009] *UCLA Law Review* 115, 163–66; CK Whitehead, 'The Evolution of Debt: Covenants, the Credit Market, and Corporate Governance' (2009) 34 *Journal of Corporation Law* 641, 662 ff.

[246] DG Baird and RK Rasmussen, 'Private Debt and the Missing Lever of Corporate Governance' (2006) 154 *University of Pennsylvania Law Review* 1209, 1244.

[247] F Tung, 'Leverage in the Board Room: The Unsung Influence of Private Lenders in Corporate Governance' [2009] *UCLA Law Review* 115, 176–78; H Hu and B Black, 'Debt and Hybrid Decoupling: An Overview' [2008] *M&A Lawyer* 1, 9; CK Whitehead, 'The Evolution of Debt: Covenants, the Credit Market, and Corporate Governance' (2009) 34 *Journal of Corporation Law* 641. See discussion at 6.4.3.

[248] See 6.4.3.

[249] CK Whitehead, 'The Evolution of Debt: Covenants, the Credit Market, and Corporate Governance' (2009) 34 *Journal of Corporation Law* 641; Y Yadav, 'The Case for a New Market in Debt Governance' (2014) 67 *Vanderbilt Law Review* 771.

problems, followed by an agreed restructuring.[250] The operation of this approach has been threatened by the fragmentation of debt (described above) and also, to some extent, by the changes in the administration procedure, which are described below.[251] The London approach developed because the UK did not have a corporate rescue procedure such as Chapter 11 of the Bankruptcy Code in the US, and to the extent that administration performs this role, the demise of the approach is probably foreseeable. However, there is clearly a place for informal restructuring when a company falls into financial difficulties. This issue is discussed further in the context of schemes of arrangement in chapter fifteen.[252]

3.3 The Relationship Between Debt and Equity in an Insolvent Company

This section examines the respective positions of shareholders and creditors when a company is insolvent or nearing insolvency. The focus of the law's protection at this point is on the creditors. The first two parts of the section discuss the ways in which some creditors can obtain protection by being paid ahead of other creditors, and also from legal rules providing redress where the pool of assets is reduced or unevenly distributed in the run-up to insolvency. The duties of the directors to creditors in the run-up to insolvency are then considered. Whether the creditors (through the liquidator or administrator) can make any claims against the directors or the shareholders is considered in the final section.

First, though, a number of general points need to be made about the term 'insolvency'. This is a term which can be used in a number of different ways. One could say that insolvency commences when formal insolvency proceedings commence. For the purposes of the transaction avoidance provisions, this is defined in section 240(3) of the Insolvency Act 1986.[253] The label used is 'the onset of insolvency'. It is at this moment that formal collectivity occurs, and from which the order of distribution discussed below applies (although if the company goes into administration, there will be no actual distribution until the administrator decides to distribute or to put the company into liquidation). Further, once insolvency proceedings have commenced the directors are dispossessed and no longer run the company. 'The onset of insolvency', used in this sense, will be a fixed point in time which is clearly identifiable, but it may arise relatively late in the day. A company can be described as being insolvent at an earlier stage, sometimes a much earlier stage.

The line between a company being solvent or insolvent is not a fixed, clear point in time, unlike the commencement of insolvency proceedings, and the line between solvency and insolvency in this sense can be hard to define. As noted above,[254] a company is said to be insolvent when it is unable to pay its debts within the meaning of section 123 of the

---

[250] For a good description of the London Approach, see J Armour and S Deakin, 'Norms in Private Insolvency: The "London Approach" to the Resolution of Financial Distress' [2001] *Journal of Corporate Law Studies* 21, 34 ff; British Bankers Association, *The London Approach* (2004), www.bba.org.uk/media/article/london-approach.

[251] V Finch, 'Corporate Rescue in a World of Debt' (2008) 8 *Journal of Business Law* 756.

[252] See 15.3.3.1.

[253] The exact moment differs depending on whether the company is wound up or put into administration, and on the process by which this occurs.

[254] See 3.2.

Insolvency Act 1986 ('section 123 insolvency'). This can be either through balance sheet insolvency or cash flow insolvency,[255] although the approach now taken is that these are two aspects of one single exercise, namely to determine whether a company is unable to pay its debts.[256] It is possible for a company to be balance sheet insolvent and not cash flow insolvent: in fact, many highly leveraged companies are in this position all the time. Such a company has borrowed more than its assets are worth, but because the repayment of the borrowing is long term, it is not cash flow insolvent;[257] if, however, a company is merely staving off insolvency by incurring more and more long-term debt, it may be seen as insolvent in a commercial sense.[258] It is much less likely that a company will be cash flow insolvent but not balance sheet insolvent, since a company with assets will usually be able to borrow funds to pay its debts. The protections for creditors described in this section are generally only activated once the company is in formal insolvency proceedings, and the actions are brought by an administrator or liquidator, but the protections arise (and liability is triggered) at an earlier point in time. One might think that the start of section 123 insolvency would be the moment when the general law started protecting creditors. However, the position is rather more complex. For example, the protection given to creditors from the reduction of the pool of assets or from uneven distribution starts on either balance sheet or cash flow insolvency.[259]

The triggering of potential liability under section 214 for wrongful trading, however, appears to commence once companies are both balance sheet insolvent and cash flow insolvent.[260] In many ways this latter approach seems more appropriate since, as discussed, many companies are balance sheet insolvent from day one.

The term 'insolvency' can therefore be used to mean both when a company is within formal insolvency proceedings and when it is section 123 insolvent. It is used in both senses in this section. However, in this section we also use the term 'insolvency' to include another situation that can arise even earlier in time. Section 3.2 dealt with solvent companies, and solvency was defined to exclude both section 123 insolvent companies and those which while technically still solvent are nevertheless on the verge of insolvency. This section therefore considers the position of shareholders and creditors in these latter two situations. Some of the issues discussed here, such as the common law duty on directors to consider the interests of creditors, arise when the company is on the verge of insolvency, although it is likely that in practice the concept of near insolvency will be interpreted to arise very late in the day, when the company is practically section 123 insolvent.[261] When reading this

---

[255] These terms are defined at 3.2.

[256] *Carman v Bucci* [2014] EWCA Civ 383 [29] per Lewison LJ.

[257] Liabilities that fall in the reasonably near future may be taken into account when determining cash flow insolvency; see *BNY Corporate Trustee Services Limited v Eurosail-UK 2007-3bl plc* [2013] UKSC 28. See 3.2.

[258] *Carman v Bucci* [2014] EWCA Civ 383 [31].

[259] This is because, in order for such transactions to be set aside, the company must be section 123 insolvent, or rendered such by the relevant transaction. See 3.3.2.1.1 and 3.3.2.2. Of course, the transaction will only be set aside if formal insolvency proceedings are commenced.

[260] The requirement of balance sheet insolvency arises from the statute (Insolvency Act 1986, s 214(6)) but the interpretation placed by the courts on the phrase 'no reasonable prospect that the company would avoid going into insolvent liquidation' in s 214(3) suggests that liability under the section will not be triggered unless the company is also cash flow insolvent. See eg *Re Purpoint Ltd* [1991] BCLC 491, discussed at 3.3.3.2.2. See also *Roberts (Liquidator of Onslow Ditchling Ltd) v Frohlich* [2011] EWHC (Ch) [110]–[113].

[261] See 3.3.3.1.

section, therefore, the reader should be aware that the precise meaning of the term 'insolvency' at any point may depend on the particular context.

3.3.1 Order of Payment Out on a Winding Up or Distribution by an Administrator

The following discussion briefly explains what happens when a company becomes insolvent. This is not a book on corporate insolvency, and so no attempt is made to give a comprehensive account of the law. However, in order to appreciate the issues that arise both in connection with how creditors of companies can protect themselves, and whether they should be protected in any way by the general law, it is necessary to understand how a company's assets are distributed on its insolvency. It is in the shadow of this order of distribution that creditors bargain for protection, both contractual and proprietary. If a corporate debtor is insolvent, an unsecured creditor will generally rank *pari passu* with other such creditors, so that if there are not sufficient assets left to pay all unsecured creditors in full, each creditor gets the same proportionate share of what is owed to it.[262] This means that an unsecured creditor obtains only a very small proportion of its claim. Creditors can avoid being in this position by obtaining proprietary protection, or, in certain cases, by being in a class of creditors which are raised higher up the distribution order by statute. The order of distribution is described in the following paragraphs, which can then act as a reference point for discussion of the principles and policy relating to proprietary creditor protection, which follows in chapter seven.

There are two formal insolvency procedures in English law: administration and winding up. There are also other possible responses to insolvency. One is administrative receivership or receivership, which is a process for the enforcement of security by a secured creditor,[263] and which is usually followed by a winding up. There are also statutory compromises, such as company voluntary arrangements and schemes of arrangement,[264] and contractual compromises with creditors.[265] A winding up, or liquidation, leads to the dissolution of the company, and involves the collection in of all the company's assets by the liquidator, which are then distributed to the company's creditors and shareholders. The order of distribution is discussed below.

In many insolvency situations, however, it is hoped that the company, or at least the business, can be rescued. The statutory or contractual compromises mentioned above can lead to rescue, but are basically private deals, and do not provide a mechanism for an outsider to manage the company in an attempt to save the business and increase the returns for unsecured creditors, nor do such mechanisms provide for a moratorium on enforcement

---

[262] Insolvency Act 1986, s 107 (winding up) and Insolvency Rules 1986, r 2.69. See further 3.3.2.2 and 6.3.4.6.2.

[263] 7.5.1.4. Administrative receivership is only available to floating charges falling within the exceptions set out in ss 72B–72GA Insolvency Act 1986: these include charges granted as part of a securitisation (capital market arrangement) and a project finance arrangement. Security is also, now, enforced in some administrations; see 6.5.3.

[264] See chapter 15, especially 15.3.3.

[265] V Finch, *Corporate Insolvency Law: Perspectives and Principles*, 2nd edn (Cambridge, Cambridge University Press, 2009) ch 7.

by creditors while a rescue is attempted.[266] For this reason, the procedure of administration was introduced in 1986, and modified in 2002. The philosophy of corporate rescue is statutorily made clear by the hierarchy of objectives which an administrator must pursue.[267] The first objective is to rescue the company as a going concern, the second is to achieve a better result for the creditors as a whole than if the company were wound up, and the third is to realise property in order to make a distribution to one or more secured or preferential creditors. The administrator must pursue the first objective unless it is not reasonably practicable, in which case he can move on to the second, and so on. In pursuing the second and third objectives, the administrator will seek to realise the assets of the company, so that they can be distributed to creditors. In order that the administrator can carry out these objectives, he is given extensive powers to do anything necessary or expedient for the management of the affairs, business or property of the company.[268] While the administration is in progress, there is a moratorium on legal process,[269] such as the enforcement of security and quasi-security, and any execution,[270] and the company cannot be wound up.[271] An administrator can distribute assets to creditors,[272] although he requires leave to distribute to unsecured non-preferential creditors. Such distribution follows the same order as a distribution in a liquidation.[273] An administration is often followed either by a company voluntary arrangement (CVA) or scheme of arrangement (if the company is to continue trading) or a liquidation (if it is not),[274] within which the distribution to unsecured creditors may take place.

The ranking for the treatment of claims against the company in a winding up and administration, and the distribution of assets in those procedures, is discussed next. Briefly, the holders of proprietary claims come first, though there are some statutory exceptions to the priority of a floating chargee.[275] The unsecured creditors share in any remaining assets *pari passu*, and if there are any further assets available, these are shared *pari passu* by the shareholders.

3.3.1.1 Holders of Proprietary Claims

On insolvency, a distribution can be made by the liquidator or administrator only out of the assets of the company. Thus, any assets which are owned outright by other persons do not fall within the insolvency process, and can be claimed by those persons. This applies to both legal ownership (for example, where property has already passed to a buyer under a contract of sale) and beneficial ownership (for example, where the company holds an asset on trust for a client). Certain financing structures involve either the reservation of an absolute interest in an asset (for example, hire purchase and finance lease transactions)[276]

---

[266] See Goode: Corporate Insolvency, 11-01.
[267] Insolvency Act 1986, Sch B1 para 3 (Sch B1 was added to Insolvency Act by Enterprise Act 2002).
[268] Ibid, para 59.
[269] Ibid, para 43.
[270] For a brief description of execution, see 7.1.1.
[271] Insolvency Act 1986, Sch B1 para 42.
[272] Ibid, para 65.
[273] Insolvency Rules 1986, Part 2 ch 10.
[274] See Goode: Corporate Insolvency, 11-85.
[275] Discussed at 3.3.1.2.
[276] See 2.3.4.4.2.

or the grant of an absolute interest (for example, receivables financing[277]).[278] In both cases, the creditor has a proprietary interest in the relevant assets and generally those assets do not fall within the insolvency process, although those with an interest based on retention of title will have to obtain the leave of an administrator or the court in order to enforce if the company is in administration.[279] Alternatively, such a creditor could wait until the assets are realised by the administrator and a distribution is made.

Similarly, if the company is being wound up, secured creditors[280] can remove the assets subject to their security interests from the pool and realise them to satisfy what is due to them, accounting to the liquidator for any surplus.[281] If the company is in administration, a secured creditor cannot enforce without the leave of the administrator or the court, but the administrator will realise the assets which are subject to the security interest and pay the secured creditor in priority to all other claims.[282] In certain circumstances prescribed by statute, assets subject to one type of security interest, the floating charge, are payable to unsecured creditors in priority to the holder of that floating charge, if the company does not have enough unencumbered assets to pay the unsecured creditors in full. The floating charge holder loses priority in three situations: first, to the expenses of the liquidation or administration, secondly, to preferential creditors and thirdly, to the prescribed part for unsecured creditors. These will be discussed in detail below. The nature of the floating charge, and the reasons behind its loss of priority on insolvency, are discussed in detail in chapter seven.[283]

What follows discusses the details of the legislation, and in particular the level of protection given to unsecured creditors on the insolvency of the corporate debtor. The priority of secured creditors (including those with an absolute interest) is not uncontroversial, and there is a detailed discussion of the policy arguments concerning this issue, particularly in relation to the protection of non-adjusting creditors, in chapter seven.[284]

3.3.1.2 Order of Priority

The order of priority of payments out of floating charge assets is, first, the expenses of the liquidation or administration,[285] second, the preferential creditors,[286] and third, the prescribed part for unsecured creditors.[287] What is left after these have been paid goes to the floating charge holder. If there is any surplus left of the floating charge assets after the floating chargee or chargees have been paid, this will go to the unsecured creditors

---

[277] See 2.3.4.1.

[278] For discussion of the distinction between the two, see 7.2.2.

[279] On the enforcement of such interests, see 7.5.2, discussing enforcement when the company is solvent, and 7.5.3, discussing the effect of administration.

[280] For detailed discussion of the different types of security see 7.3.

[281] Insolvency Rules 1986, rr 4.75(1)(g), 4.88. For detailed discussion of enforcement see 7.5.

[282] For full discussion, see 7.5.3.

[283] See 7.3.3.

[284] See 7.6.

[285] Insolvency Act 1986, s 176ZA(2)(b)(ii) provides that liquidation expenses have priority over preferential claims and s 176A(6) provides that preferential claims rank above the prescribed part. Insolvency Act Sch B1 para 99 does not expressly provide that administration expenses have priority over the preferential creditors and the prescribed part, but s 176ZA does, and the reasoning behind the latter section was to put the liquidator in the same position as an administrator (HL Deb, 3 November 2005).

[286] Insolvency Act 1986, s 175.

[287] Ibid, s 176A.

pari passu. If the company has assets which are not subject to a floating charge, or any other security interest, the position changes. The liquidation expenses are paid first out of such assets, then the preferential creditors,[288] and then the claims of the general unsecured creditors. If the expenses and the preferential creditors are satisfied out of these non-floating charge assets, then they are not paid out of floating charge assets. However, even in this situation, the prescribed part will still be deducted from the floating charge assets.[289] It should be noted that the statutory provisions described in the following paragraphs are disapplied in relation to security and title transfer interests in financial collateral.[290]

3.3.1.2.1 Liquidation or Administration Expenses

The expenses of liquidation include all costs incurred by the liquidator in the course of the liquidation and claims by creditors in relation to contracts entered into by the liquidator after liquidation.[291] The categories of expenses are set out in rule 4.128 of the Insolvency Rules 1986, which forms an exhaustive list.[292] It had been thought for many years that such expenses were payable out of floating charge assets in priority to preferential creditors and floating charge holders. The House of Lords in *Buchler v Talbot*[293] held that this interpretation was wrong, but the position was largely restored by section 1282 of the Companies Act 2006.[294] However, section 1282 did not entirely restore the position to that which applied after *Re Barleycorn Enterprises*.[295] One of the main objections of floating charge holders, who were usually banks, to the 'top-slicing' of expenses from the floating charge assets was that the costs of actions brought by the liquidator to set aside transactions entered into by the company in the run-up to insolvency often made up a large part of the liquidation expenses.[296] Not only were these actions costly (and often unsuccessful) but any recoveries were for the benefit of the unsecured creditors and not the floating charge holder. Further, such actions could be brought against the banks themselves, so that the floating charge holder could, at least in theory, be forced to foot the bill for a challenge to its own security.[297] Thus section 1282 was tempered by amendments to the Insolvency Rules 1986 to the effect that liquidators cannot incur litigation expenses in these kinds of proceedings without the consent of the floating charge holder.[298]

When the company is in administration, floating charge assets are even more vulnerable. The administrator, in the course of pursuing his statutory objectives, may well wish to keep the business of the company going. This can involve considerable expense, both in terms of meeting pre-existing obligations and in terms of incurring new obligations, and

---

[288] Ibid, s 176ZA (expenses of liquidation); Sch B1 para 99(3) (expenses of administration); s 175(2)(b) (preferential creditors in a liquidation, applied in relation to a distribution in an administration by Sch B1 para 65(2)).

[289] Ibid, s 176ZA.

[290] FCARs, regs 8 and 10. For further discussion of financial collateral see 6.3.4.

[291] Insolvency Rules 1986, r 12.2.

[292] *Re Toshoku Finance UK plc* [2002] 1 WLR 671 (HL) [14] and [38].

[293] [2004] UKHL 9.

[294] Introducing s 176ZA into Insolvency Act 1986.

[295] [1970] Ch 465.

[296] Discussed at 3.3.2 and 3.3.3.

[297] This was attempted in *Re MC Bacon Ltd* [1991] Ch 127, although the Court of Appeal avoided this unattractive result by interpreting the (then) Insolvency Rules in such a way that the litigation expenses did not fall within the 'expenses of the liquidation'.

[298] Insolvency Rules 1986, rr 4.218A–E. The proceedings covered are those brought under Insolvency Act 1986, ss 212, 213, 214, 238, 239, 244 and 423. For discussion of these, see 3.3.2 and 3.3.3.

the Insolvency Act 1986 provides that this expense is met out of floating charge assets in priority to the floating chargee. In addition to the 'top-slicing' of the administrator's expenses from the floating charge assets, the administrator is entitled to dispose of floating charge assets without the leave of the court.[299] Sometimes such a disposition will result in proceeds, for example where stock in trade is sold, in which case the floating chargee obtains the same priority in relation to such proceeds as it had in relation to the original asset.[300] More usually the asset will be used to meet expenses resulting from existing contracts (such as employment contracts), in which case there are no immediate proceeds and the assets subject to the floating charge diminish. Similarly, payments that the administrator makes under new contracts he enters into after his appointment fall within his expenses, which will be paid out of floating charge assets in priority to the claims of the floating chargee.[301] If the administrator does enable the company to trade out of its difficulties, of course, the floating chargee will be better off as there may be sufficient assets to pay all creditors, but if the rescue attempt does not succeed the floating chargee loses out considerably.[302]

3.3.1.2.2 Preferential Creditors

Prior to the Enterprise Act 2002, preferential debts comprised two main groups, namely various taxes collected by the debtor on behalf of the Crown, including some PAYE deductions, unpaid VAT, unpaid car tax, unpaid social security contributions and various other duties, and certain debts related to the insolvent's employees. The first of these categories (known as 'Crown preference') has now had its preferential status removed.[303]

The other preferential class, namely the insolvent's employees, or those subrogated to them, has been retained.[304]

3.3.1.2.3 The Prescribed Part

The Enterprise Act 2002 recognised the need for further protection for unsecured creditors by providing that a proportion of the assets subject to the floating charge should be made available for the claims of unsecured creditors.[305] The prescribed part is calculated on the

---

[299] Insolvency Act 1986, Sch B1 para 70. This paragraph does not apply to a charge falling within the FCARs.

[300] Ibid, para 70(2).

[301] Ibid, para 99(4).

[302] For further discussion see 7.3.3.3.4.

[303] Enterprise Act 2002, s 251. This followed an international trend, although Crown preference in some form is still retained in a number of countries. See B Morgan, 'Should the Sovereign be Paid First? A Comparative International Analysis of the Priority for Tax Claims in Bankruptcy' (2000) 74 *American Bankruptcy Law Journal* 461, 479–80. See 7.6.2.3.

[304] The policy reasoning behind these legislative moves can be questioned; see R Goode, 'The Death of Insolvency Law' (1980) 1 *Company Lawyer* 123, 129; R Mokal, 'Priority as Pathology: The Pari Passu Myth' [2001] *Cambridge Law Journal* 581; A Keay and P Walton, 'The Preferential Debts Regime in Liquidation Law: In the Public Interest?' [1999] *Company Financial and Insolvency Law Review* 84. See 7.6.2.3.

[305] Insolvency Act 1986, s 176A. For details of the prescribed proportion see Insolvency Act 1986 (Prescribed Part) Order 2003 (SI 2003/2097), art 3. At present, the proportion is 50% where the floating charge assets are less then £10,000 (unless the costs of distribution are disproportionate to the benefits). If the assets exceed that amount, the proportion is 50% of the first £10,000 and 20% of the rest, with a ceiling of £600,000. The amount of the prescribed part was said to relate to the amount of floating charge assets which would have fallen within Crown preference, so that the net effect on floating charge holders was zero; see R Stevens, 'Security after the Enterprise Act' in J Getzler and J Payne (eds), *Company Charges: Spectrum and Beyond* (Oxford, Oxford University Press, 2006) 162. The Enterprise Act also abolishes administrative receivership which was regarded as unfair to the unsecured creditors: White Paper, para 2.2.

amount of floating charge assets after deduction of both the liquidation or administration expenses and the claims of the preferential creditors.[306] The prescribed part therefore means that the unsecured creditors will get something, even if the entire assets of the company fall within the floating charge. If the floating charge holder is not fully paid out of the remaining floating charge assets, it cannot prove for the balance with the other unsecured creditors out of the prescribed part.[307] This is because the prescribed part is to protect the unsecured creditors at the expense of the floating charge holder.[308]

3.3.1.2.4 General Unsecured Creditors

As mentioned above, if there are sufficient assets not subject to a security interest, the liquidator's or administrator's expenses are paid first out of these, then the preferential creditors, then the other unsecured creditors share in the rest *pari passu*. The effect of the statutory prescribed part provisions is that unsecured creditors will always get something when a company is wound up (unless there are no or de minimis floating charge assets), but it is likely in most cases that they will still only recover a small proportion of what is owed to them. If the unsecured creditors with provable debts[309] are paid in full, which is very unlikely, statutory interest (on provable debts)[310] and non-provable debts[311] then rank above the shareholders.[312]

3.3.1.2.5 The Shareholders

It is clear that shareholders come last on insolvency. In general, they will only be entitled to any claim once all of the creditors' claims against the company have been satisfied, at which point shareholders will be repaid the capital they have contributed to the company,[313] and any remainder (ie the residual value of the company) will be distributed to those entitled to share in the surplus.[314]

---

[306] Insolvency Act 1986, ss 176A and 176ZA.

[307] *Re Airbase (UK) Ltd: Thorniley v Revenue and Customs Commissioners* [2008] EWHC 124 (Ch).

[308] Goode: Credit and Security, 5-70.

[309] Defined in Insolvency Rules 1986, r 12.3.

[310] Insolvency Act 1986, s 189 (liquidation) and Insolvency Rules 1986, r 2.88 (administration).

[311] These are legally enforceable claims which do not fall within the definition of 'provable debts'. See *Re Nortel GmbH* [2013] UKSC 52 and *Re Lehman Bros International (Europe) (in administration) (No 4)* [2014] EWHC 704 (Ch).

[312] *Re Nortel GmbH* [2013] UKSC 52 [39].

[313] There is a presumption that all shares rank equally with regard to the return of capital (*Welton v Saffery* [1897] AC 299, 309 per Lord Watson). Any priority intended to be attached to preference shares regarding the return of capital must be expressly stated. The fact that preference shares have priority as to dividends does not mean that the shares are presumed to have priority as to a return of capital (*Birch v Cropper* (1889) LR 14 App Cas 525). The sum repaid may be the par value of the shares, or the articles may provide for a higher sum.

[314] The default rule is that the surplus left after the paid-up capital has been repaid is distributable equally amongst the ordinary shareholders in proportion to the nominal value of their shares: *Birch v Cropper* (1889) LR 14 App Cas 525, 543 per Lord Macnaghten. As regards the right to share in the surplus capital of the company, where a share carries a preferential right to capital on insolvency, this displaces the principle of equality, and it is presumed that the express preferential right to capital is the sum total of the entitlement: *Scottish Insurance Corporation Ltd v Wilsons & Clyde Coal Co Ltd* [1949] AC 462. It is for the preference shareholders to demonstrate that a provision in the company's constitution regarding the terms of issue of the shares confers an entitlement to share in any surplus assets. It is rare to see such a provision.

There are, however, a number of claims which shareholders can bring against a company in relation to which it could be argued that the shareholders should be treated as being akin to creditors, and that their claims should, accordingly, rank higher on the order of payment out on a winding up. Three different kinds of claims can be identified. First, claims can be brought in relation to dividend payments, or other payments arising out of the statutory contract (ie the articles of association of the company).[315] Second, there are claims arising outside the statutory contract, such as a claim against the company brought by the shareholder for misrepresentations or breaches of corporate disclosure regulations, such as sections 90 and 90A FSMA, discussed in chapters ten and eleven respectively.[316] Third, there are claims relating to loans made to the company by shareholders.

3.3.1.2.5(a) Sums Due to Shareholders Arising from the Statutory Contract

As regards sums due to the shareholders in their capacity as shareholders, for example by way of declared but unpaid dividends, it is clear that these sums are not deemed to be a debt of the company for this purpose; in other words, these claims do not rank alongside the claims of the unsecured creditors, but are only due to be paid after the unsecured creditors are paid in full, to the extent that any assets remain available for distribution at this time.[317] The consequence of this provision is that if the company is insolvent, these debts to the members will not be repaid, because an insolvent company is, by definition, unable to satisfy all of its creditors' claims with its assets.

This is a clear example of the way in which Parliament seeks to ensure that on insolvency the shareholders' claims qua shareholder will always rank behind the claims of the company's creditors.[318] The courts are also keen to ensure that the statutory order of payment out is not undermined.[319] There are numerous examples of this in insolvency cases. An example of the principle at work in a company law case is the House of Lords' decision in *Johnson v Gore Wood & Co*.[320] In this case their Lordships considered whether a shareholder should be able to recover for reflective loss, ie loss which is merely a reflection of the loss suffered by the company and which will be fully compensated if the company sues successfully to recover that loss. If the shareholder is allowed to recover, then either there will be double recovery at the expense of the defendant, or the shareholder will recover at the expense of the company. The problem can be solved either by disallowing the corporate claim and allowing the shareholders to sue individually, or by disallowing the individual claims. The House of Lords preferred the latter approach. As Lord Millett explained, disallowing the corporate claim would prejudice the company's creditors if the company becomes insolvent as a result of the wrongdoing, since on insolvency it is the creditors, and not the shareholders, who primarily benefit from the corporate action. To allow a corporate asset, namely the

---

[315] Companies Act 2006, s 33, discussed at 3.2.1.3.2(b).

[316] See 10.6.2 and 11.4.1.2. The fact that shareholders are entitled to bring these claims is made clear in Companies Act 2006, s 655.

[317] Insolvency Act 1986, s 74(2)(f).

[318] It is also relevant here that the shareholders are obliged to pay any unpaid subscription on insolvency, although most shares today are fully paid up so this issue rarely arises in practice.

[319] See eg *Re Nortel GmbH* [2013] UKSC 52. This can also be seen in relation to creditors. It is one of the main justifications for the anti-deprivation principle (see 3.3.2.1.2), and is demonstrated by the rule that parties cannot contract out of insolvency set-off (see 6.3.4.6.2) although limited 'contracting out' of the order of distribution is allowed by contractual subordination (see 6.4.4.1.3).

[320] [2002] 2 AC 1.

right to sue the wrongdoers, to be given to the shareholders individually at this point would subvert the normal ordering of payments to creditors and shareholders on insolvency.

3.3.1.2.5(b) Sums Due to Shareholders Arise Outside the Statutory Contract

As regards claims arising outside the statutory contract, the decision of the House of Lords in *Soden v British & Commonwealth Holdings plc*[321] is authority for the view that in relation to these claims the shareholders rank *pari passu* with the unsecured creditors.[322] The House of Lords therefore determined that the relevant principle is not that 'members come last' but rather that the 'rights of members as members come last'. The rationale behind section 74(2)(f) of the Insolvency Act 1986 is to ensure that the rights of members as such do not compete with the rights of the general body of creditors. A member having a cause of action independent of the statutory contract is, however, claiming as a creditor and should, therefore, be in no worse position than any other creditor.

The question of whether a shareholder bringing such a claim should rank *pari passu* with the unsecured creditors highlights a collision between securities law, in particular the investor protection provided by statutory provisions such as sections 90 and 90A FSMA,[323] and insolvency law. Insolvency law is concerned predominantly with creditor protection. Subordinating the claims of shareholders creates greater certainty and, more importantly, increases the pool of capital available to creditors, particularly the unsecured creditors. However, subordinating these claims by equity investors fails to recognise that while shareholders should accept the ordinary business risk of insolvency, they do not assume the risk of corporate fraud, or violations of securities legislation. Such subordination would, arguably, punish the innocent shareholders for the misconduct of corporate management, and would undermine the goal of investor protection that provisions such as sections 90 and 90A FSMA are intended to advance. As a result, these claims are not subordinated in the UK; other jurisdictions, most notably the US, take a different approach to this issue.[324]

3.3.1.2.5(c) Shareholder Loans

In relation to loans made by shareholders, while some legal systems subordinate shareholder loans to the claims of other creditors in some circumstances, the UK provides no specific regulation of this issue.[325] Where a shareholder lends money on an unsecured basis

---

[321] [1998] AC 298.

[322] This approach finds support in a decision of the European Court of Justice, Case C-174/12 *Alfred Hirmann v Immofinanz AG*, 19 December 2013, which considered the relationship between creditor and shareholder protection in the context of investor compensation claims for breach of a company's information duties towards its shareholders (ie claims such as ss 90 and 90A FSMA). The ECJ confirmed that the Prospectus, Transparency and Market Abuse Directives do not oppose a national law which states that a company may be held liable for incorrect information and the breach of capital market law in a prospectus. Further, the ECJ stated that these compensation payments cannot be regarded as capital distributions. As a result, compensation payments to shareholders by companies under provisions such as ss 90 and 90A FSMA should therefore not be regarded as a payment in relation to the membership of the company, but rather as a third-party claim.

[323] For discussion see 10.6.2 and 11.4.1.2.

[324] See § 510(b) of the US Bankruptcy Code; *Re Telegroup Inc*, 281 F 3d 133 (3rd Cir, 2002). For discussion see J Sarra, 'From Subordination to Parity: An International Comparison of Equity Securities Claims in Insolvency Proceedings' (2007) 16 *International Insolvency Review* 181.

[325] For example, in Germany, all shareholder loans are subordinated, subject to only limited exceptions: see the German Insolvency Statute, Insolvenzordnung (InsO) § 39(1) n 5, as amended. For discussion see DA Verse, 'Shareholder Loans in Corporate Insolvency: A New Approach to an Old Problem' [2008] *German Law Journal* 1109.

to the company, he is prima facie entitled to recover that debt *pari passu* with the other unsecured creditors. Where the money is lent secured, then the shareholder's claim qua creditor will rank ahead of the claims of the unsecured creditors. The decision in *Salomon v Salomon & Co Ltd*[326] is a good example of this principle in operation.

3.3.2 Preservation of the Assets for Creditors on and During the Run-up to Insolvency

As discussed earlier, while the company is solvent the creditors are usually expected to protect themselves against the prospective losses on insolvency by taking proprietary interests or relying on insolvency set-off. It is thus usually the unsecured creditors who suffer on insolvency, as there will almost always be insufficient assets available to pay them in full, and, in fact, unsecured creditors are on average only paid a small fraction of what is owed to them.[327]

There are, however, various statutory provisions designed to prevent some kinds of reduction in the assets available to unsecured creditors both in the period running up to insolvency and after insolvency proceedings have commenced. There are also provisions to prevent some unsecured creditors getting paid before or on insolvency in a way considered unfair to other creditors, since if some creditors get paid in full, there is less to distribute *pari passu* to the other creditors. To some extent these two types of provisions overlap, although conceptually they are distinct. One type prevents reduction of the asset pool (the 'cake') while the other type prevents uneven distribution of the 'cake'. These statutory provisions are supplemented by the common law rule known as the anti-deprivation principle (which goes to the prevention of the reduction of the 'cake' at the time insolvency proceedings commence) as well as the *pari passu* principle,[328] which goes to prevention of uneven distribution of the 'cake' by a liquidator or administrator. Although these are distinct principles, there is potential for overlap in their application to particular situations.[329]

In addition, there are a number of provisions designed to increase the money available to creditors on insolvency. Some of these are statutory, for example sections 213 and 214 of the Insolvency Act 1986,[330] which allow the liquidator or administrator to pursue claims for wrongful trading or fraudulent trading against the directors and others.[331] Any successful recoveries under these sections flow to the unsecured creditors.[332] Other provisions have

---

[326] [1897] AC 22.

[327] Mokal: Insolvency Law, 130; S Frisby, *Interim Report to the Insolvency Service on Returns to Creditors from Pre- and Post-Enterprise Act Insolvency Procedures* (July 2007), 33–34.

[328] This is rooted in the statutory provisions governing distribution of assets on insolvency: Insolvency Act 1986, s 107 (voluntary liquidation); Insolvency Rules 1986, r 4.181 (compulsory liquidation), r 2.69 (administration, but only when where an administrator makes, or proposes to make, a distribution to unsecured creditors, or to a class of unsecured creditors).

[329] *Revenue and Customs Commissioners v Football League Ltd* [2012] EWHC 1372 (Ch) [104].

[330] See now also ss 246ZA and 246ZB Insolvency Act 1986.

[331] These are discussed at 3.3.3.1. In addition, s 15 Company Directors Disqualification Act 1986 allows for the possibility that a disqualified director might be made liable for the debts of the company.

[332] This has been the general understanding of these provisions—see eg *Re Oasis Merchandising Services Ltd* [1997] BCC 282. Section 119 Small Business Enterprise and Employment Act 2015 provides that recoveries from actions brought pursuant to the statutory provisions discussed in this and the previous paragraph do not form part of the net assets of the company available to a floating charge holder.

been developed by the common law, such as the general fiduciary duty owed by directors which becomes creditor-regarding once the company is insolvent, or close to insolvency.[333] Under this common law duty, in contrast to the statutory claims, the claim, and therefore any recoveries, are regarded as assets of the company.

3.3.2.1 Preventing Reduction of the Asset Pool

3.3.2.1.1 Statutory Provisions

A reduction of the assets of the company in the period running up to insolvency is addressed by section 238 of the Insolvency Act 1986. Where a company has entered into a transaction at an undervalue within two years of the onset of insolvency this provision enables a liquidator or administrator to apply to the court for relief, restoring the position to what it would have been had the company not entered into the transaction.[334] The company must have been insolvent within the meaning of section 123,[335] or have become so as a result of the transaction.[336] A transaction at an undervalue could either be a gift (or agreement to provide goods or services for no consideration), or a disposition for consideration worth less than the asset disposed of. The effect of the transaction is to diminish the assets available for creditors generally, to the benefit of one particular person. An order made under this statutory provision has the effect of restoring the value of those assets, usually at the expense of the person benefited. The scope of the order the court can make on an application under section 238 is very wide.[337] Any recovery pursuant to such an order is usually for the benefit of unsecured creditors;[338] however, it is possible to argue that if assets subject to a fixed charge have been disposed of, the recovery is for the benefit of the charge holder.[339]

Where it can be shown that a gift or a transaction at an undervalue was entered into by the company with the purpose of putting assets beyond the reach of a creditor (not an easy thing to prove), the liquidator or administrator (or the victim)[340] can apply to the court under section 423 of the Insolvency Act 1986 for an order restoring the position. The possible scope of the order is, as with an order made on an application under section 238, very wide.[341] Unlike section 238, there is no limit on the time before the onset of insolvency within which the transaction must be made.

Reduction in the assets in the period after the onset of insolvency[342] is dealt with by section 127 of the Insolvency Act 1986.[343] This section provides that any disposition of the

---

[333] See eg *West Mercia Safetywear Ltd v Dodd* [1998] BCLC 250, discussed further at 3.3.3.1.

[334] For full discussion, see Goode: Corporate Insolvency, 13-12–13-70; R Parry, J Ayliffe and S Shivji, *Transaction Avoidance in Insolvencies*, 2nd edn (Oxford, Oxford University Press, 2011) ch 4.

[335] See 3.3.

[336] Insolvency Act 1986, s 240(2). There is a rebuttable presumption that this requirement is fulfilled if the transaction is entered into with a person connected with the company.

[337] See Insolvency Act 1986, s 241.

[338] *Re Yagerphone* [1935] Ch 392; *Re MC Bacon (No 2)* [1990] BCC 430. See also s 119 Small Business, Enterprise and Employment Act 2015 (n 333).

[339] See J Armour and A Walters, 'The Proceeds of Office-Holder Actions under the Insolvency Act: Charged Assets or Free Estate?' [2006] *Lloyd's Maritime and Commercial Law Quarterly* 27, 44. This would still be a possible argument despite s 119 if the fixed charge holder was not also the holder of a floating charge.

[340] Leave of the court is required for a victim to sue; see s 424(1)(a).

[341] Insolvency Act 1986, s 425.

[342] See 3.3.

[343] For full discussion see Goode: Corporate Insolvency, 11-127–11-135; R Parry, J Ayliffe and S Shivji, *Transaction Avoidance in Insolvencies*, 2nd edn (Oxford, Oxford University Press, 2011) ch 3.

company's property after that date is void unless the court orders otherwise. Not surprisingly, the section only applies to a winding up[344] and not to anything done by an administrator (who has wide powers to carry on the company's business as mentioned earlier). If a liquidator, however, wishes to carry on the business (to a limited extent) by making dispositions, he needs to obtain the leave of the court. The litmus test for giving leave will be whether the disposition is for the benefit of creditors generally: this can either be because carrying on business is considered to be for their benefit, or because a particular disposition does not diminish the asset pool, for example if it is for full value.[345] Section 127 is disapplied in relation to dispositions of financial collateral.[346]

3.3.2.1.2 The Anti-Deprivation Principle

The common law principle known as the anti-deprivation principle renders a contractual provision void to the extent that it purports to remove assets from the debtor on insolvency, with the effect that they are not available for distribution to creditors.[347] The contract can have been entered into at any point before the onset of insolvency: there is no time limit as under the statutory sections. For the principle to be engaged, however, the contract must provide for the deprivation to take place on or after the onset of insolvency proceedings.[348] It is conceptually distinct from the mandatory statutory *pari passu* principle[349] which renders void any provision, contractual or otherwise, that has the effect of distributing assets belonging to the insolvent estate on a basis which is not *pari passu*.[350] Since the purpose of the anti-deprivation principle is to preserve the assets of the debtor, it applies equally to a company going into liquidation or administration.[351] The scope of the anti-deprivation principle is not straightforward, as the courts have tried to maintain a balance between freedom of contract (usually between the company and its counterparty) and protecting the interests of the creditors. The latter is a policy task, and is normally done by legislation (as, for example, in relation to the provisions dealing with dispositions before and after insolvency described above) and so the courts have been loath to extend the common law principle in recent years. In *Belmont Park Investments Pty Ltd v BNY Trustee Services Ltd*[352] the Supreme Court confirmed the existence of the principle but also the existence of several limitations on its scope.[353]

---

[344] And, in fact, only to a compulsory winding up by the court, and not to a voluntary winding up.

[345] See guidelines for the exercise of the court's discretion in giving leave set out in *Denney v John Hudson & Co* [1992] BCLC 901, 904 per Fox LJ.

[346] FCARs, reg 10.

[347] *Revenue Customs and Commissioners v Football League Ltd* [2012] EWHC 1372 (Ch) [100].

[348] See below.

[349] See n 329.

[350] *Revenue Customs and Commissioners v Football League Ltd* [2012] EWHC 1372 (Ch) [64]. The potential overlap between the two principles is considered below.

[351] Ibid, [100]. For the contrasting position vis-a-vis the *pari passu* principle, see 3.3.2.2.

[352] *Belmont Park Investments Pty Ltd v BNY Trustee Services Ltd* [2011] UKSC 38. See also G Moss, 'Should British Eagle be Extinct?' (2011) 24 *Insolvency Intelligence* 49; T Cleary, 'Lehman Brothers and the Anti-Deprivation Principle: Current Uncertainties and Proposals for Reform' (2011) 6 *Capital Markets Law Journal* 411; R Calnan, 'Anti-Deprivation: A Missed Opportunity' [2011] *Journal of International Banking and Financial Law* 531; S Worthington, 'Good Faith, Flawed Assets and the Emasculation of the UK Anti-Deprivation Rule' (2012) 75 *Modern Law Review* 112; R Goode, 'Flip Clauses: The End of the Affair?' (2012) 128 *Law Quarterly Review* 171.

[353] See also *Revenue Customs and Commissioners v Football League Ltd* [2012] EWHC 137; *Lomas v JFB Firth Rixson Inc and Others* [2012] EWCA Civ 419.

First, the anti-deprivation principle is a general rule of public policy which prevents fraud on the insolvency statutes.[354] As such, it requires deliberate intention to evade insolvency laws and does not apply to commercial transactions entered into in good faith.[355] Second, the assets must actually be diminished, so if the provision means that an asset is disposed of at full value,[356] or actually has no value, the provision is not unenforceable.[357] Third, the deprivation must be insolvency triggered so the principle does not apply to a diminution that takes place for reasons other than insolvency.[358] Whilst the Supreme Court did not consider it necessary to decide whether a deprivation triggered by factual insolvency rather than formal insolvency proceedings would attract the principle, to extend the principle in such a way would lead to great uncertainty, as explained by Lord Neuberger in the Court of Appeal in *Perpetual Trustee Co Ltd v BNY Corporate Trustee Services Ltd*.[359] If a company enters insolvency proceedings, this is a known fact and the date of commencement of insolvency is simple to determine. If a diminution before that time were included, issues might arise as to whether the company is insolvent at the time of the diminution, or whether the diminution should be set aside even if the company recovered. In any event section 238 is designed to deal with such diminutions.[360]

Fourth, there has long been a distinction between an asset which is inherently limited so that insolvency marks the end of the duration of the interest (a 'flawed asset') and an absolute interest granted outright then forfeited on insolvency, with some older cases indicating that the former is permitted while the latter is not.[361] The distinction is extremely problematic, and is susceptible to manipulation by clever drafting,[362] but Lord Collins in *Belmont* said that it 'would go far beyond the judicial function to hold that the distinction is indefensible'.[363] Despite this, his view appeared to be that both types of assets could potentially fall foul of the anti-deprivation principle: flawed assets are not automatically valid.[364]

---

[354] Ibid, [121].

[355] Ibid, [104]. Where an insolvent company paid for a right of indemnity, a provision for termination of that right on the company's liquidation was void as contrary to the anti-deprivation principle as it served no commercial purpose other than avoiding the insolvency legislation: *Folgate London Market Ltd v Chaucer Insurance plc* [2011] EWCA Civ 328. For criticism of this limitation see S Worthington, 'Good Faith, Flawed Assets and the Emasculation of the UK Anti-Deprivation Rule' (2012) 75 *Modern Law Review* 112.

[356] *Borland's Trustee v Steel Bros & Co Ltd* [1901] 1 Ch 279.

[357] *Money Markets International, Stockbrokers Ltd v London Stock Exchange* [2002] 1 WLR 1150 [110].

[358] *Belmont Park Investments Pty Ltd v BNY Trustee Services Ltd* [2011] UKSC 38 [80].

[359] [2009] EWCA Civ 1160 [72]. However, where a deprivation is triggered by a non-insolvency event that occurs after the commencement of insolvency proceedings, the rule should apply: *Revenue Customs and Commissioners v Football League Ltd* [2012] EWHC 137 [156] per David Richards J.

[360] It is important to maintain a clear separation between the realm of application of the statutory avoidance actions and the anti-deprivation principle, not least because s 238 creates a cause of action, subject to defences, to claw back an asset whilst the apparently more creditor friendly common law anti-deprivation principle operates to strike down a contractual right in its entirety. Having said this, an uncommercial transaction entered into within the relevant time period before the onset of insolvency, which had the effect of depriving the debtor of assets on the onset of insolvency, might fall within s 238 so that a liquidator or administrator could apply for relief, but could also fall foul of the anti-deprivation principle.

[361] See the summary in *Whitmore v Mason* (1861) 2 J & H 204, 209–10.

[362] *In re King's Trust* (1892) 29 LR Ir 401, 410; R Goode, 'Perpetual Trustee and Flip Clauses in Swap Transactions' (2011) 127 *Law Quarterly Review* 1.

[363] *Belmont Park Investments Pty Ltd v BNY Trustee Services Ltd* [2011] UKSC 38 [88] and [163].

[364] Ibid, [88], [105].

The approach is rather 'to consider each transaction on its merits to see whether the shift in interests complained of could be justified as a genuine and justifiable commercial response to the consequences of insolvency'.[365] This approach, while a laudable compromise between the principle of freedom of contract and the need to protect creditors (the balance referred to earlier), creates at least two uncertainties. The first is that where an asset is genuinely 'flawed' it is difficult to see what deprivation the debtor has suffered, since it never had any property in the first place of which it was deprived.[366] The second is that it is difficult to draw the line between a 'genuine and justifiable response' and an illegitimate one. In an analysis favoured by Lord Mance, some clarity can be added by drawing a distinction between an executed contract, where the asset of the insolvent company is the 'quid pro quo' for a performance that has already been completed, and a contract that is wholly or partially executory, where the asset is the 'quid pro quo' for the continuing performance of the contract.[367] In the latter case, there is nothing objectionable about a provision permitting a party to terminate if the other becomes insolvent.[368] This approach has the merit of explaining why the archetypal 'limited interest' case, such as where a lease terminates on insolvency, does not offend the principle.

Ultimately, these limitations confirm that the principle is of limited application and its operation can, usually, be avoided through careful drafting. However, it is difficult to think of more satisfactory boundaries to the principle. Even if it were given a statutory basis, it would still be possible (and perhaps even easier) to draft around its application.[369] Further, the most egregious cases of fraud on the insolvency statutes, involving an intent to put assets out of the reach of creditors, are already covered under section 423. This section potentially covers any transaction entered into by the company, however long before the onset of insolvency: the transaction would have to be at an undervalue to fall within the section, but given that a transaction must be 'uncommercial' in order to fall within the anti-deprivation principle, it is likely that this condition would also be fulfilled. Indeed, it is possible to argue that if section 423 was used to its full extent to catch transactions falling within it, the anti-deprivation principle would not need to be engaged.[370] Reliance on section 423, however, has to be by an application by a liquidator, administrator or victim, whereas the anti-deprivation principle is usually relied upon when the counterparty to a pre-existing transaction relies upon the terms of the contract vis-a-vis the company.

---

[365] *Lomas v JFB Firth Rixson Inc and Others* [2012] EWCA Civ 419 [86].

[366] See the reasoning in *Belmont Park Investments Pty Ltd v BNY Trustee Services Ltd* [2011] UKSC 38 [168]. The point is also illustrated by the actual decision in *Revenue Customs and Commissioners v Football League Ltd* [2012] EWHC 137, since David Richards J held that the drafting of the agreements incorporating the football creditors rule were such that there were no assets of which the defaulting club was deprived (see [151]).

[367] Ibid, [175]–[179], approving the approach taken by Briggs J in *Lomas v JFB Firth Rixson* [2010] EWHC 3372 (Ch), [2011] 2 BCLC 120 [108]–[110].

[368] Ibid, [177].

[369] For an attempt to formulate a statutory provision reflecting the anti-deprivation principle, see T Cleary, 'Lehman Brothers and the Anti-Deprivation Principle: Current Uncertainties and Proposals for Reform' (2011) 6 *Capital Markets Law Journal* 411. See also N Kulkarni, 'A Statutory Basis for the Anti-Deprivation Rule?' (2014) 23 *International Insolvency Review* 73.

[370] Cf *Belmont Park Investments Pty Ltd v BNY Trustee Services Ltd* [2011] UKSC 38 [150], where Lord Mance said that the statutory provisions cover different ground to the anti-deprivation principle.

3.3.2.2 *Preventing Uneven Distribution of the Assets*

A solvent company is free to pay its creditors in whatever order it chooses, and none of its creditors are obliged to take account of the interests of any other of its creditors: such a creditor can pursue its own interests in seeking to be paid before anyone else.[371] This changes in the run-up to and after the onset of insolvency. One of the reasons for having a collective insolvency procedure is to avoid a race to be paid first. Such a procedure will result in the maximum benefit for all creditors, by avoiding duplication of costs, wasteful splitting up of assets and a disorderly process.[372] To gain these benefits it is necessary for all creditors without proprietary claims to be treated equally in terms of the distribution of assets so that each takes a proportionate reduction in his claim if the assets are not enough to pay everyone in full. In other words, the creditors must take *pari passu*.

Once liquidation proceedings have commenced, and if and when an administrator gives notice of distribution,[373] this *pari passu* principle is enforced strictly. It is itself prescribed by statute,[374] and there are, of course, exceptions to it created by statute.[375] Some of these are described above,[376] and another, insolvency set-off, is discussed in chapter six.[377] Contractual provisions which purport to create a different distribution from the statutory scheme are unenforceable;[378] this is the case even where the provisions are commercially justifiable.[379] As with the anti-deprivation principle, the exact boundaries of this principle are hard to determine, since the same tension between freedom of contract (between two parties) and the policy of protection of the general body of creditors arises. Two areas of difficulty are set-off and subordination agreements, and these are discussed in chapter six below.[380]

In the period before the onset of insolvency, the policy of English law is to attempt to prevent a creditor obtaining an 'unfair' advantage over other creditors. Since, in insolvency proceedings, most unsecured creditors only obtain a small share of what is due to them, any creditor who is paid in full clearly obtains an advantage. Not every creditor who is paid in full in that period, however, is obliged to return the payment: only payments made to a

---

[371] D Prentice, 'Some Observations on the Law Relating to Preferences' in R Cranson (ed), *Making Commercial Law* (Oxford, Clarendon Press, 1997) 439.

[372] Mokal: Insolvency Law, ch 4; see also V Finch, 'Is Pari Passu Passé?' (2000) 5 *Insolvency Lawyer* 194, T Jackson, *The Logic and Limits of Bankruptcy Law* (Cambridge, MA, Harvard University Press, 1986, reprinted in 2002) ch 2 and Goode: Corporate Insolvency, 2-15.

[373] Insolvency Rules 1986, r 2.95. Since the purpose of the *pari passu* principle is to support the principle that a distribution to creditors must be *pari passu*, it operates only if the purpose of the insolvency proceedings is to effect a distribution: *Revenue Customs and Commissioners v Football League Ltd* [2012] EWHC 137 [89].

[374] See n 329.

[375] It is sometimes said that the institution of security is an exception to the *pari passu* principle, but this is not the case. If an asset is not part of the company's property, it does not, even prima facie, fall within the statutory provisions for *pari passu* distribution; it must be returned to the person who has the proprietary interest in that asset.

[376] 3.3.1.2.

[377] 6.3.4.6.

[378] *British Eagle International Airways Ltd v Cie National Air France* [1975] 1 WLR 758; *Revenue Customs and Commissioners v Football League Ltd* [2012] EWHC 137 [4].

[379] *Belmont Park Investments Pty Ltd v BNY Trustee Services Ltd* [2011] UKSC 38 [75].

[380] See 6.3.4.6.2 and 5.4.4.1.

creditor whom the company intends to prefer are covered. Section 239 of the Insolvency Act 1986[381] enables a liquidator or administrator to apply to a court for a remedial order[382] if a company has given a creditor a preference within a certain period of time before the onset of insolvency.[383] This only applies if the company is section 123 insolvent[384] at the time the preference is given, or becomes section 123 insolvent as a result of the preference.[385] A preference is where a creditor is put in a better position than he would be in if the company went into liquidation,[386] and in order to trigger the section, the company, in giving the preference, must have been influenced by a desire to put that creditor in that better position.[387]

It is not always apparent why the motivation of the company in making the payment is the best test of whether the advantage obtained by the creditor is 'unfair':[388] one might have thought that the intention of the creditor would be more relevant, or that intention was not relevant at all, in that it is the mere receipt of payment which is unfair.[389] Further, if a creditor puts pressure on the company to pay, the resulting payment is not a preference under section 239: it might be thought that to reward the strongest creditor is not necessarily the best way to redress unfairness, nor does it further the aim of collective proceedings (to prevent a race to be paid). The shortcomings of the English law on preferences are the subject of much academic discussion.[390]

3.3.2.3 Potential Overlap Between the Prevention of Reduction of the Asset Pool and the Prevention of Uneven Distribution of Assets

The diminution of the asset pool which the rules discussed in 3.3.2.1 are designed to prevent, nearly always benefits another person. Sometimes that other person is not a creditor of the company (for example, where assets are hived off to another company in the same group in the run-up to insolvency). In other cases the beneficiary will be a creditor of the company. This gives rise to a potential overlap between the rules discussed in 3.3.2.1 and those discussed in 3.3.2.2. Merely paying a creditor his pre-existing debt before the onset of insolvency will not diminish the asset pool, as the extinguishing of the debt cancels out the payment so that the net value of the assets is not affected. Therefore, a transaction will not normally fall within both section 238 and section 239: this will only happen if a person receives a payment partly qua creditor and partly in excess of what he is owed.[391]

---

[381] For a full discussion of the scope of the section, see Goode: Corporate Insolvency, 13-71–11-107.

[382] The possible remedies are the same as for a transaction at an undervalue; see s 241.

[383] This period is two years if the preference is given to a person who is connected with the company and six months if the preference is given to someone else (Insolvency Act 1986, s 240(1)).

[384] See 3.3.

[385] Insolvency Act 1986, s 240(2).

[386] Ibid, s 239(4).

[387] Ibid, s 239(5).

[388] The basis for this limitation is probably that preferences were originally seen as a fraud on the insolvency laws, and therefore the intention to commit fraud was relevant. See DD Prentice, 'Some Observations on the Law Relating to Preferences' in R Cranston (ed), *Making Commercial Law* (Oxford, Clarendon Press, 1997) 439, 441.

[389] There is no requirement of intention in US or Australian law. See Goode: Corporate Insolvency, 13-71.

[390] DD Prentice, 'Some Observations on the Law Relating to Preferences' in R Cranston (ed), *Making Commercial Law* (Oxford, Clarendon Press, 1997) 439; see Goode: Corporate Insolvency, 11-69; A Keay, 'Preferences in Liquidation Law: Time for a Change' [1998] *Company Financial and Insolvency Law Review* 198.

[391] Goode: Corporate Insolvency, 13-12, 13-24. See also *Re Sonatacus* [2007] EWCA Civ 31 and L Ho and R Mokal, 'Barber v CI—Preference Equals Undervalue' (2006) 22 *Insolvency Law and Practice* 183.

The position is more difficult if the removal of the asset occurs on or after the onset of insolvency. On one view, the reasoning is the same: if the beneficiary of the deprivation is a creditor then the net value of the assets is not affected, and so the *pari passu* principle is engaged but not the anti-deprivation principle.[392] Others take the view, however, that the net asset value is not relevant on or after insolvency, since the debtor's liabilities are turned into rights to prove and are therefore distinct from the assets.[393] On this view, a contractual provision can deprive a debtor of an asset which would otherwise be available for distribution to the creditors (and therefore fall within the anti-deprivation principle) whether or not the beneficiary of that deprivation is itself a creditor.[394]

One area of potential overlap between the policy of preventing reduction in the asset pool and the policy of preventing uneven distribution of assets is where a company grants a security interest during the run-up to insolvency to secure past indebtedness. The authorities here are to some extent contradictory. In *Re MC Bacon Ltd*[395] Millett J was of the view that where a charge was granted in these circumstances, there was no transaction at an undervalue within the meaning of section 238 since '[t]he mere creation of a security over a company's assets does not deplete them'. All that has happened is that the company has appropriated the charged assets to meet the secured liability, and therefore has adversely affected the rights of other creditors, but the net asset value is not diminished.[396] On that view, the grant of a security interest can only be a preference. However, this view has been doubted by the Court of Appeal in *Hill v Spread Trustee Co Ltd*,[397] a case concerning section 423 of the Insolvency Act 1986.[398] Arden LJ said, obiter, that the grant of a charge by way of legal mortgage could be a grant of a proprietary interest and so could be a transaction at an undervalue.[399] With respect, this must be right, at least where no new value is given for the grant, since the effect of the grant of a mortgage,[400] or probably even a charge,[401] is to diminish the assets available for distribution under the insolvency regime to the unsecured creditors. The 'net asset' argument does not work for the reasons given above, at least once the debtor is insolvent. Further, the value of the secured liability on insolvency is less than that of the assets appropriated to meet it, as without the security interest the liability would be met by the payment of a dividend of a great deal less than its face value.[402] This situation may be a rare example of where an application can be brought under either section 238 or 239, which can be significant because of the differences in defences and relevant time periods.

---

[392] Goode: Corporate Insolvency, 7-03.

[393] N Kulkarni, 'A Statutory Basis for the Anti-Deprivation Rule?' (2014) 23 *International Insolvency Review* 73, 87.

[394] For judicial statements that the same provision can fall foul of both principles, see *Belmont Park Investments Pty Ltd v BNY Trustee Services Ltd* [2011] UKSC 38 [1], [83], [149]; *Revenue and Customs Commissioners v Football League Ltd* [2012] EWHC 1372 (Ch) [104].

[395] [1990] BCLC 324.

[396] Goode: Corporate Insolvency, 13-38 fn 136.

[397] [2006] EWCA Civ 542.

[398] See 3.3.2.1.

[399] See J Levy and A Bowe, 'Transactions at an Undervalue—A New Departure?' (2006) 22 *Insolvency Law and Practice* 222; R Stubbs, 'Section 423 of the Insolvency Act in Practice' [2008] *Insolvency Intelligence* 17. Cf *Feakins v Department for Environment Food and Rural Affairs* [2005] EWCA Civ 1513 [72].

[400] See 7.3.2.2.

[401] 7.3.2.3.

[402] Law of Personal Property, 38-018.

This controversy also raises the question of whether section 245 of the Insolvency Act 1986 (which provides that floating charges created otherwise than for new value[403] in the run-up to insolvency[404] are invalid) is a provision preserving the asset pool or preventing uneven distribution of assets. The answer is that it probably does both: the question is significant in that it affects how section 245 falls within the statutory scheme of transaction avoidance on insolvency and also impacts on the question whether the scope of section 245 should be extended to cover other non-possessory security interests.[405] If section 245 is about preserving the asset pool, then arguably it should be subsumed into section 238 (where the time period requirements are more generous but the requirement of insolvency at the time of the transaction is stricter). Further, there would then be no need to extend section 245 to other secured transactions, since these would be covered within section 238. However, if section 245 is primarily about avoiding uneven distribution (in other words, if the *MC Bacon* reasoning is accepted), then it has a significant role: it is much wider than section 239 since the motivation of the company in granting the charge is irrelevant. This might be a reason not to extend section 245 to other secured transactions, but to continue to require the motivation requirement in those cases. It should also be noted that section 245 is disapplied in relation to charges created under a security financial collateral arrangement.[406]

3.3.2.4 *Protection of Creditors*

It will be seen from the foregoing discussion that the law starts to offer some protection to unsecured creditors from a time before the actual commencement of insolvency proceedings. However, when that time begins is only known in retrospect, once proceedings do actually commence. This has the effect that companies (and creditors) have to have provisions such as sections 238 and 239 in mind when entering into any transaction or making any transfer of assets if at the time the company might be cash flow insolvent. It is, though, unclear whether the statutory provisions operate as a very effective deterrent to creditors or other beneficiaries against most transactions or transfers. Whether any transaction or transfer is actually reversed by the court depends, first, on whether the company actually goes into insolvency proceedings, secondly, on whether the liquidator or administrator actually brings proceedings, and, thirdly, on what remedy the court orders. The remedy is not punitive or based on loss suffered, rather it is based on the benefit gained by the beneficiary of the transaction or transfer, so the worst the beneficiary can suffer is having to pay back the benefit gained. For most creditors and beneficiaries, it is worth taking the benefit at the time, in return for the moderate risk of remedial redress later, and few claims for such redress are actually made.[407] The chances of an application being made, however, may have increased now that liquidators and administrators are permitted to assign such

---

[403] For detailed discussion of this concept in this context see Goode: Corporate Insolvency, 13-114–13-118.

[404] Within two years if the recipient is connected with the company and one year if not: Insolvency Act 1986, s 245(3).

[405] This question is discussed in detail at 7.3.3.3.4.

[406] FCARs, reg 10.

[407] See Goode: Corporate Insolvency, 13-04.

claims to persons who are more likely than office holders to bring such applications on a commercial basis.[408]

3.3.3 The Balance Between Creditors and Shareholders in an Insolvent Company

It is clear from the discussion in 3.3.1.2.5 that, as between the shareholders and creditors of the company, the shareholders' claims qua shareholder rank behind those of the creditors, and that both Parliament and the courts are keen to ensure that this ranking on insolvency is not undermined. There are, however, two additional issues that will be discussed in this section that relate to the relationship between shareholders and creditors in an insolvent company, namely the issue of directors' duties in this period, and the question of whether there are any circumstances in which the veil of incorporation can be lifted or pierced so as to allow them to access the shareholders' assets in order to satisfy their claims against the company.

3.3.3.1 Directors' Duties

As discussed earlier in this chapter, the directors owe a general fiduciary duty to act in the best interests of the company.[409] When the company is solvent, this duty is an obligation on directors to act in the long-term interests of the shareholders. While the directors have to take account of other stakeholder groups in determining how to fulfil this obligation, the company's creditors are not one of the relevant stakeholder groups. However, when the company is insolvent, or when it is nearing insolvency, the focus of the directors' attention when fulfilling their general fiduciary obligation switches from the shareholders to the creditors: they have to have regard to the creditors' interests.[410]

This obligation is, however, mediated through the company: the duty is owed to the company and not to the creditors directly.[411] Directors owe no general duty of care to

---

[408] Small Business, Enterprise and Employment Act 2015, s 118. This is also the position in relation to claims brought under s 214. See 3.3.3.2.2(c).

[409] See 3.2.1.3.1. The common law duty described is owed by de jure and de facto directors. Whether it is also owed by shadow directors has been a topic of debate (see eg *Vivendi SA v Richards* [2013] EWHC 3006 (Ch) [142]–[145]; cf *Ultraframe (UK) Ltd v Fielding* [2005] EWHC 1638 (Ch)). This point has now been clarified by s 89 Small Business, Enterprise and Employment Act 2015, which provides that the general duties apply to a shadow director of a company where and to the extent that they are capable of so applying. The Act also contains a power for the Secretary of State to make provision by regulation as to which general duties apply to shadow directors and which do not.

[410] *West Mercia Safetywear Ltd v Dodd* [1998] BCLC 250 and see *Stone & Rolls v Moore Stephens* [2009] 1 AC 1391 per Lord Mance at [239] (dissenting). The continued existence of this obligation is acknowledged by Companies Act 2006, s 172(3). For discussion see *Re HLC Environmental Projects Ltd* [2013] EWHC 2876 (Ch). The Delaware courts take a slightly different approach to this issue; see eg *Quadrant Structured Products Co Ltd v Vertin*, 4 May 2015.

[411] Early cases seemed to suggest that the duty was a direct duty to creditors (eg *Winkworth v Edward Baron Development Co Ltd* [1986] 1 WLR 1512, 1516 per Lord Templeman), although subsequent academic opinion regards this duty as an indirect one (eg D Prentice, 'Creditor's Interests and Director's Duties' (1990) 10 *Oxford Journal of Legal Studies* 265, 275; S Worthington, 'Directors' Duties, Creditors' Rights and Shareholder Intervention' [1991] *Melbourne University Law Review* 121, 151; L Sealy, 'Personal Liability of Directors and Officers for Debts of Insolvent Corporations: A Jurisdictional Perspective (England)' in JS Ziegel, *Current Developments*

creditors.[412] The directors are required to have regard to the creditors' interests generally, and not to have regard to the interests of a particular creditor or section of creditors who have special rights once a winding up occurs.[413] A breach of this duty can be litigated via section 212 of the Insolvency Act 1986. One consequence of this shift from a view of the company as shareholder-focused to one which is creditor-focused is that shareholders lose their ability to ratify the wrongs that have been done to the company by the directors.[414]

This indicates that once the company is insolvent, or nearing insolvency, it is the creditors, and not the shareholders, that are in the driving seat. Once a company goes into liquidation, the shareholders cease to have any interest in the assets of the company,[415] and the interests of the company are equated with the interests of the creditors, so that the directors must act so as to maximise creditor welfare. In a solvent company the proprietary interests of the shareholders entitle them, as a general body, to be regarded as the company, but 'where a company is insolvent the interests of the creditors intrude'.[416]

This identification of the creditors with the company arises at a point before the company is insolvent, however, when the company is 'nearing insolvency'. A number of cases make reference to this duty arising in the period prior to insolvency, when the company is 'near insolvency' or of 'doubtful solvency', or if a contemplated payment or other course of action would jeopardise its solvency or would otherwise put the company in some form of dangerous financial position.[417] These terms are imprecise, and yet the trigger for the onset of this duty is important in terms of defining the scope of protection available to creditors. It is likely, however, that this shift in directors' duties from shareholders to creditors will occur only at a late stage.

This duty is significant in that it makes clear the focus of corporate law once the company is insolvent. It can, however, be questioned whether this duty provides much meaningful creditor protection in practice. Although recent cases have suggested that this duty is not

---

in *International and Comparative Corporate Insolvency Law* (Oxford, Clarendon Press, 1994) 486; A Keay, 'Formulating a Framework for Directors' Duties to Creditors: An Entity Maximisation Approach' (2005) 64 *Cambridge Law Journal* 614) and this is the approach followed by subsequent English cases, such as *Yukong Line Ltd of Korea v Rendsburg Investments Corp of Liberia* [1998] 1 WLR 294.

[412] While dictum in *Winkworth v Edward Baron Development Co Ltd* [1986] 1 WLR 1512 suggests that directors do owe a duty of care to creditors, this view has not been followed by subsequent English cases (eg *West Mercia Safetywear Ltd v Dodd* [1988] BCLC 250). Directors could owe specific duties to creditors, eg in contract (though the contract is generally between the creditor and the company and directors are agents for the company not vice versa: *Salomon v Salomon & Co Ltd* [1897] AC 22) or tort. On this latter point the House of Lords in *Williams v Natural Life Health Foods Ltd* [1998] 1 WLR 830 made it clear that a director will only be personally liable for a negligent misrepresentation made in the course of acting qua director if he has assumed responsibility for the statement to the third party. Where fraud is involved, however, the courts will not allow a director to hide behind the company in this way and the director can be liable for deceit in addition to the company: *Standard Chartered Bank v Pakistan National Shipping Corpn* [2002] UKHL 43 (and see *Contex Drouzhba Ltd v Wiseman* [2006] EWHC 2708 (QB) on the particular application of this doctrine to creditors).

[413] *Re Pantone 485 Ltd* [2002] 1 BCLC 266.

[414] *Re Horsley & Weight Ltd* [1982] Ch 442; *Nicholson v Permakraft (NZ) Ltd* [1985] 1 NZLR 242 (New Zealand Court of Appeal); *Kinsela v Russell Kinsela Pty Ltd* (1986) 4 NSWLR 722 (Sup Ct NSW).

[415] *Ayerst (Inspector of Taxes) v C & K (Construction) Ltd* [1976] AC 167.

[416] *Kinsela v Russell Kinsela Pty Ltd (in liq)* (1986) 4 NSWLR 722, 730 per Street CJ (Sup Ct NSW) and see A Keay, 'Formulating a Framework for Directors Duties to Creditors: An Entity Maximisation Approach' (2005) 64 *Cambridge Law Journal* 614.

[417] *Facia Footwear (in administration) v Hinchcliffe* [1998] 1 BCLC 218; *Re HLC Environmental Projects Ltd* [2013] EWHC 2876 (Ch).

without some teeth,[418] it contains a number of limitations. The duty only arises when the company is in, or near insolvency, despite some early cases which held that it could apply when the company was solvent.[419] It remains a duty owed by the board to the company:[420] enforcement of the duty is primarily on behalf of the company,[421] and only indirectly on behalf of the creditors, and the loss is measured according to the loss to the company. Perhaps the most significant limitation, however, is the fact that the proceeds of recoveries under section 212 go to the company, rather than to the unsecured creditors directly, and so are subject to an after-acquired property clause.

Despite these limitations, it is nevertheless clear that creditors' interests dominate at this point in time. However, it will usually be the case that many creditors, particularly the unsecured creditors, will not receive the full amount of the debt that they are owed in insolvency. In consequence, one issue that sometimes arises between the shareholders and creditors in an insolvent situation is whether the shareholders can be made liable for the debts of the company in some way. The difficulty with any claim against the shareholders for the debts of the company is the concept of separate legal personality of the company and its corollary, limited liability, which prima facie protect the shareholders from such claims. In some circumstances, however, it may be possible for the veil of incorporation to be lifted and liability for the debts of the company imposed on those standing 'behind' the company.

3.3.3.2 Lifting the Veil Between the Creditors and the Shareholders

There are a number of common law and statutory mechanisms that are available to lift or pierce the corporate veil, whereby the separate legal personality of the company can be disregarded. The two statutory provisions which are particularly relevant in this context, and which are discussed below, are sections 213 and 214 of the Insolvency Act 1986. As discussed in this section, however, lifting the veil, whether at common law or as a result of the legislative provisions, is extremely rare in the UK. These are not mechanisms which lead to any significant increase in the funds available to creditors in practice.[422]

3.3.3.2.1 Common Law Mechanisms

At common law the courts uphold the principle of limited liability almost in its entirety. The leading case is that of the Supreme Court in *Prest v Petrodel Resources Ltd*.[423] This

---

[418] Eg *GHLM Trading Ltd v Maroo* [2012] EWHC 61 (Ch); *Re HLC*, ibid.

[419] Eg *Ring v Sutton* (1980) 5 ACLR 546 (Sup Ct NSW).

[420] Cf Lord Templeman in *Winkworth v Edward Baron Development Co Ltd* [1987] 1 WLR 1512 who stated that the board, being the company's conscience, owed a duty to 'the company and the creditors of the company' to keep its property 'inviolate and available for the repayment of its debts' (at 1516). Subsequent decisions have made clear that the duty is owed to the company, but that in determining the company's interests regard shall be had to the creditors (*West Mercia Safetywear Ltd v Dodd* [1988] BCLC 250; *Re Produce Marketing Consortium Ltd* [1989] 1 WLR 745).

[421] A claim is brought by the liquidator under Insolvency Act 1986, s 212.

[422] There is one further possibility for recovery, which is aimed at directors rather than shareholders, but which might be relevant if the shareholder becomes a de facto or shadow director, namely the Company Directors Disqualification Act 1986. This Act allows actions to be brought by the Secretary of State and the proceedings are publicly funded. The Act is primarily aimed at disqualifying unfit directors of insolvent companies but there is also provision for disqualified directors to be made liable for the debts of the company: Company Directors Disqualification Act 1986, s 15, as amended by Small Business, Enterprise and Employment Act 2015.

[423] [2013] UKSC 34.

case makes it clear that the veil of incorporation can only be lifted or pierced in extremely limited circumstances involving the abuse of the corporate legal personality.[424] According to Lord Sumption, the use of the corporate form for the purpose of deliberately evading or frustrating the enforcement of an existing legal obligation is required.[425] The veil of incorporation will not be set aside by a court 'merely because it considers that justice so requires'[426] or simply because the company is a member of a group: 'the fundamental principle is that "each company in a group of companies … is a separate legal entity possessed of separate legal rights and liabilities"'.[427] The courts may lift the veil where fraud is involved, but only where the corporate entity is being used to evade a pre-existing liability.[428] The ability to use the corporate form to ensure that a particular *future* liability does not fall on a particular company is 'what incorporation is all about'.[429] To say that there is no presumption in favour of lifting the veil at common law 'may be regarded as an understatement'.[430]

Similarly, the courts will attach liability to a shareholder or director if it is found that they are the principal and that the company is acting as a mere agent for that person. However, the Court of Appeal in *Adams v Cape Industries plc*[431] defined very narrowly the circumstances in which an agency relationship will be found to exist. Effectively, an express agency agreement will be needed, and given that most companies are established in order for the business to be carried on by the company, and for the consequent liabilities to attach to the company, that kind of express agreement will be very rare.[432]

It is sometimes suggested that, even if the general principle is that the courts will not lift the corporate veil, they should be prepared to do so for certain sub-categories of unsecured creditors. The strongest arguments in favour of additional veil piercing are made in relation to non-adjusting creditors.[433] However, as is clear from the decision of the Court of Appeal in *Adams v Cape*, which did involve tort victims, no special rule is in place in the UK to deal with this category of unsecured creditor. In the UK compulsory insurance covers the

---

[424] It was even debated before the Supreme Court in *VTB Capital plc v Nutritek International Corporation* [2013] UKSC 5 whether a general common law jurisdiction to pierce the corporate veil exists at all.

[425] Ibid, [35]. For Lord Walker (at [106]), in contrast, piercing the veil is not a doctrine at all in the sense of a coherent principle but merely a rule of law. For discussion of the spectrum of views within the Supreme Court see *Gramsci Shipping Corp v Lembergs* [2013] EWCA Civ 730.

[426] *Adams v Cape Industries plc* [1990] Ch 433, 536 per Slade LJ, although his Lordship did qualify this statement with the words 'save in cases which turn on the wording of particular statutes or contracts…' (at 536). See also *Yukong Lines Ltd of Korea v Rendsburg Investments Corp of Liberia* [1998] 1 WLR 294; *Ord v Belhaven Pubs Ltd* [1998] BCC 607; *Trustor AB v Smallbone (No 2)* [2001] 3 All ER 987; cf *Re A Company* [1985] BCLC 333, 337–38 ('In our view the cases … show that the court will use its power to pierce the corporate veil if it is necessary to achieve justice…').

[427] Ibid, 532 per Slade LJ, quoting from *The Albazero* [1977] AC 774, 807 per Roskill LJ. This principle was reaffirmed by the Court of Appeal in *Ord v Belhaven Pubs Ltd* [1998] 2 BCLC 447. While little interest is shown in domestic law for regulating corporate groups, this is an issue of increasing interest at EU level: European Commission, Action Plan (COM(2012) 740), para 4.6.

[428] Eg *Jones v Lipman* [1962] 1 WLR 832; *Gilford Motor Co Ltd v Horne* [1933] Ch 935; *Kensington International Ltd v Republic of the Congo* [2005] EWHC 2684 (Comm), [2006] 2 BCLC 296. See J Payne, 'Lifting the Veil: A Reassessment of the Fraud Exception' (1997) 56 *Cambridge Law Journal* 284.

[429] *Prest v Petrodel Resources Ltd* [2013] UKSC 34 [34] per Lord Sumption.

[430] *Ord v Belhaven Pubs Ltd* [1998] 2 BCLC 447, 453 per Hobhouse LJ.

[431] [1990] Ch 433.

[432] Although such an agreement does occasionally occur; see eg *Smith, Stone & Knight Ltd v Birmingham Corporation* [1939] 4 All ER 116.

[433] H Hansmann and R Kraakman, 'Towards Unlimited Shareholder Liability for Corporate Torts' (1991) 100 *Yale Law Journal* 1879. For a discussion of the categories of non-adjusting creditors in UK law see 3.2.2.1 and 7.6.2.3.

majority of tort claims against companies, namely those arising from accidents at work and road traffic accidents.[434] As regards other forms of tort claim, the victims who claim against companies that subsequently become insolvent are in no worse position than those victims with claims against individuals who are unable to discharge the judgment debt.[435] There is no good justification for altering the current veil-piercing rules in the UK for this reason.[436]

3.3.3.2.2 Statutory Mechanisms: Sections 213 and 214 Insolvency Act 1986

There are a number of statutory mechanisms which can be used for veil piercing,[437] albeit that they tend to target those managing the company rather than shareholders per se.[438] The legislative response to the perceived need for creditor protection when the company is insolvent or on the verge of insolvency has been to impose liability on directors for fraudulent or wrongful trading, via sections 213 and 214 of the Insolvency Act 1986 respectively. Recoveries under these sections swell the assets available to the unsecured creditors.[439]

3.3.3.2.2(a) *Fraudulent Trading: Section 213 Insolvency Act 1986*

For over 60 years the UK has provided that directors who are responsible for fraudulent trading can be ordered to contribute to the asset pool, without limit of liability,[440] should the company go into insolvent liquidation.[441] The terms of this offence involve the business of the company being carried on[442] with an intent to defraud creditors of the company, or creditors of any other person, or for any fraudulent purpose.[443] Liability will attach to those who are knowingly a party to the carrying on of the business in that manner.[444] This can,

---

[434] Employers' Liability (Compulsory Insurance) Act 1969; Road Traffic Act 1988. These two acts are coupled with the Third Parties (Rights Against Insurers) Act 2010 which transfers to the injured party an insolvent company's claim against the insurer. For further discussion see 7.6.2.

[435] Tortious claims can sometimes operate as an alternative to veil-piercing; see eg *Chandler v Cape* [2012] EWCA Civ 525.

[436] This issue is discussed at 7.6.2.3.

[437] See Gower and Davies, 8-5.

[438] In small companies these will generally be the same individuals.

[439] Sections 213 and 214 were originally silent on this point, but s 119 Small Business, Enterprise and Employment Act 2015 has the effect that recoveries under these sections are not intended to be treated as the company's general property. This codifies what was assumed to be the position in any case—see eg *Re Oasis Merchandising Services Ltd* [1998] Ch 170. This may be compared to the claims under s 212, where any recovery is the company's recovery and therefore available to satisfy the claims of the security holders, discussed at 3.3.3.1.

[440] It used to be the case that the courts were prepared to countenance the inclusion of a punitive element in determining the quantum of recovery for fraudulent trading (eg *Re A Company No 001418 of 1988* [1990] BCC 526), cf wrongful trading actions (*Re Produce Marketing Consortium Ltd* [1989] 1 WLR 745). However, remarks of the Court of Appeal in *Morphitis v Bernasconi* [2003] EWCA Civ 289 make it clear that there is no power to include a punitive element in an award for fraudulent trading: the award is purely compensatory.

[441] There are two provisions relating to fraudulent trading: (i) a criminal provision, now found in Companies Act 2006, s 993 which allows an action to be brought against directors and others for fraudulent trading but does not depend upon the company being in the process of being wound up; and (ii) a civil provision, currently found in Insolvency Act 1986, s 213 which allows an action to be brought against directors and others where the company is in the process of being wound up. An action under s 213 can be brought by a liquidator or, as a result of s 117 Small Business, Enterprise and Employment Act 2015, by an administrator.

[442] This is an odd phrase that does not appear elsewhere in statute. It has been interpreted to mean that a person can only be carrying on the business of the company if they take 'positive steps of some nature' (*Re Maidstone Buildings Provisions Ltd* [1971] 1 WLR 1085, 1092 per Pennycuick VC).

[443] Companies Act 2006, s 993(1); Insolvency Act 1986, s 213(1).

[444] Ibid.

obviously, include the directors of the company, and others involved in the management of the company,[445] but it can also include outsiders,[446] provided they have actual knowledge[447] of the fraud at that time. It is also possible for a company to be made liable for fraudulent trading[448] where the knowledge of one or more individuals can be attributed to a company,[449] and it can be appropriate to attribute knowledge of a fraud to a company even though the person with knowledge of the fraud had acted dishonestly and in breach of his duty to his principal and employer.[450] Section 213 has been held to have extraterritorial effect.[451]

One significant difficulty with this test in practice is the need to determine 'actual dishonesty … involving real moral blame'.[452] This is a subjectively assessed test,[453] and therefore it is generally going to be very difficult to satisfy this requirement. This limitation was one of the predominant reasons for the introduction in 1986 of the offence of wrongful trading, which has a lower mens rea requirement, being essentially a negligence test, as discussed next.

3.3.3.2.2(b) Wrongful Trading: Section 214 Insolvency Act 1986

Section 214 of the Insolvency Act 1986 applies where a company goes into insolvent liquidation[454] and, at some time before the commencement of the winding up, the directors[455] concluded, or ought to have concluded, that there was 'no reasonable prospect'[456] that the company could avoid going into insolvent liquidation.[457] In determining whether

---

[445] An interesting question arises as to whether wealthy parent companies can be liable for fraudulent trading. In *Re Augustus Barnet & Son Ltd* [1986] BCLC 170 the parent company supplied letters of comfort to the auditors of the subsidiary and to the subsidiary's creditors to the extent that it would financially support the subsidiary. The subsidiary subsequently went into insolvent liquidation and the liquidator brought an action for fraudulent trading against the parent company. It was held that this level of involvement did not render the parent liable under the precursor to s 213.

[446] Eg *Re Gerald Cooper (Chemicals) Ltd* [1978] Ch 262.

[447] Actual knowledge of the fraud can include 'blind eye' knowledge: *Morris v Bank of India* [2005] EWCA Civ 93, ie '… a suspicion that the relevant facts do exist and a deliberate decision to avoid confirming that they exist. But … the suspicion must be firmly grounded and targeted on specific facts. The deliberate decision must be a decision to avoid obtaining confirmation of facts in whose existence the individual has good reason to believe' (*Manifest Shipping Co Ltd v Uni-Polaris Insurance Co Ltd (The Star Sea)* [2001] UKHL 1 [116] per Lord Scott).

[448] *Morris v Bank of India* [2005] EWCA Civ 693.

[449] See *Meridian Global Funds Management Asia Ltd v Securities Commission* [1995] 2 AC 500 on the issue of attribution.

[450] *Morris v Bank of India* [2005] 2 BCLC 328.

[451] *Jetivia SA v Bilta (UK) Ltd (in liquidation)* [2015] UKSC 23.

[452] *Re Patrick & Lyon Ltd* [1933] Ch 786, 790 per Maugham J.

[453] *Aktieselskabet Dansk Skibsfinansiering v Brothers* [2001] 2 BCLC 324.

[454] Insolvency Act 1986, s 214(6) states that '[f]or the purposes of this section a company goes into insolvent liquidation if it goes into liquidation at a time when its assets are insufficient for the payment of its debts and other liabilities and the expenses of winding up'—ie a balance sheet test.

[455] 'Directors' for this purpose includes shadow directors: Insolvency Act 1986, s 214(7) (for a discussion of whether or not creditors can become shadow directors see 3.2.2.4.4). In addition this term almost certainly includes de facto directors. Although s 214 is silent on this latter point, the definition of 'director' for the purposes of Insolvency Act 1986 includes 'any person occupying the position of director, by whatever name called' (s 251). It is also accepted that de facto directors are generally assumed to be subject to the same range of obligations and liabilities as de jure directors; see eg *Ultraframe (UK) Ltd v Fielding* [2005] UKHC 1638 (Ch). See also *Re Hydrodan (Corby) Ltd* [1994] 2 BCLC 180.

[456] Insolvency Act 1986, s 214(2)(a).

[457] For discussion see R Werdnik, 'Wrongful Trading Provision: Is it Efficient?' (2012) 25(6) *Insolvency Intelligence* 81; A Keay, 'Wrongful Trading: Problems and Proposals' (2014) 65(1) *Northern Ireland Legal Quarterly* 63; R Williams, 'What Can We Expect to Gain from Reforming the Wrongful Trading Remedy?' (2015) 78 *Modern Law Review* 55.

or not the company's insolvent liquidation should have been foreseen by the directors, the directors will be treated as having the knowledge and skill of a 'reasonably diligent person' having both '(a) the general knowledge, skill and experience that may reasonably be expected of a person carrying out the same functions as are carried out by that director in relation to the company, and (b) the general knowledge, skill and experience that that director has'.[458] The directors are therefore judged by the higher of these two standards. When assessing the objective element the courts will take account of the nature of the company,[459] and the nature of that director's role within that company.[460]

Perhaps the most difficult aspect of section 214 is determining when there is 'no reasonable prospect' of the company avoiding insolvent liquidation. In practice the courts have adopted a test which means that insolvency must be almost inevitable before section 214 liability is triggered.[461] On the face of the legislation a balance sheet test is adopted.[462] In practice, however, the courts seem to utilise a cash flow test when determining whether there is 'no reasonable prospect' of avoiding insolvent liquidation.[463] If there is merely a temporary cash flow problem then the directors will not be expected to put the company straight into liquidation, provided their belief that the company can avoid insolvent liquidation is not unreasonable, for example where the company continues to have the support of its major lender. This means that section 214 is triggered at a later stage, in practice, than might appear to be the case on the face of the legislation. The consequential effect is to reduce the potential for section 214 to operate as a creditor protection device.[464]

The Company Law Review Steering Group considered whether, in addition to the section 214 duty, directors should be required 'where they know or ought to recognise that there is a substantial probability of an insolvent liquidation, to take such steps as they believe, in their good judgment, appropriate to reduce the risk, without undue caution and

---

[458] Ibid, s 214(4) (emphasis added). This subsection has now been adopted to reflect the duty of care owed by directors while the company remains solvent: Companies Act 2006, s 174(2).

[459] Eg *Re Produce Marketing Consortium Ltd* [1989] 5 BCC 569: 'the general knowledge skill and experience postulated will be much less extensive in a small company in a modes way of business, with simple accounting procedures and requirements than it will be in a large company with sophisticated procedures' (per Knox J at 594–95).

[460] The duty under s 214 therefore clearly contains a significant objective element. The position regarding the general duty owed by directors when the company is insolvent, or nearing insolvency, discussed at 3.3.3.1, is not so clear. Traditionally, the common law obligation on directors to act bona fide in the best interests of the company (ie the shareholders in a solvent company and the creditors in an insolvent company) was subjectively assessed (*Re Smith & Fawcett Ltd* [1942] Ch 304, 306 per Lord Greene MR). This principle is repeated in s 172(1) Companies Act 2006: it is for a director to act in what 'he considers in good faith' to be most likely to promote the success of the company, albeit that the obligation to take account of the interests of other stakeholders may have an objectively assessed element. However, recent cases have suggested that the duty under s 172 is subject to a number of qualifications where a company is of doubtful solvency, which may require the court to apply an objective 'reasonable and honest man' test: *Re HLC Environmental Projects Ltd* [2013] EWHC 2876 (Ch) and see *Westpac v Bell* [2012] WASCA 157.

[461] *Rubin v Gunner* [2004] EWHC 316 (Ch).

[462] Insolvency Act 1986, s 214(6).

[463] See eg *Re Purpoint Ltd* [1991] BCLC 491 in which the company was balance sheet insolvent for some time but the court held the director liable under s 214 only later, once it became clear that the company could not pay its debts as they fell due. See also *Roberts v Frohlich* [2011] EWHC 257 (Ch) which suggests that the court will only find s 214 liability to exist where there has been a blatant disregard of creditors' interests.

[464] The position in the UK can be compared with that of other jurisdictions in this respect. For example, in Germany there is an automatic requirement for filing for formal insolvency without undue delay and in any event within three weeks of insolvency or overindebtedness: § 15a Insolvenzordnung (German Insolvency Statute).

thus continuing to have in mind the interests of members'.[465] This was not taken forward by the Government, and does not appear in the Companies Act 2006, as it was felt to be inconsistent with the policy of promoting a rescue culture for companies in financial difficulty.[466] Indeed, it is easy to see how such a provision would be problematic, not only because of the difficult balancing decision that would be required, but also because of the potentially stultifying effect that such a provision could have on companies. Such an approach might well lead to the precipitate closure of otherwise viable concerns, and directors failing to take risky decisions that would otherwise be in the interests of the company's creditors and shareholders. There would also be a social cost attached to the premature closure of otherwise viable concerns.

One of the benefits of section 214 is the fact that no specific course of action is mandated by the section. It does not require the directors to put the company into insolvency when the company is in financial difficulties, or even where the company is balance sheet insolvent. The directors' actions will be judged by the court ex post by reference to the standard of the reasonable director. The directors will be able to escape liability if they behave reasonably, and there is a defence if they take 'every step with a view to minimising the potential loss to the company's creditors as … [they] ought to have taken'.[467] If the directors put in place reasonable and sensible defence plans they will escape liability, even if the plans subsequently fail and the company does go into insolvent liquidation.[468] Section 214 does not create a strict liability offence.

The principal liability of a director who is found to have breached section 214 is to make such contribution as the court thinks proper to the assets of the insolvent company, which are then available for distribution to creditors.[469]

3.3.3.2.2(c) Low Level of Claims Under Sections 213 and 214

Despite the protection for creditors provided on paper by sections 213 and 214, in practice relatively few claims are actually brought under these sections. There are a number of limitations within these sections that help to explain the relative scarcity of cases. The action in both cases can be brought by a liquidator or administrator[470] acting on behalf of the creditors as a general body. More significantly, perhaps, these actions have traditionally been funded from the pot of money available to pay the (unsecured) creditors and, as a result, office holders would not commence an action unless there was a strong prospect that the money recovered would exceed the expenses of the litigation.[471] This had the effect

---

[465] Company Law Review Steering Group, *Modernising Company Law for a Competitive Economy: Final Report* (URN 01/942, July 2001), para 3.17.

[466] DTI, *Modernising Company Law* (July 2002), Cmnd 5553-I, para 3.11.

[467] Insolvency Act 1986, s 214(3).

[468] Eg *Re Continental Assurance Co of London plc* [2001] BPIR 733.

[469] Insolvency Act 1986, s 214(1) and *Re Produce Marketing Consortium Ltd* [1989] BCLC 520.

[470] Ibid, ss 213(2), 214(1). These actions were originally confined to liquidators, in contrast to an action for breach of the directors' general fiduciary duty which on insolvency is a duty owed to the creditors as a whole (discussed at 3.3.3.1), and actions under ss 238 and 239 Insolvency Act 1986, which can be brought by liquidators or administrators. Small Business, Enterprise and Employment Act 2015, s 117 extends the actions under ss 213 and 214 to administrators.

[471] In addition, in *Re Oasis Merchandising Services Ltd* [1997] BCC 282, the transfer of s 214 claims to a third party (willing to take up risky claims which the company is unwilling to pursue) by the liquidator was held to infringe the rule against champerty. The Small Business, Enterprise and Employment Act 2015 now allows liquidators and administrators to assign causes of action under ss 213 and 214 (s 118).

of keeping the number of section 213 and section 214 actions very low.[472] Amendments to the Insolvency Rules mean that the costs of litigation for civil recovery actions under the Insolvency Act 1986 are recoverable from the insolvent's estate as part of the expenses that an office holder incurs in the proper execution of their duty.[473] Consequently, it may be that where the costs of recovery are likely to be high, and the assets of the company are limited, insolvency practitioners may feel unable to pursue civil recovery proceedings.[474] Furthermore, in order to incur litigation expenses of this kind they will need to obtain the consent of the floating charge holder.[475] In addition, these changes do not alter the fact that directors of insolvent companies may have little or nothing by way of funds which it is worth the insolvency practitioner's while to pursue. As a result it is unlikely that the number of section 213 or section 214 actions will increase significantly in the future.[476]

3.4 Conclusion

The thesis of this chapter has been that shareholders are pre-eminent within a solvent company, because it is the shareholders, or at least the ordinary shareholders, that are the residual claimants of the company, but that on insolvency there is a shift such that the creditors' interests dominate. It is suggested that this shift is entirely appropriate. In a solvent company, because the creditors' returns are fixed, they would tend to prefer excessively low risk projects as compared to the shareholders. Directors' duties are rightly shareholder-regarding at this point, since, broadly, what is in the long-term interests of the shareholders will also be in the interests of the creditors at this time. If the creditors wish to have additional influence in this period then there are a number of different corporate governance rights for which they can bargain, and which can potentially provide them with a significant monitoring role.

On insolvency, however, there is a potential problem since at that point the shareholders 'come last' and yet, if the directors are too closely aligned with the shareholders, they might favour excessively risky projects that would potentially benefit the shareholders (who would take any upside of the decision, but have nothing to lose if the risk does not pay off) at

---

[472] This can be compared to the number of actions brought against directors by the Secretary of State under the Company Directors Disqualification Act 1986. During 2013–14, for example, 1,273 disqualification orders or undertakings against directors of failed companies were secured: Insolvency Service Annual Report and Accounts 2013–14, July 2014, 18. These actions are not confined to situations where the company is insolvent, though that is the usual scenario. In addition to a disqualification order (s 6) the Secretary of State can seek to impose personal liability for the company's debts in some circumstances (s 15). Disqualification actions are funded by the State.

[473] Insolvency Rules 1986, r 4.218 as amended by Insolvency (Amendment) Rules 2008 (SI 2008/737). See 3.3.1.2.1.

[474] For discussion see R Williams, 'What Can We Expect to Gain from Reforming the Insolvent Trading Remedy?' (2015) 78 *Modern Law Review* 55.

[475] Insolvency Rules, rr 4218A–E; see 7.3.3.3.4.

[476] A recent change to the law allows the Secretary of State to seek civil recovery from disqualified directors under the Company Directors Disqualification Act 1986, via the insertion of a new section 15A (see Small Business, Enterprise and Employment Act 2015, s 110). This will potentially deal with the issue of costs, since it will be the state paying the costs, but it cannot tackle the fact that directors of insolvent companies may have little by way of funds available to pay such orders. For discussion see R Williams, 'Civil Recovery from Delinquent Directors' (2015) 15 *Journal of Corporate Law Studies*, forthcoming.

the expense of the creditors. The dominant interest on insolvency is, therefore, that of the creditors, as the discussion in 3.3 above demonstrates. At this point in time shareholders completely drop out of the picture, and therefore it does seem entirely appropriate that when the company is in insolvency, or in the vicinity of insolvency, the focus should shift from a shareholder-focused conception of the company to a creditor-focused one.

This chapter has examined the means by which the general law seeks to regulate the conflict between creditors and shareholders when the company is insolvent, and to impose an orderly procedure whereby creditors' claims can be met to the extent possible. Chapter five will discuss the mechanisms put in place by the law while the company remains solvent in order to regulate this conflict between creditors and shareholders. Creditors who are able to adjust, however, will seek to protect themselves against other creditors ex ante, by either or both of the contractual and proprietary means described in chapter two and in this chapter, and discussed in more detail in chapters six and seven. The extent to which creditors can or should be prevented from putting in place this ex ante protection will also be discussed, but it will be seen that, except to the extent discussed in this chapter, English law largely adopts a view based on freedom of contract, so that adjusting creditors can avail themselves of very substantial protection against the competing claims of other creditors by having proprietary claims against what would otherwise be the company's assets.

4

Issuing Shares

4.1 Introduction

When directors decide to finance a company via the issue of shares, they face a number of constraints on their ability to do so. This chapter considers the limitations imposed by company law. For public offers of shares these company law constraints are supplemented by a large number of additional requirements imposed via securities regulation. These provisions are dealt with in later chapters of the book.[1]

The issuing of shares is essentially a three-step process. First, the company must decide to make an offer of shares, and set the terms of the offer. This offer may be a public or a non-public offer,[2] though only public companies have the option of making a public offer.[3] Second, some person(s) must agree with the company to take the shares. At this point the shares are said to have been 'allotted'. Third, the contract between the company and those to whom the shares have been allotted must be implemented, making them members of the company and thereby completing the issuance process. The second and third stages of this process are discussed in this chapter, together with methods of holding shares, and the transferability of shares once these stages are complete.

The company law constraints that form the focus of this chapter are imposed in order to provide protection for shareholders. The starting point is therefore to consider why shareholders might be in need of protection from the law at the point when new shares are issued.

4.2 Shareholder Protection when Shares are Issued

4.2.1 The Need for Shareholder Protection

Shareholders may be apprehensive about a number of matters when new shares are issued. Principally they may be concerned (i) that the new issue may result in the dilution of their interest in the company, and (ii) that the directors may use the share issue for some ulterior purpose.

---

[1] See, in particular, chapter 10, which examines the rules imposed on companies when they seek to list companies for the first time.

[2] For the definition of what is a public offer for this purpose see Companies Act 2006, s 756. This is not identical to the definition of public offer for other purposes, including the definition of public offer in the Prospectus Directive (Directive 2003/71/EC as amended by Directive 2010/73/EU), discussed further at 10.5.2.1.

[3] Companies Act 2006, s 755 (which prohibits private companies offering securities to the public either directly or through an offer for sale via an intermediary—see 10.3.2 for further discussion of this distinction). If a private

4.2.1.1 Dilution of Existing Shareholders' Interests

This can take the form of voting dilution and/or value dilution. As regards the first of these, a dilution in the control rights of existing shareholders can occur if their voting strength diminishes. This concern will clearly only arise if a shareholder holds shares that carry a right to vote, and if this control right is meaningful to the shareholder. Take the example of a shareholder, A, who currently holds 26 per cent of the ordinary shares of a company with a one share-one vote structure. This shareholder can therefore block any special resolution put forward, for example a resolution to alter the articles of the company.[4] If more ordinary shares are issued and A does not have the opportunity to acquire enough new shares to enable her to retain 26 per cent of the ordinary shares, then the option of exercising this blocking control will be lost. If the company is a publicly traded company and if the offer is simply an offer to the public, then, of course, the ability to retain this percentage interest may be said to be within A's control, since A can purchase the requisite number of shares in the market. It may not, however, be straightforward for A to protect herself in this way in practice—she may, for example, lack the finances to do so. Furthermore, this argument will not apply where the company is a private company, where the shares are not openly traded, or where the shares are not offered to the public, for example where the shares are offered via a placing,[5] or there is otherwise a lack of liquidity in relation to the shares. In such circumstances, the law may need to intervene to enable shareholders to protect themselves against such dilution.

Shareholders may also be concerned about value dilution—in other words, the issue of new shares may amount to a wealth transfer from existing shareholders to the new share-holders in a company. This can arise because new shares are generally issued at a discount to the price at which a company's existing shares are trading. The price at which new shares should be issued is a matter for the directors' commercial judgement. Directors have a duty to obtain the best price available for those new shares, but it is accepted that it may be justifiable for them to issue shares at a discount in order to ensure that the issue is a success.[6] In practice it is very common for new shares to be issued at a significant discount to market price.[7] If this discount is not offered to existing shareholders, this will result in the reduction in the value of their investment in the company.[8] Take a shareholder, B, who currently holds all 100 ordinary shares in a company, and those shares currently trade at £1 each. If 50 new shares are issued by the directors at 80 pence each, and B is not given the opportunity to purchase these shares, and thus share in the discount, then after the issue the value of the shares in the company will be just over 93 pence per share $((100 \times 1 + 50 \times 0.8)/150)$; that is, B will have lost approximately 7 pence per share in value.

---

company does make a public offer, the validity of any agreement to sell or allot securities or any sale or allotment is not affected by the breach of the provision (s 755(1) and s 760), but the court has a wide range of powers to deal with the consequences of the breach, including requiring the company to re-register as a public company (s 758(2)), ordering the winding up of the company or imposing a remedial order (s 758(3)).

[4] Ibid, s 21.
[5] For discussion see 10.3.2.2.
[6] *Shearer v Bercain* [1980] 3 All ER 295; *Re Sunrise Radio Ltd* [2009] EWHC 2893 (Ch).
[7] See ABI, *Encouraging Equity Investment: Facilitation of Efficient Equity Capital Raising in the UK Market* (July 2013), 32.
[8] For a discussion of the loss suffered by shareholders (and by the company) when shares are issued for inadequate consideration see *Pilmer v Duke Group Ltd* [2001] 2 BCLC 773 (Aust HC).

A further possible concern regarding value dilution might arise if shareholders have concerns about the dilution of their future income stream. Bringing in new shareholders will mean that there are more claimants on the company's capital, which may be a concern if shareholders have doubts about the directors' willingness or capacity to invest the capital acquired in return for the new shares in projects yielding a return at least equivalent to the return on investments prior to the new issue.

4.2.1.2 *Misuse by the Directors of the Power to Issue New Shares*

A second concern may be that the directors will use the issue of new shares for some ulterior purpose, namely, for some purpose other than raising new capital for the company. Shareholders may fear that the directors will issue shares to 'friendly' shareholders who support them, or to individuals who favour a particular corporate strategy. For example, directors may use an issue of new shares to attempt to block a potential takeover bid, by issuing shares to a favoured bidder or to individuals who are opposed to the bid.[9]

Alternatively, the directors may issue shares in order to disrupt the balance of power between the majority and the minority within the company. For instance, in relation to the example with shareholder A in 4.2.1.1 above, the directors may be aligned with the majority shareholders or may come under pressure from the majority to reduce the control rights of the minority shareholder, A, in order to boost the position of the majority shareholders within the company.

4.2.2 Existing Company Law Mechanisms that Operate to Protect Shareholders

In general, company law regards the management of the company's affairs, including, therefore, the question of the issue of new shares, as being under the general responsibility of the board of directors.[10] A number of company law mechanisms do, however, exist that may operate to protect shareholders when new shares are issued.

4.2.2.1 *Directors' Duties*

The first company law mechanism that might provide shareholders with protection in this context is directors' duties.[11] In issuing shares, directors must comply with their directors' duties, including an obligation (i) to act in good faith in order 'to promote the success of the company for the benefit of the members as a whole'[12] and (ii) to exercise their powers for a proper purpose.[13]

---

[9] See 14.3.2, particularly 14.3.2.1.

[10] Shareholders do, of course, have various corporate governance rights which they may be able to utilise if they are unhappy with the decisions taken by directors; for example, shareholders have the right to remove directors at any time by ordinary resolution: Companies Act 2006, s 168(1).

[11] Before the UK implemented the provisions of the Second Company Law Directive (Directive 2012/30/EU, a recast of Council Directive 77/91/EEC), this was the main protection from abuse of managerial power offered by company law to shareholders concerned about these issues, although the Listing Rules of the London Stock Exchange also imposed some protections for shareholders, via the imposition of pre-emption rights.

[12] Companies Act 2006, s 172(1).

[13] Ibid, s 171(b).

The first duty provides some protection for shareholders concerned about value dilution. In particular, the duty to act in the best interests of the company operates as a constraint on the directors' commercial judgement when setting the price of the new share issue. The courts have, however, interpreted the directors' obligation to obtain the best price available for the shares as being compatible with a discount (potentially a deep discount) being offered on those shares, as discussed at 4.2.1.1 above. Consequently, this is a weak constraint and shareholders concerned about value dilution are unlikely to receive much comfort from this duty.

The duty to act for a proper purpose may provide more valuable protection for shareholders. This duty can potentially prevent directors using share issues to preserve their own control of the company or to advantage themselves in some other way. In *Howard Smith Ltd v Ampol Petroleum Ltd*,[14] for example, a majority shareholder (Ampol) wished to make an offer to acquire the remaining shares in the company. The directors of the company preferred a takeover offer from Howard Smith, but this offer could not succeed while Ampol remained a majority shareholder. The directors therefore caused the company to issue enough new shares to Howard Smith so that Ampol was reduced to a minority holding, and Howard Smith could launch its takeover offer with some hope of success. It was argued that the only proper purpose of a new issue of shares is to raise capital when a company needs it. This was rejected as too narrow.[15] There may well be other purposes for the issue of new shares that are perfectly proper, such as to secure the financial stability of the company.[16] Further, the courts have accepted that where the purpose is a proper one, the mere fact that an incidental (and desired) result is to deprive a shareholder of his voting majority or to defeat a takeover bid will not be sufficient to make the purpose improper. The proper purpose test must therefore be applied to the dominant or primary purpose of the directors.[17] Nevertheless, where the dominant purpose of the directors in issuing the new shares is clearly improper, they will be in breach of their directors' duties. In *Howard Smith v Ampol*, the predominant purpose of the directors was to dilute the majority voting power so as to enable Howard Smith's takeover offer to proceed. The purpose was to defeat Ampol's bid rather than to raise fresh capital. The court was clear that this was an improper purpose and a breach of the directors' duties.[18] As regards directors' attempts to block takeover bids, the provisions of the City Code on Takeovers and Mergers ('the Takeover Code') also operate to constrain directors' behaviour once a bid is imminent.[19]

---

[14] [1974] AC 821 (PC).

[15] Ibid, 835–36.

[16] See eg *Harlowe's Nominees Pty Ltd v Woodside Oil Co* (1968) 121 CLR 483 (Aust HC); *Teck Corp Ltd v Miller* (1972) 33 DLR (3d) 288 (BC Sup Ct).

[17] *Hirsche v Sims* [1894] AC 654 (PC).

[18] *Howard Smith Ltd v Ampol Petroleum Ltd* [1974] AC 821 (PC), 835–36. Notably, the court reached this conclusion even though the directors were not motivated by a desire to obtain a personal advantage and they considered that they were acting in the best interests of the company. See also *Hogg v Cramphorn Ltd* [1967] Ch 254; *Bamford v Bamford* [1970] Ch 212. However, it is not necessarily the case that every attempt by the directors to block or discourage a takeover will be a breach of their directors' duties, as discussed by the court in *Criterion Properties plc v Stratford UK Properties LLC* [2002] 2 BCLC 151, [2002] EWCA Civ 1883, [2004] UKHL 28 (see further 14.3.2.1.1).

[19] City Code on Takeovers and Mergers, GP 3 and r 21, discussed further at 14.3.2.2.1.

4.2.2.2 *Minority Shareholder Protection*

Company law also provides remedies for minority shareholders if they can demonstrate that their rights have been affected by a share issue. Establishing this may not be straight-forward for shareholders, however. These issues were explored in *Mutual Life Insurance Co of New York v The Rank Organisation Ltd.*[20] This case involved a decision by the directors of a company to exclude from a share issue shareholders holding 53 per cent of the company's equity. These shareholders were all resident in the US and Canada. They sought to challenge this decision on the basis that it was a breach of the contract between the company and its shareholders; specifically it was a breach of the requirement within the articles that all shareholders of the same class should be treated equally. Goulding J rejected this challenge for a number of reasons. First, he held that no shareholder has an absolute right to expect their interest to remain constant forever.[21] Second, the exclusion of the overseas sharehold-ers from the right to acquire the new shares did not affect the existence of their shares or the rights attached to them. This view accords with the approach adopted by English courts to the issue of variation of class rights: no variation will be said to occur if it is only the enjoy-ment of rights and not the rights themselves that have been altered. Accordingly, English company law takes the view that a decision to allot shares ranking alongside (or ahead of) existing shares does not amount to a variation of the rights of existing shareholders, so that their consent is not required under the variation of rights procedure laid down in the Companies Act 2006,[22] even though the practical effect of such an issue is to reduce the value of the existing shares.[23] This is on the basis that the rights of the existing shareholders (for example, the right to one vote per share) remain unchanged, albeit that the enjoyment of those rights (the economic value of the share) has been affected.[24] Third, Goulding J emphasised that the directors had acted bona fide in the company's interests in making the allotment, that there was no suggestion that the terms of the offer were improvident, and that there were good reasons for the differential treatment proposed by the company (related to the regulatory requirements of the relevant overseas jurisdiction). Consequently, it is clear that fair treatment may not require equal treatment, especially where some good objective justification can be provided for the differential treatment. Following this deci-sion, it has become very common to exclude overseas shareholders from rights issues.[25]

---

[20] [1985] BCLC 11.

[21] This contrasts with the view of the Advocate General to the Court of Justice of the EU, who has described a shareholders' right to retain their proportional share of the company's capital as inherent in being a shareholder (Case C-42/95 *Siemens AG v Henry Nold* [1996] ECR I-6017, Opinion of Advocate General Tesauro, para 15).

[22] Companies Act 2006, ss 630–31.

[23] *White v Bristol Aeroplane Co* [1953] Ch 65; *Re John Smith's Tadcaster Brewery Co* [1963] Ch 308.

[24] It is possible to deal with this issue by including within the articles the fact that this scenario should be treated as a variation of the rights of existing shareholders, thus requiring approval under the statutory procedure laid down in ss 630–31 Companies Act 2006; however explicit wording within a company's articles will be needed, to the effect that such a clause is intended to protect not only the shareholders' rights but also their economic inter-ests (see *Re Northern Engineering Industries plc* [1994] 2 BCLC 704; cf *White v Bristol Aeroplane Co* [1953] Ch 65; *Re John Smith's Tadcaster Brewery Co* [1963] Ch 308).

[25] Note that where shareholders are based outside the UK but within the EEA, the analysis put forward in *Mutual Life* is likely to be more difficult to utilise, in part because of the operation of art 46 Second Company Law Directive, but also because the justification for differential treatment in *Mutual Life*, namely that a different regulatory regime would apply, will be harder to establish as a result of the increasingly harmonised EU capital markets (discussed further at 4.4.3).

Alternatively, minority shareholders may be able to make use of the unfair prejudice remedy in section 994 of the Companies Act 2006 to deal with some of these concerns. This will not necessarily assist minority shareholders. Even though unfair prejudice was not alleged in *Mutual Life*, Goulding J was clear that there was no unfairness to the shareholders in that case, and it is unlikely that a petition on that basis would have succeeded.[26] Unfair prejudice is not a magic cure-all for shareholders in this scenario.[27] However, in some circumstances it may be valuable. An example of such a case is *Re Sunrise Radio Ltd*,[28] in which a minority shareholder in a private company successfully petitioned under section 994 in relation to an issue of new shares in the company. The minority shareholder, K, held 15 per cent of the shares in the company. As a result of the rights issue, the shares were allotted to X, a company owned by one of the directors of the company. The shares were issued at par, a price which was well below their value. As a consequence of this issue, K's shareholding was reduced to 8.3 per cent. The court held that although the reason for the rights issue offer had been the company's genuine need for cash, rather than the dilution of K's shareholding, nevertheless the directors had acted in breach of their directors' duty. Where, as was the case here, the directors know or can foresee that the minority shareholder will not or might not have the money or inclination to subscribe, the directors should, in fulfilment of the requirement of fairness, consider what price could and should be extracted from those willing and able to subscribe. The directors' failure to give proper consideration to the share price could amount to a breach of fiduciary duty. On the facts, it had not been a proper exercise of the directors' power to allot shares at par, because that resulted in a significant discrepancy between their value and the price paid. Consequently, the allotment of shares at par involved a breach of fiduciary duty which was unfairly prejudicial to K.

So, shareholders concerned about the effect of new share issues are not left completely unprotected by company law, and more specialised regulation such as the Takeover Code (discussed further in chapter fourteen). The question is the extent to which further specific protection at the point when shares are allotted is needed and is justified.

4.2.3 Justification for Additional Protection in Relation to Share Issues

Shareholders may well feel that the protections provided by general company law are rather flimsy, and that more specific protections are needed at the point of allotment. However, a desire on the part of the shareholders for some level of control over the allotment process needs to be balanced with other considerations which might suggest that leaving this issue in the hands of the directors is desirable. In particular, shareholders may be too focused on short-term concerns in relation to issues of new shares (specifically the concern that there may be wealth transfers to new shareholders), whereas directors may be in a better position to assess the company's long-term financing needs, which may be served by issuing shares to existing shareholders, but may be better fulfilled by other means. For example, there may be good reasons for expanding the pool of shareholders and broadening the investor base

---

[26] See also *Re BSB Holdings Ltd (No 2)* [1996] 1 BCLC 155 in which unfair prejudice was alleged, but Arden J adopted similar reasoning to Goulding J in *Mutual Life* to reject the unfair prejudice petition.

[27] See eg *Re Unisoft Group Ltd (No 3)* [1994] BCC 766; *Re Coroin Ltd* [2013] EWCA Civ 781.

[28] [2009] EWHC 2893 (Ch), aff'd [2013] EWCA Civ 667. See also *Graham v Every* [2014] EWCA Civ 191.

by allotting shares to new, external shareholders. Increasing the pool of investors to whom the company may turn for equity finance is likely to reduce the cost of equity finance for the company. Additionally, allowing shareholders to be part of the process of allotment necessarily adds to the time required to issue shares, and this may be problematic if the company needs to raise money quickly, particularly where market conditions are volatile. A good example of the problems that can arise is provided by the difficulties faced by UK banks in 2008, which sought to raise new equity quickly in very difficult market conditions. However, the legal and regulatory constraints in place, discussed at 4.3 and 4.4, add time and cost to the process. Although the banks were ultimately successful in raising the equity financing they sought, the added difficulties of doing so imposed by these legal and regulatory constraints raised questions about the desirability of these restrictions. Ultimately, provisions intended to protect shareholders could prove problematic if companies are not able to obtain the equity finance they need in the time frame within which they need it.[29]

A balance is therefore required. Shareholders understandably desire protection when new shares are issued, particularly against the danger of dilution. The agency issue that arises between directors and shareholders may be seen as particularly acute in relation to this matter. Weighed against that, companies also need to be able to raise money cheaply, efficiently and quickly, and undue interference by shareholders in the process of allotment might undermine companies' ability to do so.[30]

The approach adopted by the EU, in the context of public companies at least, is weighted in favour of shareholders. EU law, in the form of the Second Company Law Directive,[31] provides some significant shareholder protections in the context of new share issues for shareholders in public companies. So, for example, this directive provides that the consent of public shareholders to new share issues is required.[32] As a result, UK law contains some significant protections for shareholders, both in terms of directors' authority to allot shares and pre-emption rights. In neither case are these rights absolute: shareholders do not have an absolute veto over new share issues, but rather their consent is by majority vote, and pre-emption rights come with an in-built waiver mechanism that can again be operated via majority vote.[33] Nevertheless, these represent potentially important protective mechanisms for shareholders, as discussed at 4.3 and 4.4, particularly when it is appreciated that the UK has gold-plated the requirements of the directive and extended these protections to shareholders in private companies to some extent. Other jurisdictions tackle these issues in different ways. For example, pre-emption rights have largely been abandoned in the US.

There is no single correct balance to be struck between the shareholders' desire for protection and companies' need to raise equity capital quickly and easily. In recent years in the UK there has been a reassessment of the balance between these two competing issues, and a recognition that some adjustment of this balance, in favour of flexible capital-raising by companies, may be required.

---

[29] See E Ferran, 'What's Wrong with Rights Issues?' (2008) 2 *Law and Financial Markets Review* 523; Rights Issue Review Group, *A Report to the Chancellor of the Exchequer*, November 2008; FSA, *Rights Issue Subscription Periods* (CP09/14).

[30] For a discussion of the need for balance see eg P Myners, *Pre-Emption Rights: Final Report* (URN 05/679, February 2005), 3.

[31] Directive 2012/30/EU (a recast of Council Directive 77/91/EEC).

[32] Ibid, art 25.

[33] For discussion see 4.3 (as regards directors' authority to allot) and 4.4 (as regards pre-emption rights).

4.3 Directors' Authority to Allot Shares

In order to issue new shares, directors need to have authority to allot those shares.[34] Directors need to obtain the power to allot shares from the shareholders.[35] The rules regarding authorisation are different for different types of companies.[36] Directors of private companies with a single class of shares have authority to allot shares of that class unless the articles prohibit them from doing so.[37] For all other companies, directors can allot shares if they are authorised to do so by the company's articles, or by ordinary resolution.[38] The more permissive approach for private companies with one class of shares was introduced in the Companies Act 2006, following the recommendation of the Company Law Review process that preceded that Act.[39] This approach is based on the view that the requirement of shareholder consent is likely to be a formality in many private companies, in which directors and shareholders tend to be the same people. By contrast, there is a greater risk of opportunism where a company has more than one class of shares, and therefore at this point the shareholder consent requirement for private companies can serve a useful function.

Not to obtain the requisite consent is a criminal offence on the part of the directors knowingly involved,[40] but it does not affect the validity of the allotment.[41] This consent requirement applies to an allotment of shares, but also applies to the grant of rights to subscribe for, or to convert a security into, new shares in the company (such as a convertible bond) in order to avoid the consent requirement being circumvented by the issue of debt securities convertible into equity at a later stage.[42]

Directors may seek authorisation for 'a particular use of the power' to allot shares, for example where the issue is to raise capital for a specific project, or they may seek a more general authorisation, to be given in advance of the funds being required for any specific purpose.[43] The Act permits such an authorisation to be given for a period of up to five

---

[34] Prior to the Companies Act 2006, there was also a limit on the number of shares that directors were entitled to allot: the maximum authorised capital (Companies Act 1985, s 80). This concept has now been removed and is not found in the Companies Act 2006.

[35] These provisions apply to all types of shares, except shares allotted in pursuance of an employees' share scheme: Companies Act 2006, ss 549(1)(2).

[36] Companies Act 2006, s 549.

[37] Ibid, s 550.

[38] Ibid, s 551.

[39] Company Law Review Steering Group, *Modern Company Law for a Competitive Economy: Final Report* (URN 01/942), para 4.5. Prior to the 2006 Act, special authorisation requirements for share issues applied to all companies. These provisions were first introduced in the Companies Act 1980, when the UK implemented the Second Company Law Directive 77/91/EEC, art 29 (thereby gold-plating the directive's provisions, which applied only to public companies). The Companies Act 1980 provisions on this issue were subsequently consolidated into the Companies Act 1985, although an opt-out for regime for private companies was inserted via Companies Act 1989, s 115(1).

[40] Companies Act 2006, ss 549(3)–(4).

[41] Ibid, s 549(6). However, if in failing to comply with this section the directors act in breach of their general duties when making an allotment, its validity may then be challenged on that ground: *Hogg v Cramphorn* [1967] Ch 254; *Howard Smith Ltd v Ampol Petroleum Ltd* [1974] AC 821 (PC).

[42] Companies Act 2006, s 549(1). The requirement of shareholder consent is at the point of issuance of the convertible security, and not at the point of conversion (s 549(3)).

[43] Ibid, s 551(2). Additionally, the authorisation may be either unconditional, or subject to conditions.

years,[44] renewable for further five-year periods.[45] Whether the authorisation is general or specific it must state the maximum amount of shares that can be allotted under it by the directors, and the date on which the authority will expire.[46]

For companies other than private companies with a single class of shares, the need for the directors to go to the shareholders for their authority to allot shares is potentially important. Shareholders have the opportunity to exert control over share allotments, and they have flexibility as to how much control they wish to exercise, depending on the extent of the authorisation that they give to the directors. Where the authorisation given is extensive, for example five years in duration and for a large number of shares, then the level of control that shareholders will have via this mechanism will be very limited.

Institutional shareholders attach importance to this form of shareholder protection.[47] The Investment Association issues guidance for institutional investors on the authority that directors should be given to allot new shares.[48] Until 2008 this was the lesser of (i) the company's unissued ordinary share capital or (ii) one-third of the company's issued ordinary share capital. However, as discussed at 4.2.3, difficulties arose in 2008 for UK banks that sought to raise equity finance quickly, as they found that this constraint on their ability to allot shares compromised their ability to do so. As a result, the current guidance from the Investment Association provides more flexibility to companies: requests to allot a further one-third of the company's issued ordinary share capital will be regarded as routine, provided that the additional one-third is issued on a pre-emptive basis and is valid for a maximum of one year.[49] In addition, the grant of this additional 'headroom' is subject to the condition that if the directors exercise this power, and the aggregate actual usage of the authority exceeds one-third, and the monetary proceeds exceed one-third of the pre-issue market capitalisation, then members of the board wishing to remain in office need to stand for re-election at the next AGM.

4.4 Pre-Emption Rights

A second, significant, control mechanism that shareholders have over share issues is via pre-emption rights. Broadly, pre-emption rights provide an opportunity for existing shareholders to subscribe for securities in a new issue in proportion to their existing holdings. Predominantly this is intended to address shareholders' concerns about dilution. Although pre-emption rights can be disapplied, or even excluded entirely in some circumstances,[50]

---

[44] Ibid, s 551(3)(b).

[45] Ibid, s 551(4).

[46] Ibid, s 551(3). Where an allotment relates to convertible securities, the maximum number of shares that can be allotted subject to the rights allotted must be stated: s 551(6).

[47] See eg NAPF, *Corporate Governance Policy and Voting Guidelines* (November 2013), 36.

[48] The Investment Association was formed from the merger of the Investment Affairs Division of the Association of British Insurers (ABI) and the Investment Managers Association (IMA) in 2014, at which point it assumed the role of issuing guidance previously issued by the ABI.

[49] IMA, *Share Capital Management Guidelines*, July 2014, endorsing the approach adopted by the ABI in 2009: ABI, *Directors' Power to Allot Share Capital and Dis-Apply Shareholders' Pre-Emption Rights*, December 2009.

[50] See 4.4.3.

the UK regime essentially operates an opt-out structure for all companies, including private companies with only one class of shares;[51] in other words, the default rule for all companies is that pre-emption rights will apply.

4.4.1 Scope of Pre-Emption Rights

Under section 561 of the Companies Act 2006, any proposed allotment of equity securities[52] must first be offered to existing shareholders on a pre-emptive basis—that is, the company must offer those securities first on the same or more favourable terms to existing shareholders in proportion to their existing holdings.[53] This applies to both voting and non-voting shares. Pre-emption rights are therefore a form of option to acquire those shares before they are allotted to other people. The offer must be in writing and kept open for a minimum of 14 days.[54] Pre-emption offers can now be communicated to shareholders electronically.[55]

There are, however, a number of important exemptions in relation to these pre-emption rules. On the whole these exemptions are eminently sensible. For example, an issue of bonus shares is excluded, on the basis that no pre-emption problem arises.[56] It is also understandable that an issue of shares held under an employees' share scheme is excluded, since such schemes would be unworkable if every time a further allotment was made pursuant to the scheme all equity shareholders had to be offered pre-emptive rights.[57] More problematic is the fact that pre-emption rights are only triggered where the proposed issue is exclusively for cash.[58] This can have beneficial effects: for instance it facilitates share-for-share takeovers and other transactions in which companies use their shares as consideration for an acquisition. In such circumstances it would be impractical for companies to make a pre-emptive offer to existing shareholders on the same terms.

---

[51] See now Companies Act 2006, ch 3 of Part 17. Pre-emption rights were first introduced into company law in Companies Act 1980, s 17 to give effect to art 33 Second Company Law Directive 77/91/EEC (thereby gold-plating the directive's requirement by extending the obligation from public companies to include private companies). The pre-emption provisions of the Companies Act 1980 were replaced by Companies Act 1985, s 89, and later the provisions in the 2006 Act.

[52] The term 'equity securities' is defined in Companies Act 2006, s 560(1) as being ordinary shares in the company or rights to subscribe for, or convert securities into, ordinary shares in the company. The definition of ordinary shares is 'shares other than shares that as respects dividends and capital carry a right to participate only up to a specified amount in a distribution' (s 560(1)).

[53] For the definition of 'allotment of equity securities' see ibid, s 560(2)(3).

[54] Ibid, s 562(5). This period was initially 21 days, but the Myners Report on Pre-Emption Rights (DTI, *Pre-Emption Rights: Final: A Study by Paul Myners into the Impact of Shareholders' Pre-Emption Rights on a Public Company's Ability to Raise New Capital* (URN 05/679, February 2005)) recommended that the period for acceptances be reduced to 14 days, on the basis that the existing procedure was too lengthy and cumbersome. The 2006 Act included a facility for the Secretary of State to reduce the period to less than 21 days (but not less than 14 days) by statutory instrument: s 562(6). The reduction of the period from 21 to 14 days was effected by the Companies (Share Capital and Acquisition by Company of its Own Shares) Regulations 2009 (SI 2009/2022) with effect from 1 October 2009.

[55] Companies Act 2006, s 562(2). Whatever form of communication is used, companies will have to communicate offers to all shareholders with a registered address in an EEA state, not merely those with a registered address in the UK (s 562(3)).

[56] Ibid, s 564. This is because an issue of bonus shares involves the capitalisation of the company's reserves, no payment is made to shareholders and, in general, the shares must be allotted pro rata to those entitled to the reserve, were it to be distributed.

[57] Ibid, s 566.

[58] Ibid, s 565.

The restriction of statutory pre-emption provisions in this way, however, creates a potentially significant gap in the regime designed to protect shareholders against dilution.[59] It is possible for this exemption to be used to avoid or evade the statutory pre-emption rules. The inclusion of any element of non-cash consideration will mean that the pre-emption rules do not apply. For example, vendor placings are a common way to avoid the pre-emption provisions. In these transactions a purchaser allots new shares to the vendor in consideration for an asset (and the issue of those shares therefore falls within the non-cash exemption), and the new shares are then immediately sold on the market, the result being that the vendor receives cash for the asset and the company acquires the asset without having to go to its existing shareholders for finance or for permission to raise the finds on a non-pre-emptive basis. In practice such structures are generally regarded as unexceptional, as long as the issue of shares is not too large and the discount to the market price at which the shares are issued is reasonably modest. For listed companies, the Listing Rules, drawn up by the FCA to deal with companies with a listing on the Main Market,[60] limit the discount to 10 per cent of the market price unless the shareholders have approved a larger discount.[61] In addition, guidelines created by institutional investors seek to constrain directors in this regard, both as to the size of the issue and as to the size of the discount offered.[62]

Another possibility is a cashbox structure. Pre-emption rights do not apply to the cashbox structure because, instead of receiving cash in consideration of the issue of the new shares, the company will receive the entire issued share capital of a cashbox company, a company whose only assets are cash reserves (that is, the issue is structured as a non-cash issue). In such a structure the company wishing to raise equity finance will set up a newco (often a Jersey company for tax reasons) and newco's share capital will comprise ordinary and redeemable preference shares. An offer of newco ordinary and preference shares is made to the company's investment bank or broker, which will undertake to pay the subscription price for those shares. The bank or broker will then agree to transfer the newco ordinary and preference shares to the company in consideration for the allotment of shares in the company to placees found by the bank. The placing by the company is thus an issue for non-cash consideration. The bank or broker receives and uses the net proceeds of the placing to discharge its undertaking to pay the subscription price to newco. The preference shares and the ordinary shares in newco issued to the bank or broker are transferred to the company in consideration of the issue of the new shares to the placees. Newco is then a wholly owned subsidiary of the company. The redeemable preference shares are redeemed and the cash returned to the company. Typically newco is then liquidated by the directors. Cashbox structures raise concerns regarding the potential circumvention of the statutory

---

[59] Some protection against financial dilution is potentially provided by the provisions that require independent valuation of non-cash consideration received for the shares of public companies, discussed at 5.3.2.2.2, but there are some gaps in this statutory protection (for example, it does not apply to takeovers and mergers) and it does not provide shareholders with any individual rights, unlike pre-emption rights.

[60] See 10.3.3.1 for a discussion of the major UK equity markets for publicly traded shares.

[61] FCA Handbook, LR 9.5.10.

[62] See eg ABI, *Shareholders' Pre-Emption Rights and Vendor Placings* (1999), which provides that in vendor placings existing shareholders are entitled to expect a clawback (ie a right to subscribe for a share of an issue at a pre-arranged price) where the size of the issue is greater than 10% of the issue share capital or the discount greater than 5%. In practice vendor placings with clawbacks are rare: ABI, *Encouraging Equity Investment: Facilitation of Efficient Equity Capital Raising in the UK market* (July 2013), 33.

pre-emption provisions. The predominant constraints on directors using this kind of structure are imposed via guidelines produced by institutional investors.[63]

Where statutory pre-emption procedures are not followed, the company and every officer of it who knowingly permitted or authorised the contravention are jointly and severally liable to compensate any person to whom the offer should have been made for any loss, damage, costs or expenses which that person incurred as a result of the contravention.[64] Such failure does not, however, invalidate the allotment of shares.[65]

4.4.2 Renounceable Letters of Allotment

Pre-emption rights only protect shareholders from the possibility of dilution if they are financially in a position to take up the shares on offer. The use of renounceable letters of allotment can protect shareholders who cannot afford to do so, at least from value dilution if not from voting dilution.[66] Such letters enable the shareholder to transfer the right to subscribe for the new shares to a third party. Where a renounceable letter of allotment is issued, the shareholder can protect herself by accepting the right to acquire the new shares from the company and then renouncing that right via an assignment of it to a third party who wishes to buy the new shares. The payment that the shareholder receives for the shares should compensate her for her value dilution. Another possibility may be for the shareholder to maintain the value of her shares in the company, but not the proportion of shares held, by selling part of the rights offered—an action referred to as 'tail-swallowing'.

The use of renounceable letters of this kind is permitted, but not required, by the Companies Act 2006.[67] The 2006 Act therefore only protects shareholders from dilution to the extent that they take up the shares offered to them. However, the FCA Listing Rules require that where a listed company conducts a rights issue the issuer must make the offer to existing shareholders on the basis of a renounceable letter or equivalent document that can be traded by the shareholder during the offer period.[68] Such a rights issue may be contrasted with an 'open offer', whereby the shareholder is given the option of simply taking the shares at the price offered or forgoing the offer.[69] In practice, rights issues are the form of pre-emptive offering preferred by investors and therefore, in listed companies at least, pre-emptive offers are commonly made on a renounceable basis.

---

[63] ABI, *Encouraging Equity Investment*, ibid, 34–37.

[64] Companies Act 2006, s 563.

[65] However, in some circumstances the court may exercise its power under s 125 Companies Act 2006 to order the rectification of the register of members by removing the names of those to whom the shares were wrongfully allotted: see eg *Re Thundercrest Ltd* [1995] BCLC 117.

[66] See 4.2.1.1.

[67] Companies Act 2006, s 561(2).

[68] See FCA Handbook, Glossary Definitions. An additional protection provided to shareholders by the Listing Rules is that where in a rights issue existing shareholders do not take up their right to subscribe, the shares must be placed in the market at the end of the period, and any premium obtained over the purchase price (net of expenses) is to be held for the account of the holders, subject to a £5 per holder de minimis which may be retained for the company's benefit: FCA Handbook, LR 9.5.4. The equivalent protection for existing shareholders under an open offer is LR 9.5.8A.

[69] Ibid, LR 9.5.7–9.5.8.

4.4.3 Waiver of Pre-Emption Rights

Pre-emption rights can be excluded or disapplied by a collective decision of the shareholders. As regards exclusion, in private companies this can be achieved by a provision in the articles.[70] By contrast, in public companies exclusion is only possible where the articles provide a pre-emption alternative to the statutory scheme.[71]

As regards disapplication, both public and private companies can disapply pre-emption rights by a provision to that effect in their articles or by a special resolution.[72] These provisions relate to the provisions regarding directors' authority to allot, discussed at 4.3 above. Where directors do not need shareholder authorisation to issue the shares (ie the company is a private company with one class of shares), or the authorisation is needed but has already been given by the shareholders (via a general authorisation), then either the articles or a special resolution can disapply the pre-emption rights entirely or can give the directors discretion to apply them with modifications.[73] Where the directors have a general authority to act, the disapplication can only last as long as the underlying general authority.[74] Where, however, authorisation is required of the shareholders in relation to the issue, then a special resolution will be needed to disapply the statutory provisions in relation to a particular issue of shares, or to allow the directors to apply the statutory provisions subject to the modifications set out in the resolution.[75]

In practice it is common for companies to make use of these disapplication provisions. There are a number of reasons for this. One might be a desire to exclude certain overseas shareholders from the offer. This is common in the case of US shareholders, since under US federal securities legislation a company may have to register with the SEC if it extends the offer to such shareholders. The Listing Rules specifically permit pre-emptive offers to exclude shareholders whom the company considers it necessary to exclude on account of the laws or regulatory requirements of another country,[76] and this form of exclusion has also been upheld by the English courts.[77] Such an outcome would be harder to sustain in relation to shareholders outside the UK but within the EEA, both because equality of treatment for shareholders in public companies is mandated by the Second Company Law Directive[78] and because the broadly harmonised state of EU capital markets means that there is reduced scope for an argument for differential treatment based on some quirk of foreign laws or regulatory requirements.

Additional requirements are put in place for publicly listed companies: the Listing Rules impose some constraints,[79] and a set of guidelines drawn up by institutional investors

---

[70] Companies Act 2006, s 567.

[71] Ibid, s 568.

[72] Ibid, ss 570–71.

[73] Ibid, ss 569–70.

[74] Ibid, s 570(3) and s 571(3).

[75] Ibid, s 571. Special procedural requirements apply to this special resolution: ss 571(5)–(7) and 572.

[76] FCA Handbook, LR 9.3.12.

[77] *Mutual Life Assurance Co of New York v Rank Organisation Ltd* [1985] BCLC 11, discussed at 4.2.2.2.

[78] Directive 2012/30/EU (a recast of Directive 77/91/EEC), art 46 and note also the requirements of the Transparency Directive (Directive 2004/109/EC as amended by Directive 2013/50/EU) as regards equality of treatment for shareholders with respect to information requirements (implemented via FCA Handbook, DTR 6.1.3).

[79] For example, the maximum discount at which a company can issue shares by way of a rights issue is 10% of the prevailing market price, unless shareholders agree to a larger discount: FCA Handbook, LR 9.5.10 (see also 4.4.1).

impose further restrictions. A Statement of Principles drawn up by the Stock Exchange Pre-Emption Group[80] provides guidance on the circumstances in which institutional investors should vote in favour of a resolution disapplying pre-emption rights.[81] The principles apply to all issues of equity securities that are undertaken to raise cash for the issuer or its subsidiaries, irrespective of the legal form of the transaction.[82] A request for a general disapplication is likely to be supported where it meets the criteria as to size and duration set out in the principles.[83] As to size, the starting point is that the company should not seek to issue more than 5 per cent of its issued share capital non-pre-emptively in any given year. However, an additional 5 per cent may be permitted to be issued non-pre-emptively if the company confirms in its AGM circular that it intends to use it only in connection with an acquisition or a specified capital investment which is announced at the same time as the issue, or which has taken place in the preceding six-month period and is disclosed in the announcement of the issue.[84] This is also subject to the total shares issued non-preemptively over three years being 7.5 per cent or less of the issued ordinary share capital.[85] Issuing shares at a discount is noted to be a concern. If a discount is used, companies should restrict it to a maximum of 5 per cent.[86] Where the company wishes to seek a disapplication of pre-emption rights that fall outside these parameters, shareholders will need to be consulted. The Statement of Principles details a number of considerations that are then likely to be relevant for shareholders in determining whether to approve the request, including the strength of the business case, the stewardship and governance of the company, other financing options, the level of dilution that the issue will entail for existing shareholders, and contingency plans in case the request is not granted.[87]

This Statement of Principles has a significant impact on the disapplication of pre-emption rights in practice. Whilst it does not have the force of law, this document represents the views of the majority of major UK institutional investors.[88]

---

[80] The Pre-Emption Group comprises representatives of institutional investors, investment banks and listed companies.

[81] See Pre-Emption Group, *Disapplying Pre-Emption Rights: Statement of Principles*, 2015. See also IMA, *Share Capital Management Guidelines*, July 2014, which endorses the application of these principles. The principles apply to companies (wherever incorporated) with shares admitted to the premium listing segment of the Official List. Standard listed issuers and AIM issuers are also encouraged to adopt these principles.

[82] Pre-Emption Group, *Disapplying Pre-Emption Rights: Statement of Principles*, 2015, Part 1 para 2. So, for example, transactions which are structured so that an issue of shares for non-cash consideration falls outside the scope of the pre-emption (discussed in 4.4.1) are subject to the principles. This is a change from the previous version of the Statement of Principles, issued in 2008. Vendor placings remain outside the scope of the principles, however (but shareholders will nonetheless expect a right of clawback in respect of any vendor placing that represents more than 10% of ordinary share capital or that is undertaken at a discount of more than 5%: Part 1 para 3).

[83] Ibid, Part 2A para 2.

[84] Ibid, Part 2A para 3. The reference to the additional 5% is new to the 2015 Statement of Principles and did not appear in the 2008 version. It is intended to provide more flexibility to companies in their capital raising endeavours in relation to acquisitions and capital investments. It does not apply to a non pre-emptive offering that is raising capital for the purposes of a 'war-chest' for potential future acquisitions.

[85] Ibid, Part 2B para 1 (this limit excludes any equity securities issued pursuant to a specific disapplication of pre-emption rights, and any equity securities issued pursuant to a general disapplication of pre-emption rights in connection with an acquisition or specified capital investment as described in para 3 of Part 2A).

[86] Ibid, Part 2B para 5. This figure must include expenses, such as underwriting commissions, brokerage fees and professional advisers' fees. This is a change from the 2008 Statement of Principles.

[87] Ibid, Part 3.

[88] See generally DTI, *Pre-Emption Rights: Final: A Study by Paul Myners into the Impact of Shareholders' Pre-Emption Rights on a Public Company's Ability to Raise New Capital* (URN 05/679, February 2005).

4.4.4 Is the Current Balance Correct as Between Shareholder Protection and the Company's Capital-Raising Needs?

In general, of the two forms of shareholder protection provided by company law specifically in relation to share issues, namely the requirement for directors to seek authority to allot from shareholders and pre-emption rights, the latter tends to provide shareholders with a greater measure of protection. This is in part due to the way authority to allot operates in practice, with authorisation being given for long periods and for large numbers of shares. It is also due to the fact that pre-emption rights deliver to the shareholders either the ability to avoid dilution by purchasing shares in an issue (or trading the right to subscribe, if that option is offered), or an opportunity to engage in dialogue with the directors if a waiver of pre-emption rights is sought. This opportunity for dialogue is potentially significant. Indeed, when Paul Myners reviewed this issue in 2005 it was the corporate governance benefits of pre-emption rights that he regarded as being particularly valuable.[89] An influential report by Julian Franks and Colin Mayer has suggested that pre-emption rights can have an important disciplinary effect on underperforming management, by limiting their access to equity.[90] From this perspective, an advantage of the UK's opt-out system of pre-emption rights, as compared to the US system of opt-in rights, is the fact that the directors have to go to the shareholders to get pre-emption rights disapplied. This opportunity for dialogue can be valuable for shareholders, particularly institutional investors in publicly listed companies who will need to be consulted by directors, as least where the disapplication is not routine. Further, the need to obtain approval for a disapplication of pre-emption rights may help to deter companies from launching inappropriate issues of capital, the proceeds of which may fail to generate value.

Accordingly, pre-emption rights can provide shareholders with an important protection against dilution and may additionally perform a valuable corporate governance role. However, as discussed at 4.2.3, from the perspective of those seeking to finance companies, pre-emption rights can be problematic, both in terms of restricting the pool of investors to existing shareholders and increasing the time required for equity financing to take place. These issues came to the fore after the financial crisis. Difficulties faced by companies seeking to raise equity finance quickly post-crisis were examined by the Rights Issue Review Group in 2008. The main recommendation of this group was to reduce the time involved in rights issues.[91] Steps have been taken to deal with this point, with the period during which pre-emption offers remain open being reduced from 21 days to 14 days in 2009.[92] The guidance provided to institutional investors has also been relaxed, in light of these difficulties, in order to provide further flexibility to companies seeking to raise equity finance.[93]

Concerns about these matters persist, although to date it has been left to the market to provide further solutions to these problems. For example, a timing difficulty arises for companies engaged in rights issues, due to the fact that if the company needs to obtain

---

[89] Ibid.

[90] J Franks and C Mayer, 'Governance as a Source of Managerial Discipline', www.nbb.be/doc/ts/publications/WP/WP31En.pdf.

[91] *A Report to the Chancellor of the Exchequer by the Rights Issue Review Group*, November 2008.

[92] Companies (Share Capital and Acquisition by Company of its Own Shares) Regulations 2009 (SI 2009/2022), amending Companies Act 2006, s 562(5).

[93] See 4.3.

shareholder approval (for instance because the directors do not have authority to allot the shares, or because shareholder consent to disapply the pre-emption provisions is required) then that period for obtaining this consent does not run concurrently with the 14-day period that the shareholders have in which to consider the offer. This is because as soon as the offer is made, trading in the rights will begin, but if shareholder approval is not ultimately obtained, all of these trades will need to be unwound. This, therefore, extends the time required for a rights issue.[94] The use of open offers avoids this problem, since no trading in the rights takes place, and therefore the two periods can run simultaneously, but of course shareholders are not protected from dilution in an open offer if they cannot take up the offer. Market practice responded to this difficulty by developing the use of 'compensatory open offers', whereby shares not taken up by a shareholder are sold by the company into the market, and any premium over the offer price is paid to the shareholder who did not take up the offer. This development allows the two periods to run concurrently, reducing the period required to raise equity capital without reducing shareholder protection.

Ensuring a balance between shareholder protection and the needs of the company is not straightforward, and it is unsurprising that this balance comes under pressure in times of severe economic difficulties. In general, the approach of UK company law, which follows the lead of the EU Second Company Law Directive, leans heavily in favour of shareholder protection. Changes to the guidelines for institutional investors and market developments have been able to deal well with the difficulties facing companies. The tweaks made to existing company law provisions, such as shortening the time period for shareholders to make their decision, are sensible, and little further legislative change seems to be required at present.

4.5 Registration of Shares

The process of becoming a shareholder involves two steps: the first involves a contract of allotment between the company and the investor, and the second involves the registration of the member.[95] Allotment alone does not make a person a member of a company. Entry on the register is also needed to give the allottee legal title to the shares.[96] Registration by the company should be 'as soon as practicable' and in any event within two months of the date of allotment.[97]

Companies issuing registered shares must keep a register containing the names of the members.[98] Traditionally, company registers have only recorded those with legal title to the shares.[99] On this analysis, the company's relationship is with the person who is registered

---

[94] Although the Rights Issue Review Group suggested tackling this problem by having the periods run simultaneously, but this was not recommended by the FSA: FSA, *Report to HM Treasury on the Implementation of the Rights Issue Review Group*, April 2010.

[95] See eg *National Westminster Bank plc v IRC* [1995] 1 AC 111, 126 per Lord Templeman.

[96] See eg Companies Act 2006, s 112(2).

[97] Ibid, s 554. Non-compliance with this obligation constitutes a criminal offence for the company and every officer in default: s 554(3).

[98] Companies Act 2006, s 113. This applies to all shares, whether certificated or dematerialised, but in the latter case the shares are also registered in the CREST register, which is the root of legal title. See 4.6.2.

[99] Companies Act 2006, s 126. It is very common for shares to be held beneficially. For example, shares may be the subject of a traditional trust. Alternatively, the investor could chose to hold dematerialised shares indirectly,

as a member of the company, who is the legal owner of the shares. In such circumstances, a transfer of beneficial interest in the shares requires an agreement to sell and a transfer, but does not involve the company's register. The beneficial owner has a relationship with its trustee and not with the company.[100] However, the Small Business, Enterprise and Employment Act 2015 introduces a new requirement for a central registry of those with significant control over certain companies.[101] This new requirement applies to all UK private and public companies, other than those publicly traded companies which already report under the Disclosure and Transparency Rules in the FCA Handbook.[102] 'Significant control' for this purpose includes those with a beneficial interest in more than 25 per cent of the shares or voting rights in a company, as well as those who otherwise exercise control over the company and its management, for example by having the right, directly or indirectly, to appoint or remove the majority of the board of directors.[103] This information will be publicly available. For beneficial shareholders falling within the ambit of this new requirement, the traditional model of beneficial ownership is therefore replaced. Instead, these new provisions place obligations on companies (to investigate and obtain information on those with 'significant control' and to keep that information up to date)[104] and also on those whose interests are now registrable as a result of the new provisions (to provide information to the company).[105] Transfers of shares may therefore also require changes to the new register of those with significant control within the company.

4.6 Methods of Holding Shares

4.6.1 Certificated Shares

Shares can be held in certificated or uncertificated form.[106] Until 1996, all shares were held in certificated form, which involves every shareholder, in addition to having their name in the

---

via an intermediary (see 11.2.2.1.2), or the investor could invest in a financial product (such as a pension or a unit trust) which involves individuals investing in the stock market via a financial institution which holds the legal title to the shares in question. In the case of pension funds, for example, the pension scheme will usually be constituted as a trust, separate from the sponsoring entity. The beneficiaries of the scheme are, collectively, the ultimate beneficial owners of the scheme's equity investors. In these circumstances the private investor will hold indirectly via an intermediary, and indeed it is likely that the intermediary is holding for very many private investors in this way.

[100] The trustee will have to account to the beneficiary for any dividends it receives, and it is a well-established principle that the beneficial owner of shares, if absolutely entitled as against the registered owner, can instruct the registered owner how to deal with the shares, and how votes should be cast: *Kirby v Wilkins* [1929] 2 Ch 444, 454 per Romer J, and see also the discussion at 11.2.2.1.2.

[101] Small Business, Enterprise and Employment Act 2015, s 81 and Sch 3 (for discussion see BIS, *Transparency & Trust: Enhancing the Transparency of UK Company Ownership and Increasing Trust in UK Business*, Government Response, April 2014, 18–39).

[102] See FCA Handbook, DTR 5, discussed at 11.3.2.3 (consequently, for example, companies listed on the London Main Market are exempt from this requirement).

[103] Small Business, Enterprise and Employment Act 2015, Sch 3 inserting a new Chapter 21A and Sch 1A into Companies Act 2006; see in particular Companies Act 2006, Sch 1A paras 2–3.

[104] See Companies Act 2006, ss 790D–790E. Failure to do so will be a criminal offence on the part of both the company and its officers: s 790F.

[105] Ibid, ss 790G–790H.

[106] For further discussion of these issues see *Law of Personal Property*, ch 23.

share register of the company, having a paper certificate evidencing their shareholding.[107] Where shares are certificated, the primary record of the ownership of company shares is the register of members.[108] However, in 1996 it became possible for shares to be held in uncertificated form, thereby avoiding the generation and transfer of large volumes of paper which the certificated method involves. As a consequence, shares may be dematerialised and held through CREST.[109]

It should also be noted that if shares are not issued in the UK, they may be held in the form of a globalised share certificate, in a similar form to a global note representing an issue of debt securities.[110]

4.6.2 Uncertificated (Dematerialised) Shares

CREST is a system operated by Euroclear UK and Ireland Ltd (EUI), which was set up to enable certificated securities to be converted to uncertificated ones, and for new securities to be issued in uncertificated form.[111] 'Uncertificated' securities are also known as 'dematerialised' securities, and it is the latter nomenclature that will be used in this section. Both shares and debt securities may be held through CREST, provided that certain requirements are met.[112] EUI maintains the CREST register, on which the securities are registered and which is the root of legal title for a CREST member,[113] although, in relation to shares, the issuer is also obliged to keep a register which must be reconciled to the CREST register.[114] The registration must be in the name of a CREST member, who can be either a direct member[115] or a sponsored member.[116] The securities are transferred between members[117] by an entry in the CREST system. EUI has no proprietary interest in the securities: the registered member is the legal owner. It is also possible for companies or individuals to hold dematerialised securities through an intermediary who is a CREST member.[118] At present,

---

[107] If the shares are held in certificated form, the company has an obligation to issue a share certificate within two months of the entry of the shareholder onto the register of members: Companies Act 2006, s 769.

[108] Companies Act 2006, s 112.

[109] For an account of the CREST system see *Mills (joint administrators of Kaupthing Singer & Friedlander Ltd) v Sportsdirect.com Retail Ltd* [2010] EWHC 1072 (Ch) [5]–[6].

[110] See 8.3.2.3.2(b).

[111] The CREST system is governed by the Uncertificated Securities Regulations 2001 (SI 2001/3755) (USR), as amended by the Uncertificated Securities (Amendment) (Eligible Debt Securities) Regulations 2003 (SI 2003/1633), which extended the scope of CREST to include debt securities, the Uncertificated Securities (Amendment) Regulations 2007 (SI 2007/124) and the Uncertificated Securities (Amendment) Regulations 2013 (SI 2013/632). EUI also operates a clearing and settlement system which is used by members and their clients to trade and transfer securities.

[112] In relation to shares see USR, regs 14 to 16. In relation to other securities see USR, reg 19. For a discussion of this issue in the context of debt securities see 8.3.2.1.

[113] USR, regs 24(2) and (3).

[114] USR, reg 20 (see 4.5 above). If there is a conflict between the two registers, the CREST register prevails: USR, regs 20(5) and 24(2).

[115] An institution which has an electronic connection directly with the settlement system.

[116] This can be anyone (including any individual) who has a sponsorship arrangement with a direct member.

[117] It is only possible to transfer between members, but any buyer who is not a member can become a sponsored member, or have a member hold for him as an intermediary.

[118] See 4.6.4.

only listed companies are obliged to have dematerialised shares,[119] but this method of holding is now common in the UK.

4.6.3 Bearer Shares

Until 2015, the Companies Act 2006 allowed companies, if permitted by their articles, to create bearer shares, that is to issue warrants in relation to any fully paid shares stating that the bearer of the warrant was entitled to the shares specified in it.[120] Bearer shares thus provided an exception to the principles of registration described in this section so far. Title to such shares passed via manual delivery of the warrant, a negotiable instrument.[121] The bearer of the warrant was therefore a shareholder, but whether they were also to be regarded as a member of the company depended on the provisions in the company's articles.[122] Bearer shares were hardly ever issued, and the Small Business, Enterprise and Employment Act 2015 prohibits the creation of new bearer shares and provides a nine-month surrender period for existing issued bearer shares.[123]

4.6.4 Shares Held Through an Intermediary[124]

It is now very common for shareholders to hold shares indirectly through an intermediary, rather than being registered owners of certificated or dematerialised shares. This method of holding shares is usual in the international capital markets, although the precise model used varies from jurisdiction to jurisdiction.[125] This pattern of holding is also very common for debt securities.[126] There are many sorts of investor and patterns of holding: the following, taken from an analysis by Joanna Benjamin,[127] describes some archetypes, but the reality is, in fact, that there are investors on a spectrum between these archetypes. At one end of the spectrum are long-term investors, comprising both individual and institutional investors.

---

[119] All shares traded on the London Stock Exchange must be eligible for electronic trading, ie must be potentially available in uncertificated (ie dematerialised) form: FCA Handbook, LR 6.1.23–6.1.24.

[120] Companies Act 2006, s 779.

[121] Ibid, s 779(2). See also *Webb, Hale and Co v Alexandrina Water Co Ltd* (1905) 21 TLR 572.

[122] Companies Act 2006, s 122(3).

[123] Small Business, Enterprise and Employment Act 2015, s 84 and Sch 4 (and see BIS, *Transparency & Trust: Enhancing the Transparency of UK Company Ownership and Increasing Trust in UK Business, Government Response*, April 2014, 40–44).

[124] For detailed analysis and discussion see Benjamin: Interests in Securities; R Goode, 'The Nature and Transfer of Right in Dematerialised and Immobilised Securities' [1996] *Journal of International Banking and Financial Law* 167; Law Commission, *The UNIDROIT Convention on Substantive Rules regarding Intermediated Securities: Further Updated Advice to the Treasury* (May 2008); Goode: Credit and Security; L Gullifer, 'Protection of Investors in Intermediated Securities' in J Armour and J Payne (eds), *Rationality in Company Law* (Oxford, Hart Publishing, 2009); L Gullifer and J Payne (eds), *Intermediated Securities: Legal Problems and Practical Issues* (Oxford, Hart Publishing, 2010) chs 1, 2 and 3.

[125] The widespread cross-border holding of intermediated securities has caused international concern and has led to calls for harmonisation; see 8.3.2.3.2.2(b).

[126] See 8.3.2.3.2(b).

[127] See J Benjamin, 'The Law and Regulation Of Custody Securities: Cutting the Gordian Knot' (2014) 9 *Capital Markets Law Journal* 327.

They are interested in the growth in the value of the securities and in receiving dividends.[128] They may be interested in being involved in the governance of the issuer.[129] The benefits, for these investors, of holding securities in this way are the management and administration services provided by the intermediary, as well as the custodial security. Further, transfers, when they take place, can be done easily and securely. These investors are best served by the intermediary recording their holding in a segregated account, as this usually provides them with maximum protection in the event of the insolvency of the intermediary.

At the other end of the spectrum are hedge funds and other institutions that acquire and hold securities in order to trade them, and to make profits through arbitrage. These investors hold securities through intermediaries because of the speed and ease of transfer through the use of pooled accounts, and because intermediaries (such as prime brokers) will often provide the finance required to buy the securities, secured on the securities themselves. Many institutions (not just hedge funds) require the method by which their securities are held to generate income for them: they are willing to sacrifice some security for this. Therefore, they agree that their securities will be held in pooled accounts and that the intermediary has a right to use their securities in income earning transactions, such as stock lending. In a stock lending transaction,[130] the 'lender' transfers title to securities to the 'borrower', and the 'borrower' undertakes to re-transfer equivalent securities at a later date, and to pay a fee. The 'borrower' will usually provide money collateral to the 'lender' to secure its obligation to return the securities.[131] Since the intermediary is able to lend very large blocks of securities (because they are held in pooled accounts) it can earn considerable fees this way, which are passed on to its clients, the investors.

The legal analysis of the holding of securities through an intermediary under English law is discussed in detail in chapter eight in the context of debt securities.[132] The legal owner of debt securities is typically the depositary holding a global note which represents the entire issue of the securities. In the UK, shares are not issued as global certificates, and so the legal owners of any one (dematerialised) issue are likely to be a mixture of first tier intermediaries (banks, which are likely to be direct members of CREST) and investors (institutions or individuals who are likely to be sponsored members of CREST). The intermediaries hold the securities for their account holders, who will either be intermediaries themselves or investors. In each case, the first tier intermediary holds the securities to which it has the legal title on trust for its account holders. If an account holder is itself an intermediary, it will hold its beneficial title under that trust on a sub-trust for its own account holders. This analysis has been approved in a number of decisions, and can safely be said to represent English law.[133]

---

[128] Or interest, in the case of debt securities.

[129] See 11.2.1.2.

[130] For a fuller description see *Re Lehman Brothers International (Europe) (In Administration)* [2010] EWHC 2914 (Ch) [80]–[81].

[131] The purpose of a stock lending transaction is usually to enable the 'borrower' to cover a short selling position; see 12.3.2.1.

[132] 8.3.2.3.2(b).

[133] See *Re Lehman Brothers International (Europe) (in administration)* [2010] EWHC 2914 (Ch) [226]; *Re Lehman Brothers International (Europe) (in administration)* [2012] EWHC 2997 (Ch) [163].

4.7 Transfer of Shares

As discussed in chapter two,[134] once a shareholder has purchased shares in a company, exit will generally only be possible if the company buys back the shares, or if the shareholder finds a purchaser to buy the shares. In practical terms, companies will only infrequently repurchase shares, and will only do so if the shares are issued as redeemable shares, or if the rules regarding the purchase of shares by a company are observed.[135] In either event the capital maintenance rules discussed in chapter five must be observed.[136] If a shareholder wishes to realise its investment, the ability to transfer the shares will therefore be important.

Broadly, share transfers involve two stages. First the buyer and seller conclude a sales contract in which they agree the price of the shares and the other terms of the agreement. The second stage is the transfer of the shares to the buyer, and the buyer becomes the owner of the shares.[137]

The process at the first stage of this procedure is likely to vary according to the size and nature of the company involved. In small private companies, the importance of shares is not predominantly as a source of financing for the company, but rather as a device for allocating control within the company.[138] As a result, the transfer of shares in such companies will often be subject to restrictions in the company's articles.[139] Common restrictions include a requirement that the permission of the board is obtained before the shares can be transferred, and that the shares are offered first to the existing shareholders of the company.[140] Shares that are not publicly traded have no market as such, and therefore agreeing the price of shares in a private company is not generally straightforward. By contrast, such restrictions are not permitted in publicly listed companies: it is a requirement of the FCA Listing Rules that listed securities are freely transferable.[141] In addition, again in contrast to the shares of a private company, there is a ready market for the shares of such companies; indeed this is one of the predominant reasons for companies to seek a listing for their shares in the first place.[142] In order to sell listed shares an investor will generally enlist the services of a broker, who will sell the shares through the electronic trading system operated by the London Stock Exchange, or by making contact with another financial services provider.

As regards the second stage in the procedure, the process will depend on whether the shares are certificated or uncertificated.[143] Where shares are certificated, in order to transfer

---

[134] See 2.2.1.

[135] See 5.4.2.2 and 5.4.2.3.

[136] See 5.4.2.

[137] For detailed consideration of the transfer of shares see Law of Personal Property, ch 32.

[138] See 2.2.2.

[139] Companies Act 2006, s 544. See Gower and Davies, 988–91.

[140] This is a form of pre-emption, but these pre-emption rights arise only on transfer and only bind the selling shareholder as a matter of agreement between the parties (albeit that the agreement may be contained in the articles of association). This may be compared to the pre-emption rights discussed at 4.4 above which arise when the company issues new shares, and bind the company as a result of statute.

[141] FCA Handbook, LR 2.2.4(1).

[142] See 10.2.1.3.

[143] See 4.5. Note that, as described at 4.5, in contrast to the description of transfer contained in this section, bearer shares are transferred by manual deliver of the share warrant, which is a negotiable instrument: Companies Act 2006, s 779(2).

the shares the seller completes and signs a transfer form[144] and delivers this, together with the share certificate, to the buyer. The buyer then lodges the certificate with the company in order to have his name entered onto the share register.[145] The company must generally have new share certificates ready for delivery to the buyer within two months.[146] Only once the buyer has his name entered onto the register of members does he become a member of the company. However, the beneficial interest in the shares may well already have passed before this point.[147] When the company agrees to register the buyer's name in the register of members, it appears that this effects a novation, not simply an assignment, of the transferor's rights to the transferee.[148]

The process and legal analysis of transferring securities (including shares) through CREST is discussed in detail at 9.2.6.3,[149] and there is a similar discussion (at 9.2.6.2) of the transfer of securities held through an intermediary.

4.8 Conclusion

For shareholders, the issuance, registration and transferability of shares is important. As discussed in this chapter, shareholders will wish to have control over the process of the issue of shares, in order to ensure that their interest in the company is protected. This desire of the shareholders for protection is counterbalanced by a need on the part of the company for its equity-raising process to be as quick and efficient as possible—something which is often at odds with significant control of the process being given to the shareholders. A balance is therefore required, and this balance will need readjustment from time to time, as the aftermath of the global financial crisis has demonstrated. EU law has determined this issue largely in favour of shareholders, at least as far as public companies are concerned. The UK has followed suit, and indeed has extended much of this protection to shareholders in private companies. Of the two mechanisms created by company law to deal specifically with this scenario, namely the requirement for directors to obtain authority to allot and pre-emption rights, it is the latter which tends to provide shareholders with the greatest protection. Pre-emption rights can be a valuable protection for shareholders in both private and public companies. Where the issue is by a public company making a public offer of shares, the rules discussed in this chapter are supplemented by a significant amount of securities legislation, discussed in chapter ten.

---

[144] See Companies Act 2006, s 770(1).

[145] Even entry onto the register is only prima facie evidence of title (Companies Act 2006, s 127) and rectification of the register is possible: Gower and Davies, 1003–05.

[146] Companies Act 2006, s 776.

[147] The delivery of the signed transfer form and certificate to the seller and payment by the buyer is generally accepted to effect a transfer of the beneficial interest, and the beneficial interest may even pass before that point, on the agreement to sell, if that agreement is held to be specifically enforceable: *Michaels v Harley House (Marylebone) Ltd* [1997] 2 BCLC 166; *Kilnoore Ltd (in liq) Unidare plc v Cohen* [2006] 1 Ch 489.

[148] Gower and Davies, 986, citing *Ashby v Blackwell* (1765) 2 Eden 299, 302–03; 28 ER 913, 914; *Simm v Anglo-American Telegraph Company* (1879) 5 QBD 188, 204; RR Pennington, *Company Law*, 8th edn (Oxford, Oxford University Press, 2001) 398–99; Benjamin: Interests in Securities, 3.05; E Micheler, 'Legal Title and the Transfer of Shares in a Paperless World—Farewell Quasi-Negotiability' [2002] *Journal of Business Law* 358.

[149] 9.2.6.3.

5

Legal Capital

5.1 Introduction

The legal capital rules are a set of provisions that constrain corporate activity by reference to the shareholders' capital investment. Broadly, these rules fall into two categories: those that regulate how capital can be raised from shareholders, and in particular how much capital shareholders must invest into a company; and those that regulate whether and how capital can be returned to the shareholders. The primary purpose of these rules is to regulate the conflict that exists between creditors and shareholders regarding how to allocate a company's capital.[1] This conflict is obvious once the company is insolvent and, consequently, the company has insufficient money to meet all of its financial obligations.[2] At that point, as discussed in chapter three, the interests of the creditors dominate and the shareholders 'come last'.[3] However, UK company law also regulates this conflict, in favour of creditors, by imposing legal capital rules when a company is solvent. The function and substance of the legal capital rules currently in place in the UK are assessed in this chapter. These rules are analysed, to determine how well they operate to fulfil their purpose. The chapter then examines alternatives to the legal capital rules, and assesses the desirability of a change in the law in this context.

5.2 Function of the Legal Capital Rules

It is well understood that the interests of those who contribute to a company's cash flow may come into conflict. The most obvious potential conflict is that between the creditors and the shareholders of a company, although of course others can exist, not least between different classes of shareholders, and between different creditors.[4] The primary

---

[1] See Company Law Review Steering Group, *Modern Company Law for a Competitive Economy: The Strategic Framework* (URN 99/654, February 1999), 81.

[2] For discussion see eg Goode: Corporate Insolvency, ch 4.

[3] *Soden v British & Commonwealth Holdings plc* [1998] AC 298, 308. For discussion see 3.3, in particular 3.3.1.2.5.

[4] Disputes between creditors arise most acutely on insolvency, as a result of their respective priorities: see 3.3.1. As discussed in chapters 2 and 3, adjusting creditors can protect themselves by contractual or proprietary means: see 3.2.2 and chapters 6 and 7.

rationale of the legal capital rules is the regulation of this conflict between shareholders and creditors, and the purpose of these rules has been to resolve the conflict in favour of the creditors.[5]

5.2.1 Conflict Between Shareholders and Creditors

The operations of a solvent company can create risks for creditors.[6] The particular risks that are relevant in this chapter are those that arise from the fact that whilst a company is solvent the shareholders generally control the operation of a company, directly through the general meeting, and indirectly through the directors. They are in a position to benefit themselves at the expense of the creditors in a number of ways.[7] They can withdraw assets from the pool available to the creditors for repayment (asset diversion). Common examples of this include distributions to themselves, such as dividend payments and share buy-backs. They can manipulate the investment profile of the company in a way which disadvantages creditors—for example the company takes on riskier projects than the creditors contemplated when they extended credit to it (risk shifting),[8] or the company abandons projects with a net positive value where the only benefit attaches to the creditors (underinvestment).[9] They may also disadvantage the existing creditors of a company if the company incurs additional debts to others which do not result in an equivalent increase in assets (claim dilution). This could result in a benefit to shareholders if the directors use the borrowed money to invest in risky projects that benefit shareholders at the expense of creditors.[10] Of course, creditors can also, potentially, engage in behaviour which advantages themselves at the expense of the shareholders, such as requiring the company to repay loans early or requiring it to decline to pay a dividend. Creditors could also encourage the company to invest in projects that are less risky than originally envisaged when the creditors invested, or not to invest in projects likely to accrue benefits only for the shareholders. The extent to which these situations might occur in practice is discussed in chapter three.[11]

---

[5] Some of the rules discussed in this chapter are said to have functions in addition to their creditor-protection roles. For example, the rules relating to the consideration provided by shareholders are also said to have a shareholder-protection role (see 5.3.2.4 for discussion), and the rules restricting share repurchases have been said to have a role in protecting market integrity (see eg *The Purchase by a Company of its Own Shares* (Cm 7944, 1980)).

[6] See 3.2.2.2.

[7] CW Smith and JB Warner, 'On Financial Contracting: An Analysis of Bond Covenants' (1979) 7 *Journal of Financial Economics* 117, 118–19.

[8] The evidence regarding the empirical significance of risk shifting is mixed: eg KH Daigle and MT Maloney, 'Residual Claims in Bankruptcy: An Agency Theory Explanation' (1994) 37 *Journal of Law and Economics* 157; G Andrade and S Kaplan, 'How Costly is Financial (not Economic) Distress? Evidence from Highly Leveraged Transactions that Became Distressed' (1998) 53 *Journal of Finance* 1443; A Eisendorfer, 'Empirical Evidence of Risk Shifting in Financially Distressed Firms' (2008) 63 *Journal of Finance* 609.

[9] SC Myers, 'Determinants of Corporate Borrowing' (1977) 5 *Journal of Financial Economics* 147.

[10] See 3.2.2.2. For discussion see MC Jensen and WH Meckling, 'Theory of the Firm: Managerial Behaviour, Agency Costs and Ownership Structure' (1976) 3 *Journal of Financial Economics* 305.

[11] See chapter 3, particularly 3.2.

5.2.2 Policy Response to the Conflict

The US and Europe have traditionally adopted different responses to the potential conflict between creditors and shareholders regarding the allocation of a company's legal capital. In the US, the legal capital rules have evolved to provide maximum flexibility to shareholders, and creditor protection devices are noticeable largely by their absence in some state corporate laws.[12] Some creditor protection is provided by the federal 'fraudulent transfer laws',[13] but the primary tool available to creditors who wish to protect themselves from opportunistic shareholders is contract.

By contrast, the European model has regarded the threat to creditors from shareholders as real and credible. This is the model on which the UK depends heavily, because of the need to implement the Second Company Law Directive.[14] On this view the shareholders obtain the benefit of limited liability when they invest in a company, but this comes at a cost to the creditors. In the UK, common law exceptions to the principle of limited liability are rare and, where they do exist, very narrowly constrained.[15] The principal statutory exception, section 214 of the Insolvency Act 1986, is powerful in theory,[16] but difficulties with the operation of these actions, including their funding, has meant that this section has rarely been invoked in practice.[17]

Consequently, the principle of limited liability is very much intact in the UK. Undoubtedly, this principle constrains the amount available to creditors on insolvency. In Europe this has resulted in the view that creditors need to be compensated, and that this compensation should be provided by law, rather than being left to contract. The idea that creditors need protection is of significant longevity in the UK. The form of this protection has been rules that constrain corporate activity by reference to the shareholders' capital investment, principally by prescribing a minimum level of capital to be invested in a company by the shareholders, and a restriction on transfers to shareholders in some circumstances. The point is that creditors rank ahead of shareholders in a winding up,[18] and the purpose of the capital maintenance rules is to ensure that shareholders do not undermine that principle by improperly distributing assets to themselves, not only when the company is insolvent, but also while the company remains solvent.

Of the various potential dangers which shareholders pose to creditors, namely asset diversion, altering the investment profile of the firm and claim dilution by issuing additional debt, the focus of the Second Company Law Directive, and UK company law, has

---

[12] L Enriques and JR Macey 'Creditors Versus Capital Formation: The Case Against the European Legal Capital Rules' (2001) 86 *Cornell Law Review* 1165.

[13] RC Clark, 'The Duties of the Corporate Debtor to its Creditors' (1977) 90 *Harvard Law Review* 505. In the UK the equivalent provisions are Insolvency Act 1986, ss 238 and 423.

[14] Directive 2012/30/EU (a recast of Directive (EC) 77/91 [1977] OJ L26/1, as amended) ('Second Company Law Directive').

[15] See *Prest v Petrodel Resources Ltd* [2013] UKSC 34. For discussion see 3.3.3.2.1.

[16] See 3.3.3.2.2(b).

[17] For discussion see 3.3.3.2.2(c).

[18] See 3.3.1, particularly 3.3.1.2.5.

been on preventing the first one. Both regimes concentrate on creating and maintaining an equity cushion to protect the creditors in the event of insolvency, and one of the key factors in this approach has been the prevention of capital return to the shareholders. A rules-based approach[19] has been adopted to regulate this issue. These rules are examined at 5.3 and 5.4.

The focus on asset diversion by the Second Company Law Directive, and UK company law, is not altogether surprising. The idea of capital as a fund available to meet creditors' claims is well embedded.[20] When this view developed in the nineteenth century there was little in the way of publicly available information for creditors to use to assess the creditworthiness of companies, other than statements about the company's capital, and it is perhaps understandable that the courts placed emphasis on the retention of this fund. However, much more information is now available to creditors. There has been a significant expansion in the amount of information that is made available about a company via its annual report and accounts, and publicly traded companies are, in addition, under significant continuing disclosure obligations, as discussed in chapter eleven.[21] In addition, it is generally recognised that many creditors can and will seek additional information from the company in order to determine whether, and on what terms, to lend.[22] Given these changes, a continuing commitment to capital rules as a creditor protection device needs to be examined closely. Of the three potential forms of abuse, asset diversion is one of the easier ones for the creditors, or at least the adjusting creditors, to monitor and to control.[23] In particular, creditors may have contractual rights to prevent asset diversions, such as contractual restrictions on disposals,[24] and the control rights which come from having fixed security.[25]

By contrast, in relation to the potential abuse of altering the investment profile of the company to the creditors' disadvantage, a standards-based approach has been adopted. This has been regarded as a matter for the directors, and regulated primarily through the duties imposed on them. In particular, directors are under an obligation to make investment decisions bona fide in the best interests of the company, an obligation that has been subjectively assessed by the UK courts to date.[26] As discussed in chapter three, where the company is solvent this has traditionally meant acting in the interests of the shareholders as a whole.[27] Section 172 of the Companies Act 2006 potentially alters this, by adding a requirement that directors consider the interests of various other groups, such as employees and customers, when fulfilling this obligation. The position of the company's creditors does not, however, form part of this analysis.[28] Only where the company is insolvent, or

---

[19] For discussion of this terminology see R Kraakman et al, *The Anatomy of Corporate Law: A Comparative and Functional Approach*, 2nd edn (Oxford, Oxford University Press, 2009) ch 2.

[20] In the UK see eg *Ooregum Gold Mining Co of India v Roper* [1892] AC 125, 133 per Lord Halsbury ('[t]he capital is fixed and certain, and every creditor of the company is entitled to look to that capital as his security').

[21] See 11.3. The continuing disclosure obligations regarding debt securities are discussed at 13.3.

[22] See 6.3.2 and 13.2.8.

[23] This issue is discussed further at 6.3.2.

[24] See 6.3.1.1.

[25] See 7.3.3.1.

[26] *Re Smith & Fawcett Ltd* [1942] Ch 304, 306 per Lord Greene MR; cf Companies Act 2006, s 172, which puts this obligation on a statutory footing. For discussion see 3.2.1.3.1.

[27] See 3.2.1.3.1.

[28] Companies Act 2006, s 172, particularly s 172(3).

nearing insolvency, must the directors take account of the creditors' interests.[29] As regards the danger of claim dilution, it is largely left to creditors to protect themselves by contract where the company is solvent, by taking security[30] and using negative pledge clauses which protect their priority,[31] and by using covenants restricting borrowing and requiring certain gearing ratios.[32]

5.2.3 The UK's Legal Capital Regime

Most of the UK's legal capital rules are now in statutory form, and are found primarily in the Companies Act 2006.[33] Many of the rules have their origins in the nineteenth century, in the legal capital rules developed principally by way of case law to deal with the perceived conflicts between shareholders and creditors in all companies. More recently, EU legislation, principally the Second Company Law Directive,[34] has had an important role to play in this regard. This directive requires legal capital rules to be put in place for public companies. When the UK implemented the directive, it went beyond its strict requirements, extending many of the restrictions to private companies, and gold-plating the regime in places.[35]

---

[29] For discussion see 3.3.3.1.

[30] See chapter 7.

[31] See 6.3.1.

[32] See 6.3.1.1 and 6.3.2.2.

[33] This Act was preceded by a substantial review of UK company law. The legal capital rules in place in the Companies Act 1985 and in the common law were carefully scrutinised by an independent body, the Company Law Review Steering Group, as part of this process. The Steering Group produced a large number of papers which considered the issue of legal capital, either specifically or as part of the overall package of possible reforms (see Company Law Review Steering Group, *Modern Company Law for a Competitive Economy: The Strategic Framework* (URN 99/654, February 1999); *Company Formation and Capital Maintenance* (URN 99/1145, October 1999); *Developing the Framework* (URN 00/656, March 2000); *Completing the Structure* (URN 00/1335, November 2000); *Final Report* (URN 01/942–3, July 2001). These reforms were then considered and further amended by the Government in its response to these proposals (see DTI, *Modernising Company Law* (Cm 5553-I and Cm 5553-II, July 2002) and DTI, *Company Law Reform* (Cm 6456, March 2005)). Although the Steering Group made a large number of recommendations for the reform of the legal capital rules of both private and public companies, many of these recommendations did not find their way into the final Act. This was in part as a result of the continuing obligation to implement the legal capital requirements of the Second Company Law Directive for public companies.

[34] Directive 2012/30/EU (a recast of Council Directive 77/91/EEC). Reviews of the legal capital rules have also taken place in Europe: see eg Commission (EC), 'Simpler Legislation for the Single Market (SLIM): Extension to a Fourth Phase', SEC (1998) 1944 (Commission Staff Working Paper of 16 November 1998); High Level Group of Company Law Experts, *Modern Regulatory Framework for Company Law in Europe* (Brussels, 4 November 2002) (the Winter Group Report); European Commission, *Consultation on the Future of European Company Law* (2011). See also KPMG, 'Feasibility Study on an Alternative to the Capital Maintenance Regime established by the Second Company Law Directive', 2008. To date only modest amendments have been forthcoming—see eg Directive 2006/68/EC [2006] OJ L69/27 (these amendments are incorporated into the recast Directive 2012/30/EU) and this is clearly not a present priority for the European Commission: European Commission, *Action Plan: European Company Law and Corporate Governance—A Modern Legal Framework for More Engaged Shareholders and Sustainable Companies* (COM(2012) 740. For comment on the very limited changes to date see European Company Law Experts (ECLE), 'The Future of European Company Law', Columbia Law and Economics Research Paper No 420, 1 May 2012, www.ssrn.com/abstract=2075034.

[35] For example, par value shares are required for both public and private companies in the UK, although the Second Company Law Directive only requires them for public companies. For discussion see 5.3.2.1.

Some of this gold-plating was removed by the Companies Act 2006,[36] but it remains the case that the UK regime goes further than is strictly required by the provisions of the directive.[37]

The rules relating to company capital discussed in this chapter, which seek to deal with the potential conflict between creditors and shareholders, can be broadly divided into two parts.[38] These are, first, provisions that are intended to ensure that a certain guaranteed cushion is created for creditors by ensuring that shareholders pay a certain amount into a company; and, second, those which attempt to ensure that this cushion is not returned to the shareholders in certain circumstances (maintenance of capital). These are discussed in turn in the following sections.

5.3 Rules Regulating the Amount of Money Paid In by Shareholders

The rules regulating the amount of money that must be paid in to the company by shareholders can be regarded as falling into two broad categories: requirements as to the amount which must be invested by shareholders before business can be commenced; and rules governing the measurement of the consideration provided by the shareholders when they acquire shares.[39]

5.3.1 Entry Price for Limited Liability: Minimum Capital Rules

The Companies Act 2006 imposes an obligation on public companies to have a minimum share capital of £50,000.[40] No minimum share capital is required for private companies in the UK.[41]

---

[36] For example, the financial assistance rules applied to both public and private companies when the Second Company Law Directive was first implemented (Companies Act 1985, ss 151–53, albeit with a whitewash procedure in place for private companies: ss 155–58). The ban on providing financial assistance for the purchase of a company's own shares was removed by Companies Act 2006 for private companies but left in place for public companies (see Companies Act 2006, ss 677–82), discussed at 5.4.4.

[37] For example, the definition of capital for the purposes of Companies Act 2006 includes share premiums and any capital redemption reserve, although this is not required by the Second Company Law Directive: Companies Act 2006, s 610(4) and ss 733(5)(6).

[38] A further set of rules relating to the raising of capital, which may be regarded as creditor-neutral, are dealt with separately in chapter 4.

[39] Note that additional regulatory requirements regarding capital are imposed on certain kinds of financial institutions, such as banks (discussed at 2.3.1.3): see eg K Alexander, 'The Role of Capital in Supporting Financial Stability' in N Moloney, E Ferran and J Payne (eds), *The Oxford Handbook of Financial Regulation* (Oxford, Oxford University Press, 2015).

[40] Companies Act 2006, ss 761, 763(1). This requirement gold-plates the requirement of the Second Company Law Directive in this regard (art 6), which specifies just €25,000. A quarter of this share capital needs to be paid up: Companies Act 2006, s 586.

[41] This position differs across Europe, although regulatory competition following the decision in C-212/97 *Centros Ltd v Erhvers-og Selskabsstyrelsen* [1999] ECR I-1459 has led a number of other Member States to reduce their minimum capital levels. For discussion see M Becht, C Mayer and HF Wagner, 'Where Do Firms Incorporate? Deregulation and the Cost of Entry' (2008) 14 *Journal of Corporate Finance* 241.

Broadly, the idea behind these rules is to provide the creditors with the comfort of a guaranteed equity 'cushion'. These rules are ineffective for this purpose, however. The rules adopt a 'one size fits all' approach which does not take account of the size of the debt that the company may incur, or the riskiness of its activities. The minimum capital requirement for public companies is minuscule compared to the size of the debts of most such companies. Indeed, if this figure was ever meaningful, it is notable that the original figure of €25,000 included in the Second Company Law Directive in 1977 has never been amended or updated, rendering it increasingly trivial. In addition, the 2006 Act imposes no minimum capital requirement for private companies, which are just as likely to have creditors potentially in need of protection. For private companies there is no legal bar to them having little or no legal capital, and many private companies in the UK have very low levels of equity invested in the business.[42]

There is also no ongoing obligation on the shareholders to retain this level of investment in the company. The 2006 Act does provide that if the net assets of a public company fall to half, or less than half, of its called up share capital, then the directors must call a general meeting to consider whether any steps must be taken to deal with the situation.[43] However, this offers little or nothing by way of protection for the creditors. This rule is only likely to be invoked in situations of extreme financial distress, when the shareholders' investment in the company has already been substantially depleted. Given that this calculation will generally depend on a complex accounting calculation, it may be difficult to discern when this point is reached. Furthermore, the provision imposes no obligation on the shareholders to inject any additional capital,[44] nor does it require any particular form of action to occur at this point in time. The damage to the company's reputation as a result of calling such a meeting may be significant, and the meeting must be held even if the fall is only temporary.

The discussion here relates to the sorts of companies identified in chapter one, namely general commercial companies. There are other companies, not covered by this book, which have different rules as to capital adequacy. In particular, banks are subject to significant regulation relating to the minimum capital that they must hold.[45] This is usually expressed as a capital adequacy ratio of equity that must be held as a percentage of risk-weighted assets. There is not, therefore, a single, generic figure that all banks are required to hold as a minimum level of capital. The figure will be different for each bank depending on its risk-weighted assets. These requirements are put in place to ensure that these institutions do not take on excess leverage and become insolvent, providing a cushion of cash, reserves, equity and subordinated liabilities available to the bank to absorb losses during periods of financial stress. This cushion can consist of tiers of capital, with each layer displaying varying

---

[42] Companies House, Statistical Tables 2013/14, Table B1.

[43] Companies Act 2006, s 656, implementing Second Company Law Directive, art 17. This may be contrasted with some other European countries which have a rule of this kind in place. For instance, if the net assets of a Swedish company fall below half its share capital, then the shareholders must either inject fresh equity to restore the new asset level, or liquidate the company (see J Armour, 'Share Capital and Creditor Protection: Efficient Rules for a Modern Company Law' (2000) 63 *Modern Law Review* 355, 371).

[44] Any obligation on the shareholders to inject further capital at this point would presumably undermine the principle of limited liability.

[45] See eg the Basel Accords (Basel III is being gradually phased in between 2013 and 2019) and within the EU see the Capital Requirements Regulation (Regulation EU No 575/2013) and Directive (Directive 2013/36/EU). For discussion see 2.3.1.3.

degrees of permanence, flexibility regarding distributions and subordination. There is a significant cost to these measures, both for the regulators, which must determine how much capital each bank is required to hold and must monitor banks to ensure that they hold the correct amount, and for banks as regards the costs of compliance. These costs can be justified given the nature of the banking industry and, in particular, the systemic risks posed by it. No such justification exists to support the cost of a similar default regime for the companies covered by this book.

Of course, higher levels of minimum capital can be put in place for individual companies: as discussed in chapter six, an alternative method for ensuring capital adequacy is via the imposition of financial ratios by contractual means.[46]

5.3.2 Measurement of Consideration: Payment for Shares

5.3.2.1 *Shares must have a Par Value*

A second way in which the amount of money paid in to a company by shareholders is regulated is in relation to the payment for shares. In order to ensure that appropriate consideration is received in return for shares, the Companies Act 2006 requires that all shares in a limited company having share capital must have a fixed nominal value,[47] sometimes called the par value, and that companies may not issue shares at a discount to this nominal value.[48] Thus, if companies issue 50,000 shares with a par value of £1, the shares cannot be issued for less than £1 each.[49] Companies can have their shares denominated in any currency, or in several currencies.[50]

This nominal value is a somewhat arbitrary figure that is attached to the shares. It bears no relation to the market value of the shares at the time of issue, or later. The legal consequence of attaching a par value to a share is that this is the minimum price at which that share can then be allotted. Due to the existence of this rule, companies often set the nominal value of their shares at a very low level. There is no prescribed minimum par value in respect of the shares of private or public companies. It is very common, therefore, for the issue price of shares to be well in excess of the nominal value. As long as the shares are issued above the nominal value, the Companies Act 2006 is silent as to the actual price at which the shares are issued. Instead, this is a matter for directors' duties

---

[46] See 6.3.2.2.

[47] Companies Act 2006, s 542. An allotment of a share that does not have a fixed nominal value is void, and criminal sanctions will attach to every officer of the company who is in default, in the event of a purported allotment: ss 542(2), (4)–(5).

[48] Ibid, s 580; *Ooregum Gold Mining Co of India v Roper* [1892] AC 125. This is a requirement of the Second Company Law Directive, art 8(1).

[49] The par value must be a monetary amount, but it does not need to be an amount capable of legal tender, ie it can be a fraction or percentage of a monetary amount: *Re Scandinavian Bank Group plc* [1988] Ch 87.

[50] In order to obtain a trading certificate as a public company, however, or to re-register as a public company, a company must have its authorised minimum capital denominated either in sterling or in euros, but not in a mixture of the two: Companies Act 2006, s 765(1). The par value of any one share cannot be stated in two or more currencies, but different shares of the same company can be stated in different currencies: s 542(3).

(the directors must act bona fide in the best interests of the company when setting the price), and a matter for negotiation with the new investor.[51] The price can be below the market price as long as the directors do not breach their fiduciary duties in determining that price.[52] Any difference between the nominal price and the issue price is referred to as a share premium, and is treated in much the same way as capital. It is available to finance the company's activities, but is not generally available to distribute to shareholders as a dividend.[53]

It is unfortunate that the anachronistic concept of par value remains entrenched in the Companies Act 2006. The question of whether no par value shares should be introduced in the UK has been around for some time.[54] In the review that preceded the introduction of the 2006 Act, the Company Law Review Steering Group stated that no par value shares should be introduced, on the basis that there is no reason to impose any particular limit below which the issue price cannot fall, as long as all the proceeds of the issue are retained in an undistributable capital account.[55] After all, it is the capital employed by the company, and not the paid up share capital, that is the true value of the undertaking. No par value shares represent a share for what it is, namely a fraction of the equity of the company, and do not purport to represent a notional token of value. The Second Company Law Directive prevents these reforms being introduced for public companies, however.[56] Consequently, although the Company Law Review Steering Group initially recommended the introduction of no par value shares,[57] these proposals were eventually dropped for both public and private companies.[58] This is a great shame. Par value is a meaningless and valueless concept whose continued existence in the UK is difficult to justify, except insofar as the Second

---

[51] *Shearer v Bercain* [1980] 3 All ER 295; *Re Sunrise Radio Ltd* [2010] 1 BCLC 367. For discussion see chapter 4, especially 4.2.1.1.

[52] *Mutual Life Insurance Co of New York v Rank Organisation Ltd* [1985] BCLC 11.

[53] Companies Act 2006, s 610; note that the share premium account can be used by the company in paying up unissued shares to be allotted to members as fully paid shares (s 610(3)) and a company may write off the expenses of that issue and any commission paid on that issue against the sum transferred to the share premium account in respect of that specific issue (s 610(2)). The Second Company Law Directive does not require share premiums to be treated in the same way as share capital and, therefore, it is open to the UK Government to change the treatment of share premiums for private and public companies. This opportunity has not been taken to date.

[54] See eg Gedge Committee, *Report of the Committee on Shares of No Par Value* (Cmnd 9112, 1954); Jenkins Committee, *Report of the Company Law Committee* (Cmnd 1749, 1962), paras 32–34.

[55] See Company Law Review Steering Group, *Modern Company Law for a Competitive Economy: The Strategic Framework* (URN 99/654, February 1999), 88–91.

[56] Although the Second Company Law Directive, art 8 provides a no par share alternative for public companies, it requires that no par value shares of public companies should not be issued below their 'accountable par', whereby the fixed value of individual shares is determined by reference to the percentage or fraction of the subscribed capital that they represent. As a result, although some European countries have introduced no par value shares, by exploiting this 'accountable par' alternative, these are not true no par value shares. For discussion see J Rickford et al, 'Reforming Capital: Report to the Interdisciplinary Group on Capital Maintenance' (2004) 15 *European Business Law Review* 919, 929.

[57] Company Law Review Steering Group, *Modern Company Law for a Competitive Economy—Company Formation and Capital Maintenance* (URN 99/1145), para 3.8.

[58] See Company Law Review Steering Group, *Modern Company Law for a Competitive Economy: Final Report* (URN 01/942–3, July 2001), para 10.7. The concern was that having different regimes for public and private companies could act as a barrier to growth, and would hamper the process of conversion from a private to a public company.

Company Law Directive continues to require it for public companies.[59] By contrast, no par value shares are widely recognised elsewhere.[60]

5.3.2.2 'No Issue at a Discount' Rule

The legal capital rules regarding payment for shares provide that companies may not issue shares at a discount to their nominal value. In general, it is possible for companies to accept either cash or non-cash consideration for their shares.[61] The precise application of the 'no issue at a discount' rule will depend upon whether the consideration provided is cash or non-cash consideration.

5.3.2.2.1 Cash Consideration

The 'no issue at a discount' rule is generally easier to apply where cash consideration is received for the shares. However, the definition of cash consideration for this purpose is wider than might at first be supposed. The list of scenarios in which a share will be deemed to be paid up in cash or allotted for cash contained in the Companies Act 2006 includes not only the obvious one, namely that cash is received by the company,[62] but also a number of other situations. These include the following: (i) a cheque is received by the company in good faith, which its directors have no reason to suspect will not be paid;[63] (ii) a liability of the company is released for a liquidated sum;[64] (iii) an undertaking is given to pay cash at a later date;[65] and (iv) there is payment by some other means giving rise to a present and future entitlement (of the company or of a person acting on the company's behalf) to a payment, or a credit equivalent to payment, in cash.[66] The 2006 Act makes it clear that

---

[59] Although discussion of the reform of the Second Company Law Directive has been ongoing within the EU, no changes to the par value rules have been implemented to date. Further reform of the Second Company Law Directive does not appear to be a current priority (see European Commission, *Action Plan: European Company Law and Corporate Governance—A Modern Legal Framework for More Engaged Shareholders and Sustainable Companies* (COM(2012) 740)).

[60] Eg Australian Corporations Law, s 254C, inserted by Company Law Review Act 1998; New Zealand Companies Act 1993, s 38. No par value shares are also common in the US and Canada.

[61] Companies Act 2006, s 582(1), although note the exception for subscribers to the memorandum of a public company, who must pay cash: s 584.

[62] Ibid, s 583(3)(a).

[63] Ibid, s 583(3)(b).

[64] Ibid, s 583(3)(c). Where the company owes the investor a sum of money, the release by the investor of the company from that obligation in exchange for the shares amounts to the provision of a cash consideration for them, since it falls within s 583(3)(c): *EIC Services Ltd v Phipps* [2004] 2 BCLC 589 [36]–[52]. This provision can be used to good effect to enable debt-equity swaps to take place. As long as the face value of the liability released is at or above the par value of the shares, the courts appear to be satisfied, even if the market value of the liability is below this level because the company is facing insolvency: *Mercantile Trading Co, Schroeder's Case* (1871) LR 11 Eq 13; *Pro-Image Studios v Commonwealth Bank of Australia* (1990–91) 4 ACSR 586 (Sup Ct Victoria), cf *Re Jarass Pty Ltd* (1988) 13 ACSR 728 (Sup Ct NSW). In the absence of deceit or fraud there appears to be no option for the court to inquire into the financial capacity of the issuing company to pay to the creditor-allottee the amount of the presently payable debt. This is subject to the proviso that the debt must have been genuinely created in the course of the company's business, and must be immediately payable.

[65] Companies Act 2006, s 583(3)(d). Where pre-existing debts are assigned to the company in return for the allotment of shares, this has been held not to constitute an undertaking to pay cash at a later date within s 583(3)(d), since this subsection requires an undertaking to be given to the company in return for the allotment: *System Controls plc v Munro Corporate plc* [1990] BCC 386. This case suggests, however, that as long as the undertaking is given to the company in return for the allotment, there is no apparent limit on the future date that may be fixed for the actual payment (in contrast to the five-year limit in s 587).

[66] Companies Act 2006, s 583(3)(e).

cash for this purpose includes foreign currency.[67] It is also stated that payment of cash or an undertaking to pay cash to any person other than the company is a form of non-cash consideration.[68]

In some circumstances the allotment of shares on the conversion of convertible debentures will be regarded as being for cash consideration. This will occur where the issuer of the convertible securities and of the shares into which they convert are the same company, since an allotment of shares in exchange for the release of a liquidated debt represented by the convertibles involves a release of a liquidated debt, and is an allotment of shares for cash according to the Companies Act 2006.[69]

5.3.2.2.2 Non-Cash Consideration

As regards shares issued for non-cash consideration in private companies, the assessment of the amount of consideration is a matter for the directors' business judgement.[70] This includes the situation where shares are issued in return for an asset of some kind. In general, the courts show a lack of interest in assessing the worth of non-cash consideration received by private companies as long as it is 'not clearly colourable nor illusory'.[71]

By contrast, for public companies the Second Company Law Directive provides a stricter rule.[72] As a result, the Companies Act 2006 requires a mandatory valuation of non-cash consideration received by public companies.[73] A detailed report[74] is required by an independent valuer during the six months preceding the allotment.[75] The report must include a description of the asset, the method and the date of valuation, and it must support the conclusion that the consideration received by the company is not less than the nominal value of the shares plus any premium.[76] A copy of the report must be sent to the allottee before

---

[67] Ibid, s 583(6).

[68] Ibid, s 583(5). Payments through an electronic settlement system are deemed to be payments in cash for the purposes of s 583(3)(e): s 383(4) and Companies (Shares and Share Capital) Order 2009, SI 2009/388, art 4.

[69] Companies Act 2006, s 583(3)(c). However, this analysis will not necessarily hold where the conversion involves the cancellation of the liquidated debt represented by the convertibles (see eg *Mosely v Koffyfontein Mines Ltd* [1904] 2 Ch 108, 119 per Cozens–Hardy LJ). Consequently, whether shares allotted on the conversion of convertibles are allotted for cash may depend upon the conversion mechanism.

[70] *Re Wragg Ltd* [1897] 1 Ch 796.

[71] Ibid, 835 per Smith LJ.

[72] Directive 2006/68/EC amended the Second Company Law Directive (and these changes are incorporated into Directive 2012/30/EU). Directive 2006/68/EC sought to simplify the requirements of the Second Company Law Directive, making it possible for Member States to dispense with the requirement for independent valuation of non-cash consideration for shares in public limited companies in some circumstances, including where the consideration comprises transferable securities that are valued by reference to the price at which the have been trading on a regulated market or assets that have been subject to a recent independent expert's report or valuation for the purpose of audited accounts. However, the directive still required the publication of certain matters (including a description of the consideration and the source of the valuation) and shareholders holding at least 5% of the issued share capital were still able to request an independent expert's report. Member States were given the option whether to implement the revised rules in the 2006 directive. The UK Government took the view that it was not worthwhile to take advantage of the option provided by the 2006 directive to amend its regime in this regard.

[73] Companies Act 2006, s 593 (implementing the Second Company Law Directive, arts 10, 31(2)). There are exceptions (see ss 594–95) which are derived from the Second Company Law Directive, art 31(3), which permits Member States not to apply the valuation requirement to increases in capital made in order to give effect to a merger, division or public offer.

[74] Companies Act 2006, s 596.

[75] The company must appoint as the independent valuer someone who would be qualified to be its auditor, and may appoint its current auditor (ss 1150–51).

[76] Companies Act 2006, s 596(3).

the allotment,[77] and must be delivered to the registrar of companies when the company files the return of allotment of the shares.[78]

The Companies Act 2006 appears, therefore, to place some weight on the differentiation of consideration into cash consideration (not requiring these valuation rules to be followed) and non-cash consideration (which, for public companies, does require independent valuation as detailed above). However, it has been suggested that it is relatively easy for companies to structure their transactions in order to avoid the application of these valuation rules.[79] For example, the company could agree to purchase an asset for cash and the vendor could agree to release the company from an obligation to pay for the asset in return for an allotment of shares. Since the release of a liability for a liquidated sum is treated as cash for these purposes,[80] this would be regarded as an allotment of the shares for cash consideration and, consequently, these valuation provisions need not be followed.[81] Further, if these rules are intended to protect creditors then it is worth noting that important statutory carve-outs are created within the 2006 Act, in the shape of a takeovers exemption and a mergers exemption, both derived from the Second Company Law Directive.[82]

In addition to these valuation provisions, some forms of non-cash consideration are prohibited altogether for public companies. Most notably the Companies Act 2006 prohibits a public company from accepting an undertaking to do work or to perform services in consideration for its shares.[83] This is on the basis that this form of non-cash consideration is not capable of economic assessment. Public companies are also prohibited from accepting any sort of undertaking to provide non-cash consideration which need not be performed until after five years from the date of allotment.[84]

5.3.2.3 Consequences of a Breach of the Provisions

In general, where these provisions regarding the consideration received for shares are breached, the allottee will be liable to pay the company an amount equal to the amount of the discount, plus interest. In some circumstances the allottee may be required to pay not

---

[77] Ibid, s 593(1)(c).

[78] Ibid, s 597. Where the company allots shares in contravention of these requirements, the allottee can be liable to pay an amount equal to the aggregate of the nominal value of the shares and the whole of any premium, plus interest: s 593(3). This is in addition to the original consideration provided for the shares, and therefore the allottee may be required to pay twice (but see s 606 as regards possible relief from the harshness of this provision). Subsequent holders of shares allotted in contravention of these provisions may be liable to pay for the shares in cash in some circumstances: ss 605, 606. For discussion of the consequences of breach of these provisions see 5.3.2.3.

[79] J Rickford et al, 'Reforming Capital: Report to the Interdisciplinary Group on Capital Maintenance' (2004) 15 *European Business Law Review* 919, 935.

[80] Companies Act 2006, s 583(3)(c).

[81] It is possible that the courts might scrutinise such transactions and regard them as artificial, and might therefore look through such arrangements (see *Re Bradford Investments plc (No 2)* [1991] BCC 379).

[82] Companies Act 2006, ss 594–95, giving effect to Second Company Law Directive, art 31(3). Companies Act 2006 also makes it clear that bonus issues fall outside the valuation provisions: s 593(2).

[83] Companies Act 2006, s 585, as required by Second Company Law Directive, art 7.

[84] Companies Act 2006, s 587(1). If the company accepts such undertakings, the holder of the shares is liable to pay up to the company an amount equal to the amount treated as paid up by the undertaking, together with interest: s 585(2). The enforceability of the undertakings is not affected: s 591. Subsequent holders may also incur liability: s 588 (but note the power of the court to grant relief in s 589). For further discussion of the consequences of breach of these provisions see 5.3.2.3.

only the amount of the discount, but the whole of the nominal value of the shares plus any premium plus interest.[85] This is in addition to the original consideration provided for the shares, and therefore the allottee may be required to pay twice. The sanctions as regards allottees may have harsh consequences in some instances, particularly where the breach is technical. Consequently, the court has the power to grant relief against the liability to make a payment to the company in most circumstances.[86]

Subsequent holders of shares allotted in contravention of these provisions may also be liable to pay for the shares in cash in some circumstances.[87] The policy of the Act is generally to impose liability jointly and severally with the allottee on the subsequent holder of the shares. This is, however, subject to a defence where the subsequent holder is a purchaser for value in good faith of the securities, or someone who derives title from such a purchaser.[88] In general, therefore, where shares have been traded on a public market, the current holder of shares will not be liable. In addition, directors who authorise the allotment may be liable for breach of fiduciary duty,[89] and the company and any officer of it who is in default are liable to a fine.[90]

One question that arises is what remedy the company will have if it issues shares for non-cash consideration on the strength of an expert valuation that subsequently turns out to be negligent, so that the non-cash consideration is worth less than expected. This issue has arisen particularly in the context of share-for-share exchanges, where, in a takeover of a target company, the consideration paid to the target shareholders by the bidder is not cash but shares in the bidder company. The shares in the target company clearly comprise non-cash consideration, paid by the bidder company. If the shares in the target turn out to be worth less than expected, the question arises as to whether the company has a claim for the difference between what it paid (the value of the shares it allotted to the target shareholders) and what it obtained.

It has been held, in the Australian case of *Pilmer v Duke Group Ltd*,[91] that a company does not have a proprietary interest in its own shares. A company, Kia Ora (the bidder), successfully made a share exchange offer with a cash component for another company, Western (the target). Kia Ora retained accountants, Nelson Wheeler, to prepare a report on Western. The acquisition of Western proved disastrous and Kia Ora went into liquidation. In an action by the liquidator against Nelson Wheeler, one question for the High Court of Australia was the measure of damages payable by Nelson Wheeler in contract and tort arising from their incompetence in preparing the report on Western. Kia Ora argued that the loss it suffered was the difference in value between the shares it allotted to the Western shareholders (as consideration) and the shares of Western that it acquired from Western's shareholders.

---

[85] Ibid, ss 593(3), 585(2), 587(2).

[86] Ibid, ss 589, 606 (but note the limits on the court's power to grant relief: ss 589(5) and 606(4)). There is no relief power in relation to the allottee in the case of issuance of shares at a discount or breach of the paying-up requirements: s 589(1).

[87] Ibid, ss 588, 605.

[88] Ibid, ss 588(2), 605(3).

[89] *Hirsche v Sims* [1894] AC 654; *Lowry (Inspector of Taxes) v Consolidated African Selection Trust Ltd* [1940] AC 648.

[90] Companies Act 2006, ss 590, 607.

[91] (2001) 75 ALJR 1067, (2001) 38 ACSR 121; [2001] 2 BCLC 773 (HC Aust).

One approach to this issue is to regard the company as having no proprietary interest in its own shares.[92] On this analysis, shares are not regarded as an asset of the company *prior* to the issue. When a company issues shares it does create a proprietary interest, but that interest is a bundle of rights which are vested in the shareholder.[93] Accordingly, once issued it is the shareholder and not the company that has a proprietary interest in the share; there is nothing that the company can turn to its own benefit. If correct, this approach has significant consequences. In a share-for-share exchange in a takeover situation, such as that in *Pilmer v Duke*, it would mean that a company such as Kia Ora should be regarded as having lost nothing, where the shares are worth less than expected. This was the approach taken by the High Court of Australia in *Pilmer v Duke*. Since Kia Ora had lost nothing, the court held that there was no basis for finding liability on the part of Nelson Wheeler in either contract or tort. If this is correct, then it suggests that companies would also find it difficult to recover compensation from negligent expert valuers where they issue shares for non-cash consideration, since they have similarly lost 'nothing'.[94]

It is to be hoped that the English courts would not follow this approach. There are at least two bases for regarding the company as having suffered loss in these circumstances. First, the primary purpose of a company issuing shares is as a capital raising exercise. It is clear that while shares are an asset of the shareholders, the capital raised by the issue of shares belongs to the company.[95] A company can receive consideration for the issue of its shares by a variety of means, including the receipt of cash or non-cash assets, which can include the shares in another company. It was recognised in *Pilmer* that Kia Ora was entitled to recover the cash component of its offer. If Kia Ora had acquired all the target shares for cash, it could have obtained substantial damages. This distinction is difficult to justify. Once it is accepted that the company is employing its own capital in a share exchange takeover, it follows that if the company does not receive full value it suffers exactly the same loss as would have occurred if only cash had been paid.[96] Second, the company can be regarded as having suffered an opportunity cost—it has lost the opportunity to enter into a different (better) bargain with the allottees, or to enter a different bargain altogether. The negligent advice

---

[92] See F Oditah, 'Takeovers, Share Exchanges and the Meaning of Loss' (1996) 112 *Law Quarterly Review* 424 (cf KR Handley, 'Takeovers, Share Exchanges and the Meaning of Loss' (1997) 113 *Law Quarterly Review* 51); DD Prentice and R Nolan, 'The Issue of Shares—Compensating the Company for Loss' (2002) 118 *Law Quarterly Review* 180.

[93] For discussion see 3.2.1.3.2.

[94] Of course, the shareholders in the bidder company can be said to have suffered a loss, or at least the existing shareholders in the bidder at the time of the new issue can be said to have suffered a loss as a result of the ensuing dilution of their shareholdings. They may be able to bring a claim against the expert valuer for this loss, based on *Caparo Industries plc v Dickman* [1990] 2 AC 605 (if they can show, inter alia, that this was the purpose of the expert's report, that the expert knew that the advice would be communicated to the existing shareholders, and that the expert knew that the shareholders were likely to rely on that advice). Normally, the reflective loss principle would prevent such a claim by the shareholders (*Johnson v Gore Wood & Co* [2002] 2 AC 1) but this principle only applies where the company and the shareholder(s) both have claims arising out of the same set of facts, so that where the company has no claim, the principle does not apply.

[95] *Bradbury v English Sewing Cotton Co Ltd* [1923] AC 744, 767 per Lord Wrenbury.

[96] It may be noted that where directors issue shares at a discount, the discount is recoverable (*Hirsche v Sims* [1894] AC 654). This may be attributable to capital maintenance rules, but it does indicate that when a company issues shares it can be considered to have suffered a loss. For discussion see DD Prentice and R Nolan, 'The Issue of Shares' (2002) 118 *Law Quarterly Review* 180, 181–82.

prevents the company from disposing of the shares in another manner, and these forgone alternatives are its loss.[97]

5.3.2.4 Efficacy of the Rules as a Form of Shareholder Protection

Two explanations can be advanced to justify in policy terms these rules which seek to regulate the amount of consideration received by a company in exchange for an issue of shares. The first is that the rules protect the existing shareholders of the company from dilution of the value of their interest in the company, while the second suggests that they provide an important creditor protection function. The first will be considered in this section, and the second in the next section.

It was noted in chapter four that issues of new shares can impact on the existing shareholders in a company. In particular, the issue of new shares can have a dilutive effect on the value of the existing shares of the company, if inadequate consideration is received for those shares.[98] Pre-emption rights can perform a valuable role in preventing this dilution,[99] but the protection provided by pre-emption rights is limited in a number of ways. First, preemption rights do not apply where the issue is for non-cash consideration.[100] Second, preemption rights can be waived, and so do not necessarily protect minority shareholders.[101] Third, they only protect existing shareholders to the extent that they can afford to take up the issue of shares offered to them, unless renounceable letters of allotment are used. These can protect shareholders from value dilution, if not from voting dilution, since they enable the shareholder to transfer the right to subscribe for the new shares to a third party. However, they are not required by the Companies Act 2006.[102]

It is sometimes suggested that the rules regarding the adequacy of consideration received by the company in return for shares can have a role in protecting shareholders against dilution. However, these rules are not effective for this purpose. All that they seek to ensure is that the directors receive at least par value for the shares. If the market value of the shares is below par value, the existing shareholders are not disadvantaged by an issue below par, as long as the issue is at, or close to, the market price. Equally, the shareholders are not protected by this rule where the market price is significantly above the par value. Shareholders would be protected from dilution by a rule that required directors to issue shares at their market value. This is not a duty to which directors are subject, but they are required to obtain the best price they can for share issues.[103] This directors' duty is likely to be more valuable to shareholders than the 'no issue at a discount' rule in terms of protecting them against dilution. The rules requiring expert valuations of

---

[97] This argument is particularly powerful where the bidder is in the market to raise funds and it chooses the wrong option, although it may be difficult to run the argument in relation to a bidder acquiring shares in another company since it may more appropriately be viewed as in the market to acquire assets (the shares in the target) rather than for fundraising purposes per se: F Oditah, 'Takeovers, Share Exchanges and the Meaning of Loss' (1996) 112 *Law Quarterly Review* 424, 441–44. Of course, quantifying the resultant loss will not be straightforward.

[98] See 4.2.1.1.

[99] Companies Act 2006, s 561 and see discussion at 4.4.

[100] Ibid, s 565 and see 4.4.1.

[101] See 4.4.3.

[102] See 4.4.2.

[103] *Shearer v Bercain* [1980] 3 All ER 295; *Re Sunrise Radio Ltd* [2009] EWHC 2893 (Ch).

non-cash consideration might provide the shareholders with some information to help them determine whether the directors are in breach of their duties, but these rules are a cumbersome and expensive way to achieve that end. It is accepted that it may be justifiable for directors to issue shares at a discount in order to ensure that the issue is a success. Where the discount is deep, shareholders will only be protected against value dilution where the obligation placed on directors as regards price is combined with an ability on the part of the shareholders to either participate in the offer or trade their right to subscribe for new shares to a third party.

5.3.2.5 *Efficacy of the Rules as a Form of Creditor Protection*

The rules regarding the payment for shares are also sometimes said to be necessary as a form of creditor protection. However, it is hard to see what meaningful protection is provided to creditors in this regard. On one view the issue of the measure of consideration received by a company for its shares may be of little relevance or interest to the creditors. For example, in a case like *Ooregum Gold Mining Co of India v Roper*,[104] where the shares were allotted at 75 per cent of the par value, since the shares were then trading at a discount to the par value, it is difficult to see why this impacts on creditors in any negative way: any money contributed to this company by the shareholders expands the potential pool of assets for creditors, even if issued at below the par value of the shares.[105]

If, however, it is accepted that creditors do care about this matter and are harmed by an issue of shares below the par value of those shares, then the rules within the Companies Act 2006 do not appear to provide any significant protection for creditors on this point. For example, take the situation where shares are issued in consideration for the release of a debt, which constitutes cash consideration under the Companies Act 2006 since it involves the release of a liability of a company for a liquidated sum.[106] Where the company owes A £120 and the company issues to A 100 shares of nominal value £1, this will be regarded as cash consideration and will not infringe the no-discount rule, as long as the debt released is greater than the nominal value of the shares. This appears to be the case even if the company is insolvent at the time, and the amount that the creditor is actually likely to receive is substantially below the nominal value of the shares issued.[107] So, even if in the winding up the creditor will only receive 50 pence in the pound, ie just £60 in the above example, this does not infringe the no-discount rule. In the absence of deceit or fraud the court will not inquire into the financial capacity of the issuing company to pay to the creditor-allottee the amount of the presently payable debt. This is subject to the proviso that the debt must have been genuinely created in the course of the company's business, and must be immediately payable.

---

[104] [1892] AC 125.

[105] This argument may have had less weight in earlier stages of company law development when mandatory accounting disclosures did not exist and creditors might have had little information other than par value to rely on. At that point future creditors of the company could potentially have been prejudiced if they relied on the par value as a measure of the capital actually subscribed. It is difficult to imagine that any creditors, present or future, would rely on par value in this way today.

[106] Companies Act 2006, s 583(3)(c).

[107] *Pro-Image Studios v Commonwealth Bank of Australia* (1990–91) 4 ACSR 586 (Sup Ct Victoria); cf *Re Jarass Pty Ltd* (1988) 13 ACSR 728 (Sup Ct NSW).

Even if the rules are effective in ensuring that the value received by the company is in fact equal to the par value of the shares, this guarantee is not a very valuable one as far as creditors are concerned. First, as discussed, the par value of the shares may in fact be well below their market value. Second, all that the rules aim to guarantee is that the value of the item on receipt is equal to the par value of the shares at that moment in time. For many items this will bear little relation to the value of the item at the future point in time when the creditors seek to realise their debts.[108]

In fact, these valuation rules can be regarded as being costly for companies both in money, in that the independent reports need to be paid for, and in time, as they delay company formation and increases in capital through the issue of new shares. The prohibition on issuing shares in exchange for future services contained in the Second Company Law Directive is also regarded as problematic in the context of the financing of high tech start-up companies. Creditors deciding whether to lend to a company, and on what terms, will be interested in the net worth of the company, which will include the existing share capital of the company. In assessing this they will need to examine the current value of the firm's assets, rather than the value of the assets at the moment of purchase, as measured against the par value of the shares.[109]

5.4 Maintenance of Capital

In the Companies Act 2006, the starting point for maintenance of capital issues is that any form of distribution of corporate assets to shareholders is prohibited except where the value of the distribution is less than that of the assets available for distribution. Distributions can be made to the shareholders in a number of ways, such as via the payment of dividends, via the redemption or repurchase of the company's own shares, or through a reduction of share capital. Each of these mechanisms is explored in this section.

There are good reasons for companies to make use of these various mechanisms in some circumstances, but these distributions can also be used by shareholders to advantage themselves at the creditors' expense, as discussed at 5.2. As a consequence, a number of constraints are placed on the use of these mechanisms. The central idea is that capital must not be returned to the shareholders. There is a longstanding common law rule that prohibits the return of capital to shareholders, which allows courts to strike down those that are inappropriate on the basis that they amount to a fraud on the company's creditors.[110] There are also statutory controls in place which place constraints on the use of dividends, share repurchases, share redemptions and reductions of capital. Although these mechanisms can

---

[108] Many assets devalue quickly (eg computers) and may have little or no value at a later date. In addition, the 'independent' experts in this regard are repeat players in the market and will not wish to lose current or prospective clients by acting too independently in this regard. So long as the assets are not outrageously over-valued, it is likely that the non-cash consideration will be approved.

[109] Clearly creditors are interested in just these issues in practice: see the discussion at 6.3.2 (regarding the initial information required by creditors) and chapter 13 (regarding the information required in relation to debt securities).

[110] See eg *Ridge Securities Ltd v IRC* [1964] 1 WLR 479; *Re Halt Garage (1964) Ltd* [1982] 3 All ER 1016; *Barclays Bank plc v British & Commonwealth Holdings plc* [1995] BCC 19.

in many ways be regarded as alternative methods of returning value to shareholders, the statutory controls on these concepts differ in many respects.[111]

5.4.1 Dividend Payments

The decision whether or not to pay dividends generally lies with the directors.[112] The procedure for the declaration and payment of dividends is set out in the articles of association. These usually provide for final dividends to be declared by shareholders, but only following the recommendation of the directors, and for interim dividends to be determined by directors without recourse to the shareholders for approval.[113] Generally, articles will prevent shareholders from declaring a larger dividend than that recommended by directors, and it is unusual for shareholders to approve a lesser sum, so in practice it is the directors who determine the size of dividend payments.

5.4.1.1 *Potential Benefits of Dividend Payments*

There may be good reasons for directors to recommend the payment of a dividend. In particular, such payments may be necessary to meet shareholder expectations, and therefore to encourage investment in the company.[114] In addition, dividends can perform a valuable role as a signalling device, to represent to the market the financial health of the company. Paying healthy consistent dividends is a way for managers to indicate to the market that they have long-term confidence in the business. These issues are discussed further at 2.5.

5.4.1.2 *Constraints on Dividend Payments*

Despite these potential benefits, the approach in the UK has been to seek to constrain the directors' discretion to make dividend payments, with a view to regulating the conflict between creditors and shareholders highlighted in 5.2. After all, one of the obvious ways in which shareholders could potentially be advantaged at the expense of creditors is for large distributions to be paid to them in the form of dividends. Consequently, there is a common law rule of long standing that a distribution of assets to a shareholder, except in accordance with specific statutory procedures, is a return of capital which is unlawful and ultra vires for the company.[115]

---

[111] Other differences between these mechanisms are also observable; for example, their tax treatment varies somewhat.

[112] See 2.2.1, 3.2.1.

[113] See eg Model Articles for Private Companies Limited by Shares, art 30; Model Articles for Public Companies, art 70. It has been suggested that directors who only ever utilise interim dividends, without recourse to the shareholders, may not be properly exercising the power conferred by the articles in this regard: *Re Paycheck Services 3 Ltd; Revenue and Customs Commissioners v Holland* [2010] UKSC 51.

[114] For a discussion of the income rights generally attached to ordinary and preference shares see 3.2.1.1.2 and 3.2.1.2.2 respectively.

[115] Eg *Re Halt Garage (1964) Ltd* [1982] 3 All ER 1016. For a recent discussion of this principle see *Progress Property Co Ltd v Moorgarth Group Ltd* [2010] UKSC 55. This rule also prevents disguised distributions: *Aveling Barford Ltd v Perion Ltd* [1989] 1 WLR 360, although see now Companies Act 2006, ss 845–46.

This common law rule operates in tandem with the statutory rules, now contained in the Companies Act 2006, which lay down rules determining how companies may pay dividends.[116] The 2006 Act provides that dividends can only be made out of a company's distributable profits, which are the company's 'accumulated, realised profits … less its accumulated, realised losses'.[117] For public companies an additional hurdle is imposed: a dividend may only be paid when the amount of its net assets[118] is not less than the aggregate of its called up share capital and undistributable reserves, and only if, and to the extent that, the distribution does not reduce the amount of those assets to less than the aggregate.[119] The undistributable reserves for this purpose include the share premium account, the capital redemption reserve, the amount by which accumulated unrealised profits exceed accumulated unrealised losses, and any other reserve which the company is prohibited from distributing by any enactment or by its articles.[120] Companies must pay dividends in cash unless dividends in kind are authorised by the articles[121]—something that is commonly included.[122]

The amount of dividend that can be paid is therefore determined by reference to the company's financial position in its relevant accounts,[123] generally its last annual accounts.[124] There are a number of potential problems with this approach. The first is that the test is backward-looking, based on historical information about the company and its assets and liabilities. This may be contrasted with the forward-looking solvency-based test that has been suggested by some commentators as an alternative test for determining whether and how much may be distributed to shareholders by way of dividends. This solvency-based test is discussed further at 5.5.3 below. Second, these rules depend upon the accounts of the company accurately identifying the profits that may be distributed to shareholders under the legal rules. There may, however, be a divergence between the aims of accounting rules (which can be regarded as providing information relevant to investment decisions) and the legal rules regarding dividend distribution (which are focused on creditor protection issues).[125] Unsurprisingly, these rules may not always be in sync. The present link between a company's accounts and its dividend-paying capacity may, therefore, be questioned.

In the event of an unlawful dividend being paid, the recipient is personally liable to repay the dividend, but only if they have knowledge of the unlawfulness of the payment.[126]

---

[116] Note that there is often a contractual restriction on dividend payments in loans to private companies: see 6.3.1.3.

[117] Companies Act 2006, s 830(2).

[118] The definition of 'net assets' for this purpose is the aggregate of the company's assets less the aggregate of its liabilities: ibid, s 831(2).

[119] Ibid, s 831, giving effect to the Second Company Law Directive, art 17(1). Detailed guidance on these issues is provided by the accounting profession: see ICAEW & ICAS, *Guidance on the Determination of Realised Profits and Losses in the Context of Distributions under the Companies Act 2006* (TECH 02/10).

[120] Companies Act 2006, s 831(4).

[121] *Wood v Odessa Waterworks Co* (1889) 42 Ch D 636.

[122] Model Articles for Private Companies Limited by Shares, art 34; Model Articles for Public Companies, art 76.

[123] Companies Act 2006, s 836(1).

[124] Ibid, s 836(2). See also s 837.

[125] For discussion see eg G Strampelli, 'The IAS/IFRS After the Crisis: Limiting the Impact of Fair Value Accounting on Companies' Capital' (2011) 8 *European Company and Financial Law Review* 1.

[126] Companies Act 2006, s 847(2) and see *Precision Dippings Ltd v Precision Dippings Marketing Ltd* [1986] 1 Ch 447; cf J Payne, 'Unjust Enrichment, Trusts and Recipient Liability for Unlawful Dividends' (2003) 119 *Law Quarterly Review* 583. The recipient must have knowledge of the facts giving rise to the contravention and does not need to know that the payment is a breach of the Act: *It's a Wrap (UK) Ltd v Gula* [2006] EWCA Civ 544.

In addition, the directors who authorise the unlawful dividend payment will be liable to the company for those sums.[127] It remains unclear whether the directors are strictly liable to repay the money, or whether the liability is fault-based and depends upon whether the directors have acted under an honest and reasonable belief that the facts justified the payment, such as where the directors base their decision in good faith on accounts which are later found to be defective.[128]

5.4.2 Repurchases and Redemptions of Shares

There is a general rule that companies are not permitted to acquire their own shares.[129] However, the Companies Act 2006 contains a number of important exceptions to this rule. In particular, both redemptions and repurchases of shares are permitted in certain circumstances.[130] There are some significant similarities between these forms of distribution, which both involve a purchase of shares from a shareholder by the company. The procedures for financing the purchase of shares are broadly similar, as is the use of the capital redemption reserve as a mechanism for preserving the company's capital, although the details of the two regimes do differ. The essential difference between the two is the fact that as regards repurchases of shares the agreement of both parties is required at the time of the purchase, and the terms of the purchase are set at that time, whereas for redeemable shares the terms are generally set in the articles and may not require the consent of both parties.

5.4.2.1 Potential Benefits of Repurchases and Redemptions of Shares

Repurchases and redemptions of shares can be extremely beneficial, especially in small companies with little or no active market for the company's shares, as they provide an exit route for shareholders. They can therefore deal with the problems of capital lock-in that shareholders in such companies can otherwise face. Offering an opportunity to exit the company in this way may, therefore, facilitate investment into the company. Redeemable shares, in particular, can be attractive to investors for this reason, as they provide a measure of certainty about the ability to exit the investment in the future.

Even in larger companies, these mechanisms can be a useful tool where the company has surplus cash which it wants to return to its shareholders. There are other ways in

---

[127] *Flitcroft's Case* (1882) LR 21 Ch D 519; *Precision Dippings Ltd v Precision Dippings Marketing Ltd* [1986] 1 Ch 447.

[128] Eg *Hilton International Ltd v Hilton* [1989] 1 NZLR 442, although in that case the directors failed to obtain a proper set of accounts, and therefore were held liable to refund the amount of the dividend. See also *Re Paycheck Services 3 Ltd* [2010] UKSC 55 [46]–[47] per Lord Hope, obiter, who acknowledged that there are two lines of authority on this issue, namely a strict view of the liability of directors and one which depends on fault; his Lordship's view was that the trend of modern authority supported the former (see also Lord Walker at [28]). For discussion see E Ferran, 'Directors' Liability for Unlawful Dividends' (2011) 70 *Cambridge Law Journal* 321.

[129] Companies Act 2006, s 658(1); *Trevor v Whitworth* (1887) LR 12 App Cas 409.

[130] See Companies Act 2006, s 659, and in particular ss 684–89 as regards redemptions of shares and ss 690–708 as regards purchases of own shares.

which a company could achieve this outcome, for example by paying dividends to the shareholders, but there may be reasons for preferring a share buy-back to achieve this goal. For example, where dividends are utilised as a signalling device, directors tend to prefer to keep dividend payments stable and therefore to make a one-off payment via an alternative mechanism that will not raise expectations about future payouts.[131] Share buy-backs can also provide a signalling function, however, and may be utilised by directors to indicate their belief that the share price is undervalued based on the expected future performance of the company.[132] Another potentially valuable use of these mechanisms is to facilitate a reorganisation of the company's capital, for example by getting rid of a class of shares entirely, such as the preference shares. This may be because the company wishes to replace one class of shares with another, or because it wishes to replace some of its equity financing with cheaper debt. They also facilitate employee share schemes as they make it possible for the company to purchase the shares when the employee leaves the company.[133]

Consequently, there are many good reasons why companies may want to make use of repurchases or redemptions of shares. However, because these mechanisms potentially infringe the maintenance of capital principle, their use has been curtailed by legislation.[134] It is notable that many of the constraints regarding the use of these mechanisms have gradually been relaxed over time, although the Second Company Law Directive continues to require certain conditions where public companies seek to issue redeemable shares or to repurchase shares.[135]

5.4.2.2 Repurchases of Shares

5.4.2.2.1 Rules Applicable to All Companies

Share buy-backs are possible, provided the company satisfies the legislative requirements and any restrictions included in its articles.[136] For a share buy-back it is not necessary

---

[131] For discussion see 2.5. There may also be tax advantages for the company if it structures the return of surplus cash to shareholders via a share buy-back rather than a dividend payment: R Moore, B Ward, B Phillips and S Stewart, 'Returning Value to Shareholders: Giving Something Back' (2012) 23(8) *PLC* 23.

[132] Of course, it is possible that share buy-backs could therefore be used by directors to manipulate the share price in a way that is designed to mislead the market. Market manipulation of this kind is both a criminal and an administrative offence in the UK. For discussion see 12.2.

[133] See, in this regard, Companies Act 2006 (Amendment of Part 18) Regulations 2013 (SI 2013/999) as amended by SI 2015/532, which aim to promote employee share ownership by improving the operation of internal share markets within companies (see BIS, *Employee Ownership and Share Buy Backs: Implementation of Nuttall Review—Recommendation V: Government Response to Consultation* (February 2013)).

[134] Share buy-backs also give rise to other concerns, most notably the concern that they might be used by the company to bolster or stabilise the share price. These concerns are best dealt with via the specific provisions concerning market manipulation: Financial Services Act 2012, ss 89–91; Financial Services and Markets Act 2000, s 118 (discussed further at 12.2.2.2 and 12.2.2.3).

[135] Second Company Law Directive, art 21(1) as amended by Directive 2006/68/EC, which introduced some relaxations into the regime.

[136] Companies Act 2006, s 690(1). Section 690(2) provides that a company must not purchase its own shares where to do so would result in there being no member of the company holding shares other than redeemable shares or shares held as treasury shares.

for a company proposing to purchase its own shares to have the authority to do so in its articles,[137] however a shareholder resolution is required to authorise the buy-back.[138]

Where the purchase is a 'market' purchase,[139] this needs to be an ordinary resolution.[140] A market purchase occurs where the purchase is made on a recognised investment exchange provided the shares are subject to a marketing arrangement on that exchange.[141] This would include shares purchased on the Main Market in London or on the AIM market.[142] Until 2013, an 'off-market' purchase required a special resolution, but this form of purchase now requires only an ordinary resolution.[143] Repurchases must be funded out of distributable profits or a fresh issue of shares in order not to reduce share capital.[144] Where the buy-back is funded wholly out of the company's profits, the amount by which the capital of the company is reduced must be transferred to a capital redemption reserve,[145] and this reserve is treated for most purposes as though it is share capital.[146] In addition to these company law requirements, the Listing Rules create some extra requirements for listed companies.[147]

5.4.2.2.2 Additional Flexibility for Private Companies

For private companies, the legislation creates additional flexibility when it comes to repurchasing its own shares. In 2013 it became possible for private companies seeking to repurchase small amounts of shares to do so without having to specify that the cash for the

---

[137] However, the articles may restrict or prohibit the company's purchase of its own shares (ibid, s 690(1)).

[138] Shareholders cannot rely on the *Re Duomatic* principle of unanimous consent as an alternative to a resolution passed in a general meeting in this instance: *Re RW Peak (Kings Lynn) Ltd* [1998] BCC 596 (affirmed in *Wright v Atlas Wright (Europe) Ltd* [1999] 2 BCLC 301). The statutory protections are intended to protect the creditors as well as the shareholders and therefore it is not acceptable for the shareholders to waive that statutory protection. However, if it can be demonstrated that a particular provision is intended to protect the shareholders rather than the creditors, it may be open to the shareholders to act unanimously in order to waive compliance: *Kinlan v Crimmin* [2006] EWHC 779 (Ch).

[139] Companies Act 2006, s 701. The authority may be general and not linked to any particular purchase of shares (cf off-market purchases). The maximum length of an authority is five years: s 701(5) (as amended by Companies (Share Capital and Acquisition of its Own Shares) Regulations 2009 (SI 2009/2022)).

[140] In practice, listed companies often use a special resolution for this purpose as this is preferred by institutional investors. For discussion see E Ferran and LC Ho, *Principles of Corporate Finance Law*, 2nd edn (Oxford, Oxford University Press, 2014) 189.

[141] Companies Act 2006, s 693(4).

[142] As regards shares admitted to trading on the Main Market see s 693(3)(a), and as regards shares admitted to trading on AIM see s 693(3)(b).

[143] Companies Act 2006, s 694, as amended by Companies Act 2006 (Amendment of Part 18) Regulations 2013 (SI 2013/999) and SI 2015/532. A general authorisation is not acceptable (unless the buy-back relates to a private company and is connected to an employee share scheme: s 693A, as amended by SI 2013/999). Accordingly, the shareholders must approve the specific terms of the contract by which the shares are purchased before it is entered into, or the contract must provide that no shares may be purchased until its terms have been authorised by a special resolution of the company: s 694(2). The resolution may be of unlimited duration if a private company is involved (cf public companies: s 695(5)). A resolution approving an off-market purchase of own shares will not be effective if any shareholder holding shares to which the resolution relates exercised the voting rights carried by those shares in voting on the resolution and the resolution would not have been passed if he had not done so: s 695(3).

[144] Companies Act 2006, s 692(2).

[145] Ibid, s 733(2). Where the buy-back is funded from a fresh issue of shares see s 733(3): normally the nominal value of the issued capital available to creditors will remain intact because the new shares will simply replace those being bought back.

[146] The exception to this situation is that the capital redemption reserve may be used to pay up fully paid bonus shares: ibid, s 733(5).

[147] See generally FCA Handbook, LR 12.

repurchase is from distributable reserves, as long as there is provision to this effect in the company's articles.[148] The threshold for this provision is the lower of £15,000 or the equivalent of 5 per cent of the share capital of the company in any given year.

In addition, a private company can buy back its own shares out of capital in certain circumstances.[149] In particular, the directors must make a statement as to the solvency of the company.[150] The directors must state that they have formed the opinion that, if the payment is made, the company will be able to pay its debts as they fall due for the coming 12 months, taking account of the company's liabilities, including its contingent and prospective liabilities.[151] Annexed to this statement must be a report by the company's auditors stating that they are not aware of anything to indicate that the directors' opinion is unreasonable.[152] The directors commit a criminal offence with a maximum term of imprisonment of two years if they make their statement 'without having reasonable grounds for the opinion expressed in it'.[153] A special resolution approving the payment is also required,[154] and the directors' statement and auditors' report must be made available to the shareholders prior to their vote.[155] The fact that the company has passed a resolution for payment out of capital must be publicised.[156] The legislation includes the right for creditors, or members who did not vote in favour of the repurchase, within five weeks of the special resolution, to apply to court in relation to the repurchase.[157] Consequently, the payment out of capital must be made no earlier than five weeks after the special resolution.[158]

Repurchased shares may be held by the company as treasury shares, which involves the company being entered onto the register of members in respect of those shares.[159] During this period the company cannot exercise any rights in relation to the shares (such as the right to vote) and no dividends may be paid on them.[160] The company may then dispose

---

[148] Companies Act 2006, s 692(1)(b), as amended by Companies Act 2006 (Amendment of Part 18) Regulations 2013 (SI 2013/999) and Companies Act 2006 (Amendment of Part 18) Regulations 2015 (SI 2015/532).

[149] The procedure is modified for buy-backs in connection with an employee share scheme: ibid, ss 720A–720B, as amended by Companies Act 2006 (Amendment of Part 18) Regulations 2013 (SI 2013/999) and SI 2015/532.

[150] Companies Act 2006, s 714.

[151] Ibid, s 714(3)(4).

[152] Ibid, s 714(6).

[153] Ibid, s 715.

[154] Ibid, s 716. The votes of any member holding shares to which the resolution relates will be discounted for the purposes of determining whether the resolution has passed: s 717.

[155] Ibid, s 718.

[156] Ibid, s 719.

[157] Ibid, s 721. On hearing the application the court must make an order either confirming or cancelling the resolution.

[158] Ibid, s 723.

[159] Treasury shares were introduced for publicly quoted companies in 2003 (see G Morse, 'The Introduction of Treasury Shares into English Law and Practice' [2004] *Journal of Business Law* 303), and were extended to unquoted public companies and private companies in 2013: Companies Act 2006, s 724 as amended by Companies Act 2006 (Amendment of Part 18) Regulations 2013 (SI 2013/999). For shares to be treated as treasury shares, the purchase must be made out of distributable profits or with cash, where permitted in relation to private companies (s 724(1), as amended). Additional requirements are imposed by the Listing Rules on a premium listed company in relation to treasury shares: FCA Handbook, LR 12.6.

[160] Companies Act 2006, ss 726(2)–(3).

of the treasury shares, for example by selling the shares for cash consideration or for the purposes of an employees' share scheme,[161] or it may cancel the shares.[162] Treasury shares can have a number of advantages for companies, including giving a company the ability to manage the demand and supply for its shares.

5.4.2.3 Redemption of Shares

The Companies Act 2006 permits the existence of redeemable shares—that is, shares which are to be redeemed, or are liable to be redeemed, at the option of the company or of the shareholder.[163] Any class of shares may be issued as redeemable, and redeemable ordinary shares and redeemable preference shares are both common. The issue of redeemable shares by public companies can only occur if there is prior authorisation in the articles;[164] this is not a requirement for private companies.[165]

One matter that arises is whether the terms and manner of the redemption need to be specified in the articles of the company. The 2006 Act allows the directors of both public and private companies to determine the terms and manner of the redemption at the time of the issue of the redeemable shares, provided they are authorised to do so under the articles or by an ordinary resolution.[166] In other words, the terms of the redemption need not be specified precisely in the articles, unless the directors are not provided with this authorisation.[167]

The financing of redemptions broadly follows that of repurchases.[168] Redemptions must be funded out of distributable profits or a fresh issue of shares, in order not to reduce share capital,[169] but private companies are permitted to redeem shares out of capital if they follow the solvency statement procedure set out in the Act.[170] Unlike share repurchases, redeemed shares must be cancelled, and may not be held in treasury,[171] so that redeeming shares will have the effect of reducing the company's share capital.

---

[161] Ibid, s 727. To the extent that the proceeds are equal to or less than the amount paid by the company for the shares, they are treated as a realised profit, and to the extent to which they exceed this figure they are treated as a share premium: ibid, s 731.

[162] Where treasury shares are cancelled, the amount of the share capital is reduced accordingly by the nominal amount of the shares cancelled and the equivalent amount is transferred to the capital redemption reserve: ibid, ss 729, 733.

[163] Ibid, s 684.

[164] Ibid, s 684(3).

[165] It is, however, possible for the articles to exclude or restrict the use of redeemable shares: ibid, s 684(2).

[166] Ibid, s 685. If the directors have such authority, they must determine the terms, conditions and manner of redemption before the shares are allotted and the details must be disclosed in a statement of capital: s 685(3). The terms of redemption do not, however, have to provide for payment on redemption (s 686) so payment can be at a later date (s 686(2)). If the company fails to redeem shares in accordance with their terms the holder may seek specific performance but not damages: s 735.

[167] In this case, the terms, details and manner of redemption must be specified in the articles: ibid, s 685(4).

[168] One difference between redemptions and repurchases is that stamp duty is payable on a redemption, unlike a buy-back of shares where no stamp duty is payable.

[169] Companies Act 2006, s 687(2).

[170] Ibid, s 687(1). The exception created for private companies engaged in small repurchases of shares in s 692(1)(b) as amended is not extended to share redemptions.

[171] Ibid, s 688.

5.4.3 Reductions of Capital

5.4.3.1 *Potential Benefits of a Reduction of Capital*

Reductions of capital may be valuable to companies in a number of scenarios. First, a company may have surplus assets, that is, assets that are in excess of the needs of the business, and it may therefore wish to return some of this surplus to shareholders. A reduction of capital is one of the methods by which it might do so, alongside a dividend payment, or a share repurchase or redemption of shares.[172] Unlike a dividend payment, the effect of a reduction of capital, a share buy-back or a redemption of shares is to reduce the number of shares in issue. The mechanism for a reduction of shares is more complex than these other methods, however, as it requires court approval for public companies, and private companies often opt for the court approval mechanism too, although they also have a solvency statement mechanism available to them, which allows them to avoid this requirement.[173]

A second use for a reduction of shares can be to facilitate a reorganisation of capital of the company, for example by enabling the company to get rid of a class of shares, such as the preference shares, entirely. Share repurchases and redemptions can also be utilised for this purpose.[174] One benefit that reductions might provide to the company in this regard, however, is that they can potentially be used to get rid of shareholders even where they do not consent. This is in contrast to both share repurchases and share redemptions, which require the consent of the shareholder to the sale, either at the time of the issue of shares or at the time of the sale.[175]

A third use of a reduction of capital is to convert undistributable reserves in the company into a reserve that is capable of being distributed. The reserve arising from a reduction of capital that has been confirmed by the court is treated as a realised profit, and is therefore distributable, unless the court orders otherwise,[176] and a reduction of capital following the solvency statement mechanism can also be treated as a realised profit in certain circumstances.[177] Such a reduction is often done in combination with a scheme of arrangement.[178]

Finally, a reduction of capital may be valuable as a way of reflecting the actual assets of the company, where losses have resulted in the capital of the company no longer reflecting the reality of the situation. Such a reduction will not be accompanied by any payment to the shareholders.

---

[172] Discussed at 5.4.1 and 5.4.2.

[173] See 5.4.3.2 and 5.4.3.3.

[174] See 5.4.2.

[175] See 5.4.2.

[176] Companies (Reduction of Share Capital) Order 2008 (SI 2008/1915), art 3.

[177] This requires an order under s 654 Companies Act 2006 to be made: Companies (Reduction of Share Capital) Order 2008 (SI 2008/1915), art 3(2).

[178] See chapter 15, especially 15.3.2. For an example of this use of a reduction of capital see *Re Mann Group plc* [2012] EWHC 4089 (Ch), and for further discussion see J Payne, *Schemes of Arrangement: Theory, Structure and Operation* (Cambridge, Cambridge University Press, 2014) ch 4.

5.4.3.2   Court Approval Route Available to All Companies

The Companies Act 2006 allows court-approved reductions of capital for both public and private companies. Section 641 of the Companies Act 2006 allows both public and private companies to reduce their capital by way of a special resolution, which is subsequently confirmed by the court.[179]

Creditors are entitled to object to the reduction where their interests may be adversely affected, such as where the reduction involves a repayment to shareholders,[180] rather than merely cancelling share capital which is unrepresented by a company's available assets.[181] The basis of the creditor's objection is that he or she must show that there is a real likelihood that the reduction would result in the company being unable to discharge the debt when it fell due.[182] Once the list of objecting creditors has been settled by the court, the court may not confirm the reduction unless all the objecting creditors have consented to the reduction, or their claims have been discharged or secured.[183] In practice, companies will generally structure the reduction of capital in such a way as to deal with these creditor protection issues and to persuade the court to disapply this statutory protection, for example by demonstrating that after the reduction they will continue to have sufficient cash to pay their existing creditors, including contingent creditors, or by arranging for a guarantee of their creditors' debts. Alternatively, companies may seek the consent of creditors to the reduction, since the court will dispense with these statutory creditor protection requirements to the extent that creditors have consented to it.

In determining whether to approve the reduction, the court will also be interested in the issue of shareholder protection.[184] In particular, the court will wish to see that there was full disclosure of the relevant issues to the shareholders before the vote, so that they were aware what they were agreeing to. Where the shareholders comprise more than one class, the court will have regard to whether the reduction infringes class rights.[185] The issue will often turn on whether the proposed reduction involves the fulfilment of the class right, as set out in the articles, or is a variation of that right, in which case the consent of the class may be required.[186] These issues will often turn on the court's interpretation of the rights set out in the articles. Where, for example, the reduction of capital involves paying off the preference shareholders, if the articles specify a right to a preferential dividend, and priority with regard to a return of capital but no right to participate in surplus and no other protection, then the courts have interpreted the reduction of capital to be a fulfilment and not a variation of their class rights.[187] No consent will therefore be required from the preference shareholders, and they will not be able to object to being paid off in this manner.

---

[179]   The company is required to apply to the court for an order confirming the reduction: Companies Act 2006, s 645(1). The court can reject the confirmation, or confirm it on any terms that it thinks fit: s 648.

[180]   Ibid, ss 645(2), 645(4) and 646 (as amended by Companies (Share Capital and Acquisition by Company of its Own Shares) Regulations 2009 (SI 2009/2022)).

[181]   Companies Act 2006, s 645(3).

[182]   Ibid, s 646. For discussion of the requirement of 'real likelihood' in this scenario see *Re Liberty International plc* [2010] EWHC 1060 (Ch).

[183]   Companies Act 2006, s 648; *Prudential Assurance Co Ltd v Chatterley-Whitfield Collieries Co Ltd* [1949] AC 512.

[184]   See *Scottish Insurance Corp v Wilsons & Clyde Coal Co Ltd* [1949] AC 462.

[185]   See Companies Act 2006, s 641(6) and *Re Northern Engineering Industries plc* [1994] BCC 618.

[186]   See 3.2.1 for a discussion of the variation of class rights.

[187]   See eg *Scottish Insurance Corp v Wilsons & Clyde Coal Co Ltd* [1949] AC 462.

If the court approves the reduction, a copy of the court's order, together with a statement of capital setting out the details of the company's new share capital, must be lodged with the registrar of companies.[188]

5.4.3.3 Solvency Statement Mechanism for Private Companies

The Companies Act 2006 introduced a new method of reducing capital for private companies by way of a special resolution coupled with a solvency statement from the directors.[189] The Company Law Review Steering Group initially recommended that this method should replace the court approval method for private companies, although this recommendation was later dropped.[190] The Steering Group also recommended that public companies be allowed to reduce their capital on this basis, without having to seek court approval.[191] However, the Government decided against introducing this change for public companies.[192]

There are close similarities between this solvency statement and that required of directors in the procedure whereby private companies can repurchase their shares from capital,[193] although one difference is that the required statement for a reduction of capital does not need to be accompanied by an auditors' report.[194] The directors are required to state that they have formed the opinion that, as regards the company's position at the date of the statement, there is no ground on which the company will be found to be unable to pay its debts, and that the company will be able to pay its debts as they fall due during the following year.[195] The statement must be made by all directors, and the directors must take account of prospective and contingent liabilities of the company.[196] Making a statutory statement without having reasonable grounds for the opinions expressed in it is a criminal offence for which the maximum penalty is imprisonment for up to two years.[197] The special resolution, solvency statement and statement of capital must all be delivered to the registrar within 15 days of the special resolution.[198]

---

[188] Companies Act 2006, s 649.

[189] In one scenario, however, private companies are not able to make use of this mechanism, namely where the result of the reduction would be to leave the company with no member of the company holding shares other than redeemable shares: ibid, s 641(1)(2).

[190] See Company Law Review Steering Group, *Modern Company Law for a Competitive Economy: The Strategic Framework* (URN 99/654, February 1999); *Company Formation and Capital Maintenance* (URN 99/1145, October 1999), para 3.27; Company Law Review Steering Group, *Completing the Structure* (URN 00/1335, November 2000), para 7.9.

[191] *Company Formation and Capital Maintenance*, ibid, paras 3.27–3.35. Compliance with the Second Company Law Directive requirement that creditors whose claims antedate the publication of the decision to reduce capital should be entitled to have a right to obtain security for their claims (Second Company Law Directive, art 32) would have been achieved by providing creditors with the opportunity, at their initiative, to challenge a reduction in court.

[192] DTI, *Company Law Reform* (Cm 6456, 2005).

[193] Companies Act 2006, ss 709–23 (discussed at 5.4.2.2.2).

[194] Ibid, s 643.

[195] Ibid, s 643 and Companies (Reduction of Share Capital) Order 2008 (SI 2008/1915), art 2. If the company is intended to be wound up within the next 12 months, this statement is modified: s 643(1)(b)(i).

[196] Companies Act 2006, ss 643(1) and (2).

[197] Ibid, ss 643(4) and (5).

[198] Ibid, s 644. The directors must also deliver to the registrar a statement confirming that the solvency statement was made not more than 15 days before the special resolution (s 644(5)). There are criminal sanctions for non-compliance with these registration requirements: s 644(8)(9).

Although this procedure offers a measure of deregulation for private companies, there are a number of reasons, both presentational and practical, why private companies may still wish to follow the more cumbersome and expensive court approval route. These include the desire to draw as complete a line as possible under a particular change of share capital, and the desire to obtain the court's approval for an unusual reduction,[199] in circumstances where the directors are faced with a difficulty in forming the opinion required for the solvency statement.[200] Concerns amongst directors about the criminal sanctions that attach to the solvency statement mechanism, that are absent in the court approval route, may also incline directors to prefer the latter option.

5.4.4 Prohibition on Financial Assistance

The rules regarding financial assistance deal with the scenario in which a company financially supports the purchase of its own shares. The rules prohibiting companies providing assistance for the acquisition of their own shares have traditionally been regarded as part of the legal capital rules, but the root of these provisions has little in common with the rest of the capital maintenance provisions. In particular, creditor protection does not seem to be a strong driver behind these rules. Indeed, the link between capital maintenance and financial assistance is tenuous.[201] The concerns regarding the use of financial assistance often seem to be focused elsewhere. One mischief at which these sections are aimed is not abuse of creditors per se, but rather the prevention of the use of target company resources in a leveraged buy-out to assist the acquisition of shares.[202] In many instances, for example where the form of assistance is a loan, no harm to the creditors will result from the assistance. Indeed, the Company Law Review Steering Group concluded that the prohibition 'can only endanger the interests of creditors in a situation of potential insolvency, when the directors' duties and the provisions on fraudulent and wrongful trading are likely to be relevant'.[203] It may also be noted that even though the ban on financial assistance is often said to be an impediment to leveraged buy-outs, it has not prevented the development of a significant

[199] A private company cannot reduce its capital to zero except with court approval: s 641(2).

[200] When the new solvency statement method for reducing capital was introduced, it was anticipated that reserves arising as a result of this procedure might be treated differently from (and less favourably than) reserves arising from a court-approved reduction of capital. However, the Secretary of State has made use of powers within the 2006 Act (specifically s 654) to introduce delegated legislation to clarify this issue. The Companies (Reduction of Capital) Order 2008 (SI 2008/1915) provides that when a company reduces its share capital by any means, a reserve arising from that reduction is to be treated as a realised profit for the purposes of the rules on distributions of companies assets set out in Part 23 of the 2006 Act unless, in the case of a court-approved reduction, the court orders otherwise.

[201] This was recognised by the Jenkins Committee in 1962: *Report of the Company Law Committee* (Cmnd 1749, 1962), paras 173–76.

[202] J Armour, 'Share Capital and Creditor Protection: Efficient Rules for a Modern Company Law' (2000) 63 *Modern Law Review* 355, 378.

[203] See Company Law Review Steering Group, *Modern Company Law for a Competitive Economy: The Strategic Framework* (URN 99/654, February 1999); *Company Formation and Capital Maintenance* (URN 99/1145, October 1999), 39.

European leveraged buy-out market.[204] Other concerns regarding financial assistance centre on its potential use to bolster the share price of the company giving the assistance.[205] Manipulating the share price of the company is, however, an offence with both criminal and administrative sanctions attached to it, so it is questionable whether a separate regime is needed to deal with particular scenario.[206] The financial assistance rules are therefore best seen as an 'offshoot' of the legal capital rules, as they have only a limited overlap with the idea that a company should maintain its capital.

The financial assistance rules have been subject to substantial criticism as a result of both the complexity of the rules and the costs associated with complying with them.[207] Until 2006 the rules prohibiting financial assistance applied to public and to private companies, although private companies had the option of a 'whitewash' procedure.[208] Reform proposals were suggested by the Company Law Review Steering Group[209] and, as a result, the ban on financial assistance no longer applies to private companies, unless they are subsidiaries of public companies.[210] Public companies, however, remain subject to a prohibition on the giving of financial assistance for the purchase of their own shares.[211] In large part this is due to the need to implement the requirements of the Second Company Law Directive.[212]

The concept of 'financial assistance' is construed broadly, to include not only assistance which directly or indirectly helps to pay the price of the shares but also other steps which merely smooth the path, for example the payment of concurrent benefits such as accountants' fees.[213] The assistance must be financial in nature and it must fall within the forms of financial assistance specified in section 677 of the Companies Act 2006, since only these forms of assistance are banned. These include, for example, financial assistance given by

---

[204] L Enriques, 'EC Company Law Directives and Regulations: How Trivial Are They?' in J Armour and JA McCahery (eds), *After Enron: Improving Corporate Law and Modernising Securities Regulation in Europe and the US* (Oxford, Hart Publishing, 2006). For further discussion see chapter 16.

[205] See eg *Report of the Company Law Amendment Committee* (the Greene Committee) (Cmd 2657, 1926), para 30.

[206] See 12.2.

[207] See eg E Ferran, 'Simplification of European Company Law on Financial Assistance' (2005) 6 *European Business Organization Law Review* 93.

[208] Companies Act 1985, ss 155–58.

[209] Company Law Review Steering Group, *Company Formation and Capital Maintenance* (URN 99/1145, October 1999), paras 3.42–3.43.

[210] Since the rules on maintenance of capital continue to apply to private companies, there is a danger that some corporate actions that would have infringed the ban on financial assistance will remain unlawful notwithstanding this repeal, because they are contrary to the maintenance of capital regime. The Government agreed to make it clear in a saving provision under Companies Act 2006, s 1296 that the removal of the prohibition on private companies giving financial assistance for the purchase of own shares will not prevent private companies entering into transactions which they could lawfully have entered into under the whitewash procedure: see Companies Act 2006 (Commencement No 5, Transitional Provisions and Savings) Order 2007 (SI 2007/3495), para 52.

[211] Companies Act 2006, ss 677–83.

[212] Second Company Law Directive, art 25.

[213] There is no legislative definition of this term, so it has been left to the courts to determine this issue. See eg *Chaston v SWP Group plc* [2002] EWCA Civ 1999; cf *MT Realisations Ltd v Digital Equipment Co Ltd* [2002] EWHC 1628 (Ch); *Re Uniq plc* [2011] EWHC 749 (Ch). See generally E Ferran, 'Corporate Transactions and Financial Assistance: Shifting Policy Perceptions but Static Law' (2004) 63 *Cambridge Law Journal* 225.

way of gift,[214] by way of guarantee, security or indemnity,[215] or by waiver[216] or loan,[217] and include the catch-all of 'any other financial assistance given by a company where … the net assets of the company are [thereby] reduced to a material extent'.[218] Finally, it must be ascertained whether the assistance is given for the purpose of the acquisition of shares,[219] or for the purpose of reducing or discharging a liability incurred for the purpose of an acquisition.[220] The assistance will not be caught by the provisions of the 2006 Act if the 'company's principal purpose in giving the assistance is not to give it for the purpose of any such acquisition' or is only an incidental part of some larger scheme.[221] The concepts of 'larger' or 'principal' purpose have, however, been construed very narrowly by the courts.[222] In addition, some statutory exceptions are provided.[223]

Criminal penalties follow from the provision of unlawful assistance: the company is liable to a fine and every officer of the company who is in default is also guilty of a criminal offence and liable to imprisonment for up to two years, or a fine, or both.[224] In addition, any transaction constituting unlawful assistance is illegal, and any obligations undertaken by the company will be unenforceable.[225] If the company has actually given the unlawful financial assistance, the transaction will be void. The directors who are a party to the breach of the financial assistance provisions will be in breach of their directors' duties and liable to the company for any losses incurred by it as a result of the default.[226]

The law relating to financial assistance is riddled with uncertainty, which leads to significant costs for companies as they seek legal advice regarding whether transactions will fall foul of these provisions and, if so, how to structure transactions so as to avoid this prohibition. Cost considerations were certainly part of the reason why the ban was removed for private companies in the 2006 Act.[227] Also relevant, however, was the fact that there are other rules in place that can be called upon to provide protection for any of the groups that might be harmed by a company providing financial assistance, including general company

---

[214] Companies Act 2006, s 677(1)(a).

[215] Ibid, s 677(1)(b)(i).

[216] Ibid, s 677(1)(b)(ii).

[217] Ibid, s 677(1)(c)(i).

[218] Ibid, s 677(1)(d)(i).

[219] Ibid, s 678(1). For discussion see *Dyment v Boyden* [2004] EWCA Civ 1586.

[220] Companies Act 2006, s 678(3).

[221] Ibid, ss 678(2), 678(4).

[222] *Brady v Brady* [1989] AC 755; *Chaston v SWP Group plc* [2002] EWCA Civ 1999; *Re Uniq plc* [2011] EWHC 749 (Ch).

[223] Companies Act 2006, ss 681–82.

[224] Ibid, s 680. The Company Law Review considered whether to remove these criminal penalties for financial assistance, but in the end the recommendation was to retain them: Company Law Review Steering Group, *Final Report* (URN 01/942–3, July 2001), para 15.18.

[225] *Brady v Brady* [1989] AC 755. The illegality of the financial assistance will not, however, taint other connected transactions, such as the agreement by the person assisted to acquire the shares, unless the obligation to acquire the shares and to provide the assistance form part of a single, composite transaction (see eg *Carney v Herbert* [1985] AC 301 (PC)).

[226] See eg *Belmont Finance Corp v Williams Furniture Ltd (No 2)* [1980] All ER 393. Liability for third parties may also arise as a result of assistance that they provide to the directors in the giving of unlawful financial assistance or if they receive funds of the company that have been misapplied by directors with knowledge of the breach.

[227] DTI, *Company Law Reform* (Cm 6456, 2005), 41. The Company Law Review Steering Group estimated that the cost of legal advice regarding the financial assistance provisions amounted to £20 million per annum (see Company Law Review Steering Group, *Modern Company Law for a Competitive Economy: The Strategic Framework* (URN 99/654, February 1999), para 5.4.21), a figure which is regarded by some practitioners as an underestimate.

law principles (in particular directors' duties and minority shareholder protection), take-over regulation,[228] market manipulation provisions,[229] and the rules designed to protect creditors in the run-up to insolvency,[230] including wrongful trading[231] and fraudulent trading.[232] It is hard to justify the continued existence of these rules for public companies, except for the need to comply with the requirements of the Second Company Law Directive in this regard.

5.4.5 Efficacy of the Rules as a Form of Creditor Protection

The capital maintenance rules appear to offer more protection to creditors than the minimum capital rules, since they aim to restrict distributions to shareholders and reductions of capital. In reality, however, little if any protection is actually afforded by the rules. There are a number of reasons for this failure. The comments here focus, in particular, on the rules regarding dividends, repurchases and redemptions of shares and reductions of capital, since these all represent methods by which cash can be returned to shareholders and raise the creditor-shareholder conflict discussed in 5.2. The financial assistance rules seem to have a different rationale, and can be regarded as concerned with creditor protection only tangentially.[233]

One difficulty with the distribution rules as a form of creditor protection is that distributions to shareholders are regulated by imposing a balance sheet test.[234] Consequently, only that portion of the net assets that exceeds the capital and the undistributable reserves[235] can be paid out to shareholders, irrespective of whether the payments will threaten the creditors' expectations of repayment. This balance-sheet information bears little relation to the company's true financial position.[236] It is calibrated by reference to historic contributions by shareholders, rather than by any calculation of a company's assets or financial needs on a going concern basis.[237] In addition, using the company's accounts as a basis for determining whether the company can return assets to shareholders without unduly disadvantaging the creditors is problematic when the accounts are focused not on creditor protection but on the distinct goal of providing information relevant to investment decisions.[238] As a result, there is a disjunction between a company's real capacity to make distributions to

---

[228] See chapter 14.

[229] See 12.2.2.2 and 12.2.2.3.

[230] See 3.3.2 and 3.3.3.

[231] Insolvency Act 1986, s 214 and see 3.3.3.2.2(b).

[232] Ibid, s 213 and see 3.3.3.2.2(a).

[233] See 5.4.4.

[234] Second Company Law Directive, art 17(1) and see Companies Act 2006, Part 23.

[235] Although the Second Company Law Directive only requires the subscribed capital, or par value, to be undistributable, the UK has gold-plated these provisions so that share premium and capital redemption reserves are also, generally, undistributable.

[236] L Enriques and JR Macey, 'Creditors Versus Capital Formation: The Case Against the European Legal Capital Rules' (2001) 86 *Cornell Law Review* 1165, 1190; J Rickford, 'Reforming Capital: Report of the Interdisciplinary Group on Capital Maintenance' (2004) 15 *European Business Law Review* 919.

[237] Companies Act 2006, s 831 comes closer to an asset test, but this only applies to public companies. A similar point arises regarding the effectiveness of capital ratio tests, as opposed to cash flow tests: see 6.3.2.2.

[238] See 5.4.1.2.

shareholders, and the result under the maintenance of capital rules, which may produce either an unduly generous or unduly restrictive outcome.[239] It is likely that more effective controls on distributions can be put in place by other means.[240]

Where a company has no positive net present value projects in which to invest, an inability to distribute its surplus to shareholders can be regarded as a waste of resources. There are often good reasons for a company to be able to return its capital to its shareholders, via a dividend payment, a repurchase or redemption of shares or a reduction of capital.[241] For example, to the extent that the payment of dividends is a method by which companies can signal particular information to the marketplace,[242] an unduly restrictive policy on dividend payment constrains the company's ability to make use of this facility. An inability to do so can potentially have a negative impact on the efficiency of the equity market.[243] Undue constraints on a company's ability to make use of these mechanisms should therefore be avoided.

Another difficulty with the distribution rules is that they comprise only a narrow set of circumstances in which capital cannot be returned to the shareholders.[244] They do not prevent assets being distributed to shareholders in other ways, such as the payment of excessive compensation for shareholders who are also directors of the company. In the UK, directors of private companies can avoid the rules preventing the payment of dividends out of capital by returning capital to the shareholders by means of a share repurchase or a reduction of capital, provided the directors declare that the company will remain solvent for 12 months.[245] Neither do the capital maintenance rules prevent the assets being lost in other ways, for example through poor investments taken by directors, fraud by directors, or simply unfortunate market conditions.

Not only do the legal capital rules not provide any significant levels of creditor protection, they also impose burdens on companies. One example of this relates to reductions of capital. If the company has to go to court to carry out the reduction,[246] this becomes a costly exercise. The amount of protection afforded to creditors via this procedure, where the company is undeniably solvent, is minimal. Although the court has to have regard to the creditors' interests when determining whether to allow the reduction, the evidence that the creditors' interests are protected is usually demonstrated by the company providing the court with evidence of a bank guarantee for all existing debts.

The legal capital rules also impose other costs on companies. For example, costs sometimes arise because transactions have to be ingeniously structured so as to avoid a particular legal capital rule. The legal capital rules rarely prevent transactions altogether.

---

[239] J Rickford, 'Reforming Capital: Report of the Interdisciplinary Group on Capital Maintenance' (2004) 15 *European Business Law Review* 919; cf W Schön, 'Balance Sheet Tests or Solvency Tests—or Both' (2006) 7 *European Business Organization Law Review* 181.

[240] See 5.5.

[241] See 5.4.1, 5.4.2 and 5.4.3.

[242] Eg A Brav, JR Graham, CR Harvey and R Michaely, 'Payout Policy in the 21st Century' (2005) 77 *Journal of Financial Economics* 483.

[243] The use of dividend policy as a signalling device is discussed at 2.5.

[244] It has been argued that this is a situation that particularly merits intervention (J Armour, 'Share Capital and Creditor Protection: Efficient Rules for a Modern Company Law' (2000) 63 *Modern Law Review* 355) since dividends may be seen as harming only creditors whereas other kinds of losses (arising, for example, through poor investment decisions or unfortunate market conditions) harm shareholders too.

[245] See 5.4.2.2.2 and 5.4.3.3.

[246] See 5.4.3.2.

There are generally ways around the rules, although these often require expensive legal advice and may require court orders,[247] and are therefore costly in terms of both time and money. The complexity of the system, and the fact that these alternative mechanisms for returning value of shareholders, namely dividends, share repurchases and redemptions and reductions of capital, all have different statutory controls and different requirements, is hard to justify.

5.5 Alternatives to the Legal Capital Rules

In light of the apparent failure of the legal capital regime to provide meaningful creditor protection, a failure acknowledged by many academics[248] and even accepted by the ECJ (now the CJEU), at least as regards minimum capital requirements,[249] alternatives to the current regime need to be investigated. This section assesses creditor protection via contract and via insolvency law, before analysing the possibility of the introduction of a general solvency-based approach to these issues.

5.5.1 Creditor Protection via Contract

One suggested alternative approach is that adopted by many US states, namely that the law need not and should not regulate this issue. Creditor protection, to the extent that it is required, can be provided via contract.[250] On this view, there is no need for any protection to be provided to the creditors beyond what they might be able to bargain for themselves. To the extent that there is a danger of abuse by the shareholders,[251] the adjusting creditors have the opportunity to protect their own interests, by building in adequate interest rates to take account of the risk of lending, by taking some form of control rights over the company to monitor the directors' behaviour, and by taking security to protect themselves in the event of insolvency.[252] Chapters six and seven analyse in detail the forms of protection that creditors can bargain for themselves.

---

[247] For example, companies can sidestep the distribution rules by reducing the capital of the company and returning the capital to the shareholders in this way. A public company will require a court order to reduce its capital. A private company may do so through the solvency statement procedure, although, as discussed, it is likely that many private companies will still opt for the court approval route.

[248] See eg European Company Law Experts, 'The Future of European Company Law', 1 May 2012, www.ssrn.com/abstract=2075034.

[249] Case C-212/97 *Centros Ltd v Erhvervs-og Selskabsstyrelsen* [1999] ECR I-1459.

[250] See generally chapter 6. Specifically in relation to the ability of contract law to restrict the payment of dividends see 6.3.1.3.

[251] It is questionable whether the dangers of shareholder abuse on which these rules are predicated are as acute as is supposed. Companies that engage in behaviour which systematically harms creditors are soon going to find that future creditors will refuse to extend credit to the company at competitive rates. This particularly applies to the danger of asset diversion, since this form of shareholder abuse is the most easily detectable by creditors. Borrowing is a repeat game for companies. Although only a subset of creditors will be able to adjust their behaviour in this way, these adjusting creditors are likely to be the most crucial to a company's future financial success.

[252] See 3.2.2.

Against this approach, it is sometimes suggested that the legal rules mimic what can be achieved through contractual bargaining and that, because they provide a ready-made solution, they reduce transaction costs.[253] There seems little evidence for this in practice,[254] however, and even if there were, this does not present a compelling argument for retaining them as mandatory rather than optional rules. As Professor Ferran points out:

> A justification for legal capital rules that is based on their function as a transaction cost-reducing mechanism is only plausible where market participants are allowed the flexibility to choose between the ready-made model provided by the law or a contractual model that may cost more to negotiate but which may be cheaper in the long run because of lower interest charges or otherwise more favourable financing terms.[255]

Contract-based systems have a flexibility and adaptability which is hard, if not impossible, to mimic in a statutory model. It is difficult to see why official lawmakers are in a better position to supply the terms for loans and debt securities than the users of such instruments in practice, and if standard terms are needed it seems sensible to leave it to the market participants themselves to generate them.

One further argument that is sometimes raised against the proposition that creditor protection can be left to contract is the fact that only some creditors are in a contractual relationship with the company and, of those, only a subset will have the incentive, bargaining power and resources necessary to improve their position by taking security or by other contractual means.[256] Even non-adjusting creditors,[257] however, may be able to free-ride on the covenants imposed by more sophisticated creditors.[258] This may not always work perfectly in practice, and the benefits to weaker creditors will only arise where the contractual negotiation or creditor monitoring processes of the adjusting creditors works effectively. Nevertheless, this system allows for the possibility of some protection for the non-adjusting creditors, and there are other mechanisms available to protect these creditors.[259]

As regards involuntary creditors, compulsory insurance schemes cover the majority of tort claims against companies, namely those arising from accidents at work and road traffic accidents.[260] Employees are covered by a range of employment legislation to protect them,

---

[253] Many loan agreements do already follow a standard form (for example, syndicated loans follow the LMA form) so there is already a ready-made solution for these contracts, which also has the advantage of some flexibility.

[254] Although see in this regard, for example, C Leuz et al, 'An International Comparison of Accounting-Based Payout Restrictions in the United States, United Kingdom and Germany' (1998) 28 *Accounting & Business Research* 111; M Bradley and MR Roberts, 'Are Bond Covenants Priced?', www.repec.org/esNASM04/up.21166.1069857472. pdf where the authors argue that dividend restrictions in state corporate law codes in the US are associated with better credit ratings for bonds issued by firms incorporated in those jurisdictions. However, these findings should be treated with care, not only because the results themselves may be questioned (in the Bradley and Roberts study many codes restricted dividends, but not other forms of return of capital and so it is difficult to see how they could have any real effect) but also because, even if there are some potential cost savings via this form of collective bargaining, it is not clear whether these are captured by the capital maintenance doctrine, and indeed the doctrine itself has a significant cost element.

[255] E Ferran, 'The Place for Creditor Protection on the Agenda for Modernisation of Company Law in the European Union' (2006) 3 *European Company and Financial Law Review* 178, 189.

[256] See 3.2.2.1 and 7.6.2.3.

[257] See 3.2.2.1 for a discussion of non-adjusting creditors.

[258] Eg L Enriques and JR Macey, 'Creditors Versus Capital Formation: The Case Against the European Legal Capital Rules' (2001) 86 *Cornell Law Review* 1165, 1172. For a specific example see 6.3.1.3.

[259] See 3.2.2.1.

[260] Employers' Liability (Compulsory Insurance) Act 1969; Road Traffic Act 1988. These claims are protected on insolvency: Third Parties (Rights Against Insurers) Act 2010. See 7.6.2.3 for further discussion.

and are placed in the category of preferred creditors on a winding up as regards the payment of at least some of the money owed to them. This raises an important issue. Creditors are principally in need of protection from shareholders when the company is insolvent, and the protections that adjusting creditors can bargain for themselves are of primary benefit in the event of insolvency. By the same token, non-adjusting creditors are most in need of protection when the company is insolvent. The availability of creditor protection once the company is insolvent is dealt with in the next section.

5.5.2 Creditor Protection via Insolvency Law

Protection of the creditors from the shareholders is of principal importance when the company is insolvent.[261] At that point there will generally be insufficient money to satisfy all the claims against the company and the conflict between the shareholders and the creditors will be clear. On insolvency, however, the creditors are put in the driving seat, and insolvency law protects the creditors from the shareholders' claims. As discussed in chapter three,[262] statutory provisions are in place to ensure that the shareholders do not undermine the principle that creditors rank ahead of the shareholders at this point in time. In particular, section 74(2)(f) of the Insolvency Act 1986 provides that claims by a member in his character as a member by way of dividends, profits or otherwise are deemed not to be a debt of the company, so that on a winding up these claims are subordinated to the claims of the unsecured creditors. The courts are also keen to ensure that the statutory order of payment out on a winding up is not undermined.[263] On insolvency, then, the rules regulating the order of payment out on a winding up or distribution by an administrator are effective at protecting creditors from the claims of shareholders, which is the principal concern of the legal capital rules. The protection of some types of creditors from the claims of other, more powerful creditors is discussed in chapters three and seven.[264]

The suggestion is, therefore, that while the company remains solvent, creditors are not in need of any special protection from the law. It is notable that at this point the law does not separate creditors' interests from those of the shareholders in determining the scope of directors' duties. Section 172 of the Companies Act 2006 does separate a number of other stakeholder groups which require consideration by directors when determining what is 'most likely to promote the success of the company for the benefit of its members as a whole'.[265] However, creditors are absent from this list, and rightly so.[266] The creditors' primary interest in the company is the return of their investment, and while there is adequate money to pay them they have no need of additional protection from the law.[267] This

---

[261] This issue is discussed at 3.3, particularly 3.3.1.2.5.

[262] See 3.3.1.2.5.

[263] *Soden v British & Commonwealth Holdings plc* [1998] AC 298. For discussion see 3.3.1.2.5.

[264] 3.3.1, 3.3.2 and 7.6.2.3.

[265] Companies Act 2006, s 172(1), discussed at 3.2.1.3.1.

[266] See chapter 3, particularly 3.3.

[267] One gloss could be added to this: if the riskiness of the company's business increases dramatically this will increase the probability of default and may reduce the market value of debt claims, even if the company never does default. However, if the company remains solvent this does not impact on the likelihood of the creditors being repaid and so this does not seem to be an area in which the law needs to intervene.

changes only where the company is insolvent, or on the threshold of insolvency. Where the company is insolvent, although the creditors do need protection from the shareholders, this protection is provided by insolvency law.

One argument that could be raised against this approach is that the definition of insolvency is notoriously difficult,[268] and therefore it should not be used as a hard boundary between creditor protection being provided by law and no such creditor protection. There is obviously a period just prior to insolvency when the creditors do become in need of protection, although formal insolvency procedures have not begun. The law recognises this grey area already.[269] The directors' duty to have regard to the creditors' interests operates when the company is *nearing* insolvency,[270] and many of the provisions in the Insolvency Act 1986 take account of behaviour in the period before insolvency. In particular, section 214 of the Insolvency Act 1986 operates once the directors have concluded, or ought to have concluded, that there is 'no reasonable prospect' that the company can avoid going into insolvent liquidation.[271] This provision is important because it acts as a disincentive to directors to dispose of assets, or to trade wrongfully, and because it allows the creditors to obtain redress against those directors.[272] There are also provisions operating in the period prior to insolvency which enable the liquidator to get back the assets from the person to whom the assets were disposed,[273] although whether these sections deter dissipation of the assets in the first place is more difficult, since directors do not suffer any specific detriment as a result of an action under these provisions.[274]

If there is a concern that the boundary between solvency and insolvency means that creditors are potentially left unprotected in this twilight zone, it would be better to focus on providing more protection for creditors at this time, or clarifying the definition of insolvency, rather than legislating for the entire period when a company is solvent. However, there is a danger of over-regulation of this area.[275] The Company Law Review, which preceded the 2006 Act, did consider increasing directors' obligations to creditors. One early suggestion was that the common law duty on directors to consider creditors' interests at or near insolvency should be moved further back into the solvent life of the company, so that this obligation should kick in when insolvency was merely in prospect. This was dropped due to fears that it would have a 'chilling effect'—that is, it would encourage directors to move too precipitously to put companies into liquidation, and not to risk trying to trade out of their difficulties with the attendant risk of being sued by the liquidator on the creditors' behalf

---

[268] For discussion see eg Goode: Corporate Insolvency Law, ch 4. This is also discussed at 3.3.

[269] See 3.3.2 and 3.3.3.

[270] *West Mercia Safetywear Ltd v Dodd* [1988] BCLC 250, although the courts are not always consistent in their terminology. See 3.3.3.1.

[271] Insolvency Act 1986, s 214(2)(b) and see 3.3.3.2.2(b) for a discussion of when section 214 liability is triggered.

[272] See also the fraudulent trading provisions in Insolvency Act 1986, s 213, which allow personal liability to be attached to those carrying on the business of the company in certain circumstances, discussed at 3.3.3.2.2(a).

[273] See 3.3.2.1 and 3.3.2.2.

[274] See 3.3.2.4.

[275] See eg B Cheffins, *Company Law: Theory, Structure and Operation* (Oxford, Oxford University Press, 1997) 540–48.

if they failed and worsened the creditors' position in the meantime.[276] The Companies Act 2006 maintains the previous position regarding directors' duties to creditors.[277]

It is sometimes suggested that the rules relating to piercing the corporate veil need to be reconsidered in order to allow the creditors on insolvency to claim from the shareholders above and beyond the limit of their contributions to the company.[278] These arguments are not concerned with the need to ensure that the creditors rank ahead of the shareholders on a winding up, rather they question whether it is acceptable to undermine the concept of limited liability in some circumstances. The strongest arguments in favour of additional veil-piercing are made in relation to involuntary creditors.[279] Yet, in the UK compulsory insurance covers the majority of tort claims against companies, namely those arising from accidents at work and road traffic accidents.[280] There is no good justification for altering the veil-piercing rules in the UK on this basis.[281]

Another counter-argument is that, even if the company does not become insolvent as a result of the distributions to shareholders, the creditors' interests can nevertheless be harmed because the distributions reduce the company's net assets, and therefore expose them to a greater risk of default.[282] Creditors, it could be argued, are still prejudiced if the risk of default increases above that at which they priced it, and if the value of their debt claim matters to them as an asset.[283] A restriction on the return of capital to shareholders could potentially bring some benefits to creditors, especially the adjusting creditors, who, after all, are the group able to price the risk of the default they believe they are facing and factor that into their relationship with the company. This is, however, a group which is in a position to protect itself by contract. It may be questioned whether this concern justifies the imposition of the legal capital rules in a solvent situation, particularly when these inefficiencies are weighed against the costs of the legal capital rules themselves.

The suggestion, therefore, is that most creditors are able to protect themselves by contract, and that creditors only need additional protection from the law on insolvency, at which point the insolvency provisions do provide that protection.[284] A natural follow-on from this proposition is the solvency statement approach, discussed in the next section, which is an approach that gives the directors considerable freedom to manipulate the company's capital while the company is solvent, subject to the agreement of the company's

---

[276] DTI, *Modernising Company Law* (Cm 5553-I, 2002), paras 3.8–3.14. For discussion see 3.3.3.2.2.

[277] Companies Act 2006, s 172(3) states that the duty imposed on directors by s 172 to promote the success of the company is subject to any enactment (eg Insolvency Act 1986, s 214) or rule of law (eg the common law duty to creditors: *West Mercia Safetywear Ltd v Dodd* [1988] BCLC 250).

[278] See 3.3.3.2.1.

[279] Eg H Hansmann and R Kraakman, 'Towards Unlimited Shareholder Liability for Corporate Torts' (1991) 100 *Yale Law Journal* 1879. See 3.3.3.2.1.

[280] Employers' Liability (Compulsory Insurance) Act 1969; Road Traffic Act 1988. These claims are protected on insolvency: Third Parties (Rights Against Insurers) Act 2010. This issue is discussed further at 7.6.2.3.

[281] See 3.3.3.2.1.

[282] See J Armour, 'Legal Capital: An Outdated Concept?' [2006] *European Business Organization Law Review* 5, 11–15.

[283] For example, where the creditor wishes to realise the value of the loan before maturity, as with bonds, factoring of book debts etc.

[284] If the insolvency rules are inadequate in this regard (see, for example, in relation to s 214 Insolvency Act 1986, R Williams, 'What Can We Gain from Reforming the Wrongful Trading Remedy?' (2015) 78 *Modern Law Review* 55) it may be preferable to reform the insolvency rules rather than concentrate on the legal capital rules.

shareholders. On this analysis, no specific creditor protection is provided by law while the company remains solvent.

5.5.3 Solvency Statement Approach

The solvency statement approach starts from the proposition that creditors only need protection when the company is insolvent. The law should provide protection for the creditors at that point, and it does so via insolvency provisions, but there is no need for the law to provide any protection while the company is solvent. Obviously, there is a difficult period just prior to insolvency where the law may need to intervene, when the company is technically solvent but creditors are in need of some protection against abuse from the shareholders, but the UK already has provisions in place to deal with this period.[285] The value of the UK's regulations in this regard has been recognised within Europe. When the Winter Group considered whether a general solvency statement should be adopted at EU level, it was suggested that *should* a solvency statement-based system be put in place then a wrongful trading provision akin to section 214 of the Insolvency Act 1986 would be desirable throughout Europe.[286] In terms of regulating the relationship between creditors and shareholders, which, after all, is all that the legal capital rules aim to achieve, the existing provisions are reasonably effective. Even if some creditors are not protected against other creditors on insolvency, they are nevertheless protected against the possibility of shareholders ranking ahead of them, which is all that the legal capital rules aim to prevent.

The basis of the solvency statement approach is that solvent companies should be left unconstrained by the legal capital rules as regards the manipulation of their own capital. As long as a company is solvent, the directors should be able to make distributions of capital, including dividend payments, reductions of capital, repurchases and redemptions. Indeed the directors should be able to manipulate the company's capital as they see appropriate, without the need to have regard to creditors' interests, while the company remains solvent. That is not to say that constraints would not exist. Directors would be constrained by the need to gain shareholder approval for the measures they propose, and by the need to comply with their directors' duties in proposing and carrying out those measures, that is, a standards-based approach. In addition, in relation to public companies, the market would act as a constraint on the company's management. In particular, the institutional shareholders within the UK have the potential to act as an important check and balance on management action. This has already been discussed in the context of pre-emption rights at 4.4.3 above, and the corporate governance role of institutional shareholders is discussed further in chapter eleven.[287] Furthermore, to the extent that the company has debt finance, the directors' behaviour will be considerably constrained by covenants.[288]

---

[285] For discussion of these issues see 3.3.2 and 3.3.3.

[286] Report of the High Level Group of Company Law Experts, *A Modern Regulatory Framework for Company Law in Europe* (Winter Group Report), ch IV.

[287] See 11.2.2.2.

[288] See 3.2.2.4 and 6.3.1.

A general solvency test approach has been adopted elsewhere to deal with these issues.[289] It has already been adopted in the UK to deal with specific aspects of legal capital regulation, namely allowing private companies to repurchase shares out of capital and to reduce their capital without the need to go to court.[290] However, in order for this approach to be a successful tool in regulating company capital on the wholesale basis suggested above, it will need careful application. In particular, careful thought needs to be given to the appropriate solvency test, to the imposition of liability on directors, and to the consequences that should flow from unlawful payments.

5.5.3.1 The Test of Solvency

The solvency test to be applied in this context needs to be carefully considered. In contrast to the balance sheet test that forms the basis of the current distribution rules, discussed at 5.4, the starting point for a solvency-based approach is a test which focuses on whether the company is able to pay its debts as they fall due. This is, therefore, a forward-looking approach.[291] On this basis, the directors are required to reach a view that for the reasonably foreseeable future, taking account of the company's expected prospects in the ordinary course of business, it could reasonably be expected to meet its liabilities.[292]

The test of solvency currently adopted by the Companies Act 2006, in relation to repurchases of shares out of capital by a private company, is a good starting point. This test requires the directors to form an opinion about the company's ability to pay its debts at the time of making the solvency statement, and to look forward over the coming 12 months in order to determine whether, after making the proposed distribution, the company will be able to pay its debts as they fall due over that period (or to pay its debts in full if it is wound up within that period).[293] This test requires directors to take account of 'contingent or prospective' liabilities, in addition to existing liabilities, when making this assessment.[294] Rickford et al have suggested that 'contingent or prospective' liabilities should not be interpreted too narrowly in this context.[295] This phrase should not be confined to contingent liabilities that have already vested, or prospective liabilities that have already accrued. An overly technical interpretation would reduce the value of this solvency test as a creditor protection device. Instead, directors should take account of all the liabilities which the

---

[289] See eg New Zealand Companies Act 1993, s 4; US Model Business Corporation Act, § 6.40, although in both cases an additional net assets test is added as a requirement.

[290] As regards the procedure whereby private companies can repurchase their shares from capital: Companies Act 2006, ss 709–23. As regards the method by which private companies can reduce their capital without going to court: ss 642–44. For discussion see 5.4.2.2.2 and 5.4.3.3.

[291] In *BNY Corporate Trustee Services Ltd v Eurosail-UK 2007-3BL plc* [2013] UKSC 28 Lord Walker noted that any attempt to apply the cash flow test will become speculative once the test moves beyond the reasonably near future.

[292] If a company is funded by debt, it is likely that it will already have to report on its solvency as part of its contractual covenants: see discussion at 6.3.2.2.

[293] Companies Act 2006, s 643(1); cf s 714(3) (regarding repurchases) which encompasses similar ideas, but which is expressed in different terms.

[294] Ibid, ss 643(2) 714(4).

[295] J Rickford, 'Reforming Capital: Report of the Interdisciplinary Group on Capital Maintenance' (2004) 15 *European Business Law Review* 919, 979–80.

company will face in the following period, encompassing all of the normal trading prospects of the company.

One issue that arises is the appropriate time horizon for the application of this test. Too short a period could potentially reduce the level of creditor protection, and concerns are sometimes voiced about the inability of a solvency-based test to address long-term liabilities, such as pension obligations. By contrast, too long a time horizon increases the uncertainty of the issues which directors are being asked to assess. In general, the 12-month period that is found within the Companies Act 2006 at present seems to be accepted as a reasonable minimum period for this purpose.[296]

It is generally accepted that a cash flow test, that is, one which focuses on the debts of the company as they fall due, will be a more useful starting point for a solvency test approach than a balance sheet test. The question arises, however, as to whether this cash flow test should be combined with some form of asset-based test in order to provide creditors with the requisite level of protection. The general solvency-based regime introduced in New Zealand, for example, requires certification of solvency by the directors based on both a cash flow test and a bare net assets test.[297] A bare net assets test simply requires that the company's assets should exceed its liabilities. This test differs from the asset-based test created for distributions by the Second Company Law Directive, which requires that the assets exceed the liabilities by a 'margin',[298] that margin being the amount of the company's legal capital. This chapter has argued that the legal capital rules do not provide any meaningful creditor protection, and as a result the addition of this 'margin' is unnecessary and indeed has costs attached to it. However, the question arises as to whether a net assets test without this additional margin is a meaningful form of creditor protection and should, therefore, be combined with a cash flow test in this regard.

There appears to be some support for the view that the introduction of a general solvency-based approach in Europe should utilise both the cash flow test and some form of bare net assets test. One argument in favour of this approach is that it can potentially provide more information to the directors when they are determining whether they can legitimately make a distribution.[299] However, the addition of an asset-based test potentially faces the same problems as those discussed in the context of the current balance sheet-based approach, namely that the information provided by the net assets test, linked as it is to historical balance sheet information, does not per se provide useful information about whether a company should make a distribution, since '[n]et assets tests are not well suited to covering these important forward looking indicators of the true financial position'.[300] Such a test would therefore need to be implemented with care to avoid these concerns. One way to address these difficulties

---

[296] See eg Federation of European Accountants, *Discussion Paper on Alternatives to Capital Maintenance Regimes*, September 2007, 28.

[297] New Zealand Companies Act 1993, s 4.

[298] J Rickford, 'Reforming Capital: Report of the Interdisciplinary Group on Capital Maintenance' (2004) 15 *European Business Law Review* 919, 970.

[299] Federation of European Accountants, *Discussion Paper on Alternatives to Capital Maintenance Regimes*, September 2007.

[300] J Rickford, 'Reforming Capital: Report of the Interdisciplinary Group on Capital Maintenance' (2004) 15 *European Business Law Review* 919, 976.

would be to ensure that any net assets test is applied in a flexible way, which takes account of these issues and subjects the accounting figures to proper business appraisal. However, if this approach is followed, there may be very little difference between an assessment of the net position of a company and an assessment of solvency using the cash flow test.[301]

Once the decision is taken as to which solvency test to use, the next issue is how to apply that test in practice. In particular, the question arises as to whether this solvency statement by the directors should be audited. Of the two examples of the solvency statement method at work within the Companies Act 2006, one does require the statement to be audited,[302] and the other does not.[303] In practice, this distinction may not be significant, since directors will often want to obtain the advice of the company's auditors before making a solvency statement, and therefore the auditors will be potentially liable both in contract and in tort if they act negligently. Therefore, although the auditors may not be liable on the face of the statute for negligent advice, in practice the auditors are likely to be joined in any action against the directors arising from an inaccurate solvency statement.

5.5.3.2 Liability of the Directors

The solvency statement approach rests heavily on the ability and willingness of directors to produce accurate assessments of the solvency of the company. The second important component of an effective system based on a solvency statement method is to ensure that directors are made suitably accountable for their solvency statements. This requires a consideration of both the law on the books and the enforcement regime that exists, to ensure that directors behave appropriately in practice.

Again, the solvency statement test currently utilised in the Companies Act 2006 provides a useful starting point. All directors are required to make the statement. Any directors unhappy about making the statement would have to resign or be removed from office before the procedure could be used.[304] If the directors make a solvency statement without having reasonable grounds for the opinions expressed in it, every director in default commits a criminal offence.[305]

The difficulty with imposing a criminal sanction is that, although the aim of imposing criminal liability has the effect of focusing the directors' minds on the issue at hand, over-penalising this issue may not achieve the desired result. If the effect is to dissuade directors from manipulating the company's capital, by repurchasing the company's shares for example, this could be problematic. There may be good reasons for directors to make use

---

[301] If that is correct, then the additional net assets test may add little to a solvency statement approach based on a cash flow test. For discussion see Rickford, ibid, 977–78.

[302] Companies Act 2006, s 714.

[303] Ibid, s 643. This is despite initial recommendations of the Company Law Review Steering Group (see *Company Formation and Capital Maintenance* (URN 99/1145, October 1999), para 3.30). This recommendation was later dropped: see Company Law Review Steering Group, *Developing the Framework* (URN 00/656, March 2000), para 7.26; *Completing the Structure* (URN 00/1335, November 2000), para 7.10.

[304] If such a resignation is effected merely for the purposes of escaping liability for the solvency statement and the individual continues as a de facto director, this might call into question the validity of the solvency statement procedure: *Re In A Flap Envelope Co Ltd* [2003] EWHC 3047 (Ch).

[305] Companies Act 2006, ss 643(4)(5), 715.

of the company's capital, and if the capital is left unused and the company has no positive net value projects in which to invest, this could lead to a waste of the company's resources. By contrast, if the criminal provisions are rarely or never enforced, it may be questioned how much of a deterrent effect they will have in practice. In relation to the criminal liability imposed for breach of the financial assistance provisions, for example, the view has tended to be that this is an over-penalisation of the issue.[306]

An alternative mechanism would be to impose some form of civil rather than criminal liability on the directors, perhaps adopting an approach similar to that in relation to section 214 of the Insolvency Act 1986 whereby 'the court ... may declare that [the director] is to be liable to make such contribution (if any) to the company's assets as the court thinks proper'.[307] This form of liability is not without difficulty either. Often directors of insolvent companies will have few personal assets available to satisfy such claims, either because they have invested their personal wealth into the company or because they have been carefully advised to place their assets elsewhere to protect them. If these payments are funded by directors' and officers' liability insurance (D & O insurance) rather than out of the directors' own pockets, the deterrent effect of such liability will be weakened.

Directors are also likely to view civil liability as an unattractive potential consequence of the solvency statement approach, and this form of liability could also deter them from facilitating distributions that would be valuable to the company. However, directors face civil consequences for unlawful distributions at present,[308] and if the company breaches any financial ratios laid down in its debt covenants, the creditors who have the benefit of those covenants will have the option of accelerating and terminating the loan, or could engage in dialogue with the company with the purpose of improving its position, for example by replacing the existing management.[309] These issues can also have an incentivising effect on the directors. It may be that facing civil consequences for negligently authorising distributions would not overly deter directors in this regard.

Some attention would also need to be paid to the enforcement regime that would support these provisions. In general, the level of litigation against directors in the UK tends to be very low, both when the company remains solvent and also as regards the claims faced by directors on insolvency, such as claims under section 213 and 214 of the Insolvency Act 1986.[310] A lack of enforcement could have the effect of undermining whatever liability regime is put in place in this context.

---

[306] The Company Law Review considered decriminalising this offence, but after receiving mixed views on this point it eventually recommended retention of the criminal sanctions: Company Law Review Steering Group, *Completing the Structure* (URN 00/1335, November 2000), para 13.42. In the event, criminal liability was retained in the Companies Act 2006: s 680(2).

[307] Insolvency Act 1986, s 214(1); *Re Produce Marketing Consortium Ltd (No 2)* [1989] BCLC 520.

[308] While directors face civil consequences for unlawful distributions at present (see eg *Flitcroft's Case* (1882) LR 21 Ch D 519; *Bairstow v Queens Moat Houses plc* [2001] EWCA Civ 712), it has been suggested that directors might consider a rule-based system (such as the current rules) easier to comply with than one based on a standard (the proposed solvency statement test): Gower and Davies, 317.

[309] See 3.2.2.4.

[310] See 3.3.3.2.2(c).

5.5.3.3 *Recovery of Unlawful Payments*

The third component of such a system is to ensure that effective mechanisms for the recovery of wrongful payments are put in place. The current solvency tests within the Companies Act 2006 do not provide a good basis for the determination of this issue. The 2006 Act is silent on the civil consequences of a distribution to shareholders paid consequent upon a false or inaccurate solvency statement. There is case law to the effect that an unlawful return of capital is void,[311] and this is so even where the failing is purely procedural, so it is likely that a flawed solvency statement would invalidate a distribution in a similar manner. In addition, the common law has established that the responsible directors are in breach of their duties to the company.[312] However, in order for the solvency statement method to operate as an effective way of protecting the company's capital, a system of ensuring that the wrongful payments are returned to the company should be put in place.

The present position regarding dividends is clear: recipients are only liable to repay if they know or have reasonable grounds for believing that the payment is made unlawfully.[313] Recipient liability for other forms of distribution to shareholders is dealt with by the common law, but the position is the same.[314] The requirement of knowledge means that few shareholders will be held liable to repay. Generally, only shareholder-directors and parent companies are likely to have the requisite knowledge to render them potentially liable to repay. This has a significant impact on the ability of the company to recover these payments. Of course, the directors who authorise the payments may be liable to compensate the company unless they acted under an honest and reasonable belief that the facts justified the payment,[315] but this relies on the company having an appetite to sue its directors, and on the directors having the capacity to compensate the company should the company be successful in its claim. This seems to be an inappropriate way of dealing with this issue. There should be strict liability on those receiving wrongful payments, requiring those payments to be returned, with relief only if the recipients are in good faith, if they have changed their position, and if it would be unfair to insist upon recovery.

There are theoretical arguments in favour of such an approach, rather than the present knowledge-based system.[316] There are also policy arguments available to support this approach, since the purpose of these rules is creditor protection and that is best served (if the rules are breached) by ensuring that the wrongfully paid sums are returned to the company for the benefit of the creditors. It is notable that in other jurisdictions that have

---

[311] *MacPherson v European Strategic Bureau Ltd* [2000] 2 BCLC 683.

[312] *Aveling Barford Ltd v Perion Ltd* [1989] BCLC 626.

[313] Companies Act 2006, s 847(2). This means knowledge of the facts giving rise to the contravention. It is not necessary for the recipients to appreciate that the payment involves a contravention of the Companies Acts: *It's A Wrap (UK) Ltd v Gula* [2006] EWCA Civ 544.

[314] *Re Halt Garage (1964) Ltd* [1982] 3 All ER 1016.

[315] *Flitcroft's Case* (1882) LR 21 Ch D 519; *Precision Dippings Ltd v Precision Dippings Marketing Ltd* [1986] 1 Ch 447.

[316] J Payne, 'Unjust Enrichment, Trusts and Recipient Liability for Unlawful Dividends' (2003) 119 *Law Quarterly Review* 583; cf CH Tham, 'Unjust Enrichment and Unlawful Dividends: A Step Too Far?' (2005) 64 *Cambridge Law Journal* 177, 182.

adopted a solvency-based approach, a much tougher statutory approach towards recipients of wrongful payments has been adopted than is present in the UK system.[317]

5.5.3.4 Potential for Reform

A solvency test has some significant attractions when compared to the present legal capital system, and adopting such an approach would bring the EU in line with the trend in other industrialised economies.[318] There is academic support for a relaxation of the legal capital rules in this way,[319] but there can be no adoption of a full solvency statement approach for public companies while the Second Company Law Directive remains in its current form. In the UK, the Government has unequivocally stated its support for more flexibility than is permitted by the Second Company Law Directive.[320]

There have been some signs of a shift away from the view that it is the role of company law at the European level to protect creditors,[321] and the European Court of Justice (now the CJEU) has stated that there is no unique value in the minimum capital rules as a creditor protection device.[322] In addition, the *Centros* decision has led to a substantial number of entrepreneurs living and trading on the continent establishing private companies in the UK in order to take advantage of the comparatively more relaxed capital regime for private companies in the UK.[323] In turn this has led to a process of negative harmonisation and a relaxation of capital maintenance regimes in Europe.[324] However, these changes have not resulted in any meaningful changes to the content of the Second Company Law Directive. The 2006 changes to this directive were minimal,[325] and the 2012 recast of the directive is therefore in very similar terms to the original 1977 version. The Company Law Action Plan published in 2012 suggests that reform of the directive is not high on the European

---

[317] Eg Companies Act 1993, s 56(1) (New Zealand).

[318] See eg ibid, s 4; US Model Business Corporation Act, § 6.40, although in both cases an additional net assets test is added as a requirement.

[319] Eg J Armour, 'Share Capital and Creditor Protection: Efficient Rules for a Modern Company Law' (2000) 63 *Modern Law Review* 35; E Ferran, 'The Place for Creditor Protection on the Agenda for Modernisation of Company Law in the European Union' (2006) 3 *European Company and Financial Law Review* 178; J Rickford (ed), 'Reforming Capital' (2004) 4 *European Business Law Review*; J Payne, 'Legal Capital in the UK following the Companies Act 2006' in J Armour and J Payne (eds), *Rationality in Company Law: Essays in Honour of DD Prentice* (Oxford, Hart Publishing, 2008); European Company Law Experts (ECLE), 'The Future of Company Law', 1 May 2012, www.ssrn.com/abstract=2075034.

[320] DTI, *Company Law Reform* (White Paper) (Cm 6456, 2005), 42–43.

[321] Commission (EC), 'Modernising Company Law and Enhancing Corporate Governance in the European Union' (Communication) COM(2003) 284 final (21 May 2003).

[322] Case C-212/97 *Centros Ltd v Erhvervs-og Selskabsstyrelsen* [1999] ECR I-1459.

[323] M Becht, C Mayer and HF Wagner, 'Where Do Firms Incorporate? Deregulation and the Cost of Entry' (2008) 14 *Journal of Corporate Finance* 241.

[324] J Simon, 'A Comparative Approach to Capital Maintenance: France' (2004) 15 *European Business Law Review* 1037.

[325] Directive 2006/68/EC allowed a relaxation of the rules governing the need for an expert valuation when non-cash consideration is received by public companies in exchange for their shares, a relaxation of the rules governing financial assistance, and a relaxation as regards the rules governing a public company's ability to purchase its own shares.

Commission's priority list.[326] Meaningful reform of the Second Company Law Directive is not, therefore, foreseeable at present.

5.6 Conclusion

This chapter has set out the legal capital rules that have been put in place to deal with a perceived conflict between creditors and shareholders. It has been suggested that these rules are largely misplaced. It is difficult to justify the imposition of costly and burdensome legal capital rules constraining a company's actions while solvent, when the need for creditor protection arises predominantly on insolvency. The rules are also difficult to justify when many creditors are in a position to protect themselves by contract, and even those that are not able to do so are often able to free-ride on the actions of adjusting creditors to some extent. Even if the needs of non-adjusting creditors are not met via free-riding, the legal capital rules do not provide them with any meaningful protection. In short, the legal capital rules in place under the Second Company Law Directive, and implemented into UK law by the Companies Act 2006, are expensive and largely ineffective as creditor protection devices. Even if some benefits are obtained, these are likely to be outweighed by the costs of the system.

There is a compelling case for reforming the legal capital regime. Ideally, most of the current regime should be dismantled, for both public and private companies. No par value shares should be introduced for all companies. The minimum capital rules should be abolished for public companies, as should the 'no issue at a discount rule' for all companies, since they fulfil no significant role as regards creditor protection at the present time. In relation to distributions of capital, provided the company is solvent, and not in the twilight period just before insolvency, the law should not intervene to protect creditors. As this chapter has suggested, careful thought would need to be put into the operation of a general solvency statement approach, and into the regulation of the pre-insolvency twilight period, but in principle such an approach is superior to the majority of the existing legal capital rules. Unfortunately, while the Second Company Law Directive remains in place such a regime cannot be implemented for public companies, and no change to this directive appears to be on the horizon.

---

[326]   COM(2012) 740. The idea that the Second Directive should be amended was first raised as part of 'Simpler Legislation for the Single Market (SLIM): Extension to a Fourth Phase', SEC (1998) 1944 (Commission Staff Working Paper of 16 November 1998), and was later added to the agenda for the Commission's High Level Group of Company Law Experts: *Modern Regulatory Framework for Company Law in Europe* (Brussels, 4 November 2002) (Winter Group Report). However, a study on an alternative to the capital maintenance system of the Second Company Law Directive, commissioned by the European Commission in 2006, concluded that the minimum legal capital requirements and rules on capital maintenance do not constitute a major hurdle to dividend distribution: KPMG, 'Feasibility Study on an Alternative to the Capital Maintenance Regime established by the Second Company Law Directive', http://ec.europa.eu/internal_market/company/capital/index_en.htm. This seems to have removed the impetus for reform within the European Commission: European Commission, *Results of the External Study on the Feasibility of an Alternative to the Capital Maintenance Regime of the Second Company Law Directive and the Impact and Adoption of IFRS on Profit Distribution* (2008).

6

Creditor Protection: Contractual

6.1 Introduction

In chapter two, the various ways in which a company might be financed through debt were considered, and the possibilities for mitigating the credit risk to the creditor were discussed.[1] The risks faced by creditors were discussed further in chapter three,[2] and it was pointed out that, although there is some very limited protection for creditors under the general law,[3] most creditors are expected to protect themselves by proprietary or contractual means, or both.[4] Not all creditors are in a position to obtain such protection: the extent to which creditors can adjust is discussed in chapter three,[5] and the policy issues surrounding the protection of non-adjusting creditors are discussed in chapter seven below.[6]

Adjusting creditors who are in a position to obtain proprietary protection are in a strong position. The advantages of such protection are discussed below,[7] but it should be noted at this point that all creditors who obtain proprietary protection also have contractual rights against the debtor company, quite often of a very extensive nature. Broadly speaking, such contractual rights give protection while the company is solvent,[8] while proprietary protection is most useful when the company is insolvent, although there can also be significant advantages to proprietary protection even outside insolvency.[9] Contractual rights against the debtor company itself are of less use once the company is insolvent, but creditors can often also obtain contractual rights against third parties, which will be effective protection unless the third party is also insolvent.

In this chapter some of the main contractual provisions for reducing credit risk are discussed, both as against the debtor company and as against third parties. Rights against the debtor company itself include covenants and other contractual terms, as well as set-off, which arises under the general law but can be extended or reduced by contract. Rights against third parties include rights permitting redress against (more solvent) third parties, such as guarantees, indemnities, performance bonds, credit insurance and credit default swaps, and intercreditor rights, whereby the order of priority of payment is determined by agreement so that some creditors are subordinated to others.

---

[1] 2.3.1.2 and 2.3.1.3.
[2] 3.2.2.2.
[3] The requirements for legal capital are discussed in chapter 5, and regulation is discussed in chapter 13.
[4] 3.2.2.2.
[5] 3.2.2.1.
[6] 7.6.2.3.
[7] 7.1.1.
[8] See 3.2.2.4.
[9] See 7.1.1.

In most cases, these contractual rights will form part of complex documentation. How a court or other dispute resolution body will interpret these agreements is of the utmost importance to lenders and borrowers: it affects not only their rights on default or if there is a dispute, but also the drafting and negotiation process. First, then, the law on the interpretation of commercial contracts will be considered briefly, before consideration of the various contractual rights in more detail.

6.2 Interpretation of Commercial Contracts

6.2.1 Introduction

This section will consider the way in which courts interpret commercial and, particularly, financial contracts. This is a complicated area of the law on which there are many detailed texts to which the reader is referred;[10] all that will be attempted here is a summary of the relevant principles. These are important in the context of the contractual protection of creditors for a number of reasons. Financial contracts are drafted and agreed, usually by transaction lawyers, in the course of finalising the relevant transaction. They are there to set out the agreement between the parties, partly for their own benefit, but largely to govern the position if something goes wrong. Very many disputes in relation to finance contracts boil down to a matter of construction of the agreements involved, and parties often use arguments based on construction to attempt to avoid liabilities or other undesirable consequences. It is therefore important for those drafting financial contracts to consider how those contracts will be interpreted by a court or an arbitral tribunal and, ideally, to draft accordingly. Focusing on the construction of contracts also highlights the tension between the virtues of freedom of contract, certainty and predictability and other virtues such as protection of certain parties and general fairness. It is important to consider how the balance between these principles is struck in the context of commercial and financial contracts: while freedom of contract is very significant, protection of weaker parties is built into some parts of the law.[11] There are also special considerations relating to financial contracts. These are often based on standard form agreements, which are used not only in the UK market but more widely. The fact that many contracts of loan and, of course, debt securities are transferred to other parties also affects the way in which they are to be interpreted.

6.2.2 Basic Principle

The summary given by Lord Hoffmann in *Investors Compensation Scheme v West Bromwich Building Society*[12] is the best starting point. He said that 'Interpretation is the ascertainment

---

[10] G McMeel, *The Construction of Contracts: Interpretation, Implication, and Rectification* (Oxford, Oxford University Press, 2011); K Lewison, *The Interpretation of Contracts*, 5th edn (London, Sweet & Maxwell, 2011); R Calnan, *Principles of Contractual Interpretation* (Oxford, Oxford University Press, 2013); J Carter, *The Construction of Commercial Contracts* (Oxford, Hart Publishing, 2013).

[11] See, for example, the position in relation to sureties (6.4.1.3.1) and the exclusion of set-off (6.3.4.5).

[12] [1998] 1 WLR 896, 912.

of the meaning which the document would convey to a reasonable person having all the background knowledge which would reasonably have been available to the parties in the situation in which they were at the time of the contract'. By including a reference to background knowledge, the law thus steers a middle path between a subjective approach (which would in any event be meaningless in the context of financial contracts, which are agreed between large companies and drafted by lawyers)[13] and a purely objective approach. In the context of commercial contracts, there is a gloss on the meaning of background knowledge, in that it is that which 'would reasonably be available to the audience to whom the instrument is addressed'.[14] Thus, where a contract has been or is likely to be transferred to a number of different people, only circumstances which are known to all of them should be taken into account in interpreting the wording.[15] In determining the background to the contract, the court is free to look at the 'matrix of fact',[16] which, according to Lord Hoffmann, 'includes absolutely anything that would have affected the way in which the language of the document would have been understood by a reasonable man'.[17] There are some exclusions, however. Evidence of pre-contractual negotiations is not admissible, except where rectification of an agreement is claimed,[18] nor is the post-contractual conduct of the parties, except where it is alleged that the agreement is a sham.[19]

6.2.3 The Meaning of Words

It is often said that the court will give the words used in a contract their 'natural and ordinary meaning'.[20] While this is difficult to achieve, even in a simple contract, it becomes nearly impossible in many financial agreements. The difficulty is the tension between what the words appear to mean, and the result of applying them to the situation before the court. This result may seem to be uncommercial, and not, therefore, what the parties would have intended. There is high authority that if the wording of a contractual provision is unambiguous, it will be given effect even if the meaning is uncommercial,[21] and there is certainly no overriding construction criterion of 'commercial common sense'.[22] The commercial (and financial) background of the agreement, though, is highly relevant and may overcome a detailed literal analysis of the words used. 'Detailed semantic analysis must give way to business common sense.'[23] In many cases the words considered can be interpreted in two different ways; after all, where there is a dispute as to the meaning of a contract, each side will

---

[13] See Bamford: Financial Law, 11.29–11.31.

[14] *Re Financing No 3 Ltd v Excalibur Funding No 1 plc* [2011] EWHC 2111 (Ch) [42].

[15] *Re Sigma Finance Corp* [2009] UKSC 2 [37] per Lord Collins; *Torre Asset Funding Ltd v Royal Bank of Scotland plc* [2013] EWHC 2670 (Ch) [151].

[16] *Reardon Smith Line Ltd v Yngvar Hansen-Tangen* [1976] 1 WLR 989, 997.

[17] *Investors Compensation Scheme v West Bromwich Building Society* [1998] 1 WLR 896, 912.

[18] *Chartbrook Ltd v Persimmon Homes Ltd* [2009] 1 AC 1101 [41].

[19] *James Miller v Whitworth Street Estates* [1970] AC 583, 603.

[20] *Robertson v French* (1803) 4 East 130, 135 and see Chitty 12-051.

[21] *Rainy Sky v Kookmin Bank* [2011] UKSC 50 [23].

[22] *Jackson v Dear* [2012] EWHC 2060 (Ch) [40].

[23] *Re Sigma Finance Corp* [2009] UKSC 2 [37] per Lord Collins, citing *The Antaios* [1985] AC 191, 201 per Lord Diplock. Cf *Arnold v Britton* [2015] UKSC 36 [17]–[23].

have put forward an alternative interpretation. In that case, 'the court is entitled to prefer the construction which is consistent with business common sense and to reject the other'.[24]

Although the court will not easily accept that the parties have made a mistake in drafting,[25] sometimes errors are made so that the language may give an absurdly uncommercial interpretation. There seems little doubt that the court can correct the mistake, either by interpretation[26] or by rectification.[27] The onus is on the party alleging the mistake to show that it is absurd.[28]

6.2.4 Implication of Terms

The implication of terms in a commercial contract is closely associated with construction; it takes place, however, where a contract is silent about a particular point. The court takes a very restrictive attitude when implying terms into a contract, except where they are implied in law by statute or, sometimes, by common law. When the court is asked to imply a term in fact to 'fill a gap' in a contract, 'the most usual inference in such a case is that nothing is to happen. If the parties had intended something to happen, the instrument would have said so. Otherwise, the express provisions of the instrument are to continue to operate undisturbed. If the event has caused loss to one or other of the parties, the loss lies where it falls.'[29] It is, therefore, only in limited cases that the court will imply a term (in fact) into a contract. There have been a number of tests set out in cases over the years: for example that it is 'necessary to give business efficacy to the contract',[30] or 'so obvious it goes without saying'.[31] These and other tests have now all been rationalised by Lord Hoffmann in *Attorney-General of Belize v Belize Telecom Ltd*[32] as being ways of expressing 'the central idea that the proposed implied term must spell out what the contract actually means, or in which they have explained why they did not think that it did so'.[33]

In relation to financial contracts, in particular, a term will not be implied merely because it is reasonable, but only because it is necessary.[34] It must also be capable of being expressed with precision.[35] Where the contract is in a standard form, there is a strong presumption that the parties' agreement is complete and therefore a term should not be implied.[36]

---

[24] *Rainy Sky v Kookmin Bank* [2011] UKSC 50 [21]; *Barclays Bank plc v HHY Luxembourg SARL* [2010] EWCA Civ 1248 [25].

[25] *Chartbrook Ltd v Persimmon Homes Ltd* [2009] 1 AC 1101 [20]; *Re Financing No 3 Ltd v Excalibur Funding No 1 plc* [2011] EWHC 2111 (Ch) [45].

[26] *Chartbrook Ltd v Persimmon Homes Ltd* [2009] 1 AC 1101 [22]–[25].

[27] Where documents are public, for example where they are registered, this should be dealt with by rectification and not interpretation: see *Cherry Tree Investments Ltd v Landmain Ltd* [2012] EWCA Civ 736 [124]–[130].

[28] *Re Financing No 3 Ltd v Excalibur Funding No 1 plc* [2011] EWHC 2111 (Ch) [48].

[29] *AG of Belize v Belize Telecom Ltd* [2009] UKPC 10 [17].

[30] *The Moorcock* (1889) 14 PD 64, 68; *Equitable Life Assurance Society v Hyman* [2002] 1 AC 408, 459.

[31] *Shirlaw v Southern Foundries (1926) Ltd* [1939] 2 KB 206, 227.

[32] [2009] UKPC 10.

[33] Ibid, [27].

[34] Chitty 13-010; *Mediterranean Salvage & Towage v Seamar Trading & Commerce Inc* [2009] EWCA Civ 531 [15]–[18].

[35] *BP Refinery (Westernport) Pty Ltd v Shire of Hastings* (1977) 180 CLR 266, 282–83; *Cassa di Risparmio della Repubblica di San Marino SpA v Barclays Bank Ltd* [2011] EWHC 484 (Comm) [544].

[36] *Greatship (India) Limited v Oceanografia SA de CV* [2012] EWHC 3468 (Comm) [41].

There is no general concept of good faith in English contract law,[37] although similar ideas have been included in certain situations and certain types of contracts in a piece-meal fashion.[38] Recently, however, there have been indications that courts will be willing to imply limited duties of good faith into specific contracts. Where a contracting party has to exercise a discretion, the courts have implied a term that it should be exercised not unreasonably, capriciously or arbitrarily.[39] Further, in *Yam Seng Pte Limited v International Trade Corporation Limited*[40] Leggatt J considered the cases in which a duty of honesty and aspects of a duty of good faith had been implied into contracts, then decided that two such aspects should be implied into the contract in that case: a duty of honesty in the provision of information and a duty not to approve a domestic retail price for a product which under-cut the duty free retail price.[41] This approach of implying good faith duties into long-term relational contracts has already been followed in some cases, though not yet in the financial sphere.[42] However, the courts have made it clear that where the parties to the contract are sophisticated parties negotiating at arms' length, a term obliging the parties to act in good faith is unlikely to be necessary and therefore is unlikely to be implied.[43]

6.3 Contractual Rights Against the Borrower

The most basic contractual right that a lender has against the borrower is the right to be repaid, plus (usually) a right to some form of additional payment, often periodic, which represents payment for the making of the loan. Although this can come in many forms, we can loosely call this 'interest'.[44] As discussed in chapter three,[45] the contractual provisions considered in the current chapter are included in debt agreements in order to protect the lender from the risk of non-payment. This protection is achieved by restricting the borrower's activities, by requiring the borrower to meet certain financial ratios, and by requiring the borrower to provide information (usually financial) both at the time the loan is made and throughout the life of the loan. These covenants are discussed in 6.3.1 and 6.3.2 below. It should be noted that where a guarantee is taken,[46] similar covenants may be included against the guarantor in the guarantee agreement, and where the borrowing company is part of a group, the financial covenants and events of default are likely to apply to all group companies. Breach of any requirement, or any other specified event of default,

---

[37] Chitty 1-039.

[38] *Interfoto Picture Library Ltd v Stiletto Visual Programmes Ltd* [1989] 1 QB 433, 439.

[39] *Gan Insurance Co Ltd v Tai Ping Insurance Co Ltd (No 2)* [2001] EWCA Civ 1047 [64]; *Socimer International Bank Ltd v Standard Bank London Ltd* [2008] EWCA Civ 116 [66]. See R Hooley, 'Controlling Contractual Discretion' (2013) 72 *Cambridge Law Journal* 65.

[40] [2013] EWHC 111 (QB) [119]–[154].

[41] Ibid, [165].

[42] *Bristol Groundschool Limited, Intelligent Data Capture Limited v Alexander John Whittingham* [2014] EWHC 2145 (Ch) [196]; *D&G Cars Limited v Essex Police Authority* [2015] EWHC 226 (QB); cf *Mid Essex Hospital Services NHS Trust v Compass Group UK and Ireland Ltd* [2013] EWCA Civ 200.

[43] *Greenclose Limited v National Westminster Bank plc* [2014] EWHC 1156 (Ch) [150]; *Dennis Edward Myers v Kestrel Acquisitions Limited* [2015] EWHC 916 (Ch) [53]–[63].

[44] See 3.2.2.

[45] See 3.2.2.4.1.

[46] See 6.4.1.

will give the lender the right to accelerate the loan and terminate the agreement. These rights are discussed in 6.3.3 below. The way in which these contractual rights are used by lenders to influence the running of the borrower company is discussed in some detail in chapter three.[47]

The discussion of debt covenants focuses on provisions which are included in agreements specifically for the provision of finance, typically loan agreements and (to a limited extent) issues of debt securities,[48] rather than all extensions of credit. Thus, except where otherwise indicated, the debtor is referred to throughout this chapter as the 'borrower' and the creditor as the 'lender'.[49] Not all of the covenants discussed will be included in all debt agreements: this will depend, inter alia, on the type of borrowing, the creditworthiness of the debtor and the respective bargaining powers of each party, as well as the state of the market.[50] In particular, the level of covenants in debt securities is generally lower than in loan agreements, with the possible exception of high-yield bonds.[51] For ease of reference, the term 'loan agreement' will be used throughout. Many of the provisions discussed (or variations of them) are contained in standard forms and precedents used by lenders and those extending credit, including standard contracts produced by organisations such as the Loan Market Association (LMA) for use in syndicated loans.[52] It should also be noted that debt agreements will also include many other terms which are not discussed in this chapter, for example provisions for interest, provisions concerning taxation and other administrative provisions. The purpose of the discussion in this chapter is to focus on the main means of contractual protection used by lenders, and to consider some important legal issues which impact on the effectiveness of that protection. It is not a comprehensive guide to drafting covenants in debt agreements: for this the reader is referred to more specialist literature.[53]

At 6.3.4 we consider rights of set-off and netting which a lender may have in respect of the borrower's indebtedness. These rights can have a very considerable impact on the protection of a lender from credit risk, particularly since set-off is available on the insolvency of the borrower. Although some rights of set-off arise under the general law, these have limits, and financing agreements often include specific provisions relating to set-off. These may either extend its availability or restrict it. In addition, agreements may include provisions for netting which operate in conjunction with set-off to reduce risk. Set-off which operates on insolvency gives protection that is as powerful as proprietary protection, and in some cases more powerful, but it is reasonably clear that under English law set-off is not a proprietary interest, and so its discussion is included in this chapter and not in chapter seven, which deals with proprietary protection.

---

[47] 3.2.2.4.

[48] Other agreements such as asset finance agreements (see 2.3.4.4.2) may also include similar clauses.

[49] The term 'lender' includes situations where there are, in fact, multiple lenders, such as syndicated loans and bond issues. For ease of exposition, other terminology is used when discussing specialised areas, such as guarantees: this is explained at 6.4.1.1.

[50] These issues are discussed in more detail in chapter 3 at 3.2.2.2.

[51] See 3.2.2.3, where the reasons for this are discussed and it is pointed out that the purpose of covenants in debt securities is often to protect the value of the bond rather than directly against the risk of non-payment.

[52] See 8.4.1.

[53] For example, see Fuller, Corporate Borrowing; Encyclopaedia of Banking Law; Wood, Loans and Bonds. For precedents see the *Encyclopaedia of Forms and Precedents* (London, Butterworths Tolley), vol 4(1) (Banking).

6.3.1 Restrictions on the Borrower's Activities[54]

6.3.1.1 Restrictions on Borrowing

These covenants directly address the risks to creditors which arise because of the different interests of creditors and shareholders. These risks are identified and discussed in chapter three above:[55] in general terms they are that the borrower may incur further debts after borrowing from the lender, or may dispose of assets which otherwise would be available to pay the lender. Future borrowing can, broadly speaking, be controlled in two ways.[56] One is by the inclusion of a general financial covenant, which requires the borrowing company (and often the entire group of companies) to comply with a specified gearing ratio. These seek to ensure that there is sufficient value in the company generally to repay the borrowing and are discussed below.[57] The second is by using a specific covenant restricting borrowing which conflicts with that of the lender, usually borrowing which ranks ahead of that from the lender. This will usually be secured borrowing, and so it is likely also to fall foul of a negative pledge clause. Broadly speaking, a negative pledge clause prevents the borrowing company from granting security over its assets. It comes in a number of forms, and gives significant protection to a lender. However, its use also raises a number of interesting legal issues, which are discussed below,[58] after a brief discussion of other forms of restrictive covenants which are used to protect lenders.

6.3.1.2 Restrictions on Asset Disposal

It is common for a lender to include a clause restricting the disposal of substantially all of the assets of the company: disposals in the ordinary course of trading, those for which full value is received and those with the consent of the lender are likely to be excluded.[59] It is possible that a restriction on disposal would be interpreted as including restricting the grant of security to another lender (and could in particular include quasi-security structures which include the disposal of assets, such as the sale of receivables[60] or sale and lease-back devices[61]).[62] However, these transactions are much better dealt with by a negative pledge clause which covers them specifically, and a clause restricting disposal will usually be coupled with a negative pledge clause. A restriction on disposal is particularly important if the lending is unsecured. If the lender is protected by a fixed charge or mortgage, there

---

[54] See 3.2.2.3.

[55] 3.2.2.2.

[56] See the analysis by Fuller: Corporate Borrowing, 168, who calls these the outer and the inner borrowing limits.

[57] 6.3.2.2.

[58] 6.3.1.6.

[59] For further details see Wood: Loans and Bonds, 5-030–5-032; *Encyclopaedia of Forms and Precedents* (London, Butterworths Tolley), vol 4(1) (Banking) [204] cl 19.10. This clause is known as a 'Tickler' clause after the case of *Commercial Union Assurance Co Ltd v TG Tickler Ltd* (unreported, 4 March 1959), in which it was held that the sale of a factory was not a sale of part of the company's 'undertaking': a specific contractual restriction was therefore required to prevent such actions: see Fuller: Corporate Borrowing, 181.

[60] 2.3.4.1.

[61] 2.3.4.4.1.

[62] See Wood: Loans and Bonds, 5-030. Fuller: Corporate Borrowing, 181 points out that this would depend on the interpretation of the contract.

is no need to restrict disposal of those assets expressly, since it is in the nature of a fixed charge that the chargor cannot dispose of the charged assets without the consent of the chargee.[63] However, in relation to assets over which a lender has a floating charge,[64] there is some point in including the clause, since, without further restriction, the chargor is free to dispose of assets in the ordinary course of business, and this is given a very wide definition in the context of a floating charge.[65] The exact scope of the restrictions can then be a product of the negotiations between the borrower and the lender, and will represent a balance between protection of the lender and the freedom required to enable the borrower to carry on its business successfully.[66] Restrictions on disposal are particularly important where the borrower company is part of a group, since intra-group transfers are common, and yet, if made between the borrowing company and another company in the group, potentially damaging to the lender. If the borrower is the holding company, transfers between the subsidiary companies do not damage the lender, but a disposal of assets by a subsidiary company outside the group would be damaging and would be prohibited by a covenant restricting disposals.[67]

6.3.1.3 Restrictions on Dividend Payments

The payment of dividends or other distributions to shareholders by the borrower company may also be restricted to a particular percentage of net profits.[68] Such a clause is less common when the borrower is a public company. This may be because public companies tend to present less credit risk, but also may be because dividend distributions by public companies are regulated further than those by private companies.[69] This is an example of where a 'default' level of protection is given to creditors by statute, rather than expecting creditors to bargain for their own protection. Whether statutory regulation is a better means of protecting creditors than contractual protection is discussed above.[70] In addition to the points made in that discussion, it will appear from the current chapter that there is a complicated, and potentially varied, mix of covenants in loan agreements, which supplement the limited statutory protection available. It thus might seem odd to provide such limited protection for creditors of public companies, when the major creditors are extremely likely to bargain for additional covenants anyway and so could easily include, for example, a covenant restricting dividend payments. Moreover, covenants can be more closely tailored to

---

[63] See 7.3.3.1.

[64] See 7.3.3 for discussion of the floating charge.

[65] For the scope of 'ordinary course of business' in a floating charge see *Ashborder BV v Green Gas Power Ltd* [2004] EWHC 1517 (Ch) and 7.3.3.1.

[66] A McKnight, 'Restrictions on Dealing with Assets in Financing Documents: Their Role, Meaning and Effect' (2002) 17 *Journal of International Banking Law* 193.

[67] E Ferran and LC Ho, *Principles of Corporate Finance Law*, 2nd edn (Oxford, Oxford University Press, 2014) 287.

[68] See Wood: Loans and Bonds, 5-045.

[69] In relation to all companies, dividends can only be paid out of distributable profits: see Companies Act 2006, s 830 and 5.4.1.2. Distributions to public companies are also subject to Companies Act 2006, s 831: see 5.4.1.2.

[70] 5.5.1. See also DP Miller and N Reisel, 'Do Country-Level Investor Protections Affect Security-Level Contract Design? Evidence from Foreign Bond Covenants' (2012) 23 *Review of Financial Studies* 408, a study finding that the use of restrictive covenants in Yankee bonds is more prevalent in countries with weak creditor protection laws; and E Black, T Carnes, M Mosebach and S Moyer, 'Regulatory Monitoring as a Substitute for Debt Covenants' (2004) 37 *Journal of Accounting and Economics* 367, a study of debt issues by banks which finds a reduction in the level of covenants when federal monitoring increases.

the particular requirements of the lender and the situation of the borrower. They can also overcome the shortcomings of the statutory tests, so that, for example, a clause restricting dividend payments can depend on cash flow tests rather than the historic balance sheet tests used by the Companies Act 2006.[71] Further, breach of a covenant leads to the right to accelerate the loan and terminate the contract, while breach of the statutory provisions only leads to a rather restricted ability to recover the payment.[72] Non-adjusting creditors (who, arguably, are the group that the statutory protection seeks to protect) would then be able to free-ride on the benefits of the contractual protection.[73]

6.3.1.4 Change of Control Covenants

Sometimes covenants are also included which prohibit a substantial change of business of the borrower company, or prohibit mergers or change or control.[74] A change in the type of business carried out can greatly affect the credit risk faced by the lender: the new business may be much riskier, which may be good for the shareholders who will benefit from any increased gains, but bad for the creditors who will not benefit from gains, but who will suffer if the company becomes insolvent.[75] A merger or change of control will not necessarily affect the credit risk, but it may be perceived to do so, and so may affect the current value of the loan. This is especially important for bondholders, who may wish to sell their bonds, but also, maybe, for syndicated lenders, who may wish to transfer their interest.[76] For these reasons, the consequences are often not triggered unless the change of control is also accompanied by a downgrading in credit rating.[77]

Often the provisions referred to in the previous paragraph are not drafted as restrictive covenants, but as events which give rise to certain consequences. In a loan agreement, this could be an event of default[78] or, in order not to trigger a cross-default, it could be a trigger for mandatory prepayment.[79] In bond issues, such events are not usually breaches as such, but trigger a 'put option'. This gives the bondholders the right to require the issuer to redeem the bonds.[80] To the extent that such a provision acts as a disincentive to a takeover, it can be seen as a kind of poison pill,[81] and care would need to be taken by the directors of the borrowing company that, in agreeing to it, they were not in breach of their duties.[82]

---

[71] For a critique of the balance sheet test imposed by the statute see 5.4.5.

[72] See 5.4.5.

[73] The free-riding argument is discussed further in chapter 3, especially at 3.2.2.4.5. There is also the possibility of free-riding by bondholders, whose covenants are less extensive, probably because of the difficulties of enforcement: see P Wood, 'Bondholders and Banks: Why the Difference in Protection?' [2011] *Capital Markets Law Journal* 188.

[74] For a description of the ways changes of control can be effected see 2.2.2.

[75] See 3.2.2.2.

[76] For a discussion of transferred debt see chapter 9.

[77] M Hartley, 'Beyond Change of Control' [2006] *Journal of International Banking and Financial Law* 475. See 2.3.3.3 and 13.7 for a discussion of credit rating.

[78] 6.3.3.

[79] See *Encyclopaedia of Banking Law*, F3238.

[80] See Fuller: Corporate Borrowing, 8.52–8.53; M Hartley, 'Beyond Change of Control' [2006] *Journal of International Banking and Financial Law* 475; M Hartley, 'Bondholder Protections Revisited' [2010] *Journal of International Banking and Financial Law* 219. L Hornuf, M Reps and S Schaferling, 'Covenants in European Investment-Grade Corporate Bonds' (2010), http://papers.ssrn.com/sol3/papers.cfm?abstract_id=2393291 states that a 2010 study of corporate bonds by HSBC found that 57% of UK bonds in the sample included such put options.

[81] See Wood: Loans and Bonds, 6-025.

[82] For discussion see 14.3.2.1.1.

6.3.1.5 Debt Buybacks

Another area of debtor activity which may be restricted in a loan agreement is that of pre-payment[83] or repurchase of the loan. Borrowers are usually permitted to prepay subject to certain restrictions, such as timing and the giving of notice.[84] Repurchase by the borrower of the whole or part of a syndicated loan has become more common since the financial crisis, as loans often trade at below their face value and the borrower can thus, effectively, repay the loan at a discount, or, if the price of the loan goes up again, can sell at a profit.[85] Further, it can enable the borrower to have a say in any restructuring of the indebtedness. However, this causes problems with the democratic governance of the syndicate,[86] which lenders may wish to avoid. Thus the LMA documentation now contains an optional clause prohibiting or restricting debt buy-backs in the leveraged loan facilities agreement.[87]

It should be noted that there are likely to be exceptions to the restrictions contained in a loan agreement. This is in order to maintain the balance between the protection of the creditor and the need for the borrower to have flexibility to run its business.

6.3.1.6 Negative Pledge Clause

A negative pledge clause provides important protection where a loan is unsecured. Where a lender takes fixed security, there is no need for a negative pledge clause, since the mortgagor or chargor is automatically prohibited from disposing of the secured assets (including creating security interests over them) without the consent of the mortgagee or chargee.[88] This is not the case where the lender takes a floating charge, and it is very common for a negative pledge clause to be included in such a charge. The effect of this is considered in chapter seven below.[89] The following discussion is limited to the use of a negative pledge clause in unsecured lending. The primary purpose of such a clause is to protect the ability of the lender to enforce the loan against the assets of the borrower in the latter's insolvency: even though it may be an unsecured creditor and have to rank *pari passu* with all other unsecured creditors, at least all the assets of the company will be available for distribution if there are no secured creditors. In bond issues, a negative pledge clause is usually combined with a *pari passu* clause, the purpose of which is to ensure both that the bondholders rank equally among themselves and that no other creditors rank above them.[90] Coupled with

---

[83]   This is called repayment, in the case of loans, and redemption, in the case of debt securities.

[84]   For detailed discussion see Fuller: Corporate Borrowing, 5.5–5.16. Prepayment provisions in relation to a syndicated loan or bond issue usually include a system for sharing the prepayment pro rata among the multiple lenders: see 7.4.1.

[85]   S Samuel, 'Debt Buybacks: Simply Not Cricket?' [2009] *Journal of International Banking and Financial Law* 24: P Clark and A Barker, 'The Evolution of Debt Buybacks' [2009] *Journal of International Banking and Financial Law* 359.

[86]   See 8.4.6.

[87]   At cl 30, inserted in September 2008. It seems that this clause was little used at first: see P Wood, 'Life after Lehmans: Survey of Changes in Market Practice' [2009] *Journal of International Banking and Financial Law* 579. This may be beginning to change: see A Ward and K Fevzi, 'The European Leveraged Loan Market Must Continue to Evolve to Survive' [2013] *Journal of International Banking and Financial Law* 500.

[88]   See 7.3.3.1.

[89]   See 7.4.4.

[90]   This is achieved by both a representation as to the position at the date of issue that there are no creditors ranking above the bond, and an undertaking that this will not happen in the future: see Fuller: Capital Markets, 9.04 ff.

extensive rights to information about the company's financial position,[91] which enables a lender to take steps to accelerate and enforce a loan if the borrower gets into financial difficulties, a negative pledge clause gives good protection. Thus the lender may be able to complete enforcement before the borrower becomes insolvent,[92] and even if this is not possible, may be able to prevent dissipation of assets before insolvency, so that the lender is likely to be able to recover all or most of the amount owed. Moreover, it is when the borrower is in financial difficulties that it will need to give security in order to raise new money.[93] If the grant of security is prohibited by a negative pledge clause, this enables the original lender to protect its interests either by refusing permission or by giving consent on terms, such as limiting the amount of new borrowing.[94] This argument only works, of course, if the borrower asks for permission to breach the clause.[95] A breach of the clause would be an event of default, and thus would enable the lender to take protective action at a point when its interests are threatened.[96] It should also be noted that a secured lender tends to have considerable power and influence on insolvency,[97] particularly in a restructuring: by preventing there from being any secured creditors the lender increases its chances of being in a position to exercise influence itself.[98]

It might be asked why a lender would lend unsecured using the protection of a negative pledge clause, which, while valuable, is only a contractual right and not a proprietary right, when it could take security, which is a proprietary right. Where the borrower is a very large creditworthy company, the balance of bargaining power will be in favour of the borrower, and it can dictate the terms of the loan. Furthermore, the cost of taking security can be very considerable, especially in complicated international transactions, and where the borrower appears very creditworthy that cost seems unnecessary.[99] Despite conferring merely a contractual right, a negative pledge can be very effective, as a borrower will not wish to breach it and trigger an event of default. For many companies this is a very serious occurrence, as not only will it entitle the lender to accelerate or terminate the loan,[100] but it may also put the borrower in breach of cross-default clauses in other agreements, and could have the effect of ruining the borrower's financial reputation.[101] Thus the clause regulates the borrower's behaviour by deterring breach: if, however, the borrower does breach the clause the remedies for the lender are rather limited.[102]

---

[91] See 6.3.2.2.

[92] If there is sufficient pressure from the lender, it is unlikely that payment would count as a preference under Insolvency Act 1986, s 239: see 3.3.2.2.

[93] See Wood: Loans and Bonds, 5-009.

[94] If the lender actually wants to control the amount of liabilities incurred by the borrower more generally, it is probably more effective to do this by a direct covenant restricting borrowing; see Wood: Loans and Bonds, 5-009, and see 6.3.1.1.

[95] The lender's options if the borrower breaches without permission are discussed at 6.3.1.6.2.

[96] J Arkins, '"OK—So You've Promised, Right?" The Negative Pledge Clause and the "Security" it Provides' (2000) 15 *Journal of International Banking Law* 198, 199. See 6.3.3.

[97] This is particularly true of a holder of a floating charge, although the position has changed somewhat recently. See 7.3.3.3.4 and 7.5.1.4.

[98] See Wood: Loans and Bonds, 5-009.

[99] J Arkins, '"OK—So You've Promised, Right?" The Negative Pledge Clause and the "Security" it Provides' (2000) 15 *Journal of International Banking Law* 198, 199.

[100] 6.3.3.

[101] Benjamin calls it a 'financial death sentence': Benjamin: Financial Law, 8.25.

[102] See 6.3.1.6.2.

In a eurobond issue, the purpose of a negative pledge clause is rather different. Rather than attempting to preserve priority over all the borrower's assets by preventing security being given for any borrowing, the object of the clause is to protect the trading value of the issue by preventing the issuer from issuing secured bonds into the same market, which would have the effect of making the unsecured issue less attractive and therefore less valuable.[103]

6.3.1.6.1 Forms of Negative Pledge Clause

There are three possible forms of negative pledge clause in unsecured lending (although the wording of each will, of course, vary). The first is a basic agreement not to grant security to any other person. Alternatively, the agreement could provide that the debtor can grant security to another person only if it grants matching security to the original lender. This can be drafted either so that the provision of matching security is a non-promissory condition of the granting of security to a third party, or so that there is a positive promise to grant matching security.[104] Further, the agreement could provide that if security is given to a third party, a matching security in favour of the original lenders automatically attaches to the same asset. As mentioned above, negative pledge clauses are included in bond issues for a different purpose from loan agreements. While all forms of the clause are typically found in loan agreements, bonds tend to include the second type of clause,[105] which then only covers the granting of security for issues of securities rather than for all kinds of debt.[106]

One challenge in drafting such a clause is to make sure that a wide enough class of trans-actions is prohibited to protect the lender, while not prohibiting transactions which the bor-rower needs to undertake in order to carry on its business.[107] This can be done by limiting the transactions to those creating security interests, but this will not catch 'quasi-security' transactions such as asset-based finance transactions,[108] so the clause is often extended to include these.[109] The balance can also be achieved by limiting the assets which are involved, so that the borrower is prohibited from alienating some, but not all, assets.[110]

6.3.1.6.2 Enforcement of Restrictive Covenants

The possible remedies of the lender for breach of the restrictive covenants discussed above fall into three classes: first, a personal (contractual) remedy against the borrower; second, a personal remedy (probably in tort) against the party to whom the disposition was made, or the security was granted, or who made the prohibited loan ('the third party'); and, third, a proprietary remedy. A distinction needs to be made between those situations where the lender monitors the borrower's conduct extensively and those, for example in bond issues, where monitoring is very limited.[111] If there is extensive monitoring, then enforcement of a

---

[103] Fuller: Capital Markets, 9.24–9.25; see Wood: Loans and Bonds, 12-012; P Wood, 'Bondholders and Banks: Why the Difference in Protection?' (2011) *Capital Markets Law Journal* 188.

[104] Goode: Credit and Security, 1-80.

[105] See Fuller: Corporate Borrowing, 8.24.

[106] For a discussion of when an 'all monies' negative pledge clause might be used in a bond issue see M Hartley, 'Bondholder Protections Revisited' [2010] *Journal of International Banking and Financial Law* 219.

[107] Hudson: Finance, 19-59.

[108] 2.3.4.3.

[109] For an example of a negative pledge clause see Fuller: Corporate Borrowing, 9.33. See also Wood: Loans and Bonds, 5-013.

[110] See Hudson: Finance, 19-59.

[111] For discussion of monitoring see 3.2.2.4.2, 6.3.2.2 and 8.3.4.2.2.

negative pledge clause by contractual remedies is not a problem. If the lender knew or suspected in advance that a breach was going to occur, then in theory it could obtain injunctive relief to prevent it, or maybe even (at least in the case of an unauthorised disposition
or security interest) appoint a receiver.[112] However, this is very unlikely to happen unless
there is extensive monitoring. If the lender does not know about the breach for some time,
the personal remedies will be of less use. It has, of course, the right to rely on the event of
default, to accelerate the loan and terminate the contract. If the borrower is solvent, then the
threat of doing this might force the borrower to renegotiate the terms of the loan: this use
of a breach of covenant is discussed above in chapter three as a method of corporate governance.[113] However, in a situation where, because of the borrower's fragile financial state,
the lender is seriously concerned about a disposal of assets or a grant of security, it is likely
that exercising its rights to accelerate and terminate will force the borrower into insolvency.
Faced with an insolvent borrower, the lender's personal rights are of little use. In theory, it
has a right to damages for breach, but this does not put it in a better position than its contractual right to repayment of the loan: both are unsecured claims.[114]

The lender might, therefore, wish to assert a remedy which will be effective against the
third party. A possibility under all forms of the clause is that there is a tort action against the
third party for inducing breach of contract or interference with contractual relations. This
action is discussed in this paragraph in the context of a breach of a negative pledge clause,
since that is the context in which it is most likely that a lender might wish to obtain such
a remedy, but the same reasoning would apply to breaches of other restrictive covenants.
The possibility of such an action in tort has been the subject of some debate,[115] and recent
developments in the law of the economic torts have made it unlikely that it would succeed.
It has been established that there is no independent tort of interference with contractual
relations and that the two torts that remain are inducing breach of contract and causing
economic loss by unlawful means.[116] There are clearly no unlawful means in the situation
considered here: all the third party has done is enter into a secured transaction with the
borrower. Therefore the only possibility is the tort of inducing breach of contract. This,
however, requires an intention on the part of the defendant to induce breach, which means
that the defendant has to know of the term breached (it is not enough that he ought to
have known) and to have intended the breach either as an end or as a means to an end (not
merely as a foreseeable consequence of his actions).[117] Although it is not impossible that
these criteria could be fulfilled where security is granted to a third party in breach of a negative pledge clause, it would be very rare.[118]

---

[112] D Allen, 'Negative Pledge Lending' [1990] *Journal of International Banking Law* 330.

[113] 3.2.2.4.

[114] It is possible that a disposal of assets at an undervalue in the run-up to insolvency could be avoided under
s 238 Insolvency Act 1986: see 3.3.2.1.1.

[115] J Stone, 'Negative Pledges and the Tort of Interference with Contractual Relations' (1991) 8 *Journal of Inter-
national Banking Law* 310; TC Han, 'The Negative Pledge as a Security Device' [1996] *Singapore Journal of Legal
Studies* 415; L Wo, 'Negative Pledges and their Effect on a Third Party' (1999) 14 *Journal of International Banking
Law* 360.

[116] *OBG Ltd v Allan* [2007] UKHL 21 [189].

[117] Ibid, [39]–[43].

[118] The possibility of a tort action was accepted by the Singapore Court of Appeal in *DBS Bank v Tam Chee
Chong* [2011] SGCA 47 [55]. For discussion of the position in the UK, see T Matuda and S Thompson, 'He Who
Procures the Wrong is a Joint Wrongdoer: Tortious Liability for Inducing Breach of Contract in the Context of a
Bond Restructuring' [2012] *Journal of International Banking and Financial Law* 442.

A third possible remedy for breach of a negative pledge clause is a proprietary remedy against the borrower's assets (which, being proprietary, may bind the third party to whom security is granted). Such a remedy is a possibility where the clause is in the second or third forms discussed above which purport to give the lender a security interest if one is granted to the third party: if successful this would make the lender a secured creditor with a proprietary right against the borrower's assets which ranked above or equally with that of the third party. Let us initially consider the case where the clause provides for automatic attachment of security. First, it is necessary to identify the asset over which security is given[119] so that if the clause only provides for 'matching security' this will not be enough and the clause will be ineffective.[120] If there is sufficient identification, all the lender has at the time of the contract is a contractual right and not an inchoate security,[121] since an agreement to grant security on a contingency is not in itself a security interest.[122] If it were a security interest, it would be immediately registrable.

Can the security interest in favour of the lender then attach automatically on the occurrence of the contingency, that is, the granting of the security to the third party? There is considerable debate about this, focusing on whether fresh consideration is required at that point.[123] One view[124] is that consideration must be executed at the time the security interest comes into existence, and since there is no new money extended at the time the contingency occurs, the security interest in favour of the lender cannot arise or attach. The opposite view[125] is that the original loan by the lender is sufficient consideration. There are no direct English authorities.[126] Although there are dicta from the Singapore Court of Appeal supporting the view that no further consideration is required, this was not part of the ratio of the case, and, arguably, only refers to the obligation of the debtor to provide security rather than the automatic attachment of a security interest.[127]

---

[119] See 7.3.2.1.

[120] See Goode: Credit and Security, 1-80. However, it is not difficult to draft a clause which does sufficiently identify the assets; J Stone, 'The Affirmative Negative Pledge' (1991) 6 *Journal of International Banking Law* 364, 368.

[121] For further discussion of inchoate security see 7.3.2.1.

[122] See Goode: Credit and Security, 1-81; and see the decision of the Singapore Court of Appeal in *The Asiatic Enterprises (Pte) Ltd v United Overseas Bank Ltd* [2000] 1 SLR 300 [16]. For a view that, at least in relation to land, a negative pledge clause in this form does create an immediate security interest which is registrable as a floating charge, see G Hill, 'Negative Pledge with Provision for "Automatic Security" on Breach: A Form of Floating Charge?' [2008] *Journal of International Banking and Financial Law* 528. This view has some support from an obiter dictum of Lord Scott in *Smith v Bridgend County Borough Council* [2002] UKHL 58 [61]–[63].

[123] The need for executed consideration for the grant of a security interest in equity is discussed in 7.3.2.1.

[124] See Goode: Credit and Security, 1-81; J Maxton, 'Negative Pledges and Equitable Principles' [1993] *Journal of Business Law* 458; P Ali, *The Law of Secured Finance* (Oxford, Oxford University Press, 2002) 3.20–3.24; A McKnight, 'Restrictions on Dealing with Assets in Financing Documents: Their Role, Meaning and Effect' (2002) 17 *Journal of International Banking Law* 193, 203.

[125] P Gabriel, *Legal Aspects of Syndicated Loans* (London, Butterworths, 1986) 86–90; J Stone, 'The Affirmative Negative Pledge' (1991) 6 *Journal of International Banking Law* 364; Security and Title-Based Financing, 8.81; CH Tan, 'Charges, Contingency and Registration' (2002) 2 *Journal of Corporate Law Studies* 191.

[126] Two cases (*Re Jackson & Bassford Ltd* [1906] 2 Ch 467; *In re Gregory Love & Co* [1916] 1 Ch 203) which have been relied upon by proponents of both sides of the argument are not directly on the point since in both the security interest was expressly executed and did not arise automatically, and, further, was executed by deed so consideration was irrelevant; see Goode: Credit and Security, 1-81.

[127] *The Asiatic Enterprises (Pte) Ltd v United Overseas Bank Ltd* [2000] 1 SLR 300 [18]: 'Where it is part of the agreement that the debtor will in certain events provide a certain security or further security, then upon the happening of that event, the debtor will be obliged to provide such security and no fresh consideration from the creditor is called for.'

Even if fresh consideration is required, it could be argued that since the breach of the negative pledge clause is an event of default, consideration is provided at that point by the lender by refraining from making a demand for payment.[128] The main problem with this argument is that the lender will normally be unaware that the breach has occurred: if it were aware, as would be the case had it been monitoring extensively, it would usually immediately exercise its right to terminate the loan agreement, but if it is unaware, how can the lender be said to have refrained from making a demand?[129] It might also be possible to avoid the requirement for fresh consideration by making the original loan agreement by deed. However, it is difficult to see how the requirement for a further deed can be avoided if fresh consideration would, otherwise, be required. Further, the deed would only operate in relation to property owned by the borrower at the time of execution of the deed.[130]

If fresh consideration is not required, there are still further problems for the lender. First, the security interest created is likely to be registrable within 21 days.[131] Since the lender is unlikely to know that the interest has arisen, it will not know to register the charge,[132] and the prospect of the lender having to monitor the borrower's activities so as to know if it needs to register a charge is unattractive to some lenders. Second, the lender will only gain priority over the security interest granted to the third party if the lender's interest predates that of the third party. If the trigger for the lender's interest is the grant to the third party, the lender will lose priority. Therefore, if the lender wants priority, the clause would have to be drafted so that an earlier point (for example, the attempt to grant a security interest to a third party) was the trigger.[133] Third, there is still a possibility that the security interest in favour of the lender would be set aside as a preference under section 239 of the Insolvency Act 1986 if the borrower became insolvent within the relevant time.[134] The value given by the lender at the time of the original loan will not count as new value[135] even if it did count as sufficient consideration to support the grant of the security interest.

Given all these difficulties, it is unlikely that an 'automatic security' clause would be effective to create a security interest in favour of the lender. An unsecured lender that does not monitor, and that relies on a negative pledge clause to give quasi-proprietary protection, is likely to fall into difficulty. If coupled with effective monitoring, however, the contractual remedies available for breach of negative pledge clauses and other restrictive covenants are likely to act as a deterrent against breach, and might provide adequate protection, particularly if an injunction could, if necessary, be obtained.

---

[128] CH Tan, 'Charges, Contingency and Registration' (2002) 2 *Journal of Corporate Law Studies* 191, 199.

[129] See Goode: Credit and Security, 1-81; A McKnight, 'Restrictions on Dealing with Assets in Financing Documents: Their Role, Meaning and Effect' (2002) 17 *Journal of International Banking Law* 193, 203.

[130] See P Ali, *The Law of Secured Finance* (Oxford, Oxford University Press, 2002) 3.57.

[131] Companies Act 2006, s 859A: see 7.4.2. It would be registrable unless it were a security financial collateral arrangement (see 7.3.4).

[132] Any leave for late registration would be given subject to the priority of other charges already created: see 7.4.2.

[133] Such drafting has succeeded in the context of automatic crystallisation: see *Re Manurewa Transport Limited* [1971] NZLR 909 (Sup Ct Auckland); *Fire Nymph Products Ltd v The Heating Centre Pty Ltd* (1992) 7 ACSR 365 (Sp Ct NSW CA). However, it has been doubted by some writers that this analogy would be accepted by the courts: see J Arkins, '"OK—So You've Promised, Right?" The Negative Pledge Clause and the "Security" it Provides' (2000) 15 *Journal of International Banking Law* 198.

[134] This is two years where a preference is given to a connected person and six months for any other person: see 3.3.2.2.

[135] The presence of new value would prevent the security interest being a preference; see Goode: Corporate Insolvency, 13-83.

In addition to the technical reasons discussed above, there are good policy reasons why it should not be possible for a security interest to arise automatically on a particular contingency, when that contingency is not a public event. If the interest did arise, it would not be visible to the outside world, nor to the third party grantee of the security interest which triggered the clause, whose security would be severely cut down by the lender's interest. If there is fresh executed consideration for the lender's interest at the time it arises, at least the assets of the borrower are swelled and the third party's position is not so adversely affected: thus there is a policy justification for the requirement of fresh consideration. In any event, there is also an argument in favour of registration of the new interest at the time of its creation (so that other potential creditors are put on notice) and also, maybe, for registration at the time the loan agreement is entered into, so that third parties know that an interest may arise. Of course, if such registration is required, some of the benefits of lending unsecured are lost and the lender might as well take a security interest in the first place.

Depending on the construction of the clause, even if there is no automatic security there is likely to be an obligation on the borrower to grant the lender security if security is granted to a third party. If the borrower were to grant such security, it would have to be by deed,[136] or be over present but not future property, or there would have to be valid executed consideration.[137] It would also have to be registered, unless it were a security financial collateral arrangement. It would not have priority over the security granted to the third party as it would have been created after that security interest. Given these drawbacks, it is only in certain circumstances that a right to be granted security is of benefit to a lender in the context of a negative pledge clause.

6.3.2 Rights to Information and Financial Covenants

The creditworthiness of a borrower, that is, its ability to pay interest payments and eventually to repay the loan, is of critical importance to a lender at all stages during the currency of the loan. The lender will want to be able to check the position throughout, and to be able to take action if the creditworthiness of the borrower deteriorates. This section examines the lender's rights to information at various stages of the loan, which enables the lender to monitor both the borrower's creditworthiness, and also whether the borrower's business is being conducted in a way which may jeopardise the interests of creditors.[138] The lender's ability to take protective action is also examined, as are the contractual provisions which trigger these rights. The method of protection is different before and after the loan is made, and the discussion is split up accordingly. After the loan is made, the protective rights are triggered by breaches of covenants and events of default, many of which involve the maintenance of certain financial standards. The covenants specifying such financial standards (financial covenants) are examined in section 6.3.2.2.

---

[136] As in *Re Jackson & Bassford Ltd* [1906] 2 Ch 467 and *In re Gregory Love & Co* [1916] 1 Ch 203.

[137] The need for executed consideration for a security interest over future property is discussed at 7.3.2.1.

[138] See 3.2.2.2 for a discussion of the risks creditors face, particularly where the interests of shareholders and creditors diverge.

6.3.2.1 *Rights at the Time of Making the Loan*[139]

At this stage the lender wishes to be in a position to make an informed decision as to whether to lend, and also, if it does decide to lend, as to the amount of risk it will take on. In theory, the greater the risk the more the lender can charge for lending, but in practice the interest rate is often not very negotiable, either because there are multiple lenders and the rate is already fixed, or because the weight of the bargaining power is tipped towards the borrower. The lender will then have to decide whether the risk is worth taking for the reward it will bring. On assessment of the risk the lender will also be able to decide what other protection it needs, such as the level of proprietary protection and also the level of contractual protection, although the amount it can actually get also depends on the balance of bargaining power between the parties.[140] The bottom line for many lenders is, therefore, that they will not lend if the information shows that the risk is too great for the combination of interest and protection they are able to obtain.

Where loans are transferable, however, the ability to transfer the loan for a good price may be more important to the lender than the absolute credit risk, since the lender may have little intention of keeping the loan until it is due to be repaid. This may make a lender less concerned about the details of the borrower's financial position and more concerned about the marketability of that sort of loan. For example, in a securitisation structure where loans are bundled together and repackaged into securities which are then tranched,[141] the absolute credit risk of each loan becomes much less important than the likelihood of enough securities being sold to finance the purchase of the loans from the lender. Arguably, this decoupling of absolute credit risk from the lender can lead to less assiduous assessment of credit risk and loans being made to borrowers who cannot repay or on terms which do not accurately reflect the credit risk.[142]

The initial information on which a lender will make a decision will, in the case of a securities issue or a syndicated loan, be provided by a standard document produced for all potential bondholders or syndicated lenders. In the case of a publicly listed securities issue, this will be a prospectus or listing particulars which will have to comply with the appropriate regulations and which will be publicly available.[143] In relation to a non-listed offer of securities (which will be made to a limited number of potential investors) or a syndicated loan, information will be contained in an offering circular, an invitation letter or an information memorandum.[144] Further, those purchasing debt securities and entering into syndicated loans will take into account the credit ratings of a borrower produced by the credit rating agencies.[145] A single bank lender, however, will have to obtain information from the borrower itself, although a considerable amount of historic information about a company's

---

[139] See also discussion at 13.2.8.

[140] Borrowers may also prefer to agree to stricter covenants rather than let the whole risk be reflected in the interest rate: see 3.2.2.2 and also A Choi and G Triantis, 'The Effect of Bargaining Power on Contract Design' (2012) 98 *Virginia Law Review* 1665.

[141] 9.3.3.

[142] See also the discussion at 3.2.2.4.6.

[143] See 8.3.1 and 13.2 where the regulation of initial issues of debt securities is discussed.

[144] See 8.3.1 and 8.4.2. The question of redress for false statements in such documents is discussed in 8.4.4 (in relation to syndicated loans) and 13.2.7 (in relation to debt securities).

[145] See 2.3.3.3 and 13.7.

financial position is often publicly available.[146] In this form of relationship lending, which is usually undertaken by banks to SMEs, the lender will take steps to know the borrower's business well. The lending will usually be at least partly on the basis of an overdraft and so the bank's exposure at any one time will not necessarily be great, and the bank will put great store by its own knowledge of the customer in deciding whether to loan and what the overdraft limit should be.

At this initial stage, the contractual protection a lender has is in the form of conditions precedent in the agreement. These relate to a number of matters which, from the lender's point of view, have to be in place before the loan will be made. For example, it will be a condition precedent that the borrower has capacity to enter into the loan and has delivered documents which prove this.[147] Another example of a condition precedent, if the loan is secured, will be that the security has been validly created and perfected, and again that supporting documentation has been delivered.[148] Another important condition precedent will be that the representations and warranties made by the borrower are true, that there has been no material adverse change in circumstances since the date of the information provided, for example in the audited accounts, and that no event of default has occurred.[149] The term 'representations and warranties' relates to the information, provided by the borrower, on which the lender makes the lending decision. Usually, representations are statements of fact and warranties are promises that certain representations are true or that certain acts have been done.[150] The problem with all information provided is that the situation may change between the provision of the information and the time the creditor actually acts on it. This time lag is dealt with by the condition precedent mechanism.

There is a distinction in contract law between a promissory condition and a contingent condition.[151] The former is a promise made by one party to a contract, and failure to perform it entitles the other party to terminate the contract and sue the other party for breach.[152] A contingent condition, however, is a state of facts which has to be fulfilled, which may or may not be something within a party's control: if it is the former, the party is not obliged to bring that state of facts about, but (usually) must not prevent it coming about.[153] The exact consequences if the state of facts is not fulfilled is a matter of interpretation of the contract,[154] although the effect will always be that one party is not obliged to perform some or all of his obligations under the contract until the state of facts is fulfilled. In the present context, this means that the lender is not obliged to advance funds unless and

---

[146] This will vary according to the size of the company and whether it is public or private and whether it is listed or not: see 11.3.1.1 and 11.3.1.2. Any security interests granted by the company will be registered in the company charges register: see 7.4.1.

[147] See Wood: Loans and Bonds, 3-008; Fuller: Corporate Borrowing, 2.7.

[148] Wood: Loans and Bonds, 3-009.

[149] Fuller: Corporate Borrowing, 2.7.

[150] Note that a distinction can be made between legal warranties, which are promises that legal prerequisites and formalities have been complied with in order for the loan agreement to be valid, and commercial warranties, which are promises about the financial position of the borrower at the relevant time: Wood: Loans and Bonds, 4-003.

[151] Chitty 12-027; *Trans-Trust SPRL v Danubian Trading Co Ltd* [1952] 2 QB 297, 304.

[152] Contractual promises may also be warranties, breach of which entitles the innocent party only to damages and not to termination, or they may be intermediate terms, breach of which may entitle the innocent party to termination depending on the seriousness of the breach. See Chitty, ch 12 s 2.

[153] Treitel 2-108.

[154] *Total Gas Marketing Ltd v Arco British Ltd* [1998] 2 Lloyd's Rep 209, 215.

until the condition precedents are fulfilled. However, there are various possibilities as to the state of the contract between the parties if the condition precedent is not fulfilled. One is that the contract never comes into existence at all,[155] or that if there is a contract, both parties are discharged, so that either party can withdraw from the contract. Another is that one party can withdraw but the other cannot,[156] and a further possibility is that the contract is binding on both, but the obligations of one or both are suspended pending the fulfilment of the condition.[157] The position in relation to conditions precedent in loan agreements appears to be the third of these: the lender is not obliged to lend if a condition precedent is not fulfilled, but the contract to lend (the underlying facility agreement) remains valid and binding unless there is an event of default.[158] Of course, non-fulfilment of a condition precedent may well be an event of default. It should also be remembered that in many loan facilities the advances are made in stages, so that each time the lender is called upon to make an advance it will be able to refuse if a condition precedent is not fulfilled, for example if the financial state of the company has changed.

6.3.2.2 Ongoing Rights

After an advance has been made, a lender wants to protect itself against changes in circumstances which would make the borrower less likely to be able to repay the loan. Obviously, once the loan has been made, the technique of a condition precedent cannot be used, so the loan agreement will also contain financial covenants, breach of which is an event of default which will entitle the lender to accelerate the loan and terminate the loan agreement.[159] The agreement will also list events of default which are not breaches, but which again give the lender the right to accelerate and terminate.[160] One type of covenant seeks to enable the lender to take action if early warning signs of financial weakness appear: while drastic action, such as acceleration, could be taken, the lender's response is far more likely to involve a dialogue with the directors of the company which may culminate in the renegotiation of the loan.[161] Alternatively, a lender of tradable debt such as a debt security or a tradable loan may choose to 'exit' via sale. The actual content of these covenants will vary according to the circumstances, particularly in relation to the creditworthiness of the

---

[155] Treitel 2-106; *Pym v Campbell* (1856) 6 E & B 370.

[156] Chitty 12-028.

[157] Ibid.

[158] Wood: Loans and Bonds, 3-011; P Rawlings, 'Avoiding the Obligation to Lend' [2012] *Journal of Business Law* 89, 97. cf *Bryan Court Limited v National Westminster Bank plc* [2012] EWHC 2035 (QB), where a lender was held to be obliged to make further advances despite non-fulfilment of the condition precedent, as the lender had already advanced some funds pursuant to the agreement.

[159] 6.3.3.1. For detailed empirical research on covenants see P Taylor and J Day, 'Evidence on the Practices of UK Bankers in Contracting for Medium-Term Debt' [1995] *Journal of International Banking Law* 394; P Taylor and J Day, 'Bankers' Perspectives on the Role of Covenants in Debt Contracts' [1996] *Journal of International Banking Law* 201; P Taylor and J Day, 'Loan Contracting by UK Corporate Borrowers' [1996] *Journal of International Banking Law* 318; P Taylor and J Day, 'Loan Documentation in the Market for UK Corporate Debt: Current Practice and Future Prospects' [1997] *Journal of International Banking Law* 7; P Taylor and J Day, 'Financial Distress in Small Firms: The Role Played by Debt Covenants and Other Monitoring Devices' (2001) 3 *Insolvency Lawyer* 97; J Day, P Ormrod and P Taylor, 'Implications for Lending Decisions and Debt Contracting of the Adoption of International Financial Reporting Standards' (2004) 19 *Journal of International Banking Law and Regulation* 475.

[160] 6.3.3.1.

[161] See 3.2.2.4.

borrower,[162] and the type of debt.[163] However, covenants usually require the company to meet particular financial targets, usually expressed as ratios.[164] The ratio requirements can often relate to the consolidated position of the corporate group rather than the individual borrowing company.

One type of ratio relates to the capital worth of the company. As explained earlier, a company will be balance sheet insolvent if its assets are insufficient to discharge its liabilities.[165] A financial covenant could use this measure and prescribe a minimum net worth of a certain amount.[166] Alternatively, a covenant could provide that the company must meet a particular gearing ratio (borrowings expressed as a percentage of net worth). The balance of debt and equity in a company's financial structure was discussed earlier from the point of view of the company.[167] From the point of view of a lender, too high a level of debt can lead to insolvency risk, although a certain level is desirable because of the discipline it exerts on the directors. As mentioned above,[168] gearing covenants can act as a general restriction on borrowing, which mitigates the debt dilution risk that lenders face.[169] The main problem with reliance on capital ratios alone is that they are calculated historically and are susceptible to manipulation by the borrower[170] (although some control is exercised by the requirement of auditing).

Another type of ratio relates to the income of the company. A covenant may require that the ratio of the profit of the company to the interest payments that it has to make to service its debt is not less than a certain amount.[171] An alternative is to use a cash flow-based ratio, such as the relationship between cash inflow and the costs of the business (including funding).[172] This has the advantage that it is not a historic measure, and cash flow information can be required from the borrower company at intervals more frequent than other financial information. It can, though, be difficult to draft effective covenants based on cash flow.[173] All these financial covenants are heavily dependent on the accounting methods used to calculate the ratios,[174] and changes in accounting standards can lead to covenants

---

[162] Loans to very highly rated investment grade companies may not include any financial covenants at all.

[163] High-yield bonds, for example, rarely include covenants requiring compliance with financial ratios; see J Macdonald, 'High Yield Bonds: An Introduction to Material Covenants and Terms' [2014] *Journal of International Banking and Financial Law* 242. In certain markets, such as the leveraged buy-out market, loans are following suit: see Z Thomas, 'Is the Cov-Lite Party Over?' *International Financial Law Review* (29 May 2014).

[164] P Taylor and J Day, 'Evidence on the Practices of UK Bankers in Contracting for Medium-Term Debt' [1995] *Journal of International Banking Law* 394, 397.

[165] See 3.2.

[166] Minimum net worth is what would be left if all the assets were sold and all the liabilities paid: Valdez: Financial Markets, 104. This would be of interest to a lender in asset-based lending.

[167] 2.6.

[168] See 6.3.1.1.

[169] See 3.2.2.2.

[170] See Hudson: Finance, 32-28; Hughes: Banking, 15.

[171] See Valdez: Financial Markets, 104; Hudson, 32-27. This covenant is particularly relevant to cash flow lending (overdraft and invoice discounting): P Taylor and J Day, 'Evidence on the Practices of UK Bankers' [1995] *Journal of International Banking Law* 394, 397. The way the components of this ratio are calculated can be a matter of considerable negotiation (See Wood: Loans and Bonds, 5-040 ff). One common measure for 'profit' is EBITDA (earnings before interest, tax, depreciation and amortisation) or EBIT (earnings before interest and tax).

[172] See Hudson: Finance, 32-28.

[173] P Taylor and J Day, 'Evidence on the Practices of UK Bankers in Contracting for Medium-Term Debt' [1995] *Journal of International Banking Law* 394, 397.

[174] P Taylor and J Day, 'Loan Documentation in the Market for UK Corporate Debt: Current Practice and Future Prospects' [1997] *Journal of International Banking Law* 7, 10.

operating in different ways from that originally intended.[175] The warranties relating to the pre-loan representations may also continue, so that the borrower warrants that there is no change in its financial position.[176] If a ratio is not met, this will enable the lender to decide what to do: it will not necessarily terminate the arrangement but might use its power to do so to put pressure on the borrower to improve the position, and, if necessary, to renegotiate the loan with more protection for the lender.[177] The agreement might also provide for a 'pricing grid', so that if the risk for the lender increases because of the poor financial performance of the borrower, the interest payable on the loan rises.[178]

Another possible trigger is a downgrade in the rating of the borrower.[179] Clauses based on a rating trigger can provide for one or more of the following consequences: an obligation to post more collateral, an obligation to increase the rate of interest, a right to accelerate the loan, a requirement that the borrower buy back the debt, or even an event of default. While these triggers can be highly effective, they give rise to concerns (most notably that the existence of the trigger itself affects the rating of the borrower but the existence of the trigger is not always known to the rating agency).[180]

The clauses mentioned above all specify particular financial criteria, but often a more general clause covering any 'material adverse change' (MAC) is also included: there is either a representation that no such change has occurred plus a continuing warranty that no such change will occur, or a provision that such a change is an event of default.[181] The flexibility that such a clause gives can be useful, but, as with any clause requiring an assessment of materiality,[182] it can also lead to serious uncertainty.[183] MAC clauses have been subject to considerable academic scrutiny[184] and, recently, the High Court considered the interpretation of such a clause.[185] Blair J reached some general conclusions on the basis of authority regarding the interpretation of a MAC clause taking the form of a representation by the borrower that there had been no MAC in its financial position since the date of the loan agreement.[186] He concluded that the starting point for showing a MAC is the borrower's

---

[175] See J Day, P Ormrod and P Taylor, 'Implications for Lending Decisions and Debt Contracting of the Adoption of International Financial Reporting Standards' (2004) 19 *Journal of International Banking Law and Regulation* 475 on the effects of the change from the GAAP standard to the IFRS standard.

[176] These are known as 'evergreen' covenants: see Wood: Loans and Bonds, 4-007.

[177] P Taylor and J Day, 'Evidence on the Practices of UK Bankers in Contracting for Medium-Term Debt' [1995] *Journal of International Banking Law* 394, 399. See 3.2.2.4.2.

[178] This works both ways: if the financial position of the borrower improves, the interest payable will reduce. See C Whitehead, 'Creditors and Debt Governance' in C Hill, J Krusemark, B McDonnell and S Robbins (eds), *Research Handbook on the Economics of Corporate Law* (Cheltenham, Edward Elgar, 2002) 72.

[179] This could be the downgrade from investment grade to speculative grade, but it could also be a more finely tuned trigger. It should also be noted that some high-yield bonds may include covenants which fall away when the borrower's rating is upgraded to investment grade: see K Clowry, 'European Credit Documentation Trends: Covenant-Lite or Covenant Empty?' [2014] *Journal of International Banking and Financial Law* 296.

[180] For a full discussion see F Parmeggiani, 'Ratings Triggers, Market Risk and the Need for More Regulation' (2013) 14(3) *European Business Organisation Law Review* 425.

[181] J Day and E Kontor, 'Corporate Lending in an Intangibles Economy: Potential Solutions' [2002] *Journal of International Banking Law* 174, 177; Wood: Loans and Bonds, 6-018–6-022.

[182] Note the difficulties experienced by a bond trustee who has to certify that an event of default is 'materially prejudicial' to the bondholders, discussed at 8.3.4.2.3.

[183] See, for example, the problems caused by a similar clause in the *Elektrim* litigation, discussed at 8.3.4.2.3.

[184] R Zakrzewski, 'Material Adverse Change and Material Adverse Effect Provisions: Construction and Application' (2011) 5 *Law and Financial Markets Review* 344; P Rawlings, 'Avoiding the Obligation to Lend' [2012] *Journal of Business Law* 89, 96–97.

[185] *Grupo Hotelero Urvasco SA v Carey Value Added SL* [2013] EWHC 1039 (Comm).

[186] Ibid, [364].

own financial information, but the enquiry will not be limited to this if there is other compelling evidence, that the test for materiality is whether the change significantly affects the borrower's ability to repay the loan in question,[187] and that the burden of proof of the breach is on the lender.

He also considered whether the clause could be breached when the lender could foresee the change that had taken place. This issue is contentious. There is English law authority that the fact that the causes of the change were known, or ought to have been known, will not prevent there being breach of the clause,[188] but there is US authority that a MAC clause only applies to 'unknown events',[189] and this is supported by some commentators.[190] Blair J took the view that 'a lender cannot trigger such a clause on the basis of circumstances of which it was aware at the time of the agreement'. However, whether the MAC was foreseeable must be a matter of degree. Mere knowledge of the causes may not mean that the precise event relied on was foreseeable, and in these circumstances it seems wrong that the clause is not triggered.[191] Further, it must be a matter of interpretation of the contract whether the lender intended to take on the risk of the event. A similar approach applies in relation to force majeure clauses[192] and frustration of contracts.[193] Having said this, lenders will generally include a MAC clause as a general safety net to catch any events which they have not been able to foresee in the future, but will combine it with specific covenants and events of default dealing with foreseeable risks.[194]

Coupled with financial covenants are obligations to provide information, so that the lender can monitor the borrower's financial position. The effectiveness of these depends on the information being timely and reliable,[195] and also on the company being willing to provide the information.[196] The minimum information would be that which is publicly available, such as the information periodically made available by companies.[197] However, most of this information is historic,[198] and so further timely and up-to-date information may be required to be provided by the management.[199]

---

[187] See also R Zakrzewski, 'Material Adverse Change and Material Adverse Effect Provisions: Construction and Application' (2011) 5 *Law and Financial Markets Review* 344, 349–50.

[188] *Levison v Farin* [1978] 2 All ER 1149.

[189] *IBP Inc v Tyson Foods Inc* 789 A2d 14 (Del Ch 2001), 65.

[190] R Hooley, 'Material Adverse Change Clauses After 9/11' in S Worthington (ed), *Commercial Law & Commercial Practice* (Oxford, Hart Publishing, 2003); P Rawlings, 'Avoiding the Obligation to Lend' [2012] *Journal of Business Law* 89, 97.

[191] J Woolrich, 'MAC Clauses, Change and *Grupo Hotelero*' (2014) 29 *Journal of International Banking Law and Regulation* 373.

[192] *SHV Gas Supply & Trading SAS v Naftomar Shipping and Trading Co Ltd Inc* [2005] EWHC 2528 (Comm) 163 [29]. For discussion of the similarity of MAC clauses and force majeure clauses see R Zakrzewski, 'When is a MAC Clause a Force Majeure Clause?' [2012] *Journal of International Banking and Financial Law* 547.

[193] Chitty 23-059–23-060.

[194] R Youard, 'Default in International Loan Agreements: Part 2' [1986] *Journal of International Banking Law* 378, 390.

[195] P Taylor and J Day, 'Financial Distress in Small Firms: The Role Played by Debt Covenants and Other Monitoring Devices' (2001) 3 *Insolvency Lawyer* 97, 111.

[196] Thus very large companies may have the bargaining power to restrict the information provided to that which is publicly available: see P Taylor and J Day, 'Loan Contracting by UK Corporate Borrowers' [1996] *Journal of International Banking Law* 318, 323.

[197] See 11.3. In relation to debt securities which are listed on the GEFIM or the PSM, certain levels of ongoing disclosure are required: see 13.3.1.

[198] Hughes: Banking, 2.10. Not all the information disclosed to the markets is historic, however: see 11.3.2.5.

[199] Such a requirement is not always very effective: see P Taylor and J Day, 'Loan Documentation in the Market for UK Corporate Debt: Current Practice and Future Prospects' [1997] *Journal of International Banking Law* 7, 13.

6.3.3 Termination and Acceleration Rights

As mentioned above, debt contracts usually stipulate a number of 'events of default', the occurrence of which entitles the lender to accelerate repayment of the loan and/or to terminate the loan contract (which has the same effect, but which also releases the lender from the obligation to make further advances).[200] For a lender this is a very significant right: it should, however, be noted that it is only a right, which the lender can decide not to rely on, and that acceleration or termination does not happen automatically.[201] A lender has a choice whether to waive a breach or to enforce it. The best way of exercising this choice is by making a positive communication to the borrower: there is often a concern that inaction may be seen as a waiver, and so an agreement will often contain a 'no-waiver' clause. Such a clause, though useful, does not completely block a successful argument of waiver by estoppel when the facts support this.[202] The lender's choice is an absolute one, not a matter of discretion which could, in some circumstances, be subject to a requirement that it be exercised reasonably or in good faith.[203]

At its strongest, when it includes a 'cross-default' clause so that any default on any borrowing by the borrower is an event of default,[204] a right to accelerate or terminate enables a lender to drive a borrower into insolvency very quickly.[205] It means that a lender can, if it wishes, seek to get paid (or to enforce its liability against the assets of the company) at the first sign of financial trouble, or, at least, to have a seat at the 'restructuring' table.[206] A cross-default clause might be thought to be a way to 'steal a march' on other creditors, although if all the borrower's credit agreements include similar clauses this will not be successful, as all other creditors will also be able to accelerate their claims, thus driving the borrower into insolvency. Conversely, the cross-default clause can lead to inertia as there is no incentive on any particular lender to take action.[207]

---

[200] Wood: Loans and Bonds, 6-001. Where a loan is secured, events of default are usually also triggers for crystallisation of a floating charge: see P Mather, 'The Determinants of Financial Covenants in Bank-Loan Contracts' (2004) 19 *Journal of International Banking Law and Regulation* 33, 35. For further discussion of crystallisation see 7.3.3.2.

[201] R Youard, 'Default in International Loan Agreements' [1986] *Journal of International Banking Law* 276, 278. Note that the decision whether to accelerate a loan can be complicated where there are multiple lenders. In a bond issue, a trustee usually has discretion as to whether to waive a breach, and also has the power to accelerate a loan if it decides that an event of default is materially prejudicial to the bondholders, and is obliged to do so if instructed by the bondholders and is satisfactorily indemnified. The difficulties this can cause are discussed at 8.3.4.2.3. In a syndicated loan, the decision whether to waive the breach or accelerate can be taken by a majority of lenders, except in relation to breaches of certain provisions, such as conditions precedent. See 8.4.6.

[202] *Tele2 International Card Company SA and others v Post Office Limited* [2009] EWCA Civ 9; see also E Nalbantian, M Brown, H Territt and N Davies, 'Drowning about Waiving?' [2010] *Journal of International Banking and Financial Law* 195.

[203] *Sucden Financial Limited v Fluxo-Cane Overseas Limited, Manoel Fernando Garcia* [2010] EWHC 2133 (Comm) [50]; R Hooley, 'Controlling Contractual Discretion' (2013) 72 *Cambridge Law Journal* 65, 85. See also 6.2.4.

[204] In bonds, the clause usually provides for cross-acceleration rather than cross-default.

[205] See Benjamin: Financial Law, 8.25; Hudson: Finance, 19.49; K Clark and A Taylor, 'Events of Default in Eurocurrency Loan Agreements' (1982) 1 *International Financial Law Review* 12, 13, who point out that the effectiveness of cross-default clauses can be limited by banks' standards of secrecy, so that one lender will not necessarily know of a default on another loan.

[206] C Wells and A Doulai, 'Till Default Do Us Part: Facility Agreements and Acceleration' [2013] *Journal of International Banking and Financial Law* 571.

[207] Wood: Loans and Bonds, 6-013. In *Rahman v HSBC Bank* [2012] EWHC 11 (Ch) the judge found that a cross-default clause was not unfair for the purposes of the Consumer Credit Act 1974.

The acceleration clause also, however, enables a lender to force a renegotiation of the loan as a price for not activating the clause:[208] most lenders would prefer to do this as they are more likely to get paid if the borrower overcomes its financial troubles. The right is obviously of most use in term loans where the amount outstanding is considerable. The right to terminate its own further obligations to lend is also important to the lender, especially where the facility is revolving rather than for a term. A lender will have no desire to advance further funds when the likelihood of being repaid the funds already advanced is reduced. Further, the ability to refuse to advance further funds is an important way of forcing a renegotiation. The forced renegotiation may be on terms which include changes in the way the company is managed, thus giving a lender an important corporate governance role when the company is in difficulties.[209]

6.3.3.1 Events of Default

The loan contract will stipulate such events of default as, from the lenders' view, are thought to be suitable indications of the borrower's inability to repay the loan, and, from the borrower's view, are not so easily triggered as to make it impossible to carry on its business. This balancing exercise is difficult, and is often the product of considerable negotiation. Some events of default will be breaches of the agreement, but others will be events outside the control of the borrower and will not amount to breach (so that they will not, for example, give rise to a right to damages). The most obvious breach is failure to pay the lender amounts due, whether of principal or interest.[210] Since a failure to pay can arise from a minor administrative error, there is usually a short grace period.[211] Any breach of warranty (including the warranty that all representations remain accurate) or breach of covenant will also be an event of default. These events, and a failure to pay, amount to breaches. Non-breach events may include insolvency proceedings, or actual insolvency, default on other loan or other types of contracts (these are cross-default clauses)[212] and any change in circumstances which might have a materially adverse effect on the financial condition of the borrower.[213] Often, a loan agreement will provide that a breach of a financial covenant can be cured by the provision of more equity. This is termed an 'equity cure'.[214] Sometimes, the cure can be effected by debt rather than equity: this can lead to a rather odd situation where debt is 'recycled'. If this comes within the terms of the equity cure clause

---

[208] Lenders also often charge a fee for waiving a breach or an event of default: see L Hornuf, M Reps and S Schaferling 'Covenants in European Investment-Grade Corporate Bonds' (2010), http://papers.ssrn.com/sol3/papers.cfm?abstract_id=2393291.

[209] See 3.2.2.4.

[210] It should be noted that loans payable on demand do not require an acceleration clause: see R Youard, 'Default in International Loan Agreements' [1986] *Journal of International Banking Law* 276, 276.

[211] S Lear and M Lower, 'Events of Default', *Law Society Gazette*, 21 April 1993, 90 at (31); Wood: Loans and Bonds, 6-009; K Clark and A Taylor, 'Events of Default in Eurocurrency Loan Agreements' (1982) 1 *International Financial Law Review* 12. The typical 'grace' period in an English law agreement is very short, while a longer period is typical in an agreement governed by New York law: see C Wells and A Doulai, 'Till Default Do Us Part: Facility Agreements and Acceleration' [2013] *Journal of International Banking and Financial Law* 571.

[212] Such clauses can be justified on the basis that a default in meeting the obligations to one creditor is a good advance warning of financial difficulty: R Youard, 'Default in International Loan Agreements' [1986] *Journal of Business Law* 378, 384.

[213] Wood: Loans and Bonds, 6-018. See 6.3.2.2.

[214] See C Kerrigan, 'Equity Cure Rights' [2010] *Journal of International Banking and Financial Law* 196.

(interpreted according to the principles discussed above),[215] it can be effective to cure an event of default.[216]

6.3.3.2 Effect of Wrongful Acceleration

In some circumstances, especially where the event of default in question requires the lender to interpret a widely drafted clause, such as to decide whether an adverse change of circumstances is 'material', a borrower may allege that the lender has sought to exercise its right to accelerate wrongfully. It appears from the House of Lords decision in *Concord Trust v Law Debenture Trust Corporation plc*[217] that a wrongful exercise of the right to accelerate is of no legal effect. This means that it is ineffective to achieve an acceleration,[218] and that, in the absence of an implied term to the effect that the lender agreed not to give an invalid notice of acceleration, the lender is not contractually liable for doing so. Such a term would only be implied if it were necessary to give business efficacy to the contract[219] and this is unlikely to be the case in most circumstances.[220] It would, of course, be a breach of contract if the lender refused, on the basis of the wrongful acceleration, to make further advances which it was contractually obliged to do, or if it wrongfully enforced security.[221]

There are other possible causes of action for which a lender might be liable for wrongful acceleration. A discussion of these and of the policy implications of the *Concord* decision can be found in chapter eight in the context of the obligations of bond trustees.[222]

6.3.3.3 Validity of Acceleration Clauses

When the trigger for the acceleration of the payment obligation is a breach of contract,[223] the question arises as to whether the clause can be challenged as contrary to the rule against penalties. The penalty jurisdiction is an exception to the general rule that the courts should uphold the terms of the contract as agreed between the parties.[224] A clause providing for sums payable[225] on breach[226] will be struck down as a penalty if its primary contractual

---

[215] 6.2.

[216] *Strategic Value Master Fund Ltd v Ideal Standard International Acquisition SARL* [2011] EWHC 171 (Ch).

[217] *Concord Trust v Law Debenture Trust Corporation plc* [2005] UKHL 27.

[218] See the decision of the Court of Appeal in the same case at [2004] EWCA Civ 1001 [71] (Jonathan Parker LJ), approved by Lord Scott at [2005] UKHL 27 [37].

[219] *The Moorcock* (1889) LR 14 PD 64, 68.

[220] This is clear both from the House of Lords decision in the *Concord* case and from the decision of *BNP Paribas SA v Yukos Oil Company* [2005] EWHC 1321 (Ch), in which the approach of the House of Lords was followed.

[221] *Concord Trust v Law Debenture Trust Corporation plc* [2005] UKHL 27 [41]; E Peel, 'No Liability for Service of an Invalid Notice of "Event of Default"' (2006) 122 *Law Quarterly Review* 179, 182–83.

[222] See 8.3.4.2.3.

[223] The rule against penalties applies only to sums payable on breach of contract and not to sums specified as payable on other non-breach events: *Export Credits Guarantee Department v Universal Oil Products Co* [1983] 1 WLR 399.

[224] *Robophone Facilities v Blank* [1966] 1 WLR 1428, 1446–47; *Murray v Leisureplay plc* [2005] EWCA Civ 963 [29]; *Makdessi v Cavendish Square Holdings BV* [2013] EWCA Civ 1539 [44].

[225] Or benefits forgone: see *Makdessi v Cavendish Square Holdings BV* [2013] EWCA Civ 1539.

[226] It is still the position in English law that the rule only applies to clauses triggered by breach, despite the contrary decision of the High Court of Australia in *Andrews v Australia & New Zealand Banking Group Ltd* [2012] HCA 30.

function is deterrence of breach, and not compensation of the innocent party for the breach.[227] The primary test for this is whether the amount payable under the clause is a genuine pre-estimate of the loss flowing from the breach.[228]

It is clear that the mere fact that the loan becomes repayable early does not make it a penalty, as long as no extra interest is payable other than that which has already accrued and continues to accrue.[229] This seems to be the case despite the fact that early payment is usually more expensive for the payer and more valuable to the payee, at least where there is a positive rate of inflation.[230] If, however, the obligation accelerated includes unaccrued interest,[231] or there is provision for an additional rate of interest after default, either of these might potentially be struck down as a penalty.

It appears from the judgment of Colman J in *Lordsvale Finance v Bank of Zambia*[232] that being a genuine pre-estimate of loss is not the only reason why a payment on breach provided for by a contractual clause might not be a penalty: it will not be a penalty if there is another good commercial reason why the dominant contractual purpose of the clause is not to deter breach.[233] This approach has been confirmed in the decision of the Court of Appeal in *Makdessi v Cavendish Square Holdings BV.*[234] That case concerned the breach of a share sale agreement by the seller, giving rise to an entitlement on the part of the buyer not to make further payments, and also triggering a call option whereby the buyer could buy the seller's remaining shares at a disadvantageous price. It was held that, because the result of the provisions was so disadvantageous to the seller, and the buyer suffered no recoverable loss, the provisions were neither a genuine pre-estimate of loss nor were they commercial, since their function was to deter breach.[235] The actual decision has given rise to considerable adverse comment,[236] but it does not seem to change the current position in relation to an increase in the rate of interest charged on a loan after default, which was established in the *Lordsvale* case.

In *Lordsvale*, the increase was of 1 per cent. Colman J explained that this was explicable since the credit risk of the borrower had increased after the default, and that interest rates were generally higher where credit risk was higher. Thus an increase was to be expected and could not be said to be for the dominant purpose of deterring default.[237] It is, however, a question of degree. In *Jeancharm Ltd v Barnet Football Club Ltd*,[238] default interest was

[227] *Lordsvale Finance plc v Bank of Zambia* [1996] QB 752, 762.

[228] *Dunlop Pneumatic Tyre Co Ltd v New Garage & Motor Co Ltd* [1915] AC 79, 86.

[229] *Oresundsvarvet AB v Lemos (The Angelic Star)* [1988] 1 Lloyd's Rep 122; *Wadham Stringer Finance Ltd v Meaney* [1981] 1 WLR 39; *O'Dea v Allstates Leasing Systems (WA) Pty Ltd* (1983) 152 CLR 359 (HC Aust); GA Muir, 'Stipulations for the Payment of Agreed Sums' (1985) 10 *Sydney Law Review* 503; *AMEV-UDC Finance Ltd v Austin* (1986) 162 CLR 170 (HC Aust); *BNP Paribas v Wockhardt EU Operations (Swiss) AG* [2009] EWHC 3116 (Comm); cf *Esanda Finance Corp Ltd v Plessing* (1989) 166 CLR 131 (HC Aust), (1989) 63 ALJ 238.

[230] M Furmston (ed), *The Law of Contract*, 4th edn (London, Butterworths, 2010) para 8.118.

[231] *Oresundsvarvet AB v Lemos (The Angelic Star)* [1988] 1 Lloyd's Rep 122, 125; *County Leasing Limited v Richard John East* [2007] EWHC 2907 (QB) [112]–[117].

[232] [1996] QB 752. See also Hughes: Banking, 2.4–2.5.

[233] Ibid, 763; *Cine Bes Filmcilik ve Yapimcilik AS v United International Pictures* [2003] EWCA Civ 1669 [15].

[234] [2013] EWCA Civ 1539 esp at [103].

[235] [2013] EWCA Civ 1539 [119]–[120].

[236] E Peel, 'Unjustified Penalties or an Unjustified Rule Against Penalties?' (2014) 130 *Law Quarterly Review* 365; J O'Sullivan, 'Lost on Penalties' (2014) 73 *Cambridge Law Journal* 480; W Day, 'Penalty Clauses Revisited' [2014] *Journal of Business Law* 512.

[237] This approach appears to be approved of in *Makdessi* at [87] and [120].

[238] [2003] EWCA Civ 58.

charged at an uplift of 5 per cent: this was held to be a penalty on the grounds that it could not be justified on the basis that the credit risk of the borrower had increased, and also that it was not a genuine pre-estimate of loss.[239]

It should be noted that, in *Lordsvale*, the judge took account not only of the protection against increased credit risk, but also of the prevalence of default interest clauses in international loan agreements and the attitude of the courts of other countries to them. In particular, he took account of the fact that the law of New York upheld such clauses, and commented that

> It would be highly regrettable if the English courts were to refuse to give effect to such prevalent provisions while the courts of New York are prepared to enforce them. In the absence of compelling reasons of principle or binding authority to the contrary there can be no doubt that the courts of this country should adopt in international trade law that approach to the problem which is consistent with that which operates in that nation which is the other major participant in the trade in question. For there to be disparity between the law applicable in London and New York on this point would be of great disservice to international banking.[240]

This pragmatic attitude to terms in commercial contracts has been much approved by those in practice,[241] although it is not entirely clear that such a wide view of what amounts to commerciality is consistent with the decision of the Court of Appeal in *Makdessi*.

It should, in addition, be mentioned that the penalty jurisdiction has also been applied to acceleration clauses in hire purchase and conditional sale agreements.[242] The relevant principles are now well-established and tend to be followed in the drafting of all such clauses. The question of relief against forfeiture of the subject matter of a finance lease has also been considered, and this will be discussed in chapter seven.[243]

The penalty clause jurisdiction does not apply when the trigger for acceleration is not a breach of contract. Where the event of default is that formal insolvency proceedings have been commenced against the borrower company, however, the question arises as to whether the acceleration clause falls foul of the anti-deprivation principle.[244] The first question to ask is whether the effect of the clause is to deprive the insolvent company of an asset it would otherwise have. It could be said that by accelerating the loan, the company becomes liable for a sum for which it would not otherwise be liable, and that increasing a company's liabilities has the same effect as diminishing its assets.[245] However, on insolvency all future and contingent debts become immediately provable anyway,[246] which means that they are, in effect, accelerated. Thus, unless the acceleration clause contained some element of penalty for acceleration (that is, an extra payment which was only to be made if the loan were

---

[239] Ibid, [16], [22] and [29]. Jacob J took the view that the interest rate in *Lordsvale* was a genuine pre-estimate of loss (see [16]).

[240] [1996] QB 752, 767.

[241] Hughes: Banking, 2.5. See also *BNP Paribas v Wockhardt EU Operations (Swiss) AG* [2009] EWHC 3116 (Comm) [23]–[25].

[242] *Bridge v Campbell Discount Co Ltd* [1962] AC 600. For the possible application of the principle to finance leases see R Goode, 'Penalties in Finance Leases' (1988) 104 *Law Quarterly Review* 25.

[243] 7.5.2.1.

[244] See 3.3.2.1.2.

[245] *In re Johns, Worrell v Johns* [1928] 1 Ch 737. See also *Ex p Mackay* (1873) LR 8 Ch App 643, 647 and *Belmont Park Investments Pty Ltd v BNY Corporate Trustee Services Ltd* [2011] UKSC 38 [149].

[246] Insolvency Rules 1986, rr 11.13, 12.3(1), 13.12.

accelerated) there cannot be said to be a deprivation. It should be noted that an acceleration clause is often combined with a right of set-off on insolvency, but even here the principle will not be contravened provided that the right of set-off falls within insolvency set-off.[247]

If the acceleration clause is coupled with the termination of the right to call for future advances, this, in theory, could amount to a divesting of an asset of the company on insolvency. However, since the insolvency is bound to be an anticipatory breach by the borrower (since it will be unable to repay the loan),[248] this brings the obligation of the lender to make the loan to an end, and a clause stating that this is the case (or terminating the contract before the actual onset of insolvency) cannot be said to divest the company of any asset which would otherwise be available to creditors.[249]

6.3.4 Set-Off[250]

Set-off can arise in a number of forms, but the basic idea is the same. If A owes money to B and B owes money to A, the two debts can be set off against each other so that only the balance is payable. Set-off operates both outside and within insolvency, although in the latter situation it is restricted by statutory criteria. Set-off can operate to the advantage or disadvantage[251] of a creditor in a number of ways. Outside insolvency, its prime function is to avoid circuity of action, so that instead of a creditor having to sue a debtor for the debt, it can (in certain circumstances) merely cancel its own debt to the debtor. This not only saves litigation and enforcement costs, but can also reduce the creditor's exposure to the debtor's credit risk (both actually and in its books, which can have an effect on capital adequacy) as well as the creditor's own debts. When combined with netting,[252] set-off is extensively used by those who trade on the financial markets (especially the derivatives markets) to reduce exposure and risk, and also to reduce the volume of settlements.[253] Although set-off operates by operation of law, its limits (outside insolvency) can be extended or reduced by agreement between the parties. Thus, with agreement, a lender can set off the debt owed by a borrower against a debt the lender owes to a third party, such as a parent company of the borrower.[254]

Conversely, the parties can exclude the right of set-off, so that, for example, loans[255] and bonds may provide that payment must be made without set-off, so that they can be more

---

[247] See 6.3.4.6.2. For a decision that an acceleration provision, coupled with a provision that the payment of the loan must be by way of set-off, did not contravene the anti-deprivation principle, see *Re Mistral Finance Ltd (In Liquidation)* [2001] BCC 27 [56]–[61].

[248] *Sale Continuation Ltd v Austin Taylor & Co Ltd* [1968] 2 QB 849.

[249] F Oditah, 'Assets and the Treatment of Claims in Insolvency' (1992) 108 *Law Quarterly Review* 459, 494–99. See also Goode: Corporate Insolvency, 8-09 and the reasoning of Lord Mance in *Belmont Park Investments Pty Ltd v BNY Corporate Trustee Services Ltd* [2011] UKSC 38 [177].

[250] See, generally, Derham: Set-Off; Goode: Credit and Security, ch 7; Wood: Set-Off and Netting, ch 1; L Gullifer and P Pichonnaz, *Set-Off in Arbitration and Commercial Transactions* (Oxford, Oxford University Press, 2014).

[251] Where it is to the disadvantage of the creditor, it is possible to exclude all but insolvency set-off: see 6.3.4.6.2.

[252] See 6.3.4.5.

[253] Benjamin: Financial Law, 8.25; Hudson: Banking Law, 22-99–22-104.

[254] Such an agreement would normally be coupled with a guarantee from the parent company.

[255] Wood: Loans and Bonds, 3-058.

easily traded.[256] While such a clause is valid outside insolvency, it does not apply within insolvency as insolvency set-off is mandatory.[257]

6.3.4.1 Use of Set-Off and Flawed Asset Structures in Lending

If the borrower becomes insolvent, set-off has an important protective function for the lender. Under English law, mutual debts are set off on insolvency so that only the balance due to the solvent party is provable. Thus, if a borrower owes £1 million to the lender, and the lender owes £750,000 to the borrower, the lender's liability to the borrower is discharged and the lender need only prove for the £250,000 balance. If it proves for a debt in the debtor's insolvency, a lender is very unlikely to receive the full amount owed, but the effect of insolvency set-off is that it does 'receive' the full £750,000 which is set off, as it no longer has to pay this to the borrower. Insolvency set-off, therefore, puts the lender in the same economic position as if the debt were secured: it gets the full amount in priority to the unsecured creditors. In fact, it is in a better position than, for example, the holder of a floating charge, since the liquidator's costs, preferential creditors and the prescribed part for the unsecured creditors are paid out of floating charge assets in priority to the floating chargee.[258] It is even in a better position than a fixed chargee, in that no enforcement of security is necessary: insolvency set-off operates automatically.

Lenders, especially bank lenders, may structure transactions to enable themselves to be 'paid' by set-off if the borrower becomes insolvent. Thus, to give a very simple example, if a borrower has a deposit account with a bank, the bank will rely on being able to set off its debt to the borrower against the amount due on the loan if the borrower becomes insolvent. The bank may seek to protect itself further by a provision in the deposit agreement that the deposited funds cannot be withdrawn while the loan remains extant. This changes the nature of the bank's obligation to pay the borrower into a conditional debt, often known as a 'flawed asset'. The debt remains conditional ('flawed') even if the borrower is insolvent,[259] so the flawed asset arrangement continues to provide protection to the lender unless it contravenes the anti-deprivation principle, or is an unregistered but registrable charge.

There are a number of reasons why this structure does not contravene the anti-deprivation principle, despite the fact that it was made clear in the *Belmont* case that flawed assets can, in theory, fall foul of that principle, since a 'substance over form' approach was to be adopted.[260] First, and most importantly, the 'flaw' is not triggered by the onset of insolvency proceedings.[261] The payment to the depositor is conditional upon non-payment of the loan. While the possibility of payment may be exacerbated by insolvency, actual non-payment occurs both before and after the onset of insolvency, and is certainly not triggered

---

[256] This is a requirement for any debt securities traded through CREST (see 9.2.6.3) and is also invariably included in issues of stock (see 9.2.6.1). This was not necessarily the case for bearer bonds, which were negotiable instruments, since they were transferred free from equities including set-off (see 9.2.3 and Fuller: Corporate Borrowing, 323).

[257] *National Westminster Bank Ltd v Halesowen Presswork and Assemblies Ltd* [1972] AC 785.

[258] 3.3.1.2.

[259] *In re Bank of Credit and Commerce International SA (No 8)* [1996] Ch 245, 262–63.

[260] *Belmont Park Investments Pty Ltd v BNY Corporate Trustee Services Ltd* [2011] UKSC 38 [89]–[90]; *Lomas v JFB Firth Rixson* [2012] EWCA Civ 419 [86].

[261] *Belmont Park Investments Pty Ltd v BNY Corporate Trustee Services Ltd* [2011] UKSC 38 [14]; *Revenue and Customs Commissioners v Football League Ltd* [2012] EWHC 1372 (Ch) [67]. See 3.3.2.1.2.

by it.[262] Second, even on a 'substance over form' test, the asset is limited from the beginning. It is not, even in substance, an asset which is granted to the company and then removed at a later date. Third, the clause is commercially justifiable.[263]

Although it will depend on the precise words used, it is also unlikely that the arrangement will constitute a charge.[264] The bank acquires no rights in the deposit: it is merely entitled to withhold payment.[265] Even when combined with a contractual set-off provision, it is unlikely that an English court would conclude that a charge is created, since the rights created are purely personal.[266]

Where the depositor and the borrower are the same person, the flawed asset device merely preserves the value of the deposit so that the lender can benefit from the application of insolvency set-off if the borrower becomes insolvent. If the deposit is by another party, such as a parent company, insolvency set-off will not apply, and so the flawed asset has independent value. As explained by Rose LJ in the Court of Appeal decision in *BCCI (No 8)*,[267]

> It will almost invariably be in the interests of the general body of creditors for [the depositor's liquidator] to permit the bank to recoup itself out of the deposit, take delivery of any other securities which the bank holds for the principal debt, and seek to recover from the principal debtor.

However, if the depositor has guaranteed the borrowing, insolvency set-off will apply in any case since the obligation under the guarantee will be set off against the deposit.[268] In the past it was frequently the practice of bank lenders to take a 'triple cocktail' of protection: a flawed asset, a contractual set-off and a charge-back (a charge taken by the lender over the deposit). This represented a 'belt and braces' approach, which was perhaps appropriate when there was doubt about the validity of charge-backs[269] and the scope of insolvency set-off was more limited.[270] Triple cocktails, and, indeed, flawed assets, are now much less common.[271]

Whether the advantage insolvency set-off gives to a creditor is justified in policy terms will be discussed below.[272] First, the various types of set-off and netting outside insolvency will be briefly discussed. The labels for these types sometimes vary: the titles used here are those coined by Philip Wood, which are now widely used.[273]

---

[262] This is in contrast to the 'flaw' in cl 2(a)(iii) of the ISDA Master Agreement, which has been challenged as contrary to the anti-deprivation principle (*Lomas v JFB Firth Rixson* [2012] EWCA Civ 419). There, the flaw was that no event of default had occurred, and the event of default was the commencement of the administration of the relevant party.

[263] *Belmont Park Investments Pty Ltd v BNY Corporate Trustee Services Ltd* [2011] UKSC 38 [102]–[104].

[264] In two cases the courts have held that flawed asset arrangements in different contexts did create a charge: see *Fraser v Oystertec plc* [2004] EWHC 1582 (Ch) [7]–[12]; *Re Lehman Brothers International (Europe) (In Administration)* [2012] EWHC 2997 (Ch) [47]–[48].

[265] Goode: Credit and Security, 1-23.

[266] Cf *Caisse Populaire Desjardins de l'Est de Drummond v Canada* [2009] SCC 29, discussed in Goode: Credit and Security, 1-21.

[267] [1996] Ch 245, 263.

[268] This is now so even if there has been no demand under the guarantee: see Goode: Credit and Security, 7-98.

[269] Now resolved: see 7.3.2.4.

[270] In particular, contingent debts owed to the insolvent party could not be the subject of set-off. This has now changed: see Insolvency Rules 1986, rr 2.85(4) and 4.90(4) as amended by the Insolvency (Amendment) Rules (SI 2005/527).

[271] R Calnan, *Taking Security: Law and Practice*, 2nd edn (London, Jordan Publishing, 2012) 12-30; P Ali, *The Law of Secured Finance* (Oxford, Oxford University Press, 2002) 280.

[272] See 6.3.4.6.3.

[273] P Wood, *English and International Set-Off* (London, Sweet & Maxwell, 1989). See also Goode: Credit and Security, 7-03.

6.3.4.2 Independent Set-Off

This originated from the Statutes of Set-Off, and is sometimes called statutory set-off. Now it also includes that form of set-off which was applied by analogy where one of the claims was equitable—which, confusingly, was called legal set-off. It is really a procedural defence: where a claim for a liquidated sum is brought, a cross-claim for a liquidated sum can be asserted to extinguish or reduce the judgment that the claimant can obtain.[274] The significance of this is that it only applies where an action has actually been brought: where the claimant seeks to exercise a self-help remedy, independent set-off does not apply. Thus, for example, a borrower cannot rely on independent set-off to reduce the amount payable on an instalment of a loan, or an instalment under a hire purchase agreement. If it did so, the lender could invoke an acceleration clause,[275] or could terminate the agreement and repossess the goods, on the grounds that an instalment had not been fully paid.[276]

Independent set-off has significant other limitations, in that it can only apply to debts (liquidated claims for money) and not to claims for damages, and only to debts due at the start of the action. For these reasons, it is rarely relied upon, since transaction set-off is more liberal. There is one situation, however, where independent set-off can be used when transaction set-off cannot be. Independent set-off applies even where the claim and the cross-claim are unconnected, whereas transaction set-off, which is based on the principle that it is inequitable for the claimant to succeed on the claim without giving credit for the cross-claim, requires a very close connection.

6.3.4.3 Transaction Set-Off

This form of set-off operates where there is sufficient connection between the claim and the cross-claim. Like independent set-off, transaction set-off does not extinguish or reduce the claim or cross-claim until judgment or agreement,[277] but this does not prevent transaction set-off being relied upon as a substantive defence.[278] Thus (unlike the situation in relation independent set-off discussed above) where a payment is made taking account of transaction set-off, a self-help remedy for underpayment is not triggered.[279] If a creditor ignores the asserted set-off and goes ahead with the self-help remedy, he acts 'at his peril':[280] if the set-off is upheld, the creditor will be liable for wrongfully doing whatever the self-help remedy would otherwise entitle him to do.[281] The borrower must, however, assert the set-off

---

[274] Independent set-off is not a defence, although it is usually pleaded as such (CPR r 16.6), and thus does not actually reduce the defendant's liability but only takes effect on and from the date of judgment: *Glencore Grain Ltd v Agros Trading* [1999] 2 Lloyd's Rep 410 [28].

[275] See 6.3.3.

[276] See Goode: Credit and Security, 7-37–7-38. If the borrower had sufficient bargaining power, it could, of course, include contractual set-off with a wider scope in the agreement.

[277] *Fearns v Anglo-Dutch Paint & Chemical Co Ltd* [2010] EWHC 2366 (Ch) [50(1)], recently followed in *Equitas Ltd & Another v Walsham Bros Co Ltd* [2013] EWHC 3264 (Comm) [175]–[185].

[278] *Fearns v Anglo-Dutch Paint & Chemical Co Ltd* [2010] EWHC 2366 (Ch) [50(3)].

[279] Goode: Credit and Security, 7-54.

[280] See *Federal Commerce & Navigation Co Ltd v Molena Alpha Inc (The 'Nanfri')* [1978] 2 QB 927, 974 (per Lord Denning); *Equitas Ltd & Another v Walsham Bros Co Ltd* [2013] EWHC 3264 (Comm) [179].

[281] See *Federal Commerce & Navigation Co Ltd v Molena Alpha Inc (The 'Nanfri')* [1978] 2 QB 927, 974 where Lord Denning refers to liability in damages for wrongful exercise of a right to withdraw a ship; *Fuller v Happy Shopper Markets Ltd* [2001] 1 WLR 1681, liability for wrongful distress for rent.

before it can act as a defence in this way,[282] although its cross-claim need not be definitively quantified provided that the assertion is made reasonably and in good faith.[283]

The availability of a self-help remedy by the assertion of transaction set-off creates considerable uncertainty in practice as to the operation of an acceleration or termination clause. This is a strong reason for providing that payments under a loan agreement or in an issue of securities should be made without set-off.[284]

For a transaction set-off to arise, the claim and cross-claim must be so closely connected that it would be unjust to enforce the main claim without taking the cross-claim. There are two elements to the test: the 'formal' requirement of close connection, and the 'functional' requirement, which is the part relating to injustice.[285] The test relates to the substance rather than the form of the claims, so even if the claims arise out of the same transaction this does not necessarily mean that they are sufficiently connected, while claims arising out of separate contracts may qualify if they are sufficiently connected. Provided there is sufficient connection, it does not matter that one claim is liquidated and the other unliquidated (for example, a claim for damages).[286]

Further, the claims must be mutual, although in determining mutuality account is taken of equitable interests as well as legal interests. Thus, if a beneficiary is sued, it can set off a claim held on trust for him by a trustee.[287]

6.3.4.4 Banker's Right to Combine Accounts

For bank lenders, a significant part of the law of set-off is the right to combine current accounts. This is probably best analysed as an implied contractual right to set off the credit balance on one account (a debt due by the bank to the customer) against a debit balance on another account.[288] This is because there is no obligation on the banker to combine accounts,[289] and the right to do so can be excluded by express or implied agreement. Where a customer has a loan account and a current account, it will be presumed that there is no right to combine without express agreement.[290] This makes obvious sense, since the customer will normally want to carry on its business by writing cheques on its current account, even though it has borrowed from the bank. However, the bank will want, and will have, a right of set-off on insolvency (since insolvency set-off cannot be excluded) and will often provide for a contractual right of set-off under certain circumstances.

---

[282] *Equitas Ltd & Another v Walsham Bros Co Ltd* [2013] EWHC 3264 (Comm) [179].

[283] *Federal Commerce & Navigation Co Ltd v Molena Alpha Inc (The 'Nanfri')* [1978] 2 QB 927, 975; *Santiren Shipping Ltd v Unimarine SA (The 'Chrysovalandou Dyo')* [1981] 1 Lloyd's Rep 159.

[284] The advantages of an acceleration clause depend on speed and certainty, and if a paying borrower could claim to pay less than the due amount on the grounds of set-off, this would prevent the timely operation of the clause, even if the cross-claim turned out later to be without merit.

[285] *Geldof Metaalconstructie NV v Simon Carves Ltd* [2010] EWCA Civ 667 [43].

[286] *Hanak v Green* [1958] 2 QB 9.

[287] *Cochrane v Green* (1860) 9 CB (NS) 448.

[288] Goode: Credit and Security, 7-31. cf Derham: Set-Off, 15.03 ff.

[289] *Halesowen Presswork and Assemblies Ltd v National Westminster Bank Ltd* [1971] 1 QB 1, 34; *Re EJ Morel Ltd* [1962] Ch 21, 31.

[290] *Bradford Old Bank Ltd v Sutcliffe* [1918] 2 KB 833.

6.3.4.5 *Contractual Set-Off and Exclusion of Set-Off*

Although in many circumstances a lender might be sufficiently protected by relying on set-off which arises under the general law, it is likely to wish to provide in the agreement for the precise application of set-off to the transaction. This is as much in the interests of certainty as in order to extend or reduce the application of set-off, although this may also be desired. However, as can be seen even from the brief discussion above, the scope of independent and transaction set-off or the application of set-off to a particular transaction is not always absolutely clear, and providing for the precise operation of set-off in the agreement prevents any possible dispute as to whether set-off is available.

Contractual set-off can also be used to provide for set-off to occur where otherwise it would not. For example, an agreement can provide that unconnected debts between the same parties can be set off in such a way that the amount payable is reduced, either immediately or at a later date at the option of one party.[291] This is significantly beyond the application of independent set-off, where such debts can only be set off once litigation has commenced. Independent and transaction set-off do not constitute payment, but contractual set-off can do so immediately (depending on the terms of the contract). Thus, when combined with netting, contractual set-off is a useful tool to reduce the number of settlements and exposure risk.

Netting comes in various forms, which are closely related to but distinct from set-off.[292] It encompasses various contractual provisions which change the nature of the parties' obligations to each other, either to have the effect of set-off or so that set-off (contractually provided for) can take place. Novation netting is an agreement whereby all contracts between the parties are consolidated into one single contract, with one payment obligation.[293] Usually, as each new contract is entered into, it is consolidated with the single contract so that there is only ever one balance payable. The actual time of payment is provided for separately by the contract. One use of this technique is where there is a clearing house in a market. The clearing house rules usually provide that each time two members of the market trade with each other, each transaction is novated to the clearing house (so that the clearing house then has two contracts, one with each party) and consolidated with each party's other obligations to and rights against the clearing house so that only one balance is payable either to or from the clearing house.[294]

Settlement netting relates purely to payment, so that when amounts become due from and to two or more parties, they are netted out so that only one sum is payable. Thus it is distinct from novation netting, which can apply to executory contracts. The purpose of settlement netting is to deal with the rather specific risk that A will pay the gross amount to B, but B will not be able to pay the gross amount due back to A: the operation of settlement netting means that A's risk of B's non-payment is limited to the net amount.[295]

---

[291] Derham: Set-Off, 741.

[292] Goode: Credit and Security, 7-17–7-21.

[293] To the extent that the contracts are executory, only those with the same payment date can be amalgamated; accrued obligations can be combined into one balance payable on a specified date.

[294] See description of rules of the London Clearing House (LCH Clearnet Ltd) in Goode: Credit and Security, 7-19. LCH Clearnet Ltd assumes the risk that a member might default on payment and become insolvent, and therefore requires members to post margin with it as security.

[295] *Enron Europe Ltd (In Administration) v Revenue and Customs Commissioners* [2006] EWHC 824 (Ch) [22].

It is often used in the settlement of payment through a clearing house, although, as will be seen, novation netting is a safer method in the event of the insolvency of one of the members.

Close-out netting is the most significant type of netting in terms of protecting against credit risk. It is a vital component of the ISDA Master Agreement, which governs most derivatives transactions, as well as of repos and securities lending transactions. Its purpose is to reduce all present, future and contingent indebtedness to a single net balance in the event of a party's insolvency: this means that the exposure of the other party is limited irrespective of the applicable insolvency laws, which otherwise might allow an insolvency officer to elect not to perform the insolvent's side of the bargain, leaving the other party as an unsecured creditor.[296] Given the wide scope of insolvency set-off under English law, the functions of close-out netting are to turn non-monetary obligations into monetary obligations (so that insolvency set-off can operate), to avoid the uncertainty caused by the valuation of future or contingent debts by a liquidator or administrator, and to avoid market fluctuations which may apply between the onset of insolvency and the time at which set-off is actually calculated. Close-out netting provisions typically provide that on the occurrence of a specified event (either insolvency or default or some other such event) the contracts between the parties are terminated or accelerated so that money claims become due either way. The calculation of the amount due on non-monetary obligations is normally carried out using the usual principle of contractual damages: the difference between the contract price and the market price. These money claims are then set off so that only a net sum is payable.[297] Close-out netting provisions are extensively used in the financial markets and are found in many master agreements governing such transactions.[298]

Another way in which the scope of set-off which arises by operation of law can be extended by contract is to provide that set-off will occur even where there is no mutuality of parties. Thus, a lender could have the right to set off a claim owed to party B against the obligation of borrower A.

There is no problem with the effectiveness of any of these provisions outside of insolvency, since parties have freedom of contract.[299] If, however, a party becomes insolvent, as a general rule any contractual terms providing for set-off which operate more widely than insolvency set-off are unenforceable. Further, any attempt to rely on them may be set aside as a preference or a transaction at an undervalue.[300] Insolvency set-off is mandatory and parties cannot contract out of it.[301] Mutuality of parties is required for insolvency set-off. Where this exists, however, insolvency set-off is very wide in scope, and includes unrelated, future and contingent claims. Therefore, the main situation where contractual set-off is

---

[296] The laws on close-out netting vary considerably from country to country; UNIDROIT has recently adopted a set of Principles on the Operation of Close-Out Netting in order to provide an international legislative standard.

[297] See definitions of close-out netting in FCD, art 2(1)(n); FCARs, reg 3.

[298] For example, Global Master Securities Lending Agreement 2010, cl 11 (securities lending); Global Master Repurchase Agreement 2011, cl 10 (repos); ISDA Master Agreement, s 6(e)(i).

[299] There are some limits, however, on the effectiveness of set-off against third parties: see Goode: Credit and Security, 7-27–7-29. For example, no new set-off (contractual or otherwise) can arise between debtor and creditor once the debtor has had notice that the debt has been assigned: see 9.2.2.3.

[300] Provisions which do fall within insolvency set-off cannot have this result: see *Re Washington Diamond Mining Co* [1893] 3 Ch 95, 104. See Derham: Set-Off, 16.06.

[301] *National Westminster Bank Ltd v Halesowen Presswork & Assemblies Ltd* [1972] AC 785.

likely to be unenforceable is where it is sought to set off debts where there is no mutuality. The mandatory nature of insolvency set-off is discussed further in the next section.

Set-off can also work to the disadvantage of a lender in that the borrower may seek to rely on it to avoid making repayments in full or at all. Obviously, if a cross-claim exists the lender will eventually have to pay the borrower, but it may not wish to have to do so immediately. For example, the lender may have itself to make back-to-back payments on its own arrangements for financing the loan, such as a securitisation, or it may wish to have the ability to challenge the cross-claim as a defendant rather than as a claimant,[302] or it may wish to take away from the borrower any incentive to make spurious cross-claims. Alternatively, if the debt obligation is transferable, there may be doubt as to whether it can be transferred free from equities, including set-off.[303] Thus the lender may wish to exclude the operation of set-off by contractual terms, so that payment will take place in full.

Outside insolvency, there now seems little doubt that such a clause is effective.[304] Although the width of application of the exclusion will depend in each case on the exact wording of the term, independent set-off can be excluded as well as transaction set-off, and it seems that there is no policy objection to this.[305] This is also the case where the exclusion is by reason of the CREST rules (incorporated into the contract):[306] this is particularly important as the operation of the CREST system depends upon the immediate completion of bargains without regard to any other transactions between the parties.[307] There is, however, a presumption that parties to an agreement do not intend to abandon remedies for breach which arise by operation of law, and clear words must be used to rebut this.[308]

Generally, therefore, set-off cannot be excluded without clear words, although in deciding whether a more general clause (which does not use the word 'set-off') excludes it, the whole contractual context will be considered.[309] Despite this, it is clear that where a debt security is sought to be transferred through the CREST system an exclusion of set-off will be incorporated even without express words.[310]

---

[302] There are great advantages to being a defendant: most notably, the defendant has, at least temporarily, the money that is being claimed. Further, if a cross-claim cannot be set up as a defence, the lender can obtain summary judgment under Civil Procedure Rules, r 24 which is quicker and much less expensive than a defended claim. A similar advantage is obtained by the payee of a negotiable instrument, in that only cross-claims which amount to a total or partial failure of consideration can be defences to a claim on such an instrument by an immediate party: see Goode: Commercial Law, 561–62.

[303] This is unlikely to be the case where the debt obligation is a bearer security (a negotiable instrument), but will be the case where the transfer is by way of assignment, and may be the case when there is a novation: see 9.2.4.2.5. Therefore issues of stock usually include a clause excluding set-off (see *Hilger Analytical Ltd v Rank Precision Industries Ltd* [1984] BCLC 301), and the CREST rules provide that a security traded through the system must be 'transferable free from any equity, set-off or counterclaim between the issuer and the original or any intermediate holder of the security' (r 7 3.2). These issues are discussed in more detail in chapter 9.

[304] *Hong Kong and Shanghai Banking Corporation v Kloeckner & Co AG* [1990] 2 QB 514, 521; *Coca-Cola Financial Corp v Finsat International Ltd (The Ira)* [1998] QB 43.

[305] *The Ira*, ibid, 52.

[306] *Re Kaupthing Singer and Friedlander Ltd (In Administration)* [2009] EWHC 740 (Ch).

[307] Ibid, [19]. See 9.2.6.3.

[308] *Gilbert-Ash (Northern) Ltd v Modern Engineering (Bristol) Ltd* [1974] AC 689, 717.

[309] *BOC Group plc v Centeon LLC* [1999] CLC 497, 503. For a full discussion see Derham: Set-Off, 5.78–5.99.

[310] See 9.2.6.3.

6.3.4.6 *Insolvency Set-Off*

6.3.4.6.1 The Limits and Operation of Insolvency Set-Off[311]

Insolvency set-off applies both on liquidation and in administration where the administrator chooses to make a distribution.[312] The idea is that an account is taken of mutual dealings between the insolvency company and a creditor to produce a net balance: if a debit balance, the creditor may only prove for that balance in the liquidation or administration.

Insolvency set-off is mandatory and as such operates automatically.[313] This means that there needs to be a specific cut-off date early on in the insolvency process when it (theoretically) operates. However, the actual accounting process and the actual amounts to be taken into the calculation will not be known until later, when the liquidator has been appointed and is able to do the necessary work.[314] Two principles[315] deal with this problem: the retro-activity principle and the hindsight principle. The former deems the account to be taken at the 'date of the account' even though it does not actually happen till later. The latter means that the liquidator or administrator can take into account events that occur after the date of the account when calculating the balance due.[316]

Two specific issues are of particular interest in the context of this chapter. The first is the inclusion of contingent debts in insolvency set-off.[317] Contingent debts are provable in a liquidation or administration,[318] and there is a procedure for estimating their value, since otherwise the process would be unduly protracted pending the contingencies eventuating. Contingent claims by the company (against the creditor) are included, although if the account results in a balance payable to the company by the creditor, this does not need to be paid until it becomes due, if it ever does.[319] The liquidator or administrator estimates the value of a contingent claim, taking into account both the possible amount of the debt and the probability of it arising.[320]

The second issue is whether the mutuality required for insolvency set-off is destroyed by the presence of a charge-back. A charge-back, it will be recalled, is a charge taken by a lender over a debt owed by it, usually a credit balance in an account held with it. It might be thought that such a charge is not required, since the lender is in any event protected by set-off, but despite this many lenders do take such a charge. One reason for this is that the

---

[311] For detailed discussion see Goode: Credit and Security, 7-75–7-103.

[312] The relevant rule in liquidation is r 4.90 of the Insolvency Rules 1986, and, in administration, r 2.85. Amendments in 2005 brought the two regimes in line as far as possible, although there are significant, though inescapable, differences: see Goode: Credit and Security, 7-85.

[313] *Stein v Blake* [1996] 1 AC 243, 254–55; *Gye v McIntyre* (1991) 171 CLR 609, 622 (HC Aust). The mandatory nature of insolvency set-off is discussed at 6.3.4.6.2.

[314] The process is even more protracted in an administration.

[315] Articulated by Hoffmann LJ (as he then was) in *MS Fashions Ltd. v Bank of Credit and Commerce International SA (No 2)* [1993] Ch 425, 432–33.

[316] Goode: Credit and Security, 7-79 and 7-80.

[317] rr 4.90(4)(c) and 2.85(4)(c). As to what is included in contingent debts, see *Re Nortel Companies* [2013] UKSC 52.

[318] Insolvency Rules 1986, r 12(3)(1).

[319] Ibid, r 2.85(4) and (8) and r 4.90(4) and (8).

[320] rr 2.81 and 2.85(5) (administration) and rr 4.86 and 4.90(5) (liquidation). Under current practice, an office holder will often wait for a contingency to occur, but this is likely to change in the light of the decision of the Court of Appeal in *In re Danka Business Systems plc* [2013] EWCA Civ 92. See M Cohen and G Jacobs, 'Contingent Creditors: Are Liquidators Going Down in their Estimation?' [2013] *Corporate Rescue and Insolvency* 119.

lender wishes to have a choice whether and when to enforce the security, rather than having it operate automatically by insolvency set-off. A lender might wish to have this choice, for example, where the debt and the credit balance are in different currencies and it is sought to exploit the varying exchange rates to the lender's advantage.[321] However, this choice will not be available unless mutuality is destroyed by the charge.

Where the solvent party has security for a debt, there are two views as to the position. On one view, insolvency set-off operates automatically unless the secured creditor has already enforced its security by the onset of insolvency proceedings.[322] On the other view, the secured creditor has a choice either to enforce its security, in which case insolvency set-off will not apply, or to prove in the liquidation.[323] On this view, the problem is that at the date of the account it is not known whether the creditor will enforce the security or prove in the liquidation. However, if the creditor does enforce the security by the time of the actual taking of the account then the liquidator, by application of the hindsight principle, must conclude that the mutuality is broken and automatic insolvency set-off does not apply. One could go further and say that the mere potential ability of the creditor to enforce the security means that the mutuality is broken at the date of the account, but that this lack of mutuality can be reversed if the creditor makes it clear by the time the account is actually taken that it intends to prove and not to rely on its security. The position in relation to charge-backs has been left open by authority. Hoffmann LJ and the Court of Appeal in *MS Fashions Ltd v Bank of Credit and Commerce International SA (No 2)*[324] appeared to take the view (in a slightly different context) that a charge-back did not break the mutuality or prevent set-off. However, Lord Hoffmann in *BCCI (No 8)*[325] left the point open, and did not appear to have a firm view in support of the views expressed in *MS Fashions*. There is strong academic and practitioner opinion to support the view that mutuality is destroyed, at least unless the creditor chooses to submit a proof, and this view seems preferable.[326]

6.3.4.6.2 The Mandatory and Exclusive Nature of Insolvency Set-Off

It will be recalled that it is a basic principle of insolvency law that the insolvent company's assets are to be distributed *pari passu* to its unsecured creditors.[327] This principle, however, applies to such a limited extent in practice that many commentators have suggested that it

---

[321] M Evans, 'Triple Cocktail Becomes a Single Malt' (1998) 13 *Journal of International Banking Law* 115, 116; R Calnan, 'The Insolvent Bank and Security Over Deposits' [1996] *Journal of International Banking and Financial Law* 174, 177.

[322] Goode: Corporate Insolvency; L Ho, 'Book Review' [2008] *Journal of International Banking and Financial Law* 426. See also *Totty, Moss & Segal on Insolvency* (London, Sweet & Maxwell, looseleaf) H10-09.

[323] *Re Norman Holding Co Ltd* [1991] 1 WLR 10; *Stewart v Scottish Widows and Life Assurance Society plc* [2005] EWHC 1831 (QB) [185] (appealed [2006] EWCA Civ 999, but not on this point). See also *Re Bank of Credit and Commerce International SA (In Liquidation) (No 8)* [1996] Ch 245, 256; L Gullifer and P Pichonnaz, *Set-Off in Arbitration and Commercial Transactions* (Oxford, Oxford University Press, 2014) 12.86; Derham: Set-Off, 6.178.

[324] [1993] Ch 425, 438, 446.

[325] [1998] AC 214, 225.

[326] Derham: Set-Off, 16.83–16.88; M Evans, 'Triple Cocktail Becomes a Single Malt' [1998] *Journal of International Banking Law* 115; C Farner, 'Charges over Bank Accounts' [1998] *Journal of International Banking and Financial Law* 85; R Calnan, 'The Insolvent Bank and Security Over Deposits' [1996] *Journal of International Banking and Financial Law* 185.

[327] See 3.3.1.

does not exist,[328] or that it should be reformulated.[329] Any creditor with a proprietary claim falls outside the principle (an alternative formulation of this is that since the asset is no longer owned by the company, the principle does not apply to it), and there are significant statutory exceptions.[330] Insolvency set-off can be seen as another exception to the principle, in that it enables some unsecured creditors to recover the whole or part of their claim in full.[331] Whether it is justifiable to have such an exception is discussed in detail below.[332] However, because it is an exception to the principle, its limits are clearly defined by statute, as discussed above.

Where a contractual arrangement falls outside the boundaries of insolvency set-off, it is vulnerable to being declared void in the insolvency of a party as contrary to the *pari passu* principle or the anti-deprivation principle.[333] The *pari passu* principle operates regardless of the intention of either the insolvent party or the contractual counterparties, and there is no requirement that the contractual provision is triggered by the insolvency.[334] Since it relates to the distribution made to creditors, it applies when this is the overriding purpose of insolvency proceedings, that is, to liquidation and to administration once a notice of distribution has been issued.[335] Any contractual arrangements which have their effect before the company enters liquidation, or before a notice of distribution is issued by an administrator (collectively, 'the relevant date'), will not be rendered void by the principle.[336] Because of the wide scope of insolvency set-off, it is relatively unlikely that any contractual set-off would fall foul of the *pari passu* principle unless it provided for set-off between non-mutual parties.

An example of this is the case of *British Eagle International Air Lines Ltd v Compagnie Nationale Air France*.[337] In that case, amounts due to and from airlines which were members of a clearing house (IATA) were netted out by the clearing house each month, at which point the clearing house would pay or receive the net balances to or from the airlines (a form of settlement netting). British Eagle became insolvent and was owed a sum by Air France. The question was whether the liquidator could claim this amount in full, or whether it could only claim the net balance from IATA, taking into account the sums that British Eagle owed other airlines.

The crucial question was whether British Eagle's claim to payment was against Air France directly (in which case the arrangements netting it off against the claims of other clearing house members contravened the *pari passu* principle)[338] or whether British Eagle merely

---

[328] R Mokal, 'Priority as Pathology: The Pari Passu Myth' (2000) 60 *Cambridge Law Journal* 581 (esp 616–21); P Wood, 'The Bankruptcy Ladder of Priorities' (2013) 14(3) *Business Law International* 209.

[329] L Ho, 'The Principle Against Divestiture in Insolvency Revisited: Fraser v Oystertec' [2004] 19 *Journal of International Banking and Financial Law* 54. 'Unfair' unequal distribution before insolvency is dealt with by Insolvency Act 1986, s 239, which is discussed at 3.3.2.2.

[330] These are discussed at 3.3.1.2.

[331] See 6.3.4.1.

[332] 6.3.4.6.3.

[333] See 3.3.2.2 and 3.3.2.1.2.

[334] *Revenue and Customs Commissioners v Football League Ltd* [2012] EWHC 1372 (Ch) [65].

[335] Under r 2.95.

[336] *Revenue and Customs Commissioners v Football League Ltd* [2012] EWHC 1372 (Ch) [76]–[90]. Such arrangements may, however, constitute a preference or a transaction at an undervalue: see 3.3.2.1.1 and 3.3.2.2.

[337] [1975] 1 WLR 758.

[338] The decision is now seen as a clear application of the *pari passu* principle rather than the anti-deprivation principle: *Belmont Park Investments Pty Ltd v BNY Corporate Trustee Services Ltd* [2011] UKSC 38.

had a claim directly against IATA, after taking into account all the debits and credits owed to and from other airlines. The majority favoured the former view, while the minority took the latter view, with the consequence that payment to British Eagle of the net balance would not contravene the principle, since IATA could set off against sums it owed to British Eagle claims it had against the insolvent company.

There are several ways to structure the transaction so that British Eagle only ever has a claim against IATA. One is for the rules of the clearing house to provide that all inter-member claims are immediately novated to the clearing house (novation netting).[339] Another method, which has been successful in Australia, is for the rules to provide that no claims ever arose between members but only between members and the clearing house.[340] Concerns about the invalidity of settlement netting in clearing house arrangements in insolvency (bilateral settlement netting would fall within insolvency set-off and would therefore be valid) have led to statutory intervention, so that settlement netting arrangements in financial markets are statutorily protected on insolvency.[341]

Absent such contractual workarounds, a provision for non-mutual set-off would be invalid on insolvency.[342] Such a provision could take one of two forms, both of which would contravene the *pari passu* principle. One is that a liability of the insolvent company (C) to A should be set off against the liability of A to B.[343] The other is that a liability of A to C should be set off against the liability of the insolvent company to B.[344] A close-out netting provision,[345] by itself,[346] is relatively unlikely to violate either the *pari passu* principle or the anti-deprivation principle, since it will have the same effect as the operation of insolvency set-off, which applies to future and contingent debts as well as present debts. However, obligations to do something other than pay money (such as delivery obligations) cannot be set off in insolvency against money obligations,[347] and so to the extent that a close-out netting provision has this effect, it could be said not to be protected by being within insolvency set-off.[348] Absent any close-out netting provision, the obligation to deliver is merely contractual unless property in the items to be delivered has already passed. If it is

---

[339] Goode: Credit and Security, 7-92. Such an arrangement would be unlikely to appeal to a body such as the IATA as it would then bear the risk of a member's insolvency itself. Such a body would be unlikely to be able to call for margin as security, unlike the London Clearing House (see n 294).

[340] *Ansett Australia Holdings Ltd v International Air Transport Association* [2008] HCA 3 (HC Aust).

[341] Companies Act 1989, s 159 and Financial Markets and Insolvency (Settlement Finality) Regulations 1999, reg 14, enacting the 1998 Settlement Finality Directive (EC 98/26), art 3(2).

[342] *Re Bank of Credit and Commerce International SA (In Liquidation) (No 8)* [1996] Ch 245, 272–73.

[343] This can be illustrated by a rather basic example: C owes £50 to A. A owes £50 to B. If the two debts can be 'set off' then the effect is that A does not have to pay B. A therefore obtains the benefit of £50, rather than merely receiving the proportion it would have received if it had proved in C's liquidation. In effect, B is paying C's debt, but, when C is insolvent, this could be seen as contrary to *pari passu*, since if B wished to make a gift of £50 to C, it should become part of C's assets and be available to all of C's creditors.

[344] In this example, A owes £50 to C and C owes £50 to B. This time, A does not have to pay C, and B forgoes its payment, that is, 'pays' C's debt to A. Again, on C's insolvency, the *pari passu* principle could be said to prescribe that B's gift should be available to all of C's creditors.

[345] See 6.3.4.5.

[346] Provisions which are used in the ISDA Master Agreement to have the same protective effect as close-out netting, such as the use of a master agreement and the 'flawed asset' cl 2(a)(iii), might be thought to be more vulnerable: see the discussion in Goode: Credit and Security, 7-93.

[347] See Goode: Credit and Security, 7-86.

[348] R Derham, 'Set-Off and Netting of Foreign Exchange Contracts in the Liquidation of a Counterparty: Part 2. Netting' [1991] *Journal of Business Law* 536, 40.

the insolvent party that is obliged to deliver, an insolvency officer could choose to breach (or disclaim) the contract,[349] or to perform it. Breach or disclaimer would turn the obligation into a money claim, which could be the subject of set-off, but performance would mean that the solvent counterparty would be obliged to pay its money obligation in full. A close-out netting provision effectively takes from the insolvency officer the choice of performance, and imposes a solution similar to that on breach or disclaimer. While this could, theoretically, be a deprivation[350] it is unlikely to fall foul of the anti-deprivation principle for two reasons. First, the 'deprivation' is for full value, which is a well-recognised exception to the anti-deprivation principle;[351] this is also a good reason why the provision does not offend the *pari passu* principle. Second, there are good commercial reasons for the provision, namely increase in certainty and reduction in credit and systemic risk: the anti-deprivation principle therefore does not apply.[352]

To the extent that close-out netting provisions might be seen as violating either principle, such provisions in certain types of contracts are rendered valid in insolvency by statute.[353]

As mentioned above, set-off can also be excluded contractually for various reasons.[354] However, when the borrower becomes insolvent, the exclusion is ineffective.[355] This is strange, in that, where the borrower is insolvent, set-off almost invariably operates to the advantage of the creditor, so by excluding it the creditor is swelling the assets available for the unsecured creditors and taking its chance by proving for the full amount in the insolvency.[356] The justifications for the rule appear to be that the insolvency set-off legislation is beneficial for the orderly administration of insolvent estates[357] and that, if the creditor did not pay, the liquidation proceedings might be held up by lengthy and costly litigation against it.[358] This justification, weak even on its face,[359] does not counterbalance the freedom of contract argument allowing a creditor to exclude set-off if it wishes.[360]

---

[349] An administrator has no power to disclaim.

[350] Derham: Set-Off, 16.38. Derham points out that this will not be objectionable if there is only one contract (relying on *Shipton, Anderson & Co (1927) Ltd v Micks, Lambert & Co* [1936] 2 All ER 1032), but might be objectionable where the close-out netting provisions relate to a number of contracts. This issue may not arise where there is a master agreement clause.

[351] *Borland's Trustee v Steel Bros & Co Ltd* [1901] 1 Ch 279.

[352] See 3.3.2.1.2.

[353] Companies Act 1989, Part VII s 159 in relation to 'market contracts' and the default rules of recognised investment exchanges and clearing houses; Financial Markets and Insolvency (Settlement Finality) Regulations 1999, reg 14 in relation to systems used for settlement and payment of transfers of securities; FCARs, reg 12 in relation to financial collateral arrangements. Carve-outs such as this are justified by the benefits of set-off and netting in the financial markets: see 6.3.4.6.3.

[354] See 6.3.4.5.

[355] *National Westminster Bank Ltd v Halesowen Presswork and Assemblies Ltd* [1972] AC 785; *John Dee Group Ltd v WMH (21) Ltd* [1998] BCC 972, 976.

[356] Take the following examples: (1) lender (L) owes borrower (B) £100, B owes L £200. If B is insolvent and insolvency set-off operates, L can prove for £100 and is released from its debt (so gets 'paid' £100 and pays nothing). If insolvency set-off does not operate, L must pay B £100 and prove for £200. (2) L owes B £200, B owes L £100. If insolvency set-off operates, L must pay £100 and is released from £100 of its debt (so gets 'paid' £100). If insolvency set-off does not operate, L must pay £200 and prove for £100.

[357] *National Westminster Bank Ltd v Halesowen Presswork and Assemblies Ltd* [1972] AC 785, 808–09.

[358] *Re Maxwell Communications Corp plc (No 2)* [1993] 1 WLR 1402, 1411.

[359] See the critique in Derham: Set-Off, 6.112. The quantification of claims in insolvency is complicated whether or not there is set-off, especially now that contingent claims (which must be quantified) can be set off in both directions.

[360] A term which excluded set-off outside insolvency would, in any case, only operate within insolvency if it was clear that it was intended to do so: *National Westminster Bank Ltd v Halesowen Presswork and Assemblies Ltd* [1972] AC 785.

Further, in one specific situation there is a strong argument for allowing such exclusion. This is where an insolvent company, in the course of restructuring under an agreed moratorium with creditors, opens a current account with a bank which has lent to it in order to pay in its earnings. If the bank did not agree to exclude insolvency set-off, all credits to that account would go to reduce the company's indebtedness to the bank, and would not be available for creditors generally.[361] For this reason the Cork Committee on Insolvency Law and Policy recommended that the prohibition on contracting out of insolvency set-off be reversed.[362] However, no legislation has resulted from this.

6.3.4.6.3 Policy Justifications for Insolvency Set-Off

As has been mentioned earlier, insolvency set-off is a significant exception to the *pari passu* principle of insolvency law that all creditors within a particular class should be treated alike.

The policy justifications for this are varied. It can be argued that, since the parties have given credit to each other outside of insolvency on the basis that they would be able to rely on set-off to ensure payment, it would be unfair to deprive the creditor of this benefit on the insolvency of the other party.[363] One problem with this argument is that, to the extent that the set-off relied on is contractual (rather than independent or transaction set-off), reliance on it is no different from reliance on any other contractual term which seeks to give a creditor an advantage in insolvency. A right to set-off is not a proprietary right like a security interest:[364] secured creditors are clearly in a different class, and the line between proprietary and personal rights is (relatively) easily drawn and justified. A line between contractual rights which survive insolvency and those which do not is both less easy to draw and harder to justify. Further, many contractual provisions (such as close-out netting) are designed merely to protect the creditor in the event of the debtor's insolvency, and so an argument based on reliance on the use of set-off outside insolvency does not apply. If the reliance argument applies to a creditor who has, by the use of contractual terms, attempted to put himself in a better position than other creditors on the insolvency of the debtor, then this argument should result in all such bargains being effective in insolvency. In fact, the reverse is true: a desire to improve a creditor's position on insolvency is a reason for transfers being set aside.[365]

---

[361] This problem can be avoided by opening the current account with a bank other than the original financier, but such a bank has less incentive to take on an insolvent client.

[362] *Report of the Review Committee of Insolvency Law and Practice* (Cork Report) (Cmnd 8558, 1982), para 1342.

[363] Goode: Corporate Insolvency, 9-01.

[364] This is clearly explained in a Singaporean case of *Electro-Magnetic (S) Ltd (Under Judicial Management) v Development Bank of Singapore Ltd* [1994] 1 SLR 734, 738 (Sing CA), where LP Thean JA said: 'A security over a property consists of some real or proprietary interest, legal or equitable, in the property as distinguished from a personal right or claim thereon. A right of set-off is a personal right; it is a right given by contract or by law to set one claim against the other and arrive at a balance.' See also Goode: Credit and Security, 1-20, the 2nd edition of which was cited with approval in that case. When Lord Hoffmann in *Stein v Blake* [1996] AC 243, 251 described insolvency set-off as 'a form of security', he was clearly describing its functional use rather than classifying it as a security interest. However, see now the Canadian Supreme Court decision in *Caisse Populaire Desjardins de l'Est de Drummond v Canada* [2009] SCC 29, where a majority of the court held that a right to set off an amount deposited with the lender bank against the loan was held to be a 'security interest' within the meaning of the Income Taxes Act. This decision turned on the particular wording of the contractual provisions, and also (arguably) on the functional view of 'security interest' which applies in the Canadian Personal Property Securities Acts. See also Goode: Credit and Security, 1-21.

[365] As transactions at an undervalue under Insolvency Act 1986, s 238 and as preferences under s 239 Insolvency Act 1986: see 3.3.2.

The argument is stronger, in a way, in relation to set-off which would have arisen outside insolvency by operation of law: reliance on this surviving insolvency is, perhaps, more justifiable, although if the law did not allow set-off on insolvency (as is the case in many jurisdictions)[366] parties would be expected to know this and not to rely on pre-insolvency law. Further, in many cases the possibility of set-off, or even of there being a cross-claim, is not in the parties' minds at the time of entering into the transaction, so that the reliance argument does not apply.[367] Thus, we should look for other justifications for insolvency set-off to bolster the reliance argument.

A related justification is that if an insolvent company can receive the full amount of a claim due from another person, it is only fair that that person should be able to receive its claim against the company in full.[368] This justification was noted by Lord Hoffmann in his masterly analysis of insolvency set-off in *Stein v Blake*,[369] where he pointed out that, for example, in *Forster v Wilson*,[370] Parke B said that the purpose of insolvency set-off was 'to do substantial justice between the parties'. It is difficult to see how, in the absence of reliance (which is discussed above), it is any fairer to pay a person with a cross-claim in full than any other creditor. The amount which that creditor receives over and above the proportion that all unsecured creditors receive is an amount that those unsecured creditors do not receive, so the 'fairness' in favour of the cross-claimant is balanced out by the unfairness to the other creditors.[371] Lord Hoffmann also pointed out, perhaps by way of justification, that the rule was of extreme longevity in that it had been part of the law of England since the time of Queen Elizabeth I.[372]

Another justification, which is articulated by the House of Lords in *National Westminster Bank Ltd v Halesowen Presswork and Assemblies Ltd*, is that insolvency set-off simplifies the liquidation process so that the estate of an insolvent company can be administered in a 'proper and orderly way'.[373] Unfortunately, the decision gives no further explanation of what is meant by this, but it can be surmised that the reduction of claims to net claims would relieve the liquidator's burden of having to deal with the gross payments. However, even to administer the net claims requires the liquidator to value each claim before set-off, and it is difficult to see that a great deal of time and costs are saved, especially now that contingent claims can be set off. It should be remembered that the effect of insolvency set-off is that other creditors who do not have the benefit of set-off lose out as the proportion of their own claims which are recoverable is reduced. Thus the justification for insolvency set-off needs to be strong, and it is hard to see that the saving in costs and time for a liquidator outweighs the disadvantages to the other creditors.

A further, and much more significant, justification is that set-off on insolvency is critical to the management of risk in the financial markets, as well as more generally in the commercial world. Philip Wood points out that the effect in reducing exposure is huge,[374]

---

[366] See Wood: Set-Off and Netting, 1-015 for a summary of insolvency set-off and netting worldwide.

[367] Derham: Set-Off, 6.21.

[368] *National Westminster Bank Ltd v Halesowen Presswork and Assemblies Ltd* [1972] AC 785, 813 (Lord Cross).

[369] [1996] 1 AC 243, 251.

[370] (1843) 12 M & W 191, 204.

[371] See Derham: Set-Off, 6.20, who points out that the existence of a cross-claim may be wholly fortuitous and not the result of forethought on the part of the benefited party at all.

[372] [1996] 1 AC 243, 251.

[373] [1972] AC 785, 809 (Lord Simon).

[374] 95% in the foreign exchange markets.

and without it the risk of systemic collapse, with the concomitant cost to the public purse, is greatly increased.[375] One effect of this reduction in risk is that less collateral has to be held against exposure, both in relation to individual transactions, which frees up capital and improves the liquidity and capacity of the markets,[376] and also in relation to the general exposure of banks as capital adequacy requirements are reduced.[377] Wood thus argues that 'the economic advantages of insolvency set-off seem overwhelming'.[378] The question is whether the undoubted advantages in the financial markets outweigh the disadvantages to unsecured creditors elsewhere in the commercial world.

If the justifications for insolvency set-off do not obviously outweigh the disadvantages, should it be permitted? The answer is probably that it should be allowed in certain circumstances, but the difficulty is drawing the lines around those circumstances. One way is to provide by statute that certain contractual provisions which limit market risk are valid, within the context of that particular market, which has been done in the cases of settlement of market transactions and financial collateral arrangements.[379] Apart from such provisions, the limits on set-off in insolvency under English law are in theory the *pari passu* and anti-deprivation principles. In practice, this broadly means that any contractual provisions for set-off which are wider in scope than the statutory limits of insolvency set-off are unenforceable on insolvency. These statutory limits are now quite extensive, having been widened by legislation over the years, but it is hard to rationalise these limits on the basis of any of the justifications of insolvency set-off discussed above.

6.4 Contractual Rights Against Third Parties

As will be clear from the above discussion, contractual rights against the borrower have one major drawback: on the insolvency of the borrower the lender will only be able to prove in the insolvency for a fraction of the amount due (set-off, as explained above, is an exception to this). One way of overcoming this problem is for the lender to have a contractual

---

[375] Wood: Set-Off and Netting, 1-012. To give an idea of scale, in 2012 the Gross Market Value of outstanding over-the-counter (OTC) derivatives products was $24.7 trillion whereas after netting it was $3.6 trillion, 14.3% of Gross Market Value and of 0.6% of Notional Value (source: ISDA OTC Derivatives Market Analysis end-year 2012, based on data from Bank for International Settlements semiannual review and ISDA research (June 2013)). When Lehman Brothers collapsed, it owed £400 billion to counterparties of credit default swaps, but, after netting, the total amount actually payable was $5.2 billion: see *The Future Regulation of Derivatives Markets: Is the EU on the Right Track?*, House of Lords 10th Report 2009–10 (31 March 2010), 20, citing Evidence from the Association for Financial Markets in Europe (AFME), British Banking Association (BBA) and International Swaps and Derivatives Association (ISDA), para 4.4 (annexed to report at annex 1)).

[376] The use of central counterparties has now become compulsory for certain derivatives transactions (see EMIR). The posting of collateral by both parties to a transaction is now compulsory, but the use of netting in relation to transactions entered into through the same clearing house will reduce the amount required considerably: see L Gullifer, 'Compulsory Central Clearing of OTC Derivatives: The Changing Face of the Provision of Collateral' in L Gullifer and S Vogenauer (eds), *English and European Perspectives in Contract and Commercial Law* (Oxford, Hart Publishing, 2014).

[377] It is now thought, however, that larger capital adequacy requirements would assist in preventing a financial collapse such as that which happened in 2007–09, and the Basel III framework requires more and better quality capital in banks: see 2.3.1.4.

[378] Wood: Set-Off and Netting, 1-012.

[379] 6.3.4.6.2.

right against a third party who is more likely to remain solvent.[380] The lender can also take security over the assets of the third party, or take other steps to protect itself against the third party's credit risk.[381] There are two main categories of third parties: those who are connected to the borrower and who give the protection without payment, such as a parent company or a director, and those whose do so for a fee, such as a financial company or bank whose business is providing credit protection.

There are other related benefits which accrue, some to the borrower and some to the lender. First, in a bond issue or securitisation, the fact that such protection exists will make the securities more marketable and also more valuable.[382] Second, the existence of such protection may mean that the borrower can borrow on more advantageous terms. Third, where the person giving the credit protection has some control over the behaviour of the borrower, for example a parent company or a director, the existence of the credit protection aligns the interests of that person with those of the lender and helps to ensure that the borrower does not conduct itself in a way which makes it less likely that the loan will be repaid.[383] This is most graphically illustrated in the case of small private companies, where the directors are a small number of natural persons. If a director gives a guarantee of a loan or overdraft, backed up with a charge over his or her home, he or she has a large incentive to take steps to make sure that the lending bank is repaid. Fourth, a protection right against a third party is useful if the lender wishes to exercise rights of set-off against that third party in any circumstances, for example, in order to net all the accounts of a group company or in the event of the insolvency of both the borrower and the third party.[384] Fifth, for tax reasons the borrower may be a particular member of a group of companies; that member then on-lends the money to a trading company that really needs it: that latter company then guarantees the original loan.[385] Sixth, in certain transactions the creditor or lender will wish to know that it is getting paid irrespective of any underlying dispute over whether payment is due: this gives that party a procedural advantage so that it becomes the defendant in any subsequent litigation rather than the claimant.[386] It also means that payment is made on the due date (when the creditor or lender may need the money to pay another party) rather than being postponed while the dispute is resolved. Third parties who give credit protection for a fee sometimes prefer this sort of structure, since they know that they will have to pay under any circumstances, rather than having the uncertainty of waiting until a dispute is resolved. Since the third party will normally have a right of indemnity against the debtor, upon which it can call immediately on payment to the creditor, the third party will only be out of its money for a short time. Examples of this structure are performance bonds (also called demand guarantees) and standby credits.

---

[380] This is neatly put by Wood: Loans and Bonds, 18-002, who says: 'Guarantees are usually taken to provide a second pocket to pay if the first should be empty.' See also B Adler and M Kahan, 'The Technology of Creditor Protection' (2013) 161 *University of Pennsylvania Law Review* 1773.

[381] For a description of techniques for doing this where the third party is a bank, see C Kerrigan and J Wyatt, 'The Strength of a Bank Guarantee: A Credit Risk?' [2009] *Journal of International Banking and Financial Law* 488.

[382] Fuller: Corporate Borrowing, 9.01.

[383] Wood: Loans and Bonds, 18-003.

[384] Ibid, 18-006. Note that set-off will only be effective in insolvency if there is mutuality: see 6.3.4.6.2.

[385] See 2.3.5.2.

[386] See n 302.

Rights against a third party take a number of forms, some of which are very similar to each other. They can be called, variously, guarantees, indemnities, performance bonds, standby credits and insurance. Further, there are less formal arrangements, such as comfort letters. The different forms are considered below at 6.4.1 and 6.4.2. A structure that is in some ways similar to a guarantee is a credit default swap, which is a form of credit derivative. It has the effect of shifting the risk of default, or part of the risk, onto a third party for a fee. The credit default swap is considered below at 6.4.3, together with a brief discussion of other derivatives which are used to manage risk.

Another technique used by creditors to improve their chances of being paid out of the insolvent borrower's limited assets is to agree with another creditor, such as a parent company or a member of the same group, that the latter's claim will be subordinated to that of the creditor. This technique, known as subordination, is also used extensively to enable lenders to take a specific amount of credit risk in, for example, a bond issue, where lower ranking lenders will receive a higher rate of return as they are taking on more risk than those to whom they are subordinated.[387] Subordination is considered below at 6.4.4.

6.4.1 Guarantees, Indemnities and Performance Bonds[388]

6.4.1.1 Introduction

There are numerous different kinds of contract which can fall within the loose category of 'guarantees', in that they a give a creditor a contractual right against a third party which is referable to the borrower's obligation.[389] This section will consider suretyship guarantees, indemnities, performance bonds and standby credits, which can all be used for similar purposes but which have different legal characteristics. The next section will consider credit insurance. The differences between the various legal forms have significant consequences, so that although the legal effect of any such contract will depend on its terms, it is sometimes necessary for the court to characterise the agreement as being of a particular form. Each of the different legal forms has disadvantages for one or more parties.[390] Lawyers try to draft agreements to obtain the maximum advantage without the concomitant disadvantages, while trying to avoid the agreement being recharacterised. Some of the techniques used are considered below, as well as the approach of the courts to construction and characterisation.

In this chapter, to aid comparison between the various legal forms, the following terminology will be used. The lender, who might be investors in a bond issue,[391] or a syndicate of lenders, or a single bank, or a company extending credit to another company, will be called

---

[387] This is called 'tranching': for a fuller description see 9.3.3.

[388] What follows is of necessity a very brief discussion of the voluminous law surrounding guarantees. For a full discussion see Andrews and Millett: Guarantees; G Moss and D Marks, *Rowlatt on Principal and Surety*, 6th edn (London, Sweet & Maxwell, 2011); J Phillips and J O'Donovan, *The Modern Contract of Guarantee*, 2nd English edn (London, Sweet & Maxwell, 2010); KP McGuinness, *The Law of Guarantee*, 3rd edn (Toronto, Carswell, 2013).

[389] For a list of such contracts, see Wood: Loans and Bonds, 18-007.

[390] These are discussed at 6.4.1.3.1–6.4.1.4.

[391] When a guarantee is given for a bond issue where there is a trustee, the guarantor is a party to the trust deed and the trustee holds the benefit of the guarantee on trust for the holders of the securities: Fuller: Corporate Borrowing, 9.03. Bond issues are discussed in chapter 8.

the 'creditor'. The borrower, who is the recipient of the loan or credit in such transactions, will be called the 'principal debtor'. The third party, who is the provider of the credit protection, will be called the 'third party', rather than variously described as the guarantor, the indemnifier and so on.

6.4.1.2 *Important Distinctions*

One major distinction is between contracts where the liability of the third party is triggered by a default on the part of the principal debtor, and those where the trigger is a demand by the creditor, often coupled with other requirements, such as the presentation of documents. Examples of the latter type of contracts are performance bonds (also known as demand guarantees) and standby letters of credit. The former type can be subdivided into suretyship guarantees, where the third party agrees to pay the principal debtor's outstanding liability if the principal debtor does not pay, and indemnities, where the third party agrees to make good any loss suffered by the creditor,[392] so that liability is triggered by the loss caused by the failure of the principal debtor to pay the creditor.

The third party's obligation under a suretyship guarantee is a secondary liability, while liability under the other types of transaction referred to above is primary. This means that under a suretyship guarantee the third party's liability only arises when the principal debtor defaults.[393] The liability is co-extensive with that of the principal debtor, that is, it is for the same amount,[394] and it cannot be enforced if the obligation of the principal debtor cannot (for example if it is illegal or void or released by the creditor). Further, if the third party pays, it is entitled to be subrogated to the rights that the creditor had against the principal debtor.[395] If those rights are changed, either by agreement between the creditor and the principal debtor or because of the conduct of the creditor, the surety is protected by being discharged.[396]

Where the third party's obligation is primary,[397] this means that it is independent of that of the principal debtor and arises whether or not there is default. In the case of an indemnity, it is the loss caused by default against which the creditor is indemnified: if there is no default there will be no loss. In the case of a performance bond or a standby credit, the obligation to pay arises on demand irrespective of whether a default has occurred. Where the obligation is primary, the third party's liability is not usually affected by matters affecting the contract between the creditor and the principal debtor. It is this point that is the principal consequence of the distinction between guarantees and indemnities, and on which many of the cases turn. Another consequence is that contracts of guarantee must be in writing and signed by the guarantor to be enforceable.[398] Since most modern credit

---

[392] *Yeoman Credit Ltd v Latter* [1961] 1 WLR 828. This means that the liability on an indemnity is unliquidated: Goode: Credit and Security, 367.

[393] *Ex p Gardom* (1808) 15 Ves 286; Andrews and Millett: Guarantees, 7-001.

[394] The actual amount for which the third party is liable may be modified by the terms of the contract of guarantee.

[395] *Davies v Humphreys* (1840) 6 M & W 153.

[396] See 6.4.1.3.2.

[397] For example, in the case of an indemnity, a performance bond or a standby letter of credit.

[398] Statute of Frauds 1677, s 4.

protection contracts with third parties will be in writing and signed, this is rarely of much importance.[399]

Another distinction, which can be important in practice, is whether the liability of a third party is in debt or damages. If the claim is for damages, the creditor has to prove its loss, and will have to take reasonable steps to mitigate its damage, whereas a claim in debt is for a liquidated sum. Further, claims for contribution under section 1 of the Civil Liability (Contribution) Act 1978 (between co-sureties) can be made in respect of damages claims but not claims in debt, and therefore a different limitation period applies to such claims.[400] Again, the position depends on the true construction of the agreement. Two possible constructions were identified by Lord Reid in *Moschi v Lep Air Services Ltd.*[401] The first is that there is an undertaking that if the principal debtor fails to pay the debt the third party will pay it.[402] The third party's obligation, which would be in debt, would arise on the principal debtor's failure to pay. The second is that the third party promises that the principal debtor will fulfil its obligation: if it fails to do so, the third party will be in breach of contract and liable for damages.[403] The first construction causes difficulties if, for example, payments are to be made by instalments and the principal debtor fails to pay one instalment. This is often a repudiatory breach or triggers a termination clause so that the contract is terminated, and the principal debtor is no longer liable to pay the rest of the instalments, but is liable in damages for the creditor's loss caused by the termination. On the first construction, the debt in relation to the rest of the instalments never falls due, so the third party is not liable to pay it, whereas on the second construction the third party is also in breach and therefore liable for damages. It should be remembered, though, that in relation to the instalments that have already accrued, the third party is liable in debt.[404]

---

[399] For an example where s 4 of the Statute of Frauds was not complied with, see *Actionstrength Ltd v International Glass Engineering In.GL.en SpA* [2003] UKHL 17. For criticism of the writing requirement in the context of modern commercial guarantees, see J Phillips, 'Guarantees: Protecting the Bankers' [2012] *Journal of Business Law* 248, 250–52.

[400] Limitation Act 1980, s 10; *Hampton v Minns* [2002] 1 WLR 1. A further consequence relates to the application of s 237 Insolvency Act 1986 (presentation of a bankruptcy petition against an individual surety): see Goode: Credit and Security, 8-10.

[401] [1973] 1 AC 331, 344–45. Later cases have considered and followed this distinction: see *General Produce Co v United Bank Ltd* [1979] 2 Lloyd's Rep 255, 258; *Hampton v Minns* [2002] 1 WLR 1 (where the guarantee was said to be of the first construction); *Carlton Communications plc v The Football League* [2002] EWHC 1650 (Comm) [84] (where the second construction was preferred). See also *Barnicoat v Knight* [2004] EWHC 330 (Ch) and *Nearfield Ltd v Lincoln Nominees Ltd* [2006] EWHC 2421 (Ch). See Goode: Credit and Security, 8-09; Andrews and Millett: Guarantees, 6-002; Fuller: Corporate Borrowing, 9.08.

[402] Termed a 'conditional payment obligation' in *McGuinness v Norwich and Peterborough Building Society* [2011] EWCA Civ 1286.

[403] Termed a 'see to it' obligation in *McGuinness*, ibid. Note that many standard guarantees include both types of obligation in two separate clauses: see X Lok, 'Guarantees and Indemnities: The Issues' [2007] *Journal of International Banking and Financial Law* 491; J Phillips, 'Guarantees: Protecting the Bankers' [2012] *Journal of Business Law* 248, 267–68.

[404] *Chatterton v Maclean* [1951] 1 All ER 761; *Moschi v Lep Air Services Ltd* [1973] 1 AC 331, 354–55; *Hyundai Heavy Industries Co Ltd v Papadopoulous* [1980] 1 WLR 1129, 1136–37.

6.4.1.3 Guarantees

6.4.1.3.1 Protection of the Third Party: Construction of the Guarantee

The main disadvantage of a guarantee to a creditor is that the law protects a third-party guarantor in several ways. The first of these is that, traditionally, the guarantee agreement is construed strictly against the creditor.[405] This is, at least in part, because the balance of bargaining power usually favours the creditor, who will normally draft the contract,[406] and also because a third-party guarantor often receives no direct benefit for his guarantee.[407] The 'modern' approach to contractual construction, which is exemplified in the approaches of Lord Hoffmann in *ICS Ltd v West Bromwich Building Society*[408] and Lord Clarke in *Rainy Sky SA v Kookmin Bank*,[409] is discussed earlier in this chapter.[410] This latter approach is rather different from the strict approach to guarantees,[411] and, while not all the cases are easy to reconcile, there appears to be an attempt to steer a middle course in relation to the construction of guarantees. Thus, while in general the modern approach applies to guarantees,[412] clear words are still necessary to derogate from the normal incidents of suretyship,[413] at least when the document 'admits of doubt'.[414]

In the event of any ambiguity, it might be possible for a creditor to argue that the strict approach is inapplicable, since the reasons for the law's fiercely protective attitude towards third-party guarantors is not necessary where the third party is, for example, a well advised parent company.[415] This argument, however, is unlikely to work where the third party is an individual director, or a member of his or her family. A creditor cannot avoid the strict construction approach by drafting the agreement as an indemnity, since the principle of strict construction applies equally to indemnities as to guarantees.[416]

6.4.1.3.2 Protection of the Third Party: Disclosure

A contract of suretyship is not a contract of the utmost good faith, in contrast (until now) to a contract of insurance.[417] There is, however, a limited duty imposed on a creditor to

---

[405] *Trafalgar House Construction (Regions) Ltd v General Surety & Guarantee Co Ltd* [1996] AC 199, 208; Chitty 44-061.

[406] *Eastern Counties Building Society v Russell* [1947] 1 All ER 500; Andrews and Millett: Guarantees, 4-002.

[407] *Blest v Brown* (1862) 4 De GF & J 367. It should be borne in mind, however, that there are often considerable indirect benefits, especially when the third party is part of the same corporate group.

[408] [1998] 1 WLR 1257.

[409] [2011] UKSC 50.

[410] 6.2.

[411] The two lines of authority were discussed in *Meritz Fire, Marine Insurance Co Ltd v Jan de Nul NV* [2010] EWHC 3362 (Comm) [55]–[62] and *John Spencer Harvey v Dunbar Assets plc* [2013] EWCA Civ 952 [28]–[32].

[412] *Static Control Components (Europe) Ltd v Egan* [2004] EWCA Civ 392 [12], [37]; *John Spencer Harvey v Dunbar Assets plc* [2013] EWCA Civ 952 [28]; *National Merchant Building Society Ltd v Bellamy* [2013] EWCA Civ 452 [39].

[413] *Liberty Mutual Insurance Co (UK) Ltd v HSBC Bank plc* [2002] EWCA Civ 691 [56]–[59]; *Barclays Bank plc v Kingston* [2006] EWHC 533 (QB).

[414] *Static Control Components (Europe) Ltd v Egan* [2004] EWCA Civ 392 [12], [37].

[415] Chitty 44-061.

[416] Andrews and Millett: Guarantees, 4-003.

[417] 6.4.2. The duty of disclosure of an insured party is changing to a duty of fair presentation: see Insurance Act 2015, Part 2.

disclose 'unusual features of the contractual relationship between the creditor and the debtor, or between the creditor and other creditors of the debtor'.[418] This duty of disclosure does not extend to other matters, such as investigation of the debtors for embezzlement, or the fact that their bank accounts had been frozen.[419] If the duty would otherwise arise, it is not a sufficient defence to non-disclosure that the creditor thought that the surety knew the facts already.[420] The duty of disclosure, therefore, is wider than in an ordinary contract, but it is not the primary means by which a surety is protected, unlike in a contract of insurance.

6.4.1.3.3 Protection of the Third Party: Discharge of the Third Party

Another principle protecting a third-party guarantor is that his liability is discharged if the liability of the principal debtor is void or voidable[421] (and avoided) or unenforceable[422] or discharged[423] or released by the creditor.[424] This comes from the co-extensiveness principle, so that if the principal debtor is not liable, the third party cannot be either. Further, the third party loses its right of indemnity and subrogation against the principal debtor if the latter is released.[425]

Another related principle, sometimes called the rule in *Holme v Brunskill*,[426] is that a third-party guarantor is discharged if the creditor varies the terms of its contract with the principal debtor without the third party's consent, including giving the principal debtor extra time to pay.[427] The rationale of this principle is the protection of the third party, who is taken to have agreed only to guarantee the precise liabilities that were in the original agreement and no other.[428] Further, the third party's rights of indemnity and subrogation could be damaged by an agreement between the creditor and the principal debtor, which the third party may not know about and has no ability to affect. The rule, however, takes little account of whether the variation of the contract causes any actual damage to the third party. Unless the creditor can show that the variation is 'unsubstantial or that it cannot be otherwise than beneficial to the [third party]',[429] the third party is discharged: there is no requirement for it to show detriment or for a court to inquire into whether there is such detriment. However, the variation must affect the risk of non-fulfilment of the guaranteed obligation:[430] if it merely affects the amount for which the third party is liable, the third

---

[418] *Royal Bank of Scotland v Etridge (No 2)* [2001] UKHL 44, [2002] AC 773 [188]; *North Shore Ventures Ltd v Anstead Holdings Inc* [2011] EWCA Civ 230 [31].

[419] *North Shore Ventures*, ibid.

[420] Ibid, [37].

[421] Andrews and Millett: Guarantees, 6-024.

[422] For example, time-barred: see Andrews and Millett: Guarantees, 6-027.

[423] By the acceptance by the principal debtor of a repudiatory breach by the creditor: *Watts v Shuttleworth* (1861) 7 H & N 353. The position where the principal debtor affirms the contract after a repudiatory breach is less clear, but it is probably that the third-party guarantor's liability remains: see Andrews and Millett: Guarantees, 9-017.

[424] *Mahant Singh v U Ba Yi* [1939] AC 601.

[425] For the third party's right of indemnity see 6.4.1.3.4.

[426] (1878) 3 QBD 495.

[427] *Swire v Redman* (1876) 1 QBD 536, 541.

[428] A Choy, 'Discharge of Guarantees: The Rule in *Holme v Brunskill* Revisited' [2007] *Journal of International Banking and Financial Law* 450.

[429] *Holme v Brunskill* (1878) 3 QBD 495, 505; *Ankhar Pty Ltd v National Westminster Finance (Australia) Ltd* (1987) 162 CLR 549, 559 (HC Aust); *Topland Portfolio No 1 Ltd v Smith News Trading Ltd* [2014] EWCA Civ 18 [20].

[430] Andrews and Millett: Guarantees, 9-024.

party will only be discharged in relation to the amount by which the liability is increased.[431] The risk of non-fulfilment can, though, be affected even if the amount for which the third party is liable is not changed, for example where there is a cap.

It can be seen that the application of the rule in *Holme v Brunskill* can be very detrimental to creditors in corporate finance transactions. It effectively means that any restructuring of financing arrangements will potentially discharge the third party unless the latter's consent is obtained.[432] This, however, introduces a moral hazard problem, as the third party has an incentive to withhold consent to a variation if it would like to be discharged from the guarantee, or to extract concessions as a price for giving consent.[433]

The rule in *Holme v Brunskill* has been criticised for its breadth, and it has been suggested that it would be sufficient to protect a third party for it to be discharged pro tanto for any detriment it suffers from the variation of the principal contract.[434] This seems a sensible way forward. Even if the variation affects the general risk of non-payment rather than a specific risk, the pricing of risks by the markets is well developed, and it should be possible for a court, with appropriate expert evidence, to quantify the increased risk and adjust the third party's liabilities accordingly.

The rule in *Holme v Brunskill*, and the related rules protecting sureties, have also given rise to problems of construction, which introduce some very unwelcome uncertainty into the law, particularly on restructuring of debt. One issue is whether the original guarantee covers a new loan or other debt: if it does not, the third party is not bound in relation to that debt.[435] Another issue is whether a clause, inserted to avoid the rule, covers what has actually happened: the 'purview' doctrine usually limits such a clause to covering matters which fall 'within the general purview of the original guarantee'.[436] In relation to both issues, the original guarantee and the new agreements fall to be interpreted, and the line between a restructuring which varies the existing agreement and one which creates a new contract is notoriously unclear.[437] Further, a clause may be interpreted to cover situations where the

---

[431] So that, for example, where security held for the debt by the creditor was sold at an undervalue, the third party was *pro tanto* released: *Skipton Building Society v Stott* [2001] QB 261 [21]. If the creditor's actions were repudiatory, however, the third party might be fully discharged: [22]. See also *Barclays Bank plc v Kingston* [2006] EWHC 533 (QB).

[432] Consent probably requires both an actual assent by the guarantor and communication to the creditor: see *Polak v Everett* (1876) 1 QBD 669; *Wittmann (UK) Ltd v Willdav Engineering SA* [2007] EWCA Civ 824 [27]; *Hickory Developments Pty Ltd v Brunswick Retail Investment Pty Ltd* [2012] VSC 224 [44]–[61].

[433] A Choy, 'Discharge of Guarantees: The Rule in *Holme v Brunskill* Revisited' [2007] *Journal of International Banking and Financial Law* 450.

[434] Ibid, relying on the Court of Appeal's decision in *Mercers Co v New Hampshire Insurance Co* [1992] 2 Lloyd's Rep 365, 377. See also A Berg, 'Suretyship: *Holme v. Brunskill* and Related Rules' (2006) 122 *Law Quarterly Review* 42.

[435] *The Nefeli* [1986] 1 Lloyd's Rep 339; see also *Triodos Bank NV v Dobbs* [2005] EWCA Civ 630.

[436] *Trade Indemnity Company Limited v Workington Harbour and Dock Board* [1937] AC 1, 21 discussed in *CIMC Raffles Offshore (Singapore) Limited v Schahin Holding SA* [2013] EWCA Civ 644. See also *Hackney Empire Ltd v Aviva Insurance Ltd* [2012] EWCA Civ 1716.

[437] The most egregious example of this is *Triodos Bank NV v Dobbs* [2005] EWCA Civ 630, which has been heavily criticised as an uncommercial decision: see A Berg, 'Suretyship: *Holme v. Brunskill* and Related Rules' (2006) 122 *Law Quarterly Review* 42; J Phillips, 'Guarantees: Protecting the Bankers' [2012] 3 *Journal of Business Law* 248, 262–64; I Wilson, 'Debt Restructuring: Putting the Security at Risk' [2012] *Journal of International Banking and Financial Law* 334; Andrews and Millett: Guarantees, 4-026.

principal debtor's liability is discharged or released, but not where the principal agreement is void because it is prohibited by statute.[438]

Due to the difficulties discussed in this section, it has become standard practice to insert a clause into a guarantee to exclude the operation of the rule in *Holme v Brunskill*, as well as the principle, discussed earlier, that a third party is discharged if the principal debtor's liability is void or discharged. The 'indulgence' clauses can take a number of forms. One is a direct provision that the liability of the third party is not to be prejudiced or diminished if certain listed events occur (including defects in the principal contract, discharge or release of the principal debtor and variations to the principal contract).[439] Alternatively, the agreement may provide for consent in advance by the third party to any variation of the principal contract, or that the creditor has authority to agree to a variation without reference to the third party. Yet another possibility is to provide that the third party is deemed to be liable as a principal debtor. The insertion of these protective clauses, especially a principal debtor clause, might also have the effect that the agreement is recharacterised as an indemnity.

6.4.1.3.4 Protection of the Third Party: Third Party's Rights Against the Principal Debtor

A third-party guarantor is protected by having an indemnity against the principal debtor, which arises by either express or implied agreement between the third party and the principal debtor or in restitution.[440] There cannot be any such agreement, or such a right to restitution, where the guarantee is not given at the request of the principal debtor but is arranged solely between the creditor and the third party.[441] In addition to any indemnity, when a third party has paid the principal debtor's liability, it is subrogated to the rights of the creditor against the principal debtor, which includes the right to any security which the creditor holds.[442] Although this is an equitable right, the right to security is also contained in section 5 of the Mercantile Law Amendment Act 1856. This is important since the equitable right of subrogation may well not be available to a third party where the principal debtor does not request the guarantee, but it would seem that the statutory right is not so limited.[443]

6.4.1.4 Indemnity and Performance Bond

As mentioned above, uncertainty remains regarding the effectiveness of the methods used by creditors to preserve a third party's liability under a guarantee when that of the principal debtor is discharged or varied. Creditors often, therefore, seek to take an indemnity either instead of, or as well as, a guarantee.[444] It is also possible that attempts to exclude

---

[438] *Heald v O'Connor* [1971] 1 WLR 497. cf *General Produce Co v United Bank Ltd* [1979] 2 Lloyd's Rep 255, where the third party was held to remain liable despite the release of the principal debtor by operation of law.

[439] For examples of such clauses, which are often drafted so as to be very comprehensive, see Wood: Loans and Bonds, 19-018; Fuller: Corporate Borrowing, 9.77.

[440] Andrews and Millett: Guarantees, 10-002.

[441] *Owen v Tate* [1976] QB 402. This rule is subject to some exceptions, for example where the guarantee is given in cases of necessity.

[442] *Craythorne v Swinburne* (1807) 14 Ves 160.

[443] Andrews and Millett: Guarantees, 11-019.

[444] A common combination is that of a pure guarantee (the second 'Moschi' category giving rise to a liability in damages), a conditional payment guarantee (the first 'Moschi' category giving rise to a liability in debt) and an indemnity: this is included in the LMA standard syndicated loan agreements. See Fuller: Corporate Borrowing,

the protection given by the general law to third-party guarantors have the effect of turning a guarantee into an indemnity. It should be remembered that there is no hard and fast line between guarantees and indemnities. Neither are they completely distinct concepts.[445] As mentioned above, there are two main reasons why a court might need to distinguish one from the other. The first is to decide whether the third party's liability is co-extensive with that of the principal debtor. If it is, it can take advantage of defences available to the principal debtor,[446] it will not be liable if the principal debtor is not, and the rule in *Holme v Brunskill* will apply.[447] The second is to decide whether the requirement of writing under the Statute of Frauds applies. It is only in the latter context that a bright line has to be drawn: the contract either falls within the statute or it does not. The line in the former context can be more blurred.

A considerable jurisprudence has grown up surrounding the distinction.[448] The distinction was described in one Statute of Frauds case in the following terms: 'An indemnity is a contract by one party to keep the other harmless against loss, but a contract of guarantee is a contract to answer for the debt, default or miscarriage of another who is to be primarily liable to the promisee.'[449] It will be seen that the chief differentiating feature, therefore, is whether the third party's liability is primary or secondary; there are, however, other touchstones that have been used to answer this question in this context, such as whether the third party is separate from or 'interested in' the transaction.[450]

Where the issue to be determined is whether defences apply or whether the third party's liability is discharged by the discharge of the principal debtor or under the rule in *Holme v Brunskill*, the question could be said to have become circular: (a) the third party is discharged if its liability is secondary, (b) it is secondary if the contract is one of guarantee, (c) the contract is one of guarantee if the liability of the third party is secondary. The knot can be untied by treating the issue as one of construction of the particular agreement in these cases, without the court having to make a decision as to whether the contract is one of guarantee or of indemnity. Thus the labels used by the parties are not conclusive,[451] and the courts will look at the rights and obligations created by the words used.[452] This approach means that clauses such as those referred to earlier[453] can be successful in preventing a third

---

9.13, and for further discussion of the 'Moschi' categories see 6.4.1.2. Of these three elements, the first two create secondary liability on the third party: A Berg, 'Rethinking Indemnities' [2002] *Journal of International Banking and Financial Law* 360, 403. Whether contracts which include both a guarantee and an indemnity are treated as giving rise to two separate obligations (one secondary and one primary) or just one secondary obligation is a matter of construction: Andrews and Millett: Guarantees, 1-014; *Western Credit Ltd v Albery* [1964] 2 All ER 938; *Stadium Finance Co Ltd v Helm* (1965) 109 Sol Jo 471; *Citicorp Australia Ltd v Hendry* [1985] 4 NSWLR 1 (Sup Ct NSW CA).

[445] For a review of the contractual possibilities, see *Vossloh Aktiengesellschaft v Alpha Trains (UK) Limited* [2010] EWHC 2443 (Ch) [34].

[446] *IIG Capital LLC v Van Der Merwe* [2008] EWCA Civ 542; *Carey Value Added SL v Grupo Urvasco SA* [2010] EWHC 1905 (Comm).

[447] *ABM AMRO Commercial Finance plc v Ambrose McGinn* [2014] EWHC 1674 (Comm).

[448] Andrews and Millett: Guarantees, 3-006–3-016.

[449] *Yeoman Credit Ltd v Latter* [1961] 1 WLR 828, 831.

[450] *Sutton & Co v Grey* [1894] 1 QB 285; *Pitts v Jones* [2007] EWCA Civ 1301.

[451] *Seaton v Heath* [1899] 1 QB 782, 792; *Gold Coast Ltd v Caja de Ahorros del Mediterraneo* [2001] EWCA Civ 1806 [21]; *Vossloh Aktiengesellschaft v Alpha Trains (UK) Limited* [2010] EWHC 2443 (Ch) [20].

[452] See eg *Associated British Ports v Ferryways NV* [2009] EWCA Civ 189.

[453] 6.4.1.3.3.

party being discharged from liability without that party's liability necessarily being characterised as primary, and without the agreement being characterised as one of indemnity.[454]

An indemnity, being a contract to keep another harmless against loss, will normally result in the indemnifier being liable in damages rather than in debt.[455] Difficult questions of quantification can arise, particularly where the creditor is said to be contributorily negligent, or has failed to mitigate its loss, but in practice these are usually overcome by the inclusion of a liquidated damages clause.[456] In corporate finance transactions, the usual position is that the principal debtor is itself liable in debt, and so the indemnity analysis is not attractive.

There is, however, another possible analysis. This is that a third party can undertake liability in debt (on the basis of a similar construction to the first category suggested by Lord Diplock in the *Moschi* case)[457] but in such a way that it is not discharged if the principal debtor is.[458] The difficulty with this construction is that it is not clear how the third party's obligation can be a principal and not a secondary liability if it is dependent upon failure to pay by the principal debtor. If it is not so dependent, then it becomes akin to a performance bond. This in itself would not be so much of a problem were it not for the 'presumption' that is said to exist against a contract being a performance bond if the third party is anything other than a bank. This comes from the case of *Marubeni Hong Kong and South China Ltd v Government of Mongolia*,[459] where the Court of Appeal made it clear that specific language would be required in the agreement to displace this presumption.[460] This presumption has been much criticised,[461] and rightly so, as although performance bonds are chiefly given by banks as a 'guarantee' (in a loose sense) of performance of non-monetary obligations such as those under a construction contract[462] or in a contract for international sale of goods,[463] there is no reason why they cannot be used in the context of corporate finance as a 'guarantee' of performance of a loan contract. They offer more protection to the creditor than a true guarantee as the creditor is assured of payment and does not need to prove loss even for non-accrued liabilities.[464] While the courts are prepared to displace the *Marubeni* presumption in some circumstances, for example where the agreement included a clause providing that the third party was liable as principal debtor coupled with provision for a certificate of the amount payable by the third party to be conclusive in

[454] *General Produce Co v United Bank Ltd* [1979] 2 Lloyd's Rep 255; A Berg, 'Rethinking Indemnities' [2002] *Journal of International Banking and Financial Law* 403.
[455] *Firma C-Trade SA v Newcastle Protection and Indemnity Association (The Fanti)* [1991] 2 AC 1.
[456] Ibid.
[457] *Moschi v Lep Air Services Ltd* [1973] 1 AC 331, 344–45.
[458] Fuller: Corporate Borrowing, 9.09.
[459] [2005] EWCA Civ 395.
[460] Ibid, [30]. Where the third party is a bank, however, the courts seem happy to go the other way and characterise an agreement labelled as a guarantee as a performance bond (*Gold Coast Limited v Caja de Ahorros del Mediterraneo* [2001] EWCA Civ 1806).
[461] Hughes: Banking, 15.12; A Berg, 'Suretyship: *Holme v. Brunskill* and Related Rules' (2006) 122 *Law Quarterly Review* 42; P McGrath, 'The Nature of Modern Guarantees: *IIG v Van Der Merwes*' (2009) 2 *Corporate Rescue and Insolvency* 10. For a discussion of how the courts have and should use the *Marubeni* presumption, see T Evans, 'Guarantees and Performance Bonds: Problems of Drafting and Interpretation' [2013] *Journal of International Banking and Financial Law* 614.
[462] Andrews and Millett: Guarantees, 16-004.
[463] Ibid, 16-005.
[464] Hughes: Banking, 15.12, postscript to ch 5.

the absence of manifest error,[465] in other cases the courts have held that the presumption is not rebutted.[466]

The above discussion is predicated on the basis that, if the third party's liability is primary, there is no danger that it will be discharged under the rule in *Holme v Brunskill*. This, however, was doubted (obiter) by Cresswell J in the *Marubeni* case,[467] and it has even been argued that the rule should apply to a performance bond as well.[468] To the extent that the rule in *Holme v Brunskill* (and the related rules on discharge of the third party when the contract with the principal debtor is void, or discharged) depends on the secondary nature of the third party's liability, this argument is clearly fallacious.[469] But to the extent that the purpose of the rule is to protect the ability of the third party to have recourse against the principal debtor, it might be said that the third party needs as much protection where its liability is primary as where it is secondary.[470] One counter-argument is that where the third party is being paid (by the principal debtor) to take on primary liability, it can make whatever arrangements it likes concerning reimbursement, and these need not depend upon the liability of the principal debtor to the creditor. It is only really where the third party and the surety do not involve the principal debtor in the transaction that the third party is obliged to rely on its rights under the general law for reimbursement[471] and therefore needs the protection of the general law, such as the rule in *Holme v Brunskill*.

Under a contract of indemnity it seems (although there is no direct authority) that the third party has a right of indemnity against the principal debtor, in a similar way to that of a third-party guarantor.[472] With a performance bond, an indemnity will usually be given expressly by the principal debtor as a condition of the third party giving the performance bond,[473] and in the absence of an express indemnity, it seems that one will be implied.[474]

The principal drawback of a performance bond, from the point of view of the principal debtor (and maybe the third party) is that the third party is still obliged to pay even if the creditor makes a demand when nothing is due from the debtor. If, for example, the third party's liability is fixed by a conclusive certificate, it is possible that the amount paid may eventually be seen to be too much. This loss will usually fall on the principal debtor, who will be obliged to indemnify the third party: the principal debtor will also have a right of restitution against the creditor as regards the overpayment, to which the third party will be subrogated.[475] In the first place, though, the absolute nature of the third party's obligation

---

[465] *IIG Capital LLC v Van Der Merwe* [2008] EWCA Civ 542. This approach was distinguished in *North Shore Ventures Ltd v Anstead Holdings Inc* [2011] EWCA Civ 230.

[466] *Carey Value Added SL v Grupo Urvasco SA* [2010] EWHC 1905 (Comm); *Vossloh Aktiengesellschaft v Alpha Trains (UK) Limited* [2010] EWHC 2443 (Ch). For a more nuanced approach, see *Wuhan Guoyu Logistics Group Co Ltd v Emporiki Bank of Greece SA* [2012] EWCA Civ 1629.

[467] *Marubeni Hong Kong and South China Ltd v Government of Mongolia* [2004] EWHC 472 (Comm) [142]. This point was not considered by the Court of Appeal in that case.

[468] G Bhattacharyya, V Reynolds and A White, 'Differentiating and Identifying Primary and Secondary Liability Instruments in the Law of Guarantees' (2005) 20 *Journal of International Banking Law and Regulation* 488. See *CIMC Raffles Offshore (Singapore) Limited v Schahin Holding SA* [2013] EWCA Civ 644 [57].

[469] See *ABM AMRO Commercial Finance plc v Ambrose McGinn* [2014] EWHC 1674 (Comm) [36].

[470] For the ability of a third party under an indemnity and a performance bond to recover against the principal debtor, see below.

[471] Whether by indemnity or by subrogation.

[472] Andrews and Millett: Guarantees, 10-002.

[473] Ibid, 16-012.

[474] *IIG Capital LLC v Van Der Merwe* [2008] EWCA Civ 542 [26]–[27].

[475] Ibid, [27].

means that it is obliged to pay. This is the case even if nothing is due and the demand is made fraudulently. In this situation, it is very unlikely that the debtor will be able to obtain an injunction stopping the third party from paying,[476] although in a case of fraud there does appear to be a possibility of obtaining an injunction to prevent the creditor from making the demand in the first place.[477] The contract between the creditor and debtor could include an express term prohibiting the creditor from making an unjustified demand: in these circumstances an injunction to prevent demand may be obtained.[478] While a term is unlikely to be implied,[479] it has been held that if there is a strong case that the beneficiary is in breach of contract and so is not entitled to payment, the court will issue an interim injunction to prevent demand.[480] There will, in any case, be a duty on the creditor to account for any sums received to which it is not entitled under the debt contract:[481] this could be on the basis of an implied term,[482] or on restitutionary grounds.[483]

6.4.2 Credit Insurance

Where a company extends credit to customers, which are usually other companies, there is always a risk that the customers will not pay their debts. If the creditor is supplying goods, it may be able to protect itself by using retention of title terms,[484] but this may not always be possible, for example because the goods are to be immediately used in manufacture or sold on. Alternatively, the creditor may be supplying not goods but services. In these circumstances, a creditor will usually take out credit insurance, whereby an insurance company agrees to pay the creditor the insured sum if the debtor becomes insolvent. To avoid the moral hazard of creditors who, if they were able to claim the full amount of the loss, would not perform proper credit checks on their customers, the amount covered is usually only about 80–95 per cent of the debts.[485] The insurance can cover some or all of the creditor's debtors: whether an insurance company will be prepared to cover any particular debtor will depend on that debtor's credit rating.[486] The fact that a company has credit insurance also makes it easier for that company to obtain receivables financing, as it makes it more likely that the receivables will be paid. Credit insurance can also be used to protect other lenders, such as those investing in securities issued in a securitisation.[487] In the context of

---

[476] Andrews and Millett: Guarantees, 16-021.

[477] *Themehelp Ltd v West* [1996] QB 84; Andrews and Millett: Guarantees, 16-025.

[478] *Simon Carves Limited v Ensus UK Limited* [2011] EWHC 657 (TCC).

[479] *The State Trading Corporation of India Ltd v ED & F Man (Sugar) Limited and The State Bank of India* [1981] Com LR 235 per Shaw LJ; Andrews and Millett: Guarantees, 16-026.

[480] *Doosan Babcock Limited v Comercializadora de Equipos y Materiales Mabe Limitada* [2013] EWHC 3201 (TCC). This decision has been criticised, in the context of the construction industry, as undermining the ability of a beneficiary to call on a bond without investigating any underlying dispute and thus destroying the commercial usefulness of such bonds: see L Adams, 'New Clots in the Lifeblood of International Construction Projects: Enjoining Employers' Calls on Performance Bonds' (2014) 30 *Constitutional Law Journal* 325.

[481] *Cargill International SA v Bangladesh Sugar and Food Industries Corp* [1998] 1 WLR 461.

[482] *Tradigrain SA v State Trading Corporation of India* [2005] EWHC 2206 (Comm) [26].

[483] Andrews and Millett: Guarantees, 16-033.

[484] 2.3.4.4.4.

[485] J Wright, 'Insuring against Insolvency' (2009) 20 *Construction Law* 26.

[486] *Close Invoice Finance Ltd v Watts* [2009] All ER (D) 09 (Sep) (unreported).

[487] Fuller: Corporate Borrowing, 4.81. For an example of credit insurance being used to cover the exposure of a bank under derivative transactions, see *Merrill Lynch International Bank Ltd (formerly Merrill Lynch Capital Markets Bank Ltd) v Winterthur Swiss Insurance Co* [2007] EWHC 893 (Comm).

exporting goods, UK Export Finance provides insurance against non-payment by foreign counterparties.

Credit insurance performs a similar function to a guarantee, and in certain cases it may be difficult to tell whether the contract in question is one or the other. It is important to distinguish between the two, however, since the protection that the law gives to the insurer is different to that given to the guarantor.[488] As discussed above, the secondary nature of the guarantor's liability means that release of the principal debtor or variations to the principal's contract discharges the guarantor. By contrast, the insurer's protection consists of the law providing every possibility of assessing the risk it is taking correctly. Thus, until recently, an insured party was under an obligation to make full disclosure of all material facts, meaning that the contract was one of the utmost good faith (*uberrimae fidae*). This is different from most contracts, where there is no duty of disclosure but only liability for misrepresentation. This strict duty has now changed in relation to consumer insurance,[489] and will soon change in relation to commercial insurance. The Insurance Act 2015[490] introduces a duty of fair presentation of the risk, which requires accurate presentation of material facts, but does not require presentation of facts which diminish the risk, or facts that the insurer knows or ought to know, or of which the insurer waives the need to be told. The insurer no longer has the absolute right to set aside the contract for any breach: it has a remedy[491] only if, but for the breach, it would not have entered into the contract at all, or would have entered into it on different terms.

The difference in protection for the third party between a contract of guarantee and a contract of insurance is justified by the usual background to the two types of contract: an insurer is normally at arm's length from the insured party, and is paid a premium for taking the risk, which it must therefore assess accurately. The guarantor, in contrast, is usually not paid for giving the guarantee, and frequently knows the debtor well, so that it is in a good position to assess the risk it is taking on.[492] It is clear that the label given to the transaction by the parties is not determinative of the characterisation issue,[493] but that the distinction depends on the 'substantial character' of the transaction.[494] Unfortunately, this does not mean that there are any definitive touchstones for characterisation, but it appears[495] that the courts will look at whether the guarantor/insurer is paid,[496] whether the guarantor/insurer deals with the creditor (which would make it a contract of insurance) or the debtor (which would make it a contract of guarantee),[497] and whether the guarantor/insurer has easy means of discovering the creditworthiness of the debtor.[498]

---

[488] Hughes: Banking, 5.25.

[489] The Consumer Insurance (Disclosure and Representations) Act 2012 introduces a duty on consumers to take reasonable care not to make misrepresentations during pre-contract negotiations, the remedy for which will vary according to the state of mind of the consumer and the reliance placed upon the misrepresentation by the insurance company.

[490] This was enacted on 12 February 2015 and comes into force on 12 August 2016.

[491] The remedies, too, are on a sliding scale: see Insurance Act 2015, Sch 1.

[492] *Seaton v Heath* [1899] 1 QB 782, 793 per Romer LJ. This distinction breaks down when considering some of the examples of guarantees discussed earlier.

[493] Ibid, 792.

[494] Ibid.

[495] Benjamin: Financial Law, 5.129.

[496] Although guarantors do sometimes get fees, Hughes: Banking, 5.25.

[497] This is not always conclusive: see *In re Denton's Estate* [1904] 2 Ch 178, 189.

[498] This is not always the case with guarantors: see Hughes: Banking, 5.25.

It should also be pointed out that insurance is a regulated activity within FSMA,[499] so that, unlike the provision of guarantees, anyone providing it in the course of a business must be authorised or exempt.[500]

6.4.3 Derivatives and Credit Default Swaps[501]

6.4.3.1 *Management of Risk by the Use of Derivatives*

Although structurally different, credit default swaps can perform a similar function to guarantees. They are a mechanism for transferring risk of default from one party to another. They are part of a broader category of transactions known as financial derivatives, which are parasitic transactions which derive value from an underlying product, and which are used for management of risk, both on the financial markets and in other areas.[502] The main types of derivatives are options, forwards, futures and swaps. Options are either a right to buy something (a call option) or to sell something (a put option) at a specified price during a specified time period. A forward contract is an agreement to buy or sell something in the future at a specified price on a specified date: these are usually specific to the parties and are largely agreed over the counter (OTC). If a forward contract is traded on an exchange it is known as a futures contract: it is likely to be standardised and regulated. Swaps are contracts where a party agrees to exchange with a counterparty the financial effects of a contract the first party has with the financial effects of another position actually or notionally undertaken by the counterparty.

Many types of derivatives are used by lenders and corporate borrowers to manage the risks inherent in the financing process. One example is the use of interest rate swaps to manage the fluctuation of interest rates. If the borrower is borrowing at a floating interest rate, but it considers that interest rates are going to rise, it will enter into a swap with a financial counterparty. The swap agreement will provide that, periodically, the company will pay a fixed rate of interest to the counterparty, and the counterparty will pay it the floating rate that the company has to pay to its lender.[503] In fact, the obligations will be set off against each other, so that a net payment is made at each payment date, either by the company to the counterparty or vice versa, depending on the actual floating rate on that day. The company is also likely to have paid the counterparty a fee for the transaction, although it may be that the counterparty takes a different view as to which way interest rates are going to move for the duration of the loan, and thus hopes to make a profit out of the swap.[504]

Another example is the use of foreign currency forwards by a borrower to manage the risk of the value of its exports diminishing while it still has to pay the costs of its borrowing. A company could manage the risk of an increase in the price of a commodity by entering

---

[499] s 22 and Sch 2 para 20.

[500] FSMA, s 19.

[501] The law relating to credit default swaps, and derivatives in general, is complex and only a few issues are discussed in this section. For detailed discussion, see S Firth, *Derivatives: Law and Practice* (London, Sweet & Maxwell, 2012); A Hudson, *The Law on Financial Derivatives*, 5th edn (London, Sweet & Maxwell, 2012).

[502] Hudson: Finance, 40-02. See Hudson ch 40 for a general discussion of derivative products.

[503] For a worked example, see www.isda.org/educat/pdf/IRS-Diagram1.pdf.

[504] See ISDA, 'An Introduction to the Documentation of OTC Derivatives' at www.isda.org/educat/pdf/documentation_of_derivatives.pdf and Benjamin: Financial Law, 4.37 for further explanations of interest rate swaps.

into a futures contract to buy that commodity in the future at a price fixed at the time of the contract (or entering into an option to buy that commodity at a fixed price). Alternatively, it could enter into a futures contract or option to sell that commodity at a fixed price: if the market price then rises, the profit on the futures sale will cancel out the loss on the actual purchase price paid.[505]

All derivatives, including credit derivatives, have two possible functions. Those entering into such a transaction may want to protect themselves against risk resulting from a particular transaction. This process is known as 'hedging'. Alternatively, derivatives can be used to make money through speculation and trading.[506] Credit derivatives can be divided into end-user instruments, which relate to a specific asset, and trading instruments, which relate to the general creditworthiness of the reference entity.[507] Here, we are largely concerned with end-user instruments, which are used by lenders to protect themselves in a corporate finance transaction against risk of default by the borrower.

6.4.3.2 Credit Default Swaps

In a typical credit default swap (CDS), the buyer of protection (in our case, the lender) enters into a contract with the seller of protection whereby the latter agrees to bear the credit risk of a particular entity ('the reference entity') and pay on certain events of default (but is under no obligation to pay unless such an event occurs).[508] These events could be a failure to make an instalment payment on a loan, or a bond, or could be any material breach of covenant, including financial covenants.[509] The seller of protection is paid a fee by the buyer of protection for taking on the risk. It can be seen that the protection given to the lender is similar in many ways to that under a guarantee or indemnity: the lender is protected against the credit risk of the borrower, but is exposed to the credit risk of the seller of protection, as it is to the credit risk of the third party in a guarantee.[510] Unlike a guarantee, which is usually seen as a means of credit enhancement to be used in conjunction with the taking of security and other methods of reducing credit risk,[511] a CDS can be seen as an alternative to transferring the debt,[512] so that the lender is no longer economically involved

---

[505] See further D Abbey, 'The Use of Derivatives in the Airline Industry' (2007) 5 *Journal of Business and Economics Research* 7. Abbey notes a large discrepancy in the amount of hedging used by different airline companies against a rise in the price of fuel, ranging from 0% to 85% of liabilities.

[506] Hudson: Finance, 40-10 ff.

[507] S Henderson, 'Credit Derivatives—At a Crossroads?' [2001] *Journal of International Banking and Financial Law* 211. It should be realised that those who provide protection under a CDS may also protect themselves by entering into a CDS with another entity: S Henderson, 'Regulation of Credit Derivatives: To What Effect and For Whose Benefit? Part 5' [2009] *Journal of International Banking and Financial Law* 413.

[508] Benjamin: Financial Law, 4.59; see also *Cassa di Risparmio della Repubblica di San Marino SpA v Barclays Bank Ltd* [2011] EWHC 484 (Comm) [22]–[28].

[509] Hudson: Finance, 430-44–40-46. As noted above, a credit event can also refer to the creditworthiness of a particular entity, so that the trigger for payment is the insolvency of that entity or a downgrade in its credit rating, Hudson: Finance, 40-47. However, this is usually a feature of trading instruments, which are not considered here.

[510] For discussion of more complex uses of credit derivatives, see Benjamin: Financial Law, 4.4.6; S Henderson, 'Regulation of Credit Derivatives: To What Effect and For Whose Benefit? Part 5' [2009] *Journal of International Banking and Financial Law* 413.

[511] Such as due diligence in assessing the credit risk of the borrower, and monitoring of the borrower.

[512] M Todd Henderson, 'Credit Derivatives are Not "Insurance"' University of Chicago Law & Economics, Olin Working Paper No 476, www.ssrn.com/abstract=1440945; A Morrison, 'Credit Derivatives, Disintermediation and Investment Decisions' Oxford Financial Research Centre Working Paper 2001-FE-01, www.ssrn.com/abstract=270269. See 9.3.2.

in the debt, even though it retains its relationship with the borrower.[513] The disadvantage, from the lender's point of view, compared to an outright transfer of the debt is that it still retains the credit risk of the counterparty to the CDS.[514]

CDSs are merely contracts, and many legal issues will largely be a matter of construction of the contract. Most CDSs, like other derivatives, will be entered into in the form of the ISDA Master Agreement, which governs the entire relationship between the parties, a confirmation, which relates to an individual transaction, and a credit support annexe dealing with collateralisation.[515] When interpreting the ISDA Master Agreement, the courts, while taking account of the normal principles of interpretation of commercial contracts,[516] are also acutely aware that it is an important standard form contract used throughout the world, so that '[i]t is axiomatic that it should, as far as possible, be interpreted in a way that serves the objectives of clarity, certainty and predictability, so that the very large number of parties using it should know where they stand'.[517]

6.4.3.3 Are Credit Default Swaps Insurance?

In the past, an important issue was whether a credit derivative was a gaming contract, as such contracts were unenforceable,[518] but this is no longer the case.[519] It is still, though, important to consider whether a credit derivative contract is one of insurance. There are two reasons why this is of significance. If a CDS were an insurance contract, those who sold protection would be required to be authorised by the FCA and PRA to carry on insurance business.[520] Sellers of protection, such as banks and hedge funds, are of course authorised by the FCA and PRA to carry on various functions. However, the regulation of insurance companies is different from the regulation of these other financial institutions,[521] so that, for example, a bank authorised to carry on banking business will not be authorised to carry on insurance business. Further, if a bank were to seek such authorisation, it would be prohibited from carrying on any business other than insurance.[522] For this reason, banks would not wish to be authorised to carry on insurance business.[523]

---

[513] This may have consequences for the corporate governance of the borrower: see 3.2.2.4.6.

[514] Benjamin: Financial Law, 18.32; Fuller: Corporate Borrowing, 4.77. This risk is usually covered by the provision of collateral by the counterparty.

[515] A Hudson, *The Law on Financial Derivatives*, 5th edn (London, Sweet & Maxwell, 2012) 2-01.

[516] See 6.2.

[517] *Lomas v JFB Firth Rixson* [2010] EWHC 3372 (Ch) [53] per Briggs J. See also *Greenclose Limited v National Westminster Bank plc* [2014] EWHC 1156 (Ch) [90]; J Golden, 'Interpreting ISDA Terms: When Market Practice is Relevant, as of When is it Relevant?' (2014) 9 *Capital Markets Law Journal* 299, discussing both the need to take market practice into account when interpreting the ISDA Master Agreement and the difficulties of doing so.

[518] See Benjamin: Financial Law, 5.135–5.143.

[519] Gambling Act 2005, s 335.

[520] Financial Services and Markets Act 2000 (Regulated Activities) Order 2001 (SI 2001/544) ('Regulated Activities Order'), art 10. See 13.1.1 for a brief account of the regulatory process.

[521] On 1 April 2013 the PRA took over responsibility for the prudential regulation of insurance companies and banks. The insurance regime is set out in the Prudential Sourcebook for Insurers (INSPRU), whereas banks are now regulated primarily under the CRR and CRD, known collectively as CRD IV. Most hedge funds must be authorised by the FCA and are regulated under the Alternative Investment Fund Managers Regulations 2013 (No 1773), discussed further in chapter 16.

[522] 1.5.13 INSPRU.

[523] M Smith, 'The Legal Nature of Credit Default Swaps' [2010] *Lloyd's Maritime and Commercial Law Quarterly* 386, 387.

Secondly, as mentioned above,[524] an insured party[525] is subject to specific disclosure obligations: at present this is a duty of the utmost good faith, but will soon change to a duty of fair presentation. However, this would not be the case if the swap were not an insurance contract. The basic structure of a CDS does seem very similar to that of an insurance contract: the buyer pays the seller to pay it if an event occurs. In considering whether it is an insurance contract, it is first important to consider precisely what such a contract involves.

There is no statutory definition of an insurance contract, nor any very satisfactory common law one.[526] One description is found in *Prudential Insurance Company v Commissioners of Inland Revenue*.[527] This stresses three aspects: first, it is a contract whereby one secures for oneself a sum of money upon the happening of an uncertain event; secondly, the insured must have an insurable interest; and, thirdly, the sum of money is to meet a loss or detriment which will occur because of the event. While the first is certainly the case in CDSs, the second two are not necessarily the case. It is quite possible to have a CDS where the buyer of protection has no interest in the underlying loan, and even when it does in fact have such an interest, its rights depend on the contract between the parties and not on the existence of that interest. Further, the obligation on the seller of protection to pay is not dependent on any loss on the part of the buyer of protection: it is an absolute obligation which arises on the event of default (rather like the obligation to pay on a performance bond), and the amount may be fixed without reference to the amount of future loss.[528]

These two technical differences between a CDS and a contract of insurance were relied upon in an opinion given to the International Swaps and Derivatives Association in 1997 by the late Robin Potts QC, which has been relied upon by the entire industry ever since as conclusive, at least as to English law.[529] However, the presence of an insurable interest and the fact that the payment meets a loss are not strictly speaking necessary for a contract to be a contract of insurance. Some further explanation is required. Many types of insurance are 'indemnity insurance', where the insurer pays out a sum of money representing the loss suffered by the insured on the occurrence of the insured event. There are also many types of 'non-indemnity' insurance, however, such as life insurance, where the amount paid out is fixed in advance and does not depend on loss.[530] The fact, then, that a CDS does not provide for an indemnity does not prevent it being a contract of insurance.[531]

Whether an insurable interest is a requirement for a contract to be a contract of insurance is more complicated. If a contract is an indemnity insurance contract, payment is only made if the insured suffers loss: the insured, then, must have an interest in the subject matter of the insurance for there to be any loss.[532] In non-indemnity insurance contracts, this

---

[524] See 6.4.2.

[525] Here this would be the buyer of protection, ie the lender.

[526] FCA, Perimeter Guidance Manual ('PERG'), 6.3.

[527] [1904] 2 KB 658.

[528] JJ de Vries Robbe, *Securitisation Law and Practice in the Face of the Credit Crunch* (Alphen aan den Rijn, Kluwer Law International, 2008) 3.42.1.

[529] Benjamin: Financial Law 5.140–5.142. The opinion has been criticised: see M Smith, 'The Legal Nature of Credit Default Swaps' [2010] *Lloyd's Maritime and Commercial Law Quarterly* 386; O Juurikkala, 'Credit Default Swaps and Insurance: Against the Potts Opinion' [2011] *Journal of International Banking Law and Regulation* 128.

[530] For a full analysis, see Law Commission, *Insurable Interest Issues Paper 4* (January 2008), 1.14–1.18 and ch 3.

[531] M Smith, 'The Legal Nature of Credit Default Swaps' [2010] *Lloyd's Maritime and Commercial Law Quarterly* 386, 405.

[532] See Law Commission, *Insurable Interest Issues Paper 4* (January 2008), 1.16.

is not the case. In order to distinguish such contracts from wagers, which used to be (as a matter of policy) unenforceable,[533] and in order to prevent moral hazard,[534] statute requires an insurable interest for non-indemnity insurance contracts to be enforceable.[535]

An insurable interest, however, is not a requirement at common law for a contract to be a contract of insurance.[536] In fact, if it were, there would have been no point in statutorily providing that an insurable interest is necessary for a contract of non-indemnity insurance to be enforceable.[537] Thus the two differences identified by Robin Potts QC do not appear to prevent a CDS being a contract of insurance.[538] Of course, the kind of CDS we are concerned with in this book does include an insurable interest, in that the buyer of protection will be protecting its credit risk under a loan to a company. Thus it will not fall foul of the statutory requirement in the Life Assurance Act 1774. However, there is no insurable interest in 'naked' CDSs entered into for speculative purposes, and so these could potentially be void under English law.[539] If a CDS is a contract of insurance at common law, then the requirement of full disclosure[540] will apply. Even more significantly, it is possible that the insurance regulatory regime of the PRA and FCA will apply.

The lack of clarity as to the definition of a contract of insurance prompted the FCA to issue guidance as to what they consider relevant when deciding whether a contract is a contract of insurance, for the purposes of deciding whether authorisation is required under FSMA.[541] The FCA's guidance lists a number of general principles as to characterisation, such as the dominance of substance over form,[542] which apply in most contexts,[543] as well as more specific factors which are said to be indicative of a contract of insurance. Three that seem relevant to the question of credit derivatives are whether the provider 'assumes risk',[544] whether the amount paid by the 'recipient' is related to the likelihood of the event occurring or the seriousness of the event,[545] and whether the provider may either make

---

[533] This is not the case now: see fn [518].

[534] Such as the risk that A, who insured the life of B, might murder B to claim on the insurance policy.

[535] The statutory provisions are complicated and the law is not entirely clear: see Law Commission, *Insurable Interest Issues Paper 4* (January 2008), part 2 for an account of the history of the statutory requirements and the resulting lack of clarity. It is, however, clear that the Life Assurance Act 1774 requires an insurable interest for non-indemnity insurance that does not cover goods, merchandise and ships.

[536] FSA Policy Statement 04/19, 2004. See also O Juurikkala, 'Credit Default Swaps and Insurance: Against the Potts Opinion' [2011] *Journal of International Banking Law and Regulation* 128, 132.

[537] M Smith, 'The Legal Nature of Credit Default Swaps' [2010] *Lloyd's Maritime and Commercial Law Quarterly* 386, 397.

[538] Ibid, 409; O Juurikkala, 'Credit Default Swaps and Insurance: Against the Potts Opinion' [2011] *Journal of International Banking Law and Regulation* 128, 135, who finds the Potts opinion inconclusive.

[539] This depends on the scope of Life Assurance Act 1774, s 3. This section has been held not to apply to contracts not in the form of a 'policy' of insurance (see N Legh-Jones, J Birds and D Owen (eds), *MacGillivray on Insurance Law*, 11th edn (London, Sweet & Maxwell, 2008) 1.030) and so may well not apply to naked CDSs.

[540] See 6.4.2.

[541] PERG 6: 'Guidance on the Identification of Contracts of Insurance', www.fca.gov.uk. Prior to this the FSA issued Consultation Paper No 150 on Draft Guidance on the Identification of Contracts of Insurance (2002) and Policy Statement 04/19, 2004 dealing with the responses. Further, the lack of clarity as regards the statutory requirement of an insurable interest led the Law Commission to issue an Issues Paper on the subject (Law Commission, *Insurable Interest Issues Paper 4* (January 2008)).

[542] PERG 6.5.4. Despite this, a relevant factor is whether the contract is described as one of insurance: see PERG 6.6.8(3).

[543] See, for example, the characterisation of an interest as an absolute or a security interest, discussed at 6.2, and the characterisation of fixed and floating charges, discussed at 6.3.3.3.2.

[544] PERG 6.6.2.

[545] PERG 6.6.8(1).

a profit or bear a loss (a 'speculative risk') or only bear a loss (a 'pure' risk).[546] It will be seen that the lack or presence of an insurable interest is not part of the test, although the emphasis on 'assuming risk' might lead to the inference that the provider is 'assuming' a risk the 'recipient' has, and there would only be such risk if the 'recipient' had some form of interest which could be damaged in some way.[547] The FCA also lists as relevant whether the contract is described as an insurance contract, and whether it includes terms (such as obligations of the utmost good faith) which are usually found in insurance contracts.[548] However, the absence of usual terms is not conclusive, since the test is one of substance rather than form.[549] The exact interpretation of this substance test may be crucial in deciding whether CDSs are insurance contracts. If a similar approach is followed to that of the courts when deciding whether an interest is an absolute or a security interest,[550] namely whether the rights and obligations created are consistent with the label put on the transaction by the parties, then it is likely that they will not be held to be insurance contracts. If the approach is similar to that followed when deciding whether a charge is fixed or floating, namely that the rights and obligations created by the contract are decided using the usual rules of interpretation, and then the contract is characterised in law ignoring the labels used by the parties,[551] then it seems much more strongly arguable that CDSs are insurance contracts. This could have very far-reaching consequences, however. For example, if an agreement to pay a specific sum on a contingency were an insurance contract, then this would surely include some types of performance bond, as well as other contingent debts.[552] A court is, therefore, unlikely to characterise a CDS as an insurance contract.

6.4.3.4 Regulation of CDSs

It could be argued that the discussion above is an overly technical approach to the question, and that the real question is whether CDSs should be treated as insurance contracts from a regulatory point of view. Here there are two questions: the first is whether CDSs should be regulated in the same way as insurance contracts, and the second is whether they should be regulated at all. This latter point is complex, and will be dealt with briefly below. In relation to the former point, it is necessary to consider why insurance contracts are regulated in the way that they are. Reasons include the fact that insurance companies have particular corporate governance problems in that they take premiums up front, and deliver the 'product' (paying out on claims) later, so that there is a particular need to ensure that they are in a position to pay out.[553] Further, many insurance contracts are entered into by consumers who need protection against entering into contracts which they do not understand.[554] The second of these arguments does not apply to CDSs, since buyers of protection are either

---

[546] PERG 6.6.8(2).

[547] Law Commission, *Insurable Interest Issues Paper 4* (January 2008), 7.17.

[548] PERG 6.6.8 (3).

[549] PERG 6.6.8(4).

[550] See 7.2.2.

[551] *Agnew v Commissioner of Inland Revenue* [2001] UKPC 28 [32]; see 7.3.3.3.3.

[552] See 6.4.4.1.2 for discussion of the use of contingent debts in debt subordination.

[553] M Todd Henderson, 'Credit Derivatives are Not "Insurance"' University of Chicago Law & Economics, Olin Working Paper No 476, www.ssrn.com/abstract=1440945.

[554] Ibid. Both of these reasons are similar to those that apply to the regulation of public issues of securities, which is discussed in 10.4.

lenders or sophisticated investors. The risk for the buyer of protection is counterparty risk, that is, that the seller of protection will not pay. This is a very significant risk, and in one sense is analogous to the risk borne by an insured party that an insurance company will not pay on an insurance contract.[555] The seller faces the risk of moral hazard, in that the lender that has divested itself of risk using a CDS will have little incentive to monitor the borrower,[556] which may affect the likelihood of payment out by the seller of protection.

It can be argued that these risks apply to many transactions, not just to those CDSs. To the extent that all a CDS is doing is transferring risk, this is done by many types of transactions, both debt and equity,[557] which are not regulated or are regulated in a different way to insurance contracts. If it were sought to regulate CDSs that looked like insurance in the same way that insurance is regulated, there would be great difficulty drawing lines to decide which CDSs looked like insurance and which did not. Further, parties would then contract around those lines and enter into synthetic transactions which had the same economic effect but a different legal structure.[558] It is more satisfactory to make a decision about regulating the entire credit derivatives market. This issue is considered briefly in the next paragraph, but first it should be pointed out that, from a regulatory perspective, CDSs which protect a lender against credit risk are seen as the 'safest' kind, since they are limited in scope to protection against actual risks in relation to actual transactions.[559]

The question of whether the entire CDS market should be regulated was much debated in the wake of the financial crisis.[560] This resulted in an agreement by the G20 nations in relation to how the derivatives market should be regulated.[561] The main problems identified were lack of transparency and counterparty risk. Both problems stemmed largely from

---

[555] P Vasudev, 'Credit Derivatives and Risk Management: Corporate Governance in the Sarbanes-Oxley World' [2009] *Journal of Business Law* 331, 337. This counterparty risk is ameliorated by the posting of collateral by the seller of the swap. This may be adequate in the case of the simple credit support discussed in this section. In relation to CDSs relating to complicated portfolios, the requirement to post collateral is marked to market, and increases as the value of the portfolio diminishes. In the financial crisis this requirement became excessively onerous for some swap counterparties, such as American International Group (AIG), which, ironically, was an insurance company. See S Henderson, 'Regulation of Credit Derivatives: To What Effect, and For Whose Benefit? Part 6' [2009] *Journal of International Banking and Financial Law* 480.

[556] See 3.2.2.4.6.

[557] M Todd Henderson, 'Credit Derivatives are Not "Insurance"' University of Chicago Law & Economics, Olin Working Paper No 476, www.ssrn.com/abstract=1440945, arguing that the issuing of shares is just another way for a company to transfer risk, except that the sequence of payments is reversed, in that the shareholders pay the amount relating to the risk up front (but will lose it if the company becomes insolvent) while the 'price' is paid periodically in dividends.

[558] Ibid.

[559] S Henderson, 'Regulation of Credit Derivatives: To What Effect, and For Whose Benefit? (Part 6)' [2009] *Journal of International Banking and Financial Law* 480.

[560] The matter was considered in the Turner Review: Lord Turner, *The Turner Review: A Regulatory Response to the Global Banking Crisis* (March 2009), 3.1. Further discussion in the UK included Financial Services Authority and HM Treasury, *Reforming OTC Derivatives Markets: A UK Perspective* (December 2009); *The Future Regulation of Derivatives Markets: Is the EU on the Right Track?*, House of Lords 10th report 2009–10 (31 March 2010); S Henderson, 'Regulation of Credit Derivatives: To What Effect, and For Whose Benefit?' [2009] *Journal of International Banking and Financial Law* 413, 480, 679; T Strong and I Wilkinson, 'Derailing Derivatives' [2009] *Journal of International Banking and Financial Law* 666; R Ayadi and P Behr, 'On the Necessity to Regulate the Credit Derivatives Markets' (2009) 10 *Journal of Banking Regulation* 179. There was also an extensive debate in Europe and the US.

[561] This was part of the agreement at the Pittsburg summit held on 25 September 2009: see www.g20. org/Documents/pittsburgh_summit_leaders_statement_250909.pdf at para 13. The commitment to achieve these goals by the end of 2012 was reaffirmed at the Toronto summit on 27 June 2010: see www.g20.org/Documents/ g20_declaration_en.pdf at para 25.

the fact that most credit derivative contracts were not traded on a market with a central counterparty but 'over the counter' (OTC). It was thought that lack of transparency could lead to systemic risk, since it was not clear to parties what their counterparties' total exposure is, nor could such exposure be monitored by regulatory agencies, so dangerous levels of risk could pass unnoticed.[562] More transparency, it was said, would increase the utility of credit default swap pricing in signalling credit risk to the market and to other creditors of the reference entity.[563] Counterparty risk, as mentioned above, was a significant danger both to individual contracting parties and more generally, since if one counterparty failed to pay, there was a danger of a domino effect. The G20 agreement stated that these problems should be dealt with by greater standardisation of contracts, by (where possible) requiring derivatives to be traded on exchanges and cleared through central counterparties, for contracts to be reported to trade repositories and for there to be higher capital requirements for non-exchange derivative contracts.

In the US these proposals were addressed through the Dodd-Frank Act.[564] In the EU, reforms are being implemented through EMIR,[565] which introduces two new requirements: a 'clearing obligation' and a 'reporting obligation'. The 'clearing obligation' requires all OTC derivative contracts, subject to exemptions, to be cleared through central counterparties (CCPs),[566] which are akin to clearing houses. The CCP guarantees the performance of the contract and so bears the market risk of the trade, while the original parties to the trade bear the counterparty risk of the CCP. The 'reporting obligation' requires all counterparties, post-trade, to report contract details to a trade repository.[567] The European Securities and Markets Authority (ESMA) is responsible for implementing EMIR, monitoring trade repositories and exchanging information with competent authorities that monitor CCPs. MIFIR,[568] when implemented, will introduce an additional 'trading obligation' that will require certain derivative contracts that are sufficiently liquid and are subject to the EMIR clearing obligation to trade on a 'trading venue'. These requirements, whilst intended to reduce systemic risk, will undoubtedly lead to increased costs,[569] and the efficacy of a system that concentrates the market risk of the OTC derivatives market in clearing houses can be called into question.

6.4.4 Subordination

A lender can protect itself against the credit risk of the borrower by ensuring that it will get paid before other creditors. One way of doing this is to take security over the borrower's

---

[562] *The Future Regulation of Derivatives Markets: Is the EU on the Right Track?*, House of Lords 10th report 2009–10 (31 March 2010), 18.

[563] See 3.2.2.4.6, where the role of credit default swap pricing in corporate governance is discussed.

[564] Dodd-Frank Wall Street Reform and Consumer Protection Act 2010.

[565] Regulation (EU) 648/2012.

[566] EMIR, art 4.

[567] Ibid, art 9.

[568] Regulation (EU) No 600/2014.

[569] Deloitte estimate that the clearing requirement will lead to an additional cost of €15.5 billion for the OTC market in the EU: see www2.deloitte.com/content/dam/Deloitte/uk/Documents/financial-services/deloitte-uk-fs-otc-derivatives-april-14.pdf.

assets;[570] another is to achieve a higher ranking by means of subordination, so that subordinated creditors are not paid until the lender has been paid in full. While this is particularly important on the insolvency of the borrower, it may also have cash flow implications while the borrower is still solvent. Subordination can be used to allocate risk among different lenders in a particular funding structure: those lenders taking the greater risk gain a higher reward. One example of its use is in a leveraged buy-out,[571] where the subordination is usually achieved by using a chain structure of several companies.[572] The legal effects of this structural subordination are discussed at 6.4.4.1.4 below. Another common example of its use is in a securitised bond issue,[573] where the different tranches of securities rank in order: this can be achieved by using a turnover trust or by contractual subordination, or by providing that the senior ranked tranches are secured but the lowest rank is not.[574] Intercreditor agreements providing for ranking of lenders are very common in syndicated loan transactions, and are often in the standard LMA form.[575] It is also common for a parent company to agree that its loan be subordinated to others lending to a subsidiary company. Where a company is in difficulties, lenders may agree to be subordinated to a party who is willing to lend in an attempt to enable the company to trade out of its difficulties. Deeply subordinated debt is a hybrid security used by financial institutions to comply with capital adequacy requirements.[576]

A subordination agreement can be made between both secured and unsecured lenders. Where the lenders are secured, the agreement determines their priority, which would otherwise be determined by the general law.[577] Such agreements are very common. A lender taking a charge over the borrower's assets will normally know of any earlier charges, either because the borrower has informed it of these or because it has searched the register: the lender will, if it can, make a subordination agreement with the previous secured creditor. There is no need to obtain the borrower's consent or to make it party to the subordination agreement.[578] It is usually advisable for the lenders to agree to subordinate the debt as well as the security interest, so that the senior lender is protected even if the security is ineffective or insufficient.[579]

Where a subordination agreement is made between unsecured lenders, the main question is whether it will be effective on the insolvency of the borrower. Unless the borrower

---

[570] Discussed in chapter 7.

[571] Discussed in chapter 16.

[572] See 16.4.

[573] See 9.3.3.

[574] It should be noted that in a tranched securitisation, the order of payment outside insolvency is controlled by a 'waterfall' clause. This may provide for sequential payments (top tranches first) or pro rata payments (each tranche gets paid something): see Fuller: Corporate Borrowing, 4.67. These clauses can be very complex and their interpretation has been the subject of much litigation. See eg *Re Sigma Finance Corp (in administrative receivership)* [2009] UKSC 2; *LB Re Financing No 3 Limited v Excalibur Funding No 1 plc* [2011] EWHC 2111 (Ch); *In re Lehman Bros International (Europe) (In Administration) (No 4)* [2014] EWHC 704 (Ch).

[575] Not surprisingly, issues of interpretation of intercreditor agreements have also been considered frequently by the courts. See eg *Saltri Iii Limited v MD Mezzanine Sa Sicar* [2012] EWHC 3025 (Comm); *Torre Asset Funding Limited v Royal Bank of Scotland plc* [2013] EWHC 2670 (Ch); *US Bank Trustees Limited v Titan Europe 2007-1 (NHP) Limited* [2014] EWHC 1189 (Ch).

[576] See 2.4 and *In re Lehman Bros International (Europe) (In Administration) (No 4)* [2014] EWHC 704 (Ch) [35]–[47].

[577] See 7.4.4.

[578] *Cheah Theam Swee v Equiticorp Finance Group Ltd* [1992] 1 AC 472.

[579] Wood: Project Finance, 10-031.

is insolvent, the order of payment of lenders is not critical, since all will be paid eventually, although timing of payments can make a difference to cash flow. In insolvency, though, the order of payments is likely to make the difference, for some lenders, between being paid and not being paid. It will be recalled that the default rule for distribution of assets in insolvency to unsecured creditors is *pari passu* and that it is not possible to contract out of the operation of the *pari passu* principle by agreeing that insolvency set-off should not apply to particular debts.[580] There has been concern that contractual subordination would be likewise ineffective as an attempt to contract out of *pari passu* distribution, on the basis of both the *Halesowen case*[581] and the *British Eagle* case.[582]

6.4.4.1 Types of Subordination

In order to assess this concern, it is necessary to consider the various types of subordination which have been developed. In this analysis, the subordinated lender is known as the junior creditor, and the lender that benefits from the subordination is known as the senior creditor. In reality, the senior or junior creditor could be one or many creditors, or could be all other debt owed by the borrower (so that one or more junior creditor can be subordinated to all other creditors, for example). The subordination may also be 'springing', in that it only takes effect if a particular event happens, such as the insolvency of the borrower,[583] or it can apply at all times (a 'complete' subordination).[584]

6.4.4.1.1 Turnover Trust

One type of subordination is known as a turnover subordination. Here, the junior creditor assigns to the senior creditor or declares a trust for him of the proceeds of the debt it is owed (including dividends paid in the borrower's insolvency) until the senior creditor is paid in full.[585] In both methods, the junior creditor proves as normal in the borrower's insolvency, and thus the *pari passu* principle cannot be said to be infringed.[586] The senior creditor, in fact, is greatly benefited by this method, since it gets a 'double dividend' in the borrower's insolvency.[587] To illustrate this, suppose that the borrower's assets were £1 million and its liabilities £10 million, of which £1 million was owed to the senior creditor, £1 million to the junior creditor and the rest to other unsecured creditors. Each creditor would therefore obtain a dividend of one tenth. The senior creditor would, under the turnover method, obtain £200,000: £100,000 from each of its own dividend and that of the junior creditor.

---

[580] See 3.2.2 and 6.3.4.6.2.

[581] *National Westminster Bank Ltd v Halesowen Presswork & Assemblies Ltd* [1972] AC 785.

[582] *British Eagle International Air Lines Ltd v Compagnie Nationale Air France* [1975] 1 WLR 758.

[583] This is the common form in relation to subordinated securities issues: see Fuller: Corporate Borrowing, 10.38.

[584] This is more likely to be the situation where the subordinated creditor is a parent company or otherwise connected with the borrower: Fuller: Corporate Borrowing, 10.38.

[585] Alternatively, the junior creditor merely agrees to pay over such proceeds or dividends as it receives to the senior creditor until the latter is paid in full. It will be seen that this second method is less attractive to the senior creditor as it takes the risk of the junior creditor's insolvency, and so it is rarely used: Wood: Project Finance, 10-022.

[586] *Re NIAA Corp Ltd* (1993) 12 ACSR 141 (Sup Ct NSW); Security and Title-Based Financing, 8.111.

[587] Goode: Credit and Security, 8-24; *Re SSSL Realisations* [2004] EWHC 1760 (Ch) [27], affirmed on appeal sub nom *Squires v AIG Europe Ltd* [2006] EWCA Civ 7.

Under other methods of contractual subordination, the junior creditor would not prove, or its proof would be assessed as nil, and so there would be £1 million to be distributed among nine creditors, so that each would get a dividend of one ninth: under this method the senior creditor would therefore get £111,111.[588] It is possible, though, that under the turnover trust method, the junior creditor's debt could be reduced by the operation of insolvency set-off, so that the proceeds held on trust would also be reduced.[589]

There is no problem with an agreement by a creditor to hold the proceeds of a debt on trust for another party: this cannot violate the *pari passu* principle. An issue does arise, however, as to whether the trust is absolute or by way of security. If it is a security interest,[590] it will be registrable.[591] Further, entering into the agreement might be a breach of a negative pledge clause in another agreement to which the junior creditor is a party.[592] When characterising a transfer of an asset as absolute or by way of security, the court will look at whether the indicia of security are present, namely, the right of the transferee to any surplus value over and above the underlying obligation, the obligation of the transferor to pay the balance if the transfer does not fulfil the underlying obligation, and the right of the transferor to redeem the security if the underlying obligation is fulfilled in another way.[593] One analysis of a turnover trust is that the junior creditor has an underlying obligation to pay to the senior creditor such amount of the proceeds or dividend as will result in the senior creditor being fully paid. That amount might be all, or only some, of the proceeds received by the junior creditor. It cannot be more, so the second indicia of security cannot be present. If the amount due is only some of the proceeds, but the entire proceeds are assigned or held on trust, the junior creditor has a right to the surplus or an equity of redemption (the first and third indicia of security). But this will not be the case if the trust is only over that portion of the proceeds that is equal to the amount required to enable the senior creditor to be paid in full. To some extent, therefore, the question of whether a charge is created will depend on the wording of the declaration of trust. In *Re SSSL Realisations*[594] Lloyd J held that, on construction of the relevant clause, the trust obligation was limited to the sums due to the senior creditor, and therefore was not a charge.[595]

While this seems an eminently sensible solution, it does entail an analysis that there can be a trust of part of a fund, in this case the proceeds or dividend received by the junior creditor.[596] One could argue that this falls foul of the requirement of certainty of trusts,[597] particularly since the sums held on trust are not segregated from the assets of the trustee

---

[588] See Wood: Project Finance, 10-027 for a similar worked example.

[589] M Fealy, 'Can Set-Off Prejudice a Debt Subordination Agreement?' [2009] *Journal of International Banking and Financial Law* 64.

[590] Such a security interest could be an equitable mortgage, created by an equitable assignment of the proceeds, or a charge. The term 'charge' in the Companies Act includes both a mortgage and a charge, so either would potentially be registrable.

[591] Companies Act 2006, s 859A.

[592] Wood: Project Finance, 11-017.

[593] 7.2.2.

[594] [2004] EWHC 1760 (Ch) [49], [51].

[595] This was upheld by the Court of Appeal in *Re SSSL Realisations, sub nom Squires v AIG Europe (UK) Ltd* [2006] EWCA Civ 7 [122].

[596] This may be a debt due to the junior creditor, if it is paid into its bank account, or it will be a debt to the junior creditor from the liquidator, who is usually mandated to distribute the amount due directly to the senior creditor. Fuller: Corporate Borrowing, 10.59.

[597] Discussed in 8.2.1.3.3.

(the balance of the fund). The argument is that a person cannot declare a trust of an amount of money it owns (whether in cash or in a bank account) without separating out that sum of money from any other money by, for example, transferring it to a separate bank account.[598] The main authority cited in support of this is *MacJordan Construction Ltd v Brookmount Erostin Ltd*[599] where, pursuant to a contract between a developer and a builder, the developer was to make interim payments to the builders on production of an architect's certificate, but was entitled to retain 3 per cent of each amount, which sum it was to hold on trust for the builder. The Court of Appeal held that the developer was under a contractual obligation to separate and set aside the 3 per cent as a trust fund. This was never done, and any money retained was kept by the developer among its own assets. The Court of Appeal held that the builder could have no proprietary remedy against the insolvent developer, since no trust had been validly created, and there was no equity which bound the bank (which had a floating charge over the developer's assets) to set aside the amount that should have been separated. This decision was followed in *Re Global Trader Europe Ltd*,[600] where client money which should have been segregated by a broker was not, and was mixed with the broker's own funds: it was held that the clients had no proprietary claim on the insolvency of the broker. However, it could be said that the situation in both of these cases fell foul of the certainty requirement in two ways: not only was the trust money not segregated from the trustee's money, but it was also unidentifiable by any means, since it formed part of the trustee's general assets. It was not an unsegregated part of a particular fund.[601]

The difference between being part of a fund and being part of the trustee's general assets can be explained by reference to the argument made by Professor Goode. He starts from the premise that money is not fungible, in that although a debt is enumerated in units of currency, say, £100, those units cannot be split off from the debt in the way that bottles of wine can be taken out of a bulk.[602] Each debt, he says, is capable of separate ownership, but when part of a debt is assigned this results in co-ownership of the debt. It is clear that part of a debt can be assigned in equity, though not by statutory assignment,[603] and Professor Goode explains that because of the lack of fungibility of the subject matter, such an assignment can only result in (equitable) co-ownership of the debt.[604] If this is correct, there is no problem of certainty or identification with a declaration of trust over part of a debt, for example a bank account, by the person to whom the debt is owed. The trustee then holds the debt on trust for himself and the beneficiary. In certain circumstances, the trustee may be under an express or implied obligation to segregate money held on trust for others from money held

---

[598] D Hayton, 'Uncertainty of Subject-Matter of Trusts' (1994) 110 *Law Quarterly Review* 335, 337; Hudson: Finance, 21–16.

[599] [1994] CLC 581.

[600] [2009] EWHC 602 (Ch).

[601] Thus, for example, the situation can be distinguished from that in *Hunter v Moss* [1994] 1 WLR 452, which is discussed in detail at 8.2.1.3.3. This view also obtains some support from the judgment of Arden LJ in *Lehman Brothers International (Europe) (In Administration)* [2010] EWCA Civ 917 [171] (upheld on different grounds in *Re Lehman Brothers International Europe (In Administration)* [2012] UKSC 6).

[602] R Goode, 'Are Intangible Assets Fungible?' [2003] *Lloyd's Maritime and Commercial Law Quarterly* 379.

[603] *Re Steel Wing Co Ltd* [1921] 1 Ch 349. See 9.2.2.4.

[604] This analysis is supported by discussion in recent cases: see *In the Matter of Lehman Brothers International (Europe) (In Administration)* [2009] EWHC 2545 (Ch) [56]; *Lehman Brothers International (Europe) (in admin)* [2010] EWCA Civ 917 [171]; *Re Lehman Brothers International (Europe) (In Administration)* [2010] EWHC 2914 (Ch) [232]–[239].

for himself. An example is where this is required by the FCA Rules if the money belongs to a client of the trustee:[605] the trustee must pay that money into a separate bank account. Where this is not the case, segregation is not necessary to constitute a trust, provided that the intention to create a trust is clear. This view is supported by considerable authority to the effect that the main relevance of segregation is as evidence of intention, so that an obligation to segregate money, and/or actual segregation, shows that it was intended to declare a trust, while if there is no obligation to segregate then this is evidence that a trust was not intended.[606] Where, however, there is a very clear intention to create a trust, actual segregation is not essential to create a trust provided that the trust assets can be identified.[607] This identification can take place where the trust relates to part of a specified debt, as the obligations of the trustee are clearly defined in relation to that debt.[608]

So far we have considered whether a trust over part of the proceeds is conceptually possible, but in any particular case, it is also necessary for a court to consider whether it is intended to create such a trust,[609] as opposed to creating a charge over the whole of the proceeds. The two questions are intertwined: if a trust is not possible, the intention of the parties to create a proprietary interest would mean that the court is likely to hold that a charge has been created. If a trust of part of the proceeds is possible, however, the question is reduced to ascertainment of the intention of the parties. For example, in *Re ILG Travel Ltd*, Jonathan Parker J held that the parties in fact intended to create a charge,[610] although he accepted that it was possible for parties to intend to create a 'bare trust' where beneficiaries' money was mixed with that of the trustee.[611] In other cases where a separate bank account was set up into which money held on trust was paid, the fact that some of the money paid in belonged to the trustee did not prevent the trust being valid.[612] If the intention to create a trust over part of the proceeds is made clear enough in a turnover trust, it should be upheld by the court.[613] This was the view of the High Court of Australia in the case of *Associated*

---

[605] CASS 5.5; CASS 7.4.

[606] *Henry v Hammond* [1913] 2 KB 515, 521; also *Re Nanwa Gold Mines Ltd* [1955] 1 WLR 1080; *R v Clowes* [1994] 2 All ER 316, 325.

[607] In *Re Kayford Ltd* [1975] 1 WLR 279, 282; *R v Clowes* [1994] 2 All ER 316; *Re ILG Travel Ltd (in administration)* [1995] 2 BCLC 128; *Re Lewis's of Leicester Ltd* [1995] BCC 514; *Stephens Travel Service International Pty Ltd (Receivers & Managers Appointed) v Qantas Airways Ltd* (1988) 13 NSWLR 331 (CA) (at 348 Hope JA specifically distinguished *Henry v Hammond* as dealing merely with the case where intention is unclear); *Air Canada v M & C Travel Ltd* (1991) 77 DLR (4th) 536 (Sup Ct Canada). See also *In the Matter of Lehman Brothers International (Europe) (In Administration)* [2009] EWHC 2545 (Ch) [54].

[608] This view has been supported by a number of commentators; see P Parkinson, 'Reeconceptualising the Express Trust' (2002) 61 *Cambridge Law Journal* 657, 668; J Martin, 'Certainty of Subject Matter: a Defence of *Hunter v Moss*' [1996] *Conveyancer* 223; S Worthington, 'Sorting Out Ownership Interests in a Bulk: Gifts, Sales and Trusts' [1999] *Journal of Business Law* 1; A Dilnot and L Harris, 'Ownership of a Fund' [2012] *Journal of International Banking and Financial Law* 272.

[609] The arguments made here only really work if the proceeds are in the form of a debt owed to the junior creditor. It is submitted that this is inevitably the case: either the debt is owed by the liquidator (although note that a dividend paid by a liquidator is not a debt it the sense that it can be recovered by action) or the money is paid into the junior creditor's bank account, in which case the debt is owed by the bank. The analysis would be more difficult were the proceeds to be paid in cash (that is, legal tender), but this possibility is so unlikely that it can be dismissed.

[610] [1995] 2 BCLC 128, 156–57.

[611] An example given was the Australian case of *Stephens Travel Service International Pty Ltd (Receivers & Managers Appointed) v Qantas Airways Ltd* (1988) 13 NSWLR 331 (CA).

[612] *Re Kayford Ltd* [1975] 1 WLR 279; *Re Lewis's of Leicester* [1995] BCC 514.

[613] See, in support of this view, L Ho, 'A Matter of Contractual and Trust Subordination' (2004) 19 *Journal of International Banking Law and Regulation* 494.

Alloys Pty Ltd v ACN 001 452 106 Pty Ltd.[614] Here a contract for the sale of goods on retention of title provided that such part of the proceeds of such goods as equalled the amount
due from the buyer to the seller was to be held on trust by the buyer for the seller. The High
Court held that the trust took effect when the proceeds were received by the buyer, so that
the constitution of the trust over the relevant part of the cash or bank account amounted to
fulfilment of the buyer's obligation to pay the seller under the contract of sale.[615]

    Even if the turnover trust does create a charge and not a trust, it will only be registrable
if it is not a security financial collateral arrangement, that is, a security interest over cash
or securities, of which the secured party has possession or over which it has control.[616] It
might be such an arrangement if the charge is over the junior creditor's bank account and
the junior creditor is not permitted to withdraw cash so as to leave less than the balance due
to the senior creditor in the account, and the bank has been notified of this (so that there
is practical control).[617]

6.4.4.1.2 Contingent Debt

Another way of structuring a subordination so that it does not infringe the *pari passu* principle is as a contingent debt. There are various drafting techniques, but the basic idea is that
the junior creditor and the borrower agree that if the borrower is insolvent[618] the junior
creditor will not recover (or will be treated as a holder of preference shares) unless the
senior creditor has been paid in full.[619] In order to create a contingent debt, it is important
that the borrower is a party to the agreement: this is usually the case in, for example, a
securities issue. Contingent claims are, of course, provable in a liquidation,[620] but they are
valued by the liquidator, and if the junior creditor is not going to receive anything under
the arrangement, the conditional debt will be valued at nil (and if it is valued at more than
this, it is because it is entitled to recover on a *pari passu* basis with the other creditors).[621]

6.4.4.1.3 Contractual Subordination

Another formulation is for the junior creditor to agree with the senior creditor that it will
not claim until the senior debt has been paid in full,[622] or to agree with the debtor that
the senior creditors are entitled to be paid in full before any payments are made to the
junior creditor.[623] Potentially, this could infringe the *pari passu* principle, although it has

---

[614] [2000] 202 CLR 588 [34].

[615] It is true that it is unlikely that the actual decision would be followed in this country, but this is because it is
unlikely that the courts would interpret a contract of sale to have the effect that the buyer could pay the seller only
out of the proceeds of sale (as opposed to any other source of payment), rather than because of the reasoning in
relation to the effectiveness of the trust. See 7.3.4.

[616] See 7.3.4.

[617] For discussion of the requirements of possession and control, see 7.3.4.2.

[618] The test for insolvency may be defined so as to exclude the liabilities owed to the junior creditor: Fuller:
Corporate Borrowing, 10.49.

[619] Wood: Project Finance, 10-024; Fuller: Corporate Borrowing, 10.49; Security and Title-Based Financing,
8.102. For examples of clauses, see Wood: Loans and Bonds, 10-024–10-025.

[620] Insolvency Rules 1986, r 12.3(1).

[621] Fuller: Corporate Borrowing, 10.49; Security and Title-Based Financing, 8.117.

[622] This was the position in *Re SSSL Realisations* [2004] EWHC 1760 (Ch) [27], affirmed on appeal sub nom
Squires v AIG Europe Ltd [2006] EWCA Civ 7.

[623] This was the formulation in *Re Maxwell Communications Corp plc (No 2)* [1993] 1 WLR 1402, 1411–12.

now been held in three cases that it does not.[624] Various arguments persuaded the judge in *Re Maxwell Communications Corporation plc*, where the parties to the agreement included the debtor.[625] First, if a creditor can waive its right to prove in the liquidation after it has commenced, there is no reason why it cannot do so in advance, and partially (in case any assets remain once the senior creditor has been paid in full). Secondly, to disallow contractual subordination would have widespread repercussions.[626] Thirdly, since a subordination can be achieved by the use of the trust formulation, to disallow contractual subordination would 'represent a triumph of form over substance'.[627] Fourthly, since other jurisdictions give effect to such a form of subordination, it would be 'a matter of grave concern' if English law did not.[628]

Other arguments can also be marshalled. One is that the *pari passu* principle is designed to prevent one unsecured creditor obtaining an advantage over another in the distribution on insolvency, and there is no objection to one creditor agreeing to be paid after all the other creditors, as this merely gives that creditor a disadvantage.[629] It could be said that although this argument makes some sense where the agreement is only between the creditors, it is less successful where the borrower is also a party.[630] However, Lloyd J in *Re SSSL Realisations* thought that it made no difference to the validity of the agreement that the borrower was a party,[631] and it is difficult to see why this should be the case where it is the *pari passu* principle itself which is in issue.[632] It is, however, hard to see why the principle should render such agreement void if all creditors have consented to it, unless the true meaning of *National Westminster Bank v Halesowen*[633] is that consent is irrelevant in relation to any attempt to contract out of insolvency distribution.

One could argue that the anti-deprivation principle[634] applies where both the borrower and the junior creditor are insolvent, as in the *Re SSSL Realisations* case. In this situation, the creditors of the junior creditor are effectively deprived of an asset (the debt owed by the borrower to the junior creditor) as a result of the subordination agreement. This argument was (strongly) made in the *Re SSSL Realisations* case in relation to the debtor's insolvency, and rejected on the sensible grounds that the insolvency of each company had to be looked at separately.[635] Thus, on that view the principle clearly did not apply in the insolvency of the debtor.

---

[624] *Re Maxwell Communications* [1993] 1 WLR 1402; *Re SSSL Realisations* [2004] EWHC 1760 (Ch). The latter decision was confirmed by the Court of Appeal at [2006] EWCA Civ 7. See also *In re Lehman Bros International (Europe) (in administration) (No 4)* [2014] EWHC 704 (Ch) [84].

[625] [1993] 1 WLR 1402, 1406.

[626] Ibid, 1416. This argument may have been too strong, in that subordinations were, and still usually are, drafted as turnover trusts or contingent debt subordinations because of the uncertainty about the validity of contractual subordinations, so the use of the latter was not widespread.

[627] Ibid, 1417.

[628] Ibid, 1420.

[629] Wood: Loans and Bonds, 11-025.

[630] Security and Title-Based Financing, 8.117.

[631] [2004] EWHC 1760 (Ch) [45].

[632] This view appears to be supported by the analysis of the *pari passu* principle by David Richard J in *Revenue and Customs Commissioners v Football League Ltd* [2012] EWHC 1372 (Ch) [64], where he says that it 'applies to *any contractual or other provision* which has the effect of distributing assets belonging to the insolvent estate on a basis which is not pari passu' (emphasis added).

[633] [1972] AC 785.

[634] 3.3.2.1.2.

[635] [2004] EWHC 1760 (Ch) [45]. See L Ho, 'A Matter of Contractual and Trust Subordination' (2004) 19 *Journal of International Banking Law and Regulation* 496.

In relation to the insolvency of the junior creditor, the judge in *SSSL Realisations* at first instance held that the subordination agreement did not contravene the anti-deprivation principle.[636] The point was not raised on appeal. However, the matter did not appear to be analysed in detail. The subordination considered was a contractual agreement, and such a provision could be seen as a deprivation, in that the junior creditor had an asset (the debt) and agreed with the other creditors not to enforce it. One of the limitations of the principle may still apply, though. For example, there might be full value for the deprivation.[637] Further, the timing might be such that the diminution takes place before the junior creditor's insolvency.[638] Thirdly, the subordination could be seen as an inherent limitation of the debt,[639] if the whole arrangement was entered into under one contract.

If a subordination agreement is structured as a turnover trust, the analysis is likely to be that the junior creditor has disposed of an asset (the proceeds of its claim against the debtor), but the disposition has happened before the insolvency of the junior creditor. Thus the issue is governed not by the anti-deprivation principle, but by section 238 of the Insolvency Act 1986 covering transactions at an undervalue.[640] If the subordination is structured as a contingent debt, then this will probably be seen as a flawed asset. The reasoning above in relation to flawed assets will therefore apply.[641]

6.4.4.1.4 Structural Subordination

Debt can also be subordinated structurally: this is particularly common in private equity transactions,[642] but also in other lending to and within group companies. Structural subordination uses a tiered company structure whereby the senior debt is lent to company A, which will actually make use of the money, and the junior debt is lent to a company B. Company B owns 100 per cent of company A. As result the senior creditor has a direct debt claim against company A, whereas the junior creditor only has a debt claim against company B. Company B's claim against company A is a qua shareholder claim and is thus subordinated to all of the creditor claims of company A (including of course that of the senior creditor).[643] This has the effect that the junior creditors will only receive some value (maybe not to the full amount) if the senior creditor has been paid in full.

---

[636] [2004] EWHC 1760 (Ch) [45]. This appears to be what was meant, although the judge referred to the principle as the *pari passu* principle. Both the judge and the Court of Appeal (at [2006] EWCA Civ 7) held that the subordination agreement could not be disclaimed as an onerous contract.

[637] See 3.3.2.1.2. This appears to have been the case in *SSSL Realisations*, where the judge pointed out, in the context of establishing whether the subordination was an onerous contract, that the disability was part of the price paid for the financing of the group of companies (at [88]). It could also be the case where, for example, the subordinated creditor obtains a higher interest rate, which will occur where there are various tranches of debt.

[638] See 3.3.2.1.2

[639] See 3.3.2.1.2.

[640] F Oditah, 'Assets and the Treatment of Claims in Insolvency' (1992) 108 *Law Quarterly Review* 478; L Ho, 'A Matter of Contractual and Trust Subordination' (2004) 19 *Journal of International Banking Law and Regulation* 498. Whether the transaction was at an undervalue would depend on a number of circumstances which will not be reviewed here. See further 3.3.2.1.1.

[641] See 6.3.4.1.

[642] See 16.4.

[643] 3.3.1.2.5.

6.5 Conclusion

This chapter has examined various ways in which creditors can be protected by contractual means. It is clear that, at least for all creditors who are able to adjust by using contractual protection, the protection against the risks posed by the actions of directors which favour shareholders is superior to that provided by the general law under the legal capital rules discussed in chapter five. In relation to such risks, non-adjusting creditors may well be able to free-ride and obtain some protection. Much of the protection discussed in this chapter, then, deals with the risks posed to a particular creditor by other creditors in the event of the borrower's insolvency. Insolvency set-off, for example, enables a creditor to recover its debt or part of it pound-for-pound in a situation where most unsecured creditors would receive a mere proportion of what is owed to them. By obtaining contractual rights against solvent third parties, a creditor is able to safeguard its position when the borrower is insolvent. A creditor can also neutralise the competition that other creditors pose when the borrower is insolvent, by using covenants against further borrowing, restrictive debt/equity ratios and negative pledge clauses, as well as by obtaining agreement from other creditors that they will subordinate their claims. Of course, none of this protection is available to a creditor unless it is able to adjust.[644] Non-adjusting creditors may need some protection under the general law, but this is better dealt with on insolvency and is discussed below at 7.6.2.3.

Despite all these devices, a creditor is still better off obtaining proprietary protection if it can. The benefits of proprietary protection, as compared to contractual protection, are discussed in the next chapter.[645] It is important to realise, however, that the two are not mutually exclusive. In fact, virtually all secured creditors will also take extensive contractual protection, in the form of both covenants and rights against third parties, such as guarantees, and will usually seek to take security interests over the assets of the guarantor as well. Most lenders want as much protection as they can get, and the only restraining factors relate to the bargaining power of the borrower,[646] the availability of assets over which to take security, and the availability of third parties who can give contractual protection.

---

[644] See 3.2.2.1 for a discussion of which creditors can and cannot adjust, and of ways of adjusting which are not covered in this chapter, such as adjusting the price, diversification, refusing to contract and requiring payment in advance.

[645] 7.1.1.

[646] This can be considerable; large public companies rarely borrow on a secured basis.

7

Creditor Protection: Proprietary

7.1 Introduction

This chapter considers the proprietary protection that a creditor might have. The advantages of proprietary protection are very considerable, and are discussed at 7.1.1. However, the very advantages that a proprietary interest gives to a lender are potential disadvantages to other, less protected lenders and other creditors. For this reason, there are some limits on the freedom of lenders to demand proprietary protection. These limits take two main forms. The first is the statutory alteration of priorities on insolvency: this device is used to protect non-adjusting creditors. The details of this have already been set out in chapter three,[1] while the policy considerations are dealt with below in 7.6.[2] The second is the statutory disclosure of certain types of proprietary interests, in order to enable subsequent lenders and creditors to make adjustments so as to protect themselves.[3] The current system of registration of security interests, and the priority scheme which relates to it, is discussed throughout this chapter, but particularly in 7.4.

It is very important that a legal system enables creditors to protect themselves by taking proprietary interests: this is vital for the availability of credit. There are certain basic attributes which a law should have in this regard. One such attribute is that the law is clear, certain and easily accessible. Another is that it should be possible to obtain a proprietary right over any asset of a borrower, and that the process of doing so should be as easy and cheap as possible. Further, it must be possible to acquire proprietary rights over both the present and future assets of the borrower, without any additional formalities in the future, and to acquire a non-possessory proprietary interest which does not prevent the borrower from disposing of the asset subject to that interest in the ordinary course of business. It should be possible for any creditor (with or without proprietary protection) to find out sufficient information to enable it to adjust adequately to the risks it takes in advancing credit.[4] There should also be a simple and straightforward way for a creditor taking a proprietary interest to protect itself from losing priority to a future creditor taking a proprietary interest in the same asset. Further, it should be possible to enforce a proprietary claim effectively, whether or not the borrower is insolvent.

It is important to bear these ideal attributes in mind when considering the English law discussed in this chapter. In 7.7 the theme of an ideal law is reintroduced. In that section,

---

[1] 3.3.1.2.
[2] Especially at 7.6.2.3.
[3] For discussion of possible adjustments see 3.2.2.1.
[4] Non-adjusting creditors are discussed at 3.2.2.1 and 7.6.2.3.

the extent to which English law shapes up to that ideal is considered and a possible alternative system is discussed.

As this is a lengthy chapter, a more systematic description of the sections is in order. The rest of this section looks at the advantages to a creditor of obtaining a proprietary interest and various distinctions relating to that interest. 7.2 considers the important distinction between absolute and security interests. 7.3 discusses the types of security interests, concentrating mainly on non-possessory true security interests (mortgages and fixed and floating charges). The registration requirements are considered in 7.4, including the extent to which registration constitutes notice, as well as priority between two or more security interests, and between a security interest and an absolute interest. 7.5 discusses briefly the enforcement of security and quasi-security interests. 7.6 discusses the various economic justifications for secured credit, from both the US and the UK standpoint. 7.7 considers the arguments for and against reform of the law of personal property security in England and Wales.

7.1.1 Purpose of Obtaining Proprietary Rights

In chapter six the various ways in which a creditor[5] can protect itself by obtaining contractual rights were considered. In many of the situations discussed, an important question is whether those contractual rights give the creditor sufficient protection should the debtor became insolvent. In some cases, such as set-off, the protection given is indeed extensive. As a general rule, however, one of the main drawbacks of contractual protection is that contractual rights merely entitle a creditor to prove in the liquidation of the insolvent debtor, which generally results in recovery of little or none of the outstanding debt. In contrast, a creditor who has proprietary rights[6] is in a position to enforce them either outside of the liquidation altogether, or, at least, in priority to the claims of most of the general body of creditors. The acquisition of proprietary rights is, then, a very significant part of the protection of creditors in corporate finance. However, it should be noted that only adjusting creditors are able to protect themselves in this way.[7]

The ease of enforcement of a proprietary interest is also a significant advantage, whether or not the debtor is insolvent. If a creditor merely has a contractual right to payment, and the debtor will not pay, the creditor has to sue it for the debt. If the creditor obtains a

---

[5] In this chapter the terms 'creditor' and 'lender' will be used when appropriate in the context. When specific situations of corporate finance are discussed, the term 'lender' will be used, even where the transaction involves the retention or grant of an absolute interest. This is because the position of the financier in these cases is analogous, and is often compared to, that of a financier making a secured loan.

[6] There is considerable academic discussion about the nature of property and proprietary rights. For a brief discussion see M Bridge, *Personal Property Law*, 4th edn (Oxford, Oxford University Press, 2015) 12–13. For more detailed discussion see AW Scott, 'The Nature of the Rights of the Cestui Que Trust' (1917) 17 *Columbia Law Review* 269; JW Harris, 'Trust, Power and Duty' (1971) 87 *Law Quarterly Review* 31; A Honoré, 'Trusts: The Inessentials' in J Getzler (ed), *Rationalising Property, Equity and Trusts* (Oxford, Oxford University Press, 2003) 1; P Birks, 'Personal Property: Proprietary Rights and Remedies' (2000) 11 *King's College Law Journal* 1; R Nolan, 'Equitable Property' (2006) 122 *Law Quarterly Review* 232; R Nolan, 'Understanding the Limits of Equitable Property' (2006) 1 *Journal of Equity* 18; B McFarlane, *The Structure of Property Law* (Oxford, Hart Publishing, 2008); Law of Personal Property.

[7] See 3.2.2.1.

judgment against the debtor, and the debtor still will not pay, the creditor has to execute that judgment, either by obtaining seizure and sale of goods by a sheriff or other enforcement officer,[8] or by obtaining an attachment of debts in third-party proceedings,[9] or by obtaining a charging order.[10] The creditor then becomes an execution creditor, and obtains proprietary rights against the company's assets, giving priority over unsecured creditors on insolvency. A creditor that already has a proprietary interest is in a position (subject to contractual restriction) to enforce its interest on default even if the debtor is not insolvent, without going through this process. The threat of this is often enough to persuade a recalcitrant debtor to pay. Further, if the debtor is insolvent, the procedure for enforcing a proprietary interest is often quicker and easier than proving in a liquidation, although it should be noted that if the debtor goes into administration, there will be a moratorium on the enforcement of nearly all proprietary interests, whether absolute interests or security interests.[11]

There are other significant advantages in having proprietary rights, even outside insolvency. Such rights will usually enable the creditor to monitor what the company does with the assets over which it has such rights and, if the rights are broad enough, to monitor the entire operation of the company.[12] These monitoring rights are coupled with the right to control what the company does with the assets. The ability to control does depend, to some extent, on the nature of the proprietary rights. The holder of a fixed charge, for example, has to give consent each time a charged asset is disposed of by the company, while assets subject to a floating charge can be disposed of without the charge holder's consent. The 'ultimate weapon' of the floating charge holder, namely the ability to appoint an administrative receiver to manage the company if the charge holder's interests were threatened, has now been removed by statute[13] and so, arguably, the control power of the floating charge holder has been significantly diminished.[14] It can be said that the control power of a creditor with proprietary rights is analogous to that of an unsecured creditor with detailed financial covenants in its loan agreement, coupled with strict events of default and an effective termination and acceleration clause.[15] Security, though, gives a creditor an additional advantage, since the secured creditor is in a position to enforce against the secured assets on default without having to go through an execution process, and is also in a position to influence insolvency proceedings.[16] The extent to which a floating charge holder can still influence insolvency proceedings is discussed below.[17]

---

[8] County Courts Act 1984, Part V; Courts Act 2003, Sch 7 paras 6–11.

[9] Civil Procedure Rules, Part 72.

[10] Charging Orders Act 1979; Civil Procedure Rules, Part 73.

[11] Insolvency Act 1986, Sch B1 para 43. See 7.5.3.

[12] It is, of course, possible for a creditor to have extensive contractual monitoring rights without a security interest: see 3.2.2.4 and 6.3.2.2.

[13] Insolvency Act 1986, s 72A, as inserted by Enterprise Act 2002, s 250.

[14] This will be discussed in more detail later in the chapter: see 7.3.3.4 and 7.5.1.4.

[15] Secured loan agreements often include such provisions as well: the control power of proprietary rights comes from the general law, but lenders prefer to have the details spelled out in the agreement in the interests of clarity and certainty.

[16] J Armour, 'The Law and Economics Debate about Secured Lending: Lessons for European Lawmaking?' (2008) 5 *European Company and Financial Law Review* 3, 8–9. Other advantages of security are discussed at 7.6.2.

[17] See 7.3.3.4.

7.1.2 Absolute Interests

So far we have talked generically about proprietary rights. However, as will be recalled from the discussion in chapter three,[18] a distinction should be made between absolute interests and security interests. Under English law, the difference between the two is not the purpose for which the interest is obtained, but the legal form of it. <u>Many absolute interests are obtained by creditors, either by grant or by reservation,[19] for exactly the same purpose for which a creditor would obtain a security interest.</u> Such interests are often called 'quasi-security' interests, and there is a strong argument that they should be treated in the same way as security interests, at least in some respects, such as the requirement of registration. This argument will be considered later.[20] Other absolute interests are obtained by grant or reservation for other reasons—for example, an absolute interest in goods is granted to a buyer of those goods, and the absolute interest in goods which are hired to a company is retained by the hire company. Although the purpose of these transactions is not security for an advance (in the first example the grantee of the interest is a debtor of the company, though in the second the party reserving the interest is a creditor), the effect on the insolvency of the company is the same: the party that has the absolute interest can claim the asset irrespective of the insolvency.[21]

7.1.3 Distinctions in Relation to a Company's Assets

There are a number of important distinctions to bear in mind in relation to the types of assets which a company may have and over which a creditor can obtain a proprietary interest. The first distinction is between tangible and intangible property. Tangible property[22] has a corporeal existence. Put briefly, it comprises things that can be touched. In the context of corporate assets, tangible assets will usually include equipment, raw materials (if the company is a manufacturing company) and stock in trade[23] (manufactured goods or goods bought by the company for resale or to hire to others). It also includes land, but, as will be explained below, land falls into a slightly different category. The most significant point about tangible assets is that they can be possessed, and that there is no necessary link between who has possession and who has another proprietary interest in those assets.[24]

Although, in the absence of other evidence, possession is evidence of title, there is no problem in English law with the creation of non-possessory proprietary interests, whether absolute or security interests, if there is contrary agreement. This is critically important in

---

[18] 3.3.1.1.

[19] 3.3.1.1.

[20] 7.7.4.1.

[21] The examples that are given are of absolute legal interests, but the same point applies to absolute equitable interests—in other words, to the interest of a beneficiary under a trust.

[22] Such property can also be called choses in possession, although this term does not include land; see Law of Personal Property, 1-015.

[23] This may also be called inventory.

[24] Possession can be seen as a proprietary interest; see Goode: Commercial Law, 45–49; Law of Personal Property, 2-045. cf W Swadling, 'The Proprietary Effect of a Hire of Goods' in N Palmer and E McKendrick (eds), *Interests in Goods* Interests in Goods 2nd edn (London, Lloyd's of London Press, 1998).

relation to corporate financing, since, in relation to tangible assets, it is usually important for the company to have possession of the assets in which the creditor has a proprietary interest.[25] This is because those assets are used by the company in its business, as equipment, raw materials, or as stock in trade. For many companies, though, most of their wealth will be found in their intangible assets. These are assets which cannot be possessed, and which form a residual category of assets once the category of tangible assets has been taken out.[26] Intangible assets are usually rights against other people, either a specific person (such as a right to sue that person for a sum of money),[27] known as a 'thing in action', or people in general (such as the various forms of intellectual property),[28] usually known as 'other intangible property'.[29] In relation to this type of property there is clearly no problem about a split between who has possession and who has proprietary rights, but the question of how these rights are transferred does have to be addressed.[30] There is one case where there is a distinct overlap between tangible and intangible property: where intangible rights are contained in a document so that they can be transferred by transfer of that document, much of the law governing tangible property applies to that document. In the context of corporate finance, negotiable instruments, such as bills of exchange and bearer bonds,[31] come into this category.

The next important distinction is between real and personal property. Real property comprises land, or rights to land, and personal property comprises everything else. This distinction is largely historical, and this is reflected in different rules for, for example, the creation of security interests in land and the transfer of rights to land. However, much of the difference is technical, and will not be addressed in this book except to the extent that it impinges on the actual use of proprietary rights in land as protection for creditors. Usually, creditors are very happy to obtain proprietary rights in land owned by a company. Land is seen as a safe asset, the value of which is reasonably stable (although the experience of subprime mortgages in the US and in the UK during the financial crisis has shown that this is not always the case).

Another distinction, which has to be approached with considerable care, is between fixed and circulating. Fixed assets are assets which a company does not dispose of in the ordinary course of business, while circulating assets are acquired by the company with the

---

[25] Empirical research has shown that there is a strong correlation between the introduction of non-possessory security and an increase in bank lending in the transition economies of Eastern Europe: J Armour, 'The Law and Economics Debate about Secured Lending: Lessons for European Lawmaking?' (2008) 5 *European Company and Financial Law Review* 3, 15, citing R Haselmann, K Pistor and V Vig, 'How Law Affects Lending', Columbia Law and Economics Working Paper No 285 (2006) and M Afavuab and S Sharma, 'When Do Creditors' Rights Work?', World Bank Policy Research Working Paper No 4296 (2007), 36 (Table 8). See also M Campello and M Larrain, 'Enhancing the Contracting Space: Collateral Menus, Access to Credit and Economic Activity', Columbia Business Research Paper 13-86, http://papers.ssrn.com/sol3/papers.cfm?abstract_id=2358183.

[26] Law of Personal Property, 1-021 ff. It should be pointed out that not all writers accept that intangible property is actually property: see A Pretto, *Boundaries of Personal Property: Shares and Sub-Shares* (Oxford, Hart Publishing, 2005).

[27] In other words, a debt, including cash in a bank account.

[28] For example trade marks, patents and copyright.

[29] This category can also include such assets as export quotas (see *Attorney-General of Hong Kong v Nai-Keung* [1987] 1 WLR 1339, PC) and carbon trading units (see *Armstrong DLW GmbH v Winnington Networks Ltd* [2012] EWHC 10 (Ch)).

[30] This question is addressed in chapter 9.

[31] Discussed at 9.2.3.

aim of disposing of them in the course of its business. The characteristics of circulating assets are that they are usually only in the ownership (and/or possession) of the company for a relatively short time, they are disposed of for a greater price than the price at which they were acquired, and more, similar, assets are acquired on a regular basis. Examples of circulating assets that fit this description are raw materials and stock in trade. However, receivables can also be seen as circulating assets. They fit a different part of the cycle, in that they include the profit obtained by disposal of tangible circulating assets (if this is the business of the company) but the company has them for a relatively short time, until they are paid. The company obtains new receivables on a regular basis. Many companies, of course, have no circulating tangible assets: the business of the company may be providing services, or making loans, or creating intellectual property, but most have circulating receivables in some form or other.[32]

The distinction between fixed and circulating assets is not a hard and fast one, and can cause considerable confusion. First, most companies will dispose of their fixed assets from time to time, either to replace them or to raise money, or, because their operation has changed, so that the assets are no longer needed. Assets which are replaced regularly, such as information technology (IT) equipment, may be owned by the company for not much longer than circulating assets, as defined above (although if this is the case, most companies would use some form of hire to obtain such equipment rather than obtaining full ownership). Second, a particular type of asset, such as a car, may be a circulating asset for one company (a car sale or hire company) but a fixed asset for another company (a taxi company). Third, the structure of a transaction may affect whether a company owns one asset or many circulating assets. For example, a company may hire equipment to other companies either under a number of separate consecutive contracts or under one long-term contract. The receivables stemming from this transaction (an asset of the leasing company) could in the first instance be seen as a long-term fixed asset and in the second instance be seen as circulating assets. The points made in this paragraph need to be borne in mind when considering the distinction between fixed and floating charges, which is discussed below.[33] They show that there is a danger in characterising a charge merely by looking at the type of assets it covers.

A further, related distinction is between present and future assets. If a lender lends money generally to a company,[34] it will usually want proprietary rights not only in the assets presently owned by the company, but also in the assets to be owned by the company in the future. This is particularly true of circulating assets (they are constantly being disposed of, so eventually there will be nothing left of those assets which were 'present assets' at the time of the loan) but also of 'fixed' assets, since these will be replaced over time or new ones will be acquired. The ability of creditors to take proprietary rights over future assets is therefore critical to an effective law of corporate finance, and the way in which it has been achieved in English law will be discussed in detail later on in this chapter.[35]

It should also be noted that security interests over financial collateral (bank accounts, debt and equity securities, and credit claims by banks that grant credit in the form of loans)

---

[32] This is not necessarily true of investment companies.
[33] 7.3.3.3.2.
[34] As opposed to lending specifically for the acquisition of a particular asset.
[35] 7.3.2.1.

are treated somewhat differently from security interests over other kinds of assets. This stems from the Financial Collateral Directive (FCD),[36] enacted in the UK as the Financial Collateral Arrangements (No 2) Regulations 2003 (FCARs),[37] although some of the provisions largely reflect the preceding law. The FCARs disapply certain formality requirements (including registration)[38] and insolvency provisions.[39] They also provide that certain provisions often found in such arrangements, such as a provision for close-out netting,[40] a right of use and a right of appropriation,[41] are effective.[42] The provisions of the regulations apply both to absolute interests (called title transfer financial collateral arrangements) and to security interests (called security financial collateral arrangements) over financial collateral. A security financial collateral arrangement is one where the collateral holder has possession or control of the collateral.[43] The precise meaning of this is a matter of much debate[44] and the position in English law is uncertain. The issue is discussed in detail below.[45] The policy behind the special treatment of interests in financial collateral is to improve the efficiency and stability of the financial markets, by reducing administrative burdens, promoting certainty and harmonising the position in relation to financial collateral across the EU.[46]

7.2 Absolute and Security Interests

7.2.1 What is a Security Interest?[47]

A security interest is a proprietary interest that A obtains in relation to property owned by B to secure an obligation owed to A[48] by B or, more rarely, by C. In relation to corporate finance, this obligation is nearly always an obligation to pay money, and it is on this that

---

[36] Directive 2002/47/EC as amended by Directive 2009/44/EC.

[37] SI 2003/3226 as amended by SI 2010/2993.

[38] Ibid, reg 4.

[39] Ibid, regs 8 and 10.

[40] See 6.3.4.5.

[41] 7.5.1.2.

[42] FCARs, regs 12 and 16–18.

[43] Ibid, reg 3.

[44] Law Commission No 296, *Company Security Interests: Final Report* (Cm 6654, 2005), ch 5; Goode: Credit and Security, 6-32 ff; Security and Title-Based Financing, ch 3; M Hughes, 'The Financial Collateral Regulations' (2006) 21 *Journal of International Banking and Financial Law* 64; D Turing, 'New Growth in the Financial Collateral Garden' (2005) 20 *Journal of International Banking and Financial Law* 4; A Zacaroli, 'Taking Security over Intermediated Securities: Chapter V of the UNIDROIT (Geneva) Convention on Intermediated Securities' in L Gullifer and J Payne (eds), *Intermediated Securities: Legal Problems and Practical Issues* (Oxford, Hart Publishing, 2010) 167; R Parsons and M Dening, 'Financial Collateral—An Opportunity Missed' (2011) 5 *Law and Financial Markets Review* 164; S Goldsworthy, 'Taking Possession and Control to Excess: Issues with Financial Collateral Arrangements under English Law' [2013] *Journal of International Banking and Financial Law* 71; LC Ho, 'The Financial Collateral Directive's Practice in England' (2011) 26 *Journal of International Banking Law and Regulation* 151.

[45] 7.3.4.

[46] See the recitals to the FCD, especially 3, 5, 9 and 10. For comment see L Gullifer, 'What Shall We Do about Financial Collateral?' (2012) 65 *Current Legal Problems* 377.

[47] See Goode: Credit and Security, 1-17–1-42.

[48] It has been held that it is also possible for a valid security interest to be granted to A to secure an obligation owed to a third party (D): *In the matter of Lehman Brothers International (Europe) (In Administration)* [2012] EWHC 2997 (Ch) [43] and [44].

this book will concentrate. Therefore, A can be called the creditor,[49] and B the debtor. There are various forms of consensual security interest (pledge, contractual lien, mortgage and charge):[50] the first two are possessory and the second two are non-possessory. They will be discussed in more detail below: the discussion of a security interest in this section is generalised and largely applies to all types of security interest.

In English law it is the location of ownership that determines whether an interest is absolute or by way of security (as mentioned above, the actual purpose of the transaction is largely irrelevant). Ownership is an illusive concept.[51] There are a number of rights which a person may have in relation to a thing, including the right to use it, to possess it, to dispose of it and so on. An owner of a thing may have all these rights in relation to that thing, but it can also give away most of these rights, and still remain the owner.[52] For example, a seller of goods may retain title (ownership) in those goods when the buyer has possession and use of those goods and is permitted (by contract) to dispose of them as it wishes.[53] Ownership can therefore be seen as the residual right: that which remains when other rights in respect of the thing have been given away. On this view, the location of ownership could be seen as a matter merely of the intentions of the parties and to bear no relation to the rights that each party to the transaction actually has. However, as we shall see, the courts do not allow parties complete freedom of contract to decide on the location of ownership if it is felt that the 'reality' is truly otherwise.

If a creditor has a proprietary interest in assets which are still owned by the debtor, then that interest is a security interest if it is granted or arises by operation of law for the purpose of securing an obligation. There are various features, known as the indicia, or incidents, of security,[54] that an interest is likely to have if it is a security interest, and which, if present, indicate that an interest is a security interest. The first is that if the asset in question is realised in order to meet the secured debt, and the amount realised is more than the debt, the debtor has a right to that surplus. The second is that if the amount realised is less than the secured debt, the debtor remains liable for the balance. The third is that the debtor is always able to rid the asset of the creditor's proprietary interest by paying the debt by means other than by the realisation of the asset: this is known as the 'right to redeem'. Another main feature of a security interest is that it can only be created by grant and not by reservation.[55] If a debtor grants an interest to a creditor, therefore, this can either be an absolute interest or a security interest: which it is will depend on whether the incidents of security are present. If a creditor reserves an interest, however, this can only be an absolute interest, even if the debtor is granted many of the rights that usually go with ownership, such as the right to possess, the right to use and the right to dispose of the asset.

---

[49] The term 'creditor' will be used throughout this chapter rather than the term 'lender' which is used in other chapters.

[50] *Re Cosslett (Contractors) Ltd* [1998] Ch 495, 508 (Millett LJ).

[51] See discussion in Law of Personal Property, 2-002 ff.

[52] M Bridge, *Personal Property Law*, 4th edn (Oxford, Oxford University Press, 2015); A Honoré, 'Ownership' in A Guest (ed), *Oxford Essays in Jurisprudence* (Oxford, Clarendon Press, 1961) 107, 126–28.

[53] For further discussion and more examples see Security and Title-Based Financing, 4.07–4.11.

[54] *Re George Inglefield* [1933] Ch 1, 27–28.

[55] *McEntire v Crossley Brothers Ltd* [1895] AC 457, 462; *Clough Mill v Martin* [1985] 1 WLR 111, 116, 119, 120–21 (CA); *Armour v Thyssen Edelstahlwerke AG* [1991] 2 AC 339, 351–52 per Lord Keith, 354 per Lord Jauncey. See Security and Title-Based Financing, 4.22 for further discussion of this proposition.

This discussion, which might be thought rather theoretical, is important for at least two reasons. First, since there are a number of statutory and other consequences where an interest is a security interest, most notably that most security interests are required to be registered, a creditor may attempt to avoid creating a security interest. This conclusion may be challenged by other creditors if the debtor is insolvent, and the courts have on a number of occasions had to decide whether a particular interest is absolute or by way of security. This process of characterisation will be examined shortly. The second is that in many countries the technical differences between some absolute interests and security interests have been statutorily abolished, and all transactions which have the purpose of security are treated in the same way. Such systems will be examined later in this chapter in the course of a discussion as to whether the same route should be followed in England and Wales.[56]

7.2.2 Characterisation of Interests as Absolute or Security Interests

Courts have to characterise in many contexts, usually where a concept appears in a statute. Particular consequences may flow from the characterisation of a contract (for example, as a contract of service or for services), of a person (for example, whether a company is an enemy alien),[57] of a tangible asset (for example, whether it is a motor vehicle)[58] and so on. We are concerned here with the characterisation of a proprietary interest. This means that, possibly unlike other types of characterisation, the result of the court's decision is likely to affect not only the parties to the transaction by which the interest was created, but other parties as well.[59] In the context of security interests, this is usually because the debtor is insolvent, and the general creditors are competing for the scarce resources. Thus, if an interest is a security interest but is unenforceable against the liquidator as it has not been registered,[60] this increases the assets available for distribution to the general creditors. It should be noted that the courts have also had to characterise charges as fixed or floating since, as will be recalled, preferential creditors, the prescribed part and the expenses of the insolvency are paid out of floating charge assets in priority to the floating chargee, but not out of fixed charge assets.[61] This characterisation process will be discussed later in the chapter.[62] It is important, however, to appreciate that where third parties are affected by the characterisation of an interest, an argument can be made that the parties creating that interest cannot have total freedom of contract in labelling that interest, so that they cannot have the benefits of a certain type of interest without suffering the detriment that follows from having that type of interest. This argument has been much more strongly endorsed by the courts in the context of the fixed/floating charge characterisation than in the context of absolute/security interest characterisation.

---

56 7.7.

57 *Daimler Company Ltd v Continental Tyre and Rubber Company (Great Britain) Ltd* [1916] 2 AC 307.

58 Hire Purchase Act 1964, s 29(1).

59 This is not necessarily the case. For example, in theory characterisation may be necessary in order to determine whether a party is in breach of a negative pledge clause by creating a security interest. This would only affect the position between the parties to the negative pledge clause (see 6.3.1.6.).

60 Companies Act 2006, s 859H.

61 3.3.1.2.

62 7.3.3.3.2.

In relation to the absolute/security interest characterisation, the courts have identified two approaches, called the 'external approach' and the 'internal approach' by Staughton LJ in *Welsh Development Agency v Export Finance Co Ltd*.[63] In both approaches, the court has to determine what rights and obligations are actually created by the contract:[64] the labels put on the rights and obligations by the parties, and the label attached to the interest created, are not determinative at this stage, although they can be taken into account. The 'external approach' is where it is contended that the parties did not intend to create the rights and obligations that the contract purports to create.[65] If this is made out, the document is said to be a 'sham' and will be recharacterised or declared a nullity. In order to determine this question, the court can look at evidence external to the agreement itself, including evidence of what the parties have done after the date of the contract.[66] If there is no evidence of sham, the court will look at the rights and obligations actually created by the contract and decide whether they give rise to an absolute or a security interest (the 'internal approach').[67] Since a finding of a sham involves a finding of at least some dishonesty, the courts are slow to come to this conclusion,[68] and, in the context of corporate finance, the internal approach is more likely to be followed. This does not mean, however, that the courts will never consider whether a commercial agreement is a sham.[69] It should also be pointed out that doubt has been cast on the analysis of Staughton LJ by Lord Walker in *Re Spectrum Plus*[70] and by later commentators, particularly as to whether it covers all possible cases.[71] It is certainly true that parties can change the nature of an agreement after it has been made by variation, waiver or estoppel. Such an analysis may be a halfway house between a court finding a sham and not recharacterising at all, in a situation where post-contractual conduct is inconsistent with the interest that appears to have been created by the agreement.[72]

There is a strong argument that the courts' approach to characterisation of security interests differs between the absolute/security interest cases and the fixed/floating charge cases. One reason is that there is a reasonably clear touchstone as to whether a charge is fixed or floating—namely, whether the chargee has control over the charged assets[73]—whereas the

[63] *Welsh Development Agency v Export Finance Co Ltd* [1992] BCLC 148, 186.

[64] The principles of interpretation of contracts discussed at 6.2 should be borne in mind in this regard.

[65] *Snook v London and West Riding Investments Ltd* [1967] 2 QB 786, 802C–802E. For discussion of the concept of 'sham' in relation to security interests see A Berg, 'Recharacterization' (2001) 16 *Journal of International Banking and Financial Law* 346; J Vella, 'Sham Transactions' [2008] *Lloyd's Maritime and Commercial Law Quarterly* 488; Lord Neuberger, 'Sham Doctrine and Company Charges' in E Simpson and M Stewart (eds), *Sham Transactions* (Oxford, Oxford University Press, 2013).

[66] When construing a contract, the normal rule is that the court cannot look at evidence of post-contractual conduct: *James Miller & Partners Ltd v Whitworth Street Estates (Manchester) Ltd* [1970] AC 583, 603, 611, 614. See 7.3.3.3.2.

[67] This method is also advocated in relation to the fixed/floating charge characterisation by Lord Millett in *Re Brumark Investments Ltd* [2001] 2 AC 710 [32], and was approved by the House of Lords in *Re Spectrum Plus Ltd (In Liquidation)* [2005] 2 AC 68 (see Lord Walker at [141]).

[68] *National Westminster Bank v Jones* [2001] 1 BCLC 98 [46] per Neuberger J.

[69] See 7.3.3.3.2.

[70] [2005] 2 AC 680 [160].

[71] S Atherton and R Mokal, 'Charges over Chattels: Issues in the Fixed/Floating Jurisprudence' (2005) 26 *Company Lawyer* 10; A Berg, 'The Cuckoo in the Nest of Corporate Insolvency: Some Aspects of the *Spectrum* Case' [2006] *Journal of Banking Law* 47.

[72] This approach is problematic in the context of fixed and floating charges, however, because of Insolvency Act 1986, s 251 which provides that the Insolvency Act consequences of a charge being floating apply to the charge 'as created': see 7.3.3.3.2.

[73] 7.3.3.3.2. This touchstone may, of course, be difficult to apply in practice.

position is much less clear in relation to the absolute/security interest cases. Another is that even if a charge which is labelled fixed is recharacterised as floating, the consequences for the chargee (loss of priority) are not as drastic as where an unregistered 'absolute' interest is recharacterised as a security interest and is therefore void. The result appears to be that in the latter cases, the courts tend to ask whether the rights and obligations created are consistent with the label put on the transaction by the parties,[74] rather than the more open question 'what is the correct legal label to put on the rights and obligations created in this agreement?' This is despite the fact that the rhetoric of the courts in the absolute/security interest cases is that they are looking at the substance and not the form of the agreement.[75] This, of course, does not mean the economic substance: it is quite clear that under English law the parties can choose whatever legal form they wish to achieve an economic result.[76]

7.2.3 Reasons for Choosing a Structure Based on an Absolute or a Security Interest

Before discussing the policy considerations that apply to the absolute/security interest characterisation process, we should consider why companies, and their lenders, choose a structure involving retention or grant of an absolute interest rather than a security interest. One reason which applies to all such structures is that there is no registration requirement under the Companies Act 2006 in relation to absolute interests. Other reasons are more transaction specific. In relation to devices based on retention of title, these usually give the lender priority over secured creditors.[77] Certain structures, such as hire purchase arrangements,[78] also give the lender priority over bona fide purchasers of the asset. The lender may be interested in having the surplus value in the asset, for example, this is the case in an operating lease. A lender may perceive that an absolute interest is a 'stronger' interest than a security interest.[79] Where the company has already borrowed on terms which include a negative pledge clause, a transaction involving an absolute interest may not be in breach of this clause.[80] A lender may prefer to finance receivables by factoring or invoice discounting because of the difficulties in creating a fixed charge over receivables,[81] whilst a floating charge is unattractive for the reasons discussed in chapter three and below.[82] Where

---

[74] *Orion Finance Ltd v Crown Financial Management Ltd (No 1)* [1996] BCC 621, 625–26.

[75] *McEntire v Crossley* [1895] AC 457, 462; *Helby v Matthews* [1895] AC 471, 475; *In re George Inglefield Ltd* [1933] Ch 1, 27. For an attack on that rhetoric see A Berg, 'Recharacterisation after Enron' [2003] *Journal of Business Law* 205, 237.

[76] *Re Polly Peck International plc* [1996] BCC 486, 495; *Chow Yoong Hong v Choong Fah Rubber Manufactory* [1962] AC 209, 216–17; *Beconwood Securities Pty Ltd v Australia and New Zealand Banking Group Limited* [2008] FCA 594 [53].

[77] See 7.4.4; *Welsh Development Agency v Export Finance Co Ltd* [1992] BCC 270, 300G.

[78] Except in relation to motor vehicles; see Hire Purchase Act 1964, Part III.

[79] See eg BLM30015, HM Customs and Excise, Finance Leasing Manual: 'Lessors are therefore more prepared to lend to less solid businesses and, perhaps, to lend cheaper than ordinary lenders (even leaving aside tax considerations).'

[80] See *Welsh Development Agency v Exfinco* [1992] BCLC 148, 154. Clauses, however, are usually now drafted widely enough to catch absolute interests: see 6.3.1.6.1.

[81] See 7.3.3.3.2.

[82] See 7.3.3.3.4 and 2.3.4.1.

the borrower is in administration, security interests cannot be enforced by a lender without the permission of the administrator or without the leave of the court.[83] The same applies to certain absolute interests created by retention of title.[84] However, the 'enforcement' of other absolute interests is free of these restrictions, which may make them more attractive to certain lenders.

For both parties there may be tax advantages, although these have been steadily whittled away by the Inland Revenue.[85] They depend on whether the criteria in the relevant legislation are fulfilled; whether the interest created is absolute or by way of security is either irrelevant or only partially relevant.

From the borrower's point of view, certain structures, such as securitisation, are attractive in that assets are removed from the borrower's balance sheet, since an absolute interest is granted to the lender. This may improve the borrower's debt to equity ratio,[86] or, in the case of a bank or financial institution, affect how much capital has to be retained to comply with capital adequacy requirements.[87] However, like tax, accounting and capital adequacy are governed by particular and strict rules and are not specifically dependent on the nature of the transaction. For example, International Accounting Standard 39 'de-recognises' assets if the originator has 'no continuing involvement' in them, and this can be the case either if there is a true sale or if there is a 'pass-through' arrangement, which need not be a true sale.[88]

In the context of the provision of collateral for capital market transactions, particularly derivatives, title transfer collateral arrangements are very common in Europe.[89] This is largely because the collateral taker is thereby free to use (rehypothecate) the collateral, can enforce by retention or appropriation of the collateral, can rely on close-out netting, and does not need to register the interest created. These advantages also arise if a security collateral arrangement falls within the FCARs, but it can be difficult to identify when this is the case.[90] Title transfer arrangements such as repos are commonly used to borrow money using securities are collateral.[91]

It may be that a structure involving an absolute interest is the only way a lender is prepared to lend, or that the terms, such as the rate of interest, may be more attractive than borrowing on security. However, such a structure is riskier for a borrower than a straight loan on security. Depending on the terms of the transaction, the borrower may lose any surplus value in the asset if it defaults. Further, even if there is a contractual obligation on the lender to repay any surplus to the borrower, the borrower takes the credit risk of the

---

[83] Insolvency Act 1986, Sch B1 para 43(2).

[84] Insolvency Act 1986, Sch B1 para 43(3) is in similar terms to para 43(2) and applies to hire purchase agreements (defined in Sch B1 para 111(1) as including 'a conditional sale agreement, a chattel leasing agreement and a retention of title agreement').

[85] For example, a finance lease is much less advantageous from a tax point of view than it used to be; see 2.3.4.4.2.

[86] Wood: Project Finance, 6.010.

[87] See 2.3.1.4.

[88] Implemented in the UK by FRS 26 (Financial Reporting Standard). Note also that the economic effects of other receivables financing transactions such as invoice discounting must be reflected in accounts: see FRS 5.

[89] Thus the ISDA Credit Support Annex (English law) gives rise to a title transfer collateral arrangement, while the ISDA Credit Support Annex (New York) law gives rise to a security interest arrangement. There is a Credit Support Deed (English law) which gives rise to a security interest, but this is much less commonly used.

[90] 7.3.4.

[91] See Goode: Credit and Security, 6-27 ff.

lender in relation to this, and if the lender becomes insolvent the borrower will only have an unsecured claim.[92] In contrast, where a secured creditor enforces security it holds any surplus value on trust for the borrower.[93]

7.2.4 Policy Considerations

The process of recharacterisation is not a merely technical one: there are significant policy issues to be considered. On one hand there is the policy of freedom of contract: this has to be the default position in a commercial contract unless there is any reason to qualify it. Of course, freedom of contract cannot permit parties to create contracts which are internally inconsistent, or to put a label on an interest which is completely inappropriate. Having said this, where only the parties to the contract are affected, they are (sometimes) allowed to agree that black is white,[94] but the position is different when third parties are affected. Then, a policy in favour of publicity of interests (where those interests are not readily apparent by external examination) must be weighed against the policy of freedom of contract. Those dealing with companies should have a simple means of discovering their true financial state, and this includes knowing whether the assets they appear to have are encumbered by security interests or actually belong to other parties. At present, however, only security interests are registrable, and not absolute interests, despite the fact that assets which appear to belong to the company actually belong to a financier. This distinction will be discussed in detail below,[95] but it is important to note at present that where an English court characterises an interest as absolute this means that it is not registrable, and is therefore 'hidden'.[96]

It should be remembered, however, that there are ways of discovering the state of a company's finances other than by consulting the company charges register. The company produces annual accounts which are public,[97] and if a company has sold an asset, such as its receivables, in theory the balance sheet will show that the company's assets are reduced. However, the assets will be increased by the purchase price obtained for the receivables. Often this cash will be used to pay other liabilities, so that these will reduce (and the assets will also reduce). Thus, although the balance sheet will reflect the transaction, it may not be obvious to those looking at it that the receivables have been sold.[98] It can also be argued

---

[92] This risk is now well appreciated in the capital markets, particularly in relation to derivative transactions. A similar risk arises where the collateral taker under a security collateral arrangement has a right of use, permitted under reg 16 FCARs. Various regulatory steps can be taken to mitigate the risk. See, in the context of central clearing of derivative transactions, L Gullifer, 'Compulsory Central Clearing of OTC Derivatives: The Changing Face of the Provision of Collateral' in L Gullifer and S Vogenauer (eds), *English and European Perspectives on Contract and Commercial Law* (Oxford, Hart Publishing, 2014). Title transfer collateral arrangements with retail clients are banned under art 16(10) MiFID II, which was adopted by the European Council in May 2014 and came into force in July 2014.

[93] *Charles v Jones* (1887) 35 Ch D 544, 549.

[94] One example of this is a non-reliance clause in a contract, where both parties know that there actually was reliance: the clause is effective on the basis of contractual estoppel. See *Peekay Intermark Ltd v Australia and New Zealand Banking Group Ltd* [2006] EWCA Civ 386 [56]—[57]; *Springwell Navigation Corporation v JP Morgan Chase Bank* [2010] EWCA Civ 1221 [169] and [177]. See also 8.4.4.

[95] 7.7.

[96] *Associated Alloys Pty Ltd v ACN 001 452 106 Pty Ltd* (2000) 202 CLR 588 [95] (HC Aust).

[97] See 11.3.1.1. Note that listed companies are required to produce more frequent reports (see 11.3.1.2).

[98] Also balance sheets are historic so do not necessarily give an up-to-date picture.

that if a capital asset, such as a machine, is acquired using a retention of title device such as a finance lease, the company will not be able to produce documentation proving ownership if asked to do so as part of a due diligence exercise, whereas it would be able to do so if the machine were charged. Thus, absolute interests are discoverable with sufficient due diligence; however, this is expensive. A system of registration, on the other hand, provides a cheap and accurate method of publicising and discovering the existence of interests. If publicity of interests is considered important, it can be argued that companies should not be able to 'hide' interests by entering into transactions which create absolute interests rather than security interests, when the purposes are virtually identical.

One argument that is made in relation to characterisation of fixed and floating charges is that the very benefit parties want when they take a floating charge, namely the ability to take a wide-ranging charge over circulating assets of the company, is the reason for the statutory consequences which chargees seek to avoid by attempting to create a fixed charge.[99] Thus, a policy justification for recharacterisation is that lenders cannot have the benefit without having the statutory detriment which Parliament has decided goes with it. It is not so clear, however, that this argument can be applied to the sale/charge characterisation. It can be argued that the legislature has decided what interests are registrable, and provided that the parties have actually created an absolute interest, the policy of publicity should not affect characterisation: it is up to the legislature to further this policy by widening the category of registrable interests, not the courts by recharacterising interests.[100]

It is also significant that many of the financing transactions that operate on the basis of a grant or reservation of an absolute interest are in forms that are used extensively on a daily basis in the financial world and account for many billions of pounds' worth of lending every year. Thus the recharacterisation of a 'true sale' securitisation[101] or an invoice discounting transaction as a registrable security interest would have very widespread consequences. However, the strength of this argument should be doubted. The courts should not determine the boundaries of concepts on the basis of the damage done or not done to the financing industry by their decisions. Therefore, if there is serious concern, the better course may be express legislation to deal with the problem, such as a 'safe harbour' for securitisations,[102] or a reform of the registration requirements.[103]

7.2.5 Process of Characterisation in Relation to Particular Structures[104]

In this section the party providing the finance is called the 'lender' and the company receiving the finance is called the 'borrower' despite the form of the transaction. This is to aid comparison with structures involving 'true' security interests. Of course, if the transaction is not recharacterised as a secured loan, the parties are not lenders and borrowers in law.

---

[99] See *Re Spectrum Plus* [2005] UKHL 41 [111], [141].

[100] *McEntire v Crossley Brothers* [1895] AC 457, 466; *Helby v Matthews* [1895] AC 471, 477; *Associated Alloys Ltd v ACN 001 452 106 Pty Ltd* (2000) 202 CLR 588 [49]–[51].

[101] See 9.3.3.

[102] V Seldam, 'Recharacterisation in "True Sale" Securitisations: The "Substance Over Form" Delusion' [2006] *Journal of Business Law* 637, 643.

[103] See 7.7.

[104] For detailed discussion of the law in this area see Security and Title-Based Financing, 4.28–4.35.

7.2.5.1 Grant and Grant-Back

The structure of sale and lease-back[105] constitutes a grant by the company of an absolute interest in an asset to the lender, and a grant-back by the lender of a possessory interest to the company. The economic purpose of the transaction is (virtually) always for the lender to provide finance to the borrower. However, as we have seen, the economic purpose is irrelevant to the legal process of characterisation. In relation to this structure, the court will look at the transaction as a whole;[106] this is important since if the constituent parts were examined separately it could not be a secured transaction: the grant-back involves the retention of an absolute interest and cannot be a security interest.[107] In fact, the courts have only recharacterised such agreements as secured loans in what appear to be sham cases;[108] where the borrower genuinely intends to enter into a sale and lease-back, the courts have upheld the structure.[109] Where, however, a transaction was completely circular (a sale and sale-back) the court did recharacterise it as a secured loan.[110] This is generally seen as a one-off case which turned on some (rather unclear) terms in the agreement. The fact that there was an obligation to repurchase the same assets as were sold to the financier meant that there was exact mutuality.[111] It can be argued that in other sale and sale-back transactions, such as repos and securities lending transactions, the obligation is to transfer equivalent securities and so exact mutuality is not present.[112]

7.2.5.2 Grant

At least two structures fall into the category of grant. One is the very common receivables financing transaction;[113] the other is the sale of goods to a financier who then sells as an undisclosed agent.[114] Since the relevant interest is granted to the lender, it can potentially be either absolute or by way of security.[115] One might think, then, that the courts would approach characterisation by looking at the rights and obligations created and deciding whether they created an absolute or a security interest. In fact, in the case of both structures, the courts have looked at the legal form of the transaction (as creating an absolute interest)

---

[105] Described above at 2.3.4.4.1.

[106] *Re Curtain Dream Ltd* [1990] BCLC 925, 934.

[107] See 7.2.1.

[108] For example, *Re Watson* (1890) 25 QBD 27; *Polsky v S and A Services* [1951] 1 All ER 185; *North Western Central Wagon Finance Co Ltd v Brailsford* [1962] 1 WLR 1288.

[109] *Yorkshire Railway Wagon Co v Maclure* (1882) 21 Ch D 309.

[110] *Re Curtain Dream Ltd* [1990] BCLC 925.

[111] Ibid, 939.

[112] This was one of the reasons given by Finkelstein J for not recharacterising a securities lending transaction as a mortgage in *Beconwood Securities Pty Ltd v Australia and New Zealand Banking Group Limited* [2008] FCA 594 [50]. However, if it is right that shares and bonds are fractional interests (see 8.2.1.3.3 and Goode: Credit and Security, 6.14) this may need some qualification: G Tolhurst, 'Securities Lending in Australia' (2009) 1 *Corporate Rescue and Insolvency* 22. Another way of analysing the issue is as follows. Shares and bonds are fractional interests (so that there is no identification problem in relation to a declaration of trust) but different 'parcels' of shares or bonds acquire a different history over time. These different 'parcels' can then be seen as distinct, so that they can be seen as 'equivalent' rather than the 'same'. See Goode: Credit and Security, 6.14. For detailed discussion of the recharacterisation of repos and securities lending agreements see Security and Title-Based Financing, 4.30.

[113] 2.3.4.1.

[114] *Welsh Development Agency v Export Finance Co Ltd* [1992] BCLC 148.

[115] See 7.2.1.

and then looked to see if the exact terms of the agreement are consistent with that form. The difference is, perhaps, subtle but has had the effect that no agreement in this category has actually been recharacterised by the courts, despite the fact that in both structures there are provisions which, looked at from a different perspective, could be seen as indicia of security.[116]

In a receivables financing transaction, for example, the sale of the receivables is often with recourse, so that the credit risk of non-payment by the debtors is on the borrower and not the lender.[117] This might be seen as indicative of the second of the indicia of security discussed above: that the borrower is always liable for the balance if the 'security' does not realise enough to repay the 'loan'. However, the courts have taken the view that this does not convert a contract expressed to be a sale into a charge.[118] Further, a receivables financing agreement will often provide for the borrower to retain any surplus generated by the debtors over and above the original purchase price and the discount charge, which resembles the first indicium of security.[119] Despite this, the courts have held that this provision is consistent with a sale rather than a charge.[120] Receivables financing has also increased hugely in popularity in the last 20 years.[121] This is partly because asset-based lending is seen as a safer finance model than cash flow lending, particularly since the moratorium on enforcement of security in an administration does not apply to outright assignments.[122] However, the growth in popularity is also a result of the uncertainty as to characterisation of fixed and floating charges engendered by the *Spectrum* decision:[123] there is very little danger of an absolute interest being recharacterised as a floating charge.

The other structure, where goods are sold to a financier and then sold by the company as undisclosed agent, was considered in the important case of *Welsh Development Agency v Export Finance Co Ltd*.[124] The Court of Appeal again took the view that freedom of contract was to be upheld, and features which might have been thought to indicate security, such as a 'right of redemption', were said not to be inconsistent with the structure of the transaction by the parties as a sale.[125]

---

[116] See 7.2.1.

[117] This is done by the borrower guaranteeing the debts, or agreeing to repurchase debts which are not paid within a certain period.

[118] *Lloyds & Scottish Finance Ltd v Cyril Lord Carpets Sales Ltd* [1992] BCLC 609, 616.

[119] See 7.2.1.

[120] *In re George Inglefield Ltd* [1933] Ch 1, 20; *Olds Discount Co Ltd v John Playfair Ltd* [1938] 3 All ER 275, 276–77.

[121] 2.3.4.

[122] Insolvency Act 1986, Sch B1 para 43.

[123] J Armour, 'Should We Redistribute in Insolvency?' in J Getzler and J Payne (eds), *Company Charges: Spectrum and Beyond* (Oxford, Oxford University Press, 2006); S Frisby, '*In re Spectrum Plus—Less a Bang than a Whimper*' in P Omar (ed), *International Insolvency Law: Themes and Perspectives* (Aldershot, Ashgate, 2008). For discussion of the *Spectrum* decision see 7.3.3.3.2.

[124] [1992] BCLC 148. See also *In re Lovegrove* [1935] Ch 464; *Palette Shoes Pty Ltd v Krohn* (1937) 58 CLR 1 (HC Aust).

[125] [1992] BCLC 148, 168–69, 189. Indeed, Dillon LJ said that the parties were 'entitled to choose' how to raise finance, and Ralph Gibson LJ stated that '[i]f any mischief arising from off balance sheet financing is judged to be serious it could be prohibited by legislation'.

7.2.5.3 Retention of Title

Structures such as credit sales on retention of title (ROT) terms,[126] hire purchase and conditional sale agreements and finance leases[127] all depend on the device of retaining title. Since a security interest cannot be created by the retention (as opposed to the grant) of title, such transactions will not be recharacterised as creating a security interest even if they include terms which otherwise would appear to be indications of security, such as a right to the surplus.[128] However, many contracts of sale on ROT terms also provide that the seller shall 'retain' title in any products made with the goods sold, or in any proceeds of resale. Whether such a provision creates an absolute or a security interest in the products or proceeds depends on the precise terms of the contract in question, but certain general propositions can be stated. Let us first consider products. If the product is a new thing,[129] then it is initially owned by the producer (the buyer). The actual effect of the 'retention' provision is that the buyer grants an interest in the product to the seller. Being by grant, that interest can be either an absolute or a security interest. However, it is likely that the parties intended the buyer to have the right to any surplus value over and above the purchase price, and to be able to pay the purchase price from any source of finance, after which it will own the product outright. These are the first and third indicia of security mentioned above,[130] and therefore the transaction will be characterised as a security interest.[131]

Next, we will consider a provision that the seller 'retains' an interest in the proceeds of a sub-sale. It is even clearer here that the seller's interest is by grant from the buyer, since the sub-buyer clearly intends to transfer ownership in the proceeds to the buyer. Therefore, any interest of the seller is granted by the buyer, and the test is once again whether the indicia of security are present. Since the sub-sale is likely to be at a profit, the buyer will be entitled to any surplus, and will be able to pay the seller's purchase price from other funds, thus 'redeeming' the sub-sale proceeds: thus the two indicia of security are present. The seller's interest in the proceeds will be recharacterised as a charge.[132] One case in which the opposite result was reached is the Australian case of *Associated Alloys Pty Ltd v ACN 001 452*

---

[126] 2.3.4.4.4.

[127] See 2.3.4.4.2.

[128] See *Clough Mill v Martin* [1985] 1 WLR 111, 117, where there was held to be an obligation to account, and *McEntire v Crossley* [1895] AC 457, 465 per Lord Herschell. In that case the same effect was specifically provided for in the contract. See also the agreement in *Kinloch Damph Ltd v Nordvik Salmon Farms Ltd* (1999) Outer House Case, June 30, 1999, where the seller's right to repossess was limited to the amount outstanding under the contract. Similar reasoning applies where the contract provides that title will not pass until all monies due from the buyer to the seller have been paid.

[129] That is, the goods sold cannot be removed from the product: where this is the case then title continues to be retained; see *Hendy Lennox (Industrial Engines) Ltd v Grahame Puttick Ltd* [1984] 1 WLR 485.

[130] 7.2.1.

[131] See eg *Clough Mill v Martin* [1985] 1 WLR 111; *Ian Chisholm Textiles v Griffiths* [1994] 2 BCLC 291; *Modelboard Ltd v Outer Box Ltd* [1993] BCLC 623.

[132] *E Pfeiffer Weinkellerei-Weineinkauf GmbH & Co v Arbuthnot Factors Ltd* [1988] 1 WLR 150; *Tatung (UK) Ltd v Galex Telesure Ltd* (1988) 5 BCC 325; *Compaq Computers Ltd v Abercorn Group Ltd* [1993] BCLC 602. If the contract provides that the buyer is selling as the seller's agent, the seller may be entitled to the whole sub-purchase price, in which case the seller's interest is not by way of charge: *Caterpillar (NI) Limited (Formerly Known as) FG Wilson (Engineering) Limited v John Holt & Company (Liverpool) Limited* [2013] EWCA (Civ) 1232. For criticism see L Gullifer, 'The Interpretation of Retention of Title Clauses: *Wilson v Holt* Generates Some Difficulties' [2014] *Lloyd's Maritime and Commercial Law Quarterly* 564.

106 Pty Limited.[133] In that case, the purchase price was expressed to be payable by a trust which arose over the proceeds of the sub-sale as soon as they were received, but the trust only extended to the amount of the purchase price due. It is unlikely that this result would be achieved in other cases, since the courts would probably not interpret a contract of sale to have the effect that the buyer could pay the seller only out of the proceeds of sale (as opposed to any other source of payment).

7.2.5.4 *Quistclose Trusts*

A device which has sometimes been said to be a security interest is that under a 'Quistclose' trust.[134] This device is sometimes used to protect a lender against the insolvency of a borrower where money is lent for a specific purpose, often in a corporate restructuring. The security-like purpose of the device was noted by Lord Millett in *Twinsectra Ltd v Yardley*, where he commented on its similarity to a ROT clause, in that the lender 'enables the borrower to have recourse to the lender's money for a particular purpose without entrenching on the lender's property rights more than necessary to enable the purpose to be achieved'.[135] Lord Millett's analysis in that case was that where a lender makes it clear that money is lent for a specific purpose, the courts are likely to hold that the borrower holds the money on resulting trust for the lender, in circumstances that the lender's beneficial interest is qualified by a power of the borrower to use the money for the specified purpose. If the purpose fails, the power disappears and the money is held on the original unqualified resulting trust.[136] It will be seen that the trust cannot be said to be a security interest, as there is no separate obligation to be secured: the borrower's obligation to pay the money to the lender comes from the trust itself.[137] A different analysis may apply where the trust is not created by the payment from the lender to the borrower, but is declared by the borrower after the payment has been made (in order to protect the lender). This is more analogous to the extended reservation of title cases discussed above, since the lender's interest is granted by the borrower, and also appears to secure a separate and pre-existing obligation to repay.[138]

---

[133] [2000] 202 CLR 588 [34], discussed at 6.4.4.1.1.

[134] So called because this form of trust was first recognised in *Barclays Bank Ltd v Quistclose Investments Ltd* [1970] AC 567. See also M Bridge, 'The Quistclose Trust in a World of Secured Transactions' [1992] *Oxford Journal of Legal Studies* 383.

[135] [2002] UKHL 12 [81].

[136] Ibid, [100]. However, the resulting trust analysis has been doubted by some academics. See eg R Chambers, *Resulting Trusts* (Oxford, Oxford University Press, 1997) ch 3; see generally W Swadling (ed), *The Quistclose Trust: Critical Essays* (Oxford, Hart Publishing, 2004). It may be that different analyses are appropriate for different versions of a 'Quistclose' type agreement: J McGhee, *Snell's Equity*, 32nd edn (Sweet & Maxwell, 2010) para 25-036.

[137] Security and Title-Based Financing, 8.153. See J Glister, 'Trusts as Quasi-Securities? The Law Commission's Proposals for the Registration of Security Interests' [2004] *Lloyd's Maritime and Commercial Law Quarterly* 460; Law Commission Consultation Paper No 164, *Registration of Security Interests: Company Charges and Property other than Land* (July 2002), Part VII.

[138] Security and Title-Based Financing, 6.155.

7.3 Types of Security Interest

7.3.1 Introduction

This section is concerned solely with 'true' security interests, that is, those interests characterised in English law as security interests. There are four types of consensual security interests, which can be said to form a *numerus clausus* so that no new forms of security interest will be recognised. These are the pledge, the contractual lien, the mortgage and the charge.[139] There are also other variants of security interest which arise by operation of law, for example the possessory lien and the equitable lien, but these will not be considered further here.[140] The pledge and the contractual lien are both possessory interests. The latter arises where possession is given for a purpose other than security (such as storage), and is really a contractual extension of the possessory lien, giving security for sums due from the owner to the party in possession. The pledge is created when possession of goods is given to the pledgee for the purpose of securing an obligation owed by the pledgor to the pledge. Pledges and liens are relatively little used in corporate finance,[141] although the pledge of documents of title to goods is important in the financing of international trade,[142] and the pledge of negotiable instruments is of considerable importance where debt instruments are in negotiable form.[143] Since in English law pledges are only created by the transfer of possession, there cannot be a pledge of an intangible that is not a documentary intangible. If the intangible is evidenced by a piece of paper this can be pledged, but the pledge does not entail entitlement to the underlying contractual rights.[144] The term 'pledge' is often used in practice in relation to financial collateral: this is a non-technical use meaning 'security interest'.

The other two types of security interest, mortgage and charge, are non-possessory. This makes them far more suitable for most kinds of corporate secured lending. First, since many corporate assets are intangibles, this is the only type of security interest that can be taken over them. Second, even over tangible assets, a non-possessory security interest allows the borrower to have the use of the assets and yet use them as security. For most tangible assets, including land, this is vital.[145]

This section discusses non-possessory security interests in general, then the floating charge in particular. It concludes with a discussion of security financial collateral arrangements,

---

[139] *Re Cosslett (Contractors) Ltd* [1998] Ch 495, 508.

[140] For further discussion of these interests see Security and Title-Based Financing, 5.57–5.77 and 6.140–6.163.

[141] The amount secured by a lien is rarely significant, but a lien can arise over goods of a very high value, such as aircraft. See *Bristol Airport plc v Powdrill* [1990] Ch 744.

[142] See Security and Title-Based Financing, 5.34–5.40; for detailed discussion see R Jack, A Malek and D Quest, *Documentary Credits*, 4th edn (London, Butterworths, 2010) ch 11; R King, *Gutteridge and Megrah's Law of Bankers' Commercial Credits*, 8th edn (London, Europa, 2001) ch 8.

[143] For a discussion of the form in which debt securities are now usually held see 8.3.2.3.2(b). Negotiable instruments are discussed below at 9.2.3.

[144] Goode: Credit and Security, 1-48 fn 216.

[145] See 7.1.3.

which, though not a type of security interest in the same sense, comprise a category of security interests which attracts its own rules, and the categorisation of which raises considerable problems.

7.3.2 Non-Possessory Security Interests

7.3.2.1 Security Over Future Property

The ability to take security over future property of a company is critical for a lender. If this were not possible, the lender's security would be limited to the assets the borrower had at the time of the loan, and each new asset acquired would necessitate a new security agreement.[146] Of course, there are some situations where a security interest will be limited to assets owned by the borrower at the time of the loan, for example a security interest over a particular item to secure money advanced to finance that particular purchase. The bulk of security interests are more general than this, however, and even fixed security interests (where the consent of the security holder is required for disposal of any assets) would normally cover future assets: even 'fixed' assets such as land or equipment are usually replaced from time to time.[147] Where a security interest is floating, so that the secured assets can be disposed of without the consent of the security holder, the need for the security interest to cover future property is self-evident.

It has for many years been straightforward to create a security interest over future assets under English law.[148] However, this is not possible under common law. At law it is only possible to transfer assets which exist at the time of transfer. An agreement can be made at law to transfer future assets, but there will only be an actual transfer when there is a new act of transfer, such as the taking of possession.[149] However, in equity an agreement to transfer future assets will have the effect that the assets are transferred automatically without a future act. This was confirmed in the nineteenth-century case of *Holroyd v Marshall*.[150] The basis for this is the doctrine that 'equity considers as done that which ought to be done',[151] coupled with the fact that equity will specifically enforce the agreement to transfer.[152] This does not mean, however, that all the criteria for specific performance must be fulfilled: that would be overly restrictive and technical.[153] It is necessary, however, for the consideration for the transfer to be executed, which will usually mean that at least some of the loan must

---

[146] This is one of the reasons why pledges are of such limited use in corporate finance.

[147] See 7.1.3.

[148] This has not been the case in the past in other jurisdictions, as illustrated by the following examples. In France, assets subject to security interests had to be specifically described, which limited the ability of the borrower to pledge its future assets. The position in France has now been amended by the new book IV of the Code Civil (2006), especially arts 2333 and 2355. Denmark amended its law in 2006 so that security over some future assets, especially receivables, could be created. In Slovakia, reform of the law in 2002 allowed future assets to be used as security.

[149] *Robinson v Macdonnell* (1816) 5 M & S 228; *Holroyd v Marshall* (1861–62) 10 HL Cas 191, 210–11 per Lord Westbury.

[150] (1862) 10 HL Cas 191.

[151] *Tailby v Official Receiver* (1888) 13 App Cas 523, 546.

[152] *Holroyd v Marshall* (1862) 10 HL Cas 191, 210–11.

[153] *Tailby v Official Receiver* (1888) 13 App Cas 523, 547.

have been advanced, and that the assets in question be identifiable. The latter criterion can be fulfilled by a general description such as 'all the book debts due and owing or which may during the continuance of this security become due and owing to the said mortgagor'.[154]

Another remarkable feature of the *Holroyd v Marshall* doctrine is that it has the effect that the security interest arises at the time that it is created, rather than at the time at which each asset is acquired. Of course, this does not tell the whole story, since obviously a secured lender cannot have a proprietary interest in an asset until it is acquired by the borrower: it is therefore often said that the security interest does not 'attach' to the asset until it is acquired. However, for priority purposes at least, once the asset is acquired the security interest is treated as having arisen at the time it was created.[155] This is very important, since if the priority point in relation to each asset was the date on which it was acquired, this would lead to considerable complexity.[156]

On this reasoning, where a security interest covers present and future assets, it is clearly a valid security interest at the time of creation, which attaches to the future assets as they are acquired by the borrower. However, if the security interest only covers future assets, or where the borrower owns no assets falling within the description at the time of creation, the question arises as to whether the lender has any sort of security interest at that time. There seems little doubt that the effect of *Holroyd v Marshall* in this situation is that as soon as an asset falling within the description is acquired by the borrower the security interest immediately attaches to that asset in the same way as if a security interest over present and future assets had been created. Before that moment, though, the lender can have no interest in that particular asset.[157] But does the secured lender have some sort of inchoate security interest dating from the time the security agreement is executed? The question could be said to be hypothetical, in that until an asset is acquired, no secured lender would wish or be able to enforce the security interest, and so the nature of it, or whether it exists at all, is irrelevant. It is not irrelevant, however, once assets are acquired. The date of the creation of the security interest is relevant for a number of reasons. First, it may affect priority. Second, unless it falls within section 859A(6) of the Companies Act 2006 it is necessary to register it within 21 days of creation. Third, some event may occur between the date of execution of the document creating the security interest and the date the borrower first acquires any assets, which would affect certain types of rights and not others. For example, if the borrower were not a company, the discharge from bankruptcy of the borrower would terminate any contractual rights.

In relation to priority, it is clear from *Re Lind*[158] that the 'priority point' in this situation is the date of the agreement creating the security interest and not the date the assets are acquired. In that case, L mortgaged property he expected to receive under his mother's will to N in 1905 and to A in 1908. Ignoring his intervening bankruptcy (for the purposes of the

---

[154] Ibid.

[155] Ibid, 533 per Lord Watson; Security and Title-Based Financing, 6.15; Goode: Credit and Security, 2–13.

[156] This, of course, is on the basis that the priority point is the date of creation of the security interest: see 7.4.4. As to reform of the law on this point, see 7.7.

[157] This has led some commentators to say that a charge cannot be created over a future asset; see Security and Title-Based Financing, 8.91.

[158] *Re Lind* [1915] 2 Ch 345.

discussion in this paragraph), he then assigned the property to P in 1911. His mother died in February 1914, L obtained the property and he assigned it (again) to P in May 1914. The mortgages to N and A were held to have priority over the assignment to P. On its own this could be said to have a number of explanations: one is that once the asset is acquired, the date of priority 'relates back' to the date of execution; another is that although each person's interest attaches automatically at the time the asset is acquired, they attach in the order of the purported assignments. A third would be that the secured lender has an inchoate interest from the moment of execution.[159] This last analysis is the most attractive.

In relation to registration, the position is now determined by statute. Section 859E of the Companies Act 2006 provides that, for the purposes of the registration requirements, a charge is created when the deed creating it is delivered, or when the document creating it is executed.[160]

The other context in which this issue has arisen is where the assignor's bankruptcy has intervened between the execution of the security agreement and the acquisition of the asset. Once a bankrupt has been discharged, all merely contractual rights anyone had against him will be terminated. Therefore, if all the assignee had was a contract to assign the asset, this would not survive the discharge of the bankruptcy.[161] In *Re Lind*, L became bankrupt in 1908 and was discharged in 1910. It was held by the Court of Appeal that N's and A's mortgages survived the bankruptcy so that when the asset was finally acquired, it was automatically subject to their mortgages.[162] The alternative, that they had a contractual right only, was rejected, and a case in which this had been held, *Collyer v Isaacs*,[163] was distinguished[164] (and, to the extent that it could be said to be inconsistent with the ruling in *Re Lind*, overruled).[165] The nature of the assignee's right, then, is that it is a right 'higher' than a contractual right[166]—'something in the nature of an estate or interest'.[167] This is not a very exact description, but maybe no more precision is possible.[168]

---

[159] Goode: Credit and Security, 2-13. This view was cited with approval by the Supreme Court of Canada in *Royal Bank of Canada v Radius Credit Union Ltd*, 2010 SCC 48, 325 DLR (4th) 635 [20]. The Supreme Court used this analysis in support of the conclusion that the Canadian Bank Act 1991 gave 'statutory recognition to this notion of "inchoate interest from the date of execution" that had long been recognized by courts of equity' (at [21]).

[160] Provision is also made for situations where the effectiveness of the deed of document is postponed by agreement.

[161] *Re Lind* [1915] 2 Ch 345, 364 per Phillimore LJ.

[162] The actual debt was, of course, discharged by the bankruptcy, but the right of the mortgagee in relation to the future property was not merely ancillary to this debt: ibid, 370 per Bankes LJ.

[163] (1881) 19 Ch D 342.

[164] Ibid, 363 per Swinfen Eady LJ.

[165] *Re Lind* [1915] 2 Ch 345, 375 per Bankes LJ. RP Meagher, JD Heydon and MJ Leeming (eds), *Meagher, Gummow and Lehane's Equity, Doctrine and Remedies*, 4th edn (Sydney, Butterworths LexisNexis, 2002) suggest that it is more satisfactory to see *Collyer v Isaacs* as overruled, a view which has some support from the judgment of Neuberger J in *Peer International Corporation and others v Termidor Music Publishers Ltd* [2002] EWHC 2675 [79].

[166] Ibid, 365 per Phillimore LJ.

[167] Ibid, 364 per Phillimore LJ. It should be borne in mind that Phillimore LJ was not particularly happy with the conclusion as he thought it would be better as a matter of policy that all assignments of bare futurities should be made impossible.

[168] See RP Meagher, JD Heydon and MJ Leeming (eds), *Meagher, Gummow and Lehane's Equity, Doctrine and Remedies*, 4th edn (Sydney, Butterworths LexisNexis, 2002) 256 where it is called a sui generis right. For an analysis concluding that the interest of the assignee is 'an equity' see Tolhurst: Assignment, 4.33.

7.3.2.2 Mortgage

In a mortgage, title in the mortgaged assets passes from the mortgagor to the mortgagee with an obligation to re-transfer on payment of the secured obligation.[169] Where legal title is transferred to the mortgagee, the mortgage is a legal mortgage. The right to re-transfer will be enforced by equity, and is seen as an equitable interest in its own right: the equity of redemption.[170] This is a proprietary interest in the assets, which the mortgagor can encumber and even alienate, for example to a second mortgagee.[171] The value of the equity of redemption will, of course, depend on the amount outstanding on the secured obligation at any time. Arguably, if the mortgagee is undersecured, so that the amount of the loan is more than the value of the mortgaged assets, the mortgagor has no interest in the assets. However, this misstates the position as the mortgagor always has the ability to redeem the mortgage by paying off the loan, and the better view is that, in equity, the mortgagor owns the assets subject to the mortgage.[172]

A legal mortgage is, in one sense, the 'best' security which can be taken: its priority position is advantageous in that no subsequent interest can gain priority over it without the agreement of the mortgagee, and the legal mortgagee can in theory enforce by foreclosure and obtain full legal ownership of the assets.[173] These advantages are somewhat illusory, however, in that the legal mortgagee will still take subject to any prior legal interest and some prior equitable interests[174] and foreclosure is only obtained by applying to court, which has various powers to enable the mortgagee to take steps to protect its equity of redemption.[175] Obtaining a legal mortgage can involve formal steps, depending on the nature of the asset mortgaged, so that, for example, a legal mortgage of shares requires a transfer to the mortgagee in the issuer's register[176] or in the CREST register[177] and a legal mortgage of debts requires transfer by statutory assignment[178] or novation.[179] If the formal steps are not followed, the mortgage usually will take effect as an equitable mortgage.

An equitable mortgage involves the transfer of equitable title to the mortgagee, subject, again, to the mortgagor's right to re-transfer, which is the mortgagor's equity of redemption. A mortgage will be equitable in the following three situations. First, if the mortgagor only has an equitable title in the first place (for example, as a beneficiary under a trust);

---

[169] *Santley v Wilde* [1899] 2 Ch 474.

[170] *Paulett v AG* (1667) Hard 465, 469; *In re Sir Thomas Spencer Wells* [1933] Ch 29, 44, 46.

[171] Although that mortgage will of necessity be equitable: *King v Hussain* 2411/05, 2005 NSWSC 1076 (Sup Ct NSW).

[172] *In re Sir Thomas Spencer Wells* [1933] Ch 29, 52; *Cunliffe Engineering Ltd v English Industrial Estates Corp* [1994] BCC 972, 976; cf *Railton v Wood* (1890) LR 15 App Cas 363.

[173] See 7.5.1.1 for a brief account of foreclosure.

[174] Any prior legal interest would have priority under the *nemo dat* rule, and the legal mortgagee would have constructive notice of any prior registered equitable security interest and would therefore take subject to it; see 7.4.4.

[175] See 7.5.1.1.

[176] See 4.6.

[177] 9.6.2.3.

[178] See 9.2.2.2.

[179] 9.2.1. Other legal mortgages also require entries in the relevant register, such as mortgages of ships (s 16 and Sch 1 Merchant Shipping Act 1995), aircraft (Mortgaging of Aircraft Order 1972, SI 1972/1268) and intellectual property (Patents Act 1977, ss 30–33; Trade Marks Act 1994, s 25; Registered Designs Act 1949, s 19).

second, if it is a second mortgage and legal title has already been transferred to the first mortgagee; and third, if the formalities required to create a legal mortgage have not been carried out.

One significant advantage of an equitable mortgage over a legal mortgage is that the former can be taken over future assets.[180] The lack of formal requirements can also be seen as an advantage, so that, for example, an equitable mortgage can be taken over intellectual property without registering it,[181] and it is possible to create an equitable mortgage over debts without giving notice to the debtor.[182] However, the concomitant disadvantage is that the equitable mortgagee is more likely to lose priority to later interests than a legal mortgagee.[183]

7.3.2.3 Charge

Unlike a mortgage, a charge is a security interest which entails no transfer of title to the chargee. Despite this, it is a proprietary interest and fully enforceable on insolvency. It is a 'mere encumbrance', whereby the charged property is appropriated to the discharge of an obligation.[184] A charge is always equitable, and is clearly different from a legal mortgage, which entails a transfer of legal ownership. The difference between a charge and an equitable mortgage is sometimes illusory and difficult to draw, in that the law treats both in the same way for certain purposes. For example, the priority position of a fixed charge is virtually identical to that of an equitable mortgage, and the registration requirements are the same, so that the word 'charge' in Part 25 of the Companies Act 2006 includes a mortgage.[185] The chief practical (as opposed to conceptual) difference arises on enforcement. Even in the absence of specific words in the agreement creating the security agreement, a mortgagee, by virtue of its ownership, can enforce the mortgage by foreclosure[186] or by taking possession of, and selling, the asset. A chargee may not foreclose or take possession, and will only have a right of sale or to appoint a receiver[187] if the charge is made by deed[188] or if it applies to the court for an order for sale or the appointment of a receiver. However, power to take possession, to sell the assets and to appoint a receiver are routinely included in the document creating a charge, and in these circumstances it is hard to know whether the document creates a charge or an equitable mortgage. Since the situations in

---

[180] See discussion at 7.3.2.1.

[181] Security and Title-Based Financing, 14.62–14.63, 14.69. However, registration is a priority point, and an unregistered equitable mortgage will lose priority to a later registered mortgage or charge, whether legal or equitable.

[182] This is by equitable assignment; see discussion at 9.2.2.2.

[183] See 7.4.4.

[184] *Carreras Rothmans Ltd v Freeman Mathews Treasure Ltd* [1985] Ch 207, 227.

[185] Companies Act 2006, s 859A(7). In s 205(1)(xvi) Law of Property Act 1925, the word 'mortgage' includes a charge. In many judgments, the court uses the two terms interchangeably: see Security and Title-Based Financing, 6.56 fn 289.

[186] Foreclosure is where the mortgagee's ownership interest is made absolute, and the mortgagor's equity of redemption is extinguished. See 7.5.1.1.

[187] A receiver is a person appointed to take control of the asset(s) which are the subject matter of the security interest, in order to realise their value or to receive the income from them. See 7.5.1.4.

[188] By virtue of Law of Property Act 1925, s 101 which also applies to a mortgage. The right of sale given by this section is limited to certain situations by s 103.

which it is necessary to distinguish between the two are very limited,[189] the courts have paid little attention to this particular characterisation.[190]

7.3.2.4 Security Interest Over Lender's Own Indebtedness

A bank that lends to a company often wishes to take a security interest over any account the company has with that bank. The account is, of course, only a debt owed by the bank to the account holder;[191] thus the security interest is taken over the lender's own indebtedness. There was much debate over whether such a security interest is valid, which was put to rest by the decision of the House of Lords in *BCCI (No 8)*.[192] There a bank's charge over its own indebtedness was held to be a valid proprietary interest, a decision which was greatly welcomed by the banking industry, which had been taking such charges for some time. One objection had been that if the debt owed by the bank was assigned to the bank, the debt would be released:[193] this objection might still apply to a mortgage-back, but not if the security interest were a mere charge.[194]

Another objection was that if the secured obligation was owed by the account holder, the charge was indistinguishable from a set-off,[195] and if it was owed by a third party, this undermined insolvency set-off.[196] The question of whether a charge-back breaks the mutuality required by insolvency set-off is discussed above.[197]

7.3.3 The Floating Charge

7.3.3.1 Introduction

A charge can be fixed or floating. A fixed charge is a security interest which attaches to specific assets either on creation of the charge or, in the case of future property, when the relevant asset is acquired by the chargor. This means that the charge can be enforced on default without any further action by the chargee and that the chargor cannot dispose of the charged assets without the consent of the chargee. These characteristics of a fixed charge mean that anyone who takes the asset under an unauthorised disposition takes subject to the charge, unless that person is a good faith purchaser of the legal interest without notice of the fixed charge.[198] A fixed charge also operates like a negative pledge clause so that any unauthorised disposition is a breach of contract, which may give the lender the right to accelerate and terminate the loan.[199] Thus, taking fixed security enables a creditor to

---

[189] See Security and Title-Based Financing, 6.54–6.67.
[190] The matter is discussed by Ferris J in *Re ELS Ltd* [1995] Ch 11, 24.
[191] *Foley v Hill* (1848) 2 HL Cas 28.
[192] *Re Bank of Credit and Commerce International SA (No 8)* [1998] AC 214, 227.
[193] *Re Charge Card Services Ltd* [1987] 1 Ch 150, 175.
[194] This was made clear by Lord Hoffmann in the *BCCI* case, [1998] AC 214, 226: 'A charge is a security interest created without any transfer of title or possession to the beneficiary.'
[195] R Goode, *Legal Problems of Credit and Security*, 2nd edn (London, Sweet & Maxwell, 1988) 128.
[196] R Goode, *Commercial Law*, 2nd edn (London, Butterworths, 1995) 660.
[197] 6.3.4.6.1.
[198] See 7.4.4.
[199] 6.3.1.6.

prevent asset diversion, one of the main dangers faced by creditors.[200] It is clear that, as mentioned above, there is very little difference between a fixed charge and an equitable mortgage.

However, the inability of the chargor to dispose of the charged assets in the ordinary course of business means that there are severe practical restrictions regarding the kinds of assets that can be the subject of a fixed charge. It will be recalled that earlier there was discussion of a distinction between fixed and circulating assets.[201] Although this distinction is by no means hard and fast, it will be seen that it is vital for a company to be able to dispose of circulating assets such as raw materials and stock in trade quickly and easily, and also to be able to use the proceeds of receivables (themselves the proceeds of the disposition of the other circulating assets) to meet current expenses, such as the wage bill. Thus, in order to be able to give security over the entire undertaking of the company, the floating charge developed in the nineteenth century.[202] The floating chargor had a power to dispose of the charged assets either absolutely or by way of security in the ordinary course of business. This power could be express but was usually implied as a necessary incident of a charge over the whole undertaking of the company.[203] Nowadays, such a power is inherent where a charge is expressed to be 'floating'. When security is taken over all the assets of a company, fixed charges will be taken over fixed assets and floating charges over circulating assets. Although the power only authorises dispositions in the ordinary course of business, this concept has been interpreted very widely in this particular context to include exceptional and unusual transactions, particularly if they are necessary for the survival of the business[204] (but not transactions which are intended to bring the business to an end or which have this effect).

The benefit of having a security interest which can be taken over all the assets of the company was initially important because it gave the secured creditor priority over other creditors of the company. This was coupled with the right to appoint a receiver over the charged assets, which was included in the charge agreement and developed into a right to appoint a 'receiver and manager' (later 'administrative receiver') of the company. Thus, the secured creditor with an 'all assets' charge could, on default, take control of the whole business, and dispose of it either in its entirety or piecemeal in order to pay the secured creditor. The whole process was outside formal insolvency proceedings.[205] Even outside insolvency, there are benefits, from a corporate governance perspective, in having a single bank lender,[206] and the ability to take security over all the company's assets encourages this model.

These benefits have, to some extent, been eroded over the years. First, Parliament decided to give certain creditors priority over the 'all assets' secured creditor in relation to assets

---

[200] See 3.2.2.2. Asset diversion is the main danger against which the legal capital rules seek to protect a company: see 5.2.

[201] See 7.1.3.

[202] Its origins were the mortgage over the company's undertaking sanctioned by the Companies Clauses Consolidation Act 1845. For accounts of the history of the floating charge see R Pennington, 'The Genesis of the Floating Charge' (1960) 23 *Modern Law Review* 63; R Gregory and P Walton, 'Fixed and Floating Charges—a Revelation' [2000] *Lloyd's Maritime and Commercial Law Quarterly* 123.

[203] *In re Panama, New Zealand and Australian Royal Mail Company* (1870) 5 Ch App 318, 322; *In re Florence and Public Works Company* (1878) 10 Ch D 530, 546.

[204] *Ashborder BV v Green Gas Power Ltd* [2004] EWHC 1517 (Ch); *Re Borax Ltd* [1901] 1 Ch 326.

[205] See Goode: Corporate Insolvency, 10-02.

[206] 3.2.2.4.5.

covered by a floating charge.[207] Second, the ability of most such creditors to appoint an administrative receiver has been abolished in favour of a power to appoint an administrator and therefore to put the company into formal insolvency proceedings. As will appear from the discussion below, the floating charge per se has become less popular, and lenders are seeking to use other forms of security and quasi-security over circulating assets. However, the importance of being able to take security over all the company's assets still remains.[208]

7.3.3.2 Crystallisation[209]

An important feature of the early floating charge was that it could not be enforced until the company had ceased to be a going concern, whereas a fixed charge or mortgage could be enforced against any charged or mortgaged assets immediately on default. Thus, before enforcement, the floating charge had to crystallise, that is, attach to specific assets. Until fairly recently, crystallisation could only occur on events which signalled the end of the ordinary course of business of the company,[210] that is, winding up, cessation of business, or active intervention by the chargee, for example by taking possession or appointing a receiver. The appointment of an administrator, however, probably does not in itself crystallise a floating charge, since this does not necessarily denote cessation of trading[211] or the taking of control by the chargee.[212]

It is now possible for the charge agreement to provide that a floating charge will crystallise by the giving of notice by the chargee to the chargor[213] (semi-automatic crystallisation) or on the occurrence of an event which does not involve the intervention of the chargee (automatic crystallisation). Such events are often similar to the events of default that enable the lender to accelerate the loan,[214] for example the giving of security to another creditor, the levying of execution by another creditor, a cross-default,[215] or the breach of a prescribed financial ratio.[216] Automatic crystallisation clauses, although contentious, are likely to be held to be valid on the grounds that the parties are free to agree any trigger for crystallisation.[217] The policy ramifications of this are considered below.

The effect of crystallisation is that the floating charge becomes a fixed charge.[218] Practically, this means that the chargor no longer has the power to dispose of the charged assets (including the creation of a security interest over them) without the consent of the chargee. If the chargor does make such a disposition, this is a breach of contract, and may trigger a right to accelerate or terminate the loan, and will also give the chargee the right to restrain

---

[207] See 3.3.1.2.

[208] For discussion on the future of the floating charge see 7.3.3.4.

[209] For detailed discussion see Goode: Credit and Security, 4-31–4-64.

[210] See ibid, 4-34–4-40.

[211] See ibid, 4-40.

[212] See ibid, 4-45.

[213] *Re Brightlife Ltd* [1987] Ch 200.

[214] See 6.3.3.1.

[215] See 6.3.3.

[216] See 6.3.2.2.

[217] See *Re Brightlife Ltd* [1987] Ch 200. There are also Australian and New Zealand cases supporting this proposition, but these are inapplicable in these countries since the enactment of the Australian and New Zealand Personal Property Securities Acts. See 7.7.3.

[218] *Evans v Rival Granite Quarries Ltd* [1910] 2 KB 979, 999 per Buckley LJ.

such a breach by injunction.[219] In theory, the disponee will take subject to the charge, but this may not actually be the case since one or both of the following analyses may apply. First, the disponee may acquire the legal interest for value without notice of the charge, and so will take free of the prior equitable interest.[220] This is likely to be the case if the disposition is a sale of stock in trade in the ordinary course of business, or the payment of a trade bill in cash. Thus, although in theory crystallisation prevents the chargor from carrying on business, in practice it is possible to do so, at least if the chargee waives the breaches of contract.[221] Second, there is a strong argument that a disponee will not take subject to the charge unless it has notice that the authority of the chargor to dispose of the assets free of the charge has been terminated, that is, that the charge has crystallised.[222] It is very unlikely that the disponee will have such notice if the crystallisation is automatic. However, an unsecured creditor who does not complete execution until after crystallisation will lose priority to the crystallised charge.[223] This priority rule applies whether or not the execution creditor has notice of the charge, or of the fact that it has crystallised;[224] the execution creditor is therefore not prejudiced by the secret nature of the crystallisation itself, but by the fact that a charge can crystallise automatically and yet the chargor can continue trading.[225]

The conceptual effect of crystallisation is a matter of some debate, as this depends on how the nature of the floating charge before crystallisation is seen.[226] One view is that until crystallisation the chargee does not have any form of proprietary interest.[227] On crystallisation, therefore, the chargee obtains such an interest. Although this view has met with some support in Australia,[228] it does not appear to represent English law. Another is that, prior to crystallisation, the floating chargee has an interest in a fund rather than in specific assets.[229] The composition of the fund can change, but the interest remains the same. On this view, it does not matter whether the fund is closed so that no further assets can be added, or open so as to include future assets. On crystallisation the charge attaches to the assets which

---

[219] This would only have practical effect if the chargee were able to obtain an injunction before the disposition was made.

[220] See below 7.4.4.

[221] This may result in refloatation of the charge; see below.

[222] Goode: Credit and Security, 5-51; WJ Gough, *Company Charges*, 2nd edn (London, Butterworths, 1996) 255–56.

[223] *Evans v Rival Granite Quarries Ltd* [1901] 2 KB 979. Berger J considered that the effect of a valid automatic crystallisation clause was that 'the debenture-holder would be able to arrange the affairs of the company in such a way as to render it immune from executions': *R v Consolidated Churchill Copper Corp* (1978) 90 DL (3d) 357 [22]. Obtaining priority over execution creditors is now one of the main purposes for which automatic crystallisation clauses are now included in charge documents.

[224] WJ Gough, *Company Charges*, 2nd edn (London, Butterworths, 1996) 319–20.

[225] Goode: Credit and Security, 4-53. One other reason, which is no longer valid, is that a charge which crystallised before winding up did not count as a floating charge in the statutory provisions applicable on insolvency (see 7.3.3.3.1), such as those giving priority to preferential creditors (see 3.3.1.2.2). This was changed in 1986 so that the statutory provisions apply to a charge which 'as created' was a floating charge (Insolvency Act 1986, s 251).

[226] For a full discussion see Security and Title-Based Financing, 6.71–6.77.

[227] WJ Gough, *Company Charges*, 2nd edn (London, Butterworths, 1996) 97–101, 341–48.

[228] *Tricontinental Corporation Ltd v Federal Commissioner of Taxation* (1987) 73 ALR 433, 444 per Williams LJ (Queensland CA); *Lyford v Commonwealth Bank of Australia* (1995) 17 ACSR 211, 218 per Nicholson J (Federal Court of Australia). These authorities are no longer applicable in Australia: see 7.7.3

[229] Goode: Credit and Security, 4-03–4-04.

are presently in the fund.[230] Another view is that the nature of the charge before and after crystallisation remains the same, so that the chargee has a proprietary interest in each of the charged assets at all times. However, on this view the chargee's interest before crystallisation is qualified in that (on one view)[231] it is defeasible and disappears on permitted dealings, or in that (on another view)[232] it is overreachable so that on disposition the disponee obtains good title. Both of these views are hard to reconcile with the reasoning in many of the cases, which is based on the idea that the charge attaches to specific assets on crystallisation, and which specifically denies that a floating charge is a fixed charge with a licence to deal.[233] Therefore the 'interest in a fund' theory is the most attractive explanation of the present law.[234] In terms of conceptual purity, however, there is a great deal to be said for the idea of a single type of charge under whose terms the chargor has a limited or full power to dispose of the charged assets. If the law were to be reformed on the lines discussed below,[235] the usefulness of the floating charge could be retained on this basis, without the complicated conceptual structure of crystallisation or the difficulties of categorising a charge as fixed or floating.[236]

Does the conceptual debate discussed above have any practical significance? Generally it does not, but there are three areas on which it has some bearing. First is the effect of decrystallisation.[237] Second, if the nature of the charge when floating is different from a fixed charge, it makes sense for there to be a bright line between a fixed and a floating charge which can be determined by the courts rather than by the intentions of the parties. If the nature of the charge is the same, however, it makes more sense for the incidents of that charge to be solely a matter for the parties. Third, in the rare case where a disponee takes subject to an uncrystallised floating charge, the priority position will depend on the nature of that charge.[238] However, this is rarely significant as usually the charge will have crystallised by the time the chargee wishes to enforce the charge.

Although, over the years, drafters have tried to manipulate the concept of crystallisation to achieve maximum protection and flexibility for secured creditors, this technique has not been successful in preserving the priority of a floating chargee, except, perhaps, in relation to execution creditors. Priority over other disponees would only be achieved if there was a way of giving them notice of crystallisation, and the operation of semi-automatic and

---

[230] Of course, if the charge is expressed to cover future assets, assets acquired by the chargor will continue to fall within the charge after crystallisation, in the same way as if the charge had been a fixed charge from the start: *NW Robbie & Co Ltd v Witney Warehouse Co Ltd* [1963] 1 WLR 1324.

[231] S Worthington, *Proprietary Interests in Commercial Transactions* (Oxford, Clarendon Press, 1996) 81.

[232] R Nolan, 'Property in a Fund' (2004) 120 *Law Quarterly Review* 108.

[233] *Evans v Rival Granite Quarries Limited* [1910] 2 KB 979, 999; *In re Colonial Trusts Corporation, ex p Bradshaw* (1879) 15 Ch D 465, 472. See also other cases on priority of execution creditors, such as *In re Standard Manufacturing Company* [1891] 1 Ch 627, 639–41; *In re Opera Ltd* [1891] 3 Ch 260; *Taunton v Sheriff of Warwickshire* [1895] 2 Ch 319, 323; and on distress for rates *Re ELS Ltd* [1995] Ch 11.

[234] There is some support for this view from Lord Walker in *Re Spectrum Plus* [2005] 2 AC 680 [139], although immediately afterwards he cites with apparent approval the analysis by Professor Worthington in *Proprietary Interests in Commercial Transactions* (Oxford, Clarendon Press, 1996) 74–77, which suggests the theory of the defeasible fixed charge.

[235] 7.7.

[236] Discussed at 7.3.3.3.2 and 7.3.3.3.3.

[237] Discussed below.

[238] See Goode: Credit and Security, 5-41.

automatic crystallisation clauses is, by its nature, private. In fact, a chargee may well not know that automatic crystallisation has occurred. It is therefore not practicable to make such crystallisation registrable, and all attempts to do so have failed.[239] By contrast, now that a negative pledge clause in a floating charge is registrable,[240] this provides a much better method of preserving priority over subsequent security interests for a floating chargee.

There is also a danger that an automatic (or semi-automatic) crystallisation clause can be drawn too widely, so that the charge crystallises on an event which is not so serious that the company stops trading. Matters may then improve so that the continuance of trading is the preferred option for all parties, but for this to take place the chargee either has to consent actively to all dispositions (which is impractical) or, if it just stands by and does nothing, may well be taken to have waived the crystallisation.[241] The effect of such a waiver is unclear: it may mean that the charge never crystallises or that it decrystallises. Decrystallisation, by notice or on certain events, may also be provided for expressly in the charge agreement, so that if the situation that caused the crystallisation (such as the breach of a financial ratio) improves, the company can continue trading.[242]

The actual effect of decrystallisation is untested in the courts, and is unclear. One possibility is that the charge can move from floating to fixed to floating at the will of the parties: it is purely a matter of freedom of contract.[243] Another is that, on decrystallisation, the assets are released from the fixed charge and a new floating charge is created.[244] This is based on the view that when a floating charge crystallises, its nature changes so that it becomes a charge over specific assets as opposed to an interest in a fund (or in no assets at all), so that once it has attached to specific assets its nature cannot be reversed.[245] If the charge is of the same nature before and after crystallisation, then there seems to be no objection to the 'licence to deal' being imposed or removed at the will of the parties, so that a new charge is not created.

The debate also raises the wider question, which also arises in the context of the characterisation of fixed and floating charges, as to how far the parties can be free to determine the incidents of the charge without regard to specific legal concepts or the interests of third parties. If the effects of crystallisation applied only to the parties themselves, then there would be no objection to an approach based solely on freedom of contact, but to the extent that third parties are affected such freedom should be controlled. The effect of

---

[239] Companies Act 1989, s 100 introducing a new s 410 into Insolvency Act 1986 (Companies Act 1989 never came into force); see also Company Law Review Steering Group, *Modern Company Law for a Competitive Economy: Final Report* (URN 01/942, July 2001), para 12.28; Law Commission, *Registration of Security Interests: Company Charges and Property other than Land*, Consultation Paper No 164 (2002) para 4.143; BIS, *Registration of Charges Created by Companies and Limited Liability Partnerships: Proposals to Amend the Current Scheme and relating to Specialist Registers*, 12 March 2010, paras 25–27. The latter proposal was not included in the final reforms.

[240] See 7.4.2.

[241] For detailed discussion see Security and Title-Based Financing, 6.87.

[242] See Encyclopaedia of Forms and Precedents, vol 4(1) Banking 1016.

[243] See WJ Gough, *Company Charges*, 2nd edn (London, Butterworths, 1996) 404–06; R Pennington, 'Recent Developments in the Law and Practice relating to the Creation of Security for Companies' Indebtedness' (2009) 30 *Company Lawyer* 163.

[244] R Grantham, 'Refloating a Floating Charge' [1997] *Company Financial and Insolvency Law Review* 53; CH Tan, 'Automatic Crystallization, De-Crystallization and Convertibility of Charges' [1998] *Company Financial and Insolvency Law Review* 41.

[245] See the previous discussion of the nature of the uncrystallised charge.

decrystallisation on third parties, on one level, is minimal, since if the powers of the chargor to dispose of the charged assets are restored, disponees taking after that date will take free of the charge anyway, and it does not matter to them whether the charge is new or the original charge. Previous disponees might benefit if the charge is new, in that date of creation affects priorities.[246] However, if it were possible to decrystallise a charge with no adverse consequences, this would act as an incentive to chargees to include 'hair trigger' automatic crystallisation clauses in their charges, which might have an adverse effect on other creditors. If the effect of decrystallisation were to create a new charge, however, this would act as a disincentive on its use, since the new charge might require a new registration[247] and could be set aside under section 245 of the Insolvency Act 1986 if created within one year of the chargor's insolvency.

A further problem arises if it is possible to decrystallise a fixed charge, for example by the fixed chargee standing by and permitting disposal of assets by the chargor. If this creates a new floating charge, the issues of registration and priorities mentioned above arise. If, however, the same charge remains, then arguably it is a charge which is, as created, a fixed charge and so does not fall within the statutory definition of a floating charge in section 251 of the Insolvency Act, despite the ability of the chargor to dispose of the assets without the permission of the chargee. Such a result would be very unfortunate, as the statutory provisions on insolvency which apply to floating charges[248] would not apply here. Thus, there is a strong policy argument for the effect of the decrystallisation of a fixed charge to be to create a new floating charge.

Another way to disincentivise the use of widely drafted automatic crystallisation clauses is for them to be strictly construed by the courts. The only English cases on the subject have upheld the validity of clauses providing for crystallisation by notice, but they did not specify the actual effects of that crystallisation.[249] However, in a recent Irish case,[250] the court construed the contract, disregarding the 'crystallisation' label, to discover the rights and obligations of the parties after the service of the notice. Since those rights and obligations did not include any express restriction on the chargor's dealing powers over the charged assets, and since the express obligation to carry on the business in a proper manner still applied, the Irish High Court held that the charge remained floating, despite the service of the notice. The approach of the court was similar to that used in the *Spectrum* decision,[251] and it remains distinctly possible that an English court could take the same approach. This would certainly have the beneficial effect of incentivising much more careful drafting of automatic and semi-automatic crystallisation clauses.

---

[246] See 7.4.4.

[247] B Collier, 'Conversion of a Fixed Charge to a Floating Charge by Operation of Contract: Is it Possible?' (1995) 4 *American Journal of Comparative Law* 488; CH Tan, 'Automatic Crystallization, De-Crystallization and Convertibility of Charges' [1998] *Company Financial and Insolvency Law Review* 41, 45. It has been argued that, even if a new charge is created, it will not fall within s 860 Companies Act 2006 as it was not 'created by the company': see A Berg, 'The Cuckoo in the Nest of Corporate Insolvency: Some Aspects of the *Spectrum* Case' [2006] *Journal of Banking Law* 42.

[248] Discussed at 3.3.1.2; see also 7.3.3.3.1.

[249] *Re Woodroffes (Musical Instruments) Ltd* [1986] Ch 366 (where the validity of the clause was conceded); *Re Brightlife Ltd* [1987] Ch 200.

[250] *Re JD Brian Ltd (in liquidation)* [2011] IEHC 283. For a more detailed analysis see Goode: Credit and Security, 4-60.

[251] [2005] 2 AC 680. See 7.3.3.3.2.

7.3.3.3 Distinction Between Fixed and Floating Charges

7.3.3.3.1 Introduction

As discussed in chapter three,[252] statute provides that certain creditors of the company have priority over the floating (but not fixed) chargee in relation to charged assets, namely, the liquidator or administrator in relation to expenses, the preferential creditors and the unsecured creditors to the extent of the prescribed part. There are also other statutory provisions which apply only to floating charges and not to fixed charges. These include the provision that floating charges created in the run-up to the insolvency of the chargor are set aside on insolvency, unless for new value,[253] and the ability of an administrator to dispose of floating charge assets without the leave of the court.[254] Thus it may become necessary for the court to decide whether a charge is fixed or floating in order to know whether these provisions apply.[255] This process has spawned a great deal of litigation. It should be remembered, though, that the cases are primarily about statutory interpretation—that is, what is meant by 'floating charge' in the statute in question.[256] Because of this, the court has to take a black or white view on the substance of the interest created by the parties: the charge must be either fixed or floating. However, if there were a different trigger (or triggers) for the statutory consequences, it would be possible to permit the parties to decide the incidents of a charge for themselves, so that it had some features of a fixed charge and some of a floating charge.

7.3.3.3.2 Defining Features of Fixed Charges and Floating Charges

The statutory consequences of a charge being floating have acted as a strong incentive to chargees to draft charge documents which create fixed charges over as many of the chargor's assets as possible. In the past, charges, labelled as fixed charges, were created over not only fixed assets but circulating assets as well. As we have seen from the earlier discussion,[257] there is no problem with there being a fixed charge over future assets as well as present assets; however, practically, the chargor will also need to dispose of circulating assets and a power to do so without the chargee's consent will, under current authority, lead to the charge being characterised as floating. This is established by the decision of the Privy Council in *Agnew v Commissioner of Inland Revenue*[258] and of the House of Lords in *Re Spectrum Plus*.[259] These confirmed that the defining characteristic of a floating charge is the third of the characteristics identified by Romer LJ in *Re Yorkshire Woolcombers Association Ltd*,[260] namely the ability of the company to 'carry on business in the ordinary way' in relation to those assets.

---

[252] 3.3.1.2.
[253] Insolvency Act 1986, s 245.
[254] Ibid, Sch B1 para 70.
[255] Note that in relation to security financial collateral arrangements these provisions are disapplied: see 7.3.4.
[256] L Gullifer and J Payne, 'The Characterization of Fixed and Floating Charges' in J Getzler and J Payne (eds), *Company Charges: Spectrum and Beyond* (Oxford, Oxford University Press, 2006) 63; P Turner, 'Floating Charges, a "No-Theory" Theory' [2004] *Lloyd's Maritime and Commercial Law Quarterly* 319.
[257] 7.3.2.1.
[258] [2001] UKPC 28.
[259] [2005] UKHL 41.
[260] [1903] 2 Ch D 284, 295.

What amounts to 'carrying on business in the ordinary way' has been further refined by these cases to mean disposal of the relevant assets free from the charge.[261] The other two characteristics identified by Romer LJ,[262] while often present in a floating charge, appear not to be definitive. Thus, a charge can be floating even if it is over a present and unchanging asset, provided that the chargor has the power to dispose of it without the consent of the chargee. Lord Scott in the *Spectrum* case illustrated this by giving the example of a floating charge over a specific debt.[263] This point is also illustrated by the decision of the House of Lords in *Smith v Bridgend County Borough Council*,[264] where a charge over two huge coal washing plants (which took years to install) was held to be floating because the chargor had, in theory, the ability to replace them.[265]

A charge is floating if the chargor has the power to dispose of the charged assets without the consent of the chargee, and is fixed if it does not have this power, or, in other words, if the chargee has control of the charged assets. Of course, the terms of a charge are often not this clear cut. For example, most floating charges will contain a negative pledge provision prohibiting the creation of security interests over the charged assets which rank in priority to that of the chargee,[266] but will permit the chargor to dispose of the charged assets by sale, and many other charges will include more complex mixtures of prohibitions and permissions. The application of the *Spectrum* test can thus be uncertain. It is not always clear what amounts to the 'charged assets' over which the chargee must have control, nor is it clear what amounts to control.

7.3.3.3.2(a)   The Charged Assets

First, let us consider what is meant by 'the charged assets'. If the charge is over a debt, it appears that the chargee must exercise control over both the debt and its proceeds, on the basis that the proceeds are the traceable assets of the debt and represent its entire value.[267]

In both the *Agnew* and the *Spectrum* cases, the chargor collected the proceeds from the debtors and was free to dispose of those proceeds, though not the debts themselves. As a result, the charges were held to be floating. The result of these two decisions is that there are only two effective ways for a chargee to take control of the proceeds: either the chargee itself must collect in the debts for its own benefit, or the chargor must pay the proceeds into

---

[261] *Agnew v Commissioner of Inland Revenue* [2001] UKPC 28 [32].

[262] 'If it is a charge on a class of assets of a company present and future' and 'if that class is one which, in the ordinary course of the business of the company, would be changing from time to time': *Re Yorkshire Woolcombers Association Ltd* [1903] 2 Ch D 284, 295.

[263] *Re Spectrum Plus* [2005] UKHL 41 [107]. He also confirmed (at [111]) that the essential characteristic of the floating charge was that until crystallisation 'the chargor is left free to use the charged asset and to remove it from the security'.

[264] [2001] UKHL 58.

[265] Ibid, [44] per Lord Hoffmann. The plants were also included in a description which included assets more likely to be replaced.

[266] For the priority effect of such a provision see 7.44.

[267] *Agnew v Commissioner of Inland Revenue* [2001] UKPC 28 [46]. This view is not universally accepted: see D Henderson, 'Problems in the Law of Property after *Spectrum Plus*' [2006] *International Company and Commercial Law Review* 30; R Pennington, 'Recent Developments in the Law and Practice Relating to the Creation of Security for Companies' Indebtedness' (2009) 30 *Company Lawyer* 163.

a blocked bank account (either with the chargee or with another bank).[268] It can be seen that these options are usually unattractive to a company granting security to a lender over its receivables, since the proceeds from receivables will usually be used by the company to pay its ongoing expenses, such as rent, wages and utilities bills.

The structure of the lending, however, must be considered. If the loan is a term loan, or represents capital start-up funding which cannot easily be repaid, it would seem impossible for fixed security over receivables to be given, for the reasons set out above.[269] If the lending is purely to provide cash flow, so that the amount that is lent is roughly equivalent to the receivables owed to the company, the lending can be repaid by the incoming receivables (either collected by the lender or by the borrower on behalf of the lender) and ongoing expenses can be funded by further borrowing. This, of course, is the economic structure of receivables financing and can be achieved either by outright assignment of receivables or by lending secured by a fixed charge over those receivables using one of the methods outlined above. Both of these methods are used in invoice discounting, that is, non-notification receivables financing.[270] One effect of the *Agnew* and *Spectrum* decisions has been that much financing of SMEs is by invoice discounting rather than by an overdraft secured by charges over all the assets of the company.[271]

Most charged assets generate income (or proceeds) or have the potential to do so. Whether it is necessary for the chargee to control the income as well as the asset for a charge over that asset to be fixed depends on a number of factors.[272] One is how directly the generation of income is connected to the asset. Machinery, for example, enables the company to make things to generate income but there would be no need for the chargee to control the products made by the machinery to have a fixed charge over the machinery itself. Another is how close the generation of proceeds or income comes to being the sole value of the asset.[273] Yet another is whether the asset is destroyed in the generation of the proceeds or income; for example, this is true of a receivable.[274] One analogy that is often used in relation to the destruction of a receivable is that of a caterpillar becoming a butterfly: this is distinguished from a tree which bears fruit.[275] The tree remains (and thus is a separate asset from the fruit) while the chrysalis becomes the butterfly. Examples of 'tree and fruit' cases

---

[268] This is a summary of the account given by Lord Hope in *Spectrum Plus* [2005] UKHL 41 [54]. See also S Worthington and I Mitchkovska, 'Floating Charges: The Current State of Play' (2008) 23 *Journal of International Banking and Financial Law* 467.

[269] See G Yeowart, 'Why *Spectrum Plus* is Bad News for Banks' (2005) 24 *International Financial Law Review* 19.

[270] See 2.3.4.1.

[271] J Armour, 'Should We Redistribute in Insolvency?' in J Getzler and J Payne (eds), *Company Charges: Spectrum and Beyond* (Oxford, Oxford University Press, 2006); S Frisby, '*In re Spectrum Plus*—Less a Bang than a Whimper' in P Omar (ed), *International Insolvency Law: Themes and Perspectives* (Aldershot, Ashgate, 2008).

[272] See Security and Title-Based Financing, 6.130.

[273] For example, Lord Millett pointed out that the whole value of a receivable was its proceeds: see *Agnew Commissioner of Inland Revenue* [2001] UKPC 28 [46].

[274] For an argument that this is the sole criterion for whether control over proceeds is required for a fixed charge over the asset see N Frome and K Gibbons, '*Spectrum*—an End to the Conflict or the Signal for a New Campaign?' in J Getzler and J Payne (eds), *Company Charges: Spectrum and Beyond* (Oxford, Oxford University Press, 2006).

[275] See R Stevens, 'Security after the Enterprise Act' in J Getzler and J Payne (eds), *Company Charges: Spectrum and Beyond* (Oxford, Oxford University Press, 2006) 165–66.

include land and the rent from it,[276] and shares and the dividends from them.[277] It is possible therefore to grant a fixed charge over the land, or shares, and a floating charge over the income stream derived from them.

However, these analogies are only useful to illustrate the distinction between two extremes: they do not help with intermediate cases which resemble neither the tree nor the chrysalis. One example of this is a long-term income-producing contract, such as a chattel lease charged by the lessor[278] or a contract to operate an infrastructure project for a limited period charged by the operator in a project finance transaction. Both of these contracts generate the proceeds directly, and only exist economically as income-producing assets, so that the payments due represent the whole of their value. However, the asset survives separately from the payments made, until the end of its term: on this basis it could be said to have a separate existence. It has been argued that such contracts are to be treated as receivables payable over a long period of time, so that for a charge over such a contract to be fixed the chargee must control the proceeds as well as the contract itself.[279] This is an unpalatable view for those who provide finance for special purpose vehicles and other companies whose sole assets are income-producing long-term contracts.[280] Whilst all the proceeds from such contracts are not usually used to pay running expenses, there is often some form of payment waterfall whereby the destinations of the incoming payments are agreed in advance and not all the destinations will be under the control of the lender.[281] The preferable view is that whether the income from a long-term contract is a 'separate asset' is a matter of degree, depending on the length of time over which payments are to be made and the extent to which the assets is treated as separate on capital and other markets. If it is a separate asset, a chargor can grant a fixed charge over the contract even if it has a right to dispose of the income.[282]

7.3.3.3.2(b)   Control

The level of control required on the part of the chargee for the charge to be fixed will now be considered. It is necessary for the chargee's actual consent to be required for every disposition of the charged assets: it is not enough for consent to be given in advance or for the chargee to be obliged to give consent.[283] This is made very clear by the reasoning in

---

[276] *Rhodes v Allied Dunbar Pension Services Ltd* [1989] 1 WLR 800, 807 (also referred to as *Offshore Ventilation Ltd* [1989] 5 BCC 160). The decision in this case is not straightforward as it may depend on the special position of a chargee of a leasehold interest in land; see Security and Title-Based Financing, 6.132.

[277] *Arthur D Little Ltd (in administration) v Ableco Finance LLC* [2003] Ch 217.

[278] In *Re Atlantic Computer Systems Ltd* [1992] Ch 505, the Court of Appeal held that a charge over sub-leases of computers was fixed despite the right of the chargor to use the income in the ordinary course of business. This case was followed in *Re Atlantic Medical Ltd* [1993] BCLC 386, but it is now widely accepted that both cases must be seen as wrong in light of the *Agnew* and *Spectrum* decisions. See eg F Oditah, 'Fixed Charges and Recycling of Proceeds of Receivables' (2004) 120 *Law Quarterly Review* 533.

[279] S Worthington and I Mitchkovska, 'Floating Charges: The Current State of Play' (2008) 23 *Journal of International Banking and Financial Law* 467.

[280] It should, however, be pointed out that it is still possible for such lenders to take floating charges over such contracts. Note also that Insolvency Act 1986, s 176A does not apply to many project finance arrangements.

[281] Payment waterfalls are common in project finance transactions and also in securitisations: see 2.3.5.1 and 9.3.3.

[282] For detailed discussion see Security and Title-Based Financing, 6.138–6.139.

[283] Ibid, 6.110–6.112.

Agnew[284] and *Spectrum*,[285] which seems to overrule the reasoning in *Queen's Moat Houses plc v Capita*.[286] In that case, a chargor's right to require the chargee to release the charged property from the charge was considered consistent with the charge being fixed.[287] Thus, where the proceeds of charged receivables are paid to the chargor, they must be paid into a blocked account, that is, an account from which the chargor cannot withdraw without the consent of the chargee.[288]

Four practical issues arise from this. First, are the restrictions on the use of proceeds contained in a payment waterfall enough to give a chargee (if a party to the waterfall agreement) sufficient control for a charge to be fixed? While it is true that the waterfall clause does control the application of the proceeds so that the chargor does not have an unfettered right to their disposition, the control is not sufficient.[289] The clause amounts to consent to disposal in advance, and furthermore it is often the case that at least the residual amount of the proceeds is paid to the chargor, who then has control over its disposition.[290]

Second, can a fixed charge can be created over receivables by a 'two-account' structure?[291] This structure consists of a blocked account, into which the charge requires the proceeds of the charged receivables to be paid, and another current account. The chargee may then permit the chargor to transfer funds from the blocked account to the current account so long as a certain level of funds remains to the credit of the account. Once transferred, the chargor obtains free use of the funds, thus enabling it to meet cash flow expenses. The requirement that the proceeds be paid into a blocked account is clearly consistent with the chargee having sufficient control, but it would also be necessary for consent to every transfer to the current account to be an independent act of will by the chargee. The chargee must not be under any obligation to permit transfers.[292] There are, however, practical problems with this structure. First, it is expensive and time-consuming for the chargee[293] and, secondly, it has the effect that the chargor cannot be assured of having cash available to meet the

---

[284] [2001] UKPC 28 [27] and [22]: in the latter paragraph Lord Millett cited with approval Henchy J in *Re Keenan Bros Ltd* [1986] BCLC 242, 246, where he said that where assets were 'made undisposable save at the absolute discretion of the debenture holder' this had the distinguishing features of a fixed charge.

[285] [2005] UKHL 41 [138] (where Lord Walker stated that under a fixed charge 'the assets can be released from the charge only with the active concurrence of the chargee') and [140]. Lord Walker also made it very clear (at [158]) that agreements other than the charge agreement can be taken into account when characterising a charge, so it will not make any difference if consent in advance is given in another agreement.

[286] [2004] EWHC 868 (Ch).

[287] *Gray v G-T-P Group Ltd* [2010] EWHC 1772 (Ch) [38]. In that case a charge was held to be floating where the chargor was entitled to require the chargee to transfer some or all of the charged assets to it on request.

[288] *Agnew v Commissioner of Inland Revenue* [2001] UKPC 28 [48]; *Re Spectrum Plus* [2005] UKHL 41 [54].

[289] See A Berg, 'The Cuckoo in the Nest of Corporate Insolvency: Some Aspects of the *Spectrum* Case' [2006] *Journal of Banking Law* 33. For a contrary argument see N Frome and K Gibbons, '*Spectrum*—an End to the Conflict or the Signal for a New Campaign?' in J Getzler and J Payne (eds), *Company Charges: Spectrum and Beyond* (Oxford, Oxford University Press, 2006).

[290] An example of such a provision is a project finance waterfall clause, where the residual sum left after all obligations have been paid is earmarked for dividends to the sponsor shareholders, since there is no obligation on the special purpose vehicle to pay dividends.

[291] Such as that considered in *Re Keenan Brothers Ltd* [1986] BCLC 242.

[292] In *Re Keenan*, an attempt was made to do this by providing in the charge document that the chargee was under no obligation to permit transfers, and the fact that it might do so on any number of occasions should not be taken or construed as giving rise to any express or implied right to the company to do so: see first instance decision at [1985] BCLC 302, 305.

[293] G Yeowart, 'Why *Spectrum Plus* is Bad News for Banks' (2005) 24 *International Financial Law Review* 19.

expenses it incurs in the ordinary course of business. This is not only inconvenient; it could mean that the continuation of business under these circumstances constitutes a breach of duty by the directors of the chargor company.[294]

It might be argued that, so long as the balance of the funds which must remain in the blocked account is more than the secured indebtedness, this amounts to sufficient control for a fixed charge. However, this argument is fallacious. What is being characterised (usually) is the charge over the book debts, and the question is whether there is sufficient control of 'the charged assets': this includes the debts and the proceeds. To obtain a fixed charge over all the book debts, it is necessary to control all the proceeds. It makes no logical sense to say that there is a fixed charge over all the book debts but control only over part of the proceeds. In addition, there is the simple point that in characterising a charge, the court looks at control over the charged assets, which may at any time be worth more (or less) than the secured indebtedness. Whether it is possible to have a fixed charge over part of a fund of debts or money and a floating charge over the rest is an interesting question. In theory it must be possible, but only if the part is sufficiently identified. This raises the issues of identification that are discussed in different contexts throughout this book.[295] Identification issues do not usually arise in relation to a security interest, since a security interest can be taken over a body of assets worth more than the secured debt, and, therefore, such assets can be generically defined.[296]

In past cases where the characterisation of fixed and floating charges has been considered, there has usually not been a credit balance in the bank account into which receivables proceeds are paid, since the chargor has had the ability to dispose of the funds, and has used them to pay bills. The asset that was in issue in these cases was the receivables themselves. If an attempt is made to block or partially block an account, however, there may be a credit balance. It should be noted that it is likely that that the charge in relation to the credit balance at the bank (though not in relation to the receivables) is a financial collateral security arrangement and therefore the insolvency provisions are disapplied, thus removing one of the main reasons why a chargee would want a fixed charge.[297]

The third issue concerning control arises from the dictum of Lord Millett in the *Agnew* case that the question of whether the chargee had sufficient control is not determined merely by the wording of the charge document, but by the post-contractual conduct of the parties. Thus, it is not enough to provide contractually for a blocked account if it is not operated as one in fact.[298] The difficulties stemming from this proposition are largely caused by the fact that, because of section 251 of the Insolvency Act 1986, it is the nature of the charge *as created* that is relevant to whether the statutory consequences on insolvency apply. Thus, *prima facie*, the courts are deciding whether the transaction entered into by the parties created a fixed or floating charge. This depends on the construction of the agreement between the parties. Usually, however, the conduct of parties after a contract is made

---

[294] A Berg, 'The Cuckoo in the Nest of Corporate Insolvency: Some Aspects of the *Spectrum* Case' [2006] *Journal of Banking Law* 45.

[295] 6.4.4.1.1 and 8.2.1.3.3.

[296] For example, 'all existing and future book debts' as in *Tailby v Official Receiver* (1888) 13 App Cas 523.

[297] regs 8 and 10 FCARs (as amended)

[298] *Agnew v Commissioner of Inland Revenue* [2001] UKPC 28 [48].

cannot be taken into account in construing that contract.[299] One exception to this is where the court is considering whether the original agreement is a sham,[300] so that if an account is never treated as blocked this is good evidence that the blocking provision was not intended by the parties to represent the rights and obligations between them. In this situation, the court would have no difficulty in characterising the charge as floating. However, such a clear case will be rare, and since a finding of a sham involves a finding of dishonesty, it is unlikely that the court will reach this conclusion if there is evidence that the parties did, at least initially, intend to create a blocked account or other structure which gave the chargee sufficient control.

If the court does not find a sham, the failure of the chargee to exercise the potential control given to it by the charge document could give rise to a variation of the original agreement,[301] or a waiver of the chargee's rights,[302] either of which could have the effect of decrystallising the fixed charge created by the original agreement.[303] As pointed out earlier, whether decrystallisation creates a new floating charge or merely changes the incidents of the existing fixed one is not entirely clear. In the present context, however, unless a new charge is created, a charge which is operated as a floating charge is still a fixed charge 'as created' and the statutory consequences on insolvency do not apply to it. This is highly undesirable from a policy point of view.[304] If a new charge is created, it will be void against the liquidator and secured creditors unless it is registered within 21 days of its creation.[305] This could lead to a paradox: if the court finds a sham, the charge will be floating not fixed, but will be valid in insolvency, while if the court finds that there has been a waiver of rights, leading to a new floating charge, this charge could be void for non-registration.

A fourth issue relating to control is whether a charge can be fixed when the chargor cannot dispose of the charged assets generally but has the right to substitute other assets for the charged assets without the consent of the chargee. This is of significance in relation to financial collateral, where a right to substitute is very common indeed, but can also be relevant in relation to machinery, for example, which the chargor may wish to update. It is, of course, not the right to acquire new assets that is the problem, but the concomitant

---

[299] *James Miller & Partners Ltd v Whitworth Street Estates (Manchester) Ltd* [1970] AC 583, 603, 611, 614; *L Schuler AG v Wickman Machine Tool Sales Ltd* [1974] AC 235, 252, 260–61, 265–68, 272–73; *Dunlop Tyres Ltd v Blows* [2001] EWCA Civ 1032 [21]–[22].

[300] *AG Securities v Vaughan* [1990] 1 AC 417, 466 and see 7.2.2.

[301] For example, by an agreement that the chargee will give consent to withdrawals or dispositions in the future.

[302] For example, by the chargee's failure to prevent a withdrawal or a disposition. While one waiver would not result in decrystallisation, repeated waivers could create a representation leading to an estoppel which would prevent the chargee from relying on its control in the future. cf A Berg, 'The Cuckoo in the Nest of Corporate Insolvency: Some Aspects of the *Spectrum* Case' [2006] *Journal of Banking Law* 43, who sees the operation of an estoppel as likely to be only temporary.

[303] S Atherton and R Mokal, 'Charges over Chattels: Issues in the Fixed/Floating Jurisprudence' (2005) 26 *Company Lawyer* 10, 17. It should be pointed out that in the reverse situation, where proceeds subject to a floating charge were paid into a blocked account from four months after the charge was created, this conduct was ignored and the charge was held to be 'floating as created': see *Fanshaw v Amav Industries Ltd* [2006] EWHC 486 (Ch). The question of whether payment into the blocked account had the effect of crystallising the charge was not considered. Where a charge was created as fixed, the charge document gave the chargee the option of requiring payment into a blocked account and this was actually done, the charge was characterised as fixed: see *In the matter of Harmony Care Homes Ltd* [2009] EWHC 1961 (Ch).

[304] It would mean that those who take the 'benefit' of a floating charge are not also taking the burden of the statutory consequences.

[305] Companies Act 2006, s 859H.

right to dispose of the old assets without the chargee's consent that could be inconsistent with the necessary level of chargee control. The authorities are inconclusive.[306] The right to substitute would normally require that the value of the charged assets remains constant, or at least above the level of the secured borrowing, with the result that, to that extent, the chargee is retaining control over its security. However, there seems to be no suggestion in *Agnew* and *Spectrum* that the necessary control is limited to charged assets to the value of the borrowing: it appears that it must extend to all the charged assets, and, as discussed above, in normal circumstances it would be very difficult to limit control to a certain part of the charged assets. For this reason, it would seem that a general power to substitute assets is not consistent with a fixed charge, and to achieve the necessary control the chargee would have to give consent to every substitution. A more specific power to substitute with very strict criteria for substitution might be sufficient. This could relate to machinery, for instance, which required periodic updating. It would be necessary for the chargor to be obliged to add new substitute assets to the charged assets before disposing of old assets.[307]

7.3.3.3.3 Methodology of Characterising a Charge as Fixed or Floating

It is now necessary to address the actual process of characterisation carried out by the courts in this context. The approach is somewhat different from that in relation to characterising a transaction as a sale or charge; the possible reasons for these differences are discussed above.[308] Lord Millett laid down some very specific methodology in *Agnew*.[309] In the first stage, the court construes the agreement between the parties to ascertain what rights and obligations are intended to be created by the parties. In the second stage, the court characterises the charge as fixed or floating, based on the criteria discussed above, but without reference to the label put on the transaction by the parties. To what extent, then, is the intention of one or both parties to create a particular type of transaction relevant to the process? It can be relevant during the first stage (in conjunction with other factors such as the nature of the assets charged) in ascertaining the parties' intentions as to the rights and obligations created, if these are not fully spelled out in the charge document.[310] Otherwise it is not relevant: it is clear that the characteristics of fixed and floating charges are matters of law and cannot be changed by the agreement of the parties. Thus, in this particular characterisation process, policy considerations trump those of freedom of contract. In characterising a charge as floating, the courts are deciding that certain statutory consequences apply, and so the line drawn by the courts should reflect the policy reasons for those statutory consequences. It is to these that we now turn.

7.3.3.3.4 Should Floating Charges be Treated Differently?

Floating charges are treated differently from other security interests on the insolvency of the chargor. Three categories of claims have priority over the floating chargee in relation

---

[306] See Security and Title-Based Financing, 6.120–6.127 and the authorities discussed therein.
[307] Ibid, 6.127.
[308] See 7.2.2.
[309] *Agnew v Commissioner of Inland Revenue* [2001] UKPC 28, [2001] AC 710 [32].
[310] S Atherton and R Mokal, 'Charges over Chattels: Issues in the Fixed/Floating Jurisprudence' (2005) 26 *Company Lawyer* 10, 15.

to floating charge assets.[311] For this reason, there is every incentive for secured lenders, and their advisers, to try to avoid creating floating, as opposed to fixed, charges. This involves unproductive and wasteful costs. The position is made even worse by the uncertainties caused by the characterisation process previously discussed. Lawyers are unable to advise definitively as to whether a charge is fixed or floating: this increases legal risk (and therefore cost) and may make it more difficult for certain structures to obtain a favourable rating.

This section discusses various arguments that arise from this state of affairs. First, the policy reasons why certain classes of claims have priority in relation to floating charge (but not fixed charge) assets are analysed; secondly, the viability of an alternative statutory trigger for the insolvency consequences is considered; thirdly, the statutory provision that floating charges created in the run-up to insolvency is invalid if not for new value is discussed.

7.3.3.3.4(a) *Priority of Certain Classes of Claims Over Floating Charges*

The class of preferential creditors is now limited to employees of the company,[312] but unsecured creditors generally have some protection through the prescribed part. This is a percentage of floating charge assets which is set aside for unsecured creditors.[313] The policy arguments in favour of protecting unsecured creditors in the insolvency of the debtor largely focus on their inability to adjust.[314] The difference between fixed and floating security interests is irrelevant to these arguments. Therefore, to justify giving unsecured creditors limited priority over only floating charges, different arguments are required. Several such arguments have been made, particularly when such priority was first introduced. First, a floating charge can be given over all the assets of the company, so that there is nothing left for the unsecured creditors.[315] Second, the existence of the floating charge does not prevent the company from trading and thus incurring further debts to unsecured creditors.[316] Third, the raw materials and stock in trade of the company increase in value by virtue of the work performed on it by the workers, and therefore the workers' unpaid wages should have priority over the claims of the debenture holders.[317] These arguments are all premised on the fact that, by being able to take a floating charge, a chargee will have priority over assets which would otherwise be available to the unsecured creditors: in other words, it comes from the 'floating' nature of the floating charge. The ability to take a fixed security interest, however, is seen as part of the law of property: the debtor can grant a proprietary interest in its own assets, and little distinction is made, for the sake of this argument, between absolute

---

[311] 7.3.3.3.1.

[312] Crown preference was abolished in 2002: see 3.3.1.2.2.

[313] See 3.3.1.2.3 and, for detailed discussion, Security and Title-Based Financing, 20.24–20.33. The more general arguments about protection of unsecured creditors are discussed at 7.6.

[314] See 7.6.

[315] See eg speech by Lord Davey, HL Deb vol 87 cols 400–01 (2 August 1900), who suggested priority for all trade creditors for debts incurred within three months before winding up (this suggestion was rejected). A similar comment, and suggestion, was made by Lord Macnaghten in *Salomon v A Salomon & Co Ltd* [1897] AC 22, 53.

[316] L Gullifer and J Payne, 'The Characterization of Fixed and Floating Charges' in J Getzler and J Payne (eds), *Company Charges: Spectrum and Beyond* (Oxford, Oxford University Press, 2006) 80.

[317] HC Deb vol 46 col 73 (10 February 1897) (debating the Preferential Payments in Bankruptcy Act (1888) Amendment Bill). It should be noted that in 1897 floating charges were not registrable: this was also seen as detrimental to employees, and unsecured creditors more generally (HC Deb vol 46 col 80 (10 February 1897); registration was introduced in 1900 (see Companies Act 1900).

and security interests.[318] This type of argument justifying the different treatment of fixed and floating charges is evident in the rejection of proposals, in 1897, to give preferential creditors priority over all security interests, whether specific or floating,[319] and is still evident today.

Mokal makes another argument bearing on fixed charge priority, although he concludes that the floating charge should now be abolished.[320] He argues that, while fixed security interests bring positive benefits to unsecured creditors (by increasing the chances of the company's survival, by helping to control the behaviour of managers and by making it more likely that the chargee will continue to lend if the company becomes distressed), floating charges bring none of these benefits. The benefit previously brought by the existence of the floating charge, namely the ability of the chargee to appoint an administrative receiver which kept the debtor's estate together and prevented a race to enforce, has now disappeared.[321] Therefore, he argues, it should not be possible to for a creditor to obtain priority over circulating assets by taking a floating charge. An extrapolation of his argument leads to the conclusion that, if unsecured creditors are to have priority over any security interests,[322] this should be over floating charge assets.

These arguments are contradicted by other arguments leading to two opposite conclusions. Some argue that priority for unsecured creditors (limited as appropriate) should be over all assets subject to security interests.[323] Others argue that the benefits of priority for some, or maybe all, unsecured creditors are so small that they are outweighed by the costs of determining over which assets priority should occur.[324] It can also be argued that employees can be, and are, better protected by their direct claim against the Secretary of State,[325] and that the benefits obtained by the Government from subrogation of employees' preferential creditor claims are not great enough to outweigh the costs of maintaining the fixed/floating charge distinction mentioned above.

The main problem with the current uncertainty, though, does not relate to the priority of unsecured creditors. It is relatively straightforward to calculate the amount that will be deducted from floating charge assets for employees and the prescribed part: secured lenders will therefore just ensure that they are oversecured by at least that amount. This, of course, reduces the amount of credit available to the company, but, as a matter if policy, this is a direct trade-off against the benefits obtained to those unsecured creditors. A far greater degree of uncertainty, however, comes from the use of floating charge assets to fund the insolvency proceedings.[326] This is achieved, in administration, by top-slicing the

---

[318] Nor, perhaps, between interests created by grant and those created by reservation.

[319] HC Deb vol 46 cols 80, 83, 87 (10 February 1897).

[320] R Mokal, *Corporate Insolvency Law: Theory and Application* (Oxford, Oxford University Press, 2005) ch 6.

[321] Following the reforms brought about by the Enterprise Act 2002; see 7.5.

[322] Mokal also criticises the current priority for employees and the prescribed part; see R Mokal, *Corporate Insolvency Law: Theory and Application* (Oxford, Oxford University Press, 2005) 4.7.

[323] See R Calnan, 'Floating Charges: A Proposal for Reform' (2004) 19 *Journal of International Banking and Financial Law* 341.

[324] See J Armour, 'Should We Redistribute in Insolvency?' in J Getzler and J Payne (eds), *Company Charges: Spectrum and Beyond* (Oxford, Oxford University Press, 2006).

[325] See 7.6.2.3.

[326] R Calnan, 'Floating Charges: A Proposal for Reform' (2004) 19 *Butterworth's Journal of International Banking and Financial Law* 341.

administrator's expenses out of floating charge assets and by the statutory power of the administrator to use and dispose of floating charge assets without the leave of the court.[327] In a liquidation, the liquidator's expenses are top-sliced, subject to the floating chargee's veto on certain litigation expenses.[328] The categories of expenses are very wide. They include not only the insolvency practitioner's fees, which can be considerable, but any debts arising from contracts entered into by the insolvency practitioner: these can be for legal or other services, or contracts necessary to keep the business going pending a sale or as part of a corporate rescue attempt. Of course, floating chargees, who are usually banks, make considerable efforts to control fees and to monitor the incurring of other expenses,[329] but the overall cost may depend on the necessity to react to events which are unforeseeable even at the time the insolvency commences, and certainly unforeseeable at the time the security is taken. It is thus very hard for lenders to adjust accurately ex ante, especially when it is unclear which asset pool will be used to pay these expenses.

7.3.3.3.4(b) Who Should Fund the Insolvency Process

It is therefore important to consider who should fund the insolvency process, and out of what pool of assets. Different justifications apply for the use of floating charge assets in funding liquidation and administration. Administration is, at least in theory, a corporate rescue process. The administrator, to the extent that he is seeking to rescue the company, should be able to operate in the ordinary course of business, in the same way as the company operated before administration. This will include disposing of circulating assets such as stock in trade, making payments to creditors, employees and utilities and entering into new contracts, which, arguably, he should be able to do using assets which the company was able to use before administration.[330] Further, the floating charge holder is most likely to gain from a rescue of the company, since its lending is provided on the basis that it will be paid out of income rather than out of specific assets,[331] so arguably it makes more sense that it should fund the rescue attempt.[332]

Many administrations are not rescue attempts, however: they are pre-packaged administrations ('pre-packs')[333] or other forms of realisation of assets for distribution. Much of the administrator's work relates not to the floating charge assets, but to assets subject to the bank's fixed charge, or to other secured creditors' interests. One might ask why this work should be funded merely from floating charge assets. Moreover, liquidations are far more

---

[327] Insolvency Act 1986, Sch B1 paras 70 and 99; see 3.3.1.2.1. Paragraph 71 provides that an administrator requires the leave of the court to dispose of assets subject to a fixed charge.

[328] Ibid, s 176ZA, and see 3.3.1.2.1.

[329] See E Kempson, *Review of Insolvency Practitioner Fees: Report to the Insolvency Service* (July 2013), 4.2.1.

[330] This was the view of the Law Commission: see Report No 296, *Company Security Interests: Final Report* (Cm 6654) at 3.166 fn 205, in relation to the power of the administrator to use floating charge assets without the leave of the court (Insolvency Act 1986, Sch B1 para 70).

[331] See the discussion of the distinction between relationship lending and asset-based lending at 2.3.4.3.

[332] It should be noted that the floating charge assets would not necessarily fund the rescue attempt directly, but would be used to pay the costs of additional finance raised by the administrator. Of course, if the rescue attempt failed, the repayment costs would form part of the administration expenses. A proposal to rank finance costs above all other administration expenses, in an attempt to assist corporate rescue, was made by the Insolvency Service in *Encouraging Corporate Rescue—A Consultation* (June 2009) Proposal C, but this has not been taken further.

[333] See 7.5.1.4.

numerous than administrations,[334] and in many cases companies exit administration by going into creditors' voluntary liquidation (CVL).[335] A floating chargee may gain no, or little, immediate benefit from a liquidation.[336] It can, of course, be argued that banks and other repeat players gain a general benefit from the orderly conduct of a collective insolvency procedure.[337] Further, there are good policy reasons to have the same funding regime for administration and liquidation, as otherwise there are perverse incentives to choose one over the other.[338] However, these arguments lead just as persuasively to a regime of funding by all secured creditors, rather than the present regime.

Under the present system, of course, expenses (as well as the prescribed part and preferential creditors) are paid only from assets subject to a floating charge. An SME's principal assets are usually its receivables, and if these are subject to receivables financing (as is now often the case), there are few if any assets subject to the floating charge. This has two consequences. First, there is often little left for the prescribed part.[339] Second, in reality much of the funding of insolvency proceedings by banks is 'voluntary' (ie, not taken out of assets which would otherwise meet the bank's claim): this means that the bank's consent is required before the expenses are incurred, which gives banks much more control over the insolvency process.

7.3.3.3.4(c) Possible Statutory Triggers for Priority

The suggestion made by the City of London Law Society's Financial Law Committee, and particularly by its chair, Richard Calnan, is that the costs of the insolvency process should be paid by taking a percentage out of all assets subject to a security interest, subject to a cap (using the same method as for the prescribed part).[340] This proposal has the obvious benefit that the need to distinguish between fixed and floating charges would disappear (or be greatly reduced). However, there are considerable difficulties in fixing the value of the percentage or the cap, and there is also the problem that lenders might seek to avoid falling within the levy's scope, by taking absolute rather than security interests for proprietary protection.

Another possible solution is to redefine the statutory trigger for priority so that it becomes easier to administer and less easy to avoid, while keeping roughly the same outcome so that the same assets are subject to the statutory priority consequences as at the moment.

---

[334] In 2013 there were 2,365 administrations and 14,990 liquidations (figures from Insolvency Service).

[335] There were 947 instances of administrations being followed by a CVL in 2013 (figures from Insolvency Service).

[336] If it does, there is an obvious reason why it should pay the costs.

[337] L Gullifer, 'The Reforms of the Enterprise Act 2002 and the Floating Charge as a Security Device' in L Gullifer, W-G Ringe and P Théry (eds), *Current Issues in European Financial and Insolvency Law* (Oxford, Oxford University Press, 2009) 34.

[338] Ibid, 35–36.

[339] This statement is based on *Pre-Pack Empirical Research: Characteristic and Outcome Analysis of Pre-Pack Administration* (July 2014), para 84, a report produced by the University of Wolverhampton for the Graham Review of pre-packs. The study examined 500 administrations in 2010, and the need for further research in this area was noted in the Graham Review (para 8.31).

[340] Discussion paper produced by City of London Law Society Financial Law Committee, 24 February 2014, www.citysolicitors.org.uk/attachments/article/121/20140219%20Secured%20Transactions%20Reform%20 Discussion%20Paper%202%20Fixed%20and%20floating%20charges%20v2.pdf. See also R Calnan, 'Floating Charges: A Proposal for Reform' (2004) 19 *Butterworth's Journal of International Banking and Financial Law* 341.

A contender is the criterion used in New Zealand, which is that priority is given over charges over accounts receivable and inventory of the company.[341] Although there will always be arguments at the edges of the definition of 'accounts receivable' and 'inventory', there is a clear core area which will always be included. Further, by concentrating on the type of assets over which the charge is given, it is much more difficult for creditors to avoid the trigger by clever drafting. Another contender is the definition in the Australian Personal Property Securities Act 2009, which replaces 'floating charge' with 'circulating security interest', that is, a security interest over circulating assets. 'Circulating assets' are defined as certain types of assets, such as inventory, currency, bank accounts and receivables, but an asset will not be a circulating asset if the secured party has either possession or control of it. 'Control' in this context is specifically defined in relation to specific types of assets.[342]

If there is to be any statutory trigger that differentiates between charges for the purpose of priority for certain unsecured creditors, it should reflect the reasons for this differentiation, namely, those referred to above. The *Spectrum* criterion, that is the ability of the chargor to dispose of any of the charged assets without the consent of the chargee, is over-inclusive in that it does not just include charges which cover all the assets of the company or those which permit the company to trade. Is a differentiation that depends on the type of assets charged more appropriate? In many situations, in order to trade a company needs to dispose of inventory and (the proceeds of) receivables, and so a charge over these assets is necessarily floating. Under modern financing techniques, however, both of these types of assets can be the subject of an absolute disposition which does not stop the company trading. Most obviously, receivables can be sold to a financier, and, less commonly, inventory also can be sold to a financier and then sold to customers by the company as an undisclosed agent.[343] Even if the statutory trigger were changed, such dispositions would not be included. Nor, arguably, should they be. These sales bring new money into the company, and the financier's interest relates only to that money, while assets subject to a floating charge are security for all past and future borrowing.[344]

The question of the statutory trigger for priority provisions is a difficult and somewhat intractable question, on which the experience of other jurisdictions is invaluable. Care must be taken, however, to look at each jurisdiction's experience in the context of its own insolvency procedures: the funding of such procedures is only one piece in a very complicated policy-driven jigsaw.

---

[341] New Zealand Personal Property Securities Amendment Act 2001, Sch 1, amending cl 9 of Sch 7 to Companies Act 1993. This criterion only relates to priority over preferential creditors, and no other insolvency consequences.

[342] In the five-year review of the Australian Personal Property Securities Act 2009, it was recommended that the provisions on 'circulating assets' and 'control' be replaced with wording similar to the New Zealand provisions. See B Whittaker, *Review of the Personal Property Securities Act: Final Report* (2015), 9.2.1. For criticism of the current legislation see D Turner, 'Fixed Charges over Receivables and the Personal Property Securities Act' (2011) 19 *Insolvency Law Journal* 71.

[343] As in *Welsh Development Agency v Exfinco* [1992] BCLC 148. See 7.2.5.2.

[344] A financier's interest which is acquired for new money is excluded from the New Zealand definition of security interests over which preferential creditors have priority (in New Zealand 'security interests' include some outright transfers). The same effect is achieved in Australia by the definition of 'control': see A Duggan and D Brown, *Australian Personal Property Securities Law* (LexisNexis Butterworths Australia, 2012) 13.23.

7.3.3.3.4(d) Invalidity of a Floating Charge in the Period Before Insolvency

The last difference in treatment to be considered is that a floating, but not a fixed, charge created in the run-up to insolvency can be set aside if not given for new value.[345] It is difficult to discern a coherent rationale for this.[346] The argument for this provision is that a lender that takes a charge when the borrower is in financial difficulties improves its position significantly vis-à-vis all the other creditors. This improvement in position can only be justified if, and to the extent that, the lender provides the borrower with new value. First, new value may enable the borrower to keep trading so that its financial position improves and all creditors benefit. Second, although the lender taking the charge is then in a better position than other creditors, the borrower itself is no worse off. However, both of these arguments apply equally to fixed and floating charges. Further, even if no new value is given, a lender that refrains from enforcing the debt due because a charge is granted to it is enabling the borrower to continue trading. This is true for both fixed and floating charges.

The Cork Committee supported the present position by arguing that the grant of a floating charge (as opposed to a fixed charge) was more damaging to unsecured creditors because of the breadth of the charge, and because it encompassed future assets which could be acquired on credit by the borrower, thus prioritising the floating chargee over the unpaid vendors.[347] This latter argument is open to several objections. First, both fixed and floating charges can cover future assets, although it is true that future circulating assets are more likely only to be the subject of a floating charge. Second, unpaid vendors are in a position to protect themselves,[348] and if they fail to do so when a borrower has granted a (registered) floating charge it is hard to see why insolvency law should protect them. In fact, it is the unsecured creditors existing at the time the charge was granted who are worse off, since they did not know of the existence of the charge when they extended credit. Again, though, this argument applies to both fixed and floating charges. The only justification for the existing breadth of section 245 is that floating charges are wider in scope than fixed charges, and this does not seem a good enough reason to limit section 245 to floating charges.[349]

7.3.3.4 The Future of the Floating Charge[350]

The floating charge has suffered many blows over the years, and yet retains its popularity amongst lenders. To some extent, this is hard to fathom. As a priority device, it is severely limited, as discussed above.[351] Admittedly, the *Spectrum* decision has meant that there are now assets over which it is very hard to take a fixed charge, and so there may be more assets within the scope of floating charges than there used to be. As discussed above, however,

---

[345] Insolvency Act 1986, s 245.

[346] For a full discussion see L Gullifer and J Payne, 'The Characterization of Fixed and Floating Charges' in J Getzler and J Payne (eds), *Company Charges: Spectrum and Beyond* (Oxford, Oxford University Press, 2006) 85–87. See further 3.3.2.3.

[347] *Report of the Review Committee on Insolvency Law and Practice* (Cmnd 8558, June 1982), para 1553.

[348] See 3.3.2.1.

[349] See R Mokal, *Corporate Insolvency Law: Theory and Application* (Oxford, Oxford University Press, 2005) 186.

[350] See R Goode, 'The Case for the Abolition of the Floating Charge' in J Getzler and J Payne (eds), *Company Charges: Spectrum and Beyond* (Oxford, Oxford University Press, 2006).

[351] R Mokal, *Corporate Insolvency Law: Theory and Application* (Oxford, Oxford University Press, 2005).

lenders are developing new ways of obtaining proprietary protection in relation to such assets, by using receivables financing and other asset-based techniques involving the transfer of an absolute and not a security interest.

The main benefit of taking a floating charge used to be the ability to take control of enforcement, by the appointment of an administrative receiver, and floating charges were taken for control rather than for priority. Except in certain circumstances, this is now not possible.[352] Instead, the floating chargee can appoint an administrator out of court. This right is still valuable to a lender, although in fact many administrators are now appointed by the directors or the company.[353] Despite the legislative rhetoric that the administrator's duties are owed to all creditors, the appointing lender still has considerable influence over the conduct of the administrator. First, the lender is in a position to choose the identity of the administrator. This means that it can choose an insolvency practitioner sympathetic to the interests of banks, and also that the chosen person has an incentive to comply with the lender's wishes to ensure future business. Second, the administration is funded by the principal lender, through the top-slicing of expenses and the unrestricted use of floating charge assets. Thus the lender has a strong incentive to monitor the actions of the administrator closely.[354] An argument could also now be made that the growth of pre-packaged administration[355] has meant that, at least in some cases, the position of the floating chargee is now very similar to the position it was in when it had a right to appoint an administrative receiver, in that it can broker a decision to sell the business with little or no consultation with the other creditors.[356]

The presence of a monitoring lead creditor is valuable to other creditors both within and outside insolvency.[357] In English law, the traditional way of identifying a lead creditor is to see who has fixed and floating charges over all the assets of the company. The growth in asset-based lending in recent years could threaten this structure, but only where different financiers have lent against different assets.[358] To the extent that one financier lends against all the assets of the company, as in 'true' asset-based lending,[359] this replicates the lead creditor. Since an asset-based lender takes a mixture of absolute interests and charges, it may end up qualifying to appoint an administrator, since it will have charges over all the assets of the company (any other assets are already owned by the asset-based financier).[360]

---

[352] It should not be forgotten, though, that in those exceptional cases, for example project finance, the ability to appoint an administrative receiver is still very important.

[353] S Frisby, 'Not Quite Warp Factor 2 Yet? The Enterprise Act and Corporate Insolvency (Pt 1)' (2007) 22 *Journal of International Banking and Financial Law* 327. This seems to be for public relations purposes, to prevent the banks looking too predatory. Of course, the directors are under great pressure from the lender to make the appointment, and the lender exercises control over the identity of the administrator.

[354] And does so: see E Kempson, *Review of Insolvency Practitioner Fees: Report to the Insolvency Service* (July 2013), 4.2.1.

[355] See 7.5.1.4.

[356] See *Graham Review into Pre-Pack Administration* (June 2014), para 7.36. For discussion of the pre-pack see 7.5.1.4.

[357] See 7.6.2.1.

[358] S Frisby, *Report on Insolvency Outcomes, prepared for the Insolvency Service* (June 2006), 9, 39–43.

[359] See 2.3.4.3.

[360] At least one charge must be floating, however: see Insolvency Act 1986, Sch B1 para 14.

Where, then, does this leave the floating charge? Probably still with a residual role: largely to enable the appointment of an administrator, but also for priority where nothing else is possible. A lender is likely to prefer to have a floating charge rather than being unsecured, despite the disadvantages of this form of security. It should be remembered that when it comes to taking security, lenders will usually try to have security over every asset possible (the 'crown jewels'); if a floating charge is the only way to achieve this, then this is the route that they will take.

7.3.4 Security Financial Collateral Arrangements[361]

7.3.4.1 Introduction

The Financial Collateral Directive (FCD) was entered into partly to harmonise rules for the taking of collateral in financial market transactions between different Member States, partly to make the taking of such collateral easier in some Member States, and partly to ensure that the rules applicable to security arrangements have the same effect as those applying to title transfer arrangements.[362] The FCD was implemented in the UK by the FCARs. The FCARs disapply various provisions which would otherwise apply under English law. To make it more straightforward to create a valid collateral arrangement, formal requirements, including registration requirements,[363] are disapplied.[364] Insolvency provisions which might inhibit enforcement of collateral arrangements are also disapplied,[365] and, for security collateral arrangements, uncertainty is removed in relation to common market practices, which would be effective in title transfer arrangements: these are close-out netting, the right of use and appropriation.[366] Financial collateral comprises money in accounts, securities and claims for repayment of a loan made by a bank or credit institution.[367]

As discussed earlier,[368] in a title transfer financial collateral arrangement ownership of the collateral is transferred to the collateral taker, who owes a personal obligation to return 'equivalent collateral' to the collateral provider.[369] A security financial collateral arrangement is an arrangement which creates a security interest, and where the collateral is 'delivered, transferred, held, registered or otherwise designated so as to be *in the possession or under the control* of the collateral taker' (emphasis added).[370] The question of what amounts to 'possession or control' is not straightforward, and has attracted a great deal of

---

[361] For detailed discussion see Goode: Credit and Security, ch 6.

[362] Proposal for the Financial Collateral Directive (COM(2001) 168 final, 27.03.2001).

[363] It should be remembered that, before the 2013 reforms, fixed charges over securities were not registrable (though floating charges were).

[364] FCARs, reg 4.

[365] Ibid, regs 8 and 10.

[366] Ibid, regs 12, 16 and 17.

[367] See Goode: Credit and Security, 6-04–6.06 for detailed discussion.

[368] 7.2.3.

[369] FCARs, reg 3.

[370] Ibid; see also FCD art 2(2).

practitioner and academic comment.[371] It should be remembered that if the 'possession or control' requirement is fulfilled, the security arrangement attracts all the protection of the FCARs, so that not only is registration not required, but insolvency provisions are disapplied, and appropriation and the right of use are available if included in the security agreement.[372] Thus 'possession or control' is not merely a method of perfection.

The 'possession or control' requirement is qualified in the FCARs, in that '[a]ny right of the collateral-provider to substitute financial collateral of the same or greater value, or withdraw excess collateral or to collect the proceeds of credit claims until further notice shall not prevent the financial collateral being in the possession or under the control of the collateral taker'.[373] This exception, which was included to reflect market practice, clearly enables at least some floating charges to fall within the FCARs, but its precise scope is unclear.

The policy reasons for imposing the 'possession or control' requirement do appear to centre on finding an easily fulfilled replacement for the 'administrative burdens' which the FCD disapplies.[374] It was sought to strike 'a balance between market efficiency and the safety of the parties to the arrangement and third parties, thereby avoiding *inter alia* the risk of fraud', the balance being struck by the directive covering only collateral arrangements which provided for some sort of 'dispossession' and which were evidenced in writing.[375] Based on this, it is possible to argue that 'possession or control' should be interpreted as requiring sufficiently objective conduct both to prevent fraudulent assertion of a security interest by one party against another, and to provide third parties with a means of discovery of the security interest.[376] However, current English law does not fully reflect this argument, as will become clear from the discussion that follows, despite the fact that it has been held that the phrase 'possession or control' must be given an autonomous meaning rather than one necessarily derived from ordinary English law.[377]

First, it is helpful to consider two distinctions that can be drawn in relation to 'control', since the meaning of the term is not self-evident.[378] One is between positive and negative

---

[371] Law Commission No 296, *Company Security Interests: Final Report* (Cm 6654, 2005), ch 5; Goode: Credit and Security, 6-32–6-37; Security and Title-Based Financing, ch 3; M Hughes, 'The Financial Collateral Regulations' (2006) 21 *Journal of International Banking and Financial Law* 64; D Turing, 'New Growth in the Financial Collateral Garden' (2005) 20 *Journal of International Banking and Financial Law*; A Zacaroli, 'Taking Security over Intermediated Securities: Chapter V of the UNIDROIT (Geneva) Convention on Intermediated Securities' in L Gullifer and J Payne (eds), *Intermediated Securities: Legal Problems and Practical Issues* (Oxford, Hart Publishing, 2010) 167; LC Ho, 'The Financial Collateral Directive's Practice in England' (2011) 26 *Journal of International Banking Law and Regulation* 151; R Parsons and M Dening, 'Financial Collateral—An Opportunity Missed' (2011) 5 *Law and Financial Markets Review* 164; S Goldsworthy, 'Taking Possession and Control to Excess: Issues with Financial Collateral Arrangements under English Law' [2013] *Journal of International Banking and Finance Law* 71; L Gullifer, 'Piecemeal Reform: Is It the Answer?' in F Dahan (ed), *Secured Lending in Commercial Transactions* (Cheltenham, Edward Elgar, 2015). See also Financial Markets Law Committee, *Analysis of Uncertainty regarding the Meaning of 'Possession or … Control' and 'Excess Financial Collateral' under the Financial Collateral Arrangements (No 2) Regulations 2003*, FMLC Paper: Issue 1 (2012).
[372] Close-out netting is likely to be available anyway under English law, but the provision in FCARs precludes any uncertainty, though its scope is not entirely clear. See R Parsons and M Dening, 'Financial Collateral—An Opportunity Missed' (2011) 5 *Law and Financial Markets Review* 164.
[373] FCARs, reg 3.
[374] FCD, recital 9.
[375] Ibid, recital 10.
[376] See L Gullifer, 'Piecemeal Reform: Is It the Answer?' in F Dahan (ed), *Secured Lending in Commercial Transactions* (Cheltenham, Edward Elgar, 2015).
[377] *Re Lehman Brothers International (Europe) (In Administration)* [2012] EWHC 2997 (Ch) [105].
[378] Benjamin: Financial Law, 478 fn 192.

control,[379] and the other is between legal and operational control. Positive control is where the collateral taker has the right to dispose of the collateral without any further reference to the collateral provider, and negative control is where the collateral provider is prohibited from disposing of the collateral without the consent of the collateral taker. Legal control refers to control established by the rights and prohibitions in the security agreement, while operational control refers to the practical ability of the collateral taker to dispose of the collateral, or to prevent the collateral provider disposing of it, as the case may be.

7.3.4.2 Current English Law

The current English position can be summarised as follows. It might be thought that the concept of possession only applies to tangible assets. Possession by the collateral taker of bearer securities, for example, both evidences the arrangement and gives sufficient publicity of the security interest. Although the view that the concept of possession (under English law) was limited to tangible collateral was accepted in the case of *Gray v G-T-P Group Ltd*,[380] this caused disquiet among market participants.[381] The reason for this was that in *Gray* an arrangement whereby the collateral was in the collateral taker's name (in a bank account) was held not to be a security financial collateral arrangement because the collateral taker had only operational control and not legal control. The collateral taker held the collateral in a bank account in its name, on trust for the collateral provider. The collateral provider had the right to call for funds to be transferred to it from the account (by the collateral taker) until an event of default occurred, at which point the collateral taker was entitled to withdraw unpaid fees from the account.[382] It was strongly pointed out by market commentators that the collateral taker in *Gray* had the equivalent of possession of the collateral—that is, the account was in its name.[383] The collateral provider could not deal with the funds without them being transferred back to it, which could only occur with the cooperation of the collateral taker, who could then alert a third-party potential transferee to the existence of the charge.[384]

The decision in *Gray* was followed by that of Briggs J in *Re Lehman Brothers International (Europe) (In Administration)*,[385] which postdated the amendments discussed below but was decided in relation to the unamended FCARs. In that case, in which the points were argued at much greater length, the collateral was held by the collateral taker as custodian for the

---

[379] This distinction is also made by the Law Commission in *Company Security Interests: Final Report* No 296 (Cm 6654, 2005), para 5.46.

[380] *Gray v G-T-P Group Ltd (Re F2G Realisations Ltd)* [2010] EWHC 1772 (Ch).

[381] Financial Markets Law Committee paper Issue 87—control 'Gray v G-T-P Ltd' (Dec 2010); R Parsons and M Dening, 'Financial Collateral—An Opportunity Missed' (2011) 5 *Law and Financial Markets Review* 164.

[382] It would appear that the subject matter of the charge was the beneficial interest of the chargor in the debt owed to the chargee by the bank, which the chargee held on trust for the chargor (although this was not spelled out in these terms in the judgment). This does raise conceptual problems as to whether the requirement of possession or control can apply to a beneficial interest; see L Gullifer, 'Piecemeal Reform: Is It the Answer?' in F Dahan (ed), *Secured Lending in Commercial Transactions* (Cheltenham, Edward Elgar, 2015).

[383] Financial Markets Law Committee paper Issue 87—control 'Gray v G-T-P Ltd' (Dec 2010), 4.8–4.12.

[384] Even if the 'collateral' were the beneficial interest of the collateral provider, which could be dealt with without the consent of the trustee, the fact that the interest was under a trust would at least alert third parties to consult the trustee if they wished. This reasoning is rather similar to that underlying the rule in *Dearle v Hall*; see 7.4.4.

[385] [2012] EWHC 2997 (Ch).

collateral provider,[386] and the relevant charge secured not only the collateral provider's debt to the collateral taker but also debts owed to its affiliates. The collateral provider had the right to withdraw collateral which was not required to cover the debts due to the collateral taker. Since the collateral provider could withdraw collateral which 'covered' the debts due to the affiliates, it was held that the collateral taker was not in 'possession or control' of the collateral. The argument that there was sufficient possession if the collateral was in the name of the collateral taker was expressly rejected.[387]

As a result of market pressure, when the FCARs were amended in 2010, a wider definition of 'possession' was included to cover the situation where the collateral was placed in an account in the name of the collateral taker.[388] Unfortunately, though, the definition did not end there but included a proviso:

> … provided that any rights the collateral-provider may have in relation to that financial collateral are limited to the right to substitute financial collateral of the same or greater value or to withdraw excess financial collateral.

The focus of this proviso on the rights (or lack of them) of the collateral provider introduces a requirement of negative legal control into the test for possession. The existence of additional rights would not prevent the mitigation of invisibility and fraudulent assertion risk required by the recitals to the directive. The inclusion of the proviso was explained on the grounds that it was 'the intention of the FCD that only those financial collateral arrangements providing for some form of dispossession should be within the scope of the Directive'.[389] This begs the question of what is meant by 'possession' (and therefore 'dispossession') in the directive, and also fails to grapple with the fact that 'dispossession' is stated in the recitals to be required only to the extent necessary to mitigate the risks analysed above. Furthermore, the proviso introduces a great deal of uncertainty, especially relating to the definition of 'excess collateral'. As this is also relevant to 'control', it will be discussed below.

Given the wider definition of 'possession', the concept of 'control' is of most importance when collateral is held in the name of the collateral provider, or in the name of a third party: the latter is a common way of holding collateral to avoid the insolvency risk of the collateral taker.[390] It is reasonably clear from *Gray*, *Lehman* and the approach taken in the 'possession' amendment to the FCARs that the critical rights are those of the collateral provider rather than those of the collateral taker. Negative and legal control is clearly required, and operational control is not enough. Thus, a security arrangement will only fall within the FCARs if, within the terms of the security agreement, the collateral provider has no rights in relation to the collateral except to substitute and to withdraw excess collateral. Is negative legal control sufficient without more? It is sufficient for negative legal control if the collateral

---

[386] Presumably it was held by the collateral taker in its own account with an intermediary or a CSD.

[387] [2012] EWHC 2997 (Ch) [129]–[134]. Briggs J did accept that 'possession' in this context could apply to intangibles (at [131]).

[388] The definition is expressly not exclusive.

[389] HM Treasury, *A Consultation on the Implementation of the amending EU Directive 2009/44/EC: Summary of Responses* (2010), para 2.20.

[390] S Goldsworthy, 'Taking Possession and Control to Excess: Issues with Financial Collateral Arrangements under English Law' [2013] *Journal of International Banking and Financial Law* 71; A Gordon-Orr, 'The benefits and pitfalls of tripartite collateral arrangements' [2013] *Journal of International Banking and Financial Law* 627.

provider is prohibited by the charge document from disposing of the assets, without any mechanism actually to prevent him actually making such a disposal. This control would not be apparent to the outside world, nor could it be said to amount to 'dispossession'.[391] In order to achieve the aims set out in the recitals, arguably some sort of operational control is required.[392]

Practical examples serve to illustrate the principles set out above.[393] One example of negative operational control is where money is held in a blocked bank account, as discussed earlier in relation to floating charges.[394] In fact, negative operational control is often coupled with positive operational control, for example where the collateral taker is registered as the owner of shares in the books of the company, or in the CREST register.[395] Another example, in relation to intermediated securities,[396] is where the intermediary is the collateral taker,[397] or is notified of the charge by the collateral taker, or where the securities are transferred to the collateral taker's account.[398] Of course, each of these examples will only fall within the FCARs where the collateral provider's rights are limited to rights of substitution and withdrawal of excess collateral.

The precise boundaries of the permitted rights of the collateral provider are uncertain, and it is unclear whether certain rights common in collateral arrangements will be fatal.[399] It is also unclear what is meant by the right to withdraw 'excess collateral'. Briggs J defined excess collateral, in the context of the *Lehman* case, as 'property in the Custody Account in excess of the property which the custodian believes will be sufficient to cover any exposure that the custodian has to the client'. This begs a number of questions. What is meant by 'exposure': does it include contingent and future debts? And can the parties agree that it does not? Moreover, can the parties agree that less than the full value of exposure need be left in the account? And can they agree a method of valuation? On one view, the question of what amounts to 'excess collateral' should be a matter of freedom of contract for the parties to define, so long as the agreement is clear. If the 'possession or control' requirement is to have any bite at all, there must probably be limits on what the parties can agree, but the extent of these limits is not clear.

---

[391] See A Zacaroli, 'Taking Security over Intermediated Securities: Chapter V of the UNIDROIT (Geneva) Convention on Intermediated Securities' in L Gullifer and J Payne (eds), *Intermediated Securities: Legal Problems and Practical Issues* (Oxford, Hart Publishing, 2010) 167.

[392] cf *Re Lehman Brothers International (Europe) (In Administration)* [2012] EWHC 2997 (Ch), where Briggs J gave an example which appears to constitute merely legal control.

[393] For more practical examples see Goode: Credit and Security, 6-38–6-45.

[394] 7.3.3.3.2(b).

[395] For an account of CREST see 4.6.2. There are other methods of taking security in relation to securities held through CREST which have a similar effect; see Security and Title-Based Financing, 3-48.

[396] See 8.3.2.3.2(b).

[397] Of course, there may not be sufficient negative control if the investor has the right to give instructions to the intermediary in relation to the collateral, for example where the securities are held under a prime brokerage agreement and it is envisaged that the securities will be used to execute trades as instructed by the client. The answer in practice may well turn on the definition of 'excess collateral'.

[398] These methods are those listed by the Law Commission as amounting to control under the scheme it proposed. See Law Commission No 296, *Company Security Interests: Final Report* (Cm 6654, 2005), para 5.20.

[399] For full discussion see S Goldsworthy, 'Taking Possession and Control to Excess: Issues with Financial Collateral Arrangements under English Law' [2013] *Journal of International Banking and Finance Law* 71.

It can be seen that, as a general rule, a floating charge will not fall within the FCARs as there will not be sufficient negative legal control. However, a charge may be floating merely because there is a right to substitute or to withdraw excess collateral, in which case it will meet the requirements. Thus the disapplication of insolvency provisions which apply only to floating charges has some meaning. Further, if a floating charge is crystallised by the chargee acquiring control (operational, and probably both positive and negative), the FCARs apply at that stage. This probably means that the insolvency provisions are disapplied, and may even mean that the charge is valid against an administrator or liquidator even though it has not been registered.[400]

Although the thrust of the argument so far has been that the FCARs are probably too narrow, there is one respect in which they are too broad in scope. The UK chose to 'gold-plate' the implementation of the FCD, so that the FCARs apply to any collateral arrangement between non-natural persons.[401] While this avoids the complications of the limits found in the FCD,[402] it does mean that the registration, and particularly the insolvency, regimes are disapplied in respect of arrangements which are far from the capital market arrangements the financial collateral scheme was designed to protect.[403]

7.3.4.3 Registration

So far we have considered whether a security arrangement falls within the FCARs so as to be exempt from registration requirements. Such requirements are often seen as burdensome where arrangements are part of trading on capital markets. However, there may be situations where a lender taking security over a bank account or over securities would like to register its interest, so as to give effective notice to other parties, and maybe to overcome any uncertainty as to whether the arrangement falls within the FCARs. Unfortunately, the wording of the registration reforms of 2013 raises the question of whether such a charge can be registered if it falls within the FCARs. Section 859A sets out the situations in which the registrar must register charges, but it expressly does not apply to charges excluded from its application by legislation. There is no provision expressly giving the registrar power to register charges which do not fall within section 859A.

This could be dismissed as a drafting error of no consequence, were it not for two matters. The first is that fixed charges over securities were not registrable before the 2013 reforms, and neither (probably) were fixed charges over bank accounts.[404] The second is that under the UCC Article 9 system, the only method of perfecting security interests

---

[400] Security and Title-Based Financing, 3.68, 3.78–3.79, apparently approved in *Gray v G-T-P Group Ltd (Re F2G Realisations Ltd)* [2010] EWHC 1772 (Ch) [51].

[401] FCARs, reg 3.

[402] The FCD applies only to arrangements where a regulated or public financial institution is at least one party: FCD, art 1(2).

[403] For further discussion see Goode: Credit and Security, 6-25.

[404] See H Beale, M Bridge, L Gullifer and E Lomnicka, *The Law of Personal Property Security*, 1st edn (Oxford, Oxford University Press, 2007) 10.23, where, however, it is noted that charges over bank accounts are often registered as a precaution.

in bank accounts is by 'control',[405] and, although security interests over securities can be perfected by registration, one perfected by control will have priority.[406] Under the Australian PPSA a security interest in a bank account or in securities can be perfected by control or registration, and the former will have priority over the latter.[407] The rationale for the priority rule is that a secured party taking control will not need to search the register, since they know they will obtain priority over any registered interests.[408] Thus, in systems where security over financial collateral can be perfected by control, perfection by registration is 'downgraded' and is only used by those prepared to take a risk. It is not at all clear that the priority position would be the same under English law, and, given the wide scope of the FCARs, it is desirable that registration is an alternative means of perfection to taking 'possession or control'.

7.4 Registration and Priorities[409]

7.4.1 The Requirement of Registration

Under English law, non-possessory security interests created by companies are required to be registered in the register of company charges. The purpose of this requirement is to give publicity to security interests the existence of which would not otherwise be obvious to third parties, including any person taking an interest in the assets and others extending credit to the company. For this reason, only non-possessory security interests are registrable, since possession is seen as sufficient publicity in itself.[410] As mentioned above, the registration requirements were amended in 2013. One of the chief reforms was to make all company charges[411] registrable, except for security financial collateral arrangements and security interests operating by operation of law.[412]

---

[405] UCC 9-312(b) and 9-314. There is 'control' under art 9 in relation to a bank account where the bank is the secured party, where the secured party becomes the account holder, or where the secured party, the bank and the collateral provider enter into an agreement that the secured party has positive control (see 9-104).

[406] UCC 9-328. Registration of security interests over securities was only introduced in the 1999 revision of art 9, and this priority rule reflected the pre-existing practice, which was not to search the register. See Official Comment to UCC 9-328. 'Control' is positive control.

[407] ss 25, 26, 27 and 57. 'Control', again, is positive control.

[408] A Duggan and D Brown, *Australian Personal Property Securities Law* (LexisNexis Butterworths Australia, 2012).

[409] For a detailed overview of the new registration system see P Graham, 'Registration of Company Charges' [2014] *Journal of Business Law* 175; for criticism see L Gullifer, 'Piecemeal Reform: Is It the Answer?' in F Dahan (ed), *Secured Lending in Commercial Transactions* (Cheltenham, Edward Elgar, 2015).

[410] Law Commission, *Registration of Security Interests: Company Charges and Property other than Land*, Consultation Paper No 164 (2002), para 1.6.

[411] The term 'charge' in this section includes a mortgage (s 859A(7)), and is used in this sense throughout this section.

[412] Other, very limited, exceptions are listed in Companies Act 2006, s 859A(6).

There are also other registers in which charges created by companies over certain assets (such as registered land,[413] unregistered land,[414] ships,[415] aircraft,[416] patents,[417] trade marks,[418] and registered designs)[419] are either required to be registered or can be registered (usually to obtain priority over subsequent charges). The position is complex and varies according to the type of asset in question.[420]

7.4.2 The Registration Process[421]

Charges can only be registered once created, and must be registered within 21 days of creation if they are not to attract the sanctions for non-registration.[422] Registration involves delivering a statement of particulars and a certified copy of the charge instrument (if there is one) to the registrar.[423] The registrar gives the charge a unique identification code, which enables the particulars, the instrument and any other documents filed to be 'tied' together on the register. The registrar includes in the register all documents filed which are required to be filed (section 859I), including the entire charge instrument. Some personal information can be redacted (section 859G). The registrar must give a certificate of registration to the person delivering the particulars, which is conclusive evidence that the documents required were delivered to the registrar before the end of the period allowed for delivery.[424]

The matters that must be set out in the statement of particulars are listed in section 859D and include not only the details of the chargor and chargee and the date of creation of the charge, but also details of the property charged, whether the charge is fixed or floating, and whether the terms of the charge include a negative pledge clause.[425] Much of this information is provided by using drop-down menus or tick boxes.

Late registration is only permitted on application to the court,[426] although leave will usually be granted on terms that no one taking a security interest between the date of creation of the charge and the date of the late registration will be prejudiced. However, unsecured creditors who have relied on the absence of registration are not generally protected, although they are if the company is in liquidation (when late registration will not be ordered). Further, the imminence of insolvency is a matter for the court to take into account when making the order for late registration.[427]

---

[413] That is, land registered under Land Registration Act 2002.
[414] Maintained in the Land Charges Registry under Land Charges Act 1972.
[415] Merchant Shipping Act 1995, Sch 1.
[416] Maintained under Mortgaging of Aircraft Order 1972, SI 1972/1268.
[417] Patents Act 1977, s 33.
[418] Trade Marks Act 1994, s 25.
[419] Registered Designs Act 1949, s 19.
[420] For detailed discussion see Security and Title-Based Financing, 14.34–14.77.
[421] This section reflects the reformed system, which came into force on 6 April 2013.
[422] Companies Act 2006, ss 859A and 859H.
[423] Delivery may, but need not, be done electronically.
[424] Companies Act 2006, s 859I(6).
[425] It is not clear what should be registered if the negative pledge clause is in another document from the charge document, as is often the case. We are indebted to Marisa Chan of Clifford Chance for this point.
[426] Companies Act 2006, s 859F.
[427] *Re Ashpurton Estates Ltd* [1983] Ch 110.

7.4.3 The Effect of Registration

7.4.3.1 Consequences of Failure to Register

In relation to the effect of registration, two issues require discussion. The first is the consequence of failure to register a charge, and the second is the extent to which registration amounts to notice to third parties. This section deals with the first issue, which is provided for in the Companies Act 2006.[428]

An unregistered charge is void against 'a liquidator [or] an administrator … [or] a creditor of the company'.[429] This provision requires some explanation. The word 'creditor' appears to mean a creditor taking a proprietary interest in the company's assets, that is, either a secured creditor[430] or a creditor who has completed execution.[431] Thus, before the onset of insolvency proceedings, if such a creditor enforces its proprietary interest it does not have to pay the proceeds to a prior unregistered chargee. An unregistered charge, however, is not void against the company (or unsecured creditors) before the onset of insolvency, so that an unsecured creditor cannot prevent an unregistered chargee enforcing its security.[432]

Once insolvency proceedings have commenced,[433] the unregistered charge is void against the company in liquidation or in administration.[434] This effectively means that it is void against the unsecured creditors, so that the unregistered chargee itself becomes an unsecured creditor. It is not clear what the position is regarding a purchaser of assets which are subject to an unregistered charge.[435] Usually, such a person will take free of the charge as they are obtaining the legal interest for value without notice of the charge.[436]

Where, however, a financier purchases receivables by taking an absolute assignment, yet an unregistered chargee is the first to give notice to the obligors and so obtains priority under the rule in *Dearle v Hall*,[437] the question arises as to whether the unregistered charge is void against the purchaser.[438] The section is silent on this matter, and the position should be clarified.[439] One suggestion is that the word 'creditor' could be interpreted to include 'purchaser', but this seems to do violence to the language.[440]

---

[428] Companies Act 2006, s 859H. Note that the criminal sanction has now been abolished.

[429] Ibid, s 859H.

[430] *Re Monolithic Building Co* [1915] 1 Ch 643, 662.

[431] *Re Ashpurton Estates Ltd* [1983] Ch 110, 123.

[432] *Re Ehrmann Bros Ltd* [1906] 2 Ch 697, 708.

[433] That is, when a winding up petition has been presented (Insolvency Act 1986, s 129) or when an administrator is appointed (Insolvency Act 1986, Sch B1 paras 10, 19, 31).

[434] *Smith (Administrator of Cosslett (Contractors) Ltd) v Bridgend County Borough Council* [2001] UKHL 58 [21], [31].

[435] The opportunity to clarify this point in the reformed regime was not taken; see L Gullifer, 'Piecemeal Reform: Is It the Answer?' in F Dahan (ed), *Secured Lending in Commercial Transactions* (Cheltenham, Edward Elgar, 2015).

[436] See 7.4.4. If the absolute transfer is first in time, the chargor will not have notice of it since it is not registrable.

[437] (1828) 3 Russ 1. See 7.4.4 for a discussion of the rule in *Dearle v Hall*.

[438] In theory the question arose in *E Pfeiffer Weinkellerei-Weineinkauf GmbH & Co v Arbuthnot Factors Ltd* [1988] 1 WLR 150, where an extended ROT clause over proceeds of sale (receivables) was held to be a registrable charge, and competed with an absolute assignment of receivables to a financier. The argument that the unregistered charge was valid against the purchaser appears not to have been taken and the case appears to have been dealt with on the basis that the purchaser was a 'creditor of the company' (at 155).

[439] The opportunity to clarify this point in the reformed regime was not taken. See L Gullifer, 'Piecemeal Reform: Is It the Answer?' in F Dahan (ed), *Secured Lending in Commercial Transactions* (Cheltenham, Edward Elgar, 2015).

[440] See also the restricted interpretation of 'creditor' in another context in *Re Lehman Brothers International (Europe) (in administration)* [2009] EWCA Civ 1161 [169]–[177]; see also 15.2.2.4.

When a charge becomes void under section 859H, the money secured by the charge becomes immediately payable.[441] This provision helps to protect secured creditors by giving the company a strong incentive to grant another security interest, which can then be registered. This is often a quicker and cheaper way of dealing with an oversight resulting in non-registration than an application for late registration.

7.4.3.2 Registration as Notice

The main point of registration is to enable other parties who may be affected by a security interest to find out about it easily, quickly and cheaply without having to rely on the honesty of the company that has granted the interest, or on expensive due diligence exercises.[442] The company charges register can be searched electronically, by inputting the name or number of the relevant company. Those lending to companies[443] will usually search the register, and will be able to see both the particulars and the charge document. This means that the searcher will see, and will, therefore, have notice of, whether the charges are described as fixed or floating, and any negative pledge clauses as well as the details of the property charged.[444] The party searching can then make adjustments in light of that information. This could include refusing to lend at all, entering into agreements with other chargees, taking security interests over different assets from the ones originally contemplated, charging more for the loan, or limiting the amount lent. If it does lend, the fact that it has notice may affect its priority position.[445] However, since a chargee has 21 days in which to register, it is possible that a second chargee may search the register before a previous charge is registered, yet the previous charge, registered later yet within 21 days of creation, has priority. To avoid this, chargees sometimes do not advance any funds until 21 days after the creation of a charge, and check the register before making such an advance.[446] It will, of course, be an event of default[447] for a borrower to have created a charge ranking in priority to the charge in question.

Since notice may be relevant to priorities, it is necessary also to consider the position where a person taking a proprietary interest does not search the register. It should be stressed that in the case of commercial lenders, this is very unlikely to occur: most lenders will search before advancing any funds. This is fortunate, since the law as to whether such a person has constructive notice of a registered interest is unclear.[448] The best attempt at rationalising the law is that registration is constructive notice to those who would reasonably be expected to search the register. Unfortunately, there is no direct authority on the point, nor any

---

[441] Companies Act 2006, s 859H(4).

[442] Other benefits of registration may be that there is an objective record of the security interest, the combating of fraud between the parties, and enabling an insolvency officer to know quickly and easily what security interests have been created in the company's property.

[443] This includes those extending credit to companies, although it is less clear that trade creditors will actually search the register. However, if they do not, they will rely on credit rating agencies, which do.

[444] If the particulars do not accurately reflect the charge document, it would seem that the risk of such inaccuracy is on the searcher (this was the case under the previous regime—see *National Provincial and Union Bank of England v Charnley* [1924] 1 KB 431). It would be more appropriate, though, for the risk of inaccuracy to be on the person registering, that is, the chargee.

[445] See 7.4.4.

[446] However, quite often lenders will just take the risk of another interest having been created.

[447] Enabling the lender to accelerate the loan and terminate the charge agreement: see 6.3.3.

[448] For detailed discussion see Goode: Credit and Security, 2-25–2-31.

provision in the Companies Act 2006.[449] The contrary view, that registration is notice to all the world, would appear to lead to unreasonable and undesirable results.[450] This still leaves open, however, the question of who would reasonably be expected to search the register.

While it seems clear that those taking registrable charges fall within this category, and that trade purchasers in the ordinary course of business do not, the position is far less clear in relation to those taking non-registrable security interests (such as pledges) and those taking absolute transfers made in the financing context (such as absolute assignments of receivables). It is strongly arguable, however, that those in the latter category must be expected to search the register and so will have constructive notice, since they are financiers operating in a similar way to those making secured loans.

Of what is registration constructive notice? The position established by the cases is that a party has constructive notice of particulars which are required to be included on the register.[451] Since it is now required both to indicate in the particulars whether the terms of the charge include a negative pledge and to register a copy of the whole charge document, in theory anyone taking a subsequent security interest will have actual or constructive notice of a negative pledge clause,[452] thus doing away with much previous uncertainty.[453] However, some uncertainties remain, most notably whether there is constructive notice of the entire charge document, and what the position is if the particulars do not accurately reflect the charge document.[454]

7.4.4 Priorities

In this section we consider the position where more than one person has a competing proprietary interest in assets which have some sort of connection with a company. This language is very loose, but it is hard to be more precise, since proprietary claimants may be purchasers from the company, sellers to the company who have reserved title, those for whom the company holds an asset on trust, those who have a security interest (possessory or non-possessory) granted to them by the company, or creditors who have executed judgment against the company's assets. It is thus not possible to say with precision whose assets are the subject of the competing claims, as this would prejudge the issue.

Even if we leave aside the priority consequences of non-registration, the English law rules on priority are highly technical and complex. It is not proposed to do more than give an outline of them here.[455] The complexity of these rules is one of the key arguments for

---

[449] Clarification of this issue was not included in the 2013 reforms; see L Gullifer, 'Piecemeal Reform: Is It the Answer?' in F Dahan (ed), *Secured Lending in Commercial Transactions* (Cheltenham, Edward Elgar, 2015).

[450] WJ Gough, *Company Charges*, 2nd edn (London, Butterworths, 1996) 842.

[451] *English and Scottish Mercantile Investment Co v Brunton* [1892] 2 QB 700; *Standard Rotary Machine Co Ltd* (1906) 95 LT 829; *Wilson v Kelland* [1910] 2 Ch 306; *G & T Earle Ltd v Hemsworth* (1928) 44 TLR 605; *Siebe Gorman & Co Ltd v Barclays Bank Ltd* [1979] 2 Lloyd's Rep 142, 160; *Welch v Bowmaker (Ireland) Ltd* [1980] IR 251 (Sup Ct Ireland); *Re Salthill Properties Limited* (2004) IEHC 145 (HC Ireland).

[452] For the consequences of this see 7.4.4.

[453] See Security and Title-Based Financing, ch 12.

[454] See P Graham, 'Registration of Company Charges' [2014] *Journal of Business Law* 175, 191–92.

[455] For detailed discussion see Security and Title-Based Financing, chs 12–17; Goode: Credit and Security, ch 5; R Calnan, *Taking Security: Law and Practice*, 3rd edn (Bristol, Jordans, 2013) ch 7.

reform, which are addressed below.[456] It should be pointed out, however, that these are only default rules, and are rarely relied upon in their raw state by commercial parties. Instead, most of the sophisticated lenders we consider in this book will ensure that the priority of their interests is determined contractually, by using the register and performing due diligence to discover what other proprietary interests there may be and, if necessary, by making agreements with those with competing interests.[457] In fact, for this very reason there are few cases on the default rules, which, in turn, is a major reason why the law in this area is so uncertain. It should be pointed out, though, that agreement is not always possible, particularly where discovering the existence of those with a prior claim would be expensive or time-consuming. This might be, for example, where their consensual interests are not registered, where interests arise by operation of law, or where the register does not give an up-to-date position (for example, where a floating charge has crystallised automatically). For a secured lender, there is also the danger of further security interests being created in the future over the same assets, and an understanding of the priority rules is necessary so that the lender can protect itself against this danger. Such protection may take the form of a negative pledge clause,[458] or of attempting to take the 'strongest' security interest possible.

The basic priority point in English law is the date of creation. This is articulated in relation to legal interests by the maxim *nemo dat quod non habet* (you cannot give what you have not got), and in relation to equitable interests by the proposition that the first in time has priority. There are a number of exceptions to this basic rule. First, if A acquires an equitable interest in an asset, and B then acquires a legal interest, B will take free of A's interest if B acquired its interest in good faith, for value and without notice of A's interest. An example of this rule in the corporate finance context is that a purchaser of goods or other assets in the ordinary course of business will nearly always take free from a prior equitable charge, since the purchaser will not search the register nor be expected to do so, and thus will not have constructive notice of the charge. Trade buyers of stock in trade would fall into the category of 'purchaser of goods in the ordinary course of business', but it is less clear whether buyers of equipment or other movable corporate infrastructure would do so.[459] A lender taking a legal mortgage would be expected to search the register and so would take subject to a prior equitable security interest.

However, where B is a statutory assignee[460] of a debt, the reasoning is different. Since section 136 of the Law of Property Act 1925 provides that a statutory assignment is 'subject to equities', the legal interest exception does not apply and the governing rule is, instead, the rule in *Dearle v Hall*.[461] This rule is the second exception to the basic first in time doctrine. It provides that, where there are successive assignments of a debt or chose in action, the first assignee to give notice to the obligor gains priority, provided that that assignee did not take

---

[456] 7.7.

[457] See R Calnan, 'Taking Security in England' in M Bridge and R Stevens (eds), *Cross-Border Security and Insolvency* (Oxford, Oxford University Press, 2001) 33. Secured lenders can agree amongst themselves to reverse the default priorities without obtaining the borrower's consent or, indeed, even informing it: *Cheah Theam Swee v Equiticorp Finance Group Ltd* [1992] 1 AC 472.

[458] See 6.3.1.6.

[459] Law Commission, *Registration of Security Interests: Company Charges and Property other than Land*, Consultation Paper No 164 (2002), para 2.61.

[460] 9.2.2.3.

[461] (1828) 3 Russ 1.

its assignment with notice of the other assignment.[462] If B takes a statutory assignment, it will have given notice to the obligor, whereas if A (the prior assignee) has an equitable assignment this is probably because it has not given notice.[463]

However, B will not necessarily win. If A's assignment is a registrable charge, which A has registered, and B is a financial institution, it is likely to have searched the register and so will have notice of A's assignment, and A will have priority.[464] If B has not searched the register, it may have constructive notice of A's interest, if B would reasonably be expected to search the register.[465] The position is even less straightforward where A's interest is not registered, for example where it has taken an absolute assignment which is not registrable. Here B will only be able to find out about A's interest by obtaining information from the borrower, C, or by asking the debtor. Making enquiries of the debtor is impractical where the assignment is of a large number of debts.[466] If C does not disclose A's interest, and B has not discovered it by a due diligence exercise, then B will lose priority to A (since A is first in time), unless B has given notice to the debtor first. B can, of course, protect itself to some extent by taking a warranty from C that there have been no previous assignments of the debts, and making breach of that warranty an event of default. Breach would then enable B to accelerate any obligations C has and to terminate the agreement. However, this will not fully protect B if C is insolvent.

Another situation which creates a potential exception to the first in time rule is where a lender has taken a security interest over (present and) future property of the borrower, and the borrower then acquires an asset solely with finance provided by another lender, who wishes to take a security interest over that asset. There are a number of reasons why that second secured party should have priority over the first. The asset is a 'windfall' to the first chargee: it merely increases its security when it has done nothing to assist its acquisition. Further, if the first chargee could just keep increasing its security in this way, there would be no incentive for subsequent lenders to lend on security at all. A subsequent lender who lent in relation to a particular asset might be a specialist in the field, and therefore able to lend at a more advantageous rate than the original lender.[467] In many cases of corporate finance, of course, the second lender will be an asset financier, who will supply the asset on retention of title terms.[468] Since the second lender's interest is a legal interest by retention, the borrower never acquires any interest at all, and so the asset cannot fall within the after-acquired property clause in the original charge. Therefore the second lender has priority in relation to that asset. However, if the second lender does take a charge, it will lose priority to the

---

[462] This proviso is known as the 'second limb' of the rule and was added by cases decided after *Dearle v Hall*, ibid.

[463] 9.2.2.4. If A has given notice, its assignment is likely to have become statutory, at least in relation to present debts.

[464] This is an application of the 'second limb' of the rule. B could, of course, have made a priority agreement with A.

[465] See 7.4.3.2.

[466] Also, the debtor is under no obligation to provide any information (*Ward v Duncombe* [1893] AC 396, 387, 393–94 per Lord McNaghten) and is not liable for negligence for any inaccurate information given (*Low v Bouverie* [1891] 3 Ch 82).

[467] For further discussion see C Walsh, 'The Floating Charge is Dead; Long Live the Floating Charge' in A Mugasha (ed), *Perspectives in Commercial Law* (Sydney, Prospect, 2000) 134. See also 7.2.4.3, where purchase money security interest (PMSI) super-priority in a notice filing scheme is discussed.

[468] This includes a conditional sale, hire purchase or finance lease: see 2.3.4.4.

first charge, since on acquisition there is a *scintilla temporis* (a tiny amount of time) when the asset belongs to the borrower before the grant of the charge to the second lender, within which time the asset falls within the after-acquired property clause in the first charge. There have been a few cases in which a *scintilla temporis* has been held not to exist,[469] but the law in this area is still unclear.[470]

Another category of exceptions to the first in time doctrine is the series of exceptions to the *nemo dat* rule contained in sections 21–25 of the Sale of Goods Act 1979. These exceptions relate only to priority between legal interests in goods[471] and apply to situations where a person who is not the owner of goods appears to be in a position to dispose of them, usually because that person is in possession of the goods. There is no general principle that a good-faith disponee obtains good title in these circumstances, but the Act contains a series of specific situations where this is the result. Only some are relevant to the proprietary protection taken by lenders discussed in this book. One situation is where the goods are disposed of with the authority or consent of the owner.[472]

This is commonly the case where goods are sold on ROT of title terms, but the contract provides that the buyer has the power to sell the goods in the ordinary course of business. The sub-buyer thus obtains good title, free of any interest of the original seller. Another situation is where a retention of title device is used but there is no power to sell the goods, for example in asset financing.[473] If the device is a conditional sale, section 25 of the Sale of Goods Act 1979 provides that a good-faith disponee taking delivery of the goods similarly obtains good title. Asset financing by means of a hire purchase agreement[474] or a finance lease, however, is not included, so a disponee takes subject to those interests. To take another example, if a legal mortgagor of goods sells them to a good-faith buyer, the *nemo dat* rule applies so that the buyer takes subject to the mortgage. Section 24 of the Sale of Goods Act 1979, which provides that a good-faith buyer from a seller in possession takes free of the first buyer's interest, does not apply here.[475]

More generally, a third party taking an interest in assets subject to a security interest (a disponee) will take free of that security interest if the grant of the interest to the disponee is made with the authority or consent of the secured lender. The extent of authority or consent may be made clear ex ante in the security agreement (as in the case of a floating charge) or may be given at the time of the grant (as where assets are subject to a fixed charge but consent to a particular disposition is made). The disponee takes in priority to the prior security interest; in other words, the first in time rule does not apply. For example, let us take the situation where an asset subject to a fixed charge is sold by the chargor to a disponee who has actual or constructive notice of the charge. On the priority rules set out above (*nemo dat* and first in time), the disponee will take subject to the charge. If, however,

---

[469] For example, *Abbey National v Cann* [1991] 1 AC 56; *Wilson v Kelland* [1910] 2 Ch 306; *Security Trustee Co v Royal Bank of Canada* [1976] AC 503.

[470] See Goode: Credit and Security, 5-63–5-67.

[471] Priority between a prior equitable interest and a subsequent legal interest has already been dealt with.

[472] Sale of Goods Act 1979, s 21.

[473] 2.3.4.4.2.

[474] *Helby v Matthews* [1895] AC 471. The position is different (and more complicated) where the goods are a motor vehicle: this is governed by Hire Purchase Act 1964, s 27.

[475] Sale of Goods Act 1979, s 62(4), which provides that provisions in the Act concerning contracts of sale do not apply to mortgages or charges.

the chargee has consented to the disposition and given the chargor power to dispose of the asset, then the disponee will take free of the charge.

This reasoning can also explain the position of a party taking an interest in an asset falling within a floating charge. The chargor has power to dispose of the asset in the ordinary course of business, so the disponee takes free of the charge. Thus where a floating chargor creates a subsequent fixed charge over the assets subject to the floating charge, the fixed charge has priority; a floating chargee is taken to have power to create fixed charges ranking in priority to the floating charge.[476] This is also true of an absolute assignment of receivables: the rule in *Dearle v Hall* does not apply.[477] However, if the disposition were outside the ordinary course of business, the disponee would take subject to the charge.[478] The chargor's powers to dispose are, though, commonly limited in the charge agreement.[479] In this situation, the disponee will take subject to the charge, but only if it has notice (actual or constructive) of the limitation of power. Otherwise, the disponee is entitled to assume that the floating chargor has the power to dispose of the asset free of the charge, and will therefore take free of the charge. A floating charge will commonly contain a negative pledge clause, prohibiting the creation of any charge ranking in priority to the floating charge. A party taking a subsequent fixed charge with notice of the negative pledge clause will cede priority to the floating charge, but if the fixed chargee does not have notice it will take free of, and in priority to, the floating charge.[480] In practice, most parties taking a charge will search the register, and will know of the restriction,[481] so that they can either adjust to the loss of priority or overcome it by means of a subordination agreement.[482]

In the same way, where a floating charge has crystallised automatically or by notice (as opposed to by a more public trigger, such as cessation of business) a third party acquiring an interest who does not know of the crystallisation is entitled to assume that the floating chargor has the power to dispose of the charged assets free of the charge, and will therefore take free of the charge.[483] If the third party has searched the register and read the registered charge document, it will know that the charge includes an automatic crystallisation clause, but it will not know of a 'private' crystallisation. To safeguard its position, it must make enquiries of any prior chargee and, perhaps, enter into an agreement as to priorities.

Having discussed priority issues involving floating charges which depend on authority reasoning, we now turn to other priority issues where such reasoning is wholly or partially

---

[476] *Wheatley v Silkstone and Haigh Moor Coal Company* (1884) 29 Ch D 715; *Cox Moore v Peruvian Corporation Ltd* [1908] 1 Ch 604. This power is usually restricted in the charge agreement; see discussion later in the paragraph.

[477] *Ward v Royal Exchange Shipping Co Ltd* (1887) 58 LT 174; *Re Ind Coope & Co Ltd* [1911] 2 Ch 223.

[478] For a discussion of what effect this actually has, see Goode: Credit and Security, 5-40–5-41. This situation would, though, be very rare since 'the ordinary course of business' is very widely defined: see *Ashborder BV v Green Gas Power Ltd* [2004] EWHC 1517 (Ch); *Re Borax Ltd* [1901] 1 Ch 326.

[479] It should be borne in mind that a charge where nearly all, but not all, dispositions without the consent of the chargee are prohibited will still be characterised as floating as a result of the *Spectrum* decision.

[480] *English and Scottish Mercantile Investment Co v Brunton* [1892] 2 QB 700; *Welch v Bowmaker (Ireland) Ltd* [1980] IR 251(Sup Ct Ireland).

[481] Which must now be included in the registered particulars: see 7.4.2.

[482] See 7.4.3.2 for a discussion of constructive notice of a negative pledge clause.

[483] See 7.3.3.2.

absent. An execution creditor will not obtain priority over a floating charge unless it has completed execution by the time the charge crystallises.[484] Similarly, a local authority cannot distrain for rates once a floating charge has crystallised, unless the charge is a 'mere charge' and not by way of equitable mortgage.[485] A landlord, however, can levy distress for rent on the goods of a company whether or not a floating charge over those goods has crystallised.[486] Obtaining priority over execution creditors is one of the main reasons why automatic crystallisation clauses are included in floating charges. Even if an execution creditor has no notice of crystallisation, it still takes subject to a crystallised floating charge.[487] Creditors obtaining rights of set-off before a floating charge over the debt set-off has crystallised take free of the charge;[488] this is also the case where the right of set-off arises after crystallisation but before notice of the charge to the person asserting the set-off.[489]

So far in discussing priorities between charges we have assumed that the loan secured is made at the time of the creation of the charge, or at least before the competing charge is granted. If, however, the first chargee makes a further loan or advances credit after the second charge is created, this potentially prejudices the position of the second chargee, who cannot adjust specifically in relation to such an advance, but can only adjust generally ex ante.[490] English law gives limited protection to the second chargee, in that the first chargee cannot 'tack' further advances onto its original security interest once it has notice of the second charge, unless it is obliged to make the further advance in its charge agreement.[491] The boundaries of the 'rule against tacking' are very complex and riddled with uncertainties.[492] Therefore, as in so many contexts in relation to the law of priorities, the answer is for the default position to be circumvented by agreement.

As can be seen from this discussion of the principal priority rules, the English law in this area is complex and, to a large extent, uncertain. The ability of parties to overcome this uncertainty by agreement is not a sufficient justification for the law to remain in its present state. Agreements are not costless, and the law should reflect an easily ascertained default position—that is, the priority position most usually adopted by parties—so that the costs of negotiating around that position are minimised. Reform of the law in this area, and in relation to registration, are discussed below.[493]

---

[484] *Re Opera Ltd* [1891] 3 Ch 260; *Robson v Smith* [1895] 2 Ch 118; *Evans v Rival Granite Quarries Ltd* [1910] 2 KB 979.

[485] *Re ELS Ltd* [1995] Ch 11.

[486] *Re Coal Consumers Association* (1876) LR 4 Ch D 625; *Cunliffe Engineering Ltd v English Industrial Estates Corporation* [1994] BCC 972.

[487] *Robson v Smith* [1895] 2 Ch 118.

[488] *Biggerstaff v Rowatt's Wharf Ltd* [1896] 2 Ch 93.

[489] *Business Computers Ltd v Anglo-African Leasing Ltd* [1977] 2 All ER 741.

[490] This could be either by charging a higher interest rate (which is unlikely to be a fine-tuned adjustment) or by including a covenant prohibiting future borrowing. However, such a covenant (at least in a bald state) may be difficult to include in a loan agreement. See 6.3.1.1.

[491] Law of Property Act 1925, s 94.

[492] For discussion see Security and Title-Based Financing, 14.78–14.102; Goode: Credit and Security, 5-17–5-23.

[493] See 7.7.

7.5 Enforcement

One of the advantages of security is that the secured lender can usually enforce its proprietary rights without using a court process. This can be contrasted with the position of an
unsecured creditor, which has to obtain a judgment on its claim and then execute it.[494] If
winding up of the company commences before execution is complete, however, the unsecured creditor loses the benefit of the execution and is merely entitled to prove *pari passu*
with all the other unsecured creditors.[495] The benefits of security as a means of protecting against credit risk are only as good as the ability of the secured lender to enforce its
security.[496] A secured creditor must, therefore, have remedies which enable it to assert its
proprietary rights effectively and to turn non-cash assets into money out of which it can
pay itself. Although the best protection for the secured creditor is if it can enforce without
needing to go to court (and this, largely, is the position under UK law, although not in many
other countries),[497] there need to be effective court procedures as a longstop, including
collective insolvency proceedings.

The freedom of a secured creditor to enforce its proprietary rights needs to be balanced
against the interests of all those who have an actual or potential interest in the relevant
assets. Although this is prima facie the debtor company, the company is likely to be insolvent at the time of enforcement, so the interests that are protected are those of its creditors.
Those most closely interested in the particular asset against which enforcement is being
made are creditors who also have a security interest in that asset (either senior or junior
to the enforcing creditor) and any surety of the secured debt, since a surety will have a
right to the security if it pays the debt.[498] It is only if there is surplus value in the asset once
these parties have been paid that the unsecured creditors (for whom the term 'debtor' is
often used as a shorthand) are interested. The danger for all these parties is that the asset
will decline in value, through mismanagement, or will be sold or otherwise realised at an
undervalue. It will be seen that English law provides a certain level of protection against this
danger, but it is by no means comprehensive.

Another danger for all the company's creditors is that enforcement of security results
in individual assets being sold at a lower value than if all the assets of the company, or
indeed the whole business of the company, were sold together. The former type of sale is
often referred to as a 'fire sale'. One way of preventing this is to have one lead secured creditor, who runs the enforcement process.[499] Another response, however, is for there to be a

---

[494]   For the forms of execution see 7.1.1.

[495]   Insolvency Act 1986, s 183.

[496]   See eg F Dahan, E Kutenicova and J Simpson, 'Enforcing Secured Transactions in Central and Eastern
Europe: An Empirical Study, Part 1' (2004) 19 *Journal of International Banking and Financial Law* 253.

[497]   In civil law jurisdictions the original position was that security could only be enforced by a judicially monitored public auction, in order to protect the debtor. Although this position has changed substantially in recent
years, so that private sales are permitted under certain circumstances, the court still plays an important part in
enforcement in many countries. For an overview see P Wood, *Comparative Law of Security Interests and Title
Finance*, 2nd edn (London, Sweet & Maxwell, 2007) 20–026–20–037.

[498]   See 6.4.1.3.3.

[499]   This benefit of a lead creditor is discussed at 7.6.2.1 and also at 7.3.3.4 in the context of the benefits of the
floating charge.

collective insolvency procedure, which involves a stay on enforcement of security interests while attempts are made either to rescue the company or to sell the business as a whole.[500]

In the UK, there has been a recent move away from the first situation to the second. Before 2003, the bank, which would typically have fixed and floating charges over all the company's assets, would enforce outside any insolvency proceedings by appointing an administrative receiver. The company would then go into liquidation, and any assets which were not included within the charge, or which were left over once the chargee had enforced, would be distributed by the liquidator. The Enterprise Act 2002 abolished the power of the floating chargee to appoint an administrative receiver,[501] and instead provided a power for the floating chargee to appoint an administrator out of court.[502]

Administration is a collective insolvency procedure, as referred to above, and a moratorium on the enforcement of security and quasi-security is imposed on the appointment of an administrator.[503] The moratorium enables the administrator to attempt to rescue the company, but if this is not possible (and it rarely is) the administrator will realise the assets, often by selling the business as a going concern, and distribute the proceeds to such secured creditors as are entitled.[504] If there is any surplus for unsecured creditors, the administrator can distribute this to them,[505] or can put the company into liquidation.[506]

Although certain rights to enforce security interests come from the general law, these are usually extended by provisions in the secured loan documentation. The right to enforce security will normally arise on default in payment, and also on acceleration as a result of an event of default.[507] The loan documentation will usually provide for a wide variety of enforcement powers which will enable the creditor to do anything permissible to obtain the value of the secured assets, including taking possession, selling the assets, collecting receivables and other debts, notifying the debtor (in order to turn an equitable assignment into a statutory one), and appointing a receiver.[508]

A secured creditor is not obliged to enforce its security. It can choose to enforce as an unsecured creditor or pursue contractual rights it has against third parties, such as claiming under a guarantee or a credit default swap.[509] Unless it is restricted by contract, it has a totally free choice as to its actions: it does not owe a duty to the debtor or to any counterparty to act in a particular way.[510] To the extent that one form of enforcement does not fully satisfy the debt, usually the creditor can pursue another form, unless there is a contractual

---

[500] For a global overview of such procedures see P Wood, *Comparative Law of Security Interests and Title Finance*, 2nd edn (London, Sweet & Maxwell, 2007) 21–011–21–022.

[501] Insolvency Act 1986, s 72A inserted by Enterprise Act 2002, s 250. There are some exceptions to this; see ss 72B–72GA.

[502] Insolvency Act 1986, Sch B1 para 14. The directors or the company can also appoint an administrator out of court (Insolvency Act 1986, Sch B1 para 22).

[503] Ibid, para 43.

[504] The administrator has power to distribute to the secured and preferential creditors under Insolvency Act 1986, Sch B1 para 65.

[505] Leave of the court is required: ibid, Sch B1 para 65(3).

[506] A reasonably high number of administrations end in this way; see 7.3.3.4.

[507] Such an event may not be a breach, but will give the creditor the right to accelerate the loan; see 6.3.3.1.

[508] For an example of a clause providing for very wide powers of enforcement see P Wood, *Comparative Law of Security Interests and Title Finance*, 2nd edn (London, Sweet & Maxwell, 2007) 32–086.

[509] See 6.4.

[510] *China & South Sea Bank Ltd v Tan* [1990] 1 AC 536, 545; *Cheah Theam Swee v Equiticorp Finance Group Ltd* [1992] 1 AC 472, 476; *White v Davenham Trust Ltd* [2010] EWHC 2748 (Ch) [32]–[34].

restriction on this.[511] However, if a creditor has security over several assets (A, B and C) and another creditor has security over only one of those assets (A), the doctrine of marshalling operates to prevent the first creditor enforcing over asset A, and leaving the second creditor unsecured.[512]

As discussed earlier in this chapter, a creditor can have proprietary protection in the form of either a security interest or an absolute interest. While the foregoing two paragraphs apply to both kinds of proprietary protection, the details of enforcement vary. One of the chief differences is that on enforcement of a security interest there is an obligation to account for any surplus,[513] that is, the amount of any proceeds over and above the sum required to pay off the secured debt.[514] This obligation is expressly included in section 105 of the Law of Property Act 1925 in relation to a sale by a mortgagee or chargee under the power of sale provided for in that Act.[515] This section rarely applies, since enforcement is usually under the terms of the mortgage or charge rather than under the Act, but the same principle applies, and is usually provided for expressly in the terms of the loan agreement.[516] The right of the debtor to the surplus is a proprietary right, that is, it is a right to be paid out of the proceeds of the enforcement themselves; it is not just a personal right to be paid the equivalent of the surplus.[517] This is of considerable importance if the enforcing creditor is itself insolvent.

If another creditor also has a security interest in the asset, which ranks below that of the enforcing creditor, then the enforcing creditor is obliged to pay the surplus to the subordinate creditor.[518] Although it will normally be the most senior secured creditor that enforces, in theory a subordinate (or junior) creditor can do so, either with the consent of the senior secured creditor, in which case it is liable to account to the senior creditor before meeting the costs of enforcement and its own claim,[519] or without consent, in which case the sale is subject to the interest of the senior creditor, which can enforce its interest against that of the buyer.[520] Apart from these general points, the legal position in relation to enforcement varies according to the kind of interest that is being enforced. The discussion that follows will concentrate on non-possessory interests, both security interests and absolute interests.

The various means of enforcement outside insolvency proceedings are discussed first. These are still available to a secured creditor even if the company is being wound up, but if an administrator has been appointed, there is a statutory moratorium which prevents

---

[511] This statement may need some qualification in relation to title finance agreements; see 7.5.2.1.

[512] For details see Security and Title-Based Financing, 18.05–18.09; *Szepietowski v National Crime Agency* [2013] UKSC 65 [28]–[38], [79].

[513] See 7.2.1.

[514] This does not apply on foreclosure: see 7.5.1.1.

[515] Law of Property Act 1925, s 101 provides that a mortgage (or charge) made by deed includes such a power of sale.

[516] P Wood, *Comparative Law of Security Interests and Title Finance*, 2nd edn (London, Sweet & Maxwell, 2007) 32–089.

[517] Law of Property Act 1925, s 105; *Charles v Jones* (1887) 35 Ch D 544, 549. The loan agreement may provide that the proceeds are held on trust.

[518] Law of Property Act 1925, s 105. An obligation to account to subordinate secured creditors is often also included in the loan agreement: P Wood, *Comparative Law of Security Interests and Title Finance*, 2nd edn (London, Sweet & Maxwell, 2007) 32–089.

[519] Law of Property Act 1925, s 105. This is usually also provided for in the loan agreement.

[520] *Manser v Dix* (1857) 8 De GM & G 703. Such a sale would not be in the ordinary course of business, and so it is very unlikely indeed that a buyer would be a bona fide purchaser without notice of the prior security interest.

the enforcement of any security interest (and some quasi-security interests) without the leave of the court. The circumstances in which such leave will be given are briefly discussed below.[521]

7.5.1 Methods of Enforcement: Security Interests

7.5.1.1 Foreclosure

Foreclosure is a remedy only available to a mortgagee; it is not available to a chargee. It will be recalled that legal or equitable title is transferred to the mortgagee, subject to the mortgagor's right to redeem and equity of redemption.[522] On foreclosure, the mortgagor loses its rights, so that the mortgagee becomes the absolute legal or equitable owner of the assets. It will be seen that, if the assets are worth more than the secured indebtedness, this remedy is greatly to the disadvantage of the mortgagor, who loses the surplus. For this reason, foreclosure is only available by order of the court.[523] Foreclosure is a remedy with many difficulties and few advantages, and in fact is very rarely used.[524]

7.5.1.2 Appropriation of Financial Collateral

This is a remedy which is only available for a security financial collateral arrangement.[525] If the terms of the security interest include a power for the collateral taker to appropriate the collateral, this power can be exercised without any order of the court. The collateral taker appropriates the collateral by becoming absolute owner. On doing this, it is obliged to value the collateral in a commercially reasonable manner, and account to the collateral giver for any surplus value.[526] If the value of the collateral is insufficient to meet the secured obligation, the collateral provider remains obliged to pay the outstanding amount.[527]

These features make the remedy crucially different from foreclosure: it is a novel remedy, previously unknown to English law.[528] It is closer to a sale by the secured party to itself,[529] previously prohibited under English law:[530] sale, as will be seen below, is subject to an equitable duty to take reasonable care to obtain true market value.[531] Furthermore, appropriation can be of the absolute legal title (if the mortgage is legal) or the absolute equitable title

---

[521] 7.5.3.

[522] 7.3.2.2.

[523] For details see Security and Title-Based Financing, 18.21–18.26.

[524] It has been described by the Privy Council as 'obsolescent' (*Cukurova Finance International Ltd v Alfa Telecom Turkey Ltd* [2009] UKPC 19 [13]).

[525] See 7.3.4.

[526] FCARs, reg 18(2).

[527] Ibid, reg 18(3).

[528] *Cukurova Finance International Ltd v Alfa Telecom Turkey Ltd* [2009] 1 CLC 701 [14] (CA British Virgin Islands). In very rare cases, relief against forfeiture can be given against an appropriation: *Cukurova Finance International Ltd v Alfa Telecom Turkey Ltd* [2013] UKPC 2.

[529] Ibid, [27].

[530] *Martinson v Clowes* (1882) 21 Ch D 857.

[531] *Cuckmere Brick Co v Mutual Finance Ltd* [1971] Ch 949, 965, 972, 977.

(if the mortgage is equitable).[532] The nature of appropriation as a sale to the mortgagee, however, means that the obligation to account for the surplus is not proprietary but is merely a personal obligation to pay the surplus to the collateral giver. This puts the collateral giver at risk of the collateral taker's insolvency, and stands in contrast to enforcement by sale to a third party or other means. It should be remembered, though, that appropriation is only available if the mortgagor has agreed to it in the security agreement.

7.5.1.3 Possession and Sale

A mortgagee or chargee may enforce its interest itself by taking possession of the assets and, if necessary to realise their value, selling them. A legal mortgagee has a right to take possession,[533] but an equitable mortgagee may not, and a chargee does not. Generally, though, the security agreement will make express provision both for a right to take possession and for a right to sue to enforce charged choses in action (such as receivables).

The right of sale of a mortgagee or chargee may arise under the general law,[534] but virtually all security agreements will include a wide express power. The mortgagee[535] is under no duty to enforce in a particular way, or even to enforce at all. There is a basic duty to act in good faith;[536] apart from this, the secured party is free to act in its own interests, subject to certain equitable duties. These duties are imposed only when the secured party actually takes steps to enforce, and are owed not only to the mortgagor, but also to other secured creditors,[537] and sureties,[538] all of whom are affected by diminution in the value of the assets. There is no duty on a mortgagee to sell the assets[539] or to sell at any particular time,[540] even if those decisions result in detriment to the mortgagor. Generally, the duties of a mortgagee only arise where their imposition would not result in a conflict of interest between it and the mortgagor. Where there is such a conflict, the mortgagee is entitled to protect its own interests.[541]

When a mortgagee takes possession of the mortgaged assets, it is under a duty to take reasonable care to manage[542] and preserve them, the standard of care being a flexible one

---

[532] *Cukurova Finance International Ltd v Alfa Telecom Turkey Ltd* [2009] 1 CLC 701 [34]–[36]. It is, however, necessary that there is a positive act evincing the intention to appropriate, which is communicated to the collateral giver.

[533] *Four-Maids Ltd v Dudley Marshall (Properties) Ltd* [1957] Ch 317, 320. The agreement normally provides that this right only arises on default: *Johnson v Diprose* [1893] 1 QB 512; *Birmingham Citizens Permanent Building Society v Caunt* [1962] Ch 883.

[534] A power of sale on default under a mortgage is implied by law: *Re Morritt* (1886) 18 QBD 222, 233; where a mortgage or charge is made by deed there is a statutory power of sale under Law of Property Act 1925, s 101.

[535] The analysis in this and the following paragraphs applies equally to a mortgagee and a charge; for clarity only the term 'mortgagee' will be used.

[536] *Downsview Nominees Ltd v First City Corporation Ltd* [1993] AC 295, 317.

[537] *Tomlin v Luce* (1889) 43 Ch D 191; *Downsview Nominees Ltd v First City Corporation Ltd* [1993] AC 295, 311.

[538] *American Express International Banking Corporation v Hurley* [1986] BCLC 52, 61.

[539] *Raja v Austin-Gray* [2002] EWCA Civ 1965 [55]; *Silven Properties Ltd v Royal Bank of Scotland plc* [2003] EWCA Civ 1409 [14].

[540] *Cuckmere Brick Co v Mutual Finance Ltd* [1971] Ch 949, 965; *Tse Kwong Lam v Wong Chit Sen* [1983] 1 LR 1349, 1355.

[541] *Cuckmere Brick Co v Mutual Finance Ltd* [1971] Ch 949, 965; *Shamji v Johnson Matthey Bankers Ltd* [1991] BCLC 36, 42. See Security and Title-Based Financing, 18.38.

[542] *Palk v Mortgage Services Funding plc* [1993] Ch 330, 338 per Sir Donald Nicholls VC; *McHugh v Union Bank of Canada* [1913] AC 299.

of reasonable competence.[543] If a mortgagee decides to sell the mortgaged assets, it comes under a duty to take reasonable care to obtain the true market value at the time of sale.[544] The mortgagee will not be liable just because a higher price could be obtained: it is enough if it obtained a 'proper price',[545] and it is under no duty to improve the assets to obtain a higher price.[546]

7.5.1.4 Appointment of a Receiver

The (albeit light) duties imposed on a mortgagee in possession have meant that in the past most mortgagees have preferred to appoint a receiver over the mortgaged or charged assets rather than take possession themselves. The mortgagee is protected from liability, since, usually, the receiver is the agent of the mortgagor. The mortgagee can act totally in its own interests in deciding whether or not to appoint a receiver[547] (provided that it acts in good faith), although if it does decide to appoint it is probably under some sort of minimal duty to appoint a competent person.[548] Where a mortgage or charge is made by deed, the mortgagee or chargee has a right to appoint a receiver (though with limited powers) under section 101 of the Law of Property Act 1925: there is usually a much wider power included in the mortgage or charge agreement.[549] In the past, a floating chargee would routinely appoint a receiver over all the assets of the company, latterly known as an administrative receiver.[550] However, except in limited cases, the power to appoint an administrative receiver has been abolished,[551] and a floating chargee can, instead, appoint an administrator out of court.[552] A mortgagee or chargee, however, can still appoint a receiver over part of the company's assets under section 101 Law of Property Act 1925 or under a power in the security agreement.

Despite the fact that, after the Enterprise Act 2002 came into force, chargees under charges created before 15 September 2003 were able to appoint administrative receivers, there was a rapid dropoff in receiverships after 2003, coupled with a rapid rise in administrations, indicating that chargees were preferring to appoint administrators rather than administrative receivers, even where they had the right to appoint the latter.[553] However, in 2008 and 2009 the number of receiverships increased considerably, and continued to remain high until 2013.[554] The number of administrations rose (unsurprisingly) in 2008

---

[543] *Medforth v Blake* [1999] EWCA Civ 1482.

[544] *Cuckmere Brick Co v Mutual Finance Ltd* [1971] Ch 949, 965, 972, 977.

[545] *Parker-Tweedale v Dunbar Bank plc* [1991] Ch 12.

[546] *Silven Properties Ltd v Royal Bank of Scotland plc* [2003] EWCA Civ 1409.

[547] *In re Potters Oils Ltd* [1986] 1 WLR 201, 206; *Shamji v Johnson Matthey Bankers* [1991] BCLC 36, 42.

[548] *Shamji v Johnson Matthey Bankers* [1991] BCLC 36, 42.

[549] There is also a residual power to apply to the court for the appointment of a receiver, but again this will be superseded by the express power in the agreement.

[550] See 7.5.

[551] See below for the reasons for this; for more discussion see L Gullifer, 'The Reforms of the Enterprise Act 2002 and the Floating Charge as a Security Device' in L Gullifer, W-G Ringe and P Théry (eds), *Current Issues in European Financial and Insolvency Law* (Oxford, Oxford University Press, 2009).

[552] Insolvency Act 1986, Sch B1 para 14.

[553] Insolvency Service statistics, Receiverships, Administrations and Company Voluntary Arrangements.

[554] The increase was from 337 in 2007 to 1,468 in 2009, remaining at a level of around 1,300 until 2013, when there was a drop to 914. The drop has continued: there were 724 receiverships in 2014, and only 142 in Q1 2015, the lowest quarterly figure since Q4 2007. (figures from Insolvency Service statistics).

and 2009, probably as a result of the financial crisis, but have since diminished.[555] The statistics do not distinguish between administrative receiverships and receivers appointed in relation to part of the assets.[556] One possible explanation, therefore, is that more secured creditors are appointing receivers over part of the assets (particularly land) as an alternative to putting companies into administration.[557] The advantage of doing this is that enforcement can take place straight away, unless another creditor[558] or a company's directors[559] appoint an administrator, in which case the moratorium will apply.[560]

It should be pointed out that the cases in which a floating chargee can still appoint an administrative receiver are significant in terms of the sums involved. These cases are set out in sections 72B–72GA of the Insolvency Act 1986, and broadly cover two areas: charges in relation to the capital and financial markets, and those in relation to project finance, including projects in the public sector. The carve-outs were included as a result of considerable lobbying from interested parties, and as such are connected more by policy considerations than by matters of principle.

A receiver is usually the agent of the mortgagor and not the mortgagee.[561] The agency is not a usual one, however.[562] The relationship is tripartite, comprising the receiver, the mortgagee and the mortgagor.[563] The receiver owes duties (which are equitable, not common law duties) both to the mortgagee and to all those interested in the equity of redemption, which includes the mortgagor and other creditors. The receiver owes a duty of good faith, and other duties which vary depending on the circumstances. If the receiver chooses to manage the mortgaged assets, he owes an equitable duty of care, the primary duty of which is to bring about a situation in which the secured debt is repaid.[564] In relation to sale of the mortgaged assets, the receiver owes the same duties as the mortgagee.[565] Since the receiver is the agent of the mortgagor, the mortgagee will not be liable for the receiver's acts, unless the mortgagee treats him as an agent,[566] or specifically directs him to do particular acts.[567]

It will be seen that, apart from a general duty of good faith and some limited duties if he actually manages or sells the property, a receiver is free to act in the interests of the

---

[555] 4,161 in 2009 and 2,365 in 2013.

[556] Under s 101 Law of Property Act 1925 or under a power in the security agreement.

[557] See V Finch, 'Reinvigorating Corporate Rescue' [2003] *Journal of Business Law* 526, 537; R Stevens, 'Security after the Enterprise Act' in J Getzler and J Payne (eds), *Company Charges: Spectrum and Beyond* (Oxford, Oxford University Press, 2006) 166–67.

[558] A creditor can only appoint an administrator by application to the court under Insolvency Act 1986, Sch B1 para 12.

[559] The company's directors can appoint an administrator out of court under Insolvency Act 1986, Sch B1 para 22. The company can also make such an appointment where there is a resolution of shareholders to that effect (Insolvency Rules 1986, r 2.22).

[560] Insolvency Act 1986, Sch B1 para 43. See further 7.5.3

[561] Law of Property Act 1925, s 109(2), where the receiver is appointed under s 101; Insolvency Act 1986, s 44 in relation to administrative receivers. The security agreement will also usually provide that the receiver is the agent of the mortgagor.

[562] Although it is a real agency: *Rhodes v Allied Dunbar Pension Services Ltd* [1989] 1 WLR 800, 807.

[563] The relationship and the duties arising from it are considered in *Silven Properties Ltd v Royal Bank of Scotland plc* [2003] EWCA Civ 1409 [27].

[564] *Medforth v Blake* [2000] Ch 86, 102.

[565] Ibid, 99. See 7.5.1.3.

[566] *American Express International Banking Corporation v Hurley* [1986] BCLC 52, 57.

[567] *Standard Chartered Bank v Walker* [1982] 1 WLR 1410, 1418; *Medforth v Blake* [2000] Ch 86, 95.

mortgagee, and, to some extent, to protect his own interests by not taking on tasks which might leave him open to liability.[568] In relation to administrative receivers, it was this focus on furthering the interests of the floating chargee, rather than on operating for the benefit of all the creditors, which persuaded the Government that there was too little protection for unsecured creditors.[569] This was especially the case where the floating chargee was oversecured, as there was no incentive for the administrative receiver to do anything other than realise from the charged assets the amount due to the floating chargee.[570] The Government responded by abolishing administrative receivership and replacing the floating chargee's remedy with a fast-track into administration. The administrator, unlike a receiver, owes a duty to act in the interests of all the company's creditors,[571] unless he has decided that he cannot either rescue the company or achieve a better result for the company's creditors as a whole than if it were wound up.[572] If he does so decide, he can pursue the tertiary objective of realising property in order to distribute to secured and preferential creditors, but even so he is under a duty not to harm unnecessarily the interests of the creditors of the company as a whole.[573] Thus, in theory, the administrator's duties when realising security are more onerous than those of an administrative receiver, but this is unlikely to make much difference in the application of those duties in practice.

In practice, many administrations[574] are now conducted as pre-packaged administrations ('pre-packs'). In a pre-pack, a sale of part or all of the company's undertaking is arranged before the administration commences and takes place as soon as the administrator is appointed.[575] Very often, the floating chargee, that is, the secured creditor with an all-assets security interest, is the driving force behind a pre-pack, and a beneficiary in the sense that costs are reduced and access to funds is rapid. Returns are, at least in theory, increased by a sale which takes place without the damaging publicity of the commencement of insolvency proceedings. However, pre-packs have been much criticised for lack of transparency, for damaging the interests of unsecured creditors, who have no means of affecting their outcome, and for enabling connected parties to buy businesses at a low price. A Statement of Insolvency Practice (SIP 16) was issued in 2009 in order to improve transparency, and a wholesale review of pre-packs took place in mid-2014.[576] The review found that pre-packs had a valuable role to play, but that a certain amount of 'cleaning up' was needed, and made various recommendations to be implemented by the market, mainly related to 'connected party' pre-packs.

---

[568] R Stevens, 'Security after the Enterprise Act' in J Getzler and J Payne (eds), *Company Charges: Spectrum and Beyond* (Oxford, Oxford University Press, 2006) 159.

[569] Insolvency Service, *Insolvency—A Second Chance* (Cm 5234, 2001), para 2.2, 2.3.

[570] R Mokal, *Corporate Insolvency Law: Theory and Application* (Oxford, Oxford University Press, 2005) 212.

[571] Insolvency Act 1986, Sch B1 para 3(2).

[572] Ibid, para 3.

[573] Ibid, para 3(4).

[574] There are probably around 750 pre-packs a year, which is roughly a third of all administrations (see Graham Review into Pre-Pack Administration (June 2014)).

[575] See the working definition in para 5.15 of the Graham Review into Pre-Pack Administration (June 2014) and, for detailed discussion, Goode: Corporate Insolvency, 11-37 ff.

[576] Graham Review into Pre-Pack Administration (June 2014).

7.5.2 Methods of Enforcement: Absolute Interests

7.5.2.1 Devices Based on Retention of Title[577]

Where the lender[578] has retained title to goods, enforcement consists of the retaking of possession. For this to occur, the borrower's contractual right to possession must revert to the lender, either because the lender accepts the borrower's repudiatory breach or under a provision in the agreement.[579] The effect on the borrower of retaking the goods will vary depending on two linked matters: the current value of the goods (whether they are worth more or less than the amount agreed to be paid) and the amount already paid by the borrower to the lender pursuant to the agreement. If the value of the goods has risen, or (perhaps more likely to be the case) a substantial amount has already been paid pursuant to the agreement, the borrower will be left 'out of pocket' by the retaking. Prima facie the lender, as owner, has no obligation to account to the borrower for any surplus value of the goods over and above the outstanding debt. This issue is dealt with in various ways in the current law.

One technique is for the parties to provide in the agreement that the surplus, or part of it, will be returned to the borrower. Since the transaction involves a reservation of title rather than a grant of an interest, this will not result in the interest being recharacterised as a security interest.[580] In conditional sale, hire purchase and finance lease transactions, which have a fixed amount of payments due over a particular term, there are usually provisions which have the effect that the seller is to be put into the same position as if the buyer had committed a repudiatory breach of contract. Thus the lender is compensated for the loss of bargain, but has to give credit for the amount realised by the sale of the repossessed goods, and for early repayment of the outstanding debt. The borrower is, to some extent, protected by the rule against penalties,[581] and also, in some situations, by the ability to obtain relief against forfeiture of sums already paid.[582]

The courts have been more willing to grant relief against forfeiture of goods, however, where a lender seeks repossession. The jurisdiction to grant relief exists where there is a transfer of possessory or proprietary rights[583] (in the situations discussed in this section

---

[577] Sales on ROT terms, conditional sales, hire purchase agreements and finance leases. For discussion of these devices see 2.3.4.4. For detailed discussion of enforcement in relation to such devices see Security and Title-Based Financing, ch 19.

[578] The word 'lender' will be used throughout this section to refer to the financier who extends credit, either for the acquisition of assets on the basis of retention of title (see 2.3.4.4.2) or by buying assets from the borrower company who then buys or leases them back (see 2.3.4.4.1). The word 'borrower' will be used for the borrower company.

[579] An agreement may provide that the lender has the right to terminate the right to possession on a particular breach (such as non-payment of an instalment) or event (such as insolvency of the lessee or indication of financial distress).

[580] See 7.2.1 and 7.2.5.3.

[581] Although it should be noted that the scope of this rule is limited to sums paid on breach, and so does not extend to sums payable on a non-breach event which entitles the lender to terminate the contract: *Bridge v Campbell Discount Co Ltd* [1962] AC 600; cf *Andrews v Australia and New Zealand Banking Group Limited* [2012] HCA 30.

[582] The law on this is technical and complicated, and still, to a certain extent, unclear. See Chitty, ch 26 s 10(b); Security and Title-Based Financing, 19-16, 19.28, 19.38; L Gullifer, 'Agreed Remedies' in A Burrows and E Peel (eds), *Commercial Remedies* (Oxford, Oxford University Press, 2007) 200.

[583] *The Scaptrade* [1983] 2 AC 694.

the rights transferred are possessory) and where the object of the transaction and the insertion of the right to forfeit is essentially to secure the payment of money.[584] These criteria are fulfilled in the cases of conditional sale, hire purchase and finance lease transactions,[585] although not in the case of an operating lease.[586] The relief is discretionary, and will only be granted if the lender can be protected financially, either by the continuation of periodic payments[587] or by the payment of all outstanding debts.[588] The conduct of the borrower is also relevant (repeated default is a reason not to grant relief),[589] as is the size of any windfall the lender would obtain were relief not to be given.[590]

At least in situations where relief is granted on payment of the outstanding amount, this jurisdiction can be seen as treating a device based on retention of absolute title like a security interest, since the borrower is effectively given a right to redeem.[591] This is particularly striking in a case like *On Demand Information plc v Michael Gerson (Finance) plc*,[592] where relief was given despite the fact that the goods themselves had been sold, so that all that was being protected was the borrower's financial position—that is, the surplus value in the goods over and above the outstanding debt. The result is analogous to that where a security interest is enforced. In a case where the borrower is entitled to retain the goods themselves, this can be seen as enabling the borrower to use the goods in its business.[593] Protection of this non-financial interest was the original reason for granting relief against forfeiture, in the context of interests in land, and to the extent that this is the reason for giving relief in retention of title cases, it is less easy to see the grant of such relief as treating the lender's interest as a security interest. After all, if a secured party has the right to take possession and sell the collateral on default,[594] the borrower cannot ask the court for relief against the loss of the use of the asset.

Apart from the situation where the borrower is insolvent[595] (where use of the goods may be temporarily critical to enable the business to be sold quickly), it is hard to see why relief should be given for non-financial reasons where the subject matter of the contract is goods, which are not unique, as opposed to land, which is unique. It should always be

---

[584] *Shiloh Spinners Ltd v Harding* [1973] AC 691, 722.

[585] Hire purchase: see *Transag Haulage Ltd v Leyland DAF Finance plc and others* [1994] 2 BCLC 88; Finance lease: see *On Demand Information plc v Michael Gerson (Finance) plc* [2003] 1 AC 368.

[586] *Celestial Aviation Trading 71 Ltd v Paramount Airways Private Ltd* [2010] EWHC 185 (Comm).

[587] This was offered in *More OG Romsdal Fylkesbatar AS v The Demise Charterers of the Ship 'Jotunheim'* [2004] EWHC 671 (Comm), although the court decided not to award relief on other grounds.

[588] *Transag Haulage Ltd v Leyland DAF Finance plc* [1994] 2 BCLC 88. This was also effectively the position in *On Demand Information plc v Michael Gerson (Finance) plc* [2003] 1 AC 368.

[589] *Goker v NWS Bank plc* (unreported, 1 August 1990); *More OG Romsdal Fylkesbatar AS v The Demise Charterers of the Ship 'Jotunheim'* [2004] EWHC 671 (Comm).

[590] *Transag Haulage Ltd v Leyland DAF Finance plc* [1994] 2 BCLC 88, 101.

[591] L Smith, 'Relief Against Forfeiture: A Restatement' (2001) 60 *Cambridge Law Journal* 178. See also *Celestial Aviation Trading 71 Ltd v Paramount Airways Private Ltd* [2010] EWHC 185 (Comm) [53] where Hamblen J described the interest of a lessor under a finance lease as 'more of a security interest than an ownership interest'.

[592] [2003] 1 AC 368.

[593] This was the reason for seeking relief in *Transag Haulage Ltd v Leyland DAF Finance plc* [1994] 2 BCLC 88 since the borrower's business could not be carried on and sold as a going concern without the use of the fleet of lorries which was the subject of the application.

[594] See 7.5.1.3.

[595] A similar effect to relief against forfeiture is achieved within insolvency by the moratorium imposed on the appointment of an administrator (see 7.5.3), since the borrower is enabled to retain the goods provided that the administrator pays the rent or other periodic payments.

possible for the borrower to refinance and acquire replacement goods, and if it is not, this indicates that the lender will be disadvantaged by being forced to continue in a relationship with the borrower. This type of reasoning underlay the decision in *Celestial Aviation Trading 71 Ltd v Paramount Airways Private Ltd*,[596] where the court decided that there was no jurisdiction to give relief against forfeiture in relation to an operating lease, since the point of the termination provisions was not just to secure the payment of rent. In that case, a stark distinction was drawn between the retention of title devices discussed above, which were treated as security interests, and an operating lease, where the interest of the lessor was in more than merely getting paid: it was also in receiving back the aircraft that was the subject of the lease.[597]

7.5.2.2 Devices Based on the Grant of an Absolute Interest[598]

As discussed at 2.3.4.1, there are two possible types of receivables financing structure which involve the transfer of an absolute interest to the lender: factoring and invoice discounting. A factor, which takes a statutory assignment of the debts and provides a debt collection service to the borrower, is in a position to sue any non-paying debtor in its own name.[599] In an invoice discounting arrangement, the lender normally takes only an equitable assignment and the debtors are not notified.[600] The borrower thus collects in the debts itself, but will hold the proceeds on trust for the lender. As trustee, the borrower will be obliged to account to the lender for the proceeds, and, in relation to those proceeds, the lender will have priority over all other claimants to the borrower's assets if the borrower is insolvent. In most invoice discounting agreements, the lender will have the right to give notice to the debtors and convert its equitable assignment into a statutory assignment, so that it can sue the non-paying debtors itself. As mentioned above, many receivables financing transactions contain terms giving the lender a right effectively to recover any shortfall and an obligation effectively to account for a surplus to the borrower, but this has not led the courts to recharacterise the arrangement as a charge.[601]

7.5.3 The Effect of Administration

If an administrator is appointed, the effect on enforcement by secured creditors is immediate and dramatic: there is a moratorium on the enforcement of security and the repossession of goods under hire purchase agreements, as well as other legal process against the property of the company.[602] The imposition of the moratorium means that no steps may

---

[596] [2010] EWHC 185 (Comm).

[597] Ibid, [64].

[598] The term 'lender' is used in this section to mean the receivables financier (the purchaser of the receivables) and the term 'borrower' for the seller of the receivables.

[599] See 9.2.2.2.

[600] See 9.2.2.4.

[601] See 7.2.5.2.

[602] Insolvency Act 1986, Sch B1 para 43. An interim moratorium, which has the same effect, takes effect while certain procedural steps prior to the appointment of an administrator are being taken (Insolvency Act 1986, Sch B1 para 44).

be taken to enforce security or repossess goods without the consent of the administrator or the leave of the court while the company is in administration. The effect of the moratorium is merely procedural: the secured creditor retains its proprietary rights.[603] The purpose of the moratorium is to permit the administrator during the temporary period of the administration to use the company's property to carry on the business with a view to rescue, or to carrying out one of his other purposes.[604] It will be recalled that the administrator, in order to further the purposes of the administration, also has the power to dispose of floating charge assets without leave of the court,[605] and to dispose of assets subject to fixed charges and hire purchase property with the leave of the court,[606] in which case the secured party is protected by obtaining an interest in the proceeds.[607] There is thus a balance between the rights of the secured creditors to enforce against the secured assets and the benefits that come to all the creditors from keeping the assets together, as well as from allowing the administrator freedom to act.[608]

Two further points need to be made about the moratorium. First, it extends not just to the enforcement of true security interests, but to title retention devices as well.[609] Second, a secured creditor (used in the wide sense) can ask the administrator for permission to enforce, and, if this is not forthcoming, apply to the court for leave.

The principles on which permission and leave should be granted were set out in *Re Atlantic Computer Systems plc*.[610] The Court of Appeal gave this guidance in order to assist administrators and parties. It stressed that the decision whether to agree to enforcement should usually be that of the administrator, and that applications to court should be the exception rather than the rule. This has proved to be the case. The general principles set out related to the previous legislation,[611] but the wording of the current legislation is the same,[612] and recent cases have applied the *Re Atlantic Computers* guidance to applications under the current legislation.[613]

The guidelines make it clear that it is for the secured creditor to make out a case for permission to enforce, but that the moratorium is imposed so as to enable the administrator to carry out the purpose of the administration;[614] so, if enforcement will not interfere with that purpose, then it will normally be permitted. If it will interfere with the purpose, then

---

[603] *Centre Reinsurance International Co v Freakley* [2006] UKHL 45 [7], [16].

[604] See 7.5.1.4. His purpose may be, or may become, the realisation of assets for distribution to the secured creditors.

[605] Insolvency Act 1986, Sch B1 para 70.

[606] Ibid, para 71(1).

[607] The nature of this interest varies according to the type of security or quasi-security: ibid, paras 70(2), 71(3) and 72(3).

[608] R Mokal, *Corporate Insolvency Law: Theory and Application* (Oxford, Oxford University Press, 2005) 254.

[609] Paragraph 43(3) prohibits repossession, without leave of the court, under a 'hire-purchase agreement'. 'Hire-purchase agreement' is defined in para 111(1) of Sch B1 to the Insolvency Act 1986 as including a conditional sale agreement, a chattel leasing agreement and a retention of title agreement.

[610] [1992] Ch 505, 541 ff.

[611] Insolvency Act 1986, s 11(3)(c).

[612] Ibid, Sch B1 paras 43(2) and (3).

[613] *Fashoff (UK) Ltd v Linton* [2008] EWHC 537 (Ch); *Innovate Logistics Ltd v Sunberry Properties Ltd* [2008] EWCA Civ 1321.

[614] The possible purposes are now set out in Insolvency Act 1986, Sch B1 para 3. See 7.5.1.4. The administrator must, as soon as practicable after the company enters administration, identify which purpose is achievable and explain how he envisages that it is to be achieved (Insolvency Act 1986, Sch B1 para 49; Insolvency Rules 1986, r 2.33(2)).

the administrator, or the court, has to carry out a balancing exercise between the interests of the secured creditor and those of the other creditors of the company, including
an assessment of the likely loss that will be caused to each party by granting permission.
Although the exercise is one of balance, there appears to be a considerable amount of extra
weight given to the interests of those creditors with proprietary protection (the guidelines
in *Re Atlantic Computers* were given in relation to the whole moratorium, which also covers
enforcement by unsecured creditors).[615] However, the administrator or court should also
take into account the extent of the creditor's proprietary protection: if the creditor is undersecured, a delay in enforcement is more likely to be prejudicial than if it is fully secured.[616]
Permission, or leave, can be given on terms, and terms can also be imposed by the court if
no leave is given, in that the court can give directions to the administrator. Thus a secured
or quasi-secured creditor can be protected even though it cannot enforce immediately, by
terms which oblige the administrator to continue to pay rent (in the case of, for example, a
finance lease or hire purchase) or interest payments.

In common with many other insolvency provisions, the moratorium provisions are
disapplied in relation to financial collateral arrangements.[617] The purpose of the disapplication of these provisions is said to be to prevent systemic risk and to promote the certainty of
such arrangements, by taking away the various insolvency provisions in different Member
States which inhibit effective realisation of financial collateral.[618] Thus, even if the borrower
company is in administration, secured or quasi-secured creditors can freely enforce their
interests over securities, and also over cash in bank accounts provided that their security
interest meets the criterion of 'control' in the FCARs.[619] In relation to a bank account, an
ability of the chargor to withdraw cash if the credit is over the amount of the secured debt
would probably not prevent the chargee having such control.[620]

7.6 Economic Arguments Concerning Secured Credit

So far it has been assumed that companies should generally be free to grant proprietary
interests in their assets (both absolute and by way of security), although we have noted that
English law places some restrictions on this, both in terms of registration requirements
and (in relation to the floating charge) in terms of loss of priority and other effects on
the insolvency of the chargor. We now turn to the question of whether the institution of
secured credit is desirable at all from an economic point of view and, if it is, what system
achieves the best economic outcome, in the sense of eliminating inefficiencies and maximising added value.

---

[615] Insolvency Act 1986, Sch B1 para 43(4) covers the right of forfeiture by peaceful re-entry by a landlord,
and para 43(6) covers all legal proceedings as well as execution.
[616] *Re Atlantic Computer Systems plc* [1992] Ch 505, 544.
[617] FCARs, reg 8.
[618] FCD, recital 5 and art 4.
[619] Discussed at 7.3.4.2.
[620] This would be a right to withdraw excess collateral; see FCARs, reg 3 and 7.3.4.2.

The strongest argument in favour of a system of secured credit is that it increases access to credit and lowers the cost of credit. Theoretical arguments as to whether this is the case are discussed below. There is, however, a great deal of empirical evidence from around the world indicating that where an effective system of secured transactions is introduced, the availability of credit increases and economic growth results.[621] Agencies such as the World Bank, the International Finance Corporation and the European Bank for Reconstruction and Development have been extremely active in encouraging and enabling reform of secured transactions law around the world to capture these economic benefits.

7.6.1 Means of Assessing a System of Secured Credit

There is extensive literature on this subject, mainly generated by scholars from the United States.[622] It is necessary to appreciate that there are different criteria as to what is a 'good' system. One criterion is that of economic efficiency. This can be judged by one of two standards: the Kaldor-Hicks test, which sees an activity as efficient if it maximises value overall even if some participants are worse off, and the Pareto test, which only sees it as efficient if it maximises overall value without any participants being worse off.[623] At first sight, a system of secured credit clearly does make some participants worse off, as the priority of secured creditors in insolvency automatically means that the unsecured creditors do not recover in full. If it can be argued, however, that the unsecured creditors are either made better off by the general institution of security, or that they are not made worse off by the grant of a security interest in a specific situation, then the system is potentially efficient even on the Pareto test.

Another possible criterion is that of fairness to the unsecured creditors of the borrower, particularly when the latter is insolvent.[624] This can be seen as an extended application of the Pareto test: it can be unfair for some creditors to suffer for a system which brings overall benefit. It can also include other kinds of arguments, however, such as the argument that the employees of a company have contributed towards the assets and so should share in them.[625] A third possible criterion is the extent to which the system upholds freedom of contract:[626] on this view the borrower's right to alienate its own property is critical, and the system would be judged on how well it facilitated the granting of security (and other)

---

[621] See J Simpson and F Dahan (eds), *Secured Transactions Reform and Access to Credit* (Cheltenham, Edward Elgar, 2008); A Alvarez de la Campa, *Increasing Access to Credit by Reforming Secured Transaction Law in the MENA Region* (World Bank Policy Research, Working Paper no 5613, 2011), 3–6 and papers cited in the footnotes thereto; M Campello and M Larrain, 'Enhancing the Contracting Space: Collateral Menus, Access to Credit and Economic Activity', Columbia Business Research Paper 13-86, http://papers.ssrn.com/sol3/papers.cfm?abstract_id=2358183.

[622] For an interesting overview of much of the literature see G McCormack, *Secured Credit under English and American Law* (Cambridge, Cambridge University Press, 2004) ch 1.

[623] Ibid, 23.

[624] See eg E Warren, 'Making Policy with Imperfect Information: The Article 9 Full Priority Debates' (1997) 82 *Cornell Law Review* 1373; V Finch, 'Security, Insolvency and Risk: Who Pays the Price?' (1999) 62 *Modern Law Review* 633.

[625] See 7.3.3.3.4.

[626] See eg S Harris and C Mooney, 'A Property-Based Theory of Security Interests' (1994) 80 *Virginia Law Review* 2021.

interests by borrowers.[627] Another possible line of enquiry is to consider whether there are benefits in the institution of secured credit which are not available (or are available only at greater cost) if creditors solely protect themselves by means of contractual protection such as covenants.[628] In considering the US literature, it needs to be remembered that the US system is very different from that of the UK, both in terms of the law of secured transactions[629] and in terms of the general law.[630]

It is useful, however, to consider some of the arguments made and to apply them to current English law as well as to any proposals for reform.

7.6.2 The Puzzle of Secured Credit

7.6.2.1 *Monitoring*

A 'puzzle' addressed by the law and economics scholars is why debtors grant security interests. They argue that because of the advantages of security to a creditor, a secured loan attracts a lower rate of interest than an unsecured one, but this is offset exactly by a raising of interest rates by unsecured creditors.[631] They therefore look for other possible benefits of secured credit. One possible benefit is monitoring. All creditors need to protect themselves against two dangers: the first is that the borrower will deplete its assets either by diminishing their value or by substituting for its safe assets more risky ones,[632] and the second is that it will dilute the value of the creditor's debt by adding more liabilities without correspondingly increasing the asset pool.[633] To achieve this protection, unsecured creditors need to have extensive covenants which give them the ability to monitor the entire business of the borrower and, in conjunction with that monitoring, to stop the borrower depleting the asset pool or increasing liabilities.[634] The same benefits can be achieved by taking a security interest, but this has the added benefit that the creditor's monitoring can be focused solely on the asset which is given as security, and therefore monitoring costs are reduced.[635] Asset withdrawal and substitution can be prevented more effectively by a security interest than by covenants, since the secured creditor has not only the right to prevent disposition (if it knows about it in advance) but also the right to 'follow' the asset so that the person who takes the asset may take subject to the security interest.[636] Furthermore, certain creditors

---

[627] This is not necessarily the best criterion, however. One could produce an effective and efficient system for the buying and selling of slaves: this does not make it desirable. See P Shupack, 'Solving the Puzzle of Secured Transactions' (1988) 41 *Rutgers Law Review* 1067, 1072 fn 15.

[628] For contractual protection by covenants see chapters 3 and 6.

[629] Which is governed in the US by UCC art 9.

[630] For example, the position in relation to tort claims.

[631] TH Jackson and AT Kronman, 'Secured Financing and Priority among Creditors' (1989) 88 *Yale Law Journal* 1143; A Schwartz, 'Security Interests and Bankruptcy Priorities' (1981) 10 *Journal of Legal Studies* 1.

[632] This is a concern as creditors do not benefit from any increase in value which may come from risky projects, while shareholders do, while creditors are more likely to suffer first from any loss. Shareholders thus have an incentive to indulge in risky projects, and creditors wish to prevent them. See 3.2.2.2.

[633] For a helpful analysis of these dangers see R Squires, 'The Case for Symmetry in Creditors' Rights' (2009) 118 *Yale Law Journal* 806, 819–20. For further discussion of the points made in the text see 3.2.2.2.

[634] The benefits of monitoring and the use of covenants in this regard are discussed in more detail at 3.2.2.3.

[635] TH Jackson and AT Kronman, 'Secured Financing and Priority among Creditors' (1989) 88 *Yale Law Journal* 1143, 1153.

[636] This depends on the rules of priority, which are discussed at 7.4.4.

can reduce monitoring costs further by taking security over assets in respect of which they have specialised knowledge. The reduction in costs lowers the cost of credit, and therefore, it is argued, the taking of security is efficient.

Against this argument it could be said that the savings in monitoring costs from the taking of security are equalled by the increase in monitoring required by unsecured creditors in relation to the assets that are not subject to security.[637] However, this is not necessarily the case. It can be argued that, if the assets monitored by the secured creditor were representative of the health of the business, unsecured creditors could 'free-ride' on that monitoring and could save the costs of monitoring themselves.[638] Shareholders could also benefit from this free-riding.[639] Taking this argument to its logical conclusion, the most effective monitoring can be done by a creditor with a security interest over all the assets of the company, since its interests are most closely aligned with both the shareholders and the unsecured creditors (who are the residual claimants unless there is a surplus).[640] It is unclear, however, whether the taking of security is an essential element in this argument. Would the benefits of having a 'lead' creditor to monitor not be just as great if that lead creditor were unsecured?[641]

To reach a negative answer to this question it is necessary to focus on the issue of enforcement, either in the run-up to insolvency, or on insolvency itself. While the company is solvent a secured lead creditor would only be more efficient if it could be shown that the secured creditor charged a lower interest rate because of the security, and this was not offset by higher rates charged by the unsecured creditors. This could be the case if some of the unsecured creditors did not adjust fully.[642] On enforcement the existence of the 'lead' secured creditor can, however, be shown to have a beneficial impact on all creditors. There is a danger for unsecured creditors as a whole that, on insolvency, the total assets of the company will be depleted by a 'race to be first' by specific creditors who are in a position to enforce before others. Obviously, this has distributive effects (in that there is less for the other creditors) but it also may have an effect on the overall size of the pot, in that the value of the assets is lower when broken up than when held together as a whole.

The presence of a lead secured creditor can help in several ways. First, by being able to make an effective threat to remove assets from the business (as well as to accelerate the loan) the secured lead creditor is more likely to be able to force the company to make the necessary restructuring to keep it going. This will be to the benefit of all creditors. Second, other creditors know that they cannot enforce against assets subject to security and so the 'race to be first' is deterred.[643] Third, if security gives 'control' rights (such as the right to appoint an administrative receiver under English law, now abolished for all but certain categories

---

[637] A Schwartz, 'Security Interests and Bankruptcy Priorities' (1981) 10 *Journal of Legal Studies* 1.

[638] S Levmore, 'Monitors and Freeriders in Commercial and Corporate Settings (1982) 92 *Yale Law Journal* 49.

[639] Ibid, 50, 68–71.

[640] R Scott, 'A Relational Theory of Secured Financing' (1986) 876 *Columbia Law Review* 901. The single creditor can also be more efficient as it can negotiate with the borrower as a proxy for the other creditors, thus saving duplication of costs. See J Armour and S Frisby, 'Rethinking Receivership' (2001) 21 *Oxford Journal of Legal Studies* 73, 84.

[641] P Shupack, 'Solving the Puzzle of Secured Transactions' (1988) 41 *Rutgers Law Review* 1067.

[642] This argument is examined at 7.6.2.3.

[643] J Armour and S Frisby, 'Rethinking Receivership' (2001) 21 *Oxford Journal of Legal Studies* 73, 87. This argument is of limited value in relation to assets over which the lead creditor has a floating charge, as execution creditors who complete execution before crystallisation obtain priority over the floating chargee. See 7.4.4.

of floating chargee) this enables the lead creditor to take control of the whole enterprise, to keep the business going and realise maximum value by selling it as a going concern, or, at least, not disposing of assets in a piecemeal fashion.[644] The extent to which this is still an advantage of a floating charge is discussed above.[645] Fourth, if the lead creditor is secured, its incentive to intervene in the running of the company and, eventually, to enforce, is increased as the company's financial position deteriorates, since until that stage the secured creditor's 'cushion' of assets may be sufficient to avoid the need to take action.[646] Since it is at this stage that lead creditor intervention is most useful to other creditors, this can be seen as a factor in favour of the lead creditor being secured.

7.6.2.2 Signalling

Another possible benefit from security is said to be that it acts as a signal to other creditors. One view is that the grant of security signals that the borrower is of good quality. This is because security is costly to grant, and so a company will only be prepared to incur those costs if it has faith in its projects and wishes to signal to the market that its projects are worthwhile, that is, more worthwhile than the market is likely to think on the basis of other information that is available.[647] The main problem with this argument is that it does not reflect the real world. In fact, security is demanded by creditors rather than offered by borrowers, and is demanded in those situations where it is of most use, that is, where the borrower's creditworthiness is weak.[648] Thus to the extent that it is a signal, it is a signal that the borrower is of poor quality. It is difficult to see the value of this signal as significant enough to explain why security is efficient.

7.6.2.3 Non-Adjusting Creditors

A third explanation often put forward as to why the lower cost of secured lending is not completely outweighed by the higher cost to the borrower of unsecured credit is that some unsecured creditors cannot adjust, and therefore the full cost of the security interest is not reflected in the increased costs of unsecured credit. This argument has been used by some commentators to conclude that secured lenders and borrowers are deliberately exploiting non-adjusting creditors to obtain more advantageous rates on secured lending than would be the case were these creditors to adjust fully.[649] Empirical studies appear to show no support for the deliberate exploitation thesis.[650] It is, however, said to be the case that

---

[644] R Mokal, 'Administrative Receivership and the Floating Charge' in R Mokal, *Corporate Insolvency Law: Theory and Application* (Oxford, Oxford University Press, 2005); J Armour and S Frisby, 'Rethinking Receivership' (2001) 21 *Oxford Journal of Legal Studies* 73.

[645] 7.3.3.4.

[646] J Armour, 'The Law and Economics Debate about Secured Credit: Lessons for European Law-Making' (2008) 5 *European Company and Financial Law Review* 3.

[647] A Schwartz, 'Security Interests and Bankruptcy Priorities' (1981) 10 *Journal of Legal Studies* 1.

[648] For this and other arguments against the signalling theory see V Finch, 'Security, Insolvency and Risk: Who Pays the Price?' (1999) 62 *Modern Law Review* 633, 649.

[649] L LoPucki, 'The Unsecured Creditors' Bargain' (1994) 80 *Virginia Law Review* 1887; Finch, ibid, 645.

[650] R Mokal, 'The Priority of Secured Credit' in R Mokal, *Corporate Insolvency Law: Theory and Application* (Oxford, Oxford University Press, 2005); Y Listokin, 'Is Secured Debt Used to Redistribute Value from Tort Claimants in Bankruptcy? An Empirical Analysis' (2008) 57 *Duke Law Journal* 1037.

the presence of security does damage the position of unsecured creditors, and that some unsecured creditors are not in a position to adjust fully.[651]

This bald statement of fact deserves examination. Let us consider the categories of creditors discussed in chapter three.[652] The first category is those who choose to extend credit to the company. Of these, some may be secured creditors (in the wide sense of having proprietary protection) and others may adjust by using the contractual means outlined in chapter six.[653] If a creditor chooses to contract with a company, it has the means of discovering what security interests that company has granted over its assets (either by checking the register or by using a credit rating agency, which uses the information held in the company charges register to compile its ratings).[654] If the company has assets over which it could grant security in the future, the creditor can adjust either by taking security itself or by attempting to prevent security being granted to any other creditor by use of a negative pledge clause,[655] or by charging more for its loan to reflect the increased risk of security being given in the future. A creditor also has the capacity to adjust by the various means discussed in 3.2.2.1: by adjusting the price (either for this particular company or for all of its customers), by not extending credit, by diversification, or by refusing to contract with companies that appear to be in financial difficulties.

One could argue that if a creditor (such as a trade creditor) is not able to adjust to the presence of security using one of these means, then it clearly cannot adjust to the other risks that are in the market, and the fact that such a creditor may itself become insolvent as a result of non-payment by the company is not a cause for great concern.[656] It should also be mentioned that many loans made by directors and group companies are unsecured. This may well be because of agreements with other creditors (such loans may also be subordinated) and is a product, therefore, of conscious choice. Such loans are often made when the company is in difficulties, and these lenders have a strong incentive to benefit the company, and therefore will knowingly take on the risk of being unsecured. They are also in a strong position to monitor and to take steps to improve the financial position of the company.

It is possible to have more sympathy for the second category of creditors, namely those who, while they chose to have dealings with the company, did not choose to extend credit but have become creditors because the company has become liable to them, usually for breach of contract or in tort.[657] Although it is possible for such creditors to protect themselves (for example, by refusing to pay for goods until they have been examined thoroughly to make sure they conform to the contract, or by keeping running accounts with the company so

---

[651] V Finch, 'Security, Insolvency and Risk: Who Pays the Price?' (1999) 62 *Modern Law Review* 633.

[652] 3.2.2.1.

[653] These include set-off, insurance and guarantees, as well as contractual terms.

[654] The use of information held in the company charges register by credit rating agencies (on whose information unsecured creditors rely) was made clear to the Law Commission during its consultation on the reform of the registration of company charges. See Law Commission, *Company Security Interests: A Consultative Report*, Consultation Paper No 176(2004), 3.152 and fn 200. The ease with which this information can be procured by a creditor depends on the efficiency of the registration system: this argument has more weight where there is an effective, low-cost system of registration.

[655] 6.3.1.6. Note that a negative pledge clause can also be included in a floating charge. See 7.4.4.

[656] R Mokal, 'The Priority of Secured Credit' in R Mokal, *Corporate Insolvency Law: Theory and Application* (Oxford, Oxford University Press, 2005) 152 ff.

[657] Utility companies could also be included here, as well as the tax authorities. See below for discussion of these.

that they can assert set-off), this is not always possible. They are therefore in a similar position to the third category of claimants—those who have no prior contact with the company before becoming creditors (such as tort claimants).

In relation to tort claimants,[658] there is a distinction between the US position and that in the UK.[659] Much of the US literature focuses on the weak position of tort claimants. However, in the UK, tort claimants are not a substantial category of unsecured creditor in most insolvencies.[660] There are a number of differences between the UK and the US systems which may explain this, and which mean that the arguments made about tort claimants in the US context must be treated with care in the UK. The structure and funding of class actions is different in the US, and as a result such actions are much more common there than in the UK. Coupled with this is the quantum of damages, which is much larger in the US as damages include a punitive element which is usually assessed by a jury. The quantum of damages for personal injury is also affected by the difference in provision of health care and social security between the two countries.[661]

Many tort claimants are the victims of accidents at work or road accidents. In the UK liability insurance is compulsory for employers and drivers respectively in respect of both of these types of claims.[662] Further, if the insured company is insolvent, victims have the right to claim direct against the insurance company by a statutory transfer of the insured company's rights to the victim.[663] This right to claim direct may also benefit other tort and contract claimants, since the company may well be insured for liability other than for employment and road accidents, such as liability for defective products, and damage caused to third parties through polluting or other dangerous activities. These kinds of tort claims figure significantly in the US literature.[664] Thus, in the UK, tort victims have much greater protection in the insolvency of the company than appears to be the case in the US. It should be pointed out, though, that (in the UK), the insured is free to charge or assign the proceeds of a non-compulsory third-party insurance policy to a lender. If this security or absolute interest is not a floating charge, the lender will have priority over the victim in respect of the proceeds of the insurance policy.[665]

---

[658] See also the discussion at 3.3.3.2 and 5.5.2.

[659] R Mokal, 'The Priority of Secured Credit' in R Mokal, *Corporate Insolvency Law: Theory and Application* (Oxford, Oxford University Press, 2005) 151–52.

[660] Although it is not necessarily the case that tort claimants figure extensively in most US insolvencies either. See R Mokal, 'The Priority of Secured Credit' in R Mokal, *Corporate Insolvency Law: Theory and Application* (Oxford, Oxford University Press, 2005) 138–52; C Hill, 'Is Secured Debt Efficient?' (2002) 80 *Texas Law Review* 1117 fn 241.

[661] Most health care in the UK is provided by the National Health Service, and although there is a certain degree of 'claw-back' from tortfeasors in relation to liability for road traffic accidents (Road Traffic Act 1988 ss 157–58), this is limited. The Law Commission recommended a much wider claw-back (see Law Commission Report No 262, *Damages for Personal Injury: Medical, Nursing and Other Expenses* (1999), paras 3.19–3.43) but this recommendation has not been enacted. However, the state does have the right to claw back certain social security payments made to an injured person from a tortfeasor (Social Security (Recovery of Benefits) Act 1997). Obviously, any payments clawed back can form part of the victim's claim against the tortfeasor.

[662] Employers' Liability (Compulsory Insurance) Act 1969, s 1; Road Traffic Act 1988, s 143.

[663] Third Party (Rights against Insurers) Act 2010. This is also provided by statute in some US states, such Louisiana, Wisconsin and New York.

[664] L LoPucki, 'The Unsecured Creditors' Bargain' (1994) 80 *Virginia Law Review* 1887, 1897.

[665] Law Commission Report 272, Third Parties—Rights against Insurers (2001), paras 7.13–7.14.

Two types of non-adjusting creditors deserve special mention. First, employees of the company are not in a position to take security or, usually, to adjust in any meaningful way. Most employees cannot negotiate their level of wages, especially once they have commenced employment, and it may be difficult for them to leave the company and obtain another job. Second, the tax authorities and utility companies cannot adjust (for example, by charging higher interest rates), except by being more aggressive in enforcing debts. However, this course of action may send the company into insolvency, and so the authorities have to balance the negative effects of this against their own protection.

Those who consider that there is a transfer of wealth from secured lenders to non-adjusting creditors suggest various ways to protect the latter. One possibility is for certain classes of non-adjusting creditors to be given priority over secured lenders (or a class of secured lenders).[666] This suffers from the objection that it does not assist all non-adjusting creditors, but could be worth considering for particular disadvantaged groups. In the UK there are arguments against this course of action for the three main groups in contention. First, tort claimants are protected to some extent by a direct claim against an insurance company, as discussed above. Second, although the priority course is in fact followed to some extent for employees, who have preferential status above floating charge holders, employees themselves actually have a much better route for recovery. They are entitled to claim a sum direct from the Secretary of State, who is then subrogated to their preferential claim against the company.[667] This directly claimed sum is greater than the amount of the employees' preferential claim.[668] Third, the tax authorities used to have preferential status above floating charge holders until 2002 (Crown preference), when this was abolished in order to fund the 'prescribed part', the theory of which is discussed in the next paragraphs.[669] Many countries have totally or partially abolished tax preference, largely because the tax authorities can protect themselves to a considerable extent via more efficient enforcement mechanisms.[670] The strongest argument in favour of tax preference relates to tax collected or withheld by the company from others (for example, employees' income tax and value added tax paid by customers). This tax, in one sense, has already been collected and 'belongs' to the tax authorities, and it is hard to see why it should be available for the unsecured creditors.[671] However, it was the preferential status in relation to this tax that was given up by the UK Government in 2002,[672] as it was considered more important for this asset to be available to the unsecured creditors generally.

---

[666] L LoPucki, 'The Unsecured Creditors' Bargain' (1994) 80 *Virginia Law Review* 1887, 1908 ff discusses this possibility in relation to tort claimants. For an argument that a similar system, operating in maritime law, has not had an adverse effect on the provision of secured credit, see K van der Biezenbos, 'A Sea Change in Creditor Priorities' (2015) 48 *University of Michigan Journal of Law Reform* 595.

[667] The claim against the Secretary of State is for a maximum of eight weeks at £475 per week: Employment Rights Act 1996, ss 182–86. The weekly limit is raised regularly: the current limit is imposed by SI 2015/226 Sch 1.

[668] An employee's preferential claim relates to wages for four months before the date of administration or winding up, with a maximum of £800, plus any accrued holiday pay within certain limits (Insolvency Act 1986, Sch 6; Insolvency Proceedings (Monetary Limits) Order 1986 (SI 1986/1996), para 4).

[669] See also 3.3.1.2.3.

[670] B Morgan, 'Should the Sovereign be Paid First? A Comparative International Analysis of the Priority for Tax Claims in Bankruptcy' (2000) 74 *American Bankruptcy Law Journal* 461, 505–06. (This needs to be balanced against the risk of sending the company into insolvency; see above.)

[671] Report of the Review Committee, *Insolvency Law and Practice* (Cmnd 8558, 1982) (The Cork Report), on which the Insolvency Act 1986 is based, para 1418.

[672] Preferential status for taxes paid directly by the company was abolished in 1986.

Another possible mechanism for protecting non-adjusting creditors is to set aside a certain percentage of assets subject to a security interest for those creditors. Various such schemes have been suggested. One is for secured creditors to cede some priority to unsecured creditors who were non-adjusting in respect of the particular secured claim asserted by the secured creditors.[673] The problem with this idea is that it is very difficult (and costly) to identify who the non-adjusting, as opposed to adjusting, unsecured creditors are.[674] Another scheme considered by US writers is the 'fixed-fraction' scheme, whereby secured creditors are only secured for a specific fraction of their secured claim, and the balance of the assets forming security are available for unsecured creditors.[675] This can be contrasted with the actual position in the UK, where the prescribed part (available to all unsecured creditors) is a fixed fraction of the assets subject to the floating charge, whatever the amount of the debt owed to the floating chargee.[676] Both schemes can be criticised on the basis that they will increase the cost of credit, either because lenders will charge more for credit (as their recovery is diminished) or because they will lend less. The latter danger is more likely in the UK, where a floating charge lender can protect itself by oversecuring, that is, attempting to ensure that there is a 'cushion' of floating charge assets which exceed the value of the debt, and which are available for the preferential creditors and the prescribed part. In fact, a floating chargee is better off under the present scheme than when there was Crown preference, since the amount of the prescribed part is easily calculated in advance, as is the amount payable to preferential creditors, which depends largely on the number of employees the borrower company has. The amount due to the Crown, of course, was more difficult to predict, since it depended on how effective the Crown was in enforcing the sums due to it.

Another problem with a partial priority scheme is that the costs of redistribution may not outweigh the benefits to the non-adjusting unsecured creditors. First, as all unsecured creditors benefit equally, those who do adjust will obtain a double benefit. Those who could have adjusted but chose not to (for whatever reason) will also benefit. This could act as a disincentive to adjustment.[677] The amount left for genuine involuntary creditors is therefore small.[678] If there is real concern about such creditors, and a desire to ensure that costs of torts are internalised within the borrower company, a better route is likely to be compulsory insurance against such liability.[679] The premiums that the company has to pay thus

---

[673] L Bebchuk and J Fried, 'The Uneasy Case for the Priority of Secured Claims in Bankruptcy' (1996) 105 *Yale Law Journal* 857, 905.

[674] Ibid, 908.

[675] L Bebchuk and J Fried, 'The Uneasy Case for the Priority of Secured Claims in Bankruptcy: Further Thoughts and a Reply to Critics' (1997) 82 *Cornell Law Review* 1279, 1323.

[676] Insolvency Act 1986, ss 176A and 176ZA; see 3.3.1.2.3.

[677] However, at least on the UK figures, the benefits from the prescribed part to individual creditors are unlikely to be significant enough to preclude adjustment.

[678] It is likely that the actual benefit of the prescribed part to unsecured creditors generally will, on average, be tiny. See R Mokal, 'The Priority of Secured Credit' in R Mokal, *Corporate Insolvency Law: Theory and Application* (Oxford, Oxford University Press, 2005) 129–30.

[679] This would need to be coupled with a right of the tort claimant to sue the insurance company direct, as currently exists under the Third Party (Rights against Insurers) Act 2010, although at present there is the danger of loss of priority to secured lenders for non-compulsory insurance. See discussion at 7.6.2.3.

internalise the cost, and provide a disincentive against risky behaviour.[680] Second, a rule of partial priority provides an incentive for secured creditors to structure their transactions so that the rule does not apply to them. This is particularly marked in the UK, where lenders have developed structures which do not include taking a floating charge,[681] but is also a danger in the US.[682]

Other methods for improving the position of unsecured creditors should also be mentioned. Transactions in the run-up to insolvency likely to damage unsecured creditors, including the grant of security for existing debt, attract remedies which are usually purely for the benefit of unsecured creditors.[683] Such transactions potentially damage all unsecured creditors, as it is difficult to adjust accurately in relation to such transactions.[684]

Strengthening these provisions (such as by extending section 245 of the Insolvency Act 1986 to cover fixed charges)[685] would protect unsecured creditors in a way that is targeted at the most objectionable types of security or other interests.[686] Another possibility is to make it easier for unsecured creditors to adjust accurately, by improving transparency and reducing the cost of obtaining information about the credit of the borrowing company. Arguably the reforms discussed in the next section would do this.

7.7 Reform

Over the last 40 years, there has been much discussion about the need to reform the law governing personal property security in England and Wales.[687] There has been some limited reform, for example in relation to the details of the registration system[688] and in relation to the registration of charges created by overseas companies over property within the UK,[689] but no wholesale reform. There is still ongoing consideration of reform in the practitioner

[680] S Block-Lieb, 'The Unsecured Creditors' Bargain: A Reply' (1994) 80 *Virginia Law Review* 1989, 2002; R Mokal, 'The Priority of Secured Credit' in R Mokal, *Corporate Insolvency Law: Theory and Application* (Oxford, Oxford University Press, 2005) 151.

[681] See 7.3.3.3.4.

[682] C Hill, 'Is Secured Debt Efficient?' (2002) 80 *Texas Law Review* 1176.

[683] See 3.3.2. Note that the remedies do not always only benefit unsecured creditors as they can involve the setting aside of the transaction: if a security interest is set aside, this may benefit another creditor who holds a security interest over the same asset.

[684] This is because adjustment usually has to be done before the transaction takes place, and therefore can only reflect the chance of it happening. If such a transaction were prohibited, unsecured creditors would not need to make such a speculative adjustment.

[685] See 7.3.3.3.4.

[686] R Mokal, 'The Priority of Secured Credit' in R Mokal, *Corporate Insolvency Law: Theory and Application* (Oxford, Oxford University Press, 2005) 186.

[687] The discussion in this section relates solely to the law of England and Wales. The Scottish law of security is different and the considerations in relation to reform are not the same. For a detailed list of the various reports and recommendations for reform, see http://securedtransactionslawreformproject.org/reform-in-the-uk/history-of-reform.

[688] Discussed at 7.4.2.

[689] The previous regime, introduced by the Overseas Companies Regulations 2009 (SI 2009/1801), was abolished by the Overseas Companies (Execution of Documents and Registration of Charges) (Amendment) Regulations 2011 (SI 2011/2194).

and academic fields.[690] In the following section, we set out the arguments for and against reform, and give a brief description of what a reformed system might look like. It is not possible to include a detailed discussion in a book of this size, and the reader is referred to the relevant Law Commission papers and more specialist literature.[691]

7.7.1 Attributes of an Ideal Law

It is important, first, to consider what the most desirable attributes of a law governing the proprietary protection of creditors are. One such attribute is that the law is clear, certain and easily accessible. As discussed in this chapter, proprietary protection lowers the cost of credit, and, in order to price such reduction accurately, lenders need to be able to predict their position in law if the borrower defaults. There should be certainty as to whether a proprietary interest is effective against third parties, both when the borrower is solvent and on its insolvency, and as to whether that interest is subject to any other interest in the same asset. In other words, the priority rules must be clear. Another attribute is that it should be possible to obtain a proprietary right over any asset of a borrower, and that the process of doing so should be as easy and cheap as possible. A further attribute is that it must be possible to acquire proprietary rights over both the present and future assets of the borrower, without any additional formalities in the future, and to acquire a non-possessory proprietary interest which does not prevent the borrower from disposing of the asset subject to that interest in the ordinary course of business.

Further, it should be possible for any creditor (with or without proprietary protection) to find out sufficient information to enable it to adjust adequately to the risks it takes in advancing credit.[692] This means both that it should have accurate information about the extent of the borrower's assets at the time it advances credit, and that it should be able to monitor what happens to those assets during the time it is exposed to the credit risk of the borrower, that is, after it has advanced credit but before it is paid. There should also be a simple and straightforward way for a creditor taking a proprietary interest to protect itself from losing priority to a future creditor taking a proprietary interest in the same asset. Further, it should be possible to enforce a proprietary claim effectively whether or not the borrower is insolvent. Lastly, although it should be possible for creditors to contract out of most default rules in relation to priority and enforcement, that default position should be the one most likely to be required in general, so as to minimise transaction costs. It will be noticed that these attributes refer to a 'proprietary interest' rather than to 'security'. That is because if a lender relies on such an interest to protect it in the event of a borrower's default, the desirable attributes of the relevant law are the same whether or not the interest is a 'true' security interest or an absolute one.

---

[690] Secured Transactions Law Reform Project, http://securedtransactionslawreformproject.org/. See also the work of a committee set up by the City of London Law Society Financial Law Committee, www.citysolicitors.org.uk/index.php?option=com_content&view=category&id=129&Itemid=469.

[691] Security and Title-Based Financing, ch 23; J de Lacy (ed), *The Reform of UK Personal Property Security Law* (Abingdon, Routledge-Cavendish, 2010).

[692] See 7.6.2.3.

7.7.2 Unsatisfactory Aspects of English Law

With these desirable attributes in mind, it can be said that the English law of personal property security is unsatisfactory from a practical point of view for several reasons. First, it is difficult to access. Most English personal property security law is found not in statute, but in case law dating from the middle of the nineteenth century. One example of this is the rule in *Dearle v Hall* governing the priority of successive assignments.[693] The fact that so much of the law consists of case law, rather than legislation, means that substantial amounts of time and money are spent on research. In addition, the absence of a modern statute means that the UK has no exportable product; this limits its ability to influence the future shape of the law in Continental Europe.[694]

Secondly, once located, the law in this regard is confusing and over-complicated. English law has a range of devices which fulfil a security function, such as legal and equitable mortgages, legal and equitable charges, title transfer and title retention devices, and hire purchase agreements. For each there exist separate creation, perfection and priority rules. The complexity of the priority rules is apparent from the discussion earlier in this chapter.[695] The law is also unclear in many respects. For example, the relation between registration and priority is complex, the scope of constructive notice arising from registration is uncertain,[696] and the effect of non-registration is likewise uncertain.[697] The difficult distinction between the fixed and the floating charge has considerable priority and insolvency consequences. Priority of competing assignments of receivables is governed by the *Dearle v Hall* rule, criticised above, and a lender taking an absolute assignment of receivables cannot protect its priority position by registration.[698] Where a debtor wrongly disposes of property, the priority rules are different according to whether the creditor is a legal or equitable mortgagee or chargee, a seller under a conditional sale agreement, or the owner under a hire purchase agreement. The lack of clarity has been exacerbated by the introduction of the FCARs, which are uncertain in their scope and application.[699]

Thirdly, the system of registration is flawed in a number of ways. The process itself is cumbersome and expensive, and, although searching can now be done electronically, registration includes the submission of the original charge document in paper or electronic form, as well as particulars. The risk of mistakes in the particulars appears to be on those who subsequently search the register, rather than the person registering.[700] The register itself can be misleading, and does not include all non-possessory interests which could affect secured or unsecured creditors.[701] Further, the requirement of registration within a

---

[693] See 7.4.4.

[694] For example, the Draft Common Frame of Reference Book IX relates to personal property security, but draws little on English law.

[695] 7.4.4.

[696] 7.4 3.2. This continues to be the case even after the recent reforms.

[697] 7.4.3.1.

[698] See 7.4.4.

[699] 7.3.4.2.

[700] See 7.4.3.2.

[701] While the scope of registrable interests has widened, interests created by retention of title and absolute transfer are still omitted.

21-day period leads to the invisibility period of 21 days[702] and, if parties fail to register in time, they face unnecessary costs in order to obtain a court order to register out of time.[703]

The fact that there are specialist registers for particular types of assets also makes the system more complex.

7.7.3 Options for Reform

As appears from the discussion earlier in this chapter, the 2013 reforms to the registration system did not address most of these criticisms, and were of a very limited nature. There are, therefore, still several options for reform. The first, which is very limited, is for some of the specific criticisms of the 2013 reforms to be met, such as the lack of clarity in relation to constructive notice, and in relation to the position where the particulars are not consistent with the charge agreement. Another possible option is to make amendments to English law in a wider area than just registration of company charges. This could include the law relating to priority, not just between security interests but including absolute interests as well. It could also include the law of insolvency, so that, for example, the trigger for various statutory consequences could be something other than the distinction between fixed and floating charges.[704]

While, obviously, there could be considerable discussion about the content of such amendments, and they could be quite far-reaching, the resulting system would still fall foul of the first and second criticisms of English law set out above. Unless the whole system were codified, it would still be difficult to know what the law was (and an exportable product would still be lacking), and, even if it were codified (if that were possible), the distinctions between the different types of interests would remain.

A third option is wholesale reform of the English system, similar to that adopted recently in some other common law jurisdictions, namely a notice filing system, which utilises a functional approach when determining when its rules apply, where priority is usually determined by date of filing, and where there are common rules on enforcement for all interests falling within the scheme. Such a scheme was first introduced in the United States in Article 9 of the Uniform Commercial Code (UCC),[705] and has been broadly followed in the Personal Property Security Acts (PPSAs) of Canada,[706] New Zealand,[707] Australia[708] and,

---

[702] See 7.4.3.2.

[703] See 7.4.3.1.

[704] See eg R Calnan, 'What is Wrong with the Law of Security' in J de Lacy (ed), *The Reform of UK Personal Property Security Law* (Abingdon, Routledge-Cavendish, 2010). For general discussion see also Security and Title-Based Financing, 23.55–23.69.

[705] Now art 9 (revised).

[706] The first such Act was the Ontario PPSA in 1967. There are PPSAs in nine of the ten provinces and the three territories. See R Cuming, C Walsh and R Wood, *Personal Property Security Law* (Toronto, Irwin Law, 2012).

[707] New Zealand Personal Property Securities Act 1999, which introduces a wholly electronic registration system. For detailed commentaries see M Gedye, R Cuming and R Wood, *Personal Property Securities in New Zealand* (New Zealand, Brookers, 2002); L Widdup, *Personal Property Securities Act: A Conceptual Approach*, 3rd edn (Wellington, LexisNexis Butterworths, 2012).

[708] Personal Property Securities Act 2009, which came into force in January 2012. For detailed discussion see A Duggan and D Brown, *Australian Personal Property Securities Law* (LexisNexis Butterworths Australia, 2012); B Whittaker, *Review of the Personal Property Securities Act: Final Report* (2015).

recently, Jersey.[709] The Law Commission, in its Consultative Report of 2005,[710] set out a version of a PPSA scheme for England and Wales. The following discussion sets out the main features of such a scheme, and seeks to point out where there would be significant change were such a scheme to be introduced in England and Wales.

7.7.4 Outline of Notice Filing Scheme[711]

7.7.4.1 Functional Approach

All interests created by agreement that have the function of security are included within the scheme, and are largely treated the same way. Differences of form are, therefore, disregarded. Thus the rules apply equally to pledges, liens, mortgages and charges,[712] and also to title retention devices such as sales on ROT terms, conditional sales, hire purchase agreements and finance leases. Transactions with the function of security where title is transferred are also included. Title retention and title transfer devices for the purposes of security can be referred to as 'quasi-security' interests. Furthermore, two forms of transaction which do not perform the function of security are included in the rules governing registration and priorities,[713] because of their similarity to transactions which do have a security function: these transactions are known as 'deemed security interests'. They are absolute assignment of receivables[714] and (operating) leases for over a year.[715]

The functional approach is often justified on the basis that these transactions all have a common function and so should be treated alike.[716] The approach brings simplicity and clarity to a system where otherwise there would be a number of different ways of doing the same thing, each with slightly different legal consequences, which can be exploited by those aware of them, and which confuse those who are not. However, it also could be argued that the different forms of transactions do involve genuine (though, in some cases minor) differences and so the decision to treat them alike in law is a policy choice, which requires further justification. Such justification has to be made in relation to each area of

---

[709] Security Interests (Jersey) Law 2012. This relates to intangible property; consultation in relation to the law governing tangible property is still underway.

[710] Law Commission Consultation Paper No 176, *Company Security Interests: A Consultative Report* (2004).

[711] The references that are given are to art 9 (revised) UCC, Ontario PPSA (OPPSA), Saskatchewan PPSA (SPPSA), which was used as a model for the New Zealand Act, New Zealand PPSA (NZPPSA) and Australian PPSA (APPSA).

[712] Although possessory interests do not require registration.

[713] But not the rules relating to enforcement: UCC (revised) art 9-601(g), SPPSA s 55(2)(a), NZPPSA s 105, APPSA s 109(1).

[714] UCC (revised) 1-201(37), OPPSA s 1(1), SPPSA s 2(1)(qq), NZPPSA s 17(1)(b), APPSA s 12(3). Certain types of assignments of receivables are excluded, such as those taking place on the sale of a business, and those that take place only to facilitate collection: UCC (revised) 9-109(d), OPPSA s 4, SPPSA ss 4(g) and (h), NZPPSA ss 23(e)(viii)–(x), APPSA ss 8(f)(vi)–(x).

[715] OPPSA s 2(c) (added by amendment in 2006), SPPSA s 2(1)(qq), NZPPSA s 17(b), APPSA ss 12(3) and 13. Operating leases are not deemed security interests under UCC art 9, although they are very often registered anyway (Law Commission Consultation Paper No 176, *Company Security Interests: A Consultative Report* (2004), para 3-37).

[716] See eg JS Ziegel, 'The New Provincial Chattel Security Law Regimes' (1990) 70 *Canada Barereview* 681, 685–86.

law (registration, priorities and enforcement) and, in some cases, exceptions to uniform treatment are themselves justified. Thus, for example, in the PPSA scheme registration is not required for possessory interests, and the priority position of purchase money security interests is different from that of other security interests.[717] It should be noted, however, that in relation to generalised arguments about secured credit (such as those discussed in 7.6 above), all creditors with a proprietary interest are treated alike, but are differentiated from unsecured creditors.

In relation to registration, parity of treatment for non-possessory interests with the function of security can be justified on the basis of publicity and ostensible ownership—that is, the fact that the borrower appears to own more assets than he actually does. Against this, it can be argued that lenders know that borrowers usually encumber their assets (either with true security interests or quasi-security interests), and so can discover this by due diligence exercises, coupled with warranties in lending agreements, so that a register is not necessary. Even if it is accepted that there is little danger of an interest being so hidden that it is impossible to discover it, registration which is cheap to do and easy to access can cut the costs of taking security (including quasi-security) since an accurate register can form the basis of enquiries and prevent unnecessary investigation. Thus, for example, if a lender is lending against equipment which may be the subject of quasi-security interests, it is cheaper to undertake the necessary investigations (for example, as to how much is left to pay under the agreement) when there is a definitive list available which does not depend on the veracity of the borrower.

7.7.4.2 Registration

All interests within the scheme require 'perfection' if they are to be enforceable against third parties. 'Enforceable' in this context means having priority over unperfected interests and later registered interests, and being enforceable against a liquidator or administrator in the insolvency of the debtor. Possessory interests are perfected by the taking of possession (in English law pledges and liens are not created until possession is taken, so perfection and creation would be simultaneous).[718] Some schemes provide that interests over financial collateral may be perfected by control.[719]

Most other security interests are perfected by registration, which means the filing of a financing statement giving certain minimum details about the identity of the debtor and of the secured party and a description of the collateral.[720] In most schemes this information can be (or must be) submitted electronically by completing an online form.[721] There is no need to submit (in any form) the agreement creating the interest, or to include details of its terms. The information is submitted directly to the register, and the risk of any errors is on the person submitting it, usually the secured party, since registration is conclusive evidence

---

[717] See 7.7.4.3.

[718] NZPPSA s 41, UCC (revised) art 9-313, OPPSA s 22, SPPSA s 24, APPSA s 21(2).

[719] UCC (revised) art 9-312, 9-314, APPSA s 21(2)(c). What amounts to control is defined in APSSA, ss 25–29.

[720] The information varies from system to system, but see UCC (revised) art 9-502(a), NZPPSA s 142, APPSA, s 153.

[721] The New Zealand system is wholly electronic, as is the Australian system.

of the scope of the security interest.[722] Although the information is relatively sparse, it is sufficient to enable any interested party to make enquiries of the registered secured party, who is obliged to provide fairly extensive further information.[723] The financing statement can be filed at any time before or after the creation of the security interest. This is so that a secured party can protect itself from the time that a security interest is envisaged, and removes the problem of the invisibility period.[724]

The secured party is not obliged to file at any particular time, but if it files after creation it risks losing priority to another secured party who files earlier. To avoid the risk of a filing being entered or remaining on the register if no security interest is actually granted, most systems require the debtor to be notified of the filing,[725] and give the debtor power to remove an incorrect filing, or to require the filing of a statement correcting the position.[726]

Only one financing statement is required to be filed in relation to all security interests taken by the secured party over the assets specified. This means that where there are likely to be multiple interests (such as when goods are sold on ROT terms), only one registration is required.

One of the advantages of a modern notice filing system, such as those established in New Zealand and Australia, is that it is wholly electronic—security interests are registered online, and the register can be searched online. The New Zealand computer system, for example, is cheap and easy to use,[727] and requires very little maintenance. Further, such a system can be linked up to other registers, such as, in England, those relating to land, ships and aircraft, so that information registered on one register can be forwarded to another.[728] A notice filing system would also address the other problems inherent in the current system identified above.[729] Those relying on the register would be protected from mistaken registration, and there would not be any period during which a subsequent interest could lose priority to a prior invisible interest. There would also be no need for a secured creditor to apply for permission to register late, since registration can take place at any time. There would still be a significant incentive to register, since unregistered interests would be void against unsecured creditors in insolvency,[730] and would lose priority to all registered security interests in the same assets.

7.7.4.3 Priorities

The basic priority rule is very simple: where interests in relation to any particular asset are perfected, priority is determined by the date of perfection. In most cases, this will mean

---

[722] Thus, if certain collateral is omitted, the security interest is valid in relation to the collateral mentioned, but not in relation to the omitted collateral. NZPPSA s 152, SPPSA s 43(9), APPSA s 164(3). This is in contrast to the current English system, where the risk of error in the particulars appears to be on subsequent persons searching the register, although now the entire charge document is registrable and can therefore be read.

[723] NZPPSA s 177, SPPSA s 18, OPPSA s 18, UCC (revised) art 9-210, APPSA s 275.

[724] See 7.4.3.2.

[725] NZPPSA s 148, SPPSA s 43(12), OPPSA s 46(6), APPSA s 157, UCC (revised) art 9-509 (requires the debtor's authorisation for filing, but this is usually by being bound by the security agreement).

[726] NZPPSA s 162, UCC (revised) art 9-518, SPPSA s 50, OPPSA s 56, APPSA s 178.

[727] Registration costs $3 and search of the register costs $1.

[728] There is power in Companies Act 2006 to introduce such a system to the current register: see s 893.

[729] See 7.7.2.

[730] This is not the position in New Zealand.

that priority is by date of registration. The date of creation of the interest is irrelevant. A perfected interest has priority over an unperfected one, and unperfected ones rank in order of attachment.[731] These rules determine the priority of security interests in relation to all advances made by the secured party, at whatever time, so that the rules on tacking do not apply.

Although these are the basic rules, there are some exceptions. In some systems, where one interest in an asset is perfected by registration and another by control, the interest perfected by control has priority, regardless of the dates of perfection.[732] The parties can agree a different order of priority from that laid down by the basic rules. This can either be done by means of a subordination agreement, or by the debtor being given specific permission by a secured party to create security interests ranking in priority to that of the secured party. However, unlike a floating charge, a security agreement which merely gives the debtor permission to dispose of the assets in the ordinary course of business will only relate to dispositions which are not for the purpose of security, and will not (without more) cover the creation of subsequent security interests. Since the default position is that priority is by date of registration, there is no need for negative pledge clauses or automatic crystallisation to protect the position of a 'floating chargee'.[733] The troublesome question of whether registration constitutes constructive notice also disappears.[734]

An interest in an asset to secure an advance made to acquire that asset (a purchase money security interest, PMSI) has priority over a previously perfected interest which would attach to that asset under an after-acquired property clause. Most interests created by retention of title, such as conditional sale agreements and finance leases, fall into the category of PMSI, since title is retained to secure the purchase price. Leases which are deemed security interests are also treated as PMSIs.[735] Some schemes also permit cross-collateralisation, so that an interest retains PMSI status not only to the extent that it secures the obligation to pay or repay the purchase price of that asset, but also to the extent that it secures all obligations owing from the debtor to the creditor;[736] this is, in effect, an 'all monies' clause. Other schemes limit PMSI status to the obligation securing the purchase price of that asset.[737] To obtain PMSI status, the interest must usually be registered within a certain (short) period following its attachment[738] or following the debtor taking possession of the relevant asset, and some schemes require notice to be given to holders of prior registered interests when the PMSI is in inventory.[739] Many schemes also provide that the perfected interest (together

---

[731] Attachment is the moment when the security interest is effective as against the debtor and any creditors against whom an unperfected interest is not void, for example unsecured creditors before insolvency. It is defined in the PPSAs, as are the conditions that are necessary for an interest to attach, which are usually that value is given and that the debtor has rights in the collateral. NZPPSA s 40, SPPSA s 12, OPPSA s 11, UCC (revised) art 9-203, APPSA s 17.

[732] APPSA s 57(1).

[733] In most schemes, perfected security interests have priority over execution creditors who execute later than the date of perfection, thus removing another reason for automatic crystallisation. See 7.4.4.

[734] UCC (revised) art 9–331(c), OPPSA s 46(5), SPPSA s 47, NZPPSA s 20, APPSA s 300.

[735] APPSA s 14(1)(c).

[736] UCC art 9-103(b)(2).

[737] APPSA s 14(3).

[738] UCC (revised) art 9-324, SPPSA s 34, OPPSA s 33, NZPPSA s 74, APPSA s 62. In all these schemes, in the case inventory, the registration must be before attachment or possession.

[739] UCC (revised) art 9-324(b) and (c), OPPSA s 33(1), SPPSA s 34(3).

with its PMSI status) automatically continues to the proceeds of sale of the asset or to products made from it. In relation to proceeds in the form of receivables, this causes a conflict with a financier financing the debtor's receivables, over whom the PMSI holder would, without more, have priority. Many jurisdictions have recognised this tension and, as a matter of policy, have provided that, in this particular case, the PMSI super-priority should not apply and that priority should be by date of registration. Even this does not fully solve the conflict, since if the debtor refinances with a new receivables financier, who registers after the PMSI is registered (and it must be remembered that a supplier of raw materials only needs to register once to cover all its future ROT supply contracts), the ROT supplier will still have priority over the receivables financier. Arguably, this could raise the cost of receivables financing, since the financier will, in order for its financing to be effective, have to make subordination agreements with all the debtor's suppliers.[740]

There are many policy reasons for the PMSI super-priority.[741] These include preventing the first registered financier having a monopoly on lending to a debtor (since one registration covers all future advances, any subsequent non-PMSI lenders would have to obtain a subordination agreement from the first lender in order to get priority) and considerations of fairness, as the PMSI lender swells the debtor's assets by the amount lent, and if the asset falls within the first financier's security interest, that financier obtains a 'windfall'. PMSI lending is also seen as efficient, since those who lend on this basis are specialists in the field, and not only price the credit more accurately than a general financier, but also are in a better position to realise the asset if there is a default, and therefore can reflect this in the price of credit.

The circumstances in which a buyer[742] would take free of security interests are specified separately from the rules governing priority between security interests. Basically, a buyer takes assets subject to any prior security interests unless the sale is permitted in the security agreement (a type of floating charge) or either the security interest is unperfected or the disposition is of goods sold in the ordinary course of business of the debtor. The schemes vary as to whether the buyer's knowledge of the security interest, or that the disposition is in breach of the security agreement, prevents the buyer taking free.

7.7.4.4 Enforcement

The schemes also normally provide a default code for enforcement outside insolvency.[743] This will provide for various methods of enforcement, which will vary according to the type of asset, but which broadly speaking involve the secured party taking control of the asset and then realising its value. A form of foreclosure, called retention, is also usually included. The debtor and other secured creditors (who may have an interest in the asset) are safeguarded by notice requirements. The default code will also include general obligations,

---

[740] The APPSA has a notice system which swings the balance further in favour of a receivables financier: see APPSA s 64; see also A Duggan and D Brown, *Australian Personal Property Securities Law* (LexisNexis Butterworths Australia, 2012) 8.41.

[741] For a full discussion see L Gullifer, 'Retention of Title Clauses: A Question of Balance' in A Burrows and E Peel (eds), *Contract Terms* (Oxford, Oxford University Press, 2007) 287–89. See also 7.4.4.

[742] Similar rules apply to lessors.

[743] See UCC Part 6, OPPSA Part V, SPPSA Part V, NZPPSA Part 9, APPSA ch 4.

such as the obligation to obtain market value when realising collateral and an obligation to act with commercial reasonableness.[744] Further, the order of distribution on realisation will be prescribed, including an obligation to account to the debtor for any surplus after the enforcing secured creditor and all other secured parties with an interest in the collateral have been paid. To some extent, the parties can contract out of these enforcement provisions, but not if third parties are affected. Further, there are certain provisions, such as the debtor's right to the surplus and the right to redeem, which are mandatory.[745]

7.7.5 Assessment of Reform

The attributes of an ideal system, and an assessment of how English law fails to match up to this, are set out above. There is a strong case for reform, and for wholesale reform which not only produces a modern, wholly electronic registration system, but involves a rational and integrated system of registration and priorities, together with a codification of the law on enforcement.[746] What arguments, then, can be made against this? The most general argument (which can be expressed in a variety of ways) is that the current system is not broken enough to warrant the costs of wholesale reform. It is said that the problems identified above can, largely, be overcome by drafting and devices which are now very familiar to the legal profession, and that the uncertainties, which are unsatisfactory in theory, rarely cause important or expensive problems in practice. The costs of a wholly new system would be considerable; not so much in terms of setting up the central system but in terms of re-educating the users of that system (both lenders and borrowers and their lawyers) and the inevitable uncertainty that comes with a new system, even if the final result is law that is more certain. To some extent, an assessment of this argument is an empirical matter, since the actual extent of problems caused by the present law across the entire spectrum of borrowers and lenders is largely unknown, and the actual costs of reform can only be estimated. It should be borne in mind, though, that the transitional costs of any reform are immediate but transitory, while reform (if it is worthwhile) lasts for generations.

One way to assess the situation is to look at other countries, where the need for reform has been accepted and reform has been introduced relatively recently. The New Zealand experience has been largely favourable.[747] In Australia the general benefits of reform have been appreciated, although there is still concern about the complexity of the Australian

---

[744] UCC (revised) art 9-610(b), OPPSA s 63(1), SPPSA s 65(3), NZPPSA s 110, APPSA ss 111 and 131.

[745] It will be recalled that these two rights are indicia of security under English law (see 7.2.1). The precise position varies among the jurisdictions. Some legislation lists the provisions that may be contracted out of (eg NZPPSA s 107, APPSA s 115), some lists the provisions that may not be contracted out of (UCC (revised) art 9-602), and some do both (SPPSA s 56(3), which provides that there can be no waiver or variation by agreement of the enforcement provisions, with some limited exceptions, such as that in s 59(4) that the payment for collateral disposed may be deferred if agreed in the security agreement). The order of distribution can also be changed, but only by agreement of all interested parties after default, not by the security agreement (s 60(2)).

[746] See also the Secured Transactions Law Reform Project's case for reform, http://securedtransactions lawreformproject.org/the-case-for-reform.

[747] See S Flynn, 'Personal Property Securities Reform' (INSOL World—Second Quarter 2008); G Brodie, 'Personal Property Securities: A New Zealand Maritime Perspective' (2008) 22 *Australia & New Zealand Maritime Law Journal*; P Wells, 'Personal Property Securities: Possibilities, Problems and Peculiarities' [2008] *Journal of the Australasian Law Teachers Association* 335.

legislation and there is still much to do to educate small businesses. The conclusion reached in the review of the reforms is that they are still to achieve their potential to unlock value for businesses, though this is partly because of the initial transitional costs and the complexity of the legislation, which it is proposed should be simplified.[748]

Other arguments are made against wholesale reform. One is that the current English law has the benefit of flexibility and upholds freedom of contract. Thus the 'hierarchy' of interests between a legal and an equitable interest means that the parties can choose a more formal approach to creation and have the priority protection of a legal interest, or can choose the more informal and flexible approach of equity, and still have an interest which is effective in insolvency and has relative priority against other interests.[749] Further, new security devices can be created to deal with specific problems, in the way that the floating charge was developed over time to deal with circulating assets.[750]

However, these concerns can be met within a reformed system. The functional approach means that all interests with the purpose of security are treated alike in relation to registration and priorities, but within that approach there is freedom for the parties to agree whatever terms they like in the security agreement. The floating charge, in function if not in name, can remain and, in fact, aspects of it are built into the system.[751] As mentioned above, the priority rules are largely default rules which can be varied by the parties, but the advantage is that the default position is that which most parties would wish to adopt.[752] There is no predetermined extent to which the parties can contract out of the enforcement scheme: this varies within the established schemes, and so could be very extensive in an English scheme. The present system, where only specified interests are registrable, is in some ways restrictive of the development of new interests, in that there is uncertainty as to whether such interests are registrable or not. For example, over the years many attempts have been made to draft clauses in relation to the proceeds of sale of goods sold on ROT terms which do not require registration, since they are, at present, difficult or impossible to register, and any interests created are void if they are not registered as they are likely to be characterised as charges.[753] If the position in relation to registration were clear, such interests could have been developed more readily.

A further argument made against reform is that, although superficially simple, a notice filing system is actually too complex. It is true that there have to be some exceptions to the simple general rules to cover particular situations, for example the PMSI exception, and this does add complexity. The experience of other jurisdictions is relevant here. At least some of the complexity comes from the way that legislation is drafted rather than from the rules themselves. UCC Article 9 seems, to English eyes, to be rather impenetrable, and

---

[748] B Whittaker, *Review of the Personal Property Securities Act: Final Report* (2015), www.ag.gov.au/consultations/pages/StatutoryreviewofthePersonalPropertySecuritiesAct2009.aspx.

[749] City of London Law Society Financial Law Panel commentary on the Law Commission, *Company Security Interests: A Consultative Report*, Consultation Paper No 176 (2004), para 1.19.

[750] Ibid, para 1.16.

[751] Such as the priority of a purchaser in the ordinary course of business over a secured party; see 7.7.4.3.

[752] Unlike, for example, the present position in relation to floating charges, where, to obtain priority over a fixed charge, an effective negative pledge clause is necessary.

[753] See 7.2.5.3.

the Australian Act, which tries to cover every possible situation, is long and detailed.[754] However, the Canadian PPSAs, the New Zealand Act and the Jersey Law are relatively short and are drafted in a straightforward manner, as was the draft suggested by the Law Commission. To some extent there is a trade-off between having enough rules, so that the law is certain and clear in most situations, and simplicity. Since the principles behind a notice filing scheme are clear and straightforward, it can be argued that adding further detail does not detract from the basic clarity of the scheme.

One other objection is that the amount of information on the register is reduced in a notice filing scheme. This is undoubtedly true, in that at present virtually all the terms of the original charge are copied and pasted into the form that constitutes the basis of registration. However, the point of notice filing is that it gives the searcher notice of the interests registered, so that further enquiries can be made. As was pointed out earlier, it provides a definitive list of interests which need to be investigated, and therefore cuts the cost and risk of investigations rather than precluding the need for them altogether.

The weighing up of the advantages and disadvantages of wholesale reform depends, to some extent, on the perspective from which one comes. From a theoretical point of view, there is a strong case for adopting a codified system based on rational and coherent principles. From a practical point of view, too, an electronic notice filing scheme is attractive and has proved successful in a number of jurisdictions similar to our own. There would be some costs and disruption while the system was changed, and so, from the perspective of those familiar with the existing system, change can be seen as undesirable. In assessing the impact of change, the experience of Australia in introducing their reforms is instructive and is worth monitoring closely.[755]

Are the arguments for wholesale reform stronger than those for a more piecemeal approach to reform of the registration system, or the wider law as discussed above?[756] If one is replacing the current system with an electronic one, reforming the list of registrable charges and changing the priority structure to make registration a priority point, for example, it could be said that it is much more conceptually coherent to take on the whole jurisprudence of notice filing, rather than trying to 'bolt' some of its ideas onto our current law. It could be said that a wholly new system would also involve working out how it fitted with the rest of the English law of personal property, and so achieving total conceptual coherence is never possible. However, other jurisdictions with similar common law jurisprudence to our own have incorporated notice filing schemes, and the experience of Canada and New Zealand is that, after some transition, they fit well into the rest of the existing law. Changing the law to deal with a few particular problems would only be a temporary solution, in that new problems would emerge and new changes would then need to be made: this would mean that the law would be forever in a state of flux, which in the end is inimical to certainty.[757]

---

[754] See B Whittaker, *Review of the Personal Property Securities Act: Final Report* (2015), www.ag.gov.au/consultations/pages/StatutoryreviewofthePersonalPropertySecuritiesAct2009.aspx.

[755] See now the five-year review, ibid.

[756] See 7.7.3.

[757] See also L Gullifer, 'Piecemeal Reform: Is It the Answer?' in F Dahan (ed), *Secured Lending in Commercial Transactions* (Cheltenham, Edward Elgar, 2015).

7.8 Conclusion

Taking a proprietary interest in assets gives a creditor very strong protection against the credit risk of a debtor. This process, however, is not without its difficulties and technicalities. The system of taking proprietary protection, both by way of an absolute interest and by way of security, under English law has been critically discussed in this chapter. Many aspects of the law are uncertain, including whether interests purporting to be of one kind are likely to be recharacterised as another kind. This is a particularly keen issue in relation to the floating charge. The benefits in terms of corporate governance of having one lead creditor have already been pointed out,[758] and the concept of the floating charge not only facilitates this but enables security to be taken over circulating assets which otherwise could not be used as collateral for borrowing. These beneficial features of the floating charge are offset by its treatment in insolvency and the uncertainty surrounding both the floating concept and recharacterisation. The future of the floating charge is therefore the subject of much debate.

Another area of uncertainty relates to the scope of the disapplication regime applying to security financial collateral arrangements: as enacted in the UK, the scheme is wider than is justified by its effect on the financial markets, and its precise boundaries are still unclear. Yet more uncertainty arises in relation to the priority rules, and still, to some extent, in relation to the registration system, despite recent reforms.

It has been argued in this chapter that the institution of security (widely interpreted to include some absolute proprietary interests) does increase the availability and decrease the cost of credit. While security does have a deleterious effect on unsecured creditors, most can bargain for protection, and there are targeted ways of protecting those who cannot, including state payments to employees, compulsory insurance coupled with direct rights against the insurance company, and the prescribed part.

Finally, the options for reform of the system of taking security under English law have been considered. Many countries have undertaken wholesale reform of their systems, introducing codification and an electronic notice filing system. The arguments for and against such reform in this country have been considered, and it is concluded that wholesale reform is better in the long term than taking a piecemeal approach.

---

[758] 3.2.2.4.2.

8

Multiple Lenders

8.1 Introduction

Where a company borrows money from one lender, such as a bank, the organisation of the loan is relatively straightforward. The loan agreement is a contract between the borrower and the lender, and the terms of it govern their relationship. As we have seen, this relationship may include contractual protection for the lender, which can be enforced by the lender taking whatever action the provisions allow. This could involve refusing to lend because a condition precedent has not been fulfilled, acceleration of the loan, relying on a right of set-off (outside or within insolvency), or obtaining an injunction to prevent the borrower from breaching a covenant. Alternatively, it may entail the lender suing the borrower for the debt owed, or for breach of contract. Again, if the lender has rights against a third party, it can enforce these directly against that third party. Similarly, if the lender has proprietary protection, such as a security interest, that means that the lender itself has a proprietary right in a particular asset or assets, and can assert this under the circumstances envisaged in the loan agreement either outside or within the insolvency of the borrower. A single bank lender is likely to have monitoring rights in relation to the borrower's business and assets, and this means that the transaction is often seen as a relationship between lender and borrower (and is often referred to as 'relationship lending').[1]

Where a company wishes to access funds from more than one lender, it can take out a series of loans or other borrowing. An example of this is where each loan or borrowing is secured on a different asset. Such sequential lending can cause problems of priority, which can be dealt with by subordination agreements (where the borrowing is unsecured)[2] and the general law of priority, usually modified by priority agreements, where the borrowing is secured.[3] If a company is large and requires considerable funds, however, it will want to access a number of lenders simultaneously, either by taking out a syndicated loan or by issuing debt securities.

Having multiple lenders raises a number of issues which do not arise where there is a single lender. First, there needs to be an organisational structure whereby one (legal) person sets up the transaction, collects in and distributes payments and is able to set in train the enforcement procedure, maybe even enforcing the debt obligation on behalf of all the

---

[1] It is not always the case that finance from a single lender will be in the form of 'relationship lending'. Asset-based finance, which is discussed at 2.3.4.3, depends less on the relationship between lender and borrower since it is not based on cash flow. However, the lender will monitor the assets of the company closely to ensure that it retains its proprietary protection.

[2] 6.4.4.

[3] 7.4.4.

lenders.[4] There are considerable advantages to the borrower in having only one person to deal with, especially where the lenders are numerous and diverse, as in a bond issue. It is usually necessary to have some sort of decision-making procedure included in the structure of the transaction, and often having one person who can make relatively minor decisions on behalf of the lenders is advantageous to all.[5] A decision-making procedure also has to deal with the potential problem of one lender holding out against the rest, since if one person can exercise termination provisions against the wishes of the others, this may well affect everyone due to the operation of cross-default clauses.[6] Further, if each lender can enforce on its own, there is a danger that those who get in early will recover all that the issuer has, leaving the other bondholders to prove against an insolvent issuer.[7] As will be seen below, these problems are overcome in whole or in part by the use of agents or trustees.

Secondly, in order to attract lenders there needs to be a mechanism for conveying information to potential lenders. In relation to both syndicated loans and issues of debt securities fairly standard mechanisms have developed, which involve the use of specialist advisers, usually investment banks. There is considerable regulation of this process in relation to debt securities, but not in relation to syndicated loans. The content of this regulation, and the reasons for the difference in approach, are discussed below in chapter thirteen, while the operation of the mechanisms themselves is discussed in this chapter.

Thirdly, although not essential, it is desirable to have a system for transferring the company's obligation to pay from one lender to another, both so that the potential pool of lenders can be increased and also to attract more lenders in the first place. The ways in which transfer of debt can be effected are discussed in chapter nine.

Issues similar to those discussed above arise in relation to shares as well as debt. Shareholders, especially in publicly traded companies, can be numerous, and can have diverse interests, and therefore the issue of who makes decisions on behalf of the shareholders as a whole, and the question of potential minority abuse, arise in that context just as they do with debt securities. Subject to that, issues of collective enforcement do not arise in quite the same way as they do in relation to debt. Shareholders are purchasing the 'hope' that the company will make profit rather the promise of a specific payment in the future (they are the residual claimants in the company). As a result there is no ultimate payment obligation to enforce. Shareholders can be involved, however, in the enforcement of obligations owed by the directors to the company.[8] These issues are discussed in relation to shareholders in chapter three.[9] Further, mechanisms similar to those used to attract investors in a bond issue are used in an initial public offering of shares. These mechanisms and the regulation

---

[4] Different legal persons may, in fact, perform each of these different functions.

[5] Decision-making procedures are discussed at 8.3.3 in relation to bonds and at 8.4.6 in relation to syndicated loans.

[6] See 6.3.3.

[7] This issue is dealt with by the 'no-action' clause found in debt securities, discussed at 8.3.4.2.3, and the 'pro rata' clause found in syndicated loan agreements, discussed at 8.4.1.

[8] For majority shareholders this is rarely a problem: the articles may provide them with the right to commence litigation and even if the right to commence litigation resides with the board, at the end of the day they have the right to remove the directors by ordinary resolution and thus to control the composition of the board. Minority shareholders also have the possibility of bringing such an action, by way of a derivative action: Companies Act 2006, ss 260–64 (England, Wales and Northern Ireland) and ss 265–69 (Scotland). See generally Gower and Davies, ch 17.

[9] See 3.2.

governing them are discussed in chapter ten. Transfers of shares raise similar issues to the transfer of debt securities and are discussed in chapters four[10] and nine.[11]

If the company's obligation to the lender or investor is transferable, then it has a value in the hands of the transferor, and falls within its assets. As regards third parties (both transferees and an insolvency officer of the transferor)[12] it is seen as property,[13] and the transferor is seen as having a proprietary interest in the debt due to it or in the shares. Thus the transferor is seen as the owner of the debt or shares, and can sell or create a security interest over it or them. This is true in relation to loans (even loans made by one lender). However, the idea of ownership seems even more obvious when the debt is in some way reified by being divided up into securities, so that a person can say 'I own a bond',[14] in a similar way to saying 'I own a share'. The ownership of debt securities by the holders is largely taken for granted. However, the nature of this ownership right is not always clear cut, particularly where the debt obligation is not owed directly to the actual investor, for example in an issue of stock, or where securities are held through an intermediary. These issues are discussed below.

Before dealing with the specific application of the law to syndicated loans and bond issues, it is worth considering two important legal concepts that have been used to deal with the issues relating to multiple lenders set out above. These are trust and agency.

8.2 Basic Concepts

8.2.1 Trust

8.2.1.1 Introduction

The concept of a trust is largely peculiar to common law jurisdictions.[15] It arose from the division of the law in England and Wales into that administered by the courts of common law and that administered by the Court of Chancery, which was known as equity.[16] The trust has been called 'the outstanding creation of equity'.[17] It was developed originally from

---

[10] 4.6.

[11] 9.2.6.

[12] The definition of property in Insolvency Act 1986, s 436 includes things in action.

[13] Transferability has generally been seen as a requirement for an asset to be seen as property: see *National Provincial Bank v Ainsworth* [1965] AC 1175, 1247–48. For discussion of whether transferability is a requirement for an asset to be seen as property, see Law of Personal Property, 1-004 and J Penner, *The Idea of Property in Law* (Oxford, Oxford University Press, 2000) 100–01.

[14] It is also more obvious where the securities are bearer securities, so that each debt is represented by a piece of paper.

[15] As opposed to civil law or other types of jurisdictions.

[16] For the historical background leading to the development of the trust, see P Pettit, *Equity and the Law of Trusts*, 12th edn (Oxford, Oxford University Press, 2012) ch 1; DJ Hayton and C Mitchell, *Hayton and Mitchell: Commentary and Cases on the Law of Trusts and Equitable Remedies*, 13th edn (London, Sweet & Maxwell, 2010) 1-26–1-27; J Martin (ed), *Hanbury and Martin: Modern Equity*, 19th edn (London, Thomson Reuters, 2012) 1-003–1-017.

[17] P Pettit, *Equity and the Law of Trusts*, 12th edn (Oxford, Oxford University Press, 2012) 12.

the medieval device of the use, whereby land was conveyed to a 'feoffee' by a common law conveyance, with directions to hold it for other persons, known as the 'cestui que use'.[18] Although the use was largely abolished by the Statute of Uses in 1535, the concept remained and in the seventeenth century was developed into the trust: a concept whereby one person owns property at law, but is obliged in equity to deal with it in accordance with the terms of the trust for the beneficiary (or beneficiaries) of the trust. A relatively recent statement of the basic principles of trust law was given by Lord Browne-Wilkinson in *Westdeutsche Landesbank Girozentrale v Islington LBC*:[19]

(i)   Equity operates on the conscience of the owner of the legal interest. In the case of a trust, the conscience of the legal owner requires him to carry out the purposes for which the property was vested in him (express or implied trust) or which the law imposes on him by reason of his unconscionable conduct (constructive trust).

(ii) Since the equitable jurisdiction to enforce trusts depends upon the conscience of the holder of the legal interest being affected, he cannot be a trustee of the property if and so long as he is ignorant of the facts alleged to affect his conscience, that is, until he is aware that he is intended to hold the property for the benefit of others in the case of an express or implied trust, or, in the case of a constructive trust, of the factors which are alleged to affect his conscience.

(iii) In order to establish a trust there must be identifiable trust property. The only apparent exception to this rule is a constructive trust imposed on a person who dishonestly assists in a breach of trust who may come under fiduciary duties even if he does not receive identifiable trust property.

(iv) Once a trust is established, as from the date of its establishment the beneficiary has, in equity, a proprietary interest in the trust property, which proprietary interest will be enforceable in equity against any subsequent holder of the property (whether the original property or substituted property into which it can be traced) other than a purchaser for value of the legal interest without notice.

8.2.1.2 Use of the Trust in Commercial Transactions

Although Lord Browne-Wilkinson's statement has not proved uncontroversial,[20] it is a good starting point for considering the basic features of a trust. In the eighteenth and nineteenth centuries, and for a portion of the twentieth century, the main use of a trust was in relation to the protection of family assets, but over the years, and particularly recently, it has been developed widely for use in commercial transactions,[21] including those involving

---

[18] Ibid.

[19] [1996] 1 AC 669, 705.

[20] This is especially true of the second proposition as to the role of conscience in the law of property (see W Swadling, 'Property and Conscience' (1988) 12 *Trusts Law International* 228), and as to whether a trust can arise without the trustee being aware of it (see, in relation to a resulting trust, the discussion in P Pettit, *Equity and the Law of Trusts*, 12th edn (Oxford, Oxford University Press, 2012) 14).

[21] For discussion of this phenomenon see P O'Hagan, 'The Use of Trusts in Finance Structures' [2000] *Journal of International Trust and Corporate Planning* 85; D Hayton, H Pigott and J Benjamin, 'The Use of Trusts in International Financial Transactions' [2002] *Journal of International Banking and Financial Law* 23; D Hayton, P Matthews and C Mitchell (eds), *Underhill and Hayton: Law of Trusts and Trustees*, 18th edn (London, LexisNexis Butterworths, 2010) 1.97–1.138.

multiple lenders. Its use in this field has been based upon the two main distinctive features of a trust.[22] First, there is the separation of title between the legal owner and the beneficiaries. The beneficiaries have an equitable proprietary interest in the trust property, which persists against the trustee, and also against any subsequent owner of the property, except a bona fide purchaser of the legal interest without notice, although enforcement against such an owner has to be by the trustee rather than the beneficiaries.[23] This persistence is effective even in the insolvency of the trustee or the third party, so that the beneficiaries have priority over all the other creditors of that party in relation to that asset. This persistence in insolvency is one of the main reasons why the trust structure is the best explanation of the rights of owners of securities who hold them through an intermediary. As explained below, such owners include many bondholders, where the bond is issued as a global note.[24] Moreover, the trust property can be held for any number of beneficiaries, which makes the structure particularly useful in the situation of multiple lenders. Thus, where security is given for the loan, the security can be granted to the trustee to be held on behalf of the lenders.[25]

Secondly, the fiduciary obligation owed by the trustee to the beneficiaries imposes a number of duties on the trustee. The precise nature of the trustee's duties in any situation is governed by the terms of the trust deed, and the primary duty of the trustee is to comply with those terms. However, there are some basic duties common to all trustees, such as the duty to exercise their powers in the best interests of the beneficiaries,[26] to preserve the trust fund[27] and not to put themselves in a position of conflict of interest with the beneficiaries of the trust, including obtaining unauthorised benefits from the use of the trust property.[28] Trustees also owe a duty of care to the beneficiaries of the trust, although the precise boundaries of that duty will depend upon the provisions in the trust deed, and on the status of the trustee. A professional corporate trustee owes a duty of special care and skill, because of the expertise it professes to have,[29] although the extent of this, too, will depend on the terms of the trust deed. The extent to which the trust deed can define the trustee's obligations and exclude liability is a matter of considerable debate and is discussed below in the context of bond trustees.[30]

It is the ability of the trustee to act on behalf of the beneficiaries with respect to the trust property that is of particular use in relation to issues of stock and bonds. Although

---

[22] P O'Hagan, 'The Use of Trusts in Finance Structures' [2000] *Journal of International Trust and Corporate Planning* 85. These two aspects follow the third and fourth, and then the first and second propositions of Lord Browne-Wilkinson set out above.

[23] J Martin (ed), *Hanbury and Martin: Modern Equity*, 19th edn (London, Thomson Reuters, 2012) 1–019; D Hayton, P Matthews and C Mitchell (eds), *Underhill and Hayton: Law of Trusts and Trustees*, 18th edn (London, LexisNexis Butterworths, 2010) 1-47–1-52.

[24] 8.3.2.3.2(b).

[25] See 8.3.2.3.1.

[26] *Armitage v Nurse* [1998] Ch 241. Millett LJ said at 253 that 'there is an irreducible core of obligations owed by the trustees to the beneficiaries and enforceable by them which is fundamental to the concept of a trust'. However, he considered that these did not include 'the duties of skill and care, prudence and diligence', but rather that '[t]he duty of the trustees to perform the trusts honestly and in good faith for the benefit of the beneficiaries is the minimum necessary to give substance to the trust'. For further discussion see 8.3.5.4.

[27] *Re Brogden* (1888) 38 Ch D 546 (deals with duty to safeguard trust assets); *Buttle v Saunders* [1950] 2 All ER 193 (could not accept lower offer even if felt honour bound to do so); *Jobson v Palmer* [1893] 1 Ch 71 (duty in relation to land).

[28] *Bray v Ford* [1896] AC 44; *Boardman v Phipps* [1967] 2 AC 46.

[29] *Bartlett v Barclays Bank Trust Co Ltd (No 2)* [1980] 1 Ch 515, 534.

[30] 8.3.4.

a bond trustee's powers and duties are usually limited to some extent by the trust deed,[31] it performs many functions which would be difficult or expensive for the bondholders to perform collectively, such as dealing with modifications to the terms of the bonds, receiving information from the issuer and taking action on possible events of default.[32] Further, the ability to enforce the security on behalf of bondholders or syndicated lenders is one of the main benefits of having a security trustee.

8.2.1.3 The Three Certainties

Although trusts can be created by operation of law, it is with the creation of express trusts that we are concerned here. The trust is created by a trust deed, which is one of the several documents drawn up when the bond or stock issue takes place or a secured syndicated loan is set up. In order to create an express trust, three certainties must be present: certainty of intention to create a trust, certainty of objects (that is, who is to benefit from the trust), and certainty of subject matter of the trust.[33] These will now be considered in turn.

8.2.1.3.1 Certainty of Intention to Create a Trust

The intention to create a trust must be apparent from the words of the documentation (and any surrounding circumstances) but there is no need for any particular form of words to be used.[34] This is not usually an issue where there is a trustee of a stock or bond issue, or where the security for a syndicated loan is held by a trustee, since the trust deed will expressly use the word 'trust'. However, the question might conceivably arise where it is sought to use a trust structure to explain the holding of securities by an intermediary, if the agreement is not so explicit.

8.2.1.3.2 Certainty of Objects

The need for certainty of objects means not only that it must be certain for what purpose the trust was created, but that there needs to be one or more beneficiaries who are either legal or natural persons[35] and that the identity of those 'objects' is clear. There is no need for these beneficiaries to be individually identified when the trust is created[36] so long as they form an ascertainable class.[37] Thus it can be seen how beneficial the trust structure is when there is a class of multiple lenders, the membership of which can change frequently, without the knowledge of the issuer, by transfer of the stock, bonds or loans. The issuer or borrower

---

[31] So that, for example, there is usually only a very limited duty to monitor the financial position of the borrower; see 8.3.4.2.2.

[32] See 8.3.4.2.

[33] *Knight v Knight* (1840) 3 Beav 148, 173.

[34] P Pettit, *Equity and the Law of Trusts*, 12th edn (Oxford, Oxford University Press, 2012) 8–51; *Re Kayford* [1975] WLR 279, 282.

[35] This is known as 'The Beneficiary Principle' and is discussed in Pettit, ibid, 59–60; J Martin (ed), *Hanbury and Martin: Modern Equity*, 19th edn (London, Thomson Reuters, 2012) 3–024; G Moffat, G Bean and R Probert, *Trusts Law*, 5th edn (Cambridge, Cambridge University Press, 2009) 216.

[36] J Martin (ed), *Hanbury and Martin: Modern Equity*, 19th edn (London, Thomson Reuters, 2012) 3–024; P Pettit, *Equity and the Law of Trusts*, 12th edn (Oxford, Oxford University Press, 2012) 56–57.

[37] *Inland Revenue Commissioners v Broadway Cottages Trust* [1955] Ch 20.

only has to deal with one trustee without worrying about the identity or the whereabouts of the lenders.

8.2.1.3.3 Certainty of Subject Matter

The third requirement of certainty, that of subject matter, is potentially more problematic, especially when applying a trusts analysis to securities held through an intermediary. The principle is discussed at this point, and its application discussed later on in the chapter.[38] The rule is that there cannot be a valid trust unless the subject matter of the trust can be identified.[39] The identification can be very wide, such as 'all my property', but any further act of appropriation cannot be left to be done by the trustee or a third party. The main difficulty, especially in the commercial context, arises where there is a defined pool of assets of which a part is declared to be held on trust. The argument is that there cannot be a valid trust, since it is not known which of the assets form the trust property. Thus, if A owns ten bottles of wine, he cannot declare himself trustee of five bottles of this wine for B, as it is not known which five bottles are held on trust for B.

Three cases are said to establish this proposition in relation to tangible assets, although only one in fact actually concerned a defined pool of assets. In *Re London Wine Co (Shippers) Ltd*,[40] a company which sold wine to customers buying for investment had granted a floating charge to a bank. The receiver appointed under that charge claimed that all the stocks of wine held by the company belonged to it and not to the buyers, and so were subject to the charge. No wine was ever appropriated to each customer and it was held that no property could therefore pass under a contract of sale because of section 16 of the Sale of Goods Act 1893.[41] The buyers also argued that the sellers held 'the wine that they had bought' on trust for them. This entailed arguing that the contract of sale manifested an intention to create a trust (which in itself was dubious) and that there was sufficient certainty of subject matter, on the basis that there was an identifiable mass and a declaration of trust of a quantitative interest within that mass. This argument was rejected as there was no ascertainable mass, since the company remained free to fulfil its contracts to the purchasers from any source.[42] The court said that even if there had been an identifiable mass, the declaration of trust could only have taken effect as a trust of the whole, giving effect to the proportionate interest of the beneficiary, so that, in the example above, A would hold all ten bottles of wine on trust for itself and B in equal shares.[43]

Similar reasoning applied in *Re Goldcorp Exchange Ltd*.[44] Here, customers bought gold from a company, and were led to believe that the company was storing gold in its vaults on their behalf. In fact it only stored enough gold to meet its commitments to deliver on a daily basis. Despite the customers' belief, it was clear from the contract that the sale was not out of an identified bulk, and the subject matter of the contract was therefore totally

---

[38] See 8.3.2.3.2.
[39] *Wright v National Westminster Bank plc* [2014] EWHC 3158 (Ch).
[40] [1986] PCC 121.
[41] Now Sale of Goods Act 1979, s 16, which states that when there is a contract of sale of unascertained goods, no property in goods is transferred until the goods are ascertained.
[42] *Re London Wine Co (Shippers) Ltd* [1986] PCC 121, 156. This was the ratio of the case.
[43] This possibility was not the case on the facts.
[44] [1995] 1 AC 74.

unascertained. As a result no property could pass when the contract was made,[45] nor was there any trust created when the company acquired gold from which it was going to fulfil its obligations (since there was no duty to fulfil any obligation out of the gold acquired: the company could have bought in more gold).[46]

The sale in the third case, *Re Wait*,[47] was out of an ascertained bulk, but since it was clear that property could not pass at law because of section 16 of the Sale of Goods Act, the claimants claimed that there had been an equitable assignment of part of the bulk.[48] This argument failed largely on the grounds that, where there was a contract for the sale of goods, the parties would not be taken to have intended to create equitable rights or interests in the absence of express words, especially where the creation of a legal interest failed.[49] Lord Hanworth, though, also said that the argument that there was an equitable assignment failed as the subject matter was not specific.

As can be seen, neither of the first two cases is direct authority for the proposition that there cannot be a declaration of trust of a certain number of goods out of a mass, since in neither case was there a defined mass. In fact, in both cases it was envisaged that such a trust could be declared,[50] although at least in *Re London Wine* it was envisaged that this would be a trust of the whole, held in proportionate shares. In *Re Wait*, there was no declaration of trust, nor could such a declaration be implied from the contract made. It is from these three cases, none of which is directly on the point, that the doctrine that it is not possible to declare a trust of a certain number of tangible objects out of a mass of such objects has developed. It is, though, possible for a trustee to hold a mass on trust for himself and/or others in undivided shares, that is, fractional interests in the mass.

The next series of cases involves intangible property. In *Hunter v Moss*,[51] A declared himself trustee for B of 5 per cent of the issued share capital of a company whose share capital consisted of 1,000 shares. A was the registered owner of 950 shares, so the declaration of trust was said to apply to 50 shares out of 950. Colin Rimer QC held at first instance that the trust did not fail for uncertainty of subject matter, and his judgment was upheld in the Court of Appeal. The first instance judgment is more detailed than that of the Court of Appeal, and the reasoning is easier to follow. It is based on there being a difference between a trust of tangible objects, which can be separated and which each have a different existence, and intangible assets, which cannot physically be separated or allocated, and so the requirement of certainty can be satisfied in a different way from that required in relation to tangibles. The requirement of certainty, the judge said, was based not on some immutable principle about allocation but on 'whether, immediately after the purported declaration of trust, the court could, if asked, make an order for the execution of the purported trust'.[52]

---

[45] Ibid, 91.

[46] Ibid, 96–97.

[47] [1927] 1 Ch 606.

[48] They also claimed specific performance, but this failed as the goods were not 'specific or ascertained' as required under s 52 Sale of Goods Act.

[49] Ibid, 636 (Atkin LJ).

[50] *Re Goldcorp Exchange Ltd* [1995] 1 AC 74. Lord Mustill said at 91: 'Their Lordships do not doubt that the vendor of goods sold ex-bulk can effectively declare himself trustee of the bulk in favour of the buyer, so as to confer pro tanto an equitable title.' See also *Re London Wine Co* [1986] PCC 121, 136–37.

[51] *Hunter v Moss* [1994] 1 WLR 452, upholding decision at first instance [1993] 1 WLR 934.

[52] [1993] 1 WLR 934, 945.

This was entirely possible: if the court had made such an order, 50 shares out of the 950 registered in A's name could have been transferred to B and registered in his name, and this would have executed the trust. B could not have complained that he had received the 'wrong' shares because the shares were completely indistinguishable from one another, not just contractually (as with bottles of wine, where delivery of any out of a mass might satisfy a contract of sale, but there might be real differences between them, in that one might be corked or have been stored badly and therefore have deteriorated)[53] but absolutely, so that it is not possible to separate one from another.[54]

The decision in *Hunter v Moss* has been subject to extensive criticism.[55] However, it was (rather unenthusiastically) followed in England in the subsequent case of *Re Harvard Securities Ltd*[56] and (more enthusiastically) in Hong Kong.[57] In the Australian case of *White v Shortall*, the question was considered at some length at first instance.[58] The judge supported the result in *Hunter v Moss*, though not the reasoning of the Court of Appeal. His process of reasoning is particularly interesting as he focuses on the nature of the property (shares). He points out that the choses in action which a shareholder has (and which therefore represent the value of his shareholding) are not necessarily divided up on a share-by-share basis. For example, in relation to the right to be paid a dividend he says:

> In that way, the chose in action—the thing that the law regards as a piece of property because it can be sued for—is the single right to be paid the dividend, the measure of which is the number of shares held.[59]

He then goes on to say:

> Given the types of rights that are involved in holding shares in a company, the way that rights of a shareholder need not be identified only in terms of owning particular identified shares, how identification of individual shares can be unimportant for a transfer of some of the shares in a shareholding, and how these particular shares in [the relevant company] were in any event not numbered and were held as an undifferentiated balance in a share register, there is nothing in the nature of the trust property that is inconsistent with recognising the validity of the trust.[60]

This argument reflects that which has been put forward for many years by Professor Goode;[61] namely that shares (and other intangible property) are not separate pieces of property, rather the number of shares is merely a way of determining the size of each shareholding. Thus, even the legal owner of shares does not own a number of separate pieces of

---

[53] Ibid, 940.

[54] See also Goode: Credit and Security, 6-14.

[55] P Pettit, *Equity and the Law of Trusts*, 12th edn (Oxford, Oxford University Press, 2012) 52; Hudson: Finance, 21.16–177; D Hayton, P Matthews and C Mitchell (eds), *Underhill and Hayton: Law of Trusts and Trustees*, 18th edn (London, LexisNexis Butterworths, 2010) 8.18–8.21. However, Martin in *Hanbury and Martin: Modern Equity*, 19th edn (London, Thomson Reuters, 2012) takes a different view at 3-022–3-023, arguing that the *Hunter v Moss* solution is 'fair, sensible and workable'.

[56] *Re Harvard Securities Ltd* [1997] 2 BCLC 369.

[57] *Re CA Pacific Finance Ltd* [2000] 1 BCLC 494.

[58] *White v Shortall* [2006] NSWSC 1379. As the discussion in the first instance judgment was strictly obiter, the point was not considered by the Court of Appeal of NSW, which dismissed the appeal at [2007] NSWCA 372.

[59] Ibid, [199].

[60] Ibid, [211].

[61] Goode: Credit and Security, 6-14. See also E Micheler, *Properties in Securities* (Cambridge, Cambridge University Press, 2007) 30; M Ooi, *Shares and Other Securities in the Conflict of Laws* (Oxford, Oxford University Press, 2003) 3–14.

property, but owns an undivided share in the share capital of the company. When a person is registered as the legal owner of 250 shares out of a share capital of 1,000, what he really owns is 25 per cent of the share capital.[62] If he declares himself trustee of 50 shares out of his 250 for B, the question 'of which shares is he the trustee?' does not arise. The position must be that he is holding 20 per cent of his 25 per cent for B, and therefore holds his 25 per cent for himself and B as tenants in common in the proportions 80 per cent to 20 per cent. A similar argument applies to debt securities.[63]

So far, the situation where a person declares a trust of part of his intangible property has been considered. It is more usual in commercial situations for either A to transfer property to B to hold on trust for C and D, or for C and D to transfer their property to B to hold on trust for them. As long as there is agreement that the property can be mixed, the analysis is very similar to that discussed above. In theory there is the possibility that B's own property could also be held as part of the mixture, although in practice there are usually regulatory restrictions on this.[64] In summary, there are a number of different ways of approaching the question of certainty of subject matter in the commercial context, each of which lead to a similar conclusion. These will now be examined in a little more detail.

One approach is that it is necessary for the trustee to declare that he is holding the property for the beneficiaries (which could include himself) in undivided shares as tenants in common.[65] There is no real doubt that this would be effective, though the question remains whether such a declaration would be implied if not express. It is very likely to be implied in commercial situations,[66] and the co-ownership analysis has been judicially accepted in a number of cases.[67]

A second approach is that discussed above, whereby shares, debt securities or parts of debts are characterised as fractional interests in the whole. This approach needs to be combined with the co-ownership analysis, since, in practice, each fractional interest acquires a history and if one is mixed with another, there has to be some explanation of why those histories are ignored: the co-ownership analysis provides this explanation.[68]

A third, rather different, approach is the argument that the purpose of the certainty rule is to enable the trust to be administered and executed, and so long as this is possible, then the requirement is fulfilled.[69] This view is consistent with a view of a trust as primarily concerning obligations in relation to property, rather than conferring equitable ownership

---

[62] Note that in *Hunter v Moss* [1994] 1 WLR 452, [1993] 1 WLR 934 '5% of the issued share capital' is used synonymously with '50 shares'.

[63] Goode: Credit and Security, 6-15.

[64] See CASS client money rules 7.4 and 7.13, and custody rules 6.2 (expressed in general terms rather than requiring segregation).

[65] See the approach suggested by Oliver J in *Re London Wine Co* [1986] PCC 121, 137.

[66] G Morton, 'Commentary on the Dematerialisation of Money Market Instruments' in S Worthington (ed), *Commercial Law and Commercial Practice* (Oxford, Hart Publishing, 2003);

[67] *In the matter of Lehman Brothers International (Europe) (In Administration)* [2009] EWHC 2545 (Ch) [56]; *Lehman Brothers International (Europe) (in admin)* [2010] EWCA Civ 917 [171]; *Re Lehman Brothers International (Europe) (in administration)* [2010] EWHC 2914 (Ch) [232], [2011] EWCA Civ 1544 [69] ff.

[68] Goode: Credit and Security, 6-14.

[69] This approach was taken by Campbell J in *White v Shortall* [2006] NSWSC 1379 and has a number of adherents, including S Worthington, 'Sorting Out Ownership Interests in a Bulk: Gifts, Sales and Trusts' [1999] *Journal of Business Law* 1, 18–20; P Parkinson, 'Reconceptualising the Express Trust' (2002) 61 *Cambridge Law Journal* 657; A Dilnot and L Harris, 'Ownership of a Fund' [2012] *Journal of International Banking and Financial Law* 272.

on the beneficiaries. Obviously, it is important to know in respect of which property the obligations are owed (otherwise the trust is no more than a contract); however, it is possible for the obligations to be owed in relation to part of a larger mass of property if the declaration of trust is sufficiently clear for the trustee to know what to do in any given circumstance,[70] for example, if he disposes of any of the mass, if profits accrue to the mass, or if a disposal is taxed.[71]

So far the discussion has been limited to the scenario where a trust is declared over a specified fund or account in which the intangible property remains static, or relatively static. Recent litigation has thrown up two other problems which have caused the law on certainty of subject matter to be examined. First, there is the situation, common where securities are held through intermediaries, where the trustee has the right to use the securities it holds for its own purposes so long as it replaces them with equivalent securities.[72] Such a 'right of use' has been held not to destroy the trust, and, when there are securities in the relevant account, they are held on trust despite the fact that they are not the original securities over which the trust was declared.[73] A trust can be validly declared over after-acquired property even if the trustee does not hold any property at all at the time of the declaration.[74] The important point is that the trust is declared over identified property (in this case, securities held within a particular account). A more difficult problem arises where a trust is declared over intangible property which is supposed to be segregated into an account but, in breach of trust, is not. Can property falling within the description still fall within the trust? This issue arose in the *Lehman* litigation in the context of the statutory trust over client money: Lehman had failed to segregate much of this client money but the Supreme Court held that the trust extended to identifiable client money even if it were not segregated and could not be traced.[75] This decision was, however, based on the purpose of the particular statutory scheme and the wording of the client money rules,[76] rather than laying down any general principles. Generally, if a person mixes property he holds on trust with his own, it remains trust property and can be traced,[77] but only if it can be identified according to the rules of tracing.[78] In that situation, the trustee holds the property (for example, a credit balance at a bank) partly for himself and partly for the beneficiaries rateably according to their contributions.

8.2.1.3.4 Equitable Nature of an Interest Under a Trust

An interest of a beneficiary under a trust is an equitable interest, and thus attracts certain rules which do not apply to ownership or other interests at law. One difference relates

---

[70] P Parkinson, 'Reconceptualising the Express Trust' (2002) 61 *Cambridge Law Journal* 674, 676.

[71] S Worthington, 'Sorting Out Ownership Interests in a Bulk: Gifts, Sales and Trusts' [1991] *Journal of Business Law* 18; *White v Shortall* [2006] NSWSC 1379 [251]–[263].

[72] See 4.6.4.

[73] *Re Lehman Brothers International (Europe) (in administration)* [2010] EWHC 2914 (Ch) [234], [2011] EWCA Civ 1544 [73]–[76].

[74] *Tailby v Official Receiver* (1888) 13 App Cas 523; *Re Lehman Brothers International (Europe) (in administration)* [2010] EWHC 2914 (Ch) [235].

[75] *Re Lehman Brothers International (Europe) (In Administration)* [2012] UKSC 6.

[76] Ibid, [159].

[77] *Foskett v McKeown* [2001] 1 AC 103, 110.

[78] For a summary of the rules of tracing, see Law of Personal Property, 15-136–15-170.

to formalities: transfer of an equitable interest must be in writing.[79] However, certain formalities which are necessary for a legal interest to be transferred (such as the registration of a transfer of shares at law) are not necessary in relation to the transfer of equitable interests. Another difference relates to priorities, namely that where an equitable interest is transferred to another who is unaware of an inconsistent equitable right or interest, the transferee does not take free of that right or interest, while the transferee of a legal interest in property (absolute ownership or a security interest) will take free if in good faith and without notice of the inconsistent equitable right or interest.

8.2.2 Agency

The concept of an agent is simple: it is a person who acts on behalf of another person so that the former can affect the latter's legal relations with third parties.[80] Unlike a trustee, the agent is not appointed in relation to any particular property, but the scope of his duties and powers is usually defined by an agency agreement, although it can also be wholly or partially implied from his situation, for example the nature of his employment. This scope is known as the agent's authority, and is important in two ways. First, we should consider the position as between the agent and his principal. If the agent acts outside his authority, he is in breach of contract and the principal can, in extreme cases, terminate the agency agreement. Second, we should consider the position between the agent and a third party, given that the main value of the concept of agency is that an agent can make binding contracts between the principal and third parties. Although any attempt to bind the principal to a contract in a way which is outside the agent's actual (express or implied) authority is, as between the agent and the principal, a breach of contract, it may nevertheless be successful in binding the principal to the third party. This would be the case if the principal had held the agent out as having authority (ostensible or apparent authority), and the third party had relied on that holding out, or if the principal had later ratified the unauthorised transaction. It is also possible for an agent to act on behalf of a principal without disclosing the fact that he is an agent: the principal will be bound where the agent acts within his authority and also, exceptionally, where the agent is in a position which would have given rise to apparent authority had the agent been disclosed.[81]

The position between the principal and the agent is of significance where an agent represents multiple lenders. Although the agent's authority and specific duties are defined by the agency agreement, there are certain duties which are inherent to agency, at least unless excluded by the agency agreement. Not only does an agent owe a duty of care and skill in performing his duties, but he is usually treated as a fiduciary. This has the effect that he owes a duty to his principal to act in good faith, and to avoid conflicts of interest both between his principal and any other principals he has, and between himself and his principal.

---

[79] Law of Property Act 1925, s 53(1)(c).
[80] P Watts (ed), *Bowstead and Reynolds on Agency*, 20th edn (London, Sweet & Maxwell, 2014) 1–003.
[81] *Watteau v Fenwick* [1893] 1 QB 346, although this decision has been much criticised.

8.3 Issue of Debt Securities[82]

It will be recalled from the discussion in chapter two[83] that debt securities are tradable instruments issued by a company to multiple lenders. They are tradable by nature, and are usually listed for trading on a public secondary market, although there is no requirement for them to be so. Debt securities can vary enormously in terms of the amount repayable, the term of repayment, whether and how interest is charged and so on.[84] There are also more complicated types of debt securities: those which are convertible into, or exchangeable for, equity securities,[85] those which are backed by assets,[86] and those which have equity-like features and are known as 'hybrids'.[87] The discussion in this chapter seeks to make general legal points about debt securities, although not every point will apply to every type. One crucial distinction is made, however: that between bonds (or notes) and stock.[88] These two types of securities are structured differently and so are subject to a different legal analysis in what follows.

8.3.1 Attracting Lenders

The first task in a securities issue is attracting lenders who are prepared to invest. Where the securities are listed on a regulated exchange, and sometimes in other circumstances, the process of eliciting lenders will attract regulatory supervision. Regulation of debt is dealt with in chapter thirteen and what follows is merely a short description of the varieties of process by which buyers of debt securities are found.

There are two main ways in which bond issues are sold: either by a single stand-alone issue, or under a 'programme'. Short-term securities such as commercial paper are nearly always issued under a programme,[89] and it is also common for longer-term notes to be issued in this way.[90] In a progamme, the documentation for a series of issues is drafted and agreed in advance, so that each issue only requires very limited documentation.[91] Stand-alone issues require full documentation for each issue, and are therefore more expensive and time-consuming. They are rarely used for plain 'vanilla' issues—rather they are used for more complicated issues, such as convertible or high-yield bonds requiring more negotiation.[92] Domestic stock is issued in a different way again, the most common method being a 'placing', which is a one-off process, and which can also be used for bonds.[93]

---

[82] For an analysis of the history of the international bond market see Bamford: Financial Law, ch 6.
[83] 2.3.3.
[84] The varieties of debt securities are discussed at 2.3.3, especially 2.3.3.5.
[85] See 2.4.
[86] See 2.3.3.5.
[87] 2.4.
[88] For discussion of this distinction see 8.3.2.1.
[89] Known as an ECP programme; see Fuller: Capital Markets, 1.172 ff.
[90] Known as an EMTN programme; see ibid, 1.105 ff.
[91] This has many similarities with a revolving loan facility: see above and Hughes: Banking, 4.8.
[92] M Doran, D Howe and R Pogrel, 'Debt Capital Markets: An Introduction' (2005) 16 *Practical Law Company* 21, 23–24. For a description of high-yield bonds, see 2.3.3.3.
[93] See 10.3.2.2 for a discussion of placing in relation to shares.

The basic ideas behind all issues of debt securities are the same. One or more investment banks organise the issue for the issuer: these are called 'arrangers'[94] or 'managers'[95] or 'dealers'.[96] These banks will advise the issuer on the best market for the securities. In terms of the primary market, this means whether they should be offered only to a small number of selected institutions or more widely, and in terms of the secondary market, it means whether they should be listed and admitted to trading on one of the financial markets. There is often one lead bank, which does most of the administration, but several other banks will join with the lead bank in underwriting the issue,[97] that is, agreeing to buy the bonds if no one else will, usually with a view to selling them on to investors quickly, or, alternatively, agreeing to buy all the bonds in any event, so that they can subsequently sell them on to investors.[98] This is an incentive on the banks to try to find investors, and to advise accurately on the price and terms that the market will bear.[99] By this means the issuer knows that it will obtain the financing represented by the bond issue. This, however, comes at a price, and the investment banks are well paid for taking on the underwriting risk.[100]

The most important documents are also common to all procedures. First, a mandate letter appoints the lead manager(s) or arranger. This may follow a period of bidding, where potential managers compete for the position by setting out their credentials and their suggested terms for the issue. The lead manager(s) will then prepare for the launch, by discussing with the issuer the details of the terms of the securities, and by deciding whom to appoint as trustee. At the launch, the issue is announced to potential co-managers, who will buy or underwrite the issue, and potential investors. Next comes the subscription agreement, which is an agreement between the issuer and the managers[101] including representations and warranties from the issuer and an agreement from the managers to subscribe to, or to procure others to subscribe to, the issue. The liability of the managers under this agreement is usually joint and several, so that any one of them might be liable to buy the whole issue if the other managers all fail and there are no investors.[102]

There will also be an agreement between the managers, setting out the obligations of each of them. The issue will be marketed to investors by the managers by means of an offering circular or prospectus. This is the document which must comply with the regulatory requirements, which are set out in chapter thirteen.[103] It will contain information, often prescribed

---

[94] Usually in relation to stock: Fuller: Corporate Borrowing, 13.3.

[95] Generally in relation to stand-alone issues; see Fuller: Capital Markets, 7.02.

[96] Generally in relation to programmes: see ibid.

[97] For a discussion of underwriting in relation to equity securities see 10.3.2.1.

[98] This is termed a 'bought deal'. See P Wood, *Law and Practice of International Finance* (London, Sweet & Maxwell, 2008) 11–33; Fuller: Capital Markets, 7.17. If the on-sale is to a small group of selected investors, this will be a 'private placing'.

[99] Hudson: Finance, 34-07.

[100] In early 2015 the FCA consulted on, inter alia, competition in this sector and its effect on pricing; while at the time of writing (mid-2015) the study is not yet finished, there seems to be little evidence of overpricing. See www.fca.org.uk/your-fca/documents/feedback-statements/fs15-02 and www.fca.org.uk/news/fca-publishes-terms-of-reference-investment-corporate-banking-market-study.

[101] In relation to stock this is called a placing agreement. In relation to a programme, the equivalent document is the programme agreement, but under this agreement the dealers only agree to subscribe on an uncommitted basis, so that there will be a subscription agreement for each issue as well; Fuller: Capital Markets, 7.06–7.08; M Doran, D Howe and R Pogrel, 'Debt Capital Markets: An Introduction' (2005) 16 *Practical Law Company* 21, 24.

[102] Hudson: Finance, 34-17.

[103] 13.2.

by regulation, about the issuing company and the issue itself. Other documentation which must be prepared includes the trust deed (if there is a trustee), agreements with paying and/ or fiscal agents[104] and the bond itself.

The details of the process vary according to the type of issue. With stock, a placing takes place in one day (the 'impact' day) with one arranger sending provisional invitation letters and preliminary offering circulars to potential buyers in the morning. The stock is priced later in the day on the basis of the response, and formal documents are sent out the following morning.[105]

In a stand-alone issue of eurobonds,[106] a lead manager will be appointed and the issue is launched. At this point, the preliminary offering circular is sent to potential investors and also to other potential managers (who will underwrite the issue). The price may either be specified by the issuer when appointing the lead manager, or be determined after feedback from potential investors and managers: the former is now much more common than the latter except for specialised issues.[107] The next stage is the signing of the subscription agreement, after which the sales to investors are confirmed, as are the listing and the rating (if the issue is listed and/or rated). The issue is then closed, at which time the final documents are produced, the global note is delivered to the depositary[108] and the price is paid by the buyers, via the paying agent,[109] to the issuer. In a programme issue, the general process is the same, but the offering circular and other major documentation are agreed and signed when the programme is set up, so for each issue only the price and other key terms need to be agreed and documented.

There is a danger, when a new issue of securities is launched on the market, that the price will be very volatile in the period after the launch. This is often because those who initially bought the securities (such as the managers or initial investors) may offload securities onto the market to make a quick profit, or because they have initially asked for more securities than they actually want. In order to combat such volatility, the lead manager may buy a large number of securities in the market, thus artificially pushing up the price. This process is called 'stabilisation'. It will enable itself to do this by allotting to the managers more securities than are actually being issued. The managers will not be aware of this, or, at least, not of the extent of over-allotment. The lead manager will then be able to 'buy back' the over-allotted securities before the issue is closed. This creates an artificial demand and drives up the price which otherwise would be depressed by the large amount of sales by the managers.[110] The main problem with stabilisation is that it is likely to fall foul of the statutory provisions against market abuse.[111] Since stabilisation is seen as a beneficial activity, safe harbours have been created from the market abuse offences. These are discussed in chapter thirteen.[112]

Part of the process will usually involve the rating of the issue by a rating agency.[113] The rating of the bond will affect its status (as investment grade or high yield), and

---

[104] See 8.3.2.3.1(a) and 8.3.2.3.3.

[105] Fuller: Corporate Borrowing, 13.3.

[106] For detailed description see ibid, 13.5–13.8; Wood: Loans and Bonds, 10-035; Fuller: Capital Markets, ch 7; Tolley's Company Law Service B5049–5052; M Doran, D Howe and R Pogrel, 'Debt Capital Markets: An Introduction' (2005) 16 *Practical Law Company* 21, 24.

[107] Fuller: Capital Markets, 7.16–7.19.

[108] See 8.3.2.3.2(b).

[109] See 8.3.2.3.2(a).

[110] For a full description of stabilisation see Fuller: Corporate Borrowing, 13.71–13.73; Fuller: Capital Markets, 7.199–7.205.

[111] See 12.2.

[112] 13.4.1.

[113] See 2.3.3.3 and 13.7.

therefore its price and its terms. While a company can have a rating dependent on its own creditworthiness which is irrespective of the terms of a particular bond issue (an 'issuer rating'),[114] it is also possible for there to be a rating for a particular issue of bonds, taking into account the terms of the issue, including credit enhancement.[115] The terms of the bond are then influenced by the likely rating, and there may even be negotiation between the issuer or its advisors and the rating agency.

The process will often also include an application for listing on a stock exchange, so that the bonds can be traded on a public market.[116] Not all bonds are listed,[117] but listing has certain advantages for the issuer. It provides a wider market for the bonds, including, in theory, the public. However, in order to escape certain regulatory requirements,[118] very few bonds are actually offered to members of the public; rather they are limited to sophisticated investors such as pension funds and investment funds. Much of the trading of bonds is actually done off the market (or 'over the counter' (OTC)), but many institutional investors are not permitted, either by law or by their own prudential guidelines, to invest in non-listed securities.[119] Therefore many issues are listed, although traded OTC. In addition, listing gives a benchmark price for OTC, which can be helpful to investors.[120] Further, a 'quoted eurobond', which is one that is listed on a recognised stock exchange, is exempt from the requirement to withhold tax at source when interest is paid: this is very important for investors, who would otherwise receive a heavily reduced interest payment.[121] The disadvantages of listing are the regulatory requirements, which apply not only at the listing stage but throughout the life of the bond.[122] These not only add to the expense, but are time-consuming and may delay an issue, which makes it difficult to take advantage of favourable market conditions.[123]

8.3.2 Structure of Securities Issue

8.3.2.1 Difference Between Bonds and Stock

One of the fundamental distinctions in relation to debt securities is that between bonds[124] and stock.[125] Loan stock is issued by a company to the domestic market, and comprises

---

[114] See Fuller: Capital Markets, 1.187.

[115] Ibid, 1.186.

[116] The two debt securities markets on the London Stock Exchange are the Gilt Edged and Fixed Interest Market (GEFIM), which is a regulated market, and the Professional Securities Market (PSM), which is an unregulated market. See chapter 13.

[117] For example, commercial paper is rarely listed: M Doran, D Howe and R Pogrel, 'Debt Capital Markets: An Introduction' (2005) 16 *Practical Law Company* 21, 25.

[118] See chapter 13.

[119] Wood: Loans and Bonds, 10-039; Hudson: Finance, 34-41.

[120] Wood: Loans and Bonds, 10-039.

[121] Income Tax Act 2007, s 882; Inland Revenue CTM35218.

[122] These are discussed in chapter 13.

[123] Wood: Loans and Bonds, 10-040.

[124] The term 'bonds' is used here to cover bonds of all types of maturity, including commercial paper and medium-term notes: see 2.3.3 for discussion of the different terms.

[125] See Fuller: Corporate Borrowing, 3.3–3.5. For further discussion of the differences see Fuller: Capital Markets, 1.171 ff.

just one debt obligation, held either by a trustee or created by deed poll. As it is a single obligation, it can be split up into as many parts as there are people who want to hold it (though not in units of less than £1). Loan stock originated as a debt structure seen as similar to shares,[126] and is usually long-term indebtedness which is traded in a similar way to shares.[127] Bonds (or notes), in contrast, are individual debt obligations owed by the company to each holder. Bonds of this structure were originally only issued for the international market (as eurobonds), but the bond structure is now commonly used for domestic issues as well.[128]

Another important difference between the two is that stock is usually in registered form, while bonds are usually bearer instruments.[129] This is because, in the past, this enabled the identity of the bond investor to be kept secret from the issuer.[130] This distinction is best understood by looking at the position in the UK before dematerialisation of securities.[131] The title to registered securities was derived from the register kept by the issuer, which was evidenced by a certificate issued to the holder. In order to transfer registered securities, it was necessary to execute a stock transfer form, and deliver this to the issuer together with the certificate. The issuer would then amend the register. The actual piece of paper (the certificate), however, did not give the holder any particular rights, unlike a bearer security, which is owned by the holder and transferable by delivery.[132]

Although it is in theory possible for this situation to arise today, it is unlikely. Registered securities are now usually held in dematerialised form through the CREST system.[133] Thus, stock is usually now held through CREST, although it is still possible to hold it in certificated form. Bonds can still be held as bearer bonds, but the cost of producing individual definitive notes[134] and the requirements of the US securities laws have led to them almost always being issued as global notes.[135] This means that, at least initially, only one note is issued representing the whole of the bond issue. It is held in a depositary on behalf of Euroclear (in Belgium) and/or Clearstream (in Luxembourg), which are the two major international central securities depositaries (ICSDs) in Europe.[136] The holders of the bonds are account holders with Euroclear or Clearstream (or hold through account holders who act as

---

[126] Bamford: Financial Law, 6.19.

[127] Butterworths Corporate Law Service CAF 16.17.

[128] Fuller: Corporate Borrowing, 3.2.

[129] Now, bonds are usually issued as global bearer notes. However, they are also sometimes issued in registered global note form—see 8.3.2.3.2(b). This is more likely where they are intended to be bought by US buyers, in order to comply with US tax regulations (see Fuller: Capital Markets, 13.10; Wood: Loans and Bonds, 11-008).

[130] M Doran, D Howe and R Pogrel, 'Debt Capital Markets: An Introduction' (2005) 16 *Practical Law Company* 21.

[131] Dematerialisation was brought about by the Uncertificated Securities Regulations 2001 (SI 2001/3755) (USR).

[132] A bearer instrument is likely to be a negotiable instrument, where the bona fide transferee gets a better title than the transferor; see 9.2.3.

[133] For an account of the CREST system see 4.6.2.

[134] These have complicated and expensive security features, since, as bearer securities, possession of the note confers ownership and all the rights of a holder.

[135] M Doran, D Howe and R Pogrel, 'Debt Capital Markets: An Introduction' (2005) 16 *Practical Law Company* 21; Tolley's Company Law Service B5034; Fuller: Corporate Borrowing, 1.222.

[136] It is also possible for registered securities to be held through Euroclear or Clearstream: see Fuller: Capital Markets, 1.122. The holding system and the rights of bondholders who hold through intermediaries is discussed in detail at 8.3.2.3.2(b).

intermediaries), and the securities are transferred through the clearing systems operated by those companies. Securities issued as bearer securities can also be held through CREST,[137] and this is common for money market instruments such as commercial paper.

It is now common for securities of all types to be held through an intermediary rather than directly by the owner.[138] One reason for indirect holding is, as indicated above, because a bond is issued in global form and so is held by the legal owner for the account holders. Another reason is that intermediation itself brings benefits. These include ease of settlement and transfer,[139] the use of local intermediaries in cross-border investment,[140] and services provided by the intermediaries, such as management services or financial services.[141] The legal analysis of indirect holding of securities is discussed in the context of bond issues below.[142]

In the future, securities which are traded on trading venues[143] will be obliged to be either dematerialised, or immobilised and held through intermediaries (both known as holding in 'book-entry' form)[144] in order to improve the efficiency and integrity of the settlement system.[145]

8.3.2.2 Stock

There are two possible structures for the holding of stock, both of which are consonant with it being just one single debt owed by the issuing company. The first is that the debt is owed to a trustee, and the second is that the debt is contained in a deed poll.

8.3.2.2.1 Debt Owed to a Trustee

Where there is a trustee of the stock, it[146] holds the benefit of the covenant to pay on behalf of the stockholders. No direct covenant to pay principal or interest is made with the stockholders, which means that a stockholder is not a creditor of the company.[147] The stockholders, even collectively, can have no legal title to the debt, but it is held for them as beneficiaries under a trust, so that they become equitable co-owners of the debt which they

---

[137] Tolley's Company Law Service, C4009, 4015. In order for a bearer security to become dematerialised, it in effect becomes a registered security, since the root of title becomes the CREST register: USR, regs 24(2) and (3).

[138] See 4.6.4.

[139] This is discussed at 9.2.6.2.

[140] Benjamin: Financial Law, 8.68.

[141] The provision of finance by an intermediary for the investor to buy the securities is one of the chief reasons for the prime brokerage agreement, whereby the intermediary makes an advance to the investor to buy the securities, which it (the prime broker) then holds on the investor's behalf subject to a security interest to secure the advance. See S Worthington and I Mitchkovska, 'Pitfalls with Property Claims: Lehman Bros Again' [2009] *Journal of International Banking and Financial Law* 321.

[142] See 8.3.2.3.2(b), and for discussion of the transfer of intermediated securities see 8.2.5.

[143] These are MTFs and OTFs; see 13.3.1.

[144] Regulation (EU) No 909/ 2014 on improving securities settlement in the European Union and on central securities depositories, art 3. This will apply from 1 January 2023 to transferable securities issued after that date and from 1 January 2025 to all transferable securities (Regulation (EU) No 909/ 2014, art 76).

[145] Ibid, recital 11.

[146] As in most of the situations described in this chapter, the trustee (or agent) is likely to be a department of a bank or other financial institution; thus the pronoun 'it' will be used.

[147] And therefore cannot petition for its winding up for non-payment of interest: *Re Dunderland Iron Ore Company* [1909] 1 Ch 446, 452.

hold as tenants in common in proportion to the amount of stock they own.[148] However, it is the stockholders who are entered on the register of holders kept by the company[149] and issued with certificates (if the stock is certificated) which evidence the holder's equitable interest. Moreover, the trust deed normally provides that the company recognises the holder as absolute owner of the stock.[150] If the stock is dematerialised and is admitted to CREST, a similar register is kept in the CREST system.[151]

The fact that the stockholders' interest is an equitable interest has various consequences, some of which have been mentioned above. One is that any transfer of an equitable interest has to be in writing.[152] This requirement is disapplied when securities are transferred through the CREST system.[153] Another is that a stockholder can grant only an equitable and not a legal mortgage of his stock.[154] Normally, having an equitable mortgage could present a problem to the mortgagee, since it would lose priority to a subsequent legal mortgagee.

However, since it is not possible to grant a legal mortgage, any subsequent mortgage would also be equitable, and so the first equitable mortgagee would always have priority on the grounds of being first in time.[155] Also, a transferee of stock, even if without notice, in theory takes subject to any equitable rights or interests affecting that stock.[156]

Stock can be structured in this way whether or not the company's covenant to pay is secured, but where there is security, it will be granted to the trustee to hold on behalf of the stockholders. Secured loan stock is usually called debenture stock (although this term can also be used for unsecured stock).[157] In either case, it is the trustee that has the power to enforce the covenant to pay, and also enforce the security, if any. The stockholders cannot enforce directly, but they have the power to force the trustee to enforce on their behalf, and, if he will not do so, to bring an action themselves under the *Vandepitte* procedure[158] so long as they join the trustee as co-defendant.[159] The advantages of having a trust structure as opposed to a deed poll are in many ways similar to those in relation to a eurobond issue, which are discussed below.[160]

---

[148] Goode: Credit and Security, 6-14. This satisfies any requirement as to certainty of subject matter of the trust. It is also inevitable, since there is only one obligation. No question of ascertainment of separate units can therefore arise; see 8.2.1.3.3.

[149] Note that this is different from the position in relation to shares, since no notice of a trust can be entered on the register of members of a company: Companies Act 2006, s 126 (although new provisions in the Small Business, Enterprise and Employment Act 2015 make some changes to this regime: see 4.5).

[150] Tolley's Company Law Service C4002.

[151] USR, reg 22 and Sch 4 para 14.

[152] Law of Property Act 1925, s 53(1)(c).

[153] USR, reg 38.

[154] Tolley's Company Law Service C4006, which explains that if the stock is transferred into the name of the mortgagee in the stock register, this has an effect very like a legal mortgage, because of the provision in the trust deed that the company recognises the registered holder as owner.

[155] See 7.4.4, where the relevant priority rules are discussed. The proposition in the text is potentially qualified by the application of the rule in *Dearle v Hall*, but this is unlikely to affect the result. See discussion in Tolley's Company Law Service C4029/2 and 9.2.6.1.

[156] This will rarely cause problems in practice. See the discussion at 9.2.6.1.

[157] Butterworths Corporate Law Service CAF 16.17.

[158] [1933] AC 70. For discussion of the *Vandepitte* principle, see 9.2.2.6.5(b).

[159] Tolley's Company Law Service C4002.

[160] 8.3.2.3.1.

8.3.2.2.2 Debt Contained in a Deed Poll

An alternative way to structure stock is by means of a deed poll. A deed poll is an instrument executed by one party which contains a promise that can be enforced by anyone who is benefited by the promise.[161] Thus, the company executes a deed making a promise to pay those registered as holders of the stock, which is enforceable by whoever are the holders from time to time. Although enforceable rights can now be conferred on third parties to a contract under the Contracts (Rights Against Third Parties) Act 1999, a deed poll is still significant in that it is unilateral, whereas the Act only applies to contracts made between two or more people.[162] Although it is possible to transfer stock issued by deed poll, this structure tends to be used for larger denominations of stock, where there will not be many holders and where there is not an active market. For smaller denominations, where there are many holders and an active market, the trustee structure is usually used.[163]

8.3.2.3 Eurobonds

Although this section is headed 'Eurobonds', the structure discussed is that of bonds and notes of all maturities, including short-term notes such as commercial paper. The term 'bonds' will be used throughout, unless the context demands otherwise. As mentioned above, bonds are usually bearer instruments, and, for the purpose of initial analysis, it is worth considering the position where individual bearer securities are issued, although this is very unlikely in practice, since normally a global note is issued. Each bearer security constitutes an independent debt and promise to pay the bearer.[164] This obligation is 'locked up' in the document (and passes by delivery of the document): the bond is a documentary intangible.[165] Therefore, each holder is the legal owner of the bond and the obligation locked up in it. A bearer bond is transferable by delivery and there seems little doubt that a bearer bond is a negotiable instrument.[166] Since a bond issue involves multiple lenders, the problem of coordination, and the difficulties of collective action identified earlier, arise. These are dealt with structurally in one of two ways: either a fiscal agent is appointed, or there is a trustee.

---

[161] *Moody v Condor Insurance Ltd* [2006] 1 WLR 1847 [16]; *Global Distressed Alpha Fund 1 Ltd Partnership v PT Bakrie Investindo* [2011] EWHC 256 (Comm) [7].

[162] Fuller: Corporate Borrowing, 3.8. However, if the person making the obligations intends a deed to operate as a deed poll, it will be held to do so, despite the fact that there are in fact two or more parties to the deed: *Moody v Condor Insurance Company Ltd* [2006] 1 WLR 1847, following *Chelsea and Walham Green Building Society v Armstrong* [1951] 1 Ch 853.

[163] Butterworths Corporate Law Services CAF 16.231–16.232.

[164] In a typical issue, this covenant is qualified by the bearer's promise not to enforce the issuer's debt unless the trustee refuses to sue. The question of whether the bearer can actually enforce this covenant is discussed at 8.3.4.2.3.

[165] For a discussion of documentary intangibles generally, see Goode: Commercial Law, ch 18; in relation to bearer bonds, see 611–15.

[166] See 9.2.3.

8.3.2.3.1 Advantages and Disadvantages of the Trustee Structure

8.3.2.3.1(a) Difference Between a Fiscal Agent and a Trustee Structure

There are a number of advantages to using a trustee structure, from the perspective of both the bondholders and the issuer.[167] A fiscal agent structure is cheaper, though, and is used extensively in issues of short-term securities (such as commercial paper) and plain 'vanilla' issues.[168] The main difference between a fiscal agent and a trustee is that the fiscal agent acts on behalf of the issuer, while the trustee acts on behalf of the bondholders, to whom it owes fiduciary duties. The primary function of the agent is to make payments on the bonds to the bondholders, and thus it is common for there to be a paying agent even where there is a trustee.[169] A trustee has a much more extensive role, as it is acting as the representative of all the bondholders and therefore its role includes taking all the steps one would expect a single lender to take to protect its interests. The trustee has a monitoring role,[170] is expected to consider the seriousness of events of default and, if the default is serious enough, can accelerate and enforce payment of the bonds. The trustee is also able to negotiate restructuring on behalf of the bondholders, and is able to agree minor modifications to the terms of the issue during the life of the bonds.[171]

8.3.2.3.1(b) Advantages and Disadvantages of a Trustee for the Bondholders

For the bondholders, the main advantage is having an expert person to deal with the issuer. A bond trustee will be a specialist corporate trustee[172] and will be in a position to evaluate financial information produced by the issuer. Moreover, the presence of a trustee means that the issuer is more likely to agree to disclose confidential information, when it will only be seen by the trustee. It will also be more likely to agree to include in the documentation covenants which require expert evaluation, such as financial ratio covenants, or which require a decision to be made, such as whether a breach is 'material'.[173] As we shall see, the obligations on a trustee to monitor are limited, but even so the trustee is more likely to be aware of financial difficulties or a default at an earlier stage than individual bondholders would be: this enables action to be taken which can either aid restructuring of the debt or facilitate orderly enforcement. In the case of restructuring, the trustee will be in a stronger position to negotiate than any individual bondholder, as it represents a large amount of debt. It will, however, need authority from the bondholders to agree any major

---

[167] See generally Fuller: Corporate Borrowing, 213–14; Fuller: Capital Markets, 3.73–3.76; Wood: Loans and Bonds, 16-002–16-005; Tennekoon: International Finance, 247; C Duffett, 'Using Trusts in International Finance and Commercial Transactions' (1992) 1 *Journal of International Trust and Corporate Planning* 23; P Rawlings, 'The Changing Role of the Trustee in International Bond Issue' [2007] *Journal of Business Law* 43; Financial Markets Law Committee, Issue 62, *Trustee Exemption Clauses*, 16–17.

[168] M Doran, D Howe and R Pogrel, 'Debt Capital Markets: An Introduction' (2005) 16 *Practical Law Company* 21, 24.

[169] Fuller: Corporate Borrowing, 3.02–3.04.

[170] Though note the limitations of this; see 8.3.4.2.2.

[171] See 8.3.4.2.1.

[172] As opposed to an agent, which will usually be a bank. Fuller: Capital Markets, 3.06.

[173] Wood: Loans and Bonds, 16-002.

changes. This will necessitate arrangements for obtaining the consent of a majority of the bondholders, which can either be contained in the original documentation or set up after the event.[174] Furthermore, since it is the trustee who decides when to accelerate payment on default,[175] a trustee will be in a position to waive or take no action on a minor breach. This prevents one or two 'mad bondholders' from enforcing their rights to the detriment of all the others as well as the issuer,[176] since acceleration is likely to trigger cross-default clauses in other agreements, which is likely to push the issuer into insolvency. Having a trustee also makes enforcement easier, since it is the trustee who has the right to bring enforcement proceedings: this is cheaper and more convenient where there are numerous and dispersed bondholders, and preserves the anonymity of bondholders.

Bolstering the trustee's position in relation to acceleration and enforcement is the 'no-action' clause, which provides that no bondholder can enforce its rights against the issuer unless the trustee has been directed to do so and has taken no action.[177] The other advantage brought by the no-action clause is that the proceeds recovered on enforcement are distributed rateably, as no bondholder can gain more by being the first to sue.[178]

Interestingly, the development of this clause, and the analogous clause in syndicated loans, the 'pro rata' clause, is evidence that there is substance behind the theoretical argument justifying the *pari passu* rule in insolvency: in collective situations, parties really will bargain for a pro rata distribution to avoid the race to the courtroom door, as each, when behind a veil of ignorance, will rationally perceive it to be the best outcome for it in all possible worlds.[179] Where the issuer is not in difficulties, but a change in circumstances make it desirable for a change to be made to the terms of the issue, a trustee can agree to minor changes without troubling (or having to find) the bondholders,[180] who generally do not take much interest in the administration of the bond issue, provided that the payments are made on time and the issuer is not in financial difficulties.[181]

Having a trustee poses some disadvantages for the bondholders. There is some rather minor expense. More significantly, there is a general loss of control, since the advantages listed above can only be given effect to by giving the trustee discretion to act without consulting the bondholders at every turn. Further, negotiation and restructuring on default,

---

[174] R Karia and K Hargreaves, 'Negotiating with Bondholders' [2009] *Journal of International Banking and Financial Law* 259. See 8.3.3.

[175] Subject to the power of the bondholders, if acting by a large majority, to direct acceleration if the trustee refuses to do so: see 8.3.3.

[176] It should be pointed out that such bondholders are not necessarily mad; it may be quite rational in terms of its own interests to accelerate although harmful to the collective interests of the bondholders and to the issuer. For examples of such situations see P Rawlings, 'The Changing Role of the Trustee in International Bond Issue' [2007] *Journal of Business Law* 43, 47. For further discussion of the 'no-action' clause and its use in dealing with the 'mad bondholder' problem, see 8.3.4.2.3.

[177] There is no need to use the *Vandepitte* procedure here, as there is in the case of stock (see 8.3.2.2.1), as the bondholder will have an independent obligation owed to it, albeit qualified by the no-action clause: see below.

[178] Wood: Loans and Bonds, 16-002.

[179] T Jackson, *The Logic and Limits of Bankruptcy Law* (Cambridge, MA, Harvard University Press, 1986) ch 1.

[180] See 8.3.4.2.1.

[181] R Karia and K Hargreaves, 'Negotiating with Bondholders' [2009] *Journal of International Banking and Financial Law* 259.

which are facilitated by the presence of a trustee, are not necessarily always beneficial to the bondholders, who may consider that they are better off being paid (although they will only get paid in full if the issuer is solvent).[182] Obviously, the advantages of a trustee for bondholders are greatest where the bondholders are numerous and diverse, as the problems of collective action are very great, as well as where there is no desire on the part of holders to expend their own resources on the protection of their economic interest in relation to the bond (although, of course, the trustee has to be paid). While it used to be compulsory for an issue of domestic bonds which was listed on the London Stock Exchange to have a trustee,[183] this is no longer the case.

8.3.2.3.1(c) Advantages of a Trustee for the Issuer

The presence of a trustee can also have advantages for the issuer. These advantages stem largely from the convenience of dealing with one person rather than a large number, such as the ability to agree minor modifications with the trustee alone, the ability to negotiate with the trustee alone in the event of rescheduling, and only having to deal with one person enforcing the bonds. Further, the no-action clause gives the issuer considerable protection against the 'mad bondholder' problem: an acceleration by a single bondholder on the basis of default may harm the interests of the other bondholders, but it will be even more disastrous for the issuer, as it is likely to lead to its insolvency. Many eurobond issues also permit the trustee to agree that another entity be substituted as the debtor in place of the issuer:[184] this may be desirable, for example, for tax reasons.[185]

8.3.2.3.1(d) Security Trustees

There is one situation in which the advantages of having a trustee are overwhelming: where security is given for the obligation to pay. While this is not common in eurobonds, it is fundamental to other structures, such as securitisation and project finance. If security had to be given to each bondholder, not only would this be expensive and complicated at the start, but each time a bond was transferred to another holder, a new security interest might have to be granted.[186] Further, the trustee can enforce on behalf of all the bondholders. These benefits stem from the fact that it is possible to have a trust with a changing group of beneficiaries,[187] so that the trustee holds the trust property for those who are bondholders for the time being. The free tradability of the bonds is thereby preserved. Other advantages include common terms for all secured creditors, and more efficient administration of subordination, for example turnover trusts.[188]

---

[182] Wood: Loans and Bonds, 16-002 points out that this disadvantage, if it is such, is often overcome by the creation of a committee of bondholders.

[183] Hudson: Finance, 34-22.

[184] Fuller: Corporate Borrowing, 12.8.

[185] Wood: Loans and Bonds, 16-003.

[186] P Rawlings, 'Reinforcing Collectivity: The Liability of Trustees and the Power of Investors in Finance Transactions' (2009) 23 *Trust Law International* 14, 24. See also 9.2.4.2.4 (in relation to syndicated loans).

[187] See 8.2.1.2.

[188] Hughes: Banking, 13.10–13.12.

8.3.2.3.2 Subject Matter of the Trust[189]

This section considers what it is that is held on trust by the bond trustee. It starts from the simplest case: that of a bearer bond. It then moves on to consider the more common holding pattern for bonds, where the bond is issued as an immobilised global note. This discussion inevitably involves consideration of what a bondholder owns under such a structure, and this will be discussed in some detail.

As noted earlier in the chapter, the most distinctive feature of the trust is that the obligations of the trustee are owed in relation to property. This is true of even the most 'obligation-centred' view of trust,[190] otherwise a trust would be indistinguishable from a contract. Whether a trust deed is also a contract is a matter which we will consider later,[191] but the argument that it is in no way detracts from the need for there to be some property as the subject matter of a trust. In a secured bond issue, there is no problem: the subject matter of the trust is the security interest granted to secure the issuer's obligations. However, in an unsecured bond issue there is no such obvious answer. One view is that the trustee does not hold assets like an ordinary trustee, but instead has a collective delegation of authority from the bondholders[192] or is a fiduciary representative of the bondholders.[193] This view contradicts the orthodox notion of a trust, and would appear to make the 'trustee' merely a fiduciary agent of the bondholders, whose authority could be revoked by any bondholder at any time, and who therefore could not be relied upon to bind all the bondholders when waiving the right to accelerate on breach.[194] It is, however, unnecessary to take such a radical view since, as will be discussed in the next paragraph, there is something which can be the subject matter of the trust.

8.3.2.3.2(a) Bearer Bonds

Let us start with the simpler position where individual bearer securities are issued. Here the issuer makes separate promises to pay to all the bondholders, but also a parallel covenant to the trustee, which is satisfied by payment made to the bondholders.[195] It is not the case that the trustee holds the promises to the bondholders on trust for them: this would reduce their interests to equitable interests, which would prevent the bonds being negotiable instruments.[196] However, the trustee can hold the parallel covenant made to it

---

[189] For an interesting discussion of this and the other difficulties in seeing the bond trusteeship as an orthodox trust, see A Hudson, *The Law on Investment Entities* (London, Sweet & Maxwell, 2000) ch 6.

[190] See P Parkinson, 'Reconceptualising the Express Trust' (2002) 61 *Cambridge Law Journal* 657; see also 8.2.1.3.3.

[191] See 8.3.5.

[192] Goode: Commercial Law, 166; P Rawlings, 'The Changing Role of the Trustee in International Bond Issue' [2007] *Journal of Business Law* 43, 48.

[193] P Wood, *Law and Practice of International Finance* (London, Sweet & Maxwell, 2008) 9.12(3)(b). However, Professor Wood's views have changed: see Wood: Loans and Bonds, 16-013. See also S Schwartz, 'Commercial Trusts as Business Organisations: Unravelling the Mystery' (2003) 58 *Business Lawyer* 559, 569 in relation to the US position.

[194] Tennekoon: International Finance, 227, who also takes the view that a no-action clause would be ineffective on termination of authority.

[195] Or payment to the paying agent who will then pay the bondholders: Wood: Loans and Bonds, 16-13; Fuller: Capital Markets, 3.44.

[196] Goode: Commercial Law, 614; Tennekoon: International Finance, 226; Fuller: Corporate Borrowing, 3.10.

on trust for the bondholders.[197] This makes sense: the trustee's obligations all relate to the protection of that covenant for the benefit of the bondholders, since the 'no-action' clause means that it is enforcement by the trustee which is the bondholders' route to protecting their economic interest in the bond. The structure might be seen as a little artificial or even circular, in that the covenant is given to the trustee merely so that it can hold it on trust for the bondholders, and the trustee's covenant is valuable to the bondholders purely because they agree not to enforce their own covenants unless the trustee unreasonably refuses to enforce its own covenant (which it holds on trust for the bondholders).[198] It is no more artificial, however, than many other structures, and at least it is consistent with the usual understanding of trust law. One might ask why it is necessary for the bondholders to have their own covenants: why is the transaction not structured like stock, where there is only one covenant made to the trustee? The answer is that, when bonds were issued as bearer bonds, it was seen as very important that bondholders had legal title to the bond. This was partly because legal title was necessary for the bond to be a negotiable instrument, partly because disposal of an equitable interest would require writing,[199] and partly because, as it was to be traded on the international markets, the bondholders' title would need to be recognised in countries which did not recognise or understand equitable interests.[200]

One potential difficulty with this analysis, pointed out by Tennekoon,[201] is that the promise made by the issuer to the trustee is an asset of which only the trustee can declare a trust, since the issuer is the debtor. If the trust deed (executed by the issuer) declares that the trustee holds this covenant on trust for the bondholders, is this sufficient to create a valid trust? Tennekoon's view is that such a trust should be valid,[202] but that it would be safer for the trustee itself to declare the trust. This is achieved in practice by including an express declaration of the trust in the trust deed, to which the trustee is a party.[203]

8.3.2.3.2(b) Global Notes

The current position, though, is that bonds are no longer individual bearer securities, but are constituted by a global note, which is held by a depositary (usually a bank) for a clearing

---

[197] Wood: Loans and Bonds, 16-013; Fuller: Corporate Borrowing, 3–10; Tennekoon: International Finance, 226; Hudson: Finance, 34-28. This trust is usually expressly declared in the trust deed: see Tolley's Company Law Service B5050.

[198] It would be possible to see the no-action clause as a contractual version of the *Vandepitte* procedure (based on *Vandepitte v Preferred Accident Insurance Corporation of New York* [1933] AC 70, 79) whereby the beneficiaries of a trust have the right to bring an action, joining the trustee as defendant, if the trustee unreasonably refuses to enforce the trust (see 9.2.2.6.5(b) and Fuller: Capital Markets, 1.148 and 3.45). However, this seems to assume that the trustee holds the bondholders' rights on trust as well as its own, which, for the reasons given in the text, it is argued is not the case.

[199] Hudson: Finance, 34-28. This is a not a problem with stock as registration provides the necessary writing, and the section is disapplied to CREST transfers. See 8.3.2.2.1.

[200] Tennekoon: International Finance, 226.

[201] Ibid, 226–27.

[202] There is authority for such a declaration of trust in *Fletcher v Fletcher* (1844) 4 Hare 67, although whether there was actually intention to create a trust of the promise in that case is open to doubt; see J Martin (ed), *Hanbury and Martin: Modern Equity*, 19th edn (London, Thomson Reuters, 2012) 4–020. The view expressed by Hanbury and Martin is that where there is consideration for the promise, the relevant intention to create a trust is that of the promisee, while if the promise is voluntary, the intention of the promisor will suffice.

[203] Tolley's Company Law Service B5050.

system (one or both of Clearstream and Euroclear: the ICSDs).[204] The global note is usually in the form of a bearer bond,[205] although sometimes a registered security is used: in this case all that is registered is the name of the nominee for the depositary to whom the bond is payable.[206] The note will include provision for the issue of definitive securities in certain situations, such as an event of default by the issuer or the closure of the clearing system.[207]

The precise nature of the relationship between the depositary and the ICSDs depends on whether the Classic Global Note (CGN) structure or the New Global Note (NGN) structure is used. In the CGN structure the depositary would be a commercial bank, which could be anywhere in the world.[208] The European Central Bank (ECB), which provides liquidity for banking operations in the Eurozone, and which regularly takes debt securities held as global notes as collateral, was concerned that the CGN system was not robust enough, particularly in the case of the insolvency of a depositary which might be situated outside the Eurozone.[209] As a result, the NGN system was introduced for bearer notes;[210] this is compulsory if the securities are to constitute eligible collateral for Eurosystem operations.[211] In this structure there is no depositary as such; the global note is held by a 'common safe-keeper' and the payment and other functions previously carried out by the depositary will be carried out by a 'common service provider'. The ICSD will usually be both the common safekeeper[212] and the common service provider.[213] One other change is that under the CGN structure the note showed the amount of indebtedness,[214] while under the NGN structure the indebtedness is recorded by reference to the records of the ICSDs.[215]

The ICSDs hold the global note for their account holders, which are banks. Sometimes an account holder will hold for itself, but in most cases it will hold as an intermediary for the ultimate bondholder.[216] Bondholders' rights therefore derive either from an entry in the books of the ICSD or from an entry in the books of an intermediary.[217] Trading of bonds takes place through the clearing system, again by entries in the relevant books. It is clear, then, that the bondholders do not have legal title to the bond in the way described above in relation to bearer bonds.

---

[204] See 8.3.2.1.

[205] See below for discussion of whether it is a negotiable instrument.

[206] Bamford: Financial Law, 6.62 fn 28. Registered notes are used where there are potential US buyers; see n 130.

[207] Fuller: Capital Markets, 1.127; M Doran, D Howe and R Pogrel, 'Debt Capital Markets: An Introduction' (2005) 16 *Practical Law Company* 21. The problems caused by the absence of definitive securities are discussed below and at 8.3.3.3.

[208] For a description of a CGN structure see *Secure Capital SA v Credit Suisse AG* [2015] EWHC 388 (Comm) [6]–[22].

[209] Bamford: Financial Law, 6.67–6.71.

[210] From 1 January 2007. A new safekeeping structure (NSS) was introduced for global registered notes from 30 June 2010. See J Machin, 'Registered Notes: ECB Eligible Collateral and the Proposed New Safekeeping Structure' [2010] *Journal of International Banking and Financial Law* 53.

[211] Guideline (EU) 2015/510 of the ECB of 19 December 2014 on the implementation of the Eurosystem monetary policy framework (ECB/2014/60), art 66(3)(a). Article 66(3)(b) provides that, to be eligible collateral, registered notes must be issued under the NSS structure.

[212] The actual function will be carried out by the ICSD's nominee.

[213] In order to constitute eligible collateral as above, both the common safekeeper and the common service provider must be one of the ICSDs.

[214] With provision to amend this if definitive securities were issued to any bondholders.

[215] See ICMA, New Global Note structure FAQs (January 2007), www.icmagroup.org/assets/documents/NGN004%20FAQ.pdf.

[216] It is of course possible for there to be a chain of intermediaries; see below.

[217] The holding of securities in this way is known as holding them in 'book-entry form'.

In thinking about the legal analysis of the relationships just described, it must be borne in mind that each component could be governed by a different law. For example, while it is quite common for the notes themselves to be expressly governed by English law,[218] the two ICSDs are located in Luxembourg and Belgium, and a depositary may be situated in another country, so the law relating to the relationship between these parties or to the proprietary rights may well not be English law.[219] For the purposes of analysis here, though, it will be assumed that English law applies to all components of the structure.

There are two possible analyses of the relationship between the depositary and the ICSDs in a CGN structure. Which possibility is correct in any given case may well depend upon the terms of the documentation. One analysis is that the depositary holds the obligation contained in the global note on trust for the ICSD(s). This would be on the basis that the depositary is treated by the issuer as the person entitled to receive payment (this is usually stated on the face of the security itself)[220] and since the security is a bearer security it makes sense for the holder to be the legal owner. The other possibility is that the depositary holds the global note as bailee for the ICSD(s), which then hold it on trust for the investors.[221] It is necessary, though, to consider whether the global note is an instrument in the sense that the obligation contained in it is owed to the holder as possessor of that instrument, rather than for any other reason.[222] It is reasonably clear that it is not a negotiable instrument, since it is intended to remain with the depositary and not to be transferred.[223] It is certainly assumed in the market, however, that there can be a 'holder' of the global note who is entitled to payment,[224] and this is reflected in the documentation, which usually provides that only the 'holder' is entitled to payment,[225] with the depositary being seen as 'holder'.[226] In many situations, the bond itself, or the programme under which it is issued, provides that the depositary is the owner of the global note,[227] by which is meant that the contractual obligation is owed to the depositary.[228] Thus, the analysis that this obligation is held on trust for the ICSD(s) seems preferable. It also makes more sense when the depositary holds the single global note for both ICSDs.

In the NGN structure, the status of the global note as an instrument is even more problematic, at least where the common safekeeper is the ICSD itself.[229] There will then be a

---

[218] Although the issuer would be free to choose whatever law it wanted.

[219] Note, though, that a claim characterised as a claim on the contract could be governed by English law and not by the law of the ICSD; see *Secure Capital SA v Credit Suisse AG* [2015] EWHC 388 (Comm).

[220] Fuller: Capital Markets, 1.132.

[221] Benjamin: Financial Law, 8.71.

[222] Goode: Commercial Law, 513.

[223] Ibid, 615. For more detailed discussion see Bamford: Financial Law, 6.81–6.90. Bamford's conclusion goes further: his view is that the note is not an essential element of the debt obligation and is merely evidence of it and serves to identify the payee.

[224] *Secure Capital SA v Credit Suisse AG* [2015] EWHC 388 (Comm) [9].

[225] Fuller: Capital Markets, 1.132.

[226] The question of who is the holder of eurobonds is discussed in Tennekoon: International Finance, 171–76, where the author reaches no firm conclusion. However, it should be noted that the bulk of his discussion concerns bearer bonds which are held by the depositary and not a permanent global note.

[227] *Secure Capital SA v Credit Suisse AG* [2015] EWHC 388 (Comm) [15]; *In the matter of Castle Holdco 4 Limited* [2009] EWHC 3919 (Ch) [22].

[228] *Secure Capital SA v Credit Suisse AG* [2015] EWHC 388 (Comm) [55].

[229] Bamford: Financial Law, 6.125 ff. There could be two ICSDs in this structure, but this paragraph considers the position where there is only one.

direct contractual relationship between the issuer and the ICSD, and the legally relevant record of the indebtedness of the issuer is maintained by the ICSD.[230] Under this structure, it seems even more appropriate that the ICSD is the legal owner, since it will usually hold the global note as common safekeeper. Even if it does not, it makes sense for the common safekeeper to be merely a bailee of the piece of paper. If the note is not an instrument, the true value is in the contractual obligation, which is owed to the ICSD.

In order to simplify the analysis in the next few paragraphs, it will be assumed that the ICSD is the legal owner of the obligation contained in the global note.[231] The ICSD holds the obligation on trust for all those with accounts with it in relation to securities from that particular issue. If an account holder is an intermediary, it will hold its beneficial interest on trust for its own account holders, who may be the ultimate bondholders or may be intermediaries themselves. This structure of sub-trusts is the best way under English law to explain the relationships in the holding of intermediated securities,[232] since an important feature of a sub-trust is that the sub-beneficiary only has rights against its immediate sub-trustee and not against the trustees higher up the chain.[233] In the context of intermediated securities, this is known as the 'no look through principle' and is often expressly provided for in the documentation.[234] This principle is important given that trading systems operate by trading taking place at the lowest level, so that higher-level intermediaries have no knowledge of those holding accounts with lower-tier intermediaries. The 'no look through' principle has recently been reinforced in the case of *Secure Capital SA v Credit Suisse AG*,[235] where the court denied an investor who held notes through an intermediary the right to sue the issuer for breach of the terms of the notes.[236]

The other important feature of the trust structure is the persistence of the beneficiary's interest against all others, except a bona fide purchaser of a legal interest without notice, including the insolvency officer of the trustee: in the present context this means that those

---

[230] See European Central Bank press release, 13 June 2006, www.ecb.europa.eu/press/pr/date/2006/html/pr060613.en.html.

[231] This will almost certainly be the case in an NGN structure. Under the CGN structure, it is likely that the depositary will be the legal owner, as discussed above.

[232] For detailed discussion of the position in English law in relation to intermediated securities, see Benjamin: Interests in Securities; R Goode, 'The Nature and Transfer of Right in Dematerialised and Immobilised Securities' [1996] *Journal of International Banking and Financial Law* 167; Law Commission, 'The UNIDROIT Convention on Substantive Rules regarding Intermediated Securities: Further Updated Advice to the Treasury' (May 2008); Goode: Credit and Security, ch 6; L Gullifer, 'Protection of Investors in Intermediated Securities' in J Armour and J Payne (eds), *Rationality in Company Law* (Oxford, Hart Publishing, 2009); L Gullifer and J Payne (eds), *Intermediated Securities: Legal Problems and Practical Issues* (Oxford, Hart Publishing, 2010) chs 1, 2 and 3. The structure described in the text now has judicial approval: see *Re Lehman Brothers International (Europe) (in administration)* [2010] EWHC 2914 (Ch) [226]; *Re Lehman Brothers International (Europe) (in administration)* [2012] EWHC 2997 (Ch) [163].

[233] *Hayim v Citibank NA* [1987] AC 730.

[234] *Secure Capital SA v Credit Suisse AG* [2015] EWHC 388 (Comm) [15]. This approach has been criticised on the grounds that it fails to protect the interests of investors, since intermediaries can exclude their liability to their own clients. See E Micheler, 'Intermediated Securities and Legal Certainty', LSE Working Paper 2014, www.lse.ac.uk/collections/law/wps/WPS2014-03_Micheler.pdf.

[235] [2015] EWHC 388 (Comm).

[236] See also *Eckerle v Wickeder Westfalenstahl GmbH* [2013] EWHC 68 (Ch), where shareholders holding through an intermediary (which was an account holder with Clearstream) were held not to be 'holders' for the purposes of s 98 Companies Act 2006, which permits 5% or more of holders to apply to court to cancel a resolution to delist a company.

ultimately beneficially entitled to the bonds (that is, investors) are protected against the other creditors of anyone higher up in the chain who might become insolvent. It can therefore be seen that the features of the trust discussed above[237] make it an important and useful concept in the modern methods of holding securities, designed to speed up the processes of issuance and trading.

So far we have considered the position in relation to the obligation of the issuer contained in the global security, so that what is being held on trust is the ICSD's right to sue the issuer. This right is likely to be very limited, however, because of the 'no-action' clause.[238] The important right to enforce is that of the trustee, which has its own separate covenant.[239] If, as we concluded earlier, it is this right that is the subject matter of the trust of which the bond trustee is trustee, who is the beneficiary where there is a deposited global note? Again, the best analysis appears to be that the trustee holds this right on trust for the legal owner of the global note, which then holds this interest on trust for the account holders, in addition to holding its own right to sue on trust.[240]

In order for the trust structure to work, the certainty requirements of a trust[241] need to be considered. First, is there sufficient intention to create a trust? This is likely to be expressed in documentation, but if not it will nearly always be implied, given the enormous benefits of the trust analysis and the judicial approval.[242] Secondly, is the subject matter of the trust sufficiently certain? Although the entire issue is now represented by a global security, the entitlement of individual investors is still described in money denominations. Thus, an investor can buy any number of bonds from one issue at, say, £100,000 par value from an issue of 1,000. However, where the issue is represented by one global bond, the ICSD holds the single obligation represented by the bond on trust for all the account holders as co-owners, despite the convenience of the issue being split up into denominations. This overcomes the problem of identification of subject matter when the securities are held in a pooled account, although in fact it would be the case even if the ICSD (or other intermediary) held each account holder's securities in a separate account: the interest of the account holder is of its nature a co-ownership interest, that is, a one-thousandth share of the entire issue. In practice, such securities are always held in pooled accounts, as this facilitates dealing.[243] The trust analysis, of course, is specific to English law, but the problem of identification is universal. If Belgian or Luxembourg law applies, for example, account holders are in a similar position, but without using the concept of trust: they have a proprietary co-ownership right which is proportionate to the credit of securities in their account.[244]

In practice, the clearing systems (and maybe the depositary) will be in jurisdictions which are not governed by English law, and under whose law there is no concept of trust. The problems caused by cross-border holdings of intermediated securities are outside the scope

---

[237] See 8.2.1.2.

[238] See 8.3.4.2.3.

[239] See 8.3.2.3.2(a).

[240] Hudson: Finance, 34-29.

[241] 8.2.1.3.

[242] See eg *In the matter of Lehman Brothers International (Europe) (In Administration)* [2009] EWHC 2545 (Ch) [56].

[243] Benjamin: Interests in Securities, 19-06. See 4.6.4.

[244] Tolley's Company Law Service C401.

of this book, but have been much discussed.[245] The latest attempt to deal with such issues is the UNIDROIT Convention on Substantive Rules regarding Intermediated Securities 2009 (the 'Geneva Securities Convention'),[246] which, if adopted by the relevant countries, would provide some uniformity of rules in relation to such securities. The specific issue of the obligations of bond trustees, however, is not addressed directly by this Convention. Generally, the exact analysis and classification of the obligations owed by participants in the intermediation process might be seen as less important than having a system which works efficiently and well. However, it is critical that the rights and obligations of all parties are clear and certain in the global markets, where huge amounts of securities are bought and traded. The Convention addresses this issue of certainty at an international level. Until it is adopted, however, and even if it is, a robust domestic analysis is also necessary to provide that certainty.

What is it, then, that the investor in a eurobond represented by a global note actually has? It has a beneficial co-ownership interest in the obligation represented by the global note, which is held by the ICSD as trustee pooled with other co-ownership interests. The interest of the account holder is a proprietary interest vis-a-vis the ICSD (and thus survives its insolvency) but is an interest in a contractual right against the issuer.[247] The investor may hold through another intermediary (which itself has an account with the ICSD) and in this case the investor has a beneficial interest, via a sub-trust, in the beneficial interest that its intermediary has.[248] The investor has no direct relationship with the issuer, although it may have a right (through the layers of intermediaries) to call for a definitive bond in certain circumstances.[249] In the absence of other arrangements,[250] the investor cannot, therefore, sue the issuer direct for non-payment, or for any other breach of the contract contained in the note.[251] The investor has to proceed against its intermediary, which will then have to sue up the chain. Furthermore, the bond trustee holds the covenant made to it on trust for the ICSD,[252] which holds that beneficial interest also on trust for the account holders. The investor's interest in the bond trustee's covenant is thus held under a sub-trust. If this is correct, then, technically, it is the ICSD that should give instructions to the trustee in relation to all matters where the trustee requires consent, and to whom the trustee's duties are owed. This, of course, makes no sense in that it is the ultimate investors who have the economic

---

[245] See Hague Convention on the Law Applicable to Certain Rights in Respect of Securities Held with an Intermediary 2006 ('Hague Securities Convention'); L Gullifer and J Payne (eds), *Intermediated Securities: Legal Problems and Practical Issues* (Oxford, Hart Publishing, 2010) especially chs 1, 2 and 9; P Paech, 'Intermediated Securities and Conflict of Laws' http://papers.ssrn.com/sol3/papers.cfm?abstract_id=2451030; F Garcimartin and F Guillaume, 'Conflict of Laws Rules' in T Keijser (ed), *Transnational Securities Law* (Oxford, Oxford University Press, 2014).

[246] For discussion see Gullifer and Payne, ibid. For further discussion of the Geneva Securities Convention and (so far) abortive plans for an EU Securities Law Directive, see P-H Conac, U Segna and L Thevenoz, *Intermediated Securities* (Cambridge, Cambridge University Press, 2013) and also T Keijser (ed), *Transnational Securities Law* (Oxford, Oxford University Press, 2014).

[247] The bondholder is thus exposed to the credit risk of the issuer, but not the credit risk of the ICSD.

[248] See Hughes: Banking, 4.3–4.4, who makes the point that this is a long way from the bearer bond and the basic concept of a negotiable instrument. How this affects trading of securities is discussed at 9.2.6.2.

[249] R Goode, 'The Nature and Transfer of Rights in Dematerialised and Immobilised Securities' [1996] *Journal of International Banking and Financial Law* 17.

[250] See 8.3.2.3.3.

[251] *Secure Capital SA v Credit Suisse AG* [2015] EWHC 388 (Comm).

[252] Or the depositary if it is the holder and holds on trust for the ICSD.

interest in the proper performance of the trustee's duties, so provision has to be made in the trust deed to deal with this issue.

First, the deed is likely to provide that, if a bond is held through an ICSD, a trustee must consider the interests of the account holders rather than the depositary or the clearing system.[253] Secondly, the bond itself or the trust deed may provide that account holders shown in the records of an ICSD will be treated as holders for the purposes of giving instructions to the trustee.[254] Alternatively, the depositary or ICSD is treated as the holder, and itself sets up a system for ascertaining the instructions of the account holders, which it passes on to the trustee.[255] The powers and duties of the trustee and the way in which the balance between discretion and direction from the bondholders is struck are considered below.[256]

8.3.2.3.3 Bond Issue Without Trustee

Despite the advantages of having a trustee, discussed above, some debt securities are issued without a trustee. Various administrative tasks will still be undertaken by agents:[257] this is often the case even if there is a trustee. At the very least there is likely to be a fiscal agent, who is responsible for making payments to bondholders.[258] Since any agents appointed are agents of the issuer and not of the bondholders, if the bonds are individual bearer securities there is a direct relationship between each bondholder and the issuer, which is enforceable by each bondholder. Where a global note is immobilised, however, the same structure applies as discussed above, so that the interest of each bondholder is a beneficial co-ownership interest under a trust. Enforcement therefore presents a problem, since the depositary or ICSD will be the only party entitled to enforce, on the instructions of all the bondholders. Without more, an individual bondholder will not be able to enforce on its own.

The way to overcome this is for the issuer to execute a deed poll at the time of issue, assuming a direct obligation to pay the bondholders if a default occurs. As was pointed out earlier in the context of stock,[259] a deed poll enables the issuer to undertake unilateral obligations which can be enforced by persons who are not a party to the deed.[260] In this context, however, the obligation owed to the bondholder arises at the moment of default, rather than at the time of issue, which may well be at a point when the issuer is insolvent and may even be once insolvency proceedings have started.[261] An alternative analysis, put forward by

---

[253] Financial Markets Law Committee, Issue 62, *Trustee Exemption Clauses* (2004), 27, sample clause at 1.1.12. However, this does not deal with the situation where the account holder is itself an intermediary and holds for the ultimate investor.

[254] E Cavett and J Walker, 'New Issues for Trustees in the Credit Crunch' [2009] *Journal of International Banking and Financial Law* 215. Such a provision is called a 'look through' provision: Fuller: Capital Markets, 15.19.

[255] Fuller: Capital Markets, 15.19. The way in which the instructions of the bondholders are ascertained is discussed at 8.3.3. A further alternative, mainly used in the US, is for the registered holder to issue an omnibus proxy to the trustee or paying agent, who then issues sub-proxies to account holders, who can issue them to their account holders and so on: C Maunder, 'Bondholders' Schemes of Arrangement: Playing the Numbers Game' [2003] *Insolvency Intelligence* 73, 74; Fuller: Capital Markets, 15.21.

[256] 8.3.3.

[257] For a full account of the tasks agents often undertake, see Fuller: Capital Markets, 3.13–3.37.

[258] Where the bond issue is represented by a global note, the depositary or ICSD is very often appointed as a fiscal or paying agent: Fuller: Capital Markets, 3.20.

[259] 8.3.2.2.2.

[260] Fuller: Capital Markets, 1-129.

[261] Hughes: Banking, 4.11; Tolley's Company Law Service B5038.

Martin Hughes, is that the Contract (Rights of Third Parties) Act 1999 can be used, so that the bond can provide that the benefit of the obligation owed to the holder (the depositary or ICSD) is enforceable by the bondholders as a class.[262] Another possibility would be for the bondholder to call for the issue of a definitive security, which is a right usually exercisable in the event of a continuing default.[263]

It is also necessary to have a system in place to deal with any modifications the issuer wishes to make to the terms of the securities. Such modifications potentially affect all bondholders, and so each should have the opportunity to express a view as to whether they should be allowed. As will be seen later, where there is a trustee, it will be given powers to agree to minor modifications.[264] Where there is no trustee it is common for a fiscal agent to have similar but more limited powers.[265] However, with regard to more far-reaching modifications, the bond will provide that the bondholders' views are expressed through the requirement for majority approval at a bondholders' meeting, which will now be discussed. The following discussion applies both to issues where there is a trustee and to issues where there is not: in the former case any resulting decision will constitute instructions to the trustee to act, rather than approval direct to the issuer.

8.3.3 Ascertaining the Views of Holders[266]

8.3.3.1 *The Decision-Making Process*

Where there are multiple lenders there is always the danger that a course of action which is in the interests of some will not be in the interests of others. Although there has to be a decision-making process, it must include some protection for those who might be disadvantaged by the proposed course of action. This is the case whether the proposed action relates to modification of the terms of the issue, to acceleration or enforcement, or to restructuring within or outside insolvency. In relation to decisions outside insolvency proceedings, the bond or the trust deed will normally specify that decisions shall be taken at a bondholders' meeting. All bondholders are entitled to attend, and there will be a procedure for giving notice,[267] thus protecting the opportunity of all to take part in the decision-making process. Where bonds are held through a clearing system, notice is given through that system. Bondholders can attend the meeting or appoint a proxy.[268] Since most bonds

---

[262] Hughes: Banking, 4.14. It is not clear, however, that this would work where the right is conferred unilaterally by the issuer rather than as a result of agreement between two parties, and because of this doubt, the deed poll remains the most popular method used in practice (Fuller: Capital Markets, 1-129 fn 2) and the Contracts (Rights of Third Parties) Act 1999 is usually excluded (Fuller: Capital Markets, 1-152).

[263] Fuller: Capital Markets, 1-127. It is one of the functions of a fiscal agent to receive the definitive security from the issuer and to pass it on to the bondholder: Fuller: Corporate Borrowing, 3.19. For the relevance of this right to voting in a scheme of arrangement, see 8.3.3.3.

[264] See 8.3.4.2.1.

[265] Fuller: Corporate Borrowing, 14.04, 14.09.

[266] This discussion also applies to stock. For detailed discussion of the meeting of holders, see Fuller: Capital Markets, 15.10–15.38.

[267] Fuller: Capital Markets, 15.24. Where the securities are listed, LR 17.3.10 and 17.3.12 prescribe certain matters which must be included in the notice.

[268] Note that the Standard Provisions for Meetings and Voting in relation to notes/bonds recently produced by the International Capital Market Services Association include provision for electronic voting; see www.icmsa.org/news/111/59/.

are easily traded without the knowledge of the issuer, notice might be given to the wrong party. To ensure that those voting are entitled to vote, where the bonds are held through a clearing system the holder has to 'block' its account. In the case of bearer bonds, the holder must either produce them at the meeting or, if appearing by proxy, deposit the bonds with the paying agent until the meeting is completed.[269] This system ensures that those voting are those entitled to vote, although in the case of bonds held indirectly it only works in relation to the account holders at the ICSDs, who may themselves be intermediaries for investors or for other intermediaries. Unless the blocking system works all the way down the chain, there is no guarantee that the ultimate beneficial owners of the bonds are actually those giving voting instructions: whether this is the case will depend on the position between each intermediary and its clients.[270]

The interests of bondholders are also protected by both quorum and majority requirements. A meeting is only valid if the quorum requirements are met: these vary according to the type of business, but most require a quorum of a majority, with changes to fundamental terms (known as entrenched terms) requiring a higher number, which can be as much as 75 per cent.[271] In each case, the numbers are calculated on the nominal amount of bonds held by those present, in person or by proxy.[272] A resolution will be binding if 75 per cent of those present vote in favour.[273]

8.3.3.2 Protection of the Minority

It is very important, in order that decisions can be made and a course of action taken, that the majority of voting bondholders can bind the minority. However, this has to be tempered by protecting the minority against oppressive conduct by the majority. Thus, it is well established in case law[274] that the majority must act in good faith[275] and for the purpose of benefiting the class of bondholders as a whole.[276] This is similar to the obligation owed by shareholders to one another when voting to change the articles of association.[277] This obligation is not as onerous as it might sound, since it is recognised that not all bondholders will have identical interests, and each is entitled to vote according to its own interests.[278] Since it takes effect as an implied term qualifying the contractual provision that the majority

---

[269] E Cavett and J Walker, 'New Issues for Trustees in the Credit Crunch' [2009] *Journal of International Banking and Financial Law* 215; Fuller: Capital Markets, 15.28, 15.30.

[270] For discussion of similar issues in relation to shares, see 11.2.2.1.2.

[271] See Fuller: Corporate Borrowing, 14.34; Wood: Loans and Bonds, 16-043.

[272] There may in fact only be one person present, since where the bonds are held through a clearing system and the depositary or ICSD is treated as holder, its representative will be the only person voting, although in accordance with the account holders' wishes.

[273] Lower percentages to quorum and majority apply to meetings adjourned for lack of quorum. In practice, the combination of quorum and majority percentages mean that quite a low percentage of holders can bind a majority: see R Wedderburn-Day and P Phelps, 'The Enfranchisement of Bondholders in the Marconi Schemes of Arrangement' [2003] *Journal of International Banking and Financial Law* 421.

[274] Briggs J traced the principle back to Justinian's *Institutes*: see *Assénagon Asset Management SA v Irish Bank Resolution Corporation Ltd* [2012] EWHC 2090 (Ch) [41].

[275] *Goodfellow v Nelson Line (Liverpool) Ltd* [1912] 2 Ch 324, 333.

[276] *British America Nickel Corporation Ltd v MJ O'Brien* [1927] AC 369, 371; *Greenhalgh v Arderne Cinemas Ltd* [1951] Ch 286, 291, which, although it related to shareholders, was applied to syndicated loans in *Redwood Master Fund Ltd v TD Bank Europe Ltd* [2002] EWHC 2703 [84]. See also *Law Debenture Trust Corporation plc v Concord Trust* [2007] EWHC 1380 [123].

[277] *Allen v Gold Reefs of West Africa Ltd* [1900] 1 Ch 656. See generally 3.2.

[278] *Goodfellow v Nelson Line (Liverpool) Ltd* [1912] 2 Ch 324, 333.

can bind the minority, it is subject to qualification by the express terms of the contract.[279] The position is very similar to that relating to syndicated lenders[280] and the principle established in *Redwood Master Fund Ltd v TD Bank Europe*[281] applies here, namely that where the documentation specifies different classes of lenders there is no need for each to vote in the interests of the lenders as a whole so long as they act in good faith. One possible difference, however, is that the difficulties of coordination among bondholders are even greater than among syndicated lenders. Bondholders may have little or no idea who the other bondholders are, and information as to their identity and their voting intentions is hard to obtain. On the other hand, it should be remembered that there are few retail bondholders in the UK, and that most are institutional investors who are repeat players and who are in a position, if they wish to do so, to talk to other institutional investors and even form bondholder committees and pressure groups.[282]

Ascertaining the views of holders, and making decisions about how to proceed, are issues that are particularly troublesome in the context of restructuring bond issues. Although major decisions require the calling of a meeting and formal resolutions, in complicated transactions trustees like to consult bondholders on a more informal basis, and there is increasing use of bondholder committees to sound out views more informally.[283]

Various techniques have developed to encourage, and even coerce, bondholders to vote in favour of an issuer's proposal for modification or restructuring, even when it does not necessarily appear to be in their interests to do so. Some of these techniques seek to exploit the lack of coordination and information just mentioned. The techniques were first developed in the US, where it is necessary to obtain unanimous consent in order to amend terms affecting the rights of bondholders to interest and capital:[284] this has resulted in some creditors using 'hold-out' strategies to prevent restructuring.[285] These techniques have survived judicial scrutiny in the US.[286] They are also used in the UK to obtain the necessary consents in order to effect a consensual restructuring, rather than having to use formal insolvency proceedings. While these techniques can be beneficial in facilitating such restructuring, the UK courts have taken a stricter line than in the US.

---

[279] *Assénagon Asset Management SA v Irish Bank Resolution Corporation Ltd* [2012] EWHC 2090 (Ch) [46]. The contractual power of the majority may also be reduced by construction of agreement; see *Mercantile Investment and General Trust Co v International Company of Mexico* [1893] 1 Ch 484, 489.

[280] 8.4.4.

[281] [2002] EWHC 2703.

[282] See R Peel, 'Assessing the Legality of Coercive Restructuring Tactics in UK Exchange Offers' (2015) 4 *UCL Journal of Law and Jurisprudence* 162, 171. Some institutional investors in the UK have formed the Bond Covenant Group, which has produced a model set of covenants: see 3.2.2.3.

[283] E Cavett and J Walker, 'New Issues for Trustees in the Credit Crunch' [2009] *Journal of International Banking and Financial Law* 215; R Karia and K Hargreaves, 'Negotiating with Bondholders across Multiple European Jurisdictions: What Are the Key Issues?' [2009] *Journal of International Banking and Financial Law* 259, 261; M Dakin, F Diminich, P Hertz and G Ruiz, 'Getting into Bed with Bondholders' [2012] *Corporate Restructuring and Insolvency* 120, 121.

[284] Trust Indenture Act 1939, s 316.

[285] See R Peel, 'Assessing the Legality of Coercive Restructuring Tactics in UK Exchange Offers' (2015) 4 *UCL Journal of Law and Jurisprudence* 162, 163.

[286] See the two cases in the Delaware courts: *Katz v Oak Industries Inc*, 508 A.2d 873 (1986); *Kass v Eastern Airlines Inc* [1986] WL 13008.

One technique is for the issuer to offer a payment to all bondholders who consent to the restructuring. This was considered in the case of *Azevedo v IMCOPA*,[287] where the Court of Appeal rejected an argument that it amounted to bribery, since the offer was fully disclosed and open to every bondholder to accept.[288] A more contentious technique, considered in the case of *Assénagon Asset Management SA v Irish Bank Resolution Corporation Limited*,[289] is that of 'exit consent', which is used to procure consent to an exchange of existing bonds for new ones on different terms, which are less favourable, at least to some. Bondholders who agree to exchange their bonds are required to vote for a resolution to amend the bonds of those who do not vote in favour to make them much less valuable or worthless.[290] This technique exploits the coordination problem and raises a 'prisoner's dilemma'.[291] The best outcome for a bondholder would be if he refuses to exchange and the majority does the same, and the worst would be if he refuses to exchange and a majority agree to exchange, as his bond would then be worthless. If the bondholder agrees to exchange, the best outcome applies if the majority refuse to exchange; if the majority agree to exchange, the bond-holder's bonds, while less valuable than before, would not be worthless. Since no individual bondholder knows how the others are going to behave, each takes the safest option, which is to agree to exchange. Bondholders are thus 'coerced' into agreeing to the exchange when they would be better off not agreeing. Obviously, if enough bondholders could get together and agree not to exchange, this would avoid the coercion, but in the *Assénagon* case the time between the offer and the decision was so short that this was not possible.[292] In that case, Briggs J decided that the exit consent was an abuse of the power of the majority, and contrary to the implied term mentioned above. The resolution (which in that case made the bonds worthless) was clearly expropriatory of the interests of the minority, and by the time the vote for it occurred, those voting in favour could not be said to be acting fairly as they were obliged to do so by their decision to exchange the bonds. That decision was also not a free one, because of the deliberately created 'prisoner's dilemma' discussed above.[293] If, however, those who had decided not to exchange their bonds had been given an opportunity to change their minds once they had seen that a majority had decided to do so, this would not have been an abuse of power,[294] although it would also not have been so effective in obtaining consent.

8.3.3.3 Schemes of Arrangement

It may be desirable to have the sanction of the court for a restructuring, either in a scheme of arrangement under section 895 of the Companies Act 2006[295] or by a company voluntary

---

[287] [2013] EWCA Civ 364.
[288] Ibid, [63], [69], [71].
[289] [2012] EWHC 2090 (Ch).
[290] Ibid, [1].
[291] See www.prisoners-dilemma.com/.
[292] *Assénagon Asset Management SA v Irish Bank Resolution Corporation Limited* [2012] EWHC 2090 (Ch) [4].
[293] Ibid, [84]. See also R Nolan, 'Debt Restructurings: The Use and Abuse of Power' (2013) 129 *Law Quarterly Review* 161.
[294] *Assénagon Asset Management SA v Irish Bank Resolution Corporation Limited* [2012] EWHC 2090 (Ch) [75].
[295] See the discussion of schemes of arrangement in chapter 15.

arrangement.[296] In these situations, statute provides that a majority of the creditors (if over 75 per cent in value) can bind the minority.[297] However, the requirement for 'a majority of the creditors' for scheme purposes requires a majority in number in addition to 75 per cent in value,[298] which may cause problems where the bond issue is represented by a global bond as it is not entirely clear who the 'creditors' are. As discussed earlier, the holder is either the depositary or the ISCD; it is not those beneficially entitled to the bonds. The trustee, if there is one, is also a creditor, but in many cases it is the same entity as the depositary. If there is a trustee, there is even a doubt as to whether the depositary (or ICSD) is a creditor, since the 'no-action' clause means that it cannot enforce the obligation owed to it unless the trustee refuses to act.[299] A 'no-action' provision did not prevent bondholders taking part in safeguard proceedings in France, which are similar to a scheme of arrangement in the UK.[300] However, who counts as a creditor is ultimately a matter of interpretation of the relevant UK statutory provisions.

This means that, where there is a global bond, there is likely to be only one creditor or maybe two, in which case a majority in number seems impossible, even though the depositary and/or trustee can represent the wishes of the beneficial holders who have instructed it, and can exercise its vote split as to value.[301] One possible way of avoiding this problem is for the issuer to issue definitive bonds to all the beneficial bondholders. However, whether this is possible will depend on the terms of the global note, and in any event it is slow and expensive as the definitive instruments have to be security printed.[302] Another method, which is now quite widely used, is for beneficial bondholders to be characterised as 'contingent creditors' on the basis of their right to receive definitive notes.[303]

While these techniques illustrate the potential difficulties arising from the intermediated system of holding securities, they also illustrate the inventiveness of lawyers in overcoming such problems. Nevertheless, it might have been better had the Companies Act been amended to remove the 'majority in number' requirement for schemes, as recommended by

---

[296] Goode: Corporate Insolvency, 12-12 (schemes of arrangement), 12-26–12-55 (company voluntary arrangements).

[297] It is notable that in schemes of arrangement the creditors may need to meet in order to consider and vote on the scheme in classes (see 15.2.2.2), whereas there is no such requirement for company voluntary arrangements (CVAs). Further, the ability of the majority to bind the minority differs slightly as between schemes and CVAs; for example, schemes can bind dissenting secured creditors in some circumstances but CVAs cannot. For discussion see J Payne, *Schemes of Arrangement: Theory, Structure and Operation* (Cambridge, Cambridge University Press, 2014) 5.5.1, 5.5.2.

[298] Companies Act 2006, s 899(1).

[299] Fuller: Corporate Borrowing, 3.10. Where there is only one obligation owed to the trustee, as in the case of stock, the trustee is the only creditor who can petition for winding up: *Re Dunderland Ore* [1909] 1 Ch 446.

[300] *Elliott International LP v Law Debenture Trustees Ltd* [2006] EWHC 3063.

[301] C Maunder, 'Bondholders' Schemes of Arrangement: Playing the Numbers Game' [2003] *Insolvency Intelligence* 73, 75.

[302] This is true at least where the issue is listed on a recognised stock exchange. For details of the way this problem was overcome in the Marconi scheme of arrangement, see R Wedderburn-Day and P Phelps, 'The Enfranchisement of Bondholders in the Marconi Schemes of Arrangement' [2003] *Journal of International Banking and Financial Law* 421. Even though definitive notes were issued in the Marconi scheme, the bond trustees were treated as scheme creditors. Despite attempts by the ICSDs to track them down, some ultimate bondholders were unable to be traced, giving rise to difficulties as to how the bondholders' entitlement was to be distributed: see *Re Marconi* [2013] EWHC 324 (Ch).

[303] *Re Castle Holdco 4 Ltd* [2009] EWHC 1347 (Ch) [23]; *In the matter of Gallery Capital SA* (unreported, High Court of Justice, Ch D, 21 April 2010) [11]; *In the matter of the Co-Operative Bank plc* [2013] EWHC 4074 (Ch) [38].

the Company Law Review, leaving just the 'majority in value' requirement, especially since any minority is protected by the power of the court to refuse the scheme.[304]

8.3.4 Trustees' Obligations[305]

8.3.4.1 Introduction

The large number and dispersed nature of bondholders means that the trustee plays a pivotal role in the way the bond issue is administered. Although its obligations are owed to the bondholders, the trust structure would seem to be of most use if the trustee is given enough discretion to deal with most matters without having to consult the bondholders. On the other hand, as a fiduciary, the trustee is not only accountable to the bondholders for its actions, but ought to take account of the wishes of the bondholders. The balance between these two objectives in the present context is largely driven by market practice, and is affected by a number of factors. One factor is that the trustee's powers and obligations (or lack of them) are laid down in the trust deed, which is a document executed by the issuer and negotiated with the trustee, but not necessarily with the original bondholders, and certainly not with any bondholders who acquire securities in the secondary market. Another relevant factor is the difficulty in obtaining consent via the complex process of calling a meeting, discussed at 8.3.3.1: this is time-consuming and causes delay, and the coordination problems mentioned earlier mean that it is difficult both to identify the bondholders and to spur them into action.[306] Yet another factor is cost: trustees at present charge low fees, but this is on the basis that they do very little and are indemnified for every action or decision they have to take. The influence of these factors on the nature of bond trustees' duties in the current market is discussed below.

8.3.4.2 The Functions of a Trustee

The three main functions of a trustee are to deal with modifications to the terms of the securities or the trust deed, to receive information from the issuer which indicates whether it is able to comply with its obligations, and to take action on possible events of default.[307] The first two can be dealt with reasonably swiftly, but the third requires more discussion.

8.3.4.2.1 Modifications to the Terms of the Securities or Trust Deed

It is likely that, if the issue of securities is for a reasonable duration, the issuer will want minor modifications to the terms of the securities to be made at some point. If all or a

---

[304] For discussion see 15.2.2.5.2.

[305] This discussion applies to both stock and bond issues, except where the context makes clear to the contrary.

[306] Recent techniques to overcome this problem include provisions for negative consent, whereby the trustee notifies bondholders that it intends to exercise its discretion in a particular way unless objected to within a specified time period. See E Cavett, 'When the Music Starts Again: How Should Trustees Conduct Themselves in the New World?' [2010] *Journal of International Banking and Financial Law* 469; *Market Principles for Issuing European CBMS* (Commercial Real Estate Finance Council Europe, November 2012).

[307] Financial Markets Law Committee, Issue 62, *Trustee Exemption Clauses* (2004), 17.

majority of the bondholders were required to agree to every modification, this would be very cumbersome. While bondholders are often prepared to play an active part in making decisions if the issuer gets into financial difficulties, until then they usually wish to remain passive, and often anonymous. This is accentuated where the securities are held through intermediaries, since the issuer does not know who the ultimate bondholders are, and it is difficult and time-consuming to discover this information. The trustee is therefore given power to agree modifications when, in its opinion, they are not materially prejudicial to the interests of bondholders or they are to correct a manifest error or they are of a formal, minor or technical nature.[308] Any other sort of modification will require the consent of the bondholders.[309]

8.3.4.2.2 Receiving Information from the Issuer

One might have thought that a useful role that a bond trustee might play would be to monitor whether the issuer has complied with its obligations, and whether it looks as though it can comply with them in the future. In one sense, the trustee is in a position to do this, as it is usually the recipient of considerable financial information that the issuer is obliged to provide under the bond covenants. However, the monitoring role of the trustee is greatly limited by provisions in the trust deed. These usually provide that the trustee is under no duty to take any steps to discover whether an event of default has happened and is entitled to assume that no event of default or potential event of default has occurred unless it has actual notice of this occurrence.[310] In practice, this means that the trustee relies on certificates issued by the directors of the issuer that no default has occurred.[311] While this will be satisfactory for the holders so long as the directors are diligent and honest, it does mean that there will be no advance warning of a deliberate breach. Some such breaches are difficult to remedy if the issuer becomes insolvent, such as a breach of a negative pledge clause.[312]

This limited monitoring role can be justified by arguing that trustees are not accountants or financial analysts, that market practice does not demand such monitoring, and that the fees charged reflect the limited level of service provided.[313] It must be remembered,

---

[308] Fuller: Corporate Borrowing, 12.8. For detailed discussion of these three concepts see P Regan and N Ganguly, 'How Corporate Trustees Exercise Discretion' (parts 1 and 2) [2014] *Journal of International Banking and Financial Law* 105 and 172. For an example of the breadth of the 'material prejudice' discretion, see *Re SMP Trustees Ltd* [2012] EWHC 772 (Ch).

[309] On the procedures for this, see 8.3.3.1.

[310] Fuller: Corporate Borrowing, 12.28; P Rawlings, 'The Changing Role of the Trustee in International Bond Issue' [2007] *Journal of Business Law* 43, 54; P Ali, 'Security Trustees' in P Ali (ed), *Secured Finance Transactions: Key Assets and Emerging Markets* (London, Globe Business Publishing, 2007) 33–34. For alternative formulations of these provisions see Financial Markets Law Committee, Issue 62, *Trustee Exemption Clauses* (2004), ch 4, sample cll 1.1.2, 1.1.8 and 1.1.11.

[311] The trustee does have to exercise reasonable care and skill in examining the certificate: see Fuller: Corporate Borrowing, 12.19.

[312] P Rawlings, 'The Changing Role of the Trustee in International Bond Issue' [2007] *Journal of Business Law* 43, 55, and see 6.3.1.6 for the effectiveness of certain types of negative pledge clauses in providing security for the lender. If the grantee of the security has no notice of the breach, it is likely to have priority over the holders. In this case there may be little left if the issuer becomes insolvent. This may well happen as a result of acceleration of the bond, this being the only remedy left to the holders except to sue the directors for fraud (which may be a possibility if the certificate is deliberately untrue).

[313] Financial Markets Law Committee, Issue 62, *Trustee Exemption Clauses* (2004), ch 4, comment to 1.1.8 and p 18.

however, that trustees (in this context) are professionals who provide a service: the real question is as to who should decide what service is provided. If those benefiting from a service are happy with low fees and minimal obligations, and are given a genuine choice as to the level of service provided and the level of fees, then there can be no complaint. It is true that the terms of the trust deed are negotiated between the issuer and the trustee, and the bondholders have no say in the matter, but the participants in the bond markets are sophisticated investors who will investigate the terms of the trust deed before buying the bonds.[314] Further, it is possible to make a distinction between contractual terms which limit the obligations undertaken by a party and contractual terms which exclude or limit liability for breach of obligations which a party does undertake.[315] The arguments in favour of controlling the latter are stronger, since the former allow flexibility in the actual subject matter of the contract. The same arguments apply in relation to trusts (which in any event can usually be seen as contracts),[316] as can be seen by the operation of section 750 of the Companies Act 2006, which is discussed below.[317]

8.3.4.2.3 Taking Action on Event of Default

The trustee plays a particularly important role if there is a breach of the terms of the securities, and/or if an event of default has occurred.[318] It is common for a trust deed to provide that most events of default do not entitle the trustee to accelerate payment of the securities unless it has certified that the event of default in question is materially prejudicial to the interests of the holders.[319] As pointed out above, the trustee is not obliged to monitor to check whether a breach or event of default has occurred. If it does have actual notice of a breach, however, it usually has two (linked) areas of discretion, which it is obliged at least to consider whether to exercise,[320] though only where it is satisfied that it will be indemnified by the holders.[321] First, it has discretion as to whether to waive the breach, and, second, it has discretion as to whether or not to certify that the event of default is materially prejudicial to the holders. If the trustee does not so certify, and the event of default is not a breach, this means that no further action can be taken; if it is a breach, then, in theory at least, the

---

[314] Law Commission Report No 301, *Trustee Exemption Clauses* (2006), Appendix C, C36.

[315] For example, only the latter are controlled by Unfair Contract Terms Act 1977, although both are controlled in relation to consumers under Unfair Terms in Consumer Contract Regulations 1999. See the reasoning of Gloster J in *JP Morgan Chase Bank (formerly Chase Manhattan Bank) v Springwell Navigation Corp* [2008] EWHC 1186 [602] (affirmed on appeal [2010] EWCA Civ 1221), discussed at n 481.

[316] Hughes: Banking, 13.3. For an application of such arguments to clauses limiting obligations in trust deeds, see Law Commission Report No 301, *Trustee Exemption Clauses* (2006), 5.46–5.91. It must be remembered, of course, that the same clause may include both limitations of obligations and limitation or exclusion of liability.

[317] 8.3.5.

[318] Not all events of default are breaches: see 6.3.2.2, and see 6.3.3 for a discussion of acceleration and termination rights generally.

[319] Certain events of default are exempt from this provision, such as failure to pay or the winding up of the issuer: see P Rawlings, 'The Changing Role of the Trustee in International Bond Issue' [2007] *Journal of Business Law* 43, 49. For a sample clause see Fuller: Corporate Borrowing, 5.19.

[320] Trustees who are given discretionary powers must give consideration to the exercise of those powers: see J Martin (ed), *Hanbury and Martin: Modern Equity*, 19th edn (London, Thomson Reuters, 2012) 6–006; *Re Manisty's Settlement* [1974] Ch 17, 25.

[321] See Financial Markets Law Committee, Issue 62, *Trustee Exemption Clauses* (2004), pp 20–23 and ch 4 1.3.2; *Concord Trust v Law Debenture Trust Corporation plc* [2004] EWHC 1216 [33].

decision has to be taken whether or not to waive it, since otherwise the issuer is potentially liable for damages even though no acceleration will take place.

If the trustee does certify material prejudice, it will then usually have the power to accelerate payment. It has the obligation to do this if it is directed to do so by the holders[322] and indemnified to its satisfaction.[323] Once accelerated, it is for the trustee to enforce the issuer's obligations, although, again, it is only obliged to do so if directed by the holders and indemnified. The 'no-action' clause will normally mean that only the trustee can enforce the issuer's obligations and the holders are not permitted to do so, unless the trustee fails to enforce within a reasonable time of being instructed.[324]

It can be seen that this scheme strikes a balance between the convenience of allowing the trustee to deal with less serious matters on its own, and granting it the power to consult the holders on critical matters such as acceleration and enforcement. The operation of this balance depends largely on the extent to which the trustee is prepared to act on its own, without the instructions of the holders. There are two particular concerns for trustees. The first is that, given the complex financial matters that have to be considered in exercising its discretion, it may have to incur considerable expenditure in obtaining expert advice. As pointed out above, trustees' fees are often set at a reasonably low level,[325] and so a trustee would look to be indemnified for any additional expenditure. While a trustee has a statutory right to be indemnified out of a trust fund,[326] in this case there is no trust fund as such,[327] only the issuer's obligation to pay. If the trustee eventually recovers the amount due from the issuer, it will normally have a right to deduct its expenses before paying the balance to the holders.[328] However, the discretions we are talking about arise in the context of a possible default, and it may not be at all clear when or if payment will be made by the issuer. A trustee is not required to make a personal loss out of acting in accordance with the trust[329] and trust deeds invariably make provision for the trustee to be indemnified to its satisfaction before exercising these discretions.[330]

What amounts to satisfactory indemnification can be open to question. In *Concord Trust v Law Debenture Corporation Ltd*,[331] which was part of the *Elektrim* litigation discussed below, the trustee refused to accelerate the bond on the grounds that the indemnity offered was not satisfactory, for two main reasons. The first, argued only at first instance, was that the conditions of the indemnity were not satisfactory, in that it was not joint and several

---

[322] The way in which decisions such as whether to accelerate can be taken by holders is discussed at 8.3.3.1.

[323] Fuller: Corporate Borrowing, 216.

[324] For a sample clause see ibid. Note that if the issuer is in repudiatory breach of the bond, and this had been accepted, it is at least arguable that it cannot rely on the no-action clause to prevent an action by a bondholder; see *Azevedo v Imcopa* [2012] EWHC 1849 (Comm) [38], [2013] EWCA Civ 364 [73].

[325] For example, in the *Concord* case discussed below, the trustees' fees were an initial acceptance fee of £2,000 and an annual management fee of £2,500 ([2004] EWCA Civ 1001 [38]) in relation to a bond issue of €510 million par value.

[326] Trustee Act 2000, s 31(1).

[327] This is true even for a security trustee, since the security is only available on enforcement of the issuer's obligations.

[328] This is known as 'top-slicing'; see Fuller: Corporate Borrowing, 217 for a sample clause.

[329] *Re Grimthorpe* [1958] Ch 615, 623, cited by Sir Andrew Morritt V-C in *Concord Trust v Law Debenture Trust Corporation plc* [2004] EWHC 1216 [33].

[330] Financial Markets Law Committee, Issue 62, *Trustee Exemption Clauses* (2004), ch 4 1.2.3 and 1.3.2.

[331] [2004] EWHC 1216, [2004] EWCA Civ 1001, [2005] UKHL 27.

(between the holders and the guarantor) and the creditworthiness of one of the major bondholders was in doubt. The second related to the amount of the indemnity: the trustee contended that it could be liable to the issuer for very considerable damages if it was held not to be entitled to accelerate the bond.[332] It is clear from the decisions of all the courts in the *Concord* case[333] that a trustee is entitled to refuse to act on the grounds that the indemnity offered is unsatisfactory, provided that the decision to refuse is not unreasonable according to the *Wednesbury*[334] principle (that is, that no reasonable trustee could have come to it).[335] Although the actual decision (especially in the Court of Appeal and the House of Lords) related to the amount of the indemnity, it seems reasonably clear that this principle applies to any aspect of the indemnity to which a trustee could reasonably object.[336]

As well as concern about being indemnified against expenditure, a trustee will also worry that its actions may expose it to considerable liability, and that the indemnity offered may not be enough to cover this. Unlike an indemnity against expenditure, here there is real uncertainty as to whether the liability will ever eventuate, and, if so, how much it would be.[337] It is clear from the *Concord Trust* litigation that, although the amount of possible liability will be looked at on a 'worst-case scenario' basis, a trustee cannot insist on an indemnity against a risk unless it is 'more than fanciful'.[338] Concern about possible liability may also act as a disincentive to a trustee to exercise its discretionary power to accelerate rather than to ask the holders for instructions.[339]

It is worth considering in more detail what a trustee's rights and obligations are when deciding some of the matters mentioned above. First, the trustee is likely to have to decide whether an event of default is 'materially prejudicial to the interests of bondholders'.[340] In the first case in the *Elektrim* litigation ('the *Acciona* case')[341] the relevant event of default was the suspension of the bondholders' nominated director (of the issuer), which was a clear breach of the terms of the trust deed. The bondholders contended that it was materially prejudicial. The issuer suggested to the trustee that, in financial terms, it was not. The trustee, presumably in an attempt to protect itself, asked the court for directions as to the meaning of the phrase 'materially prejudicial to the interests of the bondholders'. The steps which Peter Smith J held to be necessary seem fairly self-evident: the trustee must ascertain whether there is a breach, and, if there is, it must ascertain the consequences of that breach. It must then decide whether the interests of the bondholders (defined as the interests in being paid under the bond, and any ancillary interests which protect that right, such as

---

[332] This issue is discussed below.

[333] That is, the High Court, the Court of Appeal and the House of Lords.

[334] *Associated Provincial Picture Houses Ltd v Wednesbury Corporation* [1948] 1 KB 223.

[335] The burden of proof is on the party or parties challenging the decision, who in that case were the bondholders.

[336] For example, the failure to provide security if the creditworthiness of the bondholders was very suspect, or a provision that the bondholders' liability was several, rather than joint and several.

[337] It is reasonably clear from the *Concord* litigation that an indemnity would have to cover possible costs if there was a chance of the issuer or a third party commencing proceedings: see [2005] UKHL 27 [34].

[338] Ibid.

[339] P Rawlings, 'The Changing Role of the Trustee in International Bond Issue' [2007] *Journal of Business Law* 43, 50.

[340] It may also, at times, have to consider whether a proposed modification is materially prejudicial.

[341] *Law Debenture Trust Corporation plc v Acciona SA* [2004] EWHC 270. The subsequent case was the *Concord Trust* case discussed above.

security) have been materially prejudiced.[342] Sometimes this will involve extensive factual investigation and sometimes it will be self-evident (as it was held to be in this case).

It will be noted that the only parties to the *Acciona* case were the trustee and the bond-holders. The issuer, therefore, was not bound by the decision, and was free to challenge it. The trustee duly issued a certificate of material prejudice and was instructed by the bondholders to accelerate liability, but then refused to accelerate as it was concerned about a possible challenge by the issuer, and was not satisfied with the indemnity offered, as discussed above. The House of Lords[343] held that it was very unlikely that a wrong-ful acceleration would give the issuer a valid cause of action, since it had no contractual effect. Such an acceleration did not actually have the effect of accelerating the liability;[344] there was no need to imply a term prohibiting the service of such a notice, of which a wrongful acceleration would be a breach.[345] Nor was there an action in tort, since there was no duty of care owed, and no intention to found a conspiracy or other economic tort claim.[346]

It might be thought that this is an unfortunate state of the law. If a trustee, and therefore the bondholders, were to be liable for wrongful acceleration, this would act as a deterrent against opportunist interpretations of 'events of default' clauses in order to trigger renego-tiations, and would preserve some sort of balance between issuer and bondholders.[347] In a difficult economic climate there is a greater incentive for bondholders to seek to renegoti-ate, and therefore to become more activist, which is likely to result in more trustees being instructed to serve acceleration notices. Even if, technically, it has no legal effect, a wrongful acceleration can have deleterious effects on an issuer, especially if it becomes public knowl-edge either through an obligation to disclose[348] or in any other way. Such information might discourage other lenders or other companies from doing business with the issuer. Further-more, the mere service of a notice might constitute default in other agreements the issuer may have, although this would depend on the wording of the particular agreements. There are two possible lines of argument left open by the House of Lords' decision. The first is that the service of the notice gives rise to a cause of action in defamation.[349] The second, which would be far more likely to apply where the lending was by way of syndicated or other loan, is that by serving the notice the lenders are evincing an intent not to make further advances

---

[342] [2004] EWHC 270 [42] and [48]. The judge found that there was material prejudice. For discussion as to what amounts to material prejudice, see P Regan and N Ganguly, 'How Corporate Trustees Exercise Discretion (Part 2)' [2014] *Journal of International Banking and Financial Law* 172.

[343] *Concord Trust v Law Debenture Trust Corp plc* [2005] UKHL 27.

[344] This follows the position already established in *Bournemouth and Boscombe Athletic Football Club v Lloyds TSB Bank plc* [2003] EWCA Civ 1755 (see A McKnight, 'A Review of Developments in English Case Law during 2004: Part 1' [2005] *Journal of International Banking Law and Regulation* 105).

[345] [2005] UKHL 27 [37]. This has been followed in two cases: *Jafari-Fini v Skillglass Ltd* [2007] EWCA Civ 261 and *BNP Paribas v Yukos Oil Company* [2005] EWHC 1321. For comment see D Whitehead, 'Pride or Prejudice' (2011) 30(5) *International Financial Law Review* 32.

[346] [2005] UKHL 27 [38]–[43].

[347] S Wright, 'Making Lenders Liable for Damage Caused by "Wrongful Acceleration" of Loans' (2006) 27 *Company Lawyer* 123.

[348] See 13.3.1.

[349] E Peel, 'No Liability for Service of an Invalid Notice of "Event of Default"' (2006) 122 *Law Quarterly Review* 179, 183; Hughes: Banking Law, 11.20.

to the borrower. If they are contractually obliged to do so, this in itself would be a breach, maybe even a repudiatory breach.[350]

On the other side of the coin, the issuer has some protection against bondholder activism through the 'no-action' clause. The point of such a clause is to prevent what is called the 'hold-out' problem: where one or a small number of bondholders wish to take action which is damaging to the interests of the bondholders as a whole, or which is unmeritorious and potentially damaging to the issuer who has to defend the action (and therefore is also damaging to the interests of the bondholders as a whole).[351] The clause also stops multiplicity of actions, as only the trustee can enforce.[352] An example of its use can be found in the case of *Re Colt Telecom Group plc*,[353] where one hedge fund acquired 7 per cent of the bonds at a discount and sought to put the company into administration, with a view to making a profit if the value of the bonds rose as a result of restructuring. None of the other bondholders supported the petition. The court held that the no-action clause prevented all enforcement, including 'noncontractual claims', that is, those not based on a breach of contract, and also enforcement where there had not been an event of default.[354] It was argued that if the no-action clauses were interpreted in this way, this could lead to situations where no one could enforce, not even the trustee.[355] Whether this would be the case, of course, would depend not only on the construction of the no-action clause but also on the construction of the powers of the trustee as set out in the trust deed. In the situation in *Colt Telecom*, however, the trustee, as a creditor, would have been able to petition for administration or liquidation, both under the Insolvency Act, and so would have been able to enforce.

In subsequent cases it has also been held that a no-action clause covers 'any claim designed to vindicate the rights of a bondholder in his capacity as such', including claims in both contract and tort,[356] although not the bringing of opposition proceedings to

---

[350] A McKnight, 'A Review of Developments in English Case Law during 2004: Part 1' [2005] *Journal of International Banking Law and Regulation* 117, 117–18. See *Essentially Different Ltd v Bank of Scotland plc* [2011] EWHC 475 (Comm) for a case where a failure to make a loan led to a successful claim for damages. See also P Rawlings, 'Avoiding the Obligation to Lend' [2012] *Journal of Business Law* 89.

[351] *Feldbaum v McCrory Corporation*, 18 Del J Corp L 630, 642; *Elektrim SA v Vivendi Holdings 1 Corp* [2008] EWCA Civ 1178 [1]–[4]. See 8.3.2.3.1(b) for discussion of the mad bondholder problem.

[352] *Elektrim SA v Vivendi Holdings 1 Corp* [2008] EWCA Civ 1178 [91], [101].

[353] *Re Colt Telecom Group plc* [2002] EWHC 2815.

[354] The bonds were governed by New York law, and so this was actually a decision on what the law of New York was, but the cogent reasoning supporting this decision, namely that the limitations argued for gave rise to distinctions which were illogical, would surely also apply to English law.

[355] This argument was based on M Kahan, 'Rethinking Corporate Bonds: The Trade-Off between Individual and Collective Rights' (2002) 77 *New York University Law Review* 1040. Professor Kahan was called as an expert in the case. See also P Rawlings, 'Reinforcing Collectivity: The Liability of Trustees and the Power of Investors in Finance Transactions' (2009) 23 *Trust Law International* 14, 24.

[356] *Elektrim SA v Vivendi Holdings 1 Corp* [2008] EWCA Civ 1178 [92]–[93]. It should be remembered, however, that a no-action clause does not prevent the bondholders bringing actions which are not related to enforcing the obligations in the bonds, such as a misrepresentation action against the issuer in relation to statements made in the prospectus (either at common law or for a breach of the regulatory regime under s 90 FSMA: see 13.2.7) or against other parties, such as a negligent intermediary, or an action for breach of trust against the trustee: see P Rawlings, 'Reinforcing Collectivity: The Liability of Trustees and the Power of Investors in Finance Transactions' (2009) 23 *Trust Law International* 14, 22.

safeguard proceedings[357] in the French Commercial Court.[358] The court also held in the *Colt Telecom* litigation that there was no rule of English public policy prohibiting the use of such clauses.[359] It is difficult to see how the argument that there was such a rule could stand any chance of success. It was based on an argument that any creditor should be free to wind up a company, and that this freedom could not be bargained away. There are other instances of such bargains, though, and no absolute right exists, statutory or otherwise, to bring insolvency proceedings. Further, the advantages of the no-action clause are clear and well established. The fact that the courts are prepared to interpret the scope of such clauses expansively means that a no-action clause gives wide and strong protection; when combined with the existence of a bond trustee (who will hold any payments made by the issuer on trust for the bondholders), it has been described as a 'robust fortress against holdout litigation'.[360]

These cases demonstrate that there appears to be an increase in the appetite of bondholders and issuers to become involved in the acceleration and enforcement of bonds, either by seeking to take action themselves or by mobilising themselves to give directions to the trustee, and for issuers to oppose this, either through the courts or by putting pressure on the trustee in other ways. It may well be that one reason is the large number of junk or high-yield bonds in circulation:[361] the return is higher, which attracts more aggressive investors, but default is more likely,[362] so the stakes are also higher and the perceived benefits of interference are greater. The trustee is left in the middle of this surge of activism and, not unexpectedly, tries to protect itself against liability and challenge as much as possible. It is to this that we now turn.

8.3.5 Excluding Trustees' Duties

8.3.5.1 Forms of Exclusion Clauses

As mentioned above, trustees are under various duties to the beneficiaries of the trust in relation to the trust property. A trustee owes a duty to carry out its administration of the trust with care and skill, the standard being higher in relation to professional trustees, depending on the level of expertise they hold themselves out as having.[363] Bond trustees

---

[357] Safeguard proceedings are corporate rescue proceedings in French law, which are somewhat similar to administration proceedings in the UK.

[358] *Elliott International LP v Law Debenture Trustees Ltd* [2006] EWHC 3063.

[359] *Re Colt Telecom Group plc* [2002] EWHC 2815 [62]–[77].

[360] N Ishikawa, 'Towards the Holy Grail of Orderly Sovereign Debt Restructuring. Part 2: Optimum Architecture of Collective Action Clauses' [2007] *Journal of International Banking and Financial Law* 404. See also P Rawlings, 'Reinforcing Collectivity: The Liability of Trustees and the Power of Investors in Finance Transactions' (2009) 23 *Trust Law International* 14, 32, who argues that this gives the issuer too much protection to the detriment of minority bondholders.

[361] P Rawlings, 'The Changing Role of the Trustee in International Bond Issue' [2007] *Journal of Business Law* 43, 65. See also M Dakin, F Diminich, P Hertz and G Ruiz, 'Getting into Bed with Bondholders' [2012] *Corporate Restructuring and Insolvency* 120.

[362] Both because of the nature of the issuer and because the covenants are likely to be stricter: see 2.3.3.3 and 3.2.2.3.

[363] *Bartlett v Barclays Bank Trust Co Ltd (No 2)* [1980] 1 Ch 515, 534. There is also a limited duty of care and skill imposed by s 1 Trustee Act 2000, which is wider than the *Bartlett* duty in that the test of knowledge and

are invariably professional trustees, and will of necessity have held themselves out to have certain types of expertise in order to be used in the first place. Since the duty will have prima facie arisen, any protection from liability has to be achieved by means of an exclusion or limitation clause.[364] However, in relation to bond issues, section 750(1) of the Companies Act 2006[365] provides that:

> Any provision contained in (a) a trust deed for securing an issue of debentures, or (b) any contract with the holders of debentures secured by a trust deed, is void in so far as it would have the effect of exempting a trustee of the deed from, or indemnifying him against, liability for breach of trust where he fails to show the degree of care and diligence required of him as trustee, having regard to the provisions of the trust deed conferring on him any powers, authorities or discretions.

For the purposes of the Companies Act, 'debenture' is defined as including debenture stock, bonds and any other securities of a company, whether or not constituting a charge on the assets of the company.[366] This is a wide definition and will cover most bond and stock issues, although only those issued by UK companies because of the jurisdiction of the Act.[367] The effect of this section is that any clause which expressly excludes liability for breach of the equitable duty of care and skill[368] will be void, and as a result such clauses are not included in bond issue trust deeds. However, the last part of section 750(1), 'having regard to the provisions of the trust deed conferring on him any powers, authorities or discretions', indicates that the section is limited to actual exclusion clauses and does not cover clauses which contain powers to do things which would otherwise be in breach of trust, such as taking advice from specialists or which confer discretion on the trustee or which limit the duties of the trustee.[369] Such clauses were described by the Law Commission, in its consultation paper on trustee exemption clauses, as extended powers or authorisation clauses, and duty exclusion clauses,[370] but despite their difference in structure, their actual effect is to protect trustees from liability.[371] Bond issue trust deeds, therefore, include such clauses in order to give

---

expertise does not just depend on what the trustee has held itself out as having, but includes a more objective test of what it is reasonable to expect of a person acting in the course of that kind of business. This only applies to certain activities, which are set out in Sch 1 to the Act, and which do not include many of the main activities of a bond trustee, as discussed in the previous paragraphs.

[364] The statutory duty in s 1 Trustee Act 2000 does not apply where excluded by the trust deed: Sch 1 para 7.

[365] Re-enacting Companies Act 1985, s 192, which itself re-enacted Companies Act 1948, s 88, the provision having been first introduced in Companies Act 1947.

[366] Companies Act 2006, s 738. For discussion of the meaning of 'debenture' in the light of the decision in *Fons HF v Corporal Ltd* [2014] EWCA Civ 304 see 13.1.1.

[367] In practice, similar wording is included in many trust deeds for issues of international securities: Financial Markets Law Committee, Issue 62, *Trustee Exemption Clauses* (2004), 4; Fuller: Corporate Borrowing, 12.15.

[368] The duty referred to in *Bartlett v Barclays Bank Trust Co Ltd* [1980] 1 Ch 515, 534. The section does not prevent the exclusion of the statutory duty under Trustee Act 2000; Fuller: Corporate Borrowing, 12.12. This is because it is the duty that is excluded and not the liability: see Law Commission Consultation Paper No 171, 'Trustee Exemption Clauses' (2002), 82 (sample cl A3).

[369] Fuller: Corporate Borrowing, 12.14; Tennekoon: International Finance, 238. Examples of such clauses can be found in Fuller: Corporate Borrowing, 12.28; Financial Markets Law Committee, Issue 62, *Trustee Exemption Clauses* (2004), ch 4; Law Commission Consultation Paper No 171, 'Trustee Exemption Clauses' (2002), Appendix A, A3 and A4.

[370] Law Commission, ibid, ch 2, 2.5–2.6.

[371] It should be noted that the possibility of these sorts of clauses was acknowledged when Unfair Contract Terms Act 1977, which seeks to control clauses excluding contractual and other common law liability, was drafted so that some duty-defining clauses also trigger the controls: see ss 3(2)(b) and 13.

trustees a comprehensive package of protection, and it is these clauses that the following discussion considers.

There seems to be no doubt that, since the trust is created by the trust deed, the terms of the deed define the trustee's obligations. The deed can therefore impose obligations on the trustee, can define such obligations and can exclude liability for breach of obligations imposed. However, such terms only have effect within the limits of their true construction, so that the debate is partly at least about the relevant principles of construction. A second possible limit is based on public policy, so that, at least in certain situations, a trustee should not be able to restrict its obligations or liability beyond a certain point. The construction question will be considered first.

8.3.5.2 Contractual Construction of Clauses

The starting point when construing the terms of a contract[372] is that the parties are free to agree whatever rights and obligations they like, provided there are no statutory or common law controls against unfairness.[373] Most of these controls are based on protection of parties with weaker bargaining power or who do not have enough information to make an informed decision. Apart from the requirement of consideration (which usually means that there have to be reciprocal promises), there is no pre-conceived idea of the content of contractual obligations, or that one party rather than the other should owe any particular duties to anyone.[374] However, terms which exclude or restrict liability for breaches of those obligations will be construed strictly against the person relying on them (*contra proferentem*).[375] Further, the more deliberate and serious the breach, the more unlikely it is that it will be covered by an exclusion clause if the result would be against 'business common sense',[376] even if that would be the literal meaning of the word used.[377] The aim of this approach is largely to preserve internal consistency. If the parties have agreed that one party should be under a particular obligation, it makes no sense if he is not liable even for a deliberate and serious breach: it means that the obligation has no contractual content.[378]

There has been considerable discussion as to whether these principles apply to the construction of exclusion clauses in trust deeds. It can be said that a trust deed, especially in a commercial context, is like a contract. It sets out the rights and obligations as between the trustee and the settlor (here the issuer) so that, for example, the House of Lords in *Concord Trust v Law Debenture Trust Corporation plc*[379] construed the trust deed as though it were a contract, applying the usual contractual principles relating to the implication of terms

---

[372] For discussion of the law relating to interpretation of commercial contracts, see 6.2.

[373] For example, Unfair Contract Terms Act 1977 or the rule against penalties.

[374] This is, of course, subject to the qualification that in certain types of contracts there are specified duties, so that, for example, in a sale of goods contract the seller owes certain duties to the buyer and in an employment contract the employer owes certain duties to the employee. However, if the configuration of rights and obligations does not bring the contract into a particular category (for example, in a contract of barter there is no seller and no buyer), there is still an enforceable contract.

[375] See Chitty 14-005.

[376] *Photo Production Ltd v Securicor Transport Ltd* [1980] AC 827, 850–51.

[377] *Internet Broadcasting Corporation v MAR LLC* [2009] EWHC 844 [27], [32].

[378] See *Kudos Catering (UK) Limited v Manchester Central Convention Complex Ltd* [2013] EWCA Civ 38 [19].

[379] [2005] UKHL 27, discussed at 8.3.4.2.3.

and referring to breach of a possible implied term as 'breach of contract'.[380] It is, of course, possible that the same document has two functions: one as a declaration of trust and the other as (evidence of) a contract between the issuer and the trustee. Even on this analysis, though, it could be said that the contract can qualify and refine the terms of the trust.[381] In other contexts, an 'arm's-length commercial contract' can qualify the duties of a fiduciary.[382] An alternative view is that the exclusion of liability is not a matter of contract; it can only be achieved by means of equitable provisions.[383]

It is certainly true that a trust is different from a contract, and that the differences between them should qualify the application of contractual principles of construction to some extent. One rather obvious difference is that the people for whose benefit many of the duties are undertaken, and who have the capacity to enforce them, are not parties to the trust deed at all, and in theory play no part in the bargaining process.[384] As pointed out earlier, though, in the case of a bond issue, the bondholders will usually be in a position to see the terms of the trust deed before they invest[385] and although they have no bargaining power as such, they have the opportunity not to buy, or, at least in relation to bonds traded on a market, to exit from the transaction if they do not like the terms. In any event, many of the terms used are very standard, and so are familiar to everyone involved in the transaction (although, of course, this could also be said to reduce the ability of the potential bondholder to 'shop around' for better terms).

Another difference is said to be that a trust is based on a grant of property rather than an agreement.[386] This has various ramifications. One is that the terms of the trust deed bind subsequent beneficiaries as well as the original beneficiaries. This, of course, is true in relation to a bond issue, but the same arguments apply as made above, and, in addition, similar considerations apply to any traded debt, even when only purely contractual rights apply.[387] The proprietary basis of the trust also means that the beneficiaries may have remedies other than damages, such as orders for restitution of trust property and for disgorgement of profits. In relation to trusts in general this is a very telling point, and, in fact, a clause excluding liability for breach is unlikely to be held to cover either remedy.[388] In the context of a bond issue, however, it is not the misappropriation of property that is

---

[380] Ibid, [37] and see Hughes: Banking, 11.4–11.5.

[381] Financial Markets Law Committee, Issue 62, *Trustee Exemption Clauses* (2004), 1–2.

[382] *Hospital Products Ltd v United States Surgical Corporation* (1984) 156 CLR 41, 97, cited in *Kelly v Cooper* [1993] AC 205, 215; *Halton v Guernroy* [2005] EWHC 1968 [139]; in the context of the duties of a security trustee, *Saltri III Ltd v MD Mezzanine SA Sicar* [2012] EWHC 3025 (Comm) [123].

[383] A Hudson, *Equity and Trusts*, 8th edn (Abingdon, Routledge-Cavendish, 2015) 487, relying on *Re Duke of Norfolk Settlement Trusts* [1982] Ch 61, 77.

[384] M Bryan, 'Contractual Modification of the Duties of a Trustee' in S Worthington (ed), *Commercial Law and Commercial Practice* (Oxford, Hart Publishing, 2003) 513, 518.

[385] The terms of the trust deed will usually be described in the offering circular; see 8.3.1 and Law Commission Report No 301, *Trustee Exemption Clauses* (2006), Appendix C, C36.

[386] Law Commission, ibid, ch 2, 2.60–2.61.

[387] This has some influence on the way such contracts are interpreted: only the background information that would be reasonably known by all transferees should be taken into account. See 6.2.2.

[388] This will generally be the case on a straightforward construction of the clause: M Bryan, 'Contractual Modification of the Duties of a Trustee' in S Worthington (ed), *Commercial Law and Commercial Practice* (Oxford, Hart Publishing, 2003) 518–19; *Armitage v Nurse* [1998] 1 Ch 241, 253. See also Bryan at 513 and 519, where the author points out that this is especially so if unauthorised profits are seen as trust property: *Foskett v McKeown* [2001] 1 AC 102.

likely to be at issue, or covered by the exculpation provisions, but the duty to act with care and skill, or maybe the duty to avoid a conflict of interest, so this distinction from contract is not particularly relevant.

8.3.5.3 *Unfair Contract Terms Act*

If a trust deed were seen as a contract, section 2(2) of the Unfair Contract Terms Act 1977, which subjects a contract term or notice excluding liability for negligently caused economic loss to a test of reasonableness, might apply. It seems reasonably clear, however, that this section does not apply to trustee exemption clauses in bond issues, for several reasons. First, it can be argued that a trust deed is not a contract, and so the exclusion clause is not a contract term. The Law Commission thought that this was the case,[389] and it was conceded in the only case to consider the matter, *Baker v Clark*.[390] It is, of course, arguable that the Act does apply,[391] but this argument is context dependent, and there are other good reasons why section 2(2) does not apply to bond issues. One is that the duty of care and skill to which the clause relates is not a 'common law duty' as required by section 1(1) of the Unfair Contract Terms Act, but an equitable duty imposed because of the trustee's status as trustee. Where there is no explicit additional duty stated in the trust deed, this would appear to be correct.[392] Further, section 2 of the Unfair Contract Terms Act does not apply to 'any contract so far as it relates to the creation or transfer of securities or of any right or interest in securities'.[393] This reflects the freedom of contract policy in relation to the capital markets that has so far resulted in very little regulation of the actual terms of contracts[394] as well as the concerns that were expressed to the Law Commission in relation to commercial trusts.[395]

8.3.5.4 *Public Policy: Common Law Constraints*

The basis in recent case law for the courts' approach to construction of trustees' exclusion clauses has been the case of *Armitage v Nurse*.[396] In that case, the Court of Appeal had to consider whether liability for the trustee's (maybe gross) negligence was covered by a wide exclusion clause. In holding that it was, Millett LJ considered the construction of the clause, and also whether there was any public policy against the validity of a wide exemption clause

---

[389] Law Commission Consultation Paper No 171, 'Trustee Exemption Clauses' (2002), 2.60–2.61.

[390] [2006] EWCA 464, [19].

[391] Hughes: Banking, 11.5–11.6. Hughes then, however, points out that if the trust deed were to be seen as a contract simpliciter, the beneficiaries' enforcement of the duty of care and skill would be either in tort or in reliance on Contracts (Rights of Third Parties) Act 1999. Section 7(2) of that Act provides that s 2(2) Unfair Contract Terms Act does not apply where a third party is relying on the 1999 Act to enforce a breach of a contractual duty of care and skill.

[392] Law Commission Consultation Paper No 171, 'Trustee Exemption Clauses' (2002), 2.63. Although the judge assumed that there was a common law duty in *Baker v Clark* [2006] EWCA Civ 464 [20], this appears to have been because of the way the case was pleaded and argued, rather than an actual decision on this point.

[393] Unfair Contract Terms Act 1977, Sch 1 para 1(e); Fuller: Corporate Borrowing, 12.16.

[394] For a discussion of the regulation of debt more generally, see chapter 13.

[395] For example by the Financial Markets Law Committee, in Issue 62, *Trustee Exemption Clauses* (2004); Hughes: Banking, 11.7.

[396] *Armitage v Nurse* [1998] 1 Ch 241.

which purported to cover any liability except for actual fraud. In relation to construction, he appeared to be applying contractual principles. The clause excluded liability for all loss and damage unless it was caused by 'actual fraud'. Millett LJ construed the clause literally and strictly. He rejected an argument that fraud was to be given an extended meaning including gross negligence, and limited its scope to dishonesty. This approach has been followed in some subsequent cases.[397]

In relation to public policy, Millett LJ took the view that under English common law exclusion of the liability of a trustee for gross negligence was not contrary to public policy.[398] He therefore thought that any large-scale control of trustee exclusion clauses was a matter for Parliament.[399] However, he did say that there was an irreducible core of trustees' obligations which could not be excluded for there still to be a trust. This was the duty of the trustee to perform the trust honestly and in good faith for the benefit of the beneficiaries.[400] This is not so much a matter of public policy as one of definition, and herein lies an important difference between trust and contract.

As with many transactions that confer particular benefits on the parties, there are certain definitional criteria which need to be fulfilled for those benefits to be obtained. In relation to contract, the criteria are limited (agreement, consideration, some degree of certainty). However, to obtain proprietary benefits such as accrue under a trust, the criteria are stricter. The three certainties have already been discussed, but it is also the case that, for a trust to exist, the trustee must be under these minimum duties, otherwise the link between it, the property and the beneficiaries is not sufficiently strong. Without that link, the beneficiaries should not be entitled to priority in insolvency over the trustee's creditors, or to the other benefits of there being a trust. It could, of course, be said that this reasoning is undermined as the detriment of being subject to the fiduciary duties is suffered by the trustee but it is the beneficiaries who obtain the benefit. However, the whole transaction is interlinked: the higher the duties on the trustee, the more fees the beneficiaries (at least in a bond issue) have to pay.[401]

---

[397] *Bogg v Raper* (*The Times*, 22 April 1998); *Alexander v Perpetual Trustees WA Ltd* [2001] NSWCA 240; *Fattal v Walbrook Trustees (Jersey) Ltd* [2010] EWHC 2767 (Ch).

[398] *Armitage v Nurse* [1998] 1 Ch 241, 254–56. This view was considered by the Privy Council in *Spread Trustee Co Ltd v Hutcheson and others* [2011] UKPC 13. The case was an appeal from the Guernsey Court of Appeal, and the Privy Council had to consider the question of what English common law (and therefore Guernsey law) was in 1988, immediately before legislation was passed in Guernsey prohibiting exclusion of liability for gross negligence by trustees. The majority of the Privy Council agreed with Lord Millett's analysis of English law, but doubt was cast on his analysis of Scots law ([2011] UKPC 13 [48]) and, by the minority, of English law ([138] per Lady Hale and [166] per Lord Kerr). These two dissenting opinions indicate that if the issue were to come before the UK Supreme Court, it cannot be assumed that *Armitage v Nurse* would necessarily be followed. See K Loi, 'Gross Negligence and Trustee Exemption Clauses in the Privy Council: *Spread Trustee v Hutcheson*' [2011] *Conveyancer* 521.

[399] *Armitage v Nurse* [1998] 1 Ch 241, 256. Since that case, the Law Commission has considered the issue: see Law Commission Consultation Paper No 171, 'Trustee Exemption Clauses' (2002); and Law Commission Report No 301, *Trustee Exemption Clauses* (2006).

[400] *Armitage v Nurse* [1998] 1 Ch 241, 253–54. For a similar approach in Australia, see *Australian Securities and Investments Commission v Citigroup Global Markets Australia Limited* [2007] FCA 963.

[401] One could make a similar argument in relation to the fixed charge: in order to have a fixed charge it is the chargor and not the chargee who suffers the detriment of lack of ability to deal with the assets. However, the chargor will benefit from a lower rate of interest.

Even on the reasoning in *Armitage v Nurse*, it is not clear how far this idea of an irreducible core extends. It is clear that it does not cover the duty of care and skill: any form of negligence can be excluded.[402] The line between gross negligence and failure to perform the duties under the trust honestly and in good faith is, however, not always easy to draw. There must be some fiduciary duties which are fundamental to the trust structure which cannot be excluded or modified. For example, at least where the trustee holds security, it must have some management function in relation to that property, which includes monitoring its value.[403] Even where the trustee does not hold security, it has been argued that it cannot be entirely supine and 'simply follow instructions from a third party, without applying his mind to what he is doing'.[404] The case on which this argument relies,[405] however, was recently overturned on appeal, and the Court of Appeal of the Cayman Islands upheld the distinction in *Armitage v Nurse* between wilful default and negligence, saying that for the former there needs to be proof of 'a deliberate and conscious decision to act or fail to act in knowing breach of his duty; negligence, however gross, is not enough'.[406] This view appears to support the approach taken by the courts in relation to bond trustees discussed in the next paragraph.

There are certainly indications that in commercial transactions the court is prepared to interpret the 'core' very narrowly and to strive to give effect to the trust. In *Citibank NA v MBIA Assurance SA*,[407] the trust deed provided that the trustee was obliged to follow the instructions of the guarantor of a bond issue without having regard to the interests of the noteholders, and excluded the trustee from liability to the noteholders when so doing. It was argued by the noteholders that this clause reduced the obligations of the trustee below the irreducible core. However, the Court of Appeal held, having interpreted the clause, that this was not the case. The trustee continued to have an obligation of good faith, and also had discretion to act in other areas. The approach of the Court of Appeal was to lean against an interpretation that the trustee was not a trustee at all, although it did not rule out the possibility of this if it were justified on the documentation.[408] On this approach, there seems to be little 'downside' to suffer in order to get the benefit of a proprietary interest.[409]

---

[402] The distinction between the fiduciary duties of honesty and good faith (which are the irreducible core of trustee's obligations) and a duty of care (of whatever standard) was emphasised by Lord Clarke in *Spread Trustee Co Ltd v Hutcheson and others* [2011] UKPC 13 [61].

[403] J Getzler, 'Equitable Compensation and the Regulation of Fiduciary Relationships' in P Birks and F Rose (eds), *Resulting Trusts and Equitable Compensation* (London, Mansfield Press, 2000) 256; P Ali, 'Security Trustees' in P Ali (ed), *Secured Finance Transactions: Key Assets and Emerging Markets* (London, Globe Business Publishing, 2007) 38. For discussion of the duties of a security trustee in relation to enforcement of security, which were modified by the intercreditor agreement to correspond to the ordinary duties of a mortgagee, see *Saltri III Ltd v MD Mezzanine SA Sicar* [2012] EWHC 3025 (Comm).

[404] L Cohen QC and T Seymour, 'Trustee Exculpation: The Law, the Quirks and the Business Sense' (2014) 20 *Trust & Trustees* 993.

[405] *Weavering Macro Fixed Income Ltd v Peterson* (26 August 2011, Grand Court of the Cayman Islands).

[406] *Weavering Macro Fixed Income Ltd v Peterson* (2015) CICA 10 of 2011 [95].

[407] [2006] EWHC 3215.

[408] Ibid, [82].

[409] A Trukhtanov, 'The Irreducible Core of Trust Obligations' (2007) 123 *Law Quarterly Review* 342. For a comparative view in a rather wider context than that of bond trustees, see A Hofri-Winogradow, 'The Stripping of the Trust: From Evolutionary Scripts to Distributive Results' (2014) 75 *Ohio State Law Journal* 529.

That can be seen as a commercial approach to the development of the law, but it must be realised that the corollary of giving the benefit of a trust lightly is that other creditors may lose out in the event of insolvency of the trustee.

8.3.5.5 *Public Policy: Legislative Constraints?*

When the Law Commission considered the question of whether there should be statutory control of trustee exclusion clauses, it initially proposed that professional trustees should not be able to exclude liability for negligence.[410] There was considerable adverse reaction to this from those who used trusts in a commercial context, who argued that restricting the ability of trustees to have extensive protection from liability would mean that trust corporations would refuse to act as trustees, so that the use of the trust structure would die out in favour of fiscal agency, and the benefits of using the trust would therefore be lost. Furthermore, where there was a trust, the trustees would be reluctant to exercise their discretion without consulting the beneficiaries, which would make the operation of the trust much more inefficient.[411] These arguments persuaded the Law Commission that statutory control was not desirable, and in its final report it recommended merely a rule of practice that paid trustees should take reasonable steps to ensure that settlers are aware of exemption clauses included in trust deeds.[412] Such a rule is likely to have little impact in relation to bond issues, where the terms of the trust deed are already made known to both the settlor and the beneficiaries.[413] In any event, the Law Commission proposed that the rule would not apply where the trustee was already subject to statutory regulation of exemption clauses,[414] although the statutory regulation of debenture trust deeds, of course, only extends to a limited type of clause.[415]

8.3.5.6 *Conclusion*

The current position, then, in relation to bond issue trust deeds, depends on a balance. It is not possible for a trustee expressly to exclude liability for breach of the duty of care and skill but a similar effect can be achieved by indirect means, which are not subject to regulation but which are, as a matter of practice, known both to the settlor (the issuer) and to the beneficiaries (the bondholders). Such clauses are likely to be interpreted strictly, but will be enforceable unless they reduce the irreducible core of the trustee's obligations, which is very unlikely in relation to the standard type of clause. However, unusual arrangements, such as in the *Citibank* case, are potentially more open to challenge, although where the alternative to holding a clause enforceable is deciding that there is no trust, the courts are likely to be very loath to go down that route, and will probably give force to the parties' intentions.

---

[410] Law Commission Consultation Paper No 171, 'Trustee Exemption Clauses' (2002).
[411] Financial Markets Law Committee, Issue 62, *Trustee Exemption Clauses* (2004), 1–3.
[412] Law Commission Report No 301, *Trustee Exemption Clauses* (2006).
[413] Ibid, 6.81.
[414] The predecessor to s 750 Companies Act 2006, s 192 Companies Act 1985, was given as an example.
[415] See 8.3.5.1.

8.4 Syndicated Loans[416]

8.4.1 Comparison Between Agency in Syndicated Loans and Trustee Structure in Bond Issues

Like an issue of debt securities, a syndicated loan is a way of enabling the borrower to borrow from more than one lender. The impetus for this is usually that the borrower wishes to borrow more money than one lender is prepared to lend. The arranging bank thus organises a syndicate of banks, all of which participate in making the loan, thus spreading the risk of non-payment amongst them. While what is described in this section is a syndicated loan where the arranging bank finds lenders that then enter into an agreement with the borrower and amongst themselves, another method is for the loan agreement to be made with one bank, which then sells participations to a number of other banks using the methods discussed in chapter nine below.[417] Unlike bonds, syndicated loans are not of their nature tradable, but they can be transferred and there is now a well-developed secondary market in such loans.[418] The fact that the transferability of loans is an 'add-on' to their intrinsic nature,[419] however, means that their structure is more geared to lenders that intend to remain locked into the deal, and take a longer-term view, rather than bondholders who can offload their investment in the market whenever they wish.[420] This is reflected, for example, in the more extensive covenants that normally appear in a loan, whereas bonds often just include little more than a negative pledge.[421]

Another difference is that a bond issue is a one-off event: there is no obligation on the bondholders to lend more money, while a syndicated loan, even if it is a term loan, can be drawn down in tranches, so that the lenders have an obligation to lend in the future. This means, for example, that on transfer, unlike bonds, obligations are transferred as well as rights. Borrowers, therefore, may want to protect themselves against a loan being transferred to a person who would be unable to fulfil the lending obligations.[422] Having said this, even this difference between the two methods of borrowing has been eroded, in that many bonds are now issued under a programme, with common documentation for a series of issues and which enables the issuer to obtain more credit when it needs to, which in some ways is similar to a revolving loan facility.[423] There are still differences, though, since dealers in a bond programme are not obliged to subscribe for any further issues: the programme agreement is on an uncommitted basis, whereas participants in a syndicated loan are obliged to lend within the terms of the loan.

Another difference, which stems largely from their tradability, and from the identity of the investors, is that bonds are rated and, apart from high-yield issues, are issued only by

[416] For detailed discussion see Mugasha: Multi-Bank Financing.
[417] See ibid, ch 6.
[418] See 9.2.4.
[419] Hughes: Banking, 4.2, Fuller: Corporate Borrowing, 1.4.
[420] This, of course, depends on a level of liquidity in the market.
[421] Fuller: Capital Markets, 1.57; Wood: Loans and Bonds, 10-018. See 3.2.2.3.
[422] Hughes: Banking, 4.8. See 9.2.1.
[423] See 8.3.1.

investment grade companies.[424] Loans can be made to any company, although the terms on which they will be made depend on the creditworthiness of the borrower. Obviously, the size of the company to which a syndicated loan is made will be large, but that does not always ensure creditworthiness. This is another reason for the more extensive covenants in loans, and may also be a reason for the loan to be secured.

Other points of distinction between bonds and syndicated loans will emerge in the ensuing discussion. There is, though, an important similarity as well. Both structures involve multiple lenders, and one of the most important elements of the structure is the balance between the individual interests of each lender and the collective interests of the whole group.[425] One might have thought that, since syndicated lenders are less able to 'exit' and are therefore more likely to be part of the group for longer, there would be more protection for the group as a whole. This is true to some extent, but against this it must be remembered that lenders have obligations as well as rights.[426] It is the disinclination of syndicated lenders to be liable for the failure of the other participants to lend that has led to the rights (and therefore) obligations of lenders being several rather than joint.[427] Further, since the lenders are banks, and may have other relationships with the borrower, such as deposit accounts, a lender may want to be able to set off the loan debt against what it owes the borrower on the deposit account: this would not be possible if the debt were jointly owned with the other participants.[428]

The several nature of the lenders' rights means that each lender can enforce the debt owed to it individually. As we have seen, owners of debt securities are not able to do this if there is a trustee (in relation to either stock or bonds). The position of holders of stock issued under a deed poll, and of bonds issued without a trustee, is more similar to that of syndicated lenders.[429] As with a trustee structure in respect of bonds, there are advantages to having a collective procedure for enforcement.[430] Thus, the right of each lender to enforce is usually qualified in practice by a provision that acceleration can only occur after an event of default has been declared by the agent bank, on the direction of the majority lenders,[431] and also by the 'pro rata' clause discussed in the next paragraph. Instructions given to the agent bank by the majority lenders will usually override any conflicting instructions given by any other party.[432] What is less clear is whether, in the absence of an express 'no-action

---

[424] See 2.3.3.3.

[425] The balance in any individual transaction will, of course, depend on the terms of that particular transaction: Hudson: Banking, 33-12. The discussion that follows is based on some of the more usual provisions in loan agreements, found in the LMA standard form, but the situation will vary according to the context of the loan and the negotiating powers of the borrowers.

[426] For an overview of when a lender can refuse to lend, see P Rawlings, 'Avoiding the Obligation to Lend' [2012] *Journal of Business Law* 89.

[427] Fuller: Corporate Borrowing, 2.17; Hughes: Banking, 9.2. There is also no question of the syndicate being a partnership, for similar reasons: see Benjamin: Financial Law, 8.25; Hudson: Finance, 33-11–33-13; E Ellinger, E Lomnicka and C Hare, *Ellinger's Modern Banking Law*, 5th edn (Oxford, Oxford University Press, 2011) 784.

[428] Fuller: Corporate Borrowing, 2.17. Note that the contract will normally exclude the right of the borrower to rely on set-off.

[429] For details see 8.3.2.2.1 and 8.3.2.3.3.

[430] See 8.3.4.2.1.

[431] Mugasha: Multi-Bank Financing, 5.11. See LMA Leveraged Finance Facility Agreement, cl 28.20. The term 'majority lenders' is defined in the loan agreement, and may require a majority of more than 50%: see 8.6.4.

[432] See LMA Leveraged Finance Facility Agreement, cl 32(2)(c); Paget 12.38.

clause', these provisions mean that any particular lender is unable to enforce the debt due to it individually.[433] Where a syndicated loan is secured, security cannot conveniently be held separately by each lender, and it is necessary for there to be a security trustee to hold the security for the benefit of all the banks. In this situation there will be a parallel covenant to pay the security trustee, who will be responsible for enforcing this and the security on the direction of a majority of the lenders,[434] thus giving rise to a collective procedure.

Since bonds are collectively enforced, if an issuer is insolvent, each bondholder will get a pro rata share of whatever is recovered. In the case of syndicated loans, however, separate enforcement might lead to a 'race to the bottom', so that a lender that enforces early can obtain full payment while all the others recover proportionately less. The 'pro rata' clause therefore provides that if a bank recovers more than it would have done on collective enforcement, it must pay the excess to the agent who distributes it pro rata.[435] However, this clause can also operate to give the syndicated lenders a collective advantage over other creditors. As mentioned earlier, the several nature of the lenders' rights means that deposits can be set off against the borrower's obligations under the loan. If one lender has such a right of set-off, the pro rata clause means that it enures to the benefit of all the lenders, and, provided the lenders collectively have counterclaims against the borrower equal to the amount of the loan, the entire loan can be paid through set-off.[436] This may give the same effect as if the loan had been secured, although without the actual grant of security, which could infringe negative pledge clauses in other agreements with the borrower.[437] It is not entirely clear (and would in any event depend on the actual wording) whether the pro rata clause applies to a buy-back of the debt by the borrower, which has the effect of extinguishing the debt.[438] While still advantageous to the borrower, if the lender has to share the proceeds of a buy-back with the other lenders, it is no more advantageous to the lender than selling on the loan. On the other hand, if it does not, it is not consistent with the collective spirit of a syndicated loan.

A further instance of collectivism is the fact that, although the rights and obligations of the lenders are several, there is only one agreement to which all are parties, so that the terms and conditions are identical.[439] In order to simplify the drafting process for each agreement, and to save on lawyers' time and costs, the Loan Market Association has put together standardised loan agreements, which are periodically revised to reflect market practice.[440]

---

[433] See P Rawlings, 'The Management of Loan Syndicates and the Rights of Individual Lenders' (2009) 24 *Journal of International Banking Law and Regulation* 179.

[434] See 8.4.6.

[435] For examples of such a clause, see Fuller: Corporate Borrowing, 2.20; Wood: Loans and Bonds, 7-029. See 8.3.2.3.1(b) for discussion of the similarity between this and the compulsory *pari passu* rule on actual insolvency.

[436] This is by the process of double-dipping. If lender A owes the borrower more than the amount of A's share of the loan, A can set off its entire share. The excess is then shared between the other lenders, and A is subrogated to the rights of the other lenders for the amount distributed. A can then set off the balance of the debt it owes the borrower against these subrogated loans. For a full explanation see Wood: Loans and Bonds, 7-030; Encyclopaedia of Banking Law 3503.

[437] Wood: Loans and Bonds, 7-030. Whether the double-dipping would be effective in insolvency would depend on the timing of the 'dips': it is unlikely that any 'dipping' would be permitted after the onset of insolvency.

[438] S Samuel, 'Debt Buybacks: Simply Not Cricket?' [2009] *Journal of International Banking and Financial Law* 24. See also 6.3.1.5.

[439] Loan Market Association, *Guide to Syndicated Loans*, 1.

[440] Most of the changes are negotiated between the Loan Market Association and the Association of Corporate Treasurers.

Some provisions in these agreements are reasonably standard, while others are still very dependent on the position of the parties, so that the LMA form is just the starting point for negotiations.[441] A market standard agreement is also a significant advantage where there is a thriving secondary loan market, since traders are not keen to examine the terms of the loans traded, nor are they in a position to negotiate such terms.[442] There are separate standard agreements for investment grade and leveraged finance loans.

8.4.2 Finding Lenders

As with bonds, it is necessary for there to be an institution which puts together the group of lenders. In relation to a syndicated loan, this is done by an arranger, which is a bank (or more than one bank) which will also itself be a participant lender. The arranger is granted a 'mandate' to solicit other banks to join the syndicate. The arranger is not usually committed to lend at this stage, but it gives a 'best efforts' undertaking to put together a syndicate that will make the loan. It is also possible for the arranger to underwrite the loan, thereby promising to lend if no other banks can be found. In this case the underwriting obligation is likely to be subject to changes in the market, which can entitle the arranger to change the terms of the loan or even to pull out altogether.[443] The arranger advises the borrower on putting together the information memorandum. This gives information about the borrower in a similar way to a preliminary offering circular in a bond issue.[444] On the basis of this document, the arranger finds other banks to participate and the loan documentation is negotiated.[445]

8.4.3 Role of the Arranger

The legal position of the arranger will now be discussed, including whether the arranger acts as agent for the borrower or for the participant banks, and what, if any, fiduciary duties it owes and to whom. One important question is whether the arranger is liable for false statements in the information memorandum. If the borrower is insolvent, the lenders will seek to sue a 'deep-pocketed' defendant such as the arranging bank for such false statements. If the arranger owes a fiduciary duty to the lenders, this will include a duty to make full disclosure, although there are also alternative causes of action relating to false statements which are considered below.[446] The question of whether an arranging bank is a fiduciary, however,

---

[441] M Campbell, 'The LMA Recommended Form of Primary Documents' [2000] *Journal of International Banking and Financial Law* 53; K Clowry, 'LMA Credit Documentation: Recent Key Negotiation Issues' [2008] *Journal of International Banking and Financial Law* 6. Such terms include the events of default, the financial covenants and terms as to transferability.

[442] Hughes: Banking, 9.8.

[443] Fuller: Corporate Borrowing, 13.2; Wood: Loans and Bonds, 1-005–1-007; Loan Market Association, *Guide to Syndicated Loans*, 4.1.

[444] Note, however, that there are no regulations governing this document, unlike a bond prospectus. See 13.2.8.

[445] Wood: Loans and Bonds, 1-008; Loan Market Association, *Guide to Syndicated Loans*, 2–4.

[446] 8.4.4. A comparison can also be made with the liability of a manager or underwriter for misstatements in a bond prospectus. See 13.2.7.

goes further than just this type of liability. If the arranger were a fiduciary, it would be under a duty of the utmost good faith and honesty and to act in the best interests of the person to whom the duty is owed: this would include a duty to avoid conflicts of interest (which could be difficult),[447] a duty of due diligence and, maybe, a duty to account to the participants for fees received from the borrower.[448]

The arranging bank's factual position changes in the course of the transaction. In the first place, it is instructed by the borrower, with regard to drawing up the information memorandum and maybe advising the borrower on the type of transaction that is suitable for its requirements.[449] Its next task is to solicit other potential participants, but when it has done that, it negotiates the loan documentation with the borrower and appears to be acting for the participant banks as much as or more than for the borrower.

The question of whether an arranger is a fiduciary has, then, two aspects. First, does it owe fiduciary duties to anyone, and second, if so, to whom and when? The answer to the second question may throw some light on the answer to the first. Since it is impossible to owe fiduciary duties to each of two parties negotiating with each other, and it is very difficult to pinpoint a time when the duties of the arranger shift from the borrower to the lenders, the best solution is that the arranger does not owe fiduciary duties to anyone.[450] It certainly seems very unlikely that the arranger owes fiduciary duties to the borrower. Not only are such duties likely to be expressly excluded in the mandate letter,[451] but the borrower is usually in the position of a customer of the bank, and no fiduciary duties are owed by a bank to its customer.[452] There is, however, Court of Appeal authority for the proposition that the arranger owes a fiduciary duty to the participant banks. In *UBAF Ltd v European American Banking Corporation*[453] Lords Justice Ackner and Oliver stated:

> The transaction into which the plaintiffs were invited to enter, and did enter, was that of contributing to a syndicate loan where, as it seems to us, quite clearly the defendants were acting in a fiduciary capacity for all the other participants. It was the defendants who received the plaintiffs' money and it was the defendants who arranged for and held, on behalf of all the participants, the collateral security for the loan. If, therefore, it was within the defendants' knowledge at any time whilst they

---

[447] Wood: Loans and Bonds, 1-009. See, however, *Saltri III Ltd v MD Mezzanine SA Sicar* [2012] EWHC 3025 (Comm) in which it was accepted that 'a person in his position may be in a fiduciary position *quoad* a part of his activities and not *quoad* other parts' depending on the terms of the contract governing the relationship ([123]) and so, when exercising its duty to enforce the security in the manner of a mortgagee, the security trustee did not owe a duty to avoid a conflict with the mortgagor, as this would be impossible ([124]).

[448] G Skene, 'Syndicated Loans: Arranger and Participant Bank Fiduciary Theory' (2005) 20 *Journal of International Banking Law and Regulation* 269; see also E Tearle and S Buckingham, '*FHR European Ventures*: a Decision with Wider Implications for the Loan Market' [2014] *Journal of International Banking and Financial Law* 717. It can be argued, however, that in this context a fiduciary duty is only an aspect of a wider duty of care, which is often owed to participant banks in relation to certain functions: see *Henderson v Merrett Syndicates Ltd (No 1)* [1995] 2 AC 145, 205; D Halliday and R Davies, 'Risks and Responsibilities of the Agent Bank and the Arranging Bank in Syndicated Credit Facilities' (1997) 12 *Journal of International Banking Law* 182, 183. However, while it is possible to owe duties of care in relation to specific tasks to two people at once, it is surely more difficult to owe fiduciary duties to two people, especially if their interests are, to some extent, opposed.

[449] Loan Market Association, *Guide to Syndicated Loans*, 2.

[450] Wood: Loans and Bonds, 1-009.

[451] For an example, see *Barclays Bank plc v Svizera Holdings BV* [2014] EWHC 1020 (Comm) [15].

[452] *JP Morgan Chase Bank v Springwell Navigation Corp* [2008] EWHC 1186 (Comm) [573] applied in the current context in *Barclays v Svizera*, ibid, [8].

[453] *UBAF Ltd v European American Banking Corporation* [1984] QB 713.

were carrying out their fiduciary duties that the security was, as the plaintiffs allege, inadequate, it must, we think, clearly have been their duty to inform the participants of that fact and their continued failure to do so would constitute a continuing breach of their fiduciary duty.

This statement is often said to be obiter,[454] since the purpose of the application was to set aside leave to serve out of the jurisdiction. The two grounds for this were that the claims in deceit and under section 2(1) of the Misrepresentation Act 1967 were precluded by section 6 of the Statute of Frauds Amendment Act 1928 and that the claim in negligence was statute barred. No independent claim based on breach of fiduciary duty was in fact pleaded: the relevance of the existence of a fiduciary duty was that it would give rise to a duty of disclosure which might enable the claimant to rely on section 32(1)(b) of the Limitation Act 1980 (based on deliberate concealment), which would have the effect of making the limitation period run from the time when the facts were first known by the claimant. The statement quoted above does, therefore, appear to be relevant to the decision in the case (that leave should not be set aside), but despite that, it is not necessarily of general import. The claimant's case was based on false statements about the value of the collateral. The defendant was not only the arranging bank, but was also security trustee for the transaction and the agent bank. It would appear that the statement that the defendant owed fiduciary duties could be because of its role as security trustee rather than its role as arranger.[455] Furthermore, the defendant had previously acquired knowledge which put it in a different position from most arrangers.[456]

The case has never been expressly followed in the UK, and, it is submitted, should be treated with great care as an authority, since every case will depend on its own facts. First and foremost, the existence and extent of a fiduciary relationship between parties will depend on the contractual position between them.[457] The arranger will therefore seek to exclude any fiduciary duties, whether owed to the borrower or to the lending banks[458] (and will probably also seek to exclude liability in negligence and for misrepresentation):[459] to the extent that it seeks to exclude equitable duties this would not seem to fall within the Unfair Contract Terms Act[460] and would seem to be effective to prevent a fiduciary relationship

---

[454] G Bhattacharyya, 'The Duties and Liabilities of Lead Managers in Syndicated Loans' [1995] *Journal of International Banking and Financial Law* 172; D Halliday and R Davies, 'Risks and Responsibilities of the Agent Bank and the Arranging Bank in Syndicated Credit Facilities' (1997) 12 *Journal of International Banking Law* 182, 183; G Skene, 'Syndicated Loans: Arranger and Participant Bank Fiduciary Theory' (2005) 20 *Journal of International Banking Law and Regulation* 269, 273.

[455] Although note that even a security trustee does not necessarily owe fiduciary duties in respect of every aspect of its operations: this will depend on the contractual position between the relevant parties. See *Saltri III Ltd v MD Mezzanine SA Sicar* [2012] EWHC 3025 (Comm) [123]–[124].

[456] G Bhattacharyya, 'The Duties and Liabilities of Lead Managers in Syndicated Loans' [1995] *Journal of International Banking and Financial Law* 172; G Skene, 'Syndicated Loans: Arranger and Participant Bank Fiduciary Theory' (2005) 20 *Journal of International Banking Law and Regulation* 269, 273.

[457] *Henderson v Merrett Syndicates Ltd (No 1)* [1995] 2 AC 145, 206 (Lord Browne-Wilkinson); *Saltri III Ltd v MD Mezzanine SA Sicar* [2012] EWHC 3025 (Comm) [123]; *Torre Asset Funding Ltd v Royal Bank of Scotland plc* [2013] EWHC 2670 (Ch) [143]–[148].

[458] See eg LMA Leveraged Finance Facility Agreement, cl 32(5).

[459] See 8.4.4 and LMA Leveraged Finance Facility Agreement, cl 32(10). The LMA Investment Grade agreement was amended in 2014 to narrow the scope of arranger and agent liability to bring it into line with the Leveraged Finance Agreement.

[460] See 8.3.5.3.

arising.[461] This is desirable given the difficulties of analysis discussed above, and also given that the participants (both borrower and lenders) are sophisticated and experienced financial institutions which are in a good position to protect themselves.

8.4.4 Liability of the Arranger in Relation to False Statements in the Information Memorandum

The information memorandum used in syndicated loans, which is usually drawn up by or on the advice of the arranger, provides important information to potential lenders. The loan documentation will include a warranty by the borrower as to the correctness of the information in the memorandum, so that if information is found to be inaccurate, this is an event of default.[462] There would also be a claim against the borrower for misrepresentation and deceit.[463] However, an action against the borrower is unlikely, in the absence of special circumstances, to add anything to the claim for the amount due on the loan[464] and, in any event, if the borrower is unable to pay back the loan and is insolvent, there is no point suing for damages. The lenders would then look to sue other persons with deeper pockets; this might, of course, include guarantors or insurers,[465] but is likely also to include the bank that acted as arranger.[466] It should be pointed out that there is no equivalent action to that under section 90 of the Financial Services and Markets Act. This action arises where there is a misstatement in disclosure required by regulatory rules, and therefore only arises where those rules apply, namely in relation to offers of shares and debt securities.[467]

The question of whether the arranger owes a fiduciary duty to the lenders has just been discussed. There are also potential claims in tort and under the Misrepresentation Act 1967. Taking the claims in tort first, one possible cause of action is deceit, but this will depend on dishonesty on the part of the arranger, which is unlikely. Another possibility is that the arranger owes a duty of care to the lenders under the doctrine in *Hedley Byrne & Co Ltd v Heller & Partners Ltd*.[468] There are two cases in which an arranger has been held to owe a duty of care to lenders participating in a syndicated loan, although in neither was the issue merely one of negligent misstatement, and both, arguably, depend on their own facts.

---

[461] G Skene, 'Syndicated Loans: Arranger and Participant Bank Fiduciary Theory' (2005) 20 *Journal of International Banking Law and Regulation* 269, 279 takes the view that this would be the position under Australian law. It also appears to be the position under US law: see *Banque Arabe et Internationale D'Investissement v Maryland National Bank*, 810 F Supp 1282, 1296 (SDNY, 1993), aff'd 57 F 3d 146 (2d Cir 1995); *Banco Español de Crédito v Security Pacific National Bank*, 763 F Supp 36, 45 (SDNY, 1991), aff'd 973 F2d 51 (2d Cir 1992), cited by Skene at 277. See also Paget 12.20.

[462] For example clauses, see cl 23.4 LMA Investment Grade Loan Agreement and cl 28.4 LMA Leveraged Finance Facility Agreement. See also 6.2.3.1.

[463] As there is against the issuer of debt securities. See 13.2.7.1.

[464] Wood: Loans and Bonds, 1-019.

[465] See 6.4.

[466] G Bhattacharyya, 'The Duties and Liabilities of Lead Managers in Syndicated Loans' [1995] *Journal of International Banking and Financial Law* 172.

[467] See 10.6.2 and 13.2.7.2.

[468] [1964] AC 465.

In *Natwest Australia Bank Ltd v Tricontinental Corp Ltd*,[469] the arranger, which was also one of the lending banks, drew up the information memorandum but failed to disclose that the borrower had a contingent liability to it, the arranger. The claimant, another of the lending banks, had actually made enquiries of the arranger relating to this very matter and had been told that the contingent liabilities were only nominal. In these circumstances, the Supreme Court of Victoria held that the arranger owed a duty to disclose the contingent liabilities to the lending banks, of which it was in breach, and that the lending bank was not contributorily negligent in failing to pursue the matter or to make its own enquiries. The reasoning of the court depended heavily on the facts: there was said to be an assumption of responsibility based on the facts that the arranger was acting in the course of business and had been paid a substantial fee and that a prudent bank would realise that the existence of the contingent liability would be an important factor in the decision of the lending bank whether to participate in the syndicate.[470] The duty of care was not affected by the inclusion of a disclaimer in the information memorandum, which read: 'The information herein has been obtained from the borrower and other sources considered reliable. No Representation or Warranty expressed or implied is made with respect to this information.' This was interpreted as only relating to information provided, rather than information which was omitted, and also did not relate to the express question asked by the lending bank.[471] As with many such negligence cases, though, this finding of an assumption of responsibility is fact-specific. For example, the arranger actually knew about the contingent liabilities, so the duty was one of disclosure rather than a duty of care. Also, the lending bank made a specific enquiry, which meant that the arranger knew of the importance to it of the existence of contingent liabilities.[472] Moreover, the disclaimer was narrow and a wider disclaimer in the mandate agreement might have been more effective, as discussed below.

In the case of *Sumitomo v Banque Bruxelles Lambert SA*,[473] the arranger had failed to make disclosure to an insurance company which rendered mortgage indemnity guarantees, taken out to protect the security for the loan, invalid. Here, the limited contractual duties owed by the arranger to the lending banks did not prevent a duty of care arising in relation to the arrangement of the insurance policy: there was sufficient assumption of responsibility in relation to that particular task.[474] The exclusion clause in the loan agreement was interpreted only to apply to the arranger's liabilities qua agent bank and not as arranger[475] (and in fact was not wide enough even to exclude liability for negligent execution of the bank's tasks qua agent: the clause, like all exclusion clauses, was interpreted strictly).

The position therefore appears to be that, while each case will depend on its own facts, the court will be prepared to find a duty of care in relation to specific tasks if they are foreseeably important to the lenders. Whether a more widely drawn duty of care in relation to the information memorandum exists is a matter for considerable doubt. In *IFE*

---

[469] 1993 VIC LEXIS 743.

[470] Ibid, 164.

[471] Ibid, 167.

[472] G Bhattacharyya, 'The Duties and Liabilities of Lead Managers in Syndicated Loans' [1995] *Journal of International Banking and Financial Law* 172.

[473] [1997] 1 Lloyd's Rep 487. See S Sequiera, 'Syndicated Loans—Let the Arranger Beware!' [1997] *Journal of International Banking and Financial Law* 117.

[474] [1997] 1 Lloyd's Rep 487, 514.

[475] Ibid, 493.

Fund SA v Goldman Sachs International,[476] where it was made clear in the information memorandum that the arranging bank was accepting no responsibility for the accuracy of the information, the Court of Appeal held that no duty of care was owed,[477] and that the court would be very slow to 'superimpose' a duty of care where obligations between the various parties had been carefully agreed.[478]

In any event, such a duty can be satisfactorily excluded both by a notice given to the participants in relation to the information memorandum[479] and/or by a term in the loan agreement excluding liability of the arranger for representations made.[480] Such a disclaimer would be subject to the requirement of reasonableness in section 2(2) of the Unfair Contract Terms Act 1977,[481] but it is submitted that, given the relatively equal bargaining power of the parties and the fact that lending banks are sophisticated commercial institutions, such an exclusion is likely to be held to be reasonable.[482] The counter-argument to this is that the arranger is in a better position to assess the creditworthiness of the borrower,[483] and so it should bear some responsibility (apart from its own liability as lender) if disclosure is inaccurate. One could argue, however, that this concern is met, first, by the fact that the arranger would still be liable for fraud (including recklessness), since this liability cannot be excluded, and also by the fact that banks, unlike bondholders, do negotiate the agreement that includes the exclusion clauses and can put pressure on the arranger to take them out.

There is also potential liability under section 2(1) of the Misrepresentation Act 1967, which applies where a person has entered a contract after a misrepresentation has been made to him by another party thereto. This will only apply if the arranger is also a party to the loan agreement (this will usually be the case as the arranger is likely to be a lender). Liability by this route is easier for the participants to establish, in that no duty of care needs to be established, and the burden of proof of breach of duty is reversed.[484] Here, too, clauses in the information memorandum can also affect whether such liability arises. If it is made clear that the arranging bank is making no representations in relation to the information provided in the memorandum, then this is binding on the parties as a matter of contractual

---

[476] [2007] EWCA Civ 811.

[477] Ibid, [28].

[478] Waller LJ in the Court of Appeal at [28] agreed with the reasoning of the judge to this effect, set out at [17].

[479] Wood: Loans and Bonds, 1-021. For an example, see *Raiffeisen Zentralbank Osterreich AG v Royal Bank of Scotland plc* [2010] EWHC 1392 [65].

[480] See LMA Leveraged Finance Facility Agreement, cl 32(10).

[481] Note, though, that Gloster J in *JP Morgan Chase Bank (formerly Chase Manhattan Bank) v Springwell Navigation Corp* [2008] EWHC 1186 [602] said that contractual provisions which merely confirm the basis upon which the parties are transacting business are not subject to s 2(2) Unfair Contract Terms Act 1977, since '[o]therwise, every contract which contains contractual terms defining the extent of each party's obligations would have to satisfy the requirement of reasonableness'. While this makes a great deal of sense, it might still be possible to argue that such duty-defining clauses are 'excluding ... the relevant obligation or duty' under s 13 of that Act, and thus are brought within s 2. This argument does not appear to be available in relation to s 3 Misrepresentation Act 1967, to which section 13 does not apply.

[482] G Bhattacharyya, 'The Duties and Liabilities of Lead Managers in Syndicated Loans' [1995] *Journal of International Banking and Financial Law* 172. In *Raiffeisen Zentralbank Osterreich AG v Royal Bank of Scotland plc* [2010] EWHC 1392, in relation to contractual provisions in an information memorandum for a syndicated loan, the judge held that if the relevant clause did exclude liability for misrepresentation it satisfied the requirement of reasonableness in s 11 Unfair Contract Terms Act (at [319]–[327]).

[483] Hughes: Banking, 9.5.

[484] See 13.2.7.1, where s 2(1) is discussed in the context of liability of an issuer to bondholders.

estoppel[485] and there can be no liability for misrepresentation.[486] Such a clause is not subject to the requirement of reasonableness imposed by section 3 of the Misrepresentation Act 1967, as it does not exclude or restrict liability for misrepresentation.[487] If the clause provides that there is no reliance on any representations made, then this too can take effect as a contractual estoppel, but section 3 will apply,[488] and will also apply if the clause expressly excludes or restricts liability. In any event, where the lenders are experienced financial institutions, or where the wording used is common in the context of syndicated loan agreements, the clause is likely to be held to be reasonable.[489]

8.4.5 Position of the Agent Bank

The actual structure of the loan transaction reflects the need for efficient day-to-day administration, and for effective decision-making at critical moments. Again the balance is between collectivity and enabling individual banks to protect their own interests. One of the lending banks is usually appointed as the agent bank: this is largely an administrative position and does not attract such high fees as the position of arranger.[490]

The position of the agent bank may be compared with that of a trustee in a bond issue, in that it is a person that carries out functions on behalf of the lenders. In fact, however, there is a considerable difference: the agent bank is seen as mainly a functionary which deals with specific administrative tasks.[491] This is supported by the documentation, which provides for certain specific powers but also includes heavy exclusionary provisions. A loan agreement will usually state expressly that the agent bank is not a fiduciary,[492] unlike a bond trustee, and the agreement may provide for the agent to do things which would otherwise be a breach of fiduciary duty, such as receiving sums from the borrower on its own account.[493]

If an agent bank is also a security trustee, it will of course owe fiduciary duties, but many of these are usually excluded.[494] The agent is largely expected to act on the instructions of the lenders, and it is to the democratic structure of the syndicate that we now turn.

---

[485] *Peekay Intermark v Australia and New Zealand Banking Group* [2006] EWCA Civ 386; *JP Morgan Chase Bank (formerly Chase Manhattan Bank) v Springwell Navigation Corp* [2008] EWHC 1186 [558]–[568]; *Raiffeisen Zentralbank Osterreich AG v Royal Bank of Scotland plc* [2010] EWHC 1392 [250]–[255]; *Cassa di Risparmio v Barclays Bank* [2011] EWHC 484 [505].

[486] *Raiffeisen Zentralbank Osterreich AG v Royal Bank of Scotland plc* [2010] EWHC 1392 [267].

[487] Ibid, [316]. However, even this depends on the particular circumstances of the case: where a clear statement of fact is made which is (objectively) intended to be a representation and to be relied upon, but the terms of the contract state that no representation has been made, s 3 may apply: ibid, [307]–[308].

[488] Ibid, [286]. See also *EA Grimstead & Son Ltd v McGarrigan* [1999] EWCA Civ 3029 and *Government of Zanzibar v British Aerospace (Lancaster House) Ltd* [2000] 1 WLR 2333; cf *Watford Electronics Ltd v Sanderson CFL Ltd* [2001] EWCA Civ 317 and *Barclays Bank plc v Svizera Holdings BV* [2014] EWHC 1020 (Comm) [61].

[489] *Raiffeisen Zentralbank Osterreich AG v Royal Bank of Scotland plc* [2010] EWHC 1392 [319]–[327].

[490] *Torre Asset Funding Ltd v Royal Bank of Scotland plc* [2013] EWHC 2670 (Ch) [163(ii)].

[491] This is made very clear in *Torre Asset Funding*, ibid—see particularly [34]. For a list of the agent bank's functions, see Fuller: Corporate Borrowing, 22–23.

[492] LMA Leveraged Finance Facility Agreement, cl 32.5, and see cl 26.4 of the agreement considered in *Torre Asset Funding*, ibid.

[493] See clauses mentioned in the previous footnote. Such an authorisation of conflict may also be included in a trust deed: see Fuller: Corporate Borrowing, 12.28(3), but since the agent bank is usually one of the lenders, an actual conflict is much more likely to arise.

[494] See *Saltri III Ltd v MD Mezzanine SA Sicar* [2012] EWHC 3025 (Comm) [123]–[124].

8.4.6 Majority Lenders[495]

Most important matters concerning the loan will require the consent of 'the majority lenders'. This term will be defined in the loan agreement, usually consisting of holders of a majority (50 per cent or 66 per cent) of the loan outstanding.[496] The matters in question include modification of the loan agreement, waiver of breaches, determining whether an event or breach is material so as to amount to an event of default, directing the agent bank to accelerate the loan if there is an event of default, and giving consent to the provision of security by the borrower.[497] In relation to modification, certain entrenched provisions, such as the pro rata clause, definition of 'majority lenders' and subordination provisions, cannot be modified without the consent of all the lenders.[498] Certain breaches, for example of a condition precedent, cannot usually be waived by a majority.[499] Thus, despite the general idea of democratic decision-making which is discussed in the next paragraph, there is some protection for the individual lender that wishes, rationally or irrationally, to hold out against the collective view.

It is necessary for the agreement to provide expressly that the decision of the majority binds all the lenders: this is not inherent in the agreement.[500] Obviously, the effect of such a provision is potentially to damage the interests of the minority lenders, and the question arises as to whether, and in what circumstances, they should be given some protection. It now seems reasonably clear that the majority are under some constraints in terms of the way they exercise their power, and indeed their vote, but that these constraints are intended to prevent a dishonest abuse of power and nothing more. Thus, the majority must not exercise their power in a manner motivated by a desire to damage or oppress the minority,[501] nor to confer special collateral benefits on the majority. The principles in relation to syndicated loans are very similar to those applicable to bonds, which are discussed above.[502]

---

[495] For discussion of the ascertainment of the views of bondholders, see 7.3.3.

[496] Hughes: Corporate Borrowing, 9.7; Wood: Loans and Bonds, 7-014; Mugasha: Multi-Bank Financing, 5.118. Clause 1 of the LMA agreement provides for a majority of 66⅔%. Compare the position with bonds, where a numerosity requirement is more common than in syndicated loans (see 8.3.3). Again, unlike in a bond issue, voting procedures are rarely formalised in the loan agreement, so that when it becomes necessary to ascertain the views of the majority, some sort of 'de facto mechanism' has to be set up by the lenders: *Redwood Master Fund Ltd v TD Bank Europe Ltd* [2002] EWHC 2703 [97].

[497] Hughes: Banking, 9.7; Wood: Loans and Bonds, 7-014; Mugasha: Multi-Bank Financing, 5.118.

[498] Tolley's Company Law Service 5027; Mugasha: Multi-Bank Financing, 5.116; Wood: Loans and Bonds, 7-015.

[499] Wood: Loans and Bonds, 7-015. This enables an individual lender to refuse to advance further funds if such a breach occurs.

[500] This is implicit in the judgment of Lindley LJ in *Sneath v Valley Gold Ltd* [1893] 1 Ch 477, 489, where he says: 'Powers given to majorities to bind minorities are always liable to abuse; and, whilst full effect ought to be given to them in cases clearly falling within them, ambiguities of language ought not to be taken advantage of to strengthen them and make them applicable to cases not included in those which they were apparently intended to meet.' It would not have been necessary to provide either that full effect should be given to such powers, or that they should be strictly construed, unless only the express power enabled the majority to bind the minority.

[501] *Redwood Master Fund Ltd v TD Bank Europe Ltd* [2002] EWHC 2703 [105]. See 8.3.3.2. It is not, of course, easy to prove bad faith, but it may be inferred from the effect that the exercise of the power has on the minority, if the result is extreme enough. However, there is no reason why, absent bad faith, a lender should not vote according to its own interest: ibid, [105].

[502] 8.3.3.2.

There is therefore a balance between the advantages of majority rule, which is necessary to get things done and to avoid the 'holdout' problem, where one lender can prevent a beneficial course of action by refusing to consent, and the possible oppression of the minority. It is still possible, and indeed likely, that the majority vote will damage a minority lender, who is only protected by the 'good faith' requirement discussed above, and it may be that where there are several tranches of subordinated lenders, there is more likely to be a true divergence of interests than where there is only one tier of lenders,[503] where interests are more likely to be aligned and where the dissenting lender is more likely to be irrational, or, at least, trying to obtain an individual advantage which could well damage the interests of the whole.

The effect of a debt buy-back on syndicate democracy should also be noted. If the borrower buys back the loan itself, this may have the effect of extinguishing the loan, but if it does not, or if the buy-back is made by a sponsor, this gives the borrower a voice in the syndicate democracy, and can give rise to conflicts of interest.[504] Of course, where the decision requires a majority vote, it is unlikely that the borrower will have bought back enough debt for its vote to make a difference,[505] but where a unanimous decision is required, the borrower could hold out against a decision.[506]

8.5 Conclusion

The presence of more than one lender gives rise to a number of additional issues which do not need to be considered when there is only one lender. There is a need for the transaction to be structured in such a way that there can be efficient administration, without undue cost and duplication, which necessitates the use of either a trust or agency structure. This in itself necessitates the protection of individual rights, and the balance between this and collectivity is critical. One particular feature of both syndicated loans and bonds is their transferability, although there is no reason why loans by single lenders, or, indeed, any extension of credit, cannot be transferred.[507] The transfer of loans will be discussed in the next chapter.

---

[503] This is noted in *Redwood Master Fund Ltd v TD Bank Europe Ltd* [2002] EWHC 2703 [95].

[504] S Samuel, 'Debt Buybacks: Simply Not Cricket?' [2009] *Journal of International Banking and Financial Law* 24; P Clark and A Barker, 'The Evolution of Debt Buybacks' [2009] *Journal of International Banking and Financial Law* 359.

[505] A decision to accelerate the loan would normally fall into this category.

[506] This might, for example, be to improve its position in restructuring negotiations.

[507] Subject to some legal constraints, discussed in chapter 9.

9

Transferred Debt

This chapter draws together typical situations in which debt is transferred.[1] In most cases, we will be looking at transfers by and from people who are lending to companies, but the same techniques are used by companies in order to raise finance by transferring debts which are owed to them. Indeed, one technique, securitisation, is used both by companies and by lenders (which, after all, are companies whose business is finance) to raise money. One reason (among others) why a lender, or indeed a company, might want to transfer debt is to offload the credit risk of the debtor. In order to do this, there is no need actually to transfer the debt: the credit risk can be partially or wholly transferred to another party by other means, such as sub-participation or by using derivatives such as credit default swaps, or by the use of synthetic securitisation. These techniques are considered in this chapter, as well as outright transfers. Debts may also be transferred as security for a loan or other credit: this can be by way of mortgage or by way of charge.[2] Such transfers are largely discussed in chapter seven, although some of the discussion in this chapter will also apply to them (such as the discussion of clauses prohibiting assignment).[3]

9.1 Why is Debt Transferred?

The first distinction that needs to be drawn is between debt which is created to be traded, and other debt. As other debt, such as syndicated loans, has come to be transferred more frequently so that a liquid market has grown up, the distinction between the two has collapsed somewhat,[4] but it is still of some significance.[5] Historically, bonds and other debt securities, as well as other money market instruments such as bills of exchange, which were designed to be traded, were issued in bearer form and were negotiable.[6] This meant that the borrower knew that the debt was going to be transferred, and that it would have to pay the holder, whoever that might be. The relationship between the borrower and the original lender was, therefore, only temporary. These characteristics of debt securities and other

---

[1] The term 'transfer' is here used in a rather loose and non-legal sense. As will be seen, in some cases there is an actual transfer of the debt, in others a new debt arises in the place of the old debt, and in other cases still, only the credit risk is transferred and the debt remains owing to the same creditor.

[2] With a charge there is, again, technically not an actual transfer, but this is rarely of practical significance; see Security and Title-Based Financing, 6.62–6.67.

[3] 9.2.2.6.

[4] See E de Fontenay, 'Do Securities Laws Matter? The Rise of the Leveraged Loan Market', http://papers.ssrn.com/sol3/papers.cfm?abstract_id=2419668.

[5] For discussion of the differences in regulation, see 13.2.8, 13.3.3 and 13.4.2.

[6] The concept of negotiability, and its additional benefits, are discussed at 9.2.3.

money market instruments have continued, even though they are no longer commonly issued in bearer form.

Transferability has a number of ramifications for each original lender. First, it knows that, provided that the market is functioning normally, it can sell the securities at any time, and so it can afford to take a greater risk than with 'relationship' lending. Such risk includes the credit risk of the borrower, but also the liquidity risk of the lender (the risk that it might need the cash tied up in the loan for other ventures or to pay back its own debt) and, to some extent, market risk (although if the market became too adverse it might not be possible for the lender to sell the securities at all). Second, it is able to use the securities for other purposes, such as collateral for its own borrowing, in a very straightforward way as they can be mortgaged, charged or (in the case of negotiable instruments) pledged. Third, since the securities are designed to be traded on a market, there is generally a transparent pricing structure which can be used to value them at any time. Fourth, the presence of a market means not only that there are willing buyers to whom to transfer the securities, but also that there is a structure whereby these transfers can take place quickly, cheaply and easily.[7]

These factors translate into certain benefits for the issuer of the securities. The interest rate payable might well be lower than that charged by a 'relationship' lender.[8] Further, as the lenders can offload the credit risk, there is less incentive for extensive credit checks at the time of issue, or for extensive monitoring during the life of the security. Similarly, although there are covenants which the issuer has to observe, they are usually less stringent than those in relationship lending.[9] The presence of a market means not only that there is a larger pool of initial potential investors than with 'relationship' lending, but also that there is an even larger pool of investors who are potentially willing to buy the securities and therefore ensure continuing finance for the issuer. Further, the presence of a market means that even if it is only possible to issue relatively short-term debt, since long-term debt would be too expensive, there is usually a liquid enough market for replacement debt to be reissued, thus achieving a rolling over of the finance, while with a 'relationship' loan this would entail complicated and expensive refinancing negotiations. The lack of both the incentive and the capacity to investigate and monitor the financial state of the borrower in the case of traded debt is one of the main reasons for the regulation of the issue of debt listed on the Stock Exchange, and for the applicable continuing disclosure obligations. Regulation of debt is discussed below in chapter thirteen.

Other debt, which was not created in order to be traded, can also be transferred. As mentioned in chapter eight, it is common for a lender in a syndicated loan to transfer its interest. This could be for a number of reasons. It might be in order to transfer credit risk, as mentioned above. For example, if the borrower looks unlikely to be able to repay in full, the lenders might wish to 'crystallise' their loss and sell to less risk-averse institutions which

---

[7] This is referring not just to the ease of transfer by delivery, which is a feature of negotiability, but also to the presence of (originally) a physical market. Thus, not only could physical transfers take place easily but settlement of payment was also facilitated. More recently, this has been transformed by the presence of an electronic market which enables transfer and settlement to take place virtually instantaneously.

[8] A Morrison, 'Credit Derivatives, Disintermediation and Investment Decisions' (2003) 78 *Journal of Business* 621.

[9] See discussion at 3.2.2.3 and 6.3.

specialise in distressed debt.[10] Buyers of distressed debt may hope to make an eventual profit on the debt, and can spread the risk of loss by holding a wide portfolio bought at heavily discounted prices. Alternatively, they may be aiming at controlling the company by swapping debt for equity. The existence of a distressed debt market can perform a useful function in helping with the valuation of insolvent companies,[11] as well as permitting banks to lock in their loss or profit on a loan, according to its market valuation at the point of transfer.

Another reason for transfer might be that a lender decides that it wants a different risk profile for its assets, and so transfers its interest in a certain type of risk, or a certain type of borrower, in order to use the capital to lend elsewhere.[12] The lender, of course, might need capital for other reasons, or might decide that it does not want to retain any loans for their term, but wishes to sell on all its loans and use the proceeds to make more loans. This phenomenon becomes more likely as transfer of loans becomes easier and more common, which may lead to a situation where lenders 'originate to distribute'.[13] In this situation, the differences between debt issued to be traded, which is discussed above, and debt which on its face is not created to be traded, begins to collapse, and the features of the former, such as the lack of incentive to monitor, become apparent in the latter. Despite this, there is little regulation of the issue or transfer of syndicated or other loans, and any protection for lenders or buyers has to come from private law rights and remedies.[14]

Other reasons for transfer relate largely to the regulation of lenders, and in particular banks. As described in chapter two,[15] banks are required to keep a certain amount of capital against risky assets, of which loans are a category. If the loans can be removed from a bank's balance sheet by transfer, then the amount of capital that has to be held decreases.[16] Of course, the bank no longer has the source of income from the loan, but the future income will be taken into account in the pricing of the sale, discounted, of course, for the risk of default in both income and capital repayments. Further, a bank also might wish to transfer

---

[10] LMA Guide to Syndicated Loans and Leveraged Finance Transactions (October 2013), 6.A.4; Wood: Loans and Bonds, 7-019; Mugasha: Multi-Bank Financing, 2-57, 2-61. In some circumstances, a buyer of distressed debt may buy the debt in order to pursue remedies against the arranger of the syndicated loan, rather than sue the borrower, although if this is achieved by way of assignment it may be void as against public policy: A Chakrabarti and D Pygott, 'Trading Claims' [2007] *Journal of International Banking and Financial Law* 645. In certain circumstances, it might also be possible for the lender to sell at a profit, thus locking in the gain.

[11] G Smith and D King, 'How Insolvency Practitioners Value a Business' (2015) 28 *Insolvency Intelligence* 20.

[12] LMA Guide to Syndicated Loans and Leveraged Finance Transactions (October 2013), 6.A.2; Wood: Loans and Bonds, 7-019; Mugasha: Multi-Bank Financing, 2.58.

[13] This happened in the period between 2000 and 2007, leading up to the financial crisis; see D Llewellyn, 'The Global Financial Crisis: The Role of Financial Innovation' in P Booth (ed), *Verdict on the Crash: Causes and Policy Implications* (London, Institute of Economic Affairs, 2009).

[14] See 13.28 and 13.3.3. Note, though, that there is limited self-regulation of this market in relation to market abuse; see 13.4.2.

[15] See 2.3.1.4. For a view on how regulation impacts on the syndicated loan market, including the secondary market, see LMA, *Regulation and the Loan Market* (2012), www.lma.eu.com/uploads/files/LMA%20Paper%20%20 20impact%20of%20regulation%20on%20the%20loan%20market.pdf.

[16] LMA Guide to Syndicated Loans and Leveraged Finance Transactions (October 2013), 6.A.3; Wood: Loans and Bonds, 7-019; Mugasha: Multi-Bank Financing, 2-534. Removing loans may now also help banks meet the liquidity requirements under Basel III; see 2.3.1.4.

a loan to an associate or to another jurisdiction,[17] and a buyer might wish to purchase a loan to build up a set-off.[18]

Similar reasons can lead to the transfer of single lender loans, as well as other types of smaller scale financing such as credit card debts and asset-based lending. These debts tend to be transferred as part of a securitisation, where the purchase price for them is funded by an issue of securities, thus spreading the risk very widely and taking advantage of the lower cost of borrowing money by issuing securities. Of course, both bond issues and syndicated loans can also be securitised. A non-financial company can also securitise its receivables, but, at least in relation to smaller companies, financing of receivables is more easily achieved by transfer to a factor or an invoice discounter.[19] The prime motivation for a company is liquidity: receivables financing is a way of turning illiquid assets into ready cash[20] which can be used to improve the company's cash flow or generally to finance the company's operations.

9.2 Methods of Transfer

The most suitable method of transfer of a debt will depend not only on the nature of the debt, but also on the circumstances of the transfer. Detailed comparison between methods will take place as part of the discussion of each method, but there are a few general points to be made. First, the position of the borrower needs to be considered. Some methods require the borrower to consent to the transfer (either at the time of transfer or in advance). In these circumstances, a method which transfers risks and rewards but which does not involve a transfer may be preferable. Further, the parties to the transfer may not wish the borrower to know that the debt has been transferred. This may be because they wish to retain a particular relationship with the borrower, or because they think that the publicity would harm it (the lender) in its future dealings with the borrower, or more generally. Alternatively, it may just be simpler for the borrower to pay the original lender than to direct it to pay someone else, when it might make a mistake.[21]

Another relevant point is whether only rights are being transferred or whether there are obligations to transfer as well. Where a loan is a revolving facility, or has not been fully drawn down, the lender will owe the borrower an obligation to advance funds. Obligations cannot be assigned, but can be transferred by novation.[22] This is not a problem with an issue of debt securities, where there is never any outstanding obligation to advance funds.

---

[17] Wood: Loans and Bonds, 7-019.

[18] Ibid, 7-109. This is not permitted after the 'cut-off' date for insolvency set-off: see Insolvency Rules 1986, rr 2.85(2)(e) and 4.90(2)(d) (as amended); Goode: Credit and Security, 7.89.

[19] 2.3.4.1.

[20] This is often said to be the major point of all securitisations, but where financial institutions are involved, the other reasons discussed, especially capital adequacy, are also important.

[21] This would be true, for example, with some consumer debts.

[22] It will be seen that this principle is not absolute, as an obligor can be prejudiced by events after assignment. For example, once notice is given to the obligor further set-off or other equities cannot arise between the assignor and the obligor, and the obligor must pay the assignee and not the assignor.

A third question is whether there is any restriction on transfer in the original loan agreement. This will not apply in the case of securities or other negotiable instruments, where transfer is inherent in their nature, but could apply in the case of any other debt, including a loan. It may be that there is a restriction imposed by the borrower, or, though unusual, a restriction imposed by law.

A fourth potential problem is where security is given for the original loan. Transferring merely the benefit of the loan is likely to be construed as transferring the entitlement to the security as well,[23] but if there is a new obligation of the borrower to pay the transferee, then the entitlement to security will not automatically follow.[24]

In the following sections, the three main legal methods of transfer will be outlined. Their application will then be considered in the context of the transfer of loans (usually syndicated loans), receivables and securities.

9.2.1 Novation

The concept of novation is very simple: the original contract between A and B is terminated and a new one arises between B and C. Where there are mutual obligations still outstanding, the mutual agreement by A and B to release each other from these is consideration for the termination. Equally, the agreement by B and C to take on new obligations provides sufficient consideration for the new agreement. C's obligations to B can be on exactly the same terms as A's obligations to B, but they are new obligations: A's obligations are not transferred to C. Nor are A's rights against B transferred to C (as in an assignment): B takes on new obligations which are owed to C. Since C is undertaking new obligations to B, it is necessary that B consent to the novation.[25] Exactly how this is achieved in the context of a transfer of a loan or debt securities is examined below.

As the contract between B and C is entirely new, it is not automatically subject to equities which affected the old contract, though this will, of course, depend on the terms on which B has agreed to the novation,[26] and the terms on which the novation takes place. This is because the rights and obligations of each party under the new contract must be determined by the contractual agreements among all three parties to the novation.[27] The same analysis applies in relation to a situation where the title of the original lender to the debt is defective (that is, it is not owed the original debt). Usually, the terms of the debtor's consent (which may well be subject to the rules of an exchange, a clearing system or a standard form contract) will expressly or impliedly exclude consent to a transfer in such circumstances. A 'transfer' by novation, therefore, is at least capable of taking place free from equities and defects in title: whether it does so or not depends on the circumstances and the context. The way in which transfer systems incorporate these features is examined below.

---

[23] This would usually be done expressly as well; see Wood: Loans and Bonds, 9-033. There is no requirement to register the transfer of security: Security and Title-Based Financing, 10.65.

[24] Wood: Loans and Bonds, 10-32.

[25] For an analysis of various contractual methods by which the requirement of active consent can be dispensed with, see LK Ho, 'Unilateral Transfers of Contractual Obligations' (2013) 129 *Law Quarterly Review* 491.

[26] 9.2.4.2.5.

[27] There can, of course, be set-off between the obligor and the transferee.

9.2.2 Assignment[28]

9.2.2.1 Introduction

Assignment is a technique which is used in a number of different contexts. In the corporate finance context, it can be used when a company transfers an absolute or security interest in receivables to a bank or other financier in order to obtain finance. The generic term for this is receivables financing, and various types of it are discussed in chapter two.[29] It can also be used when a lender wishes to transfer the benefit of a loan it has made.

There are a number of significant differences between assignment and novation. First, an assignment is a transfer of rights: no new contract is created and none is terminated.[30] The amount of involvement the assignor retains following the assignment depends on whether the assignment takes place at law or in equity,[31] and also on whether the assignment is permitted under the terms of the original agreement.[32] Second, as mentioned above, obligations cannot be assigned, only rights. Third, the consent of the debtor[33] is not required for a valid assignment to take place. Fourth, although notice of the assignment to the debtor is required for a statutory assignment,[34] no such notice is necessary for an assignment to be valid in equity.[35] Fifth, an assignment takes place subject to equities (including rights of set-off), whereas if a loan contract is novated the new contract will not be affected by any prior dealings between the transferor and the borrower.[36] Sixth, an agreement to assign future rights is given effect in equity,[37] so that there can be a valid equitable assignment of both present debts and those that will arise in the future.[38] Seventh, there are limitations on the kinds of rights which can be assigned: rights which are personal to the assignor (so that the identity of the obligee is material to the obligor) cannot be assigned,[39] nor can rights which have been made non-assignable (or personal)[40] in the original contract,[41] nor can an assignment of a bare right of action take place.[42]

---

[28] See generally Tolhurst: Assignment and Smith; Leslie: Assignment.

[29] 2.3.4.1.

[30] The question of whether an equitable assignment is effected by a transfer or creates a new right is considered at 9.2.2.4.

[31] See 9.2.2.2 and 9.2.2.4.

[32] See 9.2.2.6.

[33] The word 'debtor' is used here as this chapter is concerned with the transfer of debt. In fact, any non-personal obligation can be assigned, including but not limited to, debts.

[34] Law of Property Act 1925, s 136.

[35] See 9.2.2.4.

[36] For a possible qualification of this, see the discussion in 9.2.4.2.45 of *Graiseley Properties Limited v Barclays Bank plc* [2013] EWCA Civ 1372.

[37] *Holroyd v Marshall* (1861–62) 10 HLC 191.

[38] This can be important in receivables financing; see 9.2.5.1.

[39] *Tolhurst v Associated Portland Cement Manufacturers (1900) Ltd* [1902] 2 KB 660, 668 per Collins MR: 'neither at law nor in equity could the burden of a contract be shifted off the shoulders of a contractor on to those of another without the consent of the contractee.'

[40] Goode: Credit and Security, 3-38.

[41] See 9.2.2.6.

[42] This amounts to champerty and is against public policy; see *Simpson v Norfolk and Norwich University Hospital NHS Trust* [2011] EWCA Civ 1149. However, if the assignee can show that he has an interest in enforcing the claim, such assignment would be permitted: *Trendtex Trading Corp v Credit Suisse* [1982] AC 679, 703. Lord Roskill required a 'genuine commercial interest' and this will certainly be the case where a debt is assigned as a

Assignment is the transfer of a chose in action, that is, a personal right to property which can only be enforced by bringing an action, as opposed to taking possession.[43] A chose in action can be either legal, that is, originally only enforceable in a court of law, or equitable, that is, enforceable in equity. Many of the debts we are considering in this chapter are legal choses in action. An interest under a trust is an equitable chose in action, which would include, for example, an interest in securities held by an intermediary or the interest of a holder of stock.

9.2.2.2 Statutory Assignments

Originally, assignment of a chose in action was not possible either at law or in equity.[44] By the beginning of the eighteenth century, however, the courts of equity recognised the rights of an assignee as against an assignor, although the latter had to bring any necessary action on the chose against the debtor.[45] Eventually, the Judicature Act 1873 provided that the assignee of a chose in action could sue on it in its own name, if certain conditions were fulfilled for the purpose of protecting the debtor and ensuring that the assignment was evidenced.[46] The present form of this provision is section 136(1) of the Law of Property Act 1925. The conditions are that the assignment is in writing, is absolute (not by way of charge only), and that written notice of the assignment has been given to the obligor. There also cannot be a statutory assignment of a future chose in action,[47] nor of part of a debt as opposed to the whole debt.[48] An assignment under section 136(1) is often called a 'legal' assignment, but this can be misleading as the section's effect is to enable the assignee to sue on the chose at law: it does not attract the priority rules which usually apply to a legal interest (the rule that a bona fide purchaser of the legal interest takes free of prior equitable interests)[49] in that the assignee takes 'subject to equities', including a prior equitable assignment.[50] Priority is instead determined by the rule in *Dearle v Hall*,[51] which is that the first assignee to give notice to the debtor has priority.[52] It is therefore better to refer to an assignment under section 136 of the Law of Property Act 1925 as a 'statutory assignment'. Whether the effect of the section is indeed procedural, as suggested above, or substantive

---

matter of property, even though the assignee has to sue on it to recover it: see *Camdex International v Bank of Zambia (No 1)* [1998] QB 22.

[43] *Torkington v Magee* [1902] 2 KB 427, 439; Smith and Leslie: Assignment, 2.72.

[44] This was, at least in part, because a transfer of claims was seen as champertous: see V Waye and V Morabito, 'The Dawning of the Age of the Litigation Entrepreneur' (2009) 26 *Civil Justice Quarterly* 389, 391. Tolhurst: Assignment, ch 2; Smith and Leslie: Assignment, ch 10.

[45] Tolhurst: Assignment, 26.

[46] Judicature Act 1873, s 25(6). This Act had the effect of enabling actions at law and in equity to be brought in the same courts.

[47] Goode: Credit and Security, 3.11. See discussion in Smith and Leslie: Assignment, 2.100–2.101.

[48] *Re Steel Wing Co Ltd* [1921] 1 Ch 349; Smith and Leslie: Assignment, 16.21. The reason for this rule is that if only part of the debt is assigned, and the 'assignee' could sue on part of the debt by reason of section 136, the debtor would be exposed to a multiplicity of suits, which could result in conflicting decisions (*Re Steel Wing Co Ltd* [1921] 1 Ch 349, 357).

[49] See 7.4.4.

[50] Treitel 15-037.

[51] *Dearle v Hall* (1828) 3 Russ 1.

[52] *Pfeiffer Weinkellerei-Weineinkauf GmbH & Co v Arbuthnot Factors Ltd* [1988] 1 WLR 150; *Compaq Computers Ltd v Abercorn Group Ltd (t/a Osiris)* [1991] BCC 484.

is a matter of some debate.[53] There seems little doubt, however, that once a debt has been statutorily assigned the assignor cannot sue on it: he has no interest in it.

9.2.2.3 Significance of Notice to the Debtor

Failure to give notice to the debtor has a number of consequences apart from (at least sometimes) preventing the assignee from suing on the debt in its own name. First, until the debtor is given notice, set-offs can continue to arise between the assignor and the debtor.[54] Second, until the debtor has received notice of assignment, it does not know to pay anyone other than the assignor, and can obtain a good discharge by so doing. Once the debtor has notice of assignment it can be made to pay again if it pays the assignor.[55] Third, until notice is given to the debtor, the debtor and assignor can agree to modify the contract and the assignee is bound by this[56] (although it might be a breach of the contract between the assignee and the assignor). Fourth, as mentioned above, until notice of an assignment is given to the debtor, the assignee may lose priority to a subsequent assignee who does give notice to the debtor under the rule in *Dearle v Hall*.[57]

9.2.2.4 Equitable Assignment

An assignment is likely to be equitable, and not statutory, for one of several reasons. One possible reason is that no notice has been given to the debtor.[58] This is usually remedied before any action is taken on the debt, at which point the assignment becomes statutory. Another possible reason is that the debt is a future debt, but this is a temporary defect: by the time it is sought to enforce the debt it will *ex hypothesi* have arisen and thus be a present debt, capable of being the subject of a statutory assignment. The only two situations where an assignment might realistically remain equitable even when notice has been given and when the debt has arisen are where the assignment is of part of the debt, and where the assignment is 'by way of charge'. In the latter case, the charge document will usually provide for the chargee to take a statutory assignment of the debt if it wishes to enforce it, thus turning the charge into a mortgage.[59] The circumstances in which an equitable assignee will want to enforce a debt are, therefore, rather limited in practice. It is still significant, though, to consider what happens when a debt is assigned in equity. This may be important for a number of reasons, such as when determining the effect of an anti-assignment clause.[60]

---

[53] Tolhurst: Assignment, ch 5.

[54] *Roxburghe v Cox* (1881) 17 Ch D 520. While set-off is specifically mentioned, this rule applies to all equities. It only applies to defences arising after notice to the debtor, and not, for example, to defences arising out of the original contract. Nor does it apply to set-off closely or inseparably connected with the original claim (transaction or equitable set-off): Goode: Credit and Security, 7-70.

[55] *Brice v Bannister* (1878) 3 QBD 569, 578. cf CH Tham, 'Notice of Assignment and Discharge by Performance' [2010] *Lloyd's Maritime and Commercial Law Quarterly* 38.

[56] *Brice v Bannister* (1878) 3 QBD 569.

[57] (1828) 3 Russ 1. This is subject to the so-called 'second limb' of the rule: if the second assignee has notice of the first assignment at the time of its assignment it will not gain priority over the first assignment.

[58] See, for example, the practice in invoice discounting, 9.2.5.1, and securitisation, 9.3.3.

[59] See Encyclopaedia of Forms and Precedents vol 10(2), F28 cl 4.7.2.

[60] See 9.2.2.6.

There are conflicting views on the nature of an equitable assignment, many of which, though conceptually coherent, are hard to reconcile with the authorities. The two main theories, of which there are several variants, are, first, that an equitable assignment takes effect by the creation of a new right which the assignee has against the assignor (similar or identical to the right of a beneficiary under a trust) and, second, that an equitable assignee has an equitable interest in the debt which, in some way, is his in his own right and so not entirely dependent upon that of the assignor. On either view, there is little doubt that the assignee obtains a proprietary interest which survives the insolvency of the assignor. If the debtor pays the debt to the assignor, the assignor holds the proceeds on trust for the assignee: the assignee would therefore have priority over the creditors of an insolvent assignor.[61] Further, if the assignor becomes insolvent before the debt is paid, the assignee again has priority over the assignor's creditors.[62]

On the first view, the assignee acquires a right to force the assignor to enforce the debt— in other words, the assignment only affects the relations between the assignor and the assignee.[63] Thus, the conclusion that the assignor holds the right to sue the debtor on trust for the assignee is interpreted to mean that the assignee's proprietary right only relates to the relationship between the assignee and the assignor.[64] On this view, the assignee has no relationship with the debtor, and cannot sue it. This view is supported by cases which require an equitable assignee to join an assignor in order to sue on the debt, many of which are now rather old.[65] This requirement is seen as substantive, flowing from the fact that only the assignor has the legal title to the debt, and so only the assignor can enforce it. This view is conceptually very attractive: it explains the concept of equitable assignment in a way that is coherent with the rest of the law of trusts. It is, however, inconsistent with the approach that has taken by the English courts for many years, which has been underlined in some very recent cases.

This second approach is based on the analysis that the requirement that the assignor be joined in an action to enforce the debt is merely procedural. It is there for a number of good reasons, to protect both the assignor (for example, so that the assignor has the opportunity to contest the assignment)[66] and the debtor, who might otherwise face double

---

[61] Goode: Credit and Security, 3-34.

[62] This means that the assignee can either force the assignor's liquidator to enforce the debt for its (the assignee's) benefit, or can sue the debtor itself, joining the assignor (or its liquidator) if necessary.

[63] Tolhurst: Assignment, 4.05–4.06; J Edelman and S Elliott, 'Two Conceptions of Equitable Assignment' (2015) 131 *Law Quarterly Review* 228; CH Tham, 'The Nature of Equitable Assignment and Anti-Assignment Clauses' in J Neyers et al (eds), *Exploring Contract Law* (Oxford, Hart Publishing, 2009).

[64] See the analysis of B McFarlane in *The Structure of Property Law* (Oxford, Hart Publishing, 2008) 1.2.2, in which he describes an equitable assignment as the acquisition by the assignee of a 'persistent right' against the assignor. This persistent right is a right against the assignor's right against the debtor. A persistent right, in McFarlane's terminology, is a right against a right which imposes a duty on the holder of the second right in favour of the holder of the persistent right, and which gives the latter a power to impose a duty on anyone acquiring a right which depends on the former's right.

[65] *Cator v Croydon Canal Company* (1747) 4 Younge and Collyer 593; *Durham Brothers v Robertson* [1898] 1 QB 765, 769–70; *EM Bowden's Patents Syndicate, Limited v Herbert Smith & Co* [1904] 2 Ch 86, 91–92; *Williams v Atlantic Assurance Company, Limited* [1933] 1 KB 81, 100. For a more recent statement, see *Warner Bros Records Inc v Rollgreen Ltd* [1976] QB 430, 443–45.

[66] *Weddell v JA Pearce & Major* [1988] Ch 26, 41; *Deposit Protection Board v Barclays Bank plc* [1994] 2 AC 367, 387.

jeopardy by being sued twice for the same debt.[67] There is even more concern when the assignment is of only part of a debt (one of the main reasons why it would be equitable and not statutory), since the debtor would face multiple actions for different parts of the debt.[68] The requirement that the assignor be joined can, however, be waived if there is no reason for the assignor to be joined:[69] this is because it is seen as a rule of procedure and not of substance.[70] This approach has led to various decisions based on the view that an equitable assignee has substantive rights against the debtor. First, where an equitable assignee brings an action in its own name without joining the assignor, this counts as commencing proceedings for the purposes of limitation.[71] Second, an action commenced by an equitable assignee is not a nullity, even though in a proper case it will be stayed for the assignor to be joined.[72] Third, the rights of an equitable assignee have been considered (as a matter of substantive law) not to be sufficiently different from those of a statutory assignee for the former not to be entitled to the protection of an Act protecting bank depositors.[73] Fourth, the assignor cannot bring an action to enforce the debt on his own, without joining the assignee and making it clear that he is suing in a representative capacity.[74] This could be seen as a mirror image procedural rule to that discussed above in relation to the joinder of the assignor, but the Court of Appeal in *Kapoor v National Westminster Bank*[75] has recently confirmed that it is a matter of substantive law.[76]

Further support for the second view, as opposed to the first (trust) view, can be found in other aspects of equitable assignment. If notice is given to the debtor, yet the assignment remains equitable only, the debtor is obliged to pay the assignee and cannot get a good discharge by paying the assignor.[77] Also, an equitable assignment is different from

---

[67] *Central Insurance Co Ltd v Seacalf Shipping Corporation (The Aiolos)* [1983] 2 Lloyd's Rep 25, 33–34; *Re Steel Wing Co Ltd* [1921] 1 Ch 349, 357.

[68] *William Brandt's Sons & Co v Dunlop Rubber Co Ltd* [1905] 2 AC 454, 462; *Performing Right Society Ltd v London Theatre of Varieties* [1924] AC 1, 14 (Viscount Cave); *Weddell v JA Pearce & Major* [1988] Ch 26, 40; *Deposit Protection Board v Barclays Bank plc* [1994] 2 AC 367, 381 (Simon Brown LJ); *Three Rivers DC v Bank of England (No 1)* [1996] QB 292, 309 (Peter Gibson LJ).

[69] *William Brandt's Sons & Co v Dunlop Rubber Co* Ltd [1905] 2 AC 454; *Sim Swee Joo Shipping Sdn Bhd v Shirlstar Container Transport Ltd* (unreported, 17 February 1994); *Raiffeisen Zentralbank Österreich AG v Five Star General Trading LLC* [2001] EWCA Civ 68 [60].

[70] *Three Rivers DC v Bank of England (No 1)* [1996] QB 292, 308 (Peter Gibson LJ); *Raiffeisen Zentralbank Österreich AG v Five Star General Trading LLC*, ibid, [60]. This view has now been confirmed by the Court of Appeal in *Kapoor v National Westminster Bank* [2011] EWCA Civ 1083 [30]–[45] (for criticism see PG Turner, 'May the Assignee of Part of a Debt Vote at a Creditors' Meeting?' (2012) 71(2) *Cambridge Law Journal* 270) and see also obiter dicta in *Roberts v Gill & Co* [2010] UKSC 22 [67] (Lord Collins), [127] (Lord Clarke).

[71] *Central Insurance Co Ltd v Seacalf Shipping Corporation (The Aiolos)* [1983] 2 Lloyd's Rep 25.

[72] *Weddell v JA Pearce & Major* [1988] Ch 26.

[73] See the decision of the Court of Appeal in *Deposit Protection Board v Barclays Bank plc* [1994] 2 AC 367. The decision was overruled by the House of Lords—not on this point but on the basis that on its true construction the relevant statute did not include any assignees in its protection.

[74] *Three Rivers DC v Bank of England (No 1)* [1996] QB 292, 308 (Peter Gibson LJ); *Bexhill UK Limited v Abdul Razzaq* [2012] EWCA Civ 1376.

[75] [2011] EWCA Civ 1083.

[76] Ibid, [30].

[77] *Jones v Farrell* (1857) 1 De G & J 208; *Brice v Bannister* (1878) 3 QBD 569; *William Brandt's Sons & Co v Dunlop Rubber Co Ltd* [1905] 2 AC 454. This conclusion has been challenged; see CH Tham, 'Notice of Assignment and Discharge by Performance' [2010] *Lloyd's Maritime and Comparative Law Quarterly* 38. See also A Trukhtanov, 'In Defence of the "No Discharge After Notice" Rule' [2010] *Lloyd's Maritime and Comparative Law Quarterly* 551 and CH Tham, 'In Defence of the "No Discharge After Notice" Rule: A Reply' [2010] *Lloyd's Maritime and Comparative Law Quarterly* 559.

a declaration of trust of the debt in that the equitable assignee can (usually) convert the equitable assignment into a statutory assignment by giving notice to the debtor, which will (on any view) have the effect of transferring the entire interest in the debt to the assignee.

The problem with the approach just discussed (the second view) is that it is hard to explain conceptually. Various theories have been put forward. One is that the equitable assignee has an equitable cause of action which can only attract equitable relief, so that in order to obtain a legal remedy the assignor has to be joined.[78] This reasoning is not reflected in most of the cases, and does not seem to be consistent with the waiver of the requirement of joinder in some cases. A more practical view, which is espoused in most of the cases, is that the courts of law will enforce the equitable rights of the assignee, provided that the position of the debtor and the legal rights of the assignor are protected (by joinder if necessary).[79] While this view accords with what most commercial parties would want and expect, it is conceptually rather difficult to explain, in that it appears that an equitable right is being treated exactly like a legal right, despite the fact that the common law has consistently refused to enforce an assignment except when made in accordance with section 136. Smith and Leslie have developed a theory that the assignee is 'enforcing the claim of the assignor but in its own name',[80] so that a variation of the *Vandepitte* principle applies.[81] The assignee is said to have a beneficial interest by transfer, leaving the assignor with a bare legal right: the content of the assignee's interest, which arises by constructive trust, is coloured by the purpose of the transaction, which is to confer substantive rights on the assignee.[82] This is a very attractive attempt to give a conceptual structure to the position reached by the courts as described above, and, although the courts do not use exactly the same reasoning, recent decisions appear to articulate the idea that the assignor is divested of nearly all rights.[83]

9.2.2.5 Assignment of Equitable Interests

Given that some of the transfers we are considering in this chapter are of equitable interests, for example interests in securities held by an intermediary and the interest of a stockholder,[84] it is helpful to consider the means of transfer of an equitable chose in action. Such a chose may be transferred in equity,[85] the result of this being that the assignee replaces the assignor as beneficiary under the trust, and can enforce the equitable chose (against the

---

[78] Tolhurst: Assignment, 88–90. This is consistent with the view of Staughton LJ in *Three Rivers DC v Bank of England (No 1)* [1996] QB 292, 303. However, this view does not necessarily seem to have been shared by the other two members of the Court of Appeal in that case.

[79] This appears to be the view put forward in most of the cases; see those cited above at n 69.

[80] Smith and Leslie: Assignment, 11.39 ff.

[81] See 9.2.2.6.5(b).

[82] Smith and Leslie: Assignment, 11.44–11.47.

[83] *Kapoor v National Westminster Bank* [2011] EWCA Civ 1083 [30]; *Roberts v Gill & Co* [2010] UKSC 22 [68] (Lord Collins).

[84] Although, in fact, the most attractive analysis in relation to intermediated securities is that these are transferred by novation: see 9.2.6.2.

[85] This would require writing, however, under Law of Property Act 1925, s 53(1)(c).

trustee) in its own name.[86] There is also authority that an equitable chose can be assigned under section 136.[87]

9.2.2.6 Clauses Prohibiting Assignment

9.2.2.6.1 Introduction

It is possible for a contract to provide that the rights created cannot be assigned, or can only be assigned under certain circumstances, such as if the debtor consents. The reasons why a debtor might want to include such a clause vary according to context and are discussed below in relation to transfer of loan contracts and transfer of receivables.[88] This section will consider the effect of such a clause under current English law and in accordance with existing principles. These are not entirely clear cut, and have been subject to much discussion by commentators.[89]

9.2.2.6.2 Construction of the Clause

First, it seems reasonably clear that any given clause has to be construed in order to determine its legal effect.[90] There are many permutations, but a common construction is that 'the term precludes or invalidates any assignment by the 'assignor' to 'the assignee' (so as to entitle the debtor to pay the debt to the 'assignor') but not so as to preclude the 'assignor' from agreeing, as between himself and the 'assignee', that he will account to the 'assignee' for what the 'assignor' receives from the 'debtor'.[91]

There now appears to be little doubt that such a clause is effective as far as the debtor is concerned, in other words, if there is such a clause in the agreement the debtor need

---

[86] *Cator v Croydon Canal Co* (1841) 4 Y & C Ex 405, 593; Treitel 15-008; Tolhurst: Assignment, 4.30; Smith and Leslie: Assignment, 11.05. There might, of course, be a good procedural reason for the assignor to be before the court, for example if only part of the equitable chose is to be transferred. However, in the cases discussed here, the assignor will be an equitable owner in common and the effect of the assignment will be that the assignee also becomes an equitable owner in common. Any rights of enforcement on the debt itself will be exercised by the trustee of the issue.

[87] *Torkington v Magee* [1902] 2 KB 427, 430–31; *Re Pain* [1919] 1 Ch 38, 44; *Compania Colombiana de Seguros v Pacific Steam Navigation Co* [1965] 1 QB 101, 121.

[88] 9.2.5.

[89] Goode, 'Inalienable Rights?' (1979) 42 *Modern Law Review* 553; B Allcock, 'Restrictions on the Assignment of Contractual Rights' (1983) 42 *Cambridge Law Journal* 328; A Tettenborn, 'Prohibitions on Assignment—Again' [2001] *Lloyd's Maritime and Commercial Law Quarterly* 472; G McMeel, 'The Modern Law of Assignment: Public Policy and Contractual Restrictions on Transferability' [2004] *Lloyd's Maritime and Commercial Law Quarterly* 483; Tolhurst: Assignment, ch 6(e); R Goode, 'Contractual Prohibitions against Assignment' [2009] *Lloyd's Maritime and Comparative Law Quarterly* 300; Smith and Leslie: Assignment, ch 25; Law of Personal Property, 29-028 ff; Goode: Credit and Security, 3-38–3-43; A Tomson and A Rose, 'No Assignment Clauses and Bank Insolvency' [2014] *Corporate Rescue and Insolvency* 228; GJ Tolhurst and JW Carter, 'Prohibitions on Assignment: A Choice to be Made' (2014) 73 *Cambridge Law Journal* 405.

[90] Further issues relating to construction are discussed at 9.2.2.6.5(c).

[91] This was one of four possibilities set out by Goode, 'Inalienable Rights?' (1979) 42 *Modern Law Review* 553 and approved by Lord Browne-Wilkinson in *Linden Gardens Trust Ltd v Lenesta Sludge Disposals Ltd* [1994] 1 AC 85, 106–09. See also G McMeel, 'The Modern Law of Assignment: Public Policy and Contractual Restrictions on Transferability' [2004] *Lloyd's Maritime and Commercial Law Quarterly* 483, 500. In this and what follows the words 'assignor' and 'assignee' are in inverted commas to reflect the uncertainty about the status of the assignment. It is still preferable to use these words rather than others, since it is easier then to compare the position where there is an anti-assignment clause with one where there is not.

not trouble itself over whom to pay. It will obtain a good discharge by paying the original creditor whether or not any attempt has been made to assign the debt. The debt cannot be the subject of a successful statutory assignment.[92] Further, the debtor retains the ability to assert rights of set-off arising even after notice of the purported assignment has been given to it.[93] The attempted assignment is also a breach of the contract between the original creditor and the debtor, although there is unlikely to be any substantive loss flowing to the debtor from this breach. It follows from this that the 'assignee' is not able to sue the debtor in order to enforce the debt: only the assignor can do this.[94] Thus the debtor is able to achieve its purpose of maintaining a relationship with the original creditor, which it knows and trusts, and the policy of allowing him to do this is achieved. However, there is the possibility that this policy will conflict with a policy against alienation, when we come to consider the position between the 'assignor' and the 'assignee'.[95]

It is necessary to distinguish between the position after the debt has been paid to the 'assignor' and the position before that time. After payment, the debtor can have no interest in preventing the 'assignee' from having proprietary rights to the proceeds. The debtor does not need to be sued: it has already paid. Thus the question of who can sue on the debt is irrelevant: the debt has been extinguished by payment. Before payment the value of the debt is both the right to sue on it and to receive the proceeds, so that in order for an 'assignee' to have some value in the debt before it is paid, it must have some means either of suing in its own name, or of forcing the 'assignor' to sue. An anti-assignment clause can prevent the first (we have just seen that), but the question is whether it can prevent the second.

9.2.2.6.3 Where the 'Assignor' has been Paid by the Debtor

With this in mind, let us first consider the position where the 'assignor' has been paid by the debtor. It is clear that as the 'assignor' has agreed, for valuable consideration, to assign the debt to the 'assignee' it cannot retain that money as against the 'assignee'. Thus even an ineffective assignment (vis-a-vis the debtor) will have the effect of causing the 'assignor' to hold any proceeds of the debt on trust for the 'assignee'.[96] Further, if a clause in the original agreement purported to prevent this occurring, it might well be void as against

---

[92] Goode: Credit and Security, 3-39; *Linden Gardens Trust Ltd v Lenesta Sludge Disposals Ltd* [1994] 1 AC 85, 106–09. Of course, the true effect of a clause will always depend on its exact wording, and the court in *Linden Gardens*, though laying down certain principles, was considering a particular form of words.

[93] Goode: Credit and Security, 3-38; Treitel 15-040; R Goode, 'Inalienable Rights?' (1979) 42 *Modern Law Review* 553, 553; *Don King Productions Ltd v Warren* [2000] Ch 291, 319. There may be difficulties if the 'assignor' successfully declares a trust of the debt; see 9.2.2.6.5.

[94] Though note that the 'assignee' might be able to force the assignor to sue the debtor; see discussion below.

[95] 9.2.2.6.5(e).

[96] Goode: Credit and Security, 3-40; *Re Turcan* (1888) 40 Ch D 5, 10–11, supported by Lord Browne-Wilkinson in *Linden Gardens Trust Ltd v Lenesta Sludge Disposal Ltd* [1994] 1 AC 85, 106 and Rix LJ in *Barbados Trust Co Ltd v Bank of Zambia* [2007] EWCA Civ 148 [77]. See also B Allcock, 'Restrictions on the Assignment of Contractual Rights' (1983) 42 *Cambridge Law Journal* 328, 335–36; G Tolhurst, 'Prohibitions on Assignment and Declaration of Trust' [2007] *Lloyd's Maritime and Commercial Law Quarterly* 278; G McMeel, 'The Modern Law of Assignment: Public Policy and Contractual Restrictions on Transferability' [2004] *Lloyd's Maritime and Commercial Law Quarterly* 483, 507–08; Smith and Leslie: Assignment, 527; P Zonneveld, 'The Effectiveness of Contractual Restrictions on the Assignment of Contractual Debts' (2007) 22 *Journal of International Business and Financial Law* 313 (relying on *Hodder & Tolley Ltd v Cornes* [1923] NZLR 876 and *Atwood & Reid Ltd v Stephens* [1932] NZLR 1332).

public policy,[97] since the debtor has no interest in preventing such a trust arising,[98] and, while it could make it a breach of contract for the creditor to alienate what has become its (the creditor's) own property, the debtor cannot stop such an alienation being effective vis-a-vis the beneficiary of the trust. If the assignment is expressed to cover both the debt and any proceeds, the assignment will be valid as regards any proceeds actually received.[99] The interest of the 'assignee' here takes effect as an assignment of future property,[100] which is reinterpreted in the light of the anti-assignment clause: since the contractual right itself cannot be assigned, the assignment takes effect only in relation to the proceeds.

9.2.2.6.4 Where the 'Assignor' has not been Paid by the Debtor

The position before the debtor pays the assignor will now be considered. Given that an anti-assignment clause can, uncontroversially, prevent a statutory assignment from taking place, we will consider its effect on an equitable assignment. It will be apparent from the discussion above[101] that the exact nature of the equitable assignee's rights is open to debate. If the assignment merely gives the assignee rights against the assignor and does not affect the relationship between the assignee and the debtor (the 'trust' view), then it must be questioned whether an anti-assignment clause can have any effect. On this view, the position between the assignor and the debtor has not changed, and so one might think that the debtor has no interest in preventing such an assignment. This analysis is wrong, though, for a number of reasons, which arise from the earlier discussion and which hold good whichever concept of equitable assignment is embraced. First, the relationship between the assignee and the debtor is affected by an equitable assignment: a debtor with notice has to pay an equitable assignee, and an equitable assignee can sue a debtor without the consent of the assignor as long as the assignor is joined.[102] Second, once notice is given to the debtor, equities such as set-off arising between the assignor and the debtor after that date will no longer bind the assignee.[103] An assignee takes subject to independent set-offs that have arisen before notice[104] and transaction set-offs affecting the debt at any time.[105] Third, once notice is given to the debtor, the debtor and the assignor cannot agree to modify the contract.[106] Therefore, it would seem that the debtor does have an interest in preventing an equitable assignment, and, indeed, a clause prohibiting the assignment of the whole or any part of a contract has been held to prohibit both a legal and an equitable assignment.[107]

---

[97] R Goode, 'Inalienable Rights?' (1979) 42 *Modern Law Review* 553.

[98] As by the time the trust arises, the debtor will already have paid the original creditor and will be discharged.

[99] *Re Turner Corporation Ltd (In Liq)* (1995) 17 ACSR 761, 767.

[100] This is valid in equity without more when the property is acquired under the principle in *Holroyd v Marshall* (1862) 10 HL Cas 191 and *Re Tailby* (1888) 13 App Cas 523; see 7.3.2.1. cf B Allcock, 'Restrictions on the Assignment of Contractual Rights' (1983) 42 *Cambridge Law Journal* 328, 335, who argues that the interest arises by way of constructive trust.

[101] 9.2.2.4.

[102] See 9.2.2.4. Even joinder may not be necessary if there is no good reason for it: see *Raiffeisen Zentralbank Österreich AG v Five Star General Trading LLC* [2001] EWCA Civ 68 [60].

[103] *Roxburghe v Cox* (1881) 17 Ch D 520.

[104] *Watson v Mid Wales Rly Co* (1866–67) LR 2 CP 593.

[105] *Government of Newfoundland v Newfoundland Rly Co* (1888) LR 13 App Cas 199 (PC); *Business Computers Ltd v Anglo-African Leasing Ltd* [1977] 1 WLR 578, 585.

[106] *Brice v Bannister* (1878) 3 QBD 569.

[107] *R v Chester and North Wales Legal Aid Area Office, ex p Floods of Queensferry Ltd* [1998] 1 WLR 1496.

This interest of the debtor would be fully protected only if the following could be achieved. First, if the debtor could always get a good discharge by paying the assignor. Second, if the debtor could be sure that the assignor always had control over enforcement of the debt. Third, if the debtor could be sure that, even it received a notice of 'assignment', set-off and other equities would always continue to arise between the assignor and the debtor, and modifications agreed between those parties would continue to be effective. An anti-assignment clause can achieve the first and the third conditions, by making any notice of assignment ineffective, in that a debtor cannot be bound by a notice of something which the assignor is contractually forbidden to do.[108] Thus the debtor could rely on a set-off arising between him and the assignor even after receiving notice of the purported 'assignment'.[109] However, it is less clear that an anti-assignment clause can prevent the second. The 'assignee' will be unable to sue in its own right, as it would be able to do if the clause was not there, by virtue of a statutory, or, the extent it has this effect, an equitable assignment. It is less clear, however, that an anti-assignment clause can prevent all types of proprietary interest in relation to the debt.

9.2.2.6.5 Declaration of Trust

9.2.2.6.5(a) Introduction

Attempts have been made, in particular, to circumvent anti-assignment clauses by using the device of a declaration of trust of the debt made by the 'assignor' in favour of the 'assignee'.[110] Whether this is possible at all will depend on the construction of two agreements: the contract of debt between the debtor and the 'assignor' (and, in particular, the restrictive clause therein) and the contract of 'assignment' between the 'assignor' and the 'assignee'. To eliminate the second of these construction points for the moment, we will initially consider the position where a trust is expressly declared.[111] Arguably, the 'assignor's' rights against the debtor are its own property, and any person can declare a trust of his own property. One practical effect of such a trust is unobjectionable: it means that the 'assignor' will hold the proceeds of the debt, once paid, on trust for the 'assignee' (as discussed above), and the debtor cannot prevent this, and has no interest in doing so.

9.2.2.6.5(b) Effect of a Declaration of Trust

However, what is the effect of such a declaration of trust before the debt is paid? First, there is no question of the 'assignee'[112] giving notice to pay to the debtor: the debtor continues to be able to pay the 'assignor' and obtain a good discharge. The position in relation to set-off, however, is more complex. As mentioned earlier, transaction set-off[113] is unaffected

---

[108] R Goode, 'Contractual Prohibitions against Assignment' [2009] *Lloyd's Maritime and Comparative Law Quarterly* 300, 360; Goode: Credit and Security, 3-38.

[109] For discussion of the position if the 'assignor' can validly declare a trust of the debt, see 9.2.2.6.5(d).

[110] *Don King Productions Ltd v Warren* [2000] Ch 291.

[111] This was the position in *Barbados Trust Co Ltd v Bank of Zambia* [2007] EWCA Civ 148.

[112] This person is no longer even a failed assignee but a beneficiary under a trust, but the term 'assignee' is used to show that it is in the same position as a failed assignee.

[113] 6.2.4.3.

by assignment, or by the claim being held on trust, as the assignee or beneficiary takes subject to this.[114] A beneficiary under a trust, like an assignee, takes subject to any rights of independent set-off[115] that have arisen before notice of the assignment or trust is given to the debtor.[116] If any notice of the trust given to the debtor is invalid (that is, if the trust is prohibited by the anti-assignment clause), independent set-offs can continue to arise. If the anti-assignment clause does not prohibit a declaration of trust, however, then a valid notice of trust can be given to the debtor, and subsequent independent set-offs can no longer arise. If the assignor becomes insolvent before the debt held on trust is paid, insolvency set-off[117] applies, which requires strict mutuality. Therefore, a claim against the 'assignor' in its own right cannot be set off against a claim which the 'assignor' holds on trust for the 'assignee'.[118]

In terms of enforcement of the debt, the 'assignee' cannot sue in its own right, as it is merely a beneficiary under a trust and it does not obtain the substantive interest that an equitable assignee obtains against the debtor.[119] Nor can it, unlike many equitable assignees, give notice to the debtor and obtain a statutory assignment which would give it an unquestionable right to sue in its own name.[120] However, as beneficiary, it can force the trustee to sue. If the trustee refuses to sue, a beneficiary can bring an action against the debtor, under the procedure established in *Vandepitte v Preferred Accident Insurance Corp of New York*.[121] Under this procedure, a beneficiary can bring what is effectively the trustee's action, but in its own name, joining the trustee as defendant.[122] It is available in 'special circumstances', since it is a short-circuiting procedure, collapsing two otherwise separate actions (one by the beneficiary against the trustee, and one by the trustee against the debtor).[123]

9.2.2.6.5(c) Construction of Anti-Assignment Clause

Does the presence of an anti-assignment clause in the contract between the debtor and the 'assignor' prevent an effective declaration of trust? This is, of course, a matter of construction of the actual clause.

It has been held that a clause which expressly prohibits only assignment will not be held to prevent a declaration of trust, since a declaration of trust is different in character from

[114] *Government of Newfoundland v Newfoundland Rly Co* (1888) LR 13 App Cas 199 (PC); *Business Computers Ltd v Anglo-African Leasing Ltd* [1977] 1 WLR 578, 585.

[115] 6.3.4.2.

[116] *Roxburghe v Cox* (1881) LR 17 Ch D 520.

[117] 6.3.4.6.

[118] Goode: Credit and Security, 7-83; R Derham, *Derham on the Law of Set-Off*, 4th edn (Oxford, Oxford University Press, 2010) 11–13; J Marshall, 'Declaring a Trust over Rights to an "Unassignable" Contract' (1999) 12 *Insolvency Intelligence* 1; A Tomson and A Rose, 'No Assignment Clauses and Bank Insolvency' [2014] *Corporate Rescue and Insolvency* 228. However, this reasoning may not apply where the 'assignor' declares a trust only of the proceeds and not of the debt itself: see M Feely, 'Can Set-Off Prejudice a Debt Subordination Agreement?' [2009] *Journal of International Banking and Financial Law* 64, which discusses this question in the context of a turnover trust (see 6.4.4.1.1) where there seems little doubt that the junior creditor holds only the proceeds on trust for the senior creditor.

[119] 9.2.2.4.

[120] This difference between a declaration of trust and an equitable assignment was noted by Waller LJ in *Barbados Trust Co Ltd v Bank of Zambia* [2007] EWCA Civ 148 [43].

[121] [1933] AC 70. See also *Harmer v Armstrong* [1934] Ch 65, 82–83.

[122] For detailed discussion, see Smith and Leslie 11.41.

[123] J Edelman and S Elliott, 'Two Conceptions of Equitable Assignment' (2015) 131 *Law Quarterly Review* 228, 240. The extent to which the *Vandepitte* procedure is available where there is an anti-assignment clause is discussed at 9.2.2.6.5(d).

an assignment.[124] There are a number of judicial statements to the effect that an equitable assignment is different from a declaration of trust,[125] and there are certainly some differences, such as the inability of a beneficiary to convert its position into that of a legal assignee by giving notice, to require the debtor to pay it direct. Further, if there is an equitable assignment, the assignor cannot sue without joining the assignee, whereas if there is a trust, the trustee can sue without joining the beneficiary,[126] and, as we have seen, an equitable assignee can, in some circumstances, sue the debtor without joining the assignor, while even if a beneficiary can sue under the *Vandepitte* procedure the trustee has to be joined. For these reasons, it seems correct that a clause which does not in its terms prohibit a declaration of trust should not necessarily be interpreted to do so. Against this it has been argued that the effect of an equitable assignment is that the assignor holds the debt on trust for the assignee, and therefore the effect of an equitable assignment and a declaration of trust is exactly the same. On this view, a clause prohibiting the former should also be held to prohibit the latter.[127] It has also been argued that the effect of an anti-assignment clause is to make the debt inalienable (in a similar way to a right that is personal to the assignor)[128] and so it cannot be the subject of ether an assignment or a declaration of trust.[129] These arguments, however, fail to take account of the differences discussed above, which, although in some cases are rather technical, demonstrate that an equitable assignment affects the position of a debtor to a greater extent than does a declaration of trust, and so a debtor might justifiably wish to prohibit the former and not the latter. Thus, if the clause does not specifically mention a declaration of trust, a court is likely to hold that this is not prohibited.[130]

9.2.2.6.5(d)   *Effect of Express Prohibition of Declaration of Trust*

Of course, a debtor might wish to prohibit both.[131] If the clause is drafted so as to prohibit a declaration of trust expressly, can this prohibition prevent a trust from arising? One possible view is that it cannot, in that an agreement between A and B cannot stop B declaring a valid trust over what is B's own property.[132] If we applied the same analysis as that applied to an anti-assignment clause, the result would be that the clause could only prevent any

---

[124] *Don King Productions Inc v Warren* [2000] Ch 291, 321; *Barbados Trust Co Ltd v Bank of Zambia* [2007] EWCA Civ 148 [43] (Waller LJ), [80]–[89] (Rix LJ).

[125] *Barbados Trust Co Ltd v Bank of Zambia*, ibid, [43] (Waller LJ); *Don King Productions Inc v Warren*, ibid, 319 (Lightman J); *Re Turcan* (1888) 40 Ch D 5, 10–11; *Devefi Pty Ltd v Mateffy Perl Nagy Pty Ltd* (1993) 113 ALR 225, 236.

[126] *Three Rivers DC v Bank of England* [1996] QB 292, 311.

[127] A McKnight, 'Contractual Restrictions on a Creditor's Right to Alienate Debts' [2003] *Journal of International Banking Law and Regulation* 1 and 43; G McMeel, 'The Modern Law of Assignment: Public Policy and Contractual Restrictions on Transferability' [2004] *Lloyd's Maritime and Commercial Law Quarterly* 48.

[128] See above, n 39.

[129] GJ Tolhurst and JW Carter, 'Prohibitions on Assignment: A Choice to be Made' (2014) 73 *Cambridge Law Journal* 405.

[130] See *Munib Masri v Consolidated Contractors International Company* [2007] EWHC 3010 (Comm) 305; *Stopjoin Projects Ltd v Balfour Beatty Engineering Services (HY) Ltd* [2014] EWHC 589 (TCC) [64].

[131] For a case where a clause was held to have this effect, see *Australian Zircon NL v Austpac Resources NL* [2011] WASC 186.

[132] As opposed to creating a trust by transferring the property to someone else, which could be prevented. See M Smith, 'Equitable Owners Enforcing Legal Rights?' (2008) 124 *Law Quarterly Review* 517, 519.

consequences from the declaration of trust which actually affected the debtor.[133] As has been pointed out, these would be few; the only one of possible substance is that the requisite mutuality for insolvency set-off might be broken.[134] Arguably, however, if there is a clause prohibiting the declaration of trust, the clause should be taken into account in assessing mutuality, so that mutuality would not be broken.[135] This would be on the basis that, although the 'assignor' held the claim on trust for the 'assignee', the debtor was not bound by that trust as, vis-a-vis the debtor, the declaration of trust was contractually prohibited. Moreover, any notice given to the debtor of the trust was ineffective, for the same reason.

A clause prohibiting both an assignment and a declaration of trust would render a declaration of trust a breach of the contract between the 'assignor' and the debtor, although whether the debtor would have suffered any loss is not clear. It is also unlikely that the debtor could obtain an injunction to prevent a declaration of trust, even if it knows about it in advance.[136] The possible adverse consequences to the debtor of the beneficiary ('assignee') being able to force the trustee ('assignor') to sue would be no greater than the consequences were there to be a change of control of the 'assignor' or if the assignor entered into a contract with a third party with reference to the debt, such as a credit default swap or a sub-participation, neither of which are in the power of the debtor to prevent.

A different view is that the clause can stop both an equitable assignment and a declaration of trust, since the two have the same effect and both affect the interest of the debtor.[137] This view is based on the fact that an anti-assignment clause does more than merely prevent the assignee having any relationship with the debtor; it actually changes the nature of the debt so that it becomes inalienable (in the same way as personal rights are inalienable).[138] The argument is that there is no policy reason against this, and, although the proceeds cannot be rendered inalienable, the rights against the debtor can. This is justified on the grounds of the freedom of contract of the debtor to protect itself. However, if this means that the 'assignee' has no proprietary (or 'persistent') rights against an insolvent 'assignor', this is very undesirable and there is a good policy argument against this state of affairs.[139] If the 'assignee' can obtain proprietary rights which give priority in insolvency, then it is difficult to see how the debt has become inalienable. This divergence of views points to a serious policy dilemma between the freedom of the debtor to protect itself and the freedom of the

---

[133] R Goode, 'Contractual Prohibitions against Assignment' [2009] *Lloyd's Maritime and Comparative Law Quarterly* 300, 362.

[134] See 9.2.2.6.5(b).

[135] J Marshall, 'Declaring a Trust over Rights to an "Unassignable" Contract' (1999) 12 *Insolvency Intelligence* 1.

[136] Goode, 'Contractual Prohibitions against Assignment' [2009] *Lloyd's Maritime and Comparative Law Quarterly* 300, 363.

[137] A McKnight, 'Contractual Restrictions on a Creditor's Right to Alienate Debts' [2003] *Journal of International Banking Law* 43; G McMeel, 'The Modern Law of Assignment: Public Policy and Contractual Restrictions on Transferability' [2004] *Lloyd's Maritime and Commercial Law Quarterly* 483; GJ Tolhurst and JW Carter, 'Prohibitions on Assignment: A Choice to be Made' (2014) 73 *Cambridge Law Journal* 405. See also the views of Rix LJ and Hooper LJ in the *Barbados Trust* case, both of which appear to think that a properly drafted clause could prevent a valid declaration of trust: [2007] EWCA Civ 148 [88] and [139]. See also *Don King Productions Inc v Warren* [2000] Ch 291, 321.

[138] *Tolhust v Associated Portland Cement Manufacturers (1900) Ltd* [1902] 2 KB 660, 668; R Goode, 'Inalienable Rights?' (1979) 42 *Modern Law Review* 553, 556–57; *Helstan Securities Ltd v Hertfordshire County Council* [1978] 3 All ER 262, 266.

[139] Goode, 'Contractual Prohibitions against Assignment' [2009] *Lloyd's Maritime and Comparative Law Quarterly* 300, 361.

'assignor' to alienate its property.[140] There are more specific policy tensions in relation to particular markets of transferred debt, and these are discussed below.[141]

9.2.2.6.5(e) An Implied Trust?

So far we have considered the position where the declaration of trust is express. Where there is a purported assignment, which has failed because of an anti-assignment clause, it is possible for the transaction to take effect as an implied declaration of trust of the debt which was the subject of the purported assignment. This was the solution adopted by the court in *Don King Productions Inc v Warren*.[142] Whether a trust will be held to exist depends on the intention of the parties: a failed assignment will not take effect as a trust automatically, since an intention to assign is not seen as necessarily the same as an intention to create a trust.[143] A powerful factor in favour of a trust being held to be present is where there is 'a manifest intention to transfer the benefit of a contract and that cannot legally be achieved except by virtue of a trust'.[144] The position is very fact-dependent and therefore considerably uncertain. In the three cases, aside from *Don King*, in which the issue has arisen, the court found the necessary intention in one,[145] held that it was arguable in another,[146] and held that it was absent in the third.[147]

9.2.2.6.5(f) The Vandepitte Procedure

One way in which a debtor would be protected from possible adverse consequences of a declaration of trust is if the court did not permit the beneficiary to make use of the *Vandepitte* procedure. This procedure, in effect, puts the beneficiary in a similar position regarding enforcement to that of an equitable assignee. There are, of course, some differences: in the *Vandepitte* procedure the beneficiary is enforcing the trustee's action, so the trustee always has to be joined, and the order made is for performance to the trustee (who will then hold any payment on trust for the beneficiary). Having said this, the use of the procedure leaves the debtor exposed to the more aggressive enforcement policies of an 'assignee', which is something against which a debtor tries to protect itself by the use of an anti-assignment clause. It would therefore be possible for the courts, as a matter of policy, to restrict the use of the procedure as inconsistent with the purpose of the clause, even though the presence of the clause may not prevent a valid declaration of trust.

In *Don King Productions Ltd*,[148] Lightman J did envisage a limit on the powers of the beneficiary to control the trustee, so that the trust would not 'abrogate the fullest protection that the parties to the contract have secured for themselves under the terms of the contact'.[149] Thus he envisaged that where there is an anti-assignment clause (let alone a

---

[140] This tension was noted by Rix LJ in *Barbados Trust Co Ltd v Bank of Zambia* [2007] EWCA Civ 148 [112].
[141] 9.2.5.
[142] [2000] Ch 291; see Lightman J at 321 and, in the Court of Appeal, Morritt LJ at [30].
[143] *Stopjoin Projects Ltd v Balfour Beatty Engineering Services (HY) Ltd* [2014] EWHC 589 (TCC) [64].
[144] *Co-Operative Group Limited v Birse Developments Limited* [2014] EWHC 530 (TCC) [88].
[145] *Explora Group plc v Hesco Bastion Ltd* [2005] EWCA Civ 646.
[146] *Stopjoin Projects Ltd v Balfour Beatty Engineering Services (HY) Ltd* [2014] EWHC 589 (TCC).
[147] *Co-Operative Group Limited v Birse Developments Limited* [2014] EWHC 530 (TCC).
[148] [2000] Ch 291.
[149] Ibid, 321.

clause prohibiting a declaration of trust) the court will disallow the *Vandepitte* procedure and the rule in *Saunders v Vautier*[150] (which enables a beneficiary to give directions to the trustee and to call for the trust to be wound up) will not apply.[151]

Since *Don King*, however, the courts have moved in favour of allowing the *Vandepitte* procedure to be used if there is a valid trust which is not prohibited. In *Barbados Trust Co Ltd v Bank of Zambia*,[152] it was argued that the anti-assignment clause, though not prohibiting a declaration of trust, prevented the use of the *Vandepitte* procedure as it laid the debtor open to an action by the 'assignee' which was the very thing that the clause was designed to prevent. Waller LJ took the view that the procedure was merely a shortcut, and should be available unless the beneficiary used it to obtain rights it would otherwise not be entitled to.[153] Rix LJ approached the matter as a balancing of interests, and concluded that in the circumstances the procedure should be available.[154]

Hooper LJ took the opposite view: the spirit of the anti-assignment clause would be contravened if the procedure were allowed.[155] Although there has been no decision directly on the point, there have been indications in other cases that the court will allow the *Vandepitte* procedure to be used where there is a valid trust, even where it is invoked to prevent a claim becoming time-barred because of the inaction of the 'assignor'.[156]

The views of the Court of Appeal in *Barbados Trust* do not give any definitive guidance on whether the *Vandepitte* procedure should be available where a clause prohibits a declaration of trust, which was not the case there. All the reasoning on the *Vandepitte* procedure was actually obiter, since a majority of the Court of Appeal held that the debt had not been properly assigned to the 'assignor' in the first place. The question is therefore an open one.

On the one side, as the effect of an anti-assignment clause is to prevent the 'assignee' suing the debtor in its own name (which would otherwise be possible),[157] then logically a clause which prohibits a declaration of trust should prevent the use of the *Vandepitte* procedure. If the right of an equitable assignee to sue the debtor in its own name (albeit joining the assignor if necessary) is seen as affecting the debtor, so that it has a justifiable interest in preventing it, then the same must be true of the *Vandepitte* procedure, which is analogous to the right of the equitable assignee to sue.

Against this, it can be argued that the *Vandepitte* procedure is merely a procedural mechanism to avoid circuity of action,[158] so that the debtor is made no worse off by the use of the *Vandepitte* procedure than by the normal operation of the rights of a beneficiary to force the trustee to enforce the trust. This recognises the technical differences between an assignment and a declaration of trust referred to earlier, but these are not particularly relevant to the position of the debtor, who only knows that he is de facto being sued by the

---

[150] (1841) 4 Beav 115.

[151] This latter point was justified on the basis that the trust was an 'active' trust, in that the trustees had duties to perform, and not a 'bare' trust to which *Saunders v Vautier* would apply.

[152] [2007] EWCA Civ 148.

[153] Ibid, [29].

[154] Ibid, [119]

[155] Ibid, [139].

[156] *Stopjoin Projects Ltd v Balfour Beatty Engineering Services (HY) Ltd* [2014] EWHC 589 (TCC) [70]; cf *Explora Group plc v Hesco Bastion Ltd* [2005] EWCA Civ 646 [119].

[157] As a statutory assignee, see 9.2.2.2.

[158] Goode, 'Contractual Prohibitions against Assignment' [2009] *Lloyd's Maritime and Comparative Law Quarterly* 300, 373. This has some support from the judgment of Waller LJ in *Barbados Trust* at [45].

'assignee', who can bring proceedings without the consent of the 'assignor'. From a policy point of view, there is much to be said for the view that there should be consistency between the position where there is an equitable assignment and that where there is a declaration of trust. A prohibition clause should not prevent the 'assignee' suing in either case, or it should prevent it in both cases.

There are two further points to make. From a practical point of view, if the 'assignor' is able to cede control over the bringing of an action to the 'assignee', so that the 'assignee' can force the 'assignor' to sue, then it could be said to make little difference to a debtor whether the ensuing action is technically brought by the 'assignee' or the 'assignor': the point is that the debtor's fate is being determined by someone other than the 'assignor'. Here the policy dilemma is clear. Either a debtor should be able to prevent an 'assignor' ceding that control (which would give the debtor all the protection it seeks and would swing the pendulum completely in the direction of the debtor's freedom of contract) or the policy of allowing people to alienate rights to their own property should prevail. This would mean that the debtor would not be able to prevent the ceding of control by the 'assignor', but could only protect itself to the extent of always being able to get a good discharge by paying the 'assignor' and always being able to maintain a right of set-off against the 'assignor'. Professor Goode favours this latter view, and points out that there are a number of other reasons why an 'assignor' could cede control over enforcement which cannot be prevented—for example, by a takeover of the 'assignor' by another company.[159] There are more specific arguments on this point regarding syndicated loans, which are discussed below.[160]

The second point stems from the actual nature of the trust. If the beneficiary under a declaration of trust cannot call for the trust property under *Saunders v Vautier*, or enforce the trustee's claim against the debtor under the *Vandepitte* procedure, arguably there is no trust and therefore no proprietary interest, so that the 'assignee' merely has a contractual right against the 'assignor' and will not obtain priority in the 'assignor's' insolvency.[161]

9.2.3 Negotiable Instruments

Probably the simplest way for the benefit of a loan contract to be transferred is for the obligation to be embodied in an instrument. An instrument is a piece of paper which not only evidences the obligation, but also entitles the holder (if it is a bearer instrument) or the indorsee (if an instrument payable to order) to payment. This means that the obligation represented by a bearer instrument can be transferred merely by delivery to another person. If the instrument is payable 'to order' it can only be transferred by delivery and indorsement (signing by the original payee). The payee can either sign and name the indorsee, in which

[159] Goode, ibid, 372. Another possibility is that other parties have become sub-participants in the loan (see 9.3.1) or have an interest as a result of a credit default swap (see 9.3.1) and so are in a position to influence enforcement. Neither of these 'transfers' of risk would be prohibited by an anti-assignment clause.

[160] 9.2.4.3.

[161] For discussion of this argument in the context of transfer of loans, see 9.2.4.3; in the context of receivables financing, see 9.2.5.2.

case a signature continues to be required for transfer, or it can just sign ('indorse in blank'), in which case the instrument becomes a bearer instrument.[162]

A negotiable instrument has an additional advantage. If it is transferred to a bona fide purchaser, the transferee obtains two benefits. It obtains good title to the obligation even if the title of the transferor is defective, and it takes the obligation free of any equities which affected it in the hands of the transferor. An instrument is negotiable if it is recognised by mercantile usage as such:[163] so long as the volume of usage is established, the courts will recognise a document as negotiable even if it is of recent origin.[164]

These two attributes (a convenient and easy manner of transfer, and negotiability) meant that such instruments played a significant part in corporate finance in the past, since they could be easily traded on open markets. A buyer would not have to investigate the provenance of the instrument, and could decide whether to buy purely on the basis of the credit risk of the promisor. For example, where companies received payment by bills of exchange or other similar instruments, these could be sold to banks or other financiers, which could easily sell the instruments on in the money markets.[165] As mentioned earlier,[166] bonds issued by companies were usually in the form of bearer bonds, which enabled them to be traded easily.[167]

It will be seen that the benefits of negotiability are not available when the technique of assignment (discussed above) is used. An assignee (statutory or equitable) takes 'subject to equities'.[168] There appear to be at least two reasons for this. One is the basic principle of *nemo dat quod non habet*: the assignor cannot transfer more than it has.[169] This principle applies to all transfers of property (including tangible property) unless there is an exception. Negotiability is one such exception, and is justified by mercantile usage and the smooth operation of markets. Another reason is a (weaker) principle that assignment should not prejudice the position of the obligor, so that the obligor is in the same position vis-a-vis the assignee as it would have been vis-a-vis the assignor. An obligor under a negotiable instrument accepts, when undertaking the obligation, that it will be liable to any holder, and that equities and defences that exist between it and the original obligee will no longer apply.

---

[162] Goode: Commercial Law, 513, 528. Note that in the case of instruments governed by Bills of Exchange Act 1882, where an order bill is transferred by delivery only, without indorsement, the transferee obtains the title that the transferor had, and also the right to obtain an indorsement from the transferor (s 31(4)).

[163] *Edelstein v Schuler & Co* [1902] 2 KB 144, 154. Bills of exchange, promissory notes and cheques (which are now rarely negotiable) are specifically covered by Bills of Exchange Act 1882, which provides that a bona fide purchaser is a 'holder in due course' and takes free of any defect of title of prior parties (ss 29, 38(2)).

[164] *Edelstein v Schuler & Co* [1902] 2 KB 144, 154. A modern example is the certificate of deposit, which is a certificate that money has been deposited with a bank. Certificates of deposit are actively traded on the money markets: see Valdez: Financial Markets, 162.

[165] For detailed discussion of the law relating to bills of exchange, see N Elliot, J Odgers and J Phillips, *Byles on Bills of Exchange* (London, Sweet & Maxwell, 2013); AG Guest, *Chalmers and Guest on Bills of Exchange, Cheques and Promissory Notes* (London, Sweet & Maxwell, 2009); Goode: Commercial Law, ch 19.

[166] Chapter 8.

[167] Hughes: Banking, 4.3.

[168] *Mangles v Dixon* (1852) 3 HLC 702, 731–32.

[169] See eg Smith and Leslie: Assignment, 26.43–26.47, citing *Phillips v Phillips* (1861) 4 De GF & J 208, 215–16.

9.2.4 Transfer of Loans

9.2.4.1 Introduction

There are four main situations in which loans will be transferred. The first is where the lender wishes to securitise its assets. This is discussed below.[170] The second is where the lender wishes to use its loans as security for an obligation. In many cases this will now fall within the FCARs (as amended) since financial collateral now includes 'credit claims',[171] which are loans made by banks.[172] The third is where a loan is made to a lead bank, which then sell parts of its interest to other participants, usually banks (a 'loan participation'). The fourth covers transfers in the secondary loan market: this will normally be by participants in a syndicated loan. Buyers may be banks, but they may be other financial institutions. Sales may be at par or near par (that is, at a price that reflects the original credit risk of the borrower) or as distressed debt (at a price which reflects the greatly increased credit risk of the borrower). Buyers in the latter market include specialist distressed debt traders and vulture funds.[173] This section will concentrate on the third and fourth of these categories.

In market terms, there are three methods of transfer of syndicated loans: novation, assignment and sub-participation. The last of these is not a transfer at all, even in a loose sense, since the original lender remains the lender of record. It is therefore discussed below in the section dealing with structures which have a similar effect to transfer.[174] Trading of syndicated loans usually takes place on standard LMA terms,[175] though individual transactions can also be affected by the terms of the loan agreement itself, which is also likely to be on LMA standard terms.[176] Thus, clause 24 of the standard LMA investment grade agreement[177] provides for 'assignment or transfer (by novation)' of the loan, and restrictions thereon. Sub-participation is not mentioned in the loan agreement, since, in theory, it does do not alter the position of the borrower, although in fact a borrower may be adversely affected by a sub-participant who is able to control the voting of the lender of record in a restructuring or enforcement.

Although trading of loans does not take place on an exchange, the standardisation of the relevant contracts, and the fact that many participants are LMA members, means that there is some degree of similarity to trading of securities. For example, certainty in the market is very important. An oral agreement to trade a loan is binding (a 'trade' is a 'trade'),[178] so that

---

[170] 9.3.3.

[171] These are defined in FCARS, reg 3 as 'pecuniary claims which arise out of an agreement whereby a credit institution, as defined in Article 4(1) of Directive 2006/48/EC ... relating to the taking up and pursuit of the business of credit institutions ... grants credit in the form of a loan'. 'Credit institutions' means deposit-taking institutions such as banks.

[172] For discussion of the FCARs, see 7.3.4.

[173] M Campbell and C Weaver, *Syndicated Lending: Practice and Documentation*, 6th edn (Euromoney Institutional Investor PLC, 2013) 488.

[174] 9.2.3.1.

[175] LMA Standard Terms and Conditions for Par and Distressed Trade Transactions.

[176] See 8.4.1.

[177] See also cl 29 of the LMA leveraged loan facility agreement.

[178] LMA Standard Terms and Conditions for Par and Distressed Debt Transactions, cl 2. See also *Bear Stearns Bank plc v Forum Global Equity Ltd* [2007] EWHC 1576 (Comm) where a binding contract was found to be made by an oral agreement to trade a loan, even though the LMA terms did not apply.

if assignment or novation is not possible (for example, if the debtor's consent is required but not forthcoming) the seller is obliged to effect the trade by sub-participation.[179] Further, where the facility agreement provides for a 'payment premium', which is a sum reflecting the lender's risk during the currency of the loan, which is payable when the loan is repaid, a buyer is not obliged under the transfer agreement to account to a seller for a payment premium it receives which (arguably) relates to the period of time when the seller was lender.[180] This has the effect that the transfer (and the price paid) is final at the time it is made, and any uplift has to be negotiated in the purchase price. Another example is that the LMA has been concerned about the use of 'inside' information in loan trading, and has issued guidelines for market participants to address this.[181]

9.2.4.2 The Use of Novation

9.2.4.2.1 Consent in Advance

It is reasonably likely that there will be outstanding further advances to be made at the point at which the loan is traded. It will be recalled that, although the rights of the creditor can be assigned, the obligations of the assignor cannot.[182] The problem is solved by the use of novation, at the 'cost' that the agreement of the borrower is necessary for the novation to take place. In fact, since all parties to a contract must consent to a novation, in a syndicated loan every party to the loan agreement (that is, the whole syndicate of lenders) will have to consent every time a novation takes place. Although this seems cumbersome, it is elegantly effected in syndicated loan agreements by including a unilateral offer (to accept a novation within the limits laid down in the agreement) in the original loan agreement made by all the parties. Strictly speaking, there are two offers: one to agree to the termination of the original contract, and another to agree to the formation of a new contract, on exactly the same terms as the old, with whomever is the purchaser of the loan.[183] A unilateral offer requires no overt acceptance, but can be accepted by the performance of an act, at which point the offeror is bound.[184] Transferability is made easy by a provision in the loan agreement that acceptance of the first unilateral offer can be effected by the delivery, by the selling bank, of a 'transfer certificate' to the agent bank, and of the second by the agreement of the transferee and the transferor to the transfer on the terms set out in the transfer certificate.[185]

---

[179] This will be riskier for the buyer than novation or assignment, as it bears the dual credit risk of the borrower and the seller: J Oldnall and M Clark, 'The Age of Consent' (2010) 25 *Journal of International Banking Law and Regulation* 89.

[180] *Tael One Partners Limited v Morgan Stanley & Co International plc* [2015] UKSC 12.

[181] See 13.4.2.

[182] See above and Hughes: Banking 9.21–9.22, 10.4–10.5.

[183] Mugasha: Multi-Bank Financing, 8.12.

[184] *Carlill v Carbolic Smoke Ball Company* [1893] 1 QB 256. The concept of a unilateral offer has been used to analyse situations when otherwise it would be difficult to explain why a party was bound, for example in *New Zealand Shipping Co Ltd v AM Satterthwaite & Co Ltd (The Eurymedon)* [1975] AC 154.

[185] See *The Argo Fund Ltd v Essar Ltd* [2005] EWHC 600 (Comm) [51]–[52], aff 'd [2006] EWCA Civ 241; *Habibson's Bank Ltd v Standard Chartered Bank (Hong Kong) Ltd* [2010] EWCA Civ 1335 [21]–[23]; *Leveraged Equities Ltd v Goodridge* (2011) 191 FCR 71 [307]–[313].

9.2.4.2.2 Restrictions on Transfer

Since novation results in the borrower being in a new relationship with a different party, including, in some cases, the party being obliged to advance further funds to the borrower, it is understandable that the borrower will wish to have some control over who that party might be. A primary motivation is to ensure that any future party to the loan is sufficiently creditworthy,[186] but there are other reasons as well: the borrower might wish to ensure that the new lender complies with regulatory requirements,[187] or might wish to retain rights of set-off against particular lenders, or might wish to ensure that lenders will be benign in their decisions as to when and how to enforce the loan.[188] As a result, loan agreements have in the past restricted 'transfer' of the loan to a 'bank or financial institution'; this was extended in 2001 in the LMA documentation to include 'a trust, fund or other entity which is regularly engaged in or established for the purpose of making, purchasing or investing in loans, securities or other financial assets'. It is sometimes possible for the borrower to negotiate specific exclusions from this very broad list, for example by negotiating a list of unacceptable institutions.[189]

The restriction 'bank or other financial institution' (without the 2001 additions) was considered by the Court of Appeal in *The Argo Fund Ltd v Essar Ltd*,[190] where the relevant loan had been transferred to a hedge fund. The Court of Appeal rejected the first instance judge's approach that the 'other financial institution' should be a lender of money which had the ability to advance the agreed loan during the draw-down period,[191] and held that 'other financial institution' meant '"a legally recognised form or being, which carries on its business in accordance with the laws of its place of creation and whose business concerns commercial finance" … whether or not its business included the lending of money on the primary or secondary lending market'.[192] This wide interpretation included the claimant hedge fund, and, in many ways, made the 2001 extension redundant (although it is still widely used).

The Court of Appeal considered that the ability of the transferee to advance any loan not drawn down at the time of the transfer was immaterial, as that would make the interpretation of the words 'other financial institution' depend on whether or not the loan had been fully drawn down at the time of the transfer.[193] This particular argument may have depended on the short draw-down period of the loan in question (45 days), but otherwise it seems strange. Given that a transfer could take place at any time, why should a borrower not wish to protect itself against transfer to an institution which could not advance funds due, thus necessitating expensive restructuring of the borrower's financing, even if such a restriction limited possible transferees throughout the period of the loan? A slightly different view was taken by Briggs J in *Carey Group plc v AIB Group (UK) plc*.[194] In that case, the

---

[186] *The Argo Fund Ltd v Essar Ltd* [2005] EWHC 600 [28]; Hughes: Banking, 9.25.

[187] Ibid, [29].

[188] These reasons also apply to a restriction on assignment.

[189] See Association of Corporate Treasurers, *Guide to the Loan Market Association Documentation for Investment Grade Borrowers* (2013), 125.

[190] [2006] EWCA Civ 241.

[191] Ibid, [32], [43]–[44].

[192] Ibid, [51].

[193] *The Argo Fund Ltd v Essar Ltd* [2006] EWCA Civ 241 [44].

[194] [2011] EWHC 567 (Ch).

borrower was applying for an injunction to prevent the transfer of the loan to NAMA, an Irish statutory body set up to acquire assets from banks (including the lender) participating in a scheme to stabilise the banking sector in Ireland. It was argued that the transfer was in breach of a clause in the same terms as the 2001 LMA version, on the grounds that either as a matter of construction or by implication of a term, the clause prevented transfer to an institution that could not offer banking services including an overdraft facility. Briggs J rejected this argument on the grounds since the overdraft facility under the loan agreement could be terminated at any time by the lenders,[195] this could be done before the transfer so that the transferee would not be under an obligation to make advances which it could not fulfil.[196] However, he did say that the position might have been different had the lenders been obliged to make an overdraft facility available for the whole of a fixed term,[197] which seems to indicate that a transferee's inability to make advances will be relevant to whether it falls within the restrictive clause.

The extent of the protection a borrower may be able to obtain at the time of negotiation of the syndicated loan agreement will depend on the strength of the bargaining power of the parties at the time of the agreement itself. The actual decision in *Argo* appears to have been motivated in part by a desire not to allow the defaulting borrower to escape from its obligations on what amounted, in the circumstances, to a technicality.[198]

9.2.4.2.3 Consent not Unreasonably Withheld

Another possible restriction is the overt requirement of consent on the part of the borrower to any transfer.[199] Such a requirement is more obviously advantageous to a borrower when a loan is assigned, as consent is not otherwise required.[200] It is, though, often included in clauses referring to 'transfer', which, because a transfer of obligations is included, must mean 'novation' rather than 'assignment'.[201] This requirement of consent is rather different from that which is required for a valid novation. It can be, and usually is, subject to contractual restrictions, such as that consent cannot be unreasonably withheld or delayed by the borrower,[202] and will be deemed to have been given if no reply is received to a request for consent after a (short) specified time period.

There is little specific guidance as to what will count as a reasonable withholding of consent by a borrower in this context,[203] although there is plenty of authority on the approach

---

[195] See 2.3.2

[196] *Carey Group plc v AIB Group (UK) plc* [2011] EWHC 567 (Ch) [41].

[197] Ibid, [38].

[198] *The Argo Fund Ltd v Essar Ltd* [2006] EWCA Civ 241 [44], [52]. It was not clear why Argo did not take an assignment of the rights of the transferring banks and sue on that, but, as it had not done so, the Court of Appeal held that it could not now argue that the transfer to it should be construed as an assignment, since assignment and novation were entirely different concepts under English law: see [62].

[199] This is very common in the investment grade market, and less so in the leveraged loan market, where liquidity is very important and where borrowers have less bargaining power. See *ACT Borrower's Guide to LMA Loan Documentation for Investment Grade Borrowers* (April 2013) produced by Slaughter and May, 127.

[200] 9.2.2.1.

[201] Paget 12.30.

[202] It could, of course, be argued that even if there were no express provision that consent should not be unreasonably withheld, such a provision should be implied, at least prohibiting a refusal of consent where no reasonable person would have refused: *Gan Insurance Co Ltd v Tai Ping Insurance Co Ltd (No 2)* [2001] EWCA Civ 1047.

[203] D Karp and A Lombardi, 'Transfer Restrictions may Create Additional Counterparty Risk for Distressed Debt Investors' [2014] *Corporate Rescue and Insolvency* 64.

of the courts to such an issue in general.[204] It is clear that the burden of showing that the consent is unreasonable is on the lender[205] and that the test is that of reasonableness, not correctness, so that different borrowers can take different views. Moreover, the borrower is permitted to take its own interests into account[206] and is not obliged to balance those interests with the interests of the lender.[207] Logically, the question of consent only arises if the transferee falls within the class of permitted transferees discussed above.[208] It has therefore been argued that to the extent that a transferee who is not able to make future advances falls within that class, that inability would not seem to be a valid reason for refusing consent.[209] However, the question of unreasonableness of refusal is fact specific, while whether the transferee falls within the class does not depend on, for example, what further advances need to be made. Therefore, it would seem appropriate that the ability of the transferee to make future advances would be a reasonable reason for refusing consent, as would concern about the aggressive nature of the transferee in enforcing obligations under the loan agreement.[210] If consent to a transfer is refused, yet the transferor and transferee have already agreed to the transfer,[211] the standard LMA terms require the transfer to be settled by subparticipation,[212] which is considerably more risky for the buyer, who takes on the credit risk of the seller as well as that of the borrower.[213]

9.2.4.2.4 Security for the Loan

A novation does not automatically transfer rights to any security given to the transferor for the original repayment obligation. This is often overcome by the security being held by a trustee on behalf of all the lenders.[214] The obligation that is secured is a parallel covenant made to the trustee[215] (again held on trust for the lenders from time to time) and the transferor's rights in respect of this can easily be assigned to the transferee (there being no obligations to the borrower to worry about in this transaction).

---

[204] There are many landlord and tenant cases on the subject, but that general approach is also suitable for commercial cases; see *British Gas Trading Limited v Eastern Electricity*, The Times, 29 November 1996, upheld on appeal [1996] EWCA Civ 1239.

[205] *Porton Capital Technology Funds v 3M UK Holdings Limited* [2011] EWHC 2895 (Comm) [223]; *Falkonera Shipping v Arcadia Energy PTE Ltd* [2012] EWHC 3678 (Comm) [85]; *BG Global Energy Limited v Talisman Sinopec Energy UK Limited* [2015] EWHC 110 (Comm) [109].

[206] *Barclays Bank plc v Unicredit Bank AG* [2014] EWCA Civ 302.

[207] *Porton Capital Technology Funds v 3M UK Holdings Limited* [2011] EWHC 2895 (Comm) [223].

[208] J Oldnall and M Clark, 'The Age of Consent' (2010) 25 *Journal of International Banking Law and Regulation* 89; P Rawlings 'Restrictions on the Transfer of Rights in Loan Contracts' [2013] *Journal of International Banking and Financial Law* 543.

[209] Rawlings, ibid.

[210] J Oldnall and M Clark, 'The Age of Consent' (2010) 25 *Journal of International Banking Law and Regulation* 89.

[211] The standard LMA terms provide that an oral agreement for a 'trade' of a loan is binding: see LMA Standard Terms and Conditions for Par and Distressed Debt Transactions, cl 2. See also *Bear Stearns Bank plc v Forum Global Equity Ltd* [2007] EWHC 1576 (Comm) where a binding contract was found to be made by an oral agreement to trade a loan, even though the LMA terms did not apply.

[212] See 9.3.1.

[213] See 9.3.1; J Oldnall and M Clark, 'The Age of Consent' (2010) 25 *Journal of International Banking Law and Regulation* 89.

[214] Mugasha: Multi-Bank Financing, 8.15; Hughes: Banking, 9.28. See 8.4.1.

[215] See 8.4.1.

9.2.4.2.5 Novation Subject to Equities?

As mentioned earlier, since the effect of a novation is to extinguish the original contract between the borrower and lender and to make a new one between the borrower and the transferee, the new contract is not subject to any equities, such as the right to rescind the original contract, to which the old contract was subject. In contrast, in assignment, the assignee takes subject to equities. From the borrower's point of view, this is a drastic effect of novation. For example, in *Graiseley Properties Limited v Barclays Bank plc*[216] the borrowers alleged that they had the right to rescind a syndicated loan agreement on the grounds that the lenders misrepresented that LIBOR (which was used as the basis of the interest payable under the agreement) had not been manipulated, when in fact it had. Transferees of the loan agreement by novation argued that the right to rescind was lost when the agreement was novated.

The form of the transfer clause in the agreement was complicated. It envisaged, on the one hand, 'assignment' and, on the other hand, 'transfer by novation or by "assignment, assumption and release"'.[217] On strict legal principles, the 'assignees' took free of the borrower's right to rescind for misrepresentation, while the 'transferees' did not. The Court of Appeal, in an interlocutory application to amend pleadings, took the view that the effect of these two modes of 'transfer' was a matter of interpretation of the agreement, so held it was arguable that, in these circumstances, the term 'novation' was not being used in the strict legal sense, so that the transferees might take subject to equities. This seems to envisage that the lender and borrower can agree, ex ante, on the effect of a transfer: whether it is a strict novation, an assignment, or a novation with 'assignment-like' features. While this might be said to blur the boundaries between the concepts of novation and assignment,[218] it must be right that the original parties to a loan contract can agree in advance the terms of any new contract to be made between the borrower and a new lender: the borrower, after all, has to consent to the new contract and can agree only to consent to a contract on some or all of the terms of the old contract, including (presumably) any rights to rescind the old contract.[219] Whether this is what is achieved by the standard terms used in loan documentation is another matter entirely. Presently, this seems counter to the expectations of the market.[220]

9.2.4.3 *The Use of Assignment*

If there are no future advances to be made at the time when it is desired to transfer the loan, the technique of assignment may be used.[221] In theory this has the benefit that the consent of the borrower is not required, but, as pointed out above, it is very common for the loan agreement to include provisions requiring borrower consent to an assignment as well as

---

[216] [2013] EWCA Civ 1372.

[217] See Encyclopaedia of Banking Law F2042.

[218] See Paget 12.30.

[219] See 9.2.1; *Langston Group Corporation v Cardiff City Football Club Limited* [2008] EWHC 535 (Ch) [48] where Briggs J appeared to countenance a partial novation.

[220] See eg a note by Berwin Leighton Paisner at www.blplaw.com/expert-legal-insights/articles/graiseley-and-unitech-four-things-you-didnt-know-about-the-libor-cases/.

[221] Although see the caveat below that what purports to be an assignment may not in fact be one.

a novation. The discussion above of what counts as unreasonable withholding of consent therefore also applies here.[222]

If the consent of the borrower is required, there will clearly be notice to the borrower of the assignment, in order to obtain that consent. Thus, the assignment will be statutory if the other requirements of section 136 of the Law of Property Act 1925 are fulfilled. It will be recalled, however, that there cannot be a statutory assignment of part of a loan.[223] Where a lead bank is selling participations in a loan, this will definitely be a transfer of part of a debt. Even sales by a syndicated lender will not necessarily be a transfer of the entirety of its rights under the loan agreement. In either case, then, the assignment will be equitable, even if the borrower is given notice of the sale.[224] This means that, were the assignee to wish to enforce its rights against the borrower, it would have to join the assignor: this is unlikely to be a situation where joinder is not required since the assignment is of part of a debt.[225] For these reasons alone, assignment is not a particularly suitable method of transfer. Further, the provisions for 'assignment' in the LMA agreement[226] envisage the release of the existing lender from all obligations to the borrower and all other lenders, and an assumption by the new lender of those obligations.[227] Given that an assignment cannot transfer obligations, the purported assignment under the LMA agreement may well not be a true assignment under English law.[228] However, a distressed debt fund might well seek to take an assignment of the loan, without taking on any obligations, if it can obtain agreement from all the parties.

The loan agreement will normally limit permitted assignment to certain types of institutions (as with novation),[229] and will usually require consent of the borrower to any permitted assignment. The purpose of such restrictions is slightly different from those restricting novation, which are primarily to ensure that any transferee can make the necessary future advances. In relation to assignment, the concerns are more likely to be a desire to preserve a relationship with the original creditor, or a similar 'bank-like' institution, which it may trust not to behave unreasonably in relation to waivers or enforcement, whereas it cannot be so sure that an assignee will behave in this way.[230] A borrower might, for example, wish to avoid the sale of distressed debt to a vulture fund.[231] There may also be concerns about increased costs, about whether a new lender will comply with regulatory provisions,[232] and

---

[222] 9.2.4.2.3.

[223] 9.2.2.2.

[224] Paget 12.30; EP Ellinger, E Lomnicka and C Hare, *Ellinger's Modern Banking Law*, 5th edn (Oxford, Oxford University Press, 2011) 787.

[225] See discussion at 9.2.2.4.

[226] Clause 24 of the investment grade agreement and cl 29 of the leveraged loan agreement.

[227] The assignment is also made conditional on the new lender confirming that it will assume these obligations to the other lenders.

[228] Paget 12.30. The LMA assignment clause may well be a relic of the arrangement that persisted before the transfer certificate was developed, which was that an assignment was made together with a side letter whereby the new lender confirmed that it was undertaking the relevant obligations to the other lenders. See M Hughes, 'Transferability in Syndicated Lending' [2007] *Law and Financial Markets Review* 21. See also Encyclopaedia of Banking Law, 1947 which sets out a similar system.

[229] See 9.2.4.2.3.

[230] R Goode, 'Contractual Prohibitions against Assignment' in J Armour and J Payne (eds), *Rationality in Company Law* (Oxford, Hart Publishing, 2009). See also *Barbados Trust Co Ltd v Bank of Zambia* [2006] EWHC 222 (Comm) [10].

[231] This appears to have been what happened in *Barbados Trust Co Ltd v Bank of Zambia* [2007] EWCA Civ 148.

[232] *The Argo Fund v Essar Steel Limited* [2005] EWHC 600 (Comm) [29].

about sale of loans to competitors of the borrower who will then use the voting rights to undermine the borrower. There will not usually be a desire to preserve set-off rights,[233] since any right of the borrower to set-off cross-claims against the repayment of the loan is usually expressly excluded, and this will also be the position against any assignee.

If a loan is assigned in breach of the restrictions, the resulting transaction may take effect as a declaration of trust.[234] The beneficiary may then be able to enforce it using the *Vandepitte* procedure. It will be recalled that the earlier discussion of whether this procedure is available included the point that it has the effect of transferring control of enforcement from the 'assignor' to the 'assignee'.[235] In the context of the transfer of syndicated loans, there are important policy reasons to facilitate the ability of a seller to transfer to a buyer rights of control over its enforcement, since no transferee would want to buy a debt which might or might not be enforced by the transferor. This is particularly true where loans are assigned in the distressed debt market, since a major point of the transaction is that the transferee is a specialist in recovering such loans, and the transferor is keen to avoid spending time and money concerning itself with this. It could be said, of course, that this is the very situation against which the debtor wishes to protect itself, and that if a declaration of trust can take effect in this way, the restrictions on assignment become worthless.

The *Barbados Trust* case concerned the assignment of a syndicated loan, and thus raised squarely the competing policy imperatives of allowing the borrower to protect itself, on the basis of freedom of contract, and developing a liquid secondary loan market. There is no doubt that the requirement of borrower consent is a barrier to liquidity in that market, and is a point of real contrast to the market in debt securities, which it mirrors in so many other ways. Although the restrictions on assignment and novation are part of the LMA standard documentation, their presence of absence in any individual agreement is a product of the bargaining power of the parties. In the absence of evidence of structural inequality of parties or market failure, there seems little reason to interfere with the contractual freedom of the parties.[236] The actual effect of the contractual provisions, however, is a matter of much argument and uncertainty, as discussed earlier, and the area could benefit from judicial clarification.

9.2.5 Transfer of Receivables

9.2.5.1 *The Use of Assignment in Receivables Financing*

This section considers the use of assignment in the financing of trade receivables—that is, receivables arising from contracts which are for the provision of goods or non-financial services.[237] As described in chapter two,[238] there are two main types of receivables financing:

---

[233] See 9.2.2.6.2.
[234] See 9.2.2.6.5.
[235] 9.2.2.6.5(e).
[236] Compare the position in relation to receivables financing, discussed at 9.2.6.
[237] This is the definition used in s 1 Small Business, Enterprise and Employment Act 2015 for the scope of the power to override anti-assignment clauses.
[238] 2.3.4.1.

factoring, which is on a notification basis and is largely used for very small businesses, and invoice discounting, which is on a non-notification basis and can be used for businesses of any size. Although there are many variations in the precise structure, a typical receivables financing arrangement[239] involves either a 'whole turnover' agreement, whereby the company being financed (which will be called the 'supplier') agrees to sell its present and future receivables to the financier, or a facultative agreement, whereby the supplier agrees to offer receivables for sale to the financier, which the financier has the option of purchasing.

The means of transfer of the receivables in this type of financing is assignment. There are two requirements of statutory assignment which may not be fulfilled initially: that notice has been given to the debtor, and that the debt is a present one. Once these are fulfilled, an assignment is likely to be statutory, as it will have been made in writing and will be absolute, that is, not by way of charge.[240] In an invoice discounting arrangement, the debtor is not notified, and the supplier collects in the debts itself, holding them on trust for the financier. Thus, the assignment will remain equitable, unless and until the financier notifies the debtor, for example, as a precursor to enforcing the debt. At that point, the assignment will become statutory, and the financier will be able to sue the debtor.

In relation to the future debts in a whole turnover arrangement, the agreement is binding on the assignor, and will have the effect that the debts will be automatically assigned (in equity) to the assignee when they do arise, provided they have been sufficiently identified.[241] To the extent that the date of assignment is relevant to priority, the date will be the date of the agreement, and not when the debts themselves arise.[242]

9.2.5.2 Anti-Assignment Clauses and Receivables Financing

Many contracts giving rise to trade receivables contain anti-assignment clauses. The reasons for this are varied. They range from the rather unmeritorious (that they are included in boilerplate documents by lawyers or that they are an attempt to prevent transfer of obligations, which, of course, assignment cannot do) to concerns about inadvertently paying the wrong party, wishing to preserve set-offs and a general desire to deal with the contracting party, particularly in relation to disputes. The existence of these clauses in trade receivables is a barrier to the financing of such receivables, both because they mean that some suppliers cannot obtain financing at all, or cannot obtain financing in respect of receivables containing such clauses, and also because the workarounds used by the industry are expensive and make the transactions more complex.[243]

In relation to factoring, in the course of which the debtor is notified of the assignment, where there is an anti-assignment clause it is likely that the debtor will refuse to pay the financier when notified, and will instead pay the supplier. This imposes the credit

---

[239] See Security and Title-Based Financing, 7.115; Goode: Commercial Law, 843–76 (draft whole turnover agreement).

[240] Even an assignment by way of a mortgage, which is a transfer of the absolute interest subject to an obligation to reassign, is absolute within the terms of s 136: *Tancred v Delagoa Bay & East Africa Railway Co* (1889) 23 QBD 239. See 7.2.5.2 for discussion of whether such an arrangement could be recharacterised as a security interest.

[241] *Tailby v Official Receiver* (1888) 13 App Cas 523. See 7.3.2.1.

[242] *Holroyd v Marshall* (1862) 10 HL Cas 191.

[243] For more detailed discussion see L Gullifer, 'Should Clauses Prohibiting Assignment be Overridden by Statute?' (2015) 4(1) *Penn State Journal of Law and International Affairs*.

risk of the supplier on the financier pending accounting for such payment.[244] As a result, financiers often refuse to finance receivables arising from contracts containing such clauses, or demand that the customer agree to a waiver.

Invoice discounters may also refuse to finance receivables containing an anti-assignment clause, but in practice they often employ other workarounds. The debtor is not notified of the assignment and, therefore, will continue to pay the supplier, although if it discovers the assignment, it might be able to terminate any contracts it has with the supplier, and is likely to refuse to do further business with it. The chief danger to the financier is that it will be unable to enforce an unpaid debt if the supplier refuses or becomes insolvent. Workarounds used by financiers include taking fixed[245] and floating charges over all the assets of the supplier, so that they can appoint an administrator if the supplier becomes insolvent: the administrator will then collect in all debts due to the supplier, and the supplier will hold the proceeds on trust for the financier. A financier may also take a power of attorney, enabling it to sue in the name of the supplier. This is unlikely to work if the supplier is insolvent, though.[246] A financier might take other forms of credit protection as well, such as a director's guarantee. All of this increases the cost of financing, which is also affected by the uncertain state of the law regarding anti-assignment clauses, discussed above.[247]

9.2.5.3 Statutory Override of Anti-Assignment Clauses

These difficulties have given rise to calls for there to be a statutory override of anti-assignment clauses in relation to trade receivables.[248] Legislation to this effect has been passed in a number of jurisdictions, although the precise scope of the override varies.[249] The case for reform depends on a balancing exercise: the removal of barriers to the provision of finance has to outweigh the resulting interference with freedom of contract. The case is strongest in relation to the financing of the trade receivables of SMEs, and the UK Government has introduced a power to introduced regulations to override anti-assignment clauses in trade receivables, excluding contracts for financial services.[250] At the time of

---

[244] The supplier may well hold the proceeds on trust for the financier, but this is no use if the supplier has dissipated the proceeds and is insolvent.

[245] 'Non-vesting' debts usually fall within the fixed charge, although it may be that this is also prohibited by a widely drawn anti-assignment clause.

[246] Powers of Attorney Act 1971, s 4 provides that for a power of attorney to be irrevocable on the insolvency of the supplier, the financier would need to have some sort of proprietary right in the receivables or would need to be owed the receivables directly.

[247] 9.2.2.6.

[248] P Zonneveld, 'The Effectiveness of Contractual Restrictions on the Assignment of Contractual Debts' [2007] *Journal of International Banking and Financial Law* 313; O Akseli, 'Contractual Prohibitions on Assignment of Receivables: An English and UN Perspective' [2009] *Journal of Banking Law* 650; Goode, 'Contractual Prohibitions against Assignment' [2009] *Lloyd's Maritime and Comparative Law Quarterly* 300; see also the work of the Secured Transactions Law Reform Project at http://securedtransactionslawreformproject.org/what-we-do/ban-on-assignment-clauses/.

[249] US Uniform Commercial Code, art 9-406; Canadian Personal Property Security Acts (see 7.7.3); Australian Personal Property Securities Act 2009, s 81; German Commercial Code HGB, s 354(a); Korean Civil Code, s 449(2); Japanese Civil Code, s 466(2); Italian Civil Code, s 1260(2); Greek Civil Code, s 466(2); Portuguese Civil Code, s 577(2); Spanish Civil Code, s 1112. See also UN Convention on the Assignment of Receivables in International Trade (2002), art 9(1); UNIDROIT Convention on International Factoring (1988), art 6(1); UNCITRAL Legislative Guide on Secured Transactions, II.107. We are indebted to Dr Woo-Jung Jon for the analysis in his MSt thesis which led to this list.

[250] Small Business, Enterprise and Employment Act 2015, ss 1 and 2.

writing (mid-2015), the Department for Business, Innovation and Skills is consulting on draft regulations, the final form of which is not yet available.

9.2.6 Transfer of Securities

Securities (both debt and equity) can be held in a number of forms, and can be traded on different kinds of markets, as well as over the counter. Equity securities are typically held in dematerialised form through CREST or (if not issued in the UK) in the form of a globalised share certificate: investors in either case are likely to hold through intermediaries.[251] While it is also possible for shares to be held in registered certificated form,[252] the holding of shares in bearer form is about to be abolished.[253] Debt securities in the form of eurobonds can be held through CREST but are more likely to be held as global notes and held through intermediaries. Shorter-term debt securities, and stock, are also likely to be held through CREST, although stock can also be certificated.

As discussed earlier, shares in public companies may be listed and traded on the public markets. Trading is subject to detailed regulatory requirements.[254] While the trading of debt securities has up to now been subject to much less regulation, the new regime brought in by MiFID II and MiFIR[255] will cover non-equity trading on regulated markets (such as the GEFIM),[256] multilateral trading facilities (such as the PSM)[257] and organised trading facilities, which includes any other kind of venue bringing together buyers and sellers. Thus the market abuse and transparency regimes apply to all such trades,[258] in contrast to the position in the secondary loan market. Over-the-counter trading is not included in these regimes, though if it is done by a system internaliser (a dealer who executes client trades against its own proprietary base, a frequent occurrence in the trading of debt securities) some regulation applies.[259]

The trading of securities and the settlement of trades are complicated matters on which there is much regulatory law, and the reader is referred to specialist texts.[260] This section will concentrate on the legal analysis of the transfer itself: this will be the same whatever venue or form is used for the trade, but will vary according to the manner in which the securities are held. The transfer of shares held in registered form is discussed in detail in chapter four above, and only the transfer of shares held in CREST or through intermediaries is discussed here: the analysis is similar whether the securities are debt or equity securities.

---

[251] See 4.6.

[252] Although shares in a publicly held company must be held in dematerialised form if they are to have a premium listing: see LR 6.1.23 and 6.1.24, which require that such shares must be eligible for electronic settlement.

[253] Small Business, Enterprise and Employment Act 2015, s 84, amending Companies Act 2006, s 779.

[254] Note that MiFIR has introduced a new requirement that all equity trading, with the only exception of ad hoc and infrequent trade between professionals, should take place on organised trading venues, which are subject to the transparency requirements: see MiFIR art 23 and Moloney: EU Regulation, 468.

[255] See 13.3.1.

[256] See 13.2.2.2.

[257] 13.2.2.2.

[258] See 13.3.1.

[259] See Moloney: EU Regulation, 440.

[260] For example, M Blair, G Walker and S Willey, *Financial Markets and Exchanges Law* (Oxford, Oxford University Press, 2012); A Hudson, *Securities Law* (London, Sweet & Maxwell, 2008).

9.2.6.1 Transfer of Stock

Stock is either transferred through CREST[261] or, if certificated, transferred by the delivery up of the certificate to the issuer's registrar together with a transfer form.[262] The legal analysis of the transfer is not entirely clear. One view is that it takes place by novation, since, by accepting the registration, the company is agreeing that the transferee should take the place of the transferor.[263] Thus the transfer of registered debt securities is seen as the same as the transfer of shares. However, this analysis requires modification in relation to stock, where there is only one obligation which cannot be novated in the ordinary sense. Where the stock is created by deed poll, the process may be seen as analogous to novation, since although the company's obligation to the original stockholder is not contractual (as it is effectuated by deed poll) it is replaced by a new obligation to the new stockholder, and the company, by registering the transfer, agrees to this transfer.[264]

In relation to stock issued under a trust deed, the interest of the stockholder is merely equitable: the legal interest in the debt is held by the trustee.[265] This may mean that there cannot be a novation, and the means of transfer is by assignment.[266] In either case, potentially the transferee takes subject to defects in title and equities. If the transfer takes place by assignment, the rule of priority will be that in *Dearle v Hall*.[267] Even this is not straightforward, since it is not clear whether notice of an assignment can be received by an issuer.[268] Such a notice cannot be received by an issuer of shares,[269] but this prohibition is based on the fact that no notice of trust shall be entered in the company's register.[270]

However, in relation to stock held on trust the registrar does enter a notice of trust, and it does appear that this entry is effective in some way. Thus, the reasoning applicable to shares may not apply here, although the position is likely to depend on the exact words used in the trust deed. Further, it is not clear whether giving notice to the issuer is sufficient to gain priority under *Dearle v Hall* if the trustee is not also given notice, since what is actually being assigned is the right against the trustee and not a direct right against the issuer.[271] Even if no qualifying notice under *Dearle v Hall* is given, the transferee who registers may well succeed against someone who acquires an earlier unregistered interest, since the first transferee has failed to take any steps to prevent the original stockholder from transferring the stock to someone else, such as dispossessing him of the certificates or stock transfer form.[272]

---

[261] For analysis of CREST transfers, see 9.2.6.3.

[262] Fuller: Corporate Borrowing, 3.3; Tolley Company Law Service C4002. If the instrument does not provide for the procedure for transfer, this is governed by Stock Transfer Act 1963.

[263] Benjamin: Interests in Securities, 3.07; Tolley Company Law Service C4029.

[264] This analysis is not without problems, as it means that a new debt arises each time the stock is transferred, which could have repercussions on, for example, insolvency; see Hughes: Banking, 4.3.

[265] 7.3.2.2.1.

[266] Although see 9.2.6.2 in relation to transfers of interests in intermediated securities.

[267] (1828) 3 Russ 1. As explained at 7.4.4, this rule is that priority is in the order in which the debtor is notified of the assignments.

[268] Tolley Company Law Service C4029(2).

[269] *Société Générale de Paris v Walker* (1885) 11 App Cas 20. See 8.2.7.

[270] Companies Act 2006, s 126.

[271] Law of Property Act 1925, s 137(2) which requires notice to a trustee in respect of an equitable interest in securities; and *Re Dallas* [1904] 2 Ch 385. Fuller: Corporate Borrowing, 15.18 notes that the trustee will usually have the right to inspect the register, and this may count as sufficient notice.

[272] Tolley Company Law Service C4029(2).

In any event, in most cases a priority battle is unlikely to arise, since the trust deed will invariably provide that, as between the company and stockholder, a registered holder is treated as the absolute owner whose claim against the issuer is free of any equities or set-offs between the company and any holder, including the current holder.[273] Such a provision will have the effect of excluding the usual rule that an assignee takes subject to equities,[274] although it is clear from cases concerning the exclusion of the right of set-off that clear words must be used,[275] and insolvency set-off cannot be excluded.[276] The effect of such a provision is that, despite the fact that the transfer is on the register rather than by delivery, and the interest of the transferor is equitable, the transaction is similar to the transfer of a negotiable instrument, in that a kind of contractual negotiability is conferred.[277]

9.2.6.2 *Transfer of Intermediated Securities*[278]

As discussed in chapters four[279] and eight, most securities are held through intermediaries.[280] Legal title is held by the entity at the top of the chain, and this is held on trust for the next intermediary down, which holds its interest under that trust on a sub-trust for its clients, who may be investors or intermediaries themselves.[281] In relation to most shares, and some bonds, the top of the holding chain in the UK is usually an account in CREST, the holder of which has legal title to the securities. In many cases, however, securities are issued in the form of an immobilised global note or share certificate, which is held by a central securities depository outside the UK or an international central securities depository, typically Euroclear in Belgium or Clearstream in Luxembourg. In relation to bonds, the global note is in the form of a bearer bond, but it is not clear whether it is a negotiable instrument, since it is never intended to be transferred.[282] In any event, what is traded is not the global note but the bondholders' entitlements, and these are co-ownership interests under a trust or sub-trust.[283] The same holds true for shares held in the intermediated system, and applies in any event where the securities at the top of the chain are held through CREST. A co-ownership interest cannot, of course, be a negotiable instrument: it is not transferred by delivery (there

---

[273] Fuller: Corporate Borrowing, 3.7(d). This provision is also required if the security if traded through CREST; see r 7 paras 3.2 and 5.

[274] *Re Blakely Ordnance Co* (1867) 3 Ch App 154; *Re Agra and Masterman's Bank* (1866–67) 2 Ch App 391; *Hilger Analytical Ltd v Rank Precision Industries Ltd* [1984] BCLC 301.

[275] *Gilbert-Ash (Northern) Ltd v Modern Engineering (Bristol) Ltd* [1974] AC 689, 717; *BOC Group plc v Centeon LLC* [1999] CLC 497; *IG Index Ltd v Ehrentreu* [2013] EWCA Civ 95. See 6.3.4.5. If the provisions in the trust deed comply with the CREST requirements, they will be effective: *Re Kaupthing Singer and Friedlander Ltd; Newcastle Building Society v Mill* [2009] EWHC 740 (Ch).

[276] *Halesowen Presswork and Assemblies Ltd v Westminster Bank Ltd* [1971] 1 QB 1; see also 6.3.4.6.2.

[277] Hughes: Banking, 4.3. This does not mean, however, that all aspects of the law applicable to negotiable instruments also apply: *Re Kaupthing Singer and Friedlander Ltd; Newcastle Building Society v Mill* [2009] EWHC 740 (Ch) [22].

[278] See Smith and Leslie: Assignment, 19.136 ff; see also, generally, W Liang, *Title and Title Conflicts in respect of Intermediated Securities under English Law* (Cambridge, Cambridge Scholars Publishing, 2013).

[279] 4.6.4.

[280] Intermediated holdings of shares are discussed at 11.2.2.1.2 in the context of corporate governance.

[281] See 8.3.2.3.2(b) for a fuller discussion.

[282] Hughes: Banking, 4.4; Goode: Commercial Law, 615; Bamford: Financial Law, 6.90.

[283] See 8.3.2.3.2(b).

is nothing to deliver).[284] So how are shareholders' or bondholders' interests (held through an intermediary) transferred?[285] And is such transfer in any way analogous to the transfer of a negotiable instrument?

To take the simplest case, where the transferor and the transferee have accounts with the same intermediary, a debit entry is made in the account of the transferor and a credit entry in the account of the transferee. The effect of these entries is that the transferee replaces the transferor (as regards the securities transferred) as a co-beneficiary under the trust whereby the intermediary holds its own co-ownership interest on trust for those of its account holders who own those particular securities. The book entries become more complicated when the parties have accounts with different intermediaries, since debit and credit entries must be made up the chain until two intermediaries have accounts with the same higher-tier intermediary,[286] but the effect is the same: the transferor ceases to be a beneficiary in relation to that co-ownership interest and the transferee becomes a beneficiary.[287] What is the best legal analysis of this event?

Clearly the transfer has not taken place by negotiation. Assignment also seems inappropriate, since it is hard to describe the transferee's interest as being the same as the transferor's, although the two are connected. The most appropriate analysis would seem to be some sort of novation, in that the transferor's beneficial interest no longer exists and has been replaced by the new beneficial interest of the transferee. This is the conclusion reached by Joanna Benjamin.[288] It is also supported by the use of netting in the settlement of securities, so that there is rarely a straight 'transfer' from A to B.[289] Of course, to achieve novation the consent of the obligor is required.[290] However, since what is being 'transferred' is the interest of a beneficiary against a trustee, it is the trustee's consent that is required, and since the trustee/intermediary makes the book entries, this requirement is satisfied.[291] The ultimate obligor, the issuing company, has no knowledge of or involvement in the transfer.[292]

Apart from the inherent problem of complexity, two specific problems potentially arise on this analysis. First, section 53(1)(c) of the Law of Property Act 1925 provides that a disposition of an equitable interest must be in writing and signed by the person disposing of the interest. It should first be noted that this provision does not apply where the transaction is a financial collateral arrangement.[293] It is not at all clear whether the transfer of an

---

[284] J Benjamin, 'Ease of Transfer and Security of Transfer in the Securities Markets' [2001] *Journal of International Banking and Financial Law* 219, 221; Law Commission Updated Advice (May 2008), 5.39.

[285] For several worked examples, see Smith and Leslie: Assignment, 19.141 ff.

[286] For a worked example, see L Gullifer, 'Protection of Investors in Intermediated Securities' in J Armour and J Payne (eds), *Rationality in Company Law* (Oxford, Hart Publishing, 2009) 232–33. This is in the context of shares held with an intermediary, but the principle is the same for debt securities.

[287] For criticism of this method of transfer and a call for structural reform, see E Micheler, 'Transfer of Intermediated Securities and Legal Certainty' in T Keijser (ed), *Transnational Securities Law* (Oxford, Oxford University Press, 2014).

[288] Benjamin: Interests in Securities, 3.27–3.33. See also Tolley Company Law Service C4029(3).

[289] See L Gullifer, 'Protection of Investors in Intermediated Securities' in J Armour and J Payne (eds), *Rationality in Company Law* (Oxford, Hart Publishing, 2009) 232–33.

[290] See 9.2.1.

[291] Law Commission, 'Issues Affecting Transferees of Intermediated Securities' (Third Seminar), http://lawcommission.justice.gov.uk/docs/Intermediated_securities_seminar_3.pdf, 1.33.

[292] Although by agreeing that the securities are to be held through CREST (if they are), the issuer will have agreed to a novation; see 9.2.6.3.

[293] FCARs, reg 4(2); *Mills v Sportsdirect.com Retail Ltd* [2010] EWHC 1072 (Ch).

interest in intermediated securities as described above is a 'disposition' within the section. It seems that what is happening is that a new interest is created[294] (or that the transferee joins the 'group' of equitable co-owners of the pool of securities held by the intermediary by way of succession rather than disposition) and on either analysis this is not a disposition.[295]

These arguments are bolstered by the fact that a straight 'transfer' rarely happens, so that unless the transferor and transferee both have accounts with the same intermediary, the operation of the tiered system, and in particular the occurrence of netting, means that the intermediary of the transferee will make a credit entry without knowing where the 'securities' it is crediting come from. However, there is very considerable uncertainty surrounding the issue, as the word 'disposition' is not defined in the Act.[296]

One rationale of the rule in section 53(1)(c) is that, where an equitable interest is transferred, the trustee ceases to owe duties to the transferor and owes them to the transferee,[297] and so any requirement which enables the trustee to discover this change in duties is helpful (although it would be more consistent with the rationale if written notice to the trustee were required, as section 136 of the Law of Property Act 1925 requires in relation to assignments).[298] This rationale does not apply in relation to transfers of intermediated securities, in that the intermediary that is the trustee in relation to the transferee is well aware of the transfer: it is the intermediary itself that makes the credit entry in the transferee's account (similarly, the transferor's intermediary is aware that it is no longer a trustee by making the debit entry). This argument could lead to the conclusion that the records of the intermediaries are sufficient 'writing' for the purposes of section 53(1)(c).[299] However, for the avoidance of doubt it is generally recognised that legislative reform is desirable.[300]

The second problem is more complex.[301] It will be recalled that the advantages of negotiability are, first, that the transferee obtains good title even if the transferor's title is

---

[294] The declaration of a new trust is not a 'disposition' under s 53(1)(c): A Hudson, *Equity and Trusts*, 8th edn (Abingdon, Routledge-Cavendish, 2015) 292–93.

[295] Benjamin: Interests in Securities, 72 at fnn 48 and 51. While setting out these arguments, Benjamin herself thinks that the position is uncertain. The application of s 53(1)(c) to an unsigned agreement creating a charge over intermediated securities was considered in *Re Lehman Brothers International (Europe)* [2012] EWHC 2997 (Ch). The section was held to have no application since the equitable interest in the intermediated securities was validly transferred to the chargee, at which point the chargee held the intermediated securities on trust for the charger, so that the charge was carved out of the chargor's beneficial interest. This was held to be analogous to the position in *Vandervell v IRC* [1967] 2 AC 291, in which s 53(1)(c) was held not to apply (although that case concerned the creation of a legal and not an equitable interest).

[296] The section was considered in *Grey v Inland Revenue Commissioners* [1960] AC 1, where the House of Lords expressed the view that 'disposition' was to be given its 'natural' meaning (at 13).

[297] Another rationale may be to protect those entitled to property from hidden transactions; see A Hudson, *Equity and Trusts*, 8th edn (Abingdon, Routledge-Cavendish, 2015) 280.

[298] B McFarlane in *The Structure of Property Law* (Oxford, Hart Publishing, 2008) 120.

[299] A Austen-Peters, *Custody of Investments: Law and Practice* (Oxford, Oxford University Press, 2000) 69.

[300] B McFarlane and R Stevens, 'Interests in Securities: Practical Problems and Conceptual Solutions' in L Gullifer and J Payne (eds), *Intermediated Securities: Legal Problems and Practical Issues* (Oxford, Hart Publishing, 2010) 54–55; Law Commission, 'The UNIDROIT Convention in Intermediated Securities: Further Updated Advice to HM Treasury' (May 2008), 4.53. See art 11(2) Geneva Securities Convention 2009, which disapplies all formalities required for a credit to a securities account to be effective. Note also that s 53(1)(c) is expressly disapplied in relation to transfers through the CREST system (considered at 8.2.6.): Uncertificated Securities Regulations (USR), reg 38(5).

[301] Law Commission, ibid, part 5; McFarlane and Stevens, ibid, 52–54; G Davies, 'Using Intermediated Securities as Collateral: Equitable Interests with Inequitable Results' [2007] *Journal of International Banking and Financial Law* 70.

defective, and, second, that the transferee takes free from equities. In the absence of the negotiability exception to the *nemo dat* rule, a transferee can only obtain as good a title as that of the transferor.[302] If, for example, a transfer of intermediated securities is not authorised by the transferor, the transferor will have a personal claim against its intermediary that made the unauthorised transfer (which amounts to a breach of trust by the intermediary), but it may also seek to assert an equitable tracing claim against the equitable interest of the transferee.[303] One possible defence to such a claim is that the recipient transferee is a bona fide purchaser of the legal interest without notice of the breach (the 'equity's darling' defence). However, since the transferee only has an equitable interest, this defence is not available.[304] It has been suggested that this result, which means that those holding securities with an intermediary are in a different position from those holding bearer securities,[305] or those holding through the CREST system,[306] or those registered as the holder of securities,[307] is unsatisfactory and that statutory reform is required.[308] It should, however, be pointed out that in practice such a tracing claim would be rare. First, the transferor has a good personal claim against its intermediary, which it is probably more convenient to bring if the intermediary is solvent.[309] Second, because of the use of netting in the settlement system, it is often difficult or impossible to track the exact recipient of 'transferred' securities. However, even a small amount of legal risk can cause systemic problems in certain circumstances and so legislative reform is desirable.[310]

---

[302] This is not necessarily the case where there is a novation, since the new obligation undertaken by the new intermediary is not necessarily the same as that given up by the old intermediary, but the position is not clear; see 9.2.4.2.5.

[303] Benjamin: Interests in Securities, 3.59 and 2.53–2.55. Since equity will trace into substitute assets as well as the original assets, the fact that the transfer takes place by novation will not prevent such a claim arising.

[304] Benjamin: Interests in Securities, 3.64; Law Commission, 'The UNIDROIT Convention in Intermediated Securities: Further Updated Advice to HM Treasury' (May 2008), 5.40–5.43. cf B McFarlane and R Stevens, 'Interests in Securities: Practical Problems and Conceptual Solutions' in L Gullifer and J Payne (eds), *Intermediated Securities: Legal Problems and Practical Issues* (Oxford, Hart Publishing, 2010) 54.

[305] Which are negotiable instruments.

[306] See 9.2.6.3.

[307] See 4.5. These are the legal owners, so that the defence does apply. For further discussion of protection of transferees of registered shares, see Law Commission, 'The UNIDROIT Convention in Intermediated Securities: Further Updated Advice to HM Treasury' (May 2008), 5.24; E Micheler, 'Farewell Quasi-Negotiability? Legal Title and Transfer of Shares in a Paperless World' [2002] *Journal of Business Law* 358; E Micheler 'The Legal Nature of Securities: Inspirations from Comparative Law' in L Gullifer and J Payne (eds), *Intermediated Securities: Legal Problems and Practical Issues* (Oxford, Hart Publishing, 2010) ch 5.

[308] Law Commission, ibid, 5.67; Financial Markets Law Commission, 'Property Interests in Investment Securities' (July 2004) Issue 3, www.fmlc.org/papers.html, 6.8; G Davies, 'Using Intermediated Securities as Collateral: Equitable Interests with Inequitable Results' [2007] *Journal of International Banking and Financial Law* 70.

[309] Intermediaries are regulated under the Financial Conduct Authority and Prudential Regulation Authority and so in theory should not become insolvent (see Law Commission, ibid, 5.5), although the recent experience of Lehman Brothers belies this point.

[310] The UNIDROIT Convention addresses this point in detail: see arts 18 and 19. See L Gullifer, 'Ownership of Securities' (26–30) and C Mooney and H Kanda, 'Core Issues under the UNIDROIT (Geneva) Convention on Intermediated Securities: Views from the United States and Japan' (94–119), both in L Gullifer and J Payne (eds), *Intermediated Securities: Legal Problems and Practical Issues* (Oxford, Hart Publishing, 2010); L Thevenoz, 'Transfer of Intermediated Securities' in PH Conac, U Segna and L Thevenoz (eds), *Intermediated Securities: The Impact of the Geneva Securities Convention and the Future European Legislation* (Cambridge, Cambridge University Press, 2013) 6.5.

To the extent that the transferee takes subject to defects in the title of the transferor, it could also be argued that it takes subject to equities (such as vitiating factors or set-off),[311] although if, as suggested above, the transfer takes place by novation, then this may not be the case.[312] In any event, most bonds provide contractually that the holder takes free from all equities between the company and any existing holder. This is a similar provision to that included in registered stock.[313] Where the bonds are held through intermediaries, the provision would have to make it clear that 'holder' includes 'account holder'.[314] It is clear that a provision excluding set-off can be effective,[315] since the party that would otherwise assert the set-off would be the issuer, which is a party to the agreement. However, it would be more difficult to provide contractually for each transferee to take free from defects in title, as this would have to bind successive bondholders so that each was prevented from pursuing any proprietary claim against transferees. Thus, as discussed above, the protection can only be given by legislation.

9.2.6.3 *Transfers via CREST*

If securities are dematerialised and held through the CREST system[316] they in effect become registered securities, since the CREST register is the root of title.[317] Until fairly recently, money market instruments, which were bearer securities, were settled through the Central Moneymarkets Office.[318] Such securities have now become 'eligible debt securities' and can be held in a dematerialised form and traded through the CREST system.[319] Shares are also often held directly through CREST.[320]

The transfer of securities through CREST takes place by an entry in the CREST register, which has the effect of transferring legal title. Only the registered legal owner can issue the relevant transfer instruction. Once the buyer and seller have established the terms of their sale, 'dematerialised instructions' to make the transfer and the payment are sent to

---

[311] Law Commission, 'The UNIDROIT Convention in Intermediated Securities: Further Updated Advice to HM Treasury' (May 2008), 5.47, where it is argued that the rule in *Phillips v Phillips* (1861) 4 De GF & J 208 (that a bona fide transferee of an equitable interest does not take subject to equities) does not apply to choses in action, including intermediated securities.

[312] See 9.2.4.2.5; E Micheler, 'Farewell Quasi-Negotiability? Legal Title and Transfer of Shares in a Paperless World?' [2002] *Journal of Business Law* 358, 360.

[313] See 9.2.6.1.

[314] As with the sample clause at 1.1.12 of Financial Markets Law Committee, Issue 62 'Trustee Exemption Clauses'.

[315] For a discussion of the effectiveness of such provisions, see 6.3.4.5. Insolvency set-off, however, cannot be excluded; see 6.3.4.6.2.

[316] This is common for some short-term bonds traded on the money market: see Tolley Company Law Service C4009. For a brief description of the CREST system see 4.6.2, and for a more detailed discussion see Tolley Company Law Service, CREST (C8001 ff).

[317] USR, regs 24(2) and (3).

[318] Benjamin: Interests in Securities, 9.72; M Evans, 'Moving to a Dematerialised Capital Market' (2003) 18 *Journal of International Banking Law and Regulation* 121.

[319] This is the effect of the amendments to the USR 2001 made by the Uncertificated Securities (Amendment) (Eligible Debt Securities) Regulations 2003 (SI 2003/1633) and the Uncertificated Securities (Amendment) Regulations 2013 (SI 2013/632).

[320] See 4.6.1.

CREST.[321] The CREST computer matches the selling and buying instructions and settles the transaction on the nominated settlement day. It is possible for an individual to have private membership in the CREST system, in which case the CREST register will indicate the name of that investor as holding legal title to the shares.

Although it is not entirely clear, the best analysis is that this transfer takes place by novation. When certificated registered shares were transferred by entries in the company's register, the conventional analysis was that they were transferred by novation.[322] On the basis that all that has changed in relation to the transfer of shares with the introduction of the CREST system is the location of the register (the definitive register is now that of CREST), it would seem to be strongly arguable that the explanation for the transfer of shares through CREST is also that of novation. This analysis though, is not universally accepted. It has been argued, in fact, that it can no longer apply as the company cannot be said to agree to a novation, since it is not involved in the transfer process.[323] The argument is then made that this means that the transferee cannot take free from equities, as the company has not agreed to waive its rights to assert equities against that transferee.[324] This then forms the basis of a new theory that shares are quasi-negotiable because of the importance that shares are freely transferable.[325]

The novation analysis is perfectly acceptable, though, when applied to debt securities which are traded through CREST. First, a security can only be an eligible debt security if the terms of issue provide that its units may only be issued in uncertificated form.[326] Although in theory securities originally issued as bearer securities can be converted to uncertificated form, this is very rare, and in any event requires the participation of the issuer.[327] Thus, the issuer must be taken to have agreed in advance to the transfer of securities through the CREST system, and, thus, to novation (if that is the legal method by which such transfer is effected). Secondly, for a security other than a share to comply with the CREST rules for entry into the system, it must be 'transferable free from any equity, set-off or counterclaim between the issuer and the original or any intermediate holder of the security'.[328]

---

[321] These instructions are sent in specified format, using specified security devices, over a specialised telecommunications network, all of which are approved by Euroclear UK and Ireland Ltd (EUI) (see 4.6.2). In addition, these instructions can only be sent by 'system participants'. Other system members, called 'sponsored members', must arrange for system participants to send instructions on their behalf.

[322] E Micheler, *Property in Securities: A Comparative Study* (Cambridge, Cambridge University Press, 2007) 2.1; RR Pennington, *Company Law*, 8th edn (Oxford University Press, 2001) 398–99; Benjamin: Interests in Securities, 3.05.

[323] E Micheler, 'Farewell Quasi-Negotiability? Legal Title and Transfer of Shares in a Paperless World' [2002] *Journal of Business Law* 358, 363; E Micheler, *Property in Securities: A Comparative Study* (Cambridge, Cambridge University Press, 2007) 5.2.3.

[324] Micheler, 'Farewell Quasi-Negotiability?', ibid.

[325] Ibid; E Micheler, *Property in Securities: A Comparative Study* (Cambridge, Cambridge University Press, 2007) chs 5 and 6.

[326] USR, reg 3.

[327] USR, reg 33.

[328] CREST r 7 3.2. Normally this would be contractually incorporated into the terms of the security and is included in the pro forma terms for an eligible debt security published by the Bank of England (see www.bankofengland.co.uk/markets/money/edsterms.pdf at 6.4); if not, it would clearly be implied. Both statutory and equitable set-off are included: see *Re Kaupthing Singer and Friedlander Ltd; Newcastle Building Society v Mill* [2009] EWHC 740 (Ch).

This provision in the CREST rules also means that one of the advantages of negotiability is maintained when a debt security is transferred through CREST. When it was proposed to include transfers of money market instruments in the CREST system, those consulted made it very clear that it was important to keep all the benefits of negotiability.[329] The other aspect of negotiability, that the transferee takes free from any defect of title of the transferor, has not been dealt with expressly in the legislation or the CREST rules as it was thought to be sufficiently covered by the existing provisions.[330] The dangers were considered to be those of a forged or otherwise defective transfer instruction (resulting in an unauthorised transfer), and adverse claims by third parties. The former is covered under USR regulation 35 in that where there is a 'properly authenticated dematerialised instruction' the purported transferor cannot deny that it was authorised, and an addressee without actual notice of a defect can accept that an instruction was sent with authority.[331] As regards the latter, competing claims could (in theory) be either legal or equitable. Since the CREST register is the definitive record of legal title,[332] a competing legal claim cannot arise: only the registered legal owner can issue the relevant transfer instruction. There could, however, be competing equitable claims, since these cannot be registered on the CREST register.[333] The transferee, though, will have the protection of the equity's darling defence unless it has notice of the competing claim: this position is similar to that where there is a negotiable instrument.[334]

9.3 Structures which have a Similar Effect to Transfer

9.3.1 Sub-Participation[335]

Another method of 'transfer' that is often used in the context of an interest in a syndicated loan is sub-participation. This is not, strictly speaking, a transfer, since the original lender remains in exactly the same legal position vis-a-vis the borrower. Instead, new contractual rights between the original lender ('lender') and the new participant ('participant') are

---

[329] Bank of England consultation paper 'The Future of Money Market Instruments' (November 1999), appendix II; Bank of England consultation paper 'The Future of Money Market Instruments: Next Steps' (March 2000), 11; Bank of England interim report 'The Future of Money Market Instruments' (January 2001), 6 (proposal (v)).

[330] 'The Future of Money Market Instruments' (November 1999), ibid, appendix II, including notes of an advice by Richard Sykes QC on this very point. cf the view of Benjamin, who argues that, as the original regulations were not designed to replicate negotiability, they only achieve integrity of the system itself; they do not prevent reversal of a transfer under the operation of the general law, for example the law of tracing: Benjamin: Interests in Securities, 213 fn 131.

[331] USR, regs 35(2)(4)(5). The requirement of actual notice may even put the transferee in a better position than where there is a negotiable instrument, since this may be narrower than the notice required to prevent a transferee being a holder in due course.

[332] USR, reg 24.

[333] USR, reg 23(3).

[334] USR, reg 35(4). See further Bank of England consultation paper 'The Future of Money Market Instruments' (November 1999), appendix II, advice of Richard Sykes QC.

[335] This method of transferring the risk and benefit of a loan without changing the contractual relationship between the lender and borrower is that used where English law applies. In the US a different legal method is used, called 'loan participation', which has very similar practical effects. For a discussion of the legal position in the US see Mugasha: Multi-Bank Financing, ch 6.

created. Since no interest is transferred, the contract between the lender and the participant can be on any terms they wish. There are, however, two main forms. Either the participant pays the lender a sum of money (equivalent to the 'price' of the debt) and the lender agrees to account to the participant for any money it receives from the borrower (this is called a 'funded sub-participation'), or no money is paid by the participant but it agrees to accept the risk of non-payment by the borrower, by giving a guarantee or indemnity of the borrower's obligations to the lender (this is called a 'risk participation').[336] This latter structure has now, in practice, largely been replaced by the use of credit derivatives.[337]

The precise legal nature of each agreement is, of course, a function of the exact words used,[338] but the usual structure is that there are two back-to-back contracts: the original loan contract between the lender and the borrower, and the contract between the lender and the participant. The participant is therefore merely an unsecured creditor of the lender and has no proprietary interest in the loan or the proceeds.[339] The result of this is that the participant takes on the credit risk of both the borrower and the lender. If the borrower does not pay, the participant does not get paid, and will only receive whatever the lender receives in the borrower's insolvency. If the lender is insolvent, as the participant has no proprietary right to proceeds of the loan already or subsequently received by the lender, all it has is an unsecured claim to the amount of those proceeds, and it has no right to sue the borrower direct.[340]

In most circumstances, the additional credit risk of the lender adds little extra risk to the transaction, since the lender is likely to be a bank or a stable financial institution. In times of financial uncertainty, however, when banks can become insolvent, this can present a concern. There are several possible ways for a participant to protect itself. One is for the participant to take a charge over the loan or the proceeds of the loan.[341] A charge over the loan itself will, without more, normally give the participant a charge over the proceeds as well, meaning that it will have priority over unsecured creditors of the lender in relation to proceeds which have been paid or which continue to be paid during insolvency.[342]

---

[336] Mugasha: Multi-Bank Financing, 7.04–7.05.

[337] Fuller: Corporate Borrowing, 15.41; Mugasha: Multi-Bank Financing, 7.02. See 9.3.2, and, for discussion of credit default swaps, see 6.4.3.

[338] *Lloyds TSB Bank plc v Clarke* [2002] UKPC 27 [14]. If the parties make it clear that a sub-participation structure is intended, the court will not recharacterise the transaction as an assignment.

[339] Ibid, especially [16] approving the description of a sub-participation agreement by Professor Wood, of which the most up to date version is Wood: Loans and Bonds, 9-039.

[340] Wood: Loans and Bonds, 9-039. Note, though, that in a risk participation where the participant guarantees the loan, the participant might, on payment under the guarantee, obtain rights against the borrower by way of subrogation. This issue is not without difficulty. The guarantee is (usually) given without the consent of the borrower and in these circumstances a surety has no right of indemnity as such (*Owen v Tate* [1976] QB 402; M Hughes, 'A Commentary on the Recent Report by the Financial Law Panel on the Secondary Debt Market' [1997] *Journal of International Banking and Financial Law* 75). However, a surety might have a right of subrogation under the Mercantile Law Amendment Act 1856 s 5, although if this does not apply it is not clear that subrogation would apply under equitable principles, see Goode: Credit and Security, 8-08.

[341] Wood: Loans and Bonds, 9-039; Loan Market Association discussion paper 'LMA Sub-Participation Agreements and Grantor Insolvency' (C Winkworth and L Watt, Richards Kibbe & Orbe LLP), http://documents. lexology.com/8cc59b5c-cc73-48f2-a5a4-da96b1428880.pdf, 2, where it is suggested that the charge would be in favour of a security trustee. See also Fuller: Corporate Borrowing, 301 fn 107.

[342] The insolvency of the lender will not stop the borrower making payments to the lender, which, in the absence of a charge, would be part of the lender's assets for distribution to all of its creditors.

There are, however, a number of potential problems with this structure. First, the obligation secured by the charge is the lender's obligation to pay the participant under the sub-participation agreement. This obligation only arises when the borrower pays the lender, at which point the subject matter of the charge (the loan) ceases to exist. There is, therefore, no equity of redemption.[343] This objection does not apply to a charge over the proceeds, as the obligation to account arises once the proceeds are received, and can be fulfilled by the payment of any money the lender has. There is, therefore, an equity of redemption in the proceeds. There is thus more sense in taking a charge over the proceeds alone, although until the borrower makes the first payment there is no secured obligation (and therefore no executed consideration so the charge cannot be enforceable in equity), nor is there any subject matter of the charge.[344]

Further, the ability of the lender to use the proceeds for its own purposes and to pay the participant the money due from any source means that if there is a charge, it is a floating one.[345] The participant will therefore lose priority to preferential creditors and the ringfenced fund,[346] unless it is a security financial collateral arrangement within the FCARs, in which case these priority provisions will be disapplied. The proceeds, which will be held in a bank account, will be financial collateral within the FCARs, but for the charge to be a security financial collateral arrangement it will be necessary for the collateral to be within the possession or control of the collateral taker, that is, the sub-participant: given the freedom of the lender to use the proceeds for its own purposes, this is unlikely.[347] Unless the charge falls within the FCARs it will also be registrable.[348]

If the lender has other secured borrowings, the chargee is likely to lose priority to earlier security holders, or, if the borrowings are unsecured, the grant of the charge is likely to be in breach of a negative pledge clause.[349] It has also been suggested that if the charge is given when the lender is in financial difficulties, it could be vulnerable to being set aside as a preference.[350] However, the giving of security for a contemporaneous or subsequent advance is not usually seen as a preference,[351] so that, at least to the extent that the charge secures the lender's obligation to pay in relation to payments not yet received from the borrower, it will not be a preference. Nor, if the charge were floating, would it be vulnerable to being set aside under section 245 of the Insolvency Act 1986.[352] It is also possible that the arrangement might be held not to be a charge at all. In this case, it is likely either to be completely ineffective or to be characterised as an absolute transfer of the loan. This is not

---

[343] M Daley, 'Funded Participations—Mitigation of Grantor Credit Risk' (2009) 24 *Journal of International Banking Law and Regulation* 288, 289.

[344] For a discussion of whether there can be a charge over purely future property, see 7.3.2.1.

[345] This seems reasonably clear in the light of *Re Spectrum Plus* [2005] UKHL 41: the question is raised in M Daley, 'Funded Participations—Mitigation of Grantor Credit Risk' (2009) 24 *Journal of International Banking Law and Regulation* 288, 290.

[346] See 3.3.1.2.

[347] See 7.3.4.2 for further discussion.

[348] Companies Act 2006, s 859A; see 7.3.4.3.

[349] Wood: Loans and Bonds, 9-039. This may also be the case if the earlier borrowing is secured by a floating charge. Note that the sub-participation agreement itself is likely to contain a promise by the lender not to create any security interest in the loan.

[350] Wood: Loans and Bonds, 9-039. For a brief discussion of preferences, see 3.3.2.2.

[351] Goode: Corporate Insolvency, 13-84.

[352] See 3.3.2.3. This section would be disapplied if the charge fell within the FCARs.

usually what the parties to the transaction intended, since the reason for using the sub-participation structure is often that an assignment has adverse consequences. These problems in taking a charge appear to have led to it being a very rare occurrence in practice.[353]

Another way for a participant to protect itself against the credit risk of the lender is to include a provision in the sub-participation agreement giving it the right to request a transfer of the loan, either to itself or to a third party,[354] such a transfer taking place by way of an assignment or a novation. The problem with this course of action is that if there is a reason not to assign or novate the loan in the first place, for example because the borrower's consent is required, then this reason may still prevent this course of action even if the lender is in financial difficulties.

As has been seen, the position of a sub-participant is considerably weaker than that of an assignee or a party to whom a loan has been novated.[355] One might, then, wonder why a participant would enter into such a structure. One reason may be that the loan contains restrictions on assignment or novation. The difficulties that such restrictions cause have been discussed earlier, and one way of bypassing them is to transfer the credit risk without transferring the loan, by means of a sub-participation or credit derivative.[356] Other reasons for using sub-participation include tax or regulatory disadvantages to the subparticipant if it became the 'lender of record'[357] or practical reasons, for example, where the loan is the subject of arbitration proceedings which require the lender of record to be registered.[358]

If the loan is syndicated, obviously the sub-participant does not acquire any rights against the agent bank or direct rights against the borrower. However, whether the loan is syndicated or not, the participant may acquire contractual rights against the lender to direct the conduct of enforcement or other administration of the loan. Thus, where an anti-assignment clause is inserted to protect the borrower against someone other than the lender having control over the enforcement of the debt, or obtaining voting rights in a restructuring, sub-participation, while not being a breach of the clause, can still have adverse effects on the borrower.[359]

9.3.2 Credit Derivatives

A similar effect to a risk sub-participation can be achieved by the use of a credit default swap. Like sub-participation, this cannot be seen as a transfer of the loan obligation itself, but involves the transfer of credit risk, so that risk is divorced from legal ownership. As with

---

[353] Wood: Loans and Bonds, 9-039. Fuller: Corporate Borrowing, 301 fn 107.

[354] Loan Market Association discussion paper, 'LMA Sub-Participation Agreements and Grantor Insolvency' (C Winkworth and L Watt, Richards Kibbe & Orbe LLP), http://documents.lexology.com/8cc59b5c-cc73-48f2-a5a4-da96b1428880.pdf, 3.

[355] For other weaknesses see Wood: Loans and Bonds, 9-040–9-047.

[356] R Goode, 'Contractual Prohibitions against Assignment' [2009] *Lloyd's Maritime and Comparative Law Quarterly* 300.

[357] Loan Market Association discussion paper, 'LMA Sub-Participation Agreements and Grantor Insolvency' (C Winkworth and L Watt, Richards Kibbe & Orbe LLP), http://documents.lexology.com/8cc59b5c-cc73-48f2-a5a4-da96b1428880.pdf, 3.

[358] M Hughes, 'Legal Liability in the Secondary Debt Market' [1997] *Journal of International Banking and Financial Law* 469, who gives such an example where the registration process was complicated and expensive.

[359] Ibid.

a sub-participation, this can have an effect on the way the lender behaves vis-a-vis the borrower, and has implications for the corporate governance of the borrower.[360] Credit default swaps are discussed in detail in chapter six.[361]

9.3.3 Securitisation[362]

Securitisation is a technique which can be used by either a company or a lender to transfer the credit risk of receivables (either (in the case of a company) trade receivables or (in the case of a lender) loan receivables or even bonds) and/or to receive immediate finance for rights to payment in the future. One of the benefits of securitisation for lenders, especially banks, is that it removes risk from the balance sheet, thus reducing the amount of capital that has to be held. 'Traditional' or 'true sale' securitisation is where receivables are transferred by their owner ('the originator') to a special purpose vehicle (SPV) in exchange for a price, and the SPV issues securities to the market to fund the acquisition.[363] The payments on the securities are funded by the income from the receivables, now owned by the SPV, and the securities are secured by a charge over the receivables for the benefit of a security trustee, who is usually also trustee of the issue.[364] The SPV (and therefore the holders of the securities) takes the risk that the receivables will not be paid, but is otherwise 'insolvency remote' so that it incurs no other risks that might render it insolvent. This is achieved by the shares in the SPV being held on trust for a charity and its directors being independent from the originator,[365] and by the fact that it is prohibited from engaging in any activities other than the securitisation and having any employees.[366] As it has no employees the actual administration of the structure and of the portfolio of assets is carried out by a service provider, which may be the originator.[367]

The securities issued are usually 'tranched'. This means that there is a pre-set order of payment to different groups of investors in the securities, laid down in a 'waterfall' clause. The senior ranking tranches are paid first (after payment to third-party service providers), followed by lower ranking tranches, which are often called 'mezzanine notes', followed by 'junior' notes (sometimes called 'equity' as the risk is analogous to an equity risk, since the holders are the first to take a loss and yet are entitled to any surplus). The greater risk in holding lower-tranched notes is offset by a higher rate of interest payment. This tranching is achieved by subordination[368] and the 'waterfall' clause will often include other payments such as tax, and an administration payment to the originator.[369]

---

[360] See 3.2.2.4.6.

[361] 6.4.3.

[362] See 2.3.3.5. For detailed discussion see Fuller: Corporate Borrowing, ch 7; Fuller: Capital Markets, ch 4; Hudson: Finance, ch 44; Wood: Project Finance, part 2.

[363] For discussion of the basic features of such a securitisation, see *MBNA Europe Bank Ltd v Revenue and Customs Commissioners* [2006] EWHC 2326 (Ch) [45]–[49].

[364] See chapter 8 for a discussion of the position of trustees.

[365] The trustee and directors will be provided by a corporate service provider, whose fees will be payable in priority to the holders of the securities.

[366] The SPV is usually situated in a low-tax jurisdiction.

[367] Fuller: Corporate Borrowing, 7.25.

[368] For the various techniques, see 6.3.4.

[369] Wood; Project Finance, 7-010.

The relationship between the SPV and the noteholders in a securitisation has been illustrated by the case of *Titan Europe 2006-3 plc v Colliers International UK plc*.[370] In that case, what was securitised were loans secured on properties, one of which had been negligently valued by the defendants, resulting in a very considerable loss when the tenant became insolvent and the property had to be sold. The action in negligence was brought by the SPV issuer, which claimed that it was the proper claimant and that it had suffered a loss when it bought the loan from the original lender at a price well above what it was worth. The valuers argued that the proper claimants were the noteholders, who actually suffered the loss, as the SPV was a mere conduit through which the payments on the loan passed. The court held that the SPV was the proper claimant: it had suffered a loss when it bought the loan, and it was irrelevant that the purchase was funded by the purchase of the notes. It was not only difficult to quantify the loss of the noteholders, as the value of the notes (based on the securitised pool of assets) was too remote from the misvaluation for there to be an accurate assessment of the loss caused,[371] but it would also undermine the contractual allocation of priorities for any noteholders to sue in their own right.[372] Since the SPV was contractually obliged to pay out the proceeds as part of the payment waterfall, this not only preserved the priorities, but also established that the SPV had suffered a loss.[373] The court dismissed the argument that the valuers might be subject to double liability, as noteholders who had (economically) suffered a loss and then sold their notes would have no right of action against the valuers: they had agreed to the contractual distribution when they bought the notes and could not go behind that, and the right to the proceeds of the action was part of the contractual claims of the present noteholders. The court stressed that the analysis was based on the wording of the contracts of the particular structure in the case, but it would seem a fairly typical securitisation structure so that the rights and liabilities are likely to be similar in most securitisations. While the decision makes perfect sense when considering the relationship between the SPV and the noteholders, it does have the effect that no defence of contributory negligence can be raised by the valuers, which would be available were the SPV to sue as assignee of the originator's claim, which it would take subject to equities.[374]

The technique usually used to transfer receivables to an SPV in a securitisation structure is that of assignment. This is because the originator does not usually want the obligors to know that the receivables have been securitised,[375] so novation is unsuitable. Since the obligors are not notified, an assignment can only be equitable.[376] This creates a number of risks and effects.[377]

---

[370] [2014] EWHC 3106 (Comm). See also N Rushton, 'The Consequences of an Issuer in a CMBS Having its Own Rights of Action' [2015] *Journal of International Banking and Financial Law* 22.

[371] *Titan Europe*, ibid, [104].

[372] Ibid, [109].

[373] Ibid, [121].

[374] N Rushton, 'The Consequences of an Issuer in a CMBS Having its Own Rights of Action' [2015] *Journal of International Banking and Financial Law* 22.

[375] This is particularly true where there is an ongoing relationship between the originator and the debtor, for example in the context of credit card receivables: see *MBNA Europe Bank Ltd v Revenue and Customs Commissioners* [2006] EWHC 2326 (Ch) [59].

[376] Of course, it is sometimes the case that the obligors do know that their obligations are being securitised, such as where a bank acts as an intermediary to obtain finance more cheaply from the securities market than a company can do so, by making a loan to the company, which is then securitised. In this case the transfer can be by novation or statutory assignment.

[377] See 9.2.2.2 and 9.2.2.4 for a discussion of statutory and equitable assignments.

First, the enforcement of the receivables has to be by the originator (the assignor). This is hardly a problem, since the originator is usually administering the collection of the receivables. However, the assignee may have to be joined to the action.[378] Second, there is in theory a risk of loss of priority if the originator assigns the receivables to someone else and gives notice. However, this will normally be in breach of, and an event of default of, the originator's sale contract with the SPV and so could cause the whole structure to terminate. Third, set-offs can continue to arise between the originator and the obligor.[379] Further, the SPV takes subject to equities between the originator and the obligor. It also means that if a receivable is not assignable, then in theory the assignment is ineffective, although, as we have seen, if the SPV can force the originator to recover from the obligor, the originator will hold the proceeds on trust for the SPV.[380] The SPV and the holders of the securities cannot be protected from these risks, or the general credit risk of the obligors, by having recourse against the originator, as would be common in a straightforward receivables financing, as this might prejudice the 'true sale' nature of the assignment, which is discussed below.[381] These risks are therefore reflected in the price paid for the receivables, which is discounted from their face value, and/or in the amount of lower rate notes issued, which bear the very high risk of being paid last. Credit enhancement, by third-party guarantees or insurance, can also cover the risk.[382]

The most important aspect of the transfer to the SPV in this form of securitisation is that it is a 'true sale'. This is critical for a number of reasons. First, if the transfer were to be recharacterised as merely granting the SPV a security interest, it would be void if not registered, and enforcement would be rendered difficult or impossible if the originator became insolvent.[383] Second, usually one reason for securitisation is to move the receivables off the balance sheet of the originator for regulatory capital adequacy purposes, and this would not be achieved if there were no true sale.[384] Third, there must be no question that the originator is collecting the receivables on its own behalf, as on its insolvency any payments made to the SPV might be set aside.

The approach of the courts in characterising transactions as an outright sale or the creation of security for a loan has been discussed above.[385] In the present context, it is absolutely clear that the form of the transaction is that of a sale. Further, the rights and obligations of the parties set out in the (usually very complicated) documentation are intended to bind the parties: there is no question of a sham. Therefore, the approach to be taken is the 'internal route',[386] that is, whether the rights and obligations created are consistent with the label

---

[378] 9.2.2.4.

[379] J Benjamin, *Financial Law* (Oxford, Oxford University Press, 2007) 406 fn 28.

[380] 9.2.2.6.3.

[381] Wood: Project Finance, 7-026; *MBNA Europe Bank Ltd v Revenue and Customs Commissioners* [2006] EWHC 2326 (Ch) [48].

[382] See 6.4.1 and 6.4.2; Benjamin: Financial Law, 18.23.

[383] Wood: Project Finance, 8-002.

[384] The criteria for a true sale which is effective under Basel III are found in arts 243 and 244 Regulation (EU) 575/2013 of 26 June 2013 on prudential requirements for credit institutions and investment firms [2013] OJ L176/1 (CRR).

[385] 7.2.2.

[386] See 7.2.2 and *Welsh Development Agency v Export Finance Co Ltd* [1992] BCLC 148, 186.

that is given to the transaction by the parties.[387] The approach of the court acknowledges that parties may structure a transaction as a sale even though the economic purpose of it is security for a loan.[388] It is only if the legal structure of the transaction (taken as a whole) amounts to the creation of a secured loan that the courts will recharacterise it.[389]

The possible features of securisation that might cause problems in relation to characterisation are where the originator still bears some of the credit risk of the receivables (for example, if the sale is to some extent with recourse) and where the originator is entitled to any surplus value generated by the receivables once the amounts due on the securities have been paid.[390] The originator often does want that benefit, and various techniques are used to achieve this: the originator may make a subordinated loan to the SPV, or may buy the 'equity' tranche of the securities,[391] or may charge high servicing fees for the administration of the receivables.[392] Neither recourse to the seller nor the ability of the seller to receive a surplus has prevented the courts upholding the characterisation of invoice discounting agreements as sales of receivables.[393] This line of cases is relied upon in the 'true sale' opinions required to be produced by lawyers in every securitisation transaction that takes place.

There are as yet however, no English cases dealing with the characterisation of a securitisation true sale. The nearest the English courts have come to considering the matter is the case of *MBNA Europe Bank Ltd v Revenue and Customs Commissioners*,[394] where the issue was whether the assignment in the course of a securitisation was a 'supply' within the VAT regime. Briggs J held that the transfer was not by way of security[395] but by way of sale, although he said that it was not a 'simple' sale[396] and did not constitute a supply under the VAT regime. The case is therefore far from conclusive, and even less so as it did not involve a securitisation as described above but a 'master trust' structure whereby the receivables are assigned to another SPV which holds them on trust for the originator and the first SPV jointly.[397] It is, however, an indication that the courts will uphold the structure of a securitisation as the parties have set it up rather than be quick to recharacterise it.[398]

If the originator does not wish to transfer receivables, it can transfer risk by making a 'whole business' securitisation,[399] where the SPV makes a loan to the company secured on the company's assets, funded by the issue of securities. It may also use a synthetic

---

[387] That, at least, seems to be the approach of the courts in the cases involving characterisation as a sale or loan: see 7.2.2. The approach in relation to characterisation of a charge as fixed or floating appears to be different, at least in emphasis.

[388] See, for example, the cases discussed at 7.2.5.1.

[389] *Re Curtain Dream* [1990] BCC 341; V Seldam, 'Recharacterisation in "True Sale" Securitisations: The "Substance Over Form" Delusion' [2006] *Journal of Business Law* 637, 641.

[390] Hudson: Finance, 44-15 fn 15.

[391] This is now required by regulation in some circumstances; see below.

[392] These and other techniques, together with the risks they pose, are discussed in Wood: Project Finance, 7-031.

[393] See 7.2.5.2.

[394] [2006] EWHC 2326 (Ch).

[395] Ibid, [95].

[396] Ibid, [98].

[397] Fuller: Capital Markets, 4.72.

[398] *MBNA Europe Bank Ltd v Revenue and Customs Commissioners* [2006] EWHC 2326 (Ch) [90]–[91].

[399] See 2.3.3.5.

securitisation structure, which achieves the same economic effect as a true sale securitisation by the use of credit derivatives but the assets remain with the administrator.[400]

In each of these structures, the original obligors play no part in the securitisation and, indeed, are often unaware of it. This is, then, another example of debt being transferred in such a way that the 'control' of it passes to a third party, who may have an adverse effect on the obligor and about which the obligor can do very little. Further, the risk of the debt moves away from the original lender, which, if it happens on a large scale, may render the lender less cautious about the loans it makes in the first place.

This shift in the incentives of the original lender towards less cautious lending, together with the lack of transparency in a securitisation structure (which makes it difficult for investors to assess accurately the risks they are taking by purchasing the securities), has led to a regulatory response. In Europe this has been achieved by requiring investors that are credit institutions (such as banks) or investment firms[401] only to invest in securitisations where the originator has disclosed to them that it has retained at least 5 per cent of the economic interest in the securitisation.[402] This can be done in a number of ways, for example, by retaining 5 per cent of each tranche, or retaining the equity tranche, but the originator is not allowed to mitigate the credit risk by the use of credit derivatives or any other hedging process. There is no direct requirement on the originator to do this,[403] although it would be impossible to find investors if it did not do so. Certain securitisations are exempt, for example where the exposures are guaranteed by governments, but an exemption under the previous directive[404] which included 'syndicated loans, purchased receivables or credit default swaps where these instruments are not used to package and/or hedge a securitisation'[405] does not appear to have been included in the more recent Capital Requirements Regulation.

The originator must also disclose information to investors to enable them to make an informed decision about whether to invest,[406] and both originators (if a credit institution or investment firm) and investors must exercise due diligence and inform the regulators that they have done so.[407] Failure to comply with these requirements means that additional risk weight is added to the transaction,[408] which has serious consequences for the capital adequacy requirements for the relevant institution.

Whether these regulations will make securitisation safer remains to be seen. It is certainly arguable that the more 'skin in the game' the originator has, the more careful it will be in analysing the risks involved in the securitisation, and the prudential requirements on both originators and investors should have an effect in preventing the market from

---

[400] For a brief outline of synthetic securitisation see *Barclays Bank plc v Unicredit Bank AG* [2012] EWHC 3655 (Comm) [9]–[11]. Synthetic securitisation can also be used for speculation purposes; see 2.3.3.5.

[401] As defined in art 4 MiFID. Note that investors who are alternative investment fund managers and who are regulated under the AIFMD (see 16.7.2) are also included; see art 17 AIFMD.

[402] CRR (Regulation (EU) No 575/2013), art 405.

[403] This is unlike the position in the US under the Dodd-Franks Act.

[404] EU Capital Requirements Directive 2006/48/EC, art 122a, as inserted by Directive 2009/111/EC (known as 'CRD2').

[405] Ibid, art 122a(3).

[406] CRR, art 409.

[407] Ibid, art 406. The treatment of securitisations as a means of taking risk from a balance sheet and thus reducing capital adequacy requirements has remained in the CRDII/CRR regime. Since the CRR is a regulation, it is directly applicable in Member States, which should reduce discrepancies.

[408] Ibid, art 407.

overheating. They cannot necessarily stop any one institution behaving in a risky way, but they are designed to reduce systemic risk in the market while allowing the benefits of securitisation—that is, the extra capital that is released by exposure to the capital markets as opposed to the banking sector—to flow to corporate borrowers.[409]

9.4 Conclusion

This chapter has sought to differentiate the various ways in which a lender's entitlement under a debt contract can be transferred, and also ways in which the credit risk can be transferred without actually transferring the debt. Although there has been some blurring of the edges, in law there are only three transfer techniques: novation, assignment and negotiation, and the advantages and disadvantages of each have been discussed. The technique of negotiation has proved valuable for market transfers in the past, and it is not surprising that attempts have been made to incorporate the advantages of negotiation into current methods of market transfer, which do not involve tangible representations of the debt obligation. Where debt is not designed to be traded, that is, when it is not incorporated into a security, a question of balance arises between the right of the borrower to prevent or limit the transfer of the debt and the right of lender to alienate its own property, namely the debt or the proceeds. This difficult issue, which has been developed by the courts over the last century, is likely to be the subject of legislation along the lines of that in many other countries, but only in a limited area, so that much of the uncertainty will remain. The transfer of risk by other methods, such as sub-participation and securitisation (which can involve actual transfer of debts) raises the question of protection of the 'transferee' against the credit risk of the 'transferor' as well as of the borrower.

The transfer of debt, or the risk of debt, can potentially lead to lower standards of risk assessment or protection on the part of the original lenders. This issue arises in different contexts throughout this book, and can be seen as one of the contributing causes of the recent global financial crisis. The regulatory response has been patchy, reflecting the balance between the ability of parties to protect themselves and the need to control systemic risk.[410] The transfer of the risk of debt also has effects on the ability of lenders to contribute to corporate governance; these are discussed in chapter three.[411]

---

[409] See O Askeli, 'Securitisation, the Financial Crisis and the Need for Effective Risk Retention' (2013) 14 *European Business Organisation Law Review* 27. Note that the EU is now consulting further on how to create a framework for simple, transparent and standardised securitisation: see http://ec.europa.eu/finance/consultations/2015/securitisation/index_en.htm. This consultation is part of the Capital Markets Union project.

[410] See above and chapter 13.

[411] 3.2.2.4.6.

10

Public Offers of Shares

10.1 Introduction

In chapter four, the rules relating to the issue of shares by companies were examined. These rules are relevant to all issues of shares, including where shares are issued to the public, and indeed some of the rules examined in chapter four, such as pre-emption rights, can be very important in this context. Where a public offer of shares is to be made, however, those rules are supplemented by extensive additional regulation, which is considered in this chapter.[1] This chapter concentrates primarily on the issues related to the initial public offer of shares (IPO). The following two chapters deal with the ongoing regulation of the market, once securities have successfully been offered to the public. Many companies will raise external equity finance only once, at the time of their IPO. Thereafter they may rely upon retained earnings and debt, either from banks or through the issue of bonds,[2] in order to finance their operations, although rights issues and seasoned equity offerings do occur once a company's shares are traded on the public markets. Furthermore, a company can also arrange to have its debt securities traded on a public market. If the company wishes to offer debt securities to the public it must satisfy most of the same requirements as when offering shares to the public. This is discussed in more detail in chapter thirteen.

The ability to offer shares to the public confers significant advantages on companies, but these advantages come at the cost of additional regulation, both of the companies themselves and of the capital markets in which those companies operate. All jurisdictions regulate capital markets to some extent, and the UK is no exception. This chapter considers why that additional regulation is thought necessary at the IPO stage, and assesses the extent to which the regulation in place in the UK achieves its goals.

10.2 Why do Companies Go Public?

10.2.1 Advantages of Going Public

There are various advantages of going public.[3] This section considers the main ones.

---

[1] This is an important issue. Although fewer than 1% of the total number of companies registered are public companies, the economic power of these companies belies this low figure (see eg Companies House Statistical Release, *Companies Register Activities 2013–14*, July 2014, 8, www.companieshouse.gov.uk).

[2] See chapter 8.

[3] For discussion see JC Brau, 'Why Do Firms Go Public?' in D Cumming (ed), *The Oxford Handbook of Entrepreneurial Finance* (Oxford, Oxford University Press, 2012); JC Brau and SE Fawcett, 'Initial Public Offerings: An Analysis of Theory and Practice' (2006) 61 *Journal of Finance* 399.

10.2.1.1 Opportunity to Raise Equity Finance from a Broader Range of Investors

One of the advantages of an offer of shares to the public is that it enables a company to raise finance from a broader range of investors than its existing shareholders. If, as is usual, the IPO involves the issue of new shares, the funds raised are received by the company as new capital. The company may want to increase its equity base in order to fund business expansion plans, to introduce new products, or to reduce borrowings. The capital required may exceed the amounts that the original shareholders can, or wish to, contribute. This will place limits on the company's development if further sources of funding are not tapped. An IPO allows the company to have access to outside investors who can invest substantially in the company.[4] Traditionally, this access to significantly increased levels of equity capital has been regarded as one of the major advantages of offering shares to the public,[5] especially when combined with an admission of the shares to listing or to trading on a public market,[6] although in recent years some doubts have been raised concerning the idea that admission to trading on a public equity market is primarily capital-raising in nature.[7]

10.2.1.2 Providing an Exit for Existing Shareholders

Another advantage of IPOs is that they allow the existing shareholders of the company to exit.[8] It is quite common for the shares sold at the IPO to consist of both newly created shares and existing shares, in order to allow the exit of existing shareholders, although it is possible for IPOs to consist of shares in just one of these categories. In a private company

---

[4] An alternative possibility that has emerged in recent years is equity crowdfunding, whereby large numbers of investors can put capital into businesses via internet-based platforms and social media sites (see eg FCA, *The FCA's Regulatory Approach to Crowdfunding over the Internet, and the Promotion of Non-Readily Realisable Securities by Other Media*, Policy statement, PS 14/4, March 2014, and see 2.2.2). The companies involved tend to be small, and the sums raised are likewise modest (the average amount raised is £199,095: FCA, *A Review of the Regulatory Regime for Crowdfunding and the Promotion of Non-Readily Realizable Securities by Other Media*, February 2015, 5). This option may be attractive to some businesses, but for larger companies seeking to raise substantial levels of equity financing an IPO will be more valuable. This chapter will focus predominantly on IPOs, although equity crowdfunding is discussed at 10.7.

[5] These issues are discussed in chapter 2, especially 2.2.2. However, most companies will also want to retain a significant debt element in their financing portfolio: see 2.6 for a discussion of 'optimal' debt to equity ratios. Research suggests that in addition to improving equity financing options, an IPO may also improve the rate at which the company can borrow from banks: M Pagano and A Röell, 'The Choice of Stock Ownership Structure: Agency Cost, Monitoring, and the Decision to Go Public' (1998) 113 *Quarterly Journal of Economics* 187.

[6] For a discussion of the difference between an admission to listing and to trading on a public market, and what this involves, see 10.3.3.

[7] See eg Kay Review of Equity Markets and Long-Term Decision Making, *Final Report*, 2012, 10 and 14; Commission Staff Working Document accompanying the Green Paper on Long-Term Financing of the European Economy (2013) (SWD (2013) 76), 22–23.

[8] See eg BS Black and RJ Gilson, 'Venture Capital and the Structure of Capital Markets: Banks versus Stock Markets' (1998) 47 *Journal of Financial Economics* 243. Studies have suggested that companies underprice their shares when going public: eg JR Ritter, 'The Costs of Going Public' (1987) 19 *Journal of Financial Economics* 269; T Jenkinson and C Mayer, 'The Privatisation Process in France and the UK' (1988) 32 *European Economic Review* 482. This would suggest that existing shareholders are not always best advised to sell their shares in the IPO as they can potentially receive higher prices by retaining their shares and selling them in the after-market. However, the validity of this proposition will depend on a number of factors, including the size of the shareholding which the shareholder wishes to sell.

the shareholders' exit options are limited. Shareholders are normally unable to exit the company unless they hold redeemable shares,[9] the company repurchases its shares,[10] the shareholder manages to find a private purchaser for the shares, or the company is wound up. Going public can, therefore, constitute an opportunity for the existing investors to realise their profits from the company.[11] Shareholders are then faced with the choice of exiting entirely or selling part of their investment while retaining a stake in the company. Even where the existing investors do not sell their stake in the company on the IPO they have a market for the shares, and the IPO may provide a means for their exit from the company at a later date. A further option is for the IPO to be a first step towards selling the company, for a higher price than might have been obtained in a private sale.[12]

10.2.1.3 Increased Flexibility and Value Attached to the Shares in a Publicly Traded Company

Going public can also increase the flexibility and value that are attached to a company's shares. The shares in a publicly traded company are generally more flexible investments than shares in private companies. Not only is there a ready market for the shares, but requirements imposed by the stock exchange mean that to be admitted to listing or trading on a public market shares must be freely transferable.[13] As a result, any restrictions on the transfer and registration of shares must be removed before the shares can be offered to the public.[14] The marketability of the shares tends of itself to increase the value of the investment and investors generally look favourably on the increased liquidity of shares. Shareholders may also find that banks will accept such shares as security for loans.

From the company's perspective, publicly traded shares can be used as a form of payment, for example as consideration in share-for-share acquisitions, thereby widening the company's financing options.[15] The liquidity associated with publicly traded shares also provides greater scope for the company to offer remuneration packages to its employees that include shares and options.

---

[9] See 5.4.2.3.

[10] See 5.4.2.2.

[11] An IPO can also be an important mechanism whereby a private equity fund exits from its investment: JC Brau, N Sutton and N Hatch, 'Dual-Track versus Single-Track Sell-Outs: An Empirical Analysis of Competing Harvest Strategies' (2010) 25 *Journal of Business Venturing* 389. This issue is discussed further in chapter 16.

[12] See M Pagano and L Zingales, 'Why Do Companies Go Public? An Empirical Analysis' (1998) 53 *Journal of Finance* 27.

[13] For shares admitted to listing, the LSE imposes this requirement via the Listing Rules: FCA Handbook, LR 2.2.4(1). For companies admitted to trading on AIM, this requirement is imposed by the admission rules for AIM: LSE, *AIM Rules for Companies*, May 2014, r 32. For a discussion of the transfer of shares see 4.7.

[14] It is common market practice for IPOs in the UK to have capital structures comprising a single class of ordinary shares adhering to the 'one-share-one-vote' principle: MJ Brennan and J Franks, 'Underpricing, Ownership and Control in Initial Public Offerings of Equity Securities in the UK' (1997) 45 *Journal of Financial Economics* 391; R Adams and D Ferreira, 'One Share-One Vote: The Empirical Evidence' (2008) 12 *Review of Finance* 51 (this latter study makes it clear that there is significant divergence between European countries in this regard). In general this has occurred due to market-based pressures, ie institutional shareholders expect this structure, rather than regulatory requirements, but in 2014 the FCA introduced changes to its premium listing regime, mandating voting equality and proportionality for premium listed shares and classes of shares (see FCA Handbook, LR 7.2).

[15] See eg JC Brau and S Fawcett, 'Initial Public Offerings: An Analysis of Theory and Practice' (2006) 61 *Journal of Finance* 399.

10.2.1.4 Corporate Governance Improvements

The change from a private company to a publicly traded company entails a number of corporate governance changes,[16] and is often a catalyst for developments in the professional management systems of a company. Key managers are often recruited and non-executive directors may be introduced. Going public may also enable some additional pressure to act in the shareholders' interests to be exerted on managers. The existence of a share price may allow managers' performance to be assessed with reference to an external variable, since share prices in large and liquid markets continuously aggregate information about a company's performance,[17] and so can be used as a tool to reward and incentivise managers' efforts. It is also sometimes suggested that an IPO will operate as a trigger for analysts to follow a company, and that such a following can increase the reputation of a firm and create shareholder value.[18]

It is common for managers in the US and UK, in particular, to use pay-for-performance strategies in order to encourage managers to pursue shareholders' interests. The issuing of share options and other similar strategies as a form of performance-based compensation is a potentially valuable tool, especially where shareholders are widely dispersed and may not be able to monitor the managers' actions effectively.[19] However, equity-based compensation schemes for directors and managers can introduce their own difficulties. In particular, such schemes increase the windfalls resulting to these individuals if they manipulate the share price of the company and therefore increase the possibility of market abuse.[20] In addition, if the strike conditions focus on short-term performance objectives, such schemes may encourage managers to take excessive short-term risks at the expense of sustainable long-term profits. Alternative tools are available to discipline poorly performing managers. In relation to UK publicly traded companies, for example, a positive relation between UK rights issues and managerial change has been found to exist.[21] In the US, takeover bids are thought to play an important role in disciplining poorly performing managers,[22] although empirical studies have concluded that in the UK takeovers do not appear to operate in the same way.[23] This is discussed further in chapter fourteen.[24]

---

[16] See FRC, *UK Corporate Governance Code*, September 2014.

[17] See 11.2.1.1.

[18] Eg DJ Bradley, BD Jordan and JR Ritter, 'Analyst Behaviour Following IPOs: The "Bubble Period" Evidence' (2008) 21 *Review of Financial Studies* 101, but see JC Brau and S Fawcett, 'Initial Public Offerings: An Analysis of Theory and Practice' (2006) 61 *Journal of Finance* 399. For discussion of the regulation of analysts see 11.5.

[19] This depends on shareholders having enough control over the process of setting the strike price of the options.

[20] For discussion see 12.2.

[21] J Franks, C Mayer and L Renneboog, 'Who Disciplines Management in Poorly Performing Companies?' (2001) 10 *Journal of Financial Intermediaries* 209; D Hillier, SC Linn and P McColgan, 'Equity Issuance, CEO Turnover and Corporate Governance' (2005) 11 *European Financial Management* 515. Discussed further at 4.4.4.

[22] Eg HG Manne, 'Mergers and the Market for Corporate Control' (1965) 73 *Journal of Political Economy* 110. For discussion of this issues see J Coffee, 'Regulating the Market for Corporate Control: A Critical Assessment of the Tender Offer's Role in Corporate Governance' (1984) 84 *Columbia Law Review* 1145.

[23] J Franks and C Mayer, 'Hostile Takeovers and the Correction of Managerial Failure' (1996) 40 *Journal of Financial Economics* 163, 180. See also B Clarke, 'Articles 9 and 11 of the Takeover Directive (2004/25) and the Market for Corporate Control' [2006] *Journal of Business Law* 355.

[24] See 14.3.2.2.2.

10.2.1.5 Prestige

Another perceived advantage of going public includes the additional prestige that is felt to attach to a company with 'plc' in its title; furthermore, an IPO is often an opportunity for publicity for the company.[25]

10.2.2 Disadvantages of Going Public

There are a number of disadvantages attached to an IPO. In particular, the process can be time-consuming, complex and costly. The cost of an IPO can be significant, with companies needing to pay underwriting fees, and fees to lawyers and other advisers.[26]

The process involved for a company to put itself in a position where it can offer its securities to the public, discussed in the next section, is a substantial one, with significant costs attached to it.[27] The additional costs and regulation do not end once the IPO is complete. For example, once a company obtains a listing on the Main Market of the London Stock Exchange, it will face significant additional regulation, not least the need to comply with the FCA's Prospectus Rules, Listing Rules, Disclosure Rules and Transparency Rules.[28] The company will face increased obligations in relation to its accounts.[29] The level of disclosure of information also increases. This disclosure occurs not only at the time of the IPO itself, but on an ongoing basis.[30] The information to be published includes important financial data such as announcements of results and dividends, events which affect the management of the company, such as changes of directors, and alterations in capital structure. Such companies must disclose any price-sensitive information to the market as soon as possible.[31] In addition, shareholders holding more than 3 per cent of the company will have to disclose the size of their holdings and any material changes in them.[32]

Directors' duties also become more onerous. Companies listed with a 'premium' listing on the Main Market become subject to the requirements of the UK Corporate Governance Code.[33] These are a set of corporate governance principles that include, inter alia, the requirements that at least half of the board should be independent non-executive

---

[25] See Eversheds (Sponsor), 'Going Public 2: A Survey of Recently Floated Companies' (London Stock Exchange plc, 2003), in which 1 in 10 respondents to a survey conducted on behalf of the LSE said that the extra credibility and profile was a major motivation in going public.

[26] Fees charged by investment banks for conducting an IPO do, however, appear to be lower in the UK than in the US: M Abrahamson, T Jenkinson and H Jones, 'Why Don't US Issuers Demand European Fees for IPOs?' (2011) 66 *Journal of Finance* 2055.

[27] Research conducted for the LSE found that flotation costs were typically 10% of the capital raised: Eversheds (Sponsor), 'Going Public 2: A Survey of Recently Floated Companies' (London Stock Exchange plc, 2003).

[28] This chapter will focus on companies admitted to trading on the Main Market. Additional regulation exists for companies admitted to trading on AIM, although this arises in large part from the rules of the stock exchange (see LSE, *AIM Rules for Companies*, May 2014) and tends to be set at a slightly lower level than the regulatory requirements for listed companies.

[29] See 11.3.1.1.

[30] Ongoing disclosure requirements are discussed in detail at 11.3.

[31] FCA Handbook, DTR 2.2, discussed further at 11.3.2.1.

[32] Ibid, DTR 5.1 (this figure is 5% for non-UK issuers: DTR 5.1.2), discussed at 11.3.2.3.

[33] FRC, *UK Corporate Governance Code*, September 2014.

directors;[34] the board should have nomination, audit and remuneration committees on which the non-executive directors are the only or dominant representatives;[35] and the chief executive and the chairman should not be the same person.[36] The Listing Rules require all companies with a premium listing of equity shares in the UK to disclose in their annual report the extent to which they have complied with the UK Corporate Governance Code in the previous 12 months and to give reasons for any non-compliance.[37] Constraints on directors' actions may also arise from the need to consider and deal with arm's-length investors, and in particular institutional investors.[38] There is also more external scrutiny of the company and the share price often becomes a barometer for the company's performance.

10.2.3 Summary

A company may go public for a variety of reasons. Often these reasons are good ones, such as enabling the company to raise new equity finance, but this may not always be the case, with some commentators suggesting that companies may sometimes go public in order to benefit from a market in which shares are over-priced.[39]

It is clear that going public will not suit all companies.[40] For many companies, however, once they reach a particular size or stage in their development, the need to access the additional funds that can be tapped in the equity capital markets by offering shares to the public, and to benefit from the reduced cost of capital which flows from the enhanced liquidity of the shares, becomes too compelling to ignore, and outweighs the attendant disadvantages.[41]

10.3 The Process of Going Public

The process of going public is complex and time-consuming. The level of complexity will, however, depend upon a number of factors, such as to whom the company wishes to offer its shares (all the public or a subset of it, such as institutional investors), whether it wishes those shares to be traded on a public market, and, if so, on which public market it wishes them to be traded.

---

[34] Ibid, B.1.2, although in companies below the FTSE-350 the requirement is only for two independent non-executive directors.

[35] Ibid, B.2.1, C.3.1, D.2.1.

[36] Ibid, A.2.1.

[37] FCA Handbook, LR 9.8.6(5) and (6), 9.8.7. Companies trading on AIM are not required to comply with the UK Corporate Governance Code.

[38] The role of institutional investors is discussed at 11.2.2.2.

[39] See M Pagano and L Zingales, 'Why Do Companies Go Public? An Empirical Analysis' (1998) 53 *Journal of Finance* 27.

[40] For discussion of equity crowdfunding as an alternative for some companies, predominantly SMEs, see 2.2.2 and 10.7.

[41] This analysis may well be different for debt and equity securities. There may be more marginal benefits to be gained from an offer of debt securities to the public, when weighed against the very considerable disadvantages that follow from a public listing. This issue is discussed further at 8.3.1 and 13.2.2.2.

10.3.1 Only Public Companies Can Offer their Shares to the Public

Private companies cannot offer shares to the public, so if such a company wishes to do so a first step will often be for it to change its status.[42] This change of status will have consequences for the way in which the company can be organised and run. The Companies Act 2006 imposes more stringent requirements on public companies. For example, the 2006 Act imposes minimum share capital requirements for public companies,[43] whereas no such requirements exist for private companies,[44] and it imposes a more onerous regime on public companies as regards their legal capital.[45] The 2006 Act also includes many other instances of additional regulation, such as: increased obligations regarding AGMs;[46] a continuing obligation to have a company secretary;[47] a requirement of a minimum of two directors rather than the single director required for private companies;[48] a requirement to lay its accounts and reports before the general meeting;[49] and an inability to make use of the written resolution procedure that is available to private companies.[50] Some of these issues may seem relatively insignificant, but cumulatively the effect is that it is administratively more complicated, and more expensive, to run a public company than a private company.

10.3.2 An Offer to the Public

Becoming a public company is only the first step, however. In addition, the company will need to make an offer to the public.[51]

There are two primary ways in which the company can offer its securities to the public for the first time: (i) by an offer for sale or subscription; or (ii) by a placing.

10.3.2.1 Offer for Sale or Subscription

For large issues the most appropriate method will generally be an offer for sale or subscription, coupled with a listing or admission to trading on a stock exchange.[52] The offer[53]

---

[42] Companies Act 2006, s 755. A private company can be converted into a public company: ss 90–96. Alternatively, a company can be set up and registered as a public company: s 4(2).

[43] Ibid, s 763 (£50,000).

[44] See 5.3.1.

[45] For discussion see 5.3 and 5.4.

[46] Companies Act 2006, s 336; cf private companies which need not have an AGM.

[47] Ibid, s 271; cf private companies which need not have a secretary: s 270.

[48] Ibid, s 154. There are also additional requirements regarding the appointment of directors of public companies: s 160.

[49] Ibid, ss 437–38; cf private companies which are not under any statutory obligation to hold an AGM or to lay accounts and reports in general meetings.

[50] Ibid, s 288.

[51] 'Offer of securities to the public' is a term which has a precise legal meaning (see FSMA, s 85(2)). While a general offer to retail investors will fall within this definition, there are various exemptions that have been created, for example where the offer is only being made to 'qualified' (ie professional) investors. For discussion see 10.4.2.1.

[52] For discussion see 10.3.3.

[53] This is not an offer in a contractual sense and any acceptance is not binding on the offeror. Rather, it is an invitation to make an offer which the company may or may not accept. This allows the offeror company (or sponsoring bank) to deal with the situation where the offer is oversubscribed, usually by accepting in full offers

is made via a prospectus, which is a lengthy and heavily regulated document, designed to provide potential investors with the information they need to decide whether or not to invest.[54] In order to ensure that the issue is fully subscribed, the offer will usually be underwritten.[55]

Underwriting is a form of insurance for the company and its shareholders if the issue does not prove popular with the market in general.[56] This can either be via a sponsoring investment bank agreeing for a fee to subscribe for the whole issue, and for it, rather than the company, to make the offer to the public (an offer for sale), or for the underwriting bank to agree to take up any securities for which the public have not subscribed (an offer for subscription).[57] There may also be sub-underwriting, whereby the lead banks seek to persuade other financial institutions to take on some of the risk. The offer price is usually stated as a fixed and pre-determined amount per share.[58] This amount will be fixed as late as possible. Pricing is difficult because each company is more or less unique, and since the offer involves, by definition, shares that have never been offered to the public before, there is no existing market price to act as a yardstick for the issue price.[59] The aim is to set the price at a level which will ensure a modest over-subscription, and that trading will open at a small premium.[60]

10.3.2.2 Placing

The second method, which may be used where smaller amounts of capital are being raised, is a placing.[61] A public offer is both expensive and time consuming, involving months of work from a team of people at the company, at the company's advising bank and at the company's solicitors' firm. Additionally, an IPO will involve paying for the services of the sponsoring investment bank, paying commissions for the underwriters and sub-underwriters

---

for small numbers of shares and scaling down large applications, the details of which would need to be set out in the prospectus.

[54] For further details on the content of the prospectus see 10.5.2.2.

[55] The offer will not always be underwritten. In difficult market conditions, for example, the lead banks may only take the shares on a 'best efforts' basis.

[56] For a discussion of underwriting in the context of debt securities see 8.3.1.

[57] Generally the sponsoring bank will attempt to arrange for the offer to be sub-underwritten by other institutions in order to spread the risk.

[58] Alternatives are available. For example, a minimum price can be stated, and applicants invited to tender at or above that price. The issue price is then fixed at the highest price that will enable the issue to be subscribed in full, all successful applicants paying that same price and those tendering below the issue price being eliminated. This method is rarely used, however.

[59] The empirical literature demonstrates that IPOs tend to be underpriced: eg RP Beatty and J Ritter, 'Investment Banking, Reputation, and the Underpricing of Initial Public Offerings' (1986) 15 *Journal of Financial Economics* 213; K Rock, 'Why New Issues are Underpriced' (1986) 15 *Journal of Financial Economics* 187; R Carter and S Manaster, 'Initial Public Offerings and Underwriter Reputation' (1990) 45 *Journal of Finance* 1045.

[60] Typically, the issue price of the securities is determined via a process called bookbuilding, whereby an indicative price range is published and a marketing process is engaged in by the underwriters in order to gauge the level of interest in the shares, before a price is finally determined. In other words, unlike a traditional underwriting process the marketing process precedes the determination of the final price (see ABI, *Encouraging Equity Investment: Facilitation of Efficient Equity Capital Raising in the UK Market* (July 2013), 13–14). For discussion see TJ Jenkinson and H Jones, 'Bids and Allocations in European IPO Bookbuilding' (2004) 59 *Journal of Finance* 2309.

[61] For a discussion of placing in the context of debt securities see 8.3.1.

and probably paying a specialist share registrar.[62] These costs are likely to be prohibitive unless a large amount of capital is being raised. A placing is a less expensive endeavour. It usually involves the investment bank obtaining firm commitments to take up the shares in the company. Generally these commitments will be from the bank's institutional investor clients. There is therefore no general offer to the public. These commitments can then be coupled with a listing or an admission to trading on a stock exchange. A variation on this method is an intermediaries' offer, where financial intermediaries take up the offer for the purpose of allocating the securities to their own clients.[63]

10.3.3 Admission to Listing or to Trading on a Public Market

An offer of shares to the public is usually accompanied by an admission of the company's securities to trading on a public market. This latter step is not vital: a company may offer its shares to the public without securing their admission to a public market. While there are approximately 8,000 public companies on the register in the UK,[64] the number of companies admitted to trading on a public market is much smaller.[65]

The distinction between an admission to listing and an admission to trading is discussed further at 10.3.3.1 below. Broadly, an admission to listing involves companies being admitted to trading on the 'Official List', which involves companies having their securities admitted to trading on certain markets (such as the Main Market of the London Stock Exchange) but not others. An admission to trading involves securities being available to be traded on a public market, but not being admitted to trading on the 'Official List'. Within the UK, an admission to trading on the Alternative Investment Market (AIM) would fall into this latter category.

The advantage of an admission to listing or to trading on a public market is the fact that it provides a secondary market for the shares, so that investors can trade the shares that they obtain in the IPO. Companies are generally able to raise money more easily and to obtain a better price if, after the initial issue of shares to the public, there is a healthy secondary market available to investors on which they can sell their shares and realise their investment, if they so choose. The lack of liquidity in the shares of a private company is one of the significant disadvantages of this form of capital and it is therefore unsurprising that many public offers are accompanied by an admission to listing or to trading. It is, however, possible that where the company does not expect or want the shares to be traded very widely it may not take this step, and will rely on investors to trade their shares privately.[66]

---

[62] For a discussion of underwriting fees see OFT, *Equity Underwriting and Associated Services: An OFT Market Study*, January 2011.

[63] Of course, once an initial public offer has taken place the company can subsequently raise new equity capital by way of a rights issue, and indeed if it is issuing new shares for cash it will be obliged to do so unless the shareholders have agreed to set aside pre-emption rights (see 4.4).

[64] As at 31 March 2014 there were 7,821 public limited companies on the UK register: Companies House Statistical Release, *Companies Register Activities 2013–14*, July 2014, 8.

[65] See LSE, List of all companies on the London Stock Exchange at the end of each month, www.londonstock-exchange.com/statistics/companies-and-issuers, which provides information on the country of incorporation of listed companies and companies admitted to trading on AIM.

[66] For a discussion of the advantages and disadvantages of listing debt see 8.3.1.

If the offer of shares to the public is coupled with the additional step of obtaining a secondary market for the shares, there are a number of options available.

10.3.3.1 Choice of UK Markets

When a company decides to apply for the securities to be traded on a stock exchange, it has available to it a number of options within the UK.[67] In particular, there is the Main Market, for well-established companies, and AIM, for less well-established companies. These markets are run by the London Stock Exchange (LSE). However, the LSE has no monopoly on the operation of public markets for securities within the UK and a number of alternative markets exist, mostly for companies wishing to raise relatively small sums of money.[68]

In general, it is the exchange that controls admission to trading on the relevant exchange.[69] For some companies it may be that they want their securities not merely to be publicly traded, but also to be admitted to listing. The concept of a 'listed' security is narrower than that of a 'traded' security: in the UK only companies admitted to trading on the 'Official List' can be said to be listed securities. By contrast, unlisted shares can still be admitted to trading on a public market, for example where those shares are traded on AIM. Admission to the Official List is controlled by the FCA, acting as the UK Listing Authority (UKLA), which sets out the requirements for inclusion in the Official List in the Listing Rules,[70] although the controlling legislation is made at EU level. In particular, the Consolidated Admissions Requirements Directive (CARD)[71] states that securities may not be admitted to official listing on a stock exchange unless certain merit requirements have been satisfied.[72]

Since only companies whose securities are in the Official List will be admitted by the LSE to its Main Market, an admission to trading on that market in practice requires companies to satisfy both requirements—that is, to seek inclusion in the Official List and to apply for admission of the securities to trading on the market, a matter governed by the LSE. This chapter focuses on the admission of securities to the Main Market.

---

[67] For a discussion of the position regarding debt securities see 13.2.2.2.

[68] Eg ISDX (the ICAP Securities and Derivatives Exchange), an independent UK stock exchange regulated by the FCA and operated by ICAP plc. ISDX specialises in smaller and growing companies (see www.isdx.com).

[69] See eg LSE, *Admission and Disclosure Standards*, April 2010 (regarding admission to the Main Market) and LSE, *AIM Rules for Companies*, May 2014 (regarding admission to AIM). While the Main Market is a regulated market for the purposes of European Community law, AIM is an exchange regulated market (see Title III of Directive 2004/39/EC on the markets in financial instruments (MiFID), a directive which is recast by the 2014 MiFID II (Directive 2014/65/EU) and supplemented by a new regulation, MiFIR (Regulation (EU) No 600/2014)). The level of regulation imposed on AIM is consequently lighter. Eligibility requirements for admission to trading on AIM are a matter for the exchange itself (unless there is also a public offer of securities) and the LSE does not lay down any general eligibility requirements, relying mainly on certification from the 'nominated adviser' that the issuer is appropriate for that market: LSE, *AIM Rules for Companies*, May 2014, r 1. Empirical evidence suggests that the lower regulatory requirements on AIM do not mean that this market caters to low quality firms, but rather that the AIM market attracts small firms that, due to their size, face disproportional regulatory costs, but are otherwise equivalent to firms listing in more regulated markets: U Nielsson, 'Do Less Regulated Markets Attract Lower Quality Firms? Evidence from the London AIM Market' (2013) 22 *Journal of Financial Intermediation* 335.

[70] FSMA, s 74. The Listing Rules are included in the FCA Handbook, www.fsahandbook.info/FSA/html/handbook.

[71] Directive 2001/34/EC on admission of securities to official stock exchange listing and on information to be published on those securities.

[72] Ibid, art 5, discussed at 10.4.3.2. In addition, the Prospectus Directive obliges Member States to enact laws requiring a prospectus to be published in relation to all offers of securities to the public (save those that are

Once a company has decided to seek to have its shares listed on the Main Market, it then faces a further option: companies listing on the Main Market, whether UK companies or overseas companies, can choose whether to obtain a 'premium' or a 'standard' listing.[73] As originally conceived, a 'standard' listing required an issuer to comply with the minimum standards required by EU legislation, whereas a number of obligations were 'super-added' for those wishing to acquire a premium listing, such as additional obligations regarding substantial and related party transactions,[74] and an obligation to 'comply or explain' with the requirements of the UK Corporate Governance Code.[75] Changes were introduced to the standard and premium regimes in 2014 which, in addition to increasing the requirements for premium-listed companies,[76] expanded the application of certain listing principles to companies with a standard listing.[77] While it is clear that the two tiers of listing impose different regulatory requirements on companies, with the premium listing requiring more of companies than the standard listing,[78] it is arguable that the requirements for standard listing now go beyond the minimum standards required by EU legislation.[79]

10.3.3.2 Choice of International Markets

There is no obligation on UK companies to secure a listing or an admission to trading of their shares on a UK market. A UK company has the freedom to decide where to seek admission

---

exempted by the directive): Directive 2003/71/EC of the European Parliament and of the Council of 4 November 2003 on the prospectus to be published when securities are offered to the public or admitted to trading on a regulated market, as amended ('Prospectus Directive'). Other EU regulations and directives will also be relevant once shares have been admitted to trading, eg Regulation (EU) No 596/2014 on market abuse and Directive 2014/57/EU on criminal sanctions for market abuse; Directive 2004/109/EC of the European Parliament and of the Council of 15 December 2004 on the harmonisation of transparency requirements in relation to information about issuers whose securities are admitted to trading on a regulated market (the Transparency Directive) as amended by Directive 2010/73/EU and Directive 2013/50/EU. The obligations imposed by these provisions are discussed in chapters 11 and 12.

[73] See the Listing Rules Sourcebook (Amendment No 3) Instrument 2009, www.fsahandbook.info/FSA/handbook/LI/2009/2009_54.pdf, and FSA, *Listing Regime Review*, CP09/24, October 2009. For further discussion see FSA, *Consultation on Amendments to the Listing Rules and Feedback on DP08/1 (A Review of the Structure of the Listing Regime)* CP 08/21, December 2008. The effective date for most of these rules was 6 April 2010, but standard listing was made available to UK companies from 6 October 2009. Prior to this date, UK companies had to apply for listing under the 'primary' listing and overseas companies applied for a 'secondary' listing. These changes to the Listing Rules were intended to create a level playing field for all companies listing on the Main Market.

[74] See FCA Handbook, LR 10 and LR 11, discussed further at 11.3.2.4.

[75] See FRC, *UK Corporate Governance Code*, September 2014.

[76] This includes, for example, additional requirements where the company has a controlling shareholder (see LR 6).

[77] See FCA, *Enhancing the Effectiveness of the Listing Regime*, CP13/15, November 2013; FCA, *Response to CP13/15—Enhancing the Effectiveness of the Listing Regime*, May 2014, PS14/8. For the listing principles that apply to standard listed companies see FCA Handbook, LR 7.2.1.

[78] In addition to the broader range of listing principles that apply to companies with a premium listing (see LR 7.2), one obvious difference between the two is the fact that in the premium listing regime companies must appoint a sponsor when they are applying for a primary listing of equity securities and on specified occasions thereafter (see LR 8), whereas no such obligation attached to companies with a standard listing.

[79] The FCA contends that the application of listing principles to companies with a standard listing is not a departure from the policy of applying the minimum standards required by EU law, since the principles in question are derived from the existing statutory framework: FCA, *Enhancing the Effectiveness of the Listing Regime*, CP13/15, November 2013, para 10.5.

for trading of its shares, either as a primary listing or as a secondary cross-listing. Equally, non-UK companies can choose to seek admission to listing or trading of their shares in London.[80] There has been an erosion of the concept of 'national' exchanges in recent years. Companies may be attracted by lower trading costs in one regime as compared to another. In addition, a particular regime may be able to offer more skilled analysts and institutional investors, more advanced technology, greater liquidity, or higher accounting standards and better shareholder rights protection than exist in the issuer's home jurisdiction.[81] Alternatively, it has been suggested that issuers might want to 'bond' themselves to a regime with higher disclosure standards and a stricter enforcement regime in order to attract investors who would otherwise be reluctant to invest.[82] Securities markets can then respond, and compete, by adopting techniques designed to persuade companies to list with them.[83] For some time, the US was regarded as a particularly popular destination for cross-listing, although the pre-eminence of the US in this regard seems to have declined in recent years. For example, in the 10 years to 2011 London attracted a significantly greater proportion of cross-border IPOs than New York.[84] There is an ongoing debate as to the cause of this shift, and in particular whether increased regulatory burdens imposed in the US as a result of the Sarbanes-Oxley Act in 2002, amongst other things, prompted firms to look elsewhere.[85]

---

[80] The EU Prospectus Directive contains arrangements, known as 'passporting' arrangements, designed to make cross-border securities issuance within the EEA easier. The passporting arrangements make it simpler for EEA companies that have had a prospectus approved in their 'home jurisdiction' (as defined in the directive) to make a public offer of securities into other EEA jurisdictions ('host jurisdictions'). They also make it simpler for EEA companies to seek admission to trading on regulated markets in other EEA 'host' jurisdictions.

[81] M Pagano, AA Röell and J Zechner, 'The Geography of Equity Listing: Why Do Companies List Abroad?' (2002) 57 *Journal of Finance* 2651.

[82] For a discussion of the bonding hypothesis see eg JC Coffee, 'The Future as History: The Prospects of Global Corporate Convergence in Corporate Governance and its Implications' (1999) 93 *Northwestern University Law Review* 641; JC Coffee, 'Racing Towards the Top?: The Impact of Cross Listings and Stock Market Competition on International Corporate Governance' (2002) 102 *Columbia Law Review* 1757; RM Stulz, 'Globalization, Corporate Finance and the Cost of Capital' (1999) 12 *Journal of Applied Corporate Finance* 8; GA Karolyi, 'Corporate Governance, Agency Problems and International Cross-Listings: A Defense of the Bonding Hypothesis' (2012) 13(4) *Emerging Markets Review* 516.

[83] According to the theory of regulatory competition, offering market participants a choice of legal regimes results in optimal regulation. For a discussion of the advantages of a regulatory competition approach see eg R Romano, 'Empowering Investors: A Market Approach to Securities Regulation' (1998) 107 *Yale Law Journal* 2359; SJ Choi and AT Guzman, 'Portable Reciprocity: Rethinking the International Reach of Securities Regulation' (1998) 71 *Southern California Law Review* 903, further developed in AT Guzman, 'Capital Market Regulation in Developing Countries: A Proposal' (1999) 39 *Virginia Journal of International Law* 607. Cf MB Fox, 'Retaining Mandatory Securities Disclosure: Why Issuer Choice is Not Investor Empowerment' (1999) 85 *Virginia Law Review* 1335.

[84] See PWC, *Equity Sans Frontières—Trends in Cross-Border IPOs and an Outlook for the Future*, November 2012. Other financial centres also seem to be gaining ground in this regard, at the expense of the US. See eg C Doidge, GA Karolyi and RM Stulz, 'Financial Globalization and the Rise of IPOs Outside the US' (2013) 110 *Journal of Financial Economics* 546.

[85] See eg K Litvak, 'The Effect of the Sarbanes-Oxley Act on Foreign Companies Cross-Listed in the US' (2007) 13 *Journal of Corporate Finance* 195. Cf C Doidge, GA Karolyi and R Stulz, 'Has New York Become Less Competitive than London in Global Markets? Evaluating Foreign Listing Choices over Time' (2009) 91 *Journal of Financial Economics* 253 (who point out that one reason for London's rise has been the success of AIM, which attracts a large number of companies, but that these are often much smaller in size than the companies that continue to make use of the opportunity to cross-list in the US).

10.4 The Theory of Regulation of Public Offers

Potentially significant advantages flow to the company from an offer of its securities to the public, as discussed at 10.2.1, but these are coupled with a number of disadvantages, including a considerable amount of additional regulation. This section considers the aims of this regulation. The following sections then assess the rules that are in place to regulate public offers of shares with a premium listing on the Main Market in the UK in the light of these goals. This chapter concentrates on the investor protection that arises from the regulation of the markets. The UK regulatory regime also regulates the providers of financial products, so that no one may carry on regulated activities without authorisation from the FCA.[86] Those acting as intermediaries in relation to issues of equity securities who carry on regulated activities, for example by advising on investments,[87] arranging deals in investments[88] or managing investments,[89] are required to be authorised. Regulating these intermediaries is another way in which a regime can seek to ensure investor protection. A full discussion of this form of regulation falls outside the parameters of this book.[90]

10.4.1 Objectives of Regulation

The overarching aim of capital market regulation at the IPO stage is undoubtedly investor protection, but the goal is not to insulate investors from sustaining losses.[91] Instead, the aim is to enable investors to make informed choices and efficient resource allocation decisions. The primary problem for investors in a public offering is valuing the offered securities. Issuers and their insiders enjoy an informational advantage over outside investors. The risk for such investors is that issuers will use this advantage to sell overvalued shares. This informational asymmetry also gives rise to potential problems for issuers. More sophisticated investors can compensate for this risk by demanding a lower price to purchase the shares, with the result that issuers would be forced to accept less for their securities than they would if investors had full information on which to value the securities. This would raise the cost of capital for issuers.

As discussed in chapter eleven, the position is more complex once the securities have been admitted to trading. It is generally accepted that at that stage there are two objectives being pursued in regulating the capital markets: the first is to ensure that the prices of publicly traded securities are reasonably well informed—that is, to promote the efficiency of the market through the promotion of efficient market pricing; and the second is to ensure that shareholders are protected by effective corporate governance institutions once they

---

[86] FSMA, s 19.
[87] Financial Services and Markets Act 2000 (Regulated Activities) Order 2001 (SI 2001/544), art 53. The same issue arises in the context of debt securities—see 13.1.2.
[88] Ibid, art 25.
[89] Ibid, art 37.
[90] For discussion of these topics see eg I MacNeil, *An Introduction to the Law on Financial Investment*, 2nd edn (Oxford, Hart Publishing, 2012).
[91] The FCA operates on 'the general principle that consumers should take responsibility for their decisions': FSMA, s 5(2)(d).

invest in publicly traded shares. The latter objective is only of significance after the IPO and will be dealt with in chapter eleven. The former objective also operates differently at the IPO stage as compared to the position in the secondary market. In the IPO there is only a market for shares once the shares have been issued and are actually available to be traded. Investors who subscribe to the offer cannot, therefore, rely on the market to ensure that the price is efficient. In order to protect them, a slightly different set of investor protection devices needs to be put in place. These devices are based on disclosure, as we shall see, but rather than relying on the market to provide the requisite level of investor protection, there are a number of structures and processes put in place that result in a partial reversal of the usual 'caveat emptor' principle.

10.4.2 The Need for Regulation

The need to protect investors in publicly traded securities stems in part from the nature of the assets in question. Securities are intangible goods which cannot be inspected in the same way as other consumer products.[92] Buying a security is not like buying a car. There is no opportunity to walk around the asset, to inspect its material condition, or to take it for a test drive. In addition, unlike other consumer products where the value of the asset depends on what has happened to it to date (to continue the car analogy, how many miles it has driven, the quality of the service history, whether it has been in any serious accidents), the value of securities is largely contingent on the expected future performance of the issuing company.

Securities are claims to the future income of companies. The quality of these securities cannot be fully assessed in advance. The problem with selling securities is that this future income is subject to many unknowns. No entrepreneur can make binding promises about the future income that will be generated by the company. Nevertheless, the directors and managers in a company are in a better position than prospective investors, certainly most outside investors, to judge the likely nature of the risks that the company will face, and how it is likely to fare under them. This creates a risk that they will misrepresent the company's prospects in order to encourage investors to invest. It is this risk, caused by the asymmetry of information between companies and market participants, that capital market regulation seeks to address.[93]

---

[92] Indeed many investors do not even want to inspect: they aim to be passive recipients of an income stream rather than active investigators in the product. Public company shareholders have traditionally been regarded as passive (for a discussion of the 'rational apathy of such shareholders' see AA Berle and GC Means, *The Modern Corporation and Private Property* (London, Transaction Publishing, 1991)). Of course, investors come in all shapes and sizes. Retail investors are classically passive investors, but institutional investors can be either passive investors (eg tracker funds) or more active (eg hedge funds). This is discussed further at 11.2.2.1.

[93] These issues operate slightly differently for debt securities. The future income of a debt security will generally be certain, in terms of the amount owed and the dates of payment, albeit that whether the lender will be repaid will depend on the financial state of the company at the time. As regards shares, however, the amount that the shareholder will receive is uncertain in all respects. As discussed at 3.2.1 there is no entitlement to dividend payments. The shareholders, or at least the ordinary shareholders, are the residual claimants on the company, taking the lion's share of the risks and rewards in the company, and this makes their income stream entirely dependent on the future fortunes of the company. In this way bonds can be said to be less informationally sensitive than shares, because their price is less likely to change with the release of new information about the company as compared to equity securities, except where the information reflects the inability of the issuer to repay the debt.

These same points could, however, be made in relation to the investments in private companies, which are not regulated in the same way. The law does put in place protections for shareholders in private companies, such as pre-emption rights.[94] It is notable, though, that these measures are in place to protect existing members of the company, not incoming shareholders, whose position is left primarily to contract law. So, what is it about publicly traded securities that makes this additional protection necessary?

The objectives of regulating the capital markets, namely market efficiency and investor protection, require the law to constrain opportunistic managers and controlling shareholders, in other words to regulate the conflict between corporate insiders and corporate outsiders. There is a general assumption that investors in private companies have some connection with the company and, consequently, that the information asymmetry between them and the managers/controllers will be less severe than that which exists for investors in publicly traded companies. This is true to some extent. In private companies with small numbers of shareholders, those shareholders are more likely to be involved in the management of the firms, and therefore to have direct knowledge of corporate affairs, but this argument tends to weaken as the size of private companies increases. Moreover, some investors in publicly traded companies can still be regarded as 'insiders' to some extent, for example where founder shareholders remain in the company following the IPO. This distinction is, therefore, an inexact one.

Another justification for differentiating between public and private companies is the idea that a fraud in a publicly traded company may impact on the prices of independent but similar companies in the market place, whereas a fraud within a private company is unlikely to have a similar spillover effect.[95] A further difference between publicly traded companies and private companies is the fact that private company share purchases are generally a matter of negotiation. Investors purchasing a significant stake in a private company are able to contract for their own protection, including their own disclosure regime.[96] The foundational documents in venture capital financing arrangements attest to the possibility that shareholders can contract for the necessary protective structures in some circumstances.[97] 'Outside' investors in private companies still need information, and will need to bargain for this disclosure themselves on a company by company basis, but this obviously comes with costs attached to it which make it unsuitable for use in the context of publicly traded companies. In such companies it is unreasonable to expect most retail investors to conduct, and pay for, their own disclosure regime. There can be a transaction cost benefit for publicly traded companies in imposing a mandatory regime of disclosure. Although a regime of this kind could be of benefit to some private companies, this type of regulatory mechanism will be too costly for most private firms to support, and therefore disclosure in private companies remains a matter for individual investors to negotiate.

---

[94] See 4.4. In addition there are general company law devices in place to protect minority shareholders in private companies, eg Companies Act 2006, ss 994–96.

[95] R Kraakman et al, *The Anatomy of Corporate Law*, 2nd edn (Oxford, Oxford University Press, 2009) 9.1.

[96] The position regarding debt securities, and the opportunity for debt investors to negotiate, is discussed at 13.1.3.

[97] Eg SN Kaplan and P Strömberg, 'Financial Contracting Theory Meets the Real World: An Empirical Analysis of Venture Capital Contracts' (2003) 70 *Review of Economic Studies* 281. The position of private equity investors is discussed further at 16.3.2.

10.4.3 Regulatory Strategies

There are three principal strategies for regulating this conflict between corporate insiders and corporate outsiders: governance strategies, affiliation strategies and mandatory disclosure.[98] While the first and second of these have a small part to play, mandatory disclosure forms the central plank of the UK's regulatory strategy.

10.4.3.1 Governance Strategies

One form of governance strategy, sometimes termed 'merit regulation', involves a disinterested third party screening companies that wish to enter the public securities market. In the UK a prospectus must be vetted by the FCA, acting in its capacity as the UK Listing Authority,[99] and section 75(5) of FSMA entitles the FCA to refuse an application for listing if that listing would be detrimental to investors.[100] Time constraints mean that this review is by no means full and comprehensive. The primary aim of this process is to ensure that the prospectus's content complies with the requirements of the Prospectus Directive, and not to ensure that the information provided is correct. The FCA can be expected to spot glaring omissions or inaccuracies in the information provided, but it cannot guarantee the completeness or accuracy of all the information in the prospectus.[101] In general, the costs of a merit regulation system are deemed to be too great to be justified in a mature market.[102] In the UK, therefore, the FCA has the role of general watchdog, rather than a more formal role of gatekeeper at entry level.

The governance strategy can also be regarded as comprising any rules designed to provide oversight of the directors in the context of publicly traded companies. On this analysis rules relating to the structure of boards, such as the need for independent directors, or rules providing shareholders with corporate governance rights in the context of publicly traded companies, could be regarded as part of the governance strategy. In the UK the Corporate Governance Code[103] is an example of the first strategy, whereas the control rights which shareholders in certain publicly traded companies have in relation to directors' remuneration is an example of the latter.[104]

---

[98] This section utilises the language adopted by R Kraakman et al, *The Anatomy of Corporate Law*, 2nd edn (Oxford, Oxford University Press, 2009) ch 9.

[99] FSMA, s 87A, implementing Prospectus Directive 2003/71/EC, art 13. The draft prospectus, and other relevant documents, must be submitted to the FCA at least 10 days prior to the intended publication date in order to allow this process to occur.

[100] In fact it is more likely that the FCA will simply require the issuer to remedy the inaccuracy, and to refuse approval only if that does not occur: FSMA, s 87J.

[101] It is worth noting that the FCA and its officers are protected from liability in damages for acts and omissions in the discharge of their functions, unless bad faith is shown or there is a breach of s 6 Human Rights Act 1998, so it will not usually be worth suing the FCA if the prospectus is incomplete or inaccurate: FSMA, s 102.

[102] For a discussion of the limited role of merit regulation within the US see SEC, *Report on the Uniformity of State Regulatory Requirements for Offerings of Securities that are Not Covered Securities* (1997), which states that approximately 40 states undertake a merit review, but acknowledges that disclosure, rather than merit review, is the dominant regulatory response in the US.

[103] FRC, *UK Corporate Governance Code*, September 2014.

[104] Companies Act 2006, ss 420–21, 439–439A (as amended by Enterprise and Regulatory Reform Act 2013, ss 79–82). These provisions apply to 'quoted companies', which are defined in Companies Act 2006, s 385 as comprising, inter alia, companies whose equity share capital is included in the Official List (s 385(2)(a)).

10.4.3.2 *Affiliation Strategies*

The affiliation strategy involves rules being introduced to govern the characteristics and behaviour of publicly traded firms, such as rules relating to the minimum size of corporate issuers, a minimum float for listed securities and a minimum history for published accounts. The UK adopts this strategy to some extent. For example, the expected market value of the equity securities to be admitted to listing[105] must be at least £700,000.[106] In addition, the company must produce audited accounts for a period of three years, ending not earlier than six months before the application for admission.[107] The company must show that it will be carrying on an independent business as its main activity,[108] and that it will have sufficient working capital to meet its requirements for the 12 months after listing.[109]

These requirements aim to ensure that issuers have a certain quality that is demonstrated by the company's trading history and size. It is clear, however, that rules of this kind can only go so far towards protecting investors from possible abuse, and very few company law rules protect matters such as the price and voting rights attached to the shares of publicly traded companies.[110] It is also notable that this is a limited list of issues compared to the very significant amount of information which a company must disclose in its prospectus as a result of the imposition of mandatory disclosure, discussed next. The value of these requirements may, therefore, be questioned. In a regime that is so heavily geared towards mandatory disclosure, an alternative approach would be to allow companies to determine these issues for themselves, so that they could, for example, include less than three years of accounting records, but then would be obliged to disclose that fact to the public.

Liability regimes for ongoing disclosure obligations, such as section 90A FSMA, can also be regarded as falling within this category, since they aim to ensure the reliability of ongoing corporate disclosures. These are discussed further in chapter eleven.[111] Liability regimes for disclosures made in prospectuses are more usually regarded as part of the disclosure strategy.

10.4.3.3 *Mandatory Disclosure*

Although the UK does make use of governance and affiliation strategies to a small extent, the primary mechanism for regulating its capital markets is via the use of mandatory

---

[105] These requirements do not, therefore, apply to an admission to trading on AIM. The exchange does put in place some requirements (see AIM, *Rules for Companies*, May 2014), but primary responsibility for assessing the suitability for admission to AIM is placed with an adviser, a 'nomad': see LSE, *AIM Rules for Nominated Advisers*, May 2014.

[106] FCA Handbook, LR 2.2.7(1)(a). The value is £200,000 for debt securities: LR 2.2.7(1)(b) (discussed further at 13.2.2.2). This is a requirement of the Consolidated Admissions Requirements Directive 2001/34/EC (CARD): CARD, arts 43 and 58. Other UK requirements, which all flow from CARD, are that the securities on offer must be admitted to listing (LR 2.2.9), the securities must be freely transferable (LR 2.2.4(1)), and, in the case of shares, a 'sufficient number' of the class of shares in question must be distributed to the public (LR 6.1.19(1)).

[107] FCA Handbook, LR 6.1.3, implementing CARD, art 44.

[108] Ibid, LR 6.1.4. This requirement does not flow from CARD.

[109] Ibid, LR 6.1.16. This requirement is subject to exceptions: LR 6.1.17, 6.1.18. These requirements do not flow from CARD and are super-added by the UK.

[110] One of the exceptions is the company law rule that, once listed in the UK, shares cannot generally be issued at more than a 10% discount to the middle market price (LR 9.5.10), unless as part of a rights issue or if the discount is specifically approved by shareholders.

[111] See 11.4.1.2.

disclosure.[112] As discussed in 10.4.2, equity securities are intangible goods, which are claims to the future income of companies, and insiders are in a better position than investors to evaluate the risks faced by the company, and its potential to overcome those risks. It is clear that to be effective a system needs to regulate the agency relationship between directors, as insiders, and investors, as outsiders, by preventing fraud by the insider. Many jurisdictions have developed anti-fraud rules to counteract this possibility. The UK was one of the first to do so, with its Directors' Liability Act of 1890. Anti-fraud regimes need to be coupled with disclosure obligations, however, to provide investors with protection, otherwise companies could avoid liability by simply staying silent.[113]

Mandatory disclosure is the strategy adopted in the UK to deal with the need both to regulate IPOs, discussed in this chapter, and also to regulate the ongoing market, once shares have been listed, discussed in chapter eleven. However, the rationale for mandatory disclosure is not identical in these two scenarios. The primary rationale to explain the need for disclosure in relation to the ongoing market is to ensure market efficiency, although disclosure can also perform other useful functions, such as allowing shareholders to exercise a corporate governance role and allowing lenders to reduce monitoring costs.[114] The efficient capital markets hypothesis (ECMH) suggests that investors (including unsophisticated investors) are protected, provided all relevant information is disclosed, as this is then reflected in the price of the securities.[115] At the IPO stage, however, no market yet exists for the securities, and therefore no market price has yet been established. The rationale for disclosure at this stage rests on the informational asymmetry that exists between corporate insiders and outsiders. Accordingly, the disclosure rules at the IPO stage seek to overcome this asymmetry by modifying the principle of caveat emptor, in order to provide investors in the public offering with the information they need to assess whether to purchase the offered shares.

This strategy, however, rests on investors actually reading and digesting the information that is provided, in order to make an informed investment decision.[116] This is in contrast to disclosures made in the secondary market whereby the operation of the ECMH allows investors to rely on the price of the securities, into which all the available information has, arguably, been impounded, rather than to have to read those disclosures for themselves.[117] Some indirect protection may be available to investors, however, via analysts' recommendations and other intermediary activity, although this is far less developed than the investor protection benefits that such intermediaries provide in the secondary market.[118]

---

[112] For discussion of mandatory disclosure as a regulatory strategy see L Enriques and S Gilotta, 'Disclosure and Financial Market Regulation' in N Moloney, E Ferran and J Payne (eds), *The Oxford Handbook of Financial Regulation* (Oxford, Oxford University Press, 2015); O Ben-Shahar and C Schneider, 'The Failure of Mandated Disclosure' (2011) 159 *University of Pennsylvania Law Review* 647.

[113] In principle, under the common law there is no liability for silence unless it makes something already said misleading: see eg *Derry v Peek* (1889) 14 App Cas 337. For further discussion see 10.6.2.1.

[114] See 11.2.

[115] See 11.2.1.1.

[116] In recognition of this fact the Prospectus Directive requires that the information in a prospectus 'shall be presented in an easily analysable and comprehensible form' (art 5(1) and see FSMA, s 87A(3)). However, the directive also recognises the fact that few retail investors will read a prospectus in full before deciding whether to invest, and therefore requires a summary to be part of the prospectus, conveying the essential elements of the securities being offered, but with a warning that the summary prospectus should only be read as an introduction to the prospectus (art 5(2) and FSMA, s 87A(5)(6)).

[117] See 11.2.1.1.

[118] For discussion see 11.2.1.1 and 11.5.

Disclosure can also be seen to be of benefit to issuers. Faced with inadequate information about companies and their securities, investors would not be able to differentiate the 'good' investments from the 'lemons'.[119] If issuers offering better quality securities are unable to distinguish themselves, investors will view all securities as average. Consequently, there will be too little investment in the good businesses, and the low-quality businesses will attract too much money.

It is generally accepted that in order to allow investors to make efficient choices about the securities in which to invest, a system of *mandatory* disclosure is required.[120] Due to the agency problem between investors and corporate insiders it is believed that managers would not have an incentive to disclose all relevant information to investors. This is not to say that managers would not have incentives to disclose voluntarily some information about their company. The managers of above average companies would, after all, have an incentive to reveal information that would allow them to differentiate the securities of their companies from those of other companies and, thereby, to receive above average prices for their securities. Furthermore, they would have an incentive to reveal at least some of the bad information about the company, as well as the good information, as a means of convincing investors that they had been told everything that was relevant, that the information provided should be trusted, and therefore that the price of the securities should not be discounted.

Alternatively, companies could attempt to differentiate their securities as a high-quality product by other means, although these all come with significant costs attached to them. For example, the company could use reputational means, a technique sometimes referred to as 'signalling'. This might involve employing a respected merchant bank or stockbroker to bring them to the market, or employing other well-respected outsiders, such as accountancy firms, to certify the accuracy of the company's representations. Investors ought to be able to trust reputable intermediaries to report truthfully, even if they do not trust the issuing companies themselves to do so because, in theory, these intermediaries are repeat players who face serious sanctions but make no significant gains from misreporting.[121] This mechanism is in use in the UK.[122]

---

[119] G Akerlof, 'The Market for "Lemons": Quality Uncertainty and the Market Mechanism' (1970) 84 *Quarterly Journal of Economics* 488.

[120] For discussion of the utility of mandatory disclosure, see generally JC Coffee, 'Market Failure and the Economic Case for a Mandatory Disclosure System' (1984) 70 *Virginia Law Review* 717; FH Easterbrook and DR Fischel, 'Mandatory Disclosure and the Protection of Investors' (1984) 70 *Virginia Law Review* 669; MB Fox, 'Retaining Mandatory Disclosure: Why Issuer Choice is Not Investor Empowerment' (1999) 85 *Virginia Law Review* 1335; R Romano, 'Empowering Investors: A Market Approach to Securities Regulation' (1998) 107 *Yale Law Journal* 2359; A Ferrell, 'The Case for Mandatory Disclosure in Securities Regulation around the World' (2007) 2 *Brooklyn Journal of Corporate Financial and Commercial Law* 81. For a summary of the empirical evidence on this issue see R Kraakman et al, *The Anatomy of Corporate Law*, 2nd edn (Oxford, Oxford University Press, 2009) 9.2.1.2.

[121] For a discussion of the role of reputational intermediaries in protecting investors see J Payne, 'The Role of Gatekeepers' in N Moloney, E Ferran and J Payne (eds), *The Oxford Handbook of Financial Regulation* (Oxford, Oxford University Press, 2015).

[122] A company applying for a premium listing of its equity securities on the Main Market must appoint a sponsor, normally an investment bank, whose role is to provide assurance to the FCA that the responsibilities of the applicant under the listing rules have been met, and to guide the applicant in understanding and meeting its responsibilities under the listing rules: FCA Handbook, LR 8.3.1. It is the sponsor who submits the application for listing to the FCA and accompanies it with a sponsor's declaration that it has fulfilled its two duties (LR 8.4.3). Where a prospectus is required, the sponsor must not submit the application unless it has come to the reasonable opinion that the applicant has also met all the requirements set out in the Prospectus Rules: LR 8.4.2 and LR 8.4.8. These obligations are super-added, and do not fall on an issuer seeking a standard listing. There is no requirement

Companies could also attempt to differentiate themselves by requiring directors to hold substantial quantities of shares (ie to have 'skin in the game'): the higher the quality of the securities, the more likely it is that directors will be prepared to hold them. Directors are likely to want to be compensated, however, if they have to hold undiversified portfolios. Alternatively, the company could make promises regarding dividend payments, or could make use of leverage in order to demonstrate their confidence in the company's prospects.

Without mandatory disclosure, information might also be made available to investors by other means. One suggestion is that differentiation between the good and bad securities could take place as a result of the efforts of financial intermediaries.[123] For example, analysts actively search for information before they invest in a company, follow up tips and look at global information such as the price of raw materials. The efforts of analysts to uncover this information can also be valuable to investors more generally, who may be able to piggyback on the analysts' efforts.[124] The absence of a mandatory disclosure regime would not, therefore, result in an absence of information for investors.

There are two weaknesses, however, with these arguments in favour of voluntary disclosure. First, it may be that voluntary disclosure would lead to less information disclosure than a mandatory regime. In determining whether to make voluntary disclosure, companies would need to weigh up the advantages of doing so, namely persuading investors to pay a higher price for their securities, against the costs. There is a financial cost involved in disclosure that cannot be ignored. In addition, revealing information may harm the company, for example by providing commercially valuable secrets to the company's competitors, and managers would need to weigh up whether the benefit of revealing the information outweighed this cost. Put simply, voluntary disclosure may lead to the underproduction of information. Mandatory, standardised disclosure can solve this problem. If every company must disclose the same things, there are reciprocal benefits for each company's investors, even though the company may be compelled to disclose information which is advantageous to its rivals. It may be that the managers would also be better off by not revealing all the information about a company, since they are then able to engage more easily in insider trading. Although, as we will see in 12.2, insider trading is prohibited, the prohibitions are imperfect, and insider trading is hard to detect. As a result, managers are unlikely to reveal *all* the information they have about a company, even if it would be relevant to investors. Furthermore, some of the information that will be relevant to investors in assessing the value of a company's securities will not be in the control of the managers, so they would not be able to reveal the information even if they wanted to do so. This would include, for example, information which is in the control of competitor companies.

for an issue of debt securities to have a sponsor: see 13.2.2.2. The sponsor therefore owes duties to its client and to the FCA. In relation to an admission to AIM the 'nominated adviser' plays a similar role in relation to the admission document required for admission to AIM; see *AIM Rules for Nominated Advisers*, May 2014.

[123] G Akerlof, 'The Market for "Lemons": Quality Uncertainty and the Market Mechanism' (1970) 84 *Quarterly Journal of Economics* 488.

[124] For discussion see J Payne, 'The Role of Gatekeepers' in N Moloney, E Ferran and J Payne (eds), *The Oxford Handbook of Financial Regulation* (Oxford, Oxford University Press, 2015), and see discussion at 11.5. The imposition of the burden of mandatory disclosure on companies, which carries a cost element with it, can be regarded as an implicit subsidy by companies to analysts working in the securities markets. See JC Coffee, 'Market Failure and the Economic Case for a Mandatory Disclosure System' (1984) 70 *Virginia Law Review* 717.

Second, a significant problem with a voluntary system, and therefore one of the most compelling arguments in favour of mandatory disclosure, is the fact that the information provided under a voluntary system would be idiosyncratic. Without standardisation of the information involved it would be more difficult for most investors to make use of it. Standardisation improves comprehensibility and comparability and thereby increases the value of the information to investors. While it is possible for standardisation of this kind to arise through private ordering, a mandatory system ought to be cheaper and quicker to establish.

Arguments in favour of voluntary disclosure can be made.[125] Furthermore, the benefits of mandatory disclosure may be questioned if it leads to an overproduction of information or the production of irrelevant information.[126] Nevertheless, most academics and regulators accept that mandatory disclosure is an essential feature of capital markets regulation. This is certainly the accepted position in the EU,[127] and it is from the EU that the UK's mandatory disclosure rules now flow, in the form of the Prospectus Directive and its implementing regulation. The content of the UK's mandatory disclosure rules is discussed next.

10.5 Regulation of Public Offers in the UK: Ex Ante Protection via Mandatory Disclosure

10.5.1 Regulatory Structure

The regulatory structure in this area is complex, being a mixture of EU legislation, UK domestic legislation, rules generated by the UK regulator (currently the FCA), and rules generated by the stock exchanges themselves.

There has been a slew of EU directives aimed at promoting the concept of a single market for financial services.[128] As far as the disclosure of information in prospectuses is concerned, the most important piece of EU law is the Prospectus Directive, whilst admission to listing is regulated by CARD.[129] The Prospectus Directive is a maximum harmonisation directive, which was introduced in order to regulate the disclosure of information required in securities prospectuses within the EU.[130] In addition, a directly applicable regulation was adopted

---

[125] For a good summary of these issues see L Enriques and S Gilotta, 'Disclosure and Financial Market Regulation' in N Moloney, E Ferran and J Payne (eds), *The Oxford Handbook of Financial Regulation* (Oxford, Oxford University Press, 2015) part II.

[126] T Parades, 'Blinded by the Light: Information Overload and its Consequences for Securities Regulation' (2003) 81 *Washington University Law Quarterly* 417.

[127] See eg *Report of the High Level Group of Company Law Experts on a Modern Regulatory Framework for Company Law in Europe*, Ch II.3 (4 November 2002).

[128] The genesis of many of these directives was the Financial Services Action Plan: European Commission, 'Financial Services: Implementing the Framework for Financial Markets: Action Plan' COM(1999) 232. For discussion see Moloney: EU Regulation, ch 1.

[129] 2001/34/EC.

[130] Directive 2003/71/EC as amended (and further amendments to this Directive are likely: see European Commission Consultation Document, *Review of the Prospectus Directive*, 18 February 2015).

at EU level, which provides over a hundred pages of detailed information regarding the information to be disclosed in public offers.[131]

The implementation of the Prospectus Directive into UK law was achieved in large part via amendments to FSMA and the FCA Handbook.[132] FSMA gave responsibility for listing matters to the FCA's predecessor, the FSA, in 2000. These responsibilities were transferred to the FCA in 2013, following a reorganisation of financial regulation in the UK.[133] The FCA now has statutory authority for these matters,[134] and is, inter alia, responsible for the FCA Handbook, which contains the Prospectus Rules, the Listing Rules and the Disclosure and Transparency Rules. It is the Prospectus Rules that are of particular importance for the purpose of IPOs.[135]

The final element of regulation exists at the level of the stock exchanges themselves, which also have an important rule-making function. As discussed, in the UK admission of securities to trading on the Main Market requires companies to seek inclusion in the Official List (currently governed by the FCA in its capacity as the UKLA) *and* to apply for admission of the securities to trading on the market (a matter governed by the London Stock Exchange). The LSE's rules governing this process are therefore of considerable importance.[136]

10.5.2 Mandatory Disclosure in the UK

The key mechanism by which UK law achieves its disclosure objectives is the prospectus. A prospectus is required whenever admission of securities to trading on a regulated market, such as the LSE's Main Market, is sought,[137] or indeed whenever a company offers its securities to the public.[138] It is unlawful to offer prescribed transferable securities to the public in the UK, or to request that they be admitted to trading on a regulated market operating within the UK, unless an approved prospectus has been made available to the public

---

[131] Commission Regulation (EC) No 809/2004 as amended (see in particular Commission Delegated Regulation (EU) No 486/2012 and Commission Delegated Regulation (EU) No 862/2012). No implementing legislation was required to give effect to this regulation in UK law, but the relevant disclosures are reproduced for ease of reference in the FCA Handbook.

[132] At EU level an important distinction is drawn between regulated and non-regulated markets. Within the UK, the Main Market of the LSE is a regulated market for the purposes of the Prospectus Directive, but the decision was taken by the LSE not to seek regulated status for AIM, which is, instead, an exchange-regulated market.

[133] See Financial Services Act 2012.

[134] FSMA, Part 6.

[135] However, note that the Listing Rules are also relevant because of the threshold requirements for a listing of securities stipulated by CARD.

[136] See LSE, *Admission and Disclosure Standards*, April 2010 (regarding admission to the Main List). Debt securities admitted to the Professional Securities Market are still part of the Official List and the admission process therefore falls within the remit of both the FCA (as the UKLA) and the LSE. This is in contrast to the position of AIM. Eligibility for admission to trading on AIM is entirely a matter for the LSE to regulate: see LSE, *AIM Rules for Companies*, May 2014. The role of the exchange in relation to securities such as those admitted to AIM is, therefore, potentially even more significant than for securities admitted to the Official List.

[137] FSMA, s 85(2). AIM is not a regulated market and therefore an admission to AIM per se will not trigger the need for a prospectus, although if the admission is accompanied by an offer to the public then a prospectus will be required: FSMA s 85(1). However, even if no prospectus is required, the LSE rules require an applicant for admission to AIM to produce a publicly available admission document which includes disclosure requirements and is in effect a slimmed down version of a prospectus (LSE, *AIM Rules for Companies*, May 2014, r 5 and Sch 2).

[138] FSMA, s 85(1).

before the offer has been made,[139] and contravention is a criminal offence.[140] There are, however, a number of exceptions and circumstances in which a prospectus is not required, because it is deemed that 'an offer of securities to the public' has not been made. This phrase therefore requires examination.

10.5.2.1 *Meaning of 'An Offer of Securities to the Public'*

An offer of transferable securities to the public in the UK is defined broadly for these purposes.[141] Communication in any form, or by any means, to any person which provides sufficient information regarding the securities and the terms of the offer to enable an investor to make an investment decision in respect of them will fall within this definition.[142] It covers both a new issue of shares by issuers as well as secondary offers, and an offer which takes place via a placing by a financial intermediary will be included.[143]

There are, however, a number of exemptions from the mandatory prospectus requirements. The idea behind these exemptions is to exclude the need to provide a prospectus, and thereby the information provided in that prospectus, where the cost of providing it would be likely to outweigh the benefits of having it provided. The strongest case for removing the obligation for companies to provide information in a prospectus is where no asymmetry exists between the investors and the corporate insiders. Some of these exemptions therefore recognise that in some circumstances the costs of mandatory disclosure are not justified because the investors already have the relevant information. For example, where shares are being issued to target shareholders in a share-exchange takeover bid it may be assumed that the shareholders will receive the necessary information as part of that transaction, and therefore have no need of additional mandatory disclosure from the company.[144] A similar rationale would appear to underlie the exemption that applies where the offerees receive the offer other than as part of a fundraising exercise by the company, for example those receiving bonus shares, and shares issued under employee or directors' share schemes.[145] Finally, no new prospectus is required where shares that are being sold or placed through a financial intermediary have previously been the subject of one or more offers to the public, provided certain conditions are satisfied, including that a relatively recent prospectus is available and the issuer, or other person responsible for drawing up the prospectus, has given written consent for its use.[146]

An alternative rationale for exempting an offer from the mandatory disclosure requirements is where investors may not already have the information, but can be assumed to be capable of evaluating the merits and risks of the potential investment for themselves, without the law's protection, and can acquire any information they need to make this

---

[139] Ibid, ss 85(1) and (2).

[140] Ibid, s 85(3). In addition, it is actionable as a breach of statutory duty by any person who suffers loss as a result of the contravention: s 85(4).

[141] For discussion of these issues in the context of debt securities see 13.2.2.

[142] Ibid, ss 102B(1) and (3). Notice that an offer made to a person within the UK is regarded as an offer to the public in the UK: s 102B(2).

[143] Ibid, s 102B(4).

[144] Ibid, s 85(5)(b) and FCA Handbook, PR 1.2.2.

[145] FSMA, s 85(5)(b).

[146] Ibid, s 86(1A), added by Prospectus Regulations 2012 (SI 2012/1538), reg 2(2) and amended by Prospectus Regulations 2013 (SI 2013/1125).

assessment. This explains the exemption that applies where the offer is addressed to 'qualified investors' only.[147] This rationale also appears to underlie the exemption from a public offers prospectus requirement for offers where an investor must pay at least €100,000 to acquire the securities,[148] and offers of securities in denominations of at least €100,000.[149] In this context wealth is being used as a rather crude proxy for financial sophistication. The purpose of these exemptions seems to be to facilitate non-retail offers.

Some of the other exemptions focus on the small size of the offering, so that there are exemptions where the total amount to be raised in the offer is no more than €5 million,[150] where the total offer consideration cannot exceed €100,000,[151] or where the offer is to fewer than 150 persons per EEA state.[152] In these circumstances, the reason for the lack of mandatory disclosure is entirely pragmatic, namely that while investors may benefit from mandatory disclosure, the cost of such disclosure is deemed to be out of proportion to the benefit that might be gained by imposing it.

Even if an offer falls within one of these exemptions, however, the need for a prospectus can still be triggered by a request for admission of securities to a regulated market, such as the Main Market in London. Although there are exemptions to this requirement too,[153] they are generally narrower in scope so that, for example, there is no 'qualified investor' exemption, which is unsurprising given that there is no mechanism for controlling the ownership of the shares once they have been admitted to the market.[154]

10.5.2.2 Form and Content of a Prospectus

The overriding purpose of the prospectus is to provide the information which is 'necessary to enable investors to make an informed assessment of (a) the assets and liabilities, financial position, profits and losses, and prospects of the issuer … and (b) the rights attaching to the transferable securities',[155] ie to provide disclosure to investors.[156]

---

[147] FSMA, s 86(1)(a), as amended by Prospectus Regulations 2011 (SI 2011/1668), implementing Directive 2010/73/EU. For the definition of 'qualified investor' see s 86(7).

[148] FSMA, s 86(1)(c) as amended by Prospectus Regulations 2011 (SI 2011/1668) and Prospectus Regulations 2012 (SI 2012/1538), implementing Directive 2010/73/EU.

[149] FSMA, s 86(1)(d) as amended by Prospectus Regulations 2011 (SI 2011/1668) and Prospectus Regulations 2012 (SI 2012/1538), implementing Directive 2010/73/EU.

[150] FSMA, s 85(5), (6) and Sch 11A para 9 (the figure was increased from €2.5 million to €5 million by Directive 2010/73/EU, implemented into UK law by SI 2011/1668).

[151] FSMA, s 85(1)(e) as amended by Prospectus Regulations 2011 (SI 2011/1668), implementing Directive 2010/73/EU. Where this exemption applies, Member States are not allowed to impose any prospectus requirements under their domestic law. This is in contrast to the €5 million exemption, under which Member States may impose their own domestic prospectus law if they choose to do so (although the UK has not done so).

[152] Ibid, s 86(1)(b), as amended by Prospectus Regulations 2011 (SI 2011/1668), implementing Directive 2010/73/EU.

[153] FCA Handbook, PR 1.2.

[154] There is, however, one exemption that exists for the 'admission of securities to a regulated market' trigger that does not exist as an exemption for the 'offer of securities to the public' trigger: FCA Handbook, PR 1.2.3 (no prospectus is required to admit shares representing less than 10% of the number of shares of the same class already admitted to trading on that regulated market, measured over a 12-month period).

[155] FSMA, s 87A(2). For discussion of these issues in the context of debt securities see 13.2.3.

[156] There is also an obligation to provide a supplementary prospectus if information arises after the prospectus has been published that requires the published information to be qualified: FSMA, s 87G (and see Commission Delegated Regulation (EU) No 383/2014, which specifies the minimum situations in which a supplementary prospectus is required).

The prospectus is intended to provide useful information to investors and, therefore, the information contained therein 'must be presented in a form which is comprehensible and easy to analyse',[157] and issuers need to provide a summary as part of the prospectus in order to further this aim.[158] The summary must present the key information in an easily accessible and understandable way. It should convey concisely, and in non-technical language, the key information relevant to the securities which are the subject of the prospectus and, when read with the rest of the prospectus, must be an aid to investors in considering whether to invest in the securities.[159] The length of the summary should not exceed 7 per cent of the length of the prospectus or 15 pages, whichever is longer.[160] A prospectus summary must, however, make it clear that it is only an introduction and that investment decisions should only be based on the prospectus.[161]

The source for the rules regarding the need for a prospectus, and the content of the prospectus, is the Prospectus Directive and its supporting Regulation.[162] Examination of the disclosure requirements[163] for a share registration document provides a good illustration of the nature of the disclosure requirements created by this Regulation.[164] Full details of the issuer itself must be given, including its legal and commercial name, its place of registration, date of incorporation and registered office,[165] as well as details regarding the existing share capital of the company,[166] including a description of the rights, preferences and restrictions attaching to each class of the existing shares.[167] The information that issuers must provide includes details of the members of the administrative, management or supervisory bodies of the company and any senior manager who is relevant to establishing that the issuer has the appropriate expertise and experience for the management of the issuer's business,[168] including their remuneration,[169] details of the company's employees,[170] and details of major shareholders within the company.[171] As might be expected, the issuer must also disclose risks which are specific to the issuer or its industry.

---

[157] FSMA, s 87A(3).

[158] Ibid, s 87A(5).

[159] Prospectus Directive, art 5(2) as amended, implemented by FSMA, ss 87A (6) and (9)–(10).

[160] Prospectus Directive, art 24 as amended, and FCA Handbook, PR 2.1.4.

[161] Commission Regulation (EC) 809/2004, Annex XXII and FCA Handbook, PR 2.1.7.

[162] Regulation (EC) 809/2004, as amended by Regulation (EU) No 486/2012, Regulation (EU) No 862/2012 and Regulation (EU) No 759/2013.

[163] Although the Prospectus Directive is a maximum harmonisation directive, Commission Regulation (EC) 809/2004 creates minimum disclosure requirements. Issuers may need to provide more information than is contained in the annexes, in order to comply with the overarching requirement to provide investors with all the necessary information in accordance with s 87A(2) FSMA.

[164] Commission Regulation (EC) 809/2004, Annex I. This annex is reproduced at FCA Handbook, PR App 3.1. This may be contrasted with the requirements for non-equity issues, set out in the other annexes to the regulation. In 2010 a proportionate disclosure regime was introduced for SMEs which adapts the disclosure regime for small and medium sized companies and requires a reduced level of disclosure in some respects: see Prospectus Directive, art 7.2(e), as amended by Directive 2010/73/EU (for the definition of SMEs for this purpose see Prospectus Directive, art 2(1)(f)). For discussion see ESMA, *Technical Advice on Possible Delegated Acts Concerning the Prospectus Directive as Amended by the Directive 2010/73/EU* (ESMA/2011/323). See also European Commission Consultation Document, *Review of the Prospectus Directive*, 18 February 2015, which contemplates further change in this regard.

[165] Commission Regulation (EC) 809/2004, Annex I, para 5.1.

[166] Ibid, para 21.

[167] Ibid, para 21.2.3.

[168] Ibid, para 14.1.

[169] Ibid, para 15.1.

[170] Ibid, para 17.

[171] Ibid, para 18.1.

Issuers are required to disclose audited historical financial information covering the latest three financial years, or such shorter period that the issuer has been in operation, and the audit report in respect of each year.[172] The names and addresses of the issuer's auditors for the period covered by the historical financial information must also be disclosed.[173] Issuers must provide, inter alia, a description of the issuer's principal investments for each financial year for the period covered by the historical financial information up to the date of the registration document;[174] a description of the nature of the issuer's operations and its principal activities;[175] a description of the principal markets in which the issuer competes;[176] details of the risks which are specific to the issuer or to its industry;[177] information regarding any existing or planned material tangible fixed assets, including leased properties, and any major encumbrances thereon;[178] the most significant recent trends in production, sales and inventory, and costs and selling prices since the end of the last financial year to the date of the registration document;[179] and a summary of each material contract for the two years immediately preceding publication of the registration document.[180]

It can be seen that the information required is predominantly historical in nature. It describes the issuer, its managers, its shareholders, and its financial situation up to the date of application for admission. For the most part the information required of issuers is not forward-looking at all.[181] It might seem surprising that the mandatory disclosure requirements focus so strongly on the provision of historical information, given that the value of the securities to the investor is in their *future* potential, and it is information about the company's future performance and profits that is likely to be of most interest to a potential investor. A recitation of specified objective facts is, however, the lowest-cost method of disclosure. It is also, arguably, the most reliable data on which to base any analysis of the company. If the costs of mandatory disclosure become excessively high, then alternative methods whereby high quality businesses can distinguish themselves, such as employing high-reputation outsiders, or promising significant dividends in the future, all start to look like more attractive options. Historical facts are also the easiest to compare across companies. Verification is cheapest, and the enforcement of an anti-fraud system works best, where it is relatively simple to verify the accuracy, or inaccuracy, of a statement made by the company. There are costs attached to both over-enforcement and inaccurate enforcement.[182]

---

[172] Ibid, para 20.1. Where the company seeks to have its shares admitted to the Official List, the Consolidated Admissions Requirements Directive specifies a minimum of three years' audited accounts: CARD, art 44 and see FCA Handbook, LR 6.1.3.

[173] Commission Regulation (EC) 809/2004, Annex I, para 2.1.

[174] Ibid, para 5.2.1.

[175] Ibid, para 6.1.1.

[176] Ibid, para 6.2.

[177] Ibid, para 4.

[178] Ibid, para 8.1.

[179] Ibid, para 12.1.

[180] Ibid, para 22.

[181] Some of the information required can be regarded as forward-looking to a minor extent. For example, issuers are required to provide information concerning their capital resources (both short- and long-term) (para 10.1) and 'information regarding any governmental, economic, fiscal, monetary or political policies or factors that have materially affected, *or could materially affect*, directly or indirectly, the issuer's operations' (para 9.2.3, emphasis added).

[182] FH Easterbrook and DR Fischel, 'Mandatory Disclosure and the Protection of Investors' (1984) 70 *Virginia Law Review* 669, 678.

There are also dangers associated with the inclusion of forward-looking information in prospectuses which do not arise from the provision of historical information. This is because forward-looking information provides the issuer's directors with an opportunity to present the company's future in an over-optimistic manner. This danger is clearly recognised by the EU's regulatory regime. In only one respect does EU legislation allow issuers to include genuinely forward-looking information in their prospectuses: issuers can choose to include profit forecasts in their prospectuses, though they are not obliged to do so.[183] These profit forecasts have the potential to be very influential for investors, particularly retail investors. As a result, the assumptions underlying profit forecasts have to be stated and a distinction made between assumptions which directors can influence and those which are outside their control. The assumptions must also be specific and precise and readily understandable by investors. In addition, the company's auditors or accountants must confirm that the forecast has been properly compiled, that the basis of the forecast is compatible with the issuer's general accounting policies, and that the forecast is compatible with the company's historical accounts.[184]

Whatever the reasons behind the provision of largely historical information, however, the effect is that this information disclosure will be of relatively limited value to investors in determining what the future value of the securities is likely to be, which, after all, is what investors are most concerned to determine. This is in contrast to the position regarding the ongoing regulation of the markets, discussed in chapter eleven, where some 'forward-looking' information is included in companies' continuing disclosure obligations.[185]

10.6 Regulation of Public Offers in the UK: Enforcement of the Mandatory Disclosure Regime

A regime that aims to provide investor protection via mandatory disclosure requires, first, that information is disclosed in order to allow the investor to make a decision whether or not to invest, and, second, that the information disclosed is accurate.

There are relatively few ex ante mechanisms in place in the UK to ensure that information disclosed in the prospectus is accurate. The FCA has a very low-level vetting role in relation to prospectuses,[186] which should prevent glaring inaccuracies and omissions getting through. This process does not guarantee the accuracy and completeness of the document, although it is sometimes suggested that the obligation to submit the prospectus to the FCA for vetting may act as a valuable discipline upon issuers and their advisers. Another form of ex ante protection arises from the need for the issuer to appoint a sponsor, who has to assure the FCA, when required, that the responsibilities of the applicant company under the Listing Rules have been met.[187]

---

[183] Commission Regulation (EC) 809/2004, Annex I (reproduced at FCA Handbook, PR App 3), para 13.

[184] Ibid, paras 13.2–13.3.

[185] See 11.3.1.1.2. The US makes greater use of forward-looking disclosure than the UK, by providing an extensive Discussion and Analysis of Financial Condition and Results of Operations (MD & A report) (Regulation S–K, Item 303) which supplements historical accounting data with narrative information on the accounts and a forward-looking review of the business.

[186] FSMA, s 87A.

[187] FCA Handbook, LR 8.4.3.

Finally, certain items of information within the prospectus will need to be verified by third parties, so that the accounts provided by the issuer need to have been audited, and the auditors, or reporting accountants, will also have to confirm that any profit forecast within the prospectus has been properly compiled.[188] These forms of ex ante review are, however, fairly light touch and the main remedies for omissions or inaccuracies in a prospectus are provided ex post. This section therefore considers the range of ex post protections on offer.

In the context of ex post remedies it has been suggested that it is not just the 'law on the books' but also the level of enforcement of those laws in practice that is important in determining the quality of a jurisdiction's regulatory regime.[189] On this analysis, the level of enforcement within a regime will depend both on the existence of rights of action by private citizens and public authorities, and on the intensity or frequency with which enforcement occurs in practice. This section discusses each of these issues in turn.[190]

10.6.1 The Aims of Enforcement

The liability regime for inaccurate information provided in securities prospectuses is a matter of choice for each jurisdiction. Even within the EU, although the Prospectus Directive requires Member States to apply 'their laws, regulation and administrative provisions on civil liability' to those responsible for the information contained in prospectuses,[191] it does not go on to stipulate the nature of the regime that should be imposed. Instead, this remains a matter of choice for individual Member States.[192] In order to judge the effectiveness of the UK's enforcement regime, it is first necessary to consider what are the aims of a liability regime. The UK's enforcement regime can then be judged according to these aims.

A liability regime is a key aspect of the capital markets regulation regime of a jurisdiction, and as such the aims of a liability regime are the same as the aims of the capital markets regulation regime set out above, namely to protect investors and, more generally, to promote the efficient allocation of financial resources in the economy as between competing projects. There are two ways in which a liability regime might contribute to these goals. First, a liability regime can encourage the accurate and timely disclosure of information by issuers by deterring misstatements, and, second, a liability regime can contribute to the goal of promoting investor confidence by providing compensation to those who suffer loss as a result of a misstatement in a prospectus.

10.6.1.1 Encouraging the Accurate and Timely Disclosure of Information

A liability regime can contribute to the goal of encouraging the disclosure of accurate and timely information by deterring misstatements. In order for a liability regime for

---

[188] Ibid, PR App 3.1; Commission Regulation (EC) 809/2004, Annex I para 13.

[189] JC Coffee, 'Law and the Market: The Impact of Enforcement' (2007–08) 156 *University of Pennsylvania Law Review* 229.

[190] For a discussion of this issue in the context of debt securities see 13.2.7.

[191] Prospectus Directive, art 6(2).

[192] See ESMA Report, *Comparison of Liability Regimes in Member States in relation to the Prospectus Directive*, ESMA 2013/619, 30 May 2013.

misstatements in prospectuses to have a deterrent effect, however, that liability needs to fall on the directors and others who actually make the statement, rather than on the company. A liability regime of this kind avoids moral hazard and is most likely to incentivise the directors and other statement-makers to exercise care when making statements. If the liability falls only on the company, that liability will then be borne by the shareholders rather than the makers of the misstatements, such as the directors. The shareholders may put pressure on the directors as a consequence of the liability imposed on the company, but such deterrence would operate only indirectly.

Where liability falls on the company, the result is that one set of shareholders recover at the expense of another set of shareholders.[193] Company liability for misstatements in those circumstances can be seen as little more than a redistribution of value among shareholders.[194] This is not to suggest that situations where liability is imposed only on the issuer can have no deterrent effect. It is possible that reputational and other losses will fall on the makers of the misstatements as a result of the company being involved in litigation, but the deterrent effect is likely to be less pronounced in this situation than where liability falls on the statement-makers directly.

Even if the liability regime does not make the directors liable to the investors, they might nevertheless be liable to the company, for breach of their directors' duties. Thus, the directors might have to reimburse the company for the loss suffered by the company in compensating the investor, but the decision to seek recovery from the directors would be a decision to be taken by or on behalf of the company.[195] The decision to bring such an action could be brought by the board, or by the shareholders. Shareholders in the UK have the ability to bring a minority shareholders' action against misbehaving directors either by way of a derivative action[196] or by way of a statutory petition for relief from unfair prejudice.[197] The level of enforcement of directors' duties by shareholder litigation is, however, close to nil for listed companies.[198]

Even where liability falls only on the company, the actions of the directors and advisers of the company will, of course, remain of primary importance since the company, while a separate legal person, is not a natural person and can only act via its human agents. Liability can generally only be imposed on the company if its agents have acted in a way which allows liability to be attributed to the company. Various bases of attribution exist to determine

---

[193] Of course the position will be different where the claim is from the purchaser of debt securities.

[194] Where the company is insolvent, it appears that the defrauded investors are allowed to compete with the other unsecured creditors of the company for a share of the assets (see *Soden v British & Commonwealth Holdings plc* [1998] AC 298), in contrast to the usual position that shareholders claims (eg to declared but unpaid dividends) are subordinated to the claims of the unsecured creditors on insolvency (Insolvency Act 1986, s 74(2)(f)). See 3.3.1.2.5.

[195] Companies Act 2006, s 463 provides that a director is liable to compensate a company for any loss it incurs as a result of an untrue or misleading statement or omission from the directors' report or the directors' remuneration report that accompany the annual accounts (or from summary financial statement derived from them). However, a director will only be liable if the untrue or misleading statement is made deliberately or recklessly or the omission amounts to dishonest concealment of a material fact (s 463(3)).

[196] Companies Act 2006, Part 11.

[197] Ibid, ss 994–96.

[198] J Armour, 'Enforcement Strategies in UK Corporate Governance' in J Armour and J Payne (eds), *Rationality in Company Law: Essays in Honour of DD Prentice* (Oxford, Hart Publishing, 2009) 79–85.

when the acts and state of mind of a natural person can be attributed to a company.[199] In the context of misstatements in a prospectus, this will often be the company's directors and senior managers. Imposing liability on the company for the misstatements of such individuals, however, is unlikely to have a significant deterrent effect on those individuals, unless they face some consequential penalty or effect, such as a breach of duty claim by the company.

In order to have a deterrent effect, therefore, liability needs to fall directly on those that make the misstatements. This will normally be the directors, but might also be the company's advisers, such as its auditors. However, even imposing liability on the directors might not secure any deterrent purpose in practice if the effect of directors and officers liability insurance (D&O insurance) is to transfer the costs of the liability back to the company. In the US, even where liability potentially falls on directors, in practice the system of D&O insurance operates so that little liability remains with the directors.[200] In the UK, D&O insurance is generally unavailable to cover fraudulent behaviour, but this difficulty may be bypassed if D&O insurance cover is extended to include directors' liabilities under settlements of claims brought by investors in which the directors do not admit liability. If this is the case, imposing liability on directors might simply add to the incentives for defendants to settle investors' claims out of court.[201] In relation to the company's auditors, provisions in the Companies Act 2006 make it possible for auditors to limit their liability by agreement with the company, as long as that agreement is fair and reasonable.[202]

One aim of a liability regime, then, might be to encourage the accurate disclosure of information through the use of deterrence. It is not necessarily the case, however, that the most appropriate way to achieve this is by imposing the maximum level of liability possible, say a strict liability regime with onerous penalties for issuers, directors and others held responsible for the misstatement, and easy access to the regime for a wide range of potential applicants. Three different issues need to be weighed in the balance.

First, the costs of any liability regime need to be borne in mind. It is generally accepted that the standard of accuracy in prospectuses is high, and that this can be attributed in part to the imposition of the significant liability regime that currently exists in the UK regarding misstatements in prospectuses.[203] It is also true, however, that the verification process to which prospectuses are subject is both time consuming and costly. It seems clear that the costs could be reduced if the standard of the liability regime were

---

[199] *Meridian Global Funds Management Asia Ltd v Securities Commission* [1995] 2 AC 500. For discussion see E Ferran, 'Corporate Attribution and the Directing Mind and Will' (2011) 127 *Law Quarterly Review* 239; J Payne, 'Corporate Attribution and the Lessons of *Meridian*' in P Davies and J Pila (eds), *The Jurisprudence of Lord Hoffmann: A Festschrift in Honour of Lord Leonard Hoffmann* (Oxford, Hart Publishing, 2015).

[200] JC Coffee, 'Reforming the Securities Class Action: An Essay on Deterrence and its Implementation' (2006) 106 *Columbia Law Review* 1534.

[201] It is also the case that the cost of the misstatements will be transferred back to the company if the company undertakes to provide the directors with an indemnity against liability to third parties, as is now permitted by Companies Act 2006, s 234.

[202] Companies Act 2006, Part 16, Ch 6. Limitation of liability by auditors is also promoted at EU level (see Commission Recommendation concerning the limitation of the civil liability of statutory auditors and audit firms, OJ L162/39, 1 June 2008).

[203] See eg HM Treasury, *Davies Review of Issuer Liability: Liability for Misstatements to the Market—A Discussion Paper* (March 2007) para 71.

reduced.[204] The benefits of imposing a particular standard for liability must therefore be weighed against the costs.

Second, it may be that a more stringent liability regime might actually reduce the incentives for issuers to make timely and full disclosure of information, even if the level of accuracy of the information disclosed increased. Concerns about liability might lead issuers to check and double check the accuracy of information before release. This might make the information actually released more accurate, but would be likely to increase costs and to slow down the release of that information. This concern regarding the speed of disclosure is not likely to be a concern regarding the publication of a prospectus for an IPO, since that document is the first information received by the public from the company and therefore any delay is unlikely to be prejudicial to the public, but it might be of concern regarding ongoing obligations to disclose.[205]

Of more concern in the context of IPOs is the fact that issuers have some control not only over the amount of checking that occurs before a statement is made but also over the content of the statement itself. In relation to many disclosure obligations the law requires that a statement be made, but does not determine how detailed that disclosure should be. The danger is that if liability regimes are too onerous then the level of detail in disclosures, and therefore the potential benefit of disclosures to investors, might actually reduce. There might, therefore, be less information in the marketplace if the liability regime is too stringent. Alternatively, the quality or utility of the information might decrease because it could conceivably be subject to qualifications, assumptions and disclaimers.

Finally, the ultimate purpose of these measures needs to be borne in mind, namely the promotion of investor confidence in the market, and of an efficient market for securities. It is generally accepted that permitting fraudulent statements to be made would have a corrosive effect on market confidence. By contrast, however, investors do not generally expect to see a strict liability regime in place, and therefore it is difficult to argue that a strict liability regime is needed to secure that confidence. The clearly stated general principle under which the FCA operates is, after all, that consumers need to take responsibility for their own decisions.[206] The issue is rather the extent to which misstatements involving some wrongdoing short of fraud should be brought within the liability regime.

10.6.1.2 *Providing Compensation to those who Suffer Loss*

The second way in which a liability regime might contribute to the goal of promoting investor confidence in the market is by providing compensation to those who suffer loss as a result of a misstatement in a prospectus. There are two elements that need to be considered. The first is what investors should be protected against. The point has already been made that regulation of the capital markets in the UK does not aim to insulate investors

---

[204] In the context of liability for misstatements for ongoing disclosures, the accountancy firm PriceWaterhouseCoopers estimates that if the current fraud-based regime (see FSMA, s 90A) were to be changed to a more onerous negligence-based regime (akin to the regime for misstatements in prospectuses), this would be likely to increase the audit costs for annual statements by a fifth, and that a similar further increase would be generated by the additional legal work that would be involved: HM Treasury, *Davies Review of Issuer Liability*, ibid.

[205] See 11.4.1.2.

[206] FSMA, s 5(2)(d).

from sustaining losses. It is expected that investors should take responsibility for their own decisions. It is well accepted, however, that investors should be protected against some misstatements made in company prospectuses. These are selling documents, intended to persuade investors to buy securities in the company, and it is unsurprising that the law has protected investors from fraudulent misstatements made in those prospectuses for over a hundred years.[207] More interesting is the question whether the law should protect investors against other forms of misstatement, namely those made negligently, or even innocently. The same points can be made here as are discussed above, namely that a balance needs to be struck between the benefits of accurate information versus the costs involved if the level of liability is set too high. As regards prospectus liability, the position in the UK is broadly that liability can be imposed for negligent misstatements in some circumstances, though generally not for innocent misstatements.

Attention also needs to be given to the amount of compensation to which investors should be entitled. If misstatements occur in a prospectus and an investor, A, buys shares for £2 which subsequently turn out to have been worth just £1.50 at the date of purchase, what should A be entitled to recover? Is it the difference between the price paid and the actual value of the shares at the date of purchase, ie 50p per share? Should A be able to recover any diminution in the future income stream of those shares, ie the reduced dividends that may flow from the misstatement? What if the shares are actually only worth £1.20 at the date when A brings a claim in relation to this wrongdoing; can the additional 30p per share be recovered by A in any circumstances? Should A in fact be able to return the shares to the issuer, and recover the entire £2 per share investment? The level of compensation available to the investor will have an impact on the value of compensation as a tool for investor protection. The definition of investor for these purposes will also be relevant. Should it include only those initial subscribers who purchase from the company or the underwriting bank, or should investors in the after-market also be included in this protection?[208]

10.6.2 Private Enforcement: Liability for Defective Prospectuses

Remedies for investors for misrepresentations that have caused loss to those who have relied on them have existed in the UK for well over a hundred years. The first remedy was provided by the common law: liability for fraudulent misrepresentations was introduced via the tort of deceit.[209] A statutory liability regime for prospectuses followed shortly afterwards.[210]

---

[207] See eg *Derry v Peek* (1889) 14 App Cas 337.

[208] For discussion see 10.6.2.4.

[209] *Derry v Peek* (1889) 14 App Cas 337. This common law liability for misstatements in prospectuses is in sharp contrast to the position regarding misstatements in disclosures made by the company once it has floated on the public market, discussed in detail in chapter 11. Perhaps the reason for this distinction is the origin of the liability regime in the tort of deceit, which, as we shall see, requires that the maker of the statement should have intended that the recipients of the statement rely on it. This reliance is easier to establish in relation to prospectuses, which are selling documents intended to persuade those that read them to buy shares in the company, than in relation to annual reports and accounts that are aimed at the shareholders of the company and are not primarily intended to induce the reader to engage in securities trading in the same way. The liability regime in relation to continuing disclosures is discussed in detail at 11.4.

[210] Directors' Liability Act 1890.

The current version of this statutory regime is to be found in section 90 FSMA.[211] In addition to the claim under this section, and liability in deceit, there are a number of other remedies that are available to investors in relation to misstatements in prospectuses. Two different claims for negligent misstatement exist: a claim under section 2(1) of the Misrepresentation Act 1967, and a claim for negligent misstatement based on the decision of the House of Lords in *Hedley Byrne & Co Ltd v Heller & Partners Ltd*.[212] The substance of this latter claim is that the defendant owes the claimant a duty of care not to cause the claimant economic loss by means of a negligent misstatement. It may, in addition, be possible for the courts to treat the misrepresentation as having been incorporated into the subsequent contract concluded between the parties, giving rise to the possibility of a breach of contract claim by the investor against the company as the other party to the contract.[213] The nature of these claims will be discussed in the next section. As will become clear, the claim under section 90 FSMA is likely to produce the most favourable result for investors on most occasions, and therefore this section will focus on an analysis of this claim, and compare and contrast the other forms of civil liability where relevant.

10.6.2.1 Nature of the Claim Under Section 90 FSMA

In principle, section 90 FSMA makes those responsible for the prospectus[214] liable to pay compensation to any person who has acquired any of the debt or equity securities to which the prospectus relates, and has suffered loss as a result of any untrue or misleading statement in it or of the omission of any matter required to be included under FSMA. Under section 90, anyone who has acquired the securities, whether for cash or otherwise, who can show that they have suffered loss as a result of the misstatement will have a prima facie case for compensation.

Under section 90 FSMA an investor can claim compensation for the distortion of the operation of the market through the provision of false information, arising either from positive statements included in the prospectus or from the omission of information required to be disclosed in the prospectus.[215] There is no requirement for the claimant to demonstrate that they relied on the misstatement, or even that they read the prospectus, in order to establish a cause of action.[216] It is enough that the error affected the market price.

---

[211] In contrast, the statutory liability regime for issuers in relation to continuing obligations to disclose was only introduced in 2006: FSMA, s 90A, introduced by Companies Act 2006, s 1270. The scope of the liability regime under s 90A is more limited than that which relates to prospectuses. For discussion see 11.4.1.2.3.

[212] [1964] AC 465.

[213] See eg *Jacobs v Batavia and General Plantations Trust Ltd* [1924] 2 Ch 329. Shareholders have faced difficulties bringing damages claims against companies in the past. Companies Act 2006, s 655 makes it clear that it is possible for a shareholder to bring such an action while continuing to hold shares in the company, ie it is not necessary for a shareholder to rescind the allotment before bringing the damages claim.

[214] This section applies to the prospectus, to any supplementary prospectus, and to listing particulars (these are required for admission to official listing where no mandatory prospectus is required (LR 4.1) and are rarely used). As regards a summary provided by the issuer, investors are unable to bring an action based on that summary unless it is untrue or misleading when read with the prospectus as a whole (FSMA s 90(11)). However, it may be possible to bring a claim where the summary does not contain the necessary key information required by FSMA ss 87A(6) and (9): s 90(12).

[215] FSMA, s 90(1)(b).

[216] Presumably, however, some causal connection will need to be shown between the misstatement or omission in the prospectus and the loss, so that the claimant who buys the shares after a significant lapse of time will find it hard to demonstrate that the prospectus continues to have any significant impact on the price of the securities.

This is sometimes described as 'fraud on the market', whereby a misstatement which has an effect on the market price can be said to cause an investor loss, even though that particular investor was not aware of the misstatement.[217]

There are defences available for those responsible for the prospectus. The defendant will be 'exempted' from liability if he reasonably believed, having made such enquiries, if any, as were reasonable, that the statement was true and not misleading, or that the matter whose omission caused the loss was properly omitted.[218] If the statement is made by an expert then the non-expert will escape liability if that person acted on the reasonable belief that the expert was competent and had consented to the inclusion of the statement in the prospectus.[219] As a result, the standard for liability is negligence liability, but a particularly strong form of negligence liability, since it is for the defendant to prove that he was not negligent rather than for the claimant to prove that he was.[220] Alternatively, he will not incur liability under section 90 FSMA if he can demonstrate that the claimant acquired the securities with knowledge that the statement was false or misleading or with knowledge of the matter omitted.[221]

The breadth of this claim can be contrasted with the far narrower claims available in relation to the other potential actions. The tort of deceit, for example, consists of the act of making a wilfully false statement with intent that the claimant will act in reliance on it, and with the result that he does so act and suffers harm as a consequence.[222] In contrast to section 90 FSMA, in order to succeed the investor must demonstrate that he was induced to act by the false statement.[223] The investor must also demonstrate that the maker of the statement knew that it was false, did not have an honest belief in its truth, or was reckless as to its accuracy.[224] By contrast, under section 90 FSMA the investor need not demonstrate that the maker of the statement knew that the statement was wrong.[225] These elements are significant and make it difficult to establish deceit claims in practice. In addition, unlike the section 90 FSMA claim, claims in deceit do not cover omissions per se, although omissions which cause the document as a whole to be misleading will be actionable.[226]

---

[217] 'Fraud on the market' class actions in securities litigation are commonplace in the US but they have come under increasing criticism in recent years; see eg WW Bratton and ML Wachter, 'The Political Economy of Fraud on the Market' (2011) 160 *University of Pennsylvania Law Review* 69.

[218] FSMA, Sch 10 para 1(2).

[219] Ibid, para 2(2).

[220] This is similar to the position under Misrepresentation Act 1967, s 2(1) but very different to the position regarding common law negligence where the burden of proof is on the claimant.

[221] FSMA, Sch 10 para 6. In this respect, the position of an investor under a s 90 claim is identical to that under the other forms of civil liability. A claim brought by an investor who knows that the information contained in the prospectus is false is likely to fail irrespective of the remedy pursued. An investor who knows that the information is false cannot claim to have been induced to act on it and a claim for deceit or misrepresentation under the Misrepresentation Act 1967 will fail for that reason. Similarly, in a case based on breach of the duty of care, an investor could not credibly claim that the mistaken advice caused loss where they were actually aware of the mistake and proceeded anyway.

[222] *Bradford Building Society v Borders* [1941] 2 All ER 205.

[223] *Smith v Chadwick* (1884) 9 App Cas 187. The statutory liability for misstatements in continuing disclosures under s 90A FSMA follows the deceit rule and requires reliance by the claimant (for discussion see 11.4.1.2.2).

[224] *Derry v Peek* (1889) 14 App Cas 337.

[225] Lack of knowledge on the part of the responsible person is relevant only to the extent that it may provide a basis for the defence that they believed on reasonable grounds that the information was true: FSMA, Sch 10 para 1.

[226] *R v Kylsant* [1932] 1 KB 442.

As regards a claim in negligence under *Hedley Byrne*, the scope of this duty was narrowly defined by the House of Lords in *Caparo Industries plc v Dickman*.[227] A claim in negligence arising from misstatements in a prospectus is a claim for pure economic loss, ie financial or pecuniary loss unrelated to physical injury or damage to property. The House of Lords in *Caparo* rejected the view that foreseeability is the touchstone of liability in such cases. In *Caparo* the claimant had acquired shares in a target company as part of a takeover. The claimant contended that it had relied on the company's accounts for the accounting year 1983–84, which had been audited by the company's accountants, Touche Ross. Caparo asserted that these accounts, although gloomy, in fact overvalued the company and that the auditors had been negligent in not detecting the irregularities or fraud which had led to the overstatements in the accounts, and in certifying the accounts as representing a true and fair view of the company's financial position. The House of Lords held that the auditors owed Caparo no duty of care in negligence. Their Lordships seemed particularly keen to avoid the imposition of 'a liability in an indeterminate amount for an indeterminate time to an indeterminate class'.[228] Instead, the House of Lords established three criteria for the imposition of a duty of care in a particular situation: foreseeability of damage, proximity of relationship and reasonableness.

Proximity—that is, the closeness and directness of the relationship between the parties— is particularly important in this context. The court will have particular regard to the purpose for which the statement is made and communicated, the knowledge of the maker of the statement and the reliance on the statement by the recipient, in determining whether the necessary proximity is established. For those claiming under *Hedley Byrne* that they have suffered loss as a result of the negligent misstatement of another it will be crucial to demonstrate that the defendant 'knew' that the advice or statement would be communicated to the claimant either directly or indirectly, and that the defendant 'knew' that that claimant was very likely to rely on that advice or statement.[229] The way in which the courts have interpreted the concept of duty of care in this context has necessarily limited the occasions on which the investor may be able to bring a negligence claim. A further limitation in negligence claims, when compared to section 90 FSMA, is that claims in negligence will not generally cover omissions.

Where the negligent misstatement claim is instead brought under the Misrepresentation Act 1967, there is again no claim for misrepresentation in relation to omissions unless silence has the effect of making what is said untrue. Another disadvantage of a claim under the Misrepresentation Act 1967, when compared to section 90 FSMA, is that, as with deceit claims, the investor must demonstrate reliance. If the evidence shows that the investor was unaware of the statement, or took no notice of it, the claim will not succeed.[230]

---

[227] [1990] 2 AC 605.

[228] *Ultramares v Touche* (1931) 255 NY 170, 179 per Cardozo CJ.

[229] In the context of the statutory accounts provisions, which were the subject matter of the decision in *Caparo*, the House of Lords determined that the purpose of these accounts, as far as the shareholders were concerned, was to put them in a position where they could effectively exercise their governance rights over the board, for example by replacing ineffective management, and not to enable them to take investment decisions. Accordingly, a duty of care did not exist in relation to purchases of shares in the company, whether by existing shareholders or by non-shareholders. On the other hand, the court also made it clear that liability could arise for auditors, and presumably others, where the financial statements were given to a known recipient for a specific purpose of which the auditors were aware and upon which the recipient had relied and acted to his detriment.

[230] *Smith v Chadwick* (1884) 9 App Cas 187.

The nature of the breach of contract claim is that the misrepresentation which appears in the prospectus has been incorporated into the subsequent contract between the parties. These claims face two significant difficulties. First, it is rare for prospectuses to make the kind of explicit promises about future value or performance that might give rise to a breach of contract claim for those future earnings. The prospectus will include representations, of course, but these are generally statements of fact rather than promises, and therefore can only protect the claimant's negative interest, not their expectation interest in future earnings. Second, there are in effect two separate contracts: the first is the contract of purchase of the shares, which may be with the company, but may alternatively be with the underwriter, depending on the method chosen by the company to offer its shares to the public;[231] and the second is the contract between the shareholder and the company, and between the shareholders inter se, comprising the company's constitution, predominantly now the company's articles of association, by which the shareholder becomes bound once entered into the company's register.[232] The two are quite separate and, even if the prospectus does contain explicit promises of the kind referred to above, the process of allotment of shares and the entry in the register are regarded as a complete novation, so that any such representations made in the prospectus will not automatically be carried through to the new contract.

The nature of the claim under section 90 FSMA is likely to be far more useful to an investor than the other private law claims. In particular, the fact that section 90 FSMA includes omissions, that the investor need not show reliance, and that the investor does not need to demonstrate knowledge on the part of the statement-maker, are all significant advantages of this claim. It is worth noting one limitation in the substance of a section 90 FSMA claim, however, as compared to the other private law actions: the statutory claim only extends to situations where the allegedly false information is contained in the prospectus. This definition includes supplementary prospectuses and the summary,[233] but does not include false information included in other documents, such as broker's circulars.[234] In relation to misstatements in such documents, the investor would have to pursue remedies other than section 90 FSMA.

10.6.2.2 Who can Claim?

Section 90 FSMA provides that those responsible for the prospectus are liable to pay compensation to any person who has acquired any of the securities to which it relates and suffered loss as a result of any untrue or misleading statement in it or of the omission of something required to be included under FSMA. The category of claimants includes both those who subscribe for securities and those who buy in the market when dealings commence, since the Act relates to all those who have 'acquired securities to which the particulars apply'.[235] Anyone who has acquired the securities whether for cash or otherwise, whether

---

[231] See 10.3.2.

[232] Companies Act 2006, s 33.

[233] However, liability in relation to the summary is restricted to situations where the summary is misleading when read together with the rest of the prospectus or where key information is not provided: FSMA, ss 90(11), (12).

[234] Although the word 'prospectus' is not defined for the purposes of s 90 FSMA, this section does not appear to apply if the misstatement appears in the Admission document required for an AIM admission.

[235] FSMA, s 90(1)(a) (and see s 90(4) as regards supplementary prospectuses). For the definition of 'acquisition' see FSMA, s 90(7).

from the company or by purchase in the after-market, will have a case for compensation if they can demonstrate loss as a result of the misstatement or omission. The requirement of a causal link between the inaccurate prospectus and the loss operates to exclude purchasers whose acquisition occurs after the distorting effect of the inaccurate information has been exhausted. Presumably this will occur once it has become public knowledge that the information in the prospectus was wrong, in which case the share price should have adjusted accordingly.

This is in contrast to the position regarding the other claims available to an investor. One of the significant limitations that exist in bringing a claim in deceit in this context is that, in general, only initial subscribers are able to bring an action. The tort of deceit consists of making a wilfully false statement with intent that the claimant will act in reliance on it, with the result that the claimant does so act and suffers harm as a consequence.[236] Subsequent purchasers in the marketplace have no cause of action even though they may have relied on the prospectus, because the purpose for which a prospectus is issued is to induce subscriptions of shares.[237] The purpose of the prospectus is, therefore, exhausted once the initial allotment is complete.[238] Drawing a distinction between subscribers and purchasers in the market in the period immediately after dealings begin is, however, highly artificial, at least in commercial terms. This is especially so where the offer is fully underwritten and the lead managers are the initial subscribers for the shares and then on-sell or place them with investors in the market. The preferable view is that this form of action should extend to the purchasers in the after-market.[239] Companies have an interest not only in the issue being fully subscribed but also in the development of a healthy secondary market for the shares so that the initial subscribers can sell their shares in the market, should they wish to do so.

As regards negligence claims, it is clear from the decision in *Caparo* that establishing proximity between the claimant and the defendant is particularly important in the context of misstatements in prospectuses. The requisite proximity is likely to be established only as between the maker of the relevant statement and persons to whom the document is specifically directed. Defining the category of those to whom a prospectus is directed is not, however, straightforward. Those responsible for prospectuses will try to restrict this category, either by contractual exclusion clauses or on the basis that their statements were only intended for a limited audience, namely the initial subscribers. Support for this latter approach can be found in *Al-Nakib Investments (Jersey) Ltd v Longcroft*,[240] in which the court held that misleading statements in a prospectus issued in connection with a rights issue could form the basis of a claim by a shareholder who took up his rights in reliance upon the prospectus, but not when the same shareholder purchased further shares in the market.

---

[236] *Bradford Building Society v Borders* [1941] 2 All ER 205.

[237] *Peek v Gurney* (1873) LR 6 HL 377.

[238] However, where the investor can demonstrate that the prospectus was only one of a series of false statements made by the defendants whose purpose was to encourage purchases in the secondary market as well as to induce initial subscribers, then subsequent purchasers may be able to maintain their claims: *Andrews v Mockford* [1896] 1 QB 372.

[239] See eg J Cartwright, *Misrepresentation, Mistake and Non-Disclosure*, 3rd edn (London, Sweet & Maxwell, 2012) para 7.52, who argues that liability should properly be regarded as extending to purchasers in the after-market as well as initial subscribers.

[240] [1990] 1 WLR 1390.

It might, however, be argued that the public at large could be expected to have sight of the prospectus. Indeed, one of the purposes of a prospectus could be said to be the creation of a healthy secondary market for the securities. On that analysis, investors in that after-market ought to be able to hold the authors of the prospectus to account in some circumstances. Support for this view can be found in *Possfund Custodian Trustee Ltd v Diamond*[241] in which Lightman J refused to strike out a claim that an additional and intended purpose of a prospectus issued in connection with a placing of securities was to inform and encourage purchasers in the after-market. This is a compelling argument. Unlike a set of company accounts, a prospectus is not a private document being prepared for the benefit of a limited class of people, but rather a public document required by statute to be prepared for the benefit of the public at large, and for the proper regulation of the securities markets. Prospectuses are known to fulfil this function by the persons responsible for preparing them, and therefore it can quite properly be said that the entire investing public is within the contemplation of the persons responsible for the content of the prospectus. If, however, the offer of securities is actually to a more restricted class of investor, such as in a placing, then it would follow that the investing public at large would not be within the contemplation of those responsible for the prospectus.

The preferable view is that where offers of securities are made to the public, then those responsible for the prospectus should be potentially liable to account to any investor for any loss suffered as a result of some misstatement in that prospectus. The present view in relation to claims in deceit or under *Hedley Byrne*, however, appears to be narrower than this, restricting claims to the initial subscribers, unless the investor in the after-market can establish that the purpose of the prospectus was also to encourage purchases in the secondary market. Where the investor's claim is based on the contractual relationship between themselves and the statement-maker, either via a claim under the Misrepresentation Act 1967 or via a claim for breach of contract, that claim can only be brought by the counterparty to the contract—that is, there is no possibility of claims by those in the secondary market.

On this analysis, then, a section 90 FSMA claim is significantly more powerful than the other possible claims because it clearly extends to purchasers in the after-market, subject to the limitation regarding causation, discussed above.

10.6.2.3 Who may be Liable?

The range of potential defendants under section 90 FSMA is much more wide-ranging than that under the other potential claims available to investors. The availability of a claim against persons other than the company will be particularly valuable as the company may be insolvent by the time the claim is made. A claim under the Misrepresentation Act 1967 and a claim for breach of contract are limited in scope, in that there must be a contractual nexus between the claimant and the defendant. This reduces the deterrent effect of this form of liability. In deceit claims the action can be against anyone who can be shown to be responsible for the statement, including the directors, accountants or other experts, but only if they have knowledge of the falsity of the statement or were reckless as to the truth.[242]

---

[241] [1996] 1 WLR 1351.

[242] Recklessness here must be understood to indicate the absence of any genuine belief in the truth of the matter rather than recklessness in the sense of gross negligence: *Derry v Peek* (1889) 14 App Cas 337, 375.

An honest, even if wholly unreasonable, belief in the truth of the statement will not amount to deceit.[243] This will be difficult to establish in practice. In a claim of negligence, the action can be brought against the company and also against directors and others, but only if they can be shown to have owed a duty of care to the claimant not to cause loss or damage caused by breach of that duty. As discussed above, the courts have adopted a restrictive test as to when this duty will arise. In practice these operate as meaningful constraints.

Under section 90 FSMA, liability falls on all those who are responsible for the prospectus.[244] For equity shares these include the issuer,[245] usually the company,[246] the directors of the issuer,[247] each person who accepts, or is stated to accept, responsibility for any part of the prospectus (but the liability only relates to that part),[248] and any other person who has authorised the content of the prospectus or any part of it (again, in relation to the part authorised).[249] Experts, such as the reporting accountant, are therefore potentially included in this list,[250] and in relation to these experts there is no need to demonstrate that the maker of the statement assumed responsibility towards the claimant. This is obviously in sharp contrast to liability under a common law negligence claim.

As discussed, a significant deterrent effect is only likely to occur where the liability falls directly on the makers of the statement, as it does in claims under section 90 FSMA, deceit claims and the negligence claim under *Hedley Byrne*. The legal and practical hurdles involved in the latter two claims, however, mean that such claims are extremely unlikely to succeed in practice. This is likely to reduce their potential deterrent effect. The deterrent effect of a section 90 FSMA claim will be undermined if D&O insurance and other devices mean that the costs of any potential liability are, in practice, transferred back to the company, and thus ultimately borne by the shareholders of the company.

10.6.2.4 Remedy

Where an investor has purchased shares as a result of misrepresentations in the prospectus, there are potentially two remedies that might be of interest: (i) financial compensation for the loss caused by the misrepresentation; and (ii) rescission of the contract, ie the investor hands back the shares and in return receives from the company the consideration paid for those shares. Under section 90 FSMA only the first of these options, namely financial compensation, is available as a remedy. If an investor wishes to rescind the contract, they must do so via one of the other bases for claim.

---

[243] *Derry v Peek*, ibid.

[244] See FCA Handbook, PR 5.5. In the case of listing particulars see Financial Services and Markets Act 2000 (Official Listing of Securities) Regulations 2001 (SI 2001/2956), reg 6. All those responsible for the prospectus must be identified in the prospectus itself as a result of Prospectus Directive, art 6.

[245] Ibid, PR 5.5.3(2)(a).

[246] The issuer will be the company where the company is making the offer (in an offer for subscription or a rights issue or open offer) or seeks admission, or has authorised these steps.

[247] FCA Handbook, PR 5.5.3(2)(b)(i) unless the prospectus was published without the director's knowledge or consent: PR 5.5.6. Liability also falls on those who authorise themselves to be named in the prospectus as a director, or who have agreed to become a director, immediately or in the future: PR 5.5.3(2)(b)(ii).

[248] Ibid, PR 5.5.3(2)(c).

[249] Ibid, PR 5.5.3(2)(f).

[250] FCA Handbook, PR 5.5.9 provides that nothing in the rules shall be construed as making a person responsible by reason only of his giving advice in a personal capacity. This is generally assumed to exclude certain professionals (eg lawyers) although not the reporting accountants, or the sponsor required by the Listing Rules.

10.6.2.4.1 Financial Compensation

Under section 90 FSMA the only remedy available is financial compensation. The section is, however, silent as to the basis on which compensation is to be assessed. There are two different matters to consider in this context: the relevant measure of damages, and the relevant remoteness test.

As regards the relevant measure of damages, there are, broadly, two options available: the tortious measure of damages and the contractual measure of damages. The first aims to restore the claimant to their former position. A tort action involves an action for a wrong done whereby the claimant was tricked out of money in his pocket. As a result the highest limit of his damages is the whole extent of his loss, and that loss is measured by the money which was in his pocket and is now in the pocket of the company. Insofar as he has received an equivalent for that money, however, that loss is diminished.[251] So, in the example set out above[252] where the investor pays £2 per share for shares which were worth £1.50 each at the time of the sale, the investor can recover 50 pence per share. This measure of damages includes no forward-looking element—in other words, there is no possibility of recovery in respect of any prospective gains which the investor may have been expecting. The tortious measure of damages applies to claims for deceit, claims under the Misrepresentation Act 1967,[253] and claims for a breach of duty in negligence under *Hedley Byrne*.[254]

By contrast, damages for breach of contract protect the investor's expectation/positive interest, which does take account of the prospective gains that the investor, under the contract, was entitled to expect. So, for example, the investor may recover for loss of the expected profits on the shares, in the shape of future dividends and capital growth, although assessing these, necessarily speculative, claims, is very difficult.[255] This difference makes a possible claim for breach of contract potentially very attractive.

In relation to the statutory compensation regime for inaccurate prospectuses which predated FSMA, the courts applied the deceit rules.[256] There is little doubt that it is the tortious measure of damages that also ought to apply to a section 90 FSMA claim.

This then raises the next issue, namely which test of remoteness ought to be applied. Again, there are two possible tests. The first is that which applies in negligence claims. In such claims the recoverable loss is defined by reference to the scope of the duty broken. In relation to claims regarding misstatements in prospectuses, it is likely that recovery will be limited to the loss caused by having a security worth less than the investor expected. So, the

---

[251] *McConnel v Wright* [1903] 1 Ch 546, 554–55 per Romer LJ. So, for example, if the fraudulent misrepresentation in the prospectus stated that the company had already acquired valuable property, but that property was only acquired afterwards, credit for the value of this subsequently acquired property will be given in assessing the damages.

[252] See 10.5.1.2.

[253] *Royscot Trust Ltd v Rogerson* [1991] 2 QB 297.

[254] In relation to claims for deceit it has been suggested that in some circumstances the claimant may be able to cover profits: *Parabola Investments Ltd v Browallia Cal Ltd* [2010] EWCA Civ 486. For example, where the claimant is deceived into entering a transaction by a fraudulent statement as to the profits to be made, and can show in addition that if he had not relied on the defendant's statement he would have made some other investment, then he may be able to recover the would-be profits that he would have made from that investment. For discussion see C Mitchell, 'Loss of Chance in Deceit' (2009) 125 *Law Quarterly Review* 12.

[255] This may lead the court to assess damages on the reliance basis, eg *Anglia Television Ltd v Reed* [1972] 1 QB 60; *McRae v Commonwealth Disposals Commission* (1951) 84 CLR 377.

[256] *Clark v Urquhart* [1930] AC 28.

investor can only recover 50 pence per share in the above example, even if something else has occurred that caused the shares to be worth only, say, £1.20 at the date of claim.

By contrast, the second possible test, which applies to claims for fraudulent misrepresentation, allows a person to claim all of the losses flowing from the misstatement. This can have important consequences, as illustrated by the facts of *Smith New Court Securities Ltd v Scrimgeour Vickers (Asset Management) Ltd.*[257] In this case the claimant, Smith New Court, was induced to buy shares in a company by the fraudulent misrepresentations of one of Scrimgeour's executive directors. The purchase price was just over 82 pence per share, but the market price of the shares on the acquisition date was 78 pence per share. Usually the measure of damages would be the difference between these two sums. The company in question was, however, subject to a substantial but entirely unrelated fraud, unknown to either the claimant or defendant, which occurred before Smith New Court's purchase. When this fraud became known the company's share price dropped considerably, so that Smith New Court was only able to sell its shares in the company for between 30 and 40 pence over a period of time. The House of Lords held that in these circumstances Scrimgeour was liable for *all* damage directly caused by the deceit. Although the normal measure of damages is the difference between the purchase price and the market price at the date of purchase, this rule should not be rigidly applied if it would do an injustice. Here it was more accurate to assess the true value as comprising only the proceeds received for the shares. It is unsurprising that distortions in the market price caused by the defendant should be taken into account by the court, as fraudulent defendants should not profit from their own wrongdoing. In some situations distortions caused by unrelated third-party frauds or other extraneous unanticipated events, such as a sudden downturn in the market,[258] will, therefore, be regarded as a risk that is borne by the fraudulent defendant.[259]

Of the possible claims available to investors that are discussed in this section, it is unsurprising that the fraudulent misrepresentation test of remoteness is applied to deceit claims, and that the negligence test of remoteness is applied to claims under *Hedley Byrne*. As regards claims under the Misrepresentation Act 1967, there is some disagreement as to whether the remoteness test should be that applied to the tort of deceit or that applied to negligence claims. The Court of Appeal in *Royscot Trust Ltd v Rogerson*[260] felt that the appropriate measure was the deceit test, but this was doubted by the House of Lords in *Smith New Court Securities Ltd v Scrimgeour Vickers (Asset Management) Ltd.*[261]

As regards claims under section 90 FSMA, the statute is silent as to the correct remoteness test to be applied. The fact that the deceit rules have been applied to the statutory liability regime in the past to determine the measure of damages[262] might suggest that it is the remoteness rules for deceit that should be applied, ie that the claimant can recover all actual losses flowing directly from the transaction, potentially including losses caused

---

[257] [1997] AC 254.

[258] See eg *Slough Estates Ltd v Welwyn-Hatfield DC* [1996] 2 PLR 50.

[259] See *Parabola Investments Ltd v Browallia Cal Ltd* [2010] EWCA Civ 486. The claimant remains under a duty to mitigate his loss, as far as it is reasonable to expect him to do so: *Smith New Court Securities Ltd v Scrimgeour Vickers (Asset Management) Ltd* [1997] AC 254, 266.

[260] [1991] 2 QB 297.

[261] [1997] AC 254.

[262] Eg *Clark v Urquhart* [1930] AC 28, and see P Davies, *Liability for Misstatements to the Market: A Discussion Paper* (HM Treasury, March 2007), para 107.

by the independent fraud of a third party. Given that the current statutory provision is a negligence-based standard, however, it is possible that a court might depart from this approach and apply the negligence test.[263]

10.6.2.4.2 Rescission

No remedy for rescission is available under section 90 FSMA. In this respect, then, the common law rules are potentially more powerful than a claim under section 90 FSMA. In particular, claimants who enter contracts as a result of a misrepresentation may be able to rescind those contracts. This is the case whether the misrepresentation is fraudulent, negligent or innocent.

Rescission involves a reversal of the contract, so that the claimant hands back the shares and the company hands back the purchase price.[264] This right is exercisable against the contracting party,[265] ie the company, if the contract for the purchase is with the company (as it will be in, for example, an offer for subscription or rights issue of some kind), or against the investment bank acting on behalf of the company (where it is an offer for sale), or against the transferor if the acquisition is from the previous holder of the shares. It will be necessary to demonstrate that the misrepresentation was made by the transferor. Where the transferor was the company, statements included in the prospectus, even if made by experts rather than the company directors, will generally be held to have been made by the company for this purpose.[266]

Two barriers stand in the way of a successful rescission claim. First, the court has discretion to substitute damages for the remedy of rescission in appropriate cases.[267] The court may decide that damages are more appropriate where it believes that the rescission claim is motivated by subsequent adverse movements in the stock market, rather than by the misrepresentation made by the defendant.

Second, there are a number of important limitations on the right to rescind. If the investor does anything that can be interpreted as an affirmation of the contract then the right of rescission will be lost. For a shareholder this might involve accepting dividends,[268] attending shareholder meetings,[269] or attempting to sell the securities after the truth has been discovered.[270] In addition, if the investor delays too long, then the contract will be taken to have been affirmed, and the right to rescind lost. The case law suggests that the investor must act promptly after the discovery of the misrepresentation or risk losing the right to rescind.[271] As might be expected, the liquidation of the company will also defeat a rescission claim, since at that point the interests of the company's creditors will intervene. Likewise, the fact that the company is insolvent will bar rescission, even if winding up has

---

[263] See J Cartwright, *Misrepresentation, Mistake and Non-Disclosure*, 3rd edn (London, Sweet & Maxwell, 2012) para 7.52.

[264] *Re Scottish Petroleum Co* (1883) 23 Ch D 413. The investor may also recover interest: *Karberg's Case* [1892] 3 Ch D 1.

[265] *Collins v Associated Greyhound Racecourse Ltd* [1930] 1 Ch 1.

[266] *Mair v Rio Grande Rubber Estates Ltd* [1913] AC 853.

[267] Misrepresentation Act 1967, s 2(2).

[268] *Scholey v Central Railway of Venezuela* (1868) LR 9 Eq 266n.

[269] *Sharpley v Louth and East Central Coast Railway Co* (1876) 2 Ch D 663.

[270] *Ex p Briggs* (1866) LR 1 Eq 483.

[271] Eg *Sharpley v Louth and East Coast Railway Co* (1876) 2 Ch D 663.

not yet commenced.[272] In addition, rescission will be barred where *restitutio in integrum* is not possible, such as where the shareholder has disposed of the securities before discovering the misrepresentation,[273] or if the investor has used the securities as security for its own borrowings, or a third party has otherwise acquired an interest in them, at least until that third-party interest has been unwound.

Although rescission appears to be a powerful remedy for investors, these difficulties mean that it has limited practical significance, and there is little evidence that this remedy is used much in practice.

10.6.2.5 Summary

On the whole, then, the statutory liability regime is more powerful than the other potential claims available to investors. It also seems to be more likely to fulfil the aims of a liability regime. Section 90 FSMA targets the makers of the statements and therefore has the potential to have a deterrent effect. It also, potentially, provides a generous level of compensation for investors. In addition, section 90 FSMA adopts a broad definition of 'investor', by allowing all acquirers the possibility of bringing an action, whether they are initial subscribers or purchasers in the after-market, although this is subject to a causation test, as described above.

10.6.3 Public Enforcement

In addition to the private enforcement mechanisms discussed in 10.6.2, there are criminal and administrative sanctions by way of public enforcement actions.

10.6.3.1 Criminal Sanctions

Under section 85 FSMA it is unlawful to make a public offer for securities or to request admission of securities to a regulated market unless an approved prospectus has been made publicly available.[274] On indictment the maximum penalty is a prison term of not more than two years or a fine or both.[275] The FCA has the power to invoke this provision.[276] In addition there are a number of other criminal offences, not specifically targeted at prospectuses, that might be utilised in this context. For example, the provisions in sections 89–90 of the Financial Services Act 2012, which provide criminal sanctions for market manipulation,

---

[272] *Tennent v City of Glasgow Bank* (1879) 4 App Cas 615. The investor must therefore have issued a writ or have had their name removed from the register before the company's insolvency or liquidation: *Oakes v Turquand* (1867) LR 2 HL 325.

[273] If the shareholder has disposed of only part of the shares it seems reasonable in principle that rescission should still be possible since the investor can go back into the market to buy substitute shares: see *Re Mount Morgan (West) Gold Mines Ltd* (1887) 3 TLR 556 and *Smith New Court Securities Ltd v Scrimgeour Vickers (Asset Management) Ltd* [1997] AC 254, 262 per Lord Browne-Wilkinson in support of this view, but cf *Re Metropolitan Coal Consumers' Association Ltd* (1890) 6 TLR 416.

[274] FSMA, s 85. See the exemptions from liability listed in s 86.

[275] Ibid, s 85(3).

[276] Ibid, s 401.

might be relevant where the prospectus contains false information, promises or forecasts, or conceals material facts.[277]

10.6.3.2 Administrative Sanctions

The primary sanctions in this area are the administrative sanctions operated by the FCA. The FCA has a number of sanctions that it can use prior to the allotment of the securities.[278] It has the power to refuse to approve a prospectus, thereby preventing the public offer or the admission to a regulated market from proceeding.[279] Alternatively, if approval has been given and the offer launched, or the admission process begun, the FCA has power to suspend further action for up to 10 days if it suspects that a provision of Part VI of FSMA, or a provision in the Prospectus Rules, or any other provision required by the Prospectus Directive, has been infringed. If it finds that such a provision has been infringed, it may require that the offer be withdrawn or that the market operator be prohibited from trading in the securities.[280] The FCA must give reasons for any suspension or prohibition decision in writing, and the applicant has the right to appeal.[281] Alternatively, the FCA can publicly censure the issuer or other person offering the securities or seeking admission for failure to comply with these requirements.[282] These are potentially very powerful weapons in the FCA's armoury for ensuring compliance with the relevant rules. The value of these sanctions is limited to breaches of the rules which the FCA picks up in advance of the offer to the public, or admission to trading. As regards misstatements in the prospectus, the review carried out by the FCA in advance of publication is very light touch and is not likely to reveal any but the most glaring inaccuracies. It is also notable that these sanctions fall predominantly on the company rather than its officers, who are likely to be the ones responsible for the misstatement or non-compliance. For these reasons the potential deterrent effect of these measures is diminished.

The FCA does, however, have the power to impose monetary penalties on the issuer or on any other person offering shares to the public, seeking approval for a prospectus or requesting their admission to trading on a regulated market.[283] This power extends to any person who was a director of a company where the director was 'knowingly concerned' in the contravention.[284] The amount of the penalty will be such amount as the FCA considers appropriate.[285] In addition, the FCA has the power to publicly censure the issuer or any other person offering securities or seeking admission in lieu of imposing a penalty.[286]

---

[277] For discussion see 12.2.2.2.

[278] It is possible for the FCA to make use of these sanctions once an admission to trading has been secured, but it is unlikely that the FCA will wish to exercise its power to prohibit trading at this point.

[279] FSMA, s 87D. This section sets out the procedure the FCA must follow if it proposes to refuse to approve a prospectus. More likely the FCA will require the inaccurate information to be corrected and will refuse permission only if that is not forthcoming (s 87J).

[280] Ibid, ss 87K and 87L.

[281] Ibid, s 87N.

[282] Ibid, s 87M. This is subject to the right to appeal to the Upper Tribunal: s 87N.

[283] Ibid, s 91(1A).

[284] Ibid, s 91(2).

[285] Ibid, s 91(1A).

[286] Ibid, s 91(3).

A proposal to impose a penalty must be communicated to the person by way of a warning notice, and a decision to impose a penalty may be appealed.[287]

10.6.4 Intensity of Enforcement

It is not just the law on the books that is significant. The enforcement of those laws is also an important consideration. There is some international and comparative research which associates the presence of deep and liquid securities markets with the presence in those jurisdictions of a vigorous system of private enforcement of obligations under securities law.[288] Other research has suggested that measures of public enforcement are more strongly associated with robust financial markets.[289] It has been suggested that enforcement intensity matters.[290]

10.6.4.1 Public Enforcement

A number of studies have considered the level of enforcement of securities law across a number of jurisdictions.[291] When these studies considered the 'outputs' of enforcement, ie the actions brought and the sanctions imposed, the UK did not fare well. In particular, the number of public enforcement actions brought by the FCA's predecessor, the FSA, was found to be a fraction of that brought by the US regulator, and even when those numbers are adjusted to reflect relative market size, the FSA was found to have brought only 60 per cent of the actions brought by the SEC.[292] The SEC was also found to have a track record of imposing criminal penalties (fines and imprisonment)[293] far in excess of those imposed by the FSA. A number of explanations have been put forward for this disparity. One suggestion is that the FSA committed fewer resources to enforcement action. One study found a significant difference between the percentage of the FSA's and SEC's budgets that was spent on enforcement activity.[294] The SEC devoted a percentage of its budget to enforcement that

---

[287] Ibid, s 92(7).

[288] R La Porta, F Lopez-de-Silanes and A Shleifer, 'What Works in Securities Laws?' (2006) 61 *Journal of Finance* 1.

[289] HE Jackson and MJ Roe, 'Public and Private Enforcement of Securities Laws: Resource-Based Evidence' (2009) 87 *Journal of Financial Economics* 207.

[290] JC Coffee, 'Law and the Market: The Impact of Enforcement' (2007) 156 *University of Pennsylvania Law Review* 229.

[291] See eg HE Jackson, 'Variation in the Intensity of Financial Regulation: Preliminary Evidence and Potential Implications' (2007) 24 *Yale Journal on Regulation* 253; JC Coffee, 'Law and the Market: The Impact of Enforcement' (2007) 156 *University of Pennsylvania Law Review* 229.

[292] Jackson, ibid, 284 (figure 10). The picture was even starker when the aggregate monetary sanctions were compared. Over a two-year period public securities enforcement monetary sanctions imposed by the US exceeded those imposed in the UK, even after adjusting for relative market size, by more than a 10 to 1 margin: Jackson, figure 11; JC Coffee, 'Law and the Market: The Impact of Enforcement' (2007) 156 *University of Pennsylvania Law Review* 229, 262. The two-year period in question was 2000–02.

[293] HE Jackson, 'Variation in the Intensity of Financial Regulation: Preliminary Evidence and Potential Implications' (2007) 24 *Yale Journal on Regulation* 253, 274–76. Criminal enforcement is carried out by the Department of Justice or the state criminal law enforcement authority.

[294] It is sometimes suggested that the US may expend more on enforcement than the UK because its corporate law gives shareholders fewer control rights than exist in the UK, so that enforcement in the US might to some extent be a substitute for weaker corporate governance.

was roughly three times that devoted by the FSA.[295] An alternative explanation put forward for these different levels of enforcement is the different regulatory styles adopted by the SEC and FSA.[296]

Since these studies were carried out, significant changes have taken place in the UK regulatory arena. As a result of the financial crisis, there has been a complete reorganisation of UK banking and securities regulation.[297] For the purposes of the material discussed in this book, the FSA has been replaced by the FCA. The FCA clearly recognises the importance of enforcement, stating that it intends to 'follow a strategy of credible deterrence, taking tough and meaningful action against the firms and individuals who break our rules'.[298] It is too early to say whether this approach will translate into higher levels of enforcement in this context.

10.6.4.2 Private Enforcement

The differentiation between levels of enforcement in the US and the UK discussed in 10.6.4.1 above continues when private enforcement is considered. Private enforcement of securities law violations is frequent in the US,[299] and it is estimated that private enforcement in the US imposes even greater financial penalties than public enforcement.[300] By contrast, in the UK the number of instances of private rights of action being brought in relation to misleading statements or omissions in disclosures since 1990 is negligible,[301] and there is no reported case of an investor succeeding in bringing a claim under section 90 FSMA or its predecessor.[302] There are a number of important differences between the two litigation systems that might help to explain this disparity. These include the absence of class actions in the UK,[303]

---

[295] JC Coffee, 'Law and the Market: The Impact of Enforcement' (2007) 156 *University of Pennsylvania Law Review* 229, 278–79.

[296] See J Armour, 'Enforcement Strategies in UK Corporate Governance: A Roadmap and Empirical Assessment' in J Armour and J Payne (eds), *Rationality in Company Law: Essays in Honour of DD Prentice* (Oxford, Hart Publishing, 2009) 85 who argues that, in contrast to the approach of the SEC, which seems to focus on ex post enforcement to a significant extent, the UK regulator's approach has been more ex ante, ie it appears to have opted for a more advisory and consultative relationship with issuers.

[297] See Financial Services Act 2012.

[298] FCA, *The FCA's Approach to Advancing its Objectives*, July 2013, 19.

[299] J Armour, B Black, BR Cheffins and R Nolan, 'Private Enforcement of Corporate Law: An Empirical Comparison of the US and UK' (2009) 6 *Journal of Empirical Legal Studies* 687.

[300] HE Jackson, 'Variation in the Intensity of Financial Regulation: Preliminary Evidence and Potential Implications' (2007) 24 *Yale Journal on Regulation* 253, 280 (table 3).

[301] J Armour, 'Enforcement Strategies in UK Company Law: A Roadmap and Empirical Assessment' in J Armour and J Payne (eds), *Rationality in Company Law: Essays in Honour of DD Prentice* (Oxford, Hart Publishing, 2009) 85.

[302] It is worth noting that a number of studies in the US suggest dissatisfaction with the system of private litigation in the US, one of the major criticisms being that levels of private enforcement in this context are too high: JC Coffee, 'Reforming the Securities Class Action: An Essay on Deterrence and its Implementation' (2006) 106 *Columbia Law Review* 1534.

[303] There have been calls for a reform of the UK collective action regimes—see eg Civil Justice Council, *Improving Access to Justice through Collective Actions*, December 2008. This has not resulted in any material change to date. This is an area in which the European Commission is becoming interested: European Commission, Commission Recommendation of 11 June 2013 on common principles for injunctive and compensatory collective redress mechanisms in the Member States concerning violations of rights granted under Union law (2013/396/EU).

and the fact that the UK operates a 'loser pays' rule.[304] Until 2013 there was also an absence of contingent fees for this type of claim in the UK.[305]

Things might be starting to change, however. From 2013, conditional fee arrangements may be used to fund claims in this area in the UK.[306] 2013 also saw the commencement of the first ever collective action under section 90 FSMA against a bank (RBS) and a number of its former directors in respect of alleged untrue misleading statements in and omissions from RBS's April 2008 £12 billion rights issue, which took place shortly before the bank imploded. The claimants allege that they suffered loss as a result of untrue and misleading statements in the prospectus, and that under section 90 FSMA RBS is liable to pay compensation to each of the claimants for its losses, amounting to the difference between the price paid for the shares and their actual value. A group litigation order has been made and claimants must opt in to this litigation.[307] Many thousands of investors are likely to be involved. This case arguably constitutes a watershed for collective shareholder actions against companies and directors in the UK, but much will turn on how the court manages the group action.

10.7 Regulation of Equity Crowdfunding

Equity crowdfunding is a relatively new phenomenon that allows unlisted companies to seek equity investment from members of the public. The operation of this form of crowdfunding is discussed at 2.2.2, and broadly involves companies, usually SMEs, seeking investors via a crowdfunding platform (generally a website).[308] Investors can invest small amounts (as little as £10 on some platforms) in order to acquire shares in these companies, often as direct shareholders, but sometimes via the crowdfunding platform holding these shares for them as nominee. Given the discussion so far in this chapter regarding the need for the law to intervene and provide investor protection when companies seek to issue shares to the public, it is unsurprising that the FCA has turned its attention to this issue[309] and

---

[304] It has also been suggested that the fact that in the UK it is relatively easy for a defendant to have the claim against it struck out at an early stage of the litigation has helped to impair the development of speculative litigation that is observed in the US; see eg HM Treasury, *Davies Review of Issuer Liability: Liability for Misstatements to the Market—A Discussion Paper* (March 2007), para 113.

[305] Since 1990 conditional fee arrangements have been permitted, which allowed lawyers to agree to no payment if the case is unsuccessful and an increase in their normal fee (but, crucially, not a share of the recoveries) if the case is successful (see now Conditional Fee Agreements Order 2013 (SI 2013/689)).

[306] From 2013 lawyers can agree not to be paid if they lose a case, but may take a percentage of the damages recovered for their client as their fee if the case is successful, ie damages-based agreements (see Damages-Based Agreements Regulation 2013 (SI 2013/609)). In claims of this kind the maximum payment that the lawyer can recover from the claimant's damages is capped at 50%.

[307] [2014] EWHC 227 (Ch).

[308] The average amount raised through equity-based crowdfunding is £199,095: FCA, *A Review of the Regulatory Regime for Crowdfunding and the Promotion of Non-Readily Realisable Securities by Other Media*, February 2015, 5.

[309] For discussion see FCA, *The FCA's Regulatory Approach to Crowdfunding (and similar activities)*, Consultation Paper CP 13/13; FCA, *The FCA's Regulatory Approach to Crowdfunding over the Internet, and the Promotion of Non-Readily Realisable Securities by Other Media*, Policy statement, PS 14/4; FCA, *A Review of the Regulatory Regime for Crowdfunding and the Promotion of Non-Readily Realisable Securities by Other Media*, February 2015.

regulations have been put in place.[310] In particular there are a number of risks presented by this model. Some of these are the same as the risks faced by investors in a traditional IPO; in particular there may be little information available regarding the business or its plans, and there is an asymmetry problem regarding the information provided, particularly in relation to retail investors, so that the securities offered via the crowdfunding platform may be hard to value.[311] There are also some additional difficulties that investors in an IPO do not face; for instance, this is an investment in an unlisted company and it is therefore illiquid. There is, at present, no real secondary market for equity crowdfunding investments (although this may be starting to change) and therefore no exit option for investors, unless the business is successful and is subsequently sold. In this way, the investment is more akin to a venture capital or private equity investment in a private company than to a purchase of shares in a company that will be publicly traded.[312] These investments are also unlike a typical IPO, in that many of the companies involved tend to be small start-up businesses. Given the high probability that such businesses will fail, they therefore represent a high-risk investment for investors.[313] There is a significant possibility that investors will lose some or all of their capital.

Some regulation was in place already—specifically, the financial activities of equity crowdfunding platforms are covered by FSMA and are subject to FCA regulation. Investment-based platforms are likely to be considered as carrying on several regulated activities, including arranging deals in investments as well as placing activities.[314] Following a review of this area,[315] in 2014 the FCA introduced two new measures designed to increase investor protection in relation to equity crowdfunding.[316]

First, the FCA imposed restrictions on those who are able to invest in the shares offered by unlisted companies via crowdfunding platforms.[317] Firms are able to offer these securities either to professional investors or to retail investors that fall within certain categories. In particular, firms can only send direct offer promotions for unlisted equity to the following: (i) retail clients who are certified or self-certify as sophisticated investors; (ii) retail

---

[310] For a discussion of the regulation of debt crowdfunding (generally referred to as peer-to-peer lending) see 13.8.

[311] See GKC Ahlers, DJ Cumming, C Guenther and D Schweizer, 'Signaling in Equity Crowdfunding', http://ssrn.com/abstract=2362340 for a discussion of the disclosure and signals that entrepreneurs use to induce (small) investors to commit financial resources in equity crowdfunding.

[312] For discussion of private equity as an investment model see chapter 16. As discussed there, retail investors do not invest directly into private equity funds, due to high minimum levels of investment and regulatory constraints (see 16.3.2).

[313] See FCA, *The FCA's Regulatory Approach to Crowdfunding (and similar activities)*, Consultation Paper CP 13/13, ch 4; ESMA, *Opinion: Investment Based Crowdfunding*, ESMA/2014/1378, 18 December 2014.

[314] FSMA, s 19 and Financial Services and Markets Act 2000 (Regulated Activities) Order 2001, arts 25(1), (2). As at February 2015, 14 firms were authorised to conduct this business and a further 10 firms had applications pending: FCA, *A Review of the Regulatory Regime for Crowdfunding and the Promotion of Non-Readily Realisable Securities by Other Media*, February 2015, 6 (this document also includes useful information on the sort of information the FCA considers important in assessing such applications for authorisation, at 6–7).

[315] FCA, *The FCA's Regulatory Approach to Crowdfunding (and similar activities)*, Consultation Paper CP 13/13.

[316] These new provisions apply to any firm that promotes and sells unlisted securities, not just electronic funding platforms.

[317] For the avoidance of doubt the FCA has clarified that these restrictions do not apply where a security is admitted or about to be admitted to an official listing, or where it is traded or soon to be traded on a recognised investment exchange or designated investment exchange. See eg FCA, *The FCA's Regulatory Approach to Crowdfunding over the Internet, and the Promotion of Non-Readily Realisable Securities by Other Media*, Policy statement, PS 14/4, 37.

clients who are certified as high net worth investors; (iii) retail clients who confirm before a promotion is made that, in relation to the investment promoted, they will receive regulated investment advice or investment management services from an authorised person; and (iv) retail clients who certify that they will not invest more than 10 per cent of their net investable portfolio in unlisted shares or unlisted debt securities (ie excluding their primary residence, pensions and life cover).[318] A survey in 2014 found that 38 per cent of equity crowdfunding investors were classified as professional or high net worth individuals, whereas 62 per cent described themselves as retail investors with no previous investment experience of early-stage or venture capital investment. The amounts invested remain small at present. The average portfolio size for high net worth and sophisticated investors is over £8,000, whereas for other retail investors it is less than £4,000.[319]

Second, firms need to ensure that the rules on appropriateness[320] are complied with before they arrange or deal in relation to the investment. Consequently, where no advice is provided, all firms must check that clients have the knowledge and experience needed to understand the risks involved before being invited to respond to an offer. This is intended to ensure that clients are assessed as having the knowledge or experience necessary to understand the risks involved before they can invest.[321]

Firms were required to begin complying with these new rules from 1 October 2014. The rules are relatively light touch compared to the regulation in place to deal with IPOs, examined in this chapter.[322] In particular, there is no equivalent to the mandatory disclosure regime that exists where companies engage in an IPO. Following a review of the regime in February 2015 the FCA stated that it had no plans to increase regulation in this area.[323] However, this is an area which has come under review by ESMA, and so there may be future regulation of this issue at EU level.[324]

10.8 Conclusion

UK capital markets regulation rests predominantly on two principles. The first is that members of the public who are offered company securities are entitled to full disclosure of the nature of what is on offer before they make a financial commitment. The second is that effective remedies should be available to redress any loss incurred as a result of failure on the part of the company to make complete or accurate disclosure.

The principle of mandatory disclosure is central to the regulatory regime regarding IPOs in the UK. Companies listing on the London Main Market have to comply with significant

---

[318] FCA Handbook, COBS 4.4.7–4.4.10.

[319] See Z Zhang, L Collins and P Baeck, *Understanding Alternative Finance: The UK Alternative Finance Industry Report 2014*, www.nesta.org.uk/sites/default/files/understanding-alternative-finance-2014.pdf.

[320] See FCA Handbook, COBS 10.

[321] Ibid, COBS 4.4.7(3).

[322] For discussion of the regulation of this issue in the US see C Steven Bradford, 'Crowdfunding and the Federal Securities Laws' [2012] *Columbia Business Law Review* 1; MB Dorff, 'The Siren Call of Equity Crowdfunding' (2013–14) 39 *Journal of Corporation Law* 493.

[323] FCA, *A Review of the Regulatory Regime for Crowdfunding and the Promotion of Non-Readily Realisable Securities by Other Media*, February 2015, 6.

[324] ESMA, Opinion: Investment Based Crowdfunding, ESMA/2014/1378, 18 December 2014.

levels of information disclosure, the content of which mainly flows from EU legislation. The vast majority of this information is backward-looking, namely historical data relating to the company, its directors, its shareholders, its advisers and its business to date. Forward-looking data carries with it the risk that directors might be over optimistic about the company's prospects, and the provision of historical data is cheaper to produce, easier to compare across companies, and easier to verify. The nature of this information provided to investors, however, necessarily limits the value of information disclosure as a device for assessing the future value of the securities on offer in an IPO.

The use of mandatory disclosure is also coupled with provisions to allow enforcement actions to be brought in the event that the information disclosed is inaccurate or incomplete. These are an important adjunct to the mandatory disclosure rules, since the value of the mandatory disclosure regime is diminished if there is no reasonable prospect that the information actually provided is full and accurate. In the context of IPOs the UK provides relatively minimal ex ante verification processes, but there is a range of ex post measures available which allows for both private and public enforcement of misstatements in prospectuses. In terms of the law on the books, the ex post enforcement measures on offer are substantive and potentially provide both compensation to the investors who have suffered loss as a result of the misstatement, and a deterrent for directors and others who may make misstatements in prospectuses in the future. Although the levels of both public and private enforcement in practice are low in the UK, this is not an issue that need necessarily be of concern. Perhaps most reassuring is the fact that despite the low levels of enforcement it is generally felt that the level of accuracy in UK securities prospectuses remains high.

In the next chapters the continuing obligations of issuers, once their shares have been listed, is discussed. In chapter thirteen these issues are examined in the context of debt securities. Although there are many similarities in the way in which the issue of debt and equity securities are regulated, particularly where debt securities are offered to the public, there are also a number of significant and important differences that require separate analysis.

11

Ongoing Regulation of the Capital Markets: Mandatory Disclosure

11.1 Introduction

In chapter ten the regulation of the primary market was analysed, whereby companies offer their shares to the public for the first time. This chapter and the next consider the distinct, but allied, topic of the regulation of the secondary market, whereby securities that have previously been issued can be resold. In the secondary market the person selling the security receives the funds; the issuer receives no new funds in this transaction. The secondary market serves two important functions for issuers, however. First, it makes it easier and quicker for the investor to sell the security for cash—that is, it makes the securities more liquid, and thus more valuable and easier for the issuer to sell in the primary market. Second, investors who buy in the primary market will not want to pay more than they think the secondary market will set for those securities in the immediate post-issue period. It is common for issuers to seek to provide a secondary market for their securities by simultaneously offering the securities to the public and applying to have the securities listed or traded on an exchange.

Broadly, two mechanisms are put in place to regulate the secondary market: a set of mandatory disclosure rules, and rules that are designed to prevent misconduct in the market, such as market abuse and short selling regulations. This chapter deals with the disclosure requirements in the secondary market that are imposed on issuers;[1] the rules regarding market misconduct are considered in chapter twelve.

In order to understand and evaluate the mandatory disclosure obligations imposed in the secondary market, the aims of these rules must first be understood. Section 11.2 considers the objectives of regulation. In 11.3 the content of the rules is examined and assessed in light of these regulatory aims. In 11.4 the ex post enforcement regime that accompanies these ex ante rules is considered. This chapter deals with the regulation of equity securities. Some of the issues raised here are also relevant to debt securities, but the extent of this overlap, and the regulation of debt securities more generally, are discussed in chapter thirteen.[2]

---

[1] In addition, a set of transparency obligations is imposed on trading venues as regards both pre-trade and post-trade transparency for equity and equity-like instruments. Discussion of this topic falls outside the scope of this chapter. See Moloney: EU Regulation, V.11.1.

[2] See 13.3.

11.2 Objectives of Regulating the Secondary Market

The main goal of regulating the secondary market is to ensure that the prices of publicly traded securities are reasonably well informed. A second objective, however, is to ensure that shareholders are protected by effective corporate governance institutions once they invest in publicly traded shares. This latter goal only really comes to the fore once the IPO has taken place.

11.2.1 Promoting an Efficient Market Price

Mandatory disclosure is used at the IPO stage in order to tackle the informational asymmetry that arises between insiders and outside investors, and to provide investors with the information they need to decide whether to purchase the securities offered by the issuer.[3] Mandatory disclosure at this point operates to modify the principle of caveat emptor (buyer beware). Once the securities have been admitted to listing or to trading, a secondary market for those securities develops. Investors are not purchasing shares from the issuer, but from other investors. There may still be informational asymmetries here—for example, investors with inside information about the issuer will know more than uninformed investors in the market.[4] The goal of regulation in the secondary market is not, however, investor protection per se; rather the focus is on maximising the informational efficiency of the market. The reason for the difference between the role of mandatory disclosure in the primary and secondary markets can be explained by considering the Efficient Capital Markets Hypothesis (ECMH).

11.2.1.1 Efficient Capital Markets Hypothesis

The ECMH is based on the idea that prices within the market at any given time 'fully reflect' available information.[5] Three different forms of efficiency have been identified: weak form efficiency, semi-strong form efficiency, and strong form efficiency.[6] In a weak form market the current prices of securities reflect all relevant historical information. In a semi-strong form efficient capital market the prices adjust rapidly to information as it becomes available. In a strong form efficient capital market the prices reflect all relevant information, including information not yet made public. There is significant support for the view that securities markets in major jurisdictions, including the US and UK, are efficient in both the

---

[3] See 10.4.1.

[4] For a discussion of the regulation of insider dealing see 12.2.

[5] EF Fama, 'Efficient Capital Markets: A Review of Theory and Empirical Work' (1970) 25 *Journal of Finance* 383. A distinction can be drawn between informational efficiency, which simply means that the price reflects information about the securities, and price accuracy or fundamental efficiency, which suggests that the price reflects the actual value of the underlying assets. For a discussion of what market efficiency means, and an assessment of ECMH after the global financial crisis, see R Gilson and R Kraakman, 'Market Efficiency After the Fall: Where Do We Stand after the Financial Crisis?' in C Hill and B McDonnell (eds), *Research Handbook on the Economics of Corporate Law* (Cheltenham, Edward Elgar, 2012).

[6] EF Fama, 'Efficient Capital Markets: A Review of Theory and Empirical Work' (1970) 25 *Journal of Finance* 383.

weak form and semi-strong form, with the semi-strong version being most favoured.[7] The major difficulty with the strong form hypothesis is the fact that profits can still be made by insider trading. The fact that insiders can make profits from information that is known to them, but which is not yet public, suggests that the market price does not reflect that non-public information, and markets are thus not strong form efficient.

Once the semi-strong form of market efficiency is accepted, this suggests that the more information that can be made available to the public, the better. Requiring issuers to produce information about themselves and their securities promotes informational efficiency, since that information, once publicly available, will help to move the prices of the securities to a new equilibrium which reflects that new information. One important consequence of this model is that investors do not need to read and digest the information in order to benefit from the disclosure. Instead, the analysis function is performed largely by securities analysts and other market professionals, such as arbitrageurs, researchers, brokers and other information traders, who spend their time acquiring and evaluating information regarding issuers and their securities.[8] The trading by these professionals moves the market price, and thereby allows the information to be assimilated into the price.[9] To the extent that the information disclosure provides investor protection, it is an indirect form of protection, mediated through the ECMH.

A deficiency of information is seen as reducing allocative efficiency.[10] Accurate information is necessary to ensure that money moves to those who can use it most effectively and that investors make optimal choices about their investment decisions. Without adequate information, investors will not be able to distinguish the 'good' investments from the 'bad' investments, and since those offering the 'better' securities will not be able to distinguish themselves, investors will view all securities as average. Therefore, higher quality securities will sell at lower prices than they would if the information were available, there will be too little investment in the good businesses, and the low quality businesses, the 'lemons', will attract too much money.[11] Investors lose because they invest in the wrong securities, and issuers lose because the high-quality shares are undervalued, and there is the possibility that investors may, in the long run, not invest at all in such a market. The disclosure of

---

[7] EF Fama, 'Efficient Capital Markets: II' (1991) 46(5) *Journal of Finance* 1575. However, some empirical studies also identify market phenomena that are inconsistent with the ECMH (for a summary see JW Brudney and WW Bratton, *Corporate Finance: Cases and Materials*, 7th edn (New York, Westbury, 2012)).

[8] RJ Gilson and RH Kraakman, 'The Mechanisms of Market Efficiency' (1984) 70 *Virginia Law Review* 549. For a discussion of the role of information traders, and a comparison with noise traders (those who make decisions without the use of fundamental data) and inside traders, see Z Goshen and G Parchomovsky, 'The Essential Role of Securities Regulation' (2006) 55 *Duke Law Journal* 711.

[9] Empirical studies demonstrate that the prices of securities have become more informative in the last few decades, in the US at least, as individual share price movements have become increasingly decoupled from overall market movements, suggesting that firm-specific factors have become more influential: R Morck et al, 'The Information Content of Stock Markets: Why Do Emerging Markets Have Synchronous Stock Price Movements?' (2000) 58 *Journal of Financial Economics* 215. This has coincided with a significant increase in the amount of disclosure made by issuers. For discussion see J Gordon, 'The Rise of Independent Directors in the United States 1950–2005: Of Shareholder Value and Stock Market Prices' (2007) 58 *Stanford Law Review* 1465, 1541–45.

[10] RJ Gilson and RH Kraakman, 'The Mechanisms of Market Efficiency' (1984) 70 *Virginia Law Review* 549.

[11] G Ackerlof, 'The Market for "Lemons": Qualitative Uncertainty and the Market Mechanism' (1970) 84 *Quarterly Journal of Economics* 488.

information about the companies concerned is a way of dealing with these issues.[12] An informed securities market enhances not only the value of high quality companies, but also the value of the marketable securities of publicly traded companies in aggregate.[13]

It is widely accepted that the efficiency of the price formation process in a securities market depends in large part on the mechanisms whereby information is produced, verified and analysed.[14] Analysis is a process that is largely left to market participants, but most jurisdictions put measures in place to regulate the production and verification of the information. It is these measures that are discussed in this chapter; however, given that much of the analysis on which individual investors actually rely is performed by intermediaries on their behalf, an additional, or alternative, form of investor protection is to regulate the intermediaries who channel the information to the investors.[15]

The ECMH, on which this theory of regulation is based, has, however, come under attack.[16] In particular, the hypothesis has come under threat following the advent of behavioural analysis.[17] The work of behavioural analysts causes difficulties for the ECMH because the hypothesis does not capture socio-psychological factors, such as herding, which may lead investors to engage in irrational trading activities that affect the prices of securities. Behavioural finance shifts attention from the analysis of the relationship between prices and information to investor behaviour, using the findings of behavioural psychologists about individuals' departures from rational decision-making. In particular, very large market changes and excessive volatility (booms and busts) are attributed to 'irrational' investors who over-react to a given flow of information.[18] Proponents of the ECMH find these bubbles particularly difficult to explain. Where irrational behaviour in the market is inconsistent, it can be expected that some investors' biases or irrational behaviour will cancel out that of others. A bubble results, however, from investors all operating according to a single or common bias.[19]

---

[12] The primary value associated with disclosure is, therefore, that of ensuring accurate share values. However, some academics also associate disclosure with other important corporate benefits: R Kraakman, 'Disclosure and Corporate Governance: An Overview Essay' in G Ferrarini et al (eds), *Reforming Company and Takeover Law in Europe* (Oxford, Oxford University Press, 2004). See 11.2.2.

[13] See RJ Gilson and RH Kraakman, 'The Mechanisms of Market Efficiency' (1984) 70 *Virginia Law Review* 549 on the role of mandatory disclosure in economising on investor information costs.

[14] RJ Gilson and RH Kraakman, 'The Mechanisms of Market Efficiency: Twenty Years Later. The Hindsight Bias' (2003) 28 *Journal of Corporation Law* 715. This proposition remains robust despite developments in behavioural science: for discussion see E Avgouleas, *The Mechanics and Regulation of Market Abuse: A Legal and Economic Analysis* (Oxford, Oxford University Press, 2005) ch 2.

[15] See 11.5 for a discussion of the regulation of analysts and 13.7 for a discussion of the regulation of credit rating agencies. For a more general discussion of the role of such intermediaries, and their regulation, see J Payne, 'The Role of Gatekeepers' in N Moloney, E Ferran and J Payne (eds), *The Oxford Handbook of Financial Regulation* (Oxford, Oxford University Press, 2015).

[16] For an overview of the literature see E Avgouleas, *The Mechanics and Regulation of Market Abuse: A Legal and Economic Analysis* (Oxford, Oxford University Press, 2005) 44–74.

[17] Eg A Shleifer, *Inefficient Markets: An Introduction to Behavioural Finance* (Oxford, Clarendon Press, 2000); GA Akerlof and RJ Shiller, *Animal Spirits: How Human Psychology Drives the Economy and Why it Matters for Global Capitalism* (Princeton, Princeton University Press, 2010).

[18] A Tversky and D Kahneman, 'Judgment under Uncertainty: Heuristics and Biases' (1974) 185 *Science* 1124.

[19] Even in a 'mispriced' market it may be that some large arbitrage traders, such as hedge funds, will enter the market and help to correct the pricing inefficiencies. However, fund managers acting for 'arbitrageurs' depend for their jobs and bonuses on performing equal to or better than the market, and will make decisions in order to make money and keep their jobs rather than to correct prices. As a result they, too, are likely to herd: A Shleifer and LH Summers, 'The Noise Trader Approach to Finance' (1990) 4 *Journal of Economic Perspectives* 19; RJ Gilson and RH Kraakman, 'The Mechanisms of Market Efficiency: Twenty Years Later. The Hindsight Bias' (2003) 28 *Journal of Corporate Law* 715.

It seems that investors do not always behave rationally and that markets can sometimes diverge from estimated economic values as a result of self-reinforcing herd and momentum effects. The view that investors can be irrational, however, does not mean that liquid and efficient markets have no benefits. The proposition that new information influences price behaviour still holds true, as does the fact that investors rely on market prices to make investment decisions. Markets still appear to be 'informationally' efficient even if we may doubt the market's fundamental efficiency, that is, whether the prices reflect the underlying value of companies. New information regarding a security is quickly incorporated into the market via the price of that security. Even in the midst of a bubble, liquid markets can provide useful and accurate price signals as to the relative attractiveness of different securities even if the overall level of prices is affected by the irrationality. Market prices may be regarded as the best indicator of value, even if they are not the most effective and accurate carriers of market information in all circumstances. A financial market system based on disclosure which aims to provide investors with accurate share prices is still a valuable and appropriate regulatory goal.[20]

11.2.1.2 Role of Mandatory Disclosure in Promoting Market Efficiency

As a consequence of the ECMH, one of the foundation stones in the regulation of the secondary market is mandatory disclosure.[21] As discussed in chapter ten, mandatory disclosure is the predominant form of regulation in place at the IPO stage. There are, however, important differences in the way that mandatory disclosure operates in the primary and secondary markets.

At the IPO stage the aim of investor protection is pursued primarily by providing investors with the information they need to make efficient resource allocation decisions and for them to be protected from fraudulent, and negligent, issuers.[22] In the UK this is primarily achieved via a combination of mandatory disclosure and anti-fraud rules. Both the mandatory disclosure and the fraud rules, discussed in chapter ten, focus on the prospectus. The information disclosed presents a picture of the company at the moment in time that the shares are offered to the public. The prospectus contains a significant amount of historical information about the company, but very little by way of future projections.[23] The focus is on a particular, and narrow, window of time. The prospectus is first and foremost a selling document. The aim is to convince investors to purchase shares in the company. The fact that the purpose of the prospectus is to promote securities to investors justifies the tough legal regime, described in chapter ten, which is in place to regulate the accuracy of statements placed in the prospectus.

---

[20] For example, although the Turner Review, which reviewed the causes and implications of the financial crisis, accepted that investor irrationality exists in certain circumstances, there was no suggestion that the UK's policy of regulation based on disclosure needed to be reconsidered: Lord Turner, *The Turner Review: A Regulatory Response to the Global Banking Crisis*, March 2009.

[21] For discussion of mandatory disclosure as a regulatory strategy see L Enriques and S Gilotta, 'Disclosure and Financial Market Regulation' in N Moloney, E Ferran and J Payne (eds), *The Oxford Handbook of Financial Regulation* (Oxford, Oxford University Press, 2015); O Ben-Shahar and C Schneider, 'The Failure of Mandated Disclosure' (2011) 159 *University of Pennsylvania Law Review* 647. These issues are discussed further at 10.4.3.3.

[22] See 10.4.

[23] See 10.5.2.2.

By contrast, periodic and ad hoc disclosures made once the company has been listed are generally expressions of routine reporting requirements, as discussed in 11.3, and do not typically coincide with a selling effort on the part of the company. That is not to say that disclosure rules are not needed at this stage. Bad news will hurt directors by reducing their compensation and diminishing their job security. The incidence of equity-based compensation schemes, such as share options, also means that directors suffer personally if the share price of the company drops. The worse the news, the less likely directors are to disclose it voluntarily, and the more likely they are to be tempted to misrepresent the company's finances.

Rules are therefore needed in the secondary market in order to increase the quality and quantity of information to which outside investors have access, so that this information can then be impounded into the price of the securities. The broader focus on market efficiency in the secondary market means that the disclosure rules are also utilised in order to prevent market misconduct which might otherwise undermine the efficiency of the market.[24] For example, one of the ad hoc disclosure rules to which companies are subject in the UK is the obligation to disclose inside information to the market as soon as possible.[25] In part this is in order to allow that information to be impounded into the price of the securities, but it is also intended to reduce the opportunities for insider trading. The regulation of the ongoing market is more complicated than at the IPO stage and, consequently, the use of disclosure regulation at this stage is also more complex.

Disclosure in the secondary market could be left to a voluntary regime, but such a system has drawbacks. In particular, there are reasons to doubt that the amount of information that would be produced under a voluntary scheme would be as large as that produced under a mandatory regime. In part this is because there are costs to attached to disclosure, and where the directors believe that the benefits gained, in terms of an increased share price, would not justify the costs, they would not disclose all of the information that could be of interest to investors. In addition, the lack of standardisation of voluntarily produced information is likely to reduce its value to investors. These are the same arguments as discussed in relation to mandatory versus voluntary disclosure at the IPO stage.[26] In one respect, however, these arguments may be distinguished. Much of the force of the argument in favour of voluntary disclosure at the IPO stage springs from the view that directors have an incentive to disclose in order to escape the 'market for lemons' and to be able to obtain above average prices for the company's securities. This argument has some merit where the directors are engaged in an explicit selling exercise at the IPO stage, but its strength diminishes in the secondary market where, as discussed, many of the disclosures made by issuers are not accompanied by a selling effort on the part of the company. On this basis, the arguments in favour of mandatory disclosure in the secondary market may be even stronger than those made in relation to the primary market.

---

[24] The regulation of market misconduct is discussed in chapter 12.
[25] See 11.3.2.1.
[26] See 10.4.3.3.

11.2.2 Promoting Corporate Governance

While a widely accepted role for mandatory disclosure is to prevent the undersupply of information necessary for the efficient pricing of securities, mandatory disclosure has also been said to perform an important function regarding the governance of publicly traded companies.[27] It has even been suggested that the governance functions of mandatory disclosure are its most important functions.[28] While this is debatable, it is certainly true that '[i]nformation and disclosure is an area where company law and securities regulation come together'.[29] Of course, some disclosures might perform both functions simultaneously, as where a director has committed a major fraud within the company. This information will be material to pricing the securities accurately, and the disclosure of this information will also be necessary in order to allow the shareholders to perform their role of monitoring the board. Other disclosure rules may be geared primarily to investors, such as the insider dealing rules, while others may have a predominantly governance-based function. For example, the rules governing self-dealing transactions between the company and its directors[30] may be triggered by transactions that are trivial in comparison to the company's asset value or market capitalisation, so will be relevant for governance reasons but are unlikely to have any material impact on share price.

Shares in publicly traded UK companies are typically dispersed amongst many holders.[31] The central problem of corporate governance for such companies is therefore holding managers accountable to the shareholders.[32] The problems have arguably been exacerbated by the advent of high frequency trading (HFT).[33] This involves the use of sophisticated technological tools and computer algorithms to rapidly trade securities. HFT uses proprietary trading strategies carried out by computers to move in and out of positions in seconds or fractions of a second.[34] HFT has taken place at least since 1999, but whereas at the turn of the twenty-first century such trades had an execution time of several seconds, by 2010 this had decreased to milli- and even micro-seconds. The volume of such trading has grown in recent years.[35] High frequency traders move in and out of short-term positions at high

---

[27] R Kraakman, 'Disclosure and Corporate Governance: An Overview Essay' in G Ferrarini et al (eds), *Reforming Company and Takeover Law in Europe* (Oxford, Oxford University Press, 2004).

[28] Ibid, 96.

[29] *Report of the High Level Group of Company Law Experts: A Modern Regulatory Framework for Company Law in Europe* (Brussels, 4 November 2002), ch II.3, 34.

[30] Companies Act 2006, ss 177–87.

[31] R La Porta, F Lopez-de-Silanes and A Shleifer, 'Corporate Ownership around the World' (1999) 54 *Journal of Finance* 471; M Becht and C Mayer, 'Introduction' in F Barca and M Becht (eds), *The Control of Corporate Europe* (Oxford, Oxford University Press, 2001). For discussion of the development of dispersed ownership in the UK see BR Cheffins, *Corporate Ownership and Control: British Business Transformed* (Oxford, Oxford University Press, 2008).

[32] See R Kraakman et al, *The Anatomy of Corporate Law*, 2nd edn (Oxford, Oxford University Press, 2009) 35–36. This is in contrast to the governance concerns in UK private companies which tend to revolve around inter-shareholder disputes and conflicts between shareholders and creditors (P Davies, *Introduction to Company Law*, 2nd edn (Oxford, Oxford University Press, 2010) ch 8.

[33] For further discussion see 12.4.

[34] See eg AJ Menkveld, 'High Frequency Trading and the New Market Makers' (2013) 16(4) *Journal of Financial Markets* 612.

[35] It is estimated that as of 2009, HFT accounted for 60–73% of all US equity trading volume, with that number falling to approximately 50% in 2012: 'Times Topics: High-Frequency Trading', *New York Times*, December 20, 2012.

volumes, aiming to capture small profits (perhaps a fraction of a penny) in profit on every trade. HFT firms do not consume significant amounts of capital, accumulate positions or hold their portfolios overnight. Concerns regarding short-termism in UK markets, and the consequential impact this might have on corporate governance in publicly traded companies, has grown in recent years, and the increase of HFT has increased this disquiet.[36]

It is well understood that shareholders have two main mechanisms for exercising their corporate governance function: 'voice' and 'exit'.[37] They can use their status to attend meetings and vote, for example to remove the directors of the company, or they can express their displeasure by selling their shares in the company, which could affect the company's share price if a large enough percentage of the shareholders adopt this tactic. Given the small size of shareholdings of most shareholders in publicly traded companies in the UK, where even institutional shareholders tend to hold less than 5 per cent, exit as a mechanism for corporate governance is not well developed. It is undoubtedly true that the disclosure of information to shareholders in a company allows them to make investment decisions about their shareholding, but English law has regarded this as being a private investment issue rather than a corporate governance matter.[38] 'Corporate governance' in the UK publicly traded company context has therefore tended to focus on issues of 'voice' rather than 'exit', but this is not to deny that exit can have a role in some circumstances.[39]

The UK has traditionally adopted a shareholder-centric approach to company law. In a solvent company directors traditionally owed their duties to the shareholders as a whole.[40] Section 172 of the Companies Act 2006 continues this approach, which requires directors to have regard to the long-term interests of the shareholders while the company remains solvent.[41]

Shareholders in UK companies have a number of governance entitlements.[42] As regards the company's board, they have the right to remove directors at any time by an ordinary resolution.[43] Further, the UK Corporate Governance Code provides that directors of

---

[36] Kay Review of UK Equity Markets and Long-Term Decision Making, *Final Report*, July 2012.

[37] AO Hirschman, *Exit, Voice, and Loyalty: Responses to Decline in Firms, Organizations and States* (Cambridge MA, Harvard University Press, 1970).

[38] *Caparo Industries plc v Dickman* [1990] 2 AC 605 and see the discussion below at 11.3.

[39] For example, if certain key investors or a large number of investors sell their shares in a company because they are dissatisfied with the company's performance, the share price will be depressed, making the company potentially vulnerable to a takeover, which is likely to result in the managers being displaced. This issue is discussed further at 14.3.2.2.2. Empirical evidence suggests that, in the UK at least, the market for corporate control does not in fact operate as a disciplinary device for poorly performing companies: J Franks and C Mayer, 'Hostile Takeovers in the UK and the Correction of Managerial Failure' (1996) 40 *Journal of Financial Economics* 163, 180.

[40] Eg *Smith and Fawcett Ltd* [1942] Ch 304, 306 per Lord Greene MR. As a rule directors do not owe duties to individual shareholders, although they may do so in specific factual circumstances: *Peskin v Anderson* [2001] 1 BCLC 372.

[41] See 3.2.1.3.1. For further discussion of the role of both shareholders and creditors when the company is solvent see 3.2 generally.

[42] These entitlements are generally recognised as being greater than their counterparts in the US: CM Bruner, 'Power and Purpose in the "Anglo-American" Corporation' (2010) 50 *Virginia Journal of International Law* 579.

[43] Companies Act 2006, s 168(1). Shareholders holding more than 5% of the company's voting rights may require the holding of a general meeting for the purpose of removing directors, and may require the proposed resolutions to be circulated to shareholders at the company's expense: Companies Act 2006, ss 303–05 (this 5% minimum stake was introduced by Companies (Shareholders' Rights) Regulations 2009 (SI 2009/1632), reg 4, implementing Shareholders Rights Directive 2007/36/EC, art 6). Shareholders holding more than 5% of the voting rights in public companies may require resolutions to be put on the agenda for the AGM, and circulated in advance, at the company's expense: Companies Act 2006, ss 338–39.

FTSE-350 companies should be re-elected annually.[44] This is in contrast to the 'staggered board' provisions, commonly used in the US, which allow US directors to entrench themselves against the possibility of shareholder removal.[45] Shareholders in UK publicly traded companies also have a significant role in relation to directors' remuneration. Such companies are required to send shareholders a directors' remuneration report each year on which an advisory vote must be taken at the AGM,[46] and must put their directors' remuneration policy to a binding shareholder vote, by ordinary resolution, at least every three years.[47] The EU Commission is also developing rules in this regard.[48]

In relation to takeovers, in the UK it is the shareholders who determine the outcome of the bid. The Takeover Code imposes a 'no frustrating action' principle upon directors of the target company. Once a bid is launched or anticipated, the directors are prohibited from taking any actions that might frustrate the bid without first obtaining the consent of the shareholders.[49] This is in contrast to the position in the US.[50]

The shareholders also have substantial control rights in relation to a number of corporate transactions. They have a significant role in approving certain categories of corporate transaction, particularly those involving a risk of conflict of interest or which are of a significant size in relation to the company. General company law requires transactions to which the counterparty is a director or connected party[51] to be approved by the shareholders.[52] These include substantial property transactions[53] and corporate loans.[54] There is also a long-standing tradition of shareholders ratifying breaches of directors' duties.[55] The UK Listing Rules add to these provisions for listed companies. All transactions of a value between 5 and 25 per cent of the company's business must be disclosed to shareholders,[56] and for

---

[44] FRC, *UK Corporate Governance Code*, September 2014, B.7.1.

[45] See eg LA Bebchuk, JC Coates and G Subramanian, 'The Powerful Antitakeover Force of Staggered Boards: Theory, Evidence and Policy' (2002) 54 *Stanford Law Review* 887.

[46] Companies Act 2006, ss 420–21, 439. There are also proposals for European 'say on pay' provisions, which would be introduced via revisions to the Shareholder Rights Directive: Proposal for a Directive of the European Parliament and of the Council amending Directive 2007/36/EC as regards the encouragement of long-term shareholder engagement and Directive 2013/34/EU as regards certain elements of the corporate governance statement, COM/2014/0213 final.

[47] Companies Act 2006, s 439A as amended by Enterprise and Regulatory Reform Act 2013, s 79. The approval must be sought at least every three years, or more often if a change to the remuneration policy is proposed. A company is not permitted to make any payment to a director unless such payment is in accordance with its most recent approved remuneration policy.

[48] See Proposal for a Directive of the European Parliament and of the Council amending Directive 2007/36/EC as regards the encouragement of long-term shareholder engagement and Directive 2013/34/EU as regards certain elements of the corporate governance statement, COM/2014/0213 final.

[49] City Code on Takeovers and Mergers, GP 3 and r 21. For discussion see 14.3.2.2.

[50] See 14.3.2.2.

[51] Companies Act 2006, ss 252, 254.

[52] Ibid, s 180, although the directors can avoid the need to do so in some circumstances, for example by declaring the interest in the proposed transaction to the other directors (s 177).

[53] Ibid, ss 190–96.

[54] Ibid, ss 197–214.

[55] See eg *North West Transportation Co Ltd v Beatty* (1887) LR 12 App Cas 589; *Atwool v Merryweather* (1867) LR 5 Eq 464, although it is now clear, contrary to some of the earlier case law, that the resolution will only be effective if it is passed without votes in favour of the resolution by the director (if a member of the company) and any shareholder connected with him: Companies Act 2006, s 239.

[56] FCA Handbook, LR 10.4.1. LR 10.2.2 sets out a series of different ratio tests to be used when applying this test. See 11.3.2.4.

transactions in excess of a 25 per cent threshold the disclosure must be supplemented by a shareholder vote on the transaction.[57] In relation to 'related party transactions'[58] there must be disclosure plus a shareholder vote.[59]

Finally, UK shareholders have control over the issue of new shares as a result of pre-emption rights. These rights are applied as default rules to all companies,[60] and are supplemented by the Listing Rules for firms with a premium listing in the UK Official List.[61] The application of these rules can be waived by shareholder authorisation.[62] In relation to listed companies, however, the grant of such a waiver is subject to a well-established set of voting guidelines adhered to by institutional investors in the UK.[63] In short, requests by a company to issue non-preemptively not more than 5 per cent of the ordinary share capital in any given year are likely to be regarded as routine (with the possibility of an additional 5 per cent if used for an acquisition or specified capital investment), provided the duration also meets the stated criteria,[64] otherwise a business case for waiver must be made.[65]

UK law therefore provides a potentially significant governance role for shareholders in publicly traded companies. Although recent studies have demonstrated that the level of enforcement of directors' duties by way of such shareholders bringing shareholder litigation is close to nil,[66] it has been suggested that these shareholders can have a significant role in corporate governance via more structural and/or informal measures, such as the control that they exercise over pre-emption rights. There will typically be a dialogue between the company and its major institutional shareholders in the period prior to a rights issue.[67] This provides an opportunity for shareholders to engage with the company and, potentially, to provide a monitoring role. Indeed, a positive relation between UK rights issues and managerial change has been found to exist.[68] In addition, in recent years, there has been a rise in activist shareholders seeking to assert control over companies for their own benefit.[69]

---

[57] Ibid, LR 10.5.1.

[58] The concept of 'related party' is defined in LR 11.1.4. See 11.3.2.4.

[59] The votes of the related party and their associates are excluded from the vote: LR 11.1.7(4).

[60] Companies Act 2006, ss 560–77. See 4.4.

[61] See FCA Handbook, LR 9.3.11–9.3.12.

[62] Companies Act 2006, ss 570–71; FCA Handbook, LR 9.3.12(1).

[63] Pre-Emption Group, *Disapplying Pre-Emption Rights: A Statement of Principles* (2015), part 2A. See 4.4.3.

[64] Ibid, part 2A, paras 1, 3 (ie the disapplication of pre-emption rights should last no more than 15 months or until the next Annual General Meeting, whichever is the shorter period).

[65] Ibid, part 3.

[66] J Armour, B Black, BR Cheffins and RC Nolan, 'Private Enforcement of Corporate Law: An Empirical Comparison of the US and UK' (2009) 6 *Journal of Empirical Legal Studies* 687; J Armour, 'Enforcement Strategies in UK Corporate Governance: A Roadmap and Empirical Assessment' in J Armour and J Payne (eds), *Rationality in Company Law: Essays in Honour of DD Prentice* (Oxford, Hart Publishing, 2009).

[67] GP Stapledon, *Institutional Shareholders and Corporate Governance* (Oxford, Clarendon Press, 1996) 129–30; Myners Report on Pre-Emption Rights (DTI, *Pre-Emption Rights: Final: A Study by Paul Myners into the Impact of Shareholders' Pre-Emption Rights on a Public Company's Ability to Raise New Capital* (URN 05/679, February 2005). See 4.3.1.

[68] J Franks, C Mayer and L Renneboog, 'Who Disciplines Management in Poorly Performing Companies?' (2001) 10 *Journal of Financial Intermediaries* 209; D Hillier, SC Linn and P McColgan, 'Equity Issuance, CEO Turnover and Corporate Governance' (2005) 11 *European Financial Management* 515. This effect is similar to the argument, discussed in chapter 3, regarding the corporate governance role of creditors which involves a dialogue between the company and the creditor following a trigger of acceleration: 3.2.2.4.

[69] See eg M Becht et al, 'Returns to Shareholder Activism: Evidence from a Clinical Study of the Hermes UK Focus Fund' (2009) 22 *Review of Financial Studies* 3093; B George and J Lorsch, 'How to Outsmart Activist Investors' (2014) 92 *Harvard Business Review* 88.

In order to assess the corporate governance role of shareholders in publicly traded companies in practice, a distinction needs to be drawn between individual investors and institutional shareholders.

11.2.2.1 Individual Investors

11.2.2.1.1 Role of Individual Investors

The percentage of publicly traded company shares in the hands of private investors has declined over the last 50 years or so, from well over 60 per cent in the late 1950s to just over 10 per cent in 2012.[70] The model of a UK publicly traded company is one with widely dispersed share ownership. Within this model, the concept of 'rational apathy' amongst the shareholders of publicly traded companies is well known.[71] Gains resulting from shareholder activism are expensive to produce, and other shareholders cannot be excluded from taking a pro rata share in the benefits created.[72] It is rational for small retail investors to utilise their 'exit' rights rather than their 'voice' rights if they are unhappy with the direction the company is taking. Accordingly, such investors traditionally do not have a significant governance role, despite being provided with a range of governance rights by the law.

11.2.2.1.2 Effect of Intermediation

Recent developments have potentially exacerbated this effect. In the UK, a large number of shareholders in publicly traded companies now hold their shares not directly, but through an intermediary. This is an issue that affects both individual investors and institutional investors.[73] In the UK there are many reasons why shares may be held indirectly by investors, whether individual or institutional, and these are discussed further at 4.6.4. The effect is that the intermediary is on the share register of the company and is the legal owner of the shares, and the underlying indirect holder's relationship is with the intermediary and not with the company.[74]

In addition, there has been a shift in recent years from certificated to uncertificated issues and transfers, driven in part by the rise in intermediation.[75] In the UK most of these are effected through the CREST computer system, operated by Euroclear UK and Ireland Ltd

---

[70] J Moyle, 'The Pattern of Ordinary Share Ownership: 1957–70', University of Cambridge Department of Applied Economics, Occasional Paper No 31, 1971, 6–7; Office for National Statistics, Statistical Bulletin, *Ownership of UK Quoted Shares 2012*, 25 September 2013.

[71] AA Berle and GC Means, *The Modern Corporation and Private Property* (New York, Macmillan, 1932), although it was Robert Clark who actually coined the phrase 'rational apathy': RC Clark, 'Vote Buying and Corporate Law' (1979) 29 *Case Western Reserve Law Review* 776, 779.

[72] FH Easterbrook and D Fischel, *The Economic Structure of Corporate Law* (Cambridge, MA, Harvard University Press, 1991).

[73] See 4.6.4.

[74] Traditionally the company remained 'blind' to the underlying indirect holder of the shares: Companies Act 2006, s 126 supplemented by Model Articles for Private Companies Limited by Shares, reg 23, and Model Articles for Public Companies, reg 45. However, from 2015 new provisions require companies to keep a register of those holding a beneficial interest with 'significant control' over the company: Small Business, Enterprise and Employment Act 2015, s 81 and Sch 3.

[75] The system of dematerialisation that exists in the UK stands in contrast to the systems in place elsewhere, most notably in the US, which involve immobilisation of a global security which is kept by a depositary.

(EUI).[76] A company which joins CREST can issue paperless shares and register transfers of those shares electronically, thereby saving money.[77] Dematerialisation does not itself affect the direct relationship between investor and issuer. Investors generally have the option of holding an account directly or through an intermediary. Even where investors have a choice, many small investors find that it is simpler to vest the legal title to their shares in a nominee who is a member of the system and then hold their shares indirectly. In practical terms a decision of a company to dematerialise its shares will involve many individual investors holding their shares indirectly and companies that have joined CREST are likely to have a large number of indirect investors. The compulsory dematerialisation of listed UK shares has been the topic of discussion for some time.[78] An EU regulation published in 2014 requires that as from 1 January 2023, all securities which are traded on regulated markets, MTFs or OTFs should be dematerialised, or immobilised and held through intermediaries.[79]

The effect of intermediation in the UK is that the indirect investor is regarded as the beneficial owner of the shares.[80] However, the governance rights attached to the share per se belong to the intermediary who is on the share register and is the legal owner of the shares.[81] This poses a potential corporate governance problem since these intermediaries gain no economic benefit from any activism. It has been recognised that these beneficial owners are in danger of being effectively disenfranchised.

It seems right that these indirect investors should not be disadvantaged by their method of holding shares. They may want to engage in the governance of the company and, if they do, their wishes should be facilitated. There are two basic mechanisms that can be used to enfranchise indirect investors: the intermediary can act in accordance with the wishes of the indirect investor, or the intermediary can delegate rights, such as the right to vote, to the indirect investor. Reforms put in place by the Companies Act 2006 aim to facilitate both of these mechanisms. In order to facilitate intermediaries exercising their vote in accordance with the instructions of the indirect investor, the 2006 Act provides that where a registered holder holds shares for more than one person, the rights attached to the shares (including the right to vote) need not all be exercised in the same way.[82] An intermediary who holds for a number of indirect investors can therefore vote in a way that accommodates the wishes of all of those underlying investors.

The depositary then holds for one or more intermediaries who hold for investors. For discussion see L Gullifer, 'The Proprietary Protection of Investors in Intermediated Securities' in J Armour and J Payne (eds), *Rationality in Company Law: Essays in Honour of DD Prentice* (Oxford, Hart Publishing, 2009). Transfers of shares are discussed further at 4.7 and, in relation to intermediated securities, 9.2.6.2.

[76] See Uncertificated Securities Regulations 2001, SI 2001/1633 (as amended) and as supplemented by CREST rules and conditions (see EUI, *CREST Reference Manual*, September 2009).

[77] For a discussion of transfers via CREST see 9.2.6.3.

[78] Other EU states, such as Denmark, France and Italy, have already adopted a system of compulsory dematerialisation.

[79] Regulation (EU) No 909/2014 of the European Parliament and of the Council of 23 July 2014 on improving securities settlement in the European Union and on central securities depositories, art 3, and amending Directives 98/26/EC and 2014/65/EU and Regulation (EU) No 236/2012.

[80] For a discussion of transfers of intermediated securities see 9.2.6.

[81] For an example of the difficulties that intermediation can cause shareholders, see *Eckerle v Wickeder West-falenstahl GmbH* [2013] EWHC 68 (Ch), where shareholders holding through an intermediary (who was an account holder with Clearstream) were held not to be 'holders' for the purposes of s 98 Companies Act 2006, which permits 5% or more of holders to apply to court to cancel a resolution to delist a company.

[82] Companies Act 2006, s 152(1).

In terms of delegating rights to the indirect investor, the 2006 Act does two things. First, it strengthens the right of registered shareholders to appoint another as a proxy,[83] and these rights can be used by intermediaries to appoint an indirect investor as a proxy and thereby give that indirect investor the right to vote in relation to its own shares. Second, the Act creates new rights for intermediaries to delegate information rights,[84] or a broader range of rights (including the right to requisition a meeting or require circulation of a resolution) to indirect investors in some circumstances.[85]

One downside of these rights, however, is that to a large extent they depend on the relationship between the indirect investor and the intermediary.[86] They do not create any rights for the indirect investor against the company; instead they allow the intermediary to take account of the indirect investor's wishes, or to delegate rights to that individual, without compelling the intermediary to do so. Whether the indirect investor can compel the intermediary will depend on the terms of the contract between them.[87] It is common for this contract to exclude the obligation to vote. Another difficulty is that these measures may facilitate the engagement of an indirect investor with the company *if* the indirect investor wishes to be engaged. However, they clearly do not tackle the more fundamental problem of rational apathy underlying the engagement between retail investors and publicly traded companies.[88]

11.2.2.2 Institutional Investors[89]

11.2.2.2.1 Role of Institutional Investors

While there has been a decline in the number of individual investors holding listed company shares over the past 50 years, there has been a corresponding increase in the number of institutional investors.[90] The proportion of UK shares owned by pension funds, insurance companies and unit trusts has risen dramatically in this period.[91] The growth of this group

---

[83] Ibid, s 324. The 2006 Act makes the ability to appoint a proxy mandatory for the first time. It also makes mandatory for the first time the right of proxies to attend, speak and vote at meetings of the company. The 2006 Act allows proxies to vote on a show of hands as well as on a poll: ss 284–85 (the text of these sections was amended by Companies (Shareholders' Rights) Regulations 2009 (SI 2009/1632), regs 2–3).

[84] Companies Act 2006, s 146 (traded companies only).

[85] Ibid, s 145 which allows any company, public or private, to amend its articles to allow any shareholder on the register to nominate someone else to exercise his rights as a shareholder in his place.

[86] Another issue is that these provisions may work for one layer of intermediation but are unsuited to much longer chains of intermediation.

[87] For discussion see J Payne, 'Intermediated Securities and the Right to Vote in the UK' in L Gullifer and J Payne (eds), *Intermediated Securities: Legal Problems and Practical Issues* (Oxford, Hart Publishing, 2010).

[88] For a discussion of the problems caused to bondholder democracy by immobilisation see 8.3.3.3.

[89] This section assumes that the institutional investor is the legal owner of the shares. Where the institutional investor holds via intermediation (something that is relatively common—see 4.6.4), the discussion at 11.2.2.1.2 will also be potentially relevant.

[90] This trend is also observable elsewhere. In the US, for example, between 1987 and 2009 institutional ownership in the top 1,000 US companies grew from 46.6% to 73%: M Tonello and S Rabinov, *The 2010 Institutional Investment Report: Trends in Asset Allocation and Portfolio Composition* (November 2010), http://ssrn.com/abstract=1707512.

[91] For a snapshot of the UK market in 2012 see Office for National Statistics, Statistical Bulletin, *Ownership of UK Quoted Shares 2012*, 25 September 2013. For a discussion of the impact of tax law on this development see BR Cheffins and SA Bank, 'Corporate Ownership and Control in the UK: The Tax Dimension' (2007) 70 *Modern Law Review* 778.

of investors challenges the model of the rationally apathetic shareholder posited by Berle and Means,[92] and the effect of institutional shareholders on corporate governance needs to be carefully assessed.

Of course, institutional investors come in various shapes and sizes, and some are likely to be more passive than others in relation to their portfolio companies. In general, institutional investors tend to vote on issues which are of general relevance to all companies, such as the introduction of non-voting shares,[93] the disapplication of pre-emption rights, issues of executive pay and board structure.[94] This allows many institutions to economise on their decision-making costs by adopting a standardised policy.[95] However, some institutions, such as hedge funds, may adopt a more interventionist approach, perhaps identifying specific business decisions that they wish the board to adopt.[96] These issues are not static. In recent years, the percentage holding of UK institutional investors in the UK listed equity market has decreased, while the percentage of foreign institutions and hedge funds has been increasing.[97] Another issue that may potentially impact this issue is the rise in high frequency trading.[98]

Institutional shareholders can perform a number of different roles in this regard. Undoubtedly, one significant impact that institutional investors have had in this context is the development of the shareholder-friendly corporate governance regime for publicly traded companies that currently exists in the UK. A number of examples of this influence can be given. First is the influence that institutional shareholders have had on the development of the UK Corporate Governance Code. This was first appended to the Listing Rules on a 'comply or explain' basis in 1992.[99] The basis for this Code, drawn up by Sir Adrian Cadbury, was the pre-existing guidelines of the Institutional Shareholders' Committee's Statement of Directors.[100] Second, the introduction of pre-emption rights into the Listing Rules pre-dated their introduction in general company law, and apparently followed

---

[92] See eg GP Stapledon, *Institutional Shareholders and Corporate Governance* (Oxford, Oxford University Press, 1996).

[93] Non-voting and dual class shares are not expressly prohibited by the Listing Rules but they are strongly discouraged by institutional investors: ibid, 58–59.

[94] P Davies, 'Institutional Investors in the UK' in DD Prentice and PRJ Holland (eds), *Contemporary Issues in Corporate Governance* (Oxford, Clarendon Press, 1993).

[95] BS Black and JC Coffee, 'Hail Britannia? Institutional Investor Behaviour under Limited Regulation' (1994) 92 *Michigan Law Review* 1997, 2034–55.

[96] WW Bratton, 'Hedge Funds and Governance Targets' (2006) 95 *Georgetown Law Journal* 1375; M Kahan and E Rock, 'Hedge Funds in Corporate Governance and Corporate Control' (2007) 155 *University of Pennsylvania Law Review* 1021; M Becht et al, 'Returns to Shareholder Activism: Evidence from a Clinical Study of the Hermes UK Focus Fund' (2009) 22 *Review of Financial Studies* 3093; B George and J Lorsch, 'How to Outsmart Activist Investors' (2014) 92 *Harvard Business Review* 88; L Bebchuk, A Brav and W Jiang, 'The Long-Term Effects of Hedge Fund Activism' (2015) 115 *Columbia Law Review*, forthcoming.

[97] See B Cheffins, 'The Stewardship Code's Achilles Heel' (2010) 73 *Modern Law Review* 1004, 1017–18.

[98] ESMA, *High-Frequency Trading Activity in EU Equity Markets*, ESMA Economic Report No 1, 2014. See also K Khashanah, I Florescu and S Yang, 'High Frequency Trading: A White Paper', IRRC Institute, September 2014, which provides an overview of the academic research in high frequency trading (HFT). This is discussed further at 12.4.

[99] It was called the 'Cadbury Code' at that time. See Committee on Corporate Governance, *Report of the Committee on the Financial Aspects of Corporate Governance* (Cadbury Report) (London, Gee, 1992).

[100] For discussion see GP Stapledon, *Institutional Shareholders and Corporate Governance* (Oxford, Oxford University Press, 1996) 67–69; J Holland, 'Self-Regulation and the Financial Aspects of Corporate Governance' [1996] *Journal of Business Law* 127.

pressure from institutional investors.[101] Institutional investors have taken a further role in regularising the position regarding pre-emption rights in publicly traded companies by drafting and publishing the Pre-Emption Guidelines,[102] which now have a significant impact on the operation of shareholder control over rights issues in such companies.[103] Third, institutional shareholders had a significant role in preparing the predecessor to the Takeover Code,[104] entrenching a pro-shareholder stance which was carried over into the setting up and operation of the Panel on Takeover and Mergers in 1968.[105] Finally, institutions were responsible for the introduction of the provisions in the Listing Rules requiring shareholder approval for significant corporate transactions.[106] It is undoubtedly the case, then, that institutional investors have had a significant role in establishing the framework of corporate governance in the UK.

A second, more direct, corporate governance role is for institutional shareholders to have oversight of directors' activities and behaviour and to intervene where necessary. As discussed already, such investors might sometimes have a role in this regard. It is common for listed companies to meet regularly with major institutional investors to discuss governance practices, strategy and financial issues.[107] For example, as discussed, the need for shareholder approval to disapply pre-emption rights provides a specific occasion for a dialogue between the shareholders, particularly the institutional investors, and the management of a company.[108] Activist investors may also use more informal mechanisms to influence the company's behaviour, perhaps through conversations with the company's senior management.[109] Somewhat more formal mechanisms do exist, however, predominantly via their right to vote.[110] Concerns have been raised about the level of voting by institutional investors.[111] Indeed, a number of reports have concluded that the level of institutional intervention in the affairs of the companies in which the institutions have invested is

---

[101] Stapledon, ibid, 56; LCB Gower, *Gower's Principles of Modern Company Law*, 4th edn (London, Stevens & Sons, 1979) 223, 343.

[102] Pre-Emption Group, *Statement of Principles*, 2015. See 4.4.

[103] P Myners, *Pre-Emption Rights: Final Report* (URN 05/679, February 2005).

[104] See Issuing Houses Association, *Notes on Amalgamation of British Businesses* (1959). For discussion see A Johnston, *The City Takeover Code* (Oxford, Oxford University Press, 1980) ch 3. For discussion see 14.2.1.

[105] J Armour and DA Skeel Jr , 'Who Writes the Rules for Hostile Takeovers, and Why? The Peculiar Divergence of US and UK Takeover Regulation' (2007) 95 *Georgetown Law Journal* 1727.

[106] GP Stapledon, *Institutional Shareholders and Corporate Governance* (Oxford, Oxford University Press, 1996) 60.

[107] Ibid, 101–06.

[108] J Franks, C Mayer and L Renneboog, 'Who Disciplines Management in Poorly Performing Companies?' (2001) 10 *Journal of Financial Intermediation* 209; D Hillier, SC Linn and P McColgan, 'Equity Issuance, CEO Turnover and Corporate Governance' (2005) 11 *European Financial Management* 515. See 4.3.1.

[109] See eg B George and J Lorsch, 'How to Outsmart Activist Investors' (2014) 92 *Harvard Business Review* 88.

[110] Given the relatively small size of the stakes of most institutional investors (2% is common), these are not particularly illiquid and therefore institutions are not locked in to their investments. Exit is therefore still an option, although some institutional investors (eg index tracking funds) have effectively abandoned exit as an option.

[111] When Paul Myners conducted his Review of the Impediments to Voting UK shares for the Shareholder Voting Working Group in 2004, voting levels at company meetings were around 50%. Improvements have been made in the interim and by the time of his fourth progress report in 2007 the level had risen to 63% for FTSE-100 companies: P Myners, *Review of the Impediments to Voting UK Shares: Fourth Report to the Shareholder Voting Working Group* (July 2007), 1.

less than optimal.[112] Greater shareholder engagement is also something that the European Commission appears to be interested in promoting.[113]

11.2.2.2.2 Encouraging Engagement by Institutional Investors

There has been a debate for a number of years about the best way to encourage institutional investors to be more active in the corporate governance of companies.[114] The Myners Report on Institutional Investment in the UK in 2001 recommended that fund managers be subject to an obligation to monitor and to engage in corporate governance where there is a reasonable expectation that such activity will increase the value of the portfolio investments.[115] The possibility of mandatory voting by institutional investors has also been discussed.[116]

There has now been a legislative response to this issue. The response does not amount to a requirement that institutions must vote their shares. This is unsurprising: there are difficulties attached to mandating shareholders to vote, and there is a longstanding tradition in English law of shares being regarded as the property of the shareholders to do with as they wish,[117] and this includes voting as they like, without being subject to fiduciary duties,[118] or not voting at all. Instead, the Companies Act 2006 introduced a power for the Secretary of State to make regulations requiring certain institutions to provide information, either to the public or to specified persons only, regarding the exercise of voting rights attached to shares.[119] The relevant institutions include unit trusts, investment trusts, pension schemes,

---

[112] Eg P Myners, *Institutional Investment in the UK: A Review* (HM Treasury, London, 2001); Company Law Review Steering Group, *Modern Company Law for a Competitive Economy: Final Report* (URN 01/942, July 2001), para 3.54; Sir David Walker, *A Review of Corporate Governance in UK Banks and Other Financial Industry Entities: Final Recommendations*, 26 November 2009.

[113] For example, recent proposals include a requirement that institutional shareholders and asset managers develop and disclose on a comply or explain basis a policy on shareholder engagement: see Proposal for a Directive of the European Parliament and of the Council amending Directive 2007/36/EC as regards the encouragement of long-term shareholder engagement and Directive 2013/34/EU as regards certain elements of the corporate governance statement, COM/2014/0213 final. For discussion see E Rock, 'Institutional Investors in Corporate Governance' in J Gordon and G Ringe (eds), *The Oxford Handbook of Corporate Law and Governance* (Oxford, Oxford University Press, 2015).

[114] Some commentators suggest that the corporate governance role of institutional investors can be increased through legal change (see eg BS Black, 'Agents Watching Agents: The Promise of Institutional Investor Voice' (1992) 39 *UCLA Law Review* 811), whereas others suggest that there are strong non-legal reasons for shareholder passivity (JC Coffee, 'Liquidity versus Control: The Institutional Investor as Corporate Monitor' (1991) 91 *Columbia Law Review* 1277). For a discussion of some of the dangers that might arise from giving institutional investors a dominant role in corporate governance see P Davies, 'Institutional Investors in the UK' in DD Prentice and PRJ Holland (eds), *Contemporary Issues in Corporate Governance* (Oxford, Clarendon Press, 1993) 78–81.

[115] P Myners, *Institutional Investment in the UK: A Review* (HM Treasury, 2001), para 5.89. This suggestion did not amount to a mandatory obligation to vote. This report did not propose that this requirement would be legislative, but rather envisaged a voluntary code being put in place to govern these issues.

[116] In 1998, the then Secretary of State for Trade and Industry, Margaret Beckett, demanded that institutional investors should vote all their shares and should annually disclose their voting policies and records so that they could be held accountable: Margaret Beckett, speech delivered at the PIRC Annual Conference, London, 4 March 1998, www.dti.gov.uk/ministers/archived/beckett040398.html.

[117] *Pender v Lushington* (1877) LR 6 Ch D 70.

[118] In limited circumstances, however, shareholders are constrained as to how they exercise their votes; for example, shareholders are required to vote their shares bona fide in the best interests of the company on an alteration of articles: *Allen v Gold Reefs of West Africa Ltd* [1900] 1 Ch 656.

[119] Companies Act 2006, s 1277.

entities carrying out long-term insurance business, and collective investment schemes.[120] Information may be required by the regulations regarding the manner in which voting rights are exercised, any exercise of voting rights by the institution's agent (for example, a fund manager), any instructions given by an institution to its agents as to the exercise of voting rights, and any delegation of voting rights by an institution.[121] However, there has been considerable opposition to these provisions,[122] and there seems little likelihood that these regulations will be introduced in the near future.[123]

11.2.2.2.3 UK Stewardship Code

To a certain extent these issues have been overtaken by the introduction in 2010 of a new code, the UK Stewardship Code. This Code, published by the Financial Reporting Council, sets out seven principles of good practice for institutional investors, intended to 'enhance the quality of engagement' between institutional investors and the companies in which they invest.[124] Whereas the UK Corporate Governance Code deals with corporate governance issues for companies, the Stewardship Code deals with corporate governance issues for institutional investors. The matters dealt with in the Code include a requirement that an institutional investor have a policy on how it will discharge its stewardship responsibilities (including its policy on voting), which must be publicly disclosed, that it should have a robust policy on managing conflicts of interest in relation to stewardship matters, and that it should periodically report on its stewardship and voting activities. The Code also suggests that institutional investors should consider obtaining an independent audit opinion on its engagement and voting processes which should be publicly disclosed. The Code follows the 'comply or explain' principle established by the UK Corporate Governance Code, requiring institutional investors to provide a statement on their website that details how the principles of the Code are applied by that investor, to disclose any information required by the Code, and explain whether and to what extent any elements of the Code have not been complied with. Whether this Code will be a catalyst for institutional investors to engage more actively in the stewardship of those companies in which they invest remains to be seen.[125]

11.2.2.3 *Role of Mandatory Disclosure in Promoting Corporate Governance*

Disclosure can play a role in promoting corporate governance in a number of ways.[126] First, and most obviously, it can address agency problems by improving the ability of

---

[120] Ibid, s 1278. The regulations may extend this provision to other forms of institution or alternatively limit the application of this provision: s 1278(2).

[121] Ibid, s 1280(1).

[122] For example, the Association of Investment Trust Companies (AITC) has expressed doubts about a real demand from retail investors and raised concerns as to the practical feasibility of a disclosure requirement, since the vast majority of trusts outsource their day-to-day fund management activities, including voting, to external fund managers: AITC Comments on Company Law Reform Bill: Draft Clauses, www.aitc.co.uk.

[123] The Government has said that it is willing to see how market practice evolves before deciding whether and how to exercise the power: HL Deb, vol 682 col 787, 23 May 2006 (Lord Sainsbury).

[124] FRC, *UK Stewardship Code*, September 2012, www.frc.org.uk. This code is based on the code on the responsibilities of institutional investors issued by the Institutional Shareholders Committee. The FRC is responsible for the oversight and development of the Stewardship Code.

[125] See, in this regard, B Cheffins, 'The Stewardship Code's Achilles' Heel' (2010) 73 *Modern Law Review* 1004.

[126] See P Mahoney, 'Mandatory Disclosure as a Solution to Agency Problems' (1995) 62 *University of Chicago Law Review* 1047.

shareholders to monitor the directors.[127] It seems indisputable that if shareholders in publicly traded companies are to make use of the various governance rights discussed above
they will need accurate and complete information from the directors in order to perform
this role. For example, in order for shareholders to exercise their function in making or
ratifying fundamental corporate decisions, they will need to have information about the
proposed transactions. Similarly, shareholders who are asked to propose a merger transaction need information which, in the absence of a legal requirement to do so, neither the
directors nor the outside party might be prepared to disclose voluntarily. Disclosure also
allows for the ex post enforcement of substantive rules, for example by bringing breaches
of directors' fiduciary duties to light.[128] Disclosure can therefore empower shareholders
and facilitate their monitoring role. More generally, disclosure can force directors to collect
and organise information and can make them aware of information of which they might
not otherwise have been aware. This increase in knowledge can have a beneficial effect on
directors' performance.[129]

Second, it has been suggested that disclosure can play an important corporate governance role by allowing directors credibly to commit to reveal all relevant information to
shareholders.[130] The fact that disclosure is mandated reduces the costs for the company and
can lower the company's cost of capital.[131]

11.2.2.4 Summary

One purpose of regulating the market on an ongoing basis is to promote market efficiency
and thereby to protect investors. Other secondary market disclosures are shareholder-
focused and are intended to provide information to shareholders in order to enable them
to perform their corporate governance function. Disclosure can also benefit groups outside
the specific focus of the disclosure. For example, lenders and other financial intermediaries
may employ corporate disclosure to reduce monitoring costs.[132] In recent years mandatory
disclosure has also been utilised by governments to facilitate wider social goals, as recent
requirements for companies to disclose information about board diversity, for example,
seem to indicate.[133]

The aims of regulation discussed in this section need to be borne in mind when considering the disclosure rules adopted by the UK to tackle these issues.

---

[127] For a discussion of the potential limitations of disclosure as a strategy in this regard see L Enriques and
S Gilotta, 'Disclosure and Financial Market Regulation' in N Moloney, E Ferran and J Payne (eds), *The Oxford
Handbook of Financial Regulation* (Oxford, Oxford University Press, 2015).

[128] See M Fox, 'Required Disclosure and Corporate Governance' (1999) 62 *Law and Contemporary Problems*
113.

[129] Ibid.

[130] Eg E Rock, 'Securities Regulation as a Lobster Trap: A Credible Commitment Theory of Mandatory
Disclosure' (2002) 23 *Cardozo Law Review* 675.

[131] R Kraakman, 'Disclosure and Corporate Governance: An Overview Essay' in G Ferrarini, K Hopt and
E Wymeersch (eds), *Reforming Company Law and Takeover Law in Europe* (Oxford, Oxford University Press, 2004).

[132] See 6.3.2.

[133] See Companies Act 2006, s 414C(8), introduced by Companies Act 2006 (Strategic Report and Directors'
Report) Regulations 2013 (SI 2013/1970). The use of disclosure to achieve broader social goals is also in evidence
in other jurisdictions; see eg the US Dodd-Frank Wall Street Reform and Consumer Protection Act, s 1502 on
Conflict Minerals.

11.3 Mandatory Disclosure in the Secondary Market

The mandatory disclosure obligations imposed on companies in the secondary market are discussed in this section. These can be divided into the disclosures that companies must make at a certain time each year (periodic disclosures), and those that must be made only as and when certain event occur (ad hoc disclosures). These announcements must be made in line with minimum standards that are set out in the Transparency Directive[134] relating to how quickly and securely the information is transmitted, and whether it is distributed to a sufficiently wide audience. Generally issuers do so by using one of a number of approved firms to distribute information on their behalf (a Recognised Information Service or 'RIS').

In addition to these issuer disclosure obligations, certain additional disclosure obligations regarding pre- and post-trade transparency of trading in the secondary markets arise for market operators as a result of MiFID I, soon to be replaced by MiFID II and MiFIR.[135] Under MiFID I these obligations apply only to shares admitted to trading on a regulated market, but this is expanded in MiFIR to include all trading venues—that is, regulated markets, MTFs and OTFs.[136] Consequently, market operators and investment firms operating a trading venue must make public current bid and offer prices, and the depth of trading interest at those prices, that are advertised through their systems for shares and similar financial instruments.[137] As regards post-trade transparency, they must also make public the price, volume and time of transactions executed in respect of shares and similar financial instruments trading on a trading venue. Discussion of these market operator-focused obligations falls outside the scope of this book.[138]

A number of important distinctions arise between mandatory disclosure at the IPO stage, discussed in chapter ten, and secondary market disclosure obligations. First, as noted at 11.2, the purpose of disclosure once the company has succeeded in offering its shares to the public is both to inform investors and to provide information to the existing shareholders of the company, whereas at the IPO stage only the first of these functions is performed. Second, and following on from that, the aim of a prospectus is solely to persuade investors to buy the company's securities, whereas the purpose of continuing disclosure is more varied, and selling the company's securities is rarely the predominant reason for such disclosure. Third, at the IPO stage the disclosure is made by the company, via its directors and advisers, to investors. By contrast, continuing disclosure comprises both disclosure by the company to its shareholders and investors, and disclosure to the company by corporate insiders or major shareholders, often with a further disclosure obligation on the company to publish these disclosures to the market. These differences alter the nature of the continuing mandatory disclosure facing companies.

---

[134] Directive 2004/109/EC as amended.

[135] Markets in Financial Instruments Directive (2004/39/EC) (MiFID I), to be replaced in 2017 by MiFID II (Directive 2014/65/EU) and MiFIR (Regulation EU No 600/2014).

[136] See MiFIR, arts 3–5 (pre-trade transparency) and art 6 (post-trade transparency). For a discussion of MTFs and OTFs see 12.2.2.3.

[137] See MiFIR, art 3(1). A number of waivers exist (art 4); for example, authorities are able to waive pre-trade transparency obligations in certain cases, such as for orders that are large in scale (art 4(1)(c)).

[138] For further discussion see Moloney: EU Regulation, V.11.1.

For a long time, secondary market disclosures were regarded as being fundamentally shareholder-focused, and the purpose of providing the shareholders with information was to enable them to exercise a corporate governance role within the company, rather than to inform their investment decisions. In *Caparo Industries plc v Dickman*,[139] for example, the House of Lords held that the purpose of the statutory accounts provisions was not to supply information to investors, but to provide information to the shareholders, and that the purpose of this information provision was to enable them to exercise their governance rights over the board effectively. There have been important changes in the context of secondary market disclosures since *Caparo*, however, in terms of both the disclosures themselves and the liability regime attaching to them. In recent years new investor-focused disclosure obligations have been added, and even some of the obligations that were traditionally regarded as shareholder-focused are now understood as having, additionally, an investor protection element. The purpose for which ongoing disclosures are being made remains a relevant consideration, and one which informs the potential liability for inaccurate statements, discussed in 11.4. As a result, it is important to consider not only the nature of the disclosure requirements in place but also the purpose of those requirements.

11.3.1 Periodic Disclosures

11.3.1.1 Annual Reports

11.3.1.1.1 Obligation to Produce Annual Reports and Accounts

UK companies have been subject to an obligation to provide annual reports and accounts since the nineteenth century. In relation to listed companies, these disclosure requirements have been supplemented by the Disclosure Rules and Transparency Rules. This is an area in which the EU now also has an important role to play.[140]

The basic periodic reporting requirements for companies whose securities are traded on regulated markets originate in EU law, via the Transparency Directive, as amended.[141] The Transparency Directive applies to companies whose securities are listed on the Official List,[142] but not to issuers whose securities are traded on an exchange regulated market,

---

[139] [1990] 2 AC 605.

[140] In relation to the required content of the annual report and accounts see Directive 2013/34/EU of the European Parliament and of the Council of 26 June 2013 on the annual financial statements, consolidated financial statements and related reports of certain types of undertakings, amending Directive 2006/43/EC and repealing Directive 78/660/EEC and Directive 83/349/EEC. This Directive also repeals and incorporates Directive 2012/6/EU on the annual accounts of micro-entities. For a discussion of the implementation of this directive into UK law see BIS, *UK Implementation of the EU Accounting Directive—Chapters 1–9: Annual Financial Statements, Consolidated Financial Statements, Related Reports of Certain Types of Undertakings and General Requirements for Audit*, September 2014.

[141] Directive 2004/109/EC on transparency requirements in relation to issuers, as amended by Directive 2013/50/EU which came into force on 26 November 2013 (Member States have two years from that date to implement the changes). For discussion see FCA, *Implementation of the Transparency Directive Amending Directive (2013/50/EU) and other Disclosure Rule and Transparency Rule Changes*, Consultation Paper CP 15/11, March 2015.

[142] This includes companies listed on the Main Market. These obligations relate both to companies with a premium listing and to those with a standard listing, following the segmentation of the UK Official List.

such as AIM.[143] Article 4 of the Transparency Directive requires the publication of audited annual accounts and reports for companies with securities listed on a regulated market.[144] To a large extent the requirements of this article are met by the rules contained in the Companies Act 2006.[145]

In general, the Companies Act 2006 imposes an obligation on the directors of companies to produce annual reports and accounts, to have financial statements and parts of the reports audited, to circulate the reports and accounts to shareholders and lay them before the shareholders in a general meeting, and to file them at Companies House.[146] However, different obligations are placed on different kinds of companies, so that, for example, a reduced regime is in place for small (private) companies.[147] The reporting obligations placed on companies outside the small company regime (which will include all public companies and some private companies) are more extensive, particularly for quoted companies.[148]

The time limit for public companies to lay their accounts before the general meeting and then file them with the registrar is six months from the end of the relevant accounting period,[149] although for listed companies the Disclosure Rules and Transparency Rules reduce this to four months.[150] For private companies the period is nine months.[151]

The general principle governing the content of annual accounts is that the accounts must give 'a true and fair view of the assets, liabilities, financial position and profit or loss'[152] of the individual company or companies included in the consolidation of the group accounts.[153]

---

[143] However, issuers on these exchanges still face periodic disclosure obligations in excess of those found in the Companies Acts, such as LSE, *AIM Rules for Companies*, May 2014, para 18 (which imposes a requirement for half yearly reports).

[144] Directive 2013/50/EU, art 1(3)(b) amends 2004/109/EC, art 4 and imposes a requirement that all annual financial reports be prepared in a single electronic format from 1 January 2020.

[145] To the extent that the directive requires more onerous reporting obligations than are found in the 2006 Act, these additional obligations have been implemented via the Disclosure Rules and Transparency Rules, eg FCA Handbook, DTR 4.1.3. In addition, because the Transparency Directive is a minimum harmonisation directive there are some 'super-equivalent requirements', ie requirements not required by the directive but imposed on listed companies by the FCA, which appear in the Listing Rules, eg LR 9.8.4.

[146] See generally Companies Act 2006, Parts 15 and 16. Note, however, that only public companies are now required to hold an AGM: Companies Act 2006, s 336.

[147] Companies Act 2006, Part 15, in particular s 381. A public company cannot be a 'small company' for these purposes: s 384(1)(a). The reduced regime means that, for example, most small private limited companies do not need an audit of their annual accounts, unless the company's articles of association say it must or enough shareholders ask for one (ss 476, 477). The reporting obligations for companies in the small company regime have been amended as a result of the need to implement Directive 2013/34/EU: see Companies, Partnerships and Groups (Accounts and Reports) Regulations 2015 (SI 2015/980), and for discussion see ICAEW, *Forthcoming Changes to UK Small Company Reporting*, January 2015. In addition, the need to implement Directive 2013/34/EU regarding the annual accounts of certain types of small companies known as micro-entities prompted the introduction of Small Companies (Micro-Entities' Accounts) Regulations 2013 (SI 2013/3008).

[148] A 'quoted company' for this purpose is a company officially listed in any EEA state or admitted to trading on the New York Stock Exchange or Nasdaq: Companies Act 2006, s 385(2). The power to review the accounts and reports of companies for compliance with the relevant requirements is one that has been delegated by the Government to the Financial Reporting Review Panel. That Panel's powers extend to all of the periodic reports required to be produced by listed companies, whether annual or otherwise. See 11.4.2.2.

[149] Companies Act 2006, s 442.

[150] FCA Handbook, DTR 4.1.3.

[151] Ibid.

[152] Companies Act 2006, s 393(1).

[153] For many years this was almost all that companies legislation said about the content of accounts. That is not the case today (see Parts 15 and 16 Companies Act 2006), but the true and fair view remains an overriding principle in this area (see eg s 393(1); s 396(4)(5); s 404(4)(5)).

Detailed guidance is provided for companies as to the specific information that needs to be included. A company which is under an obligation to produce individual accounts may choose[154] to produce accounts by reference to the rules set out in the Companies Act 2006 and the regulations made thereunder,[155] or by reference to International Financial Reporting Standards (IFRS).[156] The same choice is available to companies producing group accounts, although companies with securities traded on a regulated market must use IFRS for their group accounts.[157]

The annual accounts of most companies must be audited, although exemptions do exist, such as for companies within the small company regime.[158] Detailed guidance is laid down in this regard.[159] The auditors' report is addressed to the shareholders and must state whether in their opinion the annual accounts have been prepared in accordance with the Companies Act 2006 or IFRS and, in particular, whether they give a true and fair view.[160] In addition, auditors must state whether, in their opinion, the information given in the directors' report and strategic report is consistent with the accounts.[161]

11.3.1.1.2 Directors' Report and Strategic Report

A directors' report must accompany both individual and group accounts.[162] In addition, all companies, except those subject to a special regime for small companies, must produce a strategic report.[163] This replaces the previous requirement for a business review, which was included within the directors' report.[164] These reports require narrative reporting to accompany the financial information included in the accounts. The strategic report must contain a fair review of the company's business and a description of the principal risks and uncertainties facing the company.[165] The purpose of the strategic report is stated to be 'to inform members of the company and help them assess how directors have performed their duty under section 172 (duty to promote the success of the company)'.[166] This report may be sent to shareholders in place of the full accounts and reports, if the shareholders agree.[167]

---

[154] Companies Act 2006, s 395.

[155] Even the content of the 2006 Act and the regulations made thereunder are not sufficient to provide fully the detailed information needed to produce a set of accounts for any particular company; the provisions are supplemented by accounting standards drawn up by the Accounting Standards Board (ASB), an operating body of the Financial Reporting Council. The ASB is the body prescribed by the Secretary of State to issue accounting standards, which have statutory recognition: Companies Act 2006, s 464 and Accounting Standards (Prescribed Body) Regulations (SI 2008/651).

[156] Regulation (EC) No 1606/2002 on the Application of International Accounting Standards.

[157] Ibid, art 4, which is directly applicable, but which is noted in Companies Act 2006, s 403.

[158] Companies Act 2006, s 475 as amended by Companies and Limited Liability Partnerships (Accounts and Audit Exemptions and Change of Accounting Framework) Regulations (SI 2012/2301).

[159] Companies Act 2006, Part 16. The detailed requirements of the audit report are established by an International Standard on Auditing (United Kingdom and Ireland), ISA 700.

[160] Companies Act 2006, s 495(3). In addition, for quoted companies the auditor's report must include a report on the auditable part of the directors' remuneration report and state whether it has been properly prepared: s 497.

[161] Ibid, s 496 as amended.

[162] Most recently Companies Act 2006, s 415.

[163] For listed companies see also FCA Handbook, DTR 4.1.

[164] Companies Act 2006 (Strategic Report and Directors' Report) Regulations 2013 (SI 2013/1970), revoking Companies Act 2006, s 417 and inserting ss 414A–414D.

[165] Companies Act 2006, s 414C(2).

[166] Ibid, s 414C(1).

[167] Ibid, ss 426–426A as amended.

For quoted companies, the strategic report must deal with a number of additional matters, including the 'main trends and factors' likely to affect the future of the company's business, the impact of the company's business on the environment, information about its employees, and information about social, community and human rights issues.[168] In addition, the company must disclose a description of the company's strategy and its business model, and must include a breakdown of the number of persons of each sex who are directors, managers and employees of the company.[169] In large part these requirements match the requirements in the previous business review.[170] A further requirement, which is unchanged, is an obligation on the directors of quoted companies to prepare a directors' remuneration report.[171]

The information required for quoted companies includes a forward-looking element, and therefore is in contrast to the information disclosure obligations at the IPO stage.[172] Other jurisdictions, notably the US, require more forward-looking information from issuers than is required in the UK. In the US, the management of issuers are required to provide an extensive Management Discussion and Analysis of Financial Condition and Results of Operations (MD&A report)[173] which supplements historical accounting data with narrative information on the accounts and a forward-looking review of the business. When the US introduced provisions to allow forward-looking data to be included, concerns were expressed by directors regarding liability should their estimates prove wrong, and as a result a safe harbour rule was designed to protect directors from law suits,[174] and thereby to encourage them to provide this forward-looking material—although many managers are still reluctant to do so because of liability concerns should the estimates prove wrong. Section 463 of the Companies Act 2006 provides a similar safe harbour for directors regarding statements in the directors' report, strategic report and remuneration report.[175] Directors' liability in negligence to their company for statements in these reports is excluded, although liability for fraud is maintained.[176] However, liability to other persons is excluded entirely, even in the case of fraud.[177]

---

[168] Ibid, s 414C(7).

[169] Ibid, s 414C(8).

[170] The requirement for information about human rights issues alongside social and community issues and the requirements for the breakdown in the number of persons of each sex who are directors, managers and employees were new in 2013. The previous requirement within the business review, to disclose contractual arrangements essential to the company's business such as supply chains and outsourcing arrangements, was removed by the 2013 Regulations (SI 2013/1970).

[171] Companies Act 2006, s 420.

[172] See 10.4.2.

[173] The SEC requires extensive annual disclosure via Form 10-K. The financial date required to be disclosed is specified in Regulation S-K. The financial disclosures are supplemented by Regulation S-K, Item 303.

[174] Securities Act 1933, r 175.

[175] Section 463 therefore goes beyond protecting directors from liability in relation to forward-looking statements, since it covers all statements contained in these reports.

[176] The director is liable for untrue or misleading statements in the reports or omissions if the director has been fraudulent: ss 463(2)(3). Fraud for these purposes is defined in the same way as common law deceit: the maker of the statement must know it is untrue or misleading, or be reckless as to whether this is the case: *Derry v Peek* (1889) LR 14 App Cas 337.

[177] Companies Act 2006, s 463(4)(5). Third parties may still have a claim for fraud against the company: FSMA, s 90A, discussed at 11.4.1.2. In fact, s 463 excludes the third-party liability of any person (s 463(4)), not just directors, although in most cases it will only be the directors and the company who will be responsible for statements in the reports, and therefore only they will potentially be liable for any errors.

11.3.1.1.3 Corporate Governance Statement

European regulations require that a company whose securities are admitted to trading on a regulated market must also include a corporate governance statement in its annual report.[178] In the UK, all companies with a premium listing are required to report on how they have applied the UK Corporate Governance Code, regardless of their country of incorporation.[179] Overseas issuers with a standard listing of certain securities, including shares, need to make a corporate governance statement in their directors' report covering the governance code to which the issuer is subject, and providing certain details of its share capital.[180] The UK Corporate Governance Code establishes standards of good practice in relation to issues such as board composition and development, remuneration, accountability and audit and relations with shareholders. The Code sets out a number of principles, with which companies must comply.[181] There are then a number of lower-level, more specific provisions.[182] It is not obligatory for companies to follow these, but companies must state whether they have complied, and explain any areas of non-compliance. Although the FCA can impose sanctions for non-compliance with the Listing Rules,[183] if a company fulfils the requirements of the Listing Rules by disclosing its non-compliance with the Corporate Governance Code, this is a matter for the shareholders, as the recipients of this information, rather than the FCA.

11.3.1.2 Half Yearly Reporting

Although Article 4 of the Transparency Directive did not introduce significant changes when implemented in the UK, Article 5 did introduce a new requirement, namely for half yearly reports to be published within two months of the end of the half year for companies whose securities are admitted to trading.[184] Changes introduced in 2013 mean that from 2015 these reports need only be published within three months of the end of the half year.[185] These reports are less detailed than the annual ones and are not required to be audited.[186] The half year report contains a condensed set of financial statements, and an interim management report, which indicates the important events that have occurred during the first

---

[178] Directive 2013/34/EU, art 20.

[179] FCA Handbook, LR 9.8.6–9.8.7. For discussion see Listing Rules Sourcebook (Amendment No 3) Instrument 2009 and FSA, *Listing Regime Review*, CP09/24, October 2009. Prior to April 2010, whilst all UK companies were required to report on how they have applied this Code, overseas companies listed on the Main Market were merely required to explain whether they complied with the corporate governance code of their country of incorporation and how that code differed from the UK Corporate Governance Code.

[180] As a result overseas companies with a standard listing must comply with FCA Handbook, DTR 7.2.

[181] For example, Main Principle B.1 states: 'The board and its committees should have the appropriate balance of skills, experience, independence and knowledge of the company to enable them to discharge their respective duties and responsibilities effectively' (UK Corporate Governance Code, September 2014).

[182] For example, Principle B.1.2 states that at least half of the board as a whole should be non-executive directors, all of whom should be independent (UK Corporate Governance Code, September 2014). In companies below the FTSE-350 the requirement is only for two independent non-executive directors.

[183] See 10.4.2.1.

[184] FCA Handbook, DTR 4.2.

[185] Directive 2013/50/EU, art 1(4), amending Directive 2004/109/EC, art 5.

[186] However, if they are audited or reviewed, the audit report or review must be published: Transparency Directive 2004/109/EC, art 5(4); FCA Handbook, DTR 4.2.9.

six months of the financial year and their impact on the financial statements, plus an assessment of the principal risks and uncertainties for the remaining six months.[187]

Article 6 of the Transparency Directive initially went further and required reporting on a quarterly basis. Quarterly accounting is contentious. The potential benefit of more frequent reporting is that it might add to the efficiency of the securities markets. There is a danger, however, that it might promote an overly short-term approach amongst management. These concerns led to the removal of quarterly reporting obligations when the Transparency Directive was amended in 2013.[188] Although these amendments allowed Member States discretion to introduce more onerous rules, the FCA has already removed the requirement for companies which are subject to the FCA's Disclosure Rules and Transparency Rules to publish interim management statements.[189] This does mean, however, that the UK is now out of step with the US in this regard, since the US utilises quarterly accounting. Companies can, however, continue to report quarterly, on a voluntary basis, if they wish to do so, or, indeed, if their investors continue to expect this information.

11.3.1.3 Function of Periodic Disclosures

Periodic disclosures seem to be both investor-focused and shareholder-focused. Some of these disclosures are targeted specifically at shareholders, and address corporate governance issues. The fact that the annual accounts of a public company must be circulated to the shareholders,[190] and laid before the shareholders in general meeting,[191] suggests that the shareholders are regarded as a significant focus for these documents. Although there is no specific requirement for shareholders to consider a resolution to approve the accounts and report, shareholders in public companies must be afforded the opportunity to discuss them. It can also be seen that the auditors' report on the annual accounts and reports is addressed to the shareholders,[192] which suggests that the primary focus, of the annual reports and accounts at least, is the shareholders. Of course, the annual accounts are a public document, and they will be widely read not only by existing shareholders but also by creditors and the wider, investing public. Nevertheless, it is the corporate governance function of the annual report and accounts that was recognised and emphasised by the House of Lords in *Caparo Industries plc v Dickman*.[193]

Innovations since the decision in *Caparo* suggest that the shareholders remain the significant focus of disclosures in the annual report and accounts. For example, the requirement for the directors' remuneration report to be disclosed to shareholders, and, more particularly, the need for an advisory vote of the shareholders on this report, is a strong indicator as to the focus of this information. Even though a rejection of the remuneration report by

---

[187] See Directive 2004/109/EC, art 5.

[188] Directive 2013/50/EU, art 1.

[189] See FCA Policy statement PS14/15.

[190] Companies Act 2006, s 423(1). The obligation to circulate the company's annual report and accounts extends beyond the shareholders and includes debenture holders and others who are entitled to receive notice of general meetings.

[191] Companies Act 2006, ss 437–38; cf private companies where there is an obligation to circulate the accounts and reports but any further action is a matter for the shareholders or the company's articles.

[192] Companies Act 2006, s 495(1).

[193] [1990] 2 AC 605.

the shareholders has no effect on the directors' receipt of remuneration,[194] nevertheless this vote gives shareholders a guaranteed opportunity to express their views on directors' remuneration.[195] The fact that the purpose of the strategic report is specifically stated to be 'to inform members of the company and help them assess how directors have performed their duty under s 172'[196] also lends weight to this view.

By contrast, the half yearly disclosures are not tied to a shareholder meeting. Further, the dominant objective of the Transparency Directive appears to be investor protection rather than shareholder protection, although shareholders do benefit from these disclosures as well. It is also noticeable that although the measures regarding the annual report and accounts are largely to be found in companies legislation, the implementation of Article 5 of the Transparency Directive, introducing the half yearly disclosures, has been effected via securities legislation. This underlines the function of this disclosure requirement being primarily the disclosure of information to the market rather than to shareholders.

11.3.2 Ad Hoc Disclosures

In addition to the periodic reports required of publicly traded companies, these companies also have to make disclosure of certain information as and when it arises. Four kinds of ad hoc disclosures are considered in this section: requirements to disclose inside information, directors' shareholdings and major shareholdings, and disclosures required by the Listing Rules.

11.3.2.1 Inside Information

An obligation is placed on companies to disclose inside information to the market 'as soon as possible'. The origin of the current requirement is found in the EU market abuse provisions. Until 3 July 2016 this is the Market Abuse Directive,[197] but thereafter the 2014 Market Abuse Regulation will regulate this issue.[198] This requirement is implemented into UK law via the FCA's Disclosure Rules and Transparency Rules.[199] In general, inside information is information which is not known to the market, but if it were known would have a significant effect on the price of the company's securities because it is precise information relating either to the company or to its securities.[200] Common examples are the discovery of a fraud

---

[194] Companies Act 2006, s 439(5).

[195] Since the introduction in 2002 of the requirement to put the remuneration report to shareholders, a number of companies have faced shareholder revolts over their remunerations reports, such as GlaxoSmithKline in 2003, RBS and Shell in 2009, Aviva in 2012 and Burberry in 2014.

[196] Ibid, s 414C(1).

[197] Directive 2003/6/EC on insider trading and market abuse (Market Abuse Directive), art 6.

[198] Regulation (EU) No 596/2014 of the European Parliament and of the Council of 16 April 2014 on market abuse (repealing Directive 2003/6/EC of the European Parliament and of the Council and Commission Directives 2003/124/EC, 2003/125/EC and 2004/72/EC), art 17.

[199] FCA Handbook, DTR 2. Under the Market Abuse Directive 2003/6/EU these rules only apply to companies whose securities are admitted to a regulated market; however, ad hoc disclosure rules are imposed on AIM companies under the AIM rules: LSE, *AIM Rules for Companies*, May 2014, r 11. Under the Market Abuse Regulation (EU) No 596/2014, from July 2016 this obligation applies to securities traded on regulated markets and on MTFs such as AIM (see art 2.1(a)(b)).

[200] Directive 2003/6/EC, art 1; Regulation (EU) No 596/2014, art 7.

committed within the company or its subsidiaries, or the fact that the company is in discussions about a takeover bid.[201]

The obligation on the company is to display the information on the company's website,[202] and to release the information via a RIS.[203] The information should be disseminated to the public in all EEA Member States simultaneously[204] and it must be communicated to the FCA.[205] A further requirement, imposed by the Market Abuse Directive, is the requirement for issuers and those acting on behalf of issuers to maintain a list of all people who have access to inside information (insider lists) and to provide the list to the competent authority on request.[206]

Issuers are permitted to delay disclosure in order to protect their 'legitimate interests', subject to the riders that the non-disclosure must not be likely to mislead the public and that the company can ensure confidentiality on the part of those to whom the information will have to be disclosed.[207] On the face of the regulatory provisions the balance is very much in favour of disclosure. It is hard to see when a delay of disclosure of information which, when made public, will have a significant effect on price, will not 'mislead the public'. In addition, although the FCA accepts that a company in financial difficulties may delay disclosure of its detailed negotiations to secure its financial future, it still requires the company to disclose the fact that it is in financial difficulties and the fact that it is in negotiations.[208] The 2014 Market Abuse Regulation appears to take a stricter approach in relation to delaying disclosure. For example, a new requirement is that an issuer which delays the disclosure of information in this way must inform the relevant competent authority (the FCA in the UK) that disclosure of the information was delayed, and must provide a written explanation of how the conditions set out here were met, immediately after the information is disclosed to the public.[209]

All of these provisions suggest little leeway for an issuer that wishes to delay. A decision of the Upper Tribunal, however, seems to suggest that issuers have more room for manoeuvre on this requirement than might be expected. In *Hannam v FCA*[210] it was suggested that the issuer was within its rights to delay disclosure of inside information regarding drilling results on the basis that it was necessary to do so to protect its legitimate interests. Specifically, an expert witness asserted that such a delay was standard industry practice and therefore legitimised. While the Tribunal rejected the argument that an industry practice could

---

[201] For further discussion see 12.2.

[202] FCA Handbook, DTR 2.3.5.

[203] Ibid, DTR 2.2.1. These provisions apply to all companies whose securities are traded on the Official List (ie both premium and standard listings following the segmentation of the Official List into a two-tier system: see FCA Handbook, LR 9.8.6–9.8.7. For discussion see Listing Rules Sourcebook (Amendment No 3) Instrument 2009 and FSA, *Listing Regime Review*, CP 09/24, October 2009).

[204] FCA Handbook, DTR 6.3.4.

[205] Ibid, DTR 6.2.2.

[206] Ibid, DTR 2.8; Prior to 3 July 2016 see Market Abuse Directive 2003/6/EC, art 6(3), and from 3 July 2016 see Market Abuse Regulation (EU) No 596/2014, art 18, and ESMA 2014/809 regarding draft technical standards for these insider lists.

[207] FCA Handbook, DTR 2.5.1, implementing Market Abuse Directive 2003/6/EC, art 6(2), and see Market Abuse Regulation (EU) No 596/2014, art 17(4) which is in very similar terms.

[208] Ibid, DTR 2.5.3 and 2.5.4. Although see DTR 2.5.5A, which introduces some relaxation of this provision for issuers who approach the central bank for liquidity support.

[209] Market Abuse Regulation (EU) No 596/2014, art 17(4).

[210] [2014] UKUT 233 (TCC).

justify delay, it did accept that it was reasonable for the issuer to delay announcement of the results until it could provide information that avoided misleading the market. On the facts, although the drilling results gave considerable confidence that oil was present, they were not definitive and the issuer was permitted to delay until definitive results were available. The Tribunal assumed that the results were inside information, but stated that unless there is some exceptional event or fact that requires immediate disclosure then a listed company can reasonably delay reporting to ensure that an announcement is not misleading when it is made or to finalise its financial results.

This obligation to disclose information 'as soon as possible' has been described as the 'bedrock' of the EU regime.[211] It creates a continuous disclosure obligation which may be contrasted with regimes elsewhere that rely on periodic disclosure obligations. In the US, for example, issuers are placed under annual and quarterly periodic reporting obligations,[212] and although issuers are subject to an hoc disclosure regime,[213] this does not include a requirement to disclose inside information.[214] Companies can disclose such information voluntarily, for example when there is good news to report, but they fall under no specific SEC obligation to disclose bad news, unless failing to do so will violate Rule 10b-5 because it would render another statement made a half-truth. Courts in the US have regarded the timing of disclosure between periodic reports as a matter for the directors' business judgement—that is, disclosure may be delayed until the information is ripe, or withheld if a valid business reason exists, such as where premature disclosure would impair a contract.[215]

One aim of the ad hoc disclosure requirement is to make shareholders and investors aware of this information, since it may impact on their decision to deal in the shares. The predominant purpose of the disclosure, however, seems to be to deprive the information of its 'inside' character so as to remove the potential for gain from the insider with the information.[216] It is notable that the primary obligation here is on the company to disclose the information, unlike the second and third types of ad hoc disclosure, discussed below,[217] in which the primary obligation is on the holder of shares to disclose certain information to

---

[211] See L Enriques and S Gilotta, 'Disclosure and Financial Market Regulation' in N Moloney, E Ferran and J Payne (eds), *The Oxford Handbook of Financial Regulation* (Oxford, Oxford University Press, 2015).

[212] See Form 10-K (filed annually) and Form 10-Q (filed quarterly).

[213] Form 8-K requires companies to disclose 'on a rapid and current basis' material information regarding changes in a company's financial condition or operations.

[214] Disclosure obligations in the US have been described as a system of periodic disclosure, rather than continuous disclosure: see eg *Gallagher v Abbott Laboratories, Inc*, 269 F2d 806 (7th Cir 2001) per Judge Easterbrook.

[215] For discussion see eg J Cox, R Hillman and D Langevoort, *Securities Regulation: Cases and Materials*, 5th edn (New York, Aspen Publishers, 2006). The lack of a specific disclosure requirement for inside information in the US has been described as the black hole in the US continuous disclosure framework. However, the difference may not be quite as stark as it appears. Many issuers in the US do appear to make use of optional disclosure between Form 10-Q filings. In relation to insider information, for example, day-to-day circumstances can impose an affirmative obligation to disclose on the issuer, stemming from inquiries from the investment community for information and the issuer's motivation to keep that community apprised of current developments. Many issuers consequently adopt an affirmative policy to disclose material information, subject to exceptions such as when it is necessary to keep the information confidential or when the issuer has a legitimate business interest in not disclosing. For discussion see D Oesterle, 'The Inexorable March Toward a Continuous Disclosure Requirement for Publicly Traded Corporations: Are We There Yet?' (1998) 20 *Cardozo Law Review* 135.

[216] Insider dealing is both a criminal offence under the Criminal Justice Act 1993 and a breach of FSMA 2000 provisions; it is dealt with in detail in chapter 12.

[217] See 11.3.2.2 and 11.3.2.3.

the company, and the company's obligation to disclose to the market is secondary. In those circumstances the role of information provision *to* the company (and thereby its shareholders) is clear, whereas here the disclosure obligation is purely on the company to disclose to the market. Again, it is significant that these disclosure obligations are part of securities legislation rather than companies legislation, and it is telling that the EU requirement in this regard is found in the market abuse provisions. The main purpose of these disclosure obligations is, therefore, to provide information to the market rather than to shareholders.

11.3.2.2 Disclosure of Directors' Shareholdings

There has been a longstanding requirement in UK law for directors of companies to disclose their interests in securities of the companies of which they are directors, and over time this has been extended to the interests of spouses, civil partners and children. The rules originate in the 2003 Market Abuse Directive,[218] and are amended by the 2014 Market Abuse Regulation, which, for example, extends the scope of these provisions from companies incorporated in the UK whose securities are admitted to trading on a regulated market,[219] to include exchange regulated markets such as AIM.[220] Those discharging managerial responsibilities for these companies, and those connected with them,[221] are required to disclose their dealings in the shares, derivatives, or other financial instruments of the issuer.[222] This may include not only directors, but also senior managers who have regular access to inside information relating to the issuer and have the power to make managerial decisions affecting the issuer's development and business prospects.[223] Those discharging managerial responsibilities need to disclose transactions relating to the shares (but not the debt securities) of the issuer. This obligation captures the situation where the director has a purely economic interest in the shares and no ownership interest, for example where the transaction involves a contract for differences, in which the contracting party becomes entitled to the difference between the price of the share at two different times without actually acquiring a property interest in the share. A range of transactions is covered, including the use of shares as collateral for a financing transaction, for example as security for a loan from a bank.

Prior to the 2014 Market Abuse Regulation coming into effect in July 2016, a five-day disclosure requirement is in place: the transaction needs to be disclosed to the issuer within four business days of the transaction occurring, and the issuer must then, within one further business day, give the information to the market[224] and to the FCA.[225] This period is

---

[218] Directive 2003/6/EC.

[219] Prior to 3 July 2016 (when the Market Abuse Regulation takes effect), under the 2003 Market Abuse Directive these provisions therefore apply to all companies on the Main Market (ie both premium listed and standard listed companies). For AIM companies, the AIM rules impose a reduced set of requirements on directors (LSE, *AIM Rules for Companies*, May 2014, rr 17 and 31 and Sch 5).

[220] Regulation (EU) No 596/2014, arts 2.1(a)(b) and 19, and see ESMA 2014/809 as regards draft technical standards for the disclosure of these transactions.

[221] For the definition of 'connected person' for this purpose see FSMA, Sch 11B.

[222] Market Abuse Directive 2003/6/EC, art 6(4), implemented into UK law via FCA Handbook, DTR 3, and see Regulation (EU) No 596/2014, art 19(1).

[223] FSMA, s 96B(1).

[224] FCA Handbook, DTR 3.1.2, 3.1.4.

[225] Ibid, DTR 6.2.2.

reduced to three days by the 2014 Regulation.[226] Both the price and volume of the transaction need to be disclosed.[227] The 2014 Regulation introduces a new de minimis requirement of €5,000 before the disclosure obligation arises, in an attempt to address a concern about the excessive costs of this reporting obligation, although, if this is a concern, this threshold still appears to be rather low.[228] A further change introduced in the 2014 Regulation is a 'closed period'—that is, a prohibition on persons discharging managerial responsibilities within an issuer conducting any trading in the company's shares or debt instruments, or derivatives or financial instruments linked to them, in the period 30 calendar days before the announcement of interim financial reports or year-end accounts.[229] This requirement is common practice within major capital markets as a means of addressing high-risk periods for insider dealing.

One purpose of these disclosure rules is corporate governance-focused. The rules provide information to shareholders about a director's interests in the company, and therefore the existence of any particular financial incentives the director has to improve the performance of the company, as part of the process of shareholder monitoring of the directors' stewardship of the company.[230] The predominant purpose of the rules, however, is to curb insider trading, with the focus being on disclosure to the market rather than to shareholders. Again, it is relevant that these provisions are now found in securities legislation, whereas at one time they were regarded as part of company law.[231]

11.3.2.3 Disclosure of Major Shareholdings[232]

The idea that an interest in shares should be declared once certain size thresholds have been reached is a well-established principle of UK law.[233] While the names of the legal owners of shares are publicly available, appearing on the share register and reported to Companies House in the annual return, it is common for shares to be held beneficially, via a nominee. The dematerialisation of shares in recent years has made this even more common. While dematerialised shares can be held directly, it is also very common for them to be held indirectly.[234] Consequently, merely examining the share register will not provide a full picture of those with an interest in the shares of the company, although changes introduced by the Small Business, Enterprise and Employment Act 2015 alter this to a certain extent,

---

[226] Regulation (EU) No 596/2014, arts 19(1)–(3).

[227] FCA Handbook, DTR 3.1.3(7).

[228] Regulation (EU) No 596/2014, art 19(8), although competent authorities are able to raise this to €20,000.

[229] Ibid, art 19(11). In addition, issuers are required to draw up lists of people who discharge managerial responsibilities: art 19(5).

[230] See eg Law Commission and Scottish Law Commission, *Company Directors: Regulating Conflicts of Interest and Formulating a Statement of Duties: A Joint Consultation Paper* (Law Com Consultation Paper No 153, Scot Law Com Discussion Paper No 105, 1998), para 5.2.

[231] See Companies Act 1985, ss 324–29, repealed by Companies Act 2006 (Commencement No 1, Transitional Provisions and Savings) Order 2006 (SI 2006/3428), Sch 4.

[232] This section deals with disclosure obligations placed on shareholders and on issuers. There are, in addition, more general transparency obligations placed on trading venues in relation to pre- and post-trade transparency; discussion of this issue falls outside the scope of this chapter. See Moloney: EU Regulation, V.11.1 for discussion.

[233] See, for example, the recommendations of the Cohen Committee, *Report of the Committee on Company Law Amendment* (Cm 6659, 1945), 39–45.

[234] Discussed at 11.2.2.1.2.

as the Act introduces a requirement for companies to keep and make public a register of beneficial owners with 'significant control' over the company. [235]

The origins of the regime are, again, EU law, in this instance the Transparency Directive.[236] This directive applies only to companies whose securities are admitted to trading on a regulated market.[237] In implementing the directive into domestic law, however, the scope of the regime was broadened to include all companies with securities traded on a prescribed market.[238] This includes the Main Market of the London Stock Exchange (both premium and standard listings) and AIM. The disclosure obligation arises when the shareholder holds 3 per cent of the total voting rights in the company and at every 1 per cent increase thereafter.[239] Decreases must also be notified.[240] The shareholder must notify the percentage of shares held and the date on which the threshold was crossed.[241] Disclosure must take place as soon as possible, but in any event by the end of the second trading day following the day on which the obligation to disclose arose.[242] When issuers on a regulated market receive this information they are under an obligation to make public the information received as soon as possible, and in any event by the end of the following trading day.[243]

In order to capture the disclosure of *beneficial* interests, the rules require disclosure of voting rights arising out of a person's 'direct or indirect holding of financial instruments'.[244] So, for example, voting rights attached to shares held by a nominee on behalf of another will constitute an indirect holding of voting rights by that other person. The crucial issue is the control of the exercise of the voting rights. If the nominee has control of the exercise of these rights then it will be regarded as the direct holder for these purposes, whereas if the nominee may only act on the instructions of the beneficial holder then it is the beneficial holder who will be regarded as having a disclosable interest, if the threshold test is met.

---

[235] See s 81 and Sch 3. 'Significant control' is defined to include, inter alia, beneficially holding 25% of the shares or voting rights in a company, or the right to appoint or remove a majority of the board.

[236] Directive 2004/109/EC, as amended by Directive 2013/50/EU.

[237] Ibid, art 9(1).

[238] FSMA, ss 89A(1), 3(a); FCA Handbook, DTR 5.1.1(3).

[239] FCA Handbook, DTR 5.1.2. These disclosure triggers are more demanding than the Transparency Directive requires, which sets the thresholds at 5, 10, 15, 20, 25, 30, 50 and 75%: Transparency Directive, art 9(1) (note, however, that for a non-UK issuer the disclosure thresholds are 5, 10, 15, 20, 25, 30, 50 and 75%: DTR 5.1.2(1)). Exemptions are in place to cover certain categories, eg market makers who hold shares on their own account in order to be able to offer continuous trading opportunities for those who want to buy and sell shares, thereby increasing market liquidity (DTR 5.1.3(3) and 5.1.4), although often these exemptions are limited—for example, the market maker exemption does not apply when the market maker's holding in a particular company reaches 10% (DTR 5.1.3(3)).

[240] FCA Handbook, DTR 5.1.2.

[241] Ibid, DTR 5.8.1.

[242] Ibid, DTR 5.8.3 (the time limit is four trading days for a non-UK issuer). The obligation to disclose arises when the person 'learns of the acquisition or disposal or of the possibility of exercising voting rights' or 'having regard to the circumstances, should have learned of it' rather than the date on which the acquisition or disposal actually occurred: DTR 5.8.3(1).

[243] Ibid, DTR 5.8.12. For non-UK issuers and issuers whose securities are traded on a prescribed (but not regulated) market the period is slightly longer and they have until the end of the third trading day to disclose to the public.

[244] Ibid, DTR 5.1.2. These requirements are super-equivalent to the requirements of Transparency Directive 2004/109/EC, but changes introduced in 2013 brought the EU rules on this issue broadly into line with the UK rules (see 2013/50/EU, art 1(9), amending Directive 2004/109/EC, art 9). Changes to the Transparency Directive also seek to harmonise the notification of interests regime across Member States by removing options in the way that the Transparency Directive is implemented. In particular, it will be mandatory to aggregate holdings of voting rights with holdings of financial instruments in calculating notifiable interests (see 2013/50/EU, art 1(9)).

Similarly, it is common for institutional investors such as pension funds to vest the legal title of the shares in a custodian, but to outsource the management of their investment portfolio to a fund manager. The question of who has a potentially disclosable interest in the shares will depend on who has control of the voting rights. If, as is usual, the custodian can only vote upon instruction, it will not have to disclose. As between the fund manager and the institutional investor, it will depend on whether the instructions to the custodian come from the fund manager alone, or whether the fund manager is operating under a mandate from the institutional investor. Where the shares are held indirectly, in addition to disclosing the percentage of shares held and the date on which the threshold was crossed, details of the indirect nature of the holding are required. For example, where the shares are held by a nominee who can vote only under instructions, the name of the nominee must be disclosed by the beneficiary when making his disclosure, even though that nominee has no disclosable interest.[245] Once the issuer receives this information, it must again make disclosure of this information to the public.[246]

One of the reasons for requiring the holders of large shareholdings to disclose their interests publicly is to deter insider dealing. As with those discharging managerial responsibilities, large shareholders may be in a position to discover inside information about the company. However, this is only one aspect, and a rather minor aspect, of the role that these rules play. More important is the dissemination of information regarding those who are in positions of influence or control over the company as a result of large shareholdings. Support for this view can be found in the fact that holdings of non-voting shares do not have to be disclosed.[247] Similarly, where shares are held via a nominee, the person with the disclosable interest is the person in control of the voting rights, irrespective of whether they have the legal or beneficial title to the shares. It is the issue of control and influence, rather than the economic stake in the company per se, that seems to be an important driver behind these rules.[248] Indeed, it is notable that the origin of the current rules in this regard is the Transparency Directive and not the Market Abuse Directive.

There remains the question of whether this disclosure is shareholder-focused or market-focused. This information regarding the identity of those holding major shareholdings is certainly useful to those inside the company, particularly as an early warning signal about potential takeover bids.[249] However, the predominant concern behind the disclosure requirement now appears to be market-focused. This information can be useful to investors, in order to give them as full a picture of the company as possible when deciding whether to invest. The fact that the obligation on shareholders to disclose was moved from company law to become part of securities law when the Transparency Directive was

---

[245] FCA Handbook, DTR 5.8.1.

[246] Ibid, DTR 5.8.12.

[247] Similarly, shareholders who are only allowed to vote in certain circumstances (such as preference shareholders who can only vote if the preferential dividend has not been paid) do not have to be disclosed (see DTR 5.1.1(3)).

[248] By contrast, those exercising managerial responsibilities do have to disclose holdings in non-voting shares under the provisions requiring directors' disclosure because opportunities to engage in insider dealing can still arise in these shares, since the economic incentives to deal still arise in relation to these shares.

[249] Another device that can be used to elicit this information is the company's ability to ask any person to reveal the extent of their interest in the company's voting shares: Companies Act 2006, ss 793–96.

implemented into domestic law lends weight to this view.[250] Furthermore, the preamble to the Transparency Directive suggests that improving the functioning of the securities market is the dominant concern of the disclosure requirements contained in the Transparency Directive.

11.3.2.4 Disclosures Required by the Listing Rules

The Listing Rules impose a number of ad hoc disclosure requirements on companies with a premium listing on the Main Market.[251] Two are worth noting. First is the requirement for companies whose shares are listed on the Main Market to disclose related party transactions to their shareholders and to seek shareholder approval for these transactions.[252] Related party transactions include transactions between a listed company and any of its subsidiaries, on the one side, and, on the other, a director or shadow director of the listed company or another company within the corporate group or a person who has been such a director within the previous 12 months or an associate of such a director.[253] The requirement for shareholder approval also applies to transactions between the listed company and any person where the purpose and effect is to benefit a related party.[254] On the approval resolution the related party may not vote and the related party must take all reasonable steps to ensure that any associates do not vote either.[255] While the Listing Rules require this information to be disclosed to shareholders in a circular,[256] companies are also under an obligation to disclose this information to the market, via the RIS system.[257] Proposed changes to the Shareholder Rights Directive[258] put forward in 2014 will introduce new controls over related party transactions at EU level. In particular, transactions with related parties representing more than 5 per cent of a listed company's assets, or transactions that could have a significant impact on profits or turnover, will require shareholder approval.[259]

---

[250] Companies Act 2006, s 1266, introducing FSMA, ss 89A–89G. Previously these disclosure rules were to be found in Companies Act 1985 (repealed by Companies Act 2006 (Commencement No 1, Transitional Provisions and Savings) Order (SI 2006/3428), Sch 3). By contrast, the company's ability to request disclosure of someone's interest in the company's voting shares remains part of company legislation (Companies Act 2006, ss 793–96).

[251] Following the segmentation of the UK Official List into a two-tier regime, these obligations apply to those companies with a premium listing but not to those with a standard listing. Similar, though in general less demanding, rules may be imposed on companies listed on other UK public markets as a matter of contract between the company and the body organising the relevant exchange. For example, AIM companies are subject to similar ad hoc requirements by virtue of the AIM rules, which apply as a matter of contract between the company and the London Stock Exchange: eg, LSE, *AIM Rules for Companies*, May 2014, rr 12–13.

[252] FCA Handbook, LR 11.1. There are some exemptions, for example for small transactions: LR 11.1.6 and LR 11 Annex 1R.

[253] Ibid, LR 11.1.4.

[254] Ibid, LR 11.1.5.

[255] Ibid, LR 11.1.7(4).

[256] Ibid, LR 11.1.7(2).

[257] Ibid, LR 11.1.7(1).

[258] Directive 2007/36/EC of the European Parliament and of the Council of 11 July 2007 on the exercise of certain rights of shareholders in listed companies.

[259] Proposal for a Directive of the European Parliament and of the Council amending Directive 2007/36/EC as regards the encouragement of long-term shareholder engagement and Directive 2013/34/EU as regards certain elements of the corporate governance statement, COM/2014/0213 final, proposed new art 9c. Transactions with related parties that represent more than 1% of a company's assets will be subject to public announcement when the transaction is completed, and must be accompanied by an independent third-party report.

Second, the Listing Rules require disclosure by companies listed on the Main Market to their shareholders of certain 'significant' transactions, whether or not there is an element of self-dealing involved, and approval of some of those transactions.[260] Classification is by reference to the size of the transaction relative to the size of the issuer.[261] The general principle is that the more substantial the transaction is for the issuer, the greater the protection afforded to its shareholders either through disclosure or ultimately through consent at a general meeting. Four 'class tests' (gross assets; profits; consideration; gross capital) are used to determine the 'ratio' of the size of the transaction relative to the issuer,[262] and consequently the regulatory requirements that apply to the transaction. A Class 3 transaction is one where each percentage ratio is less than 5 per cent. A limited announcement is required in these circumstances if the consideration includes the issue of securities for which a listing will be sought,[263] or if the issuer releases any details of the transaction to the public.[264] A Class 2 transaction is one where any percentage ratio is 5 per cent or more, but each is less than 25 per cent. A more detailed announcement than a Class 3 announcement is required, the content requirements for which are set out in the Listing Rules.[265] A Class 1 transaction is one where any percentage ratio is 25 per cent or more. The issuer must comply with the Class 2 requirements and, in addition, send an explanatory circular to its shareholders[266] and obtain the prior approval of the transaction by its shareholders in a general meeting.[267] The content requirements for a Class 1 circular are again set out in the Listing Rules.[268] Following the circular to shareholders the company is also under an obligation to make disclosure to the market by way of a RIS circular.[269]

Despite the fact that the company is under an obligation to disclose the details of both significant transactions and related party transactions to the market via a RIS circular, there is little doubt that the predominant concern of these disclosure requirements is to provide information to the shareholders in order to allow them to perform their corporate governance functions. The fact that shareholder approval is required for related party transactions and the larger significant transactions makes this point clear. It is a well-established mechanism of company law to further good corporate governance by requiring shareholder approval for particular transactions, especially where the transaction is particularly sensitive or important. For example, shareholder approval is needed for the transaction if it is being entered into by directors or their associates,[270] and shareholder approval is required for the appointment of the company's auditors.[271] The Listing Rules take this principle further, extending the requirement for shareholder approval in the context of directors and their associates contracting with the company, and adding a new category of transaction

---

[260] FCA Handbook, LR 10.
[261] Ibid, LR 10.2.1.
[262] Ibid, LR 10 Annex 1.
[263] Ibid, LR 10.3.1.
[264] Ibid, LR 10.3.2.
[265] Ibid, LR 10.4.
[266] Ibid, LR 10.5.1(2).
[267] Ibid, LR 10.5.1(3).
[268] Ibid, LR 13.4 and 13.5.
[269] Ibid, LR 10.3.1; 10.4.1; 10.5.1.
[270] Companies Act 2006, Part 10, Ch 4.
[271] Ibid, Part 16, Ch 2.

where approval is necessary, based on the size of the transaction. The corporate governance focus of these rules in the Listing Rules seems clear.

11.3.2.5 Function of Ad Hoc Disclosures

Regulation of the capital markets has a number of aims. It variously seeks to inform shareholders for corporate governance purposes, to inform shareholders and investors regarding their investment decisions, and to ensure the efficient operation of the market more generally. All of these aims are now visible in the mandatory disclosure obligations that exist for publicly traded companies.

Traditionally, the emphasis was on the provision of information to the shareholders of the company with the purpose of that information being corporate governance-focused. Many of the disclosure obligations were found in the Companies Acts rather than in securities legislation, and the House of Lords in *Caparo* emphasised the governance focus of disclosures in the secondary market, particularly in the context of the annual report and accounts. The force of this argument is strong in relation to this periodic disclosure requirement,[272] and in relation to those ad hoc disclosure requirements where there is a significant internal corporate rationale, such as the disclosure of significant transactions and related party transactions by companies to their shareholders. However, other ad hoc disclosures appear to have a predominantly market-focused rationale.

There has undoubtedly been a shift in emphasis regarding the purpose of ongoing disclosure rules in recent years, allowing for the development of disclosure requirements which have little to do with corporate governance aims. EU legislation, in particular the market abuse provisions and the Transparency Directive, has had a significant impact in this area. The introduction of these legislative measures has resulted in a shift from ongoing disclosure rules being located in companies legislation to them being placed in securities legislation, and altering the emphasis to more of an investor focus. Recital 1 to the Transparency Directive for example, states that '[t]he disclosure of accurate, comprehensive and timely information about security issuers builds sustained investor confidence and allows an informed assessment of their business performance and assets. This enhances both investor protection and market efficiency.'[273] An obvious example of this approach is the disclosure of inside information. It cannot be ruled out that shareholders might obtain some information from these disclosures that might be relevant to them in making investment or governance decisions. However, the predominant purpose of these disclosures is one based on an investor protection approach.

Whatever the function of these disclosures, it is important to ensure that the information provided is accurate and reliable. As at the IPO stage, the protections in place to ensure that the information is accurate are predominantly applied ex post. There are a number of mechanisms which allow for public and private actions in the event of misstatements in ongoing disclosures. These are discussed next.

---

[272] See 11.3.1.3.
[273] 2004/109/EC.

11.4 Enforcement of Secondary Market Disclosure Obligations

11.4.1 Private Enforcement

Options exist for private enforcement by shareholders and investors in the context of ongoing disclosures. Until 2006 the only possible claim arose from a duty of care that was recognised to exist between shareholders and those responsible for producing secondary market disclosures, specifically the annual report and accounts, but only in the context of information that was governance-focused. In 2006 the options were expanded by the introduction of a new section 90A FSMA, to allow claims by investors for misleading statements in secondary market disclosures in some circumstances. This latter claim is investor-focused. In order to determine the nature and extent of any private remedy for misstatements made in ongoing disclosures, the purpose of the disclosure is therefore a relevant consideration.

11.4.1.1 *Enforcement by Shareholders of Misstatements in Governance-Based Disclosures*

Shareholders have rights to bring civil litigation claims regarding misstatements in secondary market disclosures made to them in some circumstances. The decision of the House of Lords in *Caparo Industries plc v Dickman*[274] determines the limits of this liability. As discussed, in *Caparo* the House of Lords decided that the purpose of the statutory accounts provisions is not to supply information to investors, but to inform shareholders, in order to enable them to exercise their governance rights over the board effectively.[275] Consequently, while shareholders can bring a claim in relation to misstatements in governance-based disclosures, it appears that a duty of care does not arise from the annual accounts and reports in relation to purchases of shares in the company, whether by existing shareholders or investors more generally.[276]

Since *Caparo* the number of ongoing disclosure obligations made has grown considerably. Many of these are predominantly investor-focused, with little, if any, element of governance, such as the disclosures regarding inside information.[277] The law could have developed to allow common law *Caparo*-style claims by investors in relation to these disclosures. Indeed, the fear that this might happen goes some way towards explaining the development of the new statutory liability regime, discussed at 11.4.1.2. The law has not developed in this way, however, and these investor-focused disclosures have not been regarded as giving rise to a common law claim in the event of misstatement. Where the disclosure has a strong governance element, such as the disclosures that provide the shareholders with

---

[274] [1990] 2 AC 605.

[275] See 10.6.2.1.

[276] Of course, a duty of care could arise if there is an assumption of responsibility by the maker of the statement to the claimant on the facts, ie if it can be shown that the statement-maker knew that the claimant was likely to use the statement for a particular purpose (such as a purchase of shares in the company) of which the defendant was, or ought to have been, aware. See eg *Galoo Ltd v Bright Grahame Murray* [1994] 1 WLR 1360.

[277] See 11.3.2.1.

information about significant transactions or related party transactions, as required by the Listing Rules,[278] it may be that shareholders could utlilise *Caparo* to bring a claim for negligent misstatement against the maker of the statement, most likely the directors of the company. This (negligence-based) liability to shareholders in respect of governance-based disclosures should not be impacted by the introduction of the statutory (fraud-based) liability to investors for misstatements in ongoing disclosure documents, discussed in the next section.[279] However, this is not an area in which there has been much litigation, and the exact parameters of shareholders' rights in this area are not well-defined.

One of the reasons for this lack of litigation may be the fact that the recovery will generally flow to the company rather than to the shareholder, due to the principle of reflective loss. This principle dictates that shareholders are not able to recover loss which is merely reflective of the company's loss. Where the defendant owes a duty to the company, and not to the shareholder, the claim belongs to the company to the exclusion of the shareholder,[280] and consequently the shareholder is restricted to pursuing a remedy for the company. Likewise, where the defendant breaches a duty to a shareholder and has never owed a duty to the company, then it is easy to see that the claim belongs to the shareholder to the exclusion of the company, even if the only loss suffered by the shareholder is a diminution in the value of his or her shares in the company.[281] However, the difficulty arises in circumstances where the defendant breaches separate duties to the company and to the shareholder. This will be the case where the director makes a misstatement in an ongoing disclosure since the director will owe a duty to the company, as part of his directors' duties, as well as (potentially) the duty of care to the shareholders recognised by the House of Lords in *Caparo*.

In these circumstances the House of Lords in *Johnson v Gore Wood & Co*[282] determined that the shareholder is debarred from claiming this personal loss, not because he has suffered no loss,[283] but for policy reasons. In order to avoid the spectre of double recovery, justice to the defendant requires that the claim in relation to a wrong that causes loss to both the company and the shareholder be given to one victim at the expense of the other. Their Lordships chose to give the claim to the company in order to deal with the collective action problem and to protect the interests of the company's creditors.[284] As a result, if the misstatement occurs in a circular to the shareholders regarding a significant transaction, which, say, causes the company to enter into a contract that it would not otherwise have entered into, both the company and the shareholder are likely to suffer loss (the latter through

---

[278] FCA Handbook, LR 10, LR 11 (see 11.3.2.4).

[279] HM Treasury, *Davies Review of Issuer Liability: Final Report* (June 2007), www.hm-treasury.gov.uk/media/4/7/davies_review_finalreport_040607.pdf, paras 42–45; HM Treasury, *Extension of the Statutory Regime for Issuer Liability* (July 2008), www.hm-treasury.gov.uk/media/2/5/issuerliability_170708.pdf, paras 5.12–5.15. The introduction of FSMA, Sch 10A, para 7(3)(a)(v) by Financial Services and Markets Act 2000 (Liability of Issuers) Regulations 2010 (SI 2010/1192) seems to make this point clear.

[280] Eg *Stein v Blake* [1998] 1 All ER 724.

[281] See *George Fischer (Great Britain) Ltd v Multi Construction Ltd* [1995] 1 BCLC 260.

[282] [2000] UKHL 65.

[283] Cf *Prudential Assurance Co Ltd v Newman Industries Ltd (No 2)* [1982] Ch 204, 223.

[284] Shareholders can recover if they can show that the company has never had a cause of action against the defendant or that they suffer loss which is 'separate and distinct from that suffered by the company' ([2002] 2 AC 1, 35 per Lord Bingham) as a result of the wrongdoer's action.

the reduction in share price). However, it is the company and not the shareholder that is regarded as having a claim for damages, so that the shareholder will not be able to recover damages for him/herself, even if the company chooses not to bring a claim.[285]

In practice, the incidence of such claims by shareholders is 'close to nil'.[286] Indeed, the incidence of actions by shareholders in publicly traded companies generally is almost non-existent.[287] The lack of formal enforcement of governance-based disclosures by shareholders, however, does not mean that such disclosures are unimportant, or that enforcement of these issues by shareholders does not occur at all. Shareholders, particularly institutional investors, have a number of important mechanisms whereby they can exercise control within a company, including, ultimately, requisitioning a shareholders' meeting and removing the directors. These mechanisms are likely to be more effective in ensuring compliance with governance-based disclosure requirements than a formal court hearing.

11.4.1.2 Enforcement by Shareholders and Other Investors of Misstatements in Investor-Focused Disclosures

11.4.1.2.1 Background

As discussed in chapter ten, liability to investors for misstatements in prospectuses has a long history in the UK, with a statutory liability regime in place since 1890, and common law liability existing even earlier.[288] By contrast, liability to investors for misstatements in relation to secondary market disclosures has been slow to develop.[289]

There are a number of reasons for this. As discussed, in contrast to disclosures in prospectuses, many ongoing disclosures were, until relatively recently, regarded as company law matters, with obligations to produce annual accounts, for directors to disclose their interests in the company's shares, and for major shareholders to disclose their shareholdings all being located in the Companies Acts.[290] Investor protection was not, therefore, regarded as a relevant consideration. By contrast, the need to disclose any price-sensitive information was not part of company law, but was regarded as a matter for the Stock Exchange rather than for the legislator to regulate. The Stock Exchange was not in a position to develop a wide-ranging compensation system. It is no coincidence that the introduction of a statutory remedy for investors facing misstatements in ongoing disclosures[291] has followed two important developments: (i) the transfer of disclosure obligations from companies legislation to securities legislation, and (ii) the transfer of rule-making power in this context from the London Stock Exchange to the regulator (now the FCA).

---

[285] For discussion see C Mitchell, 'Shareholders' Claims for Reflective Loss' (2004) 120 *Law Quarterly Review* 457.

[286] See J Armour, 'Enforcement Strategies in UK Corporate Governance: A Roadmap and Empirical Assessment' in J Armour and J Payne (eds), *Rationality in Company Law: Essays in Honour of DD Prentice* (Oxford, Hart Publishing, 2009) 86.

[287] Ibid, 79–86.

[288] Directors' Liability Act 1890. The common law developed a liability regime even earlier, via the tort of deceit (see 10.6.2).

[289] For these purposes, shareholders who make use of statements in ongoing disclosures to make investment decisions, rather than for governance purposes, can be regarded as investors.

[290] See 11.3.

[291] FSMA, s 90A, introduced by Companies Act 2006, s 1270, as amended by Financial Services and Markets Act 2000 (Liability of Issuers) Regulations 2010 (SI 1192/2010).

It is easy to understand why the common law has not developed in such a way as to produce a remedy for investors in this context, in contrast to the position regarding prospectuses. The tort of deceit, which provided the first common law remedy for inaccurate prospectuses, requires the recipient to demonstrate that the maker of the statement intended the recipient to rely on it. This makes sense in the context of the prospectus which is a selling document, but is not easily adapted for use in relation to secondary market disclosures. The primary ongoing obligation that existed in the late nineteenth century, when the tort of deceit was being adapted for use in prospectuses, was the obligation to produce annual reports and accounts. Yet, as developed, this obligation was intended primarily as a report to shareholders on the directors' stewardship and was not intended to induce reliance by way of securities trading. Although annual reports and accounts have undergone some significant changes in the intervening period, this statement still remains a fair reflection of these documents today. It is, therefore, unsurprising that the tort of deceit was not adapted to provide a remedy for misstatements in annual reports and accounts.[292]

The tort of negligence could have provided an alternative common law avenue for a remedy in this context. It is accepted that this tort can give rise to a remedy where misstatements made by one person fall below the standard set by the law and thereby cause purely economic loss to another. This principle could easily have been used to provide a remedy to investors where directors or their advisers were negligent in the misstatements made in a company's continuing disclosure documents and an investor relied on these statements and suffered loss as a consequence. However, as discussed, in *Caparo Industries plc v Dickman*[293] the House of Lords decided that the purpose of the statutory accounts provisions is not to supply information to investors, and to the extent that it provides information to shareholders the purpose of this information provision is to enable them to exercise their governance rights over the board effectively, rather than to enable them to take investment decisions. As a result of the way the tort of negligence has developed, it has not been available as a general remedy to investors.

Until 2006, then, there was no statutory regime for inaccurate statements other than those contained in prospectuses, and the common law offered no protection to investors unless the defendant knew that a particular person was likely to use the statement for a particular purpose (such as a purchase of shares in the company) of which the defendant was, or ought to have been, aware.[294] The position is clearly demonstrated by the decision in *Hall v Cable & Wireless plc*.[295] When Cable & Wireless sold One2One to Deutsche Telekom in August 1999, it agreed to indemnify Deutsche in respect of One2One's tax liabilities. Cable & Wireless also agreed that, if its debt rating fell below a particular level, it would either provide Deutsche with a bank guarantee in the sum of £1.5 billion or pay £1.5 billion into escrow to back up its indemnity. This obligation was not included in Cable & Wireless's announcement of the sale, or in its subsequent annual accounts. In December 2002, since Cable & Wireless's debt rating had fallen below the relevant level, it issued a press release to the effect that it was obliged to procure a bank guarantee for £1.5 billion or pay that sum into escrow. Not surprisingly, its share price then fell. Four shareholders, who had bought

---

[292] For a discussion of the tort of deceit in the context of misstatements in prospectuses see 10.6.2.
[293] [1990] 2 AC 605.
[294] See eg *Galoo Ltd v Bright Grahame Murray* [1994] 1 WLR 1360.
[295] [2009] EWHC 1793 (Comm).

shares between August 1999 and December 2002, sued the company for losses suffered on their shares alleging, inter alia, breach of statutory duty, as Cable & Wireless had failed to announce under the Listing Rules its potential obligation to obtain the guarantee.[296] The judge rejected these claims. The appropriate body to take action in these cases was the regulator (at that time the FSA), which has powers to impose penalties under FSMA, as discussed below at 11.4.2. The judge held that the shareholders did not have rights to bring such a claim directly against the company.

In 2006, however, a new statutory provision, section 90A FSMA, was introduced to provide a remedy for investors regarding misstatements in continuing disclosure documents in some circumstances.[297] With the implementation of the Transparency Directive into UK law, a concern was expressed that some kind of liability between issuers and investors arising from continuing disclosure obligations could come into existence where none had existed before. This was not due to any specific provision in the Transparency Directive.[298] Instead, the concern arose from the directive's emphasis on investor protection, rather than corporate governance, as being the dominant purpose of the disclosures. It was feared that this shift in emphasis might lead a future court to reconsider the *Caparo* decision, and to create issuer liability to investors for issuers and others (such as directors) based on misleading ongoing disclosures.[299]

The Government's response to these concerns was to introduce section 90A FSMA, which was intended to replace any common law liability for behaviour falling within the scope of the section.[300] A review of this section was then conducted by Professor Paul Davies, at the request of the Government.[301] As a result, the provisions regarding issuer liability for secondary market disclosures were substantially amended by the Financial Services and Markets Act 2000 (Liability of Issuers) Regulations 2010.[302] Section 90A remains on the statute book, but the detail of the provisions is now contained in Schedule 10A FSMA. These will be referred to here as the 'section 90A provisions'.

11.4.1.2.2 Scope of the Section 90A FSMA Provisions

11.4.1.2.2(a) Nature of the Claim under Section 90A FSMA

The section 90A provisions confirm the prior common law position of no liability in *negligence* to investors for the company, its directors or advisers for misstatements made in relation to continuing disclosure obligations.[303] In a departure from the pre-existing

---

[296] These continuing obligations are now in the Disclosure Rules and Transparency Rules.

[297] This provision was introduced via Companies Act 2006, s 1270.

[298] Transparency Directive 2004/109/EC, art 7 merely requires Member States to apply their existing liability regimes to misstatements in the disclosures required by the directive, rather than create any new ones.

[299] See eg House of Lords, European Union Committee, Fifteenth Report of Session 2003–04, *Directors' and Auditors' Liability*, HL Paper 89, May 2004.

[300] For a discussion of the comparison of the UK liability regime under this section with comparable regimes in the US, Australia and Canada see E Ferran, 'Are US-Style Investor Suits Coming to the UK?' (2009) 9 *Journal of Corporate Law Studies* 315.

[301] HM Treasury, *Davies Review of Issuer Liability: Liability for Misstatements to the Market: A Discussion Paper* (March 2007); HM Treasury, *Davies Review of Issuer Liability: Final Report* (June 2007).

[302] See Financial Services and Markets Act 2000 (Liability of Issuers) Regulations 2010 (SI 1192/2010) which substitute s 90A and insert a new Sch 10A into FSMA 2000. For discussion see HM Treasury, *Extension of the Regime for Issuer Liability: A Response to Consultation* (March 2010).

[303] FSMA, Sch 10A para 7(1). Note, however, that the liability of advisers *to* the company for negligent misstatements remains intact: Sch 10A, para 7(2).

common law principles, however, the section 90A provisions provide for the liability of issuers to investors for *fraudulent* behaviour regarding secondary market disclosures in certain circumstances.

The section 90A provisions provide three different types of potential liability for an issuer of securities.[304] First, an issuer can be liable if it makes a statement in the documents to which these provisions apply, and which a person discharging managerial responsibilities within the issuer[305] knows to be untrue or misleading, or is reckless as to whether it is untrue or misleading.[306] Second, an issuer can be liable where there is an omission of a required fact, if a person discharging managerial responsibilities within the issuer knew that the omission was a dishonest concealment of a material fact.[307] Third, the issuer can be liable if an investor suffers loss as a result of a delay by the issuer in publishing information to which these provisions apply, if a person discharging managerial responsibilities within the issuer acted dishonestly in delaying the publication of the information.[308]

The scope of liability is relatively tightly constrained. Recklessness involves deliberately disregarding an obvious risk and is not to be equated with negligence or even gross negligence.[309] For the purpose of both omissions and dishonest delay, the statute sets out the test of dishonesty to be applied: the person's conduct must be 'regarded as dishonest by persons who regularly trade on the securities market in question' and the person must be aware (or can be taken to have been aware) that it was so regarded.[310]

For the purposes of the section 90A provisions it is necessary to demonstrate that the claimant's loss is attributable to the inaccurate disclosure or dishonest delay.[311] This requirement of loss causation is also found in section 90 FSMA.[312] In addition, the claimant under section 90A must also demonstrate that in acquiring, disposing of or continuing to hold the securities, it acted in reliance on the published information, and that the reliance was reasonable.[313] This requirement of reliance is in contrast to the claim under section 90 FSMA which does not require reliance to be demonstrated, and instead utilises the concept of 'fraud on the market'.[314]

---

[304] 'Securities' means 'transferable securities' as defined in FSMA, s 102A(3): FSMA, Sch 10A para 8(1). In the case of depositary receipts and other secondary securities giving a right to acquire or sell other transferable securities, the issuer liable to pay compensation is the issuer of the underlying securities, provided that the secondary securities concerned have been admitted to trading by or with its consent. For depositary receipts and other secondary securities admitted to trading without the consent of the issuer of the underlying securities, and for all other derivative instruments, the issuer of the depositary receipts, other secondary securities or derivative instruments will be liable to pay compensation under the regime (see FSMA, Sch 10A para 8(2)).

[305] A person 'discharging managerial responsibilities' within an issuer is defined by FSMA, Sch 10A para 8(5). For most issuers these will be the directors of the company.

[306] Ibid, s 90A(a) and Sch 10A para 3(1)(2).

[307] Ibid, s 90A(a) and Sch 10A para 3(1)(3).

[308] Ibid, s 90A(b) and Sch 10A para 5. This last form of liability was introduced by the 2010 Regulations, and was one of the recommendations of the Davies Review: HM Treasury, *Davies Review of Issuer Liability: Final Report* (June 2007), paras 47–50.

[309] *Derry v Peek* (1889) 14 App Cas 337, 361; *OBG Ltd v Allan* [2007] UKHL 21 [40]–[41] per Lord Hoffmann.

[310] FSMA, Sch 10A para 6.

[311] Ibid, Sch 10A, paras 3(1)(b) and 5(1)(b).

[312] See 10.6.2.1.

[313] In general, English case law regarding misrepresentation allows reliance to be inferred from the facts: *Smith v Chadwick* (1884) 9 App Cas 187.

[314] See 10.6.2.1.

Section 90A was initially enacted to provide a statutory regime for liability in respect of only misstatements in periodic disclosures, such as annual reports and accounts and half yearly reports.[315] Following the recommendation of the Davies Review, the section was extended to cover ad hoc disclosures as well.[316] This was a sensible extension. The line between periodic disclosures and ad hoc disclosures is not always clear, since some ad hoc disclosures have to be repeated in periodic statements,[317] and therefore distinguishing between the two for section 90A purposes is hard to justify. There are also strong policy arguments for attempting to ensure that ad hoc disclosures are as accurate as possible. The avoidance of fraud seems equally important for periodic and ad hoc disclosures.

A further recommendation of the Davies Review was the extension of the regime beyond the Official List, to UK exchange-regulated markets such as AIM.[318] This change was accepted by the Government. Indeed, the Government went further, extending the statutory regime to issuers of securities admitted to trading on an EEA regulated market or MTF, where the UK is the home state for the issuer under the Transparency Directive or the issuer has its registered office in the UK.[319]

11.4.1.2.2(b) Who can Claim?

The issuer will be liable to any investor, whether already a shareholder or not, who acquires securities and suffers loss as a result of the misstatement or omission,[320] where that person relied on the information and it was reasonable for them to do so,[321] or where that person suffers loss as a result of dishonest delay.[322] The issuer is also potentially liable to investors who dispose of securities, and even to those who continue to hold securities.[323] The extension to holders of securities was controversial, and was not recommended by the Davies Review.[324] However, the statutory provisions are not unconstrained in this regard; in particular, the provisions are clear that there must be reliance by the holders of securities before they will be able to bring a claim under the section 90A provisions: there is 'a clear difference between an active holder and a passive holder—the latter will not be entitled to bring an action as they would not be able to show reliance upon the statement in making their investment decision'.[325] So, for example, it is expected that a claimant would have to demonstrate that he had instructed his broker to cancel a sell order. A holder of securities

---

[315] See 11.3.1.

[316] HM Treasury, *Davies Review of Issuer Liability: Final Report* (June 2007), paras 31–35.

[317] See eg FCA Handbook, PR 5.2.

[318] HM Treasury, *Davies Review of Issuer Liability: Final Report* (June 2007), paras 36–39. See HM Treasury, *Extension of the Regime for Issuer Liability: A Response to Consultation* (March 2010), ch 3.

[319] FSMA, Sch 10A para 1, inserted by Financial Services and Markets Act 2000 (Liability of Issuers) Regulations 2010 (SI 1192/2010).

[320] At common law, the tort of deceit only applies to omissions that render what has been said misleading; it does not apply to 'pure' omissions: *R v Kylsant* [1932] 1 KB 442. The s 90A provisions cover omissions, but it is not enough that the omission be intentional or reckless; it must also amount to a dishonest concealment of a material fact: FSMA, Sch 10A para 3(3).

[321] FSMA, Sch 10A para 3(1). There is no requirement that the issuer intended the claimant to rely on the statement. cf common law liability for deceit: *Smith v Chadwick* (1884) 9 App Cas 187.

[322] FSMA, Sch 10A para 5.

[323] Ibid, Sch 10A paras 3(1)(a), 5(1)(a). The extension to sellers was recommended by the Davies Review: HM Treasury, *Davies Review of Issuer Liability: Final Report* (June 2007), paras 51–53.

[324] For discussion see HM Treasury, *Extension of the Regime for Issuer Liability: A Response to Consultation* (March 2010), 15–16.

[325] Ibid, 15.

who continued to hold without giving the matter any thought would be considered to have held those securities passively and therefore would be unable to demonstrate the necessary reliance to bring a claim.

11.4.1.2.2(c) Who may be Liable?

A claim under section 90A may only be brought against the company. In contrast to section 90 FSMA, no liability arises under this section for directors or for advisers of the issuer in relation to misleading statements in ongoing disclosures.[326]

Where issuers are liable under section 90A, they should not be subject to any other liability in respect of any loss suffered by an investor in relation to an untrue or misleading statement, or any omission in published information or dishonest delay in publishing information covered by the section.[327] There are exceptions to this safe harbour provision, however. For example, it does not affect civil liability under section 90 FSMA, or for claims for breach of contract, or under the Misrepresentation Act 1967, or claims arising out of *Caparo Industries plc v Dickman* as discussed at 11.4.1.2.1 above.[328] Nor does this safe harbour affect the FCA's powers to impose a penalty, discussed at 11.4.2.1.

11.4.1.2.2(d) Remedy

Neither section 90A nor its accompanying schedule deal with the issue of the measure of damages to be awarded if an investor's claim is successful, or which test of remoteness to apply. It seems likely, however, that the courts will take the same approach as is followed in the case of common law claims for deceit, since the section is so closely modelled on the common law tort. The overriding aim in the assessment of damages in a deceit claim is to put the claimant in the position it would have been in if no false representation had been made. In general, the claimant is entitled to recover by way of damages the full price paid, but must give credit for any benefits received. These benefits will usually be the value of the property (the securities) at the date of the transaction, but in some circumstances the court may adopt a different method for calculating this benefit.

If the correct measure of damages is tortious, this then raises the question of which is the correct test of remoteness to apply. As discussed at 10.6.2.4.1, there are two possible tests: that for negligence claims, where the recoverable loss is defined by reference to the scope of the duty broken; and the fraudulent misrepresentation test, whereby, according to the court in *Smith New Court v Scrimgeour Vickers (Asset Management) Ltd*,[329] a person can claim all losses flowing from the misstatement, even those caused by unrelated third-party frauds. The section 90A provisions are silent as to which is the correct remoteness test to apply. The fact that section 90A appears to be modelled on a deceit claim might suggest that the fraudulent misrepresentation test may be more appropriate.

---

[326] FSMA, Sch 10A para 7(2).
[327] Ibid, Sch 10A para 7(1).
[328] Ibid, Sch 10A para 7(3).
[329] [1997] AC 254. See also *Dadourian Group International Inc v Simms* [2009] EWCA Civ 169.

11.4.1.2.3 Comparison of Section 90A FSMA and Section 90 FSMA

In a number of important respects the section 90A regime is narrower than that in place regarding statements in prospectuses in section 90 FSMA.[330] First, section 90 covers liability for negligent as well as fraudulent behaviour.[331] Professor Davies considered whether section 90A should also be extended to cover liability for negligence.[332] Two particular factors weighed against such an extension. Concerns were raised about the additional costs, in terms of time and money, that would arise from ensuring that periodic and ad hoc statements met this standard. It was also said that the imposition of such a standard could lead to delays in disclosures, as a result of increased verification, and the possibility of less useful disclosures being made by issuers in an attempt to avoid liability. In fact negligence-based liability does exist for issuers in relation to continuing disclosures. Under the rules set out in the FCA Handbook, the issuer 'must take all reasonable care to ensure that any information it notifies to a RIS is not misleading, false or deceptive and does not omit anything likely to affect the import of the information'.[333] The view of the Davies Review was that public enforcement of a negligence-based liability for ongoing disclosures, via administrative sanctions, was more appropriate than private enforcement.[334]

Second, a section 90 claim can be brought against all those responsible for the prospectus, including the company, its directors and each person who accepts, or is stated to accept, responsibility for any part of the prospectus (although liability will relate only to that part).[335] By contrast, only the issuer can be liable to investors under section 90A, not its directors or advisers.[336] Of course, the behaviour of these individuals will still be relevant, since it is the state of mind of 'a person discharging managerial responsibilities'[337] (whether knowledge or recklessness of the misleading statement, or dishonesty in concealing a material fact or dishonesty in delaying publication of information) that renders the issuer liable under this section. However, those individuals are not made personally liable to investors under the section, although directors will remain liable to their company for such behaviour,[338] and may be subject to FCA sanctions.[339]

---

[330] See 10.6.2 for detailed discussion of the claim under section 90 FSMA.

[331] Ibid, Sch 10 para 6. This is a particularly strong form of negligence liability since it is for the defendant to prove that he or she was not negligent rather than the claimant to prove that he or she was negligent. For discussion see 10.6.2.1.

[332] HM Treasury, *Davies Review of Issuer Liability: Liability for Misstatements to the Market: A Discussion Paper* (March 2007), paras 70–77. For further discussion see P Davies, 'Liability for Misstatements to the Market: Some Reflections' [2009] *Journal of Corporate Law Studies* 295, 301–04. These arguments have been accepted by the Government: HM Treasury, *Extension of the Regime for Issuer Liability: A Response to Consultation* (March 2010), 7.

[333] FCA Handbook, DTR 1.3.4 and 1A.3.2, discussed at 11.4.2.1.

[334] HM Treasury, *Davies Review of Issuer Liability: Final Report* (June 2007), para 11.

[335] FCA Handbook, PR 5.5.3(2). For discussion see 10.6.2.3.

[336] For a discussion of this point see E Ferran, 'Are US-Style Investor Suits Coming to the UK?' (2009) 9 *Journal of Corporate Law Studies* 315, 342–45.

[337] FSMA, Sch 10A paras 3(2)(3), 5(2). For definition of 'a person discharging managerial responsibilities' see para 8(5).

[338] Companies Act 2006, s 463 will not protect a director in these circumstances.

[339] For example, directors of companies on regulated markets can be subject to FCA sanctions (public censure and penalties) where the company is in breach of its disclosure obligations under the Disclosure Rules and Transparency Rules and the director is 'knowingly concerned' in the contravention on the part of the issuer: FSMA, s 91(2).

Third, in section 90 there is no requirement for the claimant to demonstrate that they have relied on the statement, or even that they have read the prospectus in order to establish a cause of action.[340] This is sometimes described as 'fraud on the market' since the misstatement can be said to have caused the investor loss even though that particular investor was unaware of the misstatement. No such fraud on the market concept has been adopted for section 90A, and for these purposes the claimant can only succeed if they can demonstrate that they relied on the publication,[341] although it is possible for an inference of reliance to be drawn from the facts.[342]

11.4.1.2.4 Assessment of Section 90A FSMA

The aims of a liability regime are the same as the aims of the capital market regulation regime.[343] In relation to the secondary market, this means the protection of investors and, more generally, the promotion of the efficient allocation of financial resources in the economy as between competing projects. There are two ways in which a liability regime might contribute to these goals. First, a liability regime can encourage the accurate and timely disclosure of information by issuers, and, second, a liability regime can contribute to the goal of promoting investor confidence by providing compensation to those who suffer loss as a result of a misstatement in a prospectus.

One way in which the goal of encouraging the disclosure of accurate and timely information may be achieved is through deterrence. In order for a liability regime for misstatements in periodic and ad hoc disclosures to have a deterrent effect, that liability needs to fall on the directors and others who actually make the statement, rather than on the company.[344] If the liability falls only on the company, that liability will then be borne by the shareholders rather than the makers of the misstatements. The shareholders may put pressure on the directors as a consequence of the liability imposed on the company, but such deterrence would operate only indirectly.[345] In practice, where liability falls on the company the result is that one set of shareholders recover at the expense of another set of shareholders. Company liability for misstatements can therefore be seen as little more than a redistribution of value among shareholders.[346] This is not to suggest that situations where liability is imposed only on the issuer can have no deterrent effect. It is possible that reputational and

---

[340] FSMA, s 90(1)(b), discussed at 10.6.2.1. No requirement of reliance is included but causation must still be established for s 90 (FSMA, Sch 10 para 6) and presumably some causal connection will need to be shown between the misstatement or omission in the prospectus and the loss, so that if the claimant buys the shares after a significant lapse of time they will find it hard to demonstrate that the prospectus has any significant impact on the price of the securities.

[341] FSMA, Sch 10A paras 3(4), 5(1)(b).

[342] *Smith v Chadwick* (1884) 9 App Cas 187.

[343] See 10.6.1.

[344] Recent studies suggest that even in regimes which prima facie allow claims by investors against directors for misstatements in ongoing disclosures, those directors are rarely held accountable for their misconduct (see eg M Klausner, 'Personal Liability of Officers in US Securities Class Actions' (2009) 9 *Journal of Corporate Law Studies* 349).

[345] Where controlling shareholders exist, it may be that imposing liability on the issuer increases the incentives of such shareholders to monitor management: M Gelter, 'Risk-Shifting through Issuer Liability and Corporate Monitoring' (2013) 14 *European Business Organization Law Review* 497.

[346] Where the company is insolvent, it appears that the defrauded investors are allowed to compete with the other unsecured creditors of the company for a share of the assets (see *Soden v British & Commonwealth Holdings Ltd* [1998] AC 298), in contrast to the usual position that shareholders' claims (eg to declared but unpaid dividends) are subordinated to the claims of the unsecured creditors on insolvency (Insolvency Act 1986, s 74(2)(f)).

other losses will fall on the makers of the misstatements as a result of the company being involved in litigation, but the deterrent effect is likely to be less pronounced in this situation than where liability falls on the statement-makers directly. In addition, even if the liability regime does not make the directors liable to the investors, the directors might nevertheless be liable to the company, for breach of their directors' duties. Thus, the director might have to reimburse the company for the loss suffered by the company in compensating the investor, but the decision to seek recovery from the director would be a decision to be taken by or on behalf of the company.[347]

The second way in which a liability regime might contribute to the goal of promoting investor confidence in the market is by providing compensation to those who suffer loss as a result of a misstatement in a prospectus.[348] There are two elements that need to be considered. The first is what investors should be protected against. The point has already been made that regulation of the capital markets in the UK does not aim to insulate investors from sustaining losses. It is expected that investors should take responsibility for their own decisions.[349] However, it is now accepted that investors should be protected against some misstatements found in periodic and ad hoc disclosures. The changes introduced to section 90A as a result of the 2010 regulations increased the reach of the regime in relation to ongoing disclosures significantly, extending it to dishonest delays, to the sellers of securities and to those who continue to hold securities in some circumstances, extending the securities to which these provisions apply, and extending it to all ongoing disclosures published by 'recognised means'. These changes are to be welcomed. Attention also needs to be given to the amount of compensation to which investors should be entitled. If, as expected, the courts adopt the measure of remoteness established in *Smith New Court* to this issue, the level of compensation to which shareholders might be entitled is potentially substantial.

As discussed, however, the cost of the damages imposed on the defendant company falls principally on the shareholders. The claimant shareholder recovers from the other shareholders with the result that this form of litigation involves pocket-shifting wealth transfers.[350] Long-term investors in the market are just as likely to be among the shareholders in the issuer that has made the misleading statement as among the investors who were misled. The benefits they might gain in the latter capacity are likely to be balanced out by the losses they suffer in the former. However, these payments will not entirely balance out in practice due to the fact that the litigation has transaction costs, such as the lawyers' fees involved in bringing and defending the litigation. For these investors the benefits of any compensation received will be minimal.[351]

[347] Companies Act 2006, s 463 does not protect the director from this liability where the director knows of the untruth of the statement or is reckless as to its truth, or acts dishonestly in relation to an omission.

[348] See MB Fox, 'Civil Liability and Mandatory Disclosure' (2009) 109 *Columbia Law Review* 237, who suggests that, although buyers in relation to a particular transaction can be regarded as having suffered a loss, looking at the operation of disclosure requirements across all transactions, no loss is suffered by investors.

[349] FSMA, s 5(2)(d).

[350] Following the amendments to FSMA, s 90A, to include sellers as well as buyers, this argument will clearly not work where the claimant is a seller.

[351] See RA Booth, 'The Future of Securities Litigation' (2009) 4 *Journal of Business and Technology Law* 129.

11.4.2 Public Enforcement

Given the low levels of private enforcement of investor protection laws, the potential for public enforcement of these laws is important.[352] The task of enforcement lies mainly with the FCA, although the Financial Reporting Review Panel also plays a role.

11.4.2.1 The FCA

The FCA has power, under Part VI of FSMA, to make the rules that appear in the FCA Handbook. In the context of ongoing disclosures, the FCA has the power to make the Disclosure Rules and Transparency Rules (which implement the Market Abuse Directive and the Transparency Directive) and the Listing Rules (which include obligations relating to related party transactions and significant transactions).[353] The FCA Handbook places an obligation on an issuer to 'take all reasonable care to ensure that any information it notifies to a RIS is not misleading, false or deceptive and does not omit anything likely to affect the import of the information'.[354] The FCA's rules thus impose liability for negligent misstatements. An issuer that fails to comply with its obligations under the Listing Rules, Disclosure Rules or Transparency Rules is liable to a penalty, to be imposed by the FCA.[355] In addition, a director of the issuer who was 'knowingly concerned' in the contravention of the rules will be liable to pay a penalty as well.[356] As an alternative to imposing a penalty, the FCA may issue a statement of censure.[357] The FCA also has the power to apply to the court for a restitution order.[358] Where someone has infringed Part VI FSMA and made a profit as a result (or caused loss to another as a result), the court can require an amount it considers just (having regard to the profit made or loss suffered) to be paid by that person to the FCA, for distribution to the persons who appear to the court to have suffered loss. Changes introduced via amendments to the Transparency Directive will have an impact in this area. These changes suggest minimum penalties for breaches of the directive.[359] In addition, for breaches of the notification of interests provisions (discussed at 11.3.2.3) a new penalty is created: competent authorities will have the power to suspend the exercise of voting rights attached to the shares of the entity or individual in breach.[360]

---

[352] For a discussion of private versus public enforcement see eg R La Porta, F Lopez-de-Silanes and A Shleifer, 'What Works in Securities Laws?' (2006) 61 *Journal of Finance* 1; HE Jackson and MJ Roe, 'Public and Private Enforcement of Securities Laws: Resource-Based Evidence' (2009) 76 *Journal of Financial Economics* 207.

[353] FSMA, Part VI. These obligations relate only to issuers whose shares are admitted to trading on a regulated market, ie not to AIM companies (cf the FCA's powers in relation to market abuse more generally, described at 12.2, which relate to securities trading on a prescribed market (see s 118(1)), thus including AIM). For discussion see P Davies, 'Liability for Misstatements to the Market: Some Reflections' (2009) 9 *Journal of Corporate Law Studies* 295, 309–11.

[354] FCA Handbook, DTR 1.3.4, 1A.3.2.

[355] FSMA, s 91(1) for the listing rules, s 91(1ZA) for the disclosure rules and s 91(1B) for the transparency rules. For an example see eg FSA Final Notice, *JJB Sports plc*, 25 January 2011.

[356] FSMA, s 91(2). Accordingly if a director knows that the issuer has failed to take due care to establish the accuracy of the statement, he or she will be liable to a penalty.

[357] Ibid, s 91(3).

[358] Ibid, s 382.

[359] For discussion see 11.4.3.1.

[360] Directive 2013/50/EU, art 1(21), inserting new art 28b into Directive 2004/109/EC.

The actions of the company in failing to disclose required information or in disclosing inaccurate information might also amount to market abuse in some circumstances.[361]

11.4.2.2 The Corporate Reporting Review

The Corporate Reporting Review (CRR) is one of several bodies operating under the Financial Reporting Council. The FRC's role in reviewing directors' reports and accounts was established in 1991.[362] The CRR carries out the work of the Conduct Committee of the FRC, investigating material departures from accounting standards by large companies (both public companies and large private companies), and persuading companies to rectify those errors where appropriate. The Conduct Committee has the power to apply to court for an order mandating the revision of those errors.[363] Initially, this role was largely reactive, responding to investors' complaints about particular financial statements. More recently, the the role has been more proactive in relation to listed firms.[364] The CRR scrutinises around 300 sets of financial statements a year, which are selected on the basis of a risk-assessment based on sectoral, firm-specific and statement-specific risk factors.[365] Most of the accounts reviewed are of listed companies. The bulk of the enforcement activity is informal.[366] Although action is taken relatively often,[367] in the vast majority of these cases the company in question remedies the defective accounting practice without the need for a public notice.[368]

11.4.3 Intensity of Enforcement

As discussed at 10.6.4, it is not just law on the books that matters; enforcement of securities laws is also an important consideration. Research suggests that the level of enforcement within the UK, when compared to jurisdictions such as the US, has historically been low.[369] These differences, which were discussed in the context of liability for misstatements in prospectuses at 10.6.4, are also observable in relation to liability for misstatements in secondary market disclosures.

---

[361] Market abuse is discussed further at 12.2. If the omissions or misstatements do amount to market abuse, the FCA will have a choice of bringing a criminal prosecution under ss 89–90 Financial Services Act 2012 (see 12.2.2.2) or imposing administrative sanctions under s 118 FSMA (see 12.2.2.3).

[362] See FRC, *The State of Financial Reporting: A Review* (London, 1991).

[363] Companies Act 2006, ss 456–57. The Conduct Committee is authorised to exercise those powers by Companies (Defective Accounts and Directors' Reports) (Authorised Person) and Supervision of Accounts and Reports (Prescribed Body) Order 2012 (SI 2012/1439).

[364] The CRR reviews FTSE 100 companies at least once every 3 years and FTSE 250 companies at least once every 4 years.

[365] See eg FRC, *Corporate Reporting Review: Annual Report 2014*, October 2014, 7.

[366] J Armour, 'Enforcement Strategies in UK Corporate Governance: A Roadmap and Empirical Assessment' in J Armour and J Payne (eds), *Rationality in Company Law: Essays in Honour of DD Prentice* (Oxford, Hart Publishing, 2009) 91; K Cearns and E Ferran, 'Non-Enforcement Led Oversight of Financial and Corporate Governance Disclosures and Auditors' (2008) 8 *Journal of Corporate Law Studies* 191.

[367] For example, there were 100 cases of action being taken in 2013–14 (out of 271 sets of reports and accounts reviewed): FRC, *Corporate Reporting Review: Annual Report 2014*, October 2014, 7.

[368] J Armour, 'Enforcement Strategies in UK Corporate Governance: A Roadmap and Empirical Assessment' in J Armour and J Payne (eds), *Rationality in Company Law: Essays in Honour of DD Prentice* (Oxford, Hart Publishing, 2009) 91.

[369] Eg JC Coffee, 'Law and the Market: The Impact of Enforcement' (2007) 156 *University of Pennsylvania Law Review* 229; HE Jackson, 'Variations in the Intensity of Financial Regulation: Preliminary Evidence and Potential Implications' (2007) 24 *Yale Journal of Regulation* 253.

11.4.3.1 Public Enforcement

The incidence of public enforcement of secondary market disclosures by the regulator has been low. When Professor Davies looked at this issue as part of his review for the Treasury in 2007,[370] he found no case in which the regulator (the FSA at that time) had used its restitution powers.[371] Looking at the four-year period 2003–07, Professor Davies found that little use was made of the regulator's criminal enforcement powers, and he found only seven sets of penalties or censures imposed over that period for misstatements or delays in disclosing information (as opposed to market abuse).[372] The regulator's lack of enforcement has been subject to criticism, and the financial crisis prompted a renewed focus on enforcement. Accordingly, the regulator (now the FCA) has recently adopted a much stronger approach to the size of penalties,[373] and has stated its intention to 'follow a strategy of credible deterrence' by taking a tough stance towards those that break the rules.[374] In general, this does seem to be translating into action, both in terms of the number of enforcement cases opened and the total value of fines levied (£425 million in 2013–14, up from £33.6 million in 2009–10).[375] The particular impact of increased activity in the specific context of secondary market disclosures is harder to gauge, and it is too soon to determine the effect of this increase in activity.

This is also an area in which the EU is taking more interest. The amended Transparency Directive requires Member States to establish rules on administrative measures and sanctions applicable to breaches of the national provisions adopted in transposition of the Transparency Directive, and to take all measures necessary to ensure that they are implemented. In particular those administrative measures and sanctions must be 'effective, proportionate and dissuasive'.[376] Furthermore, the directive sets out minimum powers to enable competent authorities to enforce its key provisions. These include the power to impose fines on issuers of up to €10 million or 5 per cent of annual turnover, or up to twice the amount of profits gained or losses avoided because of the breach, whichever is higher.[377]

11.4.3.2 Private Enforcement

The levels of private enforcement in the UK are also very low—much lower than is observable in the US, for example. The incidence of formal claims by shareholders in this context is close to nil. As regards governance-focused disclosures this is not particularly surprising, given the operation of the reflective loss principle.[378] Nor is it necessarily a cause for concern,

---

[370] These figures were updated by Professor Ferran in 2009, to show 12 enforcement actions by the FSA in relation to continuing disclosure obligations since 2002, of which only two involved the imposition of fines on directors: E Ferran, 'Are US-Style Investor Suits Coming to the UK' (2009) 9 *Journal of Corporate Law Studies* 315, 326–29.

[371] HM Treasury, *Davies Review of Issuer Liability: Liability for Misstatements to the Market: A Discussion Paper* (March 2007), para 63.

[372] Ibid, Appendix, Table 1.

[373] FCA, *Decision Procedures and Penalties Manual*, Pt 6.

[374] FCA, *The FCA's Approach to Advancing its Objectives*, July 2013, 19.

[375] FCA, *Annual Report 2013–14*, 10 July 2014.

[376] Directive 2013/50/EU, art 1(20), amending Directive 2004/109/EC, art 28.

[377] Ibid, inserting a new art 28b into Directive 2004/109/EC. There are separate minimums in place for individuals: up to €2 million or up to twice the amount of the profits gained or losses avoided, whichever is higher.

[378] See 11.4.1.1.

since to some extent shareholders, particularly institutional investors, may be able to make use of informal mechanisms to ensure compliance with the disclosure requirements.

As regards investor-focused disclosures, it is still too early to tell whether much use will be made of the new section 90A regime. However, section 90 has not been used a great deal,[379] and section 90A is narrower in scope than that regime.[380] Therefore, it would not be surprising if section 90A were not much used.[381] Again, this is not necessarily a cause for concern, given that the form of the claim is, as discussed, effectively a pocket-shifting wealth transfer between one set of shareholders and another, with the extraction of a sum along the way to pay for litigation costs. This process does not seem to be valuable for shareholders as a whole, and rational shareholders may prefer to leave the loss where it lies, given the considerable transaction costs and the fact that an investor in the market is likely to find itself, over time, on both sides of the equation. Indeed, the US system whereby investors can (and do) bring litigation claims for compensation in this regard has been criticised as excessive on this basis.[382]

11.5 Regulation of Analysts

So far this chapter has considered the use of information disclosure as a mechanism for increasing market efficiency and encouraging effective corporate governance via the use of mandatory disclosure obligations (placed predominantly on issuers), coupled with penalties for inaccurate disclosure. Another potential means of providing information to investors, and ensuring that the information provided by issuers is accurate, is via the use of securities analysts. Analysts can perform a valuable function in the equity markets at the IPO stage,[383] but it is in the secondary market that their role is particularly important. This section considers the investor protection role that analysts can provide, and whether regulation is needed to ensure that they perform this function.

Analysts act as information conduits between the companies they investigate and actual or potential investors in those companies. Specifically, they collect information about issuers, the securities they sell, and the industries in which they operate, along with general market factors. They then evaluate and synthesise the information they obtain and issue a recommendation. At their starkest these might be buy/sell/hold recommendations, but analysts use a variety of terms to describe their recommendations and there is no industry standard in this regard. Securities analysts are valuable to investors as they provide an assessment of

---

[379] See 10.6.4.2.

[380] However, two points which might suggest the alternative view are that (i) secondary market trading is much larger than primary market issuance so that the number of disappointed investors in the secondary market is likely to be much greater than in the primary market; and (ii) while prospectuses are issued only sporadically, periodic and episodic disclosures occur frequently in an issuer's life. For discussion see E Ferran, 'Are US-Style Investor Suits Coming to the UK?' (2009) 9 *Journal of Corporate Law Studies* 315.

[381] Professor Ferran has conducted a comparison of the new UK regime with the regimes in the US, Australia and Canada, and concludes that s 90A does not look likely to trigger an explosion of investor claims: Ferran, ibid.

[382] See eg MB Fox, 'Civil Liability and Mandatory Disclosure' (2009) 109 *Columbia Law Review* 237.

[383] See discussion at 10.4.3.3. For example, at the IPO stage analysts might aid investors by issuing recommendations regarding forthcoming issues of shares. Consequently, analysts can help to solve the puzzle as to why mandatory disclosure is beneficial to investors, if investors rarely read those disclosures.

the company's disclosures and an analysis of the company's prospects. Furthermore, they support the ECMH[384] by turning the information disclosed by issuers into a price on which investors can rely, without having to read and digest that information themselves.[385]

Analysts can therefore be said to be one of a group of financial intermediaries that operate between issuers and investors, commonly termed 'gatekeepers'.[386] Intermediaries are regarded as gatekeepers if they have significant reputational capital that they can pledge to verify or certify information produced by an issuer. Issuers have a problem with signalling that their disclosures are credible, since there is clearly an incentive for companies to misinform investors and to inflate the value of the company and its securities if they can. Gatekeepers can solve this problem by assuring investors of the quality of the issuer's signal. This involves the intermediary pledging its reputation, built up over many years, to vouch for the issuer in question. The idea is that investors can trust these intermediaries more than the issuer because they have less of an incentive to deceive investors. Unlike issuers, who might have nothing to lose from a fraud, especially if they expect only to raise money from investors once, and if they have little to fear from ex post enforcement measures, gatekeepers are 'repeat certifiers'. This group includes, in addition to analysts, credit rating agencies (CRAs), which perform a similar role to analysts in the debt market, auditors, underwriters and lawyers.[387] The role of gatekeepers has come under scrutiny in the last decade or so, resulting from a series of corporate scandals in the early years of this century, such as Enron, Worldcom and Parmalat, and exacerbated by the perceived shortcomings of this group of intermediaries that were revealed by the financial crisis. Consequently analysts, once a largely self-regulated profession, have increasingly fallen under the regulatory spotlight.

There are a number of different perceived problems regarding the role of analysts. These came to the fore after the corporate scandals in the early 2000s, exemplified by the fact that 16 out of the 17 analysts covering Enron's stock were still publishing buy or strong buy recommendations shortly before Enron's bankruptcy, even though publicly available information at that time already suggested that the stock was overpriced.[388] A slew of analyst regulation was imposed in the aftermath of these failures, both in the EU and in the US. Unlike CRAs, whose role in relation to structured financial products has been regarded as an important causal factor in the financial crisis, resulting in a significant intensification post-crisis of the regulatory regime to which CRAs are subject,[389] the financial crisis did not materially change the perception of the risks posed by analysts or the regulatory regime to which they should be subject.

---

[384] See 11.2.1.1.

[385] See RJ Gilson and RH Kraakman, 'The Mechanisms of Market Efficiency' (1984) 70 *Virginia Law Review* 549.

[386] See J Coffee, *Gatekeepers: The Professions and Corporate Governance* (Oxford, Oxford University Press, 2006); cf R Kraakman, 'Corporate Liability Strategies and the Costs of Legal Controls' (1984) 93 *Yale Law Journal* 857, who adopts a slightly narrower definition of 'gatekeeper'. For discussion see J Payne, 'The Role of Gatekeepers' in N Moloney, E Ferran and J Payne (eds), *The Oxford Handbook of Financial Regulation* (Oxford, Oxford University Press, 2015) Section II.

[387] CRA regulation is discussed at 13.7. Auditors have also been subject to increasing regulation within the EU and elsewhere as a result of their perceived failure as gatekeepers (see eg Directive 2006/43/EC as amended); discussion of this topic falls outside the parameters of this book. Lawyers and underwriters have not been the focus of regulatory reform in this context. For discussion see Payne, ibid, Section IV.

[388] See generally J Coffee, 'Understanding Enron: It's About the Gatekeepers, Stupid' (2002) 57 *Business Lawyer* 1403.

[389] See 13.7.

The predominant problem regarding analysts is a conflict of interest risk. Unlike other gatekeepers, analysts are not paid by issuers; several types of analysts exist in the market, differentiated according to who pays them. The most common are sell-side analysts, who work for large broker-dealer firms or investment banks. By contrast, buy-side analysts are employed by institutional investors, and engage in private proprietary research for their employers. The remainder of the market comprises a small minority of independent analysts, for example analysts working for 'independent' sell-side firms—that is, firms that do not provide investment banking services. The most significant conflict issue arises in relation to sell-side analysts and this is also where regulatory attention has been focused.[390] Sell-side analysts are generally funded by investment banks, which can then cross-subsidise this role with fees received from other services being offered to the issuer. For example, where investment banks offer underwriting services to issuers, there will generally be a value to the issuer if the investment bank's analysts follow the newly issued security in the aftermarket and provide (presumably positive) analyst coverage. So, pressure is placed on those analysts to provide positive reports.[391] Alternatively, analysts may be subsidised by brokerage commissions, and consequently there is an incentive for such analysts to make the most optimistic forecasts, in order to promote trading volume and enhance the firm's profits: analysts are more likely to generate brokerage commissions for their employer with buy recommendations than sell recommendations, since the audience for buy recommendations is necessarily larger. A further risk is that price-sensitive information regarding recommendations can be passed to favoured clients of a firm before that information is made publicly available. The risks of conflict can be exacerbated by analyst remuneration arrangements which link their remuneration to underwriting or brokerage revenues in the firm.

Another potential cause of conflicts of interest for analysts arises from the need for the analyst to maintain access to the issuer to perform her job, which can also provide an incentive for optimism amongst analysts. This incentive will be stronger if the analyst or her firm has financial interests in the issuer being assessed. All of these issues tend to result in a preponderance of optimism and buy recommendations made by analysts, particularly sell-side analysts.[392] This, in turn, tends to lead to an inflation of evaluations regarding securities, and to a problem of herding.[393]

Significant consensus has arisen regarding the central problem regarding securities analysts, namely the conflict of interest risk, and the need for regulation to address this issue.[394]

---

[390] Buy-side analysts are less vulnerable to conflict of interest risk as their incentives are more closely aligned with their in-house clients, although some conflict of interest is still possible.

[391] Eg R Michaely and KL Womack, 'Conflict of Interest and Credibility of Underwriter Analyst Recommendations' (1999) 12 *Review of Financial Studies* 653; DJ Bradley, BD Jordan and JR Ritter, 'Analyst Behaviour following IPOs: The Bubble Period Evidence' (2008) 21 *Review of Financial Studies* 101.

[392] Research into analysts suggests that a bias towards optimism outranked even overall accuracy in determining career advancement as an analyst (H Hong and J Kubik, 'Analysing the Analysts: Career Concerns and Biased Earnings Forecasts' (2003) 58 *Journal of Finance* 313). Empirical research suggests that independent analysts can be no less optimistic: A Kowan, B Groysberg and P Healy, 'Which Types of Analyst Firms are More Optimistic?' [2006] *Journal of Accounting and Economics* 119.

[393] See eg I Welch, 'Herding among Security Analysts' (2000) 58 *Journal of Financial Economics* 369.

[394] See eg FSA, Consultation Paper 205, *Conflicts of Interest: Investment Research and Issues of Securities* (2003); IOSCO, *Report on Analyst Conflicts of Interest* (2003).

Much of the UK's response to this issue is guided by regulations put in place at EU level.[395] Principles put in place by IOSCO in 2003 have also been very influential in setting the regulatory agenda in this area.[396] The EU legislative provisions[397] have been implemented in the UK via the FCA Handbook. The regulatory regime aims to ensure that the research produced by analysts is objective, clear, and not misleading. The focus is on requiring firms to identify and eliminate, manage or disclose conflicts of interest, and on supporting the integrity of analysts and investment research. The regulations fall into two broad categories: the imposition of prophylactic rules designed to minimise the possibility of a conflict arising, and disclosure obligations.

First, then, rules are imposed that seek to diminish conflicts of interest for analysts.[398] For example, the provisions state that analysts should not become involved in activities other than the preparation of investment research, where such involvement is inconsistent with the maintenance of their objectivity, for example participating in investment banking activities such as corporate finance business and underwriting;[399] firms and analysts are prohibited from accepting inducements from those with a material interest in the subject matter of the investment research; and firms and analysts are prohibited from promising issuers favourable research coverage.[400] These rules go some way towards dealing with the conflict of interest issue, but they do not address the underlying problem, namely the payment model (particularly for sell-side analysts) that leads to this problem in the first place. As such, it presents the regulator with a 'Sisyphean task': 'Prohibit one conflict and an alternative one springs up in its place. The regulator's task therefore becomes unending.'[401]

Second, disclosure is used as a tool to regulate analysts.[402] This operates in two ways. Firms come under a general obligation to disclose their interests and any conflicts of interest that may arise.[403] There are also disclosure obligations regarding the investment research itself—both a general obligation to ensure that the research recommendation is 'fairly presented'[404] and also more specific obligations to disclose the identity of the person making the recommendation and details of matters such as the source of any material

---

[395] For detailed discussion of the EU response see Moloney: EU Regulation, VII.3. For a discussion of the US response to this issue, see J Coffee, *Gatekeepers: The Professions and Corporate Governance* (Oxford, Oxford University Press, 2006) ch 7.

[396] IOSCO, *Statement of Principles for Addressing Sell-Side Analyst Conflicts of Interest* (2003).

[397] See MiFID, art 13(3) and MiFID Level 2 Directive, Commission Directive 2006/73/EC. MiFID has been superseded by MiFID II and MiFIR, with an implementation date of January 2017; this issue will be governed by MiFID II, arts 16(3) and 16(12). MiFID II, art 16(3) follows the same formula as MiFID, art 13(3), and it is expected that the 2006 Level 2 Directive will be reflected in a new set of administrative principles to be adopted under MiFID II, art 16(12). Additionally, the EU market abuse regime regulates investment research with a view to ensuring the integrity of the marketplace: see Market Abuse Directive 2003, art 6(5) (and Level 2 Investment Recommendations Directive 2003/125/EC) and Market Abuse Regulation 2014, art 20(1). From July 2016 the 2014 Market Abuse Regulation repeals Investment Recommendations Directive 2003/125/EC, and therefore new Regulatory Technical Standards are required, which are expected to be similar in design to the 2003 Directive. These provisions deal with the fair presentation of investment research and the disclosure of related conflicts of interest.

[398] See in particular FCA Handbook, COBS 12.2.

[399] Ibid, COBS 12.2.9.

[400] Ibid, COBS 12.2.5.

[401] J Coffee, *Gatekeepers: The Professions and Corporate Governance* (Oxford, Oxford University Press, 2006) 333.

[402] FCA Handbook, COBS 12.4.

[403] Ibid, COBS 12.4.4.(2), 12.4.10.

[404] Ibid, COBS 12.4.4(1).

information, and the basis of valuation or methodology used in assessing a security.[405] Further, in an attempt to counter over-confidence amongst analysts, firms are required to publish, on a quarterly basis, the proportion of its research recommendations that are 'buy', 'hold', 'sell' or equivalent terms.[406] These disclosures are undoubtedly of some value, but disclosure as a regulatory technique in this context has various limitations. Disclosure shifts the burden onto investors in terms of assessing these conflicts, and then adjusting their own behaviour appropriately, but it is not clear that investors are well placed to do so. Research suggests that disclosure may not work well as a strategy in this context, because those to whom the information is disclosed tend to assume that the intermediary will then deal with them fairly, whereas the intermediary, having disclosed, may then feel comfortable about pursuing their own interests aggressively.[407]

The regulatory burden on analysts has undoubtedly increased in recent years. It is evident, however, that the regulation of analysts is 'lighter touch' than that which applies to CRAs, discussed at 13.7. Notably, there has been no equivalent drive for securities analysts to fall under the supervision of a central regulator, such as ESMA, or for the litigation risk faced by analysts to be increased by regulation.

11.6 Conclusion

Regulators make use of two primary tools to deal with misstatements in prospectuses, namely ex ante protections in the form of mandatory disclosure rules, and ex post enforcement mechanisms in the event that the information is incomplete or inaccurate. A similar pattern is observable in relation to regulating the secondary market. Important distinctions exist, however, between the two stages. At the IPO stage the reason for imposing disclosure rules is simply to provide investors with the information they need to decide whether to buy the securities, whereas the position is more complex in the secondary market. Some disclosures are aimed at the shareholders and intend to provide them with the information they need to carry out their corporate governance functions. Other disclosures are aimed at investors more generally, and seek to ensure that the market operates efficiently. Some disclosures may fulfil more than one of these functions. Consequently, the regulatory regime in the context of secondary market disclosures is also more complex, as we have seen in this chapter.

There is greater variety in the mandatory disclosure obligations imposed on companies in the secondary market as compared to the IPO stage. The timing of these obligations varies, some being periodic and some ad hoc, as do their content and focus. An understanding of the purpose of the disclosure helps to explain these differences. Both public and private mechanisms for enforcement are put in place to provide remedies in the event that this information proves inaccurate. The purpose of the disclosure is also important at this stage since different remedies may be available according to the purpose of the disclosure

---

[405] Ibid, COBS 12.4.5, 12.4.7.
[406] Ibid, COBS 12.4.10(4).
[407] DM Cain, G Loewenstein and DA Moore, 'The Dirt on Coming Clean: Perverse Effects of Disclosing Conflicts of Interest' (2005) 34 *Journal of Legal Studies* 1.

in question. While investors have a general statutory remedy for fraudulent misstatements, corporate governance-focused disclosures give rise to a potential common law remedy for shareholders. Again, differences are observable between the IPO stage and the ongoing market. Investors have greater protection at the IPO stage, under section 90 FSMA, than exists at the later stage under section 90A, reflecting the fact that the prospectus is solely a selling document and that there is value in timely non-defensive disclosure.

The greater complexity of the ongoing market is also apparent in the fact that disclosure alone is not enough to ensure the smooth functioning of the secondary market. In addition to disclosure obligations placed on issuers, conduct rules are imposed on market participants more generally. The two most common examples of such conduct rules are market abuse rules and short selling regulation. The regulation of market misconduct is discussed in the next chapter.

12

Ongoing Regulation of the Capital Markets: Market Misconduct

12.1 Introduction

In chapter eleven the use of disclosure to regulate the secondary market was analysed. As discussed in that chapter, the primary goal of secondary market regulation is to ensure that the prices of publicly traded securities are reasonably well informed.[1] Information disclosure is needed in order to deal with the acute information asymmetry that can arise between issuers and insiders, on the one hand, and investors on the other. A lack of credible information about issuers is one reason why markets may not operate efficiently, and the disclosure obligations discussed in chapter eleven are a response to that problem. It is clear that secondary markets may operate inefficiently for other reasons, however. This chapter considers three further issues that are regarded as causing markets to operate inefficiently, namely market abuse, short selling, and algorithmic and high frequency trading, and analyses the regulations put in place to deal with these forms of market misconduct.

The disclosure obligations discussed in chapter eleven are predominantly focused on issuers. Although other market participants do, on occasion, fall under an obligation to disclose information to the company,[2] it is the issuer that is under the obligation to make this information public. By contrast, the regulations discussed in this chapter place obligations on a broader range of market participants. The range of regulatory strategies employed to tackle these issues is also wider here than in chapter eleven. Disclosure plays an important role in tackling these issues,[3] but other forms of regulatory intervention are also adopted, including bans in some circumstances.

12.2 The Regulation of Market Abuse

Within the EU there are two forms of market abuse: insider dealing and market manipulation. Both are said to impair market integrity, and the current regulatory approach is to treat both forms of misconduct under one umbrella.[4] This is distinct from other jurisdictions,

---

[1] See 11.2.

[2] See, for example, the obligation on shareholders to disclose major shareholdings, discussed at 11.3.2.3.

[3] For example, in order to tackle insider dealing, issuers are required to disclose inside information to the market 'as soon as possible': see 11.3.2.1. As regards short selling see the disclosure obligations discussed at 12.3.2.2.

[4] Prior to 3 July 2016 see Market Abuse Directive 2003/6/EC, recital 12 and art 1; from 3 July 2016 see Market Abuse Regulation (EU) No 596/2014, recital 7 and art 1.

such as the US, which treat the rationales for insider dealing and market manipulation as distinct, and therefore have no umbrella term of 'market abuse' uniting these two forms of market misconduct.

Insider dealing is the situation where those with inside information about securities use that information to make a profit or avoid a loss. An obvious example is where a director of a company knows, as a result of his position, that a takeover offer is about to be made for the company and that the price offered will be at a substantial premium to the current market price of the shares, and before that information is made public he buys more shares in the company at the current market price in order to participate in the windfall. Alternatively, the director may know that the company is about to announce substantial losses and so may sell his shares in advance of the disclosure of that information in order to avoid the inevitable drop in share price that will result from the announcement. It is not the holding of inside information that is relevant: the offence involves the use, or misuse, of that information.

Market manipulation involves the improper use of market power to interfere with the market's normal price-forming mechanism. Common examples include the dissemination of misleading information, such as the publication of false accounts, and the retention or concealment of material market information. False rumours of a possible takeover bid, for example, may be circulated in the market purely in order to drive up the share price. Alternatively, artificial transactions may take place in order to create the appearance of active trading, and to convey false information regarding the supply and demand for investments. This may be carried out by managers,[5] but it is not limited to this group, as others within the market, such as traders in investment banks or other professional advisers, can carry out this form of market abuse.

12.2.1 Justifications for Regulating Market Abuse

Despite the single explanatory rationale for regulating market abuse set out above, namely that market abuse harms the integrity of financial markets, it is helpful, for reasons explored in this section, to consider the rationales justifying the regulation of insider dealing and market manipulation separately.

12.2.1.1 Justifications for Regulating Insider Dealing

12.2.1.1.1 Relationship-Based Justifications vs Market-Based Justifications

The original justification for regulating insider dealing in the UK was that it involved an abuse of the fiduciary relationship between a director and his principal, the company. As a

---

[5] The increase in equity-based compensation packages for corporate executives has been linked with some market manipulation schemes. Share options provide a pay-off only where the price of the company's shares has moved above the strike price at which the options were granted, and the pay-off may increase exponentially based on the increase in reported earnings. Pay packages based on share options do not penalise executives when the company's shares underperform. This creates a recognised moral hazard problem and can increase incentives for market manipulation by corporate executives: JN Gordon, 'What Enron Means for the Management and Control of the Modern Business Corporation: Some Initial Reflections' (2002) 69 *University of Chicago Law Review* 1233.

result, company law rules were used to regulate it.[6] While the UK has moved away from a relationship-based rationale of this kind, other jurisdictions continue to justify the regulation of insider dealing on this basis. The insider dealing (or insider trading) regime in the US provides an example of a relationship-based rationale.

In the US the offence of insider trading is not statutorily defined, and is based on judicial and administrative interpretations of a broad anti-fraud statute, section 10(b) of the Securities Exchange Act 1934, and accompanying SEC rules. Use of material and specific inside information is not enough to constitute insider trading. Instead, the court must determine how the person trading on the basis of that information obtained the information. Where that person is a fiduciary, then if that person trades in the securities of the company of which they are a fiduciary on the basis of material inside information, they will be liable because of a breach of duty to the shareholders.[7] If the person is not a fiduciary of the company, but obtains the information in trust and confidence and breaches that understanding, then that is also a violation of the insider trading provisions, this time not because of a breach of duty to the shareholders, but rather because of a breach of duty to the source of the information.[8] The final category of potential insider trader in the US is a person who receives information and trades on the basis of that information, but is not themselves in breach of duty to the company and does not misappropriate that information (a 'tippee'). For liability to arise here, the information must be material and specific, the tippee must be aware that the information is being furnished in breach of duty, either to the company or to the source of the information, and the tipper must expect to receive some benefit from furnishing the information.[9] The US insider trading regime therefore adopts a relationship-based approach, rather than one which focuses on the possession and use of the information per se or the effect of that (mis)use on the market.[10]

The approach adopted by the EU, and consequently now adopted by the UK, is somewhat different. The rationale for regulating insider dealing at EU level is to facilitate the 'smooth functioning of securities markets'[11]—in other words, the rationale is market-based rather than relationship-based. Consequently, this approach to insider dealing defines inside information as material non-public information, irrespective of its source, and insiders are defined principally by reference to their possession of that information, not by their

---

[6] P Davies, 'The European Community's Directive on Insider Dealing: From Company Law to Securities Markets Regulation' (1991) 11 *Oxford Journal of Legal Studies* 92.

[7] *US v Chiarella*, 445 US 222 (1980). The concept of 'fiduciary' for these purposes includes directors and officers of the company, but has been expanded over time to include 'temporary insiders', ie those retained by the company, such as lawyers and accountants: *SEC v Lund*, 570 F Supp 1397 (CD Cal 1983).

[8] *United States v O'Hagan*, 521 US 642 (1997); *SEC v Cuban*, 620 F 3d 551 (5th Cir, 2010).

[9] For discussion see *SEC v Dirks*, 436 US 646 (1983). In a recent decision the US Court of Appeals for the Second Circuit overturned the conviction of two hedge fund traders, finding that a benefit required 'an exchange that is objective, consequential and represents at least a potential gain of a pecuniary or similarly valuable nature': *United States v Newman and Chiassion*, No 13-1837 (2d Cir Dec 10, 2014).

[10] For a discussion of the contrast between the US and EU positions see E Greene and O Schmid, 'Duty-Free Insider Trading?' [2013] *Columbia Business Law Review* 369; M Ventoruzzo, 'Comparing Insider Trading in the United States and in the European Union: History and Recent Developments', European Corporate Governance Institute Working Paper Series in Law, No 257/2014.

[11] Prior to 3 July 2016 see Market Abuse Directive, 2003/6/EC, recital 2; from 3 July 2016 see Market Abuse Regulation (EU) No 596/2014, recital 2.

relationship to the issuer.[12] Furthermore, insider dealing has become a securities law matter with a focus on protecting investors and the market generally, rather than a company law matter.

12.2.1.1.2 Arguments Against the Regulation of Insider Dealing

The idea that insider dealing needs to be regulated has proved controversial.[13] A number of arguments are advanced against regulating insider dealing.[14] There are those who argue that inside information is a property right of the company, allocation of which is better left to purely contractual negotiations rather than formal law. An adjunct of this argument is that the use of inside information is an appropriate way to compensate corporate personnel, particularly directors, as a mechanism for encouraging innovation.[15] This argument fits most closely with a relationship-based approach to the regulation of insider dealing, where regulation is an aspect of company law, since it focuses predominantly on insiders who are directors[16]—a view which is no longer current in the UK.[17] It also suffers from a number of defects. There is no evidence that directors are undercompensated, and, even if they are, there are many other mechanisms available for compensating them. The growth of equity-based compensation schemes, for example, might be said to be better targeted at achieving this goal. More problematically, insider dealing is a poor tool for incentivising managers. In particular, it is unpredictable since the opportunity to exploit inside information arises infrequently. In addition, managers can make just as much money from trading on bad news about the company as good news. This would create an unacceptable moral hazard, since managers would become 'indifferent between working to make the firm prosperous and working to make it bankrupt'.[18]

Another argument put forward is that insider dealing is a victimless crime.[19] Investors who trade with, or at the same time as, insiders are willing buyers or sellers. They do not know the identity of the counterparty to the transaction and would have bought or sold to someone else in any case, even if the insider had not been in the market. Since there is no inducement by the insider to trade, there is no loss in the investor's hands that can be said to have been *caused by* the insider. An argument is even mounted that investors benefit because if an insider goes into the market to buy shares it increases the demand for shares and the third-party seller of shares will therefore benefit from any consequential increase in price.

The points about causation and inducement may be relevant to determining the rationale of insider trading in a system that allows individual investors to bring civil claims against

---

[12] For discussion see 12.2.2.1.1 and 12.2.2.3.1(a).

[13] See eg A Padilla, 'Insider Trading: What is Seen and What is Not Seen' in SM Bainbridge (ed), *Research Handbook on Insider Trading* (Cheltenham, Edward Elgar, 2013).

[14] One of the arguments against regulating insider dealing is based on the perceived inability of regulators to monitor and enforce insider dealing. The enforcement of market abuse provisions is discussed below at 12.2.2.1.6, 12.2.2.2.4 and 12.2.2.3.3.

[15] HG Manne, 'In Defence of Insider Trading' (1966) 44 *Harvard Business Review* 113. For discussion see JR Macey, *Insider Trading: Economics, Politics and Policy* (Washington, DC, AEI Press, 1991).

[16] Professor Manne initially referred only to entrepreneurs but subsequently expanded his ambit to include managers: HG Manne, 'Insider Trading and the Law Professors' (1970) 23 *Vanderbilt Law Review* 547.

[17] See 12.2.1.1.1.

[18] WD Carlton and DR Fischel, 'The Regulation of Insider Trading' (1983) 35 *Stanford Law Review* 857, 873.

[19] See eg RW McGee, 'Applying Ethics to Insider Trading' (2008) 77 *Journal of Business Ethics* 205.

the insider in relation to the insider trading, but the UK has no such system.[20] Insider dealing in the UK is dealt with by way of a mixture of criminal and administrative sanctions in the UK imposed by the FCA.[21] More importantly, insider dealing is a zero-sum game—that is, the net benefits of insider dealing must equal the net losses.[22] Although individual investors may benefit from insider dealing on occasion, the fact remains that the net result to investors generally is negative. The victims are therefore all those who constitute the market, other than the insiders. The losses are real, albeit thinly spread, and the concern is that insider dealing can impact investor confidence in the accuracy of market prices and reduce investment in the market in the first place.

12.2.1.1.3 Justifying the Market-Based Approach: Enhancing Investor Confidence

Arguments in favour of regulating insider dealing often commence from the notion that insider dealing is 'unfair'. These arguments run the risk of being vague and being based predominantly on a sense of moral outrage.[23] The approach of the EU to insider dealing puts flesh on the bones of this concept. Insider dealing laws are regarded as necessary to promote fair and orderly markets. The objective of legislation against insider dealing is to ensure the integrity of EU financial markets and to enhance investor confidence in those markets.[24] Investor confidence is a key component in creating efficient markets. It is not the fact of trading with an insider per se that causes the problem, or the fact that insiders induce investors to trade at the 'wrong price'. The insider dealing itself does not harm investors. What is damaging is the non-disclosure of material information—in other words, the information asymmetry between insiders and investors in publicly traded companies.

Investors who buy and sell in the market know that they run the risk that they may deal in securities just before the issuer discloses information about the company to the market. This may have favourable or unfavourable results for the investor depending on the nature of the disclosure, and whether the investor is buying or selling. In the long run, and in the absence of insider dealing, any gains or losses should even out. The presence of insider dealing, however, undermines investor confidence by undermining investors' beliefs that the market is fair and that they have an equal chance of profiting from securities trades. The effect of insider dealing is that market prices do not reflect the true worth of securities, in a way which is unfavourable to outsiders.

Investors who believe that the system is rigged are likely either to withhold their investment or, alternatively, to build this risk into their investment decisions, by lowering the price they are prepared to pay for companies' shares. Either of these outcomes will increase companies' cost of capital.[25] The ECJ has identified the purpose of market abuse regulation as being to protect the integrity of the financial markets, to enhance investor confidence,

---

[20] See 12.2.2.4.

[21] This is discussed further at 12.2.2.

[22] M Klock, 'Mainstream Economics and the Case for Prohibiting Inside Trading' (1994) 10 *Georgia State University Law Review* 297; MP Dooley, 'Enforcement of Insider Trading Restrictions' (1980) 66 *Virginia Law Review* 1, 33.

[23] HG Manne, 'In Defence of Insider Trading' (1966) 44 *Harvard Business Review* 114.

[24] Prior to 3 July 2016 see Market Abuse Directive 2003/6/EC, recital 12; from 3 July 2016 see Market Abuse Regulation (EU) No 596/2014, recital 2.

[25] H Schmidt, 'Insider Dealing and Economic Theory' in KJ Hopt and E Wymeersch (eds), *European Insider Dealing* (London, Butterworths, 1991).

and to provide investors with the assurance that they are on an equal footing with all other investors.[26] In the UK, the Court of Appeal has similarly emphasised the view that insider dealing should not be regarded as a victimless crime; it should be seen as a crime which undermines confidence in the integrity of the market: 'The principles of confidentiality and trust, which are essential to the operations of the commercial world, are betrayed by insider dealing and public confidence in the integrity of the system which is essential to its proper function is undermined by market abuse.'[27]

Some of these claims may be met with scepticism. The market may be said to be constituted of three types of investors: insiders (those who trade with inside information), information traders, such as analysts (those who trade on the basis of accurate information, but not inside information), and noise traders (those who make decisions regarding buy and sell trades without the use of fundamental data).[28] Even without the presence of insiders in the market, the informational playing field is not level: noise traders ought to be aware that information traders will generally be at an informational advantage to them, and this knowledge does not seem to dissuade uninformed investors from entering the market. It may be that insider dealing regulation is therefore more concerned with the potential asymmetry between information traders and insiders.

In support of the view that insider dealing can have a negative effect on markets, there is some evidence that although merely adopting insider dealing laws does not affect the cost of equity in a country, enforcement of those insider dealing laws does affect the cost of equity, with the cost decreasing significantly after the first prosecution.[29]

By way of contrast with the current view within the EU that insider dealing regulation is needed in order to promote market efficiency, arguments have been put forward to suggest that the allocative efficiency of the market can be increased by *allowing* insider dealing to occur. It has been suggested that insider dealing provides a good method of channelling information to the market, including information that companies would not disclose publicly because it would be too expensive, or would not be believable, or because disclosing it publicly would destroy the value of the information.[30] Insider dealing, it is suggested, allows all information which has a bearing on the prospects of the company, not just that which is publicly available, to be factored into the price of the company's shares. This increases allocative efficiency, since the price at which the company's shares trade more accurately reflects the company's prospects.

A significant flaw in this argument is that dealing alone is an inefficient way to impart information to the marketplace,[31] so this system would only work effectively if the insider's identity, and presumably their status as an insider, is known to the market. In general, only one category of potential insiders (directors) are required to disclose their dealings in the

---

[26] Case C-45/08 *Spector Photo Group NV, Chris Van Raemdonck v Commissie voor het Bank, Financie-en Assurantiewezen* (CBFA).

[27] *R v McQuoid* [2009] EWCA Crim 1301 [8] per Lord Judge CJ.

[28] For discussion see eg Z Goshen and G Parchomovsky, 'The Essential Role of Securities Regulation' (2006) 55 *Duke Law Journal* 711.

[29] U Battacharya and H Daouk, 'The World Price of Insider Trading' (2002) 57 *Journal of Finance* 75.

[30] Eg DW Carlton and DR Fischel, 'The Regulation of Insider Trading' (1983) 35 *Stanford Law Review* 857.

[31] It is the release of new information rather than the supply of a particular security that is the primary driver of share price movements: RJ Gilson and RH Kraakman, 'The Mechanisms of Market Efficiency' (1984) 70 *Virginia Law Review* 549, 629–34.

company's securities, and even in this instance there is a significant lapse of time between the trade and the disclosure, so it does not appear that the dominant purpose of these provisions is to allow the market to monitor these transactions.[32] In practice, therefore, it is difficult for analysts and other information traders to know when an insider is in the market and trading on the basis of inside information. Even were these facts to become known, the analyst must then take the further step of trying to gauge the nature of the information from the mere fact of trading. It is not impossible that insiders trading on the basis of inside information could release information into the market that can be impounded into price, but this creates a very noisy signal. Furthermore, any gains would also have to be weighed against the cost to the system arising from loss of investor confidence and the consequential increase in the cost of capital. On balance, the current EU (and UK) rationale of regulating insider dealing in order to promote market efficiency seems justifiable.

12.2.1.2 Justifications for Regulating Market Manipulation

By contrast with the debate regarding whether and how to regulate insider dealing, little doubt is generally expressed about the economic need for a prohibition on market manipulation. Unlike the position regarding insider dealing, the rationale for prohibiting market manipulation tends to remain relatively consistent across jurisdictions, and is market focused.[33] Once one of the goals of capital market regulation is the smooth functioning of the market, the rationale for regulating market manipulation is clear.[34] Market manipulation involves the unwarranted interference in the operation of the ordinary market forces of supply and demand. It is an interference with the market's normal price-forming mechanism, and it thereby undermines the integrity and efficiency of the market.

Any doubts expressed about the regulation of market manipulation tend to relate to the form and content of the prohibition.[35] One reason for this is the potentially complex nature of this offence. Although some forms of market manipulation may be relatively straightforward, such as the spreading of false rumours, others encompass highly sophisticated and complex practices designed to increase or decrease artificially a security's trading volumes and/or to distort its price. Coupled with this is the fact that market manipulation practices are constantly evolving as new products are developed, new participants enter the market, and markets become more interconnected. Consequently, formal, detailed definitions are unlikely to capture the full range of manipulative activity, and are likely to become outdated rapidly.

---

[32] See 11.3.2.2. Prior to 3 July 2016 the window is five days (the director must disclose to the company within four days of the trade and the company has one further day to disclose to the market), but from 3 July this is reduced to three days (see Market Abuse Regulation (EU) No 596/2014, arts 19(1)–(3)).

[33] In the US, for example, in addition to the general anti-fraud provision in rule 10b-5, it is an offence to engage in a series of transactions in any security registered on a national exchange creating actual or apparent active trading in such security or raising or depressing the price of such security: s 9(a)(2) Securities Exchange Act 1934.

[34] The common law has dealt with cases of market manipulation for some time; see eg *R v De Berenger* (1814) 3 M & S 67 (KB); *R v Aspinall* (1875–76) 1 LR 730, although the courts regarded these manipulative schemes as amounting to straightforward fraud, albeit that the misrepresentations were addressed to the public at large and had no specific recipients. The creation of the modern securities law-based offence of market manipulation only arose in 1986 with Financial Services Act 1986, s 47.

[35] Eg DR Fischel and DJ Ross, 'Should the Law Prohibit "Manipulation" in Financial Markets?' (1991) 105 *Harvard Law Review* 503.

In order to devise a general definition of market manipulation, however, the regulator must pin down what is wrongful about market manipulation, which is not straightforward.[36] Some aspects of market manipulation are closely related to fraud, such as where an insider deliberately publishes misinformation in the market, but not all forms of manipulation can be categorised in this way. Take the example of a company that decides to purchase its own shares in order to push up the price of those shares, in circumstances where the shares are undervalued and the company's actions are intended to signal that fact. This action is intended to move the price of the securities, and the company would assert that this movement is beneficial from an informational efficiency perspective, since it moves the price towards its 'correct' level (although, of course, ascertaining the 'correct' level for the price of a security is notoriously difficult). For this reason some commentators suggest that although some aspects of market manipulation should be prohibited, especially where there is fraud involved, other aspects of market manipulation, particularly those based on price distorting effects, should be deregulated.[37]

It might be thought that market manipulation could be defined simply as activity that involves an interference with the market's normal price forming mechanisms. This formulation also runs into difficulties, however, since there are some instances of interfering with the market's price forming mechanisms that are regarded as acceptable, and even desirable. An example of such a situation is the operation of price stabilisation rules.[38] These rules allow lead managers to support the prices of new issues for a limited period after issue, by buying those securities in the secondary market. The injection of a large new block of securities may exert a temporary depressing influence on the market price. The price stabilisation rules allow the underwriters to 'stabilise' the price by creating an artificial demand for the securities. The economic justification for allowing this to occur is that it encourages new issues, and thus supports the raising of capital. Many jurisdictions allow price stabilisation to take place, and the EU is no exception. Unsurprisingly, given the potential for these rules to distort the market, the use of price stabilisation is regulated.[39] So, for example, those seeking to make use of price stabilisation rules must make disclosure of this fact, and the stabilisation price cannot be greater than the bid price.

One further issue when determining how to regulate market manipulation is whether the intentions of the potential manipulator should be a relevant consideration. Regulators may prefer to look at objectively assessed effects-based criteria in this context, such as whether the trades undertaken represent a significant proportion of the daily trading volume of a security, whether changes in beneficial ownership occur, whether the orders are undertaken by those with a significant buying or selling position, and whether the trades result in a significant movement in the price of the securities. These signals are clearly not perfect, however. Such activities may be evidence of entirely proper behaviour, such as a large, legitimate trade in a particular security. In practice it is common for regulators to

---

[36] For discussion see E Avgouleas, *The Mechanics and Regulation of Market Abuse* (Oxford, Oxford University Press, 2006) ch 4.

[37] DR Fischel and DJ Ross, 'Should the Law Prohibit "Manipulation" in Financial Markets?' (1991) 105 *Harvard Law Review* 503.

[38] For discussion of this issue in the context of debt see 13.4.1.

[39] Prior to 3 July 2016 see Market Abuse Directive 2003/6/EC, art 8 and Buy Back and Stabilisation Regulation (2273/2003/EC) arts 8–10; from 3 July 2016 see Market Abuse Regulation (EU) No 596/2014, art 5 (and see ESMA Consultation Paper, *Draft Technical Standards on the Market Abuse Regulation*, 15 July 2014, ESMA/2014/809

adopt a subjective test, focusing on the improper intent of the trader. In the US, for example, the person accused of market manipulation must be shown to have 'scienter', or intent to commit the manipulation, and it must be shown that they transacted with the purpose of inducing the purchase or sale of such security by others.[40] In the UK, the level of knowledge required of the potential manipulator varies according to whether it is the criminal or administrative offence of market manipulation that is being considered, and the precise nature of the offence.[41]

Forming a workable definition of market manipulation in practice, therefore, is not straightforward. It needs to capture those activities that, if left unregulated, will impede market efficiency, while excluding activity which could potentially fall within it, but which is thought valuable from a market efficiency perspective (such as price stabilisation, market making, and arbitrage activities), and indeed large price-moving trades which are perfectly legitimate. These difficulties with drawing the boundaries of market manipulation in practice, however, do not detract from the clear rationale for regulating market manipulation in principle.

12.2.2 The Offences of Insider Dealing and Market Manipulation

A number of regulatory techniques are available to deal with market abuse.[42] As discussed in chapter eleven, the dominant technique for regulating the capital markets is disclosure, and this has a role to play here too. Issuers must disclose inside information to the market 'as soon as possible', and one of the goals of this provision is to reduce the possibility of insider dealing.[43] To a lesser extent the obligation on directors to disclose their dealings in their company's shares can also be regarded as a means of regulating insider dealing.[44] This use of disclosure is important, but it can only go so far. The first provision applies only to issuers and does not comprise a more general obligation on all those with inside information to disclose it to the market. In relation to the second obligation, it is notable that only a very limited category of insiders is caught (directors) and the time lapse between the trade

---

regarding the replacement of the stabilisation measures). In the UK see FSMA, s 118A(5)(b); Financial Services Act 2012, ss 89(3)(a), 90(9)(b)(ii) and 91(3)(a); FCA Handbook, MAR 2.

[40] This is the case in the US under both s 9 and s 10(b) Securities Exchange Act 1934. This is similar to the mens rea element required for the criminal offence of market manipulation in the UK (see Financial Services Act 2012, s 90).

[41] See 12.2.2.2 (the criminal offences of market manipulation, which do require the establishment of mens rea) and 12.2.2.3 (the regulatory offences of mens rea under s 118 FSMA). Under s 118 FSMA some of the offences of market manipulation require no mens rea element on the face of the offence (see s 118(6)), whereas others impose a negligence standard (see eg s 118(7)). However, even in relation to s 118(6) the regulator can take account of the mens rea of the manipulator when determining the penalty (FSMA, ss 123(2) and 124(2)).

[42] This chapter deals with market abuse in the context of securities (predominantly equity securities; the regulation of market abuse in the context of debt securities is discussed at 13.4). However, market abuse can occur in other markets. For example, the Electricity and Gas (Market Integrity and Transparency) (Criminal Sanctions) Regulations 2015 (SI 2015/979) create new criminal offences for insider dealing and market manipulation of the wholesale energy markets. A discussion of market abuse in these wider markets falls outside the parameters of this book.

[43] 11.3.2.1.

[44] 11.3.2.2.

and the disclosure suggests that the provision of information to the market is not the predominant purpose of this provision.

The limitations of disclosure as a technique are even more apparent in relation to market manipulation. There are a number of reasons for this. First, disclosure rules impose positive obligations on insiders in relation to the information they must disclose. For example, we saw in chapters ten and eleven that issuers must disclose certain information about the company and its securities. They do not impose negative obligations, that is, obligations not to disclose misleading or false information. It is easy to appreciate, however, that allowing an insider to put a false rumour into the market, for example regarding an imminent takeover offer for the company, which then becomes reflected in the share price, will be just as problematic for investors trying to decide whether to buy, sell or hold the issuer's securities, as a failure on the company's part to disclose information about an actual takeover offer. Second, it is difficult for disclosure rules to capture situations where the provision of misinformation to the market occurs by way of actions rather than statements, for example where an investor simultaneously sells and buys the same financial instruments in order to artificially increase trading volume, giving the impression that the instrument is more in demand than it actually is. Finally, disclosure obligations have traditionally been focused on a narrow set of potential insiders. Often the obligations are predominantly focused on the issuer.[45] However, it is clear that it is just as easy, and just as problematic from an informational efficiency point of view, for someone other than the issuer, potentially someone unconnected with the company, to engage in artificial trades.

The predominant form of regulation in place in the UK to deal with market abuse is therefore not disclosure but, rather, a general ban. Within the UK, there are various market abuse offences. In particular, there is the criminal offence of insider dealing under the Criminal Justice Act 1993, the criminal offences of market manipulation under sections 89–91 of the Financial Services Act 2012, and the administrative offence of market abuse (covering both insider dealing and market manipulation) under section 118 FSMA.

This is an area that has been influenced by EU legislation. The Market Abuse Directive 2003[46] has had a significant effect in this area, and in the wake of the financial crisis a new Market Abuse Regulation and a new Market Abuse Directive, both published in 2014,[47] form a significant plank in the EU's post-crisis reform programme.[48] The Market Abuse Regulation makes a number of significant changes to the EU regime, and it repeals and replaces the 2003 Market Abuse Directive from July 2016. The fact that a regulation, rather than a directive, has been chosen as the legislative instrument means, of course, that these provisions are directly effective in Member States as from that date. One of the stated aims of the new

---

[45] Although in some instances other market participants may come under obligations too (for example, the EU rules regarding disclosure of directors' shareholdings start with an obligation on the director to disclose to the company which the issuer must then disclose to the market), the focus is on issuer disclosure.

[46] Directive 2003/6/EC. For discussion see G Ferrarini, 'The European Market Abuse Directive' (2004) 41 *Common Market Law Review* 711.

[47] Regulation (EU) No 596/2014 and Directive 2014/57/EU. For detailed discussion see Moloney: EU Regulation, ch VIII.

[48] For a discussion of the EU's programme in this regard see J Payne and E Howell, 'The Creation of a European Capital Market' in P Koutrakos and J Snell (eds), *Research Handbook on the Law of the EU's Internal Market* (Cheltenham, Edward Elgar, 2015); House of Lords, European Union Committee—Fifth Report, *The Post-Crisis EU Financial Regulatory Framework: Do the Pieces Fit?*, 27 January 2015.

Market Abuse Regulation is to 'establish a more uniform interpretation of the Union market abuse framework' and to avoid potential regulatory arbitrage.[49] The UK does not need to implement legislation to adopt this regulation, but it must review existing legislation, such as section 118 FSMA, to ensure that it is not contrary to the provisions of the new regulation.

The new Market Abuse Regulation casts a far wider regulatory net than its predecessor. Under the 2003 Market Abuse Directive, only financial instruments trading on regulated markets were covered, whereas the new regulation also encompasses trading on MTFs, such as the AIM market, and also trading on OTFs, a new category of trading venue introduced in 2014 and intended to act as a regulatory 'catch-all'.[50] Further, the reach of the provisions is extended to capture financial instruments the price or value of which depends on, or has an effect on, the price or value of a financial instrument traded on a regulated market, MTF or OTF.[51] The market manipulation provisions of the EU market abuse regime are expanded under the regulation to apply to any spot commodity contract that has, or is likely to have, or is intended to have, an effect on the price or value of a financial instrument, and any type of financial instrument that has, or is likely to have, an effect on the price or value of a spot commodity contract whose price depends upon the relevant financial instrument.[52] In light of the LIBOR and EURIBOR manipulation scandals, the regulation extends the market manipulation provisions to cover 'behaviour in relation to benchmarks'.[53] Emission allowances now come within the scope of the market abuse regime.[54] The geographical scope of these provisions is also extremely wide, since the only connection that a financial instrument must have in order to engage the regulation is that it is traded on a European regulated market, MTF or OTF or that it depends on or affects the value of a financial instrument traded on a European regulated market, MTF or OTF.[55] Neither the issuer, its counterparty nor the potential market abuser need have any connection with the EU.

The regulation imposes new obligations regarding the prevention, detection and enforcement of market abuse. For example, market operators and investment firms that operate a trading venue are required to establish and maintain effective arrangements and procedures aimed at preventing and detecting insider dealing and market manipulation.[56] The regulation also details minimum standards in relation to the sanctions to be imposed for these offences.

In contrast to these significant innovations, the key elements of the offences of insider dealing and market manipulation, such as the definition of 'inside information', are not changed significantly by the regulation. These issues are considered in more detail at 12.2.2.3. There are, however, extensions to the scope and enforcement of these offences that are important. For example, there is an increased focus on the use of algorithmic and high frequency trading,[57] and there are new offences of attempted insider dealing[58] and

---

[49] Market Abuse Regulation (EU) No 596/2014, recital 5.

[50] Ibid, arts 2(1)(a)–(c) and see MiFIR (Regulation (EU) No 600/2014), Title II.

[51] Market Abuse Regulation (EU) No 596/2014, art 2(1)(d).

[52] Ibid, arts 2(2)(a)(b).

[53] Ibid, art 2(2)(c). The UK has already introduced a criminal offence specifically relating to the manipulation of benchmarks with s 91 Financial Services Act 2012, discussed at 12.2.2.2.3.

[54] Market Abuse Regulation (EU) No 596/2014, arts 3(1)(19) and 2(1).

[55] Ibid, art 2(4).

[56] Ibid, art 16. There are also new provisions relating to whistleblowing: art 32.

[57] See eg ibid, art 12(2). For further discussion see 12.4.

[58] Ibid, art 14.

attempted market manipulation.[59] The regulation also introduces changes regarding the disclosure of inside information.[60]

The 2014 Market Abuse Directive sets out new criminal sanctions for market abuse.[61] It covers insider dealing and market manipulation, and provides for minimum sanctions of specified prison terms, depending on the nature of the infringement. The UK has announced its decision not to opt in to this directive at the present time, although it has reserved the right to do so at a later stage, since the current UK law already covers all the offences included within the directive.

12.2.2.1 The Criminal Offence of Insider Dealing Under the Criminal Justice Act 1993

The offence of insider dealing was initially based on a breach of fiduciary duty by directors. The root of the offence was in company law and as such the primary focus was on shareholder protection. The rationale for regulating insider dealing has undergone a shift, and is now regarded as market-focused, that is, as an aspect of securities law.[62] The Criminal Justice Act 1993 primarily adopts this latter, investor-focused approach to insider dealing.[63]

12.2.2.1.1 Definition of an Insider

The Act creates two categories of insiders. 'Primary insiders'[64] are those who obtain their information through being a director, employee or shareholder of an issuer of securities,[65] or have access to the information by virtue of their 'employment, office or profession',[66] such as professional advisers to the company. 'Secondary insiders' are those who obtain their information from a primary insider.[67] The secondary insider may be liable under this Act even if not actively tipped off by the primary insider, for example where the tipper (the primary insider) is unaware that they are communicating inside information to the secondary insider.

---

[59] Ibid, art 15.

[60] Ibid, art 17. See 11.3.2.

[61] Market Abuse Directive 2014/57/EU. A recent decision of the European Court of Human Rights makes it clear, however, that dual application of administrative and criminal sanctions is prohibited: *Grande Stevens v Italy*, 4/03/2014.

[62] See 12.2.1.1.

[63] *Patel v Mirza* [2014] EWCA Civ 1047 [67] per Gloster LJ: '[T]he mischief at which section 52 is directed is the deliberate and improper exploitation of unpublished price-sensitive information obtained through or from a privileged relationship, which may distort a regulated market because public disclosure of the relevant information would materially affect it—in other words, market abuse.'

[64] The terms 'primary' and 'secondary' insiders are not used in the legislation, but were endorsed by the House of Lords in *AG's Reference (No 1 of 1988)* [1989] 1 AC 971.

[65] Criminal Justice Act 1993, s 57(2)(a)(i). It has been suggested that the 'through being' test is a 'but for' test, ie that there must be a causal link between the employment and the acquisition of the information, but not in the sense that the information must be acquired in the course of the employment: Gower and Davies, 30-19.

[66] Criminal Justice Act 1993, s 57(2)(a)(ii).

[67] Ibid, s 57(2)(b). This latter group is referred to as 'tippees' in the US. For a tippee to be liable in the US, the information must be material and specific, the tippee must be aware that the information is being furnished in breach of duty by the tipper, and the tipper must expect to receive some benefit from furnishing that information: see *SEC v Dirks*, 346 US 646 (1983).

Due to the criminal nature of this offence, it is not enough for the individual to have information as an insider; that individual must also know that it is inside information, and he must have it, and know that he has it, from an inside source.[68]

12.2.2.1.2 Definition of Inside Information

Inside information is defined by section 56. It is information which (a) relates to particular securities or to a particular issuer of securities and not to securities generally or to issuers of securities generally; (b) is specific or precise; (c) has not been made public; and (d) if it were made public it would be likely to have a significant effect on the price of securities.

12.2.2.1.2(a) The Information must Relate to Particular Securities or to a Particular Issuer

Inside information must relate either to particular securities or to a particular issuer of securities,[69] such as information concerning an imminent takeover bid of a particular company—in other words, the information must not be general in nature. This information can include information that may affect the company's business prospects,[70] and can therefore include information coming from an outside source, such as a competitor company announcing a new and superior competing product. Presumably, however, information about the market sector to which a company belongs will not be inside information. So, a report from the Government intending to remove the monopoly position of a particular company would be inside information, but plans to regulate a particular market sector, or information of general application, such as the state of the economy, are unlikely to be particular enough to count as inside information. This distinction will not always be easy to draw, however, as the information may impact differentially on companies, and some information, which appears generic, may be of key significance to the securities of some companies.

12.2.2.1.2(b) The Information must be Specific or Precise

In order to be inside information, the information must be specific *or* precise.[71] Although these terms have sometimes been regarded as synonymous, the two concepts can be distinguished. Information that a company's profits are in excess of expectations would be specific (as to the company and its prospects) but not precise, if the amount of the excess is not stated.[72]

12.2.2.1.2(c) The Information must not have been Made Public

Section 58 provides a non-exhaustive definition of when information can be said to have been made public for this purpose. So, for example, information has been made public if it

---

[68] Criminal Justice Act 1993, s 57(1). As long as the secondary insider knows that the source of the inside information is a primary insider, he need not know the identity of that individual: *AG's Reference (No 1 of 1988)* [1989] 1 AC 971.

[69] Ibid, s 56(1)(a).

[70] Ibid, s 60(4).

[71] Ibid, s 56(1)(b).

[72] For a discussion of the meaning of 'precise' for the purposes of insider dealing under s 118 FSMA see 12.2.2.3.1(b).

is published in accordance with the rules of a regulated market for the purpose of informing investors and their professional advisers.[73] The definition of 'made public' is intended
to provide a generous test for analysts. Analysts are in a potentially difficult position. Their
role is to examine the information disclosed by companies and to search for further information of their own, and to use any information they acquire to their own advantage. The
Criminal Justice Act 1993 does not aim to prevent the use of informational advantages
of this kind. Indeed, on one view, analysts are crucial for the efficient functioning of the
market.[74]

Much of the information actually disclosed by companies is technical and detailed and is
not likely per se to provide very useful guidance to investors. The particular value of disclosure is that it impacts on the market price of the securities and therefore investors trading
at the market price are protected even if they never read the particular disclosures made by
the company. Analysts are one of the bridging mechanisms for turning company disclosures into a market price that reflects the true value of the securities.[75] The acquisition of
informational advantages through skill and diligence, rather than because that individual
holds a particular position, is not improper, and indeed is to be encouraged. As a result, the
Criminal Justice Act 1993 provides that 'information is made public if … it is derived from
information which has been made public'.[76] Further, information is public if that information can be 'readily acquired'[77] by those likely to deal in the securities, whether the information has in fact been acquired or not. It can be public even though it can only be acquired
by payment of a fee, it is only published outside the UK, or can only be acquired by those
exercising 'diligence or expertise'.[78]

12.2.2.1.2(d) If the Information were Made Public it would be Likely to have a Significant Effect on the Price of Securities

The final requirement is that if the information were made public it would be likely to have
a significant effect on the price of any securities.[79] This is intended to provide a de minimis test, and therefore exclude those who might obtain only trivial benefits from dealing
in inside information. No advice is provided within the Act as to the meaning of 'likely to
have a significant effect on price'. When this issue was examined recently in relation to the
same phrase in section 118C FSMA regarding the administrative offence of insider dealing,
the Upper Tribunal held that the word 'likely' should be read as meaning that there was a
real prospect of the information having a significant, rather than a de minimis, effect on
price.[80] The Tribunal found that 'significant' for these purposes was only to be contrasted
with insignificant, in the sense of trivial.

---

[73] Criminal Justice Act 1993, s 58(2)(a).
[74] See discussion at 11.2.1.1 and 11.4.
[75] See eg Z Goshen and G Parchomovsky, 'The Essential Role of Securities Regulation' (2006) 55 *Duke Law Journal* 711.
[76] Criminal Justice Act 1993, s 58(2)(d).
[77] Ibid, s 58(2)(c).
[78] Ibid, s 58(3).
[79] Ibid, s 56(1)(d).
[80] See *Hannam v FCA* [2014] UKUT 233 (TCC). For discussion see 12.2.2.3.1(b).

Under the Criminal Justice Act 1993, an 'individual who has information as an insider'[81] is guilty of the offence of insider dealing in three different circumstances: actual dealing in securities,[82] encouraging another person to deal,[83] and disclosing inside information to another person.[84]

12.2.2.1.3 The Offence of Actual Dealing in Securities

For the offence of actual dealing, the individual must have inside information as an insider and must deal[85] on a regulated market[86] or rely on a professional intermediary to do so, or themselves be acting as a professional intermediary.[87] Dealing is defined to include both acquiring and disposing of securities, so inaction is not caught by the Act. Dealing which occurs off a regulated market is not caught by these provisions, once again reinforcing the rationale of this offence as being directed towards maintaining the integrity of the markets. The individual must deal in securities that are price-affected securities in relation to that information.

The fact that this is a criminal offence means that there is a significant mens rea element to the offence. The insider must know that the information is inside information, and he must have it, and know that he has it, from an inside source. This is subjectively assessed and accordingly will be difficult to establish. A number of defences are available. The main defence for the defendant is if he can show he would have done what he did even if he had not had the information, for example he would have traded anyway to meet a pressing financial need or legal obligation.[88] There is also a defence if the defendant can show that he did not expect the dealing to result in a profit attributable to the fact that the information was price-sensitive information in relation to the securities.[89] This is likely to be narrowly construed and is unlikely to be very beneficial to defendants. Alternatively, the defendant has a defence if he can show that he believed on reasonable grounds that the information had been disclosed widely enough to ensure that none of those taking part in the dealing would be prejudiced by not having the information.[90]

---

[81] Criminal Justice Act 1993, s 52(1). This offence can only be committed by an individual, not a company (although the offence can be committed by an individual if he causes a company to deal or discloses information to it). This contrasts with the position under Financial Services Act 2012, s 89 and under FSMA, s 118, both of which can be committed by companies (see, respectively, Financial Services Act 2012, s 89(1) and FSMA, s 118(1)).

[82] Criminal Justice Act 1993, s 52(1)(3). For the definition of securities see Criminal Justice Act 1993, s 54, Sch 2 and the Insider Dealing (Securities and Regulated Markets) Order 1994 (SI 1994/187). In general the definition covers shares, debt securities, options and futures, but not units in unit trusts.

[83] Criminal Justice Act 1993, ss 52(2)(a), 52(3).

[84] Ibid, s 52(2)(b).

[85] For the definition of dealing in securities see ibid, s 55.

[86] For the definition of regulated markets see the Insider Dealing (Securities and Regulated Markets) Order 1994 (SI 1994/187). This Order extends the application of the Criminal Justice Act 1993 to securities which are officially listed in or are admitted to dealing under the rules of any investment exchange established within any of the States of the EEA, but see Criminal Justice Act 1993, s 62(1) on the need for a territorial connection with the UK.

[87] Criminal Justice Act 1993, s 52(3). For the definition of professional intermediary for these purposes see s 59.

[88] Ibid, s 53(1)(c).

[89] Ibid, s 53(1)(a).

[90] Ibid, s 53(1)(b). This defence is mainly aimed at underwriting arrangements, where those involved in the underwriting trade amongst themselves on the basis of shared knowledge about the underwriting proposal but the information is not known to the market generally.

There is also a general defence, which applies to all of the offences, for market makers. If the defendant can show that he acted in good faith in the course of his business as a market maker, he will have a defence to any of the insider dealing offences under the Act.[91]

12.2.2.1.4 The Offence of Encouraging Another Person to Deal

For the second offence, the individual will be liable if he has the information as an insider and if he encourages another person to deal in price-affected securities in relation to the information.[92] It is not necessary for dealing to actually take place. The dealing need not be on a regulated market or in reliance on a professional intermediary, although the defendant must have reasonable cause to believe that the dealing would be prohibited. The other person need not know that the securities are price-affected securities, nor need he actually receive the inside information. The mens rea element for this offence is that the individual must know or have reasonable cause to believe[93] that the dealing will take place on a regulated market or by, or in reliance on, a professional intermediary. The defences for this offence are the same as those for the actual dealing offence, set out above.[94]

12.2.2.1.5 The Offence of Disclosing Inside Information to Another Person

The final offence is the disclosing offence. The defendant must have information as an insider and must disclose that information 'otherwise than in the proper performance of the functions of his employment, office or profession'[95] to another person. Again, the individual must know that the information is inside information, and he must have it, and know that he has it, from an inside source. There is a defence if the defendant did not expect any person, because of the disclosure, to deal on a regulated market as, or in reliance on, a professional intermediary,[96] such as where the information is disclosed to a journalist to use as part of a story. There is also a defence if the defendant did not expect the dealing to result in a profit attributable to the fact that the information was price-sensitive information in relation to the securities.[97]

12.2.2.1.6 Penalties and Enforcement

The penalties for insider dealing under the Criminal Justice Act 1993 are up to seven years' imprisonment or an unlimited fine.[98] A person found guilty can also be disqualified by court order from being a company director.[99] There are no civil law consequences for a breach of these provisions: no contract is rendered void or unenforceable as a result of a breach of section 52 of the Act.[100] A court can make a compensation order requiring the

---

[91] Ibid, s 53(4) and Sch 1.
[92] Ibid, s 52(2)(a).
[93] Ibid. Since it is enough for the defendant to have 'reasonable cause to believe', an objective element is introduced to this offence (cf the purely subjective approach adopted under the actual dealing and disclosing offences).
[94] Ibid, s 53(2). See 12.2.2.1.3.
[95] Ibid, s 52(2)(b).
[96] Ibid, s 53(3)(a).
[97] Ibid, s 53(3)(b).
[98] Ibid, s 61.
[99] Company Directors Disqualification Act 1986, ss 2, 8 and see *R v Goodman* [1993] 2 All ER 789.
[100] Criminal Justice Act 1993, s 63(2).

insider to pay compensation to any person who has suffered loss as a result of the offence,[101] although it will be difficult to identify an individual who has suffered loss in the faceless transactions that occur in the modern marketplace. In addition, the FCA can make use of its range of remedies for market abuse, such as injunctions and restitution orders.[102]

The fact that this is a criminal offence raises a number of difficult enforcement issues.[103] An element of culpability is required as part of the offence: for the offence to be established, a mens rea element must be proved. In general it must be established that the individual knows that the information is inside information, and he must have it, and know that he has it, from an inside source.[104] This is subjectively assessed and, accordingly, it will be difficult to establish in court. Coupled with this is the fact that the burden of proof in criminal cases is higher than in civil cases: beyond reasonable doubt rather than merely on the balance of probabilities.

These offences have in the past needed to compete for police and prosecutor attention with other crimes that are generally regarded as more serious and worthy of attention, such as assaults and murders. However, it is now possible for the regulator (now the FCA) to prosecute an offence under the Criminal Justice Act 1993,[105] which deals with this difficulty to some extent, and adds a specialist element to the prosecution of the offence, even if the judge and jury in such trials remain non-specialists.[106] The regulator (the FSA at that time) secured its first criminal conviction for insider dealing in March 2009, and a number of other prosecutions have followed.[107] A lawyer, McQuoid, employed by a company, TTP communications plc (TTP), tipped off his father-in-law that TTP was about to be taken over. The father-in-law bought shares in TTP before the takeover was announced. Following the announcement TTP's share price soared, resulting in a profit of almost £49,000 on the shares. Both McQuoid and his father in law were given jail sentences of eight months, although the father-in-law's sentence was suspended for 12 months.[108] Dismissing McQuoid's appeal, the Court of Appeal stated that deliberate insider dealing was a species of fraud for which prosecution, rather than regulatory proceedings, would often be more appropriate.[109]

Levels of enforcement of the criminal offence of insider dealing have historically been low. Between 1997 and 2006, for example, proceedings were brought against 15 individuals, of which eight were successful.[110] Although these levels have risen in recent years,

---

[101] Powers of Criminal Courts Act 1973, s 35.

[102] FSMA, ss 380, 382.

[103] For a discussion see B Rider, 'Civilising the Law: The Use of Civil and Administrative Proceedings to Enforce Financial Services Law' [1995] *Journal of Financial Crime* 11.

[104] Criminal Justice Act 1993, s 57(1).

[105] FSMA, s 402. There is no need for the regulator to obtain the consent of the Secretary of State or the Director of Public Prosecutions before bringing a prosecution under s 402: *R (on the application of Matthew Francis Uberoi, Neel Akash Uberoi) v City of Westminster Magistrates' Court* [2008] EWHC 3191 (Admin).

[106] For a discussion of the role of juries see Home Office, *Juries in Serious Fraud Trials: A Consultation Document* (February 1998), chs 1–2.

[107] Details of these prosecutions can be found on the FCA's website. As at 29 April 2015 the statistics were 27 convictions and 10 individuals currently being prosecuted.

[108] *R v McQuoid* (unreported, Southwark Crown Court, 27 March 2009), upheld on appeal: *R v McQuoid* [2009] EWCA Crim 1301.

[109] *R v McQuoid* [2009] EWCA Crim 1301.

[110] HC Deb, vol 442 col 1635W (13 February 2006) (Parliamentary Question No 2005/3120 from Austin Mitchell).

particularly following the regulator's assumption of responsibility for this issue and the stated aim of the FCA to be tougher on financial crime,[111] the overall number of criminal prosecutions for this issue is likely to remain relatively small because of the need to establish a mens rea element and to satisfy the high criminal law burden of proof.

12.2.2.2 The Criminal Offences of Market Manipulation Under Sections 89–91 Financial Services Act 2012

While the basic concept of market manipulation and the rationale for regulating it are easy to understand, creating a definition of market manipulation is not straightforward.[112] If an overly rigid definition is adopted, new and ingenious schemes that result in a manipulation of the market may be excluded, and yet overly flexible or open-ended definitions will cause difficulties where market manipulation may result in criminal penalties. Article 7 of the European Convention on Human Rights requires the contours of criminal behaviour to be delineated with clarity. Any ambiguity needs to be resolved in favour of the accused. This suggests that a high level of definitional clarity will be needed for any criminal offence of market manipulation. Further, only Parliament can create and define criminal offences, and so amending these offences will be a slow process.[113]

The criminal offences of market manipulation are contained in sections 89–91 of the Financial Services Act 2012.[114] Previously this issue had been governed by section 397 FSMA. Under section 397 FSMA a single section had encompassed two forms of the offence: misleading statements and dishonest concealment on the one hand[115] and misleading conduct on the other.[116] The Financial Services Act 2012 repealed section 397 and replaced it with sections 89–91 of that Act.[117] Sections 89–90 of the 2012 Act broadly cover the same ground as section 397 FSMA, albeit that the two offences that were combined in section 397 are now separated, so that misleading statements and dishonest concealment are dealt with in section 89, and section 90 covers misleading conduct. There are some changes between section 397 and sections 89–90, but these are relatively small.

By contrast, section 91 introduces a new offence, extending the concept of market manipulation to deal with the manipulation of benchmarks.[118] The new section 91 offence was introduced to deal with the LIBOR scandal in 2012, which involved a series of fraudulent actions connected to LIBOR. This resulted in investigations and an independent review

---

[111] See eg FCA, *The FCA's Approach to Advancing its Objectives*, July 2013.

[112] For discussion see 12.2.1.2 and E Lomnicka, 'Preventing and Controlling the Manipulation of Financial Markets: Towards a Definition of Market Manipulation' (2001) 8 *Journal of Financial Crime* 297.

[113] Another restrictive element that exists in relation to the criminal offence of market manipulation is the fact that international law imposes territorial limits on the enforceability of criminal law, whereas global financial markets mean that market abuse may often be conducted in a number of jurisdictions. For the territorial reach of these provisions see Financial Services Act, ss 89(4), 90(10), 91(5), 91(6).

[114] Unlike the criminal offence of insider dealing, which may only be committed by individuals, the criminal offences of market manipulation may also be committed by legal entities.

[115] FSMA, s 397(1). This replicated the prohibition previously in place in Financial Services Act 1986, s 47(1).

[116] Ibid, s 397(3). This replicated the prohibition previously in place in Financial Services Act 1986, s 47(2). The two forms of the offence were not mutually exclusive: various kinds of behaviour, such as false rumours and artificial transactions, could conceivably fall within both forms of the offence.

[117] Financial Services Act 2012, s 95.

[118] This has also been an issue at EU level: as a consequence of the LIBOR scandal the market manipulation provisions in the Market Abuse Regulation (EU) No 596/2014 apply to benchmarks (art 2(2)(c)).

(the Wheatley Review).[119] Section 91 implements recommendations made in the final report of that Review. The only benchmark to which this new offence initially applied was LIBOR, but following a government consultation additional benchmarks have subsequently been added to the scope of section 91.[120]

These offences of market manipulation do not prohibit all forms of interference in market forces—some interference is accepted. In particular, it is a defence to an action for market manipulation if the actions are in conformity with the FCA's price stabilisation rules,[121] or the control of information rules,[122] or the EU exemption provisions for buy-back programmes and the stabilisation of financial instruments.[123]

12.2.2.2.1 Misleading Statements and Dishonest Concealment: Section 89 Financial Services Act 2012

Section 89 of the Financial Services Act 2012 creates a criminal offence relating to (i) the making of a statement[124] which the person making it knows[125] to be false or misleading in a material respect or is reckless[126] as to whether it is false or misleading, and (ii) the dishonest concealment of any material fact. A person commits an offence if the person makes the statement or conceals the facts with the intention of inducing, or is reckless as to whether they will induce, another person to engage in, or refrain from engaging in, market activity in relation to a relevant agreement or relevant investment.[127] This section largely restates the effect of section 397(2) FSMA.

A common example of this form of market manipulation is where brokers or other investment advisors provide misleading advice, in order to promote the sale of shares in which they make a market, or to offload securities which are marketed or have been underwritten by their firm, by 'talking up' the securities to unsuspecting investors. Another example is

---

[119] *Wheatley Review of LIBOR: Final Report*, September 2012.

[120] Financial Services and Markets Act 2000 (Regulated Activities) (Amendment) Order 2015 (SI 2015/369). See HM Treasury, *Implementing the Fair and Effective Markets Review's Recommendations on Financial Benchmarks: Response to the Consultation*, December 2014; FCA Consultation Paper CP 14/32, *Bringing Additional Benchmarks into the Regulatory and Supervisory Regime*, December 2014.

[121] Financial Services Act 2012, ss 89(3)(a), 90(9)(b)(ii), 91(3)(a). The FCA's price stabilisation rules are set out in the Code of Market Conduct in the FCA Handbook, MAR 2.

[122] Financial Services Act 2012, ss 89(3)(b), 90(9)(c), 91(3)(b).

[123] Ibid, ss 89(3)(c), 90(9)(d), 91(3)(c).

[124] Section 89 adopts slightly different language to s 397 FSMA: s 397(1)(2) refers to the making of a misleading 'statement, promise or forecast' whereas s 89 refers simply to making a misleading statement (s 89(1)). This is a curious change, since generally the intention of ss 89–91 (as compared to s 397 FSMA) seems to have been to extend the net of criminal liability. It may be that the prosecution will, in future, suggest that promises and forecasts are caught within the definition of 'statements'.

[125] Presumably, the requirement of knowledge here is the same as in relation to s 397 FSMA, ie it includes actual knowledge and wilful blindness, namely closing one's eyes to the obvious.

[126] One difference between s 397 FSMA and s 89 in this context is that in s 397 FSMA it was stated that reckless statements were caught by the provisions whether 'dishonestly made or otherwise' (s 397(1)(c)). This wording has been removed from s 89 and this may provide defendants with an argument that only dishonest forms of recklessness should now be vulnerable to prosecution. Presumably, the definition of recklessness here is the same as in relation to s 397 FSMA, ie recklessness should be given its ordinary meaning in English—a rash statement or promise made heedless of whether the person making it had any real facts on which to base it (see *Rv Grunwald* [1963] 1 QB 935 per Paull J, upheld by the Court of Appeal in *R v Page* [1996] Crim LR 821 in the context of Financial Services Act 1986, s 47).

[127] For the definitions of 'relevant agreement' and 'relevant investment' see Financial Services Act 2012, s 93(3)(5).

market rigging. An early example of this offence, which pre-dated statutory forms of market manipulation, involved a syndicate conspiring with a man (De Berenger) in order for the latter to appear at Dover as a French officer to bring the false news of Napoleon's death. This led to City stockbrokers and the public buying government debt, which pushed the prices considerably higher, while the members of the syndicate offloaded their holdings, as planned, at a considerable profit.[128] Modern variants on this practice make use of the internet to perpetrate practices resembling market rigging.[129]

For the offence of making a misleading statement either recklessly or with knowledge that it was misleading, there is no requirement that the statement be made dishonestly. In order to establish liability based on an *omission*, however, dishonesty is required. The defendant will be liable if he dishonestly conceals material facts whether in connection with a statement made by the person concealing the facts or otherwise.[130] Section 89 does not create any independent obligation to disclose and therefore the concealment must be of facts that the defendant is required by other provisions of the law to disclose, such as those created in the Disclosure Rules and Transparency Rules. The test of dishonesty is objective and is defined by reference to the ordinary standards of reasonable and honest people.[131]

In addition, the purpose of the statement or concealment must be either to induce someone, or be reckless as to whether it may induce someone, to enter into or refrain from entering into an investment agreement, or to exercise or refrain from exercising a right conferred by an investment.[132] The misleading statement or concealment must therefore be for the required purpose.

As under section 397 FSMA[133] there is a defence if the behaviour of the defendant was made in conformity with either the price stabilisation rules, the control of information rules or the EU exemption provisions for buy-back programmes and the stabilisation of financial instruments.[134]

A good example of the wrongdoing at which this section is aimed is found in *R v Bailey and Rigby*,[135] a case that pre-dates the introduction of the 2012 Act. The chief executive and chief financial officers of a company were found liable under section 397(2) FSMA. They were convicted of issuing a misleading trading statement that caused the share price to rise and investors to purchase its shares. The officers were found to have been reckless both as to the truth of this statement and as to whether investors would rely on it. They received custodial sentences of eighteen months and nine months respectively.

---

[128] *R v De Berenger* (1814) 3 M & S 67.

[129] See IOSCO, *Report on Securities Activity on the Internet III*, October 2003.

[130] Financial Services Act 2012, s 89(1)(c).

[131] *R v Ghosh* [1982] QB 1053, per Lord Lane CJ. This test was laid down for dishonesty offences under Theft Act 1968, as amended, but has been applied in the context of this offence prior to the introduction of Financial Services Act 2012 (see *R v Lockwood* (1987) 3 BCC 333) and presumably would continue to be applied under s 89.

[132] Financial Services Act 2012, s 89(2).

[133] FSMA, s 397(4).

[134] Financial Services Act 2012, s 89(3).

[135] [2006] 2 Cr App R (S) 36.

12.2.2.2.2 Misleading Impressions: Section 90 Financial Services Act 2012

Section 90 creates a criminal offence relating to doing any act or engaging in a course of conduct[136] which creates a false or misleading impression as to the market in or price or value of any relevant investment,[137] where the person doing the act or engaging in the conduct intends to create such an impression. If the person intends to induce another person to deal or refrain from dealing in the investment, the person commits an offence.[138] This provision replicates the effect of section 397(3) FSMA. As with section 397, there is also a specific defence made available to the defendant in relation to this offence: the defendant has a defence if he can demonstrate that he reasonably believed that the impression was not misleading.[139] This defence includes objective ('reasonably') as well as subjective elements, and therefore does not wholly exonerate honest defendants.[140]

Section 90, however, extends the effect of section 397(3) FSMA, and adds an additional offence: if the person knows or is reckless as to whether the impression is false or misleading and intends by creating the impression that a gain may be made or a loss avoided, the person also commits an offence.[141] This new offence can potentially capture a very wide range of behaviour.

Unlike the offence under section 89 of the 2012 Act, there is no need to demonstrate that the defendant had knowledge that the impression was misleading, or was reckless as to that fact, as long as it can be demonstrated that he acted for the purpose of creating an impression that was in fact misleading. It must be demonstrated that the purpose of creating the impression was to induce the other to act in a certain way.

As under section 397 FSMA[142] there is a defence if the behaviour of the defendant was made in conformity with either the price stabilisation rules, the control of information rules, or the EU exemption provisions for buy-back programmes and the stabilisation of financial instruments.[143]

Trading designed to influence (or lead) market prices, or even to mislead other market players, is a common phenomenon in competitive markets. It is only if the conduct is capable of misleading the market and affecting the price formation mechanism that such conduct should be outlawed. This form of market manipulation is rarely subject to criminal prosecution, so concrete examples are thin on the ground.[144] However, an example might

---

[136] The use of the phrase 'any course of conduct' leaves open the issue of whether both activity and inactivity on the part of the defendant could potentially fall within this offence (cf s 118(8) FSMA, which clearly includes inaction, discussed at 12.2.2.3.2).

[137] For the definition of relevant investment see Financial Services Act 2012, s 93(5).

[138] Ibid, s 90(2). The defendant must intend the consequences: it is not enough that he is reckless as to the consequences. However, nothing in the section requires the inducement to be successful. It is enough that the defendant intends to create the impression—he need not intend the impression to be false and misleading.

[139] Ibid, s 90(9)(a) and see FSMA, s 397(5)(a).

[140] This is an attenuated form of mens rea when compared to the criminal offence of insider dealing under Criminal Justice Act 1993 (see 12.2.2.1), and the offence of market manipulation under s 89 Financial Services Act 2012.

[141] Financial Services Act 2012, s 90(3). For the meaning of 'gain' and 'loss' in this context see ss 90(6)–(8).

[142] FSMA, s 397(4).

[143] Financial Services Act 2012, s 90(9)(b)(c)(d).

[144] See 12.2.2.3.2 for a discussion of the administrative offences under section 118 FSMA.

be where directors persuade the company's brokers to buy shares in the market at four times the previous market price in order to move the market price closer to that which the directors believe to be the 'true' value of the shares.[145]

12.2.2.2.3 Misleading Statements etc in Relation to Benchmarks: Section 91 Financial Services Act 2012

This new offence relating to benchmarks was added to the draft of the Financial Services Bill in October 2012 following recommendations made in the Wheatley Review.[146] The Government accepted all of the Review's recommendations, including that section 397 FSMA be extended to capture the making of misleading statements to manipulate benchmarks, such as LIBOR.[147]

Section 91 creates a new offence relating to the making of a false or misleading statement, or the creation of a false or misleading impression, in connection with the setting of a relevant benchmark.[148] The person making the statement or creating the impression must know that, or be reckless as to whether, the statement or impression is false or misleading.[149] The motive of the person is immaterial for this offence—for example, there is no requirement that the person be acting with the intention of inducing a person to engage in market activity or with the intention of making a gain or avoiding a loss. The same defences as regards price stabilisation, control of information rules etc exist here as in relation to sections 89–90 of the 2012 Act, discussed above.[150]

Given its genesis, this is a clearly targeted, and therefore narrow, provision. Section 91 certainly captures the making of misleading statements and impressions in relation to LIBOR and, now, other benchmarks.[151] It remains to be seen, however, whether this is an appropriate measure to prevent the manipulation of LIBOR and other benchmarks in the future. Although significant regulatory action has been taken by the FCA to date, and huge fines have been imposed, in relation to the manipulation of LIBOR, these have not utilised this criminal provision in order to do so.[152]

---

[145] *North v Marra Developments* (1982) 56 ALJR 106.

[146] *Wheatley Review of LIBOR: Final Report*, September 2012.

[147] The extension of market abuse provisions to capture the manipulation of benchmarks is something that has been under discussion not only at national level, but also within the EU (the new Market Abuse Regulation (EU) No 596/2014 encompasses the manipulation of benchmarks: art 2(2)(c), discussed at 12.2.2.3) and at international level (IOSCO, *Principles for Financial Benchmarks: Final Report*, July 2013).

[148] For the definition of 'relevant benchmark' see Financial Services Act 2012, s 93(4).

[149] Financial Services Act 2012, ss 91(1)(c), 91(2)(c).

[150] Ibid, s 91(3).

[151] See Financial Services and Markets Act 2000 (Regulated Activities) (Amendment) Order 2015 (SI 2015/369), which brings seven additional benchmarks within the ambit of s 91.

[152] Many of the fines for the manipulation of LIBOR were imposed before April 2013 when s 91 took effect; for example, the FSA/FCA fined Barclays Bank plc £59.5 million on 27 June 2012, UBS AG £160 million on 19 December 2012, and Royal Bank of Scotland plc £87.5 million on 6 February 2013. However, some of the fines were imposed after s 91 took effect: the FCA fined ICAP Europe Limited £14 million in September 2013, Rabobank £105 million on 29 October 2013, Martin Brokers (UK) Limited £630,000 on 15 May 2014, and Lloyds Bank and Bank of Scotland £105 million on 28 July 2014. For a full list of the fines imposed and the relevant decision notices, see www.fca.org.uk/firms/being-regulated/enforcement/fines/.

12.2.2.2.4 Penalties and Enforcement

A person guilty of an offence under sections 89–91 is liable, on conviction on indictment, to seven years' imprisonment, or a fine, or both.[153] As with the insider dealing offence discussed above, a breach of these sections does not appear to render any contract void or unenforceable.[154] In addition, the FCA can make use of its range of remedies for market abuse, such as injunctions and restitution orders.[155]

The criminal nature of these provisions creates difficulties. Chiefly, of course, the fact that this is a criminal offence means that there is a higher evidential burden than exists for a civil offence: the offence must be proved beyond reasonable doubt rather than merely on the balance of probabilities. These requirements create significant barriers for any prosecution. The changes introduced in 2012 extend the reach of the section 397 FSMA regime, with the introduction of a new offence under section 91, and the extension of the offence under section 90. However, these new sections do not make the offences less complex, and leave in place the difficulties associated with demonstrating the requisite mens rea for each offence. Despite the FCA's stated aim of bringing more criminal prosecutions in relation to financial crime, cases under these sections are likely to remain relatively rare.

12.2.2.3 The Regulatory Offence of Market Abuse Under Section 118 FSMA

The criminal offences of insider dealing and market manipulation have proved very difficult to enforce, principally due to the need to demonstrate mens rea on the part of the defendant and to satisfy the higher evidential burden imposed by the criminal law. As a result, in 2000 a new offence of market abuse was introduced in section 118 FSMA with administrative rather than criminal sanctions, and requiring a civil standard of proof.[156] It was amended in 2005 to give effect to the 2003 Market Abuse Directive.[157] These amendments involved some re-casting of the existing provisions, rather than wholesale change. The 2014 Market Abuse Regulation introduces substantial changes to this area, including extending the coverage of section 118 to include not just activity on the Main Market and MTFs, such as AIM,[158] but also trading on OTFs.[159] The Market Abuse Regulation also

---

[153] Financial Services Act 2012, s 92(1).

[154] Unlike the offence of insider dealing under Criminal Justice Act 1993 (s 63(2)) and the market abuse offence under s 118 FSMA (see FSMA, s 131), this point is not covered expressly in the legislation. However, this has been assumed to be the case in previous versions of these offences: *Aldrich v Norwich Union Life Insurance Co Ltd* [1998] CLC 1621 (Ch D) per Rimer J. In addition, there is assumed to be no possibility of a breach of statutory duty claim arising under these provisions. Again the statute is silent on this point, but this was the case under the common law, and again in *Aldrich* was assumed to be the position.

[155] FSMA, ss 380, 382.

[156] This is a point which has been debated, but was confirmed by the Upper Tribunal in *Hannam v FCA* [2014] UKUT 233 (TCC). For a discussion of the burden of proof required see A Haynes, 'The Burden of Proof in Market Abuse Cases' (2013) 20 *Journal of Financial Crime* 365.

[157] Directive 2003/6/EC. The necessary changes to FSMA were effected by Financial Services and Markets Act 2000 (Market Abuse) Regulations 2005 (SI 2005/381).

[158] Prior to the implementation of the Market Abuse Directive, s 118 FSMA applied to 'prescribed markets'. The Market Abuse Directive only required the provisions to apply to regulated markets, but in implementing the directive it was decided to retain the previous, broader coverage: Financial Services and Markets Act 2000 (Prescribed Markets and Qualifying Investments) Order 2001 (SI 2001/996), art 4.

[159] Market Abuse Regulation (EU) No 596/2014, art 2(1); for the definition of OTFs see Market in Financial Instruments Regulation, Regulation (EU) No 600/2014, Title II. See 12.2.2.

expands the financial instruments caught by the market abuse regime.[160] For example, the regulation captures financial instruments the price or value of which depends on or has an effect on the price or value of a financial instrument traded on a regulated market, MTF or OTF,[161] and the market manipulation provisions cover 'behaviour in relation to benchmarks', to address the LIBOR scandal.[162]

Whilst insider dealing and market manipulation are dealt with in a single section of FSMA (section 118), it is still useful to treat these two forms of market abuse separately for the purposes of discussion and analysis. Section 118 divides market abuse into six[163] types of behaviour. The first two relate to the use of inside information,[164] and the last four to market manipulation.[165] These offences can be committed by any person: companies fall within the ambit of these provisions.[166]

Further guidance is provided by the FCA in its Code of Market Conduct.[167] The Code does not attempt to describe exhaustively the types of conduct that may or may not constitute market abuse, but it does identify some conduct that will not amount to market abuse—that is, it creates some safe harbours.[168]

12.2.2.3.1 Insider Dealing

The types of behaviour prohibited under sections 118(2) and 118(3) FSMA are very similar to the actual dealing and disclosing offences under the Criminal Justice Act 1993.[169]

The first offence, set out in section 118(2), is committed 'where an insider deals, or attempts to deal, in a qualifying investment ... on the basis of inside information'.[170] It was made clear in *Spector Photo Group NV*,[171] a decision of the ECJ (now the CJEU) dealing with the definition of insider dealing for the purposes of Article 2 of the 2003 Market Abuse Directive, that the mere fact that a person with inside information acquires or disposes of financial instruments to which that information relates is enough—it is not necessary to

---

[160] The definition of qualifying investments is currently found in Financial Services and Markets Act 2000 (Prescribed Markets and Qualifying Investments) Order 2001 (SI 2001/996), art 5, and includes transferable securities and any other instrument admitted to trading on a regulated market. The Court of Appeal has taken a broad view of the meaning of 'qualifying investments', concluding that this term included contracts for differences which, while not themselves qualifying investments, did relate to ordinary shares, which are qualifying investments: *Canada Inc v FCA* [2013] EWCA Civ 1662.

[161] Market Abuse Regulation (EU) No 596/2014, art 2(1)(d).

[162] Ibid, art 2(2)(c). The UK has already introduced its own criminal offence specifically relating to the manipulation of benchmarks with s 91 of the Financial Services Act 2012, discussed at 12.2.2.2.3. The market manipulation provisions of the EU market abuse regime are also expanded under the regulation to apply to any spot commodity contract that has, is likely to have or is intended to have an effect on the price or value of a financial instrument, and any type of financial instrument that has or is likely to have an effect on the price or value of a spot commodity contract whose price depends upon the relevant financial instrument: art 2(2)(a)(b).

[163] Until 31 December 2014, there were seven offences under s 118, but s 118(4) ceased to have effect on that date, as discussed at 12.2.2.3.1 below.

[164] FSMA, s 118(2)(3).

[165] Ibid, ss 118(5)–(8).

[166] Ibid, s 118(1).

[167] FCA Handbook, MAR.

[168] For a discussion of the role of the Code of Market Conduct see *Winterflood v FSA* [2010] EWCA Civ 423.

[169] See Criminal Justice Act 1993, ss 52(1) and 52(2)(b), discussed at 12.2.2.1.3 and 12.2.2.1.5. There is no equivalent of Criminal Justice Act 1993, s 52(2)(a) within s 118, but encouraging another to deal is caught by FSMA, s 123(1)(b).

[170] FSMA, s 118(2).

[171] [2009] EUECJ C-45/08 (23 December 2009).

establish that the person intended to use the inside information as the basis of the trades. The Court thereby created a presumption of intention to use the inside information where a person trades while in possession of that information (a presumption which the defendant may then seek to rebut).[172] This potentially simplifies the task for the regulator in establishing breach of section 118(2).[173]

The second offence, set out in section 118(3), provides that the insider will be liable if he discloses insider information otherwise than in the proper course of the exercise of his employment, profession or duties.[174] The Code provides two examples of behaviour amounting to improper disclosure: a director of a company who discloses inside information to someone else in a social context, and directors or senior managers who selectively brief analysts.[175] In a recent decision it was held that it would never be in the proper course of a person's employment for him to disclose inside information to a third party where he knows that his employer and client would not consent to the public disclosure of that information.[176]

Until 31 December 2014 a third offence existed under section 118(4) FSMA, which was somewhat different in scope and effect to the first two offences. There was no equivalent to this offence in the Criminal Justice Act 1993; the section added a potentially significant extension to the first two forms of insider dealing. Section 118(4) was introduced in 2000 and was super-equivalent to the provisions in the 2003 Market Abuse Directive. An offence was committed where there was behaviour which was based on information 'not generally available to those using the market'[177] and the behaviour was likely to be regarded by a regular user of the market as a failure on the part of the person concerned to observe the standard of behaviour reasonably expected of a person in his position in relation to the shares.[178] This extended the reach of section 118 beyond 'inside information' to include 'information which was not generally available'. However, there was a qualification: it was necessary that the information 'if available to a regular user of the market, would be, or would be likely to be, regarded by him as relevant when deciding the terms on which transactions in

---

[172] The recitals to Market Abuse Regulation (EU) No 596/2014 reassert this rebuttable presumption, although the presumption does not explicitly appear in the substantive text of the regulation. There was some doubt at the time of the *Spector Photo* decision as to whether the UK provisions under s 118 FSMA reflected the outcome in *Spector Photo*: on one view s 118(2) together with the provisions in the Code of Market Conduct required the regulator to establish that the trading had been informed by the inside information. The FSA determined after the *Spector Photo* decision that the wording in s 118(2) FSMA ('… on the basis of …') was consistent with the ECJ decision and did not need to be amended. However, the Code of Market Conduct was amended to clarify the fact that, post-*Spector Photo*, it is not necessary for the regulator to provide evidence of a person's intention to prove insider dealing: FSA, Consultation Paper CP10/22, Quarterly consultation, October 2010, 32–33. The decision in *Spector Photo* does not have any effect on the criminal law offence of insider dealing in the Criminal Justice Act 1993 (which does clearly require a mens rea element, as described at 12.2.2.1.3–12.2.2.1.5), since that Act does not implement the EU market abuse provisions.

[173] For an example of the regulator applying the approach in *Spector Photo* in practice see FSA, Decision Notice in relation to David Einhorn, 12 January 2012.

[174] This is akin to Criminal Justice Act 1993, s 52(2)(b). The factors that will be taken into account by the FCA when determining whether disclosure of inside information was legitimate are found in MAR 1.4.5.

[175] Code of Market Conduct, MAR 1.4.2E.

[176] *Hannam v FCA* [2014] UKUT 233 (TCC). The Tribunal found that the information disclosed in that case could only be disclosed if the recipient was under an obligation of confidentiality, which was not satisfied in the present case. A mere understanding on the part of the recipient of the need to keep information confidential (had it existed) was insufficient to impose a confidentiality obligation.

[177] FSMA, s 118(4)(a).

[178] Ibid, s 118(4)(b).

qualifying investments should be effected'.[179] This might include information that is not specific enough to be defined as inside information, but which a 'regular user of the market' would regard as relevant.[180] The definition also extended the notion of insider dealing beyond 'dealing' to include behaviour generally, including, potentially, a decision not to deal (subject to significant evidentiary problems being overcome).

Section 118(4) survived the amendments to section 118 introduced to give effect to the 2003 Market Abuse Directive, because the regulator (the FSA at that time) was loath to reduce the existing scope of its jurisdiction. It was agreed, however, that over time the UK regime should be aligned with the EU regime, and consequently section 118(4) was subject to a sunset clause. This sunset clause finally expired on 31 December 2014.[181] Presumably this is because section 118(4) was wider in scope than the EU market abuse provisions which come into effect in July 2016. As a consequence, from 1 January 2015 the UK's insider trading provisions under section 118 narrowed in scope.

The Market Abuse Regulation introduces some changes to this regime.[182] In particular, the regulation extends the definition of insider dealing in two important ways. First, it prohibits the use of information for cancelling or amending an order concerning a financial instrument where the order was placed before the person possessed inside information.[183] This change is intended to ensure that the practice of withdrawing from or cancelling an existing trade in light of inside information received subsequently also constitutes insider dealing. Second, the regulation creates a separate offence of 'attempting' to engage in insider dealing, so that even an unsuccessful attempt to trade on inside information will potentially constitute insider dealing.[184]

12.2.2.3.1(a) The Meaning of 'Insiders'

Insiders are defined in section 118B to include those who have inside information as a result of being part of the management of the issuer, or as a result of holding capital in the issuer, or as a result of their employment profession or duties, or as a result of criminal activities.[185] This is similar to the definition of 'insider' found in the Criminal Justice Act 1993,[186] and therefore raises the same issue about whether analysts and other information traders and market intermediaries should be regarded as insiders. There are good policy reasons why they should not necessarily be treated as insiders and the FCA seems to recognise this, stating that market makers will not be liable for insider dealing in some circumstances even where they do possess inside information.[187]

---

[179] Ibid, s 118(4)(a).

[180] A regular user is defined as a reasonable person who regularly deals on that market in investments of the kind in question: ibid, s 130A(3).

[181] It is notable that the sunset clause attached to a similar provision dealing with market manipulation in s 118(8) was extended until 3 July 2016. See 12.2.2.3.2.

[182] This includes specific provision for insider dealing of commodity derivatives and emission allowances. See eg Market Abuse Regulation (EU) No 596/2014, arts 7(1)(b) (c).

[183] Market Abuse Regulation (EU) No 596/2014, art 8(1).

[184] Ibid, art 14.

[185] FSMA, s 118B(a)–(d). Market Abuse Regulation (EU) No 596/2014 involves no substantial changes to the definition of insiders: art 8(4).

[186] Criminal Justice Act 1993, s 57, although the reference to criminal activities is different. See 12.2.2.1.1.

[187] Code of Market Conduct, MAR 1.3.7–1.3.8.

The definition of insiders for the purposes of section 118 is extended beyond these categories, however, since under section 118B an insider is also someone who obtains inside information 'by other means and which he knows, or could reasonably be expected to know, is inside
information'.[188] Thus, an insider is someone with inside information, however obtained, but
with the qualification that the holder ought to know this fact. An example of the sort of behaviour that falls within these provisions can be found in the Final Notice issued by the FSA to
Brian Taylor in 2008.[189] In May 2007, Mr Taylor was a private retail investor. One of the stocks
that he regularly dealt in was Amerisur Resources plc. Amerisur is an oil and gas exploration
company which undertakes projects in South America. The company's shares were admitted
to trading on AIM. Blue Oar Securities plc (Blue Oar) acted as broker for Amerisur in a share
placing which took place on 24 May 2007. On 23 May 2007, Blue Oar contacted a number
of existing Amerisur shareholders, including Mr Taylor, to invite them to participate in the
placing. Blue Oar spoke to Mr Taylor at 9.35am and made Mr Taylor an insider in relation to
the placing of Amerisur shares to be announced to the market on 24 May 2007. In the course
of this conversation, Blue Oar advised Mr Taylor that the placing price was 6 pence, that the
placing would be announced the next day and that Mr Taylor was not permitted to speak to
anyone about the placing until it was announced to the market on 24 May 2007.

Following the receipt of this inside information, Mr Taylor sold 150,000 Amerisur shares
at 9.095 pence at 9.46am on 23 May 2007. Mr Taylor then purchased 500,000 shares in the
placing at 6 pence. Following the announcement of the placing on 24 May 2007 the price of
Amerisur's shares fell to 7.5 pence. By his actions, Mr Taylor realised a profit of £4,642.50.
The FSA found that Mr Taylor held this information 'by other means', because he had been
telephoned by Blue Oar and asked whether he wanted to take part in the placing, and as a
result of that conversation he could be expected to know that the information he received
was inside information. He was therefore an insider for these purposes. The FSA found Mr
Taylor liable for market abuse under section 118(2) and imposed a penalty on him designed
to strip away the whole of his profit.[190]

It may therefore be said that in a regime that has moved away from a view of insider dealing as rooted in the fiduciary relationship towards one based on a market approach, the definition of inside information is key. An insider is defined (almost) as anyone in possession
of inside information. If the definition of inside information is too lax, the market will be
impaired, but if it is too strict, this will impede legitimate information gathering and may also
have a negative impact on market efficiency.

12.2.2.3.1(b) *The Meaning of 'Inside Information'*

The definition of inside information is set out in section 118C, and implements the provisions of the 2003 Market Abuse Directive. The new Market Abuse Regulation makes very
few changes to the definition of inside information.[191]

---

[188] FSMA, s 118B(e).

[189] FSA, Final Notice, Brian Valentine Taylor, 16 October 2008.

[190] The FSA found that Mr Taylor's behaviour merited the imposition of a total penalty of £24,462.50 (being
a penalty of £20,000 plus disgorgement of Mr Taylor's profit) but because of his financial circumstances this was
reduced to £4,642.50.

[191] Market Abuse Regulation (EU) No 596/2014, art 7 (although this article does include some changes and
additions to deal with specialist circumstances, such as insider dealing regarding emission allowances in art 7(1)
(c)). An early draft of the Market Abuse Regulation (published on 20 October 2011) had included an additional

According to section 118C(2), inside information is information that is of a precise nature, is not generally available, relates directly or indirectly to one or more issuers of qualifying investments or to one or more qualifying investments, and would, if generally available, be likely to have a significant effect on the price of the qualifying investments.[192] In relation to the concept of 'precise information', section 118C(5) provides, further, that information is 'precise' for these purposes if it (a) indicates circumstances that exist or may reasonably be expected to come into existence or an event that has occurred or may reasonably be expected to occur, and (b) is specific enough to enable a conclusion to be drawn as to the possible effect of those circumstances or that event on the price of qualifying investments or related investments.[193] Additionally, section 118C provides that information is likely to have a significant effect on price if and only if it is information of a kind that a reasonable investor would be likely to use as part of the basis of his investment decisions.[194]

The meaning of 'inside information' for this purpose was examined in some detail by the Upper Tribunal in *Hannam v FCA*,[195] in the context of an application challenging a decision of the FCA that the applicant, H, had committed market abuse and should be fined £450,000. H was found to have improperly disclosed inside information in two emails that were sent otherwise than in the proper course of the exercise of his employment, in breach of section 118(3) FSMA. At the relevant time H was chairman of capital markets at an investment services firm. The information in the first email contained a potential third-party bid for H's client, an oil company (O). The second email contained a postscript that '[O] has just found oil and it is looking good' (in fact this information was not quite accurate since O had not found black oil, but had found the presence of liquid hydrocarbons). Both emails were sent to the Minister for Oil in the Kurdish Government. At the time O was mainly engaged in exploratory drilling in Uganda, but was keen to explore opportunities in Kurdistan. The particular issues raised were whether the emails disclosed inside information to another person, and if so whether the information was disclosed otherwise than in the proper course of the exercise of the applicant's employment.

The Tribunal considered the meaning of the term 'precise' as it relates to inside information for the purposes of section 118C. It considered that the question of whether information was precise gave rise to a number of issues. First, it raised the question of the extent to which information must be accurate in order to be sufficiently precise to constitute inside information. Sensibly, the Tribunal concluded that information that is not wholly accurate may, nonetheless, convey a message to the recipient, which may give the recipient an advantage over other market participants and is therefore capable of amounting to inside

category of inside information relating to relevant information not generally available to the public (RINGA). This change was proposed on the basis that information can be abused before an issuer is under an obligation to disclose it. The inclusion of this category was criticised, and RINGA does not appear in the final version of the regulation.

[192] FSMA, s 118C(2). This is similar, but not identical, to the definition under Criminal Justice Act 1993, discussed at 12.2.2.1.2.

[193] Ibid, s 118C(5). In Market Abuse Regulation (EU) No 596/2014 this issue is dealt with in art 7(1)). The regulation also provides some clarification of the meaning of 'precise' in this context, including the fact that an 'intermediate step' in a 'protracted process' that is intended to bring about a 'particular event' may also give rise to information that is sufficiently precise to be inside information: arts 7(2) and 7(3). This represents a codification of the European Court of Justice's judgment in Case C-19/11 *Markus Geltl v Daimler AG* [2012] 3 CMLR 32.

[194] FSMA, s 118C(6) (and see Market Abuse Regulation (EU) No 596/2014, art 7(4)).

[195] [2014] UKUT 233 (TCC).

information notwithstanding its inaccuracy.[196] Second, whether the information was precise was to be assessed by reference to the requirements of section 118C(5)(a) and (b). In respect of section 118C(5)(a) the information, which might not be wholly accurate, must indicate circumstances or events which actually existed or had occurred or which might reasonably be expected, when viewed objectively, to come about or occur. The test of those future events was that set out in *Geltl v Daimler AG*,[197] namely whether there was any realistic prospect that they would occur. This contrasts with the 'more likely than not' test which had been adopted by some companies for determining whether there is inside information which may have to be disclosed. This approach potentially expands the scope of uncertain future events that could amount to inside information.[198] The Tribunal also considered the meaning of 'possible effect' in the context of the requirement in section 118C(5)(b) that information should be specific enough to enable a conclusion to be drawn as to the possible effect on price. The Tribunal found that it was necessary for the information to indicate the direction of movement but not the extent to which the price might be affected. A real prospect of price movement in a known direction is sufficient: the information does not have to be such as to enable an investor to know with confidence that the price *will* move if the information is made public.

Next, the Tribunal considered the meaning of the term 'likely to have a significant effect on price'. The interaction of this requirement and the 'reasonable investor' test set out in section 118C(6) FSMA has caused some difficulties. In *David Massey v FSA*[199] the regulator succeeded in its argument that the 'reasonable investor' limb of the definition of inside information should be given primacy over the 'significant effect' limb of the definition— that is, that whether or not there was a significant effect on price, the information can be regarded as inside information if it is of a kind that a reasonable investor would be likely to use as part of the basis of his investment decision. This is a surprising decision. The approach of the Tribunal in *Hannam* is preferable, whereby the reasonable investor test in section 118C(6) must be applied in the context of the price test. In particular, the Tribunal stated that 'the reasonable investor is an investor who would take into account information which would be likely to have a significant effect on price. Conversely, he is an investor who would not take into account information which would have no effect on price at all.'[200] It might have been preferable if the Tribunal had gone yet further, and stated that the reasonable investor test is an additional condition to the requirement to demonstrate a likely price effect. Given that the Market Abuse Regulation continues to elide the concept of 'reasonable investor' and 'significant effect on price', these difficulties are likely to continue.[201]

Further, the Tribunal in *Hannam* found that 'significant' for these purposes was only to be contrasted with insignificant, in the sense of trivial. As to the meaning of 'likely', the Tribunal found that information which was 'likely' to have a significant effect on price

---

[196] It was accepted that if the information had been wholly inaccurate it could not have been inside information.

[197] Case C-19/11 *Markus Geltl v Daimler AG* [2012] 3 CMLR 32.

[198] This issue of information disclosure needs to be understood in the context of the discussion at 11.3.2.1 regarding the requirement that companies disclose inside information 'as soon as possible'. For discussion see M Green, 'Acceptable Delay in Disclosure of Inside Information' [2014] *Journal of International Banking and Financial Law* 567.

[199] [2011] UKUT 49 (TCC). See also FSA, Decision Notice in relation to David Einhorn, 12 January 2012.

[200] [2014] UKUT 233 (TCC), para 102.

[201] Market Abuse Regulation (EU) No 596/2014, art 7(4).

was information where there was a real (and not fanciful or de minimis) prospect of the information having an effect on the price of qualifying investments. It does not need to be more likely than not.

The Tribunal also addressed two additional issues of interest. First, it confirmed that information can be improperly disclosed to an individual even if the recipient is already in possession of it. Following the approach adopted in *Massey*, the Tribunal had little difficulty in accepting that information that tended to confirm a general expectation could be inside information. Second, the Tribunal reaffirmed that there is no difference in the concept of inside information when used in the context of an issuer's general obligations to disclose such information promptly and publicly[202] and when used in the context of the insider dealing offences.

The Tribunal refused H's application. Applying the *Geltl* test, the Tribunal held that the first email contained inside information and satisfied the requirements of section 118C(5), on the basis that there was a realistic prospect of an offer being made. The information enabled a conclusion to be drawn on price and a reasonable investor would use this information in making his investment decisions. The postscript in the second email was also inside information, despite its inaccuracy. There was a real prospect that the postscript would, if generally available, have a significant effect on the price of O's shares.

12.2.2.3.1(c) *Mens Rea for Insider Dealing under Section 118 FSMA*

One of the main differences between the insider dealing offences in section 118 and the criminal offence under the Criminal Justice Act 1993 is the lack of a mens rea element in sections 118(2) and 118(3). In principle, a person can be liable under section 118 if he deals with inside information even if he is unaware that the information is inside information or that he is an insider. A number of important qualifications exist, however. First, if the insider obtains the information 'by any other means' then he must know, or be reasonably expected to know, that it is inside information.[203] There are also protections created at the imposition of penalty stage. Under section 123(2) FSMA, the FCA may decide not to impose a penalty if it is satisfied that the person believed on reasonable grounds that he was not acting in breach of the insider dealing provisions, or that he had taken all reasonable precautions and exercised all due diligence to avoid the prohibition. The FCA can also take account of these factors when deciding on the amount of penalty to be imposed.[204] Mens rea is not wholly irrelevant to these offences, therefore, although it has a diminished role compared to the equivalent offences under the Criminal Justice Act 1993.

This scope and application of section 123(2) was discussed in an FSA Decision Notice relating to David Einhorn in 2012.[205] Einhorn was owner and sole portfolio manager of Greenlight Capital Inc, which held a 13 per cent stake in Punch taverns plc. Punch was considering an equity fundraising and contacted a number of shareholders and potential investors (including Greenlight and Einhorn) to gauge interest prior to an announcement.

---

[202] See 11.3.2.1.

[203] FSMA, s 118B(e), discussed at 12.2.2.3.1(a).

[204] FSMA, s 124(2).

[205] FSA, Decision Notice, David Einhorn, 12 January 2012. For discussion see J Birch, 'Mosaic Theory and Insider Trading' [2013] *Journal of International Banking and Financial Law* 173.

Greenlight and Einhorn specifically asked not to be 'wall-crossed' (which involves being made an insider, subject to a non-disclosure agreement). During the conversation inside information was disclosed, namely details of a possible equity fundraising, and immediately after the conversation Einhorn directed Greenlight to sell its stake in Punch, whereupon Greenlight reduced its stake to around 9 per cent. When Punch announced its rights issue six days after these conversations, its share price fell by almost 30 per cent and Greenlight's actions in selling its shares in advance of the announcement meant that it avoided a loss of approximately £5.8 million.

Einhorn claimed he had good reason to believe that his behaviour did not fall within the market abuse regime, on the basis that, because he asked not to be wall-crossed, he was entitled to assume that the information he received was not inside information. Accordingly, Einhorn sought to rely on section 123(2) FSMA. The regulator rejected this argument, stating that Einhorn should have been aware of the risk that the information was inside information and should have considered whether it fell into that category before acting. The regulator took account of the fact that Einhorn did not take legal advice before this dealing, even though that option was readily available. Despite the fact that the behaviour was not deliberate or reckless, nevertheless the regulator imposed a substantial financial penalty (£3,638,000) as a deterrent to other high-profile traders.[206] The defence under section 123(2) was therefore unavailable to him.

12.2.2.3.2 Market Manipulation

There are four different forms of market manipulation under section 118.[207] Some forms of behaviour that would otherwise constitute market manipulation are specifically allowed by FSMA.[208] The most obvious example is the price stabilisation rules.[209] This safe harbour is created at European level, and applies across the range of market abuse provisions in place in the UK.[210]

---

[206] The situation that arose in the Einhorn decision is dealt with by Market Abuse Regulation (EU) No 596/2014, art 11, which provides a new safe harbour where a disclosure is made to potential investors in the course of 'market soundings' conducted to gauge investment appetite and the appropriate terms for a transaction. In order for a disclosure to qualify as a market sounding, the discloser must obtain the prior consent of the disclosee and warn him that the information must remain confidential and must not be used to inform a decision to acquire or dispose of a financial instrument to which it relates. The consent and evidence of the warnings must be recorded and submitted to the competent authority upon request. However, the regulation makes clear that the disclosee must come to his own decision as to whether information disclosed is inside information. This suggests that agreeing to receive information on a 'non-wall-crossed basis' will be insufficient to protect against the improper disclosure rules. For a discussion of the commercial drivers behind wall crossing see P Bevan and K Gibson, 'Wall-Crossing post *Einhorn*' [2012] *Journal of International Banking and Financial Law* 367.

[207] In relation to Market Abuse Regulation (EU) No 596/2014, see art 12(1). The regulation goes into far greater detail in providing examples of manipulative behaviour as compared to Market Abuse Directive 2003 (see Market Abuse Regulation (EU) No 596/2014, art 12(2) for a list of behaviours that will be considered market manipulation). See also ESMA, *Final Report: ESMA's Technical Advice on Possible Delegated Acts concerning the Market Abuse Regulation*, 3 February 2015, ESMA/2015/224.

[208] FSMA, s 118A(5).

[209] For discussion see FSA, *The Price Stabilising Rules*, CP 40, January 2000.

[210] See Market Abuse Directive 2003/6/EC, art 8 and Market Abuse Regulation (EU) No 536/2014, art 5 (which also create a buy-back exemption), and ESMA Consultation Paper, ESMA/2014/809. See FSMA, s 118A(5) and Code of Market Conduct, MAR 2.

The first of the provisions dealing with market manipulation, section 118(5), involves effecting transactions or orders to trade which give, or are likely to give, a false or misleading impression about the supply of, or demand for, or the price of, qualifying investments, or which secure the price of such investments at an artificial level. A recent regulatory concern has been the use of market abuse in the context of dark pools and high frequency trading (HFT), and the first HFT enforcement action by the FCA, in July 2013, involved an action against Michael Coscia regarding manipulation of commodities markets in contravention of section 118(5).[211] This section will not apply, however, where the transactions or orders to trade were for legitimate reasons and in conformity with accepted market practices.[212] The second form of market manipulation, set out in section 118(6), involves transactions or orders to trade which employ fictitious devices or any other form of deception or contrivance.

These forms of market manipulation are similar to the behaviour caught by section 90 of the Financial Services Act 2012, that is, conduct which creates a misleading impression as to the market in or price of any relevant investments.[213] However, section 90 requires a mens rea element. It must be demonstrated that the defendant acted for the purpose of creating that impression and of thereby inducing another person to deal in the investments in some way.[214] No such element attaches to these provisions in section 118, although the FCA can take account of the mental state of the relevant person when deciding whether to impose a penalty and, if so, what the size of penalty ought to be.[215] These provisions in section 118 therefore move away from an intention-based conception of market manipulation towards one that is effects-based. One other point to note is that although section 90 of the 2012 Act is silent as to whether conduct for these purposes can include inactivity, section 118 is clear that 'behaviour' includes both action and inaction.[216]

Examples of the kind of behaviour that might fall within these sections include situations where a person simultaneously buys and sells the same qualifying investment, to give the appearance of a legitimate transfer of title or risk, or both, at a price outside the normal trading range for the qualifying investment.[217] It may be that the price of the qualifying investment is relevant to the calculation of the settlement value of an option, and the trader holds a position in the option. The trader's purpose in trading with himself in this way is therefore to position the price of the qualifying investment at a false, misleading, abnormal or artificial level, making him a profit or avoiding a loss from the option.[218] Alternatively, a series of transactions might be publicly reported for the purpose of suggesting a level of

---

[211] FCA, Final Notice, Michael Coscia, 3 July 2013. For discussion see D Connell, 'Are You Afraid of the Dark? High Frequency Trading and the Duties of Dark Pool Operators' [2014] *Journal of International Banking and Financial Law* 632. This is also a topic of interest in the US: G Shorter and RS Miller, 'Dark Pools in Equity Trading: Policy Concerns and Recent Developments' (2014), www.fas.org/sgp/crs/misc/R43739.pdf. Concerns about HFT led to this behaviour being specifically dealt with in Market Abuse Regulation (EU) No 596/2014, art 12(2)(c), which specifies the behaviours concerning algorithmic and HFT strategies that will amount to market manipulation. For further discussion of HFT see 12.4.

[212] FSMA, s 130A(3).

[213] See 12.2.2.2.2.

[214] Financial Services Act 2012, s 90(2), discussed at 12.2.2.2.2.

[215] Ibid, ss 123(2) and 124(2), and see 12.2.2.3.1(c).

[216] Ibid, s 130A(3).

[217] For an example of behaviour falling within s 118(5) see *Canada Inc v FCA* [2013] EWCA Civ 1662.

[218] Code of Market Conduct, MAR 1.6.15.

activity or price movement that does not genuinely exist. Another common form of this type of market manipulation involves a trader taking a long position on an investment and then disseminating misleading positive information about the investment to increase the price, or taking a short position and disseminating misleading negative information in order to decrease the price.[219]

The next form of market manipulation, found in section 118(7), is similar to that found in section 89 of the Financial Services Act 2012.[220] It involves disseminating information that is likely to give a false or misleading impression as to a qualifying investment by a person who knew or could reasonably be expected to have known that the information was false or misleading. Under section 89 of the 2012 Act, the person must know or be reckless as to the fact that the statement is misleading, or, in the context of concealment, that the concealment is dishonest.[221] By contrast, under section 118(7) liability can arise if the person knew or 'could reasonably be expected to have known' that the information was false or misleading. In other words, section 118 creates a negligence standard.[222] Also, in contrast to section 89, there is no need for the maker of the statement to have intended or induced someone else to rely on the statement.[223]

A good example of this form of market manipulation is provided by the FSA's prosecution of the Shell group of companies in 2004.[224] Shell was found to have made false or misleading statements in relation to its hydrocarbon reserves and reserves replacement ratios between 1998 and 2003, despite indications from 2000 to 2003 that its proved reserves as announced to the market were false or misleading. Shell did not correct its disclosures until 2004, when it announced the recategorisation of 4,470 million barrels of oil, approximately 25 per cent of Shell's proved reserves. On disclosure of this information Shell's share price fell from 401 pence to 371 pence, reducing its market capitalisation on that day by £2.9 billion. Shell was found liable for this form of market manipulation and fined £17 million.

These provisions are a way of supplementing the rules regarding the need for accurate and timely disclosures to the market, supporting the FCA's ability to bring an action against the issuer and its directors for negligently making a misleading disclosure required by the Disclosure Rules and Transparency Rules.[225] The FCA's decision to bring a market abuse action in relation to this situation, rather than just dealing with it as a misstatement issue, was due to the seriousness of the company's misconduct.

In addition to these three provisions, section 118 contains a provision that was not strictly required by the 2003 Market Abuse Directive: section 118(8). This provision is subject to a sunset clause that expires on 3 July 2016, the date on which the Market Abuse Regulation takes effect.[226] Section 118(8) only applies where behaviour does not fall within one of the

---

[219] Ibid, MAR 1.7.2.
[220] See 12.2.2.2.1.
[221] Financial Services Act 2012, s 89(1), discussed at 12.2.2.2.1.
[222] The provisions in FSMA, ss 123(2) and 124(2) are also relevant.
[223] For a discussion of s 89 Financial Services Act 2012 see 12.2.2.2.1.
[224] FSA, Final Notice, The Shell Transport and Trading Company, Royal Dutch Petroleum Company NV, 13 August 2004.
[225] FSMA, s 91.
[226] Initially, it was intended that s 118(8) would cease to have effect on 30 June 2008, but this was extended by the Treasury (for the most recent extension see Financial Services and Markets Act 2000 (Market Abuse) Regulations 2014 (SI 3081/2014), extending the date to 3 July 2016).

other forms of market manipulation. It deals with behaviour that is likely to give a regular user of the market a false or misleading impression as to the supply or demand or price of qualifying investments where the behaviour is likely to be regarded by a regular user of the market as a failure to observe the standards of behaviour reasonably expected of a person in the defendant's position.[227] It is broader than the other forms of market manipulation in that it does not require the dissemination of information,[228] and it is not limited to effecting transactions or orders.[229] However, this form of market abuse is subject to the regular user of the market test.[230] The sort of behaviour caught by this provision would be the movement of physical commodity stocks, which might create a misleading impression as to the supply of, or demand for, or price or value of, a commodity.[231]

The Market Abuse Regulation introduces some changes to this area. These include the extension of the regulatory perimeter to capture, inter alia, derivatives, algorithmic trading and benchmark manipulation.[232] In addition, as with insider dealing, the regulation contains a new offence of attempting to engage in market manipulation.[233]

12.2.2.3.3 Levels of Enforcement Under Section 118

The primary sanction for market abuse is the imposition of a penalty, such as the £17 million fine imposed on the Shell group of companies in 2004,[234] although the FCA can substitute a public censure for the penalty.[235] The FCA can also impose a prohibition order under section 56 FSMA.[236]

Prior to the Market Abuse Regulation coming into effect, the imposition of sanctions is entirely a matter for Member States. However, the regulation seeks to increase the degree of harmonisation of the market abuse regime across the EU, and one of the ways in which it attempts to do this is by imposing detailed minimum standards in relation to sanctions.[237] Under the regulation, Member States are required to ensure that they have powers that meet or exceed those listed in the regulation.[238] Member States are required to have the power to force those culpable of market abuse to disgorge their profits, the power to withdraw or suspend the authorisation of a firm, and the power to impose bans on those performing management functions.

In addition, Member States are required to ensure that they have the power to impose maximum pecuniary sanctions at least as severe as those set out in the regulation. For

---

[227] FSMA, s 118(8)(a).
[228] Cf ibid, s 118(7).
[229] Cf ibid, ss 118(5), 118(6).
[230] Ibid, s 118(8) and see s 130A for the definition of 'regular user'.
[231] Code of Market Conduct, MAR 1.9.2.
[232] Market Abuse Regulation (EU) No 596/2014, arts 25, 12(1)(2).
[233] Ibid, art 15.
[234] FSA, Final Notice, The Shell Transport and Trading Company, Royal Dutch Petroleum Company NV, 13 August 2004.
[235] FSMA, s 123(3). In addition the FCA can apply to the court for a restitution order, or impose one itself: FSMA, s 383. The FCA can also apply to court for an injunction to restrain future market abuse: FSMA, s 381.
[236] See eg *Chaligne v Financial Services Authority* [2012] All ER (D) 153 (Sep).
[237] For a comparison of the use of administrative sanctioning powers across 29 EEA Member States for 2008–10 as regards market abuse, see Report, *Actual Use of Sanctioning Powers under MAD*, 26 April 2012, ESMA/2012/270.
[238] Market Abuse Regulation (EU) No 596/2014, art 30.

individuals this includes a fine of €5 million for breach of the provisions relating to insider dealing and market manipulation set out in Articles 14 and 15 of the regulation, and €1 million for most other infringements.[239] For firms, it includes a fine of €15 million or 15 per cent of total annual turnover for breach of the provisions relating to insider dealing and market manipulation set out in Articles 14 and 15 of the regulation, and €2.5 million or 2 per cent of total annual turnover for breach of most other infringements.[240] The regulation also contains a non-exhaustive list of factors to be taken into account by national regulators when imposing penalties for market abuse.[241]

Further, the regulation contains an obligation on competent authorities to publish any decision imposing an administrative sanction or other administrative measure in relation to an infringement of the regulation on their website immediately after the person subject to that decision has been informed of that decision.[242] There is no requirement to increase enforcement resources, but a Report in the European Parliament requests that authorities have effective investigative tools.[243]

The levels of enforcement of the market abuse provisions under section 118 FSMA have been relatively low.[244] Between 2001 and 2007 the regulator (then the FSA) issued Final Notices against just eight firms and fifteen individuals for market conduct related offences.[245] When compared to other jurisdictions, the number of public enforcement actions brought by the FSA in this period appears small. In particular, the number of public enforcement actions brought by the FSA was a fraction of those brought by the US regulator in the same period, even when the numbers are adjusted to reflect the relative market size of the two jurisdictions.[246]

The relative lack of enforcement observable in the UK would not be a cause for concern if it reflected low levels of market abuse occurring in the UK market. However, a study commissioned by the FSA in 2007 on the cleanliness of the UK's market reported significant levels of unusual price movements prior to takeover announcements for UK listed firms.[247] Share price movements ahead of such announcements may reflect insider trading, although it is possible that other factors, such as good guesswork by sophisticated investors, are also relevant. Worse, for the UK regulator, this study reported that the levels of these price movements occurring prior to takeovers had not decreased since the introduction of FSMA and in particular the introduction of the regulatory offence of market abuse in section 118. This suggested that the level of enforcement engaged in by the FSA at that time in tackling market abuse was not having a significant deterrent effect.

---

[239] Ibid, art 30(2)(i).

[240] Ibid, art 30(2)(j) and also see art 30(2)(h).

[241] Ibid, art 31.

[242] Ibid, art 34.

[243] *Report on the Proposal for a Directive of the European Parliament and of the Council on criminal sanctions for insider dealing and market manipulation*, 19 October 2012.

[244] For a discussion of this issue in the context of debt securities see 13.4.1.

[245] Speech by Margaret Cole, then Director of Enforcement, FSA Securities Houses Compliance Officers Group, 29 June 2007.

[246] J Coffee, 'Law and the Market: The Impact of Enforcement' (2007) 156 *University of Pennsylvania Law Review* 229.

[247] NB Monteiro, Q Zaman and S Leitterstorf, 'Updated Measures of Market Cleanliness', FSA Occasional Paper No 25, March 2007.

These low levels of enforcement have been accepted as a problem, and the UK regulator (now the FCA) has stated an intention to follow a strategy of 'credible deterrence' by taking a tougher stance in this area.[248] There is some evidence that this is occurring. For example, the FCA's Annual Report 2013/14 states that as at 31 March 2014 there were 60 open cases of market abuse under investigation.[249] Huge fines have been imposed as a result of the manipulation of LIBOR, although in general these were imposed for breach of the FCA's Principles of Business rather than for breach of the provisions discussed in this chapter.[250] However, the regulator has also imposed substantial fines under section 118 on both firms and on individuals.[251] Recent enforcement levels at the FCA, both in terms of the number of actions and the size of penalties imposed, seem to indicate a trend towards a more muscular, intrusive approach to this issue by the regulator.[252] The most recent study conducted for the FCA on market cleanliness levels showed that after remaining close to 30 per cent for four years, this statistic decreased to 15 per cent in 2013.[253] It is too early to say whether it is the increased focus on enforcement that is causing this effect, but this seems to be an encouraging sign.

12.2.2.4 Private Enforcement of Market Abuse

The UK does not have any mechanism for the private enforcement of market manipulation or insider dealing.[254] At the present time these are dealt with entirely by way of public enforcement measures.[255] This is in contrast to other jurisdictions, most notably the US. Explicit remedies for investors for market manipulation and insider dealing exist in the Securities and Exchange Act 1934,[256] and in addition the US courts have been willing to imply rights of action from criminal law prohibitions such as SEC Rule 10b-5.[257]

Any civil claim for market abuse faces some significant obstacles. The most obvious route for a civil claim for market abuse is some kind of fraudulent misrepresentation claim. In the UK, at common law a claim for fraudulent misrepresentation requires proof that a false statement of fact (or omission of material information) was made with an intention to

---

[248] FCA, *The FCA's Approach to Advancing its Objectives*, July 2013, 19. One innovation, introduced in 2014, is the publication of warning letters as the 'first step' in the FCA's enforcement process.

[249] FCA, Annual Report 2013/14.

[250] For a full list of the fines imposed by the FSA/FCA and the Decision Notices that accompany them see www.fca.org.uk/firms/being-regulated/enforcement/fines/.

[251] Eg FCA, Final Notice, Mark Stevenson, 20 March 2014.

[252] Kinetic Partners, Global Enforcement Review 2014, www.kinetic-partners.com/wp-content/uploads/Global-Enforcement-Review-2014.pdf.

[253] 'Why Has the FCA's Market Cleanliness Statistic for Takeover Announcements Decreased since 2009?', FCA Occasional Paper No 4, July 2014.

[254] Companies Bill 1973 purported to give a right to seek compensation from insiders to contractual parties who had dealt with them and who were not in possession of insider information (cl 15(3))—ie this clause required privity. Companies Bill 1978, cl 61(1) gave a right of rescission and cl 61(2) a right to sue in damages to those directly affected by insider dealing. However, by the time Companies Act 1980 was implemented, any attempt to introduce such remedies for insider dealing had been abandoned. For a discussion of whether Market Abuse Regulation (EU) No 596/2014 will affect the private enforcement options in Member States see VD Tountopoulos, 'Market Abuse and Private Enforcement' (2014) 11 *European Company and Financial Law Review* 297.

[255] See *Hall v Cable & Wireless plc* [2009] EWHC 1793 (Comm) [23]–[24].

[256] See SJ Choi and AC Pritchard, *Securities Regulation: Cases and Analysis*, 4th edn (New York, Foundation Press, 2015) chs 5–6.

[257] See eg *Kardon v National Gypsum Co*, 69 F Supp 512 (ED Pa, 1946); *Superintendent of Insurance v Bankers Life & Casualty Co*, 404 US 6 (1971).

induce the innocent party to rely on it and enter into the injurious course of conduct. It is, in addition, necessary to demonstrate that the claimant was induced to enter into the agreement by specifically relying on the misrepresentor's statement, omission or conduct.[258] This is usually going to be difficult to demonstrate where individuals have engaged in insider dealing or manipulated the market, since these forms of wrongdoing generally arise in the context of arm's-length open market transactions. In the anonymous modern financial marketplace it is extremely unlikely that the maker of the misrepresentation or the initiator of the abusive practice and those injured by that behaviour will ever have any kind of contact. The issue of reliance is therefore likely to be very difficult to establish in most circumstances.

This problem has been solved in the US by adopting the fraud on the market theory. US courts have accepted that in a class securities fraud action involving open market transactions, the reliance element is practically impossible to prove. However, they have established that proving reliance is theoretically unimportant to the claim.[259] As originally conceived, the fraud on the market theory held that 'causation is adequately established in the context of impersonal stock markets through proof of purchase and proof of the materiality of the representations'.[260] In the court's view the proof of the materiality of the representations circumstantially established the reliance of market traders. Subsequent cases endorsed the view that purchasers do not need to rely on the misstatements, but moved away from the need to demonstrate materiality. Instead, the view has been taken that where there is a market in securities 'the market is performing a substantial part of the valuation process performed by the investor in a face-to-face transaction'.[261]

The efficient capital markets hypothesis[262] has been used to argue that since most publicly available information is reflected in market price, an investor's reliance on any public material misrepresentations can be presumed for the purposes of a Rule 10b-5 action brought by an investor.[263] Instead of having to demonstrate materiality (that is, that the price of the security was adversely affected), under this later theory of fraud on the market it is sufficient to show that the security is traded on an efficient market.[264] This presumption relieves plaintiffs of having to prove either loss causation or reliance affirmatively.[265] Instead the defendant has the burden of disproving both. This later approach has been criticised.[266]

---

[258] *Smith v Chadwick* (1884) 9 App Cas 187.

[259] *Blackie v Barrack*, 524 F 2d 891, 902 (9th Cir 1975), 429 US 816; for comment see 'Note: The Reliance Requirement in Private Actions under SEC Rule 10b-5' (1975) 88 *Harvard Law Review* 584.

[260] Ibid, 906–07.

[261] *Basic v Levinson*, 485 US 224, 244 (1988), recently re-examined and broadly upheld by the US Supreme Court in *Halliburton Co v Erica P John Fund, Inc Halliburton*, 134 S Ct 2398 (June 23, 2014) (for discussion see L Bebchuk and A Ferrell, 'Rethinking Basic' (2014) 69 *The Business Lawyer* 671).

[262] EF Fama, 'Efficient Capital Markets: A Review of Theory and Empirical Work' (1970) 25 *Journal of Finance* 383, discussed at 11.2.1.1.

[263] *Basic v Levinson*, 485 US 224, 244, 247 (1988).

[264] This presumption can be rebutted by, for example, the plaintiff's knowledge of the abuse, or the public dissemination of the information that guided the defendants' abusive actions, or statements that correct and dissipate the influence on the market of the relevant misrepresentation (eg *Basic v Levinson*, 485 US 224, 249 (1988)).

[265] However, the Supreme Court has interpreted r 10b-5 narrowly, so as to narrow the scope of the private right of action under this rule: see *Janus Capital Group v First Derivative Traders*, 131 S Ct 2296 (June 13, 2011).

[266] JR Macey and GP Miller, 'Good Finance, Bad Economics: An Analysis of the Fraud-on-the-Market Theory' (1990) 42 *Stanford Law Review* 1059. For discussion see E Avgouleas, *The Mechanics and Regulation of Market Abuse* (Oxford, Oxford University Press, 2006) 481–85.

Some commentators prefer to regard the fraud on the market presumption as a procedural device, which dispenses with the requirement to prove specific reliance, and not as a new theory of liability that replaces separate inquiries into materiality, causation and damages in securities fraud cases.[267]

The UK has now adopted the fraud on the market theory to enable investors to bring compensation claims in relation to misstatements in the prospectus.[268] Under section 90 FSMA there is no requirement for claimants to demonstrate that they have relied on the misstatement or even that they read the prospectus in order to establish a cause of action.[269] The use of the concept of fraud on the market dispenses with the need to demonstrate reliance. However, it is still necessary to demonstrate a causal link. The person claiming compensation must have suffered a loss as a result of the untrue or misleading statement in the prospectus, or the omission of information that should have been included.[270] Likewise, if the claimant is fully aware of the defect and acquired the securities anyway, there will be no causation and the claim will not be made out.[271] This is a narrower version of fraud on the market than is in use in the US.

The UK has not adopted this fraud on the market theory in the context of insider dealing and there is no civil remedy for insider dealing at present.[272] This is not surprising. There are difficulties with giving a civil remedy to the person with whom the insider dealt. Not only is it problematic to identify the particular individual, but it is difficult to justify the preferential treatment of that individual over and above all the others dealing in the market on the same day. It is just random chance that puts an investor in one category rather than another. Of course, the fraud on the market theory deals with this difficulty by providing a remedy to all those who dealt in the market on that day. However, to give a remedy to all of those individuals might be regarded as disproportionate and oppressive to the insider, and it appears to provide a windfall to those who dealt with the company's securities on the day in question. In the absence of causation it seems preferable to regard the wrong as being done to the market, but to give the cause of action to the regulatory authorities to bring an action on behalf of all investors. The FCA has a broad range of remedies at its disposal, including restitution orders if it feels that compensation needs to be made to particular individuals on the facts of a particular case.[273] As a result, any claim at common law for

---

[267] DR Fischel, 'Use of Modern Finance Theory in Securities Fraud Cases Involving Actively Traded Securities' (1982) 38 *The Business Lawyer* 1. For a discussion of the advantages and disadvantages of r 10b-5 enforcement versus exclusive public enforcement see A Rose, 'Reforming Securities Litigation Reform: Restructuring the Relationship Between Public and Private Enforcement of Rule 10b-5' (2008) 108(6) *Columbia Law Review* 1301.

[268] See 10.6.2.

[269] FSMA, s 90(1).

[270] Ibid, s 90(1)(b).

[271] Ibid, Sch 10 para 6.

[272] Early case law held that a sale of shares in breach of insider dealing regulations was unenforceable (*Chase Manhattan Equities Ltd v Goodman* [1991] BCLC 897), but subsequent changes in legislation have rendered this argument unworkable: see Criminal Justice Act 1993, s 63(2), although this provision relates only to consequences 'by reason only of' the Criminal Justice Act being contravened, and therefore if the contract is voidable at common law for misrepresentation such a consequence, not being based on the Act, is not affected by the Criminal Justice Act 1993. However any claim based on common law would still have to surmount the difficulties of demonstrating reliance and causation.

[273] FSMA, s 382.

misrepresentation based on insider dealing will fail unless both reliance and loss causation can be established. In the modern anonymous marketplace this will rarely occur.

Another circumstance in which a civil claim for insider dealing might arise, however, is where the basis of the claim is not misrepresentation but breach of fiduciary duty. The advantage of such a claim is that there is no need to show loss on the part of the investor, just that the fiduciary has made an undisclosed profit. However, generally directors do not owe fiduciary duties to those with whom they deal. Even where directors are buying from the existing shareholders in their own company they do not per se owe a duty to those shareholders. Their fiduciary duties are to the company (that is, the shareholders as a whole in a solvent company), not to individual shareholders.[274] In certain circumstances, directors can owe a duty to one or more shareholders, for example where the directors of a small company act as the agents of the individual shareholders on a takeover.[275] However, it would be unusual for this kind of relationship to arise in the listed company context.[276]

12.2.2.5 Summary

Market abuse regulation is a well-established aspect of EU, and UK, capital market regulation. Market abuse rules are needed to tackle the problem of asymmetrical information as between insiders and outsiders. The presence of market abuse undermines investor confidence by undermining investors' belief that the market is fair and that market prices reflect the true worth of securities. Investors who believe that the system is being abused by insiders are likely to either withhold their investment or build this risk into their investment decisions, by lowering the price they are prepared to pay for companies' shares. Either outcome will increase companies' cost of capital.

The law in this area has been subject to a substantial amount of change. New criminal provisions for market manipulation were introduced in the UK in 2012, and the 2014 Market Abuse Regulation introduces significant changes. One of the key issues is likely to be the enforcement of the market abuse provisions. Historically, the levels of enforcement of market abuse in the UK have been low, but this appears to be in the process of changing, and it may be that the Market Abuse Regulation will prompt further movement in this direction.

12.3 The Regulation of Short Selling

Short selling involves the practice of selling assets, usually securities,[277] that have been borrowed from a third party (in general for a fee) with the intention of buying identical assets back at a later date to return to the lender.[278] The short seller hopes to profit from a decline

---

[274] *Percival v Wright* [1902] 2 Ch 421; *Peskin v Anderson* [2001] 1 BCLC 372.

[275] Eg *Allen v Hyatt* (1914) 30 TLR 444.

[276] A final possibility is a claim for breach of confidence against someone who receives information in confidence: *Schering Chemicals Ltd v Falkman Ltd* [1982] QB 1. The potential reach of this claim is broader than that based on a fiduciary duty, but to date this civil claim has not been developed in the context of insider dealing.

[277] This chapter concentrates on the short selling of equity securities, but similar techniques also exist in other markets, including the commodities markets.

[278] IOSCO Technical Committee, *Regulation of Short Selling: Consultation Report* (March 2009), 23–24.

in the price of the securities between the sale and the repurchase, as the seller will pay less to buy the securities than the seller received on selling them. Conversely, the short seller will incur a loss if the price of the securities rises.[279] It is therefore central to the practice that the short seller wants the price of securities to fall. This can be contrasted with the more traditional conception of speculation in the capital markets, which involves the investor betting that the price of securities will rise, and therefore buying securities with the intention of selling them for a profit in the future—that is, taking a long position in a security (or 'going long'). It is worth noting that the strategy of going long in relation to investing in equity securities provides the investor with a fixed downside, namely the price paid for the shares, as long as limited liability is maintained, and an unlimited upside, at least where the shares have a right to participate in the surplus assets of the company.[280] In contrast, the strategy of short selling shares provides the investor with a fixed upside (the profit if the share price drops to zero) but a potentially unlimited downside, since the maximum price that shares might reach is not capped.[281]

Short selling is described as 'covered' where the seller has borrowed the security, or made arrangements to ensure that it can be borrowed, before the short sale. By contrast, short selling is termed 'uncovered' or 'naked' where at the time of the short sale the seller has not borrowed the security or ensured that it can be borrowed.[282] Naked short selling is possible because settlement periods exist when selling securities. In other words, there is a gap of time between the agreement to transfer the securities for a particular price, and the actual payment and transfer. Depending on the type of security traded, the length of the settlement period will differ. Settlement periods are typically quoted as T+1, T+2, T+3 etc, which means that the buyer must transfer the cash to the seller, and the seller must transfer ownership of the securities to the buyer within, respectively, 1, 2 or 3 days after the trade is made. This provides an opportunity for the short seller to acquire the shares in order to deliver them to the purchaser before the expiry of the settlement period.

In general, regulators have put in place minimal regulations to control those who wish to go long in a security. For instance, there is some use of disclosure rules in this context, for the directors of a company[283] and its major shareholders,[284] and of course there are bans on the use of inside information when going long,[285] but there is no general ban on

---

[279] Note that short selling in the debt markets can be effected in a relatively simple fashion by purchasing an uncovered or 'naked' credit default swap (CDS) (see 6.4.3 for a discussion of CDSs); the regulation of short selling in the debt markets is discussed at 13.4.3.

[280] This will generally be the ordinary shares of the company. For discussion see 3.2.1.1.

[281] For an example of the exposure that short sellers can potentially face, consider the position of short sellers in Volkswagen (VW) in October 2008. The price of the shares was expected to fall and a large number of hedge funds staked millions of euros on this bet, by short selling the stock. Unexpectedly, on 26 October 2008 new information entered the market (the fact that Porsche held a much higher percentage of the stock than had been assumed and had acquired control of the company), causing the price of VW shares to rise. The short sellers all wanted to purchase VW shares as quickly as possible to close their short positions with as small a loss as possible. Unfortunately, with only 6% of VW stock available it was quickly evident that there were not enough shares to meet the heavy demand. The price of VW shares soared, making it the world's largest company for a time (this situation can be described as a 'short squeeze'). It is estimated that short sellers lost as much as €30 billion as a result. For discussion see eg A Kammel, 'The Dilemma of Blind Spots in Capital Markets—How to Make Efficient Use of Regulatory Loopholes?' (2009) *German Law Journal* 605.

[282] See eg FSA, *Short Selling*, Discussion Paper 09/1 (February 2009), paras 2.3 and 2.4.

[283] See 11.3.2.2.

[284] See 11.3.2.3.

[285] See 12.2.

the use of going long as a strategy. In contrast, until 2008 the UK had no rules in place specifically to regulate short selling. However, the financial crisis, and in particular the market price collapse of listed financial securities following the bankruptcy of Lehman Brothers in September 2008, brought the issue of short selling regulation resolutely onto the reform agenda. The UK, in common with many other jurisdictions, introduced temporary bans on short selling shares in financial institutions in the immediate aftermath of the Lehman bankruptcy.[286] Further, a set of disclosure obligations was implemented to deal with certain instances of short selling, specifically short selling of the shares of financial institutions and short selling around the time of rights issues.[287] This is another area in which EU provisions have come to dominate, however. In 2012 the EU adopted a regulation dealing with short selling,[288] and it is the provisions within this legislative measure that now determine the regulation of this issue in the UK.

12.3.1 Justifications for Regulating Short Selling

There are a number of concerns that are voiced regarding short selling, and these became particularly pronounced in the wake of the recent financial crisis.[289] In particular it is suggested that (i) short selling destabilises orderly markets and increases market volatility;[290] (ii) short selling can be used to manipulate the market in a security, or to act profitably on inside information; and (iii) short selling involves settlement risk.[291]

12.3.1.1 Short Selling Destabilises Orderly Markets

Concerns have been raised about the effects of short selling on markets, particularly regarding the use of short selling in a falling market, where its use might push prices down even further. This issue was felt particularly strongly in September 2008 following the collapse of Lehman Brothers and the failure of other financial institutions, such as AIG, when the market became particularly concerned about the value of the securities of financial institutions. The failure of Lehman Brothers signalled to creditors and shareholders in financial

---

[286] See FSA, Short Selling (No 2) Instrument 2008, FSA 2008/50 (18 September 2008). This ban expired on 17 January 2009. On the same day the SEC put in place a similar temporary ban in the US. For discussion see J Payne, 'The Regulation of Short Selling and its Reform in Europe' (2012) 13 *European Business Organization Law Review* 413.

[287] FSA, Short Selling (No 2) Instrument 2008, FSA 2008/50 (18 September 2008). Initially the rules regarding short selling were placed within the UK's market abuse regime, in the Code of Market Conduct, but subsequently they were moved to a new section of the Handbook (the Financial Stability and Market Confidence Sourcebook, FINMAR): see Financial Stability and Market Confidence Sourcebook Instrument 2010, FSA 2010/25. New powers were also granted to the regulator in this regard in Financial Services Act 2010, s 8.

[288] Regulation (EU) No 236/2012 of the European Parliament and the Council of 14 March 2012 on short selling and certain aspects of credit default swaps. For discussion see J Payne, 'The Regulation of Short Selling and its Reform in Europe' (2012) 13 *European Business Organization Law Review* 413.

[289] For discussion see IOSCO, *Regulation of Short Selling: Final Report* (2009).

[290] Eg F Allen and D Gale, 'Arbitrage, Short Sales, and Financial Innovation' (1991) 59 *Econometrica* 1041; A Bernardo and I Welch, 'Liquidity and Financial Market Runs' (2004) 119 *Quarterly Journal of Economics* 135.

[291] See eg European Commission COM(2010) 482 final, 3. See also E Avgouleas, 'A New Framework for the Global Regulation of Short Sales: Why Prohibition is Inefficient and Disclosure Insufficient' (2009–10) 15 *Stanford Journal of Law, Business & Finance* 376.

sector firms that there was a significant possibility of large losses in their investments. The prices of these securities began to fall and stock markets in September 2008 witnessed a huge increase of short selling orders in these financial sector shares. This increase in short selling was seen as a significant cause of the downward price pressures affecting the securities, and led to temporary bans being put in place in many jurisdictions, including the US and the UK, and subsequently to more permanent measures being introduced to constrain short selling.[292]

As with insider trading,[293] however, the argument that short selling is damaging to markets, and should therefore be regulated, has been met with counter-arguments that short selling is in fact beneficial to market efficiency. In particular, it is suggested that short selling can have two important effects on markets. First, it can facilitate price corrections in overvalued securities.[294] Short sellers can therefore perform a role akin to that of securities analysts or other market professionals, who gather information about a company and analyse it, deciding whether a security is undervalued and therefore should be purchased, or overvalued and should be sold.[295] They can then exploit, through arbitrage trading, any deviations from the fundamental value of a security, and that trading will move the price to a new equilibrium. Short sellers similarly gather information about a company and analyse it, acting to short sell the security if they think it is overvalued. Empirical studies suggest that short sales do contribute to more efficient price discovery.[296] Indeed, some studies suggest that short sellers' contribution to the market's information efficiency is superior to that of securities analysts.[297] In addition, research suggests that short sellers may in fact discover and anticipate financial misconduct in firms, and as a result may convey beneficial information to the market.[298] While this suggests that short selling may be a good tool for arbitrage when the problem is a price spike, it does not necessarily answer the concern that short selling in a falling market has a negative impact, by amplifying price falls. However, this concern is not borne out by the empirical data. In fact, some studies suggest that restrictions on short selling can in fact aggravate a price fall, since the accumulated unrevealed negative information about a security only surfaces when the market begins to drop.[299]

---

[292] These constraints are discussed at 12.3.2. In fact, a study conducted by the Office of Economic Analysis in the US suggests that long sellers (those selling a stock they actually own) rather than short sellers were primarily responsible for the price falls in the aftermath of Lehman Brothers: Office of Economic Analysis, *Analysis of Short Selling Activity during the First Weeks of September 2008* (December 2008). See also E Avgouleas, 'A New Framework for the Global Regulation of Short Sales: Why Prohibition is Inefficient and Disclosure Insufficient' (2009–10) 15 *Stanford Journal of Law, Business & Finance* 376, 415.

[293] See 12.2.1.1.3.

[294] EM Miller, 'Risk, Uncertainty and Divergence of Opinion' (1977) 32 *Journal of Finance* 1151; KB Diether, K-H Lee and IM Werner, 'Short Sale Strategies and Return Predictability' (2009) 22 *Review of Financial Studies* 575.

[295] For discussion of the role of analysts in the capital markets see 11.2.1.1 and 11.5.

[296] Eg CM Jones and OA Lamont, 'Short-Sale Constraints and Stock Returns' (2002) 66 *Journal of Financial Economics* 207; A Bris, WN Goetzmann and N Zhu, 'Efficiency and the Bear: Short Sales and Markets around the World' (2007) 62 *Journal of Finance* 1029; E Boehmer, CM Jones and X Zhang, 'Which Shorts are Informed?' (2008) 63 *Journal of Finance* 491; PAC Saffi and K Sigurdsson, 'Price Efficiency and Short Selling' (2011) 24 *Review of Financial Studies* 821.

[297] MS Drake, L Lees and EP Swanson, 'Should Investors Follow the Prophets or the Bears? Evidence on the Use of Public Information by Analysts and Short Sellers' (2011) 86 *Accounting Review* 101.

[298] JM Karpoff and X Lou, 'Short Sellers and Financial Misconduct' (2010) 65 *Journal of Finance* 1879.

[299] H Hong and JC Stein, 'Differences of Opinion, Short-Sales Constraints, and Market Crashes' (2003) 16 *Review of Financial Studies* 487.

The second potential benefit that short selling can offer the market is to facilitate liquidity and trading opportunities.[300] Short selling enables investors to hedge against a decline in the prices of securities, allowing investors to take longer positions, which in turn adds liquidity to the market. Short sellers can also step in and add liquidity where there is a temporary imbalance in the market, by increasing the number of potential sellers in the market. This increases liquidity by boosting trading volumes and reducing transaction costs, through a reduction of bid/ask spreads. Naked short selling, in particular, can provide liquidity when it is otherwise scarce.

Empirical studies support the view that short selling can provide benefits to capital markets.[301] Some support for this view can be found in the studies of the effect of the periods of temporary short selling bans in 2008. For example, an independent study commissioned by the London Stock Exchange evaluated the impact of the ban on market quality by comparing the trading of 15 FTSE stocks on the restricted list with 78 stocks not on the list. This study found that the stocks on the list experienced a loss of liquidity, and that these losses in liquidity occurred independently of market-wide changes and increased volatility; in other words, the adverse impact on liquidity could be attributed to the ban.[302] This suggests that short selling does bring efficiency gains to the market, and that the short selling prohibitions of 2008 failed to stabilise securities markets or to bring about reductions in price volatility, while at the same time adversely affecting liquidity and thus pricing efficiency in the securities concerned.

12.3.1.2 The Use of Short Selling to Manipulate Markets

A second important concern relates to the use of short sales to manipulate the market, or to act profitably on inside information.[303] Short selling can be used abusively to create misleading signals about the real supply, or the correct valuation, of securities. It can also be used abusively, in conjunction with false rumours, in order to push down the price of a stock being shorted.[304] The FSA noted in its discussion paper on short selling in 2009 that the potential for abuse is particularly strong where the short sales occur before a rights issue.[305] This is because there is a potential incentive for short sellers to attempt to drive down the share price below the rights issue price so that they can both profit from their short selling

---

[300] FSA, *Short Selling*, Discussion Paper 09/1 (February 2009), para 3.4.

[301] Eg A Klein, T Bohr and P Sikles, 'Are Short Sellers Positive Feedback Traders? Evidence from the Global Financial Crisis' (2013) 9 *Journal of Financial Stability* 337; A Beber and M Pagano, 'Short Selling Bans around the World: Evidence from the 2007–09 Crisis' (2013) 68 *Journal of Finance* 343.

[302] M Clifton and M Snape, *The Effect of Short-Selling Restrictions on Liquidity: Evidence from the London Stock Exchange* (2008). See also FSA, *Temporary Short Selling Measures: Feedback on DP 09/1*, Policy Statement 09/1 (2009). Similar results emerge from studies carried out in relation to temporary bans imposed in the US in the same period: A Bris, *Short Selling Activity in Financial Stocks and the SEC July 15th Emergency Order* (2008), www. imd.ch/news/upload/Report.pdf; E Boehmer, CM Jones and X Zhang, 'Shackling Short Sellers: The 2008 Shorting Ban' (2008) 26 *Review of Financial Studies* 1363.

[303] Eg, I Goldstein and A Guembel, 'Manipulation and the Allocational Role of Prices' (2008) 75 *Review of Economic Studies* 133.

[304] FSA, *Short Selling*, Discussion Paper 09/01 (February 2009), para 3.6.

[305] Ibid, para 3.7. This explains the UK's focus in the disclosure of short selling around rights issues in its post-2008 reforms: FINMAR 2.2, which ceased to have effect on 30 October 2012.

strategy and bolster the supply of shares available for purchase (from the underwriters), thereby improving their ability to close out their short positions.[306]

These are significant concerns that need to be taken seriously. Where short selling is being used as a means to effect market abuse, however, regulators already have considerable weapons in place to tackle such behaviour, as discussed in 12.2. Importantly, such regulatory tools do not interfere with the potentially beneficial effects of short selling: they do not involve a general ban on short selling, but rather a ban on short selling when used abusively.[307]

12.3.1.3 Settlement Risk

A third concern arises from short selling, namely settlement risk. There may be settlement default if the short seller does not have a strong incentive to settle, or if the share lending market has become illiquid, so that the seller is unable to borrow the shares he sold short in order to fulfil his settlement obligations.[308] This risk arises particularly strongly in relation to naked short selling, since in that instance the shares have not been borrowed, and no arrangements have been made to borrow, at the time of the short sale. This is an important issue, since settlement risk carries with it the possibility of a disruption of orderly markets.[309] However, this is an issue that is relatively easy to tackle as long as sufficiently strict settlement rules are put in place and other strong incentives to settle are adopted, such as substantial penalties for failure to deliver.

It is worth considering the particular concerns that are raised in relation to naked short selling, as compared to covered short selling. Regulators often introduce a different, and stricter, regime to deal with naked short selling. The EU Short Selling Regulation, for example, puts in place a de facto ban on naked short selling, but imposes a lighter regime, based on disclosure, for covered short selling.[310] Both general and specific arguments are raised to justify the stricter regulation of naked short selling. On a general level, it is suggested that the potential for abusive practices is much greater with naked short selling than with covered short selling because the technique of short selling can be conducted much more aggressively. If the shares need to be borrowed first, this introduces a natural limitation of 100 per cent of the issued shares of a company that can be shorted at any time. However, with naked short selling it is possible to short more than 100 per cent of the issued shares of a company. More specifically, it is suggested that the concerns set out above manifest themselves more keenly in relation to naked short selling. So, the fact that in naked short selling the sale does not have to be covered before the settlement date means that concerns regarding settlement failure are felt more strongly. A second specific concern about naked short selling is that 'the risk of market abuse is much greater in relation to naked short

---

[306] A Saffieddine and W Wilhelm, 'An Empirical Investigation of Short-Selling Activity Prior to Seasoned Equity Offerings' (1996) 51 *Journal of Finance* 729.

[307] It should be observed that issues of market manipulation also arise for long positions. Consequently the regulatory response should target all manipulative trading rather than, for instance, singling out short sales.

[308] See eg FSA, *Short Selling*, Discussion Paper 09/01 (February 2009), para 2.5.

[309] See however V Fotak, V Ramen and PK Yadav, 'Fails-to-Deliver, Short Selling, and Market Quality' (2014) 114 *Journal of Financial Economics* 493, who find no evidence that any fails-to-deliver caused price distortions or the failure of financial firms during the 2008 financial crisis.

[310] See 12.3.2.1 and 12.3.2.3.

sales, because for covered short sales the requirement to cover (eg borrow) inhibits both the speed and extent of short selling'.[311] Although naked short selling is a more extreme form of short selling, it may be questioned whether any regulatory differentiation is justified. In relation to settlement risk, for instance, the risk posed by naked and covered short selling is the same (non-delivery) and the same response is appropriate in both cases, namely rules designed to deter settlement failure.

12.3.2 Constraints Placed on Short Selling

Before 2008 the UK did not specifically regulate short selling, although if used in the context of market manipulation or insider dealing this behaviour would potentially have been caught by the market abuse regime described at 12.2 above.[312] The collapse of Lehman Brothers triggered the imposition of temporary bans on the short selling of the shares of certain financial companies in the UK, and measures requiring the disclosure of short selling in certain instances.[313] The EU Short Selling Regulation, in force from 1 November 2012, now regulates this issue and provides the substance of the UK regime on short selling.[314] It provides a harmonised response to the perceived problems that arise as a result of short selling.[315] Given the analysis in 12.3.1, and indeed the clear recognition in many quarters that short selling can have beneficial effects on markets, the introduction of this regulation, and in particular its broad scope and content, which encompasses not only bans and constraints on the short selling of shares but also bans and constraints on sovereign credit default swaps (CDSs) and on the short selling of sovereign debt, may seem surprising. To understand why the regulation was introduced, it is necessary to appreciate that the EU agenda in this regard had become politicised. Regulators sought a way of supporting financial stability and, perhaps as importantly, wanted to be seen to be doing so. Short selling became closely associated with hedge fund activity and became entangled with the

---

[311] FSA, *Short Selling*, Discussion Paper 09/01 (February 2009), para 3.7. See also JW Christian, R Shapiro and J-P Whalen, 'Naked Short Selling: How Exposed are Investors?' (2006) 43 *Houston Law Review* 1033.

[312] This may be contrasted with other jurisdictions. The US introduced an uptick rule to regulate short selling in 1938. Although this provision was repealed in 2007, the financial crisis prompted the US to introduce a modified version of this rule (the 'alternative uptick rule') in 2010 (SEC, Amendments to Regulation SHO, Release No 34-61595, February 2010). Other tools are also utilised in the US to deal with short selling, including a locate rule and rules designed to mitigate settlement risk (see generally Regulation SHO, as amended).

[313] In particular, public disclosure was required on a one-off basis of net short positions of 0.25% or more in companies undertaking rights issues and whose shares were admitted to trading on a public market, and of net short positions in UK financial sector companies in excess of 0.25% of ordinary share capital (see FINMAR 2.2, which ceased to have effect on 30 October 2012).

[314] Regulation (EU) No 236/2012. The provisions in this Regulation are fleshed out with four delegated or implementing measures: Commission Delegated Regulation (EU) No 826/2012, Commission Implementing Regulation (EU) No 827/2012, Commission Delegated Regulation (EU) No 918/2012, and Commission Delegated Regulation (EU) No 919/2012. The Short Selling Regulation has also been subject to review by ESMA: *Final Report: ESMA's Technical Advice on the Evaluation of the Regulation (EU) 236/2012 of the European Parliament and of the Council on short selling and certain aspects of credit default swaps*, 3 June 2013, ESMA/2013/614. These findings were to assist the European Commission in preparing its own report on the operation of the regulation: European Commission, *Report on the Evaluation of the Regulation (EU) 236/2012* (December 2013).

[315] The lack of harmonised response to this issue prior to the EU regulation was regarded as a concern: European Commission, Impact Assessment SEC(2010) 1055 final, 2; Moloney: EU Regulation, 543–45.

Alternative Investment Managers Directive,[316] and the European sovereign debt crisis gave fresh impetus to reform proposals, as well as extending the remit of the measures beyond merely regulating the short selling of shares.[317]

Various mechanisms can be put in place to regulate short selling. These may be categorised as: (i) bans on short selling; (ii) disclosure rules; (iii) the use of uptick rules or circuit breakers (discussed in section 12.3.2.3); and (iv) rules designed to reduce settlement risk. The EU Short Selling Regulation makes use of options (i), (ii) and (iv) as the foundation of its short selling regime. The regulation also provides the opportunity for national regulators, and for ESMA in some circumstances, to put additional, temporary measures in place in emergency scenarios, and the use of option (iii) is raised in this context. The regulation provides potentially significant powers to ESMA, and the boundaries of these powers also need to be analysed.

In general terms the regulation relates to a broad range of financial instruments, including debt instruments issued by a Member State or by the EU, and sovereign CDSs.[318] The broad aim of the regulation is to regulate short sales of shares and sovereign debt and transactions in uncovered sovereign CDSs. This section, in common with the rest of the chapter, will concentrate on the use of the regulation to constrain the short selling of shares.

12.3.2.1 Bans on Short Selling

Article 12 of the EU Short Selling Regulation provides that a natural or legal person may enter into a short sale of shares provided that the short sale is 'covered'.[319] The regime therefore draws a fundamental distinction between covered and uncovered short sales. This requires an examination of the meaning of 'covered' for this purpose.

A short sale is regarded as covered where the person has borrowed the share, or made alternative provisions to the same effect.[320] Alternatively, it is regarded as covered if a person has entered into an agreement to borrow the share or has another 'absolutely enforceable claim' under contract or property to be transferred ownership of a corresponding number of securities of the same class so that settlement can be effected when it is due.[321] Finally, and most controversially, a sale will be regarded as covered when the 'locate' rule is met.[322] Such a rule requires the seller to be able to 'locate' the security to be sold short, in that the person

---

[316] Discussed at 16.7.2.

[317] For discussion of the background to the EU regulation see Moloney: EU Regulation, 538–51.

[318] Regulation (EU) No 236/2012, arts 1 and 2. Note that the scope of the regulation is set by the nature of the instruments traded, not by the location of the person trading, so the regulation has extraterritorial effect. See ESMA, Questions and Answers: Implementation of the Regulation on Short Selling and Certain Aspects of Credit Default Swaps, ESMA/2013/159, Question 1a. There are two major exemptions that apply within the regulation: the first relates to the geographical reach of the regulation and exempts shares admitted to trading in the EU where the 'principal venue' for the trading of the shares is located in a third country (art 16), and the second exempts market making and related activities from the scope of the regulation (art 17).

[319] The regulation also imposes constraints on uncovered short sales in sovereign debt (art 13) purchasing uncovered sovereign CDSs (arts 4 and 14).

[320] Regulation (EU) No 236/2012, art 12(1)(a).

[321] Ibid, art 12(1)(b).

[322] The European Commission and Parliament had both been particularly in favour of a 'hard locate rule' that essentially required the third party to have both 'located and reserved' the shares for lending. However, as part of the political trade-off for obtaining the effective ban on naked sovereign CDSs, the Parliament was forced to pull back from this hard rule.

has an arrangement with a third party under which that third party has confirmed that the share has been located, and has additionally taken 'measures' as regards third parties necessary for the person to have a 'reasonable' expectation that settlement can be effected when it is due.[323] The precise parameters of the 'locate' arrangements determine how close this rule comes to an absolute ban on naked short selling. This provision is dealt with in some detail in the Implementing Regulation that accompanies the EU Short Selling Regulation.[324] As a minimum, a locate confirmation (ie a confirmation from a third party that it can lend, or otherwise make available, the shares in the amount requested by the seller so as to allow settlement in due time) is required before a share can be shorted. For liquid shares or intra-day short selling, an additional confirmation needs to be obtained to the effect that the share is easy to borrow or to purchase. If the short position is in relation to an illiquid share and for a longer period, shares will need to have been 'put on hold' by the third party—that is, they must have been identified and allocated.[325] Further, the Implementing Regulation makes it clear that the third party with whom the short seller makes these arrangements must be a legally separate entity to the short seller.[326] The provisions of the regulation, and its implementing legislation, amount to a de facto ban on naked short selling.

It is notable that although the temporary bans implemented in the UK, the US and elsewhere following the demise of Lehman Brothers tended to concentrate on banning the short selling of financial stocks, in order to counter systemic risk concerns raised by declines in the share price of such stocks the ban put in place in the EU regulation is far broader, covering all shares within the ambit of the regulation.

The empirical studies discussed at 12.3.1.1 suggest that the temporary bans put in place in 2008 did not halt price falls, and in fact had a deleterious effect on market efficiency. Consequently, the value of the imposition of this broader, permanent de facto ban on naked short selling may be questioned.

12.3.2.2 Disclosure and Reporting Obligations

Disclosure and reporting requirements play a central role in the EU short selling regime.[327] The regulation aims to introduce across the EU a harmonised regime requiring the private notification and public reporting of net short positions in shares when such positions

---

[323] Regulation (EU) No 236/2012, art 12(1)(c).

[324] Commission Implementing Regulation (EU) No 827/2012.

[325] Ibid, art 6.

[326] Ibid, art 8. Note that in its Evaluation of the regulation, ESMA proposed changes to enable short sellers to obtain the necessary confirmations from parties within the same legal entity, provided the third party met with the necessary conditions set out in art 8 Implementing Regulation (it also proposed some refinements to art 8). The Commission acknowledged this suggestion but concluded that it was too early to make changes to the legislative framework: European Commission, *Report on the Evaluation of the Regulation (EU) 236/2012* (December 2013).

[327] The regulation also provides a harmonised regime for disclosure to regulators of net short positions in sovereign debt and uncovered CDSs that relate to sovereign issuers: arts 7 and 8. In contrast to the EU position, reporting and disclosure requirements do not play a large part in the US short selling regime at present. For example, the US rules contain no requirement to notify individual short positions to either the regulator or the market. Rather, they include requirements to 'mark' all sell orders of equity securities as 'short' or 'long', and the rules also provide for more general transparency obligations—for instance there are general order recording and reporting requirements.

reach, or fall below, certain specified thresholds.[328] Under the regulation, investors must report significant net short positions to regulators once these amount to 0.2 per cent of the issued share capital of a company[329] and disclose to the market at a higher 0.5 per cent threshold.[330] All changes of position should be reported in increments of 0.1 per cent, first to the regulator (at 0.3 per cent and 0.4 per cent) and then to the regulator and the market.[331]

A person's net short position is obtained by deducting any long position that a natural or legal person holds from any short position.[332] A short position is defined as either a short sale of a share issued by the company, or entry into a transaction which creates or relates to a financial instrument other than the company share, the effect of which is to confer a financial advantage on the person in the event of a decrease in the price or value of the share.[333] Notably the EU regulation requires reporting and disclosure of both direct and indirect short positions, including positions created through the use of derivatives. This is important as it provides regulators with a more complete picture and avoids any easy circumvention of the requirements.[334]

Notifications in net short positions are to be given by 3.30pm the following trading day,[335] and must include the identity of the person, the size of the relevant position, the issuer in question and the date on which the position was created, changed, or ceased to be held.[336] The regulation provides that public disclosure of information shall be made in a manner ensuring fast access to information on a non-discriminatory basis.[337] These notification and disclosure requirements apply to both natural and legal persons domiciled or established within the EU or elsewhere.[338]

Disclosure can be a valuable tool in relation to the regulation of short selling. In particular, reporting to the regulator allows the regulator to monitor and regulate potentially abusive positions.[339] The reporting requirement under the EU regulation can be seen as fulfilling this goal, and although there is a cost associated with reporting, this cost can perhaps be regarded as mitigated by the potential benefits that flow from it.

The requirement of public disclosure under the regulation is potentially more problematic. Benefits can flow from such disclosure—for instance, disclosure to the public can

---

[328] In contrast to the short sale restrictions, this aspect of the regulation was less controversial during its deliberations. This was due in particular to various national regulators introducing such requirements during the financial crisis, plus previous work that CESR had conducted with respect to developing a 'pan-EU' model for disclosure. See further CESR, *Report: Model for a Pan-European Short Selling Disclosure Regime* (March 2010).

[329] Regulation (EU) No 236/2014, art 5. In relation to sovereign debt see art 7 and Commission Delegated Regulation (EU) No 918/2012, art 21.

[330] Regulation (EU) No 236/2014, art 6.

[331] Ibid, arts 5(2) and 6(2).

[332] Ibid, art 3(4).

[333] Ibid, art 3(1).

[334] Ibid, art 3(1) and see EU Delegated Regulation (EU) No 918/2012, arts 5–7, 10.

[335] Regulation (EU) No 236/2014, art 9(2).

[336] Ibid, art 9(1). See further Commission Implementing Regulation (EU) No 826/2012, arts 2–3.

[337] Regulation (EU) No 236/2014, art 9(4). This provision provides that information shall be posted on a central website operated or supervised by the relevant competent authority. The competent authorities shall communicate the address of that website to ESMA, which, in turn, shall put a link to all such central websites on its own website (see also Commission Implementing Regulation (EU) No 827/2012, art 2).

[338] Regulation (EU) No 236/2014, art 10.

[339] See eg FSA, *Short Selling*, Discussion Paper 09/01 (February 2009), para 5.28.

provide data to the market about the impact of short sellers' price movement expectations, and therefore can contribute to more efficient pricing of stocks, if interpreted correctly.[340] Such requirements may also provide a more effective potential constraint against aggressive short selling.[341] However, the potential benefits have to be weighed against the possible deleterious effects that might result. Fearing that other players in the market may take opposite positions to frustrate its short selling strategy, a potential short seller may seek to avoid public scrutiny of their actions, and as a result might refrain from short selling entirely, or seek other mechanisms to fulfil its aims.[342] If the short seller simply uses other, unregulated mechanisms to fulfil the same goals, this will undermine the potential benefits of a disclosure regime. There is another potential problem that may arise as a result of instituting public disclosure of short selling, namely that public disclosure may actually contribute to herding behaviour, exacerbating the downward spirals that the regulations are designed to prevent.[343]

These disclosure obligations are not targeted at particular issues or scenarios that raise concerns. For instance, the UK regime that was in place prior to the EU regulation taking effect targeted short selling of financial companies (presumably due to concerns about systemic risk) and short selling of shares around the time of a rights issue, since this was one of the scenarios particularly identified by the UK regulator (then the FSA) as subject to abuse. The EU regulation, by contrast, applies to all net short positions that cross the specified thresholds of the issued share capital of companies with shares admitted to trading on an EU regulated market or MTF.[344]

12.3.2.3 Circuit Breakers and Uptick Rules

Some jurisdictions also make use of circuit breakers or uptick rules to regulate short selling. The idea of such provisions is to prevent short sales being used as a tool to accelerate price falls in a declining market. An uptick rule is a trading restriction that disallows the short selling of securities except on an 'uptick'. For the rule to be satisfied, the short sale must be either at a price above the price at which the immediately preceding sale was effected ('plus tick'), or at a price equal to the last sale price, if that price was higher than the last different price ('zero plus tick'). The US first introduced an uptick rule in 1938. This rule was

---

[340] Ibid, para 5.7.

[341] CESR, *Report: Model for a Pan-European Short Selling Disclosure Regime* (March 2010), para 31.

[342] Note that one way to deal with such concerns might be to disclose only aggregate, rather than individual, short positions. This has the benefit of not revealing information to the market about the positions of individual market participants. However, there are drawbacks: there can be inherent imperfections in the data, and there can also be considerable costs associated with such requirements that weigh heavily against the benefits (for example, there are significant costs involved in making the necessary changes to trading systems in order to implement such a system).

[343] Alternatively market participants may suffer from others who exploit the information made publicly available to manipulate the share price in order to create a short squeeze (ie this is akin to the Volkswagen/Porsche scenario observed above at n 281, where short sellers are over-extended and vulnerable to share prices rising quickly). Where this is sustained, covering short positions can drive prices up further and can lead to unlimited losses.

[344] Regulation (EU) No 236/2014, art 5. Note that the MiFID revisions now contain new rules concerning reporting transactions in financial instruments. For instance, they cover financial instruments admitted to a trading venue ('trading venue' now includes regulated markets, MTFs and OTFs). Such reports will be required to include a new short selling flag in respect of shares and sovereign debt. See MiFIR, Regulation (EU) No 609/2014, art 26. These changes come into effect in January 2017.

repealed in 2007,[345] but a modified version was introduced in 2010 (the 'alternative uptick rule'). The modified version added a circuit breaker to the equation. As a result, restrictions are only placed on short sales of a share whose price has fallen by more than 10 per cent compared to its closing price the previous day.[346] Once the circuit breaker is triggered, this rule applies to short sale orders in the affected security for the remainder of the day as well as the following day, allowing short sales to occur only where the price is above the current national best bid.[347]

The EU regulation makes only limited use of this technique: it anticipates the use by national regulators of circuit breakers as a temporary restriction in certain circumstances.[348] Where the price of a financial instrument on a trading venue has fallen significantly in value during a single trading day (in relation to the closing price on the previous trading day), the national regulator of the home Member State for that venue must consider whether it is appropriate to restrict or prohibit persons from engaging in short selling of the financial instrument on the trading venue in order to prevent the disorderly decline in the price of the financial instrument. These restrictions would be short-term (until the end of the next trading day).[349] The regulation provides that a significant fall in value for this purpose would involve a fall of 10 per cent or more in the case of liquid shares. The measure can be extended for a further two trading days if there is a further significant fall in the value of the financial instrument.[350]

12.3.2.4 Rules Designed to Mitigate Settlement Risk

Settlement failure is a potentially serious matter: it can cause disruption to the orderly operation of the market in the securities concerned. However, a number of measures can be put in place to try to reduce the risk. First, the problem is caused in large part because of the need for settlement periods. Given the nature of securities, some kind of settlement period is necessary. However, keeping settlement periods to a minimum can be beneficial. Within the EU, rules relating to settlement discipline are now contained in the EU Regulation on Improving Securities Settlement and on Central Securities Depositaries.[351] This regulation, amongst other things, harmonises the timing and conduct of securities settlement

---

[345] The uptick rule was heavily criticised in the US before its repeal in 2007: J Macey, M Mitchell and JM Netter, 'Restrictions on Short Sales: An Analysis of the Uptick Rule and its Role in View of the October 1987 Stock Market Crash' (1989) 74 *Cornell Law Review* 799. In 2004, the SEC initiated a year-long pilot that eliminated short sale price test restrictions from approximately one-third of the largest stocks. The purpose of the pilot was to study how this removal impacted the market for those securities. The SEC concluded from this study: 'The general consensus ... was that the Commission should remove price test restrictions because they modestly reduce liquidity and do not appear necessary to prevent manipulation': SEC, *SEC Votes on Regulation SHO Amendments and Proposals; Also Votes to Eliminate 'Tick Test'*, 13 June 2007.

[346] SEC, Amendments to Regulation SHO, Release No 34-61595 (February 2010) (final rule).

[347] In contrast to the original uptick rule, which pegged short sales to the price of the previous trade, the alternative uptick rule only permits short sales at a price higher than anyone is willing to pay.

[348] Regulation (EU) No 236/2012, art 23. See also art 28, which provides ESMA with powers to intervene in exceptional circumstances.

[349] Ibid, art 23(1). For further discussion see 12.3.2.5.

[350] Regulation (EU) No 236/2012, art 23(2).

[351] Regulation (EU) No 909/2014. Settlement obligations were initially introduced in Regulation (EU) No 236/2012, art 15, but these are repealed and replaced by the provisions of the 2014 Regulation.

throughout the EU. In particular, it aligns the settlement periods for transferable securities (broadly, shares and bonds) executed on trading venues across the EU to T+2.

In addition, penalties can be put in place for failure to settle, in order to provide incentives for traders. Within the EU, for example, the central securities depositories (CSDs)[352] are required to establish procedures that provide for a penalty mechanism, including cash penalties that will be calculated on a daily basis.[353] Obligations can also be placed on institutions operating securities market infrastructure to make good the failure. For instance, within the EU CSDs are required to ensure that there are adequate arrangements in place for the buy-in of securities where there is a settlement failure (or for cash compensation to be paid in the event of a buy-in proving impossible), with reimbursement from the seller.[354]

12.3.2.5 The Role of National Authorities and ESMA

The proposals set out above regarding the de facto ban on naked short selling, disclosure rules and the rules regarding settlement risk are intended to operate at all times. However, one of the triggers for the European Commission's original proposal in relation to short selling was the collapse of Lehman Brothers and its effect on banking stocks both nationally and globally. The EU regulation attempts to address the possibility of a repeat of this type of scenario by providing that in exceptional situations national financial regulators will have powers to impose a variety of temporary measures.[355] National regulators are provided with additional powers where there are adverse events or developments which constitute a serious threat to financial stability or to market confidence in the Member State concerned or in one or more other Member States and the measure in question is necessary to address the threat and will not have a detrimental effect on the efficiency of the financial markets which is disproportionate to its benefits. The regulation contemplates that in such circumstances the national authorities might, for example, impose additional disclosure obligations[356] or impose temporary bans or conditions on all forms of short sales.[357] These constraints can be imposed for an initial period of three months, extendable for three-month periods.[358]

In addition, national authorities can impose a circuit breaker as a temporary restriction on short selling where there is a significant fall in price.[359] The exercise of this power is not subject to the same qualifying condition as the exceptional powers mentioned in the previous paragraph. Where the price of a financial instrument on a trading venue has fallen significantly during a single trading day (in relation to the closing price on the previous

---

[352] Regulation (EU) No 909/2014, art 2(1).

[353] Ibid, art 7(2).

[354] Ibid, arts 7(3)–(8). In the US see eg SEC, Amendments to Regulation SHO, Release No 34-58572 (September 2008) and Release No 34-60388 (July 2009), which introduces a new rule designed to reduce the number of fails-to-deliver.

[355] Commission Delegated Regulation (EU) No 918/2012, art 24 sets out a non-exhaustive list of criteria and factors for determining when exceptional circumstances might be considered to arise.

[356] Regulation (EU) No 236/2012, art 18.

[357] Ibid, art 20.

[358] Ibid, art 24.

[359] Ibid, art 23. This is subject to time limits: art 23 restrictions must initially be imposed for not more than the trading day following the day on which the fall in price occurred and can only be extended for a further two days and only where a further significant fall has occurred: art 23(2).

trading day), the national authority of the home Member State for that venue must consider whether it is appropriate to prohibit or restrict persons from engaging in short selling of the financial instrument on the trading venue in order to prevent a disorderly decline in the price of the financial instrument. The extent of the falls that trigger this provision are set out in the regulation and its accompanying administrative measures: for liquid shares it is a fall of 10 per cent.[360]

The use by national authorities of these powers, must be notified to ESMA.[361] For the powers triggered by exceptional circumstances, ESMA must be notified not less than 24 hours before the entry into force of the measures.[362] It shall consider the information received and issue an opinion (within 24 hours) on whether the measure or proposed measure is appropriate and proportionate to address the threat, and whether measures by other competent authorities are necessary.[363] Where a competent authority takes action contrary to ESMA's opinion, it shall publish a notice giving its reasons for doing so.[364] As regards the circuit breaker power, ESMA's role is reduced, reflecting to a large extent the time sensitive nature of this power. ESMA must still be notified, however, and it may need to adopt a coordinating role where an instrument is traded on a number of venues across Member States.

Significantly, the regulation provides for an important role for ESMA in these arrangements. It is given a coordinating role in exceptional situations.[365] In addition to the notification role set out above, ESMA may itself take action where two conditions are fulfilled: where there is a threat to the orderly functioning and integrity of financial markets or the stability of the whole or part of the financial system in the EU and there are cross-border implications, and where measures have not been taken by competent authorities, or any measures taken are not sufficient, to address the threat.[366] ESMA can impose a private notification or a public disclosure obligation on the holder of a net short position in a financial instrument or class of financial instruments, or it can prohibit (or impose conditions on) entering into short sales in respect of such instruments.[367] A measure adopted by ESMA in accordance with its powers of intervention will prevail over any previous measures taken by a competent national authority.[368] A number of procedural requirements are placed on ESMA—for instance, such actions are subject to consultation with the European Systemic Risk Board;[369] however, actions can be taken without reference to the European Parliament or Council.

---

[360] Ibid. For illiquid shares and other financial instruments see Commission Delegated Regulated 918/2012.

[361] Ibid, art 26.

[362] Ibid. This period may be shorter in exceptional circumstances: art 26(3).

[363] Ibid, art 27(2). For examples of ESMA opinions in this regard to date see eg ESMA/2012/717, ESMA/2013/149 and ESMA/2013/542. Note that due to the 'urgency' behind the imposition of a circuit breaker, ESMA does not issue an opinion on whether this measure is necessary.

[364] Regulation (EU) No 236/2012, art 27(3).

[365] Ibid, art 27(1).

[366] Ibid, art 28(2) (this power does not apply in relation to sovereign debt or sovereign CDSs, but see art 29). The UK brought a case (Case C-270/12 *UK v Council and Parliament*, 22 January 2014, EU: C:2013:562) arguing that art 28 was unlawful on various grounds. The European Court of Justice upheld art 28 (despite an opinion of the Advocate General supporting certain aspects of the UK's case): see E Howell, 'The European Court of Justice: Selling Us Short' (2014) 11 *European Company and Financial Law Review* 454.

[367] Regulation (EU) No 236/2012, art 28(1).

[368] Ibid, art 28(11).

[369] Ibid, art 28(4).

Finally, the EU Short Selling Regulation provides for competent authorities to have all the powers necessary, as well as rules on administrative measures, sanctions and pecuniary measures, to enforce the proposals.[370] ESMA is also given the power to conduct inquiries into specific issues or practices relating to short selling and to publish a report setting out its findings.[371]

12.3.3 Summary

The regulation of short selling in the UK is a recent phenomenon. The justifications for regulating short selling need to be treated with some care. While short selling can be used to effect market abuse, the provisions discussed at 12.2 above should deal with these issues. The settlement risk concerns regarding short selling can be tackled by shortening settlement periods and putting in place other practical measures to mitigate this risk. The concerns regarding short selling and market destabilisation do not appear to be supported by the empirical evidence, and thus the use of bans to tackle this issue should perhaps be a cause for concern. In a report issued by ESMA in June 2013 in relation to the first five months of the regulation being in force, it observed that, as compared to a control group of US shares it found a slight decline in the volatility of EU shares, a decrease in bid-ask spreads, no significant impact on trading volumes, but a decrease in price discovery effectiveness.[372] Further, while the effective ban on naked short selling was found to have reduced the incidence of settlement failure, the report also found that the securities lending market may have been adversely affected by the locate rule.[373] Clearly this is an area that must continue to be monitored and assessed.[374]

The reporting and disclosure requirements regarding short selling are potentially less problematic, particularly the reporting to regulators. Although this has a cost attached to it, it may be justified if it helps regulators to monitor abusive short selling. In its report ESMA concluded that the reporting and disclosure thresholds in relation to shares were appropriate, but it noted that there appeared to be a reluctance to disclose short selling to the public, lending some weight to at least one of the concerns raised at 12.3.2.2 above regarding public disclosure.[375] These are early days, however, and more data is needed in order to assess the effectiveness of the provisions.

---

[370] Ibid, arts 33, 41.

[371] Ibid, art 31.

[372] ESMA, *Final Report: ESMA's Technical Advice on the Evaluation of the Regulation (EU) 236/2012 of the European Parliament and of the Council on short selling and certain aspects of credit default swaps*, 3 June 2013, ESMA/2013/614.

[373] Ibid, 21.

[374] The Commission has suggested a second review of the regulation by the end of 2016: Commission, Report of the Commission to the European Parliament and the Council on the Short Selling Regulation COM (2013) 885.

[375] ESMA found that in its assessment period (November 2012–February 2013) 74% of notifications were to national regulators and just 24% were to the public.

12.4 Algorithmic and High Frequency Trading

High frequency trading (HFT) involves the use of sophisticated technological tools and computer algorithms to trade securities rapidly, using trading strategies carried out by computers to move in and out of positions in seconds or fractions of a second.[376] HFT forms just a subset of algorithmic trading,[377] but it is HFT that has attracted the most attention in recent years.

HFT has taken place for more than a decade, but whereas at the turn of the twenty-first century HFT trades had an execution time of several seconds, by 2010 this had decreased to milli- and even micro-seconds. It is usually carried out by specialist dealers, and generally involves particular trading strategies, for example arbitrage or market making.[378] The volume of such trading has grown in recent years,[379] as have regulatory concerns about the use of this trading technique.[380]

As with the some of the other issues discussed in this chapter, specifically insider dealing and short selling, some debate arises as to whether HFT is beneficial or harmful to market efficiency. It can provide benefits to the market in the form of deeper liquidity, narrower spreads and better price discovery.[381] However, these liquidity benefits have sometimes been doubted, as HFT often leads to a decrease in trade order size rather than new liquidity, and can lead to other liquidity providers leaving the market.[382] Risks can also be generated by HFT. This was illustrated by the 'Flash Crash' on US trading venues on 6 May 2010, in which the Dow Jones Industrial Average plunged about 1,000 points (about 9 per cent) within minutes, only to recover a large part of the loss. It was the biggest one-day point decline on an intraday basis in the history of the Dow Jones Industrial Average. During a 20-minute period, over 20,000 trades, across more than 300 securities, were executed at prices which

---

[376] See eg A J Menkveld, 'High Frequency Trading and the New Market Makers' (2013) 16(4) *Journal of Financial Markets* 612; T Chordia, A Goyal, BN Lehmann and G Saar, 'High-Frequency Trading' (2013) 16(4) *Journal of Financial Markets* 637.

[377] For discussion of algorithmic trading generally see Foresight, *The Future of Computer Trading in Financial Markets: Final Project Report* (2012) (a UK government-sponsored study).

[378] See B Hagströmer and L Nordén, 'The Diversity of High Frequency Traders' (2013) 16(4) *Journal of Financial Markets* 741.

[379] The estimates vary. It has been estimated that as of 2009, HFT accounted for 60–73% of all US equity trading volume, with that number falling to approximately 50% in 2012: 'Times Topics: High-Frequency Trading', *New York Times*, 20 December 2012. The FSA estimated that it accounted for 30–50% of trading: FSA, *The FSA's Markets Regulatory Agenda* (2010), 18, whereas ESMA reported that HFT accounted for 40–70% of total equity trading volume in Q4 of 2010 in the EU equity market: ESMA, HFT Consultation, ESMA/2011/224, 49. A more recent ESMA report differentiated between the volume of orders and the number of trades executed in this context—the first being much higher than the second: ESMA, *Trends, Risks and Vulnerabilities*, Report No 1, 2014, ESMA/2014/0188, 12 March 2014.

[380] See IOSCO, *Report on Regulatory Issues Raised by the Impact of Technological Changes in Market Integrity and Efficiency* (2011).

[381] See eg T Hendershott, C Jones and A Menkveld, 'Does Algorithmic Trading Improve Liquidity?' (2011) 66 *Journal of Finance* 1; J Brogaard, T Hendershott and R Riordan, 'High-Frequency Trading and Price Discovery' (2014) 27 *Review of Financial Studies* 2267. A report commissioned by the UK Government identified four benefits of HFT: liquidity, reduced volatility, price discovery and reduced transaction costs (see Foresight, *The Future of Computer Trading in Financial Markets: Final Project Report* (2012)).

[382] G Hertig, 'MiFID and the Return to Concentration Rules' in S Grundmann, B Haar, H Merkt, P Mülbert and M Wellenhofer (eds), *Festschrift für Klaus Hopt zum 70* (Berlin, Walter de Gruyter, 2010).

were 60 per cent away from their prices at the start of the period. A joint report of the SEC and the Commodities and Future Trading Commission (CFTC) highlighted the role of algorithmic trading in this event.[383] While the effect was in one sense limited (the market was restored to normality within minutes), nevertheless this event raised concerns about HFT—in particular its effect on those investors not employing HFT, who are unable to respond with sufficient speed when market prices change rapidly in these situations, which creates an unlevel playing field. Other risks associated with HFT include concerns about the effect on markets should HFT traders withdraw in volatile market conditions, leading to a rapid reduction in liquidity, and the growth in 'dark' OTC equity trading.[384] The empirical evidence on the advantages and disadvantages of HFT on market efficiency is not clear cut.[385]

This is a new area of regulatory concern, and so far the UK's regulatory response has been largely tied to that of the EU. Within the EU, the 2014 Markets in Financial Instruments Directive (MiFID II),[386] which must be implemented in Member States by 3 January 2017, provides a legislative regime to deal with algorithmic trading. At the core of this regime are a set of requirements which impose operational requirements on the firms that engage in such trading.[387] Algorithmic trading is defined broadly as trading in the financial instruments within the scope of MiFID II, where a computer algorithm automatically determines individual parameters of orders, with limited or no human intervention.[388] A subset of rules applies to high frequency algorithmic trading.[389] These rules include a requirement for firms to have in place effective systems and risk controls to ensure that their trading systems are resilient and have sufficient capacity, are subject to appropriate trading thresholds and limits, prevent the sending of erroneous orders, and prevent their systems otherwise operating in a way that may create or contribute to a disorderly market.[390] Firms are required to have systems in place to ensure that their trading systems cannot be used for a purpose contrary to the market abuse regime. Firms must also have effective arrangements in place to deal with trading system failures. These measures complement action taken by ESMA in 2011, when it published guidelines on systems and controls in an automated trading environment for trading platforms, investment firms and competent authorities. The guidelines require firms to test and monitor algorithms, and to have procedures in place to minimise the risk that their automated trading activity will give rise to market abuse.[391]

---

[383] SEC and CFTC, *Findings regarding the Market Events of May 6 2010* (2010).

[384] See London Economics, *Understanding the Impact of MiFID in the Context of Global and National Regulatory Innovation* (2010).

[385] See eg Foresight, *The Future of Computer Trading in Financial Markets: Final Project Report* (2012); E Benos and S Sagarde, 'High-Frequency Trading Behaviour and its Impact on Market Quality: Evidence from the UK Equity Market' Bank of England Working Paper No 249 (2013), http://ssrn.com/abstract=2184302.

[386] See Directive 2014/65/EU on markets in financial instruments and amending Directive 2002/92/EC and Directive 2011/61/EU (MiFID II).

[387] MiFID II, art 17. In addition, the regime imposes specific controls on firms that, as members of trading venues, provide direct electronic access by clients to the venues: art 17(5). The scope of MiFID II has been extended to capture proprietary dealers who engage in HFT, so, for example, the exemptions that apply to proprietary dealers do not apply where the person in question applies a high frequency algorithmic trading technique (arts 2(1)(d) and (j)).

[388] Ibid, art 4(1)(39).

[389] For the definition of high frequency algorithmic trading see art 4(1)(40).

[390] Ibid, art 17(1).

[391] ESMA, *Guidelines on Systems and Controls in an Automated Trading Environment for Trading Platforms, Investment Firms and Competent Authorities*, ESMA/2011/456.

In addition, MiFID II imposes disclosure obligations on firms: they must notify their home regulator, and the regulator of the trading venue at which the investment firms is engaged in trading, of the fact that they are engaging in algorithmic trading, and the home regulator may require the firm to disclose details of its algorithmic trading practices.[392] Where a firm engages in high frequency algorithmic trading it must also store, in an approved form, accurate and time-sequenced records of all its placed orders and make these available to the regulator on request.[393] Additional conditions are imposed on the firm where it engages in algorithmic trading as part of a market-making strategy.[394] This is a new and largely untested regime, and its impact remains to be seen.

The regulatory regime for investment firms also extends beyond the MiFID II provisions. For example, the new market abuse regime includes examples of when algorithmic and high frequency trading will amount to market manipulation.[395]

12.5 Conclusion

This chapter has examined the regulation of various instances of perceived market misconduct: market abuse (comprising insider dealing and market manipulation), short selling, and algorithmic and high frequency trading. The predominant justification for regulating these forms of conduct is the same: to make the market operate more efficiently. There is some debate as to whether regulation of these activities is appropriate and necessary, or indeed whether leaving some of these forms of conduct unregulated can be beneficial to market efficiency. These are undoubtedly controversial issues. The effect of these provisions, particularly the EU Short Selling Regulation and the regulations regarding algorithmic and high frequency trading remains to be seen.

In relation to the regulation of all of these issues, the UK's regime is heavily influenced by European legislation. In relation to market abuse, the UK has its own domestic regime in relation to criminal sanctions, but its administrative provisions regarding market abuse flow from the EU regime. The 2014 Market Abuse Regulation, in force from July 2016, extends the reach of the market abuse regime and strengthens and harmonises the enforcement of the provisions. In relation to short selling, another EU Regulation, in force from 2012, regulates this issue. The shift from directive to regulation in the context of market abuse, and the use of a regulation in the context of short selling, is telling. As regards algorithmic trading and HFT, MiFID II, which requires implementation by January 2017, creates new obligations. These provisions are an important part of the EU's harmonisation programme post-crisis, and represent a further shift towards centralisation in the regulation of such issues. ESMA's powers under the Short Selling Regulation, perhaps most vividly its power of direct intervention in emergency situations, are an example of the important role that the new EU-level regulators can now assume.

---

[392] MiFID II, art 17(2). These must then be disclosed to the regulator of the trading venue at which the firm is engaged in algorithmic trading, at the request of that regulator.
[393] Ibid.
[394] Ibid, art 17(3).
[395] See 12.2.2.3.2.

13

Regulation of Debt

13.1 Introduction

So far we have considered how those who lend to companies[1] can protect themselves against credit and other risks through private adjustment. This can involve obtaining contractual and proprietary rights against the borrower or against third parties, as well as pricing the debt to reflect the risks. It can also involve a decision not to lend (or not to increase a loan) because the risks are too great. Although there are some non-adjusting creditors,[2] most creditors are able to adjust in some way. Should, then, the general law provide any protection for creditors? This issue has already been considered in certain contexts. Insolvency law provides limited specific protection for non-adjusting creditors,[3] and provides some protection for all unsecured creditors, by seeking to preserve the assets for *pari passu* distribution.[4] The legal capital rules seek to protect creditors, particularly those who cannot adjust, although their efficacy may be questioned.[5] This chapter considers the extent to which those lending to companies are protected by regulation, and the rationale behind the various kinds of regulatory protection.

Regulation can take a number of forms and can be directed at protection against different types of risk. The risk of collapse of a financial institution is a significant risk both for other financial institutions (who will be counterparties to transactions) and for borrowers (who may be counterparties, but who will also suffer from the lack of availability of credit, particularly if there is a 'knock-on' effect on other financial institutions).[6] This risk is, at least in part, addressed by the capital adequacy requirements, which are briefly described in chapter two,[7] as well as by requiring such institutions to be authorised and supervised by the FCA, and other more specific means. The regulation of financial institutions is outside the scope of this book, and is not discussed here in detail.[8] What is addressed is the regulatory response to the specific risks that lenders run in relation to loans made to corporate

---

[1] As in earlier chapters, the term 'lenders' encompasses all those who consciously extend finance to a company, including holders of debt securities, and 'loans' encompasses all finance extended. Where loan finance in particular is considered, this is made clear by the context.

[2] See 3.2.2.1 for a discussion of who these are.

[3] See 7.6.2.3.

[4] See 3.3.2.

[5] See chapter 5.

[6] Note as well that the collapse of financial institutions may affect those who finance them, which, in the case of commercial banks, will include consumers who deposit money with the bank. Depositors can be protected by deposit insurance, such as the Financial Services Compensation Scheme established by FMSA 2000, ss 212–24A.

[7] See 2.3.1.4.

[8] For more detail see Moloney: EU Regulation.

borrowers,[9] the most important of which is credit risk, that is, risk of non-payment. Many of those 'loans' are made by investors who purchase debt securities, some of which are traded on markets. In addition to credit risk, the holders of these debt securities run another risk: that the market is inefficient so that the price they pay for the securities in the secondary market is 'wrong'. This risk is also run by the holders of equity securities, as discussed in chapter twelve. The regulatory response to this risk in relation to debt securities is very similar to that which applies in the equity markets.[10]

This chapter also includes discussion of recent regulatory responses to market developments, which purport either to address market risk[11] or credit risk.[12] Other recent regulatory responses are discussed elsewhere in this book: the regulation of credit default swaps is discussed at 6.4.3.4 and the regulation of securitisation is discussed at 9.3.3.

13.1.1 General Scope of Regulation

There is discussion of the detailed scope of regulation later in the chapter, particularly the disclosure requirements. This section will discuss the basic division in the debt market between debt securities and loans.[13] Broadly speaking, the former are subject to a regulatory regime and the latter are not. The reasons for this distinction, particularly in relation to the disclosure regime, are explored below.

The regulatory structure is set out in the Financial Markets and Services Act 2000 (FSMA), which prohibits regulated activities without authorisation or exemption ('the authorisation regime').[14] There are restrictions on financial promotion, which apply to 'investment activity' ('the financial promotion regime').[15] The disclosure requirements discussed below ('the disclosure regime') are more limited: they apply only to 'transferable securities',[16] which, subject to exemptions, are those which fall within the definition in MiFID.[17] This definition comprises shares and bonds, plus hybrids, and clearly does not apply to loans. However, the scope of both 'regulated activities' and 'investment activity' include a category of 'instruments creating or acknowledging indebtedness', which, together with a list of instruments usually thought of as securities, includes the term 'debentures'.[18]

---

[9] These risks are discussed at 3.2.2.2.

[10] See 12.2. This issue is discussed in the market abuse section below.

[11] Such as the regulation of short selling (13.4.3) and, to some extent, the regulation of credit rating agencies (13.7).

[12] The regulation of peer-to-peer lending (13.8).

[13] This term includes actual loans (whether term loans or revolving facilities) and types of asset-based finance, such as receivables financing, asset-based lending or asset finance, all of which are discussed in chapter 2.

[14] FSMA, s 19. See further 13.1.2.

[15] Ibid, s 21.

[16] Ibid, s 85.

[17] Markets in Financial Instruments Directive (2004/39/EC), art 4(1)(18), to be replaced in 2017 by MiFID II (2014/65/EU), where the definition is reproduced in art 4(1)(44).

[18] FSMA, Sch II para 12; FSMA (Regulated Activities) Order 2001 (SI 2001/544), art 77; FSMA (Financial Promotion) Order 2005 (SI 2005/1529), Sch 1.

There has been doubt as to the meaning of the term 'debenture' for many years.[19] It has been used in a number of statutes but has never been definitively defined.[20] There is no definition of 'debenture' in FSMA or any of the statutory instruments issued under it, and there has been considerable academic disagreement as to whether a loan agreement falls within the term.[21]

The Court of Appeal recently considered the meaning of the term while construing a charge over 'shares' in a company, which were defined as including 'debentures' in that company owned by the chargor.[22] The court came to the conclusion that the rights of lenders under a shareholder loan agreement fell within the definition and were therefore charged. Having considered the authorities, Patten LJ held that 'the term [debenture] can apply to any document which creates or acknowledges a debt; it does not have to include some form of charge; and can be a single instrument rather than one in a series'.[23] He therefore held that the shareholder loans could, in theory, be debentures, and moreover that, on a proper construction of the charge document, they did fall into within the term, which was not limited by its being included in a list with 'other securities'. Gloster LJ overtly endorsed the view of Chitty J that a 'debenture means a document which either creates a debt or acknowledges it, and any document which fulfils either of these conditions is a debenture',[24] and dismissed as unduly technical Tennekoon's approach, namely that there is no debt until the advance is drawn down and therefore there is no instrument acknowledging indebtedness.

This decision, while made in the context of the interpretation of a particular agreement, has caused consternation in the loan markets. If the Court of Appeal's interpretation of the word 'debenture' were applied to the statutory provisions as to the scope of authorisation regime, this could mean that non-bank lenders,[25] who are not at present authorised, would be required to be authorised, and this could have a chilling effect on the shadow banking market.[26] Further, lenders would be subject to the financial promotion regime, though it is likely that most could take steps to avoid having to comply with the more onerous provisions.[27]

---

[19] See eg *Edmonds v Blaina Furnaces Company* (1887) 36 Ch D 215, 218; *Levy v Abercorris Slate and Slab Co* (1887) 37 Ch D 260, 263; *Lemon v Austin Friars Investment Trust Ltd* [1926] Ch 1, 12–13, 17; *Knightsbridge Estates Trust, Limited v Byrne* [1940] AC 613.

[20] There is a definition in s 738 Companies Act 2006, for the purposes of that statute, which provides that the term includes 'debenture stock, bonds and any other securities of a company, whether or not constituting a charge on the assets of the company'.

[21] Those who have argued that it does include A Berg, 'Syndicated Loans and the FCA' [1991] *International Financial Law Review* 27, who relies on a dictum of Lloyd J in *Slavenburg's Bank NV v Intercontinental Natural Resources Ltd* [1980] 1 All ER 955, 976; the contrary view has been taken by R Tennekoon, *The Law and Regulation of International Finance* (London, Butterworths, 1991) 124–27, Hughes: Banking, 2.2; and Mugasha: Multi-Bank Financing, 11.51, who argue that since the making of the loan gives rise to the debt rather than the agreement, which may precede the loan by some time, the loan agreement is not an instrument which creates or acknowledges indebtedness.

[22] *Fons HF (In Liquidation) v Corporal Ltd* [2014] EWCA 304.

[23] Ibid, [36].

[24] *Levy v Abercorris Slate and Slab Co* (1887) 37 Ch D 260, 263.

[25] For discussion of such lenders, see 2.3.1.1. Banks are, of course, subject to the authorisation regime as accepters of deposits: see 13.5 below.

[26] See letter of the City of London Law Society to HM Treasury dated 4 June 2014, www.citysolicitors. org.uk/attachments/article/106/20140604%20Letter%20re%20implications%20of%20decision%20in%20 matter%20of%20Fons%20HF%20(in%20liquidation)%20v%20Corporal%20Limited%20and%20Pillar%20 Securitisation%20S%20a%20r%20l%20(final).pdf.

[27] See 13.2.6 below.

However, the concern, while understandable in terms of an increase in uncertainty, is probably misplaced. The case itself was clearly focused on the interpretation of a particular document, and the wider regulatory ramifications were not put to the court at all. There is a strong argument that the meaning of a word such as 'debentures' should be contextual: it has already been interpreted in a number of different ways in different contexts, and is clearly used in the regulatory statutes to mean an instrument akin to a security.[28] There is some statutory recognition of this in the exemption of acceptance of 'an instrument creating or acknowledging indebtedness in respect of any loan' from the definition of 'regulated activity'.[29] The FCA, in reply to letters from the Loan Market Association, has confirmed that the *Fons* decision does not, in its view, change the regulatory perimeters.[30] Of course, such a view is only indicative and is not, ultimately, binding on the courts, but there are complex policy reasons behind the difference in treatment of loans and securities,[31] and it would be very unsatisfactory were a change to this balance to be effected by a case in which the regulatory position was not even discussed.

13.1.2 Methods of Regulation

There are a number of ways in which those providing finance can be protected against credit risk through regulation. One is by requiring authorisation by the FCA for those involved in the transaction and by requiring authorised persons to comply with the detailed principles set out in the FCA Handbook.[32] Thus, for example, those lending to banks by depositing money are protected by requiring banks to be authorised before they can accept deposits, which is a regulated activity.[33] This technique is rarely used in the context of corporate finance. The very limited extent to which a corporate borrower might be required to be authorised as accepting deposits is discussed below.[34] However, as with equity securities,[35] those who act as intermediaries in relation to issues of debt securities carry on regulated activities, for example by advising on investments,[36] arranging deals in investments[37]

---

[28] H Tijo, 'The Unchanging Debenture' (2014) 73 *Cambridge Law Journal* 503.

[29] FSMA (Regulated Activities Order) 2001 (SI 2001/544) ('Regulated Activities Order'), art 17. See J Roberts, 'Loans as Debentures' [2014] *Journal of International Banking and Financial Law* 431, who opines that it is unfortunate that this point was not taken in the *Fons* case.

[30] See www.citysolicitors.org.uk/attachments/article/121/20140820%20Letter%20from%20FCA%20regarding %20implications%20of%20decision%20in%20matter%20of%20Fons%20HF%20(in%20liquidation)%20v%20 Corporal%20Limited%20and%20Pillar%20Securitisation%20S%20a%20r%20l.pdf.

[31] See E de Fontenay, 'Do Securities Laws Matter? The Rise of the Leveraged Loan Market' http://papers.ssrn. com/sol3/papers.cfm?abstract_id=2419668. The arguments relating to financial promotion and disclosure generally are discussed later in this chapter.

[32] The authorisation regime administered by the FCA is complex, as is the relevant legislation. For good and concise accounts, see Benjamin: Financial Law 10.2 and I MacNeil, *An Introduction to the Law on Financial Investment*, 2nd edn (Oxford, Hart Publishing, 2012).

[33] FSMA, s 19; Regulated Activities Order, art 5. There is further protection for small-scale investors and consumers under the Financial Services Compensation Scheme, mentioned earlier.

[34] 13.5.

[35] See 11.5.

[36] Regulated Activities Order, art 53.

[37] Ibid, art 25. But note that the issue by a company of its own securities is not included: arts 18 and 34.

or managing investments,[38] and usually are required to be authorised.[39] This provides some limited protection for the buyers of those securities, in that it gives reassurance that these intermediaries will act in a proper manner, but it does not in itself moderate the credit risk of lending. Further, merely authorising persons to act does not of itself mean that they are competent, honest or reliable. What it does do is give the FCA power to call for information or to intervene in those persons' affairs, and also (in theory at least) certifies that such persons are 'fit and proper' and have adequate resources to carry on the regulated activity in question.[40]

Allied to authorisation is the concept of affiliation (discussed in 10.4.3.2) in relation to equity securities. In the context of debt finance, this involves limiting which companies can borrow in particular ways. Thus private companies cannot offer debt securities to the public[41] and there are further restrictions on which companies can list on the public markets.[42] The details of this regulation are discussed below.[43] Further, as with equity securities, there is, at least, a theoretical vetting by the FCA of companies that list debt securities on a public market.[44]

A further means of regulation is to regulate particular types of transactions, in order to reduce the risks involved in those transactions, usually by supplementing or varying the general law. An important example of this technique is the regime relating to financial collateral, discussed in chapter seven.[45] Another example is the regulation of covered bonds. These are bonds which, although payable by the issuer, are backed by a pool of assets belonging to the issuer which is ringfenced, so that if the issuer became insolvent, the payments on the bonds would continue to be made from those assets in priority to other creditors.[46] A further example is the regulation of the credit derivative market.[47]

13.1.3 Regulation by Disclosure Requirements

The main means of regulation of debt, however, is by requiring disclosure. Mandatory disclosure of information enables those advancing finance to adjust more effectively, without incurring the costs of making their own detailed enquiries. Further, if disclosure is mandatory it will be uniform in relation to all the transactions for which it is required, so that a potential lender can make a meaningful comparison of the risks of different transactions.[48] One example of mandatory disclosure, the registration of security interests, has already

---

[38] Regulated Activities Order, art 37.

[39] Benjamin: *Financial Law*, 10.28.

[40] See, for example, Part XI FSMA for the investigatory powers of the FCA, s 55J FSMA for the power of the FCA to revoke authorisation, and Sch 6 FSMA for the 'threshold conditions' for authorisation.

[41] Companies Act 2006, s 755, discussed below.

[42] See 10.4.3.2.

[43] See 13.2.2.1.

[44] See 10.4.3.1 for a discussion of this, which is a rather limited example of trusteeship.

[45] See 7.3.4.

[46] These are regulated by art 22(6) of EC Directive 85/611 on undertakings for collective investment in transferable securities, enacted in the UK as Regulated Covered Bonds Regulations (SI 2008/346) as amended by SI 2008/1714, SI 2011/2859 and SI 2012/2977.

[47] See 6.4.3.4.

[48] The benefits and drawbacks of mandatory disclosure are discussed in more detail at 10.4.3.3.

been discussed.[49] This requirement of disclosure enables lenders to adjust in the light of security interests granted by the borrower, for example by refusing to lend at all, or by adjusting the price of the loan, or by taking security over unencumbered assets, or by entering into a priority agreement with the prior secured creditor.

Registration of security interests is almost always effected by the secured creditor. In this chapter, though, we will consider disclosure by the borrowing company itself. This is important at two stages. The first is when the financier is considering whether to advance funds. The disclosed information will enable this decision to be made, and will also (if this is possible) enable the terms on which the advance is made to be adjusted. Disclosure at this stage is equivalent to disclosure at the IPO stage in relation to shares.[50] The second stage is once the advance has been made, when ongoing disclosure will inform any decision whether to advance further funds, and what steps, if any, need to be taken for protection from credit risk: whether to transfer the debt to another, whether to activate a contractual right to accelerate or to take other enforcement measures, or whether to be involved in some other way in the governance of the company.[51] This is similar to ongoing disclosure in relation to shares.[52]

As mentioned earlier, the disclosure regime only applies to (transferable) debt securities and not to loans. Instead, most lenders will, and are expected to, protect themselves by undertaking 'due diligence' enquiries and investigations into the financial state of the borrower, by relying on information from rating agencies,[53] and often by including provisions in the financing agreement. These provisions (representations and warranties) will be structured as conditions precedent, non-fulfilment of which will entitle the lender not to lend. Once the loan has been advanced, breach of the representations and warranties will be an event of default, entitling the lender to accelerate the debt or to sue for damages. Further, after the loan has been made, lenders usually require continuing disclosure by including provisions in the agreement. All these provisions are discussed above in chapter six.[54]

Where the financing takes the form of an issue of debt securities, however, disclosure is required by regulation in some circumstances. One reason for this is that where debt securities are offered to the public, or are intended to be traded among investors in an active secondary market, it is largely the issuer that sets their terms and conditions. This is in contrast to those making loans, who either impose terms and conditions or negotiate them, depending on the relative bargaining power of the parties.[55] Because the issuer of securities wants the offer to succeed, the terms and conditions of those securities will to a great extent be determined by market norms and the forces of supply and demand. As discussed in 8.3.1, the issuer will often engage and pay an investment bank to advise it in this regard, and perhaps also to underwrite the offer. Whilst there may be scope for negotiation between the issuer and the underwriters regarding the terms and conditions of the debt securities, the ultimate investor faces a 'take it or leave it' proposition, both when the securities are initially

---

[49] 7.4.
[50] Discussed in chapter 10.
[51] See the discussion of the corporate governance role of creditors in 3.2.2.4.
[52] Discussed in chapter 11.
[53] See 6.3.2.1.
[54] 6.3.2.2.
[55] See 6.3 for a discussion of the possible contractual rights a lender may have against a borrower.

issued and when they are traded afterwards in the secondary market.[56] In this regard, an offer of debt securities is not all that different from an offer of shares, and it gives rise to analogous investor protection issues. It should be pointed out, however, that, if the issuer is properly advised, the terms and conditions will reflect what the market will bear for that particular issue. To this extent, the investment bank advising the issuer will represent the interests of the investors by negotiating terms and conditions which will make the issue succeed in the market. Where there is significant credit risk, more contractual protection is likely to be included to make the debt securities more attractive to buyers.[57]

There is, however, a basic difference between debt and equity: the holder of a debt security has a different set of rights and remedies from those of a shareholder. This issue is discussed extensively in chapter three. A debt security typically gives its holder an absolute right to payment of interest and repayment of capital when due in accordance with the terms and conditions of the security, whereas a shareholder can only hope for payment of a dividend, or that there will be surplus assets available for distribution to him in a winding up after all the creditors have been paid off. Creditors will generally have powerful mechanisms to enforce payment of these sums.[58] By contrast, a shareholder's rights are much more limited, although to compensate for the residual nature of the shareholder's economic 'entitlements', shareholders are given various governance rights which are exercisable at least until the company is insolvent.[59]

While the regulation of the debt market does give the holders of securities some additional remedies for misleading statements and non-disclosure against the issuer and other parties,[60] in other respects it does not significantly alter the balance of contractual entitlements that holders of securities have against the issuer. By contrast, regulatory requirements that apply to the equity markets give shareholders, in some circumstances, additional substantive governance rights over and beyond their rights under generally applicable law, such as the right, acting by majority, to veto certain transactions with related parties and substantial acquisitions or disposals.[61] In general, debt market regulation reflects the different balance of entitlements discussed in the previous paragraph. For example, the initial disclosure requirements, where debt securities are offered to the public or admitted to trading (whether on a regulated or merely on an 'exchange-regulated' market),[62] are less onerous than those for shares. There are a number of probable reasons for this. One is that equity is inherently more risky in nature than debt, since the shareholder only has a hope of gain rather than a right to repayment, and ranks behind all creditors if the company becomes insolvent.[63]

Another reason, which does not stem from the inherent nature of debt securities, but simply from the way that the market has developed historically (at least in the UK), is that

---

[56] See 3.2.2.3 for a discussion of other reasons why there may be less contractual protection for bondholders than for those making loans.

[57] For a discussion of the process of issue of debt securities, see 8.3.1.

[58] These mechanisms are discussed in chapters 6 and 7. The position of non-adjusting creditors is discussed at 3.2.2.1.

[59] For discussion see chapter 3, in particular 3.2.1.3.3.

[60] See FSMA 2000, ss 90 and 90A, discussed at 13.2.7.1, 13.2.7.2 and 13.3.2.

[61] See 11.4.1.1.

[62] 13.2.2.2.

[63] 3.3.1.2.5.

corporate debt securities (as opposed to shares or government debt securities) are usually bought and traded by sophisticated investors:[64] this means that there can be a hierarchy of protection depending on the perceived ability of investors in particular issues to protect themselves.[65] This will be discussed later.

A third reason why the disclosure requirements for debt securities are less onerous than those for shares is that it is possible for debt securities to contain contractual protection for the holders. This will vary according to the type of security, but in situations where the credit risk is high, there can be considerable contractual protection for bondholders.[66]

Debt securities, like shares, are subject to regulatory rules relating to initial issues, and to ongoing disclosure. These will be considered separately below. It will be seen that much of the detail of the regulatory structure and requirements is the same as for shares. A great deal of what is said in chapters ten, eleven and twelve will therefore apply here, and there is therefore extensive cross-referencing. The discussion below seeks to point out the differences and similarities between the regimes for equity and debt securities, some of the reasons for which are outlined above, and also to consider the differences between the regulatory regime for debt securities and the position in relation to loans. It focuses on the regulatory regime in the UK, although much of this derives from the implementation of EU legislation. It should be noted, though, that in the context of the debt markets, UK law has been considerably shaped by the desire to attract foreign companies to list debt securities on the UK markets.

13.2 Regulation of Initial Issue of Debt Securities

13.2.1 Introduction

Regulation of initial issues of debt securities by mandatory disclosure is effected by a structure that is basically the same as that for shares, and the reader is referred to the discussion in chapter ten for a full description.[67] The general rule is that it is unlawful to offer transferrable securities to the public, or to request their admission to trading on a regulated market, unless an approved prospectus[68] has been made available to the public before the

---

[64] See 2.3.3.2 for discussion of who invests in debt securities.

[65] Indeed, that there is a sensible hierarchy of disclosure requirements is recognised by art 21(2) of the Prospectus Directive Regulation (Commission Regulation (EC) No 809/2004) ('PD Reg'), which essentially provides such a hierarchy, so that the disclosure requirements that apply to shares will also apply to debt securities, but not vice versa. The hierarchy is (1) shares (2) retail debt securities and (3) wholesale debt securities. For definitions of these terms, see 13.2.2.3.

[66] See 3.2.2.3.

[67] 10.5.1 and 10.5.2. The detailed requirements for debt securities are set out in arts 7, 8, 12 and 16 of the PD Reg (reproduced in PR 2.3) and Annexes IV, V, IX and XIII of the PD Reg (reproduced in PR 2.3.1).

[68] That is, a prospectus meeting the requirements of the Prospectus Directive (Directive 2003/71/EC) and the PD Reg. The Prospectus Directive amended by Directive 2010/73/EU ('the Amending Directive') is implemented in the UK by the Prospectus Regulations 2011 (SI 2011/1668) and the Prospectus Regulations 2012 (SI 2012/1538). The only significant amendment in relation to debt securities is the denomination threshold for wholesale securities: see 13.2.2.3 below. The requirements are set out in the Prospectus Rules in the FCA Handbook.

offer or request is made.[69] If a prospectus is not required, disclosure pursuant to the Listing Rules stipulated by the UK Listing Authority ('the Listing Rules') may nevertheless be required.[70] These two criteria—'offering to the public' and 'admitted to trading on a regulated market'—are discrete, and each has its own exceptions and qualifications. It is the ability of an issuer to take advantage of these exceptions and qualifications that is discussed in the paragraphs below.

13.2.2 Factors Affecting the Disclosure Requirements

Where disclosure is required in relation to an initial issue of debt securities, there may be considerable differences in the actual requirements, depending on a number of factors. Most of these factors are in the control of the issuer, who has to make various choices. The first choice is to whom the securities are to be offered, the second is whether the securities are to be traded on a market, and, if so, which one, and the third is the size of the denomination of the securities. The most onerous requirements apply where the securities are intended to be offered to, or traded among, retail investors,[71] either as part of the initial offer or following admission to trading on a regulated market. The issuer can therefore choose to limit the issue to sophisticated investors, and/or list the securities on an exchange-regulated market, and thereby avoid the more onerous disclosure requirements (although some disclosure still has to be made). Unlike offers of shares, where the issuer usually wishes to access the widest possible number of investors, and so little use is made of the exceptions to the rules,[72] many issuers of debt securities make a 'public offer' only to qualified investors and list the securities on the Professional Securities Market,[73] so as to attract the less onerous regime.

Of course, where the issuer is a UK public company whose shares are admitted to the Main Market, it will have had to produce a prospectus when making the IPO[74] and it will have to comply with ongoing disclosure requirements anyway.[75] Thus it might be thought that, for these companies, even the most onerous debt regulation regime does not add to their burden, and so there would be no point in trying to fall within the less onerous regime. However, it must be borne in mind that putting together a prospectus, even if some or all of the information is already public, can be costly and time-consuming. Bond issues are often put together very quickly, and so there may be advantages in not having to produce a prospectus.[76] There is one factor, though, which might lead a company (especially one who is a repeat issuer) to choose to publish a prospectus. This is that a prospectus approved by the relevant competent authority in one EEA Member State can be 'passported' to another

---

[69] FSMA 2000, s 85(2). See 10.5.2.1 for discussion of this requirement in the context of equity securities.
[70] For a summary of when each requirement applies, see 13.2.2.4.
[71] Whether this is the case is determined by a combination of whether the securities are 'offered to the public' (see 13.2.2.1) and whether the securities are 'retail securities' (see 13.2.2.3 below). The actual characteristics of those buying the securities are not in themselves determinative.
[72] Examples of exceptions relating to shares are discussed at 10.5.2.1.
[73] Discussed at 13.2.2.2.
[74] The disclosure requirements for such a prospectus are discussed at 10.5.2 above.
[75] See chapter 11.
[76] Wood: Loans and Bonds, 10-047.

EEA Member State, enabling the issuer to list the securities on a regulated market or make a public offer there without having to produce another prospectus or listing document, perhaps in a different language and complying with different local rules.[77]

13.2.2.1 To whom the Securities are Offered

It will be recalled that a company can issue shares which are not offered to the public. A private company cannot issue shares to the public, and so can only offer them to specified persons, who may well be, and usually are, connected to the company in some way. However, as is discussed in chapter ten, it is often advantageous for a company to offer shares to the public.[78] The same distinction applies to issues of debt securities. A private company cannot offer debt securities to the public.[79] Since one of the purposes of a bond issue by a public company is to reach a wider base of lenders[80] than can be achieved through a loan structure, it might be thought that most such issues would be to the public. To some extent, this is true, in that totally 'private' issues, made only to those connected to public companies, are rare.[81] However, debt securities, particularly eurobonds, are often offered only to a specific group of sophisticated investors by means of a placing, as is stock;[82] in which case there is no offer to the public. It should also be remembered that debt securities are typically purchased by institutional or other financial institutions rather than by individuals or other retail investors.[83] If this is the case, even if there is technically an offer to the public within the meaning of the definition discussed in the next paragraph, the need for onerous disclosure is less apparent, and thus, where the investors are sophisticated, there are various exceptions to the application of the disclosure requirements.

For the purposes of the mandatory disclosure requirements, an offer of transferable securities to the public is defined in section 102B of FSMA 2000 as a communication to any person which presents sufficient information on the securities and the terms on which they are offered to enable an investor to decide to buy or subscribe for the securities. This definition is extremely wide, but there are certain exceptions which narrow down its application considerably. The requirements of the Prospectus Rules do not apply to offers that fall within an exception[84] (unless the securities are also admitted to trading on a regulated market,[85] in which case the Prospectus Rules do apply). Thus the issuer can avoid the application of the Prospectus Rules if the offer is made to 'qualified investors' only,[86] or to fewer than 150 persons per EEA State.[87] The other relevant exceptions relate to the size of the offer and the denomination of the securities and are discussed below.[88]

---

[77] Prospectus Directive, art 17.

[78] See 10.2.

[79] See below.

[80] For the advantages of a bond issue as against a loan, see 2.3.3.2.

[81] Loan notes, however, are often issued to shareholders of private companies, particularly in private equity transactions. See 16.4.2.

[82] See 8.3.1.

[83] This, though, is changing: see 2.3.3.2.

[84] FSMA, s 86(1).

[85] Ie the GEFIM: see 13.2.2.2.

[86] FSMA, s 86(1)(a).

[87] Ibid, s 86(1)(b). See 10.5.2.1 for further discussion.

[88] See 13.2.2.3.

It should also be noted that the requirement to produce a prospectus may be triggered not only where securities are offered to the public by the issuer or someone on its behalf, but also by a third party to whom the securities have already been allotted (eg an underwriter).[89] Indeed, the means by which debt securities usually find their way into the hands of retail investors is via the so-called 'retail cascade', which is a process by which the debt securities are initially issued to the underwriters, who in turn sell them on to other distributors, who ultimately sell them to retail investors. While the issuer may not be obliged to prepare a prospectus if one of the exceptions applies, the secondary offeror will be obliged to do so, unless a valid prospectus is already available[90] and the person responsible for that prospectus 'consents to its use as explicitly stated in the prospectus'.[91]

The criterion of whether an offer is 'an offer to the public' is also used to trigger a separate form of regulation which is not based on disclosure. Section 755 of the Companies Act 2006 prohibits public offers of securities (both debt and equity) by private companies. The term 'offer to the public' is defined in section 756 and includes all offers of securities made to any section of the public except where the offer is made only to persons receiving the offer,[92] and/or only to persons connected with the company.[93] In relation to debt securities, it can be seen that the prohibition in section 755 protects potential investors by requiring a particular level of corporate governance and administration, and a minimal level of legal capital,[94] from a company offering such securities.[95]

13.2.2.2 *Trading on a Market*

Whether or not debt securities have been offered to the public, the issuer may well wish them to be traded on a secondary market operated by the London Stock Exchange (LSE), which will involve listing.[96] The benefits of listing are discussed in chapter eight,[97] where it is pointed out that even listed bonds are usually traded over the counter, but that the listing is important since many institutional investors are not permitted to invest in non-listed securities.[98] The main reason for this is the protection provided by the regulatory requirements of listing, which are discussed below.

---

[89] See 8.3.1.

[90] The prospectus must either be approved by the FCA or be a 'base prospectus' (see 13.2.3) and the securities must not have ceased to be issued in a continuous or repeated manner.

[91] FSMA, s 86(1A). This was added by Prospectus Regulations 2012 (SI 2012/1538), reg 2(2) and amended by Prospectus Regulations 2013 (SI 2013/1125): these Regulations implement Prospective Directive, art 3(2) as amended by the Amending Directive, art 1(3)(a)(ii).

[92] Companies Act 2006, s 756(3). In theory this exception would include a situation where an offer was made personally to thousands of people, but it seems that it is intended only to apply where the offer is made personally to a small group of people.

[93] Ibid, s 756(4). This includes shareholders and employees of the company and their immediate relatives or trustees, and existing debenture holders of the company (s 756(5)).

[94] See 10.2.2.

[95] There is further discussion of the difference between private and public companies at 10.4.2.

[96] This means that they will have to be admitted to the Official List of the UKLA, discussed at 10.3.3.1. As pointed out at 10.3.3.2, issuers can list on any market anywhere in the world if they wish. This chapter will only consider listing on the two LSE markets.

[97] See 8.3.1.

[98] A further important reason is that listed eurobonds are exempt from the requirement to withhold tax on interest at source: see Inland Revenue CTM35218.

The issuer, then, must choose whether the debt securities should be admitted to trading on a 'regulated market', admitted to trading only on an 'exchange-regulated market' or multilateral trading facility (MTF),[99] or not admitted to trading on any market at all. In the UK, the LSE's regulated market for debt securities is known as the Gilt-Edged and Fixed Interest Market (GEFIM),[100] and its MTF for debt securities is the Professional Securities Market (PSM). Both the GEFIM and the PSM are accessible to issuers incorporated in the UK or anywhere else in the world. Where debt securities are admitted to trading on the GEFIM a prospectus is required; there is no such requirement for securities admitted to trading on the PSM (unless the securities are 'offered to the public' as discussed above). However, 'listing particulars' will be required where the securities are to be admitted to trading on the PSM.

The choice of market, however, is not completely free. To list on either market, the securities must be admitted to the Official List of the UKLA. The process and requirements are very similar to those for equity securities, which are discussed in chapter ten.[101] One difference in the requirements is that debt securities may only be admitted if their aggregate expected value on admission will be at least £200,000,[102] while the equivalent amount for shares is £700,000.[103] All listings of debt securities will be standard listings.[104] This means, among other things, that the issuer is not required to appoint a sponsor, which it would be required to do in many circumstances in relation to a premium listing of its shares.

13.2.2.3 *Denomination of Securities*

As discussed above, sophisticated investors require less protection from disclosure requirements than retail investors. In the Prospectus Directive the size of the denomination of the securities is used as a rather crude proxy for the sophistication of the investors, on the basis that only sophisticated investors buy and trade large denomination securities. The critical difference is between securities with a denomination of at least €100,000 (so-called 'wholesale' debt securities) and those with a lower denomination (so-called 'retail' debt securities). Where the securities are admitted to trading on the GEFIM and/or where there is an offer to the public so that the Prospectus Rules apply, a different, and less onerous, disclosure regime applies to wholesale debt securities ('the wholesale regime') to that applying to retail debt securities ('the retail regime'). Denomination is also relevant to whether the securities are 'offered to the public' within the definition in section 102B of FSMA 2000.[105] Securities are not 'offered to the public' if they are wholesale securities[106] or if the total consideration for the securities offered in the European Union does not exceed €100,000.[107]

---

[99] See 12.2.2.

[100] This is also often called the 'Main Market', but since this term is used in chapters 10 and 11 to refer to the main equity securities market, it will not be used here.

[101] See 10.4.3 and 10.5.

[102] FCA Handbook, LR 2.2.7(1)(b).

[103] Ibid, LR 2.2.7(1)(a).

[104] Ibid, LR 1.5.1. See the discussion at 10.3.3.1 on premium and standard listings.

[105] See 13.2.2.1.

[106] FSMA 2000, s 86(1)(d).

[107] Ibid, s 86(1)(e) as amended by Prospectus Regulations 2012 (SI 2012/1538), implementing Directive 2010/73/EU.

13.2.2.4 Rationale of the Disclosure Regime

To summarise, if debt securities are admitted to trading on the GEFIM, a prospectus is required, whether they are offered to the public or not.[108] The actual content of the requirements for a prospectus will vary depending on whether the wholesale or retail regime applies. If securities are admitted to trading on the PSM, a prospectus will be required only if the securities are offered to the public *and* one of the exceptions to the 'public offer' requirement for a prospectus[109] does not apply. This, though theoretically possible, is unlikely to happen since an issuer seeking to list its securities on the PSM will wish to make sure that the issue does fall within one of those exceptions. If a prospectus is not required, the issuer need only publish 'listing particulars' pursuant to the Listing Rules. If the securities are not listed, then a prospectus will only be required if they are offered to the public and none of the exceptions apply. Otherwise, the only possible regulatory regime relating to an initial offering is that applying to financial promotion.[110] However, the secondary trading of unlisted securities on an organised trading facility (OTF)[111] will be subject to transparency requirements[112] when MIFIR and MiFID II come into effect in 2017, and the market abuse regime will apply to such securities when the Market Abuse Regulation comes into effect in 2016.[113] The regulation of the secondary market in debt securities has been greatly extended by these EU instruments, although there is still scope for some unregulated over-the-counter (OTC) trading.[114]

It would be very unlikely for debt securities to be 'offered to the public' but unlisted, since if it is sought to access a wide market on issue, it is likely that the issuer will wish to continue to access the widest possible number of potential investors in the secondary market.[115] Further, many institutional investors would not be able to buy unlisted securities: thus, issues would normally be listed unless issued to a small group of specific investors who are planning to hold the securities to maturity and are unlikely to want to trade them in the secondary market.

It will be seen, therefore, that the most onerous disclosure requirements, and therefore the most protection for lenders, comes where retail debt securities are offered to the public (and when none of the exceptions to the requirement for prior publication of a prospectus apply) and/or are traded on the GEFIM. The rationale for this seems similar to that for mandatory disclosure in relation to equity securities, namely that ordinary investors need information in order to decide whether to purchase the securities, and that mandatory disclosure is the most cost-effective method of achieving this.[116]

However, where investors are 'sophisticated' (either because they are 'qualified investors' or because the denomination of the securities is high) the disclosure requirements are less

---

[108]   FSMA 2000, s 85(5)(a) provides some limited exceptions to this, listed in FSMA 2000, Sch 11A, for example where the total consideration of the offer is less than €5 million (Sch 11A para 9). The same is true for equity securities: see 10.5.2.1.

[109]   Discussed above at 13.2.2.1 and set out in FSMA, s 86(1).

[110]   Discussed at 13.2.6.

[111]   See 12.2.2.3.

[112]   See 13.3.1.

[113]   See 13.4.1.

[114]   See Moloney: EU Regulation, 468.

[115]   For further advantages of listing, see 8.3.1.

[116]   See the argument at 10.4.3.3.

onerous. There seem to be various reasons for this. First, sophisticated investors are able to make their own enquiries, if they wish, and therefore it is less cost-effective to require extensive mandatory disclosure. Second, sophisticated investors are repeat players, and know better than retail investors what information is required. Third, sophisticated investors are generally investing large amounts of money, so that it is more cost-effective to make their own enquiries. Fourth, large investors can, if there is doubt about the creditworthiness of the issuer (which will appear from the issuer's rating),[117] put pressure on those drawing up the terms of the securities to include more contractual protection, at least indirectly, through indicating what the market will bear. It should be remembered that institutional investors are often pension funds, investment trusts or other asset managers who are investing on behalf of retail investors. Therefore those making the investment decisions are under stringent duties to scrutinise how they invest the institutions' funds.

Given that less protection is needed for such investors, there is a strong argument for reducing the amount of disclosure required, since disclosure is expensive and time-consuming.[118] Bond issues are often put together very quickly, and extensive disclosure requirements where they are not needed would have a very detrimental effect on the market.[119] Thus, the level of regulation should take into account the needs of issuers as well as the protection of the investors. In the end, at least where sophisticated investors are concerned, the optimal extent of regulation is a matter of balance: on whom should the burden of discovering information lie? It may be thought that, in relation to sophisticated investors in debt securities, this is an open question: that is, it does not really matter what the answer is, since the market will find its own equilibrium. However, there is one additional compelling point, made in chapter ten,[120] which probably tips the balance towards at least some mandatory disclosure: the benefits of standardisation. This is beneficial for investors, since they are in a better position to compare different possible investments. It is also beneficial for both issuers and investors, in that they know that they are on a 'level playing field' with others. Further, it reduces transaction costs, which makes the markets more efficient and increases transparency, which increases investor confidence.

It should also be borne in mind that there are regulatory ways to protect investors other than via mandatory disclosure per se. The first is to focus on rating agencies. When obtaining a rating for an issue of debt securities,[121] the issuer is likely to disclose more to the rating agency than it is compelled to disclose under the mandatory disclosure rules. This information, then, is distilled for the market through the intermediation of the rating agency. It will only be of benefit to the market, of course, if the rating agency gets the rating 'right'.[122] The role played here by the rating agencies raises the question as to whether and how such agencies should be regulated: this is discussed below.[123] Another method is to focus on

---

[117] See 2.3.3.3 and 13.7.

[118] The cost of compliance is felt particularly by companies with small market capitalisations, which may deter them from going to capital markets just at the point in their development at which they need access to wider pools of capital. Concern about these costs led to the amendments to the Transparency Directive (Directive 2004/109/EC) effected by Directive 2013/50/EU, which were designed to reduce the burden of reporting on small and medium-size institutions.

[119] Wood: Loans and Bonds, 10-047.

[120] See 10.4.3.3.

[121] This refers to a solicited rating, which is paid for by the issuer: see 2.3.3.3.

[122] Often an institutional investor will be required to invest in securities of a certain rating: see 13.7.

[123] 13.7.

the financial intermediaries relied upon by retail investors to advise them in their investments. Mandatorily disclosed information is then used by those intermediaries in giving their advice, who are thus a means of disseminating the information to the actual investors. It follows that these intermediaries, too, need to be regulated, which is done by requiring them to be authorised by the FCA.[124]

13.2.3 Information Required in a Prospectus[125]

The form of the required prospectus varies according to whether the securities are issued as part of a programme, or as a 'stand-alone' issue. As explained in 8.3.1, plain 'vanilla' issues of securities are usually issued under a programme, where much of the documentation is drafted in advance of the issue, and then specific updated documentation added for each issue. The Prospectus Rules facilitate this by permitting an issuer of debt securities under a programme to use a 'base prospectus', supplemented, if necessary, by a 'final terms' document.[126] Where there is a 'stand-alone' issue (which tends to be the position where more negotiation of terms is required, for example for high-yield bonds), all the information must be contained either in a composite prospectus or in a prospectus consisting of separate documents and divided into a registration document, a securities note and a summary.[127]

It will be recalled that, in order to provide useful disclosure to investors in shares, the information in a prospectus must be presented in a comprehensible form which is easy to analyse, and that, to further this aim, a summary must be provided.[128] There is a similar requirement in relation to retail debt securities, but not for wholesale debt securities provided the prospectus is published in connection with an admission to trading (as opposed to a public offer).[129] This is obviously consistent with the policy discussed earlier, in that sophisticated investors are more able to process complicated information, since they have expert analysts at their disposal. With the growth in popularity of retail bonds,[130] the usefulness of prospectuses to retail investors has become an important issue, and the FCA has issued guidance on how retail prospectuses should be drafted so as to comply with the requirement that all prospectuses be 'easily analyzable and comprehensible'.[131] The new guidance suggests using language which can be easily understood and which is jargon-free except where necessary to be accurate, sign-posting so that a potential investor can navigate through the document to find the information relevant to his particular requirements, clear calculations of the return on the securities, and clear explanations of the bondholder protections as well as features which impact on the retail investor's risks, such as subordination.[132]

---

[124] 11.5.

[125] It will be recalled that in this chapter 'prospectus' refers to a prospectus meeting the requirements of the Prospectus Directive and the Prospectus Regulation (see n 68 above).

[126] PR 2.2.7 and 2.2.8 respectively. A similar structure is permitted where the securities are issued in a 'continuous or repeated manner' by a credit institution.

[127] PR 2.2.2.

[128] See 10.5.2.2 in relation to shares.

[129] PR 2.1.3; Prospectus Directive, art 5(2).

[130] See 2.3.3.2.

[131] Prospectus Directive, art 5(1).

[132] UKLA technical note, 'Non-Equity Prospectuses Aimed at Retail Investors', UKLA/TN/632.1, issued November 2014.

In terms of the actual content of mandatory disclosure, there are, broadly, three levels required in a prospectus. The highest level is for an issue of shares, the next highest is for retail debt securities, and the least onerous is for wholesale debt securities. The reasons for this have already been explored: a few examples will now be given to illustrate the differences. Despite the differences, there is a considerable degree of overlap between all three regimes, so that, for example, all three share the overriding purpose that the prospectus must contain all information necessary to enable investors to make an informed assessment of assets and liabilities, financial position, profit and losses, the prospects of the issuer and any guarantor, and the rights attached to the securities.[133] The differences between the retail and wholesale debt regimes are largely in the amount of detail which must be disclosed in order to comply with this overriding purpose.[134]

One example relates to the disclosure of audited financial information. In the case of shares[135] and retail debt securities,[136] this information must be presented in accordance with International Financial Reporting Standards (IFRS) or an equivalent standard,[137] while for issues of wholesale debt securities, the accounts can be presented in accordance with the issuer's national accounting standards, provided that the prospectus includes a prominent statement that this is the case and a description of the key differences between the accounting standards used and IFRS.[138] At the time the Prospectus Directive came into force, the requirement to present or restate in accordance with IFRS was onerous for non-EEA issuers. This was one of the main reasons behind the retention of the PSM as an MTF, to which the Prospectus Rules do not directly apply.[139] It may be expected that as accounting standards around the world converge, the significance of this point diminishes. The information must cover the past three years in the case of a share issue, but only the last two years in the case of a debt issue.[140]

There are considerable areas of disclosure which are required under the retail regime but not at all under the wholesale regime. These include disclosure of selected historical financial information, including key figures that summarise the financial condition of the issuer,[141] information on trends, uncertainties, demands, commitments or events reasonably likely to have a material effect on the issuer's prospects for at least the current financial year,[142] and information about the issuer's board practices.[143] Interestingly, the retail regime also requires disclosure of principal recent and future investments made and to be made by the issuer, and information regarding the anticipated sources of funds needed to fulfil investment commitments.[144] Since investments may generally be funded either from

---

[133] FSMA 2000, s 87A(2) implementing Prospectus Directive, art 5(1). For shares, see 10.5.2.2.

[134] A different type of disclosure is required for asset-backed securities: this relates more to the assets themselves than to information about the issuer (see PD Reg Annexes VII and VIII).

[135] PD Reg Annex I, para 20.1. The annexes to the PD Reg are reproduced in the FCA Handbook, Prospectus Rules (PR), which includes any amendments to the PD Reg. Annex 1 relates to shares, and the other annexes to other types of securities.

[136] PD Reg Annex IV, para 13.1.

[137] The disclosure of accounts is discussed at 10.5.2.2.

[138] PD Reg Annex IX, para 11.1.

[139] Unless there is an offer to the public (and none of the exceptions apply), which is very unlikely: see 13.2.2.4.

[140] PD Reg Annex I, para 20.1 (shares); Annex IV, para 13.1 (retail debt); Annex IX, para 11.1 (wholesale debt).

[141] Ibid, Annex IV, para 3.1.

[142] Ibid, Annex IV, para 8.2.

[143] Ibid, Annex IV, para 11.

[144] Ibid, Annex IV, para 5.2.

internal cash flows or by issuing new debt or equity securities, the holders of debt securities will be interested to know whether their claims may be diluted by the company incurring further debt ranking equally with, or ahead of, their own claims.[145] As discussed earlier, the danger of claim dilution can also be addressed through covenants.[146] Although extensive covenants are unlikely to be included in most debt securities, a negative pledge covenant preventing the issue of secured bonds into the same market is very common.[147]

An example of where the regime differs between issues of shares and debt securities is in relation to the disclosure of risk. Where the prospectus relates to an issuer or offer of shares, the issuer must disclose risks which are specific to the issuer or its industry,[148] whereas in the case of both wholesale and retail debt securities, the issuer need only disclose risk factors that may affect the issuer's ability to fulfil its obligations under the securities.[149] This follows logically from the fact that debt is less risky than equity, in the sense that payment of interest is usually an obligation, whereas an investor can only hope for payment of a dividend. Further, holders of debt securities have more effective means than shareholders of enforcing the repayment obligation owed to them if the company gets into difficulties. Other types of disclosure which are required for shares,[150] but not for debt securities, include more extensive information about the issuer's business,[151] information about its property, plant and equipment,[152] its capital resources,[153] its senior management's remuneration and benefits,[154] and its employees.[155]

13.2.4 Disclosure Required for Listing on the PSM

If debt securities are listed on the PSM but are not offered to the public (or fall within one of the 'public offer' exceptions), then a prospectus is not required. Instead, the issuer is required to publish approved 'listing particulars'.[156] The general purpose of disclosure under this regime is the same as under the Prospectus Rules, namely the disclosure of all information necessary to enable investors to make an informed assessment of assets and liabilities, financial position, profit and losses, the prospects of the issuer and any guarantor, and rights attached to the securities.[157] The actual content of the disclosure requirement is generally the same as that under the wholesale regime applicable to a prospectus. Under the

---

[145] The danger of claim dilution is discussed at 3.2.2.2.

[146] See 6.3.1.1.

[147] See 6.3.1.6.

[148] PD Reg Annex I, para 4; see 10.5.2.2.

[149] Ibid, Annex IV, para 4 (retail debt) and Annex IX, para 3.1 (wholesale debt).

[150] See 10.5.2.2.

[151] Compare PD Reg Annex 1, para 6 (shares) with Annex IV, para 6 (retail debt) and Annex IX, para 5 (wholesale debt). In the case of shares, the issuer must provide detailed information about its principal markets, with revenues broken down by category of activity and geographically for each year for the period covered by the historical financial information.

[152] PD Reg Annex I, para 8 (shares) (no equivalent for debt securities).

[153] Ibid, Annex 1, para 10 (no equivalent for debt securities).

[154] Ibid, Annex 1, para 15 (no equivalent for debt securities).

[155] Ibid, Annex 1, para 17 (no equivalent for debt securities).

[156] These are in accordance with the Listing Rules, approved by the UKLA and published as part of the FCA Handbook (s 79 FSMA). The content requirements for listing particulars are set out in LR 4.

[157] FSMA 2000, s 80(1).

Listing Rules regime, though, there is no specific distinction in the requirements between retail and wholesale securities;[158] apart from certain types of securities such as hybrids and asset-backed securities, the Listing Rules merely give guidance that 'the FCA would expect issuers to follow the most appropriate schedules and building blocks in the PD Regulation to determine the minimum information to be included in listing particulars'.

13.2.5 Disclosure Requirements where Securities are not Listed

If the debt securities are not to be admitted to trading on any market at all, then neither a prospectus nor listing particulars are required unless there is an offer to the public, in which case a prospectus will be required. Therefore, issuers and their advisers will take care to ensure that the issuer and other persons connected with the financing do not inadvertently make an offer to the public. To achieve this, any hint of a public offer will be strenuously disclaimed in the documents relating to the securities, and 'selling restrictions' will be incorporated into the terms and conditions of the debt securities, which are intended to ensure that the offer falls within one of the public offer exemptions.[159]

However, even if there is no offer to the public, it is still possible that dissemination of material used for marketing such securities will constitute financial promotion, which is discussed in the next section.

13.2.6 Restrictions on Financial Promotion

Whether an issue of debt securities is listed or not, there may be materials produced in respect of the issue which are not included in a prospectus or listing particulars. There are potentially other restrictions which apply to such materials. If the Prospectus Rules apply, any advertisements must state that a prospectus will be issued, tell the readers where to find the prospectus, and make it clear that investment decisions should be based on the prospectus and not on the advertisement.[160] Further, any invitations or inducements to participate in investment activity must be approved by a person authorised under the FCA regime (such as an investment bank) unless one of the exemptions applies.[161] In order to be approved, the material has to comply with various onerous requirements,[162] and borrowers usually take steps to ensure that any materials produced are exempt.

The kinds of investments which fall within 'investment activity' are generally debt and equity securities and not bank loans. However, the inclusion of the term 'debenture' in the definition of 'investments'[163] has caused unwelcome uncertainty, which has been increased

---

[158] LR 4.2.4.
[159] Discussed above at 13.2.2.1 and 10.5.2.1.
[160] PR 3.3.2.
[161] FSMA 2000, s 21.
[162] Set out in the FCA's Conduct of Business Sourcebook at COBS 4.
[163] Financial Promotion Order, Sch 1 art 15.

by the decision in *Fons HF (In Liquidation) v Corporal Ltd*,[164] even though, as discussed earlier,[165] this case is unlikely to have a substantial effect on the meaning of 'debenture' in the regulatory context.

It certainly makes sense for loans not to be included in the scope of the term 'debenture' in the Financial Promotion Order, as this is consistent with the policy of not protecting lenders (as opposed to holders of securities) by regulatory means, but rather expecting them to protect themselves using contractual and other means.[166] Those making loans are usually banks or other large financial institutions, which can be expected to look after themselves.[167]

The uncertainty about the meaning of 'debenture', however, makes it even more important that borrowers, particularly when soliciting lenders for a syndicated loan, ensure that any information produced, such as an information circular, falls within one of the exemptions to the financial promotion restrictions.

The exemptions are wide ranging:[168] a few relevant ones are highlighted here. Any material required to be produced by the Prospectus Rules and the Listing Rules (except advertisements) is exempt,[169] as is information on how to obtain a prospectus.[170] The justification for this is clear: such material is already regulated by the mandatory disclosure rules discussed earlier.[171] Communications which are made only to investment professionals,[172] to overseas recipients,[173] or to high worth companies or unincorporated associations[174] are also exempt.[175] Again, this is consistent with the policy of not protecting those who can take care of themselves.[176] It can be seen that it is very unlikely that the restrictions will apply to the types of finance discussed in this book. Material produced in relation to debt securities will either be limited to sophisticated investors (in which case it will be exempt) or, if distributed to the public, will be in connection with a public offer of securities, which will attract the Prospectus Rules so that required material will be exempt. Even if material produced in relation to loans is prima facie included, this is very likely to be exempt where the loan is syndicated, since those to whom the material is disseminated will be investment professionals and/or high worth companies. Borrowers who borrow from a single lender very rarely produce promotional material.[177]

---

[164] [2014] EWCA Civ 304.

[165] 13.1.1.

[166] This is discussed below at 13.2.8.

[167] See Benjamin: Financial Law, 10.59.

[168] They are contained in arts 5–74 Financial Promotion Order.

[169] Ibid, art 70.

[170] Ibid, art 71.

[171] 13.2.3 and 13.2.4.

[172] Financial Promotion Order, art 19.

[173] Ibid, art 12.

[174] Ibid, art 49.

[175] For further discussion, see Fuller: Corporate Borrowing, 13.60–13.64.

[176] Although it is not clear why this argument applies to investors who are overseas: this exception, however, is part of a raft of exemptions which relate to particular types of communication rather than particular types of recipients.

[177] The regulation of peer-to-peer lending, which may well involve unsophisticated lenders, is discussed at 13.8.

13.2.7 Enforcement of the Mandatory Disclosure Regime

13.2.7.1 Claims Against the Issuer

As with the regulation of initial offers of shares, an effective enforcement regime is important if investors are to be protected. Thus the discussion in chapter ten of the aims of enforcement[178] is largely relevant here. There are, however, some crucial differences in relation to enforcement by holders of debt securities. The first is, as mentioned above, that such holders have contractual (and sometimes proprietary) rights against the issuer in respect of the debt itself,[179] and can enforce such rights, either themselves or through a trustee.[180] Thus a holder of debt securities with a nominal value of £10,000 can sue for £10,000, provided that the obligation to pay has arisen. Holders of equity securities have no such right. All they have is a hope of a dividend or an ultimate surplus. Thus, when faced with misstatements in the prospectus, all they have are common law claims or claims under section 90 FSMA[181] giving rights to damages. Given the strength of the rights of bondholders in respect of the debt, other rights that a bondholder may have against the issuer itself (such as those arising under section 90) are less significant. However, a holder may not wish to enforce the ultimate debt. If an investor buys debt securities which are less valuable that he thought they were, because of inaccurate disclosure, his loss is not the whole value of the debt represented by the securities, but the difference in value between what he paid for them and what they are really worth. Thus it is necessary to consider other remedies that a holder may have against the issuer.

It should first be noted that, as with claims relating to equity securities, the best claim for an investor against an issuer is likely to be under section 90 FSMA, for the reasons given in chapter ten above.[182] The common law claims are not so straightforward. If the holder buys the securities directly from the issuer, there will be a contract of sale between them, and thus the holder will have a claim under section 2(1) of the Misrepresentation Act 1967.[183] If the holder actually bought from a manager or underwriter, so that the contract of sale was not with the issuer,[184] the position is less clear. Section 2(1) provides that there is a remedy 'where a person has entered into a contract after a misrepresentation has been made to him by another party thereto'. The contract here would have to be the debt contract represented by the securities: if the securities are transferred by novation,[185] then the contract to which the transferee is a party is not one with the issuer.[186] Further, in many situations the party to the contract represented by the debt securities is likely to be the legal owner of the global bond, who holds the benefit of the contract on trust for investors or intermediaries as the

---

[178] 10.6.1.

[179] The most significant contractual method is probably acceleration and termination of the payment obligation, which arises on an event of default and which is discussed in 6.3.3 above.

[180] 8.3.4.2.3.

[181] See 10.6.2.

[182] See 10.6.2.1.

[183] There is also the possibility of rescission for misrepresentation: see 10.6.2.4.2.

[184] See 8.3.1 and, for a comparison in relation to shares, 10.6.2.1.

[185] For example, if they are transferred through CREST: see 9.2.6.3.

[186] See 9.2.1.

case may be,[187] and not the ultimate investor who has suffered the loss.[188] Thus, it is not at all clear that the holder has an action under section 2(1). Nevertheless this is unlikely to matter, since the holder can sue under section 90 FSMA, which, as pointed out in 10.6.2.1, is usually the claim most likely to produce a favourable result.

Should the holder have an action under section 2(1) (for example, where there is a contract of sale between itself and the issuer), it will potentially be subject to the defence that the issuer had 'reasonable ground to believe and did believe that the facts represented were true'. This reversal of the burden of proof makes a section 2(1) claim much more attractive than a claim based on common law negligence. Furthermore, unlike under section 2(1) there is a need to establish a duty of care in negligence under *Hedley Byrne & Co Ltd v Heller & Partners Ltd*,[189] which is not always straightforward. If the issuer has been fraudulent, there is the possibility of a claim in deceit, although, if the measure of damages under section 2(1) is likely to be the same,[190] there seems little point in taking on the burden of proving fraud. There is also the possibility that the representation has been incorporated into the debt contract, but this is very unlikely. Incorporation would necessitate an intention on the part of the parties that any misstatement would be a breach of contract, potentially giving the right to accelerate and enforce the debt. Given the uncertainty that this would lead to, a court would be very slow to find such an incorporation unless it were express, and, in fact, there is more likely to be a term expressly excluding it. Additionally, the amount of damages would be potentially different from that awarded in a claim for misrepresentation, as in a contractual claim the expectation interest would be protected;[191] again, an issuer will try to avoid such liability. It would be possible to include in the contract between the issuer and the holder provisions excluding liability for all the common law claims except for fraud, but an exclusion provision would be subject to the reasonableness test under the Unfair Contract Terms Act 1977.[192]

13.2.7.2 Claims Against Other Parties

In many cases where a holder has suffered loss because of inaccurate disclosure, the issuer will be insolvent or near insolvent and so a claim against it will be useless. In this situation, a holder will wish to sue another person connected with the issue of the securities, preferably one with deep pockets. Possible contenders are the directors, professionals such as auditors or lawyers, the managers or underwriters of the issue, and the person from whom the holder bought the security (if not the issuer itself).[193] The liability of the seller of the security will be governed by ordinary contract law, and it is very unlikely that the contract of

---

[187] See the discussion in 8.3.2.3.2(b).

[188] cf *Taberna Europe CDO 11 plc v Selskabet* [2015] EWHC 871 (Comm) where a purchaser of bonds in the secondary market was assumed to be in contractual relations with the issuer, so that a claim under s 2(1) against the issuer was possible (at [105]). The manner in which the bonds were held was not discussed in the case.

[189] [1964] AC 465.

[190] This depends on the status of the decision of the Court of Appeal in *Royscot Trust Ltd v Rogerson* [1991] 2 QB 297, which has been much criticised. See 10.6.2.4.1 above.

[191] See 10.6.2.4.1.

[192] In relation to contractual liability, this would fall under s 3 Unfair Contract Terms Act 1977; in relation to negligent misstatement it would fall under s 2(2) of that Act; in relation to misrepresentation, s 3 Misrepresentation Act 1967 would apply. See the discussion of exclusion of liability in the context of syndicated loans at 8.4.4.

[193] See P Wood, *Law and Practice of International Finance* (London, Sweet & Maxwell, 2008) 23-14.

sale will include a warranty that the information in the prospectus or other offering circular is accurate. Further, there will not be a claim under section 2(1) of the Misrepresentation Act unless the seller made the inaccurate statement itself.[194] In relation to the other persons mentioned, the possible causes of action are deceit, negligent misstatement (since these persons are not party to any contract with the holder, so section 2(1) cannot apply), and a claim under section 90 FSMA.

A claim under section 90 FSMA can be brought against anyone responsible for a prospectus or for listing particulars.[195] For debt securities, these are the same as for equity securities,[196] with the exception of the directors. Thus the directors can only be liable if they actually accept responsibility for the content of the prospectus or listing particulars, which is very unlikely to be the case. As pointed out in chapter ten,[197] it is likely that reporting accountants will be liable under section 90, but other experts are likely to be exempt.[198] Managers and underwriters will only be liable if they assume responsibility in the prospectus.[199]

In order to bring a claim in negligence against any of these persons, the holder will have to establish a duty of care. The relevant case law has been discussed in chapter ten,[200] and it will be seen that the court will look particularly at the purpose for which the statement was made, the knowledge of the maker of the statement and the reliance of the recipient. In relation to statements made by persons other than an issuer in a prospectus or listing particulars, it would seem clear that those who are liable under section 90 because they have assumed responsibility will also owe a common law duty of care. Whether the duty of care is wider than this is open to doubt.[201] However, the facts of each case need to be considered, and an underwriter or manager might be liable for particular statements made, either within the prospectus or otherwise, on the same basis as arranging banks have been liable.[202] The question of whether those buying securities in the secondary market would have any claim is also discussed in 10.6.2.2.

Where the prospectus rules apply, the public enforcement measures discussed in 10.6.3 also apply to issues of debt securities.

---

[194] This is a possibility if the seller were a manager or an underwriter.
[195] PR 5.5 and FSMA 2000 (Official Listing of Securities) Regulations 2001 (SI 2001/2956), reg 6.
[196] See 10.6.2.3.
[197] Ibid.
[198] PR 5.5.9.
[199] PR 5.5.4(2)(b).
[200] See 10.6.2.1.
[201] As pointed out at 10.6.2.1, in one respect the duty of care is narrower than s 90 as it does not cover omissions.
[202] See the discussion in 8.4.4; see also P Wood, *Law and Practice of International Finance* (London, Sweet & Maxwell, 2008) 23–25; Hudson: Finance, 39-14–41-16. There have also been a number of cases concerning advice given by banks to clients when selling them investments, where the courts have rejected allegations that the banks owed a duty of care to investors when dealing in investments, both on the grounds that the investors were sophisticated, so that no assumption of responsibility was made (see *JP Morgan Chase Bank (formerly Chase Manhattan Bank) v Springwell Navigation Corp* [2008] EWHC 1186 (Comm)), and on the basis that any agreement between the parties which prevented duties arising or representations being made or relied upon was conclusive (see *Springwell* and also *Titan Steel Wheels Ltd v Royal Bank of Scotland plc* [2010] EWHC 211 (Comm), David Steel J. Although not strictly on point, these cases demonstrate the unwillingness of the courts to impose liability on banks unless they actually assume responsibility).

13.2.8 Comparison of Protection by Regulation for Holders of Debt Securities and those Making Loans: Disclosure at the Initial Stage

As pointed out earlier,[203] those who provide finance through loans and by asset-based financing (who will be called 'lenders' throughout this section) face a similar credit risk in relation to the borrower to those purchasing debt securities. However, regulatory law provides no protection by mandatory disclosure for these lenders, who have to protect themselves entirely by contractual means. This section will compare contractual protection relating to the lender's initial decision whether to lend with that provided to holders of debt securities by the regulatory regime discussed above.

It should first be pointed out that, when deciding whether to lend to a corporate borrower, a certain amount of information about that borrower is likely to be publicly available, and can be used by the lender in making its decision. All companies have to produce annual reports and accounts, and there are more extensive disclosure requirements imposed on public companies, especially quoted companies.[204] Further, if the company's shares are listed on the Main Market, or if it lists retail debt securities on the GEFIM, half-yearly reports will also be available.[205] There will also be information about any security interests granted by the company available from the company charges register.[206] All of this information is, of course, also available to those purchasing debt securities.

Most lenders, however, will want further information. A single lender is usually be able to insist on information being provided by the borrower before it makes the decision to lend, so that it, or those acting on its behalf, can perform a 'due diligence' assessment of risk. Obviously, the amount of information required will vary according to the risk the lender is taking on (the size of the loan), the other protection a lender may have (such as a security or other proprietary interest, guarantees or other credit protection) and, maybe, the ability of the lender to monitor the activities of the borrower closely. The lender can protect itself against inaccuracies in the information provided by insisting that accurate information is a condition precedent of advancing funds,[207] and, in case the inaccuracies are not discovered until after the money is advanced, by requiring continuing warranties so that any inaccuracy, or material change, is an event of default.[208] As well as these contractual rights, the lender will also have the tort remedies of deceit, negligent misstatement and misrepresentation[209] discussed above, which may give rise either to an action in damages or to rescission of the loan agreement.[210] The issue of whether a lender has an action in tort against any other persons, such as the bank that arranges a syndicated loan, is discussed in 8.4.4 above.

Provided a lender can insist on obtaining information before it lends, it is in many ways no worse off than an investor protected by mandatory disclosure, and in some senses it is better off, since it can request the information that is really useful to it, rather than receiving

---

[203] See 13.1.1.
[204] See 11.3.1.1 for a full discussion.
[205] See 11.3.1.2.
[206] See 7.4.
[207] See 6.3.2.1.
[208] See 6.3.2.2.
[209] Under s 2(1) Misrepresentation Act 1967.
[210] See 13.2.7.1.

prescribed information, which may not be ideal (for example, because it is historic).[211] However, there are also benefits in having a baseline of prescribed information, particularly where it is possible to add to this baseline by negotiation. This is the position where loans are made under standard agreements, including, most obviously, those produced by the Loan Market Association (LMA).[212] As pointed out earlier, one of the benefits of regulation by disclosure is standardised information and enforcement rights: the LMA contract shows that this advantage can be obtained by private law means as well as through regulation. There is a particular advantage in standardisation where the loans are to be traded, and the development of the secondary market in loans has meant that there are considerable similarities between the position of lenders and that of holders of debt securities.[213] Given this, it might be thought strange that the regulatory position is so different, even though a similar structure has developed contractually for loans.[214] The differences provide an opportunity for regulatory arbitrage, particularly for well-informed and aggressive participants in the markets such as hedge funds.[215] There are, however, limits to the use to which hedge funds (and others) can put information disclosed to them at the time of making or purchasing a loan. These limits are imposed by the market abuse regime and are discussed below.[216]

13.3 Ongoing Regulation by Disclosure

13.3.1 Mandatory Ongoing Disclosure

There are two types of transparency requirements relating to securities which are ongoing throughout the life of the securities. The first, which imposes disclosure obligations on the issuer, relates to disclosure to the market of information concerning the issuer; the second, which imposes disclose obligations on the market venues, relates to information concerning the trading of securities in the secondary market. Until recently there was no requirement for the second type of disclosure in the non-equity markets; now, MiFID II[217] and MIFIR,[218] which will be implemented in 2017, require transparency in the secondary markets for debt securities. These two types of disclosure will now be considered in turn, the second very briefly as it falls largely outside the scope of this book.

Ongoing disclosure of issuer information to the market is required for debt securities as it is for equity securities. The purpose of requiring such disclosure in relation to debt securities is mainly to protect investors (both existing and potential) and to preserve market

---

[211] See 10.5.2.2 for a discussion of these issues in the context of equity securities.

[212] See 8.4.1.

[213] See 8.4.1 for a full comparison.

[214] For a discussion of the differences in regulation between the leveraged loan market and the securities market in the US, see E de Fontenay, 'Do Securities Laws Matter? The Rise of the Leveraged Loan Market' http://papers.ssrn.com/sol3/papers.cfm?abstract_id=2419668.

[215] See Benjamin: Financial Law, 10.6.

[216] See 13.4.2.

[217] Directive 2014/65/EU on markets in financial instruments.

[218] Regulation 600/2014 on markets in financial instruments.

integrity:[219] the additional purpose of promoting corporate governance, important in the context of equity securities,[220] is not really relevant here. As pointed out in 3.2.2.4, creditors can play a part in corporate governance, but this is largely through their reaction to breaches of covenants and events of default. Generally, provision of the information on which holders of debt securities or the bond trustee will act will be contractually required.[221] Having said this, many bond covenants will only require disclosure of information that is required to be disclosed by the Listing Rules, thus 'piggy-backing' on the statutory requirements,[222] unlike the more 'tailored' contractual requirements in syndicated loan agreements. The more limited role played by ongoing disclosure requirements in relation to debt securities is reflected in the scope of the disclosure required by regulation: material that is only relevant to corporate governance by shareholders is not required to be disclosed. It should be borne in mind, however, that such material will have to be disclosed anyway if the company lists its equity securities on the Main Market, or, to some extent, if it lists them on AIM,[223] and also that certain material has to be filed at Companies House by every UK company pursuant to the provisions of the Companies Act 2006.[224] The disclosure requirements that apply to issuers which list debt securities on the GEFIM or the PSM are only likely to prove at all onerous to non-UK companies, or to companies whose shares are not listed.

Generally, most of the Disclosure and Transparency Rules (DTR) apply to debt securities admitted to trading on either the GEFIM[225] or the PSM,[226] although the requirements are slightly different for each. This paragraph will take each category of ongoing disclosure discussed in 11.3 in turn. In relation to the first category (periodic reporting),[227] the requirements in DTR 4 to provide annual financial reports[228] and half-yearly reports[229] apply to debt securities trading on the GEFIM unless the issuer only issues wholesale securities.[230] Where an issuer only lists debt securities on the PSM, it need only publish an annual financial report within six months of the relevant financial period.[231]

In relation to ad hoc disclosure requirements, the first category (disclosure of inside information)[232] is required for issuers of all debt securities listed on either market.[233] As regards disclosure of directors' (and connected persons') shareholdings,[234] this is required where debt securities are listed on the GEFIM (as a regulated market),[235] but not where they

---

[219] See the discussion at 11.2.1.

[220] See the discussion at 11.2.2.

[221] See 6.3.2.2. For a sample set of information covenants given to a bond trustee, see Fuller: Capital Markets, 8.106.

[222] P Wood, *Law and Practice of International Finance* (London, Sweet & Maxwell, 2008) 11-18.

[223] See 11.3 for a discussion of ongoing disclosure obligations. In particular, all UK companies are required to file annual reports and accounts (see 11.3.1.1), although the content of these documents varies according to the size and complexity of the company.

[224] See 11.3.1.1.1.

[225] As a regulated market.

[226] This is the case even though the PSM is not a regulated market, by virtue of LR 17.3.

[227] See 11.3.1.

[228] FCA Handbook, DTR 4.1; see 11.3.1.1.

[229] Ibid, DTR 4.2; see 11.3.1.2.

[230] Ibid, DTR 4.4.2. For a definition of wholesale securities, see 13.2.2.3.

[231] FCA Handbook, LR 17.3.4.

[232] See 11.3.2.1.

[233] FCA Handbook, DTR 2, which applies to securities listed on the PSM by virtue of LR 17.3.9.

[234] See 11.3.2.2.

[235] FCA Handbook, DTR 3.

are only listed on the PSM. The prohibition on trading by persons discharging managerial responsibilities in the 30 days before the announcement of interim financial reports or year-end accounts applies to debt securities as well as to equity securities.[236] Since all debt security listings are standard listings, none of the disclosure requirements imposed by the Listing Rules only on companies with a premium share listing apply.

Since the financial crisis there has been concern about a lack of transparency in the secondary debt securities markets. This led to discussion as to whether Article 65 of MiFID[237] (which already required post-trade transparency in the equity markets)[238] should be extended to the bond markets. Following a consultation exercise, the Committee of European Securities Regulators (CESR) recommended this as part of the review of MiFID. The replacement legislation for MiFID (MiFID II and MIFIR) therefore requires such post-trade transparency, as well as pre-trade transparency[239] (including requirements that quotes made must be firm if certain fulfilments are fulfilled).[240] The system, which is similar to that pertaining to the equity markets, applies (with calibration) to a number of different trading venues, many more of which are brought within the regulatory net.[241] Trading venues are obliged to make public the price, volume and time of transactions traded on that venue.[242] This has to be done as soon as possible after trading unless deferred publication has been authorised based on the size and type of transaction.[243] Investment firms are also obliged to make transactions public.[244]

Thus, although there is no disclosure requirement directly equivalent to the disclosure of major shareholdings[245] (which is not surprising given that one of the main purposes of such disclosure is to give information to existing shareholders about possible takeovers), there will soon be very considerably increased transparency in the debt securities markets. Whether this will prove beneficial is not entirely clear: it has been strongly argued that it will have a chilling effect on those making markets in debt securities, and that it will have an adverse effect on liquidity.[246]

13.3.2 Enforcement of Ongoing Disclosure Requirements

The discussion in 11.4.1.2 in relation to enforcement by investors of investor-focused disclosures applies also in the context of debt securities, both in terms of common law enforcement and enforcement under section 90A FSMA. Similarly, where ongoing disclosure is required, the public enforcement discussed in 11.4.2 also applies. Since there is no

---

[236] See 11.3.2.2.
[237] Markets in Financial Instruments Directive 2004, 2002/92/EC.
[238] See 11.3.
[239] MIFIR, art 8.
[240] Ibid, art 18.
[241] Thus, not only are multilateral trading facilities (MTFs) included (including the PSM); organised trading facilities (OTFs) are also included; see 12.2.2 for details. For discussion of the OTFs see Moloney: EU Regulation, 464–67.
[242] MIFIR, art 10.
[243] Ibid, art 11.
[244] Ibid, art 21.
[245] See 11.3.2.3.
[246] R Healey, *MiFID II and Fixed-Income Price Transparency: Panacea or Problem* (TABB Group, 2012).

obligation to make governance-based disclosures in relation to debt securities, the section on private enforcement of misstatements in that context[247] does not apply. Sanctions for failure to comply with the MiFID II and MIFIR transparency requirements have yet to be specified.

13.3.3 Comparison of Protection by Regulation for Holders of Debt Securities and those Making Loans: Ongoing Disclosure

Most of what was said above[248] also applies to ongoing disclosure. Lenders are usually in a position to bargain for extensive information and monitoring rights, so that financial covenants in loans are usually far more extensive than those in debt securities. Information and financial covenants are discussed above at 6.3.2. Obviously, however, the disclosure of this information is for the benefit of those contractually entitled to it—that is, the lender or lenders. There is no general disclosure to the secondary loan market, and so prospective buyers of loans have to obtain the information they require by other means. This will usually entail obtaining at least some information from the seller of the loan. Since this information has been disclosed only to the seller, and may by its nature be sensitive information that has not been released into the public sphere, the borrower requires some protection against disclosure without its consent. Traditionally, this came from the implied duty of confidentiality between bank and customer, so that the original lender, bound by such a duty, would need the borrower's consent to disclose information,[249] and a recipient bank would be under a similar duty of confidentiality.[250]

However, now that so many non-banks, such as hedge funds, have entered the secondary loan market, an express confidentiality clause has been introduced into the LMA standard leveraged loan agreement,[251] setting out when and to whom information can be disclosed and providing that disclosure to transferees must be on condition that they enter into a confidentiality agreement.[252] How much information is actually required to be disclosed to the buyer by the seller of the loan depends, of course, on the terms of the transfer agreement. A clause in a loan transfer agreement providing that a seller was not obliged to disclose certain information and was not liable for any non-disclosure was held by the Court of Appeal to satisfy the test of reasonableness under section 2(2) of the Unfair Contract Terms Act,[253] on the grounds that the parties were of equal bargaining power and that such clauses promoted certainty. On this reasoning, it would seem that almost any clause restricting a seller's liability in relation to the transfer of a syndicated loan will be likely to be held to be reasonable, since it will be seen as an agreed apportionment of the risks of purchase.

---

[247] 11.4.1.1.

[248] 13.2.

[249] Such consent was usually given in advance in the loan agreement, but on limited terms (cl 29.8 of the pre-2008 LMA leveraged loan agreement).

[250] K Meloni, 'Lender Confidentiality Undertakings: Recent Changes to LMA Facility Documentation' [2008] *Journal of International Banking and Financial Law* 558.

[251] Clause 42.

[252] E Katz, 'Disclosure of Non-Public Information in Loan Secondary Market Trading' [2008] *Journal of International Banking and Financial Law* 585.

[253] *National Westminster Bank v Utrecht-America Finance Company* [2001] EWCA Civ 658 [59]–[62].

The dissemination of sensitive information in the secondary loan market also gives rise to concerns about market abuse, which will be discussed in the next section.

13.4 Regulation of Market Misconduct

13.4.1 Application of the Market Abuse Rules to the Debt Securities Markets

Market abuse is just as possible in relation to the trading of debt securities as in relation to equity securities. As might be expected, both the criminal regime[254] and the regulatory regime described in 12.2 apply to both debt securities markets discussed here, and little more needs to be said in this chapter about the substantive law or the policy arguments.

Up until the time of writing (mid-2015) there have been very few Final Notices enforcing breaches of the market abuse regulatory regime in relation to non-equity trading.[255] Three Final Notices were issued in 2008 and 2009 in respect of bond trading,[256] and one was issued in 2014 in respect of trading in gilts.[257] Some have also been issued in respect of trading on the commodity futures markets. The present scope of the regime is that activity can constitute market abuse if it relates to qualifying investments admitted to trading on a prescribed market.[258] The regime applies not just to trades which actually take place on the market, but also to trades of such qualifying investments which take place over the counter (OTC). This is significant, as a large amount of trading of debt securities takes place in this way: partly because there are far more different issues of debt securities traded on prescribed markets than there are equity securities, partly because the volume of a typical trade is much larger than a typical equity trade, and partly because there are far fewer trades of debt securities. Thus, liquidity has to be provided by the dealers, who typically take some securities on their

---

[254] This comprises (1) the criminal offence of insider dealing (Part V Criminal Justice Act 1993) (see 12.2.2.1): reg 4 Insider Dealing (Securities and Regulated Markets) Order 1994 (SI 1994/187) provides that Part V applies to any security which is admitted to trading on a regulated market. A regulated market is defined as any market which is established under the rules of a specified investment exchange (reg 9), which includes the London Stock Exchange (and therefore the GEFIM and the PSM). (2) The criminal offence of market manipulation under Financial Services Act 2012, ss 89–91 (see 12.2.2.2): this applies to market activity in relation to a relevant agreement or relevant investment, which, as appears from ss 93(3) and (5) Financial Services Act 2012 and the Financial Services Act 2012 (Misleading Statements and Impressions) Order 2013 (SI 2013/637), means controlled activities and investments within the meaning of Sch 1 to the Financial Promotions Order (see above, 13.2.6). Note that 'controlled investments' includes 'debentures' so that the discussion above at 13.1.1 applies.

[255] See S Parkes and T Clarke (Freshfields Bruckhaus Deringer), 'Market Abuse—Not Just an Issue for the Equities Markets' (May 2014), www.freshfields.com/uploadedFiles/SiteWide/Knowledge/Market%20abuse%20-%20 not%20just%20an%20issue%20for%20the%20equities%20markets_20Jun2014.pdf.

[256] FSA, Final Notice issued to Stephen Harrison, 8 September 2008; FSA, Final Notices issued to Christopher Parry and Darren Morton, 6 October 2009.

[257] FCA, Final Notice issued to Mark Stevenson, 20 March 2014.

[258] 'Qualifying investments' are defined in art 5 FSMA (Prescribed Markets and Qualifying Investments) Order 2001 (SI 2001/996) and include all transferable securities as defined in MiFID (see 13.1.1). 'Prescribed markets' include the GEFIM and the PSM, as markets established under the rules of a UK recognised investment exchange (art 4 of the same Order).

own books while they search for a buyer.[259] It appears that OTC trades are included so as to ensure a level playing field for the whole market: fairness would seem to require that all who trade in listed debt securities abide by the same standards, even though the trades are not technically on the market. Further, if OTC trades were not regulated, it would be very easy for those trading debt securities to avoid the market abuse regime altogether.

This scope is soon to be widened by the Market Abuse Regulation,[260] which will come into effect in July 2016. This Regulation (which has direct effect in the UK) applies the market abuse regime to financial instruments traded on regulated markets (the GEFIM), MTFs (the PSM) and OTFs,[261] as well as derivatives whose value or pricing depends on such instruments.[262]

In contrast, the criminal offence set out in Part V of the Criminal Justice Act 1993[263] is limited to situations where dealing takes place on a regulated market,[264] or where the person dealing relies on a professional intermediary or is himself acting as a professional intermediary.[265] The offence is primarily aimed at trading on formal markets, and the extension to cover dealings involving professional intermediaries was intended to cover deliberate attempts to avoid the scope of the legislation, rather than to cover all trading.[266] The 2014 Market Abuse Directive[267] introduces new criminal sanctions for market abuse, and applies to securities traded on regulated markets, MTFs and OTFs in the same way as the Market Abuse Regulation. The UK Government has decided not to opt in to this Directive, at least for the moment.[268]

There is one exception to the application of the market abuse rules which is particularly important in the context of debt securities. This is in relation to the practice of stabilisation, which is described in chapter eight.[269] Stabilisation is seen as beneficial to the market because it increases confidence in market pricing,[270] and so is thought to be worthy of protection from constituting an offence by falling within two 'safe harbours'. Without these safe harbours, stabilisation could constitute either the criminal offences or the regulatory offence discussed in chapter twelve.[271] At present, one safe harbour applies to securities admitted to trading on the GEFIM,[272] provided that there is full disclosure to the market[273] and the stabilisation takes place within a limited time period and within a limited

---

[259] See www.icmagroup.org/Regulatory-Policy-and-Market-Practice/Secondary-Markets/Bond-Market-Transparency-Wholesale-Retail/So-why-do-bonds-trade-OTC-/.

[260] Regulation (EU) No 596/2014. See 12.2.2 for more discussion.

[261] For discussion of the introduction of the wide category of OTFs to the regulatory net, see 12.2.2.

[262] Market Abuse Regulation, art 2. See 12.2.2 above.

[263] See 12.2.2.1.

[264] See n 254 above.

[265] Criminal Justice Act 1993, s 52(3).

[266] Gower and Davies, 30-11.

[267] 2014/57/EU.

[268] See 12.2.2.

[269] See 8.3.1.

[270] EU Stabilisation Regulation No 2273/2003, recital (11), currently set out in MAR 2.1.5. This regulation will be replaced by the Market Abuse Regulation, recital 11 of which states that stabilisation can be legitimate for economic reasons and therefore should be exempt from market abuse regulation under certain circumstances.

[271] See 12.2.1.2 above.

[272] Or any regulated market. The rules apply to equity securities as well, but stabilisation is particularly common in relation to eurobonds. See Fuller: Capital Markets, 13.71.

[273] Usually via a RIS (Regulated Information Service): see 11.3.

price range.[274] The other safe harbour applies to debt securities admitted to trading on the PSM.[275] The requirements are similar to those pertaining to the regulated market, except that the public disclosure requirements are less rigorous: the EU Stabilisation Regulation 2003 does not apply to them (as the PSM is not a regulated market) and so when a safe harbour regime was included in the FCA Market Abuse Rules, this was in a modified form.[276] The position once the Market Abuse Regulation comes into effect will be different. The stabilisation rules are set out in Article 5 of the Market Abuse Regulation and appear to apply to the same extent as the rest of the regulation, that is, to securities traded on regulated markets, MTFs and OTFs. The stabilisation regime is to be subject to technical standards developed by ESMA, which may clarify its scope.[277]

13.4.2 Application of the Market Abuse Rules to the Making and Transfer of Loans

The market abuse regime discussed above and in chapter twelve does not apply to the secondary loan market itself, as it is not a regulated market, nor is it subject to the FSMA regime.[278] However, it is possible that a lender or a buyer might obtain information in the course of making a loan, buying a loan, or as the owner of a traded loan, which has not been publicly disclosed to the debt and equity markets, and which that lender or buyer could use when entering those markets in a way which is contrary to the market abuse rules. For example, the purchaser of a loan to a private company may obtain non-public information about that company, and then, when the company makes an IPO of shares, may wish to subscribe for some of those shares.[279] This could amount to insider dealing, contrary to section 118 FSMA,[280] or potentially even the criminal offence.[281] Similar problems could arise where a lender is given non-public information about a company when deciding whether to make the loan, and then wishes to buy equity or debt securities which are already trading on a prescribed market,[282] or, once the Market Abuse Regulation comes into effect, an OTF.

Lenders[283] can take various steps to avoid liability for market abuse in this way. One possibility, where the lender is a large organisation, is for a Chinese Wall to be set up between

---

[274] The details of the rules are set out in MAR 2.3, reproducing the terms of the EU Stabilisation Regulation, arts 8, 9 and 10.

[275] These rules would also apply to other prescribed markets, and any listed in MAR 2 Annex 1.

[276] The requirements of the EU Stabilisation Regulation are modified in MAR 2.4.

[277] See ESMA Consultation Paper, Draft Technical Standards on the Market Abuse Regulation, 15 July 2014, ESMA/2014/809 regarding the replacement of the stabilisation measures.

[278] This will not change under the Market Abuse Regulation. It relates only to 'financial instruments' (art 2(1)) which are defined in art 4(1)(15) of MiFID II and listed in section C of Annex 1 to that Directive. The list includes transferable securities, money-market instruments, units in collective investment schemes and many derivative products, but not loans. 'Transferable securities' does not include loans: see 13.1.1.

[279] For discussion of a similar example, see S Bowles and D Fox, 'Credit Markets and Market Abuse' [2007] *Journal of International Banking and Financial Law* 209.

[280] 12.2.2.3.

[281] 12.2.2.1.

[282] A prescribed market is a market to which the market abuse regime applies: here the Main Market for equities, and the GEFIM or PSM for debt securities.

[283] The term 'lender' here includes those who purchase loans, such as hedge funds, as well as those who originate them, such as banks.

the part of the organisation dealing with lending or buying loans and the part trading on the public markets.[284] Where the lender is smaller this may not be possible, and the lender must either refrain from trading on the public markets or limit the information it obtains qua lender to that which is publicly disclosed.[285] Requests by lenders that information provided be 'scrubbed' of non-public information can potentially be very difficult for a borrower, and a practice has now developed whereby the lender agrees that a nominated third party will receive non-public information on their behalf.[286] Obviously, the more information that is disclosed publicly by the borrower, the less this question is a problem for the lender.[287]

As pointed out in chapter nine, there is increasing convergence of the secondary markets in debt securities and loans. The secondary loan market is a liquid market, and there is potential for abusive use of information, as there is in the securities markets. So far, the line has been drawn clearly in terms of the types of investments the trading of which is regulated. However, not only are many of the participants in the secondary loan market themselves regulated entities, so that they have to comply with the principles laid down by the FCA,[288] but there has also been growing concern about the lack of equality of information among all participants in the market. This has been redressed, to some extent, by guidelines issued by the LMA,[289] which, although they do not have the force of law, tend to be followed closely by market participants for fear of reputational consequences of breach.[290] The guidelines concern material information—that is, information which, if known to the whole syndicate, would significantly impact on the price of the loan.[291] They distinguish between 'borrower confidential information', which is material information not known to the whole syndicate, and 'syndicate confidential information', which is information available to the whole syndicate. The guidelines state that market participants should not trade based on borrower confidential information (even if the counterparty actually has that information); they may only trade on the basis of syndicate confidential information. In other words, information has to be disclosed to the whole syndicate before a trade can take place, though there does not seem to be any requirement that information be disclosed to a counterparty who is not a syndicate member (although that will, of course, usually be required by contract unless specifically excluded from the transfer agreement).

---

[284] P Wood, *Law and Practice of International Finance* (London, Sweet & Maxwell, 2008) 10-10.

[285] E Katz, 'Disclosure of Non-Public Information in Loan Secondary Market Trading' [2008] *Journal of International Banking and Financial Law* 585.

[286] A new clause has been inserted into the LMA leveraged loan agreement to this effect: see cl 32.13 and, further, Katz, ibid.

[287] S Bowles and D Fox, 'Credit Markets and Market Abuse' [2007] *Journal of International Banking and Financial Law* 209.

[288] The high level principles are at PRIN 2.1, and include the obligation that a firm conduct its business with integrity, and that it observe proper standards of market conduct. For more discussion of the relevance of these principles to the secondary loan market, see C Howard and B Hedger, *Restructuring Law and Practice*, 2nd edn (London, LexisNexis, 2014) 3.25.

[289] *LMA Guidelines—Transparency and the Use of Information*, first issued 6 June 2011 and amended November 2012.

[290] C Howard and B Hedger, *Restructuring Law and Practice*, 2nd edn (London, LexisNexis, 2014) 3.21, 6.30. See also D Roberts, S Baskerville and D Hamilton, 'LMA Guidelines on Transparency and the Use of Information in Distressed Debt Trading' (2011) 5 *Corporate Rescue and Insolvency* 143.

[291] Compare the meaning of 'inside information' discussed at 12.2.2.3.1.

There is, however, a tension between the desire of a borrower for confidentiality[292] and the LMA disclosure requirements. To some extent this is ameliorated if there is a confidentiality agreement between the borrower and the members of the syndicate, and any counterparty would also normally enter into such an agreement. However, it appears that borrowers regularly restrict the disclosure of information, which makes it impossible or very difficult to turn borrower confidential information into syndicate confidential information, and, in practice, has a chilling effect on trading.[293] Alternative guidelines have been produced by the Alternative Investment Management Association (AIMA)[294] as a result of dissatisfaction among its members with the LMA Guidelines, which were seen as not reflecting market practice.

13.4.3 The Regulation of Short Selling

As observed in section 12.3, short selling relates to the practice of selling an asset that a seller does not own with the aim of purchasing back identical assets at a later date for a lower price. It is not only shares that can be sold short: debt securities may also be sold short, in order to express a negative view of the evolving credit risk of an issuer. A liquid market is necessary for successful short selling; while there is clearly a secondary market in corporate bonds, it is not sufficiently liquid for short selling to take place frequently. Various features of the corporate bond market militate against a high level of liquidity.[295] One is that any one issuer is likely to have launched a number of issues of bonds, unlike shares, of which there is usually only one issue: the market for those wanting exposure to the credit risk of the issuer is thus fragmented. Another is that bonds have fixed maturity dates (unlike shares): many bondholders hold until maturity. Further, bond trades tend to be large and infrequent, so that liquidity has to be provided by dealers who take securities on their own books while they find buyers: this also means that many trades are OTC.[296] There is another, more effective way to achieve exposure to the credit risk of the bond or the issuer: to enter into a credit default swap (CDS) with a counterparty who takes a different view of the creditworthiness of the issuer, so that they are willing (for a relatively small fee) to agree to pay a large sum if the issuer defaults or becomes insolvent.[297] There is no need to own the bond in order to buy a CDS based on it: this is known as a 'naked' CDS. It is probably cheaper, and certainly simpler, to buy a CDS than to borrow bonds under a stock lending agreement[298] and to sell them short.

---

[292] See 13.3.3 above.

[293] C Howard and B Hedger, *Restructuring Law and Practice*, 2nd edn (London, LexisNexis, 2014) 3.28, 6.31.

[294] Alternative Investment Management Association, *AIMA Note on Sound Practice in the Secondary Loan Market*, March 2013.

[295] See European Commission, Impact Assessment Accompanying Document to the Proposal for a Regulation of the European Parliament and of the Council on Short Selling and Certain Aspects of Credit Default Swaps, SEC(2010) 1055, 13.

[296] See 13.4.1.

[297] For discussion of CDSs, including their regulation, see 6.4.3.

[298] See 4.6.4.

For these reasons, short selling of corporate bonds has not been a concern of the regulatory authorities.[299] However, regulatory attention has been paid to the short selling of sovereign debt (that is, bonds issued by states) and to the purchasing of CDSs based on such debt. Since this book is concerned with corporate debt and not sovereign debt, such regulation will not be considered in detail. Broadly, regulatory constraints similar to those restricting the short selling of shares (as detailed in section 12.3.2.1) govern whether a short sale of sovereign debt is 'covered' and thereby permitted, although the restrictions are deliberately lighter.[300] The restrictions on uncovered sovereign CDSs are complex: sovereign CDS transactions are banned unless the transaction is a 'permissible hedge':[301] the rules as to what counts as this are complicated. Sovereign debt is excluded from ESMA's powers of intervention.[302]

13.5 Accepting Deposits

As mentioned above,[303] accepting deposits by way of business is a regulated activity under FSMA, and can only be carried out by an authorised (or exempt) person.[304] This is potentially relevant for debt finance, since the definition of 'deposit' is very wide and could include corporate loans or debt securities, which would mean that the corporate borrowers would have to be authorised. However, there are a number of exclusions from the definition[305] which will usually mean that this form of regulation does not apply in the area considered by this book. The accepting of deposits is only a regulated activity if the money received by way of deposit is lent to others, or is used to finance the activities of the person accepting the deposit.[306] The first limb of this criterion clearly refers to the financing of banks and financial institutions, but the second limb could potentially refer to any type of corporate debt finance.[307]

A 'deposit' is defined as a sum of money paid on terms that satisfy both limbs of the following test.[308] First, the money is to be repaid on demand or at an agreed time and, second, the payment of the money is not referable to the provision of property, services or the giving of security. The words 'giving of security' in the second part of that test do not mean that money received by way of a secured loan is not a deposit. Rather, what is envisaged is that the money is paid by way of 'security' for the performance of a contract,[309] such as

---

[299] Although CDSs have been regulated: see 6.4.3.4.

[300] Council Regulation (EU) 236/2012 of the European Parliament and of the Council of 14 March 2012 on short selling and certain aspects of credit default swaps [2012] OJ L86/1, art 13.

[301] Regulation 236/2012, art 4.

[302] Ibid, art 29. For discussion of ESMA's powers in relation to the short selling of shares, see 12.3.2.5.

[303] See 13.1.2.

[304] FSMA 2000, ss 19 and 22; Financial Services and Markets Act 2000 (Regulated Activities) Order 2001 (SI 2001/544) ('Regulated Activities Order'), art 5. For details of the authorisation regime, see Benjamin: Financial Law, 10.2.

[305] Regulated Activities Order, arts 6–9.

[306] Ibid, art 5(1).

[307] Fuller: Corporate Borrowing, 10.9.

[308] Regulated Activities Order, art 5(2).

[309] Ibid, art 5(3).

when a percentage of the purchase price is paid on exchange of contracts for the purchase of a house, which will be forfeit if the purchaser fails to complete, and returned if the seller fails to convey the property.[310] So, a secured loan or debenture can still be a 'deposit'. Indeed, the definition is so broad that, as Lewison J pointed out when considering the scope of the definition in *FSA v Anderson (No 1)*, 'to call something a loan is not inconsistent with its being a deposit'.[311]

However, most debt finance considered in this book will fall within one of the exceptions to the definition of 'deposit'. Sums received as consideration for the issue of debt securities are generally excluded,[312] as are sums paid by authorised financial institutions,[313] which means that most loans to companies will not be included.

13.6 Convertible Debt Securities

So far the discussion in this chapter of the regulation of listed securities has concentrated on debt securities. However, it will be recalled that securities can start life as debt securities and be convertible into equity securities, or can be exchangeable for equity securities.[314]

The regulation of such securities reflects their hybrid nature, and is discussed in this section. Convertible debt securities are generally regulated as if they were equity securities of the issuer. For example, the rules on pre-emption apply to them.[315] They may only be admitted if the equity securities into which they are convertible are already, or will become at the same time, listed securities.[316] Where convertible debt securities are to be offered to the public or are themselves to be admitted to trading on the GEFIM (so that a prospectus is required), the content requirements are the same as for equity securities.[317] If they are not offered to the public and only admitted to trading on the PSM, then the content requirements for the necessary listing particulars follow the wholesale debt regime.[318] If the convertible debt securities are neither to be offered to the public nor admitted to trading on the GEFIM themselves, but it is intended that the equity securities into which they convert are to be admitted to trading on the Main Market, then a prospectus is not required provided that the equity securities are of the same class as equity securities of the issuer already admitted to trading on the Main Market.[319] If exchangeable debt securities are to be offered to the public or are themselves to be admitted to trading on the GEFIM, a distinction is drawn between exchangeable debt securities issued by an affiliate of the company

---

[310] This example is given by Lewison J in *FSA v Anderson* [2010] EWHC 599 (Ch) [44].

[311] Ibid, [44].

[312] Regulated Activities Order, art 9. Commercial paper with a redemption value of less than £100,000 is not excluded (arts 9(2), 9(3)): commercial paper is a form of short-term debt security. See 2.3.3.1.

[313] Ibid, art 6. Inter-company loans and loans from family members are also excluded: art 6(1)(c) and (d).

[314] See 2.4.

[315] See 4.4.

[316] FCA Handbook, LR 2.2.12.

[317] These requirements are discussed at 10.5.2.2. In the PR the term 'equity securities' is defined as including convertible securities: see PR App 1.1.1 applying Prospectus Directive, art 2(1)(b).

[318] FCA Handbook, LR 4.2.4(1).

[319] Ibid, PR 1.2.3(7).

that is the issuer of the relevant equity securities and those that are issued by a company that is not so affiliated. The former are regarded by the Prospectus Directive as equity securities, but the content requirements for the necessary prospectus would seem to follow the retail or wholesale debt regime depending on the denomination of the security.[320] The latter are regarded by the Prospectus Directive as non-equity securities,[321] and the content requirements for the necessary prospectus follow the wholesale debt regime regardless of the denomination of the security.[322] If exchangeable debt securities are not offered to the public and are to be admitted to trading only on the PSM, then the content requirements for the necessary listing particulars follow the wholesale debt regime regardless of whether the issuer is affiliated with the company that is the issuer of the relevant equity securities, and regardless of the denomination of the securities.[323] If the exchangeable debt securities are neither to be offered to the public nor admitted to trading on the GEFIM themselves, then a prospectus is not required where the equity securities for which they are exchangeable are to be admitted to trading on the Main Market.[324]

13.7 Regulation of Credit Rating Agencies

As mentioned in chapter two,[325] credit rating agencies (CRAs) play an important role in capital markets, although until recently they were largely unregulated.[326] Even before the financial crisis, some steps had been taken to regulate CRAs since they had become 'deeply embedded in investor culture'.[327] They had come to be relied on directly and indirectly not only by investors and issuers, but also by regulatory authorities. For example, investment funds[328] are often required by their mandates to invest only in listed securities, and then

---

[320] The condition in art 4(2)(2)(b) of the Prospectus Directive Regulation is not satisfied, so that art 7 applies instead.

[321] It might be wondered why this second kind of exchangeable debt security exists. Investment banks often issue debt securities that are exchangeable for shares in unaffiliated companies and which can be acquired by the bank on the market when the time comes to settle the exchange obligation. Such securities are really specialised investment products designed by the bank to cater to the demands of its sophisticated clients, rather than a significant source of finance for general corporate purposes.

[322] Prospectus Directive, art 2(1)(b).

[323] FCA Handbook, LR 4.2.4(1).

[324] Ibid, PR 1.2.3(7). This is provided that the equity securities are of the same class as those already admitted to trading on the Main Market.

[325] 2.3.3.3.

[326] Note, however, that CRAs were expected to adhere to a Statement of Principles and a (voluntary) CRA Code published by IOSCO. The first code was published in 2004 (IOSCO, Code of Conduct Fundamentals for Credit Rating Agencies, December 2004) and updated post-crisis (IOSCO, Code of Conduct Fundamentals for Credit Rating Agencies, revised May 2008). Further changes are planned: IOSCO, Code of Conduct Fundamentals for Credit Rating Agencies, Consultation Report, February 2014. This code was felt to be inadequate post-crisis, however, and therefore significant regulatory changes have been put in place in the EU (see below) and the US (see eg D Dimotrov, D Palia and L Tang, 'Impact of the Dodd-Frank Act on Credit Ratings' *Journal of Financial Economics*, forthcoming, http://ssrn.com/abstract=2444990).

[327] F Partnoy, 'Historical Perspectives on the Financial Crisis: Ivar Kreuger, the Credit-Rating Agencies, and Two Theories about the Function, and Dysfunction, of Markets' (2009) 26 *Yale Journal on Regulation* 431.

[328] Such as mutual funds and pension funds.

only in securities that carry an 'investment grade' rating issued by one or more CRA.[329] As an indicator of asset quality, banks and other lenders often value financial collateral offered to them on the basis of the credit rating assigned to it, so that investment grade bonds have more value as collateral than high-yield bonds.

Maintaining a good credit rating is also a good way for a company to signal its own creditworthiness, not only to potential investors but also to customers and suppliers. For example, a company may persuade the counterparty to a trading arrangement that it should not have to provide security for its obligations because it has an investment grade rating. Some companies positively target a particular credit rating, and this target is a management policy which is communicated to analysts.[330] Parties can incorporate credit ratings into their private arrangements by attaching consequences to a rating downgrade.[331] In *Hall v Cable & Wireless*,[332] for example, the dispute concerned an issuer's obligation to disclose to the market the fact that it might be required to provide collateral if its own credit rating was downgraded. It is easy to see how such 'ratings triggers' can become a self-fulfilling prophecy, where the downgrade both reflects and contributes to the increased likelihood of default.[333] Credit ratings are also used by regulatory authorities around the world. In most countries, for example, authorities are prepared to accept credit ratings issued by certain CRAs when determining what risk weighting to apply to assets for the purpose of the capital adequacy requirements imposed on banks and other financial institutions.[334] Securities with the safest ratings carry a low risk weighting and do not need to be funded by equity to the same extent as more risky securities.[335]

Before the financial crisis, it was considered satisfactory that CRAs were regulated by the market. It was assumed that CRAs that failed to supply accurate ratings would eventually be excluded by normal market forces, and that there was therefore no need for more intrusive regulation.[336] As a result of the financial crisis, however, questions have been raised about the role of CRAs. In particular, their expertise in rating corporate securities proved insufficient when rating the complicated asset-based securities issued in the period before the crisis.[337] The mathematical models used to rate these new products failed adequately

---

[329] 'Investment grade' securities are those with a credit rating of at least 'BBB-'. 'Speculative grade' securities have a rating of BB+ or below.

[330] See Financial Services Authority FS09/01, *Insurance Risk Management: The Path to Solvency II* (May 2009), para 5-37.

[331] See 6.3.2.2.

[332] [2009] EWHC 1793 (Comm).

[333] Such use of ratings triggers is widespread. According to a survey by Moody's, out of 771 US corporate issuers rating Ba1 or higher, only 12.5% reported no triggers, while the remaining 87.5% reported a total of 2,819 rating triggers. See Moody's Investors Service, *The Unintended Consequence of Rating Triggers* (December 2001). For further discussion of the use of rating triggers see 6.3.2.2.

[334] See 2.3.1.4.

[335] A useful cross-country comparison is found in A Estrella et al, 'Credit Ratings and Complementary Sources of Credit Quality Information', Basel Committee on Banking Supervision Working Papers (No 3, August 2000).

[336] S Phillips and A Rechtschaffen, 'International Banking Activities: The Role of the Federal Reserve Bank in Domestic Capital Markets' (1998) 21 *Fordham International Law Journal* 1754, 1762. Indeed, even in the aftermath of the global financial crisis, the Financial Stability Forum, the European Securities Market Experts Group and the Committee of European Securities Regulation argued that binding regulation was not required. However, for concerns about the role of CRAs even before the financial crisis see eg F Partnoy, 'The Siskel and Ebert of Financial Markets? Two Thumbs Down for Credit-Rating Agencies' (1999) 77 *Washington University Law Review* 619.

[337] See 2.3.3.5.

to appreciate the risk and significance of correlated default.[338] Concerns were also raised that there was a conflict of interest problem, in that CRAs were paid by investment banks sponsoring a securitisation, yet the ratings were relied upon by investors of varying levels of expertise.[339] The CRAs became involved in designing the securities themselves, so that the arranger's rating objectives could be satisfied.

As a result of these concerns, Europe has introduced new regulations for CRAs. EU regulation in relation to credit rating agencies has come in three stages since the crisis: an initial regulation in 2009, and then amending regulations in 2011 and 2013.[340] The UK's approach has largely been driven by developments at EU level.[341] The EU Regulations create a registration regime for CRAs. Registration and supervision of CRAs within the EU is in the hands of ESMA.[342] These provisions impose on CRAs certain disclosure and transparency requirements, including, for example, the obligation to disclose ratings methodologies and key ratings assumptions.[343] These Regulations also impose obligations on CRAs to identify and manage any conflicts of interest that might arise: for example CRAs cannot provide consultancy or advisory services to entities they rate, but can provide so-called 'ancillary services' provided that the nature and extent of these is prominently disclosed.[344] For certain structured products, namely re-securitisations, the regulations impose a maximum duration on the relationship between a CRA and an issuer, in order to require debt issuers to rotate between the CRAs that rate them.[345] New provisions also seek to diminish the reliance by financial institutions on external ratings.[346] The idea here is to try to ensure that financial institutions do not blindly rely on only on credit ratings when picking investment,

---

[338] FSA, *The Turner Review: A Regulatory Response to the Global Banking Crisis*, March 2009, 44, 76.

[339] F Partnoy, 'How and Why Credit Rating Agencies are Not Like Other Gatekeepers', University of San Diego Legal Studies Research Paper No 07-46, May 2006; F Partnoy, 'Overdependence on Credit Ratings was the Primary Cause of the Crisis', San Diego Legal Studies Research Paper No 09-015, 2009; J Coffee, 'Ratings Reform: The Good, the Bad and the Ugly' (2011) 1 *Harvard Business Law Review* 231; T Hurst, 'The Role of Credit Rating Agencies in the Current Worldwide Financial Crisis' (2009) 30 *Company Lawyer* 61.

[340] Regulation (EC) No 1060/2009 of the European Parliament and of the Council of 16 September 2009 on credit rating agencies (CRA I), as amended by CRA II (Regulation 513/2011) and CRA III (Regulation 462/2013). Directive 2014/51/EU also amends these provisions in relation to insurance and reinsurance undertakings (in particular the directive seeks to avoid overreliance on external rating agencies by requiring insurance undertakings to assess the appropriateness of external credit rating assessments as part of their risk management). Further, a large number of Delegated Regulations have been adopted by the European Commission, setting out Regulatory Technical Standards needed to implement key provisions of the Regulation on Credit Rating Agencies.

[341] See eg Credit Rating Agencies Regulations 2010 (SI 2010/906) (implementing CRA I) and Credit Rating Agencies (Civil Liability) Regulations 2013 (SI 2013/1637), which implements the civil liability provisions in CRA III, art 35a.

[342] See CRA II (Regulation 513/2011). ESMA is given substantial powers in this regard, including the ability to impose fines and to revoke a rating agency's licence. For a comparison of the roles of ESMA and the SEC in this regard see J Coffee, 'Ratings Reform: The Good, the Bad and the Ugly' (2011) 1 *Harvard Business Law Review* 231, 246–50.

[343] See Regulation (EC) No 1060/2009, art 8 and Annex 1. While in theory disclosure of this kind of information can be valuable in helping those wishing to make use of CRA services to assess the quality of service being provided, studies suggest that these disclosures do not seem to affect a rating agency's success in the market. See L Bai, 'The Performance Disclosures of Credit Rating Agencies: Are They Effective Reputational Sanctions?' (2010) 7 *NYU Journal of Law and Business* 47.

[344] Regulation (EC) No 1060/2009, Annex I, Section B para 4.

[345] See EU No 462/2013, inserting a new art 6b into Regulation (EC) No 1060/2009.

[346] See EU No 462/2013, inserting a new art 5a into Regulation (EC) No 1060/2009.

but also carry out their own assessments.[347] Further, the EU regulations create a new civil liability regime for CRAs.[348] The lack of an adequate remedy for investors who suffered as a result of inaccurate ratings was felt to be one of the weaknesses of the pre-crisis regime.[349] Consequently a new cause of action now allows investors to seek compensation from CRAs if they have suffered loss as a result of a flawed rating. This action is available even if there is no contractual relationship between the parties, and therefore there is no requirement to show a duty of care. The claim is available where the CRA has intentionally or with gross negligence committed an infringement of the EU CRA Regulations.[350] CRAs may, however, limit their liability where it is 'reasonable and proportionate to do so'.[351]

Whether these regulatory developments will be beneficial, and the extent to which they will actually have any effect on CRAs' business practices, remains to be seen. These reforms may be said to leave the core problems regarding CRAs untackled. In particular, they do not address the issuer-pays model which gives rise to the central conflict of interest problem.[352] It seems clear that there are concerns within the EU about the adequacy of the present response, as in January 2015 a tendering process for a study on the feasibility of alternatives to credit ratings and the state of the credit rating market was launched.[353] This is an area in which more regulatory change can be expected.

13.8 Regulation of Peer-to-Peer Lending

Peer-to-peer lending is described in chapter 2.[354] It will be recalled that, although there is a variety of methods and structures of such lending, typically the borrowers and lenders find each other through the use of an online platform, operated by a company. The platform will normally carry out some sort of credit check on potential borrowers, will publicise the borrower's requirements for a loan, will have some sort of facility for fixing the terms

---

[347] See further in this regard Financial Stability Board (FSB) principles for reducing reliance on CRA ratings, October 2010, and the Commission's response to the FSB, including an action plan: Directorate General Internal Market and Services, Staff Working Paper, EU Response to the Financial Stability Board (FSB), EU Action Plan to reduce reliance on Credit Rating Agency (CRA) Ratings, May 2014. For comment on the idea of seeking to reduce over-reliance, see J Coffee, 'Ratings Reform: The Good, the Bad and the Ugly' (2011) 1 *Harvard Business Law Review* 231, 233.

[348] See EU No 462/2013, amending Regulation (EC) No 1060/2009 and inserting a new art 35a.

[349] Very little successful litigation involving actions by investors against CRAs has emerged post-crisis. The notable exceptions to this have arisen in Australia: *Bathurst Regional Council v Local Government Financial Service Pty Ltd (No 5)* [2012] FCA 1200; *ABM AMRO Bank NV v Bathurst Regional Council* [2014] FCAFC 65.

[350] Within the UK see Credit Rating Agencies (Civil Liability) Regulations 2013 (SI 2013/1637). The explanatory memorandum to these regulations confirms that this claim is additional to the existing claim at common law in the UK for negligent misstatement.

[351] art 36(a)(3) and Credit Rating Agencies (Civil Liability) Regulations 2013 (SI 2013/1637), regs 10–12.

[352] For discussion see J Payne, 'The Role of Gatekeepers' in N Moloney, E Ferran and J Payne (eds), *The Oxford Handbook of Financial Regulation* (Oxford, Oxford University Press, 2015). In addition, Professor Partnoy has identified a key problem with CRAs as being the regulatory licence that has developed as a result of CRAs becoming hard-wired into the regulatory system (see eg F Partnoy, 'The Siskel and Ebert of Financial Markets? Two Thumbs Down for Credit-Rating Agencies' (1999) 77 *Washington University Law Review* 619). These reforms do little to address this issue, either.

[353] Call for Tender MARKT/2014/257/F for a study on the feasibility of alternatives to credit ratings and the state of the credit rating market, 5 January 2015.

[354] 2.3.2.

of the loan, and will enter into a standard form agreement with the borrower as agent for the lender. While any borrower or lender can use these crowdfunding sites, the borrowers are typically small businesses (corporate or non-corporate) that find it hard to obtain debt finance elsewhere. The peer-to-peer lending platforms provide a method of finding a much wider pool of lenders, including retail investors. Typically these are attracted by the high rate of interest offered; this, of course, reflects the high risk of many of these loans, given the small, and often immature, nature of the borrower's business.

A very comprehensive analysis of the risks involved in crowdfunding is set out in the recent review of the market by the European Banking Authority.[355] Chief among these are the credit risk of both the borrower and the lending platform. The former is a risk borne by the lender that the borrower will not repay or will become insolvent. The latter risk is borne by both the lender and the borrower, since the platform may fail while holding funds for either party or while owing money to either party.[356]

The credit risk of the borrower is, of course, no different from the credit risk borne by any other lender or holder of debt securities. However, as we have seen, most lenders protect themselves with privately enforced disclosure requirements, while investors in debt securities are protected by the regulatory disclosure regime, which is calibrated to give greater protection to less sophisticated investors. Those lending on peer-to-peer platforms are often unsophisticated, and are lending to risky businesses. They are not in a position to demand strong covenants: they are, in practice, obliged to use the standard form lending document provided by the platform. Although, in theory, they could read the agreements available on various platforms and make an informed choice between them, this is unlikely to happen in the case of retail lenders. Moreover, although, in theory, they could demand more information about the business to which they are lending, in practice they are reliant on the information provided by the borrower that is available on the platform, and on any credit checks which are carried out by the platform itself.

In the past there has been no regulation of loans made by unsophisticated lenders, apart from the rules on financial promotion, to the extent that they might apply,[357] and the general law relating to misrepresentation and fraud. Until the advent of online platforms, however, such loans were relatively rare and usually made by lenders who had some personal connection with the borrower. It is the ability conferred by the platforms to link borrowers with such lenders on a large scale that has given rise to the concern about the credit risk faced by such lenders.

In this climate, the FCA[358] was faced with various possibilities for protecting such lenders.[359] One possibility would be to have some sort of compensation scheme or insurance

---

[355] Opinion of the European Banking Authority on Lending-Based Crowdfunding, EBA/Op/2015/03 (26 February 2015), table 1, p 12.

[356] The EBA has identified many other risks, such as a liquidity risk to the borrower if the platform delays payment, for example due to technical difficulties. There is also a liquidity risk to the lender, in that it is not usually possible to exit the loan unless the platform offers a secondary market, which some do: see 2.3.2.

[357] See 13.2.6.

[358] At EU level, the European Commission is still exploring the risks and potential of crowdfunding (see http://ec.europa.eu/finance/general-policy/crowdfunding/index_en.htm). It launched a consultation in October 2013, resulting in a communication in March 2014 (COM(2014) 172 final) and the establishment of an expert group called the European Crowdfunding Stakeholder Forum.

[359] The FCA issued consultation paper CP 13/13 in October 2013 and a policy statement PS 14/4 in March 2014, setting out its regulatory response.

for possible loss. In relation to the credit risk of the borrower, this would defeat the whole purpose of the exercise: the high interest rates payable to the lender reflect the risky nature of the loan, and requiring such compensation or insurance would drastically reduce the returns to the lenders. Another possibility was to include peer-to-peer lending within the Financial Services Compensation Scheme (FSCS), which applies (chiefly) to deposits made with banks.[360] This would provide only very limited protection to lenders, as it would only apply either if the platform failed while holding money deposited by the lender (for example, prior to the loan actually being made to the borrower) or if the bank in which such funds were held failed. In the latter case, the scheme might well apply anyway, and in the former case the FCA considered that the client money rules would provide better protection.[361] It was also considered that including peer-to-peer lending in the FSCS scheme would be costly, and that the costs would be disproportionate to the benefits.[362]

Instead, the FCA's approach is to regulate the lending platforms in a number of respects, thus addressing both the credit risk of the borrower and the credit risk of the platform itself. 'Operating an electronic system in relation to lending' has been added to the list of activities regulated by FSMA.[363] Article 36H will cover lending that is peer-to-peer (P2P), business-to-peer (B2P) and peer-to-business (P2B): the focus in this chapter is on P2B. Bringing the lending platforms within the regulatory umbrella means that the High Level Standards apply to them,[364] as well as the conduct of business rules.[365]

The main approach in relation to the credit risk of the borrower is to implement a disclosure-based regime to ensure that investors have the information they require to make informed investment decisions: this is achieved by bringing the activities of lending platforms within the definition of 'controlled activities' in the Financial Promotion Order.[366] As such the high-level rules found in the COBS 4 financial promotions regime apply. Platforms must comply with general FCA guidelines, according to which all communications by the firm are fair, clear and not misleading.[367] Firms are required to consider the nature and risks of the agreement and the information needs of their customers, and to disclose relevant, accurate information. Specific disclosures in relation to crowdfunding are not mandated by the FCA, which instead prefers to leave it to the firm as to how to comply with the high-level rules regarding communication with clients. Examples of information that a firm should provide to explain the specific nature and risks of a P2P agreement include expected and actual default rates,[368] assumptions used to predict default rates,[369] a description of how

---

[360] See www.fscs.org.uk.

[361] FCA CP 13/3 para 3.6; PS 14/4 para 3.2–3.5.

[362] See HM Treasury, *ISA Qualifying Investments: Consultation on Including Peer-to-Peer Loans* (October 2014), text to question 3, www.gov.uk/government/consultations/isa-qualifying-investments-consultation-on-including-peer-to-peer-loans/isa-qualifying-investments-consultation-on-including-peer-to-peer-loans.

[363] art 36H FSMA (Regulated Activities) Order 2001/544, added by FSMA (Regulated Activities) (Amendment) (No 2) Order 2013/1881.

[364] Including the principles in PRIN2.

[365] COBS.

[366] Financial Promotion Order, Sch 1 para 4C. The provision of information in connection with peer-to-peer loans is expressly included as a controlled activity. For discussion of the financial promotion regime, see 13.2.6.

[367] PRIN 2.1.7 and COBS 4.2.1R(1).

[368] COBS 14.3.7A(1).

[369] Ibid, 14.3.7A(2).

loan risk is assessed, an explanation of the firm's procedure for dealing with default,[370] and a clear explanation of the lack of FSCS cover.

Consumer lenders have an additional safeguard, in that the cancellation rights under the Distance Marketing Directive apply.[371] Thus, a consumer can cancel within 14 days unless there is a secondary market for the loan on the platform, in which case the directive does not apply, and arguably there is less need for a cancellation right since the consumer can exit reasonably easily.[372]

The risks presented by the possible failure of the platform are addressed in a number of ways. First, lending platforms are subject to prudential standards, requiring them to hold regulatory capital. The minimum amount of capital that a loan-based crowdfunding platform will have to hold is the higher of £20,000 (rising to £50,000 on 31 March 2017) or an amount calculated by reference to the volume of funds loaned to the platform.[373] Second, by dint of such platforms' activities coming within the FSMA regime, the client money rules apply.[374] This does, however, depend upon the way in which payments are made by the lender to the borrower: some platforms do not hold client money themselves, instead using a custodian.[375] The FCA is particularly concerned to ensure that existing loans continue to be administered in the event of a platform failure. Since crowdfunding investors often contribute very small amounts, there is a risk that in the event of a platform failure borrowers will deliberately default, since it is not economically viable for investors to chase repayment. Platform operators are thus required to take reasonable steps to ensure that arrangements are in place to ensure that lending agreements will continue to be administered.[376] Third, lending platforms are subject to dispute resolution rules so that lenders and borrowers have the right to complain first to the firm, then to the Financial Ombudsman Service.[377] Fourth, platforms must report to the FCA their financial position, client money held, any complaints, and details of loans arranged each quarter.[378]

The FCA is reviewing its supervision of the market periodically,[379] and plans to carry out a full post-implementation review in 2016. So far, the market has continued to expand, and there have been few infringements and few major losses for consumer lenders. The industry is very keen to promote itself as the most conservative part of the crowdfunding spectrum, and therefore appears to be happy for the moment to comply with regulatory requirements in order to signal its quality.[380]

---

[370] Ibid, 14.3.7A(8).

[371] Directive on Distance Marketing of Consumer Financial Services (No 2002/65/EC), implemented in COBS 15.

[372] FCA 13/3, para 3.53.

[373] *Interim Prudential Sourcebook for Investment Businesses (IPRU-INV)*, 12.3, http://media.fshandbook.info/Handbook/IPRU-INV_Full_20140401_20151230.pdf.

[374] These rules are found in CASS (Client Assets Sourcebook) (see https://fshandbook.info/FS/html/FCA/CASS) and are designed to ensure adequate protection of client money when it is in the hands of the firm.

[375] FCA Policy Statement 14/4, 3.16. See also O Stacey, S Lovegrove and D Murphy, 'Crowdfunding: Possibilities and Prohibitions' (2012) 23 *Practical Law Companies* 18.

[376] Senior Management Arrangements, Systems and Controls (SYSC), 4.1.8.

[377] DISP 2.7.6R(12) found in Dispute Resolution: Complaints Sourcebook.

[378] See Supervision manual (SUP) 16.12.4.

[379] The first review took place in February 2015: see www.fca.org.uk/static/documents/crowdfunding-review.pdf.

[380] See, for example, the press release of the industry body (P2PFA) at http://p2pfa.info/p2pfa-comments-on-fca-review-into-crowdfunding-regulatory-regime.

13.9 Conclusion

The application of regulatory rules to the debt side of corporate finance is complicated and patchy. With some exceptions, the chief inconsistency, on one view, is still that, while the issuing and trading of debt securities attracts considerable disclosure requirements and some other types of regulation, there is little regulation of the making of loans, whether single lender loans or those involving multiple lenders. One reason for this could be said to be the identity of those providing the finance. Loans are usually made by banks, and they can be expected to look out for themselves.[381] However, given that most investors in debt securities are institutions of one sort or another, it is hard to see why this is a considerable point of difference. Of course, where lenders are not institutional or sophisticated, as in peer-to-peer lending, there is a great imperative to require disclosure as well as other forms of protection, and unsurprisingly this is what we have seen evolve in the last few years. Another reason for the distinction between loans and bonds, at the point at which the advance is made, is that lenders can negotiate considerable contractual (and proprietary) protection, while those purchasing debt securities take them on terms that are already fixed; again, when this ability to negotiate is effectively removed from lenders in the peer-to-peer market, regulation is required.

These points of difference are, however, not necessarily as strong as they might at first appear, especially as regards syndicated loans. First, many banks and other financial institutions buy loans which have already been made, as well as making loans themselves: there is an active secondary loan market. Second, debt securities are issued on the terms which the market will bear, and large and repeat players in the market are thus able to influence the terms generally, even if not in particular. Yet another reason for the difference in regulatory treatment is said to be the ability of lenders to investigate the borrower before lending, while it is much less cost-effective (and probably less possible) for those buying debt securities to do so. However, at least in relation to syndicated loans, lenders are given standardised disclosure in the form of the information memorandum, in the same way that potential buyers of debt securities are given a prospectus or offering circular. There are considerable similarities between debt securities issued under a programme and a syndicated loan, and it is certainly arguable that the regulatory regimes should be more similar. It can be seen, though, that where there are most similarities, in the secondary trading market, some element of self-regulation is emerging in relation to potential market abuse in the shape of industry guidelines in the secondary loan market.

As regards the regulatory regime for debt securities, this can be seen to have been influenced partly by a desire to provide some protection for investors in the market, in a way similar to the regulation of the equity markets, and partly by a desire to attract issuers of debt securities from all over the world to issue and list in the UK. This balance has led to a complex system, riddled with exceptions and distinctions. Given that most investors in debt securities have in the recent past been sophisticated investors, the approach of only requiring limited disclosure appears to be justified. The opening up of the bond market to more retail investors[382] has led to more technical guidance about the comprehensibility of

---

[381] Benjamin: Financial Law, 10.2.4.
[382] See 2.3.3.2.

retail prospectuses, but no substantive change in the law: in the end, even retail investors will have to protect themselves either by taking care themselves or by relying on (regulated) financial advisors.

There is, however, another justification for the difference between the debt securities and the equity securities regimes: debt and equity are inherently different. Debt holders have an ultimate right to sue for the amount due to them, while shareholders merely have a hope of gain, thus necessitating greater regulatory protection. In relation to continuing disclosure, this has the effect that every new piece of information is relevant to the shareholders (and therefore to the price of shares), while new pieces of information are only relevant to bondholders if they throw light on the credit risk of the issuer and if the bondholder either wants to sell the bond (as opposed to keeping it until maturity) or, in extremis, to enforce. Despite this difference, in relation to trading in the secondary market there are now considerable similarities between the regulation of equity securities and that of debt securities, particularly in relation to transparency and market abuse.

14

Takeovers

14.1 Introduction

A takeover bid is an offer by a bidder (usually a company) for shares in the target, in exchange for cash, or for securities of the bidder, or a mixture of the two. The offer is made by the bidder company to the shareholders in the target company, not to the directors of the target. There is, therefore, no obvious act of the target company upon which company law can fasten. As a result, many countries leave takeovers to be dealt with by way of securities regulation. In the UK, as this chapter will examine, takeover regulation has been developed within both company law and securities law.

The core transaction is between the bidder and the target company's shareholders, and potentially only between the bidder and a proportion of the target company's shareholders large enough to give the bidder control. A takeover will have implications for others in the company, however, because the purpose of the takeover is generally not merely a transfer of shares to the bidder but also, crucially, a transfer of control. Depending on the nature of the company, a takeover can have significant implications for the directors of the company, for the minority shareholders in the target, and for other stakeholders in the target, such as employees. The takeover may also have implications for the shareholders in the bidder company.

A takeover may be contrasted with other scenarios in which control passes to new share-holders in a company, for example as a result of the company issuing or re-purchasing shares, or where the change of control is effected via a scheme of arrangement.[1] In these scenarios a corporate decision is involved—that is, the directors take a decision for the company which is then voted on by the shareholders.[2] It is the absence of a corporate decision, and the fact that the bidder makes its offer to the target shareholders, that makes takeovers unique, and justifies their separate treatment.[3]

This chapter considers the regulatory structure in place in the UK to deal with takeovers, and analyses the substantive law governing takeovers in the UK. As with other chapters in this book, the effectiveness of the current UK regime is assessed. In order to assess its effectiveness, some consideration must first be given to what the regime is trying to achieve.

---

[1] Schemes of arrangement are discussed in detail in chapter 15.

[2] In the case of schemes of arrangement, there is also the involvement of the court: see 15.2.

[3] For a discussion of UK and European takeovers in practice see M Martynova and L Renneboog, 'The Performance of the European Market for Corporate Control: Evidence from the Fifth Takeover Wave' (2011) 17 *European Financial Management* 208.

14.1.1 Objectives of the Takeover Regulation

One possible goal of takeover regulation might be to optimise the number of takeovers that occur. Academic economists have not been able to establish that takeovers are necessarily a 'good thing', however. Indeed, there is considerable debate about whether takeovers are value maximising or efficient in a general sense. While empirical studies generally show that target shareholders gain significantly from a takeover,[4] it is less clear whether the bidder shareholders gain as a result of the takeover.[5] Some commentators suggest that the gains made by the target shareholders are a result of a redistribution of wealth of some kind, perhaps from the bidder shareholders, or from the other stakeholders in the target firm, such as long-term customers, suppliers and employees, rather than any generation of wealth as a result of the takeover.[6] The issue of whether takeovers are broadly wealth maximising remains unclear.

These concerns have not, to date, played an explicit role in determining regulatory objectives in the UK. It is specifically stated in the City Code on Takeovers and Mergers ('the Takeover Code') that it 'is not concerned with the financial or commercial advantages or disadvantages of a takeover'.[7] In the wake of the successful takeover of Cadbury by Kraft in 2010, Lord Mandelson, the then Business Secretary, suggested a number of changes to the takeover regime. These would, in his words, throw some 'extra grit' into the system, on the basis that the existing rules too often failed to create value for people other than advisers and short-term investors.[8] However, the Takeover Panel reiterated its view that the Takeover Code is not concerned with the financial or commercial advantages or disadvantages of a takeover, and that these are matters for the company and its shareholders.[9]

Instead, takeover regulation in different jurisdictions seems to pursue and advance objectives other than value-enhancement per se. Specifically, takeover regimes observable in different jurisdictions often appear to be based on different responses to the agency conflicts that arise in those jurisdictions.[10] Quite distinct issues arise where the shareholdings in the target company are concentrated in the hands of a few shareholders prior to the takeover, as compared with companies in which the shareholdings are dispersed.[11] It is now well understood that dispersed shareholdings are more common in the US and the UK,[12] and block-holdings tend to be the norm elsewhere.[13]

---

[4] For a general discussion of the empirical evidence see R Romano, 'A Guide to Takeovers: Theory, Evidence and Regulation' in KJ Hopt and E Wymeersch (eds), *European Takeovers: Law and Practice* (London, Butterworths, 1992).

[5] Eg, K Fuller, J Netter and M Stegemoller, 'What Do Returns to Acquiring Firms Tell Us? Evidence from Firms That Make Many Acquisitions' (2002) 57 *Journal of Finance* 1763.

[6] For discussion see eg JC Coffee, 'Regulating the Market for Corporate Control: A Critical Assessment of the Tender Offer's Role in Corporate Governance' (1984) 84 *Columbia Law Journal* 1145. This is discussed further in the context of stakeholders in the target company at 14.3.3.

[7] City Code on Takeovers and Mergers (Takeover Code), Introduction, A1.

[8] Lord Mandelson, speech delivered at the annual Trade and Industry dinner, Mansion House, London, 1 March 2010.

[9] Panel Statement 2010/6, *Consultation on Aspects of the Takeover Code*, 1.

[10] See eg R Kraakman et al, *The Anatomy of Corporate Law*, 2nd edn (Oxford, Oxford University Press, 2009) 8.6.

[11] Ibid, ch 8.

[12] This is primarily true of publicly traded companies. Takeovers can occur in companies whose shares are not traded, but they occur much more readily in companies whose shares are publicly traded, and as a result it is takeovers of these companies that will provide the focus for this chapter.

[13] Eg, R La Porta, F Lopez de Silanes and A Shleifer, 'Corporate Ownership Around the World' (1999) 54 *Journal of Finance* 471.

In a company with concentrated ownership, control lies with the blockholder. Therefore, the sale of shares following a successful takeover offer will effect a control shift between the seller and the acquirer. The decision whether the takeover bid is successful lies de facto with the controlling shareholder, and the primary issue for takeover regulation to determine is the need for, and extent of, any protection for the minority shareholders in the target. A detailed discussion of these issues lies outside the remit of this book.[14] By contrast, in a dispersed shareholding scenario such as that prevalent in most UK publicly traded companies, prior to the takeover de facto control of the company is likely to be with the board of directors. Consequently, the takeover results in a control shift from a third party (the directors) to the acquirer.

This disjunction creates two potential problems. The first is the role of the target directors in the bid. The incumbent directors face potentially severe conflicts of interest where a takeover offers gains to the existing shareholders, but threatens their position. The control shift consequent upon a takeover means that, often, incumbent directors will be affected personally. In many scenarios a successful takeover will result in the directors losing their jobs, an outcome they are likely to be more happy or less happy about depending on the size of the compensation package available to them. In a management buy-out (MBO) the directors will keep their jobs, but they will be just as interested in the outcome of the bid on a personal level. Moreover, the target directors are in a position to promote the bid to the shareholders (if it is an MBO, for example), or to take action to defend their position and to try to frustrate the bid. As a result of these factors, one of the key issues to be resolved in a system of dispersed share ownership, such as that in the UK, is whether to give the decision-making power in a takeover situation to the shareholders alone (since it is their shares that will be transferred), sidelining the target directors whose control will be transferred, or whether the decision should be taken by a combination of the directors and shareholders.

The second problem that arises in companies with dispersed share ownership is the fact that the bidder can potentially exploit the position of small, dispersed shareholders. The bidder can 'divide and conquer', exploiting the coordination problems that inevitably arise in such scenarios. Left to its own devices, the bidder could enter into preferential deals with some shareholders, in order to gain de facto control of the target. The bidder could then put pressure on the remaining shareholders to accept a reduced offer, the alternative for the shareholders being to remain minority shareholders in the company, with the acquirer now in charge. Consequently, another issue for takeover regulation is whether, and to what extent, to step in and regulate the relationship between the bidder and the target shareholders.[15]

These two issues, namely the amount of interference allowed by target directors in the outcome of the bid, and the amount of freedom allowed to the bidder when dealing with the target shareholders, are regarded as the two core issues for UK takeover regulation to determine, though other issues do exist. These issues could be left to the general law to address—that is, contract law, company law and securities law. However, as discussed in

---

[14] For an overview of these issues see R Kraakman et al, *The Anatomy of Corporate Law*, 2nd edn (Oxford, Oxford University Press, 2009) 8.3.

[15] In companies with concentrated share ownership similar issues exist for the minority shareholders, and the question arises as to whether they should have a right of exit when a takeover leads to a control shift, and if so, at what price.

this chapter, a significant layer of takeover regulation has been put in place to supplement the general law relating to these issues. In the UK, the first issue is resolved resoundingly in favour of the shareholders: one of the primary aims of the UK regime is to put the shareholders in the target company in control of the bid. The target directors are sidelined in this decision. The resolution of the second issue is also shareholder driven, as the UK takeover regime aims to ensure that the bidder treats all the shareholders in the target company equally.

14.1.2 Comparative Aspects

Although the focus of this chapter, in common with the rest of this book, is on the UK position, a comparison with other jurisdictions is particularly helpful in order to understand why the UK system of takeover regulation is shaped as it is, and to assess the success of this model. The implementation of the 2004 European Takeover Directive[16] has resulted in a substantial degree of harmonisation within Europe regarding the second of the core issues identified above, namely the amount of freedom given to the bidder when dealing with the target shareholders. Despite the directive needing to provide rules for one dispersed shareholding system (the UK) and many block-holding systems, the harmonised rules on this issue in the directive are based on the UK model.[17] More divergence exists on the first of the core issues identified above, namely the role of the target directors in a bid.[18] Some Member States follow the UK model, and give the decision whether to accept the bid to the shareholders. Others, most notably Germany and the Netherlands, retain a significant role in the decision-making process for the directors.

These differences between the UK's takeover regime and those of other Member States are interesting, and important. However, given that the focus of this chapter is an analysis of UK takeover law based on an assessment of how well it addresses the agency issues which arise in this context, a more useful comparison for assessing the UK regime is the US, since these are the two major jurisdictions that display dispersed share ownership patterns within their publicly traded companies. The fact that some US states (most notably Delaware) have adopted different responses to that agency conflict from those adopted in the UK raises questions as to the value of the UK regime.[19] In particular, while the UK regime gives the decision on the bid to the shareholders, in Delaware that decision-making role is allocated to the target directors in combination with the target shareholders.[20]

---

[16] 2004/25/EC.

[17] The minority shareholders in companies with concentrated ownership are in a similar position to the dispersed shareholders in UK publicly traded companies as regards this issue, although some of the solutions (eg the mandatory bid rule) have different consequences and costs when used in a concentrated ownership system. As a result many European countries have found ways to adjust the impact of these rules. These issues fall outside the remit of this chapter. For discussion see R Kraakman et al, *The Anatomy of Corporate Law*, 2nd edn (Oxford, Oxford University Press, 2009) ch 8.

[18] For discussion see eg R Skog, 'The Takeover Directive: An Endless Saga' (2002) 13 *European Business Law Review* 301.

[19] For discussion see eg J Dammann, 'The Mandatory Law Puzzle: Redefining American Exceptionalism in Corporate Law' (2014) 65(2) *Hastings Law Journal* 441.

[20] For further discussion see 14.3.2.2.2.

There are a number of reasons why such a strong shareholder-centric model might have been adopted in the UK. The UK system of company law has always been strongly shareholder-centric, particularly when compared to the position in the US, where central-ised management has been the norm. The free transferability of a shareholder's shares is regarded as an important aspect of their rights in the UK and this principle is a core tenet of the regulation of listed company shares in the UK.[21] In the UK, the board's powers have his-torically been seen as deriving from the shareholders. Shareholders have, for example, tra-ditionally had the right to remove directors at any time by ordinary resolution.[22] The other significant corporate governance rights held by UK shareholders are discussed at 11.2.2, and again can be contrasted markedly with the position in the US. In addition, the develop-ment of the system of takeover regulation in the UK coincided with a rise in institutional shareholder power. This is in sharp contrast to the development of the takeover regime in the US, and it may well be that these differences help to explain the marked contrasts in approach observable within the two systems today.[23] The next section therefore discusses the development of takeover regulation in the UK, in order to help to explain the regulation that has been put in place. The following sections then examine the substance of UK take-over regulation, comparing it, where relevant, to other jurisdictions, in particular the US.

14.2 The Regulatory Structure of Takeover Regulation in the UK

In the UK, takeovers are regulated by the Takeover Code, a body of rules that is written and administered by the Panel on Takeovers and Mergers ('the Takeover Panel').[24] For many years the Takeover Panel was an independent, self-regulating body set up by the main City institutions and organisations with an involvement in public company takeovers.[25] This system has now been underpinned by statute as a consequence of the UK's implementation of the Takeover Directive,[26] but this implementation was designed with the express objec-tive of maintaining the prior self-regulatory approach of the UK's takeover regulation to the greatest extent possible. To understand the current position regarding takeover regulation in the UK, it is necessary to appreciate the historical development of this system.

---

[21] FCA Handbook, LR 2.2.4. For companies listed on AIM see London Stock Exchange, *AIM Rules for Compa-nies*, May 2014, r 32.

[22] For the current incarnation of this rule see Companies Act 2006, s 168.

[23] J Armour and DA Skeel, Jr, 'Who Writes the Rules of Hostile Takeovers, and Why? The Peculiar Divergence of US and UK Takeover Regulation' (2009) 95 *Georgetown Law Journal* 1727; G Miller, 'Political Structure and Corporate Governance: Some Points of Contrast between the United States and England' [1998] *Columbia Business Law Review* 51.

[24] See, now, Companies Act 2006, Part 28.

[25] This self-regulatory model was undoubtedly developed in the face of clear threats of government interven-tion, should that be necessary, and has, therefore, been referred to as 'coerced self-regulation': J Black, 'Constitu-tionalising Self-Regulation' (1996) 59 *Modern Law Review* 24. For discussion of the UK model see J Armour and DA Skeel, 'Who Writes the Rules of Hostile Takeovers, and Why? The Peculiar Divergence of US and UK Takeover Regulation' (2009) 95 *Georgetown Law Journal* 1727, 1756–65.

[26] Directive 2004/25/EC (for analysis see J Rickford, 'The Emerging European Takeover Law from a British Perspective' [2004] *European Business Law Review* 1379). For the UK implementation of this Directive, see Companies Act 2006, Part 28.

14.2.1 Historical Development

The regulation of takeovers in the UK developed separately to the regulation of the securities markets.[27] The first set of rules was published in 1959,[28] followed by the first City Code on Takeovers and Mergers in 1968. These rules were drawn up in response to a wave of hostile takeovers which took place in the early 1950s. Takeovers were considered sharp practice at that time and they outraged both directors and the City establishment, who believed that takeovers were harmful for industry.[29] The first set of rules, drawn up in 1959, was not initiated or controlled by directors, however, but by a committee comprising representatives of merchant banks, institutional investors, the largest commercial banks and the London Stock Exchange. As a result, it is not surprising that the focus of these rules was not on securing the position of directors and managers, but on safeguarding the interests of the shareholders.

The 1959 guidelines were brief by modern Takeover Code standards, but they nevertheless firmly established shareholder primacy, the core principle of modern UK takeover regulation, at their centre. The guidelines emphasised that there should be no interference with the free market for shares, and that it was for shareholders themselves to decide whether to sell. Shareholders were also to be given enough information and time to make an informed decision.[30]

These guidelines were well received, and were revised and improved in 1963.[31] A significant weakness in these guidelines, however, was the lack of any mechanism for adjudication and enforcement. This was remedied in 1968. In addition to a new, and far more comprehensive, set of takeover rules, a new body was established with the task of adjudicating disputes about the application of the rules: the Takeover Panel. Until 2006 the Takeover Panel had no statutory authority, and relied for its authority on the fact that its membership represented the main parties with a material interest in takeovers.[32] The Takeover Panel's success as a regulator, therefore, depended to a large extent on the recognition that those involved in takeovers gave to it. At this time 'the City of London prided itself upon being a village community, albeit of a unique kind, which could regulate itself by pressure of professional opinion.'[33]

This short historical overview provides two insights into the development of UK takeover regulation. First, it helps to explain the shareholder-focused rather than management-focused approach that is in evidence in the UK. The Code that emerged in 1968 was

---

[27] Takeover regulation in the UK developed before the statutory regulation of the securities markets (described in chapters 10–13).

[28] Issuing Houses Association, *Notes on Amalgamation of British Businesses* (1959). For discussion see A Johnston, *The City Takeover Code* (Oxford, Oxford University Press, 1980) ch 3.

[29] For a discussion of the history of UK takeover regulation see A Johnston, 'Takeover Regulation: Historical and Theoretical Perspectives on the City Code' (2007) 66 *Cambridge Law Journal* 422; J Armour and DA Skeel, 'Who Writes the Rules of Hostile Takeovers, and Why? The Peculiar Divergence of US and UK Takeover Regulation' (2007) 95 *Georgetown Law Journal* 1727, 1756–65.

[30] Issuing Houses Association, *Notes on Amalgamation of British Businesses* (October 1958).

[31] Issuing Houses Association, *Revised Notes on Amalgamation of British Businesses* (October 1963).

[32] In addition to the chairman and deputy chairmen, the Panel consists of up to 20 members appointed by the Panel and individuals appointed by representative bodies of those involved in takeovers: Takeover Code, Introduction, A8.

[33] *R v Panel of Takeovers and Mergers ex p Datafin plc* [1987] QB 815, 835 per Sir John Donaldson MR.

significantly longer and more specific than the guidelines drawn up in 1958, but at its core it retained the concept of shareholder choice, and supplemented it with a general ban on frustrating actions by directors. This has formed the basis for the Takeover Code ever since. It is no coincidence that this shareholder-friendly model was drawn up by City institutions, and, importantly, by institutional investors who have a clear interest in rules that maximise expected gains to shareholders.[34]

By contrast, institutional investors have played a much smaller role in the development of US takeover regulation.[35] In the US, takeover regulation is only minimally the product of federal law,[36] and therefore US takeover regulation is, to a large extent, the product of state legislatures.[37] Commentators have demonstrated that state takeover legislation is a fertile ground for lobbyists in the managerial cause.[38] This is in sharp contrast to the UK position, where manager-friendly groups have had little or no part to play in the development of takeover regulation. Managers appear to have had a politically stronger and more influential role in the development of US takeover law than is observable in the UK, and this seems likely to have influenced the development of the two systems, with the US system developing in a more manager-friendly direction and the UK more shareholder-focused.

Second, this historical overview helps to explain the self-regulatory model adopted in the UK, and the relative informality of the approach adopted by the Takeover Panel. From the outset the Takeover Panel's members included representatives from the Stock Exchange, the Bank of England, the major merchant banks, and institutional investors. A decision was taken early in the Takeover Panel's existence that proactive involvement in takeover bids was better than an ex post judicial approach.[39] This is in keeping with the fact that the Takeover Panel constitutes primarily business people, rather than lawyers, and that the staff consists mainly of business and financial experts. Speed and efficiency have been at the centre of the Takeover Panel's regulatory regime, with a clear timetable for bids established from an early stage. It has also been fundamental to the operation of the Takeover Panel that it should address takeover issues as they arise in real time, imposing little or no delay on the progress of the bid.

This contrasts with the position in the US, where takeover regulation is administered by the SEC and by the courts. Far more takeover regulation is left to general corporate and fiduciary law principles in the US[40] than in the UK where, as discussed in 14.3, a significant amount of specialised takeover regulation has been put in place to supplement general corporate law principles. A consequence of the US position is that many of the rules that

---

[34] Institutional investors have also been active in other areas of corporate law in drawing up pro-shareholder rules: see 11.2.2.2.

[35] J Armour and DA Skeel, 'Who Writes the Rules of Hostile Takeovers, and Why? The Peculiar Divergence of US and UK Takeover Regulation' (2007) 95 *Georgetown Law Journal* 1727, 1767–76.

[36] Eg, 1968 Williams Act, 82 Stat 454, codified at 15 USC §§78m(d)–(e) and 78n(d)–(f), adding new §§ 13(d), 13(e) and 14(d)–(f) to the Securities Act 1934.

[37] For a detailed account of the transformation of the corporate governance landscape in the US over the past four decades see B Cheffins, 'Delaware and the Transformation of Corporate Governance' *Delaware Journal of Corporate Law* (forthcoming), http://papers.ssrn.com/sol3/papers.cfm?abstract_id=2531640.

[38] LA Bebchuk and A Ferrell, 'Federalism and Corporate Law: The Race to Protect Managers from Takeovers' (1999) 99 *Columbia Law Review* 1168.

[39] Panel on Takeovers and Mergers, Report on the year ended 31st March 1969, 4.

[40] Federal law (eg the 1968 Williams Act) and state law (eg Delaware puts in place some rules governing squeeze-out mergers) do create some specific takeover rules.

regulate takeovers in the US are judge-made, rather than developed by a regulator such as the Takeover Panel.[41] In addition, if a takeover bidder in the US is unhappy with some aspect of the bid, it will generally take the matter to the courts, resulting in a number of weeks of delay, or longer if the matter is then appealed. In the UK, a hostile bidder unhappy with the behaviour of the target's directors can lodge a protest with the Takeover Panel, which will then issue a ruling as appropriate.[42] The speed and efficiency of the manner in which the Takeover Panel deals with bids is regarded as a significant advantage of the UK system.

The advantages of the UK's system of takeover regulation when compared to traditional top-down regulation seem clear. The Takeover Panel is able to react quickly to perceived abuses, and the changes made to the Takeover Code over time reveal the Takeover Panel's ability to deal flexibly and responsively with changing circumstances.[43] The nature of the regime, in particular its self-regulatory origins, also means that it has commanded the broad assent of those who are regulated by the Takeover Panel.

Given the perceived advantages of the UK system, the requirement to harmonise UK takeover regulation with that of Europe, via implementation of the Takeover Directive,[44] was a potential concern. The next section will consider the implementation of the Takeover Directive into UK law and explain that the implementation has not undermined any of the perceived advantages of the UK system.

14.2.2 Implementation of the Takeover Directive

The Takeover Directive was adopted in 2004 and required implementation by May 2006. The implementation of the directive in the UK is achieved via the Companies Act 2006.

Prior to the implementation of the directive, a number of different takeover regimes were observable throughout Europe. This is unsurprising given that takeover regulation appears to respond to the different agency conflicts observable in different regimes.[45] As might be expected, these differences were particularly acute when comparing the UK with other European jurisdictions.[46] For some time these differences threatened to prevent agreement being reached on the final form of the directive. A compromise was finally reached, however, allowing Member States to opt out of certain substantive provisions of the directive.[47] These opt-outs allowed Member States to customise the implementation of the Takeover

---

[41] It has been suggested that the fact that the US rules are largely judge-made has made it easier for a pro-management approach to emerge: J Armour and DA Skeel, 'Who Writes the Rules of Hostile Takeovers, and Why? The Peculiar Divergence of US and UK Takeover Regulation' (2007) 95 *Georgetown Law Journal* 1727, 1793.

[42] A party unhappy with a ruling from the Panel's Executive can appeal to the Panel's Hearings Committee. A party to a hearing before the Hearing Committee may appeal to the Takeover Appeal Board, an independent body whose chairman and deputy chairman will usually have held high judicial office and whose members are experienced in takeovers: Takeover Code, Introduction, A12–A17.

[43] For discussion see A Johnston, 'Takeover Regulation: Historical and Theoretical Perspectives on the City Code' (2007) 66 *Cambridge Law Journal* 422, 442–48.

[44] Directive 2004/25/EC.

[45] See the discussion in 14.1.

[46] As discussed in 14.1, the UK generally has dispersed shareholdings within its publicly traded companies whereas in Continental Europe block-holdings are more common.

[47] Directive 2004/25/EC, arts 9, 11.

Directive to some extent. From the UK's perspective the combination of these opt-outs, together with the fact that most of the compulsory aspects of the directive were based on the existing UK regime, meant that the implementation of the directive led to very few *substantive* changes to UK takeover regulation.[48] Certainly, the implementation of the regime did not interfere with the strong shareholder-centric model of takeover regulation in place in the UK prior to implementation. The substance of UK takeover regulation is considered in 14.3.

The remainder of this section considers the effect of the Takeover Directive on the *procedural* aspects of the UK's takeover regime, and assesses the extent to which the self-regulatory model in evidence prior to implementation has survived. Key to retaining the benefits of the existing regime was the preservation of the role and status of the Takeover Panel and of the existing position regarding tactical litigation.

14.2.3 Role and Status of the Takeover Panel

The UK Government had concerns about the effect of some of the directive's provisions on the UK's regulatory regime, and in particular on the role and status of the Takeover Panel.[49] Amendments to the directive were therefore made during the drafting process in order to try to allay these fears. The implementation of the directive introduced changes to the UK's takeover regime, principally the fact that the Takeover Panel and the Takeover Code are now on a statutory footing.[50] However, the role and function of both remain largely unchanged. As regards the Takeover Code, prior to implementation it had a wide remit, wider indeed than that of the directive.[51] This wide remit has been retained. As a result, the Takeover Code applies, inter alia, to public offers to the holders of securities on a regulated market, such as the LSE's Main Market, and exchange-regulated markets, such as AIM, and indeed to all public companies, whether they have securities traded on a public market or not.[52] It also applies to other transactions which are analogous to public offers, such as schemes of arrangement.[53]

As regards the Takeover Panel, its status and composition remain unchanged by the implementation of the directive.[54] It retains its two core functions, namely rule-making

---

[48] For discussion see DTI, *Company Law Implementation of the European Directive on Takeover Bids* (URN 05/11, January 2005).

[49] Ibid.

[50] Companies Act 2006, ss 942–65. Takeover Directive 2004/25/EC, art 4.1 specifically permits the supervisory authority to be a private body, such as the Takeover Panel, although that private body needs to be 'recognised by national law', hence the need for the Takeover Panel to be put on a statutory footing.

[51] The scope of the Takeover Code is wider than that of the Takeover Directive 2004/25/EC, which applies only to public offers to the holders of securities in the target company where those securities are traded on a regulated market in the EEA and where the objective of the offer is to secure control of the target company: Directive 2004/25/EC, arts 1(1) and 2(1)(a). For discussion of situations where the Takeover Directive requires jurisdiction over a bid to be shared between different jurisdictions see Gower and Davies, 28-16.

[52] Takeover Code, Introduction, A3–A5.

[53] Ibid, Introduction, A3–A7. For schemes of arrangement see Appendix 7 (for discussion see PCP 2007/1, *Schemes of Arrangement*). The use of schemes of arrangement as an alternative to a takeover offer is discussed further in chapter 15.

[54] Ibid, Introduction, A8.

(writing the Takeover Code and keeping it up to date)[55] and a judicial function (giving rulings on the interpretation, application or effect of the rules).[56] In addition, the Companies Act 2006 provides the Takeover Panel with a right to require disclosure of information where this is 'reasonably required in connection with the exercise by the Panel of its functions'.[57]

The sanctions available to the Takeover Panel were altered slightly by the implementation of the directive. Initially, the self-regulatory nature of the Takeover Panel was evident in the sanctions it had available to it to ensure compliance with the Takeover Code. These were primarily of an informal nature: private reprimand or public censure, and a requirement that the institutions represented on the Takeover Panel withdraw the facilities of the securities market from the offender. In some circumstances the Takeover Panel can also require individuals to make compensation payments.[58] Subsequently, these sanctions have been bolstered by regulations made under FSMA, which allowed the Takeover Panel to report conduct to the regulator (initially the FSA, now the FCA).[59] In particular, FSMA introduced a 'cold-shouldering' provision which enables the FCA to target bidders and their directors indirectly via their advisers.[60] Cold-shouldering involves advisers within the scope of the FCA's powers being required not to deal with those who are likely not to observe the Takeover Code. As a result, companies that act, or are likely to act, in breach of the Takeover Code can be denied the facilities of the City of London in relation to takeover bids.[61] In addition, the 2006 Act provided the Takeover Panel with new enforcement mechanisms, such as a power to apply to the court where a person has contravened, or is reasonably likely to contravene, a requirement imposed by or under the Takeover Code, or has failed to comply with a disclosure requirement.[62]

It can be seen that, following implementation of the directive, the Takeover Panel retains its central role in the supervision of takeover bids in the UK. Despite it now being on a statutory footing, the Takeover Panel's status and role are otherwise largely unchanged.

---

[55] The Panel's powers to make rules are very widely formulated: Companies Act 2006, ss 943(2)(3), 944(1). Responsibility for the rules is assigned to a Code Committee of the Panel: Takeover Code, Introduction, A9–A10.

[56] Companies Act 2006, s 945. The Panel also has the power to make directions to ensure compliance with the rules: s 946. As a result of the introduction of the Human Rights Act 1998 the Panel's judicial and rule-making functions have been separated (for example, membership of the Panel's Code Committee and Hearings Committee does not overlap: Takeover Code, Introduction, A10).

[57] Companies Act 2006, s 947(3). See generally Companies Act 2006, ss 947–49 and Sch 2.

[58] In 1989, for example, the Takeover Panel required Guinness plc to pay compensation of around £85 million to former shareholders of the Distillers Company for breaches of the Takeover Code in failing to make a cash alternative available to them at the level required by the Takeover Code: see Panel Statement 1989/13 (The Distillers Company plc, 14 July 1989). This power is now contained in Companies Act 2006, s 954 (and see Takeover Code, Introduction, A19).

[59] The Companies Act 2006 retained these sanctions and placed them on a statutory footing: Companies Act 2006, s 952 (and see Takeover Code, Introduction, A20–A21).

[60] FCA Handbook, MAR 4.3. Direct sanctions against the directors of the bidder are not generally available to the FCA because the takeover itself is not an activity requiring FCA authorisation. However, the FCA does have oversight of the advisers to the bidder, most notably the investment banks, who need the FCA's authorisation in order to carry on their professional activities within the financial services sector.

[61] For an example see Takeover Appeal Board Statement 2010/1.

[62] Companies Act 2006, s 955. In addition, the Act created a new criminal offence for a person who knew (or was reckless as to the fact) that offer documentation did not comply with the Takeover Code's requirements and failed to take reasonable steps to ensure compliance: s 953. This offence only applies to offers for target companies whose voting securities are quoted on a regulated market: s 953(1).

14.2.4 Tactical Litigation

The ability of the Takeover Panel to make decisions in real time in relation to a bid is preserved post-2006. As discussed, the Takeover Panel's ability to give speedy, binding rulings in the course of the bid is regarded as one of the advantages of the UK system. The opportunities for the bid to be slowed down, or frustrated entirely, by tactical litigation have traditionally been very small.[63] Because there is a clear timetable laid down within which bids are to occur within the UK, as discussed in 14.3.1, delays caused by tactical litigation could effectively cause a bid to fail without the shareholders having had the chance to decide for themselves. Before the implementation of the directive there was a system of internal speedy appeal within the Takeover Panel itself. This system is retained,[64] so that decisions of the Takeover Panel Executive, giving rulings in the course of a bid, can be appealed to a Hearings Committee of the Takeover Panel in the first instance.[65]

In addition, it is accepted that the Takeover Panel's decisions are subject to judicial review.[66] The courts have, however, established narrow limits within which any judicial review of a Takeover Panel decision will operate.[67]

It is expected that parties will still have to abide by Takeover Panel rulings, even if they have indicated an intention to seek judicial review.[68] Crucially, the courts to date have been content to carry out a retrospective review of the Takeover Panel's decisions. The courts will only intervene after a bid has been concluded, and will only act to provide guidance as to how the Takeover Panel should proceed in future cases, or to relieve individuals of disciplinary sanctions. Importantly, the courts have not interfered in the course of an existing

[63] The Panel has made it clear that in general litigation designed to frustrate an offer is not acceptable. In the decision in relation to Consolidated Gold Fields plc (Panel notice 1989/7, Consolidated Gold Fields plc, 2 May 1989) the Panel ruled that the target directors should not continue litigation in the US to restrain the bid.

[64] Companies Act 2006, s 951.

[65] Takeover Code, Introduction, A12–A16. There is then the possibility of appeal to the Takeover Appeal Board, an independent body whose chairman and deputy chairman will usually have held high judicial office and whose other members will be experienced in takeovers (Takeover Code, Introduction, A16–A17). The Government considered and rejected the idea of setting up a bespoke judicial mechanism to hear issues arising from takeover proceedings: DTI, *Company Law Implementation of the European Directive on Takeover Bids: A Consultation Document* (URN 05/11, January 2005). Such a bespoke system was not required by the directive. As far as the Takeover Directive (2004/25/EC) is concerned, judicial review is required 'in appropriate circumstances' (preamble para 7) but art 4(6) leaves it to Member States to decide whether and under what circumstances the parties to a bid are entitled to bring proceedings. Article 4 also provides that the directive will not affect the power that the courts have in Member States to decline to hear legal proceedings and to decide which legal proceedings affect the outcome of the bid.

[66] *R v Panel on Takeovers and Mergers ex p Datafin* [1987] QB 815.

[67] In *Datafin* (ibid) the court established narrow parameters for a judicial review of the Panel. It was stated that 'there is little scope for complaint that the panel has promulgated rules which are ultra vires, provided only that they do not clearly violate the principle proclaimed by the panel of being based upon the concept of doing equity between one shareholder and another. This is a somewhat unlikely eventuality' (at 841 per Sir John Donaldson MR). When it comes to interpreting its own rules, the Panel 'must clearly be given considerable latitude' (at 841), primarily because, as legislator, it could change the rules at any time. Even where the court felt there was legitimate cause for complaint, the Court of Appeal in *Datafin* felt that the most appropriate response would be for the court to declare the true meaning of the rule, leaving it to the Panel to promulgate a new rule accurately expressing its intentions. Challenges to the Panel's power to grant dispensation from its rules are likely to be successful only in 'wholly exceptional' circumstances (at 841). Finally, in relation to the Panel's exercise of its disciplinary powers, the court would be 'reluctant to move in the absence of any credible allegation of lack of bona fides' (at 841). See also *Re Expro International Group plc* [2008] EWHC 1543 (Ch).

[68] *R v Panel on Takeovers and Mergers ex p Datafin* [1987] QB 815, 840–41.

bid.[69] On this basis there is very little to be gained by a party making use of litigation in the course of a takeover.

Although the judicial and appeal structure in the UK was left effectively unchanged as a result of the implementation of the directive, there was nevertheless a concern that the implementation, and in particular the new statutory footing for the Takeover Code and the Takeover Panel, might lead to an increase in tactical litigation. Various measures were put in place to try to prevent this outcome. To counteract any possibility of a new breach of statutory duty claim arising from the fact that the Takeover Panel is now a statutory body, the Companies Act 2006 specifically excludes this possibility.[70] The Takeover Panel is also given immunity from liability in damages akin to that which exists for the FCA.[71] The Act also addresses the possibility that parties may try to challenge a takeover after the event, and seeks to prevent this from occurring by providing that any contravention of any rule-based requirement does not render a transaction void or unenforceable.[72]

One further concern that has been raised relates to the grounds for judicial review. Prior to the directive, the courts had stated that arguments based on the view that the Takeover Panel had propounded rules that were ultra vires were unlikely to succeed. Might the move to place the Takeover Panel on a statutory footing alter this approach? To a large extent the wording of the Companies Act 2006 seeks to avoid future ultra vires actions by providing the Takeover Panel with very wide powers. The Takeover Panel may 'do anything that it considers necessary or expedient for the purposes of, or in connection with, its functions'.[73] As long as the courts continue to apply the same line in judicial review cases that they have maintained to date—that is, not to overturn a Takeover Panel decision or otherwise interfere in the course of a bid—it seems likely that tactical litigation will remain of little value to the parties to a bid. Nothing in the directive requires the courts to alter their existing policy in this regard[74] and there is no reason to believe that the courts will adopt a different approach in the future. This was the aim of the Government when implementing the directive.[75]

14.2.5 Summary

Despite the implementation of the Takeover Directive, which caused the Takeover Panel and the Takeover Code to be put on a statutory footing, the self-regulatory regime put in place in 1968 is still very much in evidence in the UK's takeover regime. The Takeover

---

[69] See *Datafin*, ibid; *R v Panel of Takeovers and Mergers ex p Guinness plc* [1990] 1 QB 146; *R v Panel of Takeovers and Mergers ex p Fayed* [1992] BCC 524.

[70] Companies Act 2006, s 956(1).

[71] Ibid, s 961 (as regards the Panel); FSMA, s 102 (regarding the FCA). This immunity does not extend to situations where the Panel is in bad faith or where there is a claim against it for breach of s 6(1) of the Human Rights Act 1998 (Companies Act 2006, s 961(3)).

[72] Ibid, s 956(2). It is intended that transactions can only be unravelled after the event for misrepresentation or fraud, as was the case prior to the Companies Act 2006.

[73] Companies Act 2006, s 942(2). See also ss 943, 944(1) and 945.

[74] See Takeover Directive 2004/25/EC, art 4(6) which permits the British courts to retain their existing stance in this regard.

[75] DTI, *Company Law Implementation of the European Directive on Takeover Bids* (URN 05/11, January 2005), para 2.38.

Directive did not require any significant changes to the provisions of the Takeover Code. Indeed, many of the provisions of the directive were modelled on the provisions of the Code, and the composition and discretion of the Takeover Panel are left largely unchanged by the implementation of the directive. The Government's goal of producing a situation in which the Takeover Panel could carry on much as before appears to have been achieved.

This discussion of the development of the UK regime helps to explain two key features of the UK system. First, and most importantly, it helps to explain the shareholder-centric approach adopted by UK takeover regulation, which stands in contrast to the US regime. The strong influence of shareholder-friendly groups in the development of the UK regime contrasts with the influence of manager-friendly lobby groups in the US. The shareholder-focus of the UK regime, and the consequences of adopting that approach, are discussed in the next section. The second feature is the speed of decision-making in the UK regime and the absence of tactical litigation which might otherwise be used to frustrate a bid.

The speed of decision-making is regarded as one of the significant practical benefits of the UK system and it has survived the implementation of the Takeover Directive. The absence of tactical litigation is also an important adjunct to the shareholder-focus of the UK model. The no frustration principle, discussed at 14.3.2.2 below, provides one of the foundation stones of the UK regime, and is intended to ensure that the decision on the bid is taken by the target shareholders. To allow tactical litigation which has the practical effect of frustrating the bid would significantly undermine that principle.

14.3 The Substance of Takeover Regulation in the UK

Having discussed the regulatory structure of the UK takeover regime in the previous section, this section examines the substance of the UK regime. As discussed, the UK regime is strongly shareholder-focused and operates under the twin principles that the decision-making in a bid should be left to the target shareholders, and the target directors should be sidelined (the 'no frustration principle'), and that the bidder should treat all the target shareholders equally.

14.3.1 The Procedure of a Bid

14.3.1.1 Initial Approach

Perhaps the two dominant policies at work regarding the procedure of a bid in the UK are, first, the desire to allow the shareholders of the target to have the decision-making role and for that decision to be as undistorted as possible, and, second, that the target should not be subject to a bid or bid speculation for an excessive period of time.[76]

It may therefore seem surprising that the Takeover Code provides that the offer from the bidder is put forward in the first instance not to the target shareholders, but to the target

---

[76] Takeover Code, GP 6 provides that '[a]n offeree company must not be hindered in the conduct of its affairs for longer than is reasonable by a bid for its securities'.

board or its advisers.[77] This is in order to enable the board to advise the shareholders on the bid, and to obtain independent advice on the bid, both of which the board is required to do by the Takeover Code.[78] Bidders may wish to make an informal approach before committing themselves to a formal offer. Changes introduced in 2010, however, constrain the ability of bidders to do so. In particular, the Takeover Panel became concerned about 'virtual bids' whereby bidders signal an interest in the company, but no firm offer is made. Consequently, the Takeover Code has been amended so that, except with the consent of the Panel, any publicly named potential bidder must, within 28 days, either announce a firm intention to make an offer, announce that it will not make an offer, or apply for an extension of the deadline (jointly with the target company).[79]

There is an obvious danger in this period, before a bid has been publicly announced, of insider dealing by those aware that a bid may be about to occur.[80] The Takeover Code attempts to deal with this issue by requiring that all persons privy to confidential information must treat that information as secret before a bid announcement,[81] and requiring an announcement where secrecy cannot be assured.[82] Despite these measures, various studies commissioned by the regulator into the cleanliness of the UK's market have reported significant levels of unusual price movements prior to takeover announcements for UK listed firms.[83]

14.3.1.2 *Formal Offer*

Once a 'firm intention' announcement is made, the bidder becomes obliged to proceed with the bid and to post a formal offer document to the shareholders within 28 days of the announcement.[84] The formal offer must provide shareholders with a significant amount of information about the bid, the intention being that '[s]hareholders must be given sufficient information and advice to enable them to reach a properly informed decision as to the merits or demerits of an offer'.[85] The Takeover Code sets out in detail the financial and other information which must be made available to the shareholders in order to put them in this position.[86]

---

[77] Takeover Code, r 1(a).

[78] Ibid, r 25.2 and r 3.1 respectively.

[79] Takeover Code, rr 2.6–2.8. This is similar to the pre-existing 'put up or shut up' rules, but whereas the previous provisions placed the onus on the target board to request that the Panel set a time limit, the new rules put the onus on the bidder. For discussion see Code Committee of the Takeover Panel, *Review of Certain Aspects of the Regulation of Takeover Bids*, 2010/22.

[80] UK regulation of insider dealing is discussed in chapter 12, specifically 12.2.2.1 and 12.2.2.3.1. For a discussion of this issue in the US context see A Agrawal and T Nasser, 'Insider Trading in Takeover Targets' (2012) 18 *Journal of Corporate Finance* 598.

[81] Takeover Code, r 2.1.

[82] Ibid, r 2.2.

[83] See eg NB Monteiro, Q Zaman and S Leitterstorf, 'Updated Measures of Market Cleanliness', FSA Occasional Paper No 25, 2007, although a more recent study suggests that the levels of unusual price movements dropped in 2013: 'Why Has the FCA's Market Cleanliness Statistic for Takeover Announcements Decreased since 2009?', FCA Occasional Paper No 4, July 2014, discussed at 12.2.2.3.3.

[84] Takeover Code, rr 2.7, 30.1.

[85] Ibid, r 23.

[86] Ibid, rr 24, 25. As regards the need for a bidder to comply with the FCA's prospectus requirements on a share-exchange offer see FCA Handbook, PR 1.2.2(2) and 1.2.3(3).

As with prospectuses,[87] there is a danger that any profit forecasts included in the information will prove unreliable. Thus, the Takeover Code takes particular care to ensure that the bidder is constrained as to what it can provide, and that shareholders are clear about the assumptions contained in the forecast.[88] Similar issues arise regarding the valuation of assets to be given in connection with an offer.[89] As a general principle, all documents and statements made during the course of an offer 'must be prepared with the highest standards of care and accuracy and the information given must be adequately and fairly presented'.[90] Misstatements in these documents are capable of giving rise to a negligent misstatement claim at common law on the part of the target shareholders, to whom these documents are clearly addressed,[91] alternatively the Takeover Panel has the power to award compensation.[92] Any advertisements connected with an offer which may be used to persuade shareholders to accept the offer made to them are also subject to regulation by the Takeover Code.[93] The Takeover Code attempts to keep high-pressure salesmanship techniques that otherwise might be employed by the bidder to a minimum. However, the bidder will do what it can to encourage the shareholders to accept the offer. One common technique employed by bidders is to hold meetings with institutional shareholders, financial journalists and analysts to explain their position.[94] The Code imposes significant restrictions on the ability of the bidder to impose conditions on the offer since one of its aims is that the shareholders should have a clear proposition to accept or reject.[95]

---

[87] See 10.5.2.2.

[88] Takeover Code, r 28.

[89] Ibid, r 29.

[90] Ibid, r 19.1.

[91] *Caparo Industries plc v Dickman* [1990] 2 AC 605. The Court of Appeal in *Morgan Crucible Co plc v Hill Samuel & Co Ltd* [1991] Ch 295 refused to strike out a claim by the bidder against the directors of the target that inaccurate statements made by the target company during the course of the bid had been intended to cause the bidder to raise its bid, which indeed the bidder had done. In *Partco Group Ltd v Wragg* [2002] EWCA Civ 594, however, on similar facts the Court of Appeal expressed doubt that the directors could be said to be liable since, in making the relevant statements, they had acted for the company (now owned by the bidder) and not personally. It seems clear that, in principle, bid documentation can give rise to a claim for negligent misstatement if the claimant can establish that the maker of the statement assumed responsibility for it, and made the statement knowing that it would be made available to a particular person who would rely on it for a particular type of transaction which is known (or ought to be known) to the maker of the statement (see eg *Galoo Ltd v Bright Grahame Murray* [1994] 1 WLR 1360, where the target company's accounts were sent to a potential bidder, and the auditors were aware that the accounts provided by them would be provided to that bidder and relied on by it, and the auditors intended that the bidder should rely).

[92] See Companies Act 2006, s 954 which allows the Panel to award compensation for a breach of a rule. More generally, s 952 gives the Takeover Panel power to develop a range of penalties akin to those of the FCA (for discussion see 10.6.3.2). The FCA's powers are not available in this context since the bid documentation, even in relation to a share-for share exchange, does not amount to a prospectus: PR 1.2.2(2) and 1.2.3(3).

[93] Takeover Code, r 19.4. This rule attempts to regulate not only advertisements in the press, on television, radio, video etc but also those circumstances in which shareholders are contacted by representatives of the bidder to try to persuade them to accept the offer (r 19.5, and see also r 4.3 regarding approaches to private individuals or small corporate shareholders).

[94] These are allowed, despite the potential breach of r 20.1 of the Takeover Code (which provides that '[i]nformation about parties to an offer must be made equally available to all offeree company shareholders and persons with information rights as nearly as possible at the same time and in the same manner'), provided that no new material is disclosed and no significant new opinions are expressed (see Takeover Code, Notes on r 20.1).

[95] See Takeover Code, r 13. Rules 13.1 and 13.3, for example, make it clear that the bidder must not make an offer unless financing is already in place (and see also GP 5). However, one exception to this is that the bidder may make the offer conditional on the obtaining of shareholder approval from its own shareholders to allow a fresh issue of shares in the bidder to be used to fund the bid (see Takeover Code, Notes on rr 13.1 and 13.3).

One condition that will always be present in a bid, because it is required by the Takeover Code, is that an offer for voting securities will be conditional on acceptances being secured by the bidder sufficient to give it, together with securities already held, 50 per cent of the voting rights in the target.[96] An important stage in any bid is, therefore, when it becomes 'unconditional as to acceptances', which means that it has satisfied all of its conditions (including passing the 50 per cent hurdle—or such higher hurdle as the bidder has imposed on the bid) and the bid has effectively succeeded. Once the formal offer documents have been posted to the shareholders, the bid is open to acceptance by the shareholders to whom it is addressed. The offer must be kept open for acceptance for at least 21 days.[97]

Once the offer period is underway, there is a danger that a false market in the target company's shares may be created—a danger that is specifically recognised within the Takeover Code.[98] In addition to the possibility of insider dealing, for example where the bidder comes to believe that its offer will not succeed and therefore seeks to sell its shares at the inflated price caused by the announcement of a bid, there are concerns about market manipulation. For example, the bidder could attempt to rig the market by causing a fall in the target share price, in order to make the offer look more attractive. The bidder could seek to achieve this by selling its own shares in the target. Of course, the usual rules governing insider dealing and market manipulation apply to govern these issues.[99] In addition, the Takeover Code provides some rules to try to prevent such occurrences. For example, it provides that the bidder, and those acting in concert with it, must not sell any securities in the target during the offer period without the consent of the Takeover Panel.[100] The concept of 'acting in concert' is an important one, as the Code attempts to capture not only single bidders acting alone, but also situations where two or more persons cooperate to obtain or consolidate control of a company.[101]

One common feature in many bids is the need for a bidder to revise its initial offer to the shareholders, either because its original offer proves unattractive to the shareholders or to take account of an offer from a rival bidder. At this point the Takeover Code provides that the revised offer must be kept open for a further period of at least 14 days,[102] and any shareholders who had accepted the original offer are entitled to receive the consideration contained in the revised offer.[103]

---

[96] Takeover Code, r 10. The bidder can make the offer conditional on a higher level of acceptances than 50%. In 2010 the Code Committee of the Takeover Panel consulted on whether to raise this figure to, say, 60% or two thirds of the voting rights of the target company, as part of their consideration as to whether it should be harder for hostile bids to succeed, but it ultimately determined that no amendment to the Code should be made in this regard: Code Committee of the Takeover Panel, *Review of Certain Aspects of the Regulation of Takeover Bids*, 2010/22.

[97] Ibid, r 31.1 (this can subsequently be extended). The maximum length of time the offer may remain open for acceptance is until the 60th day after the offer was posted: r 31.6.

[98] Takeover Code, GP 4 states that '[f]alse markets must not be created in the securities of the offeree company, of the offeror company or of any other company concerned by the bid in such a way that the rise or fall of the prices of the securities becomes artificial and the normal functioning of the markets is distorted'.

[99] For discussion see 12.2.

[100] Takeover Code, r 4.2. In addition, during the offer period there are stricter than usual rules in place governing disclosure (see eg Takeover Code, r 8).

[101] For the definition of 'acting in concert' for these purposes see Takeover Code, Definitions section (reflecting Takeover Directive 2004/25/EC, art 2(1)(d)). See ESMA, *Public Statement on Acting In Concert under the Takeover Bids*, ESMA/2013/1642, 12 November 2013. For discussion see M Winner, 'Active Shareholders and European Takeover Regulation' (2014) 11(3) *European Company and Financial Law Review* 364.

[102] Takeover Code, r 32.1.

[103] Ibid, r 32.3.

14.3.1.3 *Squeeze-Out*

In some circumstances the bidder will want to acquire total control of the target. This is particularly common in private equity transactions, where bidders generally want to use the target's assets to secure the loans made to the bidder to finance the bid.[104] One possibility is for the bidder to effect the takeover via a scheme of arrangement which requires a special resolution of the target shareholders, but once approved will bind all the shareholders, including the dissenting minority, to sell their shares.[105] If the change of control is effected via a traditional offer, however, then the squeeze-out rules can help the bidder to acquire 100 per cent of the target.[106] They provide that, where a single class of shares has been bid for, the offeror is entitled to acquire compulsorily the shares of the non-acceptors if the offer has been accepted by at least 90 per cent in value of the shares to which the offer relates.[107] If the shares are voting shares the acceptances also have to represent at least 90 per cent of the voting rights carried by those shares.[108] Where more than one class is bid for, the 90 per cent test is applied to each class separately.[109] A takeover offer is defined for these purposes as one to acquire all the shares[110] of the company (or all the shares of a class) which on the date of the offer the bidder does not already hold and to do so on the same terms for all the shares (or all the shares of a particular class).[111]

The successful bidder triggers the squeeze-out procedure by giving notice to the non-accepting shareholders, accompanied by a statutory declaration of its entitlement to do so,[112] within three months of the last day on which the offer could be accepted.[113] The effect of the notice is that the bidder becomes entitled and bound to acquire the shares on the

---

[104] Private equity is discussed further in chapter 16.

[105] Schemes of arrangement are discussed in detail in chapter 15.

[106] Squeeze-out rules have been present in companies legislation since 1929. The current rules are located in Companies Act 2006, Part 28 Ch 3. These rules also implement Takeover Directive 2004/25/EC, art 15 which required some amendments to the existing law governing takeovers. For discussion of the reforms in the 2006 Act see also Company Law Review Steering Group, *Modern Company Law for a Competitive Economy: Final Report* (URN 01/942–3, July 2001), 282–300.

[107] Companies Act 2006, s 979(2)(a). Note that the 90% figure does not relate to the total number of shares of the class, some of which may be held by the bidder before the bid is launched and which are therefore excluded from the calculation. This includes all shares which the bidder has already contracted to acquire unconditionally: s 975(1). As for conditional acceptances, these do not count towards the 90% except where the promise by the existing holder is to accept the offer when and if it is made (ie an irrevocable undertaking) and the undertaking is given for no significant consideration beyond the promise to make the offer (s 975(1)(2) and see Company Law Review Steering Group, *Modern Company Law for a Competitive Economy: Final Report* (URN 01/942–3, July 2001), paras 13.26–13.42). In addition, s 977(1) excludes from the definition of 'shares to which the offer relates' shares acquired by the bidder after the date of the offer but outside the bid where the bidder offers more than the final offer price for those shares.

[108] Ibid, s 979(2)(b).

[109] Ibid, ss 979(3)(4).

[110] For the definition of 'shares' for this purpose see s 974(4).

[111] Companies Act 2006, ss 974(2)(3). A concession is made as regards the need for the offer to be on the same terms for all shares by s 978, which provides for circumstances in which offers may not be communicated to target shareholders who are foreign residents (see also *Re Joseph Holt plc* [2001] EWCA Civ 770).

[112] Ibid, ss 979(4)–(8). The bidder must also send the documents to the target company: ss 980(4)–(8).

[113] Ibid, ss 980(2)–(3). Where the offer is not governed by the Takeover Code, so that there is no fixed closing date for the offer, the period is six months from the date of the offer.

final terms of the offer.[114] From the bidder's point of view the squeeze-out right is valuable as it prevents the minority exploiting their hold up power in circumstances where the bidder has good reasons to move to 100 per cent ownership. It can, therefore, be regarded as an incentive to bidders.

The effect of the squeeze-out provision is to allow for an expropriation of the shares of the minority, albeit at a fair price, and it is not surprising that the squeeze-out rule is found in legislation rather than in the Takeover Code.[115] Non-accepting shareholders can appeal to the court, objecting to the bidder's right to acquire their shares, or asking for the terms of the acquisition to be amended.[116] The expropriatory nature of these provisions has meant that the courts have tended to construe them strictly when determining whether the bidder has met the requirements for a squeeze-out to occur.[117] Once it is clear that the bidder does fulfil the requirements, however, it is for the petitioner to demonstrate that there should be no acquisition, or that the terms of the offer, such as the offer price, should be amended.[118] On this latter point, if 90 per cent of the shareholders have accepted an offer this will normally be taken by the court as evidence that the offer is fair. The courts may be prepared to amend the offer, however, or to refuse compulsory acquisition completely, if it can be shown that the 90 per cent acceptances should not be taken as an indication of the fairness of the compulsory acquisition offer to the remaining 10 per cent. Examples that emerge from the cases are where the 90 per cent acceptors were not independent of the bidder, or were not given sufficient information on which to make their decision.[119]

14.3.1.4 Sell-Out

The squeeze-out right is mirrored by a sell-out right, which allows the last 10 per cent of shareholders to leave the company rather than remain as minority shareholders.[120] Shareholders can, therefore, refuse the offer initially, with the understanding that if the bidder achieves the 90 per cent threshold, then the shareholder can accept the offer at that point.[121] The bidder must give each non-accepting shareholder notice of their entitlement to be

---

[114] Ibid, s 981(2). If the final offer gave the shareholders alternative choices of consideration then these must also be made available to the non-accepting shareholders in the squeeze-out. If the alternative is no longer available (eg, a non-cash consideration that cannot now be provided either by the bidder or by a third party) then a cash equivalent must be offered: s 981(5) (and see *Re Carlton Holdings Ltd* [1971] 1 WLR 918). One problem arises where the non-accepting shareholders cannot be traced; s 982 provides a solution to this situation.

[115] One consequence is that the Companies Act 2006 has a slightly different ambit from that of the Takeover Code, so that the squeeze-out provisions apply to all companies within the meaning of the Act, including both public and private companies: Companies Act 2006, s 974 and see *Fiske Nominees Ltd v Dwyka Diamond Ltd* [2002] EWHC 770 (Ch).

[116] Companies Act 2006, s 986(1).

[117] Eg, *Re Chez Nico (Restaurants) Ltd* [1992] BCLC 192 where Browne-Wilkinson VC construed the actions of the directors of a company as an invitation to the shareholders to offer to sell their shares to them rather than an 'offer' within the terms of the squeeze-out rules and therefore held that the squeeze-out provisions did not apply.

[118] Companies Act 2006, s 986(4).

[119] *Re Bugle Press Ltd* [1961] Ch 270; *Re Chez Nico (Restaurants) Ltd* [1992] BCLC 192; *Fiske Nominees Ltd v Dwyka Diamond Ltd* [2002] EWHC 770.

[120] The calculation of the 90% threshold operates somewhat differently in squeeze-out and sell-out. In squeeze-out the test is whether there has been a 90% level of acceptances of the offer. In sell-out, by contrast, the test is whether the bid has left the bidder holding 90% of the shares (s 983(1)).

[121] Companies Act 2006, ss 983–985. This is now a requirement of European law: Takeover Directive 2004/25/EC, art 16. For a discussion of the sell-out rule in the European context see *Report of the High Level Group of Experts on Issues Related to Takeover Bids*, Brussels, January 2002, 63.

bought out within one month of the end of the offer period, and shareholders then have three months to take up this right.[122] The effect of the notice is that the bidder is bound to acquire the shares on the final terms of the offer.[123] Either the bidder or a non-accepting shareholder may apply for the court to determine the terms of the offer.[124]

In practice the sell-out remedy is not used a great deal, since the Takeover Code requires the bidder to keep the offer open for a further 14 days once the offer has become unconditional as to acceptances,[125] and this gives shareholders an opportunity to change their mind and accept the offer, without the need to demonstrate that the bidder has reached the 90 per cent threshold, and without the need for court intervention.

The squeeze-out rules perform a potentially valuable function. They allow the bidder to achieve a 100 per cent shareholding in the target without exploitation of the last 10 per cent. They also prevent the minority shareholders exploiting their position where the bidder has good reasons to move to 100 per cent ownership. The reasons for the sell-out right are less clear.[126] Perhaps the best explanation for it is that it is seen as 'a fair counterpart for the squeeze-out right conferred on the majority shareholders and a component of the proportionality of the squeeze-out solution'.[127]

14.3.1.5 Further Offers

Where an offer has not been successful—that is, where it has not become wholly unconditional within the bid timetable, or has been withdrawn or has lapsed—neither the bidder nor any person in concert with it may make another offer for the target company within the next 12 months.[128] Further, if a person or concert party holds 50 per cent or more of the voting rights, it must not, within six months of the closure of the offer, make a second offer or acquire any shares from the shareholders on better terms than those under the previous offer.[129]

14.3.2 Relationship Between the Target Directors and the Target Shareholders

One of the fundamental issues which any system of takeover regulation needs to address is whether the decision to accept the bid should be left to the target shareholders alone, or whether the decision is one for both the target shareholders and target directors. From the

---

[122] Ibid, ss 984(1)–(4). There are criminal sanctions for the bidder and any officer in default: ss 984(5)–(7).
[123] Ibid, s 985.
[124] Ibid, s 986.
[125] Takeover Code, r 31.4.
[126] The Winter Group suggested three possible explanations for the sell-out right: protection of minority shareholders against abuse by the new controller; protection for the minority given the illiquid nature of the market for selling their shares; and promotion of undistorted choice by the shareholders (see 14.3.4 for further discussion of these issues): *Report of the High Level Group of Experts on Issues Related to Takeover Bids*, Brussels, January 2002. However, Professor Davies has doubted whether any of these explanations holds water: P Davies, 'The Notion of Equality in European Takeover Regulation' in J Payne (ed), *Takeovers in English and German Law* (Oxford, Hart Publishing, 2002) 21.
[127] *Report of the High Level Group of Experts on Issues Related to Takeover bids*, ibid, 62.
[128] Takeover Code, r 35.1.
[129] Ibid, r 35.3.

outset, the UK has given the decision to the target shareholders. The Takeover Directive gave Member States the option of opting out of the principle that shareholders should be the decision-makers on the bid. Unsurprisingly, given the UK's long adherence to this principle, the UK did not take up this opportunity.[130]

The balance of power between the target board and target shareholders in a bid is set out in the Takeover Code at General Principle 3 (GP 3) and rule 21.[131] This is sometimes referred to as the 'no frustration' principle. It states, in general terms, that the directors of the target cannot take any actions that constrain the freedom of the shareholders as a whole to decide whether to accept the offer. The general principles within the Takeover Code are taken directly from the Takeover Directive.[132] These principles are expressed in broad terms. GP 3, for example, states that '[t]he board of an offeree company must act in the interests of the company as a whole and must not deny the holders of securities the opportunity to decide on the merits of the bid'. The general principles are supplemented by more detailed rules, such as rule 21 of the Code, which puts the meat onto the bones of GP 3.

Crucially, the provisions in the Takeover Code provide that the no frustration principle applies only where the 'board has reason to believe that a bona fide offer might be imminent'.[133] A distinction has to be drawn, therefore, between the period prior to this point, when ordinary principles of company law apply to govern the situation, and the situation when a bid is imminent, or has actually been made, in which case takeover regulation applies in addition to the usual rules.[134]

14.3.2.1 Pre-Bid Defences

The Takeover Code does not apply before the point at which a bid is 'imminent'. There are two good reasons why this is the case. First, the no frustration principle involves a significant interference with normal company law principles. In general, the UK operates a system of centralised management, at least in publicly traded companies. Shareholders in UK companies have control of the board, via their ability to remove directors, as well as some potentially important corporate governance rights,[135] but, in practice, significant powers of management are delegated to the directors and the courts recognise that, as a general rule, they should not interfere with the way in which the board exercises its discretion to run the company.[136] The no frustration principle prevents the directors from taking actions that are within the usual scope of the board's powers of management. A curtailment of these powers can be justified once a bid is imminent, but to allow this infringement before that point would constitute a significant constraint on the directors' power of management.

---

[130] See DTI, *Company Law Implementation of the European Directive on Takeover Bids* (URN 05/11, January 2005), para 3.12.

[131] The Takeover Panel's Code Committee can make changes to the Rules, after public consultation: Takeover Code, Introduction, A9. The Rules are interpreted by the Panel purposively so that the spirit as well as the letter of the rules must be observed (Introduction, A2).

[132] Takeover Directive 2004/25/EC, art 3.

[133] Takeover Code, r 21.1.

[134] See D Kershaw, 'The Illusion of Importance: Reconsidering the UK's Takeover Defence Prohibition' (2007) 56 *International Comparative Law Quarterly* 267, who argues that pre-bid and post-bid approvals of defensive tactics by shareholders are functionally equivalent, so that the no frustration principle in the Code adds little or nothing to UK company law.

[135] For discussion see 11.2.2.

[136] Eg, *Automatic Self-Cleansing Filter Syndicate Co Ltd v Cuninghame* [1906] 2 Ch 34.

This would be problematic not only for directors, but also for shareholders, who benefit from the existing system of centralised management.

Second, one of the justifications for changing the rules once a bid is imminent is the fact that, in addition to the usual agency problem that exists between directors and shareholders in a typical UK publicly traded company, which general company law principles address, there is the added difficulty that the directors are likely to be personally interested in the outcome of the bid. This increases the chances that they will behave in a self-serving manner. When a bid is imminent, the particularly acute nature of the agency problem justifies the imposition of the no frustration rule; pre-bid, this justification falls away. The general company law rules governing the agency problem between directors and shareholders are felt to be sufficient to deal with the pre-bid situation, in combination with the other constraints that exist for directors at this point, discussed below.

As a result, boards have significant freedom, in theory, to put in place pre-bid measures that could prevent a future takeover attempt from succeeding. Broadly, these measures consist of two types: those designed to make the company less attractive to the bidder, and those that attempt to make it more difficult for the bidder to succeed in the bid. These are not mutually exclusive categories, however, and a measure of overlap is possible. An example of the first type of measure is the classic poison pill. This provides that the existing shareholders of a company, excluding the bidder, will receive a large amount of equity rights (shares, options etc) at a very substantial discount if one shareholder (the bidder) obtains a specified stake in the company, generally in the region of 10 to 20 per cent of the target's existing voting shares, without the approval of the target's management. Issuing discounted equity rights in this way not only destroys the hostile bidder's voting majority, but also significantly dilutes the bidder's investment.[137] Another possibility is to agree that there will be a return of cash to existing shareholders by way of a special dividend or repurchase of shares, which will have an impact on the gearing of the company and may make the target less attractive to a bidder.

Other options are for the directors to agree to sell certain assets of the company to a third party should a bid be successful (the crown jewels defence). The specified assets are ideally those of most interest to a potential hostile bidder. The directors could also enter into contracts that place the desired assets of the company outside the control of the shareholders in some other way. The directors could, alternatively, agree to make a significant acquisition in order to make the target more expensive for the bidder.[138]

Another possibility is to give certain shareholders significantly enhanced voting rights in the event of a takeover bid. The effect of this measure is to ensure that although the bidder might acquire the majority of the shares in the company, if it does not hold the shares carrying the enhanced voting rights then it will still not acquire control of the management of the target. Another mechanism for achieving much the same end is to alter the articles of the company in order to raise significantly the requisite majority for shareholder resolutions.[139]

---

[137] A twist on this defensive tactic is to issue shares to a friendly third party who wishes to see the target remain independent.

[138] An extreme form of this latter defence that can only be put in place post-bid is the 'Pacman' defence whereby the target makes an offer to acquire the bidder.

[139] A variation on this idea is to include a provision which restricts the voting rights of certain shareholders (eg the bidder) in the event of a successful bid.

In practice, there tend to be far fewer possibilities of the second type of pre-bid defences—that is, those designed to make it more difficult for the bidder to succeed in the bid. One example, however, might involve placing restrictions in the articles of the company so that share transfers are restricted, thereby giving the directors control of share transfers.

Directors' ability to make use of these defensive tactics pre-bid in the UK is by no means unconstrained. A number of different restraints exist in practice, namely the need to take account of their directors' duties, to take account of the general requirements imposed by companies and securities legislation, and to take account of the views of the shareholders, particularly the institutional shareholders.

14.3.2.1.1 Directors' Duties

There are two relevant duties that might operate as a constraint on directors considering defensive tactics in the pre-bid situation: the duty to promote the success of the company in section 172 of the Companies Act 2006, and the requirement that directors must exercise their powers for a proper purpose, in section 171 of the Companies Act 2006.

Directors must comply with the duty to promote the success of the company when putting in place any pre-bid defences. This is a subjectively assessed obligation[140] to act 'for the benefit of its members as a whole'.[141] In doing so, however, the director is required to have regard to a number of factors, such as the likely long-term consequences of the decision, and the interests of a number of different stakeholder groups, including the company's employees and customers.[142] The interests of these other stakeholder groups do not override the interests of the shareholders, but are intended to help the director to judge the long-term interests of the shareholders as a whole.[143] When putting in place any pre-bid defences, the directors will need to ensure that they are acting to promote the success of the company in the manner specified in section 172.

Directors are also required to exercise their powers for a proper purpose.[144] The proper purpose test is objective—that is, even if the directors have acted honestly they may be in breach of this duty if they have exercised their powers for a purpose outside those for which their powers were conferred upon them.[145] The courts will construe the company's articles in order to determine whether a particular purpose is proper.[146] However, the courts have acknowledged that there might be a range of purposes associated with a particular action of the directors,[147] in which case the test is applied to the dominant or primary purpose of the directors' actions.[148] As long as the directors can satisfy the court that the purpose of the action was proper, they will not be in breach of this duty, even if the incidental, and desired,

---

[140] A director must act 'in the way he considers, in good faith, would be most likely to promote the success of the company' (Companies Act 2006, s 172(1)). See *LNOC Ltd v Watford Associated* [2013] EWHC 3615 (Comm).

[141] Companies Act 2006, s 172(1).

[142] Ibid, ss 172(1)(a)–(f).

[143] See 3.2.1.3.1.

[144] Companies Act 2006, s 171(b). This reflects the prior common law position (see eg *Howard Smith Ltd v Ampol Petroleum Ltd* [1974] AC 821).

[145] *Howard Smith Ltd v Ampol Petroleum Ltd* [1974] AC 821, 834; *Punt v Symons & Co Ltd* [1903] 2 Ch 506.

[146] *Re Smith and Fawcett Ltd* [1942] Ch 304, 306.

[147] Section 171(b) provides that a director must 'only exercise powers for the *purposes* for which they are conferred' (emphasis added).

[148] *Hirsche v Sims* [1894] AC 654.

result of the particular action is to secure the directors' control of the company. This is an important restriction on the application of the proper purposes rule, and for this reason this common law rule is a weaker control than the 'no frustration principle' put in place for post-bid measures.[149] Where directors are found to have acted for an improper purpose, however, their act is voidable by the company.[150]

The application of the proper purpose rule to pre-bid defences was considered in *Criterion Properties plc v Stratford UK Properties LLC*.[151] In that case, the board of Criterion was concerned that a particular company was increasing its shareholding in Criterion and would seek to acquire control. To try to prevent this, Criterion's joint venture agreement with Stratford was amended to allow Criterion to buy out Stratford at either the market value of its interest, or for a sum calculated to give Stratford a 25 per cent per annum return on its investment, whichever was the greater. This was freely referred to by the parties as a poison pill, intended to act as a disincentive to any takeover of Criterion. Criterion later sought to rescind the variation agreement on the basis, inter alia, that it involved the directors acting for an improper purpose.

At first instance, Hart J accepted that entering into a poison pill agreement of this sort was an improper exercise of their power by Criterion's directors.[152] Particularly problematic was the fact that this poison pill was not limited to preventing a takeover by a particular unsavoury predator, but would be triggered by any takeover, even a wholly beneficial one. This poison pill seemed designed primarily to entrench the existing directors rather than to protect the company. Also problematic was the fact that the variation exposed Criterion to 'a serious contingent liability'[153] designed to 'poison' the company and therefore could not be regarded as something which was of benefit to the company as an economic unit. The Court of Appeal similarly had no difficulty finding that the directors in the instant case had acted for an improper purpose, but left open the possibility that a more limited form of poison pill, targeted at a particular predator genuinely believed to pose a threat to the company, where the measure implemented did not itself cause significant damage to the company, could be permissible.[154] The House of Lords preferred to analyse this case as turning on a different issue, namely whether the managing director of Criterion, who had signed the agreement on behalf of Criterion, had acted within the actual or apparent scope of his authority.[155] Nevertheless, Lord Scott acknowledged that this case raised an 'issue of considerable public importance', namely whether it was 'open to a board of directors of a public company to authorise the signing on the company's behalf of a "poison pill" agreement intended to deter outsiders from making offers to shareholders to purchase their shares ... where, as here, the deterrence consists of a contingent divesting of company assets'.[156] His Lordship refused to commit himself as to the validity of such devices, however,

---

[149] See 14.3.2.2.
[150] *Howard Smith Ltd v Ampol Petroleum Ltd* [1974] AC 821.
[151] [2002] EWHC 496 (Ch); [2002] EWCA Civ 1883; [2004] UKHL 28.
[152] [2002] EWHC 496 (Ch).
[153] *Criterion Properties plc v Stratford UK Properties LLC* [2002] EWHC 496 (Ch) [21] per Hart J.
[154] [2002] EWCA Civ 1883. However, the Court of Appeal came to a different conclusion to that arrived at by Hart J, and allowed the appeal, on other grounds.
[155] For discussion see DD Prentice and J Payne, 'Company Contracts and Vitiating Factors: Developments in the Law on Directors' Authority' [2005] *Lloyd's Maritime and Commercial Law Quarterly* 447.
[156] [2004] UKHL 28 [29].

simply observing that the agreement in this case went beyond deterring unwanted predators, and potentially would also deter desirable predators; indeed the primary goal of this device seemed to be to entrench the positions of the managing director and chairman.[157] His Lordship did state, however, that if actual or apparent authority did exist then he could see no reason why the agreement would not be enforceable.[158]

Consequently, while the proper purpose doctrine does impose a measure of constraint on directors seeking to put in place pre-bid defences, a well-designed measure, particularly one that is aimed at deterring a specific unwanted bidder, rather than simply entrenching the existing directors, will not necessarily fall foul of this directors' duty.

One difficulty of using these fiduciary duties to regulate pre-bid defensive measures is the fact that these duties are owed to the company, and therefore the company is the proper claimant in any action against the directors.[159] Directors of a company owe no general fiduciary duties to the shareholders.[160] However, 'in appropriate and specific circumstances' a director can owe a fiduciary duty to a shareholder,[161] and takeovers are one of those situations where fiduciary duties have sometimes been said to arise.[162] To date the types of scenarios in which a duty has arisen have involved the directors buying shares from the shareholders where the directors know a takeover is about to occur, and the takeover will have a positive impact on the share price. In these situations courts have held that the directors are under a duty to disclose that information to the shareholders.[163] These cases have not, however, acknowledged that individual shareholders can bring an action against the directors for breach of the proper purpose doctrine.

14.3.2.1.2 Share Transfer Restrictions

The management of a company can retain control of the target if they can prevent ownership of the shares being transferred. Thus, if they can impose restrictions on the transfer of shares, for instance by including such a restriction in the company's articles, then they will make the company less vulnerable to a hostile takeover. However, the Stock Exchange's Listing Rules prevent constraints being imposed on the free transferability of shares. The Listing Rules state that fully paid shares have to be free from any restrictions on the right of transfer.[164] In practice, therefore, this form of pre-bid defensive measure is not generally available in the UK.

14.3.2.1.3 Removal of Directors and Staggered Boards

In some jurisdictions, directors seek to make hostile takeovers less attractive by putting in place a staggered board structure, whereby those responsible for the management of the company are appointed for fixed terms, with a number expiring and being renewed every year.

---

[157] Ibid, [29].

[158] Ibid, [30].

[159] *Foss v Harbottle* (1843) 2 Hare 461 and see now Companies Act 2006, Part 11.

[160] *Percival v Wright* [1902] 2 Ch 421; *Peskin v Anderson* [2001] 1 BCLC 372 (CA).

[161] *Peskin v Anderson* [2000] 2 BCLC 1 (Ch), 14 per Neuberger J.

[162] *Peskin v Anderson* [2001] 1 BCLC 372 [34] per Mummery LJ (although no such duty arose on the facts of that case); *Coleman v Myers* [1977] 2 NZLR 225 (Sup Ct NZ).

[163] Eg, *Coleman v Myers,* ibid.

[164] FCA Handbook, LR 2.2.4. For companies listed on AIM see London Stock Exchange, *AIM Rules for Companies,* May 2014, r 32.

The potential difficulties caused by a delay between a bidder acquiring a controlling interest in a target and being able to implement management changes can make a hostile bid less attractive. In the UK, however, it is impossible to limit the ability of shareholders to remove directors from office at any time by ordinary resolution,[165] and so staggered boards of this kind cannot be implemented.[166]

A possible alternative is for the directors to include provisions in their service contracts which provide for substantial compensation in the event of a termination of employment following a takeover bid. If these provisions are substantial enough they may deter a bid. Provisions of this kind may be justified by the need to employ or retain certain individuals, but excessive or disproportionate payments will not be justifiable in this way. In relation to all companies in the UK, directors' service contracts have to be available for inspection.[167] For quoted companies a copy of the directors' remuneration report, including details of termination payments to directors, must be sent to the shareholders, on which an advisory vote must be taken at the AGM.[168] In addition, the directors' remuneration policy must be put to a binding shareholder vote, by ordinary resolution.[169]

Where the agreement to pay particular compensation to directors is made after a bid becomes imminent, then shareholder approval will be required.[170] A payment made without shareholder approval will be treated as held on trust by the recipient for those who have sold their shares as a result of the offer.[171] This provision also applies where the obligation to make the payment is entered into pre-bid, but 'for the purposes of, in connection with or in consequence of' the takeover.[172] Arrangements entered into in the face of a bid will therefore require specific shareholder approval, although compensation packages entered into at an earlier stage, before a specific takeover is in contemplation, are regulated only by the more general company law provisions.

---

[165] Companies Act 2006, s 168.

[166] Similarly, although it would be possible to include in the articles of association a provision giving only particular shareholders the right to appoint directors (in order to prevent the bidder from being able to do so), these rights would not override the right of the general body of shareholders to remove all directors so appointed.

[167] Companies Act 2006, s 228. Shareholders also have the right to request that a copy of the contract be sent to them (s 229).

[168] Companies Act 2006, ss 420–21, 439. There are also proposals for European 'say on pay' provisions, that would be introduced via revisions to the Shareholder Rights Directive: Proposal for a Directive of the European Parliament and of the Council amending Directive 2007/36/EC as regards the encouragement of long-term shareholder engagement and Directive 2013/34/EU as regards certain elements of the corporate governance statement COM/2014/0213 final.

[169] Ibid, s 439A as amended by the Enterprise and Regulatory Reform Act 2013, s 79. The approval must be sought at least every three years, or more often if a change to the remuneration policy is proposed. A company is not permitted to make any payment to a director unless such payment is in accordance with its most recent, approved remuneration policy.

[170] Ibid, s 219(1) (and see also ss 217–18). These provisions are drafted broadly, so as to include payments made to compensate loss of management positions as well as loss of directorships: s 215(1). They also include payments made by 'any person' (s 219(1)). Compensation is defined to include benefits other than cash (s 215(2)). There is a de minimis exception for payments that do not exceed £200 (s 221(1)(b)).

[171] Ibid, s 222(3).

[172] Ibid, s 220(3) which introduces a 'takeover' exception to the general principle that payments to directors 'in discharge of an existing legal obligation' are excluded (s 220(1)(a) and see *Taupo Totaro Timber Co v Rowe* [1978] AC 537).

14.3.2.1.4 The Role of Shareholders

Many of the types of pre-bid defensive measures described above can only be put in place with the consent or agreement of the shareholders. The provisions regarding compensation payments to directors for loss of office have already been discussed. Significant transactions, involving the sale of the company's assets or the acquisition of assets (as in *Criterion*), may well trigger the need for shareholder consent.

Any alteration of the articles, for instance to introduce non-voting shares or to include enhanced voting rights, requires a shareholders' vote.[173] It is possible for measures of this kind to be put in place in the UK, but very rare. Institutional investors have traditionally been hostile towards the introduction of non-voting shares.[174] As regards enhanced voting rights, in the dispersed shareholding structure which exists for most UK publicly traded companies it is not clear how shareholders would benefit from such provisions, and what incentive they would have to approve them. Such provisions do, however, exist in other Member States. Article 11 of the Takeover Directive, known as the 'breakthrough' rule, deals with this issue. Broadly, Article 11 allows a bidder to override certain shareholder blocking rights. In effect it provides a 'one share, one vote' rule in relation to a range of shareholder measures that could be used to entrench the incumbent management.[175] Article 11, like Article 9, was made optional by the Takeover Directive, and the British Government did opt out of Article 11.[176]

Any pre-bid measure involving the issue of shares will also require the consent of the shareholders. In public companies, shareholder authorisation is needed for decisions by the directors to issue shares or to grant rights to subscribe for or convert any security into shares.[177] Although, in principle, shareholders can provide the directors with authorisation to issue shares up to five years in advance, in practice institutional investors are unwilling to provide the directors with this kind of blank cheque.[178] In addition, if the directors plan to issue shares other than pro rata to all the existing shareholders, and in practice this will be the case where the bidder is already a shareholder, as otherwise this form of poison pill would be ineffective to reduce the incentives for the bid, then pre-emption rights will need to be disapplied.[179] In principle, pre-emption rights can be disapplied for periods of up to five years, which would give the directors considerable discretion in relation to share issues.[180] In practice, however, institutional investors prevent such wide discretion

---

[173] An alteration of articles requires a special resolution: Companies Act 2006, s 21 (if the alteration involves the variation of a class right then see Companies Act 2006, s 630).

[174] See eg J Franks, C Mayer and S Rossi, 'Spending Less Time With the Family: The Decline of Family Ownership in the UK' in RK Morck (ed), *A History of Corporate Governance Around the World: Family Business Groups to Professional Managers* (Chicago, University of Chicago Press, 2005).

[175] For example, the breakthrough rule would apply on any shareholder vote to approve a post-bid defensive measure and would apply at a general meeting called after a successful bid for the purpose of installing the bidder's nominees as directors of the company. For discussion see J Rickford, 'Emerging European Takeover Law from a British Perspective' [2004] *European Business Law Review* 1379.

[176] See DTI, *Company Law Implementation of the European Directive on Takeover Bids* (URN 05/11, January 2005), para 3.9. However, art 12 of the Takeover Directive (Directive 2004/25/EC) requires Member States that opt out to permit opting back in on a company by company basis (see Companies Act 2006, Part 28 Ch 2).

[177] Companies Act 2006, s 551. cf the stricter position once the bid is imminent: Takeover Code, r 21.1.

[178] Ibid, s 551(3)(b). For discussion see 4.3.

[179] Ibid, ss 570–71. For discussion see 4.4.

[180] See 4.4.3.

being given to the directors. A Statement of Principles drawn up by the Stock Exchange Pre-Emption Group provides guidance on the circumstances in which certain institutional investors should vote in favour of a resolution to disapply pre-emption rights.[181] In general, requests by a company to issue non-preemptively not more than 5 per cent of the ordinary share capital in any given year are likely to be regarded as routine (with the possibility of an additional 5 per cent if used for an acquisition or specified capital investment),[182] provided the duration also meets the stated criteria,[183] otherwise a business case for waiver must be made.[184] Whilst the Statement of Principles does not have the force of law, this document represents the views of the majority of major UK institutional investors. In practice, this document gives shareholders, particularly institutional investors, a level of control over the issue of new shares, which constrains directors' ability to introduce certain poison pills in the pre-bid situation.

14.3.2.1.5 Summary

Although the Takeover Code does not regulate directors' ability to put in place defensive measures before a bid is imminent, it is certainly not the case that directors in the UK are unconstrained in this period. General company law principles, particularly directors' duties, combined with securities legislation, and the powerful position of institutional investors in the UK, place significant constraints on directors in this period. Consequently, it is no surprise that the incidence of poison pills and other types of pre-bid defensive measures is very low in the UK. This stands in contrast to the position in the US, where poison pills are ubiquitous: 'every public company either has adopted a pill or can adopt one if a hostile offer is made'.[185] These devices work very effectively to provide directors with a significant role in the outcome of the bid.[186] In general, poison pills in the US are regarded as providing an opportunity for negotiation between the bidder and the target directors.[187] Rather than preventing a hostile bid entirely they are commonly seen as providing a mechanism to allow

---

[181] See Pre-Emption Group, *Disapplying Pre-Emption Rights: Statement of Principles*, 2015, discussed at 4.4.3. This Statement of Principles was formerly known as the Pre-Emption Guidelines. For discussion see *A Study by Paul Myners into the Impact of Shareholders' Pre-Emption Rights on a Public Company's Ability to Raise New Capital* (URN 05/679, February 2005), ch 3.

[182] Ibid, part 2A, paras 1, 2.

[183] Ibid, part 2A, paras 1, 3 (ie the disapplication of pre-emption rights should last no more than 15 months or until the next Annual General Meeting, whichever is the shorter period).

[184] Ibid, part 3.

[185] R Gilson, 'Unocal Fifteen Years Later (and What We Can Do About It)' (2001) 26 *Delaware Journal of Corporate Law* 491, 501. More recently, the question has been raised as to the constitutionality of poison pills: L Bebchuk and R Jackson, 'Towards a Constitutional Review of the Poison Pill' (2014) 114(6) *Columbia Law Review* 1549.

[186] For discussion see 14.3.2.2. One common tactic of US bidders is to combine a takeover offer with a proxy contest, whereby the bidder attempts to pass a shareholders' resolution to remove the incumbent directors from the board, replacing them with their own directors. Since poison pills can generally be redeemed by the directors, combining a hostile takeover with a successful proxy contest enables the pill to be disabled and the bid to proceed: LA Bebchuk, JC Coats and G Subramanian, 'The Powerful Antitakeover Force of Staggered Boards: Theory, Evidence and Policy' (2002) 54 *Stanford Law Review* 887. However, the incidence of 'staggered boards' in the US, which limits the number of directors that can be removed at any one time (typically a third), significantly reduces the efficacy of this arrangement.

[187] However, some studies suggest that the existence of certain takeover laws, such as poison pill laws, are in some instances correlated with increased hostile activity: M Cain, S McKeon and S Solomon, 'Do Takeover Laws Matter? Evidence from Five Decades of Hostile Takeovers', http://papers.ssrn.com/sol3/papers.cfm?abstract_id=2517513.

the target directors to negotiate a higher price for the shareholders.[188] Perhaps it is because these devices are so common, and are regarded as working so effectively, that other forms of takeover defence in the US are relatively rare.[189]

14.3.2.2 Post-Bid Defences

14.3.2.2.1 The No Frustration Principle

Once a bid is imminent, or has actually been made, GP 3 and rule 21 of the Takeover Code put in place a strong no frustration principle that is intended to give the decision-making role to the target shareholders and not the target directors. This is now also the position at European level as a result of Article 9 of the Takeover Directive.[190] The target board 'must not, without the approval of the shareholders in general meeting ... take any action which may result in any offer or bona fide possible offer being frustrated or in shareholders being denied the opportunity to decide on its merits'.[191] This rule is strictly applied. It is irrelevant whether the target directors had this purpose in mind in taking a particular action.[192] If the effect of their action may result in the frustration of the bid then they are in breach of the no frustration principle. GP 3 and rule 21 do not, however, require passivity on the part of the directors. Indeed, directors have an important role in the bid: they must circulate their opinion on the offer to the shareholders.[193] Further, there are some, limited defensive tactics that are open to directors.

14.3.2.2.1(a) Directors' Opinion on the Bid

The Takeover Code includes an important role for the target board post-bid, namely to circulate their opinion on the offer to the shareholders.[194] Directors must obviously act in accordance with their fiduciary duties when providing this opinion, but the Takeover Code goes further in attempting to deal with the potential conflict of interest that can arise. Any directors with a particular conflict of interest, for example those who will have a continuing role with the bidder company if the bid is successful, must not join with the rest of the board in expressing a view on the offer.[195] In addition, the board is required to obtain

---

[188] JN Gordon, 'An American Perspective on Anti-Takeover Laws in the EU: The German Example' in G Ferrarini, KJ Hopt, J Winter and E Wymeersch (eds), *Reforming Company and Takeover Law in Europe* (Oxford, Oxford University Press, 2004) 548.

[189] Ibid, 551.

[190] Article 12.1 of the Takeover Directive (2004/25/EC) allows Member States to opt out of art 9 of the directive. Even if a Member State does opt out, a company must be given the right to opt in to the no frustration principle: art 12.2. For discussion see J Rickford, 'The Emerging European Takeover Law from a British Perspective' [2004] *European Business Law Review* 1379.

[191] Takeover Code, r 21.1.

[192] This may be compared to the operation of the proper purpose rule at common law, discussed above at 14.3.2.1.1.

[193] Takeover Code, r 25.2. If the board of the target is split in its views then the minority view should also be circulated: Note 2 to r 25.2.

[194] Ibid.

[195] Rule 25.2, Note 4 and Note 5. This can cause difficulties in a management buy-out situation where all, or substantially all, of the board will continue to have a role in management if the bid is successful (see r 20.3 as part of the attempt to deal with this situation). This is discussed further in chapter 16, regarding private equity transactions (see particularly 16.5.2).

independent advice on any offer and the substance of that advice must be made known to the shareholders.[196]

14.3.2.2.1(b) *Defensive Measures Available to the Directors Post-Bid*

A number of limited, defensive tactics are open to the directors. First, they can try to persuade the shareholders that their future would be better if they retained the existing management rather than accepting the offer from the bidder company. This is one of the primary weapons available to the target directors. The bidder will claim that its offer represents a fair price and a premium to the trading value of the target's shares. The target's board may assert that the offer is inadequate and fails properly to reflect the true value of the target's shares.[197] The bid will be defeated only if the shareholders of the target are convinced that the value they will enjoy by retaining their shares is such that the price offered by the bidder is insufficient.

Second, directors can buy shares in the target in order to try to block the bid. Directors are required to disclose their purchase of shares,[198] however, and there is a more general obligation to disclose once the shareholding reaches the 3 per cent level.[199]

Third, GP 3 and rule 21 seem to be restricted to internal corporate action,[200] and therefore do not prevent the directors making use of external options to try to frustrate the bid, such as lobbying the competition authorities, at national or EU level, to take action to prohibit the bid or to subject it to conditions unacceptable to the bidder.

Fourth, the directors can seek a 'White Knight', that is, a more favourable alternative bidder, although there is no duty on them to do so. The motivation may be to encourage an auction, in order to ensure that the highest price is received by the shareholders. It may also be to find a bidder whose plans offer a better outcome for the other stakeholders, or to find a bidder who will treat the incumbent management more favourably. In the UK the practice of seeking a White Knight is generally accepted, as it is regarded as providing more choice to the target shareholders.[201] Some academics question this, suggesting that allowing directors to seek White Knights raises the costs of a successful bid, which has the effect of reducing the number of bids that will be launched, ultimately therefore reducing

---

[196] Takeover Code, r 3.1. The Code Committee of the Takeover Panel considers that the principal role of the independent adviser is to advise the board of the offeree company as to whether the financial terms of the offer are 'fair and reasonable' (for discussion see Code Committee of the Takeover Panel, Consultation Paper, PCP 2014/1, 16 July 2014, Section 11). The Code Committee has considered whether this independent advice should be given directly to shareholders rather than via the directors, but concluded that such a requirement would add little to the existing provision: Code Committee of the Takeover Panel, *Review of Certain Aspects of the Regulation of Takeover Bids*, 2010/22, paras 6.10–6.12.

[197] Any profit forecasts and asset valuations must be reported on by the target's auditors and financial adviser: Takeover Code, r 28.1.

[198] Market Abuse Directive 2003/6/EC, art 6(4) implemented into UK law via FCA Handbook, DTR 3.1.2 (and see Regulation (EU) No 596/2014, art 19(1)). For discussion see 11.3.2.2.

[199] Transparency Directive 2004/109/EC (as amended), art 9(1) implemented into UK law via FCA Handbook, DTR 5.1.2. For discussion see 11.3.2.3.

[200] See the list provided within r 21 of situations in which shareholder approval is required: Takeover Code, r 21.1(b).

[201] The Takeover Directive (2004/25/EC) also makes it clear that seeking an alternative bidder is not caught by the no frustration principle: art 9(2).

shareholder choice.[202] The empirical evidence seems to favour the view that competing bids are wealth-enhancing for the target shareholders.[203] By channelling more wealth to the target shareholders, facilitating competing bids can be regarded as a mechanism for ensuring that the gains generated by the takeover are shared between the bidder and the target shareholders.

The principal concern of any White Knight will be to avoid a bidding war with the original bidder. However, in the UK there is relatively little that can be done to protect the White Knight from a subsequent higher offer by the original bidder, or indeed by a new bidder. In the US it is common for the White Knight to be issued shares or options in the target in order to enable it to protect its position, but in the UK the rules governing share issues generally put these matters under the control of the shareholders rather than the directors.[204] Another potential option is a break fee arrangement, whereby the White Knight's costs are paid by the target company should the White Knight's bid be unsuccessful. Break fees are common in the US. Until 2010 break fee arrangements were also usual in the UK, although they were subject to a cap, imposed by the Takeover Code, of an amount equal to 1 per cent of the value of the offer.[205] Even this low sum, however, was deemed to give rise to a risk that it could provide bidders with a tactical advantage over targets.[206] In order to redress the balance in favour of the target, in 2010 a general prohibition on deal protection measures was introduced, including a general ban on break fees. Consequently, in the UK break fee arrangements are now permitted only in very limited circumstances, and with the Panel's consent.[207]

If the directors hold shares in the target themselves, then they may be able to enter into irrevocable undertakings with the White Knight (or any other bidder) to sell those shares to that bidder in order to demonstrate their support for a particular bid.[208] In *Heron International Ltd v Lord Grade*[209] there were two competing bids for a company. The target

---

[202] FH Easterbrook and DR Fischel, 'The Proper Role of a Target's Management in Responding to a Tender Offer' (1981) 94 *Harvard Law Review* 1161; R Romano, 'A Guide to Takeovers: Theory, Evidence and Regulation' (1992) 9 *Yale Journal on Regulation* 119.

[203] J Franks and R Harris, 'Shareholder Wealth Effects of Corporate Takeovers 1955–1985' in S Peck and P Temple (eds), *Mergers and Acquisitions: Critical Perspectives on Business and Management* (Oxford, Routledge, 2008).

[204] For discussion see 14.3.2.1.4.

[205] The board and its financial adviser also needed to confirm in writing to the Takeover Panel that they believed the fee arrangement to be in the best interests of the target shareholders, and the break fee arrangement needed to be disclosed.

[206] Another potential difficulty with a break fee arrangement of this kind is that, where the target is a public company, the arrangement may constitute financial assistance: Companies Act 2006, ss 677–80 (see 5.4.4). The fee is only payable if the bid fails, but the agreement to pay the fee could be regarded as entered into for the purpose of the acquisition. The view of financial assistance adopted by the Court of Appeal in *Chaston v SWP Group plc* [2002] EWCA Civ 1999 certainly seems wide enough to include an agreement to pay a break fee. However, the low level of break fee payments may mean that they can generally be brought within the de minimis exception in the Companies Act 2006, s 677(1)(d)).

[207] Takeover Code, r 21.2; for discussion see Code Committee of the Takeover Panel, *Review of Certain Aspects of the Regulation of Takeover Bids*, 2010/22. Break fees will therefore be rare: see eg Takeover Panel of the Code Committee, Review of the 2011 Amendments to the Takeover Code, 2012/8, 3.10: in the year ending 18 September 2012, there were no instances of the Executive's consent having been sought for the entering into of an inducement fee arrangement pursuant to Note 1 on r 21.2.

[208] These undertakings need to be given by deed since there is no consideration and no mutual exchange of promises. Note that irrevocable undertakings are treated as shares belonging to the bidder for the purposes of the squeeze-out rule (Companies Act 2006, s 979(2), which is a change from the previous law found in Companies Act 1985, s 428).

[209] [1983] BCLC 244.

directors held 50 per cent of the shares. The directors gave irrevocable undertakings to accept what turned out to be the lower bid, and stood by those undertakings. As a result, the higher bid was defeated. The Court of Appeal held that the directors could not sepa-rate their position as shareholders from their position as directors. The court held that the duty of the directors was to obtain the best price for the company and, further, that '[t]he directors should not commit themselves to transfer their own voting shares to a bid-der unless they are satisfied that he is offering the best price reasonably obtainable'.[210] The idea that director/shareholders are constrained as to how they may exercise their share-holder rights is out of step with the general company law view that a share is a piece of property belonging to the shareholder and that shareholders do not owe fiduciary duties as to how they exercise their shareholder rights.[211] It is also notable that the Takeover Code is silent on this issue. It does not impose an obligation on directors to deal with their shares in the target in any particular manner, and therefore leaves them free to act qua shareholder in a self-interested way if they wish.

A preferable view is that expressed by Hoffmann J in *Re a Company*.[212] The facts of this case were somewhat different. *Re a Company* involved a small private company and the issue arose in the context of an unfair prejudice petition. Nevertheless, Hoffmann J was required to consider whether directors can separate their obligations as directors of a target company when competing offers are made, from their rights as shareholders in the target. Hoffmann J did not accept that directors are under a positive duty to recommend and take all steps within their power to facilitate the highest offer, and neither did he accept that this obligation could restrict their freedom of action in relation to their own shares. The extent of their duty was an obligation, when giving advice to the shareholders under rule 25.2, to act in accordance with their fiduciary duties, and not to exercise their powers to prevent other shareholders accepting the higher offer. However, directors should be free qua share-holder to accept whichever bid they like, and to give irrevocable undertakings in advance if that is what they wish to do.

The possibility of the directors seeking a White Knight means that the initial bidder might want to try to persuade the target directors to agree not to do so. It is clear that the directors cannot commit to non-cooperation with a competing bidder, should one come forward. The Takeover Code is clear that once competing bids have arisen, the same infor-mation must be provided to each bidder by the target board, even if one of the offers is less welcome than the other(s).[213] However, a more difficult issue is whether the directors can agree not to seek an alternative bidder and, further, to recommend the original bid. It might be that the directors are acting in the best interests of the target shareholders in entering into such an agreement, for instance if the bidder would not make the bid at all without such an agreement, and if the directors genuinely believe that no other bidder will come forward. The more significant problem, however, is whether the directors can fetter their discretion in this way.

---

[210] Ibid, 265 per Lawton LJ.

[211] Some incursions have been made into this principle, both judge-made (eg *Allen v Gold Reefs of West Africa Ltd* [1900] 1 Ch 656) and created by statute (eg Companies Act 2006, s 239), but the general principle still holds good.

[212] [1986] BCLC 382.

[213] Takeover Code, r 20.2. This applies both to the information made available by the board and to the terms on which it is made available (eg the imposition of confidentiality agreements).

Section 173(2) of the Companies Act 2006 provides that the duty to exercise independent judgment is not infringed by a director acting 'in accordance with an agreement duly entered into by the company that restricts the future exercise of discretion by its directors'. This is in tune with the decision of the Court of Appeal in *Fulham Football Club Ltd v Cabra Estates plc*,[214] a decision taken prior to the Companies Act 2006. In this case the Court of Appeal held that directors can bind themselves as to the future exercise of their fiduciary powers in some circumstances. However, this decision did not arise in the context of a standard takeover bid scenario; the facts involved the directors fettering their own discretion whereas in the standard takeover context the directors are effectively attempting to restrict the shareholders' future choices. The Court of Appeal stopped short of overruling earlier decisions that cast doubt on the directors' ability to fetter their discretion in this way.[215] More significantly, section 173(2) does not override the directors' obligation to act in accordance with section 172. This suggests that directors can only bind themselves to act in the future in a way which is consistent with their duty under section 172. Should a subsequent offer emerge which the directors judge to be better than the earlier bid (taking into account the long-term interests of the shareholders) then they would presumably be under an obligation to recommend that bid, irrespective of whatever agreement they had entered into with the original bidder. This seems to be in accordance with the spirit of the Takeover Code.

14.3.2.2.2 Consequences of the UK's Adoption of the No Frustration Principle

In summary, the UK position does not require passivity on the part of the directors, but it does require that directors take no action to frustrate the bid once the bid is imminent or the offer has actually been made. This is an attempt to put the decision regarding the bid into the hands of the shareholders, sidelining the target board to the greatest extent possible.

This stands in contrast to the approach adopted in the US, where the decision-making role is allocated to the target board, in addition to the shareholders.[216] The bid cannot succeed without the consent of the shareholders, but the shareholders will not have the opportunity to decide whether to accept the offer unless the directors allow the offer to be put to them. In *Unocal Corp v Mesa Petroleum Co*[217] the Supreme Court of Delaware formulated a two-stage test to determine the legality of defensive tactics adopted by the target board.[218]

---

[214] [1994] 1 BCLC 363.

[215] Eg, *Dawson International plc v Coats Paton plc* [1991] BCC 278, although on the facts of that case it was held that the agreement not to seek, cooperate with or recommend a competing bid was not to be construed as intended to be legally binding by the parties. See also *John Crowther Group Ltd v Carpets International plc* [1990] BCLC 460, in which the board undertook to use 'all reasonable endeavours' to secure the consent of the shareholders. When a higher bid emerged the directors recommended that bid, and the initial bidder sued for breach of the agreement. The court held that 'all reasonable endeavours' did not require the directors to act contrary to their fiduciary duty.

[216] This position is not exclusive to the US. Some European states, such as Germany, provide for some form of joint decision-making in relation to takeover decisions (see eg §33(1) Übernahmegesetz, by which shareholders can authorise directors to take specified types of defensive measures in advance of a hostile offer).

[217] 493 A 2d 946 (Delaware, 1985). For discussion see RJ Gilson, 'Unocal Fifteen Years Later (and What We Can Do About It)' (2001) 26 *Delaware Journal of Corporate Law* 491; M Lipton and PK Rowe, 'Pills, Polls and Professors: A Reply to Professor Gilson' (2002) 27 *Delaware Journal of Corporate Law* 1.

[218] For discussion see M Siegel, 'The Problems and Promise of "Enhanced Business Judgement"' (2015) 17(1) *University of Pennsylvania Journal of Business Law* 48; J Grieco, 'Ever-Evolving Poison Pill: The Pill in Asset Protection and Closely-Held Corporation Cases' (2011) 36 *Delaware Journal of Corporate Law* 625.

First, did the directors have reasonable grounds for believing that the takeover endangered corporate policy and effectiveness? Second, were the defensive measures adopted by the directors reasonable in relation to the threat posed? In applying this test the courts have given considerable latitude to the target directors. The first limb of the test will be satisfied where the target board can demonstrate that the takeover threatens one of the board's existing business policies, which will be the case in the vast majority of hostile bids. If the threat is held to justify defensive action, then preventing the takeover will generally be the best way of heading off the threat, so, in practice, the second limb has not provided a significant constraint on directors either. The *Unocal* test has been applied in such a way as to give the decision-making role in a takeover first and foremost to the target board.[219] The shareholders will only have a decision-making role if the target board agrees that the offer can be put to them.[220]

It is interesting to contrast the US and UK responses to this issue.[221] The Delaware model gives significant power to the target board to determine whether a proposed takeover, and the consequent change of control, will take place. The board is, therefore, in a position to act on behalf of the shareholders to prevent opportunistic behaviour by the acquirer. It is sometimes suggested that a sale process controlled by the directors on behalf of the shareholders is likely to result in a higher premium than an uncontrolled auction.[222] If this is correct, the danger of the UK system is that uninformed or uncoordinated shareholders may sell their shares for less than they are worth. Set against this view is the strong belief in shareholder sovereignty that exists in the UK, in other words that shareholders alone should be able to decide whether or not to sell their shares. It might also be expected that, in the bid context, collective action problems will be less acute as shareholders have strong incentives to determine whether the offer price is appropriate. It is also notable that, if the issue is that the directors have superior information which allows them to determine that the offered price is insufficient, the relevant information can still be communicated to the shareholders. Indeed, in the UK directors are required to give the shareholders their opinion of the bid.[223] Studies have suggested that, in practice, the bid premia in the US and UK are very similar.[224]

A second benefit that is sometimes ascribed to the US system is that the bidder deals primarily with the board rather than the dispersed shareholders, which lessens the danger of the bidder 'dividing and conquering' the numerous dispersed shareholders; that is, the

---

[219] Eg, *Paramount Communications Inc v Time Inc*, 571 A 2d 1140 (Delaware, 1990); *Unitrin Inc v American General Corporation*, 651 A 2d 1361 (Delaware, 1995). For discussion see M Kahan, 'Jurisprudential and Transactional Developments in Takeovers' in K Hopt et al (eds), *Comparative Corporate Governance: The State of the Art and Emerging Research* (Oxford, Oxford University Press, 1998). For a more recent application of the *Unocal* test see *eBay Domestic Holdings Inc v Newmark* CA No 3705-CC (Del Ch September 9, 2010).

[220] *Revlon Inc v MacAndrews & Forbes Holdings Inc*, 506 A 2d 173 (Delaware, 1986); *Paramount Communications v QVC Network*, 637 A 2d 34 (Delaware, 1994).

[221] For discussion see K J Hopt, 'Takeover Defenses in Europe: A Comparative, Theoretical and Policy Analysis' (2014) 20(2) *Columbia Journal of European Law* 249.

[222] M Kahan and EB Rock, 'Corporate Constitutionalism: Antitakeover Charter Provisions as Precommitment' (2003) 152 *University of Pennsylvania Law Review* 473, 477; cf eg LA Bebchuk, 'The Case Against Board Veto in Corporate Takeovers' (2002) 69 *University of Chicago Law Review* 973.

[223] Takeover Code, r 25.2.

[224] JC Coates, 'M&A Break Fees: US Litigation vs US Regulation' in D Kessler (ed), *Regulation versus Litigation: Perspectives from Economics and Law* (Chicago University Press, 2011).

US model appears to face fewer collective action problems regarding the target shareholders' decision-making. On this view, the US model can better promote undistorted choice by the shareholders in their decision-making. It is certainly correct that the UK no frustration principle leaves target shareholders open to potential abuse, and that the UK model needs to deal separately with the need to protect the target shareholders from opportunistic behaviour by the bidder. The UK model does put such protections in place, as discussed below at 14.3.4, and, in practice, deals comprehensively with this issue. By contrast, although US shareholders stand in less need of protection, they are given less protection (for example there is no mandatory bid rule in either federal law or in Delaware), and therefore they are arguably worse off than their UK counterparts in this regard.[225]

Third, it is sometimes suggested that the US model also provides the directors with the opportunity to determine whether the takeover is in the best interests of the company as a whole, including stakeholder interests separate to those of the shareholders. This is discussed further below at 14.3.3. However, this model will have value in practice only if the directors use their position solely to defeat opportunistic bids, and not merely to entrench their own position. The UK no frustration principle effectively controls the acute agency problem generated by the bid, preventing the directors acting self-interestedly by sidelining them from the decision-making process. By contrast, the present application of the *Unocal* test effectively allows the board to adopt defensive tactics to preserve their own business strategy, and thereby to entrench themselves.[226]

Finally, one of the benefits sometimes ascribed to takeovers is as a mechanism for corporate accountability.[227] The operation of the market for corporate control stems from the same principles as the capital market price function.[228] The target management's laziness or self-dealing may lead the market to discount the price of the target company's shares. The precipitation for this discount may be a bid by one company which is seen by the market as a value-decreasing takeover offer. The drop in share price allows a bidder (or a second bidder in the latter scenario) to come in, purchase control of the company, remove the lazy or self-dealing directors, and put the company's assets to more profitable use.[229] On this view, the potential ability of a third party to deal directly with the shareholders, sidelining the directors, to facilitate a control shift and thereby get rid of lazy or self-seeking managers, is regarded as one benefit of hostile takeovers. The potential benefits are said to extend further, however, since the threat of a takeover may discourage the lazy or self-seeking behaviour in the first place.[230]

If this is correct, a regulatory environment needs to be conducive to the successful mounting of takeover bids (including hostile bids) in order to enable takeovers to bridge

---

[225] See eg LA Bebchuk, 'The Pressure to Tender: An Analysis and a Proposed Remedy' (1987) 12 *Delaware Journal of Corporate Law* 911.

[226] For an argument against the existence of board veto in the US, see LA Bebchuk, 'The Case Against Board Veto in Corporate Takeovers' (2002) 69 *University of Chicago Law Review* 973. For discussion see M Klausner, 'Fact and Fiction in Corporate Law and Governance' (2013) 65(6) *Stanford Law Review* 1325.

[227] Eg, HG Manne, 'Mergers and the Market for Corporate Control' (1965) 73 *Journal of Political Economy* 110. For discussion of these issues see J Coffee, 'Regulating the Market for Corporate Control: A Critical Assessment of the Tender Offer's Role in Corporate Governance' (1984) 84 *Columbia Law Review* 1145.

[228] Discussed at 10.2.1.

[229] See eg HG Manne, 'Mergers and the Market for Corporate Control' (1965) 73 *Journal of Political Economy* 110.

[230] See eg U Lel and DP Miller, 'Does Takeover Activity Cause Managerial Discipline? Evidence from International M&A Laws' (2015) 28(6) *Review of Financial Studies* 1588.

the gap between ownership and control in a large, dispersed company.[231] On this analysis, the US model is potentially at a disadvantage to the UK model.[232] Studies have shown that the number of successful hostile bids in the US in the 1990s, for example, was considerably lower than in the UK, once the relative size of the two economies is taken into account.[233] The UK model potentially provides a mechanism for addressing the agency problem that exists between directors and shareholders in a dispersed shareholding scenario, incentivising directors to prioritise the shareholders' position even when a bid is not imminent.

A note of caution needs to be added, however. First, it is not clear that takeovers necessarily provide a good corporate governance tool. There may be reasons for a bidder to make a bid other than that existing managers are lazy or self-serving, such as where the purpose of the takeover is to exploit synergies between the bidder and target company.[234]

In addition, this view of takeovers fails to explain MBOs, in which the top management are part of the acquiring team and remain in control of the company. It might also be noted that takeovers can operate as a corporate governance tool only at a very late stage in the day, when things have already gone badly wrong for the company. Takeovers are likely to serve only as a remedy of last resort where there have been massive managerial failures. Corporate acquisitions involve considerable costs and there is no guarantee that the premium available to the bidder, in taking on the under-performing company and putting the corporate assets to better use, will outweigh the total cost of the acquisition.[235]

Other, earlier-operating, more nuanced mechanisms for aligning directors' interests with those of the shareholders might well be more appropriate for incentivising directors, such as managerial compensation schemes.[236] It is unclear why the abstract possibility of a takeover is likely to operate more effectively than, say, performance-related pay, in aligning director and shareholder interests. There are also better, earlier-operating mechanisms for detecting and dealing with management failure.

The link between poorly performing managers and hostile takeovers does not appear to have been established in the UK. Empirical studies have concluded that in the UK '[t]he market for corporate control does not ... function as a disciplinary device for poorly

---

[231] Eg, FH Easterbrook and DR Fischel, *The Economic Structure of Corporate Law* (Cambridge MA, Harvard University Press, 1991).

[232] Clearly, however, the UK takeover regulation model is not designed to maximise the number of takeovers that occur. Although the approach taken on this first issue (ie the sidelining of directors from the decision-making process) will potentially increase the number of takeovers when compared to another jurisdiction which allows directors to entrench themselves, the approach adopted by the UK regime regarding the relationship between the bidder and the target shareholders, discussed at 14.3.4, has the effect of making bids more expensive, potentially decreasing the number of offers made.

[233] Eg, C Kirchner and RW Painter, 'European Takeover Law—Towards a European Modified Business Judgment Rule for Takeover Law' (2000) 2 *European Business Organization Law Review* 353, 377.

[234] For a discussion of the variety of reasons that explain why takeovers occur see R Romano, 'A Guide to Takeovers: Theory, Evidence and Regulation' (1992) 9 *Yale Journal on Regulation* 119. For a discussion of strategic versus financial bidders see AS Gorbenko and A Malenko, 'Strategic and Financial Bidders in Takeover Auctions' (2014) 69 *Journal of Finance* 2513.

[235] Eg, J Coffee, 'Regulating the Market for Corporate Control: A Critical Assessment of the Tender Offer's Role in Corporate Governance' (1984) 84 *Columbia Law Review* 1145.

[236] WG Lewellen, C Loderer and A Rosenfeld, 'Merger Decisions and Executive Stock Ownership in Acquiring Firms' (1985) 7 *Journal of Accounting and Economics* 209; DJ Denis, DK Denis and A Sarin, 'Agency Problems, Equity Ownership and Corporate Diversification' (1997) 52(1) *Journal of Finance* 135. For a UK perspective see A Cosh and A Hughes, 'Managerial Discretion and Takeover Performance', ESRC Centre for Business Research, University of Cambridge Working Paper No 216 (2001).

performing companies'.[237] The role of takeovers as a corporate governance tool appears, therefore, limited at best.[238] Instead, shareholders in the UK, particularly institutional share-holders, have an important role in monitoring management failure.[239] Franks et al have noted the key role that new equity issues appear to play in board restructurings[240]—that is, in removing poorly performing managers. As noted previously, institutional shareholders have significant control over new equity issues via pre-emption rights, which generally need to be disapplied before new shares can be issued. The constraints placed upon this process by the law, and more particularly by guidelines drawn up by the institutional investors themselves, means that directors of publicly traded companies must enter into a dialogue with shareholders before any new issue takes place.[241] In practice, this enables shareholders to express their views on issues, such as the effectiveness of current managers, and a positive relation between UK rights issues and managerial change has been found to exist.[242] It is not at all clear that hostile takeovers are necessarily the best or most cost-effective mecha-nism for ensuring corporate accountability in the UK.

14.3.3 Relationship Between the Target Directors and Other Stakeholders in the Target

One consequence of creating a shareholder-centric system of takeover regulation is that other stakeholders in the target may not be sufficiently protected in the bid process. The difficulties for stakeholders in a shareholder-centric model exist in company law generally, but the problems are potentially more acute in the event of a takeover. In general, the long-term interests of the shareholders are aligned with the interests of other stakeholders, as a result of section 172 of the Companies Act 2006. When determining the directors' duty to promote the success of the company, section 172 requires the directors to act 'for the benefit of its members as a whole' and in doing so the directors are required to have regard to a number of factors, including the interests of a number of different stakeholder groups, such as the employees. Section 172 envisages that the duty of management is a duty to promote the success of the business venture in order to benefit the members. However, these other stakeholder groups are not provided with any remedy under section 172. The only possible litigants are the board, the shareholders,[243] or a liquidator acting on behalf of an insolvent

---

[237] J Franks and C Mayer, 'Hostile Takeovers in the UK and the Correction of Managerial Failure' (1996) 40 *Journal of Financial Economics* 163, 180. See also B Clarke, 'Articles 9 and 11 of the Takeover Directive (2004/25) and the Market for Corporate Control' [2006] *Journal of Business Law* 355.

[238] See also J Coffee, 'Regulating the Market for Corporate Control: A Critical Assessment of the Tender Offer's Role in Corporate Governance' (1984) 84 *Columbia Law Review* 1145.

[239] The role of takeovers as a form of corporate governance is likely to vary according to whether the share-holding structure is generally dispersed or concentrated: S Grundmann, 'The Market for Corporate Control: The Legal Framework, Alternatives and Policy Considerations' in KJ Hopt et al (eds), *Corporate Governance in Context: Corporations, States, and Markets in Europe, Japan, and the US* (Oxford, Oxford University Press, 2005) 421.

[240] J Franks, C Mayer and L Renneboog, 'Who Disciplines Management in Poorly Performing Companies?' (2001) 10 *Journal of Financial Intermediation* 209.

[241] Discussed at 4.4.

[242] J Franks, C Mayer and L Renneboog, 'Who Disciplines Management in Poorly Performing Companies?' (2001) 10 *Journal of Financial Intermediation* 209; D Hillier, SC Linn and P McColgan, 'Equity Issuance, CEO Turnover and Corporate Governance' (2005) 11 *European Financial Management* 515.

[243] See, in the context of minority shareholders, Companies Act 2006, Part 11 (derivative action).

company. Non-shareholder stakeholders do not have any self-standing duties owed to them by the directors; their interests are subsumed generally into the directors' duty to promote the success of the company.[244]

Takeover regulation in the UK does not supplement the common law by giving any decision rights to these groups in the event of a takeover, or by creating any right of action for them. The UK position can be contrasted with that of other European jurisdictions, such as Germany and the Netherlands. In these jurisdictions, employee rights are accorded more recognition by company law generally. In Germany, for instance, employee representatives sit on the supervisory board.[245] This provides employees, though not other stakeholders, with increased protection in the event of a takeover, as it is more likely that employee interests can be taken into account in the takeover decision. In these jurisdictions, takeover regulation also supplements the general company law provisions with additional protections for employees in the event of a takeover.[246]

In a takeover situation the shareholders may have a much shorter-term focus than usual. They may only be interested in the cash that the bidder can offer them, not the future of the company, or the wellbeing of other stakeholders. A debate regarding the role, in takeovers, of stakeholders in general, and employees in particular, has questioned the value of the no frustration principle. It is suggested that the ban on defensive measures by the target board has a potentially deleterious effect on the company's relationship with its key stakeholders, and that hostile takeovers should be regarded as rent-seeking, rather than value-enhancing. Some commentators have suggested that the managerialist system of company law can encourage employees to specialise their skills, and to make investments in firm-specific human capital.[247] Where implicit contracts are put in place to encourage employees to invest in a company in this way,[248] it has been suggested that employees can in some sense be regarded as residual claimants of the company alongside the shareholders. Similar arguments can be made in relation to other stakeholders in the company, such as suppliers. Indeed, it has been acknowledged that adopting a strong shareholder-centric approach could lead to increased risks for 'employees, suppliers and others, on whom the company depends for factors of production', particularly in a takeover scenario.[249] In a hostile takeover, a change of managers allows these implicit contracts to be breached, enabling a wealth transfer between employees and shareholders to take place.[250]

---

[244] See 3.2.1.3.1.

[245] Aktiengesetz §§96, 101, 103–04.

[246] For discussion see R Kraakman et al, *The Anatomy of Corporate Law*, 2nd edn (Oxford, Oxford University Press, 2009) 8.5.

[247] MM Blair, *Ownership and Control: Rethinking Corporate Governance for the Twenty-First Century* (Washington, DC, Brookings Institution, 1995).

[248] Implicit contracts are non-binding social arrangements which are typically enforced through market forces (see eg MA O'Connor, 'Restructuring the Corporation's Nexus of Contracts: Recognizing a Fiduciary Duty to Protect Displaced Workers' (1990) 69 *North Carolina Law Review* 1189). Examples of implicit contracts include career ladders and remuneration structures that reward seniority.

[249] Company Law Review Steering Group, *Modern Company Law for a Competitive Economy: The Strategic Framework* (URN 99/654, February 1999), 42.

[250] A Shleifer and LH Summers, 'Breach of Trust in Hostile Takeovers' in AJ Auerbach (ed), *Corporate Takeovers: Causes and Consequences* (Chicago, University of Chicago Press, 1988). This could be cured in part by the use of legally binding contracts and paying employees more in the present in return for increased uncertainty about future payments.

The 'expropriation' explanation of hostile takeovers is not uncontested.[251] If it is correct, however, then takeover regulation should, arguably, contain some protection for non-shareholder stakeholder groups.[252] Some US commentators have suggested that this can be achieved by providing a degree of entrenchment for incumbent target directors, and freedom from shareholder control in the takeover scenario.[253] This would, however, be contrary to the no frustration principle of the Takeover Code. Of course, where the board is given a significant role in the takeover process, such as in the US, it is possible for the target directors to further the interests of these other stakeholder groups. Indeed, it is common in the US for statutes to expand the range of interests that directors are entitled, but not bound,[254] to take into account in responding to a takeover bid, beyond those of the shareholders.[255] However, the value of this strategy depends upon the directors actually acting protectively towards these groups in the event of a takeover, and not using their position to act in a purely self-interested way. In general, it can be expected that non-shareholder stakeholder groups will be protected only to the extent that their interests coincide with those of the directors.[256]

In the wake of the successful bid by Kraft for Cadbury in 2010, these issues were discussed in the UK. In 2009, Kraft made a hostile bid of £10.5 billion for Cadbury. This offer was not recommended by the Cadbury board, and was not accepted by the Cadbury shareholders. In January 2010, Kraft increased its offer to 840 pence per Cadbury share, consisting of 500 pence in cash, with the rest made up of Kraft shares, totalling an offer of around £11.9 billion. The Cadbury board did recommended this offer to its shareholders, and it was subsequently accepted by over 70 per cent of Cadbury shareholders. This takeover caused considerable public and political distress, one reason being that Kraft had made assurances during its bid of its intention to keep open one particular factory situated in England, but, less than a week after the offer was accepted by the Cadbury shareholders, Kraft announced the closure of this factory.[257]

This takeover prompted a consultation by the Code Committee of the Takeover Panel regarding whether it is too easy for a hostile bidder under UK takeover regulation to obtain control of more than 50 per cent of the voting rights of a target company,[258] and whether

---

[251] Eg, R Romano, 'A Guide to Takeovers: Theory, Evidence and Regulation' in KJ Hopt and E Wymeersch (eds), *European Takeovers: Law and Practice* (London, Butterworths, 1992).

[252] Some commentators suggest that protection of stakeholder interests should be left principally to the contracts between them and the company: R Daniels, 'Stakeholders and Takeovers: Can Contractarianism be Compassionate?' (1993) 43 *University of Toronto Law Journal* 315.

[253] MM Blair and LA Stout, 'A Team Production Theory of Corporate Law' (1999) 85 *Virginia Law Review* 247, but see D Millon, 'New Game Plan or Business as Usual? A Critique of the Team Production Model of Corporate Law' (2000) 86 *Virginia Law Review* 1001.

[254] A prescription to directors to take the interests of all constituencies into account 'is essentially vacuous, because it allows management to justify almost any action on the grounds that it benefits some group': O Hart, 'An Economist's View of Fiduciary Duties' (1993) 43 *University of Toronto Law Journal* 299, 303.

[255] Eg, New York Business Corporation Law, §717(b).

[256] Eg, MJ Roe, *Political Determinants of Corporate Governance: Political Context, Corporate Impact* (Oxford, Oxford University Press, 2002) 45. The increase in the use of director compensation schemes and performance-related pay means that directors are more likely to be aligned with shareholder interests (since they hold a significant part of their wealth in the form of shares and options) than with the interests of bondholders or employees (since the directors will have less of their wealth tied to bondholder or employee wealth).

[257] This led, subsequently, to the Takeover Panel reprimanding Kraft: Takeover Panel Statement, 2010/14, 26 May 2010.

[258] Panel Statement 2010/6, Consultation on Aspects of the Takeover Code.

the outcomes of takeover bids in the UK, particularly hostile bids, are unduly influenced by the actions of 'short-term' investors—that is, those investors who become interested in the shares of the target company only after the possibility of an offer has been publicly announced. One focus for this concern was the position of the stakeholders in the target company. Lord Mandelson, the then Business Secretary, said: 'it is hard to ignore the fact that the fate of the company with a long history and many tens of thousands of employees was decided by people who had not owned the company a few weeks earlier, and probably had no intention of owning it a few weeks later.'[259]

The Code Committee's consultation document considered a broad range of issues in this context, including whether the minimum acceptance condition threshold for a successful takeover offer should be raised, perhaps to 60 per cent or two-thirds of the voting rights in the target company, and whether voting rights should be withheld from shares in a target acquired during the course of an offer period so that those shares are 'disenfranchised' for the purposes of a takeover bid. The consultation also considered whether bidders should be required to provide more information in relation to the financing of takeover bids and their implications and effects, and, further, whether the boards of target companies should be required to set out their views on the bidder's intentions for the target company in greater detail.[260] The majority of these changes were not taken forward.[261] The Takeover Code makes one concession to one category of non-shareholder stakeholders: it requires information disclosure to the employees of the target company. The major change resulting from the 2010 Consultation, as far as non-shareholder stakeholders were concerned, was a limited extension of this disclosure obligation. The bidder is required to disclose its intentions regarding the future of the company, including 'its strategic plans for the offeree company, and their likely repercussions on employment' and 'its intentions with regard to the continued employment of the employees and management of the offeree company and of its subsidiaries, including any material change in the conditions of employment'.[262] In addition, when the target board gives its advice to the target shareholders regarding the bid it is required to include its views, and the reasons for those views, on the implications of the bid for the employees.[263] These documents must be made available to the employees' representatives or, in their absence, to the employees themselves.[264] Changes following the 2010 consultation mean that the bidder must now disclose greater detail on the financing of the offer.[265] None of these provisions provide the employees with any decision rights in

[259] Lord Mandelson, Speech at the annual Trade and Industry dinner, Mansion House, London, 1 March 2010.

[260] Panel Statement 2010/6, Consultation on Aspects of the Takeover Code.

[261] Code Committee of the Takeover Panel, *Review of Certain Aspects of the Regulation of Takeover Bids*, 2010/22. For discussion see J Payne, 'Minority Shareholder Protection in Public Takeovers: A UK Perspective' (2011) 8 *European Company and Financial Law Review* 145; G Tsagas 'A Long-Term Vision for UK Firms? Reconsidering Target Director's Advisory Role Post the Takeover of Cadbury's plc' (2014) 14(1) *Journal of Corporate Law Studies* 241.

[262] Takeover Code, r 24.2. Statements of intention of this kind are expected to commit the bidder to that course of action for a period of 12 months from the date on which the offer period ends (see r 19.1 n 3 and see Code Committee of the Panel, *Consultation Paper: Post Offer Undertakings and Intention Statements*, PCP 2014/2, 15 September 2014). In the wake of its takeover of Cadbury, Kraft was censured by the Takeover Panel for failing to keep its promise that it would keep the factory open.

[263] Ibid, r 25.2(a).

[264] Ibid, rr 26, 32.6.

[265] Ibid, r 24.3(f). For discussion see Code Committee of the Takeover Panel, *Review of Certain Aspects of the Regulation of Takeover Bids*, 2010/22, 19–20.

the bid. No other non-shareholder stakeholder group is provided with any protection by UK takeover regulation. Instead, protection is left to the contracts between the stakeholders and the company, and more specialist regulation, such as employment law.[266]

One other group requires brief mention, namely the creditors. Changes to the company's risk profile consequent upon a successful takeover, perhaps as a result of the bid being highly leveraged, may well have a significant impact on the company's creditors. As discussed in chapters five, six and seven, many creditors will be in a position to protect themselves against risks of this kind in their contract, either via security, or other contractual provisions such as covenants requiring the company to maintain certain debt-equity ratios. The latter type of contractual protection might also provide some protection for non-adjusting creditors, as they may be able to free-ride on the protection put in place by the adjusting creditors.

14.3.4 Relationship Between the Bidder and the Target Shareholders

The effect of the no frustration principle, discussed above at 14.3.2, means that when the bidder makes an offer for the target company, the bidder deals not with the target board but with the target shareholders. In the UK, where dispersed share ownership is the common pattern in publicly traded companies, the bidder tends to deal with the target shareholders as a class, in contrast to the position where the target company has a concentrated ownership structure, in which case the bidder will deal first and foremost with the controlling shareholders.

In the two previous categories, namely the relationship between the target directors and target shareholders, and the relationship between target directors and other stakeholders in the company, general company law principles govern these relationships and provide a base on top of which takeover regulation can be added. As discussed, a more significant top-up of general company law principles occurs in the UK in relation to the first of these two relationships. By contrast, company law has nothing to say about the relationship between the bidder and the target shareholders. In the absence of takeover regulation, the relevant principles governing this relationship are found in contract law.

The bidder deals with each target shareholder separately. In the absence of specific takeover regulation, bidders could offer different deals to different shareholders, or make offers with very short periods for acceptance. Bidders would have the opportunity to 'divide and conquer', skewing the offer in order to acquire the company at the cheapest possible price. For instance, the bidder could offer one price to those who accept the offer quickly, up until the bidder acquires control, and then could reduce the offer, leaving the remaining shareholders with the choice of accepting the lower offer or staying in the company now under the bidder's control. Shareholders would find it hard to obtain reliable information regarding the offers made to their fellow shareholders, and whether their fellow shareholders intend

---

[266] For example, where a highly leveraged bid for a target company is successful, one of the consequences may be that the risk that the company will default on its obligations under its occupational pension scheme may increase. In these circumstances the Pensions Regulator has the power to require the bidder to make extraordinary payments into the fund, in order to secure the position of the employees. If the bidder refuses to do so the offer will not proceed. See Pensions Act 2004, ss 43–51.

to accept the bid. The collective action problems faced by the target shareholders potentially increase the bargaining strength of the bidder at the target shareholders' expense. In the anonymous market that exists for publicly traded securities, it may be that the shareholder is not even aware that they are dealing with someone who is attempting to obtain control of the company.

UK takeover regulation intervenes to regulate the relationship between the bidder and the target shareholders.[267] Indeed, to a large extent these principles are now enshrined in the Takeover Directive, so that throughout Europe takeover regulation intervenes in this relationship, although there remains some variation between Member States as to how these principles operate in practice.[268] The directive provides that 'all holders of the securities of an offeree company of the same class must be afforded equivalent treatment; moreover, if a person acquires control of a company, the other holders of securities must be protected'.[269] This statement is repeated verbatim in General Principle 1 (GP 1) of the Takeover Code, although this same principle was also found in the Code prior to the implementation of the directive. The principle of equality of treatment between the shareholders in the target is an idea that has been entrenched in the Takeover Code from its inception. Broadly, this principle provides that the consideration paid by the bidder to acquire the target should be shared equally between shareholders of the same class and proportionately between shareholders of different classes.

Before considering how the UK has regulated this issue, it is important to understand why this principle is enshrined in takeover regulation. After all, the idea of equality amongst shareholders in a bid situation stands in contrast to general UK company law principles, in which shareholders must be treated fairly, but not necessarily equally.[270] Indeed, it is generally accepted that controlling shares in a company are worth more than non-controlling ones,[271] which contradicts the idea of all shareholders being paid rateably in a takeover scenario. The pursuit of equality amongst shareholders for its own sake does not seem to justify the imposition of the equality rules that are put in place during a takeover. Some other principle(s) must be at work to explain the imposition of these rules. There seem to be two principal concerns at work in this context: the need to ensure that the decision taken by the shareholders is as undistorted as possible, and a desire to protect the minority/non-controlling shareholders from abuse.[272]

---

[267] For a comparison of the protection put in place for the shareholders in a takeover effected via a scheme of arrangement see chapter 15 and J Payne, 'Schemes of Arrangement, Takeovers and Minority Shareholder Protection' (2011) 11 *Journal of Corporate Law Studies* 67.

[268] For a comparative discussion of the concept of equality in the takeover context in the UK, Austria, France, Germany, Switzerland and Italy, see P Davies, 'The Notion of Equality in European Takeover Regulation' in J Payne (ed), *Takeovers in English and German Law* (Oxford, Hart Publishing, 2002).

[269] Takeover Directive 2004/25/EC, art 3.

[270] Eg, *Mutual Life Insurance Co of New York v Rank Organisation Ltd* [1985] BCLC 11.

[271] *Short v Treasury Commissioners* [1948] AC 534.

[272] A third argument that can be made relates to a desire to equalise the position of those shareholders who are close to the market (typically institutional shareholders) and those not close to the market (typically individual shareholders): P Davies, 'The Notion of Equality in European Takeover Regulation' in J Payne (ed), *Takeovers in English and German Law* (Oxford, Hart Publishing, 2002) 18–20. However, on the whole the concerns in this context can be seen as aspects of the two principal concerns discussed in the text.

14.3.4.1 Undistorted Choice

It is clear that the bidder can use the tactics described above to put pressure on the shareholders to accept a particular offer, even if the shareholders do not think that the offer is in their interests. If the best offer is available only to those that accept quickly, there is clearly pressure on the shareholders to accept, particularly where they cannot determine the intentions of their fellow shareholders.[273] Where the decision on the outcome of the bid is given primarily to the shareholders rather than the target board, however, as it is in the UK, it is crucial that the shareholders' decision-making should be as undistorted as possible.[274] A result of the pressure to tender might be that the bidder will succeed in gaining control over a target even if the value-maximising course of action for the target shareholders would be to reject the bid. The undistorted choice argument is, therefore, an allocative efficiency argument. Efficiency requires that corporate assets be put to their most productive use. While the acquisition of some companies would produce efficiency gains, perhaps from an improvement in management, the assets of other companies are best left under existing management. A target company should be acquired if, and only if, a majority of its shareholders view the offered acquisition price as higher than the independent target's value.[275] As a result, 'ensuring undistorted choice is desirable from the perspectives of both target shareholders and society'.[276]

There are a number of provisions within the Takeover Code that can be seen as promoting undistorted choice amongst the target shareholders. First, within a class of shareholders, such as the class of equity voting shares, the offer must be the same to all those within the class.[277] The Code goes further, however, and requires an equality of protection not only within a class, but also between classes, at least in relation to equity share capital.[278] When a target company has more than one class of equity share capital, a 'comparable' offer must be made for each class, whether it carries voting rights or not.[279] The Takeover Code has rules in place to try to prevent the bidder offering disguised enhanced deals to only some of the shareholders.[280]

---

[273] The need to protect the shareholders' undistorted choice in making this decision is not based on an entitlement argument. The entitlement argument would assert that ensuring undistorted choice is necessary to protect the property rights that a target's shareholders have in the assets they own (see eg LA Bebchuk, 'Toward an Undistorted Choice and Equal Treatment in Corporate Takeovers' (1985) 98 *Harvard Law Review* 1693, 1764 fn 154). However, UK company law seems to regard shareholders as being protected by a liability rule rather than a property rule in relation to their shares, ie expropriation of shares is allowed provided a fair price is paid for those shares (see discussion at 3.2.1.3.2(b)).

[274] Even in systems that interpose the target board between the bidder and the target shareholders, such as the US, undistorted decision-making is important for those occasions on which the directors allow (or are required by the court to allow) the target shareholders to consider the bid.

[275] See eg LA Bebchuk, 'Toward an Undistorted Choice and Equal Treatment in Corporate Takeovers' (1985) 98 *Harvard Law Review* 1693; L Bebchuk, 'The Pressure to Tender: An Analysis and a Proposed Remedy' (1987) 12 *Delaware Journal of Corporate Law* 911.

[276] L Bebchuk, 'The Pressure to Tender: An Analysis and a Proposed Remedy' (1987) 12 *Delaware Journal of Corporate Law* 911, 913. The independent target's value refers to the value that the target will have if it remains, at least for the time being, independent; this value of the independent target obviously includes the value of the prospect of receiving higher acquisition offers in the future.

[277] Takeover Code, GP 1.

[278] Ibid, r 14.1. As regards classes of non-equity shares, in a voluntary bid no offer is required, unless the shares are convertible into equity shares (r 15). On a mandatory bid, an offer must be made for non-equity securities carrying voting rights, although these are rare in practice: r 9.1.

[279] Ibid, r 14.

[280] Ibid, r 16.

The definition of class for these purposes has been determined strictly. In the Eurotunnel takeover, for example, some shareholders had certain travel privileges. When a share-for-share offer was made to the Eurotunnel shareholders by a bidder company, the offer included the term that those shareholders accepting the offer would lose their travel privileges. This offer was made to all shareholders, whether they held travel privileges or not. The bidder argued that, in accordance with GP 1, it had treated all the shareholders equally. The shareholders with travel privileges argued that they were a separate class and that the offer did not take proper account of the value of their travel privileges. The Takeover Panel Executive ruled that there was no breach of the Takeover Code since these rights were personal rights only. No class rights existed in the articles of Eurotunnel and therefore the bidder had behaved properly. This decision was upheld on appeal by the Takeover Appeal Board.[281]

These rules are important, as they prevent the bidder skewing the consideration it offers, for example by offering enhanced deals to some shareholders, such as the first to accept. They thereby help to prevent a pressure to accept arising amongst those to whom the offer is made. The Takeover Code goes even further, however, in promoting equality of treatment between shareholders within the bid. If the offer is subsequently increased by the bidder, then even those who accepted the original offer are entitled to the new, higher price.[282]

The Takeover Code requires not only equality of treatment of shareholders within the bid, but also equality as between offerees and sellers outside the bid.[283] Prior to the introduction of the Takeover Code it was common practice for bidders to enter into deals with some shareholders outside the formal offer at a higher price than that offered to the shareholders in the general bid. If allowed, this would clearly undermine the equality of treatment principle that the Takeover Code seeks to protect. It is, therefore, unsurprising that the Takeover Code seeks to prevent the bidder from doing favourable deals with a few selected shareholders, either before the offer period[284] or during the offer period.[285] The Code achieves this by providing that, if the bidder makes a favourable offer to a shareholder outside the bid in this way, the bidder must raise the level of the general offer made to shareholders of that class in order to match the favourable offer made to the select few.[286]

The bidder could also seek to put pressure on the shareholders by engaging in a campaign of buying up shares in the target prior to the offer, at a higher price than the general offer it makes subsequently. The shareholders dealing with the bidder prior to the bid would feel under pressure to accept if they knew or suspected that the subsequent general offer would be lower, while the shareholders faced with the general offer might find that the bidder

---

[281] See www.thetakeoverappeal board.org.uk/statements.html.

[282] Takeover Code, r 32.3.

[283] See P Davies, 'The Notion of Equality in European Takeover Regulation' in J Payne (ed), *Takeovers in English and German Law* (Oxford, Hart Publishing, 2002).

[284] Takeover Code, r 6.1, which specifies a period of three months before the offer period, but the Panel can extend the period if it believes it is necessary to give effect to GP 1. The Panel can relax this rule if it thinks it appropriate to do so.

[285] Ibid, r 6.2.

[286] Distinctions are drawn in the Takeover Code, r 6 between purchases before the offer period begins and those made after a firm intention to make an offer has been announced. In relation to the latter, if the favourable deal to select shareholders is a cash offer, the general offer made under r 6.2 must also be a cash offer. However, the rules are more relaxed in relation to pre-offer period purchases (see r 6.1), unless r 11.1 applies.

already has de facto control of the target.[287] Consequently, the Takeover Code regulates this scenario, providing that in some circumstances purchases made by the bidder prior to the offer will impact on the required level of consideration offered by the bidder in the general offer. However, limits are set on this principle. It is not all prior purchases by the bidder that will per se have this effect, only those where the bidder, and any persons acting in concert with it, have acquired for cash shares in the target which carry at least 10 per cent of the voting rights in the 12 months prior to the offer.[288] In these circumstances the subsequent offer must be in cash or be accompanied by a cash alternative at the highest level paid outside the offer.[289] Where the initial offer is of securities, the bidder must also offer the same number of securities to the target shareholder in the general offer,[290] although generally it will be the cash alternative that will be most attractive to the target shareholders.

Perhaps the strongest expression of the equality principle at work in the Takeover Code is the mandatory bid rule.[291] The essence of this rule is that, once a person, together with anyone with whom he is acting in concert, acquires 30 per cent of the shares carrying voting rights, or holds between 30 and 50 per cent and acquires additional shares carrying voting rights, then a mandatory bid is required.[292] In other words, the mandatory bid rule is triggered when control of a company is secured, assumed for these purposes to occur when 30 per cent of the voting shares are secured, or when control is consolidated by further acquisitions above the 30 per cent level. In general, it is the first of these limbs that is most important. After all, in most cases the second limb will not be reached unless the 30 per cent threshold has been passed.[293] Once the mandatory bid is triggered, that person must extend offers to the holders of any class of equity share capital (voting or non-voting) and also to

---

[287] One issue is how easy it will be to determine whether the bidder is buying shares in the target prior to making a bid, particularly where the bidder is acting via a nominee. Of course, there is an obligation on shareholders to declare their interest in shares which is triggered when a shareholder holds 3 per cent of the total voting rights in the company, and at every 1 per cent thereafter (FCA Handbook, DTR 5.1.2 discussed at 11.3.2.3). These provisions are intended to make the interests of shareholders transparent even where the bidder is acting via a nominee. In addition, Companies Act 2006, s 793 provides that a public company (whether its shares are traded on a public market or not) may serve notice on a person whom it knows, or has reasonable cause to believe, to have been interested in the voting shares of the company at any time in the preceding three years.

[288] The Panel can exercise its discretion to trigger this requirement even where the 10% threshold has not been reached, if the equality principle requires this: r 11.1(c). The Panel has indicated that an appropriate case might be where the vendors are the directors of the target: Note 4 to r 11.

[289] Takeover Code, r 11.1.

[290] Ibid, r 11.2. This offers weaker protection than r 11.1 since it is only triggered if the prior acquisitions occurred in the three months before the bid; r 11.1 includes prior acquisitions in the 12 months before the bid.

[291] Takeover Code, r 9.1. The mandatory bid rule is now required by Takeover Directive 2004/25/EC, art 5. Implementation of this article required some minor amendments to r 9 of the Takeover Code, although the mandatory bid rule in the Code remains tougher than that required by the directive.

[292] Ibid, r 9.1. When a group of persons act in concert to acquire control of a company, r 9.2 imposes an obligation to make a general offer on the person who takes the group's shareholding over the threshold, and also on the 'principal members' of the group, if the triggering acquirer is not such a member. If, when the group decide to act, they already hold 30% of the voting shares, then the mandatory bid rule is not triggered when the group make their agreement, but any subsequent acquisition of shares by any of them will trigger the requirement (r 9.1 n 1). This includes institutional investors who come together to exercise their rights as shareholders, although no mandatory bid will be triggered if the shareholders are not seeking 'board control'. Even if the shareholder coalition is seeking to change the whole of the board it will not be regarded as seeking 'board control' if there is no relationship between the institutional shareholders and the proposed new directors (see r 9.1 n 2).

[293] There may be occasions when the mandatory bid is only triggered by the second limb, such as where the Panel waived the mandatory bid when the 30% level was passed, or where a concert party reached agreement at a time when they already held 30% of the shares between them.

the holders of any other class of transferable securities carrying voting rights.[294] The offer must be a cash offer, or with a cash alternative, and at the highest price paid by the offeror or a member of his concert party within the 12 months prior to the commencement of the offer.[295] The mandatory bid must not contain any conditions other than that it is dependent on acceptances resulting in the bidder holding 50 per cent of the voting rights.[296] The mandatory bid rule is also bolstered by a general antipathy towards partial offers, since allowing bidders to launch partial bids without restriction would quickly allow the mandatory bid rule to be undermined.[297]

The mandatory bid rule can be regarded as having an impact on the issue of undistorted shareholder choice.[298] Without this rule it may be that a shareholder would be more inclined to accept the offer, fearing that once the bidder has control it will be stuck in the target company and the value of its shares may have declined since the bidder will have no obligation to make a general offer at that point.[299] Another possible aim of the mandatory bid rule, however, is the protection of minority shareholders, discussed below at 14.3.4.2.

There are other aspects of the Takeover Code that are intended to promote undistorted choice. These include the need for the target shareholders to have adequate information upon which to base a decision, and the requirement that they should have enough time to reach a decision. An initial offer must be open for acceptance for at least 21 days,[300] and revised offers for 14 days.[301] These rules reflect General Principle 2 of the Code, which states that '[t]he holders of the securities of an offeree company must have sufficient time and information to enable them to reach a properly informed decision on the bid'. They are intended to prevent the bidder putting undue pressure on the target shareholders by keeping offers open for a very short period, which would not give shareholders time to properly assess the merits of the bid. It has been pointed out that, from an individual shareholder's perspective, there are three outcomes of an offer: the offer is rejected, the offer is accepted

---

[294] Takeover Code, r 9.1. The Panel may exercise its discretion to waive the requirement of a mandatory bid in some circumstances, either entirely, or subject to the agreement of the majority of the target shareholders. This will generally occur where the 30% threshold is breached inadvertently (and the error rectified quickly) or where the acquisition of 30% does not confer control (eg, where another shareholder holds 50% of the shares). One scenario in which the Panel will generally waive the requirement is where the actions of the company (eg, redeeming or repurchasing its shares) take a shareholder over the 30% boundary without having acted itself. In these circumstances the Panel will normally waive the bid obligation provided it is consulted in advance, the independent shareholders of the target agree and the procedure set out in Appendix 1 to the Takeover Code is followed: r 37.

[295] Takeover Code, r 9.5. The Panel can agree to an adjusted price.

[296] Ibid, r 9.3.

[297] The starting point in the Takeover Code is that partial offers will not be allowed: r 36. The Panel will usually consent to partial offers which would result in the offeror holding less than 30% of the voting rights in the target company: r 36.1. Consent will not normally be given if the offer could result in the offeror being interested in shares carrying 30% or more of the voting rights in the target company: r 36.1, but see rr 36.2–36.8 which deal with partial offers where the offeror could obtain more than 30% (in which case the partial offer is dependent, inter alia, on the bidder obtaining shareholder approval from 50% of the target shareholders: r 36.5).

[298] For discussion see E-P Schuster, 'The Mandatory Bid Rule: Efficient, After All?' (2013) 76(3) *Modern Law Review* 529.

[299] Bebchuk has argued that this rule falls short of attaining undistorted choice: 'Under the rule, a buyer will succeed in gaining control whenever it is willing to pay a per-share acquisition price that exceeds the independent target's value in the view of a sufficiently large plurality of the shareholders. According to the undistorted choice objective, however, the buyer should gain control only if such a view is held by a *majority* of the shareholders': LA Bebchuk, 'Toward an Undistorted Choice and Equal Treatment in Corporate Takeovers' (1985) 98 *Harvard Law Review* 1693, 1801.

[300] Takeover Code, r 31.1.

[301] Ibid, r 32.1.

by the majority of shareholders, including the individual, and the offer is accepted by the majority, not including the individual.[302] The shareholder may prefer the first outcome, but be so nervous about the possibility of the third outcome that he feels pressured to accept the offer. Keeping the offer open for this further period avoids this pressure to accept.[303]

In summary, therefore, undistorted choice is a crucial aspect of UK takeover regulation. In a jurisdiction such as the UK, where the target board have effectively been sidelined, and yet the shareholders are dispersed and therefore face significant coordination problems, these rules are key. Takeover regulation therefore needs to counteract this problem. This section has examined a number of the measures which seek to deal with this situation. As a result of the Takeover Directive, many of these provisions are now common throughout Europe.[304] By contrast, the position in the US gives the target directors a significant role in determining the outcome of the takeover decision and, therefore, provides the potential for the directors to protect the target shareholders from opportunistic behaviour on the part of the bidder. Accordingly, the need for specific regulation to protect the target shareholders from exploitation by the bidder is less obvious, and in practice fewer protections are put in place to deal with this issue. Two-tier offers are allowed in the US, for example.[305]

14.3.4.2 Protection of Minority Shareholders

The provisions described in 14.3.4.1 can be regarded as playing an important role in ensuring that the shareholders' decision in determining whether to accept the tender offer is as undistorted as possible. These measures are also sometimes said to be valuable as a form of minority shareholder protection. The sell-out rule, which allows the last 10 per cent of shareholders to exit the company at a fair price in some circumstances,[306] can be viewed in this light, as can the mandatory bid rule.[307]

---

[302] LA Bebchuk, 'Toward an Undistorted Choice and Equal Treatment in Corporate Takeovers' (1985) 98 *Harvard Law Review* 1693; LA Bebchuk, 'The Pressure to Tender: An Analysis and a Proposed Remedy' (1987) 12 *Delaware Journal of Corporate Law* 911, 922–31.

[303] Bebchuk points out that this provision can also cause difficulties, as it could encourage shareholders to adopt a 'wait and see' approach. A shareholder who would like the bid to proceed might decide not to tender in the 'first round'. If the bid is going to succeed regardless of his decision, then his tender decision will not matter, since shareholders who tender in the 'first round' and those who will tender in the 'second round' will be treated equally. If the bid is going to fail regardless of his decision, the shareholder will be somewhat better off holding out: since the Takeover Code requires failing bidders to return all tendered shares, tendering would lead only to unnecessary transaction costs. The outcome of bids might consequently be distorted *against* bidders: a bid might well fail even if a majority of the shareholders would prefer that it succeed: LA Bebchuk, 'Toward an Undistorted Choice and Equal Treatment in Corporate Takeovers' (1985) 98 *Harvard Law Review* 1693, 1797–98.

[304] Takeover Directive 2004/25/EC, art 3(1)(a) provides that 'all holders of the securities of an offeree company of the same class must be afforded equivalent treatment; moreover, if a person acquires control of a company, the other holders of securities must be protected' (repeated verbatim at Takeover Code, GP 1).

[305] For a discussion of the pressure that can be put on US shareholders see eg LA Bebchuk, 'Pressure to Tender: An Analysis and a Proposed Remedy' (1987) 12 *Delaware Journal of Corporate Law* 911.

[306] Companies Act 2006, ss 983–85, discussed at 14.3.1.4.

[307] According to the Winter Group, one of the reasons for putting a sell-out remedy in place is prevention of abuse for minority shareholders, ie the same reasoning as the mandatory bid rule (the other reasons being the promotion of undistorted choice and protection against an illiquid market for the company's shares): *Report of the High Level Group of Experts on Issues Related to Takeover Bids*, Brussels, January 2002, 63. However, all three of these reasons have been doubted by Professor Davies, who suggests that the more likely explanation for the sell-out right is that it is regarded as a fair counterpart to the squeeze-out rule: P Davies, 'The Notion of Equality in European Takeover Regulation' in J Payne (ed), *Takeovers in English and German Law* (Oxford, Hart Publishing, 2002) 21.

The need to provide minority shareholders with protection in this scenario requires some thought. Equal treatment of shareholders for its own sake, perhaps based on 'widely held notions of fairness',[308] does not per se justify these rules. Company law in the UK does not seek to treat shareholders equally,[309] and it accepts that in general a controlling stake in a company is worth more than a non-controlling stake, which runs contrary to the pro rata sharing of consideration which lies at the heart of the concept of equal treatment of shareholders in a takeover. Of course, this disjunction is not readily apparent in most UK companies involved in a takeover, since dispersed share ownership will be the norm in this scenario. Nevertheless, the pursuit of equality amongst shareholders for its own sake is not a goal found elsewhere in company law. An analysis of the substantive justifications for the concept of equality is required. To the extent that equal treatment of shareholders contributes to undistorted choice, this issue has been dealt with above at 14.3.4.1.

Two arguments can be made in favour of providing minority shareholders with this additional protection in a bid situation. The first is that the bidder, once successful and in control of the target, may engage in oppressive acts towards the minority, and the minority will need protection from that potential oppression. The second is that shareholders should be entitled to a right of exit when a change of control occurs following a takeover.

14.3.4.2.1 Prevention of Oppression

It is sometimes suggested that the mandatory bid rule is needed in order to prevent oppression of the minority by the bidder. Two arguments may be advanced to cast doubt on this view. First, the effect of these rules is to give the minority shareholders a remedy on the basis that they may suffer oppression in the future, not on the basis that they have indeed suffered oppression at the hands of the new controller. However, the mere fact that a company has a new controller does not usually lead to a prediction that the new controller will behave oppressively, and it is not clear why a different approach should be followed in the context of a takeover.[310] In general, remedies in company law are provided to minority shareholders on the basis that they have suffered actual abuse, and a remedy is likely to be denied to a minority shareholder who relies on merely the potential for abuse to occur in the future.[311] It is not clear why the position should be so markedly different in relation to takeovers.

Second, company law already provides remedies for minority shareholders faced with actual abuse. One justification for the mandatory bid rule is that the remedies provided generally by company law are inadequate to protect the minority shareholders following a change of control in a takeover situation, and that takeover regulation needs to step in in order to bridge the gap. The primary remedy available to shareholders provided by company law is found in section 994 of the Companies Act 2006. This provision allows minority shareholders to petition the court in the event of unfairly prejudicial conduct, the usual

---

[308] LA Bebchuk, 'Toward an Undistorted Choice and Equal Treatment in Corporate Takeovers' (1985) 98 *Harvard Law Review* 1693, 1707.

[309] Eg, *Mutual Life Insurance Co of New York v Rank Organisation Ltd* [1985] BCLC 11, discussed at 4.2.2.2.

[310] The exception might be where the bidder has a history of acting oppressively towards the minority of target shareholders.

[311] See eg *Re Astec (BSR) plc* [1998] 2 BCLC 556 (involving an unfair prejudice petition under s 459 Companies Act 1985, now restated as s 994 Companies Act 2006) where the perceived premature nature of the petition was a contributory factor in the dismissal of the petition.

remedy being that, if unfairly prejudicial conduct has occurred, the court will order the buy-out of the petitioner's shares.[312] The unfairness contemplated by section 994 'may consist in a breach of the rules or in using the rules in a manner which equity would regard as contrary to good faith'.[313]

In other words, a section 994 petition can be based on an infringement of the petitioner's legal rights, such as a breach of the articles, or on the unfair use of power which abuses the enjoyment of legal rights. Section 994 petitions generally involve small, quasi-partnership companies where the abuse falls into the second category, a typical fact pattern being that the majority are seeking to remove the minority shareholder from their position as director and, while the appropriate procedure has been followed,[314] the removal is said to be in breach of some informal agreement that the minority remain a director.

In the context of large, publicly traded companies, which is the usual scenario in which takeovers occur, while unfair prejudice petitions are possible, successful petitions are extremely rare. Indeed, the view of the courts is generally that allowing unfair prejudice petitions in such companies is a 'recipe for chaos'.[315] There are good reasons for this view. If legal rights are infringed, then a section 994 petition in the publicly traded company context is certainly possible. The sort of oppression that seems to be contemplated following a takeover, however, such as changes to the company's business strategy, seem unlikely to involve such an infringement. This leaves the second category of unfairness. The sorts of informal arrangements that can give rise to a successful section 994 action in small private companies[316] are unlikely to arise in the public company context, however, and, indeed, arguably should have no place in this context: 'If the market in a company's shares is to have any credibility members of the public dealing in that market must it seems to me be entitled to proceed on the footing that the constitution of the company is as it appears in the company's public documents, unaffected by any extraneous equitable considerations and constraints.'[317] Of course, it is possible for unfair prejudice to be felt by all members of a company,[318] so that 'universal expectations'[319] can form the basis for a petition. However, it can be difficult for judges to determine whether unfair prejudice has occurred in the absence of a clear guideline, such as an informal arrangement between the shareholders, and to date they have been reluctant to do so in the context of publicly traded companies.[320]

The other reason for the rarity of unfair prejudice petitions in the context of publicly traded companies is the existence of an active market for the company's shares, which provides unhappy shareholders with immediate access to the remedy that is most often awarded following a successful petition, namely a buy-out of the petitioner's shares at a fair price. In a publicly traded company the fair price will generally be the market price of the shares.

---

[312] Companies Act 2006, s 996 provides the court with a very wide discretion as to the remedy that it can award. Buy out of the petitioner's shares is by no means the only possibility, although it is the most common.

[313] *O'Neill v Phillips* [1999] 1 WLR 1092, 1099 per Lord Hoffmann.

[314] Ie, an ordinary resolution has been passed: Companies Act 2006, s 168.

[315] *Re Astec (BSR) plc* [1998] 2 BCLC 556, 589 per Jonathan Parker J.

[316] See eg *O'Neill v Phillips* [1999] 1 WLR 1092, albeit that the petition was unsuccessful in that case.

[317] *Re Astec (BSR) plc* [1998] 2 BCLC 556, 589 per Jonathan Parker J. Similar sentiments are expressed by Vinelott J in *Re Blue Arrow plc* [1987] BCLC 585.

[318] Companies Act 2006, s 994(1).

[319] See E Boros, *Minority Shareholders' Remedies* (Oxford, Clarendon Press, 1995) 137.

[320] See J Payne, 'Section 459 and Public Companies' (1999) 115 *Law Quarterly Review* 368.

14.3.4.2.2 An Exit Right

The second argument in favour of the mandatory bid rule is based on the idea that share-holders should be entitled to a right of exit when a change of control occurs following a takeover. This argument is based not on the view that the new controllers will behave oppressively or illegally, or that they have the potential to do so, but rather on the idea that the position of shareholders in a company depends to a significant extent on the identity of the controllers of a company. Even if the new controllers are not per se oppressive towards the minority, nevertheless the change of control has the potential to affect the minority shareholders adversely. For example, the new controller may implement a new, and less suc-cessful, business strategy. This argument is made more strongly in relation to equity share-holders, whose return from the company is more closely associated with the decisions taken by the controllers of the company, than non-equity shareholders. Take the situation where the successful bidder is part of a group of companies so that the previously independent target now also becomes part of the group. Decisions may be taken at group level which impact negatively on the target company, and its minority shareholders.

These rules, however, provide not only an exit for shareholders (after all shareholders in a publicly traded company can always sell their shares in the market), they provide an exit for the shareholders at the bid price. In the UK, therefore, the Takeover Code provides minority shareholders with a right to exit on the same terms as all other shareholders in the bid. This is potentially controversial for two reasons. First, in other areas of company law it is accepted that the holders of a majority stake in a company should obtain a premium on the sale of their shares, since they are selling control of the company.[321] No such control premium exists in a takeover situation. All the shareholders receive exactly the same pay-ment in the offer. In a system of dispersed share ownership, such as that observable in UK publicly traded companies, this is not particularly significant, but where shareholdings are concentrated this aspect of the mandatory bid rule is more difficult to justify. Where there is an existing controlling shareholder in the company the existence of the mandatory bid rule makes it less likely that they will sell to the bidder since the existing controlling shareholder may be deprived of the premium for their existing control.[322] Second, requiring the bid-der to offer for the whole share capital of the company and requiring the bidder to pay the same price for all the shares, including those bought after control is obtained, and even for the 'rump' 10 per cent under the squeeze-out and sell-out rules, means that takeover offers are more expensive than they would otherwise be, if bidders were free to make bargains with individual shareholders free from the constraints of takeover regulation. Making bids more expensive is likely to reduce the number of bids made overall.[323] If the facilitation of takeovers is desirable (for corporate governance reasons, for example), then this is poten-tially problematic.

---

[321] *Short v Treasury Commissioners* [1948] AC 534.

[322] In jurisdictions dominated by controlling blockholders, such as exist on the Continent (see eg M Becht and A Röell, 'Blockholding in Europe: An International Comparison' (1999) 43 *European Economic Review* 1049), it is common to see the mandatory bid rule being designed in a way that avoids these difficulties, in order to allow the controlling blockholder to retain some control premium. See P Davies, 'The Notion of Equality in European Takeover Regulation' in J Payne (ed), *Takeovers in English and German Law* (Oxford, Hart Publishing, 2002) 27–28.

[323] FH Easterbrook and DR Fischel, 'The Proper Role of a Target's Management in Responding to a Tender Offer' (1981) 94 *Harvard Law Review* 1161, 1174–80; LA Bebchuk, 'Toward an Undistorted Choice and Equal Treatment in Corporate Takeovers (1985) 98 *Harvard Law Review* 1693, 1740–42.

Changes of control in a company can occur in a number of ways, and other events that trigger a change of control could result in changes of policy, such as a change in the company's business activities, and could also have a detrimental effect on the minority shareholders.[324] If the argument that minority shareholders need an enhanced exit right is a good one, then it might be expected that minority shareholders would have such a right on any change of control, however it comes about. This does not occur in practice.[325]

There is one difference in the way that takeovers operate in the UK, as compared to the other scenarios outlined, that might justify the different treatment of this particular form of change of control. This is that takeovers can create a controlling shareholder where none existed before. Typically, in UK publicly traded companies shareholdings are dispersed, and there is no single shareholder with control of the company.[326] As a result of a successful takeover, however, the bidder acquires control of the company. This may be compared to the situation in which there is an existing controlling shareholder in the target which sells its shares to the bidder,[327] in which case the minority was subject to a controlling shareholder even before the successful takeover. It will still be possible for the minority shareholders to sell their shares on the open market, however, unless the majority has delisted the shares or taken the company private in the interim. Whether or not this can justify the imposition of the mandatory rule, with its attendant costs, it remains a fact that mandatory bid rules are now quite widespread outside the US.[328]

14.3.5 Relationship Between the Bidder Directors and Bidder Shareholders

In contrast to the relationship between the target directors and the target shareholders, the relationship between the bidder directors and bidder shareholders is largely unregulated by takeover rules. Rule 23 of the Takeover Code requires the bidder to provide its own shareholders with information about the bid and rule 3.2 requires the board of the bidder to obtain independent legal advice on an offer, and to make that advice known to the bidder shareholders where that offer is a reverse takeover or when the directors are faced with a conflict of interest. Otherwise this relationship is left to general company law and securities

---

[324] See chapter 15 for a discussion of how a change of control can be effected via a scheme of arrangement, and what minority protection is put in place in that instance (and see 15.3.1 for a discussion of the differences between using a scheme and an offer to effect a takeover). See also J Payne, 'Schemes of Arrangement, Takeovers and Minority Shareholder Protection' (2011) 11 *Journal of Corporate Law Studies* 67.

[325] It is also the case that even without a change of control the existing controllers might implement measures, such as deciding to embark upon a new and less successful business strategy, which can adversely affect the minority shareholders. However, no special rules are put in place to deal with issue. This is left to company law measures such as directors' duties, and rules requiring additional shareholder protection for certain transactions (eg particularly large transactions: see FCA Handbook, LR 10, discussed at 11.3.2.1).

[326] A number of institutional shareholders may, between them, have control of the company: J Franks and C Mayer, 'Governance as a Source of Managerial Discipline' (2002), www.nbb.be/doc/ts/publications/wp/wp31en. pdf.

[327] Ie, the typical UK scenario involves an acquisition of control by the bidder and not just a transfer of control: P Davies, 'The Notion of Equality in European Takeover Regulation' in J Payne (ed), *Takeovers in English and German Law* (Oxford, Hart Publishing, 2002) 25.

[328] R Kraakman et al, *The Anatomy of Corporate Law*, 2nd edn (Oxford, Oxford University Press, 2009) 8.2.5.4. For discussion see K Hopt, 'European Takeover Reform of 2012/2013—Time to Examine the Mandatory Bid' (2014) 15(2) *European Business Organization Law Review* 143.

regulations.[329] The Code Committee of the Takeover Panel raised the position of the bidder shareholders as a topic for discussion in 2010,[330] but concluded that no change to takeover regulation was required in this regard.[331]

This lack of takeover regulation may seem surprising when it is considered that the empirical evidence suggests that, while takeovers are generally wealth enhancing for the target shareholders, the position of the bidder shareholders post-takeover is at best equivocal, with a number of studies suggesting that the bidder shareholders lose out in some scenarios.[332] There are a number of reasons why this might be the case. The takeover might be carried out for reasons other than maximising the wealth of the bidder, for example because of managerial self-interest, or the bidder directors may have overpaid for the target company, or the financial structure of the bid may be deleterious to the bidder shareholders, such as where the bidder ends up highly leveraged as a result of significant debt taken on to fund the acquisition, or it may even be that takeover regulation itself, so keen to protect the target shareholders, introduces rules that secure benefits for the target shareholders at the expense of the bidder shareholders.

Despite these potential risks faced by the bidder shareholders, however, this transaction is regarded as an ordinary corporate transaction from the bidder's point of view, with none of the added potential for abuse by directors of the target company towards their shareholders (resulting from the potential loss of jobs for the directors). As a result there is felt to be no justification for overturning the usual board–shareholder relationship which is put in place by general company law principles to deal with this situation.[333]

14.4 Conclusion

The UK takeover model is dominated by the regulatory choices made in relation to two key issues: who should take the decision whether to accept the takeover, and how much

---

[329] This means that if the transaction is particularly large it may be necessary for the bidder directors to obtain shareholder consent for the transaction: see FCA Handbook, LR 10.

[330] *Review of Certain Aspects of the Regulation of Takeover Bids*, PCP 2010/2, section 7. In particular this document considered the suggestion that some protections similar to those afforded by the Takeover Code to target company shareholders should be afforded to shareholders in a bidder company. As part of this consultation, the Code Committee surveyed 16 overseas jurisdictions and found little or no evidence in those jurisdictions of equivalent levels of protection for bidder and target shareholders.

[331] Code Committee of the Takeover Panel, *Review of Certain Aspects of the Regulation of Takeover Bids*, 2010/22, 7–9.

[332] Eg, K Fuller, J Netter and M Stegemoller, 'What Do Returns to Acquiring Firms Tell Us? Evidence from Firms That Make Many Acquisitions' (2002) 57 *Journal of Finance* 1763, suggesting that in the US bidder shareholders gain when buying a closely held company, but lose when purchasing a public company. One major UK study which looked at all successful UK domestic takeovers with a bid value of over £10 million for the period 1984–92 showed that the post-takeover performance of UK companies undertaking large domestic acquisitions is, on average, negative in the long term, irrespective of the benchmark used: A Gregory, 'An Examination of the Long Run Performance of UK Acquiring Firms' (1997) 24 *Journal of Business Finance and Accounting* 971. See also M Martynova and L Renneboog, 'Mergers and Acquisitions in Europe' (2006), www.ssrn.com/abstract_id=880379). For a discussion of these points see A Kouloridas, *The Law and Economics of Takeovers: An Acquirer's Perspective* (Oxford, Hart Publishing, 2008) ch 1.

[333] For a discussion of the position of the bidder shareholders, including some suggestions as to ways in which the position of bidder shareholders could and should be better protected in a takeover, see Kouloridas, *The Law and Economics of Takeovers*, ibid.

regulation should be put in place to deal with the bidder's relationship with the target share-holders. The choices made in the UK in relation to both of these issues are resoundingly shareholder-focused. Accordingly, once a bid is imminent the target directors are sidelined and takeover regulation operates as a significant constraint on their ability to frustrate the bid. Although takeover regulation does not operate in the period before the bid is imminent, a combination of general company law, securities law and the influence and role of institutional shareholders in the UK means that in practice pre-bid defensive measures are very uncommon in the UK. In the bid itself, takeover regulation operates to require that the bidder treats all target shareholders equally, even though this equality is likely to come at a significant cost in terms of the number of takeover offers made. The shareholder focus of the UK regime also has implications for the other stakeholders in the target company. As discussed at 14.3.3 above, there is little attention given to these groups within the UK takeover regime.

The decisions adopted by the UK in relation to these issues can be compared with those of other regimes, such as Delaware, where the use of poison pills is commonplace, and directors are effectively given the power to frustrate a bid. This model, in which the decision on the outcome of the bid is shared between the target directors and shareholders, stands in sharp contrast to the shareholder-centric approach of the UK takeover regime.

15

Schemes of Arrangement

15.1 Introduction

Schemes of arrangement are a valuable tool for manipulating a company's capital. A scheme of arrangement involves a compromise or arrangement between a company[1] and its creditors or its members.[2] Schemes of arrangement can be used in a wide variety of ways. Nothing in the Companies Act 2006 prescribes the subject matter of a scheme. In theory a scheme can be a compromise or arrangement between a company and its creditors or members about anything they can properly agree amongst themselves. A company can therefore use a scheme to effect almost any kind of internal reorganisation, merger or demerger, as long as the necessary approvals have been obtained.

Schemes can offer a number of benefits to companies. In addition to their flexibility, which allows them to be tailored to a company's financing needs, they also provide a measure of finality and certainty: once the scheme is approved by members and creditors, and sanctioned by the court, it will be set aside only in very limited circumstances. A further, important, benefit is that schemes facilitate the majority imposing its views on the minority, and schemes can therefore be implemented despite dissenting members and creditors. This can be particularly valuable in the context of creditors, since, in general, creditors' rights cannot be varied without their consent, thus potentially allowing a single dissenting creditor to block a reorganisation or other arrangement between the company and its creditors. Creditors and members meet in classes to vote on whether to approve the scheme, however, and it is only the majority within a class that can impose its views on the minority of that class. A broader form of 'cramdown' of a whole class, whereby the scheme is implemented despite the opposition of a whole class of member or creditors, is not possible using a scheme alone.[3] The fact that a scheme can be imposed on dissenting members and creditors necessitates some minority protection, and this is provided via a requirement that members and creditors meet in classes to vote on the scheme, and the involvement of the court at both the class meeting stage and then in determining whether to sanction the scheme. These procedural requirements add complexity, time and cost to implementing a scheme. Despite these disadvantages, however, schemes are common, particularly when

---

[1] For the definition of 'company' for these purposes see Companies Act 2006, s 895(2).

[2] Ibid, s 895(1).

[3] See 15.2.3.1 (although see the discussion in 15.3.4.1 as to how twinning a scheme with administration can achieve a form of de facto cramdown of a whole class in some circumstances). This is in contrast to other jurisdictions which allow cramdowns of whole classes of creditors in some debt restructuring mechanisms: see eg Chapter 11 of the US Bankruptcy Code 1978. For discussion see J Payne, 'Debt Restructuring in English Law: Lessons from the US and the Need for Reform' (2014) 130 *Law Quarterly Review* 282.

utilised as an alternative to a takeover offer, and in order to reorganise the debts of financially distressed companies.[4]

In 15.2 the steps required to implement a scheme of arrangement are examined, including the division of the members and creditors into classes, and the role of the court. In 15.3 some of the most common uses of schemes are considered.

15.2 The Mechanics of a Scheme of Arrangement

There are three main steps involved in implementing a scheme of arrangement. First, a compromise or arrangement is proposed between the company and its members or creditors.[5] A scheme will generally be proposed by the board on behalf of the company. An application must then be made to court under section 896 of the Companies Act 2006 for an order that a meeting, or meetings, be summoned. Second, meetings of the members or creditors are held to seek approval of the scheme by the appropriate majorities. Third, the scheme must be sanctioned by the court, and the order sanctioning the scheme is then delivered to the Registrar of Companies.[6] As Chadwick LJ said in *Re Hawk Insurance Co Ltd*:

> It can be seen that each of those stages serves a distinct purpose. At the first stage the court directs how the meeting or meetings are to be summoned. It is concerned, at that stage, to ensure that those who are to be affected by the compromise or arrangement proposed have a proper opportunity of being present (in person or by proxy) at the meeting or meetings at which the proposals are to be considered and voted upon. The second stage ensures that the proposals are acceptable to at least a majority in number, representing three-fourths in value, of those who take the opportunity of being present (in person or by proxy) at the meeting or meetings. At the third stage the court is concerned (i) to ensure that the meeting or meetings have been summoned and held in accordance with its previous order, (ii) to ensure that the proposals have been approved by the requisite majority of those present at the meeting or meetings and (iii) to ensure that the views and interests of those who have not approved the proposals at the meeting or meetings (either because they were not present or, being present, did not vote in favour of the proposals) receive impartial consideration.[7]

15.2.1 Application to the Court for Meetings to be Summoned

Once the proposed scheme has been formulated, an application must be made to the court by, or on behalf of, the company for the court to order meetings of the creditors or the members, or classes thereof, to be summoned.[8] The court will also generally give directions about procedural matters, such as the length of notice and the forms of proxy.[9] The court

---

[4] See 15.3.1 and 15.3.4.1.

[5] Companies Act 2006, s 895(1).

[6] Ibid, ss 899(1) and (4).

[7] [2001] EWCA Civ 241 [12].

[8] Companies Act 2006, s 896(1). The application can be made by the company, by any member or creditor, or, if the company is being wound up or is in administration, by the liquidator or administrator: s 896(2).

[9] The right to vote by proxy is specified by Companies Act 2006, s 899(1).

has a wide discretion to order these meetings on such terms as it thinks fit.[10] The court is not concerned with the merits or fairness of the scheme at this stage.[11] Instead, one of the key issues for the court is deciding whether the members or creditors should be split into separate classes for the purpose of voting on the scheme.[12]

Until 2001, the court would offer no guidance to the company on the issue of class meetings at this stage, and would consider the issue at the sanctioning stage, when the only option for the court, if the wrong class meetings had been held, would be to refuse to sanction the scheme. This practice was criticised in the Company Law Review,[13] and by Chadwick LJ in *Re Hawk Insurance Co Ltd*.[14] A Practice Statement was subsequently issued, designed to produce substantive consideration of classes of creditors at this stage.[15] The onus is still on the applicant company to identify the correct classes, but it must now draw to the court's attention any potential problems at the initial application. All relevant creditors should be notified of the scheme, unless there are very good reasons for not doing so. If creditors only object at the later sanctioning hearing, the court will expect them to show good reason why the issue was not raised at the earlier stage. The position in relation to classes of members is not dealt with in this Practice Statement, but the criticisms raised by the Company Law Review and by Chadwick LJ in *Hawk Insurance* apply equally to that situation, and therefore the principles set out in the Practice Statement should also apply to the composition of classes of members.

Any notice sent out summoning the meetings must be accompanied by a statement explaining the effect of the arrangement and, in particular, stating any material interests of the directors and the effect of those interests on the scheme.[16] The court cannot waive the requirement for an explanatory statement: without this statement the court will reject the scheme for non-compliance with the statutory requirements.[17] The purpose is to provide all the information necessary to enable recipients to determine how to vote.[18] In general, the courts have applied strict standards of disclosure to this circular.[19] They have been prepared to apply a more relaxed standard, however, where it is felt that no reasonable recipient

---

[10] See eg *Re T & N Ltd (No 2)* [2005] EWHC 2870 (Ch).

[11] *Re Telewest Communications plc* [2004] EWHC 924 (Ch).

[12] The substantive issues regarding different classes of creditors and members are discussed at 15.2.2.

[13] Company Law Review Steering Group, *Modern Company Law for a Competitive Economy: Completing the Structure* (URN 00/1335, November 2000), 207. The Company Law Review also proposed other changes to the procedure at this stage (see Company Law Review Steering Group, *Modern Company Law for a Competitive Economy: Final Report* (URN 01/942, July 2001), paras 13.6–13.7) which have not been implemented. In particular, it was suggested that the court should have the discretion to sanction the scheme even if appropriate class meetings had not been held, provided the court felt that the composition of the meetings had not had a substantive effect on the outcome.

[14] [2001] EWCA Civ 241.

[15] *Practice Statement (Ch D: Schemes of Arrangement with Creditors)* [2002] 1 WLR 1345.

[16] Companies Act 2006, s 897. Where the scheme affects the rights of debenture holders the statement must give a similar explanation regarding the interests of any trustees for the debenture holders: s 897(3). The court will generally require that the notice of the class meetings convened under Part 26 of the Companies Act 2006 be advertised (see ss 897(1)(b), (4)). Breach of any of the obligations under s 897 is regarded as a criminal offence on the part of the company and any officer in default: ss 897(5)–(8).

[17] *Rankin & Blackmore Ltd* [1950] SC 218.

[18] *Re Dorman Long & Co Ltd* [1934] Ch 635, 657 per Maugham J.

[19] *Re Jessel Trust Ltd* [1985] BCLC 119, 127 per Slade J. In that case the information was correct when sent, but altered subsequently. Slade J refused to sanction the scheme despite the fact that there were substantial majorities in favour and no one appeared in court to oppose the petition.

would have changed their decision on the scheme had the information been disclosed.[20] The court is also prepared to take into account the level of sophistication of the recipients in determining whether the information provided is adequate.[21]

15.2.2 Meeting(s) of the Members or Creditors

15.2.2.1 Who Needs to Consider the Scheme?

It is only necessary for the proposed scheme to be considered and voted on by those groups affected by it. In both creditors' schemes and members' schemes it is the person who is the legal rather than the beneficial owner of the economic interest who will be party to the scheme. In the case of a members' scheme, therefore, it will be the person on the register of members, and, as regards rights attached to debt securities, the person who is the legal owner.[22]

A company is generally free to decide with whom it proposes any particular compromise or arrangement.[23] This principle can be used to exclude from the scheme any members or creditors who are so powerful that they would simply vote against the scheme if an attempt was made to vary their rights, for example commercially powerful creditors who would vote against it if they were not paid in full.

In general, it is not necessary for the company to consult with, or obtain the approval of, any class of members or creditors whose rights are unaffected by the scheme. This may be the case where, for example, the rights or interests of the constituents are not compromised or otherwise affected by the scheme. Some cases suggest that this may, alternatively, be the case where the constituents have no economic interest in the company. In *Re Tea Corporation Ltd*[24] a scheme was proposed for the sale of assets of a hopelessly insolvent company. The court directed that meetings be held, consisting of the debenture holders, the unsecured creditors, the preference shareholders and the ordinary shareholders. The first three groups voted in favour of the scheme, but the fourth did not. The fact that the company was insolvent, and the assets of the company were insufficient to generate a return to the ordinary shareholders, meant that they had no economic interest in the company. Accordingly, it was held that the court could sanction the scheme despite their dissent.

The application of these principles was discussed in relation to junior creditors in *Re Bluebrook Ltd*.[25] In this case a number of schemes of arrangement were put forward by

---

[20] *Re Minster Assets plc* [1985] BCLC 200.

[21] For example, where a scheme is proposed as an alternative to liquidation and all the known creditors are sophisticated institutions, the fact that the scheme documents do not spell out every instance in which the scheme differed from what would happen in a liquidation may not, of itself, prevent the scheme from being sanctioned: *Re Telewest Communications plc* [2004] EWHC 924 (Ch).

[22] The courts have been prepared to approve voting arrangements that allow the person with the economic interest to dictate how their vote should be cast in a scheme, and split voting has been allowed for scheme purposes, acknowledging the fact that those asked to vote may be representing a number of underlying economic rights holders: see eg *Re Equitable Life Assurance Society* [2002] EWHC 140 (Ch).

[23] See eg *Re MyTravel Group plc* [2004] EWCA Civ 1734; *Re Bluebrook Ltd* [2009] EWHC 2114 (Ch).

[24] [1904] 1 Ch 12.

[25] [2009] EWHC 2114 (Ch). See also 15.3.4.1.

the company, and agreed to by the statutory majority of the senior lenders. The schemes were not put to the mezzanine lenders, who were clearly subordinated to the senior lenders. These schemes involved the senior lenders giving up some of their debt in exchange for equity, with the business of the group being transferred to a new corporate structure in order to achieve that reorganisation. The new group would be principally owned by the senior lenders; the existing group would not retain an interest. No new rights for the mezzanine lenders were included in the schemes. No assets were left in the old group in order to pay the mezzanine lenders. The mezzanine lenders were therefore effectively shut out.

The mezzanine lenders in *Bluebrook* objected to the schemes on the basis that they deprived them of something valuable. Crucially, the rights of the mezzanine lenders were left unchanged by the schemes, in the sense that they had the same claims against the same entities before and after the scheme: their rights were not being varied or discharged. There is no suggestion that a scheme can be effected without the consent of any affected class. The argument of the mezzanine lenders was, however, that the *effect* of the scheme, and in ·particular the transfer of assets to the new entity, left them out of the picture—that is, that the court should decline to sanction the scheme on the basis that it was unfair to them. This, then, was not a question of whether the mezzanine lenders should be able to vote on the scheme at the court-approved meetings stage, but rather a question for the exercise of the court's discretion at the sanctioning stage. On any of the valuation measures looked at by the judge, it was assessed that the value of the assets was 'significantly and demonstrably' less than the value of the senior debt. The judge took the view that the mezzanine lenders, and indeed any creditors subordinated below them, had no remaining economic interest in the group, and that it was, therefore, appropriate for the court to sanction these schemes, and effectively to shut out the mezzanine lenders, without their involvement or consent.

Consequently, it seems clear that where the rights of members or creditors are unaffected by the scheme, then those constituents are not required to vote on the scheme, and while they may object to the scheme at the sanctioning stage, the court will take account of whether those constituents have any remaining economic interest in the company when assessing that objection.[26] The decision in *Re Tea Corporation* is best understood in this context. Where the rights of members or creditors are affected by the scheme then they need to be included within the scheme and given the opportunity to vote on it. If a whole class of the members or creditors votes against the scheme it is clear that the courts cannot sanction it.[27]

15.2.2.2 Separate Class Meetings: General

Once it has been determined which groups are interested in the scheme, and therefore whose consent is required, the next question is whether those groups should meet and vote to approve the scheme at a single meeting, or at separate meetings.

---

[26] See *Re MyTravel Group plc* [2004] EWCA Civ 1734.

[27] See Companies Act 2006, s 899(1), which provides that *if* the appropriate majorities of each class approve the scheme *then* the court may decide to sanction it. See further 15.2.3.1.

15.2.2.2.1 The General Test

The general test to determine whether members or creditors should meet as a whole or as separate classes is relatively easily stated, although it has proved difficult to apply in practice. The accepted test was set out by Bowen LJ in *Sovereign Life Assurance Co v Dodd*:

> It seems plain that we must give such a meaning to the term 'class' as will prevent the section being so worked as to result in confiscation and injustice, and that it must be confined to those persons whose rights are not so dissimilar as to make it impossible for them to consult together with a view to their common interest.[28]

A balancing act is required. A class with genuinely different rights requires the protection of a separate meeting, but if too many artificial distinctions are drawn then the scheme will be at the mercy of a veto by any one of the separate meetings that are held. The fewer meetings that are held, the more schemes will be approved, but this has potential consequences for the protection of minorities. In recent years, there has been a shift of emphasis in applying Bowen LJ's test, away from overzealous distinctions which give minorities strong veto rights. As Nourse J has commented: 'if one gets too picky about potential different classes, one could end up with virtually as many classes as there are members of a particular group.'[29] Clearly, the composition of class meetings should not be allowed to operate in a way that permits majority oppression either.

In *Re Hawk Insurance Ltd*[30] Chadwick LJ refined the test set out in *Sovereign Life*. That test, he said, must be applied in the context of the question 'with whom is the compromise or arrangement to be made?':

> In each case the answer to that question will depend upon analysis (i) of the rights which are to be released or varied under the scheme and (ii) the new rights (if any) which the scheme gives, by way of compromise or arrangement, to those whose rights are to be released or varied. It is in the light of that analysis that the test formulated by Bowen LJ in order to determine which creditors fall into a separate class—that is to say, that a class 'must be confined to those persons whose rights are not so dissimilar as to make it impossible for them to consult together with a view to their common interest'—has to be applied.[31]

Although *Hawk Insurance* involved creditors, this statement applies equally to schemes involving shareholders. Rather than asking whether the rights of members and creditors are sufficiently different so as to form a class, the question following *Hawk Insurance* is whether they are sufficiently similar so as not to. Chadwick LJ's judgment in *Hawk Insurance* therefore prompts a shift in emphasis. While those with genuinely dissimilar rights should be protected, overzealous distinctions which provide the minority with a veto should be avoided. The approach suggested by Chadwick LJ has been criticised,[32] but it has subsequently been applied by the courts.[33]

---

[28] [1892] 2 QB 573, 583 per Bowen LJ.
[29] *Re Anglo American Insurance Ltd* [2001] 1 BCLC 755, 764.
[30] [2001] EWCA Civ 241.
[31] Ibid, [30].
[32] See eg Company Law Review Steering Group, *Modern Company Law for a Competitive Economy: Final Report* (URN 01/942, July 2001), para 13.8; R Sykes, 'Schemes of Arrangement: The Hawk that Muddied the Waters' (2001) 12(5) *Practical Law Company* 6.
[33] Eg *Re Equitable Life Assurance Society (No 2)* [2002] EWHC 140 (Ch); *Re Telewest Communications plc* [2004] EWHC 924 (Ch), affirmed [2004] EWCA Civ 728; *Re MyTravel Group plc* [2004] EWHC 2741 (Ch).

15.2.2.2.2 Members' and Creditors' Rights

In determining whether separate class meetings should be held for members and creditors, the courts have focused on the *rights* of individuals, rather than their interests. The attitude of the courts on this issue has changed, and narrowed, over time.

Re Hellenic and General Trust Ltd[34] concerned a scheme designed to effect a change of control of a company, as an alternative to a takeover. The court in that case regarded it as necessary to separate the ordinary shareholders into two classes. Templeman J held that the shares of one shareholder in the target company, which was a wholly owned subsidiary of the bidder, needed to be treated as constituting a separate class from the shares of the other shareholders in the target. Although the rights held by all the shareholders were identical (all the shares in the target were identical), their interests in the scheme were different. The wholly owned subsidiary had a community of interest in the bidder company that the other shareholders did not. According to Templeman J, these different interests meant that they should meet separately.

In *Re BTR plc*, however, Jonathan Parker J restricted the decision in *Hellenic* to deciding only that a subsidiary's shares should be discounted.[35] He rejected the proposition that members with different interests, rather than different rights, should form a separate class:

> Shareholders with the same rights in respect of the shares which they hold may be subject to an infinite number of different interests and may therefore, assessing their own personal interests (as they are perfectly entitled to do), vote their shares in the light of those interests. But that in itself, in my judgment, is simply a fact of life: it does not lead to the conclusion that shareholders who propose to vote differently are in some way a separate class of shareholders entitled to a separate class meeting. Indeed a journey down that road would in my judgment lead to impracticality and unworkability.[36]

It is the approach in *Re BTR* that has been followed subsequently. Differences between the interests of the shareholders or creditors will not, as a result, be taken into account at the meeting stage, but might be relevant at the court sanctioning stage. One advantage of the *Re BTR* approach is that the rights of the members or creditors will generally be easier for the company to discern than their interests. It will often be difficult for the company to assess the different interests of its members without requiring a considerable amount of personal information from them. Requiring that type of information would lead to 'a wholly unworkable, and highly undesirable, situation'.[37] A consequence of this approach, however, is that fewer class meetings are likely to be held, and there is less chance of a veto of the scheme by the minority at the class meetings stage. The potential reduction in minority protection at this stage means that the court's role in scrutinising the scheme prior to sanctioning it becomes more important.

15.2.2.2.3 Selecting the Correct Comparator

The courts need to consider the correct comparator when determining the similarity or dissimilarity of the members' or creditors' rights. This issue has been of particular importance in creditor-focused schemes.

---

[34] [1976] 1 WLR 123.
[35] [1999] 2 BCLC 675.
[36] Ibid, 682–83.
[37] Ibid, 683.

Chadwick LJ stated in *Hawk Insurance* that where a company is insolvent, the starting point for determining separate classes will be the rights of those creditors on winding up. On this analysis, some groups, such as secured creditors, and preferred creditors, should meet separately. In addition, where subordinated creditors have an interest in the company which could be affected in a different way from other creditors, they will constitute a separate class.[38] Further division may also be necessary within these classes. For instance, within the category of secured creditors, differentiation will generally be required, on the basis of differing securities. A creditor whose claim is protected by a fixed charge is less vulnerable than one whose security is a floating charge.[39] Even creditors whose claims are secured over the same property may have divergent interests. A scheme that proposes the sale of a security and a transfer of the rights of the secured creditors to a substituted security might be acceptable to the first but not the second charge.

By contrast, in *Hawk Insurance* all unsecured creditors were treated as comprising one class. *Hawk Insurance* involved different types of unsecured creditors, some with vested claims and some with contingent claims, and the question arose as to whether they should be treated as being part of the same class for the purposes of voting on a proposed scheme. At first instance Arden J held that these creditors should be treated as comprising different classes.[40] Those with vested claims should be treated as being in the same class as other unsecured creditors, since they all had an accrued claim against the company which they had an immediate right to sue for in full. Those with contingent claims, however, had no such immediate right and the structure of the scheme was such that those whose claims had not yet accrued would have those claims scaled down to proportions smaller than 100 per cent. Although these creditors would rank equally on insolvency, as they were all unsecured creditors, these differences, in Arden J's opinion, meant that they should not all be treated as one class for scheme purposes. The Court of Appeal in *Hawk Insurance* disagreed with this approach. Chadwick LJ held that all the unsecured creditors, including, therefore, those with contingent rights and those with vested rights, could be treated as a single class for this purpose. All unsecured creditors had the same rights on a winding up, namely to submit their claims in the winding up, and to have those claims accepted or rejected. The only difference was that those with contingent claims held debts without a certain value, and therefore those debts would be subject to an estimate. In Chadwick LJ's view this did not mean that they should be treated as a separate class for this purpose.

Where a company is solvent, the rights of the creditors on insolvency may not be accurate comparators for the purpose of determining creditor classes.[41] In *Re British Aviation Insurance Co Ltd*, for example, Lewison J held that the appropriate comparator in that case was a continuing solvent run-off.[42] This will often have an impact on the decision of the court as to the appropriate number of class meetings to be held.

---

[38] *Re British and Commonwealth Holdings plc (No 3)* [1992] BCC 56; *Soden v British and Commonwealth Holdings plc (in administration)* [1995] BCC 531; *Re Mytravel Group plc* [2004] EWHC 2741 (Ch).

[39] See chapter 7.

[40] [2001] 2 BCLC 480.

[41] *Re British Aviation Insurance Co Ltd* [2005] EWHC 1621 (Ch); *Re Sovereign Marine and General Insurance Co Ltd* [2006] EWHC 1335.

[42] *Re British Aviation Insurance Co Ltd* [2005] EWHC 1621 (Ch) [88]. For further discussion see 15.3.5.2.

The situation in relation to debt restructurings of financially distressed companies remains somewhat unclear. Such companies may be cash flow insolvent, but if they are economically viable an argument could be made that the correct comparator is not the rights of creditors in a winding up. However, the approach of the English courts has tended to be to ask what the position would be if the scheme did not go ahead, and if the answer is that the company would go into liquidation, then the correct comparator is the rights of creditors on a winding up.[43] Nevertheless, if it could be shown that the realistic alternative to the restructuring scheme being put forward was not an insolvent liquidation but something else, such as a voluntary agreement between the parties or a different scheme, then presumably a different comparator could be held to apply.

15.2.2.3 Separate Meetings for Shareholders

The term 'member' is not defined by the Companies Act 2006 for scheme purposes, but it is clear that it is the legal owners of the shares that need to be divided into classes. In general this will be those with their names on the company's register of members.[44]

The starting point for the determination of separate meetings for shareholders is to analyse (i) the rights that are to be released or varied under the scheme and (ii) the new rights (if any) that the scheme gives to those whose rights are being released or varied.[45] Only different rights, and not different interests, should be taken into account when separating shares into classes. This test does not require *identical* treatment of members before they can be regarded as forming a single class. Rather, the focus is on the extent to which the relevant rights are dissimilar, and whether it is impossible for the relevant members to consult together in their common interest.

Where schemes involve companies with separate classes of shares in issue, for example ordinary and preference shares, these different classes may constitute different classes for scheme purposes, although 'class' for scheme purposes does not necessarily mean a class as defined in the articles of the company.[46] Often, shares that are in different classes in the articles will comprise different classes for scheme purposes, but this will not always be the case, and the exact class composition will depend on the particular circumstances of each case.[47] Conversely, the mere fact that the rights of members prior to the scheme are identical does not necessarily mean that they should be treated as one class for the purposes of the scheme. If the scheme itself proposes to treat different groups of members within a particular class differently, then it may well be that there will need to be separate meetings of these groups.[48] In short, therefore, members need to have the same rights under the constitution and under the scheme in order to be able to meet together as a single group to consider and approve the scheme.

---

[43] See eg *Re MyTravel Group plc* [2004] EWHC 2741 (Ch); *Re Telewest Telecommunications plc* [2004] EWHC 924 (Ch).

[44] Companies Act 2006, s 112. It is well established that option holders and persons holding other securities that are convertible into shares are not regarded as members of the company for scheme purposes: *Re Compania de Electricidad de la Provincia de Buenos Aires Ltd* [1980] 1 Ch 146.

[45] *Re Hawk Insurance Co Ltd* [2001] EWCA Civ 241 [30] per Chadwick LJ.

[46] See eg *Robert Stephen Holdings Ltd* [1968] 1 WLR 522.

[47] For example, where the company is hopelessly insolvent all classes of shareholders might be regarded as having the same, non-existent rights.

[48] *Re Anglo American Insurance Ltd* [2001] 1 BCLC 755.

Applying the *Re Hawk Insurance* test to members is not always straightforward. One question that has arisen in takeover schemes is whether shareholders giving irrevocable undertakings to a bidder should be treated differently to other shareholders. Dicta in *Re BTR plc* suggests that while the giving of irrevocable undertakings will not affect the ability of those target shareholders to vote at the class meeting where they have the same rights as the other shareholders, nevertheless this is an issue that can be considered at the court sanctioning stage.[49]

A second difficulty that has arisen in practice, again in the context of takeover schemes, is the position of the bidder or the bidder's subsidiaries, if they hold shares in the target company. Generally, the bidder will exclude its own shares from the scheme, or decline to vote at the court-convened member meeting which considers the scheme. The question arises, however, as to what would happen if the bidder did not do so. Would the shares of the bidder be part of the same class as all the other shares in the target company for the purposes of considering and approving the scheme? It could be argued that an application of *Re BTR* would suggest that it is only the bidder's interests that are distinct from those of the other shareholders, not its rights, although it is difficult to see how the bidder could genuinely consult with the other shareholders with a view to their common interest in such a situation. If this were the approach, then the court would have regard to the bidder's separate interest at the sanctioning hearing, at which it seems likely that the court would exclude the votes of the bidder when determining whether the class had approved the scheme by the requisite majority. As regards the shareholdings of the bidder's subsidiaries in the target, following *Re BTR* it could again be argued that the subsidiary's rights are the same as those of other shareholders, even though its interests are not the same, and that this issue should be dealt with at the sanctioning hearing instead of the class meeting stage.[50] If so, the court could, again, simply exclude the votes of the bidder's subsidiaries in determining whether the class has in fact reached the requisite majority when voting to approve the scheme. If not, then, as in *Hellenic*, the scheme is unlikely to be sanctioned.[51]

15.2.2.4 Separate Meetings for Creditors

The term 'creditor' is not defined for scheme purposes by the Companies Act 2006. Instead, the courts have developed the law on this issue. They have defined this term broadly, to include 'all persons having any pecuniary claims against the company'.[52] Thus, it includes

---

[49]   *Re BTR plc (Leave to appeal)* [2000] 1 BCLC 740, 746.

[50]   Lord Millett in *Re UDL Argos Engineering* [2001] HKCFA 54 took a slightly different approach to this issue. He was of the view that the subsidiary's shares could justifiably be treated as forming a separate class not because its rights or interests were distinct from other shareholders, but rather because the fact of the relationship between the bidder and its subsidiary might mean that the subsidiary and the other shareholders would receive different treatment under the scheme.

[51]   *Re Hellenic & General Trust Ltd* [1976] 1 WLR 123. Other jurisdictions have dealt with this issue in other ways. For example, the authorities in Hong Kong have adopted an additional regulatory requirement, to supplement the member approval requirements that otherwise apply in relation to schemes of arrangement: Companies Ordinance, Cap 622, s 674(2). This provides that in certain circumstances, including where a scheme is used to effect a takeover, the scheme can only be approved if 75% of the members vote in favour *and* the number of votes cast against the resolution to approve the scheme of arrangement is not more than 10% of the votes attaching to all 'disinterested shares'. 'Disinterested shares' for this purpose equates broadly to shares in the target company other than those owned by the bidder and its associates (see s 674(3)). See also Securities and Futures Commission, Code on Takeovers and Mergers, r 2.10.

[52]   *Re Midland Coal, Coke & Iron Co* [1895] 1 Ch 267, 277 per Lindley LJ.

actual creditors, including secured creditors,[53] as well as prospective creditors (ie, someone to whom a sum will become payable in the future, pursuant to a present obligation). It has also been accepted that it includes contingent creditors (ie, those to whom a sum may become payable in the future, dependent on the happening of some future event).[54] There are limits to this concept, however. In *Re Lehman Brothers International (Europe) (in administration)*, for example, the Court of Appeal held that the concept of 'creditor' for this purpose did not extend to beneficial owners of assets held by the company.[55] The court held that its jurisdiction under Part 26 of the Companies Act 2006 is circumscribed by the requirement that a scheme must be between a company and its creditors or members. A creditor for these purposes is someone who has a monetary claim against the company that, when payable, constitutes a debt. A proprietary claim to trust property is not a claim in respect of a debt or liability of the company. Therefore, the position of a beneficiary under a trust was held not to be analogous to the position of a secured creditor.[56]

The starting point for the division into creditor classes is that the court will consider the rights that are being varied or released under the proposed scheme and any new rights that the scheme proposes to provide to replace those removed or varied. The correct comparator must be applied in order to determine the difference that the proposed scheme would make to the rights of the creditors. This will depend on whether the company is solvent or insolvent at the time, and what the alternative is for the company if the scheme does not go ahead.[57] It will generally be the case that creditors with different levels of seniority will constitute different classes. Whether distinctions within these levels of seniority lead to separate classes will depend, to some extent, on the application of the correct comparator. This issue is likely to be especially important in relation to the lower-ranked creditors, as the decision in *Hawk Insurance* itself makes clear. The courts are alert to the danger of being too generous in their interpretation of rights, which could lead to an increase in the number of separate class meetings, and could thus provide a veto for minority groups and could open up the possibility of oppression by the minority. This issue is often of more importance in the context of creditors, since creditors generally have greater freedom to bargain for a range of rights that are distinct (potentially in relatively minor ways) from those of other creditors.[58] The rights of members, by way of contrast, tend to be more uniform. The courts have tended to adopt a commonsense approach to this issue.[59] Nevertheless, it is not

---

[53] See *Re Alabama, New Orleans, Texas & Pacific Junction Railway Co* [1891] 1 Ch 213; *Re Lehman Brothers International (Europe)* [2009] EWCA Civ 1161 [60] and [70].

[54] See eg *Re T & N Ltd (No 2)* [2005] EWHC 2870 (Ch). In this case future claimants for damages in tort attributable to asbestosis were held to be creditors for the purpose of a scheme, on proof of exposure to asbestos, even though they had no provable debt in the winding up.

[55] [2009] EWCA Civ 1161.

[56] Ibid, [82] per Lord Neuberger MR.

[57] See 15.2.2.2.3.

[58] For discussion, see chapter 2.

[59] A good example of the court's approach can be seen in the McCarthy & Stone scheme of Arrangement (2009) in which one potential class consisted of the senior term loan holders, who were all secured lenders under term loans. They each held guaranteed liabilities. They shared pari passu in all realisations and recoveries, by virtue of an intercreditor agreement. Under the proposed schemes they were each to acquire the same rights proportionate to their lendings to the companies. However, there were (minor) differences in the rates of interest payable under the facilities. The judge nevertheless viewed the interest rate differences as so small in the context of the outstanding indebtedness that separate classes were not required.

a straightforward one.[60] When the Cork Committee examined schemes of arrangement, it noted the difficulties associated with determining different classes.[61] As a result, this Committee did not recommend that separate class meetings be required for the purposes of company voluntary arrangements.[62]

As with members' meetings, difficulties can arise in relation to the distinction between rights and interests.[63] So, here again the issue arises as to whether the fact that some creditors have provided irrevocable undertakings requires their claims to be regarded as forming a separate class. Irrevocable undertakings are sometimes sought from creditors in advance of a scheme meeting, in order to provide some comfort for the company regarding the likely outcome of the meeting. In general, the fact that a creditor has given an irrevocable undertaking of this kind is regarded as affecting the interests of the creditor and not that creditor's rights and, consequently, will not give rise to the formation of a separate class.[64] In *Re Telewest Communications plc*, David Richards J stated that the position would be different if, in consideration for the agreement to vote in favour of the scheme, the creditor obtained benefits not available to other creditors of that class.[65] In practice, the courts have sometimes held that separate classes are not needed even where consideration is offered in these circumstances,[66] and in *Re Seat Pagine Gialle SpA*[67] Richards J reconsidered his earlier statements in this regard, concluding that he 'would not consider the simple fact that a benefit was conferred in return for agreement to vote in favour of the scheme as being sufficient to require the relevant parties to be constituted in a separate class'.[68] Even if these issues do not require separate class meetings to be held, they can still be relevant at the court sanctioning hearing.

---

[60] Identifying different classes of creditors is particularly challenging in the insurance industry because some creditors may have matured claims (which might be established as to liability and quantum, or liability might have been admitted but damages as yet unquantified, or an actionable condition, such as asbestosis, may have arisen, but liability and damages have yet to be established) or the condition may have been incurred but not reported (IBNR). In *Re British Aviation Insurance Co Ltd* [2005] EWHC 1621 (Ch) creditors with matured and contingent claims were grouped separately from those with IBNR claims and it was determined that separate meetings should be held for these classes. As a result of these difficulties (amongst other issues) Lewison J did not sanction the scheme in this case.

[61] See Report of the Insolvency Law Review Committee (Cork Committee), *Insolvency Law and Practice* (Cmnd 8558, 1982), paras 400 et seq.

[62] Insolvency Act 1986, ss 1–7.

[63] This issue can arise where creditors find that they are members of different classes, ie the same person is, say, both a secured creditor and an unsecured creditor. They may, therefore, have different interests as compared to other creditors in the class, but in general this will not require a separate class meeting. See eg *Re NEF Telecom Company BV* [2012] EWHC 2944 (Comm). Similarly, the fact that the same person is both a shareholder and a creditor will not require the creation of a separate class: *Re Metrovacesa SA* [2011] EWHC 1014 (Ch).

[64] See eg *Re British Aviation Insurance Company Ltd* [2005] EWHC 1621 (Ch); *Re Telewest Communications plc* [2004] EWHC 924 (Ch).

[65] *Re Telewest Communications plc* [2004] EWHC 924 (Ch) [54].

[66] See eg *DX Holdings Ltd* [2010] EWHC 1513 (Ch) [4]–[8] where relevant factors were that (i) the consideration was offered to all creditors who signed the voting agreement, (ii) the fee offered was small in relation to the common interests of the creditors in restructuring, and (iii) it was believed that the fee would not be likely to change the mind of a creditor who otherwise had determined to vote against the scheme, as not being in his interests. In *Re Primacom Holdings GmbH* [2011] EWHC 3746 (Ch), Hildyard J considered factor (ii) to be the most significant of the three factors (at [57]). See also *Assénagon Asset Management SA v Irish Bank Resolution Corporation Ltd* [2012] EWHC 2090 (Ch).

[67] [2012] EWHC 3686 (Ch).

[68] Ibid, [22].

15.2.2.5 Approval at the Class Meetings

The company needs to obtain the approval of all members or creditors, or classes thereof, that will be affected by the scheme. There is no quorum requirement for a vote on a scheme, and the vote is on a poll rather than by way of a show of hands. The level of approval required at the meeting is a majority in number, representing 75 per cent in value[69] of its creditors or members present and voting in person or by proxy.[70] Non-voting members or creditors, and those that do not turn up to the meeting, are therefore excluded for the purposes of calculating the majority.

15.2.2.5.1 The Majority in Value Requirement

The majority in value test is relatively uncontroversial. For classes of members, since each share has a nominal value, it should be comparatively easy to determine whether 75 per cent by value of each class attending the meeting in person or by proxy have voted in favour. The 75 per cent requirement aligns this shareholder vote with other major company law decisions, such as alterations of articles.[71] There is sometimes a question raised as to whether 75 per cent is a large enough majority, particularly where schemes are being used as an alternative to a takeover offer, and this issue is discussed in the context of takeover schemes at 15.3.1.2.1. For classes of creditors, it is necessary to work out in advance the amount (or a formula) in respect of which each creditor will be allowed to vote. This will depend upon the value of the debt.[72]

15.2.2.5.2 The Majority in Number Requirement

By contrast, the majority in number requirement (sometimes referred to as the 'headcount test') is potentially more problematic. This requirement was described as being 'irrelevant and burdensome' in the Company Law Review,[73] and it is not found elsewhere in the Companies Act 2006. The predominant argument in favour of this requirement seems to be that it might provide some protection for small members and creditors, to prevent the majority (or in an extreme case possibly just a single shareholder or creditor) riding roughshod over the views of the remaining shareholders or creditors.[74] However, it has the potential to result in a scheme being blocked even where the holders of the overwhelming number of shares in a company have voted in favour—in other words, it can put significant veto rights in the hands of small shareholders out of proportion to their financial involvement in the company.

---

[69] In the case of shares, each share has a nominal value. In the case of creditors, it will depend upon the value of the debt: *Re British Aviation Insurance Co Ltd* [2005] EWHC 1621 (Ch).

[70] Companies Act 2006, s 899(1).

[71] Ibid, s 21.

[72] *Re British Aviation Insurance Co Ltd* [2005] EWHC 1621 (Ch). For this reason only debts that can have an estimate placed upon them can be claimed. Given that future and contingent creditors are included within the definition of creditor (discussed at 15.2.2.4), this can give rise to some difficulties in valuing their claims for the purpose of determining whether the requisite majority has voted in favour of the scheme.

[73] Company Law Review Steering Group, *Modern Company Law for a Competitive Economy: Completing the Structure* (URN 00/1335, November 2000), 207.

[74] This was the rationale behind the introduction of this requirement for creditor schemes in 1870: see Company Law Review Steering Group, *Modern Company Law for a Competitive Economy: Completing the Structure* (URN 00/1335, November 2000), para 11.34.

For classes of shareholders, it is difficult to see why this issue should be treated differently to other decisions on fundamental corporate issues, which are determined by means of shares voted rather than the number of shareholders. Small shareholders have other protections, such as the duties of directors when proposing the scheme, and, ultimately, the fact that the court has to sanction the scheme, discussed at 15.2.3. The majority in number requirement can also be misused. For instance, in *Re PCCW Ltd*,[75] the Hong Kong Court of Appeal recognised that the majority in number requirement had only been achieved via the use of share splitting to boost the headcount. This was regarded as a form of vote manipulation and consequently the court exercised its discretion not to sanction the scheme.[76] Similar issues can arise in creditor schemes, as debts (or part of them) can potentially be assigned in order to boost the headcount.[77]

Some jurisdictions that have adopted the English scheme, such as Canada and India, have done so without incorporating the majority in number requirement.[78] Others that incorporate the headcount test do so only for creditor schemes, not for member schemes,[79] or give the court discretion to approve a scheme where the majority in value test is met but the majority in number test is not.[80] In a number of other jurisdictions there have been discussions about whether this test should be amended or abolished.[81] There are good arguments for removing the majority in number requirement in England, as recommended by the Company Law Review. Nevertheless, this test remains in place for English schemes of arrangement for the present time.

---

[75] [2009] 3 HKC 292, CA.

[76] Share splitting is a relatively common occurrence, but when this issue was debated in England, the Attorney-General stated that the theoretical possibility of such abuse in the scheme context was not a sufficient reason to justify the removal of the headcount test: HL Deb col 217 (16 May 2006).

[77] For discussion of the transfer of debt see chapter 9. The majority in number requirement can also potentially cause problems in situations where the issue is represented by a global note (for discussion see 8.3.3.3). There is some doubt as to who the 'creditor' is in a bondholder scheme of arrangement. If it is the person performing the role of common safekeeper or depositary then that will be just one person for the purposes of the majority in number test—in a scheme which seeks to compromise the bond, no majority in number will be possible. If, however, the beneficial owners are regarded as the creditor, either because they have been issued with definitive certificates or, possibly, because they are treated as contingent creditors, then this difficulty disappears. For discussion see C Maunder, 'Bondholders' Schemes of Arrangement: Playing the Numbers Game' [2003] *Insolvency Intelligence* 73. In practice the 'contingent creditor' analysis seems to have been commonly adopted to deal with this issue: see eg *Re Castle Holdco 4 Ltd* [2009] EWHC 1347 (Ch).

[78] Canadian Business Corporations Act 1985, s 192; Indian Companies Act 1956 as amended, s 391.

[79] See eg South Africa Companies Act No 71 of 2008, Ch 5. Broadly, member schemes are those focused on the transfer or reorganisation of share capital, the most common being a scheme used to effect a change of control as an alternative to a takeover offer (discussed in 15.3.1), whereas creditor schemes are concerned with the reorganisation of companies' debt capital (see 15.3.4).

[80] Australian Corporation Act 2001, s 411(d) (this discretion applies to member schemes only). A review by the Corporations and Markets Advisory Committee (CAMAC) in Australia has recommended the entire removal of the majority in number test: CAMAC, *Members' Schemes of Arrangement*, December 2009, 77–94, www.camac. gov.au.

[81] Eg, Singapore (Singapore Ministry of Finance, *Report of the Steering Committee for the Review of the Companies Act: Consultation Paper*, July 2011) and Hong Kong (the majority in number test was reformed in Hong Kong Companies Ordinance 2012, s 674).

15.2.3 The Sanction of the Court

Following the approval of the scheme in the separate class meetings, application is made to the court for approval of the scheme.[82] This application can be opposed by members and creditors who object to the scheme.[83] The Companies Act 2006 contains no details of those matters that the court should take into account when deciding whether to sanction the scheme.[84] The courts have therefore needed to determine how they should exercise their discretion to give or withhold this sanction.

As a preliminary matter, the courts will only sanction a scheme where the proposal falls within the proper scope of Part 26 of the Act. The court will not sanction a scheme the provisions of which fall outside the general law, so, for example, the court has no jurisdiction to sanction a scheme which involves an act that is ultra vires.[85] The courts will also take account of whether there is a sufficient connection between the scheme and England. In recent years, it has been increasingly common for foreign companies to seek to make use of English schemes, usually where the company is financially distressed and is seeking to use the scheme to reorganise its debts.[86] While it is clear that foreign companies can fall within the definition of 'a company' for scheme purposes,[87] the courts have developed this additional judge-made requirement, and will only, therefore, have jurisdiction to sanction a scheme involving a foreign company where a sufficient connection between the scheme and England can be demonstrated. A sufficient connection may arise as a result of a number of factors, such as where there are assets within the jurisdiction, or where the creditors' agreements with the company are governed by English law and contain an English jurisdiction clause.[88] This is an area of law that continues to evolve.[89]

---

[82] Companies Act 2006, s 899(2). The application may be from the company, any member or creditor, or, if appointed, a liquidator or administrator.

[83] There are no statutory provisions restricting who can oppose a scheme, so legitimate concerns of third parties can also be taken into account by the court: see eg *Re BAT Industries plc* (unreported, 3 September 1998). However, the court's role is not to undertake a roving commission at the suit of any objector alleging prejudice from the scheme: *Re RAC Motoring Services Ltd* [2000] 1 BCLC 307 per Neuberger J.

[84] The Act merely states that a compromise or arrangement, if agreed by the requisite creditors' and members' meetings, will be binding on the parties if the scheme is sanctioned by the court: Companies Act 2006, s 899(3).

[85] *Re Oceanic Steam Navigation Company Limited* [1939] Ch 41.

[86] See eg *Re Rodenstock GmbH* [2011] EWHC 1104 (Ch); *Primacom Holdings GmbH* [2012] EWHC 164 (Ch); *Re NEF Telecom Co BV* [2012] EWHC 2944 (Comm); *Re Cortefiel SA* [2012] EWHC 2998 (Ch); *Re Seat Pagine Gialle SpA* [2012] EWHC 3686 (Ch); *Re Vietnam Shipbuilding Industry Groups* [2013] EWHC 2476 (Ch); *Re Magyar Telecom BV* [2013] EWHC 3800 (Ch); *Re Apcoa Parking Holdings GmbH* [2014] EWHC 3849 (Ch).

[87] The Act provides that the arrangement or compromise must be between 'a company' and its members and/or creditors: Companies Act 2006, s 895. For these purposes 'a company' means 'any company liable to be wound up under the Insolvency Act 1986': s 895(2)(b). Section 221 of the Insolvency Act 1986 grants powers to the courts to wind up solvent and insolvent companies, and registered and unregistered companies. It is well established that 'unregistered company' includes foreign companies: see eg *Banque des Marchands de Moscou (Koupetschesky) v Kindersley* [1951] Ch 112. There is some debate as to whether the application of this test is affected by either the Insolvency Regulation (Council Regulation (EC) 1346/2000, and see the recast Regulation (EU) No 2015/848 which is due to take effect in 2017) or the Judgments Regulation (Council Regulation (EC) 44/2001) where the foreign company seeking to make use of the scheme is from another EU/EEA state. For discussion of this issue see J Payne, 'Cross-Border Schemes of Arrangement and Forum Shopping' (2013) 14 *European Business Organization Law Review* 563.

[88] See eg *Re Rodenstock GmbH* [2011] EWHC 1104 (Ch).

[89] See eg *Re Magyar Telecom BV* [2013] EWHC 3800 (Ch); *Re Apcoa Parking Holdings GmbH* [2014] EWHC 3849 (Ch).

Once these preliminary matters have been settled, the court will be concerned with a number of issues when determining whether to exercise its discretion to sanction the scheme.[90] The first is to ensure that the technical requirements of the Act have been complied with, such as that the requisite majorities have voted in favour of the scheme. Once these practical issues have been addressed, the court will need to exercise its broad supervisory jurisdiction in order to decide whether to sanction the scheme.[91] It will examine the fairness of the scheme as part of this process. This is often deemed to have two components: the court will be concerned to ensure that the majority fairly represented the class, and that the scheme is one which a reasonable person would approve.[92]

15.2.3.1 Have the Statutory Provisions been Complied with?

The court will want to ensure that the explanatory statement provided in relation to the scheme is adequate. If not, or if it is defective in some way, the court may not sanction the scheme. In addition, the court will want to ensure that the resolutions at the class meetings are passed by the statutory majority of each class. If this has not occurred then the court cannot approve the scheme, even if the court considers it to be fair and the scheme would otherwise have been approved.[93] The somewhat peculiar way in which approval must be obtained at these meetings (ie, the majority in number, representing 75 per cent in value of its creditors or members present and voting in person or by proxy)[94] makes this task more complicated than it might otherwise be. The fact that the scheme cannot be sanctioned without the approval of every class means that the cramdown of an entire class of members or creditors is not possible using a scheme alone, since the scheme cannot go forward without their consent. In this way, schemes are distinct from some other reorganisation mechanisms, such as Chapter 11 of the US Bankruptcy Code 1978. It is, however, possible for de facto cramdowns of classes to be achieved in some circumstances, by twinning schemes with other procedures.[95]

The court can refuse to sanction the scheme if it determines that there has been as error in the number of, or composition of, class meetings.[96] This should be rare since, following the 2002 Practice Statement, issues regarding the composition and summoning of class meetings should be resolved at an earlier stage in proceedings.[97] Creditors or members who feel unfairly treated can still raise objections to the scheme at the sanctioning stage, but the court will expect them to show good reason why they did not raise any concerns at that earlier stage.[98]

---

[90] *Re Anglo Continental Supply Co Ltd* [1922] 2 Ch 723, 733; *Re National Bank Ltd* [1966] 1 WLR 819.

[91] *Re Alabama, New Orleans, Texas & Pacific Junction Railway Co* [1891] 1 Ch 213, 238–39 per Lindley LJ.

[92] *Re Anglo Continental Supply Co Ltd* [1922] 2 Ch 723, 736; *Re National Bank Ltd* [1966] 1 WLR 819; *Re Anglo American Insurance Co Ltd* [2001] 1 BCLC 755, 762; *Re Hawk Insurance Co Ltd* [2001] EWCA Civ 241.

[93] *Re Neath and Brecon Railway* [1892] Ch 349.

[94] Companies Act 2006, s 899(1). See 15.2.2.5.

[95] See 15.3.4.1.

[96] See eg *Re British Aviation Insurance Co Ltd* [2005] EWHC 1621 (Ch), [2006] BCC 14, where the court did just that, and refused to sanction a scheme where the court convened a single meeting for the scheme's creditors when the court at the sanctioning stage held that the creditors should properly have been separated into two classes for this purpose.

[97] See 15.2.1.

[98] The courts have acknowledged that it might not always be possible to provide creditors or members with full details of the scheme, including details of class constitution, before the first court hearing, in which case it will not be reasonable to expect them to raise objections at that hearing: *Re Marconi Corporation plc v Marconi plc* [2003] EWHC 663 (Ch).

15.2.3.2 *Exercise of the Court's Discretion*

It is not enough, of itself, that the correctly constituted meetings of members or creditors have voted to approve the scheme. The court's sanction is not simply a rubber-stamping exercise. The fairness of the scheme will be a relevant consideration in the court's determination of whether to sanction it. The court has emphasised that its role is not to usurp the views of those who have properly voted in its favour, however, and the court will be strongly influenced if there is a substantial majority vote in favour of the scheme.[99] The test is not 'is this a reasonable scheme?' but rather 'could the class of creditors/members reasonably have approved it?'.

The court will consider the full commercial and factual context of the scheme. The central issue will be whether the scheme is fair between the various interests involved and so could reasonably have been approved at the meetings.[100] The court may also consider the effect on third parties.[101] In *BAT Industries plc* only the consent of members to the scheme was sought, but Neuberger J allowed prospective litigants against the company to object to the scheme.[102] The judge held that there were no statutory restrictions on whom the court could hear or what it could take into account in deciding whether to sanction a scheme. Some recent cases have seen junior lenders who had been left out of the scheme (and therefore had no vote in the scheme) objecting to it at the sanctioning stage.[103] The courts have held, however, that where the objecting creditors have no remaining economic interest in the company, this fact will be taken into account when determining whether to sanction the scheme despite these objections.[104]

The court will be concerned to ensure that the decision taken by a meeting was representative of the class as a whole.[105] The court's sanction can be refused if only a tiny minority of the class actually attended and voted. Lewison J in *Re British Aviation Insurance Co Ltd* stated that, while a low turnout at the meeting is not itself a valid reason for a court refusing to sanction the scheme, the size of turnout might be relevant in considering whether the result of the vote could have been affected by collateral factors—that is, by those members or creditors with special interests.[106]

The court may refuse to sanction where the votes necessary to secure the approval were cast in order to promote a special interest of some shareholders or creditors that was not shared by the class as a whole.[107] If the court considers that the meeting is unrepresentative, or that those voting at the meeting have done so with a special interest to promote which differs from the interests of the ordinary independent and objective creditor/member, then the court can refuse to sanction the scheme. Consequently, the votes of the majority are not treated by the court as conclusive.[108] Developments in the courts in recent years have led to a reduction in the amount of minority protection available at the class meeting stage of the

---

[99] *Re Equitable Life Assurance Society* [2002] EWHC 140 (Ch); *Re TDG plc* [2008] EWHC 2334.
[100] *Re Cape plc* [2006] EWHC 1316 (Ch).
[101] *Re RAC Motoring Services Ltd* [2000] 1 BCLC 307.
[102] Unreported, 3 September 1998.
[103] Eg, *Re Bluebrook Ltd* [2009] EWHC 2114 (Ch).
[104] Ibid. For discussion see 15.3.3.1.
[105] *Re Alabama, New Orleans, Texas & Pacific Junction Railway Co* [1891] 1 Ch 213.
[106] *Re British Aviation Insurance Co Ltd* [2005] EWHC 1621 (Ch).
[107] *Re BTR plc (Leave to appeal)* [2000] 1 BCLC 740.
[108] *Re Alabama, New Orleans, Texas & Pacific Junction Railway Co* [1891] 1 Ch 213, 244.

scheme process, making the sanctioning stage all the more important.[109] The court's scrutiny of whether the majority have fairly represented the class on a vote in a meeting under a scheme can operate as a potentially important protective device for minority shareholders and creditors.[110]

The court's role has its limits, however. Provided the scheme is fair and equitable, the court will not judge its commercial merits. The function of the court is not to determine how it would have voted on the scheme. It is not the court's role to determine whether this is the best scheme available. It is extremely rare for the court to exercise its discretion to refuse to sanction a scheme which has been approved by the correct majority of members/creditors, where the classes are completely constituted and there is no suggestion that the majority did not represent the class.[111]

15.2.3.3 Effect of the Scheme

Once the court has sanctioned the scheme, a copy of the order needs to be delivered to the Registrar of Companies. The order sanctioning the scheme takes effect at this point.[112] It then becomes binding on the company, including the liquidator/administrator if the company is in liquidation/administration,[113] and on all the relevant members and creditors. Crucially, therefore, the scheme also binds any dissentients. The court will set aside the scheme subsequently only on very limited grounds, such as where the consent has been obtained by fraud and this fraud has affected the outcome of the scheme.[114]

15.3 Uses of Schemes of Arrangement

Schemes of arrangement can be used to effect a wide variety of changes within a company. The terms 'compromise' and 'arrangement' have no precise legal meaning,[115] and should therefore be given their ordinary commercial meaning. The fact that there is no statutory definition to rely on 'does not appear to create any difficulty in practice'.[116] These terms have been construed widely by the courts.

---

[109] See discussion at 15.2.2.

[110] See eg *British Aviation Insurance Co Ltd* [2005] EWHC 1621 (Ch) [118]–[123].

[111] *British Aviation Insurance Co Ltd* [2005] EWHC 1621 (Ch) [75]–[76] per Lewison J.

[112] Companies Act 2006, s 899(4). If the order amends the company's articles or any constitutional resolution or agreement, a copy of the amended articles, resolution or agreement must be sent to the Registrar: s 901.

[113] Companies Act 2006, s 899(3). The courts have rejected the argument that a scheme that satisfies the requirements of the Act might nevertheless amount to a deprivation of possessions contrary to art 1 of the First Protocol to the European Convention on Human Rights: *Re Equitable Life Assurance Society (No 2)* [2002] EWHC 140 (Ch); *Re Waste Recycling Group plc* [2003] EWHC 2065 (Ch).

[114] *Fletcher v Royal Automobile Club Ltd* [2000] 1 BCLC 331.

[115] An 'arrangement' is partially defined in s 895(2) Companies Act 2006 as including a reorganisation of a company's share capital. This is further defined in that section as being either or both of (i) consolidating different classes of shares or (ii) dividing shares into different classes. However, this definition is clearly incomplete and schemes of arrangement encompass a far wider range of circumstances than these facts. The Court of Appeal confirmed that this is only a partial definition in *Re Lehman Brothers International (Europe) (in administration)* [2009] EWCA Civ 1161 [29] per Lord Neuberger.

[116] Company Law Review Steering Group, *Modern Company Law for a Competitive Economy: Completing the Structure* (URN 00/1335, November 2000), 206 para 11.5.

The word 'compromise' offers few difficulties of interpretation. Applying the ordinary commercial meaning of this term (the settlement of a dispute) means that, for scheme purposes, all that is required is some difficulty or dispute which the scheme seeks to resolve.[117] By contrast, the concept of 'arrangement' is wider than that of 'compromise' and is not limited to something analogous to a compromise.[118] The elements of a dispute, and an accommodation of that dispute, need not be present.[119]

For both 'compromises' and 'arrangements' the courts have required that the scheme involve some element of give and take, and not simply amount to a surrender or confiscation.[120] Therefore, in a scheme between a company and its members, where the members are simply giving up their rights, or their rights are being expropriated without any sort of compensating advantage for them, there will be no 'arrangement' or 'compromise' between the company and its members for this purpose.[121] A further limitation is that the company must be a party to the arrangement: Part 26 of the 2006 Act does not apply to arrangements or compromises between the creditors or members not involving the company. However, subject to these limitations, the courts have deliberately avoided giving the term a narrow meaning. They have been prepared to sanction arrangements where the rights of shareholders or creditors as against the company are varied, or where rights are varied between creditors or shareholders, or where those groups give up rights against third parties, such as under guarantees.[122] The breadth of the term 'arrangement' was endorsed by the Court of Appeal in *Re Lehman Brothers International (Europe) (in administration) (No 2)*.[123]

As a result, a wide range of circumstances have been held to fall within the concept of a scheme of arrangement. Some examples of the uses of schemes of arrangement in practice are discussed in this section, together with an analysis of why a scheme might prove more valuable in certain circumstances than the alternatives that might be available. This is not a closed list, however.

15.3.1 As an Alternative to a Takeover Offer

One very common use of schemes of arrangement is as an alternative to a takeover offer. Takeovers are dealt with in detail in chapter fourteen. In recent years schemes of

---

[117] *Sneath v Valley Gold Ltd* [1893] 1 Ch 477; *Re NFU Development Trust Ltd* [1972] 1 WLR 1548.

[118] No element of compromise needs to be shown in order for an arrangement to fall within s 895: *Re National Bank Ltd* [1966] 1 WLR 819, 829 per Plowman J; *Re T & N Ltd* [2006] EWHC 1447 (Ch) [46]–[50] per David Richards J.

[119] *Re Guardian Assurance Company* [1917] 1 Ch 431.

[120] *Re Savoy Hotel Ltd* [1981] Ch 351, 359–61 per Nourse J. Earlier cases had taken a more restrictive approach (eg *Re General Motor Cab Co Ltd* [1913] 1 Ch 317 (CA) but see *Re Guardian Assurance C o* [1917] 1 Ch 431). The preferable view is that adopted in the later cases, ie the term 'arrangement' is not synonymous with the term 'compromise' and should be construed more broadly.

[121] *Re NFU Development Trust Ltd* [1972] 1 WLR 1548.

[122] *Re Lehman Brothers (Europe) International* [2009] EWCA Civ 1161 [65]. The requirement that a scheme is between the company and its creditors and/or members has been widely interpreted, and can include arrangements with third parties, provided that the arrangement with the third parties is an integral part of the operation of the scheme and is part of a single proposition involving all the parties: *T & N (No 3)* [2006] EWHC 1447 (Ch). This issue has proved controversial in other jurisdictions, such as Australia: see eg *Re Opes Prime Stockbroking Ltd (No 1)* (2009) 73 ACSR 385.

[123] [2009] EWCA Civ 1161 [74].

arrangement have become the structure of choice for recommended bids.[124] If a scheme is to be used in this way then, typically, the shareholders of the target agree to the cancellation of their shares in the target company. The reserve created in the target company as a result of this arrangement is then used by the target to pay for new shares which are issued to the offeror. The shareholders of the target then receive, in exchange for their cancelled shares, cash or shares in the offeror company. This is sometimes known as a 'reduction scheme' as it combines a scheme with a reduction of capital. An alternative is a 'transfer scheme', whereby all the shares of the target not already owned by the bidder are transferred to the bidder. Reduction schemes have been more common in recent years because they require no transfer of shares, and therefore no stamp duty has been payable. A change in the law in March 2015 aims to close this stamp duty loophole by removing the reduction scheme option.[125] It remains to be seen what effect this will have on the use of takeover schemes. Reduction schemes required the target company to comply with the steps to effect the reduction of capital.[126] However, the reduction was fictitious in the sense that the credit arising in the company's accounts following the reduction was immediately applied in paying up new shares in the company, so that no creditor protection issue arose. The rules of the Takeover Panel apply to takeovers effected via schemes of arrangement, however they are effected.[127]

Although takeover offers and schemes of arrangement can be used to achieve the same end, namely a shift of control of the target company, they operate quite differently, and acquirers will need to consider carefully which mechanism is likely to suit them best. Crucially, a takeover is an offer by the bidder to the target shareholders without an action by the target company being involved,[128] whereas a scheme of arrangement is an action by the company whereby the target directors ask the target shareholders to vote in favour of the change of control.

15.3.1.1 Advantages and Disadvantages of a Scheme rather than a Takeover Offer to Effect a Change of Control

Using a scheme rather than a takeover offer to effect a change of control offers a number of advantages.[129] If it is important for the bidder to acquire 100 per cent control of the

---

[124] For example, 15 of the 19 regulated change of control transactions announced in the year ending 31 December 2012 concerning target companies listed on the Main Market of the London Stock Exchange with a deal value of at least £100 million were effected by way of a scheme of arrangement: Practical Law Company, *Public M & A: Trends and Highlights from 2012*, 4 January 2013.

[125] Companies Act 2006 (Amendment of Part 17) Regulations 2015 (SI 472/2015).

[126] This required either a shareholder resolution to approve the reduction (the meeting to pass this resolution was generally held immediately after the court-approved meeting to approve the scheme) and a court order (which could be given at the same time as the court sanctioned the scheme) (see Companies Act 2006, ss 645–49) or for private companies the reduction could be supported by a solvency statement (Companies Act 2006, ss 642–44). For discussion see 5.4.3.

[127] For detailed discussion of the way in which the Takeover Panel regulates takeovers, see chapter 14, especially 14.2. Although the Takeover Panel has always applied its rules to takeovers effected via schemes of arrangement, the practice of using schemes to effect this result has now become so common that the Panel introduced a new Appendix (Appendix 7) to the City Code on Takeovers and Mergers ('the Takeover Code') to deal specifically with this issue. For a discussion of the issues arising from the two-track approach in relation to schemes (ie the fact that they are dealt with by the courts under Part 26 of the Companies Act 2006, and the Takeover Panel as a result of the Takeover Code) see *Re Expro International Group plc* [2008] EWHC 1543 (Ch).

[128] See chapter 14.

[129] For a discussion of how the use of a scheme rather than an offer can be useful where the financial assistance rules may cause a problem see *Re Uniq plc* [2011] EWHC 749 (Ch).

target company, then bidders will often make use of a scheme of arrangement. A common scenario in which a bidder will want this level of control is in private equity transactions, where the bidder may wish to use the target company's assets to secure the loans made to the bidder to finance the bid, and for this reason it will be important for the bidder to acquire all of the target's shares.[130] A successful scheme of arrangement will always involve the bidder acquiring 100 per cent of the target, unlike a takeover offer which could involve the bidder acquiring less than 100 per cent, and indeed the offer will be successful once the bidder reaches the minimum acceptance condition (which must be at least 50 per cent).[131] It is not impossible for a bidder to achieve 100 per cent control via a takeover offer: the squeeze-out provisions allow a bidder to mop up the last of the minority shareholders, but these provisions only operate once a bidder has acquired 90 per cent in value of the shares to which the offer relates.[132] For this reason some takeover offers, where the acquisition of 100 per cent of the shares is key, will set the minimum level of acceptances at 90 per cent. In a scheme, though, the bidder can gain 100 per cent control by obtaining the agreement of a lower level of shareholders: 75 per cent by value (and a majority in number), rather than the 90 per cent required to trigger the squeeze-out provisions in an offer.[133]

In addition, tax savings have traditionally been an advantage of using a scheme (specifically a reduction scheme), rather than an offer to effect a change of control, since stamp duty is not payable (since shares are not transferred). Changes to the law in March 2015 put an end to this particular advantage.[134]

There are disadvantages to schemes, too. In particular, the court's involvement in a scheme adds to the cost of the process, and introduces an element of uncertainty regarding the exercise of the court's discretion at the sanctioning hearing. It also has implications for the time it takes to implement a scheme: six to eight weeks as a minimum. This is likely to be longer than a straightforward recommended takeover offer, where no competing offer emerges and the bidder only wishes to gain, say, 50 per cent of the target company.[135] The involvement of the court also means that there is less flexibility for dealing with new information or a new bidder: any adjournment or abandonment of a scheme meeting will require an application to court. Another disadvantage of a scheme, as compared to a takeover offer, is the need to divide the members into classes in order to vote on the scheme. The issue of class meetings is not straightforward, and if the classes are incorrectly constituted this can be a reason for the court to refuse to sanction the scheme.[136]

---

[130] For discussion of private equity transactions see chapter 16.

[131] Takeover Code, r 10. The bidder can make the offer conditional on a higher level of acceptances than 50%. For discussion see 14.3.1.2.

[132] Companies Act 2006, s 979(2)(a); for discussion see 14.3.1.3.

[133] The flipside of this is that while in an offer 50% of shareholders can block a bid, in a scheme, in theory, a shareholder holding 25% of the shares can block it. In practice, shareholders with much smaller fractions of the vote may block the scheme since (i) only shares voted at the meeting in person or by proxy are taken into account; (ii) shares held by the bidder are generally excluded from the scheme, and thus not voted at the meeting; and (iii) there may be class meetings, so that a holder of 25% of any class of shares is able to block the scheme.

[134] Companies Act 2006 (Amendment of Part 17) Regulations 2015 (SI 472/2015).

[135] However, a takeover offer may take longer to complete than a scheme, if the bid is hostile, or if a competing bid emerges, or if the bidder needs to make use of the squeeze-out procedure to obtain the rump shares.

[136] See 15.2.2.2 and 15.2.3.1.

The bidder may prefer an offer to a scheme because the offer leaves the bidder in control of the process, whereas in a scheme it is the target company that is in control. This may be important where the bidder anticipates competing bids and wishes to retain the flexibility to respond to such a bid, should it arise. It can be more difficult for the bidder to change the terms of a scheme than to change the terms of an offer.[137] Another reason for the bidder to make use of an offer rather than a scheme might be where the bid is hostile. While it is theoretically possible for a bidder to acquire shares in the target and then to use its position as shareholder to propose a hostile scheme, such schemes are difficult to organise in practice.[138] It is notable that there have not been any successful hostile schemes to date.[139]

15.3.1.2 Minority Protection in a Scheme

If a scheme is approved in each of the scheme meetings by the requisite majorities and sanctioned by the court, then all the shareholders are bound, even those that dissent. This raises the issue of minority protection in a scheme context. In a takeover offer, a number of measures are put in place to protect minority shareholders. The central principle of shareholder equality, enshrined in the City Code on Takeovers and Mergers ('the Takeover Code'),[140] gives rise to a raft of measures designed to protect shareholders in a bid, including the mandatory bid rule,[141] the squeeze-out and sell-out rules,[142] and various rules regarding the offer that bidders can make to shareholders.[143] By contrast, in a scheme, the protection in place for shareholders consists of the requirement that the members be properly informed of the details of the scheme, the fact that the members meet in classes to vote on the scheme (and the scheme cannot be sanctioned unless all the classes approve it), and the fact that the court must sanction the scheme before it becomes binding on all members.

Concerns are sometimes raised regarding the level of protection available to minorities in takeover schemes. In some countries this has led to constraints on the use of schemes in this context,[144] and to changes in the law to address these concerns.[145] These concerns may broadly be regarded as falling into two categories: (i) that the approval level for a

---

[137] There are a number of practical mechanisms that bidders can use to retain some flexibility while using a bid to effect a change of control. One possibility is to switch from a scheme to an offer if a competing bid does arise (bidders must obtain the consent of the Takeover Panel to do so: Takeover Code, App 7, s 8).

[138] See eg *Re Savoy Hotel Ltd* [1981] Ch 351. The court will not order that meetings of the members and/or creditors be held where it is clear that the company's approval will not be obtained. A shareholder attempting such an action will also face practical difficulties, such as the disclosure requirements that accompany a scheme (see Companies Act 2006, s 897).

[139] For discussion see eg *Validus Holdings Ltd v IPC Holdings Ltd and Max Capital Group Ltd* [2009] SC (Supreme Court of Bermuda) 25 Civ (13 May 2009).

[140] Takeover Code, GP 1.

[141] Ibid, r 9.1, discussed at 14.3.4.

[142] Companies Act 2006, ss 983–85; for discussion see 14.3.1.3.

[143] See 14.3.4.1.

[144] For example, in Australia s 411(17) of the Australian Corporations Act 2001 provides that a court will only have jurisdiction to approve a scheme of arrangement where either (i) the court is satisfied that the scheme has not been proposed to avoid the operation of the takeovers legislation, or (ii) a statement is received from the Australian Securities and Investment Commission (ASIC) indicating that it has no objection to the arrangement.

[145] For example, in Hong Kong takeover schemes require the approval of at least 75% of the votes of the members present and voting in person or by proxy *and* the votes cast against the scheme must not exceed 10% of the total voting rights attached to the 'disinterested shares': Hong Kong New Companies Ordinance, Cap 622, s 674(2).

takeover scheme is too low; and (ii) that the minority protection in place in takeover offers is bypassed in a scheme.[146] These arguments are considered next. It is suggested that the current stance of the English courts and the Takeover Panel in this regard, ie neutrality as to whether a change of control proceeds by way of an offer or a scheme, is correct.

15.3.1.2.1 Concerns Regarding the Approval Threshold for Schemes

Concerns have been voiced that the minority can effectively be bound by a lower percentage of the members in a scheme (a majority in number representing 75 per cent in value of the members present and voting) than in a takeover offer, where the minority cannot be forced to sell their shares unless 90 per cent of the other shareholders have already accepted the offer. It has been suggested that approving a scheme of arrangement in such circumstances should require a very high standard of proof.[147] Other jurisdictions that make use of schemes of arrangement have introduced a higher approval threshold for schemes used to effect a change of control as an alternative to a takeover offer. In Hong Kong, for example, a change in the law in 2014 introduced a requirement that in addition to 75 per cent of members voting in favour, the votes cast against the arrangement do not exceed 10 per cent of the total voting rights attached to the 'disinterested shares'.[148] This may be regarded as an attempt to equalise the approval thresholds for takeover offers and takeover schemes.

The English courts have on a number of occasions considered whether the approval level of schemes should be raised to bring it in line with the position in takeover offers, and have consistently rejected this approach.[149] The approach of the English courts is that whether a company proceeds by way of a scheme of arrangement or a takeover is a matter of choice.[150] Courts have rejected the argument that where a scheme is used as an alternative to a takeover the court should insist on a 90 per cent approval of the scheme by shareholders.[151] On this view the lower threshold in a scheme is countered by the fact that the court needs to sanction the scheme. Minority protection can therefore be ensured at that stage in the proceedings. Further, the 75 per cent (by value) approval threshold is in line with other significant member decisions, such as whether to alter the articles of the company.[152]

---

[146] A further concern that is sometimes raised regarding the use of schemes is that they do not facilitate auctions for control, and therefore do not maximise shareholder value for the target shareholders. However, if a scheme is announced, there is nothing to prevent a subsequent bidder announcing a rival offer, or a rival scheme. Indeed, it is not uncommon to see competing bids being introduced after a scheme is announced. There is also no evidence that companies are sold at lower premia under a scheme as compared to a takeover bid: see, for example, in the context of Australian deals, T Damian and A Rich, *Schemes, Takeovers and Himalayan Peaks: The Use of Schemes of Arrangement to Effect Change of Control Transactions*, 3rd edn (Ross Parsons Centre of Commercial, Corporate and Taxation Law, University of Sydney, 2013) 712–13.

[147] *Re Hellenic and General Trust* [1976] 1 WLR 123.

[148] Hong Kong New Companies Ordinance, Cap 622, s 674(2).

[149] *Re BTR plc* [1999] 2 BCLC 675, affirmed [2000] 1 BCLC 740; *Re TDG plc* [2008] EWHC 2334 (Ch). In practice, the disparity between the approval requirements in a takeover offer and a scheme may not, in fact, be as stark as it appears. This is for a variety of reasons, including the fact that in a scheme the shareholders may meet in classes, and the approval level is applied to each class, not to the shareholding body as a whole; that only the votes of those attending and voting (in person or by proxy) are counted; and that the votes of the bidder and its subsidiaries (if they are included in the scheme at all) are generally not taken into account in determining whether the threshold test is met. Consequently, even with just one class, if the bidder holds 20% of the shares and only half of the rest of the shareholders attend and vote, 10% of the 'disinterested' shareholders could block the scheme.

[150] *Re BTR plc* [1999] 2 BCLC 675, affirmed [2000] 1 BCLC 740; *Re TDG plc* [2008] EWHC 2334 (Ch).

[151] *Re National Bank* [1966] 1 WLR 819; *Re TDG plc* [2008] EWHC 2334 (Ch).

[152] Companies Act 2006, s 21. For discussion see 15.2.2.5.1.

15.3.1.2.2 Concerns Regarding the Bypassing of Minority Protection in Takeover Offers

A significant amount of minority protection is put in place in a takeover offer, often by way of specific takeover regulation, such as the Takeover Code in the UK. Concerns are raised in other jurisdictions, to the effect that the use of a scheme to effect a change of control allows bidders to bypass these protections.[153] These concerns are misplaced in the context of English schemes of arrangement.

Crucially, schemes used to effect a takeover of a company subject to the Takeover Code in the UK are subject to that regime just as much as a more traditional offer. Many of the obligations under the Takeover Code, such as disclosure requirements, apply identically to offers and schemes.[154] Where differences do exist, there are good reasons for their existence, mostly based on the structure and operation of a scheme as compared to an offer. For example, some of the minority protections that exist for shareholders in an offer, such as the mandatory bid rule and the squeeze-out and sell-out rules, do not apply in a scheme. This is however explicable and justifiable when the differences between takeover offers and schemes are considered.

Minority protection in a takeover offer is needed in order to ensure undistorted choice, and in order to prevent oppression of the minority, although the first is a far stronger justification for the minority protection devices put in place than the second.[155] By contrast, because a scheme involves a decision of the company, taken by the shareholders collectively in a meeting, there is no opportunity for the bidder to divide and conquer. The concerns regarding distorted choice do not arise, therefore, in the context of a scheme. The issue in a scheme is simply one of minority protection. Here again, though, it is important to differentiate the position regarding takeover offers. There is no need to be concerned about the minority shareholders needing a right of exit, since all shareholders are bound to transfer their shares to the bidder following a successful scheme. The bidder acquires 100 per cent of the shares and there is therefore no possibility of any shareholders being left behind who might wish to exit the target company post-bid. The possibility of oppression only arises as regards the fact that the majority decision (to sell their shares at a particular price) will bind the minority, who must also sell at that price. This form of potential oppression is therefore most akin to the position of rump shareholders who are required to sell their shares in a squeeze-out following a successful takeover.[156]

For English schemes, both the courts and the Takeover Panel play a significant role in overseeing the use of schemes to effect change of control transactions, and ensuring that minority protection is upheld. Concerns about the use of schemes to bypass the minority protections put in place in takeover offers are, therefore, misplaced.

---

[153] This concern seems to explain s 411(17) Australian Corporations Act 2001 (see n [215]). It is notable, however, that strong arguments have been made for the repeal of this section by, inter alia, the Corporations and Markets Advisory Committee (CAMAC) in Australia: CAMAC, *Members' Schemes of Arrangement*, December 2009, 95–108. For further discussion of this issue see T Damian and A Rich, *Schemes, Takeovers and Himalayan Peaks: The Use of Schemes of Arrangement to Effect Change of Control Transactions*, 3rd edn (Ross Parsons Centre of Commercial, Corporate and Taxation Law, University of Sydney, 2013) 15.2.

[154] See eg Takeover Code, r 24.

[155] See 14.3.4.

[156] See 14.3.1.3. See also J Payne, 'Schemes of Arrangement, Takeovers and Minority Shareholder Protection' (2011) 11 *Journal of Corporate Law Studies* 67.

15.3.2 To Reorganise a Corporate Group

Another common use of schemes is to reorganise a corporate group.[157] This is typically done by way of a scheme between a company and its members, which creates a new holding company for the group (often called a holdco scheme).[158] There are a number of reasons why holdco schemes are used, but two of the most common reasons are to redomicile the group to a different jurisdiction, something for which there is no mechanism within the Companies Act 2006, and to create additional distributable reserves which can then be returned to the shareholders.[159] Schemes of this kind can therefore be used in order to achieve reorganisations of the share capital that could not otherwise be effected. For instance, companies wishing to pay dividends to shareholders will face a fundamental problem if the company has insufficient distributable reserves to allow it to do so since companies may only pay dividends out of distributable reserves.[160] The benefit of a holdco scheme for a company with low distributable reserves is that it facilitates the creation of additional distributable reserves.

Member schemes can be used to add a new holding company in one of two ways: by way of a transfer scheme or by way of a reduction scheme.[161] A transfer scheme involves the members in the company that is proposing the scheme (oldco) transferring their shares in oldco to the new holding company, in exchange for shares in the new holding company. In a reduction scheme the members agree to have their existing shares in oldco cancelled in consideration for the issue to them of shares in the new holding company.[162] The introduction of the new holding company creates merger reserves for that new holding company.[163]

---

[157] For a discussion of the operation of these schemes in practice see G O'Dea et al, *Schemes of Arrangement: Law and Practice* (Oxford, Oxford University Press, 2012) 9.13–9.92. Note that under Companies Act 2006, s 900, where a scheme involves a reconstruction of any company or companies and under the scheme the whole or any part of the undertaking or property of any company concerned in the scheme is to be transferred to another company, then the court has very broad powers to make a variety of ancillary orders.

[158] See eg Rolls Royce Group plc scheme of arrangement (new holding company and reduction of capital) completed May 2011, Randall & Quilter Investment Holdings plc scheme of arrangement (new holding company and redomicile) completed July 2013.

[159] There are a number of reasons why companies might want to increase their distributable reserves in this way. It may be that in the existing structure there are very low distributable reserves, and the group wishes to unlock previously undistributable reserves in order to return capital to the shareholders, either by way of a payment of dividends or through a share buyback (see 5.4.1 and 5.4.2), or, alternatively, the group may use this route to return to the shareholders cash which has arisen from the sale of some of the group's businesses. See eg *Re Mann Group plc* [2012] EWHC 4089 (Ch) in which the scheme was effected in order to enhance the group's access to distributable reserves in order to allow the group to continue its previously stated dividend policy.

[160] See Companies Act 2006, s 830(1), discussed at 5.4.1.

[161] Reduction schemes have been more common, since they do not involve a transfer of shares and have in the past avoided the requirement to pay stamp duty. See now Companies Act 2006 (Amendment of Part 17) Regulations 2015 (SI 472/2015) (although it remains possible to effect a reduction scheme in order to insert a new holding company as part of a restructuring: reg 3).

[162] Both private and public companies tend to achieve this by way of a special resolution confirmed by the court (Companies Act 2006, s 645, discussed at 5.4.3.2), despite the fact that private companies have the option of making use of the solvency statement route, which avoids the need to go to court (see Companies Act 2006, ss 642–43, discussed at 5.4.3.3). Given that the scheme procedure involves two court hearings in any case, it is generally simpler to combine the reduction of capital and the scheme, and to comply with the requirements of both processes. Therefore, in addition to the requirements of the scheme, the company must satisfy the court that it has complied with the requirements for the reduction of capital.

[163] Companies Act 2006, s 613.

Where the scheme is intended to create additional distributable reserves a further step is then required, namely a reduction of capital of the new holding company. The reserve created by a reduction of capital is treated as a distributable reserve of the company unless the court orders otherwise.[164] Therefore, generally this reduction of capital of the new holding company will increase the distributable reserves by the amount of the reduction. If the new holding company is a UK company, this reduction will generally be by way of a court-sanctioned reduction,[165] which is conditional upon the scheme of arrangement.[166]

15.3.3 To Effect a Merger or Demerger

A scheme of arrangement can be used to effect a merger or demerger. The term 'merger' does not describe a technical legal process in English law.[167] Accordingly, it may be used to describe a number of different types of transaction. It can be used to refer to a transaction in which two separate entities merge into one legal entity, and the assets and liabilities of the target entity are transferred to the surviving entity.[168] The use of schemes in this scenario is relatively rare.[169] There are some practical reasons for this. Share sales are, on the whole, more straightforward transactions than asset sales. Only shares are transferred, as opposed to all the underlying assets of the business, for which separate transfers with different formalities may be required. In addition, on a share purchase, all of the target's liabilities will automatically pass to the buyer. On an asset purchase the buyer only acquires agreed and identified assets and liabilities, provided these can be specified with sufficient precision as a matter of fact and drafting.[170] Further, on a share purchase, the business is transferred as

---

[164] Ibid, ss 610, 612.

[165] Companies Act 2006, ss 645–49 (see 5.4.3.2). If the new holding company is not incorporated in the UK then this reduction will need to take place in accordance with the laws of the jurisdiction in which it is incorporated.

[166] The reduction of capital procedure (discussed at 5.4.3.2) is, however, simplified by reason of the fact that the new holding company will often have no creditors. As a result, the creditor protection issues that usually arise when the court considers whether to confirm a reduction of capital do not tend to arise here. The court may therefore dispense with the usual requirement that a list of creditors be settled (s 646(2)) and will generally approve a reduction where there is a bona fide commercial reason for the reduction, and creditors are adequately protected.

[167] This is not the case in other jurisdictions. In Delaware, for example, a statutory regime allows for the merger or consolidation of two or more Delaware corporations or for the merger and consolidation of one or more Delaware corporations with one or more corporations from other states in the US (Delaware General Corporation Law, §§ 251, 252).

[168] Where this kind of merger involves companies located in different Member States, see now the Cross Border Mergers Directive 2005/56/EC and, in the UK, the Companies (Cross-Border Mergers) Regulations 2007 (SI 2974/2007). In 2014 the European Commission launched a consultation on cross-border mergers and divisions in order to collect information which would allow the Commission to assess the functioning of the existing EU legal framework for cross-border operations of companies and any potential need for changes in the current rules.

[169] Where a scheme of arrangement is used to effect such a merger, s 900 Companies Act 2006 may be relevant. This section provides a number of additional powers to the court where the transaction involves a 'reconstruction' or an 'amalgamation'. However, Part 27 of the Companies Act 2006 also adds a further layer of regulation for 'mergers and divisions' of public companies.

[170] This is subject to exceptions in certain jurisdictions. For example, on the acquisition of a business as a going concern that is located in any EU jurisdiction, contracts of employees who work in the business immediately before the acquisition will automatically be transferred to the buyer (as the new employer), who must continue to employ the employees on the same terms: for the UK see Transfer of Undertakings (Protection of Employment) Regulations 2006 (SI 2006/246), which implement the European Community Acquired Rights Directive (77/187/EEC as amended by Directive 98/50/EC and consolidated in 2001/23/EC).

a going concern (subject to change of control provisions in relevant contracts). This is not necessarily the case with an asset purchase. The tax treatment of share and asset purchases is also different. Generally, transfer duties are lower on share purchases. There is little or nothing in a scheme of arrangement that can address these issues.

The word 'merger' can also be used to describe other transactions. For instance, the term might be used more generally to describe a situation in which there is effectively a takeover of one company by another, perhaps by way of a transfer of shares in the target to another company, but for commercial or presentational reasons the parties choose to call the scenario a 'merger', for example where the companies are of roughly equivalent size and they wish the transaction to be perceived as a 'merger of equals'.[171]

Schemes of arrangement can also be used to effect a division or demerger of one company into two or more companies. Demergers may be contemplated for a number of reasons, for example to streamline a group whose businesses have become too diverse, or in order to escape regulatory restrictions that affect one part of a business but not others, or as a preliminary step in a sale of one or more of a group's businesses to another company. There are various options for a group wishing to effect a demerger.[172] One option is the issue of a dividend by the company effecting the demerger to its shareholders in the form of shares in the subsidiary to be demerged. This will only be possible where the company effecting the demerger has sufficient distributable reserves, but the addition of the kind of scheme whereby a new holding company is added to the group can be a mechanism for creating sufficient distributable reserves to enable this to occur.[173] Another option is for the company to make use of section 110 of the Insolvency Act 1986, either instead of or, more usually, alongside a scheme to effect a demerger. Section 110 of the Insolvency Act 1986 allows a company to reconstruct itself by means of a voluntary liquidation, ie section 110 is designed for use when a company is solvent.[174] A typical section 110 demerger involves the company transferring its assets to two or more newly created companies in return for shares in those companies. The shares in the new companies are then distributed to the shareholders of the original company in proportion to their shareholdings in the original company, and that original company is then wound up. The shareholders may continue to own the two companies, or the companies may then be sold. The procedure to put a section 110 arrangement in place starts with a special resolution of the shareholders to wind up the company, to appoint a liquidator, to approve the section 110 reconstruction, and to authorise the liquidator to carry out the reconstruction.[175] Following the passing of this special resolution, and subject to the right of the dissenting shareholders, discussed next, the section 110 arrangement is then binding on all the members of the company.[176]

---

[171] The use of schemes in this scenario is discussed in 15.3.1.

[172] For detailed discussion of the operation of these schemes in practice see G O'Dea et al, *Schemes of Arrangement: Law and Practice* (Oxford, Oxford University Press, 2012), 9.123–9.152.

[173] See 15.3.2.

[174] A members' voluntary liquidation is one in which the directors have made a 'declaration of solvency' declaring that all the company's debts will be paid in full within 12 months (see Insolvency Act 1986, s 89). For the distinction between a members' and creditors' voluntary liquidation see Insolvency Act 1986, s 90.

[175] Insolvency Act 1986, s 110(3)(a). As to the timing of this special resolution see s 110(6).

[176] Ibid, s 110(5). Unlike a scheme of arrangement, therefore, a s 110 reconstruction of this kind does not require court approval.

Several forms of minority shareholder protection are available in a section 110 recon-struction. In a members' voluntary winding up a special resolution is required. Those that vote in favour are bound by the arrangement, but can still refuse to accept an interest in the transferee companies.[177] Those that vote against the special resolution can also refuse to accept such interests, but they have additional protection under section 111,[178] which allows a dissentient to write to the liquidator within seven days of the resolution.[179] The liquidator must then either abstain from carrying the resolution into effect, or purchase the members' interest in the transferee.[180] Since the former is only possible if there is some barrier to the transaction being carried out, in practice the liquidator will have to buy the dissentients out. The price will be that agreed by the liquidator and dissentients, or fixed by arbitration.[181] The price should take into account the value of the interest before reconstruction. Although members' rights can be varied using this form of arrangement, it will not generally be possible to make them significantly less attractive. If a number of the members elect to be bought out, the reorganisation under section 110 may well become prohibitively expensive. A reconstruction can also be challenged by a shareholders' action against the company. This action may be brought by any member that dissented, but will be brought on behalf of all shareholders.[182]

As for the protection of creditors in a section 110 reconstruction, the creditors of the transferor company remain as such, and retain all their rights against the company. It will normally be part of the arrangement in a members' winding up that the transferee agrees to meet the liabilities of the transferor, and gives an indemnity to that effect. Alternatively, the transferor may retain sufficient assets to pay its creditors. Creditors can attempt to stop a section 110 demerger from progressing by petitioning the court for a compulsory winding up order. To succeed the creditors must demonstrate either that it is just and equitable to wind up the company, or that the company is unable to pay its debts.[183] If the court orders that the company be wound up within one year of the special resolution authorising the section 110 scheme, the special resolution is not valid unless sanctioned by the court.[184] As a result, the demerger will remain open to challenge for a year after the transaction, and that challenge can be brought by any creditor whose debts are not discharged.[185] The demerger is therefore subject to a considerable period of uncertainty post-transaction, which does not exist in a scheme.[186] As a result of these disadvantages, schemes may be used along-side section 110, in which case a holdco scheme may be used to add a new holding com-pany to the group, which is then liquidated using the section 110 procedure. Since this new

---

[177] Eg, *Cleve v Financial Corporation* (1873) LR 16 Eq 363.
[178] A shareholder cannot be deprived of the rights afforded by s 111 by a provision of the company's articles: *Payne v The Cork Co Ltd* [1900] 1 Ch 308.
[179] Insolvency Act 1986, s 111(1)(2). See also *Brailey v Rhodesia Consolidated Ltd* [1910] 2 Ch 95.
[180] Ibid, s 111(2).
[181] Ibid, s 111(4).
[182] See eg *Clinch v Financial Corporation* (1868) LR 5 Eq 450; *Re Oriental Commercial Bank, Alabaster's Case* (1868–69) LR 7 273; *Re City and County Investment Co* (1879) 13 Ch D 475.
[183] See Insolvency Act 1986, s 123.
[184] Ibid, s 110(6).
[185] See eg *Re City and County Investment Co* (1879) 13 Ch D 475.
[186] See 15.2.3.3.

holding company will have no creditors, or relatively few creditors, the effect of introducing a holdco scheme is to reduce the possibility of a challenge by creditors.

15.3.4 To Effect an Arrangement Between the Company and its Creditors

When schemes of arrangement were first introduced in 1870,[187] they applied only to arrangements between a company and its creditors, and only to arrangements proposed by companies in the course of being wound up. Both of these constraints were subsequently dropped,[188] but it remains a common use of schemes of arrangement to effect a compromise between the company and its creditors.

There are a number of general reasons why a scheme may be valuable as a mechanism for amending its arrangements with its creditors. First, it allows the majority to bind the minority. It is possible for an arrangement between a company and its creditors to be effected via informal consensual arrangements between the parties. The difficulty with a contractual workout is that all creditors whose rights are being altered have to agree to the alteration. In general, the position regarding creditors is therefore distinct from that regarding shareholders. For shareholders, if the rights are in the articles, then 75 per cent of the shareholders can, in principle, bind the minority.[189] As regards creditors, the usual position is that a single dissenting creditor, even one holding only a very small percentage of the company's debts, can prevent the compromise.[190] By contrast, in a successful scheme the majority creditors within a class are able to bind the minority, provided the scheme is subsequently sanctioned by the court.[191] Second, schemes can be used whether the company is solvent or insolvent.[192] So, for example, a scheme may be used to restructure a company before insolvency in an attempt to head off liquidation. Third, schemes are also very flexible devices, and the lack of statutorily prescribed content means that schemes can be tailored to the needs of particular companies and can be used in a wide variety of ways, to modify all aspects of the creditor-debtor relationship, including security rights, to swap debt for equity, to facilitate a solvent run-off of a company, or as an alternative to liquidation or administration.

---

[187] Joint Stock Companies Arrangement Act 1870.

[188] The Companies Act 1907 extended schemes to companies not in liquidation and the Companies (Consolidation) Act 1908 extended schemes to arrangements between a company and its members or any class of them.

[189] Companies Act 2006, s 21 (regarding alterations of articles). This is subject to the common law principle that the majority must act bona fide in the best interests of the company: *Allen v Gold Reefs of West Africa Ltd* [1900] 1 Ch 656.

[190] However, this position can be varied by contract. In deeds of debt securities, for example, it is common to provide that the trustee can take action against a corporate borrower with the approval of a specified majority less than 100%. See 8.3.3. As with shareholders' ability to alter the articles, there are common law restrictions on the ability of the majority to exercise its voting power in these situations for an improper purpose: *British America Nickel Corporation v O'Brien* [1927] AC 369 (see 8.3.3.2). These can obviously only bind the parties to the contract, whereas a scheme can bind other creditors.

[191] See 15.2.

[192] See eg *Scottish Lion Insurance Co Ltd v Goodrich Corp* [2010] CSIH 6.

There are other statutory processes that can be used to effect arrangements between a company and its creditors, but a scheme of arrangement can be extremely valuable and, particularly in relation to debt restructurings of large companies, schemes have become very common.

15.3.4.1 Restructuring the Debts of Financially Distressed Companies

There are numerous ways to make use of a scheme where a company is financially distressed. One possibility is for a scheme to be used alongside, or instead of, liquidation. Schemes can provide a number of advantages in such scenarios: for example, courts have been prepared to depart from provisions that would otherwise be applied, such as the set-off rules,[193] or the pari passu principle.[194] However, in recent years a more common use of schemes has been as a debt restructuring tool.[195] Debt restructuring is a process that allows a company facing cash flow problems and financial distress to reduce and renegotiate its delinquent debts, in order to improve or restore liquidity and rehabilitate it so that it can continue its operations, possibly with a view to selling the company or its business. A typical scenario might involve a group of companies whose performance is below that forecast in its business plan. The group is unable to meet forthcoming payments on its senior debt and cannot afford to pay the interest on its junior debt. The group is cash flow positive at an operating level, ie there is a business worth saving, but the original business plan was too optimistic and the group has no chance of ever being able to repay all its senior and junior debt.

The most common restructurings involve the postponement of imminent liabilities into the more distant future; the conversion of fixed liabilities for more fluid ones, such as a debt-for-equity swap; and/or debt write-downs whereby all creditors of a particular type agree a pro rata reduction in the value of their claims. Rehabilitation of this kind will often be preferable to liquidation, and dissolution. This, of course, pre-supposes that the company is not economically distressed, but merely financially distressed, ie it is cash-flow insolvent but is nevertheless economically viable: there is a business that is worth saving, either within the present company or in a new entity. Schemes are often used alongside some of the alternative debt restructuring mechanisms open to companies.[196]

Various features of a debt restructuring regime are likely to prove valuable to a company in this exercise. The first is some kind of moratorium while the company seeks to negotiate a restructuring with its creditors,[197] which can prevent individual creditors instituting

---

[193]   *Re Anglo American Insurance Co Ltd* [2001] 1 BCLC 755.

[194]   *Re BCCI SA (No 3)* [1993] BCLC 1490.

[195]   This section will focus on the use of schemes to restructure the debts of English companies, but English schemes have increasingly been used to restructure the debts of foreign companies too. For discussion see J Payne, 'Cross-Border Schemes of Arrangement and Forum Shopping' (2013) 14 *European Business Organization Law Review* 563.

[196]   The main debt restructuring alternatives are contractual workouts, company voluntary arrangements (CVAs) and administration. For discussion see J Payne, 'Debt Restructuring in English Law: Lessons from the US and the Need for Reform' (2014) 130 *Law Quarterly Review* 282.

[197]   Different definitions of 'moratorium' can be adopted. On one view a moratorium is simply a period in which debts are not due and payable. However, a moratorium of this kind would be of relatively limited value to a company in a restructuring since it would still leave open the possibility of creditors pursuing their claims against the company in a manner which could be disruptive of the attempted restructuring, for example by seeking to have the company wound up. The definition of 'moratorium' adopted in this chapter is that utilised in the Insolvency Act 1986, which focuses on a broader concept of a statutory stay: see eg Insolvency Act 1986, Sch B1 paras 42–43 (as regards administration), Sch A1 Part III (as regards CVAs involving small companies).

enforcement actions against the company during the first stages of a restructuring, when negotiations are taking place, and thus can provide the company with breathing space in order to try to conclude a restructuring agreement with its creditors.[198] It may also be valuable for the company if it does not have to obtain the approval of every creditor but, instead, the reorganisation can go forward with the approval of a majority of creditors, ie the reorganisation can be imposed on dissenting minority creditors to some extent. Finally, it will generally be advantageous for the company if its financial distress can be dealt with at an early stage. Placing the debt restructuring mechanism in insolvency law and making insolvency a pre-condition for access to the mechanism, for example, will reduce the capacity for early intervention, and may therefore reduce the opportunity to avoid liquidation.[199]

Schemes provide a number of these features:[200] in particular, they operate pre-insolvency, and do allow the majority of a class to impose its views on the minority, although every class must vote in favour of a scheme before it can be sanctioned, ie it is not possible to cram down a whole class using a scheme alone. There is no moratorium attached to a scheme, however. Nevertheless, schemes have in recent years increasingly been used to restructure the debts of financially distressed companies, often as an alternative to liquidation or administration.

In *Re Telewest Communications plc*,[201] for example, the company was insolvent and the scheme put in place was a debt-equity swap, which was presented as a 'substantially better alternative' than the formal insolvency options open to the company.[202] A swap of this kind has the dual effect of reducing the debt levels of the company, and therefore interest payment obligations, whilst increasing the company's capital base, and so diluting the interests of existing shareholders.[203] From a creditor's point of view such a swap can look attractive, as the creditor may be offered the opportunity to participate in a future return on investment that is greater than the potential return available on liquidation. For example, an unsecured creditor facing the prospect of little or no return on liquidation might well be prepared to swap debt for equity, especially if that equity carries a preferential dividend

---

[198] In one recent case, the judge was prepared to exercise the discretion of the court to grant a stay regarding creditors' claims pending consideration of a proposed scheme of arrangement: *Bluecrest Mercantile BV; FMS Wertmanagement AÖR v Vietnam Shipbuilding Industry Group* [2013] EWHC 1146 (Comm).

[199] Another issue that might be included in this list is that of whether the directors remain in control of the company during the restructuring, which they do in schemes, for example, but do not in other restructuring mechanisms, most notably administration (see Goode: Insolvency, ch 11). This issue may have positive or negative effects. Leaving the directors in control can be advantageous, since they know the company best, have long-term relationships with creditors that may be beneficial in the renegotiations, and may be incentivised to tackle financial distress at an earlier stage if they are not concerned about being displaced in the restructuring process. However, where the directors are to some extent the cause of the company's financial distress, leaving them in control of the company is less likely to be advantageous.

[200] Schemes satisfy more of these requirements than any of the other potential restructuring tools, namely contractual workouts, CVAs and administration. For discussion see J Payne, 'Debt Restructuring in English Law: Lessons from the US and the Need for Reform' (2014) 130 *Law Quarterly Review* 282.

[201] [2004] EWHC 924 (Ch).

[202] Ibid, [7].

[203] The value of debt/equity swaps to distressed companies wishing to reorganise their affairs is well understood: DTI Consultation Paper, *Encouraging Debt/Equity Swaps* (1996). Debt-equity swaps need to comply with the relevant provisions of the articles of association and of the Companies Act 2006, regarding the issue of the new shares. For example, pre-emption rights may need to be set aside (for discussion see 4.4.3). If the company's shares are listed there will also be a requirement to comply with the Listing Rules.

rate and/or an opportunity to participate in the surplus. The upsides, in terms of potential returns, of an equity investment are, after all, potentially unlimited, and the creditor may have little to lose. This potential gain may compensate for the fact that the creditor will then lose priority on insolvency.[204] For secured creditors the bargain may not be so obvious, and the incentive to engage in the swap may be weaker. In *Telewest*, the creditors for the purpose of the scheme of arrangement included its bondholders, a subsidiary company (Telewest Jersey) in respect of a loan from the subsidiary to Telewest, and the holders of the Telewest Jersey bonds in respect of a guarantee from Telewest. The scheme proposed that the bonds, and claims arising under them, would be cancelled in exchange for 98.5 per cent of the issued share capital of a new holding company, Telewest Global Inc. All of Telewest's assets would be transferred to Telewest Global, and the remaining 1.5 per cent of its shares would be held by Telewest's existing shareholders. The scheme therefore provided for an immediate cancellation of the claims in respect of the bonds, the inter-company debt and the Telewest guarantee of the subsidiary's bonds. In consideration, each scheme creditor became entitled to receive new shares denominated in dollars in a new company, Telewest Global Inc, pro rata to their total claims. The scheme was sanctioned by the court and the company thereby avoided being placed in liquidation or administration.

While *Telewest* is an example of a scheme being used as a stand-alone mechanism, in recent years schemes have also been twinned with administration in order to overcome the two potential weaknesses in using schemes alone to restructure the debts of a company, namely a lack of moratorium and the inability to cram down a whole class of members or creditors. One significant advantage of administration is the existence of a general moratorium on the enforcement of remedies,[205] and consequently it is easy to see that twinning these procedures allows companies to access this moratorium. However, it is less immediately obvious why the addition of administration into the mix facilitates a cramdown of whole classes in a restructuring, as administration does not per se allow such a cramdown. Indeed, administration demonstrates an unwillingness to interfere with the rights of secured creditors, in particular.[206] To understand the benefit that can be gained from twinning schemes and administration it is helpful to consider the IMO Carwash restructuring.[207]

In that case, Bluebrook Ltd and two of its indirect subsidiaries were balance sheet insolvent. Rather than go into liquidation, three schemes of arrangement were devised between the companies and the lenders of the senior debt. The schemes gave effect to a restructuring arrangement whereby the business of the group was transferred to a new corporate structure via the use of a pre-pack administration, and the senior lenders effectively substituted their debt for shares in the restructured group. The junior lenders were left behind in the scheme companies and, since their rights in the scheme companies were not being altered, they were not part of the schemes and did not, therefore, have the opportunity to vote on whether the schemes should be approved.[208] The junior lenders attended the sanctioning

---

[204] Another potential disadvantage is that it may prove difficult for the creditor to realise the investment after conversion, as the sale of the shares may prove difficult.

[205] Insolvency Act 1986, Sch B1 paras 42–43.

[206] There are some exceptions, such as the moratorium on the enforcement of security interests produced by an administration.

[207] *Re Bluebrook Ltd* [2009] EWHC 2114 (Ch).

[208] See 15.2.2.1.

hearing to challenge the reorganisation, arguing that although their rights against the scheme companies were left intact, the fact that all the assets had been transferred to the new companies meant that the schemes were in fact unfair to them. The judge determined that the value of the assets of the group 'broke' in the senior debt, ie the junior creditors had no remaining economic interest in the group, and therefore that it was appropriate to sanction these schemes despite the objection of the junior creditors.[209] Consequently, this structure allowed for the de facto cramdown of the junior creditors since the reorganisation of the group could go ahead without their consent.

Some jurisdictions, most notably the US under Chapter 11 of the Bankruptcy Act 1978, provide a single, flexible debt restructuring mechanism that provides a moratorium and allows for a cramdown of whole classes.[210] Although the English scheme, when twinned with administration, can achieve the functional equivalent, this is rather unwieldy, and contains some potentially problematic elements, such as the need to transfer the assets of the company (or group) to a new entity. This gives rise to the question whether the English debt restructuring mechanisms need to be reformed, perhaps by adding a moratorium to the use of schemes when used in this context, or facilitating a cramdown of whole classes when schemes are used as a stand-alone device.[211] The Insolvency Service did propose the introduction of a restructuring moratorium in 2009, which would have attached to schemes,[212] but these proposals were shelved following what the Insolvency Service perceived to be a lukewarm response.[213] This issue may reappear on the legislative agenda as a result of developments at EU level, however, following the publication of a European Commission paper in 2014 asking Member States to facilitate the restructuring of businesses, including allowing businesses a temporary stay if need be.[214]

15.3.4.2 *Settling Claims within the Insurance Industry*

Another use of creditor schemes relates to their use to settle claims in the insurance industry. Schemes can be particularly helpful to insurance companies wanting to deal with incurred but not yet reported (IBNR) obligations. This is particularly important for insurance offered in relation to issues such as asbestos, where exposure to the harm occurs during the period covered by the policy, but the personal injury resulting from that exposure might only manifest itself years or even decades later.

---

[209] This approach places the issue of valuation at the forefront of this issue, and indeed much of the discussion in *Re Bluebrook* was concerned with this topic. The English court's handling of issues of valuation is not, however, well developed. For discussion see M Crystal and R Mokal, 'The Valuation of Distressed Companies—A Conceptual Framework' (2006) 3 *International Corporate Rescue*, 63 (Part 1) and 123 (Part 2); J Payne, 'Debt Restructuring in English Law: Lessons from the US and the Need for Reform' (2014) 130 *Law Quarterly Review* 282; S Paterson, 'Rethinking the Role of the Law of Corporate Distress in the Twenty-First Century' LSE Legal Studies Working Paper No 27/2014, http://ssrn.com/abstract=2526677.

[210] For detailed discussion of the current law and some suggested reforms of Chapter 11 see American Bankruptcy Institute, Commission to Study the Reform of Chapter 11, 2012–14, *Final Report and Recommendations*.

[211] See J Payne, 'Debt Restructuring in English Law: Lessons from the US and the Need for Reform' (2014) 130 *Law Quarterly Review* 282.

[212] Insolvency Service, *Encouraging Company Rescue: A Consultation* (London, DTI, June 2009) and see Insolvency Service, *Proposals for a Restructuring Moratorium: A Consultation* (London, DTI, July 2010).

[213] Insolvency Service, *Proposals for a Restructuring Moratorium: Summary of Responses* (London, DTI, May 2011), 5.

[214] European Commission, Commission Recommendation of 12.3.2014 on a new approach to business failure and insolvency, 12 March 2014, C(2014) 1500 final.

These schemes can be used when a company is in liquidation, as it can be a way of intro-ducing a long stop date into the submission of claims, in order to allow the liquidator to more quickly complete the process of assessing the claims against the company which must be paid, and thereby bring the liquidation to a conclusion.[215] These schemes are sometimes called cut-off schemes since they require scheme creditors to submit both their claim and their evidence for the claim to the scheme adjudicator by a specified date.

Alternatively, insurance companies may elect to stop writing certain types of coverage and go into 'run-off', meaning that the company ceases to provide that type of coverage, but it continues to remain bound by its pre-existing contractual commitments under the policies it has already issued. As long as claims continue to be presented and the company remains solvent, the claims will continue to be met in full. Run-off of insurance policies of this kind can take a long time to administer because claims may be presented for many years to come.

If a company wants to expedite this process, it could offer to commute its obligations to its policyholders, exchanging early payout for cancellation of the insurer's future obligation to pay claims as they arise in the ordinary course of business. Commutations are frequently based on actuarial calculations of the present value of future claims, determined in accord-ance with historical claims experience. An insured may be willing to accept a commutation of its policy rights if the amount of the early payout is sufficient, but only if the insurer is in a formal statutory winding up or liquidation procedure can it compel the policyholder to enter into a commutation. A policyholder with IBNR claims might refuse to commute its policy because of the extraordinary difficulty it would face trying to reach agreement with the issuer about the value of its claim. To expedite the run-off process and terminate their longstanding contractual commitments to their policyholders without entering into a formal insolvency or liquidation proceeding, and without having to enter into formal commutation with each policyholder, a number of solvent UK insurance companies have proposed schemes of arrangement.[216] These schemes can allow wholly solvent companies to manage their IBNR liabilities. The effect of a scheme in such a situation is to enable the company to achieve finality in relation to these claims, thus facilitating a release of capital to the shareholders that had previously been held against the possibility of future claims, or perhaps allowing the company to move into a new area of operation.

There are potential disadvantages to such schemes, of course, not least the fact that the claims are estimated, and therefore some policyholders or creditors will receive less (or more) than they would have received had the scheme not been implemented. The problems of estimation are obviously far more acute for IBNR claims than for those claims that have already matured. Also problematic is the fact that, in order to achieve finality, a scheme may introduce a bar date by which point creditors must submit their claims. Any creditor failing to submit a claim by this date may not receive payment under the scheme. The role of the court in ensuring creditor protection, both in determining the appropriate class meetings and in determining whether to sanction the scheme, is therefore key.[217]

---

[215] See eg *Re Pan Atlantic Insurance Co Ltd* [2003] EWHC 1696 (Ch).
[216] Eg *British Aviation Insurance Co Ltd* [2005] EWHC 1621 (Ch).
[217] Ibid.

15.4 Conclusion

Schemes of arrangement are an important tool which can be used to facilitate a wide variety of arrangements and compromises between a company and its members or creditors. Although they have been around for over a century, schemes have undergone something of a renaissance over the last decade or so. Most commonly this involves the use of schemes to effect a change of control of a company, or to restructure the debts of a financially distressed company, although schemes are capable of being used in a much wider variety of circumstances. In part the increased use of schemes in recent years has been driven by practical circumstances, such as the fact that the financial crisis has prompted companies and their advisors to be more flexible and creative in their use of debt restructuring mechanisms.

Often a scheme will be more useful than the alternative mechanisms available to the company (such as a takeover offer), although it is also possible for schemes to be used in combination with those alternatives in order to capture and maximise the benefits of both, for example where schemes are twinned with administration. The fact that schemes can facilitate the imposition of a reorganisation on a minority of creditors or members (within a class) by the majority means that an important role for the court is to ensure that minorities are properly protected. This can occur both at the class meetings stage and at the court sanctioning hearing. Developments in the operation of schemes in recent years have tended to place more emphasis on the latter stage. Courts have recognised that their role requires a balance of the rights of the minority and majority: while schemes should not be utilised in a way that rides roughshod over the minority, neither should the minority necessarily have a veto over a reorganisation that has the support of the majority of member and creditors. The pragmatic and commercially sensible approach adopted by the courts in relation to this issue, and others, is another reason why schemes have been increasingly used as a tool to reorganise company capital in recent years.

16

Private Equity

16.1 Introduction

Private equity has grown enormously in the UK in the last 20 years, to the point where it has been said to rival the public markets as a source of financing.[1] The reach of private equity has also extended in this period, so that, for instance, in 2007 Alliance Boots was the first FTSE 100 company to be purchased by a private equity firm. These developments have also raised concerns, however, most notably regarding the lack of disclosure and transparency to which private equity backed companies have traditionally been subject, and the position of non-shareholder stakeholders, particularly employees, within such companies.[2] The financial crisis, and in particular the contraction of the market for debt prompted by the collapse of Lehman Brothers in September 2008, has had a significant effect on the private equity sector. In the immediate post-crisis period the number and value of private equity deals reduced substantially,[3] although in recent years there have been signs that, fuelled by cheap debt financing, the industry is recovering.[4] If anything, the impact of the financial crisis on the private equity industry heightened calls for private equity to be regulated and, in particular, the financial crisis added a new driver to calls for regulation of the industry, namely systemic risk concerns. Consequently, the Alternative Investment Fund Managers Directive (AIFMD) entered into force in 2011, and creates new regulations for private equity firms as well as other fund managers, such as hedge funds.[5]

---

[1] In the first half of 2006, for example, UK-based private equity fund managers raised £11.2 billion of capital, compared to just £10.4 billion of funds raised via IPOs on the London Stock Exchange in the same period: FSA, *Private Equity: A Discussion of Risk and Regulatory Engagement*, Discussion Paper 06/6, November 2006, 3.

[2] For discussion see 16.7.1. It was estimated in 2006 that 8% of the UK workforce was employed in private equity-owned firms: House of Commons Treasury Committee, Tenth Report of Session 2006–07, *Private Equity*, 30 July 2007, HC 567-I, 7.

[3] See eg European Venture Capital Association (EVCA) *Buyout Report 2010, An EVCA Research Paper* (October 2010) and *Buyout Report 2011*; EVCA, *2013 European Private Equity Activity: Statistics on Fundraising, Investments & Divestments*, May 2014; Centre for Management Buy-Out Research (CMBOR), *European and UK Annual Trends*, wwwf.imperial.ac.uk/business-school/research/the-centre-for-management-buy-out-research/publications/europeanduk-equity/.

[4] See eg Bain & Co, *Global Private Equity Report 2014*, http://resultsbrief.bain.com/pdfs/Bain_and_Company_Global_Private_Equity_Report_2014.pdf; *2014 Global Prequin Private Equity Report*, www.preqin.com/docs/samples/The_2014_Preqin_Global_Private_Equity_Report_Sample_Pages.pdf.

[5] 2011/61/EU. This directive entered into force on 21 July 2011 and was implemented in the UK on 22 July 2013 primarily through the Alternative Investment Fund Managers Regulations 2013 (SI 2013/1773) ('the AIFM Regulations 2013') and updates to the FCA Handbook, but see also Alternative Investment Fund Managers (Amendment) Regulations 2013 (SI 2013/1797); Alternative Investment Fund Managers Order 2014 (SI 2014/1292). This directive is discussed further at 16.7 below.

This chapter examines the development of private equity transactions in the UK, analyses the nature of these transactions, and considers whether the concerns raised in relation to private equity are justified. Many of the conflicts and issues discussed in earlier chapters are in evidence here, and many of the techniques for protecting shareholders, creditors and other stakeholders in the company explored in those chapters are discussed in this context. First, though, a definition is required. The term 'private equity' encompasses a number of different types of transactions, the unifying theme being that the capital involved has been raised privately and will not be deployed by investing in a company which is publicly traded. Such transactions include the provision of venture capital or development capital to young or emerging companies, which typically does not involve the private equity firm obtaining a majority stake, and buy-outs, where the private equity firm buys majority control of an existing or mature firm. A variation on this latter type of funding is the buy-out of a publicly owned company which is then taken private, although the number of these transactions has diminished post-crisis. In recent years the term 'private equity' has come to be most closely associated with the buy-out transaction.

16.2 Historical Development

The core concept and model of modern private equity originated in the US. Private equity really began to develop there in the 1970s,[6] following the founding of the buy-out firm Kohlberg Kravis Roberts (KKR) and the development of the leveraged buy-out (LBO) model.[7] This model involves buying a business by borrowing money from a third party, often a bank. The company's cash flows are used to make the loan repayments and, together with the company's assets, to provide security for the lenders until the debt is repaid. Often the aim is to buy the greatest amount of assets for the smallest amount of equity investment, ie to leverage the purchase to the greatest extent possible. One important factor that contributed to the development of private equity in the US from the 1970s onwards was undoubtedly the rise of high-yield ('junk') bonds[8] which provided firms such as KKR with a highly liquid market for available debt. Over time, other forms of LBO model emerged in the US, including 'break-up' LBOs where the assets of the purchased company were seen as the main vehicle for repaying the debt, and 'strategic' LBOs where a number of single entities (perhaps loss making) were consolidated into a more attractive whole before being offered for sale.

The number of private equity firms in the US gradually increased, as did the amount of capital available to them. In addition to a liquid debt market, the firms found that a number of investors (notably the US state pension funds) wanted to make equity investments in this sector. By 1989 the sector had grown to the point where KKR was able to make a

---

[6] However, the US private equity industry existed much earlier: see eg the formation of the American Research and Development Corporation in Boston in 1946: HM Treasury, *Myners Review of Institutional Investment in the UK* (2001), para 12.30.

[7] GP Baker and GD Smith, *The New Financial Capitalists: Kohlberg Kravis Roberts and the Creation of Corporate Value* (Cambridge, Cambridge University Press, 1998).

[8] See 2.3.3.3.

$31 billion hostile takeover of the US listed foods and tobacco company RJR Nabisco/Borden. The 1990s saw the continued growth of the market, and the development of a wider variety of private equity formats. Private equity in the US had a quiet period in 2001–04, corresponding to a downturn in the global economy at that time. However, the recovery of the economy, together with low interest rates and increasing levels of cheap debt, fuelled another surge in private equity activity after 2004, until the onset of the financial crisis in 2008. The availability of cheap debt, together with the impact of the Sarbanes-Oxley Act, which arguably made private equity even more attractive than publicly traded companies, helped to fuel this increase. The private equity market slowed down in the aftermath of the financial crisis, but has subsequently started to recover, and the US remains the most important global centre for private equity transactions.[9]

Private equity was slower to develop in the UK. Although private equity in some form has existed in the UK for more than 70 years,[10] it only really started to expand in the late 1980s. At that time private equity in the UK still only comprised venture capital, whereby capital is supplied to provide funding to start-up businesses. It is also notable that in this period the transactions were management-led, ie the managers of a company would identify an opportunity they wished to pursue and they would then take their business plan to private equity organisations (venture capitalists) in order to obtain backing in the deal. These deals were therefore quite unlike the more dynamic LBO model that existed in the US at this time. It can fairly be said that at this point private equity in the UK 'operated at the fringes of corporate finance and corporate activity'.[11]

However, the intervening period has seen an enormous expansion and development of this industry in the UK. In 1984 the members of the British Venture Capital Association (BVCA) invested £190 million in 479 companies. In 2007, members of the BVCA invested £31.6 billion in more than 1,600 companies worldwide.[12] As the market developed, the deals tended to be initiated not by the management team but by the private equity funds themselves, as they sought deals to finance. This change from deals being management-led to investor-led impacted on the nature of the deals themselves. Whereas in the 1980s it was common for management to hold the majority of the shares in the private equity backed firm, this changed so that the private equity fund would hold the majority stake. Today it is uncommon for the management to hold more than 25 per cent of the equity in the company. The consequential effect of this change has been to put the portfolio company under the control of the fund rather than the management. The language used to describe these deals has also changed. Instead of referring to the transactions as 'management buy-outs' or 'management buy-ins' (where the management team joined the business at the time of the acquisition) it has become more common to refer to them as 'leveraged buy-outs', in the US style. The general term 'private equity' is used today to cover all those transactions

---

[9] See eg Bain & Co, *Global Private Equity Report 2014*, http://resultsbrief.bain.com/pdfs/Bain_and_Company_Global_Private_Equity_Report_2014.pdf.

[10] The origins of venture capital in the UK can be traced back to the 1930s at least, with the founding of Charterhouse and the identification of the 'equity gap' for smaller unquoted companies by the Macmillan Report in 1931: HM Treasury, *Myners Review of Institutional Investment in the UK* (2001), para 12.23.

[11] C Hale in C Hale (ed), *Private Equity: A Transactional Analysis*, 3rd edn (London, Globe Law and Business, 2015) 5.

[12] British Venture Capital Association (BVCA), *Private Equity and Venture Capital Report on Investment Activity 2008*, July 2009.

where investment funds managed by private equity funds are invested in private companies (or publicly traded companies that have been taken private). Although venture capital and growth capital funding are still important aspects of private equity activity in the UK, in terms of the scale of transactions buy-out activity is now the largest part of the industry, and it is this form of funding which has become synonymous with the term 'private equity' in recent years.

The amount of money invested by UK-based private equity firms has grown steadily, and reached a peak in 2007.[13] As in the US, this growth was fuelled by the availability of large amounts of cheap debt, coupled with a desire on the part of increasing numbers of investors, particularly institutional investors, to invest in this market. In the pre-crisis period the size of funds also increased, and private equity funds were prepared to cooperate on single transactions ('club deals'). In consequence, even the largest publicly traded companies became possible targets for private equity funds, as exemplified by the purchase of Alliance Boots by a KKR led consortium for £10.6 billion in 2007.

As in the US, the financial crisis and the accompanying contraction of the debt market had a significant impact on private equity in the UK in the post-crisis period. For instance, research conducted by the Centre for Management Buy-out and Private Equity Research (CMBOR) found that there were just 31 UK private equity deals in the three months to September 2009, the lowest level since 1984.[14] Since 2010 there has been a recovery from these very low levels.[15] The principal post-crisis problem was not the absence of equity—there were funds available within private equity firms.[16] Rather, it revolved around the absence of cheap available debt in the market. Although the debt to equity ratios in private equity deals have fallen from their pre-crisis levels (where ratios of 70:30 or more were common), the leveraged buy-out model depends on high levels of debt in the financing mix.

Private equity activity appears to experience boom and bust cycles.[17] After the boom in the early part of this century, which came to an end in 2008, the industry experienced one of its cyclical downturns. Private equity suffered a significant setback as a result of the contraction of the debt markets following the financial crisis. It is not surprising, therefore, that with the renewed availability of cheap debt financing the private equity market has begun to show signs of recovery.[18] There seems little doubt that private equity will continue to play an important role in the capital markets in the future.[19]

---

[13] Investment levels have dropped off since 2007: see eg BVCA, *Private Equity and Venture Capital Report on Investment Activity 2013*, Autumn 2014.

[14] CMBOR, press release, 5 October 2009.

[15] See eg CMBOR, *Third Quarter 2014 Report*; *2014 Global Preqin Private Equity Report*, www.preqin.com/docs/samples/The_2014_Preqin_Global_Private_Equity_Report_Sample_Pages.pdf.

[16] The financial crisis did not appear to significantly dent equity investors' appetite for investing in private equity. In 2014, for instance, Prequin noted a huge amount of 'dry powder' (ie capital committed to funds but not yet spent): *2014 Global Prequin Private Equity Report*, ibid.

[17] SN Kaplan and P Strömberg, 'Leveraged Buyouts and Private Equity' (2009) 23 *Journal of Economic Perspectives* 121.

[18] See BVCA, *Private Equity and Venture Capital Report on Investment Activity 2013*, Autumn 2014.

[19] For discussion see M Bishop, *The Future of Private Equity: Beyond the Mega Buyout* (London, Palgrave Macmillan, 2012).

16.3 Private Equity Funds

16.3.1 Structure of a Typical Private Equity Fund

Funds can vary enormously in terms of their size and the sorts of investments into which they will enter. Some may specialise in providing venture capital funding or buy-out funding, while others specialise in the types of company in which they will invest. However, the structure of the fund itself will generally be the same. The typical structure of a UK private equity fund is an English limited partnership,[20] although limited partnerships from other jurisdictions (for example, Guernsey, Jersey, Scotland and Delaware) may also be used. An English limited partnership lacks legal personality.[21] In a limited partnership there must be one or more partners with unlimited liability. These partners are called 'general partners'. In a private equity fund the general partner will generally be a separate vehicle, usually either an English limited company or a limited partnership, owned by the private equity firm. In theory the general partner makes the investment decisions on behalf of the limited partnership. In practice, the fund will usually be managed by a separate vehicle to the general partner, the fund manager. The fund manager, which is regulated by the FCA, then provides the limited partnership with investment advice, and makes investment decisions on behalf of the limited partnership.[22]

The general partner will usually invest equity into the fund. This ensures that the interests of the general partner are aligned with the interests of the fund investors.[23] However, the size of this investment will generally be small: the general partner's return is primarily generated from its fees. The general partner will receive an annual management fee, commonly 1.5–2.5 per cent of funds committed,[24] and a share (or 'carry') of profits made by the

---

[20] See Limited Partnership Act 1907. In 2008 the Government announced plans to repeal this Act and to introduce new provisions into the Partnership Act 1890 by way of a legislative reform order, to be implemented from 1 October 2009 (see BERR, *Reform of Limited Partnership Law: Legislative Reform Order to Repeal and Replace the Limited Partnership Act 1907: A Consultative Document*, August 2008). However, in light of responses to the consultation, the Government decided not to proceed. In March 2013, the Treasury released a report on UK investment management in which it stated that the Treasury will consult with a view to making technical changes to the 1907 Act: HM Treasury, *The UK Investment Management Strategy*, March 2013, 4.10.

[21] The Law Commission recommended a change to the law in this regard (*Limited Liability Partnerships: A Joint Consultation Paper* (Law Com Consultation Paper No 161); *Partnership Law: A Joint Report* (Law Com Report No 283, 2003)) but no change to the law has resulted.

[22] Undertaking one of a number of specified 'regulated activities' (such as advising on and managing investments) in the UK by way of business requires authorisation by the FCA (FSMA, s 19), and as regards prudential matters most private equity houses are also supervised by the FCA. FCA-authorised firms are also subject to a number of ongoing regulatory obligations that impact the way they run their business, for example regarding the amount of 'regulatory capital' they must maintain, and they are required to comply with detailed record keeping and reporting obligations and to have systems in place to ensure continued compliance with FCA rules.

[23] This alignment of interests may break down, however, if staff investment is not fully aligned with that of the investors, for example if staff are able to under- or over-commit to specific transactions—effectively cherry picking: FSA, *Private Equity: A Discussion of Risk and Regulatory Engagement*, Discussion paper 06/6, November 2006, para 4.60.

[24] These percentages have remained consistent for many years, despite the size of funds increasing dramatically. This has caused some concern since the effect can be to incentivise private equity firms to set up bigger and bigger funds. In a fund of £100 million the fee will be 10 times that of a fund of £10 million, but the workload is unlikely to be 10 times as great. However, these figures may be changing and there is some evidence that these fees are reducing (see eg 'The Cost of Investing in Alternative Assets is Falling—Slowly' *The Economist*, 8 February 2014, which suggested that the fees for investing in private equity funds were more like a '1.4 and 17' structure rather than '2 and 20').

fund as a whole (commonly 20 per cent), although this latter payment will be subject to a minimum hurdle level of return to investors, usually about 8 per cent.[25]

The other partners are the 'limited partners' and they contribute to the partnership assets a specified amount in money or money's worth, and enjoy immunity from liability beyond the amount contributed. It is an essential condition of this immunity that a limited partner shall not take part in the management of the business, and has no power to bind the firm.[26] A limited partner may inspect the books and may consult with the other partners as to the state and prospects of the business, but must not go beyond this. If the limited partner does so, even if inadvertently, or in ignorance of the law, or at the urgent request of the general partners, then he forfeits his immunity from liability.[27]

The main document governing the relationship between the general partner and the limited partner investors is therefore the partnership agreement, which will be carefully negotiated and will generally specify the types of investment that may be made by the fund, as well as specifying the management fees and other commercial terms. The limited partners will also expect to receive regular and detailed updates from the general partner on the investments made by the fund.

One of the important considerations when structuring a private equity fund is to ensure that it is tax efficient. English limited partnerships are tax transparent. As a result, the limited partners are treated for tax purposes as though they own the shares in the portfolio companies directly.[28] Since these limited partnerships are not bodies corporate and do not have legal personality separate to that of their partners, the limited partnership is afforded the same treatment elsewhere, and overseas investors should therefore be treated in their home jurisdictions as receiving dividends, interest and capital gains as though they are the direct owners of the relevant shares, and be taxed accordingly. There is no tax charge at the limited partnership level, and there is no liability to tax when the limited partnership distributes its assets to its partners.

The position of private equity funds and hedge funds may be contrasted.[29] In some ways these two forms of investment are similar. Both types of funds are managed by a team of

---

[25] To date the 'carry' has been taxed as a capital gain and has not been subject to income tax. This tax regime is under threat in the US: in February 2014, the US House Committee on Ways and Means released draft legislation, the 'Tax Reform Act of 2014', s 3621 of which would tax carried interest as ordinary income. This issue may, therefore, be reexamined in the UK context.

[26] Limited Partnership Act 1907, s 6(1).

[27] Ibid. One issue that has arisen in the past in relation to the use of the limited partnership structure for private equity firms is the extent of the involvement of the limited partners that is possible without them becoming liable to forfeit their limited liability status. The Government's proposals for the reform of limited liability partnerships in 2008 included a provision that there should be a list of activities that limited partners are allowed to undertake without jeopardising the limitation of their liability, in order to inject some clarity into this issue (BERR, *Reform of Limited Partnership Law: Legislative Reform Order to Repeal and Replace the Limited Partnership Act 1907: A Consultative Document*, August 2008, paras 20.111–20.112), but these proposals were not implemented. In comparison, several other common funds jurisdictions such as Guernsey, Jersey and Luxemburg do include safe harbours in relation to the activities of limited partners.

[28] Some changes to the regime were introduced by Finance Act 2014, s 74 and Sch 17 in an attempt to combat tax avoidance involving partnerships. For discussion see M Baldwin, 'Finance Act 2014 Notes: Section 74 and Schedule 17: Partnerships' (2014) 4 *British Tax Review* 416.

[29] See generally J Bevilacqua, 'Convergence and Divergence: Blurring the Lines Between Hedge Funds and Private Equity Funds' (2006) 54 *Buffalo Law Review* 251. It is acknowledged, however, that hedge funds are notoriously difficult to categorise and classify: see eg IOSCO, *Hedge Funds Oversight, Consultation Paper* (2009), paras 8–9.

skilled investment professionals that solicit investors directly, rather than through general advertising or a public offering. Both are commonly organised by way of limited partnerships. In both cases a management company, which acts as an investment adviser, will hold the general partnership interest of the limited partnership, and in both cases the investors (the limited partners) usually consist of high net worth individuals and families, pension funds, endowments, banks, and insurance companies. However, the investment strategies and partnership terms of these two types of investment have traditionally been quite distinct.

One of the key features of a private equity investment, certainly when compared to an investment in shares in a publicly traded company, is its illiquidity. The asset held by the limited partners is their stake in the fund. Private equity funds are typically raised with an expected life of around 10 years, a term that is established in the partnership agreement at the outset. The typical hold period for individual portfolio companies purchased by the fund is therefore shorter, typically three to five years, after which time the aim will be to exit that company, usually by way of a flotation, a trade sale, or a sale to another private equity fund.[30] A fourth exit option, which became much more prevalent post-crisis, is exit by means of a liquidation. Depending on the point in time in the boom and bust cycle of private equity, a limited secondary market for the stakes of limited partners in private equity funds may exist (for instance, it existed immediately pre-crisis, but not post-crisis), but this does not materially detract from the view that assets held by limited partners are illiquid.

By contrast, hedge funds have traditionally been open-ended, with no specified duration. This means that hedge fund managers have a quasi-permanent source of capital to be invested at their discretion, in contrast to private equity funds which must keep raising money via new funds. Unlike private equity funds, which invest only in the shares of private companies, hedge fund managers are typically subject to far fewer limitations than private equity fund managers on the types of product in which they can invest.[31] This means that they are able to invest in equity, debt with equity-like characteristics, pure debt, structured products and derivatives. Hedge funds have typically sought absolute returns, but within that framework managers tend to have wide discretion as to the investment strategies they may adopt, being able to take both long and short positions in securities as they judge appropriate.

Significantly, hedge funds have traditionally been regarded as a liquid investment, providing investors with the opportunity to enter and leave over the life of the fund. For example, it is generally possible for investors to be offered quarterly liquidity, with a 90-day notice period. As a result, managers of hedge funds have tended to be short-term investors in relatively liquid instruments in order to be able to meet any redemption requests as they arise. Management fees, which have tended to be somewhat higher than private equity fees,

---

[30] Concerns are sometimes raised about this hold period, along the lines that it encourages private equity funds to be too short-termist in their approach. However, in order for the private equity firm to be able to exit its investment and to get a good price for the company, it will have to create a company which has good long-term prospects (see eg Bank of England, Quarterly Bulletin 2013, Q1, Private Equity and Financial Stability). In addition, the three- to five-year hold period for private equity is longer in duration than the average hold period for investments in the public markets (see Kay Review of UK Equity Markets and Long-Term Decision Making, *Final Report*, July 2012).

[31] In recent years, some private equity firms have challenged this traditional model and have set up specialist funds which invest in debt, but this remains rare.

are taken at regular intervals. Typically hedge fund managers earn 2 per cent management fees and 20 per cent performance fees based on regular (current) valuations of the fund with no hurdle rate and with all fees being payable in the year they are earned.

Hedge funds are evolving, however. Some hedge funds have broadened their investment strategies to encompass typical private equity style investments, and in some instances hedge funds have invested in private equity transactions, usually by providing part of the debt component of the transaction, as discussed below at 16.4.3. This can present challenges to the hedge fund model which permits investor redemptions on a periodic basis.[32] Private equity funds are developing their investment strategies too. To some extent the distinction between hedge funds and private equity may be becoming less obvious, although differences in the partnership structures do continue to exist and differences in the nature and risk profile of the investments undertaken are still observable. There are also different systemic risk issues at work which may justify different regulatory treatment of private equity and hedge funds. This is discussed further at 16.7.1.

16.3.2 Sources of Funding for Private Equity Funds

The principal source of capital for private equity firms is institutional investors, which account for well over half of the total investment in private equity funds.[33] These include pension funds, charities, not-for-profit organisations and insurance companies. Other sources of funding include sovereign wealth funds and endowments. Of the money invested into UK private equity, a significant percentage comes from overseas sources, in particular overseas pension funds. For example, in 2013, 80 per cent of funding came from outside the UK, with 38 per cent of that coming from the US.[34] Levels of equity investment into private equity funds have remained robust despite the financial crisis.[35]

There is usually a relatively high minimum subscription for new private equity fund offerings, often £5–10 million for mid to large cap funds.[36] Even in the smaller funds, minimum subscriptions may still be in the region of £500,000. These high minimum subscriptions have a number of consequences. First, they reduce the number of investors with whom a fund manager needs to deal. This helps to reduce administrative costs. Second, it helps to ensure that the investor base is professional/expert. While retail investors can easily invest directly in publicly traded companies, the same is not true of private equity funds. Not only is the minimum subscription level a barrier to entry, but in addition regulations

---

[32] One mechanism developed by hedge funds to deal with this issue is to include 'side pockets' in a fund, ie different classes of shares within the hedge fund that are subject to a different (lesser) liquidity profile. Lock-up periods, during which time the investor cannot dispose of its investment, are used for this purpose, and gates, which place an upper limit on the absolute amount of money that can be redeemed at any one time, can be added.

[33] HM Treasury, *Myners Review of Institutional Investment in the UK* (2001), paras 12.6–12.75. Initially, many private equity organisations were wholly owned subsidiaries of large financial institutions. More recently, many of these organisations have become independent, or at least semi-captive, and therefore raise some or all of their funding from external sources. Regulatory changes have had an impact here—for instance the Volcker rule has prompted many US banks to sell their stakes in private equity funds.

[34] *Private Equity and Venture Capital Report on Investment Activity 2013*, Table 19.

[35] See eg Prequin Quarterly Update: Q2 2014 Private Equity.

[36] FSA, *Private Equity: A Discussion of Risk and Regulatory Engagement*, Discussion paper 06/6, November 2006, 23.

restrict the marketing of such investments to retail investors.[37] For many years private equity was largely self-regulated, in contrast to the heavily regulated sphere of publicly traded securities.[38] Recent years have seen private equity becoming subject to increasing regulatory scrutiny, and in particular the AIFMD, discussed in 16.7, represents a significant change in the regulatory environment.

In contrast to this traditional model of private equity, some private equity houses have also looked to the public markets for funding. There are a number of private equity funds listed on the London Stock Exchange, including buy-out funds, development capital funds, general funds, turnaround/restructuring funds, venture capital funds, and funds of funds. In addition, some private equity firms have themselves floated on the public markets. As a result the public are able to invest in the private equity firm, and thereby invest indirectly in the funds run by those private equity houses.

16.3.3 Why have Investors Wanted to Invest in Private Equity Funds?

The reason why investors have been keen to invest in private equity funds is simple: they believe they will receive superior returns compared to alternative available investment opportunities.[39] For example, Paul Myners' report for the Treasury in 2001 on institutional investment, including the private equity industry, noted that the net returns per annum to investors in UK-managed private equity funds raised between 1980 and 1995 outperformed public equity market comparators over one-, three-, five- and ten-year periods and that over the ten-year period to 2001 private equity as a whole outperformed UK equities as an investment class.[40]

However, these numbers mask wide variations between the performances of different funds. Over the 10 years to 2001, for example, the Myners Report noted that while the performance of the better funds (the top tenth percentile of private equity) had been outstanding (46.8 per cent per year), across private equity funds in the bottom tenth percentile the figures were significantly lower (6.6 per cent per year).[41] In the same period, 10-year annual returns from the FTSE All-Share stood at 14.9 per cent and UK bonds at just over 10 per cent.[42] In his comments to the House of Commons Treasury Committee on Private

---

[37] The provision of management, advisory and arranging services to a fund or its investors in or from the UK constitutes a regulated activity for the purposes of FSMA, s 19. Further, marketing restriction rules came into force in the UK on 1 January 2014, placing a general marketing restriction on the promotion of unregulated collective investment schemes (UCISs). For discussion see FCA, *Restrictions on the Retail Distribution of Unregulated Collective Investment Schemes and Close Substitutes*, PS13/3, June 2013.

[38] See chapters 10–12.

[39] Some doubt has been cast on whether superior returns do actually result: L Phallipou and O Gottschalg, 'The Performance of Private Equity Funds' (2009) 22(4) *Review of Financial Studies* 1747 find that the performance of private equity funds as reported by industry associations and previous research is overstated. They find an average net-of-fees fund performance of 3% per year below that of the S&P 500. See also SN Kaplan and A Schoar, 'Private Equity Performance: Returns, Persistence, and Capital Flows' (2005) 60(4) *Journal of Finance* 1791. Some post-crisis studies have been more favourable to PE funds, including RS Harris, T Jenkinson and SN Kaplan, 'Private Equity Performance: What Do We Know?' (2013) 69(5) *Journal of Finance* 1851.

[40] HM Treasury, *Myners Review of Institutional Investment in the UK* (2001), para 12.50.

[41] Ibid, para 12.55. See also Kay Review of UK Equity Markets and Long-Term Decision Making, *Final Report*, July 2012.

[42] HM Treasury, *Myners Review of Institutional Investment in the UK* (2001), para 12.59.

Equity, Paul Myners commented that 'on average private equity funds have produced inferior returns to public equity funds over most periods … The best private equity funds have produced very good returns; a significant number have disappointed, some very badly.'[43] There has, traditionally, been no obligation on private equity firms to disclose the information which would help an investor to distinguish between the good and not so good. The issue of mandating disclosure by private equity funds has come to the fore recently and is discussed further in 16.7.[44]

16.4 Capital Structure of a Typical Private Equity Transaction

In general a new company (newco), or more likely a series of newcos, will be incorporated to provide the structure for the private equity-acquired company. This section examines how the financing of a typical private equity transaction is structured. Generally, the financing will comprise a combination of equity, quasi-equity (either subordinated loan notes from the private equity fund or, less often, redeemable preference shares) and debt. A typical buy-out structure will contain a number of tiers of newcos. The equity investment portion of the financing (which comes from the private equity fund and the managers of the target company who are participating in the private equity deal) will be injected at the newco 1 level. Newco 1 will then hold 100 per cent of newco 2 and the debt part of the financing flowing from the private equity fund (the loan notes) will be put in at the newco 2 level. Newco 2 will then hold 100 per cent of newco 3 and the debt financing from investors other than the managers and private equity fund, such as the banks, will be put in at newco 3 level. Newco 3 will then acquire the shares in the target. If the tranching of debt involves structural rather than contractual subordination, it is possible that additional newcos will be put in place, ie the mezzanine debt would go in at newco 3 and the senior and second lien debt at newco 4 (which would then become the bid company). This structure is partly tax driven, but is also influenced by the need to structurally subordinate the loan made by the private equity fund from the loans made by the banks and other external investors.

Although private equity funding models are sensitive to the availability and cost of financing, and therefore vary over time,[45] one common feature of the funding model is the high level of debt in the package.[46] The sources of the financing also vary.[47] Accordingly,

---

[43] House of Commons Treasury Committee, Tenth Report of Session 2006–07, *Private Equity*, 30 July 2007, HC 567-I, 12–13.

[44] See also 16.6.3.

[45] For a discussion of the cyclical nature of funding in this context see P Gomper and J Lerner, *The Venture Capital Cycle*, 2nd edn (Cambridge MA, MIT Press, 2004); SN Kaplan and P Strömberg, 'Leveraged Buyouts and Private Equity' (2009) 23 *Journal of Economic Perspectives* 121.

[46] The level of leverage in private equity transactions has attracted regulatory attention in recent years, as it is sometimes suggested that it presents a risk to financial stability (see eg Bank of England Quarterly Bulletin 2013, Q1, Private Equity and Financial Stability)—this is discussed at 16.7.1.2. Following the implementation of the AIFMD, alternative investment fund managers must disclose the levels of leverage employed at the fund level, and national regulators (and in the last resort ESMA) have powers to place restrictions on the levels of leverage employed by fund managers: see 16.7.2.2.

[47] See 16.4.3.

there is no such thing as a 'typical' private equity transaction. Nevertheless this section examines the most common models, and explains the variables that tend to arise over time.

16.4.1 Equity Financing

The equity financing part of the funding occurs at the newco 1 level of the typical buy-out structure. The level of equity depends in part on the prevailing economic climate. So, for instance, in the five-year period prior to 2008 it was common to see about 30 per cent of the capital to finance a private equity transaction being provided by equity financing, whereas immediately post-crisis the percentage of equity in the deal increased to somewhere around the 50 per cent level. The leverage levels are largely a factor of the availability of debt. The number of investors putting equity into the portfolio company will be small whatever the economic conditions: generally just the private equity fund and the management team. Typically ordinary shares will be used to fund the company.[48]

A key feature of private equity has always been the involvement of management in the transaction. This is not affected by changes in economic conditions. However, in contrast to the early days of private equity deals in the UK, which saw management taking the major-ity equity stake in the company, in recent years it has been the private equity fund that has invariably led the transaction and taken the majority share. The management will be expected to invest their own money in the company to a significant extent. In return they will receive a minority stake in the company (often referred to as 'sweet equity').[49] Generally the private equity fund will hold more than 75 per cent of the equity and voting rights in the company, and the management will take the remainder. The amount that the private equity fund invests by way of equity will usually be calculated by reference to the amount that the management can contribute.[50] Consequently, the fund has control of the company. This means that the articles of association of a private equity backed company are far simpler than they used to be in management-led buy-outs, when complex provisions were inserted into the articles to protect the position of the private equity investor.

Following the private equity acquisition, the management team will be in day-to-day charge of running the company. However, the fund will expect to have considerable over-sight of this process. The investment agreement between the private equity fund and the management team will specify the substantial amount of financial and other information that the fund will expect to receive from the management team, such as regular accounts

---

[48] In the past, preference shares were often issued for tax reasons, but the abolition of advance corporation tax in 1997 meant that preference shares largely ceased to be a feature in private equity transactions. Preference shares may also have been used to provide the minority private equity investor with protection from, and priority over, the management team. However, since the private equity investor is invariably in a majority position today, the need for this form of protection has dropped away.

[49] It is called 'sweet equity' because the amount of return the management can receive on their investment can be disproportionate to the amount invested. This is because the investment by the private equity fund is by way of loan note as well as equity. The loan note, naturally, has a fixed return. Once the bank loan and loan note have been paid off, the value of the business is shared equally among the equity owners. The capital gains made by the management can therefore be disproportionate to the amount of money they put in as a percentage of the cost of acquiring the business.

[50] See 16.4.2.

and monthly board packs, including, for example, the latest balance sheet, profit and loss figures, cash position and cash flow forecast. In addition, the private equity fund will usually have at least one representative on the board of the company, and may also recommend some non-executive directors from outside the private equity fund to provide additional expertise on the board.

It is notable, therefore, that the shareholding structure of a private equity backed company, with its small number of shareholders and single controlling blockholder, looks more like a small family-owned private company than a large publicly traded company.

16.4.2 Quasi-Equity

The private equity fund will also generally invest (in newco 2 in the above structure) via a loan note. Indeed, it has become common for the majority of the fund's investment to be in this format. The scale of the fund's investment in ordinary shares in the company is usually limited by the amount of the management's investment. If the management have £100,000 available to invest in a 10 per cent stake then the maximum investment that the fund can make in ordinary shares is £900,000. If the fund wants to invest more than £900,000 it must do so in some other way. It could decide to invest via preference shares, and indeed in private equity transactions in the 1990s this was relatively common since the private equity investor could reclaim the advance corporation tax paid on these dividends, which made them more valuable. Since the abolition of advance corporation tax[51] it has become more common for funds to invest the remainder of their investment by way of a (subordinated) loan note. In the tiered newco structure described above, this loan note ranks ahead of the equity financing not only because debt ranks ahead of equity in a winding up, but also because of the structural subordination in place. This debt is also structurally subordinated to the debt financing described in 16.4.3.[52]

A loan note has a number of significant advantages over preference shares for this purpose.[53] There are tax advantages for the company, since the interest is tax deductible whereas dividends are not. There are also advantages from the fund's point of view. Whilst preference shares can be seen as a form of fixed interest security akin to debt, the position of a preference shareholder will generally be inferior to that of the company's creditors in certain crucial respects.[54] Unlike interest payments, the preferential dividend entitlement is not a debt until declared, and therefore cannot be guaranteed.[55] Even if the articles state that the dividend does not need to be declared, and specifies the due date, the payment will still be subject to distributable profits being available.[56] The preference shareholder has less security of capital than the company's creditors, who may have a charge on the assets of the

---

[51] The abolition of advance corporation tax was announced in 1997 and came into effect on 6 April 1999. For discussion see HMRC, *A Modern System for Corporation Tax Payments, A Consultative Document*, 1998, www.hmrc.gov.uk.

[52] For a description of structural subordination see 6.4.4.1.4.

[53] For a general discussion of preference shares see 3.2.1.2.

[54] See 3.2.1.2.4.

[55] *Bond v Barrow Haematite Steel Co* [1902] 1 Ch 353.

[56] See Companies Act 2006, ss 830–31. See 3.2.1.1.2.

company, although the loan note will be subordinated to the other lenders to the company. The loan note will rank ahead of the shareholders claims qua shareholder in a winding up,[57] but will be subordinated to the bank debt in order to ensure that, in the event of insolvency, the bank receives its repayment prior to the loan note being repaid.[58]

16.4.3 Debt Financing

The use of debt finance is a key tool in private equity transactions. The debt financing element will generally be inserted at newco 3 (the bid company), although it is possible for the different tranches of debt discussed below to be structurally subordinated and therefore for there to be additional newcos inserted into the structure representing different tranches of debt.

As discussed, there is no such thing as a typical debt to equity ratio in a private equity backed company. This level rarely drops below 50:50 but in certain economic conditions, when debt is plentiful and cheap, it can rise to levels of 70:30 or higher. There are a number of reasons why high levels of debt are found in private equity deals. It is cheaper than equity, particularly because the interest is tax deductible. It does not interfere with the ownership structures put in place in the newco, and while preference shares could perform the same function, they are generally less attractive to both the company and the investor for the reasons discussed in 16.4.2. High levels of leverage can have a beneficial effect on the returns to the equity investors.[59] Debt is also a far more flexible financing tool than equity, as discussed in chapter two. A wide variety of debt financing techniques have evolved in this context, which can be customised to fit the requirements of each deal. Finally, on a practical level, debt financing can often be put in place more speedily than equity financing and this can be key in private equity transactions, which are often run on a very tight timetable.

In the years prior to 2008 the debt available to private equity funds increased significantly. It is estimated that in 2006, for example, $302 billion of leverage loans were made to US and European borrowers owned by private equity sponsors.[60] The availability of this amount of debt was one of the drivers of the rapid expansion of the private equity market in the early years of this century.[61] The withdrawal of this pool of debt following the financial crisis was one of the chief reasons for the significant decrease in the number of private equity deals done after the crisis, although the renewed availability of cheap debt in recent years has fuelled a recovery of this sector.

---

[57] Insolvency Act 1986, s 74(2)(f) and see 3.3.1.2.5.

[58] In addition, for a period of time there were tax advantages to providing the investment via a loan note which made this option attractive. In essence, if the loan note was structured correctly, the company could claim tax deductibility for the interest payments due on the loan note even when the cash interest payment was deferred to a future date. Most loan note instruments would provide for payment at a future date, the idea being that both accrued interest and the capital sum would be repaid from the sale proceeds of the company on the private equity funds' exit from the investment. However, these advantages have now been removed.

[59] See 16.6.4.

[60] *Standard & Poor's Leveraged Commentary and Data*, 2006.

[61] There is support for the view that economy-wide credit conditions are the main driver of leverage and pricing in buy-outs: higher deal leverage is associated with lower buy-out fund returns, suggesting that acquirers overpay when access to credit is easier (see U Axelson, T Jenkinson and P Stromberg, 'Borrow Cheap, Buy High? The Determinants of Leverage and Pricing in Buyouts' (2013) 68(6) *Journal of Finance* 2223).

Two other developments in debt financing helped to fuel the boom in private equity transactions prior to 2008. First, although historically the majority of debt finance was provided by the major commercial and investment banks, more recently debt funding has become available from a greater variety of sources, including a wider range of banks, investment funds, hedge funds and alternative debt lenders, including specialist debt funds. Second, the variety of debt instruments on offer to fund private equity investments also developed, particularly the use of subordinated finance. It became common in large transactions to supplement the debt financing with the issuance of high-yield bonds or other forms of debt.[62] In addition, for all but the smallest private equity transactions there were likely to be two or more layers of debt, typically senior debt and mezzanine debt and, possibly, sandwiched between them, second lien debt. Each of these layers could in turn comprise a number of different tranches with slightly different lending terms and interest rates attached to them.[63] These additional layers of debt had a role in reducing the proportion of equity in the transaction. Many of these issues have been affected by the financial crisis. For instance, some of these forms of debt financing all but disappeared in the post-crisis period.

A further, general, issue is that in any but the smallest transactions, syndication of the debt is very likely.[64]

16.4.3.1 Senior Debt

This is the layer of debt which forms the core part, and invariably the largest part, of the debt finance structure. This debt will be unsubordinated and will be inserted at the bid company level (newco 3 or newco 4, depending on whether structural subordination is used to separate the tranches of external debt financing) and secured on a first-ranking basis. Generally the senior debt will be used to purchase the target company, to provide the company with the working capital it needs following the acquisition, and perhaps also to provide financing for any capital expenditure in which the company needs to engage following acquisition. The debt will comprise different forms, including several term loans and revolving credit facilities.[65] For example, the working capital will generally be provided under a revolving credit facility, often by way of an overdraft facility, whereas any capital expenditure financing will usually be provided by way of a secured term loan.

The financing required to purchase the target will generally be the largest proportion of the senior debt and may be split into different tranches, depending on the amount of financing required and the sophistication of the package put together by the lender. Different tranches of debt may have different pricing and different repayment profiles. Some of the tranches will be amortising (ie repayable in regular, fixed amounts), while others will provide for a single lump sum at maturity (sometimes called a bullet payment). Non-amortising debt has the benefit of allowing a company to use debt finance without having to eat into its short-term cash flow in order to make large debt repayments. A lack of amortisation therefore allows companies to bear a higher amount of debt financing than they might otherwise have been able to afford.

---

[62] See 2.3.3.3.

[63] For a discussion of the techniques of subordination see 6.4.4, and for a discussion of tranching in the context of securitisation see 9.3.3.

[64] For further discussion of debt syndication see 8.4.

[65] See 2.3, especially 2.3.2.

All the debt in a private equity transaction (senior, second lien and mezzanine) will invariably be supported by guarantees[66] and the taking of security.[67] Guarantees will generally be given by the newcos and may also be given by the target group (subject to possible issues of financial assistance). In terms of security, this will encompass both fixed and floating charges. The newcos will generally be shelf companies without any assets (other than, in the case of the newco which bids for and purchases the target, the shares it acquires in the target) against which the lenders could have recourse in the event of insolvency or receivership. Security will be taken over all, or substantially all, of the assets and shareholdings of the newco group. This structure will give the lenders an element of control over any restructuring, as they will be able to appoint an administrator if they hold a floating charge over all, or substantially all, of the assets of the company.[68] Where the debt is syndicated, a security trustee (often the senior lender) will usually be appointed to hold the security on trust on behalf of all the syndicate lenders.[69]

Given that the newco structure described above involves an off-the-shelf shell company with no assets of its own, other than the target company that it acquires, it can be important for the lender to ensure the creditworthiness of the target company post-acquisition. It is therefore common to see significant covenants in senior debt agreements, which are then usually repeated in the mezzanine debt and the second lien debt, if any. Some of these covenants will be of a general nature, and will restrict the company from changing its business, will restrict the creation of further security (a negative pledge clause), will restrict the company from making disposals, entering into mergers or joint ventures or issuing further debt, and will prohibit the payment of dividends or any other payments to the equity investors.[70] It is also usual for the lenders to receive an agreed package of regular financial information that will allow the lenders to monitor the performance of the target company.[71] In addition, specific financial covenants will commonly be put in place, requiring the company to operate within certain financial ratios, such as the ratio of total debt to earnings before interest, taxes, depreciation and amortisation (EBITDA) and the ratio of cash flow to total funding costs.[72] These financial covenants may well change over time, as the level of leverage in the company decreases. Failure to meet a financial covenant will lead to an event of default being triggered, which allows the lender to terminate and accelerate the loan.[73]

One development that emerged during the 2004–07 period in the UK, when there were very extensive levels of debt available to private equity firms, was 'covenant-lite' financing deals. This development arose not only from the abundance of debt (leading to a borrower-friendly market), but also because it made the loans operate much more like bonds, which have very light covenants. Some of the newer investor types in that period, such as hedge funds, were comfortable with the covenant-lite package in place in bonds. In this period

---

[66] See 6.4.1.3.
[67] See chapter 7.
[68] Insolvency Act 1986, Sch B1 paras 14–21. Although the insolvent company can also appoint an administrator, it must notify the secured creditor holding a qualifying floating charge (ie a floating charge over all, or substantially all, of the assets of the company), which may, in turn, appoint an administrator of their choice.
[69] For further discussion of this issue see 8.4.
[70] See 6.3.1.
[71] See 6.3.2.
[72] Ibid.
[73] See 6.3.3.

the market in syndicated loans also developed so that the lenders thought they could exit at the first sign of trouble (they still kept enough information covenants to enable them to do this).[74] In these deals the covenants are only tested when an event occurs, rather than being continuously tested. These types of covenant-lite financing deals disappeared in the immediate post-crisis period, but such lending appears to be on the rise once more as cheap debt again becomes available.

16.4.3.2 Second Lien Debt

Second lien debt developed in the US in the late 1990s, and began to be utilised in the UK in 2003. The abundance of debt available to private equity funds in the early part of this century facilitated the development of this additional layer of debt, which can be used as an alternative to mezzanine debt or in conjunction with it, to form a distinct third layer sandwiched between senior and mezzanine debt. One significant difference between senior debt and second lien debt is the identity of the providers of this finance. In contrast to senior debt, which is typically provided by the traditional lending banks, second lien debt was originally dominated by hedge funds, although subsequently all kinds of institutional investors became involved in providing this form of financing, and even the banks got involved and started lending in this category as well. In essence, second lien debt forms part of the senior debt, but is subordinated to the rest of the senior debt and is secured on a second-ranking basis. It is generally contractually subordinated to the senior debt.[75] In contrast to senior debt, it generally comprises just a single term loan and is non-amortised, being repayable only at maturity. This form of debt all but disappeared in the post-crisis period, but again the recovery of the debt markets has seen its return.

16.4.3.3 Mezzanine Debt

Mezzanine debt ranks after the senior debt and any second lien debt, and is secured on a second (or third) ranking basis. It is subordinated to the senior debt and second lien debt (if any), usually by way of contractual subordination (although it can also be structurally subordinated by the insertion of an additional newco into the newco tiered structure described above), but it will rank ahead of any loan notes provided by the private equity fund, and of course it ranks ahead of the equity invested into newco.[76] To compensate the lenders for this increased risk profile (as compared to the senior debt, for example), mezzanine lenders receive a higher interest rate than senior lenders. In addition, mezzanine lenders have traditionally received some kind of performance-related reward, such as warrants to subscribe for shares in newco at some point in the future, for example on the private equity fund's exit via a sale or listing (known as an 'equity kicker'). However, during periods when there has been significant liquidity in the debt markets it has not always been necessary for private equity funds to offer warrants of this kind in order to secure mezzanine financing.

---

[74] M Campbell and S Hughes, 'Leveraged Finance—Financial Covenants Under Stress' [2007] *Journal of International Banking and Financial Law* 353; J Markland, 'Cov-lite—The New Cutting Edge in Acquisition Finance' [2007] *Journal of International Banking and Financial Law* 379.

[75] See 6.4.4.1.3.

[76] Insolvency Act 1986, s 74(2)(f); for discussion see 3.3.1.2.5.

Mezzanine debt usually comprises just a single, non-amortised term loan. It generally follows the terms of the senior debt (in terms of covenants, events of default etc). If the mezzanine debt is of a sufficient size then it will be syndicated in the same way as the senior debt, either by the same arranger or by a separate arranging bank. A mezzanine lender may have the right to appoint a director to the board of the company in order to represent the interests of that lender, which could differ from the interests of the senior lender. If so, this lender could perform an important corporate governance function, especially as such lenders generally have less security than the senior lender and so may be incentivised to monitor more closely. However, where the mezzanine debt is syndicated this may reduce the likelihood of monitoring as a result of coordination difficulties.[77]

16.5 Public-to-Private Transactions

Public-to-private transactions involve the use of private equity to purchase a publicly traded company and then to take it into private ownership. In the 10 years to 2008 these transactions became relatively common in the UK. As with many other aspects of private equity transactions, the financial crisis has had an impact, and public-to-private transactions have become a rarity in the UK in recent years. In part this may be due to the lack of financing to purchase such companies, but regulatory changes may also have played a role.[78]

A public-to-private transaction is more heavily regulated than a standard private equity transaction involving the purchase of a private company. There are two principal mechanisms for these transactions: a takeover offer and a scheme of arrangement. Although takeover offers may be thought to be the more usual mechanism by which to acquire a public company, schemes of arrangement have also been a popular tool for public-to-private transactions. There are two main reasons for this. First, in general lenders will only commit the very significant sums of debt financing involved in these highly leveraged transactions if the private equity fund has carried out significant levels of due diligence on the target company. Due diligence of any depth and detail will require the cooperation of the target board, and consequently (friendly) schemes of arrangement rather than hostile takeovers have been the norm. Second, it is often crucial for the fund to purchase 100 per cent of the target in order to put in place the funding structures it requires, and a successful scheme of arrangement guarantees this outcome, provided 75 per cent by value (and a majority in number) of the shareholders (or each class of shareholders) approve the scheme and it is sanctioned by the court.[79] By contrast, a takeover offer can only guarantee this outcome if the minimum acceptance condition is set at 90 per cent, ie the shareholder acceptance threshold is higher for an offer if the bidder wishes to secure 100 per cent of the target.[80]

---

[77] The corporate governance role of debt is discussed generally at 3.2.2.4, and it is discussed in the context of private equity transactions at 16.6.2.

[78] See, for example, the changes to the City Code on Takeovers and Mergers (Takeover Code) effected in 2011, including the new rules to deal with 'virtual bids': Takeover Code, rr 2.6–2.8, discussed at 14.3.1.1.

[79] See 15.2.

[80] For discussion see 15.3.1.

Where either of these mechanisms is used to purchase a public company, the City Code on Takeovers and Mergers ('the Takeover Code') will apply in order to regulate the purchase. It is the nature of the target and not the bidding entity which determines whether the Code applies. Takeover offers were discussed extensively in chapter fourteen and schemes of arrangement in chapter fifteen, including a comparison of these two techniques as mechanisms for acquiring a company.[81] However, public-to-private transactions bring with them a specific set of issues and concerns, and therefore the application of takeover regulation to these transactions merits some analysis.

16.5.1 Financial Issues

Two issues regarding the financial aspects of the deal differ when the transaction is a public-to-private deal rather than a purely private transaction. First, the Takeover Code requires that the bidder is permitted to announce an offer only after it has ensured that it can fulfil all its obligations under the offer.[82] This means that the bidder must have made all the arrangements regarding financing (particularly its debt financing) before the offer is made. The lending banks will therefore have to commit to making the debt facilities available subject only to a very limited set of conditions. Many of the usual funding conditions will therefore have to be satisfied before the offer is made. Changes to the Takeover Code in 2011 have also increased the level of disclosure by the bidder at an earlier stage in the process, including enhanced disclosure of financing arrangements in the offer documentation.[83]

Second, financial assistance has traditionally been a tricky issue in private equity transactions.[84] It is common for the private equity fund to consider using cash in the acquired company to finance the offer. In the past this ran into difficulties with the ban on the giving of financial assistance.[85] Indeed, it is strongly arguable that the main reason for the introduction of the financial assistance provisions in the first place was to prevent leveraged buy-outs from occurring,[86] although there is little evidence that the financial assistance rules actually had this effect.[87] Prior to the Companies Act 2006 it was possible for private companies to use a whitewash procedure in order to avoid the financial assistance provisions.[88] The Companies Act 2006 abolished the ban on financial assistance for private companies, although it is retained for public companies.[89] Therefore, although funding a purchase of a private company in this way is now acceptable, cash resources in a target in

---

[81] Ibid.

[82] Takeover Code, GP 5 and r 2.7(d), which requires a third party to confirm that the bidder will have resources available to satisfy full acceptance of the offer.

[83] Takeover Code, r 2.7(c).

[84] See generally E Ferran, 'Regulation of Private Equity-Backed Leveraged Buyout Activity in Europe' ECGI Law Working Paper 084/2007, May 2007, www.ssrn.com/abstract=989748.

[85] Discussed at 5.4.4.

[86] J Armour, 'Share Capital and Creditor Protection: Efficient Rules for a Modern Company Law' (2000) 63 *Modern Law Review* 255, 378, discussed at 5.4.4.

[87] L Enriques, 'EC Company Law Directives and Regulations: How Trivial Are They?' in J Armour and JA McCahery (eds), *After Enron: Improving Corporate Law and Modernising Securities Regulation in Europe and the US* (Oxford, Hart Publishing, 2006).

[88] Companies Act 1985, ss 153–55.

[89] Ibid, ss 677–83. See 5.4.4.

a public-to-private transaction can only be extracted once the offer is completed and the company has been re-registered as a private company.[90]

16.5.2 Recommendation by the Directors

Whenever an offer is made under the Takeover Code, the target board is required to provide its opinion on the offer to the target shareholders,[91] in addition to obtaining competent independent advice on the offer which will then be made known to the target shareholders.[92] This latter requirement relates to all bids, but the Takeover Code states that this requirement is particularly important in the event of a management buy-out or similar transaction.[93]

A difficulty that arises in relation to many private equity transactions, since they often involve some form of management buy-out, is that the management of the target will face a significant conflict of interest when providing this advice. Of course, directors are subject to their normal fiduciary duties at this time, including the obligation to act in the best interests of the target, but the Takeover Code goes further and specifically regulates this issue. Rule 25.2 provides that directors with a conflict of interest should not normally take part in the recommendation process. Participants in a management buy-out are regarded as having a conflict for these purposes.[94] Indeed, any director, executive or non-executive who will have a continuing interest in the target or the bidder after a successful offer is likely to be regarded as conflicted. Where a management buy-out occurs, the target board will need to constitute an independent committee of directors, comprising those directors who do not have a conflict of interest. In some circumstances this committee may not contain any members of the existing target board, if they are all conflicted. It is this independent committee that will provide its opinion on the offer to the target shareholders. Similarly, it is this independent committee that becomes the public face of the target as far as the offer is concerned, and therefore it is this committee with which the bidder will negotiate.

16.5.3 Equality Between Bidders

One of the potential difficulties that can arise in a management buy-out scenario is ensuring that equal information is provided to all bidders. Under Rule 20.2 of the Takeover Code, any information generated by the target that is provided to the management buy-out team must, on request, be provided by the target to other competing bidders. However, the competing bidder cannot simply ask for all the information provided to earlier bidders and must make specific requests for information. Similarly, any information generated by the

---

[90] Alternatively, if the acquisition is by way of a scheme of arrangement, any actions that would otherwise be prevented by the financial assistance provisions may be approved by the court as part of the scheme. See eg *Re Uniq plc* [2011] EWHC 749 (Ch).

[91] Takeover Code, r 25.2.

[92] Ibid, r 3.1.

[93] Ibid, r 3.1 n 1.

[94] Ibid, r 25.2 n 5.

management team, or the bidder with which they are associated, and provided to potential financiers (in particular potential lenders) must be provided to the independent committee of the target if they request it.[95]

16.5.4 Equality of Treatment of Shareholders

Equality of treatment of the target shareholders is one of the key aims of the Takeover Code.[96] Particular issues arise in the context of a management buy-out because special deals may be offered to certain shareholders, namely the managers of the target who also hold shares in the company. The bidder may wish to incentivise members of the target board by rolling over their target shares, but it may wish to pay cash to all the other shareholders. Special deals of this kind are generally prohibited, and this prohibition has been interpreted to cover both the quantum and the form of consideration.[97]

There are, however, important exceptions to this principle. In particular, the Takeover Code provides an exemption for special deals for management in certain circumstances.[98] The Takeover Panel recognises that there may be a legitimate commercial interest in permitting the management of the target to remain financially involved in the business. However, a number of conditions must be satisfied before this can occur.[99] The Panel must be consulted in all cases where a special deal will be offered to management, and its consent obtained. The Panel will be particularly keen to ensure that the management is not insulated from the risks of the business. Option arrangements that guarantee the original offer price as a minimum, for example, are unlikely to be acceptable. Additionally, the independent adviser to the target company required by rule 3 of the Takeover Code must state publicly that these arrangements are fair and reasonable. Finally, these arrangements must be approved at a general meeting of the target shareholders, in a vote taken by the independent shareholders.

16.5.5 Market Abuse

The prevention of market abuse is a key aim of the regulation of the capital markets.[100] The dangers of market abuse are regarded as arising particularly keenly in the context of public-to-private transactions, due to the complexity of these transactions and the number of parties that tend to be involved.[101] The private equity firm will generally approach the directors of the target company and enter into talks with them about a possible purchase; the target company's advisors might approach other private equity managers to ascertain their level of interest; each interested private equity fund will then approach numerous

---

[95] Ibid, r 20.3.
[96] See 14.3.4.
[97] Takeover Code, r 16.
[98] Ibid, r 16.2.
[99] Ibid.
[100] See 12.2.
[101] FSA, *Private Equity: A Discussion of Risk and Regulatory Engagement,* Discussion paper 06/6, November 2006, paras 4.43–4.57.

debt providers in order to set up the complex debt financing for the transaction. This may well be done via a tendering process so that a large number of potential debt providers will receive information about the possible purchase:

> Clearly, the more parties involved in putting together the finance, the more potential there is for leakage and misuse of price sensitive information. Typically several hundred individuals will be aware of a deal, rising to over a thousand in the case of larger deals.[102]

The regulator (now the FCA) has acknowledged that the implications for market confidence of this enhanced market integrity risk in the context of private equity are significant and merit ongoing scrutiny by regulators, and enhanced vigilance and preventative action by market participants.[103]

16.6 A Comparison of Private Equity Backed Companies and Non-Private Equity Backed Companies

16.6.1 Ownership Structures

A number of important differences exist between the ownership structures in private equity backed companies (or 'portfolio companies') and many non-private equity backed companies. The shareholders in portfolio companies are typically only the directors (holding somewhere between 5 and 25 per cent of the shares) and the private equity fund. This ownership structure looks similar to that of a very small family-owned company: it appears quite unlike many larger private companies. The structure is certainly very different to that of a typical publicly traded company in which the size of the investing group is very large (the average is some 150,000 shareholders for a FTSE 100 company),[104] and the directors tend to hold a much lower equity stake in the company.

It has been suggested that one of the reasons why private equity provides (arguably) greater returns than other equity classes is that portfolio companies can resolve the problems caused by the separation of ownership and control, and the agency problems between the shareholders and directors that arise as a result. The problems associated with the separation of ownership and control are well understood.[105] One of the central problems of corporate governance for UK publicly quoted companies is how to hold managers accountable to the shareholders.[106]

There are a number of reasons why the directors (managers) and investors in a typical portfolio company may be regarded as being closely aligned. The first is the size of the

---

[102] Ibid, para 4.47.

[103] See eg *FCA Business Plan 2014/15*.

[104] D Walker, *Guidelines for Disclosure and Transparency in Private Equity*, November 2007, 8.

[105] Eg MC Jensen and WH Meckling, 'Theory of the Firm: Managerial Behavior, Agency Costs and Ownership Structure' (1976) 3 *Journal of Financial Economics* 305.

[106] R Kraakman et al, *The Anatomy of Corporate Law: A Comparative and Functional Approach*, 2nd edn (Oxford, Oxford University Press, 2009) ch 3. For a discussion of the corporate governance role of shareholders in publicly traded UK companies see 11.2.2.

directors' equity stake: they have a lot of skin in the game.[107] The fact that portfolio companies are highly leveraged allows the directors to acquire relatively large equity stakes for a relatively modest investment. The directors 'may be asked to put a few hundred thousand of their own money into the business and then, if they are successful, they can walk away in three years' time with many millions of pounds'.[108] As with the shares in all private companies, this is an illiquid investment (in contrast to an investment in a publicly traded company) and, further, a director is likely to be subject to 'bad leaver' provisions which will affect the value of her stake if she seeks to leave early without good reason or without the agreement of the fund. The illiquidity of these equity stakes reduces the directors' incentive to manipulate short-term performance. Directors will only realise the value of their equity when the scheduled exit transaction occurs, whether that is via an IPO, or a sale, or otherwise.

Second, portfolio companies have only a small number of shareholders, and those shareholders are interested in monitoring directors closely and have the capability to do so. In addition to the directors themselves the only shareholder will be the private equity fund. The fund is highly expert and used to a monitoring role of this kind. It has a strong incentive to monitor (due to its significant equity and debt investment in the company), it has the means to monitor (in addition to the significant information disclosure it will require qua shareholder it will also appoint representatives to the board) and, of course, the private equity fund will have a sufficient equity stake to remove, by ordinary resolution, any director who is perceived to be performing poorly.

It is sometimes suggested that a further benefit of the private equity ownership model, particularly compared to that of publicly traded companies, is that it can solve the free cash problem, whereby directors hang onto the 'free cash' in a company rather than distributing it to the shareholders.[109] Free cash flow is defined for these purposes as cash flow in excess of that required to fund all investment projects with positive net present values when discounted at the relevant cost of capital. Directors have incentives to retain cash in this way because cash reserves increase their autonomy as regards the capital markets.[110] This can lead to waste and inefficiency, or it might mean that the directors use the cash inappropriately, such as on self-promoting acquisitions. In a portfolio company the shareholders are in a strong position to force the directors to transfer to them any free cash that remains, should they so wish.

The empirical evidence appears to support the view that the closer alignment of director and shareholder interests, and the most concentrated ownership structure, within private equity backed companies are two of the reasons why private equity transactions generate

---

[107] The remuneration of directors in private equity backed companies is therefore far more closely related to the performance of the company. In studies carried out in the US it was found that the salary of the typical private equity backed company director was significantly more sensitive to the performance of the company than that of a typical public company director: S Kaplan, 'The Effects of Management Buyouts on Operating Performance and Value' (1989) 24 *Journal of Financial Economics* 217; MC Jensen and KJ Murphy, 'Performance Pay and Top Management Incentives' (1990) 98 *Journal of Political Economy* 225.

[108] House of Commons Treasury Committee, Tenth Report of Session 2006–07, *Private Equity*, 30 July 2007, HC 567-I, para 14, quoting Professor Tim Jenkinson.

[109] See eg MC Jensen, 'Eclipse of the Public Corporation' (1989) 67 *Harvard Business Review* 61, revised version available at www.ssrn.com/abstract=146149 (1997).

[110] See 2.4.

wealth.[111] Little evidence has, however, been found to support the free cash flow analysis per se as an explanation for the benefits provided by the private equity model.[112]

16.6.2 Board/Management Structures

A further difference between private equity backed and non-private equity backed companies relates to their different board structures. The boards of portfolio companies tend to be small and specialised. The existing managers, who are part of the buy-out, know the business well, and are supported by a private equity fund whose business it is to increase the value of the firm. There may, additionally, be a small number of expert directors appointed by the fund. The board of a portfolio company will generally also meet very regularly. This position may be contrasted with that of other companies, and is in particularly sharp contrast to the position of publicly traded companies, whose boards tend to be large (typically 12–20 members), to meet much less often,[113] and to be dominated by management-appointed outsiders.[114]

A further distinction between the boards of publicly traded companies and private equity backed companies is the nature of their role. The board of a plc is perceived as having two functions: to lead and to control the company. The latter role falls in the main to the non-executive directors. However, although the idea is that these non-executive directors will provide a disciplining function, in practice the empirical evidence does not suggest that this occurs.[115] Instead, the focus of the non-executive directors tends to be on compliance issues and committee duties. The general view is that the directors of publicly traded companies spend a great deal of time engaged in communicating with their shareholders, in investor relations and in periodic reporting. By contrast, the board of a portfolio company is freed from these burdens. It is not subject to the obligations of the UK Corporate Governance Code regarding the composition and structure of the board. While the disclosure obligations placed on portfolio companies have increased as a result of the AIFMD,[116] the levels of disclosure and compliance are relatively light, and well below the level of obligations

---

[111] L Renneboog, T Simons and M Wright, 'Why Do Public Firms Go Private in the UK? The Impact of Private Equity Investors, Incentive Realignment and Undervaluation' (2007) 13 *Journal of Corporate Finance* 591. This view has been challenged: see eg E De Fontenay, 'Private Equity Firms As Gatekeepers' (2013) 33(1) *Review of Banking and Financial Law* 115, who suggests that private equity does not create value by reducing agency costs of management; instead private equity firms create value by acting as gatekeepers in the debt markets using their reputations as repeat players with creditors to mitigate borrower adverse selection and moral hazard.

[112] Eg L Renneboog, T Simons and M Wright, 'Why Do Public Firms Go Private in the UK? The Impact of Private Equity Investors, Alignment and Undervaluation' (2007) 13 *Journal of Corporate Finance* 591.

[113] See VV Acharya, M Hahn and C Kehoe, 'Corporate Governance and Value Creation: Evidence from Private Equity' NYU Working Paper No FIN-08–032 (2010), www.ssrn.com/abstract=1354519.

[114] In terms of UK publicly listed companies, board structure is now heavily influenced by the UK Corporate Governance Code: FRC, *UK Corporate Governance Code*, September 2014. The central problem of corporate governance for UK publicly quoted companies is how to hold managers accountable to the shareholders: R Kraakman et al, *The Anatomy of Corporate Law: A Comparative and Functional Approach*, 2nd edn (Oxford, Oxford University Press, 2009) ch 3. For discussion of the corporate governance role of shareholders in publicly traded UK companies see 11.2.2.

[115] J Franks, C Mayer and L Renneboog, 'Who Disciplines Management in Poorly Performing Companies?' (2001) 10 *Journal of Financial Intermediation* 209.

[116] See 16.7.

imposed on publicly traded companies.[117] Consequently, the directors of portfolio companies have only one function, not two: they can focus on trading and strategy and do not have to concern themselves in any significant way with compliance and control. One explanation for the comparative success of private equity is that it results from these differences, which make the boards of portfolio companies more effective.[118]

16.6.3 Disclosure and Transparency

Traditionally portfolio companies have been subject to the same disclosure regime as all other private companies, ie some obligations are imposed, for instance in relation to the publication of the company's accounts on a periodic basis,[119] but these obligations are relatively light touch, certainly compared to the disclosure obligations placed on publicly traded companies. As discussed in chapters ten to thirteen, once securities are publicly traded, the issuing company becomes subject to substantial disclosure obligations to investors and reporting obligations to the regulator, both at the point when securities are issued and thereafter. These obligations relate to a wide array of issues, including periodic disclosure regarding the company's financial position and information regarding, inter alia, inside information, directors' shareholdings in the company and major shareholdings in the company.[120]

One of the aims of the increased regulation that has been imposed on the private equity industry post-crisis is to deal with this imbalance.[121] Although much of that increased disclosure has been aimed at the fund, some of the provisions of the AIFMD also require disclosure at the level of the portfolio company.[122] The Directive imposes disclosure obligations on the acquisition of major holdings (starting at 10 per cent) in non-listed EU companies.[123] More onerous disclosure obligations (to investors and to the regulator) are imposed when a private equity fund within the ambit of the AIFMD acquires a controlling interest in a non-listed company or an issuer,[124] regarding, inter alia, the identity of the fund and its policy for preventing and managing conflicts of interest.[125] Where the company is non-listed there are some additional obligations both at the time of acquisition[126]

---

[117] See 16.6.4.

[118] F Cornelli and O Karakas, 'Private Equity and Corporate Governance: Do LBOs Have More Effective Boards?', Working Paper, February 2008, www.ecgi.org. Studies of public companies suggest that smaller boards are more effective: D Yermack, 'Higher Market Valuation of Companies with a Small Board of Directors' (1996) 40(2) *Journal of Financial Economics* 185.

[119] See 11.3.1.1. Note that the Companies Act 2006 creates a reduced reporting regime for small (private) companies: Part 15, ch 1.

[120] See 11.3.

[121] See 16.7.1.1.

[122] See 16.7.2.3.

[123] Directive 2011/61/EU, art 27(1), and see the Alternative Investment Fund Managers Regulations 2013 (SI 2013/1773) (AIFM Regulations 2013), para 38.

[124] For the definition of control see Directive 2011/61/EU, art 26(5) and AIFM Regulations 2013, para 36.

[125] Directive 2011/61/EU, art 28(2) and AIFM Regulations 2013, para 39.

[126] Directive 2011/61/EU, art 28(4) and AIFM Regulations 2013, para 40. In particular, the fund must disclose its intentions with regard to the future business of the company, and the likely repercussions on employment, and provide details of the financing of the acquisition.

and on an ongoing basis.[127] These requirements increase the disclosure obligations facing portfolio companies above the level of other private companies, but these obligations are still well below the level of disclosure required in relation to publicly traded companies.

16.6.4 Debt vs Equity Levels

Portfolio companies typically have higher levels of debt than other companies. The level of debt in a private equity deal will vary according to the availability of debt in the market, so that levels may range from 50 per cent up to 70 per cent plus. In one notorious deal in 2006, Allianz sold Four Seasons Nursing Homes to a Qatari sovereign wealth fund for £1.4 billion, of which £1.3 billion was borrowed. By contrast, the level of leverage in other companies tends to be more modest. For instance, the debt-equity ratio for publicly traded companies is typically 30:70.

As discussed in chapter two, there is no ideal mix of debt and equity which will apply to all companies.[128] The amount of leverage that will suit each company will vary according to a number of factors. However, the reasons why portfolio companies regularly employ much higher levels of debt than other companies, and the potential advantages and disadvantages that may flow from that, require examination. The injection of debt can have a number of benefits. First, in the UK, the tax system favours debt over equity as a form of company funding since, although there is tax deduction for interest, there is no such favourable treatment for dividends.[129] Debt is, therefore, cheaper than equity for the company. Second, the use of leverage itself can have a beneficial effect on the returns to equity investors (the private equity fund and the directors). Take the example of a situation in which the assets of a company are £100, and the company is funded entirely by equity. If the company's assets increase to £200, the equity investors double their money. If however, the company is funded by way of 50 per cent debt and 50 per cent equity, if the assets increase to £200 the debt investors have a fixed claim of £50 (ignoring any interest payments for simplicity), whereas the remainder (£150) belongs to the equity investors, so that they triple the value of their investment. As the debt is paid down over the life of the fund, the value of the equity increases further and healthy returns can be generated, since the equity investors will take an even larger share in any gains made by realising the investment at the end of the fund. Put simply, since debt is cheaper than equity (because of the tax saving), purchasing a company and leveraging it more highly could involve tax savings, and result in gains to the company and its shareholders.[130] One common criticism of private equity is that it makes money for its investors by making use of these advantages of debt rather than by creating operational or economic value in the portfolio company.

Increasing the amount of debt increases the risks to which the company is exposed. As the proportion of debt in the company increases, it becomes more likely that the company

---

[127] Ibid, art 29 and AIFM Regulations 2013, para 42. This includes a fair review of the development of the company's business representing the situation at the end of the period covered by the annual report and an indication of the company's likely development.

[128] For discussion see 2.6.

[129] See 2.6.

[130] This is often suggested to be one of the significant gains in US public-to-private transactions: see eg SN Kaplan, 'Management Buyouts: Evidence on Taxes as a Source of Value' (1989) 44(3) *Journal of Finance* 611.

will default and enter into insolvency. Financial distress and insolvency are costly, in terms of the direct costs of lawyers, courts and insolvency practitioners, as well as the reduction in the value of the company associated with insolvency. There are also the indirect costs attached to the difficulties of running a company while going through insolvency.[131] Even if the company avoids insolvency it will still face the costs of financial distress—for example suppliers may demand more protection, creditors may charge more, and employees may leave and look for other jobs. In addition, more highly geared companies are felt to be more at risk in a recession than less highly geared companies. The financial crisis has clearly caused problems for portfolio companies, although there is no clear evidence of a higher default rate among such companies.[132]

The trade-off theory of capital structure recognises that investors will look for an enhanced return to compensate them for the increased risk of having to absorb these costs of financial distress. The addition of debt to a company's capital structure is beneficial, but only up to the point where the tax savings resulting from the debt are outweighed by the insolvency costs. The theoretical optimum is reached when the present value of the tax saving is just offset by increases in the value of the costs of financial distress.

Other relevant factors for a company will be the availability of internal funds (retained profits) as a source of financing, and the cost and availability of debt financing available to it. These principles apply to all UK companies, not just portfolio companies, but for some reason these rules have impacted differently on portfolio companies and publicly traded companies, such that the ratios of debt to equity raised by each are consistently very distinct.

One explanation for this distinction is specific to the difference between portfolio companies and publicly traded companies. Professor Jenkinson has suggested that the pattern of returns which shareholders in publicly traded companies expect, ie stable predictable dividends,[133] makes it very hard for such companies to be more highly leveraged because it is 'very difficult ... to maintain a constant dividend stream or a constant growth of dividends if you have a very highly-leveraged structure because, by its very nature, the residual profits tend to go up and down a lot with interest rates and with changes in the economy'.[134] On this view, the leverage levels in UK publicly traded companies are inefficiently low and should be increased. In other words, the effect of taking a company private is that private equity fund managers are simply transforming the companies they back into capital-efficient operations.[135]

---

[131] JB Warner, 'Bankruptcy Costs: Some Evidence' (1977) 32(2) *Journal of Finance* 337; LA Weiss, 'Bankruptcy Resolution: Direct Costs and Violation of Priority of Claims' (1990) 27 *Journal of Financial Economics* 285; EI Altman, 'A Further Investigation of the Bankruptcy Cost Question' (1984) 39(4) *Journal of Finance* 1067; G Andrade and SN Kaplan, 'How Costly is Financial (Not Economic) Distress? Evidence from Highly Leveraged Transactions that Became Distressed' (1998) 53(5) *Journal of Finance* 1443.

[132] Bank of England, Quarterly Bulletin 2013, Q1, Private Equity and Financial Stability. See also N Wilson, M Wright, D Siegal and L Scholes, 'Private Equity Portfolio Company Performance During the Recession' (2012) 18(1) *Journal of Corporate Finance* 193.

[133] See 2.5.

[134] House of Commons Treasury Committee, Tenth Report of Session 2006–07, *Private Equity*, 30 July 2007, HC 567-I, para 27, quoting Professor Tim Jenkinson.

[135] See ibid, para 45, quoting research by J Froud, S Johal, A Leaver and K Williams, Centre for Research on Socio-Cultural Change, University of Manchester, suggesting that if the debt to equity ratios of the FTSE 100 companies were changed from 30:70 to 70:30 the effect would be to increase the volatility of returns to equity, but would result in higher returns at least during upswings in the economy, albeit that the model also suggests that public company shareholders would receive poorer returns during downturns.

Another explanation for the higher leverage levels in portfolio companies is that the investors in private equity funds are more comfortable with higher levels of debt than shareholders in other companies: 'a single shareholder who has spent millions of pounds understanding the potential of a company and put great resources into exploiting it is very well placed to decide where the efficient frontier is'[136] as compared to shareholders in other companies. In the theoretical model described above whereby ideal debt to equity ratios for a company are determined, the attitude of the shareholders to debt is crucial, since it is the shareholders' need to be compensated for the increased risks of insolvency associated with debt that generally increases the costs of financing and counterbalances the tax advantages of debt. If the shareholders are comfortable with higher levels of debt (and the increased risk of insolvency that this brings) because they have carefully analysed the risks and potential of the target company, then it will be cost-effective to have higher debt levels, as compared to a company in which the shareholders do demand that compensation. This may explain why shareholders in a portfolio company are likely to be more comfortable with raised levels of debt, but it does not take account of the other stakeholders in the company who are exposed to greater risks as a result of the increased debt levels in private equity companies. Two groups in particular will be considered, namely the employees and the creditors, although other stakeholders may also be affected.

16.6.4.1 Employees

Two concerns tend to be voiced regarding the position of employees in portfolio companies. The first concern is that one of the ways in which such companies generate wealth is via wealth transfers from stakeholders, such as employees, to the shareholders, ie that portfolio companies will cut jobs and reduce wages in order to produce gains for the investors.[137] The picture suggested by the empirical studies is somewhat mixed in this regard. Some studies conclude that, on the whole, employment levels continue to increase post buy-out, but at lower levels than other firms in the industry,[138] or that employment grows at an equivalent rate but with slower wage increases.[139] Other studies accept that there are reductions following a buy-out, but that these job losses are relatively small,[140] or that while buy-outs bring about quick reductions in employment to make efficiency gains, over a three- to five-year timescale there are positive elasticities with respect to future employment.[141] These results suggest that buy-outs do not give rise to undue concerns about job destruction, and indeed they seem more consistent with the view that portfolio companies create some value

[136] Ibid, para 27, quoting Philip Yea of 3i.

[137] See eg R Cressy, F Munari and A Malipiero, 'Creative Destruction? Evidence that Buyouts Shed Jobs to Raise Returns' (2011) 13(1) *Venture Capital: An International Journal of Entrepreneurial Finance* 1.

[138] Eg SN Kaplan, 'The Effects of Management Buyouts on Operating Performance and Value' (1989) 24(2) *Journal of Financial Economics* 217; S Davis, J Haltiwanger, R Jarmin, J Lerner and J Miranda, 'Private Equity and Employment' US Census Bureau Center for Economic Studies Paper No CES-WP-08-07R (2011), www.ssrn.com/abstract=1107175.

[139] K Amess and M Wright, 'The Wage and Employment Effects of Leveraged Buyouts in the UK' (2007) 14 *International Journal of the Economics of Business* 179.

[140] S Davis, J Haltiwanger, R Jarmin, J Lerner and J Miranda, 'Private Equity and Employment', NBER Working Paper No 17399 (2011).

[141] See eg R Cressy, F Munari and A Malipiero, 'Creative Destruction? Evidence that Buyouts Shed Jobs to Raise Returns' (2011) 13(1) *Venture Capital: An International Journal of Entrepreneurial Finance* 1.

by operating more efficiently, since low levels of wage cuts and job reductions are consistent with gains in productivity and operating improvements.[142]

The second concern is that, because portfolio companies are (potentially) higher risk, the employees in these companies are at greater risk of losing their jobs. Given the number of employees in the UK workforce now employed by portfolio companies,[143] these concerns are significant. This latter concern was lent some credence in 2006 by the FSA, which stated that jobs in 'overleveraged' private equity companies looked 'increasingly precarious'.[144] Concern regarding the position of employees in portfolio companies has been one of the major drivers behind the regulation of the private equity industry,[145] and the AIFMD has led to increased disclosure obligations for the employees of some portfolio companies, but nothing more concrete.[146] Employees must look to employment law for more direct rights.

16.6.4.2 Creditors

Generally, in solvent companies, it is the interests of the shareholders that dominate. Section 172 of the Companies Act 2006 requires a director of a solvent company to act 'in the way he considers, in good faith, would be most likely to promote the success of the company for the benefit of its members as a whole' whilst also having regard to other stake-holders—although not, crucially, creditors.[147] The ordinary shareholders are the residual claimants and they have the greatest interest in monitoring the company in this period since they will take the lion's share of the loss if things go wrong (and the lion's share of the gain if the company succeeds).[148] The creditors, who are fixed claimants, are, in general, protected by the directors' shareholder-focused duties, as long as the company remains a profitable going concern. This will change, of course, once the company starts to run into financial difficulties, and directors' duties become creditor-regarding once the company is insolvent, or on the verge of insolvency.[149] To make the directors creditor-regarding at an earlier stage would generally have the effect of making directors too risk averse, since creditors are primarily interested in low-risk projects which ensure that they are repaid.

In the private equity model, however, the private equity fund takes a large equity stake in the portfolio company, but only a relatively small stake in the company's debt, and the directors in the company typically hold none of that debt. This could lead to high-risk management gambles by the directors of the portfolio company that are tolerated by the director-shareholders. If the gamble succeeds, the directors and the private equity fund will reap the rewards; if it fails, the creditors will bear the costs. The private equity scenario is

---

[142] See M Goergen, N O'Sullivan and G Woods, 'Private Equity Takeover and Employment in the UK: Some Empirical Evidence' (2011) 19(3) *Corporate Governance: An International Review* 259; R Jelic and M Wright, 'Exits, Performance, and Late Stage Private Equity: The Case of UK Management Buy-Outs' (2011) 17(3) *European Financial Management* 560.

[143] It was estimated by the BVCA in 2005 that 19% of the private sector workforce was employed by companies that had received private equity backing: BVCA, *Economic Impact of Private Equity*, 2005.

[144] FSA, *Private Equity: A Discussion of Risk and Regulatory Engagement*, Discussion paper 06/6, November 2006, para 4.22.

[145] See 16.7.1.1.

[146] See 16.7.2.3.

[147] Companies Act 2006, s 172(1). See 3.2.1.3.1.

[148] See 3.2.1.3.

[149] See 3.3.

therefore a more extreme version of the usual scenario in place for creditors of all companies, because the highly leveraged nature of the company in this instance creates greater potential for the shareholder-focused directors to use the creditors' money to fund the shareholders' (potential) gains. In most companies this conflict only becomes clearly apparent in the twilight period just prior to insolvency, when there is a possibility that the directors might gamble with the creditors' money in order to benefit the shareholders. Measures have been put in place to deal with the conflict that arises at this point.[150] This conflict has the potential to arise earlier in time in a private equity company, when no specific measures are put in place by the law to deal with this conflict.

Of course, it might be expected that the banks and other major lenders in a private equity transaction will put in place contractual and proprietary measures to protect themselves, or at least will ensure that they are properly compensated for the risks they take (and that they are in a good position to assess accurately the level of risk they are taking to ensure that the bargained-for compensation adequately covers the risk undertaken). All the major lenders (senior, second lien and mezzanine) will take security and guarantees in order to protect themselves. The lower-ranked lenders will expect their return to reflect the increased risk that they take. It is also notable that it is standard for these loans to include specific financial covenants, requiring the company to operate within certain financial ratios, such as the ratio of total debt to EBITDA and the ratio of cash flow to total funding costs.

Whilst it is open to the major lenders to put in place security packages and financial covenants in order to protect themselves, the non-adjusting creditors[151] are not in a position to do so, and are left potentially exposed. It is sometimes suggested that debt can operate as a corporate governance tool, ie the monitoring of certain lenders can have a disciplinary effect on directors such that all stakeholders in the company, including therefore the non-adjusting creditors, can benefit.

There is a general disciplining effect that can be said to flow from debt, in that, while returns to shareholders are at the discretion of directors (dividend payments, for example, only become a debt if the company has distributable profits and after the directors have declared the dividend, whatever the articles say),[152] contracted-for interest and capital payments must be met by the directors, otherwise the company can potentially be declared insolvent. Debt can be regarded as a mechanism for forcing managers to disgorge cash, albeit to the creditors rather than to the shareholders. Where most of the free cash flow is committed to debt repayments, directors are forced to adhere to strict results-oriented financial projections.[153] The higher levels of debt mean that the directors are likely to be contractually bound to distribute the free cash to the creditors. Set against this analysis are two aspects of the way portfolio companies operate in practice. First, such companies solve the owner-manager dilemma such that shareholders can force the directors to distribute free cash flows to them if they so wish. Second, in recent years it has become common for many private equity debt repayments to be payable as a single bullet payment at the end of the term, such that there is little disciplining effect on a month-to-month basis within the company. Major lenders can play a significant corporate governance role both

---

[150] Ibid.

[151] See 3.2.2.1 for discussion of non-adjusting creditors.

[152] *Bond v Barrow Haematite Steel Co* [1902] 1 Ch 353. For discussion see 3.2.1.1 and 3.2.1.2.

[153] K Palepu, 'Consequences of Leveraged Buyouts' (1990) 27 *Journal of Financial Economics* 247.

by monitoring corporate activity and by influencing it, largely using the contractual rights they have bargained for in the loan agreement.[154]

A number of aspects of the way that debt financing operates in private equity transactions in practice reduces the likelihood of this monitoring effect. Where covenant-lite financing is in place, the covenants are only tested when an event occurs, rather than being continuously tested. This will clearly diminish the potential monitoring role of the debt. Of more significance is the fact that where private equity transactions are syndicated, the potential governance role of the lender is reduced.[155] Furthermore, these loans are generally transferred by the original lender.[156] In smaller transactions the debt finance is often kept within the banking community, but in larger, more complex transactions it might be sold to participants in the institutional debt market, such as hedge funds or institutional investors. This has the effect that the ownership of the risks being undertaken in this highly leveraged system is not always clear.[157] Although the diversification of the debt market results in a reduction of individual exposure, it also reduces the capacity for monitoring and controlling the underlying risks.[158] A final mechanism whereby debt can operate as a corporate governance tool is via the use of security. This is discussed at 7.6.2.1. The senior lender in a private equity transaction will take security and will be in a position to use that security to discipline the directors, in particular by performing a monitoring role.

16.6.5 Summary

A number of explanations have been put forward to explain the success of private equity transactions, some of which have already been canvassed in this section. The first explanation is that leverage levels in portfolio companies are higher than in other companies, which leads to tax savings and could have benefits for the returns received by equity investors.[159] A second explanation is that the value arises from a reduction of agency costs within the portfolio companies as a result of the closer alignment of managers and shareholders. A third possible reason is that they generate value as a result of wealth transfers from stakeholders to shareholders. Fourth, these transactions could generate gains for the private equity fund because of reductions in transaction costs, ie the fact that regulatory and other burdens are lower, and therefore cheaper, for private equity backed companies. Fifth, the target companies may be undervalued prior to purchase by the private equity fund, ie private equity funds manage to buy the companies cheaply, and the gain is therefore their exploitation of their ability to price the company more accurately than the market.

---

[154] See 3.2.2.4.
[155] For discussion see 3.2.2.4 and chapter 8.
[156] In a study in 2006 the FSA found that, in the pre-crisis period, on average banks distributed 81% of their exposures to their largest transactions within 120 days of finalising the deal: FSA, *Private Equity: A Discussion of Risk and Regulatory Engagement*, Discussion paper 06/6, November 2006, 3–4. For discussion see also Bank of England Quarterly Bulletin, 2013, Q1, Private Equity and Financial Stability.
[157] FSA, *Private Equity*, ibid, 10.
[158] See 3.2.2.4.6.
[159] This is often suggested to be one of the significant gains in US public-to-private transactions: see eg SN Kaplan, 'Management Buyouts: Evidence on Taxes as a Source of Value' (1989) 44 *Journal of Finance* 611. See 16.6.3.

If the gains arise because of tax breaks, or because the company was underpriced, or because of wealth transfers between the stakeholders and shareholders, then private equity transactions would not appear to add any particular operational value to the company. By contrast, if the value arises as a result of financial, governance or operational changes in the target company then private equity transactions could be said to create economic value.

An empirical study conducted in 2007 found that, of the various explanations put forward for public-to-private transactions, support can be found for the view that an important source of expected shareholder wealth gains is the undervaluation of the target firms' share prices over a one-year period prior to the first public-to-private announcement. However, the study also concluded that aligning the directors and shareholders' interests was a relevant factor in the resulting gains, as was the concentration of control among a few shareholders.[160] Other studies that have investigated this issue have concluded that modest operating improvements do result from public equity transactions.[161] Whilst the picture emerging from these studies is by no means clear cut, it does appear that private equity transactions do add some economic value, although this accounts for only part of the gains made: 'It has been said that private equity made its money by leverage in the 1980s, by price/earnings arbitrage in the 1990s and since then by genuinely changing companies. In fact all three components have always played their part.'[162]

16.7 Regulation

Traditionally, private equity has been a self-regulated industry, subject to little regulatory oversight. In recent years, and particularly post-crisis, this has changed. In a survey conducted in 2014, the limited partners of private equity funds identified regulation as the biggest challenge facing the private equity community.[163] Some of these regulatory changes have not been imposed directly on the private equity industry, but will nevertheless impact on the industry. For instance, changes in the way banks are regulated means that they need to risk-weight their investments, and hold more capital against the riskier asset classes. Private equity (and venture capital) is one of the riskiest asset classes, and accordingly banks have to hold a substantial amount of capital to cover the risk of an investment in private equity.[164] The Solvency II Directive[165] will have a similar indirect effect on private equity,

---

[160] L Renneboog, T Simons and M Wright, 'Why Do Public Firms Go Private in the UK? The Impact of Private Equity Investors, Incentive Realignment and Undervaluation' (2007) 13 *Journal of Corporate Finance* 591.

[161] Eg C Weir, P Jones and M Wright, 'Public to Private Transactions, Private Equity and Performance in the UK: An Empirical Analysis of the Impact of Going Private' (2008), www.ssrn.com/abstract=1138616). Similar results emerge in a US study: S Guo, E Hotchkiss and W Song, 'Do Buyouts (Still) Create Value?' (2009), www.ssrn.com/abstract=1009281.

[162] C Hale in C Hale (ed), *Private Equity: A Transactional Analysis*, 3rd edn (London, Globe Law and Business, 2015) 8.

[163] See Prequin, *Key Issue Private Equity Investors Face in 2014*, www.preqin.com/docs/newsletters/pe/Preqin_PESL_Feb_14_Key_Issues.pdf.

[164] See the Basel Accords produced by the Basel Committee on Banking Supervision, specifically Basel II (2004) and Basel III (2010–11, as amended). The illiquidity of private equity investments also makes it harder for banks to respect the proposed liquidity ratios.

[165] Directive 2009/138/EU, due to come into force on 1 January 2016 (see Directive 2012/23/EU).

as it will require insurance firms to risk-weight their investments and only permit them to treat certain percentages of assets as capital depending on the risk weighting attributed to the asset class to which the assets belong. Again, private equity has, for these purposes, been placed in a category with a higher risk weighting than publicly quoted equities, which is likely to have an impact on the insurance sector's appetite to invest in private equity. Other EU regulations, such as MiFID II and MiFIR, are not specifically aimed at the private equity industry, but nevertheless bring this industry within their regulatory ambit, and inevitably increase the regulatory burdens on the industry.[166] There have also been other legislative changes to the tax regime in this period which will have the effect of increasing the compliance costs of private equity firms.[167]

Other regulatory reforms have been focused very directly on the private equity industry, and in particular the AIFMD[168] has brought private equity firmly within the regulatory perimeter in Europe and has had a significant impact on the industry, not least in relation to the increased costs of compliance.

16.7.1 The Need for Regulation

The lack of regulation regarding private equity pre-crisis was not, perhaps, very surprising. As regards the regulation of the fund, the investors are predominantly institutional investors, sovereign wealth funds and wealthy individuals. These are investors that can be expected to look after themselves. As regards the portfolio companies themselves, these are private companies, without direct investment by the public, and accordingly they prima facie fall under the same regime as all other private companies. However, the different regulatory response becomes very stark where a company such as the FTSE 100 company Alliance Boots is purchased by private equity and taken private, and the regulatory regime impacting the company shifts dramatically in a very short space of time.

The arguments in favour of regulation of private equity may be divided into two broad types: (1) increased transparency, and (2) concerns about systemic risk.

16.7.1.1 Increased Transparency

Traditionally, relatively little information has been available regarding the private equity industry. Many in the industry believed that 'private means private' to the point of secretiveness.[169] Calls for an increase in the levels of disclosure have not focused on the need to protect investors in the private equity fund (these are sophisticated investors and the levels of satisfaction with the information disclosed to them by the fund are generally high)[170] or investors in the portfolio company (these comprise the managers and the fund itself).

---

[166] For discussion see EVCA, *Response to ESMA Consultation Paper on MiFID II/MiFIR*, 22 May 2014, *ESMA/2014/549*; ESMA *Discussion Paper on MiFID II/MiFIR*, 22 May 2014, *ESMA/2014/548*, 29 August 2014.

[167] See eg International Tax Compliance (United States of America) Regulations 2014 (SI 2014/1506).

[168] Implemented in the UK by the AIFM Regulations 2013.

[169] See Sir David Walker, *Disclosure and Transparency in Private Equity: Consultation Document*, July 2007, 3.

[170] *Disclosure and Transparency*, ibid, 6, and see Private Equity Monitoring Group on Transactions and Disclosure, *Sixth Report*, December 2013.

Rather, the suggestion is that it is necessary to protect the non-shareholder stakeholders in the portfolio companies:

> the difference [between the reporting requirements for portfolio companies and public companies] is logical—it is rooted in the distinction between keeping a small group of private shareholders informed, and reporting to markets as a whole. Nevertheless, large businesses, and particularly those in the public eye, have a wider responsibility to engage with the community in which they operate and to meet the legitimate interests of stakeholders, both employees and the wider public, in how their operations affect them. As the private equity sector has grown and as some major companies have moved from transparent public to opaque private markets, this need has become more acute.[171]

The private equity industry has come to understand, and accept, that the growth in the volume and size of private equity transactions has introduced a wider stakeholder base into the equation that may well have a legitimate interest in the nature of the private equity firm acquiring the company. In the UK, for example, in February 2007 the BVCA asked Sir David Walker to undertake a review of the adequacy of disclosure and transparency in private equity with a view to recommending a set of voluntary guidelines. The Walker Review agreed that there was a 'major transparency and accountability gap to be filled',[172] although it did not suggest that the full array of reporting obligations imposed on publicly traded companies should also be imposed on portfolio companies. Instead, the Review suggested a set of voluntary guidelines, regulated on a comply or explain basis. These guidelines are intended to tackle the transparency and accountability gap, and largely aim to provide more information about the portfolio company, and the private equity firm behind it, to the non-shareholder stakeholders and to the wider public, rather than to the investors in the fund.[173]

The Walker Guidelines do not apply to all portfolio companies: only the largest companies are captured.[174] In 2013 it was estimated that 89 companies fell within these criteria.[175] Additional reporting requirements are imposed on these portfolio companies. For instance, the Walker Guidelines recommend that these companies should file their annual report and financial statements on their company website[176] within six months of year end rather than the nine months as otherwise provided by companies legislation for private companies.[177] That report should include information regarding the identity of the private equity fund that owns the company, the senior managers or advisers who have oversight of the fund or funds, and details on the composition of its board.[178] The guidelines also envisage more

---

[171] Speech by the then Economic Secretary to the Treasury, Ed Balls MP, to the London Business School, March 2007.

[172] Sir David Walker, *Disclosure and Transparency in Private Equity: Consultation Document*, July 2007, 6.

[173] The guidelines do not have much to say about private equity firms' reporting obligations to their investors, other than to note that private equity firms should, in their reporting to limited partners, follow established guidelines, such as those published by the EVCA, and should commit to following established guidelines in the valuation of their assets (see eg *Guidelines for Disclosure and Transparency in Private Equity: Final Report*, November 2007, 9).

[174] This remains true despite the implementation of changes recommended by the Guidelines Monitoring Group (established to review the private equity industry's conformity with the Walker Guidelines) to broaden the definition of a portfolio company and bring more companies within the disclosure regime.

[175] See Private Equity Monitoring Group on Transactions and Disclosure, *Sixth Report*, December 2013.

[176] Generally, companies legislation only places an obligation on quoted companies to make annual reports and accounts available on the company website: Companies Act 2006, s 430.

[177] Ibid, s 442(2)(a). Public companies are generally required to file their reports within six months: s 442(2)(b).

[178] None of the other corporate governance requirements regarding the composition of the board which apply to publicly listed companies are required to be adopted by portfolio companies.

information being provided regarding the private equity firms that back these particular portfolio companies.[179]

The Walker Guidelines are fairly limited in scope, both as to the number of portfolio companies that fall within their remit and as to the nature of the disclosure required of these companies. These voluntary guidelines did not quieten calls for the regulation of private equity at European level.

16.7.1.2 Systemic Risk

The other argument in favour of regulating the private equity industry is based on systemic risk. Systemic risk has been defined by the Financial Stability Board as a risk of disruption to financial services that is caused by an impairment of all or parts of the financial system and has the potential to have serious negative consequences for the real economy.[180] It is now well understood that commercial banks are not the only institutions to present systemic risk: other institutions may do so too. In particular, the provision of maturity/liquidity transformation and leverage in non-bank entities can create these risks.

'Maturity transformation' is the activity of issuing short-term liabilities (such as deposits) and transforming them into medium- to long-term assets (such as loans). 'Liquidity transformation' is the issuing of liquid liabilities to finance illiquid assets. An asset is illiquid when it cannot be easily converted into cash without a loss in nominal value. Commercial banks engage in transformation when they accept deposits from investors which are generally redeemable at very short notice (ie they borrow short) and use these funds to invest in long-term enterprises. The bank retains only a fraction of its demand deposits in cash. This system works well if only a few investors demand payment at any time. However, it will fail if many depositors call for repayment at once since the bank may run short of liquidity, and depositors will rush to withdraw their money, forcing the bank to liquidate many of its assets at a loss and eventually causing the bank to fail. A bank failure can have larger effects for the economy, since banks calling in their loans early can have a disruptive effect on business, and there can also be effects in the banking sector more generally, either because the bank run causes a loss of public confidence in banks generally (triggering further bank runs) and/or because of the interconnectedness of the failed bank with other banks in the system.

While these transformational issues can exist within the traditional hedge fund model, since these funds usually offer some liquidity to investors and will generally invest on a longer-term basis than the liquidity it offers to investors, they do not exist in the private equity model, which provides no opportunity to withdraw capital before the fund matures. The private equity model is not susceptible to the bank run scenario described above.

---

[179] Accordingly, they recommend that such private equity firms publish certain information about themselves either by way of an annual review or through regular updating of their websites. The information required includes a description of the firm's structure and investment approach, a description of the UK companies in its portfolio, an indication of the leadership of the firm in the UK and confirmation that arrangements are in place to deal with conflicts of interest, and a categorisation of its limited partners by geography and by type. The guidelines also require firms to publish a statement of their commitment to conform to the guidelines on a comply or explain basis.

[180] FSB, *Guidance to Assess the Systemic Importance of Financial Institutions, Markets and Instruments: Initial Considerations*, October 2009.

The other issue that can give rise to systemic risk is leverage. High levels of leverage can expose market participants to disruption when confidence evaporates in the markets, potentially leading to abrupt deleveraging and asset fire sales. However, unlike hedge funds, private equity funds generally do not take on leverage at the fund level. These funds generally invest in equity instruments (the shares in private companies), whereas hedge funds often invest in derivatives and other structured, synthetic products. There is, of course, leverage at the level of the portfolio companies in private equity, but this is unlikely to raise concerns from a systemic risk perspective. Neither private equity funds nor the portfolio companies are cross-collateralised, meaning that the failure of one portfolio company should have no knock-on effects for the fund or other companies held in a particular fund's portfolio. Further, negative externalities arising from the failure of a portfolio company seem to be limited due to the fact that private equity funds are generally diversified across multiple industries and tend to lack concentrated exposure to a single sector, in contrast with hedge funds.[181]

The idea that the private equity industry needed to be regulated to deal with systemic risk is somewhat problematic. Nevertheless, the European Commission's proposals for the AIFMD clearly placed the amelioration of systemic risk issues at their centre.[182] The Directive covers the management and administration of alternative investment funds generally and therefore encompasses hedge funds and private equity (and indeed other funds such as real estate funds, which fall outside the ambit of this book). It may be that private equity was swept along with a political desire to regulate hedge funds that emerged post-crisis.[183] On the plus side the AIFMD takes the first steps towards creating a European single market for the private equity industry, but it also imposes very significant additional costs on the industry for (arguably) relatively little gain.

16.7.2 The AIFMD

16.7.2.1 Scope and Authorisation Requirements

The AIFMD[184] introduces harmonised requirements for financial intermediaries engaged in the management and administration of alternative investment funds (AIFs) other than retail funds.[185] The AIFMD is implemented in the UK by the Alternative Investment

---

[181] There may be a potential concern regarding the increased failure of portfolio companies to which banks are exposed as a result of lending money to them. However, this is best dealt with by regulating the banking sector rather than the private equity industry—as indeed the Basel Accords may be perceived as doing.

[182] *Executive Summary of the Impact Assessment of the Proposed Directive*, 29 April 2009, SEC(2009) 577, 3.

[183] E Ferran, 'After the Crisis: The Regulation of Hedge Funds and Private Equity in the EU' (2011) 12 *European Business Organization Law Review* 379; T Mollers, A Harrer and T Kruger, 'The AIFM Directive and its Regulation of Hedge Funds and Private Equity' (2012) 30(1) *Journal of Law and Commerce* 87.

[184] Directive 2011/61/EU on alternative investment fund managers and amending Directives 2003/41/EC and 2009/65/EC and Regulations (EC) No 1060/2009 and (EU) No 1095/2010. For detailed discussion of this Directive see Moloney: EU Regulation, III.4.

[185] For the definition of AIF see Directive 2011/61/EU, art 4(1)(a), which defines AIFs very widely as collective investment undertakings which raise capital from a number of investors, with a view to investing it in accordance with a defined investment policy for the benefit of those investors, and which do not require authorisation under the UCITS Directive (see Directive 2014/91/EU, amending 2009/65/EC). The directive therefore covers a wide range of funds, including private equity, hedge funds, property funds and infrastructure funds.

Fund Managers Regulations,[186] which apply to UK alternative investment fund managers (AIFMs) that are permitted by the FCA to manage AIFs under the AIFMD. The focus of the directive is therefore on regulating the fund managers rather than the AIFs.[187]

The scope of the directive extends beyond entities established in a Member State of the EU which manage one or more AIFs:[188] it also applies to managers that are established outside the EU to the extent that they manage AIFs established within the EU, or market AIFs to investors domiciled in the EU. So, for example, AIFMs with a registered office outside the EU are potentially caught in relation to AIFs marketed by them in the UK. There is a de minimis exemption within the AIFMD where the fund is unleveraged and without redemption rights for five years, where the aggregate assets under management are less than €500 million; where the fund is leveraged, the exemption level is set at €100 million.[189]

An AIFM that does not fall within any of the exemptions set out in the directive[190] will not be allowed to manage an AIF unless it has been authorised to do so in accordance with the directive.[191] Once authorised, the AIFM will be permitted to provide management services to AIFs domiciled in any Member State[192] and to market the securities of those AIFs to 'professional investors'[193] across the EU.[194] The AIFMD creates a passport regime for EU AIFMs.[195]

16.7.2.2 Regulation at the Fund Level

The AIFMD imposes a number of new requirements on the private equity fund. These include new capital requirements. For example, an AIFM managing external funds will have to maintain initial capital of €125,000.[196] A self-managed fund will be required to maintain initial capital of €300,000.[197] For each fund it manages, the AIFM will need to ensure that a depository is appointed.[198] The depository's function is predominantly the safekeeping of

---

[186] Alternative Investment Fund Managers Regulations 2013 (SI 2013/1773) (AIFM Regulations 2013).

[187] It is a requirement of the directive that each AIF within its scope have a single AIFM responsible for compliance with the directive: art 5.

[188] Directive 2011/61/EU, art 2.

[189] Ibid, art 3(2) and see AIFM Regulations 2013, Part 3 (which details the regime to which such small AIFMs are subject). For discussion of the UK approach to this issue see HM Treasury, *Transposition of the Alternative Investment Fund Managers Directive*, January 2013, ch 2.

[190] Directive 2011/61/EU, art 3 and see AIFM Regulations 2013, para 4(4).

[191] Directive 2011/61/EU, arts 6–8 and see AIFM Regulations 2013, part 2. This authorisation will be via the national regulator of the Member State in which the AIFM has its registered office (the FCA in the UK). The regulator must inform ESMA on a quarterly basis of authorisations granted or withdrawn and ESMA will keep a central public register of all authorised AIFMs.

[192] Ibid, art 32.

[193] See Annex II to the Markets in Financial Instruments Directive (MiFID).

[194] Directive 2011/61/EU, art 31.

[195] Ibid, arts 31–33. A distinct regime applies in relation to non-EU AIFs.

[196] Ibid, art 9(2) and see AIFM Regulations 2013, para 5(3)(c).

[197] Directive 2011/61/EU, art 9(1) and see AIFM Regulations 2013, para 5(3)(c). There is also an own funds requirement where the fund is managed by an external AIFM, being the higher of (i) one quarter of fixed annual overheads or (ii) 0.02% of the amount by which the total value of portfolios under management exceeds €250 million, subject to a cap of €10 million (art 9(3)). Own funds must be invested with a view to short-term availability, and may not be invested speculatively.

[198] Ibid, art 21(1) (and see FCA Handbook, FUND 3.11). There are some exemptions. For example, an authorised EU AIFM marketing a non-EU AIF to professional investors on the basis of a private placement exemption will not be subject to many of the depositary requirements, and indeed a non-EU AIFM marketing EU AIFs or non-EU AIFs to professional investors on a private placement basis will not be subject to any of the depositary requirements (unless Member States impose stricter private placement rules in their territories).

the assets of the fund, and it is intended to protect investors against losses arising from fraud of the AIFM. AIFMs are also under an obligation to establish appropriate and consistent procedures for the valuation of the assets of each fund under management.[199] Both of these requirements impose costs on private equity firms, and yet it is not clear that such costs are warranted. Both measures (safekeeping and valuation) are intended to a large extent to thwart Madoff-style frauds, which makes some sense in the context of hedge funds, but the need for these provisions is less obvious in relation to private equity. The long-term illiquid nature of the assets held by the fund (the shares in private companies) virtually eliminates the potential for Madoff-style fraud. Investment and divestment in relation to these assets will be highly visible to investors and to the marketplace. The value of placing those assets with a depository can therefore be questioned. Further, as regards valuation, distributions to investors in the private equity model are typically triggered by the disposition of portfolio investments (such as via an IPO). Investor liquidity is contingent on prior disposition, which already provides a credible third-party valuation of the asset.

The directive also imposes various operational obligations on AIFMs. For example, AIFMs are under an obligation to put in place remuneration policies and practices for certain senior staff, designed to promote effective risk management.[200] More generally, the AIFMD introduces certain general principles with which AIFMs must comply on an ongoing basis.[201] For example, an AIFM shall act honestly, fairly and with due skill, care and diligence in conducting its activities and it shall act in the best interests of the fund or the fund investors and the integrity of the market.[202] These general principles are a reflection of the statements that are typically found in fund documentation in any case, but compliance with the principles will now be supervised by regulators. Measures are also imposed to ensure that AIFMs identify and manage the risks to which the AIFs they manage are exposed by virtue of their investment strategies, and to avoid conflicts of interest.[203]

The AIFMD includes a number of measures designed to increase transparency at the level of the fund. It sets out the information that must be disclosed to investors before they invest in a fund, including the investment strategy and objectives of the fund, the identity of the AIFM, its pricing methodology and valuation procedure, all fees and charges, and the latest net asset value of the fund and historic performance information, where available.[204] Much of this information is already being made available to fund investors, but this standardised approach to the information required by the AIFMD may make it easier for investors to check whether they have received the required information. The directive requires disclosure to investors and reporting to regulators on a number of issues on an ongoing basis.[205] Oversight by regulators of AIFMs is ensured as a result of various ongoing reporting obligations.[206]

---

[199] See FCA Handbook, FUND 3.9.

[200] Directive 2011/61/EU, art 13(1) and Annex II (and see FUND 3.7). See also ESMA, *Final Report: Guidelines on Sound Remuneration Policies under AIFMD*, 11 February 2013, ESMA/2013/201.

[201] Directive 2011/61/EU, art 12. See also Commission Delegated Regulation (EU) No 231/2013 of 19 December 2012.

[202] Directive 2011/61/EU, art 12(1)(a) and (b), and see FCA Handbook, COBS 18.5.

[203] Directive 2011/61/EU, arts 12(2), 14–16. See also FCA Handbook, FUND 3.7.

[204] Directive 2011/61/EU, art 20(1) (and see FCA Handbook, FUND 3.2.2). In addition, annual reports in respect of each EU fund managed by an AIFM and each fund it markets in the EU must be provided to investors, on request, and to the home Member State competent authority (art 22 and see FUND 3.3).

[205] Directive 2011/61/EU, arts 23-24 (and see FUND 3.2.5–3.2.6, 3.3).

[206] Ibid, art 24 (and see FUND 3.4). ESMA can also request national regulators to impose additional reporting requirements in some circumstances: art 24(5).

The AIFMD seeks to manage concerns about systemic risk in part by regulating leverage.[207] Information regarding leverage must be disclosed to investors both initially and on an ongoing basis[208] and reported to the regulator.[209] AIFMs are also required to set leverage limits for each AIF they manage,[210] and must demonstrate that these are reasonable and that it complies with them at all times.[211] The regulator can, if necessary, set limits on the amount of leverage that a particular fund manager can employ.[212] In the event of this occurring, ESMA, the European Systemic Risk Board and the national regulator of the AIF must be notified in advance, and ESMA must then issue advice to the relevant authority about the leverage measure that is contemplated and whether the measure is appropriate, and about the duration of the intervention.[213] ESMA has a coordination role and is also given the power to intervene in some circumstances and to issue advice to national authorities specifying remedial action, including leverage limits, where it determines that that leverage employed by an AIFM poses a substantial risk to the stability and integrity of the financial system.[214] These provisions are unlikely to be particularly beneficial in relation to private equity, given that the leverage arises only at the level of the portfolio company and raises minimal systemic risk issues.

16.7.2.3 Regulation at the Level of the Portfolio Company

The AIFMD also imposes regulation at the level of the portfolio company.[215] The Directive creates disclosure obligations on the acquisition of major holdings (starting at 10 per cent) in non-listed EU companies.[216]

More onerous obligations are imposed when an AIFM acquires a controlling interest in a non-listed company or an issuer (ie a company whose shares are admitted to trading on an EU regulated market such as the London Main Market).[217] In these circumstances, the AIFM needs to make disclosures to the regulator, and to the relevant company and its

---

[207] An AIFM managing AIFs employing leverage on a substantial basis is required to make information available to the regulator. Detailed provisions are put in place, predominantly in Commission Delegated Regulation (EU) No 231/2013 of 19 December 2012, to calculate the levels of leverage employed by AIFs. For private equity funds, ESMA has clarified that in the calculation of the leverage, any exposure that exists at the level of the investee companies should not be included (provided the AIF/AIFM's exposure is limited to its investment in the portfolio company): ESMA, *Questions and Answers: Application of the AIFMD*, 26 March 2015, 2015/ESMA/630.

[208] Directive 2011/61/EU, art 23 (see FUND 3.2.2(j) and 3.2.6(2)).

[209] Ibid, art 24 (see FUND 3.4.5). Leverage disclosure also forms part of the AIFM authorisation process: art 7(3)(a).

[210] Ibid, art 15(4).

[211] Ibid, art 25(3) (and see FUND 3.7.7–3.7.9).

[212] Ibid, art 25(3) (and see AIFM Regulations 2013, para 68). In addition, ESMA has the power to determine that the leverage employed by the fund manager poses a substantial risk to the stability and integrity of the financial system, in which case ESMA can issue advice to the AIFM's home Member State regulator specifying remedial measures (which can include leverage limits): art 25(6) and (7).

[213] Directive 2011/61/EU, art 25(3)–(6).

[214] Ibid, arts 25(5)(7)(8). Where the national authority does not follow this advice, it must notify ESMA accordingly, and ESMA can choose to make public disclosures to this effect.

[215] This regime does not apply where a non-listed portfolio company is an SME: ibid, art 26(2)(a).

[216] Ibid, art 27(1) and see AIFM Regulations 2013, para 38(1). In the UK notification to the FCA is required.

[217] Control is defined as holding more than 50% of the voting rights of a non-listed company or between 30 and 33% of the voting rights of an issuer, depending on a number of factors such as the location of the issuer's registered office (for companies listed on the London Stock Exchange it is 30%): art 26(5) (and see AIFM Regulations 2013, para 36).

shareholders, about the identity of the AIFM and its policy for preventing and managing conflicts of interest.[218] Where the target is a non-listed company, the AIFM must also disclose its intentions with regard to the future business of the company, and the likely repercussions on employment, and provide details of the financing of the acquisition.[219] These new disclosure obligations provide employees with information rights, not decision rights. They are modelled on the rights provided to target company shareholders in a takeover offer scenario, and are likely to have a similarly limited effect on employee protection.[220] For non-listed companies the AIFM must also ensure that additional information is disclosed on an annual basis. This includes a fair review of the development of the company's business representing the situation at the end of the period covered by the annual report and an indication of the company's likely development.[221]

There are also rules designed to prevent asset stripping.[222] When a private equity fund acquires a controlling interest in a non-listed company or an issuer, the AIFM shall not, within 24 months following the acquisition, be allowed to facilitate, support, instruct, or vote in favour of any distribution, capital reduction, share redemption or acquisition of own shares by the company and must use its best endeavours to prevent the same from occurring. The effect of the provisions is to 'narrow the range of options that may be used to return value to the shareholders in a tax-efficient way'.[223] Consequently, within this two-year period, private companies under the ownership of relevant AIFs will effectively be subject to the same restrictions on distributions to which public companies are subject under the Companies Act 2006, losing the benefits that are otherwise enjoyed by the more relaxed regime generally available to private companies.[224] These asset-stripping provisions are somewhat limited by the fact that, as with other capital maintenance measures, they do not limit AIFs receiving returns from, or being repaid, their shareholder loans.

16.7.2.4 Effect of the AIFMD on the Private Equity Industry

The AIFMD required implementation by July 2013, and has duly been implemented in the UK.[225] Much of the regulation imposed by the AIFMD is somewhat hard to justify in the context of the private equity industry. The main risk targeted by this directive, namely systemic risk, is not really discernible in the private equity business model examined earlier in this chapter. The AIFMD introduces some new disclosure obligations, but these provisions are unlikely to make much difference to the group identified as being most in need of protection, namely the non-shareholder stakeholders in portfolio companies. The

---

[218] Directive 2011/61/EU, art 28(2) and see AIFM Regulations 2013, para 39.

[219] Directive 2011/61/EU, art 28(4) and see AIFM Regulations 2013, para 40.

[220] See 14.3.3.

[221] Directive 2011/61/EU, art 29 and see AIFM Regulations 2013, para 42.

[222] Directive 2011/61/EU, art 30 and see AIFM Regulations 2013, para 43. See A Henderson, 'Asset Stripping under the AIFMD' [2013] *Journal of International Banking and Financial Law* 644; A Onions, 'AIFM Directive: Unfairly Targeting Private Equity?' (2014) 25(2) *Practical Law Companies* 18.

[223] E Ferran, 'After the Crisis: The Regulation of Hedge Funds and Private Equity in the EU' (2011) 12 *European Business Organization Law Review* 379, 404–05.

[224] See 5.3 and 5.4.

[225] The directive was implemented predominantly via the AIFM Regulations 2013 (SI 2013/1773), as amended, and changes to the FCA Handbook.

predominant effect of the AIFMD is likely to be a significant imposition of compliance costs: 'The AIFMD ... will add substantially to the compliance burdens of private equity. Whether the costs associated with these burdens will produce benefits that justify them remains to be seen.'[226]

16.8 Conclusion

In the period up to 2008, private equity began to be seen as a threat to the public markets, and indeed some commentators even suggested that private equity might eventually become the dominant corporate organisational form.[227] Post-crisis, the threat of private equity has diminished somewhat, but it remains the case that private equity offers an important alternative to the public markets as a source of new funds for businesses.[228] Publicly traded companies enable a large number of individuals to purchase shares and allow the risk to be borne by investors without requiring them to manage the companies they own. For very minimal stakes any individual is able to participate in the public market. Private equity, by contrast, allows a much smaller number of investors (predominantly institutional investors) to invest substantial sums via a private equity fund in mature businesses operated by private companies with a view to earning (hopefully) higher returns than can be obtained via the public markets. These returns are available as a result of a range of factors, but high levels of leverage within the portfolio company and a close alignment of the interests of managers and owners seem to play a significant role.

The private equity industry has come under substantial regulatory scrutiny in the aftermath of the financial crisis, with the AIFMD, amongst other measures, imposing new obligations, and costs, on private equity funds and the companies they own. The private equity industry suffered a significant contraction in the immediate post-crisis period, but the boom and bust cycle of this industry seems at present to be experiencing an upturn again. What recent years have demonstrated is the resilience and adaptability of this industry. Its role as a core constituent of corporate finance looks likely to continue.

---

[226] C Hale in C Hale (ed), *Private Equity: A Transactional Analysis*, 3rd edn (London, Globe Law and Business, 2015) 9.

[227] MC Jensen, 'Eclipse of the Public Corporation' (1989) 67 *Harvard Business Review* 61, revised version available at www.ssrn.com/abstract=146149 (1997).

[228] See eg Kay Review of UK Equity Markets and Long-Term Decision Making, *Final Report*, July 2012, 2.14.

INDEX

absolute interests:
  enforcement methods, 334–6
  flawed assets and, 108–9
  meaning, 22, 267
  non-registration, 276
  proprietary rights, 22
  ranking of creditors, 98–9
  retention of title, 275
  security interests and, 267, 271–81
    characterisation, 272–4
    external v internal approach, 273
    grants, 278–9
    policy considerations, 276–7
    proving, 276–7
    Quistclose trusts, 281
    reasons for choice, 274–6
    retention of title, 275, 280–1
    sale and lease-back, 278
    taxation, 275
acceleration clauses, 23, 214–18, 222, 266
accounts:
  absolute v security interests, 276
  annual accounts, 543–4
  asset finance, 44
  auditing, 489, 544
  deceit, 561
  dividend setting, 164
  false accounts, 579
  function, 547
  IFRS, 649
  pass-through arrangements, 275
  preference shares, 50
  purpose, 542
  ration requirements and, 210–11
administration:
  administrators' duties, 309, 333
  administrators' powers of disposal, 101
  distributions, 64
  enforcement of securities, 331–3, 336–8
  expenses, 100–1, 304–6, 309
  financial collateral arrangements and, 338
  fixed charges and, 337
  floating charges and, 290, 304–5, 309, 327, 331–2, 333, 337
  London approach and, 95
  moratorium, 328–9, 336–8
  objective, 98, 327
  ordinary shares and, 65
  pre-packs, 305, 333
  ranking of creditors, 97–105
  retention of title and, 337
  schemes of arrangement and, 760
  security interests and, 275
  trend, 331–2
  unregistered charges and, 318
administrative receivership, 97, 304, 331–3
affiliation strategies, 489, 638
agency:
  agency conflicts, 82, 130, 371, 680, 711
  concept, 371
  fiscal agents v trustees, 380, 411–14
  syndicated loans, 411–14
AIM, 17, 482, 658
aircraft, 317, 353
algorithmic trading, 588, 631–3
allocative efficiency, 525, 583, 718
Alternative Investment Management Association (AIMA), 665
analysts, 572–6, 596, 619
annual reports:
  accounts, 543–4
  compliance with UK Corporate Governance Code, 478
  corporate governance statements, 546
  deceit, 561
  directors' reports, 544
  EU law, 542–3, 546–7
  function, 547–8
  half-yearly reports, 546–7, 548
  requirement, 542–4
  strategic reports, 544–5, 548
anti-assignment clauses:
  construction, 434–5, 438–9
  debt paid by debtors, 435–6
  debt unpaid, 436–7
  declarations of trust and, 437–43
    express prohibition, 439–41
    implied trusts, 441
    Vandepitte procedure, 441–3
  effect, 28
  equitable assignments and, 430
  receivables, 453–5
  set-off and, 437, 438
  statutory override, 454–5
  survey, 434–43
anti-deprivation principle, 107–9, 219–20, 233, 261–2
arrangers, 94, 373–3, 414–20, 780
articles of association:
  changing, 392
  contractual rights, 10, 72–6
  distributions, 12
  enforcing, 103, 508
  private equity, 774
  share distributions, 163

share rights, 10, 63
share transfer, 144
asset-based finance:
asset-based lending, 42–3
asset-based securities, 38, 372
debt securities and, 656–7
overview, 40–6
receivables financing *see* receivables financing
retention of title *see* retention of title
supply chain financing, 42
asset finance:
accounting, 44
conditional sales *see* conditional sales
finance leases *see* finance leases
hire purchase *see* hire purchase
options, 44–6
asset preservation *see* disposal of assets
assets *see* disposal of assets; proprietary interests
assignment:
anti-assignment clauses, 28, 430, 434–43, 453–5
discharge of bankrupts and, 285
equitable assignments, 430–3, 436, 440–1
equitable interests, 433–4
insolvency claims, 113–14
invoice discounting and, 336
loan transfer, 445, 450–2
notice to debtors, 430
novation and, 428
reasonable consent, 451–2
receivables, 318, 324, 452–5, 468–9
set-off and, 437, 438
statutory assignments, 453
factoring, 336
meaning, 429–30
ranking, 321–2
survey, 428–43
transfer of choses in action, 429
auditing:
annual accounts, 543, 544, 547
appointment of auditors, 556
auditors as gatekeepers, 573
committees, 478
covenants and, 210
governance and, 546
IFRS, 649
independent audits, 539
IPOs and, 489, 498, 499, 500, 502, 507
liability of auditors, 654
solvency statements and, 168, 186
Australia:
notice filing system, 350, 353, 356–7, 358
registration of security interests, 316
securities over circulating assets, 307
set-off, 229

balance sheet test, 61, 80, 96, 120, 176
Bank of England, 683
bankruptcy discharge, 285
banks:
bond issues, 373
covenants, 84–5

debt/equity ratio, 56
insurance business and, 249
legal capital rules, 25–6, 152–3, 425–6
loans, 28–30
money markets, 20–1
monitoring borrowers, 88, 92–3
securitisation, 39
set-off: right to combine accounts, 222
shadow banking sector, 20
systemic risks, 797
transfer of risk, 93–4
twilight period: London approach, 94–5
Basel III, 30
bills of exchange, 29–30, 268, 423, 444
bonds
see also debt securities
ascertaining views of holders, 391–6
asset-based securities, 38
bearer instruments, 376, 379, 444
call options, 37
coordination of bondholders, 393
corporate governance and, 92
covenants, 85
change of control, 199
negative pledges, 200
wrongful acceleration, 215, 400–1
covered bonds, 39, 638
decision-making process, 391–2
default, 398–403
domestic stock, 37
early redemption, 37
equity financing or, 36
global notes, 376, 384–90
high-yield bonds, 30, 35
information rights, 397–8
insolvency and, 413
international stock, 37–8
issuing, 372
advertising, 651–2
issuers, 35–6
issuers' liability, 653–4
placing, 35–6, 372
programmes, 372, 374, 411
prospectuses, 648–50
junk bonds, 35, 403, 765
listing, 650–1
mad bondholder problem, 382
meaning, 33
minority protection, 392–4
modifying trust deeds, 396–7
OTC trading, 375
plain vanilla bonds, 37, 372, 380, 648
prospectuses, 642, 647
put options, 37, 199
rating, 38
rationale, 27
regulation, 638
retail investors, 34, 648. 649, 674–5
returns, 772
schemes of arrangement, 394–6
securitisation, 426

short selling, 665–6
stock and, 375–7
structure, 379–91
subordination, 255, 648
syndicated loans and, 411–14
tradability, 382
transfer, 28, 423–4
trust structure, 88, 364, 380–90
  bearer bonds, 383–4
  no trustee structure, 390–1
  subject matter, 383
  trustee obligations, 396–410
trustees, 88
  duties, 364–5, 396–410
  exclusion of duty clauses, 403–10
  fiscal agents v trustees, 380
  no-action clauses, 381, 402–3, 412–13
  security trustees, 382
varieties, 36–9
zero coupon bonds, 37
bonus shares, 133, 495
book debts, 284, 300
borrowers: terminology, 3
British Venture Capital Association (BVCA),
  766, 796
Business Angels, 15
buy-back programmes, 598

Cadbury, 678, 714
call options, 33, 37, 216
Canada:
  comparative law, 1
  notice filing system, 350, 358
  schemes of arrangement, 742
capital:
  equity share capital: definition, 76
  legal capital *see* capital rules
  maintenance *see* capital maintenance
  permanent capital, 26–7
capital maintenance
  see also capital reduction
  creditor protection, 162, 171, 176–8
  distributions and, 52
  dividends and, 163–5
  financial assistance prohibition, 173–6
  objective, 148
  reduction of capital and, 170–3
  rules, 162–78
  share redemption and, 169
  share repurchase, 165–9
capital market regulation:
  asymmetric information, 485, 486, 487
  disclosure obligations, 489–93
  market abuse *see* market abuse
  objectives, 485–6, 487
  public offers of shares *see* IPOs; prospectuses
  secondary market *see* financial reporting; secondary
    markets
capital reduction:
  benefits, 170
  court approval, 171–2

creditor protection, 171
  private companies, 172–3
  reduction schemes, 748, 749, 753
  share distributions, 162
  shareholder protection, 171
  solvency statements, 172–3
capital rights:
  ordinary shares, 12, 63, 65
  preference shares, 66, 68
capital rules:
  banks, 25–6, 152–3, 425–6
  contractual requirements, 153
  creditor protection, 25–7, 83, 146–7, 152, 189
  creditor protection alternatives, 178–90
    contract, 178–80
    insolvency law, 180–3
    solvency statements, 183–90
  function, 146–51
  hybrid instruments, 51
  maintenance *see* capital maintenance
  meaning, 146
  minimum capital from shareholders, 151–3, 189
  objective, 146
  payment of shares, 153–62
  private equity, 798–9
  public policies, 148–50
  shareholder/creditor conflict, 146, 147
  UK regime, 150–1
cash flow test, 61, 96, 120, 185
Central Moneymarkets Office, 461
certainty principle, 348
charge-backs, 226–7, 288
charges:
  banks over accounts, 288
  charge-backs, 220, 226–7
  enforcement, 328, 330–1
    receivers, 331–3
  fixed *see* fixed charges
  floating *see* floating charges
  mortgages and, 287
  non-possessory security interests, 271
  registration, 205, 285
  security interests, 22, 287–8
charities, 2, 467, 771
Chinese Walls, 663–4
choses in action, 330, 368, 429
circulating assets, 268–9, 295, 305, 307
claim dilution, 82, 650
class actions, 344, 518
clearing house rules, 223–4, 229
Clearstream, 376, 385, 457
close-out netting, 224, 229–30, 231, 270, 275, 310
commercial paper:
  bonds and, 36
  CREST registration, 377
  issue, 372
  meaning, 21, 32
  structure, 379–91
  swinglines, 29
Committee of European Securities Regulators
  (CESR), 659

companies:
  19th century law, 71
  business categories, 3–4
  legal personality, 71, 116–18
  limited by guarantee, 2, 8
  limited liability, 9, 15–16, 116–17, 148, 151–3
  size, 4–5
  UK wide company law, 2
Company Law Review:
  capital reduction, 172
  directors' duties to creditors, 181
  financial assistance prohibition, 173, 174
  par value of shares, 154
  schemes of arrangement, 731, 742
  share allotment, 131
  wrongful trading, 120–1
company voluntary arrangements, 97, 98, 394–5, 740
competition, 21, 42, 263, 705
conditional sales, 45, 46, 48, 280, 323, 334, 335
conflicts of interest:
  agency conflicts, 82, 130, 371, 680, 711
  analysts, 574–6
  arrangers, 415
  corporate transactions, 531
  credit rating agencies, 670, 671
  mortgages, 330
  private equity, 782, 787, 800, 802
  syndicated loans, 415, 422
  takeovers, 679, 704, 726, 782
  trustees, 364, 407
  UK Stewardship Code, 539
contingent convertible securities (CoCos), 51
contingent debts, 171, 172, 184, 217, 224, 226, 229,
  260, 262, 395, 418, 736, 739
contingent fees, 519
contract:
  articles of association, 10, 72–3
  breach
    damages, 512
    penalties, 215–16
    rescission, 514–15
    security interests and, 343–4
  capital rules, 153
  compromises with creditors, 97
  construction *see* interpretation of contracts
  contractual subordination, 260–2
  covenants *see* covenants
  creditor protection, 3, 22, 23–5
    alternative to capital rules, 178–80
    drawbacks, 265
    rights against borrowers, 195–233
    solvent companies, 79, 191
  debt securities, 641, 653–5
  estoppel, 419–20
  exclusion clauses *see* exclusion clauses
  freedom of contract, 107, 109, 110, 192, 198, 230,
    276, 279, 293, 339
  interpretation *see* interpretation of contracts
  misrepresentation: prospectuses, 508
  novation *see* novation
  priority of proprietary interests over, 321

  secured creditors and, 343
  set-off *see* set-off
  shareholder theory, 10–11, 76
  sharia law and, 48–9
  standard forms, 194
  third parties and *see* third parties
  trust deeds and, 405, 407
convertible debt securities, 49, 50, 51, 156, 372, 667–8
Cork Report (1982), 231, 308, 740
corporate finance: meaning, 2–3, 8
corporate governance *see* governance
Corporate Governance Code, 477–8, 483, 488, 530–1
Corporate Reporting Review (CRR), 570
corporate veil *see* piercing corporate veil
corporation tax, 56, 775
covenants:
  acceleration clauses, 23, 214–18, 222, 266
  alternative to capital rules, 178–80
  bonds, 85, 658
  borrowing restrictions, 197
  breach
    automatic security clauses, 205–6
    enforcement, 202–6
    equity cure, 214–15
    lender influence, 88–91
    termination/acceleration, 213–18
  change of control, 199
  claim dilution and, 650
  creditor protection, 84–6, 87, 195–233
  cross-default clauses, 213
  debt buybacks, 200
  debt covenants, 195–233
  debt-equity ratios, 51, 380
  debt securities, 24, 196
  default interest clauses, 217
  dividend payments, 87, 198–9
  events of default, 87, 206, 209, 212, 213, 214–15
  free-riders, 85, 92, 179, 199, 341, 716
  information rights, 206–12, 658
  loans v debt securities, 34
  meaning, 23–4
  monitoring, 340–1
  negative pledges, 87, 197, 200–6, 202–6
  no-waiver clauses, 213
  non-adjusting creditors and, 179
  non-assignment *see* anti-assignment clauses
  non-disposal of assets, 87, 197–8
  number of lenders and, 84–5
  penalties, 215–16
  private equity securities, 778–9, 793
  set-off *see* set-off
credit card companies, 39, 647
credit default swaps:
  alternative to debt transfer, 466–7
  clearing obligation, 254
  credit enhancement, 23
  EU law, 622
  G20 agreement, 254
  mechanism, 248–9
  regulation, 252–4
  reporting obligation, 254

risk management, 247–8
short selling and, 665–6
whether insurance, 249–52
credit derivatives:
   alternative to debt transfer, 466–7
   close-out netting, 224
   creditor protection, 247–54
   effect on governance, 94
   lack of transparency, 94
   regulation, 638
   risk management, 247–8
   set-off, 218
   transfer of collateral arrangements, 275
   transfer of risk, 93
   types, 247
credit enhancement, 23
credit insurance *see* insurance
credit rating *see* rating
credit rating agencies, 573, 668–71
creditors:
   agency problems, 82
   asset preservation, 105–14
   capital maintenance and *see* capital maintenance
   capital rules and *see* capital rules
   categories, 80
   compromises with, 97
   contingent creditors, 739
   contract *see* contract
   corporate veil and *see* piercing corporate veil
   covenants *see* covenants
   credit risk, 635
   debt regulation and, 634
   directors' duties to, 114–16
   diversification, 81, 148–9
   governance and *see* governance
   insolvent companies and
      asset preservation, 105–14
      creditors v shareholders, 59–61, 114–22
      ranking *see* ranking of creditors
   lead creditors, 309, 341–2
   meaning, 3, 738–9
   non-adjusting *see* non-adjusting creditors
   pre-insolvency period
      alternative to capital rules, 181–2
      anti-deprivation principle, 107–9, 219–20, 233, 261–2
      asset preservation, 107–14
      unfair preferences, 110–13
   pre-paying customers, 80, 81
   private equity companies and, 791–3
   proprietary rights, 22, 79–80, 191
   ranking *see* ranking of creditors
   regulation, 25–7
   risk transfer, 93–4
   schemes of arrangement *see* schemes of arrangement
   secured creditors *see* debt securities; security interests
   share payment rules and, 161–2
   solvent companies and
      agency problems, 82

      asset pool reduction, 83
      claim dilution, 82, 650
      contractual rights, 79, 191
      creditor risks, 82–4
      governance role, 86–95
      non-adjusting creditors, 80–1
      position, 59–61
      pricing risk, 83
      proprietary rights, 79–80
      restriction on company activities, 84–6
      twilight period, 94–5
      underinvestment, 83
   takeover bids and, 716
   tax authorities, 80, 81
   third parties and *see* third parties
   trade creditors, 5, 79, 80–1, 343
creditors' voluntary liquidations (CVLs), 306
CREST:
   debt securities, 462–3
   dematerialisation of shares, 141–2
   eurobonds, 37, 455
   governance and, 533–4
   intermediated securities, 457, 460
   loan stock, 378
   members, 143
   mortgages and, 286
   registered securities, 376, 461
   set-off and, 225
   shares, 145, 455
   stock trading, 456
   transfer mechanism, 461–3
cross-default clauses, 213
crowdfunding, 17–18, 519–21, 672
crown jewels defence, 310, 697
Crown preference, 101, 345
currency:
   bonds, 37
   par value of shares, 153
   risk management, 247–8
   share payment, 156

damages:
   breach of contract, 512
   defective prospectuses, 502–3, 511–15
   inaccurate financial reporting, 565, 568
   insider dealing, 593–4
   market abuse, 615–16
Davies Report (2007), 564, 566, 571
debentures:
   debenture stock, 378, 404
   deposits, 667
   meaning, 404, 636–7, 651–2
   regulation, 635
debt buybacks, 200, 422
debt/equity ratios:
   covenants, 51, 380
   hybrid instruments, 51–2
   information covenants, 210–11
   internal finance, 57
   models, 55–8
   Modgliani-Miller theory, 55–6

private equity, 767, 773, 776, 788–93, 798, 801
securitisation and, 275
trade-off theory, 57
debt financing:
asset-based *see* asset-based finance
cash flow, 19
categories, 19–49
choice of transactions, 20–2
creditor protection, 22–7, 634
debt securities *see* debt securities
factors, 20–2
loans *see* loans
multiple lenders *see* multiple lenders
overview, 19–49
private equity, 20, 776–80
regulation, 634–76
    disclosure requirements, 638–41
    methods, 637–8
    scope, 635–7
shortage, 7
sources, 19–20, 777
transfer of debts *see* transfer of debts
debt securities:
ascertaining views of holders, 391–6
bonds *see* bonds; eurobonds
bonds v stock, 375–7
claim dilution, 650
contractual rights, 641, 653–5
convertible securities, 49, 50, 51, 156, 372, 667–8
covenants, 24, 196
decision-making process, 391–2
deed polls, 379, 390
default: trustees' duties, 398–403
disclosure requirements, 639–41
    claims against third parties, 654–5
    factors, 642–8
    loans v securities, 656–7
    new issues, 642–57
    private enforcement, 653–5
    prospectuses, 648–50
    PSM listing, 650–1
    rationale, 646–8
    secondary markets, 644–5
    targeted purchasers, 643–4
    unlisted securities, 651
equity financing and, 36, 640–1
eurobonds *see* eurobonds
fractional interests, 369
global notes, 376
government securities, 32
hybrid instruments *see* hybrid instruments
ICSDs, 376–7, 385–91, 392, 395, 457
information rights, 207–8
institutional investors, 19
intermediaries: pooled accounts, 142–3
issue
    advertising, 651–2
    arrangers, 373
    dealers, 373
    disclosure requirements, 639–57
    Eurobonds, 374

impact days, 374
information from issuers, 397–8
initial issues, 641–57
issuers, 35–6
issuers' liability, 653–4
Listing Rules, 642
managers, 373
mandate letters, 373
marketing, 373–4
placing, 372
price, 374, 375
process, 372–5
programmes, 372, 374, 411, 648
size of offers, 645
stabilisation, 374
subscription agreements, 373
survey, 372–410
target purchasers, 643–4
vanilla issues, 648
large companies, 5
listing, 375, 650–1
loans v securities, 33–4
    initial disclosures, 656–7
    ongoing disclosures, 660–1
market abuse, 374, 661–3
minority protection, 392–4
modifying trust deeds, 396–7
money markets, 32–3
no trustee structure, 390–1
notes, 33, 379–91
overview, 32–9
primary market, 32
prospectuses *see* prospectuses
rating, 207, 374–5
registration, 376
regulation, 25, 635–57
schemes of arrangement, 394–6
secondary markets, 32, 36, 372, 644–5
    lack of transparency, 659
short-selling, 665–6
stock *see* loan stock
structures, 375–91
subordination, 51, 255, 648
taxation, 36
tradability, 34, 36, 372, 424
transfer, 423–4, 456–63, 635
transferable securities: definition, 635
trust structure, 379–90
trustees' obligations, 396–410
    exclusion clauses, 403–10
types, 32–3, 372
deceit:
bond issues, 654
burden of proof, 561
defective prospectuses, 510–11, 512
lender protection, 656
locus standi, 510
meaning, 506, 509
deed polls, 379, 390, 456
demergers, 755–7
deposits, 20, 637, 666–7

derivatives *see* credit derivatives
directors:
  breach of covenants and, 89–91
  capital maintenance, 52
  criminal offences
    financial assistance, 175
    share allotment, 131
    solvency statements, 168, 172, 173, 186–7
  debt securities: disclosures, 658–9
  D&O insurance, 502
  duties
    to creditors, 114–16, 180–2
    enforcement, 361
    fiduciary *see* fiduciaries
    insolvency, 114–16
    minority shareholders, 742
    new share issues, 126–7
    public companies, 477–8
    shareholder enforcement, 361, 536
    shareholders' interests, 69–70, 149, 530, 791
    stakeholder interests, 69, 86, 114, 149, 180
    statutory duties, 69–70
  election, 531
  financial reporting *see* financial reporting
  fraud, 82
  fraudulent trading *see* fraudulent trading
  guarantees, 80
  insider dealing, 579, 581, 616
  insolvency and, 95, 114–16
  lenders as directors, 91–2
  liabilities
    defective prospectuses, 511, 516
    strategic reports, 545
    unlawful dividends, 165
  loans to companies, 80
  non-executive directors, 86, 87, 88, 476, 477–8,
    775, 786
  powers
    dividends, 163, 165
    misuse, 126
    new share allotment, 9, 126, 131–2, 138
    share redemption, 169
  private equity, 782, 785, 786–7
  related party transactions, 78, 531, 532, 555
  removal, 77–8, 90–1, 700–1
  remuneration, 581, 701
  remuneration reports, 531, 545, 547–8, 701
  reports, 544
  risks from, 82
  self-dealing, 529, 556, 710
  shadow directors, 91–2, 93
  share options, 476
  shareholdings, 492
    dealings, 583–4, 586–7
    disclosure, 551–2
    private equity, 785
  solvency statements *see* solvency statements
  staggered boards, 700–1
  takeover bids and, 531, 679
    directors' opinions, 704–5, 782
    post-bid defences, 705–12

    pre-bid defences, 696–704
    protests, 684
    staggered boards, 700–1
    target directors v shareholders, 695–712
    target directors v stakeholders, 698, 712–16, 790
  wrongdoing: shareholder ratification, 78
  wrongful trading, 91, 96, 105, 118, 119–22
disposal of assets:
  consent, 266
  floating charges and, 289
  non-disposal covenants, 87, 197–8
  preventing asset pool reduction, 83, 105
    anti-deprivation principle, 107–9, 219–20, 233,
     261–2
    creditor protection, 106–9, 181
    statutory provisions, 106–7
    unfair preferences and, 111–13
    undervalue transactions, 106
distress for rent, 325
distressed debt, 28, 425
dividends *see* share distributions

efficient market prices:
  algorithmic trading and, 632
  efficient capital markets hypothesis (ECMH), 490,
    524–7, 573, 614
  insider dealing and, 583
  mandatory disclosures and, 527–8
emissions allowances, 588
employees:
  capital rules and, 179–80
  compulsory employer insurance, 344
  preferential creditors, 101, 179–80, 303
  private equity companies, 790–1
  security interests and, 345
  shares schemes, 133
  takeover bids and, 713, 715–16
equitable assignments, 430–3, 436, 440–1
equitable interests:
  assignment, 433–4
  transfer, 371, 378, 458–9
  trusts, 370–1
equity analysts, 572–6, 596, 619
equity crowdfunding, 17–18, 519–21
equity cure, 214–15
equity finance:
  crowdfunding, 18
  debt securities or, 36, 640–1
  hybrid instruments *see* hybrid instruments
  minimum capital, 9
  options, 4–5, 9
  private equity *see* private equity
  shares *see* shares
  sources, 14–18
  survey, 8–18
estoppel, 419–20
EURIBOR, 588
eurobonds:
  ascertaining views of holders, 391–6
  CREST transfer, 37, 455
  global notes, 384–90

international finance, 37–8
issue, 374
negative pledges, 202
no trustee structure, 390–1
quoted eurobonds, 375
structure, 376, 379–91
tax withholding, 375
trust structure, 380–90
   advantages, 380–2
   bearer bonds, 383–4
   subject matter, 383
   trustee obligations, 396–410
Euroclear, 141, 376, 385, 457, 533–4
European Banking Authority, 672
European Central Bank, 385
European Convention on Human Rights, 595
European Securities and Market Authorities (ESMA):
   algorithmic trading and, 632
   functions, 254
   price stabilisation, 663
   private equity and, 801
   short selling and, 623, 629–30
European Systemic Risk Board, 629, 801
European Union:
   algorithmic trading, 632–3
   analysts, 575
   capital rules, 148–9, 150, 152, 154–5, 189
   Company Law Action Plan, 189–90
   credit derivatives, 94, 254, 275, 622
   credit rating regulation, 670–1
   equity trading, 455
   financial assistance prohibition, 174
   financial collateral arrangements, 270, 310
   financial reporting
      activism, 571
      corporate governance statements, 546
      directors' shareholdings, 551
      impact, 557
      inside information, 550
      liabilities, 562
      major shareholders, 553
      mandatory disclosures, 541
      periodic reports, 542–3, 546–7
      related party transactions, 555
   hedge funds, 764
   increased regulation, 7
   legal relevance, 1
   listing rules, 482, 493
   market abuse, 578, 587–8, 589, 603
      insider dealing, 580–1, 582–4
      market manipulation, 608, 610, 611–12
      sanctions, 662
      short selling, 621, 622–30
   new share issues, 130
   pre-emption rights, 136
   private equity, 764, 772
      AIFMD, 798–803
      disclosures, 787–8, 791, 800–1
   prospectuses, 1, 494, 497, 500, 668
   public offers of shares, 493–4
   securitisation, 471

share payment, 156, 157
share value, 154–5
shareholder protection, 139
solvency statements and, 183
solvency test, 185
sovereign debt crisis, 623
takeovers, 680, 681, 684–5, 702, 704, 717, 722
Eurozone, 385
exclusion clauses:
   construction, 405–7
   debt securities, 403–10
   forms, 403–5
   public policy and, 405, 407–10
   syndicated loans, 416–17, 418, 419, 420
   unfair contract terms, 407, 419, 654, 660

factoring, 41, 274, 336, 426, 452–3
false statements:
   bond issues, 653–4
   financial reporting, 558–72
   lender protection, 656–7
   market manipulation *see* market manipulation
   prospectuses, 500–15
   syndicated loans, 417–20
   takeover bids, 691
feudalism, 363
fiduciaries:
   directors' duties, 114
      insider dealing and, 616
      insolvency, 106
      insolvent companies, 106
      pricing shares, 154
      private equity takeovers, 782
      takeover bids and, 700, 708
   lenders as, 92–3
   security trustees, 380, 396–410, 420
   syndicated loan arrangers, 414–17
   trustees, 364–5, 380
finance leases:
   absolute or security interests, 280
   forfeiture, 334, 335
   long-funded leases, 45
   mechanism, 44–5
   ranking of creditors, 98
   small companies, 20
   taxation, 45
financial assistance prohibition, 173–6, 781
financial collateral arrangements:
   administration and, 338
   appropriation, 329–30
   confused law, 349
   EU law, 270, 310
   overview, 269–70, 310–16
   regulation technique, 638
   sub-participation, 465
   terminology, 282
Financial Conduct Authority (FCA):
   capital rules, 26
   Code of Market Conduct, 601, 602, 603
   credit default swaps and, 249, 251, 252
   debt regulation, 637, 638, 651

defective prospectuses: sanctions, 516–17
equity crowdfunding and, 520–1
financial reporting, 566, 569–70
fund management regulation, 768
Handbook, 494
  compliance, 637
  transparency, 140
immunity, 688
insider dealing, 594, 602, 603
Listing Rules *see* Listing Rules
market abuse
  approach, 595
  remedies, 594, 600, 615
  Rules, 663
market manipulation: enforcement, 610, 611–13
peer-to-peer lending and, 672–4
price stabilisation rules and, 596
private equity takeovers, 784
prospectus vetting, 488, 499
takeovers and, 686
turnover trusts, 259
UK Listing Authority, 482, 494, 560
financial crisis:
  administration numbers, 332
  asset-based lending and, 43
  bank share issues, 130, 132
  credit default swaps and, 253–4
  credit rating agencies and, 669–70
  effects, 7
  financial regulation and, 518
  intermediaries and, 573
  new forms of financing and, 24–5
  private equity and, 764, 767, 771, 777, 780
  secondary debt securities market and, 659
  short selling and, 618
Financial Ombudsman, 674
financial reporting:
  accounts *see* accounts
  annual reports *see* annual reports
  debt securities, 635, 638–41
    ad hoc disclosures, 658–9
    enforcement, 659–60
    periodic disclosures, 658
    rationale, 657–8
    requirements, 657–9
  equities
    ad hoc disclosures, 548–57, 564
    directors' shareholdings, 551–2
    enforcement, 558–72
    equities, 541–57
    EU law, 541, 550, 557, 562, 571
    major shareholders, 552–5
    major transactions, 531–2, 556
    objectives, 524–40
    periodic disclosures, 542–8
    related party transactions, 555
  equity enforcement, 558–72
    level, 570–2
    private enforcement, 558–68
    public enforcement, 569–70
  governance objective

civil liabilities, 558–60
  obligations, 556–7
  rationale, 539–40
IFRS, 649
inside information, 548–51
limitations, 586–7
Listing Rules requirements, 555–7
market abuse and, 570
market efficiency and, 527–8
market manipulation *see* market manipulation
private enforcement
  damages, 565
  defendants, 565
  equities, 558–68
  fraud, 562–8
  governance-based disclosures, 558–60
  investor-focused disclosures, 560–8
  level, 571–2
  s 90A FSMA, 562–8
private equity companies, 787–8
public enforcement
  Corporate Reporting Review, 570
  equities, 570–1
  FCA, 569–70
  lack of enforcement, 571
short selling, 617–18, 624–6
value, 591
voluntary reporting, 528
Financial Reporting Council, 539, 570
Financial Services Compensation Scheme (FSCS), 673
Financial Stability Board, 797
fixed assets, 43, 268–9
fixed charges:
  administration and, 337
  charged assets, 296–8
  consent to disposal of assets, 266
  control power, 298–302
  floating charges or, 272, 273, 277, 288
    characterising methodology, 302
    defining features, 295–302
    different treatment, 302–3
    distinction, 295–310, 349
    ranking, 302–5
  meaning, 22
  negative pledges and, 288–9
  non-disposal covenants, 198
  private equity, 778
  ranking, 287, 306–7
flawed assets, 108–9, 219–20
floating charges:
  abolishing, 304
  administration and, 290, 309, 327, 331–2, 333, 337
  benefits, 289–90, 304, 309
  carrying on business in ordinary way, 295–6
  charged assets, 296–8
  collateral, 315
  control power, 266, 298–302, 309
  crystallisation, 290–4
    law reform, 354
  decrystallisation, 293–4, 301
  disposal of assets, 289

fixed charges or, 272, 273, 277, 288
　characterising methodology, 302
　defining features, 295–302
　different treatment, 302–3
　distinction, 295–310, 349
　pre-insolvency period, 308
　ranking, 302–5
future, 308–10
judicial interpretation, 294
law reform, 357
meaning, 22
negative pledges, 200
pre-insolvency period, 308
private equity, 778
ranking of creditors, 99–105, 302–5, 323–5
　statutory trigger for priority, 306–7
security interests, 288–310
set-off and, 219, 325
unattractive structure, 274
unsecured creditors and, 99, 289–90, 295
foreclosure, 286, 287, 329, 355
forfeiture, 334–6
forwards, 247
fraud:
　bond issues, 654
　directors, 82
　fraud on the market theory, 614–16
　insider dealing, 490, 594
　insolvency distributions, 108
　issuers, 573
　market abuse, 613–16
　market manipulation, 585, 595–600
　performance bonds, 245
　piercing corporate veil, 117
　private equity, 800
　prospectuses, 507
　public companies, 487
　　disclosure, 548–9
　　financial reporting, 562–8
　strategic reports and, 545
　syndicated loans, 419
　trading *see* fraudulent trading
fraudulent misrepresentation:
　market abuse, 613–14
　prospectuses, 504, 513
fraudulent trading, 105, 118–19, 121–2, 148, 173, 176, 187
future property, 19, 283–5, 287, 288, 348, 436
futures, 247

G20, 7, 254
gaming contracts, 249
gatekeepers, 573
GEFIM, 455, 645–6, 656, 658, 662, 667–8
Geneva Securities Convention, 389
Germany: takeovers, 680, 713
gifts: undervalue transactions, 106
global notes, 376, 384–90
good faith:
　agency, 371
　bondholders, 392–3

contract, 195
directors, 69, 126, 165, 791
majority shareholders, 392, 422
mortgagees, 331
receivers, 332–3
takeovers and, 724
trustees, 408, 409
utmost good faith, 238, 246, 250, 252, 415
governance:
　corporate governance statements, 546
　creditors' role, 86–95
　　breach of covenants, 88–91
　　debt covenants, 87
　　debt securities, 658
　　dividends, 87
　　efficiency issue, 92–3
　　monitoring, 88
　　private equity and, 792–3
　　shadow directors, 91–2
　　transfer of risk, 93–4
　　twilight period, 94–5
　directors' shareholdings and, 552
　financial reporting and
　　civil liabilities, 558–60
　　debt securities, 658
　　obligations, 556–7
　　rationale, 529–40
　pre-emption rights and, 138, 183, 532
　private equity companies, 77, 786, 792–3
　public companies, 476, 488, 529–40
　　mandatory disclosures and, 539–40
　public v private companies, 476
　shareholders' role, 77–8, 86, 530–3
　　enforcement of directors' obligations, 361, 536, 558–60
　　financial reporting and, 556–7
　　individual investors, 533
　　institutional investors, 535–9
　　intermediaries, 533–5
　　public companies, 529–40
　　UK Stewardship Code, 539
　takeovers and, 710–12
　UK Corporate Governance Code, 477–8, 483, 488, 530–1, 536, 539, 546
group companies:
　financing, 47–8
　guarantors, 80
　intra-group transfers of assets, 198
　reorganisation schemes, 753–4
　structural subordination, 262
　subordination, 255
　taxation, 234
guarantees:
　construction, 238
　credit enhancement, 23, 248
　directors' guarantees, 80
　discharge, 239–41
　disclosures, 238–9
　indemnities and, 241–2
　indulgence clauses, 241
　private equity, 778

small companies, 23
subrogation, 239
surety guarantees, 235–41
third party protection, 238–41
Guernsey, 768

hedge funds, 20, 143, 402, 622–3, 660, 764, 769–71, 797–8, 800
hedging, 248
herding, 526
high frequency trading, 529–30, 588, 609, 631–3
hire purchase:
  absolute or security interests, 280
  bona fide purchasers and, 274
  forfeiture, 334, 335
  mechanism, 44, 45
  ranking of creditors, 98
  small companies, 20
  stock finance, 46
Hong Kong, 751
hybrid instruments, 372
  capital adequacy rules and, 51
  convertible securities, 49, 50, 51, 156, 372, 667–8
  maturity dates, 51
  overview, 49–52
  preference shares, 49–50
  rating, 51
  subordination, 51–2, 79, 255
  taxation, 50
  tier two capital, 27
  twilight zone, 36

immoral activities, 48
impact days, 374
implied terms, 194–5, 405–6
indemnities, 235–7, 241–4
India: schemes of arrangement, 742
information:
  capital market regulation, 489–93
  costs, 498
  covenants *see* information covenants
  debt securities, 207–8, 397–8
    covenants, 206–12, 658
    issues, 373–4, 641–57
    loans v securities, 656–7
    ongoing disclosures, 657–61
  ECMH and, 525–7
  equity crowdfunding, 520
  financial reporting *see* financial reporting
  inside information
    see also insider dealing
    definition, 588, 590–2, 604–7
    disclosure, 548–51, 593
  loans, 663–5
  multiple lending, 361
  private equity, 795–7
  prospectuses *see* prospectuses
  public offers of shares *see* IPOs
  Recognised Information Services (RISs), 541, 549, 555, 556, 566, 569
  security interests and, 348

syndicated loans, 415, 417–20
  takeover bids, 715
information covenants:
  accounting methods, 210–11
  financial covenants, 206–12, 658
  initial lenders' rights, 207–9
  material adverse changes, 211–12
  ongoing rights, 209–12
  promissory v contingent conditions, 208–9
  rating changes, 211
  ratios, 210–11
  representations and warranties, 208
initial public offers of shares *see* IPOs
injunctions, 203, 205, 245, 291, 360, 440, 448, 594, 600
inside information, 548–51, 588, 590–3, 604–7
insider dealing:
  administrative offence, 591, 601–8
  attempts, 588–9
  compensation, 593–4
  convictions, 594
  criminal offence, 589–95
    actual dealing, 592–3
    disclosing inside information, 593
    encouraging dealing, 593
  defences, 592–3
  disclosure of inside information, 548–51
  enforcement levels, 594–5
  EU law, 580–1, 582–4
  FCA Code of Market Conduct, 602, 603
  inside information: definition, 588, 590–2, 604–7
  insiders: meaning, 589–90, 603–4
  investor confidence, 582–4
  limits of disclosures, 586–7
  loans, 663–4
  meaning, 579
  mens rea, 592, 594, 600, 602, 607–8
  non-public information, 590–1
  penalties, 593
  price impact, 591–2, 606–7
  primary insiders, 589
  private enforcement, 615–16
  regulation, 490, 529
    arguments against, 581–2
    arguments for, 579–81
    market-based approach, 582–4
    relationship v market based, 579–81
  secondary insiders, 589
  specific information, 590, 605–6
  takeovers and, 594, 692
  victimless crime, 581, 583
  zero-sum game, 582
insolvency:
  acceleration clauses and, 217–18
  administration *see* administration
  asset-based test, 185–6
  asset preservation, 105–14
  balance sheet test, 61, 80, 96, 120, 176
  cash flow test, 61, 96, 120, 185
  creditors v shareholders, 95–123
  distribution of assets *see* ranking of creditors
  expenses: funding, 305–6, 309

insolvency law or capital rules, 180–3
   meaning, 95–7
   piercing corporate veil, 116–22
   proprietary interests and, 191, 264
   ranking *see* ranking of creditors
   rescue, 97–8
   schemes of arrangement and, 736
   set-off *see* set-off
   solvency statements *see* solvency statements
   subordination and, 255–6, 260–2
   tests, 120, 184–6
   twilight period *see* pre-insolvency period
   winding-up *see* liquidations
institutional investors:
   CREST members, 143
   debt securities, 19
   eurobonds, 38
   financial reporting and, 572
   fund management, 554
   governance role, 535–9
   Myners Report (2001), 772
   new share issues and, 10
   non-listed securities and, 375
   placing shares with, 481
   pre-emption rights and, 137, 183
   private equity investors, 771, 795
   takeovers and, 537, 702–3
   voting rights, 554
insurance:
   companies, 19, 34, 771, 795
   compulsory insurance, 117–18, 179, 344, 345
   credit default swaps and, 249–52
   credit insurance, 23, 245–7
   definition, 250
   D&O insurance, 502
   IBNR claims, 761–2
   regulation, 249, 252
   schemes of arrangement, 761–2
   third party rights, 81
   tort claims, 81, 117–18
   utmost good faith, 250
intangible property:
   equity securities, 490
   pledges, 282
   security interests, 282
   shares, 72
   tangible property and, 267–8
   trusts of, 367–9
intellectual property, 43, 268, 317
interest:
   breach of covenants and, 89
   default interest clauses, 217
   Islamic finance and, 48
   secured credit, 340
interest rate swaps, 247
intermediaries:
   debt securities, 377, 433
   gatekeepers, 573
   governance of public companies and, 533–5
   regulation, 485, 637–8
   right to use securities, 370

   shareholding, 142–3
   transfer of intermediated securities, 457–61
   voting rights, 553
international central securities depositaries (ICSDs),
   376–7, 385–91, 392, 395, 457
International Financial Reporting Standards
   (IFRS), 649
International Organization of Securities Commissions
   (IOSCO), 575
International Swaps and Derivatives Association
   (ISDA), 224, 249, 250
interpretation of contracts:
   anti-assignment clauses, 434–5, 438–9
   basic principle, 192–3
   business common sense, 405
   duty exclusion clauses, 405–7
   good faith, 195
   implied terms, 194–5, 405–6
   meaning of words, 193–4
   standard forms, 194
   survey, overview
Investment Association, 132
investment banks, 361, 373, 480–1, 574, 575, 639–40,
   651, 670
invoice discounting, 38, 40–2, 274, 277, 297, 336, 426,
   453, 454
IPOs:
   change of company status, 479
   costs, 477
   disclosure obligations, 642
      asymmetric information, 485, 486, 487, 490
      costs, 477
      enforcement, 499–519
      exemptions, 495–6
      ongoing obligations, 489
      prospectuses *see* prospectuses
      rationale, 489–93
   ex-post enforcement, 504–22
   exit for existing shareholders, 474–5
   IPO process, 478–84
   methods, 479–81
   offers for sale, 479–80
   options, 5
   placing, 480–1
   pros and cons, 473–8
   regulation
      affiliation strategies, 489, 638
      European Union, 493–4
      governance strategies, 488
      justification, 486–7
      objectives, 485–6, 487
      theory, 485–93
      UK regulation, 493–9
   share price, 480
   size of offers, 496
   subscription, 479–80
   survey, 473–522
   UK regulation
      exemptions, 495–6
      overview, 493–9
      prospectuses *see* prospectuses

scope, 495–6
    structure, 493–4
  underwriting, 480
irrational behaviour, 526–7
ISDA Master Agreement, 224, 249
Islamic finance, 22, 48–9

Jersey, 134, 351, 358, 768
joint stock companies, 71
junk bonds, 35, 403, 765

Kalder-Hicks test, 339

land, 43, 268, 317, 363
Law Commission:
  notice filing system, 351, 358
  securities, 348
  trustee exclusion clauses, 404, 407, 410
lead creditors, 309, 341–2
leases:
  finance leases, 20, 44–5, 98, 280, 334, 335
  Islamic finance, 48
  operating leases, 44, 274, 335, 336, 351
  sale and leaseback, 44, 278
legal capital rules *see* capital rules
legal personality, 71, 116–18, 768
lenders: terminology, 3
leveraged buy-outs, 15, 30, 765, 766, 781
LIBOR, 450, 588, 595–6, 599, 613
liens, 22, 81, 271, 779
limited liability:
  capital rules and, 148, 151–3
  exceptions, 148
  principle, 9, 15–16, 116–17
limited liability partnerships, 2
limited partnerships, 768–70
liquidations:
  administration and, 98
  by creditors, 70
  creditors' voluntary liquidations (CVLs), 306
  demergers, 756
  disposal of assets before, 107
  distributions and, 64
  expenses, 100–1, 305, 305–6
  floating charges and, 290
  late registration of security interests and, 317
  litigation: consent by floating charge holders, 100, 305
  meaning, 97
  ordinary shares and, 65
  preference shares and, 66
  ranking of creditors, 97–105, 736
  retrieving assets, 181
  schemes of arrangement and, 756, 762
  shareholders' powers, 78
  unregistered charges, 318
liquidity transformation, 797
listing:
  admission, 481–4
  choice of international markets, 17, 483–4
  choice of UK markets, 482–3

debt securities, 375, 650–1
effect, 5
EU law, 482, 493
FCA control, 482, 488, 494
listed v traded securities, 481, 482
Listing Rules *see* Listing Rules
regulation costs, 477
Listing Rules:
  annual reports, 478
  debt securities: disclosures, 642
  discount on new shares, 134
  FCA control, 482
  mandatory disclosures, 555–7
    major transactions, 531–2, 556
    related party transactions, 555
  pre-emption rights, 136–7, 536–7
  renounceable letters of allotment, 135
  share repurchase, 167
  UK Corporate Governance Code and, 536
litigation costs, 100, 122, 305, 519, 568, 572
Loan Market Association (LMA):
  Agreements, 24, 196, 200, 255, 413, 445, 447, 448, 451, 657, 660
  debentures and, 637
  guidelines, 664–5
loan notes, 775–6, 779
loan stock:
  asset-based lending, 43
  bonds and, 375–7
  debenture stock, 378, 404
  debts owed to trustees, 376, 377–8
  deed polls, 379
  eurobonds and, 37–8
  finance, 46
  overview, 377–9
  registration, 376
  secured loan stock, 378
  transfer, 456–7
  use by intermediaries, 143
loan transfer:
  assignment, 445, 450–2
  methods, 445
  novation, 445, 446–50
  restrictions on transfer, 447–8
  situations, 445
  sub-participation, 423, 445, 446, 463–6
  survey, 445–52
loans:
  acceleration, 89
  bank loans, 28–30
    bills of exchange, 29–30
    committed facilities, 29
    facility letters, 29
    on-demand, 28–9
    overdrafts, 28–9
    repayment methods, 29
  covenants, 89, 196
  debentures and, 636, 652
  debt buybacks, 200
  debt securities v loans, 33–4
    initial disclosures, 656–7
    ongoing disclosures, 660–1

insider dealing, 663–4
large companies, 5
market abuse, 663–5
multiple lenders *see* multiple lenders
option, 28–32
peer-to-peer lending, 20, 31–2, 671–4
regulation, 635, 652
revolving facilities, 21, 29, 89, 91, 214, 426, 777
secondary market, 600–1, 664
shareholder loans: ranking, 104–5
standard agreements, 657
stock *see* loan stock
syndicated *see* syndicated loans
term loans, 29
termination, 89
transfer *see* loan transfer
local authorities, 325
London approach, 94–5
London Stock Exchange:
  AIM, 17, 482, 658
  bond market, 37–8
  GEFIM, 455, 645–6, 656, 658, 662, 667–8
  Main Market, 17, 482–3, 658, 667
  ORB platform, 34
  Pre-Emption Group, 703
  private equity, 772
  PSM, 645, 646, 649, 650–1, 658–9, 662, 668
  short-selling and, 620
  Takeover Code and, 682
  Takeover Panel membership, 683
  transfer of regulation to FCA, 560

management buy-ins, 43, 766
management buy-outs, 15, 43, 679, 711, 766, 782, 783
market abuse
  see also short selling
  administrative offences, 600–13
  algorithmic trading and, 632
  criminal offences, 589–600
  debt securities, 374, 661–3
  emissions allowances and, 588
  EU law, 578, 587–8, 589, 603, 662
  FCA Code of Market Conduct, 601, 602, 603
  fraud on the market, 614–16
  insider dealing *see* insider dealing
  justifying regulation, 579–86
  limits of disclosures, 586–7
  loans, 663–5
  manipulation *see* market manipulation
  mens rea, 600
  private enforcement, 613–16
  private equity takeovers, 783–4
  regulation, 578–616
  remedies, 594
  safe harbours, 374, 608, 662–3
  short selling, 620–1
market manipulation:
  administrative offence, 600–1, 608–13
  attempts, 589
  burden of proof, 600

concealment of facts, 596–7
criminal offence, 515–16, 595–600
damages, 614–15
definition, 584–6, 595, 596–9
enforcement level, 600, 611–13
EU law, 608, 610, 611–12
forms, 584
intentions, 585–6, 597, 598, 600
justifying regulation, 584–6
LIBOR, 588, 595–6, 599, 613
manipulation of benchmarks, 595–6, 599
meaning, 579
misleading financial reporting, 570, 579
misleading impressions, 598–9, 609–10
misleading statements, 596–7
negligence, 610
penalties, 600, 612
price stabilisation rules and, 585, 586, 596, 599, 608, 662–3
safe harbour, 608
short selling, 620–1
market rigging, 597
maturity transformation, 797
mergers:
  covenant restrictions, 87, 199, 778
  mandatory disclosures and, 540
  meaning, 754–5
  payment of shares, 157
  schemes of arrangement, 529, 753–5
merit regulation, 488
mezzanine debt, 773, 779–80
minority shareholders:
  claims against directors, 501
  demergers, 756
  litigation, 69
  schemes of arrangement, 729, 742, 750–2
  share issues, 128–9
  takeover bids and, 717, 722–6, 750–2
  unfair prejudice petitions, 74–5, 129, 723–4
misrepresentation:
  articles of association and, 72–3
  credit insurance, 246
  prospectuses, 507–11
  shareholder claims, 103
  syndicated loans, 417–20
mistake: articles of association and, 73
monitoring:
  bond trustees, 380, 397–8
  costs, 341
  covenants, 88, 92–3, 340–1
  free-riders, 85, 92, 341
  security interests, 340–2
moral hazard, 240, 245, 251, 253, 501, 581
mortgages:
  charges and, 287
  enforcement, 329–31
  equitable mortgages, 286–7, 378
  foreclosure, 329
  future assets, 287
  legal mortgages, 286–7
  non-possessory security interests, 271

possession and sale, 328, 330–1
receivership, 331
redemption, 286
security interests, 286–7
shares, 286
multiple lenders:
  agents, 371
  covenants, 84–5
  debt securities *see* debt securities
  information mechanisms, 361
  issues, 360–2
  methods, 30
  structures, 360–1
  subordination, 28, 30, 360
  syndicated loans *see* syndicated loans
  transfer of debt, 27–8, 361
  trusts *see* trusts
mutual funds, 2

National Health Service: pharmacies, 42
negative pledges:
  absolute v security interests, 274
  debt covenants, 197, 200–6
  effect of breach, 201
  enforcement, 202–6
  fixed charges and, 288–9
  floating charges, 200
  forms, 202
  law reform, 354
  private equity, 778
  registration and, 320
negligence:
  burden of proof, 506, 654
  credit rating agencies, 671
  exclusion clauses, 407–10, 416
  financial reporting, 545, 559, 561–8
  market manipulation, 610
  prospectuses, 507, 511–14, 655
  proximity, 509
  pure economic loss, 507
  securitisation, 468
  wrongful trading, 119
negotiable instruments, 282, 443–5
nemo dat quod non habet, 321, 323, 444, 460
Netherlands: takeovers, 680, 713
netting, 24, 196, 218, 223–4, 229–31, 270, 275, 310,
  458, 459, 460
New Zealand:
  comparative law, 1
  notice filing system, 350, 353, 356, 358
  ranking of creditors, 307
  solvency statements, 185
no-action clauses, 381, 402–3, 412–13
non-adjusting creditors:
  capital rules and, 179–80
  covenants and, 179, 199
  insolvency law and, 634
  private equity and, 792
  security interests and, 342–7
  solvent companies and, 80–1
  takeovers and, 716

tort claims, 80, 81
  veil piercing and, 117, 182
non-executive directors, 86, 87, 88, 476, 477–8,
  775, 786
Northern Ireland, 1
notes, 33, 379–91
notice filing system, 350–8
novation:
  assignment and, 428
  consent in advance, 446
  loan transfer, 445, 446–50
  meaning, 427
  reasonable consent, 448–9, 451
  restrictions on transfer, 447–8
  securitisation and, 468
  security for loan, 448
  stock transfer, 456
  subject to equities, 450
  transfer certificates, 446
  transfer of securities, 462
novation netting, 223–4, 229

online platforms, 25, 34
operating leases, 44, 274, 335, 336, 351
opportunity costs, 159–60
options, 247
ordinary shares:
  capital rights, 12, 63, 65
  distributions, 11–12, 63–4, 65
  features, 11–12
  flexibility, 12
  preference shares and, 68
  small companies, 12
  voting rights, 12, 64–5
OTC trading, 38, 455
overdafts, 21, 28–9
ownership: concept, 271

pari passu principle:
  contingent debts and, 260
  contractual subordination and, 260–1
  insolvency set-off and, 227–30, 233
  set-off and, 110
partnerships, 2, 9, 11, 14, 48, 52–3, 77–8, 724, 768–70
patents, 317
peer-to-peer lending, 20, 31–2, 671–4
pension funds, 19, 34
performance bonds, 23, 235–7, 243–5
personal property, 268
piercing corporate veil:
  common law mechanisms, 116–18
  fraudulent trading, 118–19, 121–2
  insolvent companies, 116–22, 187
  law reform, 182
  statutory mechanisms, 118–22
  wrongful trading, 119–22
pipelines, 47
plant and machinery, 43, 44, 297, 301–2
pledges:
  negative pledges *see* negative pledges
  non registration, 320

possessory security interests, 22, 282
security interests, 271
terminology, 282
poison pills, 697, 699–700, 702–4
portfolio companies *see* private equity
possession, 267–8, 269
possession and sale, 330–1
Pre-Emption Group, 9–10
pre-emption rights:
    cash transactions, 133
    cashbox structure, 134–5
    compensatory open offers, 139
    disapplying, 9, 17, 136–7, 702–3
    discounts, 134
    exemptions, 133
        bonus shares, 133
        employees' share schemes, 133
        non-cash consideration, 160
    governance and, 138, 183, 532
    Listing Rules, 136–7, 536–7
    objectives, 487
    renounceable letters of allotment, 135
    scope, 133–5
    shareholder protection, 132–9, 160
    Statement of Principles, 137
    takeover bids and, 702–3
    UK regulation, 130
    vendor placings and, 134
    waiver, 136–7
pre-insolvency period:
    asset preservation, 107–14
    creditor protection, 113–14, 181–2
    creditors' role, 94–5
    floating charges, 308
    preventing uneven distribution of assets, 110–13
    twilight period, 61–2
preference shares:
    accounting, 50
    capital rights, 66, 68
    distributions, 13–14, 50, 65, 67
    features, 13–14
    hybrid instruments, 49–50
    ordinary shares and, 68
    private equity and, 775
    ranking, 50
    rights in solvent companies, 67–8, 70
    voting rights, 13, 67–8
price stabilisation rules, 585, 586, 596, 599, 608, 662–3
primary markets *see* IPOs
prime brokers, 143
private companies:
    capital reduction, 172–3
    capital rules, 151, 152
    equity capital, 9
    exit options, 474–5
    financial assistance, 781
    lack of liquidity, 475, 481
    options, 4–5
    public v private companies, 473–8
    regulation, 487
    share allotment, 131

share repurchase, 167–9
share transfer, 144
shares: liquidity, 4, 16
private equity:
    asset stripping, 802
    capital structure, 773–80
        debt/equity ratios, 767, 773, 776, 788–93,
            798, 801
        debt financing, 20, 776–80
        equity financing, 774–5
        mezzanine debt, 773, 779–80
        quasi-equity, 775–6
        second lien debts, 779
        senior debt, 777–9
    covenants, 778–9, 793
    empirical studies, 794
    EU regulation, 764, 772
        AIFMD, 798–803
        disclosures, 787–8, 791
        effect, 794–5
    financial crisis and, 764, 767, 771, 777, 780
    fraud, 800
    free cash flow, 785
    fund management, 768
    governance, 77, 786, 792–3
    growth, 764, 767, 776–7
    hedge funds and, 769–71
    history, 765–7
    investors' motivations, 772–3
    limited partnerships, 768–70
    liquidity, 785
    loan notes, 775–6
    meaning, 765, 766–7
    minimum subscriptions, 771–2
    public companies and
        board structures, 786–7
        comparisons, 784–94
        creditors, 791–3
        debt/equity ratios, 788–93
        employees, 790–1
        ownership structures, 784–6
        transparency obligations, 787–8, 795–8
    public-to-private takeovers
        bidders' equality, 782–3
        directors' recommendations, 782
        financing, 781–2
        issues, 780–4
        market abuse, 783–4
        shareholder equality, 783
    regulation, 772
        AIFMD, 798–803
        authorisation requirements, 798–9
        capital rules, 798–9
        compliance costs, 803
        disclosures, 800–1
        effect, 780, 794–5, 802–3
        fund level, 798–801
        need, 795–8
        overview, 794–803
        portfolio company level, 801–2
        protection of stakeholders, 790–2, 796, 802

risk management, 800–1
  systemic risk, 797–8, 801, 802
  transparency gap, 795–7
retail investors, 771–2
returns, 772–3, 784
schemes of arrangement, 780
securities, 778
shelf companies, 778
sources of funds, 771–2, 795
structure of funds, 768–71
subordinated finance, 262, 777
success, 793
survey, 764–803
syndicated loans, 779
taxation, 769, 775, 788, 789, 794
venture capital, 766–7, 772
Walker Report (2007), 796–7
private placement market, 35–6
pro-rata clauses, 381, 413
Professional Securities Market (PSM), 645, 646, 649,
  650–1, 658–9, 662, 668
project finance, 4, 47, 382
proprietary interests:
  absolute interests *see* absolute interests
  absolute or security interests, 267, 271–81
  advantages, 264, 265–6
  creditor protection, 264–359
  enforcement, 265–6, 326–38
  financial collateral arrangements,
    269–70, 282
  fixed v circulating assets, 268–9
  forms, 271
  insolvency and, 191, 264
  meaning, 22
  possession, 267–8, 269, 271
  present and future assets, 269
  priorities, 320–5
  ranking of creditors, 98–9
  real and personal property, 268
  security interests *see* security interests
  set-off, 231
  share issues and, 158–9
  tangible and intangible property, 267
  trusts, 363
  types of assets and, 267–70
prospectuses:
  debt securities
    contents, 648–50
    convertible securities, 667
    factors, 642–8
    form, 648
    historical information, 649
    IFRS, 649
    private enforcement, 653–5
    rationale, 646–8
    regulation, 641–50
    retail investors, 648, 649
    risk factors, 650
    size of offers, 645
    summaries, 648
    target investors, 643–4, 649
  defective share prospectuses

administrative sanctions, 516–17, 517–18
  aims of sanctions, 500–4
  civil liability, 504–15, 518–19, 560–1
  compensation for losses, 502–3, 512–14
  criminal sanctions, 515–16, 517–18
  defences, 506
  defendants, 510–11
  fraudulent misrepresentation, 504
  intensity of enforcement, 517–19
  locus standi, 508–10
  misstatements, 500–3
  remedies, 511–15
  rescission, 514–15
  UK sanctions, 499–519
IPOs, 493–519, 642
  accurate and timely disclosure, 500–3
  costs, 477
  EU law, 1, 494, 497, 500, 668
  EU passporting, 642–3
  ex-post enforcement, 504–22, 557
  exemptions, 495–6
  FCA vetting, 488, 499
  form and content, 496–9
  forward-looking information, 499
  historical information, 498, 527
  industry risk, 650
  objectives, 489–93, 510, 527, 561
  offers for sale, 480
  regulation, 207
  summaries, 497
  UK regulation, 494–9
Prudential Regulation Authority (PRA), 249, 251
public companies:
  administrative burdens, 16–17
  advantages, 473–7
  broader range of investors, 474
  capital reduction, 172
  covenants: dividend payments, 198
  disadvantages, 477–8
  distribution policy, 53–5
  flexibility, 475
  governance, 476, 488, 529–40
  liquidity, 475
  listing *see* listing
  minimum capital, 151–3
  Model Articles: capital rights, 63
  prestige, 477
  private equity companies: comparisons, 784–94
  public v private companies, 473–8
  regulation theory, 485–93
  share payment, 157
  share repurchase, 55, 166–7
  shareholder apathy, 78, 86, 533
  websites, 549
public offers of shares *see* IPOs
public policy:
  anti-deprivation principle, 108, 233
  duty exclusion clauses and, 405, 407–10
  insolvency set-off, 231–3
  ranking of creditors, 303
purchase money security interests (PMSIs), 354–5, 357
put options, 37, 199, 247

quasi-equity, 773, 775–6
quasi-partnerships, 9, 11, 14, 52–3, 77–8, 724
quasi-security interests, 4, 30, 197, 202, 267, 351, 352
Quistclose trusts, 281

ranking of creditors:
　administration expenses, 100–1
　Crown preference, 101, 345
　employees, 101
　floating charge assets, 99–105, 289–90, 295, 302–5,
　　323–4
　liquidation expenses, 100–1
　loan notes, 776, 779
　pari passu principle, 110, 227–30, 233, 260–1
　preferential creditors, 101, 179–80, 303
　prescribed part, 101–2
　proprietary interests and, 98–9, 264
　schemes of arrangement and, 736
　secured creditors, 320–5
　　date of creation, 321–4
　　execution creditors, 325
　　floating charges, 323–5
　　law reform, 353–5
　　non-adjusting creditors and, 346–7
　　retention of title and, 323
　　statutory assignees, 321–2
　　third parties and, 323–4
　　uncertainty, 325
　　windfalls, 322–3
　shareholders, 102–5
　　shareholder loans, 104–5
　　statutory contract, 103–4
　statutory trigger for priority, 306–7
　survey, 97–105
　unfair preferences, 110–13
　unsecured creditors, 99–105
　　priority order, 99–100
　　security interests and, 346–7
rating:
　bonds, 38
　credit rating agencies, 573, 668–71
　debt securities, 207, 374–5, 647
　hybrid instruments, 51
　issuer ratings, 375
real property, 43, 268, 317, 363
receivables financing:
　absolute or security interests, 278–9
　alternatives for SMEs, 41–2
　assignment of receivables, 452–5
　　anti-assignment clauses, 453–5
　　ranking, 324
　　unregistered charges, 318
　charges, 299, 306
　credit insurance, 245
　enforcement of interests, 336
　extensive use, 28
　increase, 279
　meaning, 428
　overview, 40–2
　ranking of creditors, 99
　securitisation *see* securitisation

types, 40–1, 450–1
　unregistered charges, 318
receivership, 97, 304, 331–3
Recognised Information Services (RISs), 541,
　549, 555, 556, 566, 569
redeemable shares, 12, 134, 144, 165, 166,
　169, 773
redemption rights: bonds, 37
reduction schemes, 748, 749, 753
reflective loss, 559
registered designs, 317
registration of security interests:
　certificates, 317
　constructive notice, 319–20, 350
　creditor protection, 25
　effect, 318–20
　failure to register, 318–19
　law reform, 347, 349–50, 352–3
　non-possessory interests, 316
　process, 317
　registration of arrangements, 315–16
　regulation technique, 638–9
　requirement, 272, 276, 316–17
　statements of particulars, 317
　time limits, 317, 319
　transparency, 277
repos, 21, 224, 275, 278
restitution orders, 406, 569, 594, 600, 615
retained profits, 52–5
retention of title:
　absolute or security interests, 275, 280–1
　administration and, 337
　asset finance, 44–5
　creditor protection, 23–4
　financial devices, 43–6
　forfeiture, 334–6
　meaning, 271
　proving, 277
　ranking of creditors and, 323
　sale and leaseback, 44, 278
　sale of goods: law reform, 357
　sales on retention terms, 46
　stock finance, 46
　trade creditors, 81
　trade finance, 48
reward crowdfunding, 17–18
Rights Issue Review Group, 138

sale and leaseback, 44, 278
sale of goods:
　absolute or security interests, 278–9
　good faith buyers, 323
　retention of title: law reform, 357
scandals, 573
schemes of arrangement:
　administration and, 98
　approval, 394–6
　arrangements, 730, 747
　benefits, 729–30
　class meetings
　　approval, 741–2, 751

comparators, 735–7, 739
creditors, 738–40
errors, 731, 744
general test, 734
identification, 731, 732–3
notices, 731–2
separate meetings, 733–40
shareholders, 737–8
summoning, 730–2
compromises, 730, 747
creditors, 729
debt restructuring, 757–62
demergers, 756–7
financially distressed companies, 758–61
identification, 732–3
meetings, 738–40
moratoriums, 758–9, 761
Practice Statement, 731
rights, 735–7
secured creditors, 736
unsecured creditors, 736
debt-equity swaps, 759–60
insolvency and, 736–7
judicial sanction
costs, 749
discretion, 745–6
overview, 743–6
preliminary issues, 743
reasonableness, 745
refusal, 731, 744
statutory compliance, 744
summoning meetings, 730–2
meaning, 729
mechanism, 730–46
minority protection, 729, 742, 750–2
option, 97
private equity, 780
reduction schemes, 748, 749, 753
registration, 746
shareholders
minority shareholders, 750–2
rights, 735
separate meetings, 737–8
subsidiaries, 738
solvent companies, 736
stages, 730
survey, 729–63
takeovers or, 747–52
third parties and, 745
transfer schemes, 748, 753
uses, 729, 746–62
alternative to takeovers, 747–52
debt restructuring, 757–62
demergers, 755–7
group reorganisation, 753–4
mergers, 754–5
settling insurance claims, 761–2
Scots law, 1–2, 768
secondary markets:
debt securities, 25, 32, 36, 372, 644–5
disclosure requirements, 657–61

efficient market prices, 524–8
equity disclosures, 523
ad hoc disclosures, 548–57
enforcement, 558–72
EU law, 541
governance and, 539–40
market efficiency and, 527–8
periodic disclosures, 542–8
private enforcement, 558–68
reporting *see* financial reporting
survey, 541–57
governance promotion, 529–40
loan market, 660–1, 664
market abuse *see* market abuse
regulation, 523–77
mechanisms, 523
objectives, 524–40
syndicated loans, 411
securities:
debt securities *see* debt securities
intermediated securities *see* intermediaries
market *see* capital market regulation
shares *see* shares
stock *see* loan stock
transfer, 455–63
securitisation:
absolute or security interests, 277
alternative to debt transfer, 467–72
attractions, 275
business securitisation, 39
credit insurance, 245
EU law, 471
extensive use, 28
information rights, 207
Islamic finance, 48
lack of transparency, 471
mechanism, 38–9
objectives, 423
outright sale, 469–70
receivables financing, 41, 467–72
security trustees, 382
SPVs, 38–9, 467–70
subordination, 255
synthetic securitisation, 423, 470–1
tranching, 467
transfer of risk, 93, 426
whole business securitisation, 470
security interests:
absolute interests and, 267, 271–81
characterisation, 272–4
external v internal approach, 273
grants, 278–9
policy issues, 276–7
Quistclose trusts, 281
reasons for choice, 274–6
retention of title, 275, 280–1
sale and lease-back, 278
taxation, 275
charges *see* charges
collateral arrangements *see* financial collateral
arrangements

decline in value, 326
economic arguments
　assessment, 338–47
　availability of credit, 339
　efficiency, 339
　fairness, 339–40
　monitoring, 340–2
　non-adjusting creditors, 342–7
　puzzle, 340–7
　signalling, 342
enforcement
　administration, 331–3, 336–8
　alternatives, 327–8
　appropriation, 329–30
　events of default, 327
　foreclosure, 329, 355
　law reform, 355–6
　methods, 326–33
　possession and sale, 330–1
　receivers, 331–3
　subordination and, 328
future property, 283–5
indicia, 271
law reform
　access issues, 349
　arguments, 347–58
　assessment, 356–8
　certainty, 348
　confused present law, 349
　enforcement, 355–6
　future assets, 348
　ideal, 348, 356
　notice filing system, 350–8
　options, 350–1
　PMSIs, 354–5, 357
　priorities, 353–5
　registration, 347, 349–50, 352–3
　transaction costs, 348
　transparency, 348
　unsatisfactory English law, 349–50
liens, 22, 81, 271, 779
meaning, 22, 270–2
mortgages *see* mortgages
non-possessory interests, 282–310
pledges *see* pledges
possessory interests, 282
priorities, 99, 320–5
　contract, 321
　date of creation, 321–4
　default rules, 321
　execution creditors, 325
　fixed charges, 287
　floating charges, 323–5
　law reform, 353–5
　securitisation, 469
　statutory assignment, 321–2
　sub-participation, 465
　third party acquisition, 323–4
　uncertainty, 325
　windfalls, 322–3
private equity, 778

quasi-security interests, 4, 30, 197, 202, 267, 351, 352
redeeming, 271
registration *see* registration of security interests
schemes of arrangement and, 736
types, 282–316
self-dealing, 529, 556, 710
sell-outs, 694–5, 722, 725, 750, 752
set-off:
　anti-assignment clauses and, 437, 438
　assignment and, 452
　bankers' right to combine accounts, 222
　contingent debts, 226, 232
　contractual set-off, 223–5
　creditor protection, 24, 196, 218–33
　excluding, 218–19, 225, 230–3
　flawed asset structures and, 219–20
　floating charges and, 219, 325
　independent set-off, 221, 223
　insolvency set-off, 222, 224, 226–33
　　automatic operation, 226, 227
　　charge-backs and, 226–7, 288
　　contingent debts, 226
　　mandatory nature, 227–31
　　pari passu principle and, 227–30, 233
　　policy justifications, 231–3
　　secured creditors, 227
　legal set-off, 221
　mechanism, 218
　netting and, 218, 223–4, 229–30, 231
　pari passu principle and, 110, 227–30, 233
　pre-paying customers, 81
　proprietary right, 231
　statutory set-off, 221
　transaction set-off, 221–2, 223
settlement netting, 223–4, 458, 460
shadow banking sector, 20
shadow directors, 91–2, 93
sham transactions, 273, 278, 301
share distributions:
　administration, 64
　balance sheet test, 176
　capital maintenance and, 52, 162–78
　capital reduction method, 162
　creditor protection, 176–8
　debt covenants and, 87, 198–9
　dividends, 177
　　capital maintenance and, 163–5
　　covenant restrictions, 87, 198–9
　　directors' recommendations, 163
　　group companies, 753
　　in kind, 64
　finance theory, 54
　interim dividends, 64
　IPO promises, 492
　liquidations and, 64
　methods, 162
　ordinary shares, 11–12, 63–4, 65
　preference shares, 13–14, 50, 65, 67
　public companies, 53–5
　quasi-partnerships, 52–3

ranking on insolvency, 103
takeover bids and, 697
taxation, 36
share issues:
  agency problems, 130
  allotment, 124
    directors' authority, 9, 126, 131–2, 138
    renounceable letters of allotment, 135
  dilution of shareholder interests, 125–6, 132
  directors' powers, 9
  discounts, 125
  EU regulation, 130
  improper purpose, 126, 127
  IPOs *see* IPOs
  pre-emption rights *see* pre-emption rights
  price, 125, 129
  process, 124
  proprietary interests and, 158–9
  public offers *see* IPOs
  shareholder protection, 124–30
    additional protection needed, 129–30
    balance of powers, 138–9
    directors' duties, 126–7
    minority shareholders, 128–9
    need for protection, 124–6
    pre-emption rights, 132–9
  value dilution, 125–6, 127, 160
share options, 476, 528
share repurchase:
  benefits, 165–6
  creditor protection, 168
  distribution option, 162
  effect, 170
  general restrictions, 166–7
  general rule, 165
  market purchases, 167
  off-market purchases, 167
  private companies, 167–9
  public companies, 55, 166–7
  share redemption and, 165
  small companies, 52
  takeover bids and, 697
share transfer:
  EU law, 455
  hedge funds, 143
  issues, 362
  liquidity, 16, 475, 481
  mechanism, 144–5, 455
  mergers, 755–6
  restrictions, 144, 700
  stock lending, 143
  takeover bids and, 700
shareholders:
  agency problems, 82
  agreements, 10–11
  apathy, 78, 86, 533
  blockholdings, 678–9
  contractual rights, 10, 72–3, 76
  creditor/shareholder conflict, 146–51
  directors' duties to, 69–70, 149, 530, 791
  directors' holdings, 492, 583–4, 586–7, 785

dispersed shareholdings, 678–9, 709–10, 716, 726
governance role *see* governance
inaccurate financial reporting and, 103, 560–8
insolvent companies
  creditors v shareholders, 114–22
insolvent companies: creditors v shareholders,
  59–61
institutional investors *see* institutional investors
liquidation powers, 70
loans: ranking, 104–5
major shareholdings: disclosure, 552–5
minority shareholders *see* minority shareholders
new share issues and, 9–10
powers
  liquidations, 78
  ratification of transactions, 78
  ratification of wrongdoing, 78
  removal of directors, 77–8
  share allotment, 132
protection
  capital market regulation, 485–6
  capital reduction, 171
  debt securities and, 640–1
  dilution of interests, 125–6, 127, 160
  pre-emption rights, 132–9, 160
  share issues, 124–39
  share payment rules, 160–1
public companies
  apathy, 78, 86, 533
  governance, 529–40
ranking on insolvency, 102–5
reflective loss, 559
return of capital to, 162, 163–4
schemes of arrangement and, 735, 737–8
solvent companies
  balance, 59–61
  governance, 77–8
  owners of capitalised income stream, 72–5
  owners of companies, 70–2
  ownership debate, 75–6
  pre-eminence, 70–7, 70–8
  residual claimants, 76–7
  role, 69–78
  s 172, Companies Act (2006), 69–70
statutory protection, 3
takeover bids and
  bidder directors and bidder shareholders, 726–7
  bidders and target shareholders, 716–26
  equality principle, 717–22, 783
  pre-bid defences, 702–3
  private equity, 783
  shareholder focus, 680, 681, 682–3, 689, 696
  short-termism, 713, 714–15
  target directors v shareholders, 695–725
  undistorted choice, 718–22
  types, 142–3
shares:
  bearer shares, 142
  capital rights, 11, 62
  certificates, 140–1, 144–5
  consideration

breach of rules, 157–60
cash, 155–6
creditor protection, 161–2
currency, 153, 156
financial assistance, 173–6
no discount rule, 155–7, 161
non-cash, 156–7, 158, 160–1, 162
par value, 153–5
rules, 153–62
sanctions, 157–60
shareholder protection, 160–1
debentures and, 636
debt securities and, 36, 640–1
dematerialisation, 141–2
global certificates, 143
income rights, 11, 62
intangible property, 72, 490
intermediaries, 142–3
issues *see* share issues
legal capital rules *see* capital rules
liquidity, 4, 16
mortgages, 286
ordinary shares *see* ordinary shares
pre-emption *see* pre-emption rights
preference shares *see* preference shares
price manipulation, 174
public offers *see* IPOs
redemption, 165–6, 169, 170
registration, 40, 139, 142
rights, 11, 62, 73
secondary markets *see* secondary markets
shareholding methods, 140–3
transfer *see* share transfer
trusts, 367–9
types, 10–14, 62–3
voting rights, 11, 62
Sharia law, 22, 48–9
shelf companies, 778
ships: securities, 317
short selling:
bans, 618, 623–4
circuit breakers, 626–7
covered selling, 617, 623–4
debt securities, 665–6
distabilisation of markets, 618–20
ESMA role, 629–30
EU law, 621, 622–30
justifying regulation, 618–22
mandatory disclosures, 617–18, 624–6
market abuse, 620–1
meaning, 616–17
naked short selling, 617, 621–2
national authorities and, 628–9
settlement periods, 617
settlement risk, 621–2, 627–8
uncovered selling, 617, 621–2
upstick rules, 626–7
signalling, 54, 163, 166, 254, 342, 491
single-member companies, 14
small companies:
capital rights, 63

equity capital, 9
equity crowdfunding, 17–18, 519–21
equity finance, 14
finance leases, 20
guarantees, 23
hire purchase, 20
options, 4, 58
overdrafts, 28–9
peer-to-peer lending, 31
receivables financing, 40–2
share issues, 12
share repurchase, 52
supply chain financing, 42
sole traders, 2
solvency statements:
alternative to capital rules, 183–90
auditing, 186
capital reduction, 172–3
civil liability, 187
criminal liability, 168, 172, 173, 186–7
law reform, 189–90
recovering unlawful payments, 188–9
share repurchases, 168
solvency test, 184–6
sophisticated investors, 38, 253, 375, 398, 485, 520–1,
641, 642, 643, 645–7, 648, 652, 795
sovereign wealth funds, 771, 795
special purpose vehicles (SPVs):
asset-based securities, 38
Islamic finance, 48–9
project finance, 4, 47
securitisation, 38–9, 467–70
squeeze-outs, 693–4, 725, 749, 750, 752
stakeholders:
directors' duties, 69, 86, 114, 149, 180
private equity and, 790–2, 796, 802
takeovers and, 698, 712–16, 790
stamp duty, 748
standby credits, 235, 236
stock *see* loan stock
Stock Exchange Pre-Emption Group, 137
structural subordination, 255, 262
sub-participation, 423, 445, 446, 463–6
subordination:
administration, 382
asset-based lending, 43
contingent debts, 260, 262
contractual subordination, 260–2
creditor protection, 254–62
debt securities, 51, 255, 648
effect, 328
hybrid instruments, 51–2, 79
insolvency and, 255–6
meaning, 235, 254–5
multiple lenders, 28, 30, 360
pari passu principle and, 110, 260–1
private equity, 262, 777
schemes of arrangement and, 736
shareholder claims on insolvency, 104
structural subordination, 255, 262
turnover trusts, 256–60, 262

types, 256–62
subprime mortgages, 268
subrogation, 80, 101, 236, 239, 241, 304, 345
supply chain financing: meaning, 42
swaps, 247
swinglines, 29
syndicated loans:
  arrangers, 414–17
  bonds and, 411–14
  covenants, 84–5, 199, 660
  debt buybacks, 200, 422
  democratic structure, 420, 421–2
  duty exclusion clauses, 416–17, 418, 419, 420
  fiduciary duties of arrangers, 414–17
  fiscal agents v trustees, 411–14
  information memoranda, 415, 417–20, 418
  information rights, 207–8
  majority lenders, 421–2
  meaning, 30
  modification of agreements, 421
  monitoring borrowers and, 88, 92
  overview, 411–22
  position of agent banks, 420
  private equity, 779
  pro-rata clauses, 381, 413
  secondary market, 28, 411
  securitisation, 426
  standard terms, 24
  sub-participation, 423, 445, 446, 463–6
  transfer, 93, 411, 423, 424–5, 445, 452
  underwriting, 414
  uses, 27
  waiver of breach, 421

takeover bids:
  advertising, 691
  agency conflict, 680, 697, 711
  allocative efficiency, 718
  bidder directors and bidder shareholders, 726–7
  bidders and target shareholders, 716–26
    equality principle, 717, 719–20
    EU law, 717
    undistorted choice, 718–22
  breakthrough rule, 702
  City Code, 127, 537
    amending, 684, 714–15
    break fee arrangements, 706
    competing bids, 707
    directors' opinions, 704–5, 782
    equal treatment, 782, 783
    formal offers, 690–2
    further offers, 695
    information to bidder shareholders, 726
    initial approaches, 689–90
    minority shareholders, 717, 725, 750
    objectives, 678
    origins, 682–3
    pre-bid defences, 703
    private equity takeovers, 781
    role, 681
    sanctions, 686

  schemes of arrangement, 748, 752
  sell-outs, 695
  shareholders v directors, 696
  undistorted choice, 718–22
  creditors and, 716
  effect, 476
  employee rights, 713, 715–16
  EU regulation, 680, 681, 684–5, 702, 722
  formal offers, 690–2
  further offers, 695
  hostile bids, 682, 684, 697, 700–1, 709, 710–15, 714, 780
  initial approaches, 689–90
  insider dealing, 594, 692
  international comparisons, 678, 680–1
  law reform, 678, 714–16
  mandatory bids, 720–1
  meaning, 677
  minority shareholders
    bypassing, 752
    exit rights, 725–6
    prevention of oppression, 723–4
    protection, 717, 722–6
  no frustration principle, 531, 689, 696, 704–5
    effect, 708–12
    EU law, 704
    stakeholders and, 714
    UK v US, 709–11
    Unocal test, 708–9
  overpayment, 727
  post-bid defences, 704–12
    directors' opinions, 704–5, 782
    directors' share purchase, 705
    insufficient price, 705
    White Knights, 704–7
  pre-bid defences
    crown jewels defence, 697
    directors' duties, 698–700
    directors v shareholders, 696–704
    new share issues, 126, 127
    poison pills, 697, 699–700, 702–4
    removal of directors, 700–1
    special dividends, 697
    staggered boards, 700–1
    voting rights, 697, 702
  principles, 689
  process, 689–95
  profit forecasts, 691
  promises, 714
  regulatory objectives, 678–80
  sell-outs, 694–5, 722, 725, 750, 752
  shareholder-centric model, 680, 681, 682–3, 689, 696
  short-termism, 713, 714–15
  squeeze-outs, 693–4, 725, 749, 750, 752
  tactical litigation, 687–8
  target directors v shareholders, 695–712
  target stakeholders and, 698, 712–16, 790
  time limits, 690, 692
  UK regulatory structure
    flexibility, 684

history, 682–4
overview, 681–9
speed, 684, 689
Takeover Panel:
    appeals to, 684, 687–8
    bidder shareholders and, 727
    Eurotunnel decision, 719
    immunity, 688
    institutional investors and, 537
    judicial review, 687–8
    membership, 683, 685–6
    objectives, 678
    origins, 682
    private equity takeovers and, 783
    role, 681, 685–6
    sanctions, 686, 691
    schemes of arrangement and, 748, 752
    short-termism and, 714–15
    speedy reactions, 684
    status, 685–6, 688
takeovers:
    bids *see* takeover bids
    dispersed shareholdings and, 678–9, 709–10,
        716, 726
    effect, 678, 726, 727
    governance and, 710–12
    Panel *see* Takeover Panel
    public-to-private takeovers, 780–4
    schemes of arrangement or, 747–52
    share-exchange, 495
tangible property, 267
taxation:
    absolute or security interests, 275
    corporation tax, 56, 775
    Crown preference, 101, 345
    debt securities, 36
    dividends, 36
    eurobonds, 375
    finance leases, 45
    group companies, 234
    hybrid instruments, 50
    non-adjusting creditors, 80, 81
    private equity, 769, 775, 788, 789, 794
    schemes of arrangement, 749
    significance, 5
third parties:
    absolute or security interests and, 272, 276
    breach of covenants and, 203–4
    contractual rights against, 23, 233–62, 379
        benefits, 234
        bonds, 391
        categories of parties, 234
        credit insurance, 23, 245–7
        derivatives *see* credit derivatives
        forms, 235
        guarantees *see* guarantees
        indemnities, 235–7, 241–4
        nature of liability, 237
        performance bonds, 23, 235–7, 243–5
        subordination *see* subordination
    floating charges and, 293–4

insurance, 81
multiple lenders and, 362
ranking of security interests and, 323–4
schemes of arrangement and, 745
tort claims:
    breach of covenants, 202–3
    class actions, 344
    compulsory insurance, 117–18
    deceit *see* deceit
    defective prospectuses, 502–14
    importance, 3
    misrepresentation: syndicated loans, 417–19
    non-adjusting creditors, 80, 81
    rights, 79
    security interests and, 344
    US v UK, 344
trade creditors, 5, 79, 80–1, 343
trade finance, 48
trade marks, 317
transaction costs, 56, 179, 348, 487, 568, 572, 620, 647
transfer of debts:
    alternative structures, 463–72
    assignment *see* assignment
    borrowers' knowledge, 426
    debt securities *see* debt securities
    intermediated securities, 457–61
    loans *see* loan transfer
    methods, 426–63
    multiple lenders, 27–8, 361
    negotiable instruments, 443–5
    novation, 6, 427, 446–50
    price transparency, 424
    reasons, 423–6
    receivables, 452–5
    restrictions, 427
    security transfer, 427
    shares *see* share transfer
    survey, 423–72
    syndicated loans, 93, 411, 423, 424–5,
        445, 452
    transfer of obligations, 426–7
transferable securities:
    bonds *see* bonds
    debentures *see* debentures
    definition, 635
    hybrids *see* hybrid instruments
    mandatory disclosures, 635, 638–41
    shares *see* shares
treasury shares, 168–9
trustees:
    bonds, 364–5, 380–2, 396–410, 420
    conflicts of interest, 364, 407
    debt securities
        events of default, 398–403
        excluding duties, 403–10
        functions, 396–403
        information rights, 397–8
        modifying trust deeds, 396–7
        monitoring, 380, 397–8
        no-action clauses, 381, 402–3, 412–13
        obligations, 396–410

duty exclusion clauses
  construction, 405–7
  debt securities, 403–10
  forms, 403–5
  public policy, 407–10
  unfair contract terms, 407
fiduciary duties, 364–5
  bonds, 380, 396–410, 420
fiscal agents v trustees, 380, 411–14
loan stock, 376, 377–8
professional corporate trustees, 364, 403–4
security trustees, 382, 420
trusts:
  anti-assignment clauses and, 435–6, 437–43
  bonds, 88, 364, 380–90
    advantages, 380–2
    bearer bonds, 383–4
    subject matter, 383
  certainty of intention, 365
  certainty of objects, 365–6
  certainty of subject matter, 366–70, 383
  concept, 362–3
  equitable interests, 370–1
  equity, 362–3
  implied trusts, 441
  multiple lenders and, 364
  pre-payments, 81
  property, 363
  proprietary interests, 363
  Quistclose trusts, 281
  shares, 367–9
  turnover trusts, 256–60, 262, 382
  use in commercial transactions, 363–5
turnover trusts, 256–60, 262, 382

UK Stewardship Code, 539
underinvestment, 83
undervalue transactions, 106, 109, 112, 224, 262
undue influence, 73
unfair contract terms, 407, 419, 654, 660
unfair preferences, 110–11, 224
UNIDROIT: Geneva Securities Convention, 389
United States:
  algorithmic trading, 632
  asset-based lending, 42
  banks: monitoring borrowers, 92
  bonds: minority protection, 393
  class actions, 344
  comparative law, 1
  corporate rescue procedure, 95
  credit default swaps, 254
  creditor governance role, 86
  creditor protection: contract, 178
  cross-listing, 484
  debt restructuring, 761
  debt securities, 376
  Delaware, 709–10, 768
  dispersed shareholdings, 678, 709–10

D&O insurance, 502
financial crisis, 767
financial reporting, 545, 550, 572
Flash Crash (2010), 631–2
fraud on the market, 614
inside information, 550
insider dealing, 579, 580
junk bonds, 765
legal capital, 148
leveraged buy-outs, 765, 766
market manipulation, 579, 613
notice filing system, 350, 357
pay-for-performance, 476
pre-emption rights, 136, 138
private equity, 765–6, 767, 779
private placement market, 35
prospectuses: criminal enforcement,
  517–18
Sarbanes-Oxley Act, 484
security interests, 315–16, 344, 346
staggered boards, 531
subprime mortgages, 268
takeover bids, 476
  1990s, 711
  administration, 683–4
  agency conflict, 680–1
  defences, 709–11
  Delaware model, 709–10
  poison pills, 703–4
  stakeholders, 714
tort claims, 344
unlimited companies, 8
unsecured creditors *see* ranking of creditors

Vandepitte procedure, 441–3
venture capital, 4, 11, 15, 57, 487, 765, 766–7, 768,
  772, 794
voting rights:
  dilution, 125
  institutional investors, 554
  intermediaries, 553
  ordinary shares, 12, 64–5
  preference shares, 13, 67–8
  takeover bids and, 697, 702

waiver: no-waiver clauses, 213
Walker Report (2007), 796–7
warranties *see* covenants
waterfall clauses, 47, 299, 467
websites, 549
Wheatley Report (2012), 596, 599
White Knights, 704–7
winding up *see* liquidations
Winter Group Report, 183
wrongful trading, 91, 96, 105, 118, 119–22, 173,
  176, 183

zero coupon bonds, 37